A Theology of John's Gospel and Letters

Biblical Theology of the New Testament

Andreas J. Köstenberger

ZONDERVAN ACADEMIC

A Theology of John's Gospel and Letters
Copyright © 2009 by Andreas J. Köstenberger

Published in Grand Rapids, Michigan, by Zondervan. Zondervan is a registered trademark of The Zondervan Corporation, L.L.C., a wholly owned subsidiary of HarperCollins Christian Publishing, Inc.

Requests for information should be addressed to customercare@harpercollins.com.

Zondervan titles may be purchased in bulk for educational, business, fundraising, or sales promotional use. For information, please email SpecialMarkets@Zondervan.com.

Library of Congress Cataloging-in-Publication Data

Köstenberger, Andreas J., 1957-
    A theology of John's Gospel and letters : the Word, the Christ, the Son of God / Andreas J. Köstenberger.
        p. cm. - (Biblical theology of the New Testament)
    Includes bibliographical references and indexes.
    ISBN 978-0-310-26986-1 (hardcover, printed)
    1. Bible. N.T. John - Theology. 2. Bible. N.T. Epistles of John - Theology. I. Title.
BS2601.K67 2009
226.5'065 - dc22   2009028347

Scripture quotations marked TNIV are taken from the Holy Bible, Today's New International® Version TNIV®. Copyright © 2001, 2005 by International Bible Society.® Used by permission of International Bible Society.® All rights reserved worldwide. "TNIV" and "Today's New International Version" are trademarks registered in the United States Patent and Trademark Office by International Bible Society.®

Any Internet addresses (websites, blogs, etc.) and telephone numbers in this book are offered as a resource. They are not intended in any way to be or imply an endorsement by Zondervan, nor does Zondervan vouch for the content of these sites and numbers for the life of this book.

All rights reserved. No part of this publication may be reproduced, stored in a retrieval system, or transmitted in any form or by any means — electronic, mechanical, photocopy, recording, or any other — except for brief quotations in printed reviews, without the prior permission of the publisher.

Cover and interior design: Mark Sheeres

Printed in the United States of America

PRAISE FOR A THEOLOGY OF JOHN'S GOSPEL AND LETTERS

For the comprehensiveness of its coverage in the field of Johannine theology (gospel and letters), there is nothing to compare to this work.

D. A. CARSON, research professor of New Testament,
Trinity Evangelical Divinity School

This book is a "first" in many ways: the first volume that sets the pattern for the quality and style of the new Biblical Theology of the New Testament series published by Zondervan; the first major volume to be devoted specifically to the theology of John's gospel and letters at a high academic level; and the first volume to offer a thorough interpretation of the theology of an eyewitness of the life and passion of Jesus. Andreas Köstenberger has already laid a foundation for his study with his careful, detailed commentary on the gospel of John, and here presents a self-standing study that gathers together the thought of the Evangelist in a systematic and complete manner. I particularly welcome the way in which the book sets out John's theological story in the gospel and letters before giving a detailed, thematic study

I. HOWARD MARSHALL, emeritus professor of New Testament exegesis and
honorary research professor,
University of Aberdeen

Massive and masterful, this book presents Johannine theology in encyclopedic fullness. Arguing for apostolic authorship of John's gospel and epistles, Andreas Köstenberger gives due weight to historical, literary, linguistic, and thematic matters in careful interaction with other scholars. Yet pastors and advanced students will also find the discussion accessible. We find here a new benchmark in synthetic treatment of these priceless writings of Christ's beloved disciple.

ROBERT W. YARBROUGH, professor of New Testament,
Trinity Evangelical Divinity School

To the Word-Made-Flesh

"And since they all [i.e. all four canonical Gospels]
had the same object, to show Christ,
the first three exhibit His body,
if I may be permitted to put it like that,
but John shows His soul."

—*John Calvin, 1553*

Contents

Contents (Detailed) 10
List of Figures 25
Series Preface 26
Author's Preface 28
Abbreviations 30

Part 1
The Historical Framework for Johannine Theology 35

Chapter 1
Johannine Theology and the Historical Setting of John's Gospel and Letters 37
  1 Johannine and Biblical Theology 38
  2 The Historical Setting of John's Gospel and Letters 51

Part 2
Literary Foundations for Johannine Theology 101

Chapter 2
The Genre of John's Gospel and Letters 103
  3 The Genre of John's Gospel 104
  4 The Genre of John's Letters 125

Chapter 3
Linguistic and Literary Dimensions of John's Gospel and Letters 127
  5 Johannine Vocabulary 129
  6 Johannine Style 130
  7 Johannine Literary Devices 135
  8 The Structure of John's Gospel 167
  9 The Structure of John's Letters 171

Chapter 4
A Literary-Theological Reading of John's Gospel 175
  10 A Literary-Theological Reading of John's Gospel 175

Chapter 5
A Literary-Theological Reading of John's Letters 263
  11 A Literary-Theological Reading of John's Letters 263

Part 3
Major Themes in Johannine Theology 273

A. Prolegomena

Chapter 6
John's Worldview and Use of Scripture 275
    12 John's Worldview 277
    13 John's Use of Scripture 298

B. The End (Purpose; 20:30–31)

Chapter 7
The Messiah and His Signs 311
    14 The Messiah 312
    15 The Signs 323

C. The Beginning (Introduction; 1:1–18)

Chapter 8
The Word: Creation and New Creation 336
    16 New Creation: The Word, Life, and Light 337

Chapter 9
God: Father, Son, and Spirit 355
    17 John, Jesus, and Jewish Monotheism 356
    18 God 361
    19 The Father 370
    20 The Son 380
    21 The Spirit 393

Chapter 10
Salvation History: Jesus' Fulfillment of Festal Symbolism 403
    22 Salvation History 403
    23 Jesus' Fulfillment of Festal Symbolism 413
    24 Jesus as the New Temple 422

Chapter 11
The Cosmic Trial Motif: The World, the Jews, and the Witnesses to Jesus 436
    25 The Cosmic Trial Motif 437

Chapter 12
The New Messianic Community: Divine Sovereignty and Human Responsibility 457
    26 Divine Election and Predestination 458
    27 Sin and Judgment 464
    28 Believing and the New Birth 470
    29 The New Messianic Community 481

D. The Middle (Preamble to Part Two; 13:1–3)

Chapter 13
The Johannine Love Ethic 509
   30 John's Moral Vision 510

Chapter 14
John's Theology of the Cross 525
   31 The Nature of Jesus' Coming 526
   32 The Nature of Jesus' Work 532

Chapter 15
John's Trinitarian Mission Theology 539
   33 John and Mission 539

Part 4
Johannine Theology and the Canon of Scripture 547

Chapter 16
The Theology of John and Other New Testament Voices 549
   34 The Theology of John Compared to the Synoptics 550
   35 Johannine and Pauline Theology and the Theology of the Other
      New Testament Writings 563

   Conclusion 566
   Bibliography 568
   Scripture Index 615
   Index of Extrabiblical Literature 640
   Subject Index 644
   Author Index 647

Contents (Detailed)

Series Preface 26
Author's Preface 28
Abbreviations 30

Part 1
The Historical Framework for Johannine Theology 35

Chapter 1
Johannine Theology and the Historical Setting of John's Gospel and Letters 37
- 1. . . . . Johannine and Biblical Theology 38
- 1.1 . . . . Introduction 38
- 1.2 . . . . The "Spiritual Gospel" 38
- 1.2.1 . . . . History of Scholarship 38
- 1.2.2 . . . . The Road Ahead 41
- 1.3 . . . . Prolegomena 42
- 1.3.1 . . . . The Hermeneutical Triad 42
- 1.3.2 . . . . The Plan of This Book 45
- 1.3.2.1 . . . . Three Areas: Historical Investigation, Literary Study, Theological Reflection 45
- 1.3.2.2 . . . . Major Theological Themes Chosen and Criteria for Selection 47
- 2. . . . . The Historical Setting of John's Gospel and Letters 51
- 2.1 . . . . The Gospel 51
- 2.1.1 . . . . Introduction 51
- 2.1.2 . . . . The Quest for the Historical Setting of John's Gospel 53
- 2.1.2.1 . . . . Introduction 53
- 2.1.2.1.1 . . . . . The Traditional Setting of John 53
- 2.1.2.1.2 . . . . . Enlightenment Disputes 54
- 2.1.2.1.3 . . . . . The Johannine Community Hypothesis 55
- 2.1.2.1.4 . . . . . The Johannine Community Hypothesis Undermined 56
- 2.1.2.1.5 . . . . . Back to the Future 59
- 2.1.2.2 . . . . The Destruction of the Temple as a Plausible Historical Setting for John's Gospel 60
- 2.1.2.2.1 . . . . . Date of Destruction Relative to John 60
- 2.1.2.2.2 . . . . . Impact of the Destruction 61
- 2.1.2.3 . . . . The Gospel of John and Other Responses to the Loss of the Temple 63
- 2.1.2.3.1 . . . . . Jewish Strategies for Coping with the Loss of the Temple 63
- 2.1.2.3.2 . . . . . John's Gospel as Jewish Response to the Destruction of the Temple 65
- 2.1.2.3.3 . . . . . "Letting John Be John" 67
- 2.1.2.3.4 . . . . . "Points of Sensitivity" in John's Gospel 68
- 2.1.2.3.5 . . . . . Jewish Messianic Expectations and Jews Doing without a Temple 70
- 2.1.2.3.6 . . . . . Conclusion 71
- 2.1.3 . . . . Introductory Matters 72
- 2.1.3.1 . . . . Authorship 72

2.1.3.1.1	Internal Evidence	72
2.1.3.1.2	External Evidence	74
2.1.3.1.3	Richard Bauckham's Challenge of Apostolic Authorship	75
2.1.3.2	Chronology of Jesus' Ministry in John's Gospel	79
2.1.3.3	Date, Provenance, and Destination	82
2.1.3.3.1	Date	82
2.1.3.3.2	Provenance	83
2.1.3.3.3	Destination	84
2.1.3.4	Occasion and Purpose	84
2.1.3.4.1	Occasion	84
2.1.3.4.2	Purpose	85
2.2	The Letters	86
2.2.1	Authorship	86
2.2.1.1	Internal Evidence	86
2.2.1.2	External Evidence	89
2.2.1.3	Challenges to Johannine Authorship	90
2.2.1.4	Conclusion	93
2.2.2	Date, Provenance, and Destination	93
2.2.2.1	Date	93
2.2.2.2	Provenance	94
2.2.2.3	Destination	94
2.2.3	Occasion	94
2.2.3.1	The Nature of the False Teaching	95
2.2.3.2	Conclusion	96
2.2.4	Purpose	97
2.2.5	Introductory Matters Unique to 2 and 3 John	97
2.3	Conclusion	99

PART 2
Literary Foundations for Johannine Theology 101

CHAPTER 2
The Genre of John's Gospel and Letters 103

3.	The Genre of John's Gospel	104
3.1	Background and History of Research	104
3.1.1	Introduction	104
3.1.2	History of Research	106
3.2	Differences between the Gospels and Greco-Roman Biographies	107
3.3	Jewish Historiography	108
3.3.1	Introduction	108
3.3.2	John's Gospel and Jewish Historiography	108
3.3.3	Conclusion	111
3.4	The Gospel and Greco-Roman Literary Conventions	111
3.4.1	Internal Features	112
3.4.1.1	Range of Topics	112
3.4.1.2	Ancestry	112
3.4.1.3	Great Deeds and Words	112

3.4.1.4	Death and Consequences	113
3.4.1.5	Vindication Scene	113
3.4.1.6	Emphasis and Content	113
3.4.1.7	Promotion of a Particular Hero	114
3.4.1.8	Type of Material	114
3.4.1.9	Early Use of Subject's Name	114
3.4.1.10	Style	115
3.4.1.10.1	Narrative Style	115
3.4.1.10.2	Language	115
3.4.1.10.3	Atmosphere	117
3.4.1.11	Characterization	118
3.4.2	External Features	118
3.4.2.1	Structure	118
3.4.2.1.1	Formal Preface	118
3.4.2.1.2	Postscript and Dual Conclusion	119
3.4.2.1.3	Format	119
3.4.2.1.4	Careful Arrangement	120
3.4.2.1.5	Length	120
3.4.2.2	Similarities in Historiography	120
3.4.2.2.1	General Purpose	120
3.4.2.2.2	Use of Sources	121
3.4.2.2.3	Variation in Detail	122
3.4.2.2.4	Reliability of Eyewitness Testimony	123
3.5	Conclusion	124
4.	The Genre of John's Letters	125
4.1	Second and Third John	125
4.2	First John	125
4.3	Conclusion	126

Chapter 3
Linguistic and Literary Dimensions of John's Gospel and Letters 127

5.	Johannine Vocabulary	129
5.1	Survey of Johannine Vocabulary	129
5.2	Major Semantic Domains in John's Gospel and Letters	129
5.3	Other Observations	130
6.	Johannine Style	130
6.1	Introduction	130
6.2	Background and History of Research	130
6.3	Major Johannine Style Characteristics	133
6.3.1	Introduction	133
6.3.2	Select List of Major Johannine Style Characteristics	133
6.3.3	Conclusion	134
7.	Johannine Literary Devices	135
7.1	Narrative "Asides"	135
7.1.1	Introduction	135
7.1.2	List of Johannine "Asides"	136
7.1.2.1	Translations of Aramaic or Hebrew Terms	136
7.1.2.2	Explanations of Palestinian Topography	136

7.1.2.3	Explanations of Jewish Customs	136
7.1.2.4	References to Jesus' Supernatural Insight or Foreknowledge of Events or to God's Providential Ordering of Events	137
7.1.2.5	References to Characters or Events Mentioned Earlier in the Narrative	137
7.1.2.6	References to the Fulfillment of Scripture or of Jesus' Words	138
7.1.2.7	References to a Failure to Understand	138
7.1.2.8	Clarifications of the Meaning of Statements Made by Jesus or Others	139
7.1.2.9	Statements in Relation to the Gospel Tradition	139
7.1.2.10	Numbering of Events in the Narrative	140
7.1.2.11	Extended Commentary	140
7.1.2.12	Other Clarifying or Explanatory Statements	140
7.1.3	Summary and Conclusion	140
7.2	Misunderstandings	141
7.2.1	Introduction	141
7.2.2	The Dynamic Underlying Misunderstandings	141
7.2.3	Definition and List of Johannine Misunderstandings	143
7.2.4	Summary and Conclusion	145
7.3	Alleged "Seams" (Aporias)	145
7.3.1	Introduction	145
7.3.2	Investigation of Alleged "Seams" in John's Gospel	146
7.3.2.1	Introduction	146
7.3.2.2	"Jesus … came into the Land of Judea" (3:22)	146
7.3.2.3	Jesus' "Second Sign" (4:54)	147
7.3.2.4	The Sequence of Chapters 5 and 6	147
7.3.2.5	The Pericope of the Adulterous Woman (7:53–8:11)	147
7.3.2.6	The Reference to the Anointing of Jesus by Mary of Bethany in 11:2	148
7.3.2.7	"Come Now; Let Us Leave" (14:31)	148
7.3.2.8	"None of You Asks Me, 'Where Are You Going?'" (16:5)	149
7.3.2.9	The "Ending" of 20:30–31	149
7.3.3	Summary and Conclusion	150
7.4	Irony	150
7.4.1	Introduction	150
7.4.2	The Dynamic Underlying Johannine Irony	150
7.4.3	Instances of Johannine Irony	153
7.4.4	Summary and Conclusion	155
7.5	Symbolism	155
7.5.1	Introduction	155
7.5.2	The Dynamic Underlying Johannine Symbolism	156
7.5.2.1	Nature and Characteristics of Symbolism	156
7.5.2.2	J. Louis Martyn's "Two-Level Hermeneutic": Evaluation and Critique	159
7.5.2.3	Other Hermeneutical Observations Pertaining to Johannnine Symbolism	161
7.5.3	Water Symbolism	162
7.5.3.1	Introduction	162
7.5.3.2	Narrative Survey	162
7.5.3.3	Summary and Conclusion	164

7.5.4	Bread Symbolism	165
7.5.5	Light Symbolism	166
7.5.6	Summary and Conclusion	167
8.	The Structure of John's Gospel	167
8.1	Overview	167
8.2	Act I: *Sēmeio*-Drama	168
8.3	Act II: *Cruci*-Drama	169
8.4	Proposed Structure of John's Gospel	170
9.	The Structure of John's Letters	171
9.1	Introduction	171
9.2	Structural Proposals for 1 John	172
9.2.1	Division into Two Parts	172
9.2.2	Division into Three Parts	172
9.2.3	Division into Multiple Parts	172
9.3	Proposed Outlines for 1, 2, and 3 John	172
9.3.1	Introduction	172
9.3.2	First John	173
9.3.3	Second John	173
9.3.4	Third John	173
9.4	Conclusion	174

CHAPTER 4
A Literary-Theological Reading of John's Gospel 175

10.	A Literary-Theological Reading of John's Gospel	175
10.1	Introduction: The Word Made Flesh in Jesus Christ (1:1–18)	176
10.1.1	The Function of the Introduction in Relation to the Gospel as a Whole	176
10.1.2	A Thematic and Narrative Reading of the Introduction	178
10.2	The Gospel Proper: From John's to the Evangelist's Witness (1:19–20:31)	188
10.2.1	Act I: The Messiah's Signs and Rejection by His Own (1:19–12:50)	188
10.2.1.1	From John to Jesus: The Beginnings of Jesus' Ministry (1:19–51)	188
10.2.1.1.1	John's Witness to Jesus (1:19–34)	188
10.2.1.1.2	Jesus' First Appearance and Gathering of First Followers (1:35–51)	190
10.2.1.2	From Cana to Cana: The Cana Cycle: Jesus' Ministry to a Representative Jew, Samaritan, and Gentile (2:1–4:54; Signs 1–3)	191
10.2.1.2.1	On the Third Day: The First Sign in Cana (2:1–12)	191
10.2.1.2.2	One of Jesus' Jerusalem Signs: The Temple Clearing (2:13–22)	193
10.2.1.2.3	Jesus' Witness to Nicodemus (2:23–3:21)	197
10.2.1.2.4	John's Testimony (3:22–36)	200
10.2.1.2.5	Jesus and the Samaritan Woman (4:1–42)	201
10.2.1.2.6	The Second Sign in Cana: The Healing of the (Gentile) Official's Son (4:43–54)	205
10.2.1.2.7	Summary of the Cana Cycle	206
10.2.1.3	From Jerusalem to Bethany: The Festival Cycle: The Height of Jesus' Ministry to the Jews (5:1–10:42)	206
10.2.1.3.1	Another Jerusalem Sign: The Healing of the Lame Man (5:1–47)	206

10.2.1.3.2	The Feeding of the Multitude, the Walking on the Water, and the Bread of Life Discourse (6:1–71)	209
10.2.1.3.3	Summary of John's Narrative up to 6:71	213
10.2.1.3.4	Jesus at the Festival of Tabernacles (Part 1; 7:1–52)	214
10.2.1.3.5	Jesus at the Festival of Tabernacles (Part 2; 8:12–59)	219
10.2.1.3.6	Yet Another Jerusalem Sign: The Healing of the Man Born Blind (9:1–41)	223
10.2.1.3.7	The Good Shepherd Discourse and the Festival of Dedication (10:1–42)	225
10.2.1.4	From Bethany to Jerusalem: The Climactic Sign and Final Events in Jerusalem (11:1–12:36)	228
10.2.1.4.1	The Climactic Sign: The Raising of Lazarus (11:1–57)	228
10.2.1.4.2	The Anointing of Jesus at Bethany and the Triumphal Entry into Jerusalem (12:1–19)	230
10.2.1.4.3	The Coming of the Greeks (12:20–36)	232
10.2.1.5	Conclusion: The Jewish Rejection of the Messiah despite His Many Signs (12:37–50)	233
10.2.2	Act II: The Messiah's Passion and Preparation of His Own (13:1–20:31)	235
10.2.2.1	Jesus Anticipates His Exaltation: The Footwashing, the Farewell Discourse, and Jesus' Final Prayer (13:1–17:26)	235
10.2.2.1.1	The Cleansing of the New Messianic Community (13:1–30)	235
10.2.2.1.1.1	The Literal Cleansing: The Footwashing (13:1–17)	235
10.2.2.1.1.2	The Figurative Cleansing: The Removal of the Betrayer (13:18–30)	237
10.2.2.1.2	The Farewell Discourse Proper (13:31–16:33)	238
10.2.2.1.2.1	The Farewell Discourse (Part 1; 13:31–14:31)	240
10.2.2.1.2.2	The Farewell Discourse (Part 2; 15:1–16:33)	241
10.2.2.1.2.2.1	The Illustration of the Vine and the Branches (15:1–17)	241
10.2.2.1.2.2.2	The World's Hatred of Jesus' Followers (Part 1; 15:18–27)	242
10.2.2.1.2.2.3	The World's Hatred of Jesus' Followers (Part 2; 16:1–15)	245
10.2.2.1.2.2.4	The "Little While" (16:16–33)	245
10.2.2.1.3	Jesus' Final Prayer (17:1–26)	246
10.2.2.1.3.1	Jesus' Prayer for Himself (17:1–5)	246
10.2.2.1.3.2	Jesus' Prayer for His Disciples (17:6–19)	247
10.2.2.1.3.3	Jesus' Prayer for Later Generations of Believers (17:20–26)	248
10.2.2.2	Jesus Completes His Earthly Mission: The Passion Narrative and the Purpose of the Gospel (chaps. 18–20)	249
10.2.2.2.1	Jesus' Arrest and Peter's First Denial of Jesus (18:1–18)	249
10.2.2.2.2	Jesus' Hearing before Annas and Peter's Second and Third Denials of Jesus (18:19–27)	251
10.2.2.2.3	Jesus' Trial before Pilate (18:28–19:16a)	252
10.2.2.2.4	The Crucifixion and Burial of Jesus (19:16b–42)	254
10.2.2.2.5	The Empty Tomb and Jesus' Appearances to Mary Magdalene and the Eleven (20:1–29)	257
10.2.2.2.5.1	The Empty Tomb and Jesus' Appearance to Mary Magdalene (20:1–18)	257
10.2.2.2.5.2	Jesus' Appearances to the Eleven without and with Thomas (20:19–29)	259

10.2.2.3	Conclusion: Believe in Jesus the Messiah on Account of His Signs (20:30–31)	260
10.3	The Epilogue: Jesus' Third and Final Resurrection Appearance to the Disciples and His Commissioning of Peter and of "the Disciple Whom Jesus Loved" (21:1–25)	260
10.3.1	Jesus' Third and Final Resurrection Appearance to the Disciples (21:1–14)	260
10.3.2	The Commissioning of Peter and of "the Disciple Whom Jesus Loved" (21:15–23)	262
10.3.3	Conclusion: The Signature of "the Disciple Whom Jesus Loved" (21:24–25)	262

CHAPTER 5
A Literary-Theological Reading of John's Letters 263

11.	A Literary-Theological Reading of John's Letters	263
11.1	First John	263
11.1.1	Introduction (1:1–4)	263
11.1.2	The Departure of the Secessionists (1:5–2:27)	264
11.1.3	The Measure of True Love (2:28–3:24)	267
11.1.4	The Antichrists and the Love Commandment (4:1–5:12)	269
11.1.5	Purpose Statement and Conclusion (5:13–21)	270
11.2	Second John	271
11.2.1	Introduction (1–3)	271
11.2.2	Warning against Welcoming False Teachers (4–11)	271
11.2.3	Conclusion (12–13)	272
11.3	Third John	272
11.3.1	Introduction (1–4)	272
11.3.2	Commendation of Gaius and Demetrius, Condemnation of Diotrephes (5–12)	272
11.3.3	Conclusion (13–14)	272

PART 3
Major Themes in Johannine Theology 273

A. PROLEGOMENA

CHAPTER 6
John's Worldview and Use of Scripture 275

12.	John's Worldview	277
12.1	Introduction	277
12.1.1	Worldview, Cosmology, and the "Johannine Dualism"	277
12.1.2	The Johannine Worldview: Overview	279
12.2	The Cosmic Conflict between God and His Messiah vs. Satan and the World	281
12.2.1	Satan	281
12.2.2	The World	281
12.3	Major Contrasts in John's Worldview	282

12.3.1	Introduction	282
12.3.2	Light and Darkness	283
12.3.3	Life and Death	284
12.3.4	Flesh and Spirit	287
12.3.5	Above and Below	287
12.3.6	Truth and Falsehood	288
12.3.7	Love and Hate	289
12.3.8	Trust and Unbelief	292
12.4	John's Gospel as a Cosmic Drama	293
12.5	The Glory of God in Jesus	294
12.6	Johannine Eschatology	295
12.6.1	Introduction	295
12.6.2	Survey of Scholarship	295
12.6.3	Survey of the Johannine Material	297
12.7	Conclusion	298
13.	John's Use of Scripture	298
13.1	Introduction	298
13.2	The Use of the Old Testament in John's Gospel: Overview	299
13.2.1	Explicit Old Testament Quotations in John's Gospel	299
13.2.2	Introductory Formulas in John's Gospel	300
13.2.2.1	Survey Chart	300
13.2.2.2	Discussion	300
13.2.3	Old Testament Quotations in John and the Rest of the New Testament	301
13.2.3.1	Survey Chart	301
13.2.3.2	Discussion	302
13.2.4	Alignment of Old Testament Quotations in John's Gospel with the MT or the LXX	303
13.2.4.1	Survey Chart	303
13.2.4.2	Discussion	303
13.2.5	Attribution of Old Testament Quotes in John's Gospel and Old Testament Passages Cited	304
13.2.5.1	Survey Chart	304
13.2.5.2	Discussion	305
13.2.6	Old Testament Quotations in John's Gospel in Old Testament Order	305
13.2.6.1	Survey Chart	305
13.2.6.2	Discussion	306
13.2.7	Old Testament Allusions and Verbal Parallels in John's Gospel	307
13.2.7.1	Survey Chart	307
13.2.7.2	Discussion	309
13.3	Conclusion	310

B. THE END (PURPOSE; 20:30–31)

CHAPTER 7

The Messiah and His Signs 311

14.	The Messiah	312
14.1	Background and Overview	312
14.1.1	Terminology	312

14.1.2	The Messiah in the Old Testament and Second Temple Literature	313
14.1.2.1	Old Testament References to "the Lord's Anointed"	313
14.1.2.2	The Old Testament Messianic Hope	313
14.1.2.3	The Second Temple Period	314
14.1.3	The Messiah in the New Testament	314
14.1.3.1	Overview	314
14.1.3.2	The Four Gospels	315
14.1.4	Conclusion	315
14.2	Preliminary Considerations in the Study of John's Christology	316
14.2.1	The Centrality of Christology in John's Gospel and Letters	316
14.2.2	The Limitations of a "Titles of Christ" Approach	316
14.2.3	Toward a Holistic Approach: Climactic Fulfillment in Jesus	317
14.3	Major Aspects of John's Portrayal of Jesus as Messiah	317
14.3.1	The Word, the Light	317
14.3.2	Messiah, Elijah, the Prophet	318
14.3.3	Lamb of God, King of Israel	318
14.3.4	Popular Messianic Expectations	318
14.3.5	Signs	319
14.3.6	The Coming One	319
14.4	The Narrative Unfolding of John's Presentation of Jesus as Messiah	320
14.4.1	The Introduction and the Cana Cycle: Could This Be the Messiah?	320
14.4.2	The Festival Cycle: Popular Messianic Expectations and Misconceptions	320
14.4.3	The Transition from the Book of Signs to the Book of Exaltation	321
14.4.4	The Purpose Statement	321
14.4.5	First, Second, and Third John	322
15.	The Signs	323
15.1	Introduction	323
15.2	The Six Commonly Acknowledged Signs in John's Gospel	324
15.3	Signs in the Old Testament	325
15.4	Signs in John's Gospel	326
15.5	Possible Additional Signs in John's Gospel	329
15.6	Implications for the Structure of John's Gospel	333
15.7	Conclusion	335

C. THE BEGINNING (INTRODUCTION; 1:1–18)

CHAPTER 8
The Word: Creation and New Creation 336

16.	New Creation: The Word, Life, and Light	337
16.1	Introduction	337
16.2	Creation through the Word and the Word Made Flesh	338
16.3	Life and Light	341
16.3.1	Introduction	341
16.3.1.1	References to Life in John's Gospel and Letters	342
16.3.1.2	References to Light in John's Gospel and Letters	344
16.3.1.3	Observations Regarding the Use of Life and Light Terminology in John's Gospel and Letters	345

16.3.1.4	The Old Testament Backdrop for the Life and Light Motifs in John's Gospel and Letters.	347
16.3.1.5	Conclusion	348
16.4	Creation and New Creation Theology in the Book of Signs	349
16.4.1	The First Week of Jesus' Ministry	349
16.4.2	The New Birth	350
16.4.3	The Sabbath Controversy	350
16.5	Creation and New Creation Theology in the Passion Narrative	351
16.5.1	Introduction	351
16.5.2	Possible Instances of the New Creation Motif in the Passion Narrative	352
16.5.3	The Climax of New Creation Theology in Jesus' Resurrection	353
16.6	Conclusion	353

CHAPTER 9
God: Father, Son, and Spirit ... 355

17.	John, Jesus, and Jewish Monotheism	356
17.1	John's Portrayal of Jesus in the Context of Jewish Monotheism	356
17.2	Implications for John's Gospel	360
18.	God	361
18.1	Introduction	361
18.2	The Introduction to John's Gospel	361
18.3	The Book of Signs	363
18.3.1	The Cana Cycle	363
18.3.2	The Festival Cycle	364
18.3.3	Transition from the Book of Signs to the Book of Exaltation	366
18.4	The Book of Exaltation	366
18.4.1	The Farewell Discourse	366
18.4.2	The Passion Narrative	366
18.5	First, Second, and Third John	367
18.6	Summary	368
19.	The Father	370
19.1	Introduction	370
19.2	The Introduction to John's Gospel	371
19.3	The Book of Signs	372
19.3.1	The Cana Cycle	372
19.3.2	The Festival Cycle	372
19.3.3	Transition from the Book of Signs to the Book of Exaltation	375
19.4	The Book of Exaltation	375
19.4.1	The Farewell Discourse	376
19.4.2	The Final Prayer	378
19.4.3	The Passion Narrative	379
19.5	First, Second, and Third John	379
19.6	Summary	379
20.	The Son	380
20.1	Introduction	380
20.2	One and Only Son	381
20.3	Son of God	382

20.3.1	Introduction	382
20.3.2	Jesus' Calling of His First Disciples and the Cana Cycle	383
20.3.3	The Festival Cycle	384
20.3.4	Transition from the Book of Signs to the Book of Exaltation	385
20.3.5	Conclusion	386
20.3.6	First John	386
20.4	Son of Man	386
20.4.1	Introduction	386
20.4.2	Jesus' Calling of His First Disciples	387
20.4.3	The Cana Cycle	387
20.4.4	The Festival Cycle	388
20.4.5	Transition from the Book of Signs to the Book of Exaltation	389
20.4.6	The Farewell Discourse	389
20.5	The Son	390
20.5.1	Introduction	390
20.5.2	The Cana Cycle	390
20.5.3	The Festival Cycle	390
20.5.4	The Farewell Discourse	392
20.5.5	First, Second, and Third John	392
20.6	Summary	392
21.	The Spirit	393
21.1	Introduction	393
21.2	The Book of Signs	393
21.2.1	John's and Jesus' Early Ministry	393
21.2.2	The Cana Cycle	393
21.2.3	The Festival Cycle	394
21.3	The Book of Exaltation	395
21.3.1	The Farewell Discourse	395
21.3.2	The Commissioning Scene	399
21.4	First John	400
21.5	Summary	402

CHAPTER 10
Salvation History: Jesus' Fulfillment of Festal Symbolism 403

22.	Salvation History	403
22.1	Introduction	403
22.2	Creation as the Beginning of the Covenant	405
22.3	God's Manifestation through the Law, the Tabernacle, and the Temple	406
22.4	The Coming of "A Voice Crying in the Wilderness"	407
22.5	The Manifestation of God's Glory, Grace, and Covenant-Keeping Faithfulness in Christ	408
22.6	The Offering of Isaac and God's "One and Only Son"	409
22.7	The Message of Isaiah and Jewish Unbelief	410
22.8	Davidic Typology	411
22.9	Conclusion	412
23.	Jesus' Fulfillment of Festal Symbolism	413
23.1	Introduction	413

23.2	Jesus' Fulfillment of Passover Symbolism	414
23.2.1	Jesus the "Lamb of God"	414
23.2.2	Jesus the New Temple	416
23.2.3	Jesus the Bread of Life	416
23.2.4	The Prophecy of Jesus' Vicarious Death and His Anointing for Burial	417
23.2.5	Jesus' Celebration of the Passover with the Representatives of His New Messianic Community	417
23.2.6	Jesus the Passover Sacrifice	419
23.3	Jesus' Fulfillment of Tabernacles Symbolism	420
23.4	Conclusion	422
24.	Jesus as the New Temple	422
24.1	The Johannine Temple Motif and the Historical Setting of John's Gospel	422
24.2	Jesus as Fulfillment of Temple and Related Symbolism	425
24.2.1	The Word Made Flesh: The New Tabernacle	425
24.2.2	Jesus and the Open Heaven: The New House of God	427
24.2.3	Clearing the Sanctuary: The New Temple	427
24.2.4	The Inadequacy of Physical Locations of Worship: The New Worship	429
24.2.5	Jesus at the Festival of Tabernacles: The New Provision	430
24.2.6	Jesus at the Festival of Dedication: The New Liberation	431
24.3	Jesus as the Proper Focus of Worship	431
24.3.1	Giving Sight to the Blind: A New Way of Seeing	431
24.3.2	Eliciting Faith from the Skeptic: Seeing and Believing	431
24.4	And What of the Temple?	432
24.4.1	The Destruction of the Temple as a Symbol of Jewish Religious Identity	432
24.4.2	A Telling Silence: The Setting Aside of the Temple	433
24.4.3	The Temple for the Nations	433
24.5	Conclusion	434

CHAPTER 11

The Cosmic Trial Motif: The World, the Jews, and the Witnesses to Jesus 436

25.	The Cosmic Trial Motif	437
25.1	Introduction	437
25.2	Truth and the Cosmic Trial Motif in John's Gospel	437
25.3	Jesus' Witness to the Truth: His Trial before Pilate	441
25.3.1	The Jewish leaders	441
25.3.2	Pilate	444
25.3.3	Jesus	447
25.3.4	Conclusion	452
25.4	The Cosmic Trial Motif in John's Letters	454

CHAPTER 12

The New Messianic Community: Divine Sovereignty and Human Responsibility 457

26.	Divine Election and Predestination	458
26.1	Introduction	458
26.2	Divine Sovereignty and Human Responsibility	458

26.3	The Introduction to John's Gospel	460
26.4	The Book of Signs and the Book of Exaltation	461
26.5	Conclusion	463
27.	Sin and Judgment	464
27.1	Sin	464
27.1.1	The Gospel of John	464
27.1.1.1	The Book of Signs	464
27.1.1.1.1	Jesus the "Lamb of God"	464
27.1.1.1.2	The Cana Cycle	464
27.1.1.1.3	The Festival Cycle	465
27.1.1.2	The Book of Exaltation	466
27.1.1.2.1	The Farewell Discourse	466
27.1.1.2.2	The Passion Narrative	466
27.1.2	First John	466
27.1.3	Conclusion	468
27.2	Divine Judgment	468
28.	Believing and the New Birth	470
28.1	Introduction	470
28.2	References to Believing and the New Birth in the Introduction to John's Gospel	471
28.2.1	Believing	471
28.2.2	Born of God	472
28.2.3	Conclusion	473
28.3	References to Believing and the New Birth in the Book of Signs and the Book of Exaltation	473
28.3.1	The Book of Signs	473
28.3.1.1	The Cana Cycle	473
28.3.1.1.1	Believing	473
28.3.1.1.2	Born from Above/Again	474
28.3.1.2	The Festival Cycle	476
28.3.1.3	The Transition between the Book of Signs and the Book of Exaltation	477
28.3.2	The Book of Exaltation	478
28.3.2.1	The Farewell Discourse	478
28.3.2.2	The Passion Narrative	478
28.3.3	Conclusion	478
28.4	References to Believing and the New Birth in 1 John	479
28.5	Christian Assurance in John's Gospel and Letters	480
29.	The New Messianic Community	481
29.1	Johannine Ecclesiology	481
29.2	The Characterization of Jesus' Followers in John's Gospel	482
29.2.1	The Term *Mathētēs* Designating the First Followers of Jesus in John's Gospel	483
29.2.2	The Twelve	485
29.2.3	The Widening of the Term *Mathētēs* in John's Gospel	486
29.3	The Johannine Characterization of Individual Disciples	490
29.3.1	General Observations	491
29.3.2	Peter and "the Disciple Whom Jesus Loved"	491

29.3.3	Minor Characters	497
29.3.4	Women in John's Gospel	499
29.4	Corporate Metaphors	500
29.4.1	The Shepherd and His Flock	500
29.4.2	The Vine and the Branches	502
29.5	The Disciples' Task	504
29.5.1	The "Greater Works"	504
29.5.2	Following and Being Sent	505
29.6	Conclusion	507

D. THE MIDDLE (PREAMBLE TO PART TWO; 13:1–3)

CHAPTER 13
The Johannine Love Ethic 509

30.	John's Moral Vision	510
30.1	Introduction: Does John Have an Ethic, and, If So, What Is "Wrong" with It?	510
30.2	John's Ethic of Love: Introduction	514
30.3	The Contours of John's Moral Vision	516
30.3.1	Problems with an "Incarnational Angle" on John's Moral Vision	516
30.3.2	John's Love Ethic in the Farewell Discourse	518
30.3.3	John's Love Ethic in Its Larger Context	521
30.3.4	The Interface between Love and Mission	522
30.4	Conclusion	523

CHAPTER 14
John's Theology of the Cross 525

31.	The Nature of Jesus' Coming	526
31.1	Introduction	526
31.2	Coming and Going and Descent–Ascent	526
31.3	The Son of Man	529
31.4	Conclusion	531
32.	The Nature of Jesus' Work	532
32.1	Introduction	532
32.2	Narrative Survey	532
32.3	Revelation and/or Salvation	534
32.4	Implications	537
32.5	Conclusion	538

CHAPTER 15
John's Trinitarian Mission Theology 539

33.	John and Mission	539
33.1	Introduction	539
33.2	The Father	540
33.3	The Son	540
33.4	The Spirit	542
33.5	Father, Son, and Spirit: The Three Persons of the Godhead United in One Mission	543
33.6	Conclusion	544

PART 4
Johannine Theology and the Canon of Scripture 547

CHAPTER 16
The Theology of John and Other New Testament Voices 549

34. The Theology of John Compared to the Synoptics 550
   34.1 Introduction 550
   34.2 The Historical Value of John's Gospel in Relation to the Synoptics . . . 550
      34.2.1 Introduction: Enlightenment Doubts 550
      34.2.2 The Rehabilitation of John's Historical Reliability in Recent Scholarship 551
   34.3 The Literary Relationship between John's Gospel and the Synoptics 553
      34.3.1 Survey of Scholarship 553
      34.3.2 John's Effort to Interpret, Develop, and Supplement the Synoptic Pattern 555
         34.3.2.1 Introduction 555
         34.3.2.2 List of Johannine Transpositions of the Synoptic Accounts 556
         34.3.2.3 Discussion of Transpositions 557
         34.3.2.4 Significance of Transposition-by-an-Eyewitness Proposal 561
      34.3.3 Conclusion 563
35. Johannine and Pauline Theology and the Theology of the Other New Testament Writings 563
   35.1 Relationship with the Pauline Writings 563
   35.2 Relationship with the Other New Testament Writings 564

Conclusion 566
Bibliography 568
Scripture Index 615
Index of Extrabiblical Literature 640
Subject Index 644
Author Index 647

List of Figures

1.1	The Hermeneutical Triad	42
1.2	A Working Model of Engaging in Biblical/Johannine Theology	46
2.1	The Witness of John the Baptist and "the Disciple Whom Jesus Loved"	73
2.2	The Witness of Jesus and of "the Disciple Whom Jesus Loved" and Peter	74
2.3	Chronology of Jesus' Ministry in John's Gospel	80–81
12.1	Series of Johannine Contrasts and Associated Motifs	283
12.2	"Life" and "Kingdom" in the Synoptics and in the Johannine Writings	286
12.3	The Paradoxical Nature of the "Love" and "Hate" Contrasts in John's Gospel	290
12.4	Lack of Love for Believers as Evidence for Lack of Regeneration in 1 John	291
13.1	Introductory Formulas in John's Gospel	300
13.2	OT Quotations in John and the Rest of the NT	301–302
13.3	Alignment of OT Quotations in John with MT or LXX	303
13.4	Attribution of OT Quotations in John's Gospel	304
13.5	OT Quotations in John's Gospel in OT Order	305–306
13.6	OT Allusions and Verbal Parallels in John's Gospel	307–309
16.1	Creation and New Creation Theology in John's Gospel	349
16.2	New Creation Theology and Salvation History in John's Gospel	354
20.1	Jesus as the Son in John's Gospel and Letters	380
20.2	References to Jesus as the Son of God in John's Gospel	383
20.3	References to the Son of Man in John's Gospel	387
21.1	References to the Spirit in John's Gospel	395
22.1	Jesus and Salvation History in John's Gospel	405
23.1	References to Jewish Festivals in John's Gospel	413
28.1	Evidence for a Person's Having Been "Born of God" in 1 John	480
29.1	Significant Women Characters in John's Gospel	499
29.2	Inclusios regarding Specific Individuals in John's Gospel	500
34.1	Comparison between John's Gospel and the Synoptic Pattern	556–557
34.2	The Major Discourses of Jesus in John's Gospel	560

Series Preface

The Biblical Theology of the New Testament series consists of eight distinct volumes covering the entire New Testament. Each volume is devoted to an in-depth exploration of a given New Testament writing, or group of writings, within the context of the theology of the New Testament, and ultimately of the entire Bible. While each corpus requires an approach that is suitable for the writing(s) studied, all volumes include:

(1) a survey of recent scholarship and of the state of research
(2) a treatment of the relevant introductory issues
(3) a thematic commentary following the narrative flow of the document(s)
(4) a treatment of important individual themes
(5) discussions of the relationship between a particular writing and the rest of the New Testament and the Bible

While Biblical Theology is a relatively new academic discipline and one that has often been hindered by questionable presuppositions, doubtful methodology, and/or flawed execution, the field is one of the most promising avenues of biblical and theological research today. In essence, Biblical Theology engages in the study of the biblical texts while giving careful consideration to the historical setting in which a given piece of writing originated. It seeks to locate and relate the contributions of the respective biblical documents along the lines of the continuum of God's salvation-historical program centered in the coming and salvific work of Christ. It also endeavors to ground the theological exploration of a given document in a close reading of the respective text(s), whether narrative, discourse, or some other type of literature.

By providing in-depth studies of the diverse, yet complementary perspectives of the New Testament writings, the Biblical Theology of the New Testament series aims to make a significant contribution to the study of the major interrelated themes of Scripture in a holistic, context-sensitive, and spiritually nurturing manner. Each volume is written by a scholar who has written a major commentary or monograph on the corpus covered. The generous page allotment allows for an in-depth investigation. While coming from diverse academic backgrounds and institutional affiliations, the contributors share a commitment to an evangelical faith and a respect for the authority of Scripture. They also have in common a conviction that the canon of Scripture is ultimately unified, not contradictory.

In addition to contributing to the study of individual New Testament writings and to the study of the New Testament and ultimately of Scripture as a whole, the series also seeks to make a methodological contribution, showing how Biblical Theology ought to be conducted. In each case, the way in which the volume is conceived reflects careful consideration of the nature of a given piece or body of writings.

The complex interrelationships between the three so-called "Synoptic Gospels"; the two-volume nature of Luke–Acts; the relationship between John's gospel, letters, and the book of Revelation; the thirteen letters making up the Pauline corpus; and the theologies of Peter, James, and Jude, as well as Hebrews—each of which presents unique challenges and opportunities.

In the end, it is hoped that the volumes will pay tribute to the multifaceted nature of divine revelation contained in Scripture. As G. B. Caird put it:

> The question we must ask is not whether these books all say the same thing, but whether they all bear witness to the same Jesus and through him to the many splendoured wisdom of the one God.... We shall neither attempt to press all our witnesses into a single mould nor captiously complain that one seems at some points deficient in comparison with another. What we shall do is rejoice that God has seen fit to establish His gospel at the mouth of so many independent witnesses. The music of the New Testament choir is not written to be sung in unison.[1]

In this spirit, the contributors offer their work as a humble aid to a greater appreciation of the magnificent scriptural symphony of God.

Andreas J. Köstenberger, series editor
Wake Forest, NC

---

1. G. B. Caird, *New Testament Theology*, compl. and ed. L. D. Hurst (Oxford: Clarendon, 1995), 24.

Author's Preface

The prospect of writing a Johannine theology was overwhelming at the outset. Only when I resolved to start with the text of John's gospel itself rather than with the massive amount of available secondary literature on the subject did the burden lift and the task appear more manageable. Indeed, the decision to work from the gospel and to move outward to incorporate helpful insights from the secondary literature proved critical.[2]

This volume on Johannine theology represents a kind of sequel to my Baker Exegetical Commentary on John and incorporates some material previously published in monographs and essays.[3] In light of space limitations I restricted myself in "Volume 1" (the commentary) largely to dealing with exegetical matters. Now the time has come to explore John's theology in a separate volume that builds on this interpretive spadework.

The competition for this work in the English-speaking world is not great. Unlike in Pauline studies, where several extensive works are available,[4] there is no comparable volume in the field of Johannine research. Moody Smith's *Theology of the Gospel of John* (Cambridge: Cambridge Univ. Press, 1995) is fairly brief and does not ground the discussion of John's theology in a detailed reading of the Johannine material.

Among the works that bear an affinity to the present one is Craig Koester's *Word of Life: The Theology of John's Gospel* (Grand Rapids: Eerdmans, 2008), though it is more introductory in nature. Helpful surveys are W. Hall Harris, "A Theology of John's Writings," in *A Biblical Theology of the New Testament* (ed. Roy Zuck; Chicago: Moody Press, 1994); W. Robert Cook, *The Theology of John* (Chicago: Moody Press, 1979); and George Barker Stevens, *The Johannine Theology* (New York: Scribner, 1894).

Other useful resources include Michael J. Taylor, ed., *A Companion to John* (New York: Alba House, 1977); Leon Morris, *Jesus Is the Christ* (Grand Rapids: Eerdmans, 1989); Stephen Smalley, *John: Evangelist and Interpreter* (Downers Grove, IL: InterVarsity Press, 1998); and Warren Carter, *John: Storyteller, Interpreter, Evangelist* (Peabody, MA: Hendrickson, 2006). Yet there is no full-fledged Johannine theology available of which I am aware.

At the outset, I would like to express my gratitude to the Lord Jesus Christ for seeking and finding me when I was far away from him and lost in my sin. I am

---

2. A similar approach is found in Adolf Schlatter's *New Testament Theology: The History of the Christ* and *The Theology of the Apostles* (trans. Andreas J. Köstenberger; Grand Rapids: Baker, 1997 and 1999), which in many ways continues to be exemplary in its synthetic grasp and its profundity of theological insight.

3. This is acknowledged in appropriate footnotes throughout this volume. Note that many of my publications are posted at www.biblicalfoundations.org, including many reviews of books cited in this work.

4. James D. G. Dunn, *The Theology of Paul the Apostle* (Grand Rapids: Eerdmans, 1997); Thomas R. Schreiner, *Paul, Apostle of God's Glory in Christ: A Pauline Theology* (Downers Grove, IL: InterVarsity Press, 2001).

forever grateful and have chosen to devote the rest of my life to service of him who died for me on the cross for the forgiveness of my sins. This book, and any others, are a reflection of my devotion to him together with all "those who call on the Lord out of a pure heart" (2 Tim 2:22).

I am also grateful for the support of my academic institution, Southeastern Seminary, and its generous sabbatical policy, for it is during such a sabbatical that much of this book was completed. Sabbaticals are precious, because they afford the scholar the opportunity to reflect more profoundly on Scripture and on their work while stepping back from day-to-day responsibilities, and this kind of reflection was just what was called for by this volume.

I would like to express my gratitude to my dear wife and children, who are my fellow pilgrims on this earthly journey and a precious stewardship from God. Thanks are also due my parents, Hannes and Maria; my parents-in-law, Bob and Mary Gerrard; and my church, Richland Creek Community Church, and here in particular the dedicated pastoral staff and the Kingdom Families Sunday School class.

Finally, Zondervan is to be commended for their vision in commissioning this project and the entire Biblical Theology of the New Testament (BTNT) series. I am especially grateful to Stan Gundry and Katya Covrett for their support, Verlyn Verbrugge for his editorial work, and the other contributors to the BTNT series. May these volumes nurture many serious students of Scripture as they enter more deeply into the theology of the New Testament.

Soli Deo gloria.

Abbreviations

2 Bar.	*2 Baruch*
4 Bar.	*4 Baruch*
2 Clem.	*2 Clement*
1 En.	*1 Enoch*
AB	Anchor Bible
ABD	*Anchor Bible Dictionary*
ABRL	Anchor Bible Reference Library
ACCSNT	Ancient Christian Commentary on Scripture: New Testament
AcT	*Acta theologica*
Ag. Ap.	*Against Apion* (Josephus)
AGJU	Arbeiten zur Geschichte des antiken Judentums und des Urchristentums
AnBib	Analecta biblica
Ant.	*Jewish Antiquities* (Josephus)
ANTC	Abingdon New Testament Commentary
Apoc. Ab.	*Apocalypse of Abraham*
ATANT	Abhandlungen zur Theologie des Alten und Neuen Testaments
AThR	*Anglican Theological Review*
b. Bek.	Babylonian Talmud, *Bekorot*
b. ʿErub.	Babylonian Talmud, *ʿErubin*
b. Ker.	Babylonian Talmud, *Kerithot*
b. Ketub.	Babylonian Talmud, *Ketubbot*
b. Meg.	Babylonian Talmud, *Megillah*
b. Sukkah	Babylonian Talmud, *Sukkah*
b. Taʿan.	Babylonian Talmud, *Taʿanit*
b. Yebam.	Babylonian Talmud, *Yebamot*
BBB	Bonner biblische Beiträge
BBET	Beiträge zur biblischen Exegese und Theologie
BBR	*Bulletin for Biblical Research*
BDF	Blass, Debrunner, Funk, *A Greek Grammar of the New Testament*
BECNT	Baker Exegetical Commentary on the New Testament
BETL	Bibliotheca ephemeridum theologicarum lovaniensium
BETS	*Bulletin of the Evangelical Theological Society*
BHT	Beiträge zur historischen Theologie
Bib	*Biblica*
BibLeb	*Bibel und Leben*
BIS	Biblical Interpretation Series
BJRL	*Bulletin of the John Rylands University Library of Manchester*
BJS	Brown Judaic Studies
BR	*Biblical Research*

BRev	*Bible Review*
BSac	*Bibliotheca sacra*
BSL	Biblical Studies Library
BT	*The Bible Translator*
BTB	*Biblical Theology Bulletin*
BTNT	Biblical Theology of the New Testament series
BZ	*Biblische Zeitschrift*
CBET	Contributions to Biblical Exegesis and Theology
CBQ	*Catholic Biblical Quarterly*
CBQMS	Catholic Biblical Quarterly Monograph Series
ConBNT	Coniectanea biblica: New Testament series
CS	*Chicago Studies*
CT	*Christianity Today*
CTR	*Criswell Theological Review*
CurBR	*Currents in Biblical Research*
CurTM	*Currents in Theology and Mission*
DBSJ	*Detroit Baptist Seminary Journal*
Did.	*Didache*
DSB	Daily Study Bible
DSS	Dead Sea Scrolls
EBib	Etudes bibliques
EBS	Encountering Biblical Studies
EDNT	*Exegetical Dictionary of the New Testament*
EMS	Evangelical Missiological Society
EMSS	Evangelical Missiological Society Series
ERT	*Evangelical Review of Theology*
EstBib	*Estudios bíblicos*
ESV	English Standard Version
ETL	*Ephemerides theologicae lovanienses*
EvQ	*Evangelical Quarterly*
EvT	*Evangelische Theologie*
ExpTim	*Expository Times*
FAT	Forschungen zum Alten Testament
FRLANT	Forschungen zur Religion und Literatur des Alten und Neuen Testaments
GNTE	Guides to New Testament Exegesis
Haer.	*Against Heresies* (Irenaeus)
HBS	Herders Biblische Studien
HBT	*Horizons in Biblical Theology*
HCSB	Holman Christian Standard Bible
Hist. eccl.	*Ecclesiastical History* (Eusebius)
HNT	Handbuch zum Neuen Testament
HTKNT	Herders theologischer Kommentar zum Neuen Testament

HTR	*Harvard Theological Review*
HUCA	*Hebrew Union College Annual*
ICC	International Critical Commentary
IKZ	*Internationale kirchliche Zeitschrift*
Int	*Interpretation*
IRT	Issues in Religion and Theology
ISV	International Standard Version
ITQ	*Irish Theological Quarterly*
IVPNTC	InterVarsity Press New Testament Commentary
J.W.	*Jewish War* (Josephus)
JBL	*Journal of Biblical Literature*
JETS	*Journal of the Evangelical Theological Society*
JSNT	*Journal for the Study of the New Testament*
JSNTSup	*Journal for the Study of the New Testament: Supplement Series*
JSOT	*Journal for the Study of the Old Testament*
JSOTSup	*Journal for the Study of the Old Testament: Supplement Series*
JTS	*Journal of Theological Studies*
Jub.	*Jubilees*
KD	*Kerygma und Dogma*
LEC	Library of Early Christianity
Lev. Rab.	*Leviticus Rabbah*
Life	*Life* (Josephus)
LNTS	Library of New Testament Studies
LS	*Louvain Studies*
LXX	Septuagint (Greek translation of the OT)
m. ʾAbot	Mishnah, *ʾAbot*
m. Ber.	Mishnah, *Berakot*
m. ʾOhal.	Mishnah, *ʾOhalot*
m. Pesaḥ.	Mishnah, *Pesaḥim*
m. Roš Haš.	Mishnah, *Roš Haššanah*
m. Šabb.	Mishnah, *Šabbat*
m. Sukkah	Mishnah, *Sukkah*
m. Yebam.	Mishnah, *Yebamot*
Mart. Pol.	*Martyrdom of Polycarp*
MNTC	Moffatt New Testament Commentary
ModTheol	*Modern Theology*
MT	Masoretic Test
NABPR	National Association of Baptist Professors of Religion
NAC	New American Commentary
NASB	New American Standard Bible
NDBT	*New Dictionary of Biblical Theology*
Neot	*Neotestamentica*
NET	New English Translation

NIBC	New International Bible Commentary
NICNT	New International Commentary on the New Testament
NICOT	New International Commentary on the Old Testament
NIDNTT	*New International Dictionary of New Testament Theology*
NIV	New International Version
NIVAC	NIV Application Commentary
NKJV	New King James Version
NKZ	*Neue kirchliche Zeitschrift*
NLT	New Living Translation
NovT	*Novum Testamentum*
NovTSup	Novum Testamentum Supplements
NRSV	New Revised Standard Version
NS	New Series
NSBT	New Studies in Biblical Theology
NTAbh	Neutestamentliche Abhandlungen
NTD	Das Neue Testament Deutsch
NTG	New Testament Guides
NTL	New Testament Library
NTOA	Novum Testamentum et Orbis Antiquus
NTS	*New Testament Studies*
NTSI	The New Testament and the Scriptures of Israel
OBO	Orbis biblicus et orientalis
Pesiq. Rab.	*Pesiqta Rabbati*
PNTC	Pillar New Testament Commentary
Pss. Sol.	*Psalms of Solomon*
QD	Quaestiones disputatae
Rab. Lev.	*Rabbah Leviticus*
RB	*Revue biblique*
RechBib	Recherches bibliques
ResQ	*Restoration Quarterly*
RSV	Revised Standard Version
RTR	*Reformed Theological Review*
SANT	Studien zum Alten und Neuen Testament
SB	La Sainte Bible
SBET	*Scottish Bulletin of Evangelical Theology*
SBJT	*Southern Baptist Journal of Theology*
SBL	Society of Biblical Literature
SBLABib	Society of Biblical Literature Academica Biblica
SBLDS	Society of Biblical Literature Dissertation Series
SBLMS	Society of Biblical Literature Monograph Series
SBLRBS	Society of Biblical Literature Resources for Biblical Study
SBLSBS	Society of Biblical Literature Sources for Biblical Studies
SBLSymS	Society of Biblical Literature Symposium Series

SBS	Stuttgarter Bibelstudien
SBT	Studies in Biblical Theology
SBTS	Southern Baptist Theological Seminary
Scr	*Scripture*
SE	*Studia Evangelica*
SHR	Studies in the History of Religion
Sib. Or.	*Sibylline Oracles*
SJT	*Scottish Journal of Theology*
SNTSMS	Society for New Testament Studies Monograph Series
SNTU	*Studien zur neutestamentlichen Umwelt*
SP	Sacra pagina
T. Abr.	*Testament of Abraham*
T. Benj.	*Testament of Benjamin*
T. Jos.	*Testament of Joseph*
T. Jud.	*Testament of Judah*
t. Sukkah	*Tosefta Sukkah*
TDNT	*Theological Dictionary of the New Testament*
Them	*Themelios*
ThTo	*Theology Today*
TNIV	Today's New International Version
TNTC	Tyndale New Testament Commentary
TOTC	Tyndale Old Testament Commentary
TrinJ	*Trinity Journal*
TS	*Theological Studies*
TU	Texte und Untersuchungen
TynBul	*Tyndale Bulletin*
TZ	*Theologische Zeitschrift*
VE	*Vox Evangelica*
Vir. ill.	*De viris illustribus* (Jerome)
VT	*Vetus Testamentum*
WBC	Word Biblical Commentary
WF	Wege der Forschung
WMANT	Wissenschaftliche Monographien zum Alten und Neuen Testament
WTJ	*Westminster Theological Journal*
WUNT	Wissenschaftliche Untersuchungen zum Neuen Testament
y. Ber.	Jerusalem Talmud, *Berakot*
y. Sanh.	Jerusalem Talmud, *Sanhedrin*
ZIBBC	*Zondervan Illustrated Bible Backgrounds Commentary*
ZKT	*Zeitschrift für katholische Theologie*
ZNW	*Zeitschrift für die neutestamentliche Wissenschaft*
ZRGG	*Zeitschrift fur Religions- und Geistesgeschichte*
ZTK	*Zeitschrift für Theologie und Kirche*

Part 1

The Historical Framework for Johannine Theology

Chapter 1

JOHANNINE THEOLOGY AND THE HISTORICAL SETTING OF JOHN'S GOSPEL AND LETTERS

BIBLIOGRAPHY

Bauckham, Richard, ed. *The Gospels for All Christians: Rethinking the Gospel Audiences.* Grand Rapids: Eerdmans, 1998. Idem. *Jesus and the Eyewitnesses: The Gospels as Eyewitness Testimony.* Grand Rapids: Eerdmans, 2006. **Blomberg, Craig L.** *The Historical Reliability of John's Gospel.* Leicester, UK: Inter-Varsity Press, 2002. **Bockmuehl, Markus N. A.** *Seeing the Word: Refocusing New Testament Study.* Studies in Theological Interpretation. Grand Rapids: Baker, 2006. **Warren Carter.** *John and Empire: Initial Explorations.* London: T&T Clark, 2008. **Cook, W. Robert.** *The Theology of John.* Chicago: Moody Press, 1979. **Hengel, Martin.** *Die johanneische Frage.* WUNT 67. Tübingen: Mohr-Siebeck, 1993. Idem. "Das Johannesevangelium als Quelle für die Geschichte des antiken Judentums." Pp. 293–334 in *Judaica, Hellenistica et Christiana: Kleine Schriften II.* WUNT 109. Tübingen: Mohr-Siebeck, 1999. Idem. "Eye-Witness Memory and the Writing of the Gospels." Pp. 70–96 in *The Written Gospel.* Ed. Markus Bockmuehl and Donald A. Hagner. Cambridge: Cambridge University Press, 2001. **Hill, Charles E.** *The Johannine Corpus in the Early Church.* Oxford/New York: Oxford University Press, 2004. **Hoehner, Harold W.** *Chronological Aspects of the Life of Christ.* Grand Rapids: Zondervan, 1977. Idem. "Chronology." Pp. 118–22 in *Dictionary of Jesus and the Gospels.* Ed. Joel B. Green, Scot McKnight, and I. Howard Marshall. Downers Grove, IL: InterVarsity Press, 1992. **Jackson, Howard M.** "Ancient Self-Referential Conventions and Their Implications for the Authorship and Integrity of the Gospel of John." *JTS* 50 (1999): 1–34. **Kealy, Seán P.** *John's Gospel and the History of Biblical Interpretation.* 2 vols. Mellen Biblical Press Series 60a–b. Lewiston, NY: Mellen, 2002. **Keefer, Kyle.** *The Branches of the Gospel of John: The Reception of the Fourth Gospel in the Early Church.* LNTS 332. London: T&T Clark, 2006. **Keener, Craig S.** *The Gospel of John: A Commentary.* 2 vols. Peabody, MA: Hendrickson, 2003. **Klink, Edward W. III.** *The Sheep of the Fold: The Audience and Origin of the Gospel of John.* SNTSMS 141. Cambridge: Cambridge University Press, 2007. **Koester, Craig R.** *The Word of Life: A Theology of John's Gospel.* Grand Rapids: Eerdmans, 2008. **Köstenberger, Andreas J.** "John." Pp. 1–216 in *Zondervan Illustrated Bible Backgrounds Commentary.* Ed. Clinton E. Arnold. Vol. 2: *John–Acts.* Grand Rapids: Zondervan,

2002. Idem. "Early Doubts of the Apostolic Authorship of the Fourth Gospel in the History of Modern Biblical Criticism." Pp. 17–47 in *Studies on John and Gender: A Decade of Scholarship*. Studies in Biblical Literature 38. New York: Peter Lang, 2001. **Malatesta, Edward**. *St. John's Gospel 1920–1965*. AnBib 32. Rome: Pontifical Biblical Institute, 1967. **Morris, Leon**. *Studies in the Fourth Gospel*. Grand Rapids: Eerdmans, 1969. **Stevens, George B.** *The Johannine Theology: A Study of the Doctrinal Contents of the Gospel and Epistles of the Apostle John*. New York: Scribner, 1894. **Taylor, Michael J.**, ed. *A Companion to John: Readings in Johannine Theology (John's Gospel and Epistles)*. New York: Alba House, 1977. **Thatcher, Tom**, ed. *What We Have Heard from the Beginning: The Past, Present, and Future of Johannine Studies*. Waco, TX: Baylor University Press, 2007. Idem. *Greater than Caesar: Christology and Empire in the Fourth Gospel*. Minneapolis: Fortress, 2009. **Van Belle, Gilbert**. *Johannine Bibliography 1966–1985: A Cumulative Bibliography on the Fourth Gospel*. BETL 132. Leuven: Leuven University Press/Peeters, 1988.

1 Johannine and Biblical Theology

1.1 Introduction

What a wonderful challenge and opportunity it is to write a Johannine theology! This is the body of Scripture anchored in the gospel Clement of Alexandria called a "spiritual Gospel" (*pneumatikon euangelion*),[1] and this gospel, in turn, has moved countless hearts to recognize their need for Christ and nurtured many to greater heights in their spiritual pilgrimage. Markus Bockmuehl has recently made a case for the importance of *Wirkungsgeschichte* (a study of a work's "history of effects" on later interpreters) in biblical studies,[2] and John's writings have indeed had a profound impact on Christian theology and spirituality that is second to few (if any) biblical or other works.[3]

1.2 The "Spiritual Gospel"

1.2.1 History of Scholarship

In the recent history of interpretation, Clement's reference to John as a "spiritual gospel" has frequently been taken to imply that John is less interested in histori-

---

1. See the reference to Clement's *Hypotyposeis* in Eusebius, *Hist. eccl.* 6.14. The full quotation is as follows: "But that John, last of all, conscious that the outward facts had been set forth in the Gospels, was urged on by his disciples, and, divinely moved by the Spirit, composed a spiritual Gospel."

2. Markus N. A. Bockmuehl, *Seeing the Word: Refocusing New Testament Study* (Studies in Theological Interpretation; Grand Rapids: Baker, 2006).

3. See J. N. Sanders, *The Fourth Gospel in the Early Church: Its Origin and Influence on Christian Theology up to Irenaeus* (Cambridge: Cambridge University Press, 1943); François-Marie Braun, *Jean le théologien*, Vol. 1: *Jean le théologien et son évangile dans l'église ancienne* (Paris: J. Gabalda, 1959); T. E. Pollard, *Johannine Christology and the Early Church* (SNTSMS 13; Cambridge: Cambridge University Press, 1970); Alois Grillmeier, *Christ in Christian Tradition*, Vol. 1: *From the Apostolic Age to Chalcedon (431)* (trans. John Bowden; 2nd rev. ed.; Atlanta: John Knox, 1975); R. Alan Culpepper, *John, the Son of Zebedee: The Life of a Legend* (Columbia: University of South Carolina Press, 1994; repr. Minneapolis: Fortress, 2000); Annette Volfing, *John the Evangelist in Medieval German Writing: Imitating the Inimitable* (Oxford: Oxford University Press, 2001); and Charles E. Hill, *The Johannine Corpus in the Early Church* (Oxford/New York: Oxford University Press, 2004).

cal matters than the Synoptics, and a chasm began to open up between John as a "spiritual" (i.e., nonhistorical) gospel and the Synoptics as more reliable historical accounts.[4] However, taking "spiritual" as "nonhistorical" is of doubtful merit.[5] More likely, by observing that John was "conscious that the *outward facts* had been set forth in the [Synoptic?] Gospels" already, Clement sought to draw attention to the profound theological reflection present in John's gospel without intending to disparage the historical nature of his account. Indeed, John deepens the reader's understanding of the significance of Jesus' life and work by focusing on a small number of pivotal items such as the identity of Jesus, the necessity of faith, and the universal scope of Christ's redemptive work.

Understood this way, there is every reason to believe that John, as a "spiritual gospel" — in the sense of being an *interpretive* account that brings out more fully the spiritual significance of the events and teachings it features — is grounded firmly in actual historical events, for it is only on such that theological reflection can properly be based.[6] Most likely, in his theological reflection John took his departure from the "outward facts" set forth in the Synoptics rather than disregarding or contradicting them. His account commences with the Baptist's witness to Jesus (John 1:6–8, 15) and the incarnation (1:14). These events, in turn, are grounded in previous salvation history such as the tabernacle (1:14) or the giving of the law through Moses (1:17). What is more, in framing his narrative, the evangelist uses eyewitness language to testify to these events: "The Word became flesh and made his dwelling *among us*. *We have seen* his glory, the glory of the one and only Son, who came from the Father, full of grace and truth.... For the law was given through Moses; grace and truth came through Jesus Christ" (emphasis added).[7]

In this sense, then, John is a "spiritual gospel": it is the product of profound theological reflection, which, in turn, is grounded in actual historical events through which God acted in salvation history.[8] However, the last half millennium of human thought has bequeathed several unfortunate dichotomies on biblical scholarship. The separation between history and theology has led to a gradual disparagement of John's historical reliability and moved the gospel's genre closer to myth and legend.[9]

---

4. Though historical critics have questioned many aspects of the historical reliability of the Synoptics as well. Challenges to John's historicity go back at least as far as Karl Gottlieb Bretschneider, *Probabilia de evangelii et epistolarum Joannis Apostoli indole et orgine eruditorum judiciis modeste subjicit* (Leipzig: A. Barth, 1820). See the summary in William J. Baird, *History of New Testament Research* (2 vols.; Minneapolis: Fortress, 1992, 2003), 1:312–14. More recently, see Maurice Casey, *Is John's Gospel True?* (London/New York: Routledge, 1996).

5. See Marianne Meye Thompson, "The 'Spiritual Gospel': How John the Theologian Writes History," in *John, Jesus, and History*, Volume 1: *Critical Appraisals of Critical Views* (ed. Paul N. Anderson, Felix Just, and Tom Thatcher; SBLSymS 44; Atlanta: SBL, 2007), 103–7; and the discussion below.

6. Note the "eyewitness" motif in John's gospel, on which see Richard Bauckham, *Jesus and the Eyewitnesses: The Gospels as Eyewitness Testimony* (Grand Rapids: Eerdmans, 2006). See also Acts 2:36 and 1 Cor 15:12–20.

7. The fourth evangelist's affirmation, "We have seen his glory," represents perhaps the most paradigmatic statement of the entire gospel. "We have seen" captures the eyewitness dimension, while "glory" pervades John's presentation of Jesus as the Word, the Messiah, and the Son of God from his preexistent glory to his "signs" to the "lifting up" of the Son of Man and his glorious return.

8. See the still helpful discussion by Leon Morris, "History and Theology in the Fourth Gospel," in *Studies in the Fourth Gospel* (Grand Rapids: Eerdmans, 1969), 65–138. See also D. Moody Smith, "John — Historian or Theologian?" *BRev* 20 (2004): 22–31, 45.

9. See, e.g., David Friedrich Strauss, *The Christ of Faith and the Jesus of History* (trans. and ed. Leander E. Keck; Philadelphia: Fortress, 1977 [1865]), 161: "The Gospels are to be regarded as the oldest collections of the myths which were attached around the core

Another dichotomy passed on to the contemporary interpreter is that between religion and theology. If theology is understood as reflection on actual divine revelation, religion, by contrast, is conceived as the result of the human quest for meaning and as the evolution of human consciousness of a higher power. Thus Johann Salomo Semler sought to blend pietism with rationalism by separating theology as an historical, objective academic discipline from religion, which, he held, was subjective and based on personal experience.[10]

Friedrich Schleiermacher, likewise, building on Immanuel Kant's distinction between metaphysics and practical morality, drew the same distinction between religion as a phenomenon of feeling and experience, "the sense of absolute dependence on God," and theology as intellectual reflection about God. After him, Karl Bretschneider (who in 1820 threw down the gauntlet by challenging the historical reliability of John's gospel),[11] the Tübingen School (which favored a late, second-century date for John's gospel), and others applied critical reason to the biblical documents, questioning their historical reliability, while others sought to retain the spiritual relevance of the Scriptures, including John's gospel.[12]

However, salvaging John's spiritual message appeared possible only by jettisoning his historical reliability, whether through Rudolf Bultmann's demythologization program (on which see further below) or the setting aside of the gospel in historical Jesus research. Thus this gospel, which had exerted such powerful influence throughout the centuries, not least in the formation of the early Christian creeds, was increasingly marginalized. The gospel, the emerging consensus had it, was of great devotional and theological value, but lacked a proper historical foundation. It appeared that John had suffered irreparable damage at the hands of skeptical scholars, having been dissected by critics of all stripes whether by applying source, form, redaction, or some other form of "higher" criticism.

In the past several decades, however, some have come to view this approach to John's gospel as misguided, advocating the study of the final text of John's gospel. A new breed of literary, narrative critics read the gospel holistically with a view toward appreciating its narrative features.[13] At the same time, however, this "new" way of reading John's gospel — in fact, these literary critics were by no means the first to read the gospel as story — proceeded frequently only after both "legs" of the interpreter had been amputated by historical critics, and literary readings were conducted on the basis of a self-chosen agnosticism, if not negative assessment, of John's historical nature.[14]

---

of this personality [i.e. Jesus]"; Rudolf Bultmann, *The History of the Synoptic Tradition* (trans. John Marsh; New York: Harper & Row, 1963 [1957]), 370–71: "Thus the kerygma of Christ is cultic legend and the Gospels are expanded cult legends." For an excellent (though not always unbiased) account of the history of NT research, see Baird, *History of New Testament Research*. On the genre of John's gospel, see chapter 2, sec. 3 below.

10. See Baird, *History of New Testament Research*, 1:117–27.
11. Bretschneider, *Probabilia*.
12. For a discussion of the debate regarding the apostolic authorship of John's gospel between 1790 and 1810, see Andreas J. Kös-

tenberger, "Early Doubts of the Apostolic Authorship of the Fourth Gospel in the History of Modern Biblical Criticism," in *Studies on John and Gender: A Decade of Scholarship* (Studies in Biblical Literature 38; New York: Peter Lang, 2001), 17–47.

13. See especially the now-classic work of R. Alan Culpepper, *Anatomy of the Fourth Gospel: A Study in Literary Design* (Philadelphia: Fortress, 1983). Cf. Tom Thatcher and Stephen D. Moore, eds., *Anatomies of Narrative Criticism: The Past, Present, and Futures of the Fourth Gospel as Literature* (SBLRBS 55; Atlanta: SBL, 2008).

14. See, e.g., the critique of the "new criticism" in general and of Culpepper's work in particular in D. A. Carson, *The Gospel according*

1.2.2 The Road Ahead

Where does Johannine scholarship go from here? As mentioned, the historicity of John's gospel has been widely diminished by modern scholarship. Even though some have sought to overcome its alleged lack of historical grounding by accentuating its literary nature, such efforts are ultimately unsatisfactory. If, as mentioned, the Johannine narrative were found to rest on a precarious historical foundation, this would have major negative consequences for the veracity of its theological, christological, and soteriological assertions. It is therefore imperative to assess the historical value of John's gospel, not least because mere literary readings fall short of doing full justice to the historical nature of Christianity and the gospel's claim of eyewitness testimony.

In one's scholarship, it will be essential to transcend the above-mentioned dichotomies between the spiritual and the historical, and theology and religion, and to consider the possibility that John's gospel is deeply nurturing spiritually precisely *because* it is grounded in an accurate historical portrayal of what actually took place in and through the life of Jesus Christ.[15] This does not necessarily entail the rejection of historical methodologies or literary approaches where these serve to shed light on the setting of John's writings and on the contours of John's message.

In conducting one's research, it will also be vital for one's primary loyalties not to be to the critical establishment or to the current academic guild and its scholarly paradigms and methods. In fact, anyone looking at the state of Johannine research today will observe that the field is in a considerable state of disarray. D. A. Carson has spoken of the "balkanization" of Johannine studies—that is, its lapse into increasing fragmentation and disintegration into various interpretive enclaves.[16]

In many ways, the state of Johannine studies resembles that described in George Guthrie's delightful parody of "busy boats in the bay":

> The bay has gotten crowded and we must ask what we are to do about it. As we observe the frenetic activity in the bay, it occurs to us that some connections do exist between some of the boats. They can even be seen stealing bait from one another from time to time. *Yet, for the most part, those in the boats fish in their own part of the bay either ignoring or glancing briefly at the other boats to decry what seem from a distance very small catches indeed.*[17]

---

to *John* (PNTC; Grand Rapids: Eerdmans, 1991), 63–68 (adapted from his review in *TrinJ* 4 NS (1983): 122–26).

15. See David Steinmetz, "The Superiority of Pre-critical Exegesis," *ThTo* 37 (1980): 27–38; repr. in Stephen E. Fowl, ed., *The Theological Interpretation of Scripture: Classic and Contemporary Readings* (Blackwell Readings in Modern Theology; Oxford: Blackwell, 1997), 26–38. This, of course, does not mean that precritical scholarship was necessarily more accurate, just that it was not yet beholden to this dichotomy between history and theology.

16. D. A. Carson, "The Challenge of the Balkanization of Johannine Studies," in *John, Jesus, and History*, Vol. 1: *Critical Appraisals of Critical Views* (ed. Paul N. Anderson, Felix Just, S.J., and Tom Thatcher; SBLSymS 44; Atlanta: SBL, 2007), 133–59; idem, "Reflections upon a Johannine Pilgrimage," in *What We Have Heard from the Beginning: The Past, Present, and Future of Johannine Studies* (ed. Tom Thatcher; Waco, TX: Baylor University Press, 2007), 90–92. The term "balkanization" refers to the region in Europe, including the former Yugoslavia, called "the Balkans," which was broken up in the twentieth century into ever smaller regions feuding with one another. Similarly, the field of Johannine studies has witnessed a fragmentation into various camps, whether source critics, redaction critics, literary critics, deconstructionists, postmodernists, or practitioners of other methods.

17. George H. Guthrie, "Boats in the Bay: Reflections on the Use of Linguistics and Literary Analysis in Biblical Studies," in *Linguistics and the New Testament: Critical Junctures* (ed. Stanley E. Porter and D. A. Carson; JSNTSup 168; Sheffield: Sheffield Academic Press, 1999), 24 (emphasis added).

How, then, shall John's Gospel be read? In a bold proposal, N. T. Wright calls for the adoption of a form of "critical realism" and the development of nothing less than a "new epistemology."[18] While this is not the place to flesh out this proposal, I resonate with these sentiments in many ways. As Johannine scholarship moves into the future, it should take care not to build uncritically on the dubious legacy of its historical-critical forebears. Rather than attempt to construct a new edifice on top of a structurally unsound foundation, students of John's writings will be wise to eschew false dichotomies, to acknowledge the undeniable faith dimension in biblical scholarship, and to adopt a hermeneutical model that affirms the various component parts of the interpretive process in proper balance and proportion.[19]

1.3 Prolegomena
1.3.1 The Hermeneutical Triad

Interpreters of Scripture are faced with three inescapable realities they need to address in their interpretive practice: (1) the reality of God and his revelation in Scripture (theology); (2) the existence of texts containing that revelation that require interpretation (language and literature); and (3) the reality of history, or, more specifically, salvation history, that is, the fact that God's revelation to humans, which is conveyed by the biblical texts, took place in human history. The writings of Scripture did not come into being in a vacuum; they were written by people with specific beliefs, convictions, and experiences.

In essence, therefore, the interpretive task consists of considering each of the three major elements of the "hermeneutical triad" in proper balance: history, language or literature, and theology, with the first two elements being foundational and theology occupying the apex.[20]

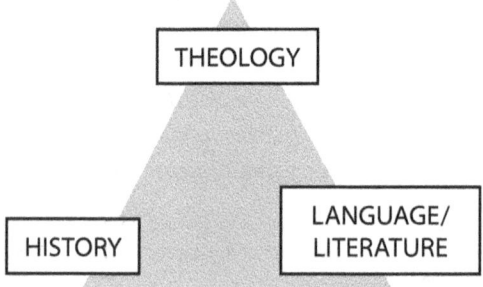

Fig. 1.1: The Hermeneutical Triad

---

18. For a very incisive, thorough discussion along similar lines see N. T. Wright, *The New Testament and the People of God* (Christian Origins and the Question of God 1; Minneapolis: Fortress, 1992), 31–144.

19. On the role of faith in the interpretive process, see Adolf Schlatter, "Atheistic Methods in Theology," in Werner Neuer, *Adolf Schlatter: A Biography of Germany's Premier Biblical Theologian* (trans. Robert W. Yarbrough; Grand Rapids: Baker, 1996 [1905]).

20. See Andreas J. Köstenberger and Richard D. Patterson, *Invitation to Biblical Interpretation* (Grand Rapids: Kregel, forthcoming).

While theology—discerning the spiritual message of Scripture—is at the pinnacle of biblical interpretation, an appreciation of both the historical-cultural background of a particular text and of the Bible's linguistic and literary features is essential. The history of interpretation has shown the flaws in approaches that neglect any one, or two, of the three poles of the "hermeneutical triad."

During the Enlightenment, many became disenchanted with the supernatural element in Scripture, such as the miracles performed by Moses or Jesus.[21] Increasingly, the very possibility of miracles was questioned, and anti-supernaturalism often prevailed. A new view of science led to the interpretation of the biblical creation and miracle stories as "myths." This included Jesus' resurrection, even though Paul and other NT writers insisted that the resurrection is essential to the Christian faith. Over time, this rationalistic mindset gave rise to a pronounced skepticism toward the scriptural data and led to the development of the historical-critical method with its commensurate criteria for assessing the historicity of biblical texts.

One particularly telling expression of this approach is the effort by the twentieth-century theologian Rudolf Bultmann to "demythologize" Scripture in order to salvage an existentialist core of the Christian message.[22] For many proponents of the historical-critical method, the question of history became detached from the biblical text, and *"Wie es eigentlich gewesen ist"*—"How it actually happened," the German theologian von Ranke's definition of history—became the preeminent preoccupation of biblical scholars. Assessing the historicity of the events recorded in Scripture largely replaced the study of the actual text of the Bible, a development trenchantly chronicled in Hans Frei's *Eclipse of Biblical Narrative*.[23] The historical-critical method therefore serves as an exemplar of an undue emphasis on history at the expense of the Bible's linguistic, literary, and theological dimensions.[24]

In the wake of Frei's work, however, the pendulum swung to the other extreme. Increasingly, historical skepticism toward the historicity of events depicted in the Bible led to a mere literary study of Scripture as any other book. In this approach, aptly labeled "aesthetic theology" by Kevin Vanhoozer, students of Scripture focused unilaterally on the various literary features of the biblical text while excluding historical questions from the scope of their investigation.[25] Biblical scholarship was transmuted into narrative criticism or various other forms of literary criticism, and while interesting literary insights were gained, Scripture's historical moorings were unduly neglected, resulting in imbalanced interpretative outcomes once again.

---

21. See, e.g., Baird, *History of New Testament Research*, 1:3–5, et passim.

22. See the perceptive discussion in Stephen Neill and Tom Wright, *The Interpretation of the New Testament 1861–1986* (2nd ed.; Oxford/New York: Oxford University Press, 1988), 237–51.

23. Hans W. Frei, *The Eclipse of Biblical Narrative* (New Haven/London: Yale University Press, 1974).

24. See in this regard Tom Thatcher, "Anatomies of the Fourth Gospel: Past, Present, and Future Probes," in *Anatomies of Narrative Criticism*, 2–4, who diagnoses a similar "eclipse of Johannine narrative" prior to the publication of R. Alan Culpepper's *Anatomy of the Fourth Gospel*.

25. Kevin J. Vanhoozer, "A Lamp in the Labyrinth: The Hermeneutics of 'Aesthetic Theology,'" *TrinJ* 8 NS (1987): 25–56. See also Andreas J. Köstenberger, "Aesthetic Theology—Blessing or Curse? An Assessment of Narrative Hermeneutics," *Faith & Mission* 15/2 (1998): 27–44.

Postmodernism, for its part, cast the very notion of truth as a mere function of sociological factors rather than in terms of correspondence to facts and reality.[26]

In assessing the merits of literary approaches to Scripture, it must be remembered that *texts* do not have a theology; *people*—authors—do.[27] This shows the limitations of methods that leave largely in abeyance the question of authorship while focusing on a written text regardless of the adjudication of authorship or other matters intrinsic to the historical setting of a given document. This does not mean that the author's larger-than-life presence should be used to override and overshadow what is expressly stated in the text; the *text* should be regarded as the place where the author expresses his theology. Yet the text is not autonomous; it did not create itself. People, including authors, for their part, are shaped by beliefs and formative experiences. N. T. Wright provides a fitting illustration of the relationship between texts and history when he compares it to eating a piece of fruit, noting that it is impossible to cleanly peel away the skin without some of the fruit attaching to it.[28] It is similar with texts that cannot be completely sanitized or divorced from history.

Yet other approaches abandoned the notion of historicity while retaining the centrality of theology. Adherents to this school of thought maintained that theological truth was not contingent on the truthfulness of Scripture in depicting various phenomena and events. The resurrection was redefined as an existential experience of new life through faith in the individual apart from the historical resurrection of Jesus following his crucifixion.[29] Personal regeneration upon faith in Christ was recast as the result of an existential encounter with God through the reading of Scripture. These examples illustrate approaches to theology that inadequately recognize the fundamental role of history in the investigation of Scripture. While, as mentioned, theology is properly placed at the pinnacle of biblical interpretation, it must be built on the foundation of a proper appreciation of the historical, linguistic, and literary dimensions of Scripture if a valid and balanced interpretive outcome is to be attained.

For this reason the "hermeneutical triad" constitutes the most satisfying overall framework from which to proceed in order to explore the theology of John's gospel and letters. Rather than being pitted against one another, history, language and literature, and theology each have a vital place in the study of Scripture. If the interpreter is willing to pay attention to each of these dimensions of biblical interpretation and is prepared to follow the text's directions rather than setting out on one's own whim, he or she will be equipped to take their proper place in submission to Scripture and affirm with young Samuel, "Speak, for your servant is listening" (1 Sam 3:10).

---

26. See on this question Andreas J. Köstenberger, ed., *Whatever Happened to Truth?* (Wheaton: Crossway, 2005).

27. See my review of Edward W. Klink III, *The Sheep of the Fold: The Audience and Origin of the Gospel of John* (SNTSMS 141; Cambridge: Cambridge University Press, 2007), in *JETS* 51 (2008): 654–56.

28. See Wright, *New Testament and the People of God*, 20, whose entire discussion in "Part II: Tools for the Task" repays careful reading.

29. See the discussion of Bultmann's program of "demythologization" and the critique in Neill and Wright mentioned above.

1.3.2 The Plan of This Book

Like any solid structure, Biblical Theology must be built on a robust foundation. In keeping with the preceding reflections, the first portion of this book will therefore be devoted to laying a firm historical and literary foundation for the proper apprehension of John's theology (Parts 1–2, chaps. 1–5). This will consist of, first, setting the enterprise of discerning Johannine theology within the larger framework of the discipline of Biblical Theology (chap. 1, sec. 1).[30] The chapter commences with a survey of the history of interpretation of John's writings, with special emphasis being given to the quest for the historical setting of the gospel and letters.[31]

This will be followed by a discussion of the major introductory matters pertaining to John's gospel and letters: their authorship and historical setting (chap. 1, sec. 2), their genre (a somewhat neglected field of inquiry; chap. 2), and various linguistic and literary dimensions of John's gospel and letters (chap. 3). Having laid the historical and literary foundations for studying John's theology, the next two chapters will be devoted to a reading of John's gospel and letters (chaps. 4–5). Under the next heading, I will discuss the nature of this reading in greater detail.

1.3.2.1 Three Areas: Historical Investigation, Literary Study, Theological Reflection

Technically speaking, as is widely recognized, introductory matters are not a part of Biblical Theology but rather inform the discipline by way of convictions derived from prior research. Exegesis, likewise, is not viewed as part of Biblical Theology as such but is presupposed.[32] Nevertheless, it will be appropriate to articulate these underlying convictions at the outset of this work.

On the basis of these assumptions and in keeping with the hermeneutical triad sketched above, the strategy in the present volume will be: (1) to investigate the historical and literary setting of John's gospel and letters (chaps. 1–3); (2) to conduct a literary-theological reading of John's gospel and letters (chaps. 4–5); and (3) to engage in theological reflection on major Johannine themes (chaps. 6–15), followed by a brief assessment of John's theology in its canonical context.

This procedure can be diagrammed as follows (read from bottom to top):

---

30. For a helpful introduction see the essays "Biblical Theology," "History of Biblical Theology," and "Challenges to Biblical Theology" by Brian S. Rosner, Charles H. H. Scobie, and Peter Balla in *New Dictionary of Biblical Theology: Exploring the Unity & Diversity of Scripture* (ed. T. Desmond Alexander and Brian S. Rosner; Leicester, UK: Inter-Varsity Press, 2000), 3–27.

31. See esp. Seán P. Kealy, *John's Gospel and the History of Biblical Interpretation* (2 vols.; Mellen Biblical Press Series 60a–b; Lewiston, NY: Mellen, 2002).

32. In the case of this present volume, this means that my BECNT commentary on John (and my other publications on John's gospel, both monographs and smaller studies) provides the exegetical foundation for this Johannine theology and that the latter is conceived as a sequel to the former. See also the helpful article by D. A. Carson, "The Role of Exegesis in Systematic Theology," in *Doing Theology in Today's World* (ed. John D. Woodbridge and Thomas E. McComiskey; Grand Rapids: Zondervan, 1991), 39–76, in which he delineates the relationship between exegesis and hermeneutics, historical theology, biblical theology, systematic theology, spiritual experience, and preaching.

BIBLICAL THEOLOGY	Theological reflection on major themes in John's theology (Part 3)
	Literary-theological reading of John's gospel and letters (Part 2)
UNDERLYING CONVICTIONS	Study of historical setting of John's gospel and letters (Part 1)
	Exegesis of individual passages in John's gospel and letters

Fig. 1.2: A Working Model of Engaging in Biblical/Johannine Theology

Note that only the theological reading and the theological reflection—the tip of the iceberg, as it were—are properly part of Biblical (here Johannine) Theology. Nevertheless, it will be helpful to provide a discussion of the assumptions regarding introductory matters that are lying beneath the surface. Exegetical matters will be discussed briefly where relevant or the reader will be directed to relevant exegetical discussions in footnotes.

How, then, will this theological reading of John's gospel and letters take place? In light of the preliminary observations registered above, this will not merely be a "literary reading" cut off from historical considerations. It will proceed on the basis of an understanding of the genre of the gospel as a theological biography written by an eyewitness[33] and of 1, 2, and 3 John as genuine first-century letters. An effort will be made to understand these writings within the context of their presumed historical setting in response to then-recent events. In this regard special attention will be given to the particular worldview reflected in these documents.

The above-sketched procedure is based on the conviction that the *theology* of a given document is revealed in the context of the specific *literary form* by which it is conveyed. This, in turn, capitalizes on the strength of Biblical Theology—its careful attention to biblical terminology and the original historical context. Further life is infused into the interpretive process through the insights of literary methods that have sharpened the reader's ability to process narratives and discourses perceptively. Especially in the case of the Gospels, this calls for considerable hermeneutical sophistication, since it is no easy task to discern the theology of a particular writer from his or her narrative.

This holistic, theological reading of John's gospel and letters will ask historical, literary, and theological questions and seek to explore them initially in the unfolding narrative or epistolary framework of John's gospel and letters. In this regard every effort will be made to be sensitive to, and to discern to the extent possible on the basis of the existing data, the plan and structure of these documents, including major and minor transitions. While paying attention to the particulars on the micro-level (i.e., individual words, phrases, and sentences), the primary focus will be on tracking John's unfolding theology on the macro-level (i.e., the larger thematic and synthetic level).

---

33. E.g., John 1:14; 19:35; 21:24–25. See esp. Bauckham, *Jesus and the Eyewitnesses*.

This simultaneous attention to the micro- and macro-level will ensure that the apprehension of Johannine theology flows organically from, and is adequately grounded in, the actual text of these writings rather than, as is sometimes the case, the text being domesticated by a scholar's larger theories regarding John's theology, on the premise that some pesky data should not be allowed to get in the way of one's grand theological scheme.[34] This would certainly not be appropriate for a book on Biblical Theology, since, as discussed below, it is intrinsic to Biblical Theology that data not be superimposed "from above" but that the process flow "from below" to the larger thematic and theological level, respecting the expression of an author's theology in a given text in his or her own idiom, style, and thought forms.

1.3.2.2 Major Theological Themes Chosen and Criteria for Selection

This attempted close theological reading of John's gospel and letters in chapters 4 and 5 will then be followed in Part 3 by sustained theological reflection on several of the most significant themes found in these documents.[35] By way of prolegomena, I will discuss the Johannine worldview and the grounding of John's theology in various strands of the OT Scriptures (chap. 6). The major theological motifs chosen for reflection are: (1) the Messiah and his signs (chap. 7); (2) creation and new creation (chap. 8); (3) God: Father, Son, and Spirit (chap. 9); (4) salvation history: Jesus' fulfillment of festal symbolism (chap. 10); (5) the cosmic trial motif (chap. 11); (6) the new messianic community (chap. 12); (7) Johannine ethics (chap. 13); (8) John's theology of the cross (chap. 14); and (9) John's trinitarian mission theology (chap. 15). In conclusion, John's theology will be set in its proper canonical context.

In the interest of full disclosure, the process by which these thematic clusters were determined can be sketched as follows. The background was set by over a decade of close working with John's gospel and letters and by engaging in a variety of exegetical and thematic studies. This repeated, reflective reading and work with John's writings resulted in an increasing grasp of John's theology and its constituent parts. As it became necessary to select the specific theological topics to be addressed, three major points of reference that emerged in the gospel were: (1) the introduction (John 1:1–18); (2) the preamble to Part 2 (13:1–3); and (3) the purpose statement (20:30–31).

Located at the beginning, the middle, and the end of John's gospel, these units represent strategically placed indicators of John's major theological purposes and

---

34. This premise has often applied to German scholarship guided by idealism. Not that Anglo-American scholarship is immune to this, however. A current example of synthesis at times illegitimately controlling exegesis might be aspects of the work of N. T. Wright.

35. In framing the present volume I have benefited particularly from the approach used in the following volumes: John W. Pryor, *John: Evangelist of the Covenant People* (Downers Grove, IL: InterVarsity Press, 1992); Charles H. H. Scobie, *The Ways of Our God:* *An Approach to Biblical Theology* (Grand Rapids: Eerdmans, 2003); and the *New Dictionary of Biblical Theology*. I have also benefited from reading several of the volumes in the NSBT series (edited by D. A. Carson) and from perusing Dunn, *Theology of Paul the Apostle*. Also, theological differences notwithstanding, Rudolf Bultmann's *Theology of the New Testament* (2 vols.; trans. Kendrick Grobel; New York: Charles Scribner's Sons, 1951, 1955) has been an inspiration as well.

thematic emphases, together with, and to a slightly lesser extent, other major or mid-level introductory, summary, or concluding sections (John 6:60–71; 12:36b–50). Indeed, it is entirely in keeping with literary theory to read a story in light of its beginning, middle, and end. These three units will therefore serve as the points of departure for the discussion of major Johannine themes in this volume. Also, since the gospel is judged to be the foundational Johannine document, it will serve as the primary basis for this study, with John's letters providing supplementary material for John's theology (though important themes in the letters will be treated in their own right).

In this manner, the present volume seeks to contribute to the question: How does one derive the theology of a particular author from a given text? Essentially, the answer given here is: (1) through repeated careful reading; and (2) through special attention being given to programmatic sections, such as a writing's introduction, purpose statement, or other sections by which an author indicates his theological emphases. What is more, not only do the beginning, middle, and end of a narrative constitute strategic junctures, it is vital to read the document in light of its purpose (the end), which is one reason why the treatment of major themes in John's gospel takes its point of departure from the Johannine purpose statement. The same is true for the letters, especially 1 John, which, as will be seen, presents its own unique challenges.

In light of the importance of reading a document with the end — its purpose — in mind, the investigation of John's theology in part 3, then, will commence with John's declared purpose, which focuses squarely on the Messiah and his signs (chap. 7): "Jesus performed many other *signs* [*sēmeia*] in the presence of his disciples, which are not recorded in this book. But these are written that you may believe that Jesus is the *Messiah*, the Son of God, and that by believing you may have life in his name" (20:30–31, emphasis added).[36] Thus the Messiah and his signs are the focal point of John's *theo*-drama, or perhaps better, his *Christo*-drama or *sēmeio*-drama (an account of the Messiah's signs).[37]

Interestingly, neither the Messiah (first as part of the expression "Jesus Christ" in John 1:17 and then describing what John the Baptist was *not* in 1:20) nor his

---

36. Note that in addition to the Messiah and his signs, "believing" and "life in his name" are also mentioned in the purpose statement. But unlike "Messiah" and "signs," "believing" and "life" form an integral part also of the introduction to the gospel, so that it seemed best to treat these latter two motifs under the rubric "beginning," below.

37. For the notion of *theo*-drama, see Kevin J. Vanhoozer, *The Drama of Doctrine: A Canonical-Linguistic Approach to Christian Theology* (Louisville: Westminster John Knox, 2005), following Hans Urs von Balthasar, *Theo-Drama: Theological Dramatic Theory* (4 vols.; trans. G. Harrison; San Francisco: Ignatius, 1988, 1990, 1992, 1994). Mark Stibbe, "Telling the Father's Story: The Gospel of John as Narrative Theology," in *Challenging Perspectives on the Gospel of John* (ed. John Lierman; WUNT 2/219; Tübingen: Mohr-Siebeck, 2006), 170, with reference to Francis J. Moloney, *The Gospel of John* (SP; Collegeville, MN: Liturgical Press, 1998), 47, says that John is "telling the Father's story," not Jesus', and cautions that "John's theology ... not ... be swallowed up in his Christology." He contends, on the basis of the reference to Jesus making God known in John 1:18, that John's gospel is not just a βίος Ἰησοῦ; it is also a βίος θεοῦ, "or, better still, a βίος πατρός" (ibid.). No one would deny that Jesus came to make God known; this is explicitly stated in 1:18. Nevertheless, it is stated plainly in 20:30–31 that it was John's purpose to demonstrate that it is *Jesus* who is the Christ and Son of God; and it is asserted in the introduction that it was Jesus *the Word* who was with God in the beginning. This amply indicates the Christocentricity of John's gospel and supports the contention that John's gospel constitutes a *theo*-drama precisely because it, as *Christo*-drama, shows that Jesus was both Messiah and Son of God.

signs are featured in the introduction.[38] This shows that they are not so much part of John's universal theological outlook but part of his particular salvation-historical message pertaining to the Jewish people. It is to them that Jesus first came as their Messiah, though they rejected him (12:36b–40). This rejection, in turn, revolves around Jesus' "signs," found only in Act I[39] of the gospel, spanning John 2 through 11. Because the Messiah and his signs are not featured in the introduction to the gospel, it may have been better to deal with them later on in the volume; yet because they are at the heart of John's purpose statement, it seemed appropriate to place the discussion of the Messiah and his signs first.

After this the exploration of John's theology starts where John starts: with protology, that is, the Word and its activity in both creation and new creation (chap. 8). Understanding John's theology as it unfolds in the Johannine narrative will turn out to be of seminal significance both methodologically and in its practical outworking. Continuing to track with John's initial remarks, it is apparent that his opening words, "In the beginning was the Word," are followed immediately by his assertion that "the Word was with God, and the Word was God" (John 1:1). This raises important questions as to the nature of God, and later in the introduction one finds references to the Father and the Son (1:14, 18), respectively (though not of the Spirit). For this reason the next topic that will be considered is God: Father, Son, and Spirit (chap. 9).

After this integrated consideration of the Godhead, the next topic that emerges organically from the unfolding fabric of John's narrative in the introduction is that of salvation history pertaining to Judaism and its various religious institutions, festivals, and holy sites, including the temple (chap. 10). This flows from the references to Jesus "pitching his tent" (cf. 1:14, an allusion to the tabernacle) and various other allusions to the exodus narrative in the latter portions of the introduction (1:14–18). In this regard, what will emerge is an integral connection between John's theology of the temple and the motif of the glory of God in Jesus the Messiah.[40]

Next in the introduction to the gospel comes John's reference to the world's rejection of its Creator upon its visitation by him (John 1:10–11)—part and parcel of the cosmic trial motif in John, which includes references to the world, the Jews, and the witnesses to Jesus—and to those who become God's children through faith and the new birth (presupposing divine election) and who thus come to form the new messianic community, Jesus' "own."[41] These two thematic clusters—the cosmic trial motif and the genesis of the new messianic community—constitute the next topics of discussion (chaps. 11 and 12, respectively).[42]

After this, the discussion moves to the middle of the Johannine narrative, the preamble to Part Two of John's *Christo*-drama. With the *sēmeio*-drama having

---

38. Though the author's affirmation, "We have seen his glory" (John 1:14), turns out to encompass the signs (2:11; 9:3–4; 11:4) as well as the cross (12:23, 28; 17:1, 4–5) in the remainder of the Johannine narrative.

39. Please note that I am using the expression "Act I" and "Part 1" as synonyms, and "Act II" and "Part 2."

40. See esp. the discussion in chap. 10, secs. 22.3, 5; and 24.

41. Compare John 1:12 with 13:1.

42. See also the reference to "believing" (as well as "life in his name") in the purpose statement (John 20:31).

drawn to a close at the end of chapter 12, chapter 13 marks the opening of the Johannine *cruci*-drama, showing how the rejection of the Messiah's signs issued in his crucifixion, which, paradoxically, constituted his glorification via the double entendre featured in the "lifted-up sayings."[43] Under this rubric, the first topic of discussion will be that of Johannine ethics (chap. 13). This is a subject that is most fully featured in the footwashing pericope, where Jesus provides an anticipatory expression of his love for his disciples and sets them an example to follow. In this way the footwashing serves as an emblem for the cross, where Jesus provides the ultimate expression of his love (John 3:16; 15:13; 1 John 3:10). Thus the Johannine ethic is shown to be an ethic of love, proving the appropriateness of the epithet for John as the "apostle of love."

Next to last, but by no means least, is John's theology of the cross (chap. 14). This is a crucial topic indeed, and, as will be shown, John's *theologia crucis* is distinctive when compared to the Synoptics (though there is, of course, considerable overlap as well). The note of redemption is sounded fairly early in the gospel (note, e.g., the Baptist's reference to "the Lamb of God" who takes away the sin of the world in John 1:29). This unit will include discussions of the nature of Jesus' coming and work and note John's contribution to the theology of the NT on this subject, a subject that has been at the center of vigorous discussion over the course of church history and again in recent years.

The final topic of investigation is one of great (albeit widely underrated) importance without which no Johannine theology would be complete: John's trinitarian mission theology (chap. 15). I have written on this subject elsewhere, so that there will be a certain amount of overlap between my treatment here and other publications, but this topic must be given its due in the present context to round out — and, indeed, culminate — John's theology, just as John's trinitarian mission theology climaxes the Johannine narrative.[44] This topic, therefore, will serve as a fitting conclusion to the exploration of John's theology.

After this set of theological reflections, one final task remains — that of considering the contribution of Johannine theology to the canon of the NT and of the entire Scriptures (chap. 16). Thus the volume is rounded out with a discussion of John's theology in comparison to the Synoptics and briefly with a comparison of Johannine theology with Pauline theology, the theology of Hebrews, and the theology of the other NT writings. A few concluding remarks and observations close out the volume. With this, the stage is set for an investigation, first, of the historical foundations for a study of John's theology.

---

43. See John 3:14; 8:28; and 12:32.
44. See John 20:21–22 (cf. 17:18), where Jesus, the Father, and the Spirit are shown to unite in their mission to the world through Jesus' commissioned followers.

2 The Historical Setting of John's Gospel and Letters

2.1 The Gospel

2.1.1 Introduction

Almost from its inception, the interpretation of John's gospel was hotly contested. In the second century AD, it was particularly the Gnostics who laid claim to this gospel, alleging that it supported their message of salvation through knowledge (revelation) apart from redemption and forgiveness of sin in Christ.[45] John's first letter may be the first to bear witness to the way in which the gospel was misunderstood if not intentionally misrepresented (e.g., 1 John 1:1–3; 4:2–3).[46] In the following centuries, John's gospel was a (if not the) major theological quarry from which both sides of Trinitarian and other controversies drew at the ecumenical councils of the church.[47]

Subsequent to the Reformation, English Deists as well as liberal German scholars initially preferred John's Gospel because of its lack of emphasis on demon exorcisms. In the wake of the Enlightenment, however, from Edward Evanson in England to Karl Bretschneider and David Friedrich Strauss in Germany, attacks were mounted alleging contradictions between John's "spiritual gospel" and the Synoptics, pitting "history" against "theology," as if a gospel that stresses the importance of eyewitness testimony and the careful evaluation of evidence must necessarily bend historical fact for the sake of theological expediency.[48] In the twentieth century, Rudolf Bultmann, as mentioned, enlisted John in his program of demythologization.[49]

In recent years, efforts were made to transfer John's gospel from the mainstream of apostolic Christianity to the margins of end-of-first-century sectarianism. The "Johannine community," "school," or "circle," rather than John the apostle, some alleged, was responsible for compiling the gospel in the wake of its struggles against a parent synagogue that expelled a portion of its members for their faith in Jesus as Messiah.[50] While as recently as 1990, this view enjoyed virtually paradigmatic

---

45. See Sanders, *Fourth Gospel*, 47–87; Pollard, *Johannine Christology*, 25. Though see Hill, *Johannine Corpus in the Early Church*, who convincingly dispels the myth of "orthodox Johannophobia" (see my review in *JETS* 48 [2005]: 390–93).

46. Though the identity of the opponents in 1 John is a hotly disputed question: see the discussion in 2.2.4 below.

47. See Andreas J. Köstenberger and Scott R. Swain, *Father, Son and Spirit: The Trinity and John's Gospel* (NSBT 24; Downers Grove, IL: InterVarsity Press, 2008), 19–22.

48. See the discussion above. On the history of Johannine scholarship in the late eighteenth and early nineteenth centuries see Köstenberger, "Early Doubts." The essays on history and theology in John's gospel and on the question of the gospel's authorship by Leon Morris (*Studies in the Fourth Gospel*, 65–292) still repay careful study. For an interesting application of Clement's statement, see Frank Thielman, "The Style of the Fourth Gospel and Ancient Literary Critical Concepts of Religious Discourse," in *Persuasive Artistry: Studies in New Testament Rhetoric in Honor of George A. Kennedy* (ed. Duane F. Watson; JSNTSup 50; Sheffield: JSOT, 1991), 183, in the context of his entire article. The reference to Clement's *Hypotyposeis* is found in Eusebius, *Hist. eccl.* 6.14. See also Thompson, "Spiritual Gospel," 103, who rightly notes that "whatever Clement meant in calling John 'a spiritual Gospel,' it is doubtful that he meant to contrast 'facts,' in the modern sense, and 'interpretation.'... A 'spiritual' Gospel gives the inner meaning of an event or reality, and hence its truth must be spiritually discerned." Thompson rightly alleges that "the modern view" that calls into question the historicity of any item in John that "stands in the service of his theological or interpretive agenda" constitutes "a very strange way to imagine how theology works, and perhaps it could only have been thought of by people actually *not* doing theology" (p. 104; emphasis original). Thompson proceeds to call for greater sophistication in biblical scholars' philosophy of history. Carson (*Gospel according to John*, 29) similarly disavows attributing to Clement a dichotomy between "spiritual" and "historical"; he suggests "spiritual" may mean "allegorical" or "symbol-laden."

49. See Carson, *Gospel according to John*, 31–33.

50. This reconstruction, it should be noted, is significantly based on the charge that the references to synagogue expulsion in John

status,[51] it has since suffered serious blows.[52] In 1993, Martin Hengel strongly criticized the hypothesis, excoriating its proponents for their virtual neglect of patristic evidence.[53]

In 1998, Richard Bauckham vehemently objected to sectarian readings of John's gospel by pointing to evidence that the early Christians were connected to each other through a network of relationships.[54] In 2002, at an annual meeting of the Society of Biblical Literature, Robert Kysar, a long-time advocate of the Johannine community hypothesis, renounced it publicly and expressed regret for ever having embraced it.[55] In 2004, Charles Hill launched a direct assault on what he called the "orthodox Johannophobia" paradigm, adducing massive evidence that the orthodox attributed the gospel to John and used it widely rather than shunning it as a result of the Gnostics' preference for it.[56] This critique, in turn, has opened the way for a thorough reassessment of the nature and origins of Johannine Christianity.[57]

Nevertheless, it must be admitted that the traditional understanding of the authorship of John's gospel, attributing the composition of this work to the apostle John, the son of Zebedee, is a minority position today.[58] In fact, the state of research

---

(esp. 9:22) are anachronistic. See J. Louis Martyn, "Glimpses into the History of the Johannine Community," in *L'Évangile de Jean: sources, rédaction, théologie* (BETL 44; ed. Marinus de Jonge; Gembloux: Duculot, 1977), 149–75; idem, *History and Theology in the Fourth Gospel* (2nd ed.; Nashville: Abingdon, 1979; 3rd ed. NTL; Louisville: Westminster John Knox, 2003); Raymond E. Brown, *The Community of the Beloved Disciple* (New York: Paulist, 1979); see also Oscar Cullmann, *The Johannine Circle* (trans. John Bowden; London: SCM, 1976).

51. See D. Moody Smith, "The Contribution of J. Louis Martyn to the Understanding of the Gospel of John," in *The Conversation Continues: Studies in Paul and John in Honor of J. Louis Martyn* (ed. Robert T. Fortna and Beverly R. Gaventa; Nashville: Abingdon, 1990), 293, n. 30: "Martyn's thesis has become a paradigm.... It is a part of what students imbibe from standard works, such as commentaries and textbooks, as knowledge generally received and held to be valid." For a helpful critique of the "Johannine community hypothesis," see Klink, *Sheep of the Fold*.

52. See already Adolf Schlatter, *Der Evangelist Johannes: Wie er spricht, glaubt und denkt* (2nd ed.; Stuttgart: Calwer, 1948), x, who commented that the term "Johannine school" appeared to him to be "completely divorced from reality" (*völlig phantastisch*).

53. Martin Hengel, *Die johanneische Frage* (WUNT 67; Tübingen: Mohr-Siebeck, 1993). Note, however, that Hengel did not return to the notion of Johannine authorship but instead postulated what he called the *Doppelantlitz* ("dual face") of John's gospel. Conceding that internal evidence seems to point to John as the author of the gospel, Hengel argued that this was what the author wanted to lead his audience to believe, but that the author himself was in fact a member of the Jerusalem aristocracy somewhat removed from Jesus' inner circle.

54. Richard Bauckham, ed., *The Gospels for All Christians: Rethinking the Gospel Audiences* (Grand Rapids: Eerdmans, 1998). Like Hengel, however, Bauckham does not affirm apostolic authorship.

55. Robert Kysar, "The Expulsion from the Synagogue: The Tale of a Theory," chap. 15 in *Voyages with John* (Waco, TX: Baylor University Press, 2005); cf. idem, "Dehistoricizing of the Gospel of John," in *John, Jesus, and History*, 75–101. Rather than rethinking his views on the historical reconstruction of John's setting, however, Kysar moved to a postmodern paradigm, which appreciates John as story and engages in various "readings" of it.

56. Hill, *Johannine Corpus in the Early Church*.

57. The integrity of John's gospel is not compromised by the inimitable Johannine style enveloping narrative as well as discourse portions. For positive assessments of the historical reliability of John's gospel, see Andreas J. Köstenberger, "John," in *Zondervan Illustrated Bible Backgrounds Commentary*, Vol. 2: *John–Acts* (ed. Clinton E. Arnold; Grand Rapids: Zondervan, 2002), 1–216; Craig L. Blomberg, "To What Extent Is John Historically Reliable?" in *Perspectives on John: Method and Interpretation in the Fourth Gospel* (ed. Robert B. Sloan and Michael C. Parsons; NABPR Special Studies Series; Lewiston, NY: Mellen, 1993), 27–56; idem, "The Historical Reliability of John: Rushing in Where Angels Fear to Tread?" in *Jesus and Johannine Tradition* (ed. Robert T. Fortna and Tom Thatcher; Louisville: Westminster John Knox, 2001), 71–82; and idem, *The Historical Reliability of John's Gospel* (Leicester, UK: Inter-Varsity Press, 2002); contra, Casey, *Is John's Gospel True?* Note also Hill, *Johannine Corpus in the Early Church*. Nevertheless, there continues to be skepticism on the part of many; see the survey by Kysar, "Expulsion from the Synagogue"; the largely positive assessment by Thompson, "Spiritual Gospel"; and the negative evaluation by Harold W. Attridge, "Response to 'The De-historicizing of the Gospel of John' by Robert Kysar" (presented at the Annual Meeting of the SBL, Toronto, November 23–26, 2002).

58. Yet, curiously, the traditional view has not so much been refuted as it has been dismissed in the wake of Enlightenment's questioning of ecclesiastical authority and long-held positions. See Köstenberger, "Early Doubts."

on the setting of this gospel is in considerable ferment today.[59] While it is unlikely that scholarship at large will return to the traditional view, the "Johannine community hypothesis" has suffered irreparable damage in recent years by the critiques of some of the world's foremost NT historians and is in the process of collapsing. Yet no new paradigm has taken its place. While many, as mentioned, agree in their criticism of the "Johannine community hypothesis," alternative proposals vary. The following discussion chronicles the quest for a plausible setting of John's gospel and proposes a constructive alternative to the "Johannine community hypothesis."

2.1.2 The Quest for the Historical Setting of John's Gospel
2.1.2.1 Introduction
2.1.2.1.1 The Traditional Setting of John

The quest for the most plausible historical setting for the composition of John's gospel has had a colorful history.[60] The traditional view is that the apostle John, at the urging of some of his disciples, put pen to papyrus and recorded his personal reminiscences of the life and times of Jesus' earthly ministry toward the end of the first century AD (Irenaeus, *Haer.* 3.1.2). The geographical setting for these developments centered on Ephesus, on the west coast of Asia Minor, a location that also features prominently in the ministry of the apostle Paul and receives mention in the letters to the seven churches in Revelation 2–3.

In the traditional reconstruction John, the son of Zebedee and one of three disciples to make up Jesus' inner circle, paired with Peter in the early portions of the book of Acts and reputed to be one of the pillars of the Jerusalem church in Galatians 2, later moved to Ephesus, perhaps just prior to the outbreak of the Jewish War, where he had a fruitful ministry that led to the establishment of several congregations, which eventually were the recipients of the three canonical Johannine letters. Still later, the same apostle was exiled to the island of Patmos, where he wrote the final book of the NT canon, the book of Revelation.

In this reconstruction John's gospel occupies a place well within the mainstream of first-century Christianity. The relationship with the other canonical gospels tends to be one of friendly supplementation rather than sharp conflict or discord. The gospel itself reflects not merely "Johannine tradition," whether independent or indebted to so-called "Synoptic tradition," but actual eyewitness testimony from one of the key participants in the actual events leading to Jesus' crucifixion by the Romans. The eyewitness claims in this gospel (e.g., John 19:35; 21:24) stem from none other than John the son of Zebedee himself, rather than being retrofitted to him by a group or community founded by him or tracing its origin back to him. While John

---

59. See the various contributions in Thatcher, ed., *What We Have Heard from the Beginning*, particularly Carson, "Reflections upon a Johannine Pilgrimage," and my brief response, "Progress and Regress in Recent Johannine Scholarship—Reflections upon the Road Ahead," 105–7.

60. "The Quest for the Historical Setting of John's Gospel" adapts material published in *Challenging Perspectives on the Gospel of John* (WUNT 2/219; ed. Johr Lierman; Tübingen: Mohr-Siebeck, 2006), 69–108, and is used with permission.

has never been viewed as the mainspring of the first-century Gentile mission—this honor was reserved for the apostle Paul—in the traditional reconstruction he participates in the mission in an apostolic capacity at Ephesus (among other locations). Hence, in this understanding the apostle serves the church prominently, both in geographical and ecclesiastical terms, and not least as an author.

2.1.2.1.2 Enlightenment Disputes

As I have documented elsewhere, the spirit of the Enlightenment, with its emphasis on the independent investigation of the biblical documents as "books like any other," led to a variety of different readings of John's gospel, with an attendant proliferation of perspectives on its likely setting.[61] The years 1790 to 1810 in particular brought considerable ferment in this regard, with some placing the date of composition well into the second century and others defending the traditional paradigm. Among those upholding a second-century composition was Edward Evanson, an English Unitarian, who found John's gospel full of legends (such as the Lazarus account) and attributed authorship to someone familiar with Platonic philosophy.[62] In a somewhat similar vein, the German pastor Karl Gottlieb Bretschneider, writing in Germany in 1820, saw the gospel against the backdrop of the Logos of Philonic Alexandrian philosophy, postulating an Egyptian provenance.[63] While some, such as Friedrich Schleiermacher, continued to advocate a more traditional approach, others, most notably David Friedrich Strauss (1835), viewed the gospel as myth, a category picked up and further developed by Rudolf Bultmann.[64]

Within this (for some) rather unsettling ferment in Johannine scholarship, voices such as B. F. Westcott's continued to flesh out more fully some of the older, more conventional notions of the composition of John's gospel. Writing only a few years after Strauss's death, Westcott sketched the occasion for writing John's gospel as follows:

> In the last quarter of the first century, the world relative to the Christian Church was a new world; and St John presents in his view of the work and Person of Christ the answers which he had found to be given in Him to the problems which were offered by the changed order. The overthrow of Jerusalem, carrying with it the destruction of the ancient service and the ancient people of God, the establishment of the Gentile congregations on the basis of St Paul's interpretation of the Gospel, the rise of a Christian philosophy (*gnōsis*) from the contact of the historic creed with Eastern and Western speculation, could not but lead one who had lived with Christ to go back once more to those days of a divine discipleship, that he might find in them, according to the promise, the anticipated replies to the questionings of a later age.[65]

---

61. Köstenberger, "Early Doubts."

62. Edward Evanson, *The Dissonance of the Four Generally Received Evangelists and the Evidence of Their Authenticity Examined* (Ipswich, 1792), cited in Köstenberger, "Early Doubts," 25–29.

63. Bretschneider, *Probabilia*, cited in Baird, *History of New Testament Research*, 1:312–14.

64. For Strauss, Jesus was "a man like others, and the Gospels ... the oldest collections of the myths which were attached around the core of this personality" (*Christ of Faith and the Jesus of History*, 161; cited in Baird, *History of New Testament Research*, 1:250).

65. B. F. Westcott, *Commentary on the Gospel according to St. John* (Grand Rapids: Eerdmans, 1975 1908.), xxxvii–xxxviii.

Contrasting John and the Synoptics, Westcott located the time of composition of John's gospel firmly in the period subsequent to the destruction of the temple:

> The Synoptic Gospels are full of warnings of judgment.... In St John all is changed. There are no prophecies of the siege of the Holy City ... the judgment has been wrought.... The task of the Evangelist was to unfold the essential causes of the catastrophe, which were significant for all time, and to shew [sic] that even through apparent ruin and failure the will of God found fulfilment. Inexorable facts had revealed the rejection of the Jews. It remained to shew [sic] that this rejection was not only foreseen, but was also morally inevitable, and that it involved no fatal loss.... The true people of God survived the ruin of the Jews: the ordinances of a new society replaced in a nobler shape the typical and transitory worship of Israel.[66]

Clearly, as far as their postulated setting of John's gospel and their evaluation of its historical value are concerned, Strauss and Westcott inhabit altogether different worlds. While Strauss assigns the Jesus of John's gospel to the category of religious myth, Westcott locates the composition of the gospel historically within the matrix of three major, then-recent phenomena: the (Pauline) Gentile mission, the destruction of the temple, and the emergence of Gnosticism. He finds in John's gospel, especially in comparison with the Synoptics, theological constructs that could best be viewed as responses to these developments. Without claiming that these phenomena are explicitly addressed in the gospel text, he defends them as eminently plausible historical inferences from the gospel's theology when it is set against historical developments in the last few decades of the first century.

While much continental Johannine scholarship in the early twentieth century followed Strauss rather than Westcott (most notably Bultmann in his celebrated 1941 John commentary), this member of the famed "Cambridge trio" (together with F. J. A. Hort and J. B. Lightfoot) has served as an important point of reference for more conservative scholars ever since. They contend that Westcott's synthesis, while frequently disputed, has never been refuted.

2.1.2.1.3 *The Johannine Community Hypothesis*

In the second half of the twentieth century, a rather novel construct of the setting of John's gospel emerged, the "Johannine community hypotheses," in its various forms and refinements. The proponent of one influential version of the hypothesis, American scholar J. Louis Martyn, used the reference to synagogue expulsion in John 9:22 as his entry point to the gospel's historical setting.[67] Martyn found in this reference an (anachronistic) pointer to something in the gospel's life setting, namely,

---

66. Ibid., xxxviii (cf. Peter W. Walker, *Jesus and the Holy City: New Testament Perspectives on Jerusalem* [Grand Rapids: Eerdmans, 1996], 197, n. 142, citing Westcott). The above references to Westcott should in no way be read as endorsing any lingering anti-Semitism, anti-Judaism, or supersessionism.

67. Martyn, *History and Theology*; idem, "Glimpses into the History."

the memory of the recent excommunication of the Johannine Christians from their parent synagogue, at the end of the first century AD.

According to Martyn, this gospel is foremost an account not of Jesus' earthly ministry, but of the history of the "Johannine community." Prominent in the latter is the struggle with the Jewish synagogue that had expelled it as a result of its belief in Jesus as Messiah. The surface language of the gospel can be decoded by the discerning reader through employment of a "two-level hermeneutic," which turns language overtly pertaining to the historical Jesus into symbolic or allegorical references to the Johannine community. An important historical datum for the full-fledged version of Martyn's Johannine community hypothesis (though not the initial version)[68] was the *birkat ha-minim* ("curse of the heretics"), which allegedly was added to Jewish synagogue liturgy around AD 90 and applied to messianic, Christian Jews.

2.1.2.1.4 The Johannine Community Hypothesis Undermined

The alleged role of the *birkat ha-minim* in the composition of John's gospel has undergone extensive critique and reevaluation. Steven Motyer, in an important monograph, helpfully summarizes the drastic turning of the tide in the post-Martyn years.[69] In 1975, Peter Schäfer argued that the *birkat ha-minim* played no significant role in the separation of Jews and Christians in the first century.[70] In 1981, Lawrence Schiffman and Reuven Kimelman contended that post-AD 70 Judaism did not close ranks against Jewish Christians and that there is no evidence that the *birkat ha-minim* was addressed toward them in particular.[71]

In 1982, Shaye Cohen wrote an essay to the effect that the Yavneh sages had a remarkably *inclusive* spirit, cursing only those unwilling to commit to ideological pluralism.[72] The same year saw the publication of William Horbury's influential study on the textual development of the Twelfth Benediction that demonstrated the insecure textual foundation of the Martyn view.[73] In 1983, Jacob Neusner showed that the Yavneh sage Eliezer ben Hyrcanus displayed a remarkably irenic spirit toward other groups within Judaism, even toward Samaritans.[74] In 1984, Steven Katz strongly opposed the view that Yavneh launched an official attack

---

68. See D. Moody Smith's response to Robert Kysar's "Expulsion from the Synagogue" at the Annual Meeting of the SBL, Toronto, November 2002, where Smith astutely observes that Martyn's 1957 Th.D. dissertation, "The Salvation-Historical Perspective in the Fourth Gospel," while displaying seeds of his two-level hermeneutic, contains no references to the *birkat ha-minim*.

69. Stephen Motyer, *"Your Father the Devil?" A New Approach to John and "the Jews"* (Carlisle, UK: Paternoster, 1997), 92–93, nn. 62–69.

70. Peter Schäfer, "Die sogenannte Synode von Jabne: Zur Trennung von Juden und Christen im ersten/zweiten Jh. n. Chr.," *Judaica* 31 (1975): 54–64, 116–24.

71. Lawrence H. Schiffman, "At the Crossroads: Tannaitic Perspectives on the Jewish-Christian Schism," in *Jewish and Christian Self-Definition*. Vol. 2: *Aspects of Judaism in the Graeco-Roman Period* (ed. E. P. Sanders; London: SCM, 1981), 115–56; Reuven Kimelman, "Birkat Ha-Minim and the Lack of Evidence for an Anti-Christian Jewish Prayer in Late Antiquity," in ibid., 226–44.

72. Shaye J. D. Cohen, "Yavneh Revisited: Pharisees, Rabbis, and the End of Jewish Sectarianism," in *SBL 1982 Seminar Papers* (ed. Kent H. Richards; Chico, CA: Scholars Press, 1982), 45–61, esp. 59.

73. William Horbury, "The Benediction of the *Minim* and Early Jewish-Christian Controversy," *JTS* 33 (1982): 19–61.

74. Jacob Neusner, "The Formation of Rabbinic Judaism: Methodological Issues and Substantive Theses," in *Formative Judaism: Religious, Historical and Literary Studies, Third Series: Torah, Pharisees, and Rabbis* (BJS 46; Chico, CA: Scholars Press, 1983), 99–144, esp. 133.

on Jewish Christians.[75] In 1985, Wayne Meeks declared (later echoed by Graham Stanton in 1992) that the *birkat ha-minim* constitutes a "red herring in Johannine [sic] research."[76]

More recently, Philip Alexander has maintained that the existence of the *birkat ha-minim* can be traced back "with some confidence to the first half of the second [but not necessarily the first] century C.E."[77] According to him, labeling someone as a *min* identified that person, not necessarily as a Christian, but as one who did not accept the authority of the rabbis, who in effect condemned all those who were not of their party, "setting themselves up as the custodians of orthodoxy." The curses, rather than singling out messianic Christians, were introduced to "establish Rabbinism as orthodoxy within the synagogue."[78]

What is more, Yavneh was in no position to force the *birkat ha-minim* on the synagogues of Palestine, "let alone of the Diaspora," so that acceptance of it as standard doubtless "would have taken some time."[79] According to Alexander, the exclusion of Christians thus was not the primary, immediate target. "The Rabbis adopted a more subtle ploy: they appear to have set out first and foremost to establish Rabbinism as orthodoxy, knowing that once that happened the exclusion of the Christians from the synagogue would inevitably follow."[80]

Alexander's view not only raises serious questions as to whether or not the *birkat ha-minim* targeted Christians, it also casts doubt on the date at which the curse was introduced into the synagogue liturgy. For this reason scholars in recent years have been far less confident than Martyn in postulating that the *birkat ha-minim* served as the key to the historical background of John's gospel.[81]

Removing the *birkat ha-minim*, of course, does not necessarily invalidate all versions of the Johannine community hypothesis (though it does cast doubt on Martyn's variety). Others, such as Martyn's colleague at Union Seminary, Raymond Brown, have managed to hold to a form of the Johannine community hypothesis without so much as mentioning the *birkat ha-minim*, which shows that the latter is not an indispensable part of such a construal of the life setting of John's

---

75. Steven T. Katz, "Issues in the Separation of Judaism and Christianity after 70 C.E.: A Reconsideration," *JBL* 103 (1984): 43–76.

76. Wayne A. Meeks, "Breaking Away: Three New Testament Pictures of Christianity's Separation from the Jewish Communities," in *"To See Ourselves as Others See Us": Christians, Jews, "Others" in Late Antiquity* (Chico, CA: Scholars Press, 1985), 93–115, esp. 102; Graham N. Stanton, *A Gospel for a New People: Studies in Matthew* (Edinburgh: T&T Clark, 1992), esp. 142.

77. Philip S. Alexander, "'The Parting of the Ways' from the Perspective of Rabbinic Judaism," in *Jews and Christians: The Parting of the Ways A.D. 70 to 135* (ed. James D. G. Dunn; Tübingen: Mohr-Siebeck, 1992), 7. Alexander refers to Justin's *Dialogue* 16.96 as "perhaps the earliest securely dated evidence for its use" (after AD 135).

78. Ibid., 9.

79. Ibid., 10. Statements such as, "The degree to which the Pharisees emerge in the fourth Gospel as the dominant force in Judaism ... is surely best explained as a reflection of the growing dominance of the rabbinic authorities within Judaism during the Jabnean period" seem therefore overconfident. Cf. James D. G. Dunn, "Let John Be John: A Gospel for Its Time," in *The Gospel and the Gospels* (ed. Peter Stuhlmacher; Grand Rapids/Cambridge: Eerdmans, 1991), 303–4.

80. Alexander, "Parting of the Ways," 11.

81. The problem is brushed aside by Dunn, "Let John Be John," 304. See Köstenberger, "John," *ZIBBC*, 2:95, who lists the following concerns: (1) the uncertainty of whether or not the twelfth of the Eighteen Benedictions included the term *noṣrim*; (2) the question of whether or not this term designated "Christians"; (3) the issue of whether a church-synagogue conflict around AD 90 was the exclusive or primary factor behind John's references to synagogue expulsion; and (4) the charge that references to synagogue expulsion in John's gospel are necessarily anachronistic. See also the detailed study by Yaakov Y. Teppler, *Birkat haMinim* (Texts and Studies in Ancient Judaism 120; trans. Susan Weingarten; Tübingen: Mohr-Siebeck, 2007).

gospel.⁸² Though he had taken a more traditional view on the setting of John in his magisterial Anchor Bible commentary (published in 1966 and 1970),⁸³ Brown subsequently postulated a five-stage trajectory of development of the "Johannine community," which he inferred from the gospel's internal evidence, that does not rely on the *birkat ha-minim*.⁸⁴

It must be pointed out, however, that quite a few versions of the Johannine community hypothesis that do without the *birkat ha-minim* also involve an essentially sectarian reading of the gospel, an approach that seems to falter in light of its manifest mission motif (e.g., John 3:16; 17:18; 20:21).⁸⁵ For this reason some advocates have tried to refine the sectarian variant of the hypothesis to accommodate this mission emphasis. Perhaps, it has been conjectured, certain elements within the Johannine community (which had been traumatized by being expelled from its parent synagogue) were ready to reach out to their persecutors, and in their gospel they exhorted the more sectarian-minded among them to embrace a more missionary outlook.⁸⁶

Nevertheless, the *birkat ha-minim* provided vital plausibility for reconstructions in the Martyn mold, and its loss throws open the door to other possibilities.⁸⁷ Moreover, besides bracketing out the *birkat ha-minim*, historians of the ancient world have raised serious doubts about other aspects of the Johannine community hypothesis, pointing to the lack of evidence for such a community in patristic literature and charging that sectarian readings of John's gospel neglect the demonstrable interconnectedness of the early Christian communities.⁸⁸

In addition, as noted above, at a session of the Johannine literature section convened under the auspices of the Society of Biblical Literature, Robert Kysar,

---

82. Brown, *Community of the Beloved Disciple*. See also Gary M. Burge, "Situating John's Gospel in History," in *Jesus in Johannine Tradition* (ed. Robert T. Fortna and Tom Thatcher; Louisville: Westminster John Knox, 2001), 39.

83. In a presentation at the Annual Meeting of the SBL in Toronto, November 2002, Robert Kysar noted that in his 1966 preface Raymond Brown called the "Johannine community" theory nothing but a "working hypothesis." As Kysar wistfully remarked, however, working hypotheses do not always work!

84. Raymond E. Brown, "'Other Sheep Not of This Fold': The Johannine Perspective on Christian Diversity in the Late First Century," *JBL* 97 (1978): 5–22; see also Wayne Meeks, "Man from Heaven in Johannine Sectarianism," *JBL* 91 (1972): 44–72.

85. For a treatment of the Johannine mission theme, see Andreas J. Köstenberger, *The Missions of Jesus and the Disciples according to the Fourth Gospel* (Grand Rapids: Eerdmans, 1998), including a discussion of the state of research and further bibliography.

86. See the discussion of the contributions of Takashi Onuki, *Gemeinde und Welt im Johannesevangelium* (WMANT 56; Neukirchen-Vluyn: Neukirchener, 1984); David Rensberger, *Johannine Faith and Liberating Community* (Philadelphia: Westminster, 1988); idem, *Overcoming the World: Politics and Community in the Gospel of John* (London: SPCK, 1988); Teresa Okure, *The Johannine Approach to Mission* (WUNT 2/31; Tübingen: Mohr-Siebeck, 1988); and others in Köstenberger, *Missions of Jesus and the Disciples*, 203–6.

87. This is recognized by Burge, "Situating John's Gospel," who has "no complaint with the notion that a Johannine Community existed and that the concerns of this community inspired the construction and shape of the Fourth Gospel," but who takes exception to the contention that such community concerns necessarily led to a severing of historical ties between the gospel and the time of Jesus' earthly ministry (p. 37). While Burge repeatedly asserts that the first stratum of the gospel is to be located well before the First Jewish War (pre-AD 66; e.g., p. 44), he does not assign a date to his "Stratum Two," the stage at which (according to Burge) John 1:19 to 20:31 was "put in written form as a single story" (ibid.). In order to evaluate Burge's proposal, however, it would be critical to know the extent to which he allows for the material in the gospel to have been shaped by the events following the destruction of the Second Temple in AD 70. Also, it is unclear how the second stratum of Burge's essay can be accommodated within the notion of editorial "seams," which Burge postulates elsewhere (see idem, "Interpreting the Gospel of John," in *Interpreting the New Testament: Essays on Methods and Issues* [ed. David Alan Black and David S. Dockery; Nashville: Broadman & Holman, 2001], 376–80; idem, *Interpreting the Gospel of John* [Guides to NT Exegesis; Grand Rapids: Baker, 1992], 62–66).

88. See Hengel, *Die johanneische Frage*, on which see my review in *JETS* 39 (1996): 154–55; and Bauckham, ed., *Gospels for All Christians*. This is not to say that on almost any reading there is some kind of community theory that needs to be adopted (whether or not this

whose encyclopedic knowledge of the scholarly literature on John's gospel is widely recognized and respected, chronicled the rise and fall of the Martyn/Brown-style "Johannine community hypothesis" and expressed regret for ever having endorsed it.[89] While Gail O'Day, in a response at that same meeting, was doubtless right to contend that the abandonment of the apostolic authorship of John's gospel has "created space" for new readings of the gospel, it is now debateable whether the paradigm that replaced the traditional one is a substantial improvement.

2.1.2.1.5 Back to the Future

Perhaps, as Richard Bauckham has recently argued, the proliferation of "community hypotheses," Johannine and otherwise, is overdue for thorough, even radical, reassessment.[90] No full-fledged critique of the multiform Johannine community hypothesis will be offered here.[91] Suffice it to say for now that the past decade has seen a remarkable shift away from a paradigm that as recently as 1990 could be labeled as "virtually established" without fear of contradiction.[92] The time has come to reassess what is the most plausible reconstruction of the historical setting surrounding the composition of John's gospel in light of the history of Johannine scholarship and recent work on the world of the first century AD.

In what follows I will take another look at one of the three historical phenomena that Westcott placed in the setting of the gospel, the destruction of the Second Temple by the Romans in AD 70. I will argue that whatever background is assigned to John, here lies a key, perhaps the key.[93] The core element occasioning the composition of John's gospel, and particularly its emphasis on Jesus as the fulfillment of Jewish festivals and institutions, including the temple, can be identified as the destruction of the Second Temple.

John's Christology would then not be tied simply to temple imagery, as others have naturally recognized, but would be formulated precisely in the context of a crisis of Jewish belief, brought on by the destruction of the temple. The gospel

---

is the best locution). After all, there is not only a gospel but three letters and an apocalypse that share remarkable commonalities of style and outlook despite the differences in genre. The Johannine letters, in particular, clearly presuppose Johannine congregations that were the result of a prolonged, fruitful ministry in a certain locale not dissimilar to Paul's. In no way does skepticism regarding the weak and subjective redaction criticism underlying many forms of the Johannine community hypothesis mean that the Johannine corpus is to be treated as cut off from concrete churches.

89. Kysar, who almost thirty years prior to this address had gone on record saying the "Johannine community hypothesis" was a "lasting contribution to end-of-twentieth-century scholarship," discusses the rise and demise of the theory in the following five stages: (1) roots; (2) first signs of flaws; (3) further erosion of confidence; (4) more outspoken criticism; and (5) the theory in a new age.

90. Note Burge's appropriation of Bauckham's work in "Situating John's Gospel," 41.

91. But see the useful monograph by Klink, *Sheep of the Fold*.

92. D. Moody Smith, "Contribution of J. Louis Martyn," 293 n. 30: "Martyn's thesis has become a paradigm, to borrow from Thomas Kuhn. It is part of what students imbibe from standard works, such as commentaries and textbooks, as knowledge generally received and held to be valid."

93. I have hinted at this possibility in *Encountering John: The Gospel in Historical, Literary, and Theological Perspective* (EBS; Grand Rapids: Baker, 1999), 25, 28, and in the entry "John" in *NDBT*, 280 = "Introduction to John's Gospel," in *Studies in John and Gender*, 7–8. For a similar thesis, see John Dennis, "Restoration in John 11,47–52: Reading the Key Motifs in Their Jewish Context," *ETL* 81 (2005): 57–86. On the history and significance of the temple in Jewish history see Paul M. Hoskins, *Jesus as the Fulfillment of the Temple in the Gospel of John* (Paternoster Biblical Monographs; Carlisle, UK: Paternoster, 2007), chap. 2; on the tabernacle in the OT and Second Temple literature see Craig R. Koester, *The Dwelling of God: The Tabernacle in the Old Testament, Intertestamental Jewish Literature, and the New Testament* (CBQMS 22; Washington, DC: Catholic Biblical Association of America, 1989), 6–75.

could then be understood, at least in part, as a response to the religious vacuum left by the temple's destruction, a response that points to a permanent solution to that vacuum: Jesus' replacement of the temple, in the religious experience of his people, by himself.

2.1.2.2 The Destruction of the Temple as a Plausible Historical Setting for John's Gospel

It would be going too far to reduce the historical setting of the composition of John's gospel to the aftermath of this one event.[94] But it seems that shining the spotlight here is justified for several reasons.[95]

2.1.2.2.1 Date of Destruction Relative to John

Unlike the *birkat ha-minim*, the destruction of the Second Temple in AD 70 is a secure, indisputable historical datum and is clearly recent from the perspective of the AD 80s or early 90s, when John's gospel is widely held to have been written.[96]

While John's gospel does not explicitly mention the destruction of the temple, this in itself provides no real help for dating John relative to the destruction, since John regularly chooses not to refer to important events (such as Jesus' baptism by John or the institution of the Lord's Supper) but opts instead for an indirect approach that brings out the theological significance of certain incidents.[97]

The replacement theme of John's gospel might be held to date it after the temple's destruction, but (attractive as this line of reasoning would be to the thesis being argued here) this also is an unreliable guide. Hebrews features a replacement theme

---

94. For example, two recent monographs have strongly stressed the backdrop of Roman imperial power as relevant for understanding the setting of John's gospel. See Warren Carter, *John and Empire: Initial Explorations* (London: T&T Clark, 2008); and Tom Thatcher, *Greater than Caesar: Christology and Empire in the Fourth Gospel* (Minneapolis: Fortress, 2009). While some of their thoughts are suggestive, however, it is far from clear that the Roman backdrop is as strong for the writing of John's gospel as these authors suggest. See further the forthcoming BTNT volume on Revelation.

95. Cf. esp. Walker, *Jesus and the Holy City*, 195, who contends that the evangelist "was almost certainly writing after AD 70, probably from somewhere in the Diaspora," and that "John and his readers would then be well aware that, since the events recorded in the Gospel, the great city of Jerusalem had fallen to the Romans; above all, the Temple was no more." Walker notes that "if Jerusalem had recently been overthrown, this would give to John and his readers a shared piece of knowledge in light of which they would understand the text" (p. 195). Earlier, see the brief but suggestive comments by Gale A. Yee, *Jewish Feasts and the Gospel of John* (Wilmington, DE: Michael Glazier, 1989), esp. 12–13 and 16–17. Even more pronounced in its agreement with the thesis of the present essay is Alan R. Kerr, *The Temple of Jesus' Body: The Temple Theme in the Gospel of John* (JSNTSup 220; Sheffield: Sheffield Academic Press, 2002).

96. See, e.g., Folker Siegert, "'Zerstört diesen Tempel...!' Jesus als 'Tempel' in den Passionsüberlieferungen," in *Zerstörungen des Jerusalemer Tempels: Geschehen–Wahrnehmung–Bewältigung* (ed. Johannes Hahn; WUNT 147; Tübingen: Mohr-Siebeck, 2002), 118, n. 20. One of the few exceptions is John A. T. Robinson, "The New Look on the Fourth Gospel," *SE* (ed. Kurt Aland et al.; TU 73; Berlin: Akademie, 1959), 342, followed by George Allen Turner, "The Date and Purpose of the Gospel of John," *BETS* 6 (1963): 82–85. See also Daniel Wallace, "John 5,2 and the Date of the Fourth Gospel," *Bib* 71 (1990): 177–205, esp. 204; idem, *Greek Grammar beyond the Basics* (Grand Rapids: Zondervan, 1996), 531, who rests his argument for a pre-AD 70 date of John's gospel primarily on the use of the present tense in John 5:2. But see the critique of Wallace's view in Andreas J. Köstenberger, *John* (BECNT; Grand Rapids: Baker, 2004), 178, n. 12, and the subsequent interaction with Wallace on my website, www.biblicalfoundations.org; see also Blomberg, *Historical Reliability of John's Gospel* (2nd ed.; Downers Grove, IL: InterVarsity Press, 2007), 43; Carson, *Gospel according to John*, 241; and Bultmann, *Gospel of John* (trans. George R. Beasley-Murray; Philadelphia: Westminster, 1971), 240, n. 4.

97. See esp. Kerr, *Temple of Jesus' Body*, 24, who, in response to John A. T. Robinson, contends that the very "nature of irony and double meaning is to make one's points with subtlety, not baldly. John could very well be working with the unexpressed, but universally known, presupposition that the Temple had fallen, in the interests of shrewdly presenting Jesus as the new Temple complex of Judaism."

similar to John's gospel, but a good case can be made that it was written before the temple's destruction. Here we will assume the most widely accepted view, that John's gospel was composed one or two decades after the destruction of the temple.

2.1.2.2.2 *Impact of the Destruction*

John's gospel very possibly originated in, and was directed to, a Jewish Diaspora context (such as the Jewish and proselyte community in Ephesus),[98] but this poses no challenge to the relevance of the fall of the temple to the gospel. As recent scholarship demonstrates, the destruction of the Second Temple, the national religious symbol of the Jewish people, deeply impacted Jews in both Palestine and the Diaspora. The impact could fairly be described as universal.[99] If the composition of the gospel is dated anytime toward the end of the first century, it is hardly conceivable that a text apparently so richly interested in the temple would not be written, as it were, in the shadow of its destruction.[100]

In an important essay, Alexander notes that "the War of 66–74 destroyed whatever existed of a centralized religious authority within Judaism."[101] According to Alexander, the events surrounding the destruction of the temple were significant in at least two important respects: first, "the debacle of the War" opened for (Jewish) Christians a "window of opportunity," sweeping away the authorities hostile to emergent Christianity and removing for the foreseeable future the threat of "being excommunicated from Israel by decree form [*sic*] Jerusalem." Moreover, "the destruction of the Temple also handed the Christians a propaganda coup, for it gave them the chance to argue that the catastrophe was a divine judgement on Israel for the rejection of Jesus."[102]

Stressing the spiritual nature of the kingdom and deemphasizing "the territorial dimension of Judaism," however, moved Christians out of step with rabbinic Judaism.[103] Ironically, the very success of the Gentile mission created an "image problem" in that "Christianity must have found it increasingly difficult to establish itself in the eyes of Jews as a *Jewish* movement."[104] Nevertheless, Alexander believes it is reasonable to assume that "the Jewish Christians never abandoned their mission to Israel."[105] Fascinatingly, he sketches the position of Jewish Christianity as "caught between Scylla and Charybdis": "the closer it moved to the Gentile Churches the less credible it would have become within the Jewish community; the more it emphasized its Jewishness the more difficult would have become its relations with the Gentile Churches."[106]

---

98. See esp. Carson, *Gospel according to John, passim*.

99. See, e.g., Jacob Neusner, "Judaism in a Time of Crisis: Four Responses to the Destruction of the Second Temple," *Judaism* 21 (1972): 313: "The destruction of the Second Temple marked a major turning in the history of Judaism in late antiquity.... The loss of the building itself was of considerable consequence ... the devastation of Jerusalem ... intensified the perplexity of the day.... The cultic altar, the Temple and the holy city, by August, 70, lay in ruins—a considerable calamity."

100. See Stefan Lücking, "Die Zerstörung des Tempels 70 n. Chr. als Krisenerfahrung der frühen Christen," in *Zerstörungen des Jerusalemer Tempels*, esp. 144–46, who relates the temple's destruction to the life setting of Mark's gospel.

101. Alexander, "Parting of the Ways," 3.

102. Ibid., 20. According to the Synoptics, this was already what Jesus himself had predicted (Matt 24:2 par.; cf. Luke 23:28–31).

103. Ibid., 23, with reference to the work of W. D. Davies.

104. Ibid.

105. Ibid., 23, n. 35.

106. Ibid., 24.

The increasing estrangement between rabbinism and Gentile Christianity left "Jewish Christianity exposed and vulnerable between the two camps."[107]

If Alexander's reconstruction is even approximately accurate, Jewish-Christian relations at the time of the gospel's composition were considerably more fluid than the rigid form of Martyn's *birkat ha-minim* hypothesis would indicate. Not only did the destruction of the temple not provoke a complete rupture of Jewish-Christian relations, it provided Christians with an opportunity for Jewish mission, a mission that, Alexander is convinced, Jewish Christians (such as John the apostle) never abandoned. The relevance of these insights to the composition and, more particularly, the purpose of John's gospel is apparent.

The data provided by Alexander's essay are supplemented by Martin Goodman in one of the most important recent studies of Diaspora reactions to the destruction of the Second Temple.[108] Goodman contends that there is "every reason to suppose that the rasing [*sic*] of the Temple horrified diaspora Jews as much as their Judaean compatriots."[109] For the Jewish historian Josephus, living in Rome, "Judaism without the Temple seems to have been unthinkable," at least initially (*Ag. Ap.* 2.193–98).[110] Thus it seems a "fair assumption" that Diaspora Jews generally "were profoundly affected" by the consequences of the first Jewish War in AD 66–70. What is more, it is not unlikely that "the large settlements of Jews in Asia Minor" acted as host for some (though probably not many) of those involved in the Judean revolt.[111] If so, the destruction of the Jerusalem temple was not just some distant event, nearly irrelevant for Diaspora Jews, but an earthquake that reverberated powerfully among Jews and proselytes who lived toward the end of the first century AD throughout the Greco-Roman world.

The *birkat ha-minim* (wherever it was actually promulgated) in all likelihood had hardly any initial impact in the Greek-speaking Diaspora. Goodman notes that it is possible "that the rabbis lacked any say in the Greek-speaking Diaspora until well into the third century AD or even later."[112] By contrast, the destruction of the temple affected Diaspora Jews in a variety of ways. First, the Romans "trumpeted their victory throughout the empire": "coins proclaimed *Judaea Capta*," and the Temple of Peace, in which spoils of the Judean wars were displayed, was dedicated on the Capitol in AD 76.[113]

Second, the ambiguity inherent in the Latin name *Iudaeus* (Greek *Ioudaios*) led to post-revolt reprisals against Jews all across the empire. The term most basically referred to Judeans, the inhabitants of Judea, but it was also the usual term for Jews wherever they lived, and thus served to tar all Jews as supporters of the revolt.

---

107. Ibid., 24, n. 37.
108. Martin Goodman, "Diaspora Reactions to the Destruction of the Temple," in *Jews and Christians: The Parting of the Ways A.D. 70 to 135*, 27–38. For the circumstances surrounding the Jewish revolt of AD 66–70, see also the same author's *The Ruling Class of Judaea: The Origins of the Jewish Revolt against Rome, A.D. 66–70* (Cambridge: Cambridge University Press, 1987), esp. 176–97.
109. Goodman, "Diaspora Reactions," 27.

110. See further below.
111. Goodman, "Diaspora Reactions," 30. On p. 36, Goodman refers to "huge numbers" of Jews in Asia Minor surviving after the Second Jewish Revolt in AD 135.
112. Ibid., 29.
113. Ibid. See also Sabine Panzram, "Der Jerusalemer Tempel und das Rom der Flavier," in *Zerstörungen des Jerusalemer Tempels*, 166–82.

Third, the Jewish "temple tax," the annual Jewish offering in support of the temple, was after its destruction converted not merely into an imperial tax (the *fiscus Judaicus*), but a tax the income of which was devoted to the Temple of Jupiter Capitolinus. The *fiscus Judaicus* was collected rigorously under Domitian (AD 81–96), under whom apparently even proselytes and Jewish apostates, which would include Jewish Christians, were subject to it (Suetonius, *Dom.* 12.2).[114] Not until Domitian's successor, Nerva (AD 96–98), did the empire begin to distinguish between Jews and Christians (cf. Pliny, *Ep.* 10.96).

The temple's ruins still cast their shadow in the days when the gospel was composed, and the echoes of its fall still rang loudly in Jewish ears everywhere. Next we turn to the Jewish reaction to the loss of their temple, and how John's gospel addresses these reactions.

2.1.2.3 The Gospel of John and Other Responses to the Loss of the Temple

The destruction of the temple evoked a variety of coping strategies among Jews. If John's gospel is a response to the temple's destruction, then it might also be characterized as a coping strategy itself, one that answers, or critiques, the coping strategies adopted by (other) Jews.

2.1.2.3.1 Jewish Strategies for Coping with the Loss of the Temple

The fall of Jerusalem in AD 70 was not the first time that the Jews were bereft of their central sanctuary. And each past instance of the destruction or loss of the temple had confronted the Jews with the need to develop coping strategies. The first such need arose for the exiles in Babylon in the years after 587/6 BC, a period that has been described as the "templeless age."[115] Intriguingly, it was not the emergent synagogue but the presence of Yahweh himself that served as a substitute for the loss of that Jerusalem temple. Yahweh contends in Ezek 11:16, "for a little while [the time of the exile] *I* have been a sanctuary for them" (emphasis added). This provides an important relativization of the function of the temple, setting it in the larger context of the manifestations of Yahweh's presence to the people of Israel and the relationship he had sustained with his people even prior to the Solomonic temple.

Not only did the Jews have to cope with the absence of the temple in exile itself, even after the remnant's return many remained in Diaspora and lived away from

---

114. Goodman, "Diaspora Reactions," 32, with reference to L. A. Thompson, "Domitian and the Jewish Tax," *Historia* 31 (1982): 329–42.

115. See Jill Middlemas, *The Templeless Age: An Introduction to the History, Literature, and Theology of the "Exile"* (Louisville: Westminster John Knox, 2007). See also Andreas Ruwe, "Die Veränderung tempeltheologischer Konzepte in Ezechiel 8–11," in *Gemeinde ohne Tempel/Community without Temple: Zur Substituierung und Transformation des Jerusalemer Tempels und seines Kults im Alten Testament,* *antiken Judentum und frühen Christentum* (WUNT 118; ed. Beate Ego, Armin Lange, and Peter Pilhofer; Tübingen: Mohr-Siebeck, 1999), 3–18; and Rainer Albertz, "Die Zerstörung des Jerusalemer Tempels 587 v. Chr.: Historische Einordnung und religionspolitische Bedeutung," and Karl-Friedrich Pohlmann, "Religion in der Krise—Krise einer Religion: Die Zerstörung des Jerusalemer Tempels 587 v. Chr.," both in *Zerstörungen des Jerusalemer Tempels,* 23–39 and 40–60.

the temple.[116] Diaspora communities acknowledged the centrality of the temple through pilgrimages and the widespread participation in the dispatch of monetary offerings to Jerusalem for the support of the temple. The Jerusalem temple nevertheless remained the central institution of the Jewish people. Complicating the picture, the Second Temple period saw the erection of rival temples at Elephantine (Upper Egypt), at Leontopolis (Lower Egypt), and in Samaria.[117] All of these were outside of Judea, however, and none rivaled the prestige of the Jerusalem sanctuary. Synagogues in Judea, for their part, were given the name *synagōgē* (rather than *proseuchē* as in the Diaspora) in order to avoid any threat to the status of the temple.[118]

Another "community without a temple" was the Qumran covenanters, who withdrew from the Jerusalem temple owing to the corruption of its worship.[119] The history of the Qumran sect anticipates the situation faced by post-AD 70 Judaism in that the sect had to face the loss of the temple earlier than other branches of Judaism. For the people of Qumran, the Jerusalem temple was "lost" owing to its corruption and the debasement of the priesthood. While there is no evidence of alternative sacrificial rites at Qumran, the covenanters viewed themselves as a virtual temple "in which, through purity regulations, prayer, and the study of God's law, it was possible to achieve the spiritual connection with the divine which had been vouchsafed to Israel in God's central sanctuary according to the Bible."[120] At the same time, the sect (presumably including former Sadduccean priests) cherished the future expectation that in the end times they would be restored to lead sacrificial worship in a purified Jerusalem temple.[121]

A fascinating glimpse of ways of coping with the loss of the Second Temple after AD 70 appears in Josephus' works *Jewish War* and *Antiquities*.[122] In the former volume, published in AD 79—almost ten years after the destruction of the temple—Josephus expresses his views in the manner of Thucydides, by placing them on the lips of the characters in his account. He features a speech by Eleazar, son of Yair, who contends that there could be no Judaism without the temple, so that the people in Masada were the final Jews on the earth (*J.W.* 7.341–88). By the

---

116. See Ina Willi-Plein, "Warum musste der Zweite Tempel gebaut werden?" in *Gemeinde ohne Tempel/Community without Temple*, 57–73.

117. See Jörg Frey, "Temple and Rival Temple—The Cases of Elephantine, Mt. Gerizim, and Leontopolis," in ibid., 171–203.

118. Ibid., 197. See also Frowald G. Hüttenmeister, "Die Synagoge: Ihre Entwicklung von einer multifunktionalen Einrichtung zum reinen Kultbau," in ibid., 357–69.

119. See esp. 4QMMT; cf. 1QS 9:3–4; CD 6:11–15.

120. Lawrence H. Schiffmann, "Community without Temple: The Qumran Community's Withdrawal from the Jerusalem Temple," in *Gemeinde ohne Tempel*, 280. On "Prayer in Qumran and the Synagogue," see the essay with this title by Esther Eshel in ibid., 323–34.

121. See esp. 1QM and 11QT. See Hermann Lichtenberger, "Der Mythos von der Unzerstörbarkeit des Tempels," in *Zerstörungen des Jerusalemer Tempels*, 100–101, citing 11QT 29.7–10; Florentino García Martínez, "Priestly Functions in a Community without Temple," in ibid., 303–19; and George J. Brooke, "Miqdash Adam, Eden, and the Qumran Community," in ibid., 285–301, who notes the importance of the community's eschatological self-understanding in coping with life without a temple. Brooke distinguishes between an earlier period featuring predominantly priestly terms and a later period that stressed the sovereignty of God and messianism. Note also Friedrich Avemarie, who proposes that John the Baptist should be viewed "as an exponent of a type of piety that had become essentially indifferent to the reality of a functioning sacrificial cult" ("Ist die Johannestaufe ein Ausdruck von Tempelkritik? Skizze eines methodischen Problems," in *Gemeinde ohne Tempel*, 395–410).

122. See Hanan Eshel, "Josephus' View on Judaism without the Temple in Light of the Discoveries at Masada and Murabbaʿat," in *Gemeinde ohne Tempel*, 229–38 (cited by Lichtenberger, "Mythos," 106). See also Kerr, *Temple of Jesus' Body*, 45, who notes that Josephus (*J.W.* 2.647–7.455 and *Life* 407–23) is the only source for most of the Jewish War and the destruction of the Second Temple.

time *Antiquities* was published thirteen years later (AD 92), Josephus had come to realize that his previous opinion had been mistaken and Judaism could continue even without the temple.

The earlier outlook of Josephus and his later shift of opinion are especially illustrative when the composition of John's gospel is placed in the same period as his writings, at the end of the first century. He shows that, at least for certain Jews, life without the temple was at first hardly imaginable. Initial shock, however, gradually gave way to coping mechanisms that overcame the absence of a temple. It may be surmised that, likewise, after initial shock waned, Christian apologetic efforts toward Jews (such as John's) emerged to address the Jews' need to fill the void left by the Second Temple's destruction.[123] The fourth evangelist's approach was to commend a permanent solution, namely, faith in Jesus the Messiah as the one who fulfilled the underlying symbolism not only of the temple, but of the entire Jewish festival calendar (not to speak of a variety of other typological substructures of OT theology, such as the serpent in the wilderness or the manna). In other words, John offered an alternative to the path chosen by mainstream (Pharisaic) Judaism, which eventually became rabbinic Judaism centered on the Mishnah and the Talmuds.[124]

2.1.2.3.2 *John's Gospel as Jewish Response to the Destruction of the Temple*

James D. G. Dunn, in his preface to the publication of the Second Durham-Tübingen Research Symposium on Earliest Christianity and Judaism (held in 1989), underscores the seminal importance for Judaism and Christianity of the late first century AD. He writes "that the years between apostolic age and post-apostolic age, between second Temple Judaism and rabbinic Judaism [AD 70–132] ... are the hinge on which major issues hung and decisive events turned."[125]

J. A. Draper draws an explicit connection between the destruction of the Second Temple and the composition of John's gospel, venturing to suggest that "John's gospel may be characterised as a fundamental response to the failed millenarian movement in 68–70 CE, which left the central symbol of the Jewish people and culture in ruins.... To most, the loss of the Temple must have seemed to be a permanent loss of the presence of God with his people."[126] Specifically, Draper dubs John's gospel

---

123. Another pertinent document illustrating this period is the book of *4 Ezra*, which was written in Hebrew shortly after the death of Domitian c. AD 100 (see Hermann Lichtenberger, "Zion and the Destruction of the Temple in 4 Ezra 9–10," in *Gemeinde ohne Tempel*, 239–49; see also Manuel Vogel, "Tempel und Tempelkult in Pseudo-Philos *Liber Antiquitatum Biblicarum*," in ibid., 251–63; and Jacob Neusner, "Formation of Rabbinic Judaism," 99–144, esp. 122). *Fourth Ezra* contains seven visions said to have been received by Ezra in the thirteenth year after the destruction of the First Temple in 587 BC. The author's solution to the loss of the temple is a return to the old law. As prior to the building of the First Temple, this time without the Second Temple ought to be characterized by renewed adherence to, and focus on, Torah.

124. See also the various essays in Hahn, ed., *Zerstörungen des Jerusalemer Tempels*, which focus on the impact that the destructions of the temple in 587 BC and AD 70 had on the identity and self-perception of both Jews and (in the case of AD 70) Christians.

125. Dunn, "Preface," in *Jews and Christians*, ix–x. See also idem, *The Partings of the Ways between Christianity and Judaism and Their Significance for the Character of Christianity* (London: SCM/Philadelphia: Trinity International, 1991), 220–29, esp. 221–22.

126. Draper, "Temple, Tabernacle and Mystical Experience in John," *Neot* 31 (1997): 285. In a basic survey article, Neusner discerns four responses to the destruction of the temple: (1) apocalyptic writers; (2) the Dead Sea community; (3) the Christian response; and (4) the Pharisees ("Judaism in a Time of Crisis," 313–27).

as an "introversionist response" to that movement, one that seeks, by drawing on "existing strands in the Jewish religion," to "open the way to direct experience of the divine presence in the heavenly realms."[127] For Draper, "the repositioning of the Temple incident in John's Gospel to the beginning of the narrative is an important clue to its central interest," with the temple serving as a "historical pivot point."[128] Draper believes that the temple's destruction must be seen as "the major turning point in the development of the Jesus movement from a movement for the physical restoration of Israel into something else."[129] Yet it was not the destruction itself that caused the crisis, but the failure of its swift restoration.[130]

While one may not agree with all of the details of Draper's reconstruction (particularly his view that John's gospel constitutes a somewhat mystical "introversionist response" to the temple's destruction), his suggestive relation of the destruction of the Second Temple to the composition of John's gospel sets the stage for other possible reconstructions.

Another scholar who explores the relationship between the destruction of the temple and the composition of John's gospel is W. D. Davies, who concurs that the fall of Jerusalem in AD 70 was an event of utmost significance in the history of Judaism.[131] In the years subsequent to the temple's destruction, the Pharisaic leaders, by a policy of consolidation and exclusion, sought to fend off both disintegration within Judaism itself and the attraction of outside forces, including paganism, Christianity, and Gnosticism. The Torah became central, and differences between rabbinic schools were minimized, a process that culminated in the codification of the Mishnah in the early third century. The synagogue replaced the temple as a symbol of Jewish unity. According to Davies, the Judaism in John's day was "vigorously adjusting to the new conditions prevailing among Jewry after 70 C.E."[132] The Johannine label "the Jews" with its equation of Judaism and Pharisaism may reflect post-AD 70 conditions.

Especially important for Davies is the notion of "holy space."[133] In discussing the replacement theme of holy places in John, Davies notes that the "poignance of that emphasis itself must, in turn, be understood in the light of the fall of Jerusalem and the devastation of The Land [sic] in the revolt against Rome. To point to Jesus the Christ as the replacement of the fallen Temple . . . as John does at a time when the war against Rome had deprived Jews of their Land and Temple and had desecrated their holy places so that their loss was constantly and painfully present, was to touch a most raw nerve."[134] Moreover, if R. Alan Culpepper is correct in identifying John 1:12 as the pivot of the Johannine introduction (and Davies thinks

---

127. Draper, "Temple, Tabernacle and Mystical Experience," 285.

128. Ibid., 263 (with further reference to 4Q174). See also the contribution by Stegemann, on which see further below.

129. Ibid., 264.

130. Ibid., with reference to y. Ber. 5a.

131. W. D. Davies, "Reflections on Aspects of the Jewish Background of the Gospel of John," in *Exploring the Gospel of John: In Honor of D. Moody Smith* (ed. R. Alan Culpepper and C. Clifton Black; Louisville: Westminster John Knox, 1996), 43–64.

132. Ibid., 51.

133. Cf. W. D. Davies, *The Gospel and the Land: Early Christianity and Jewish Territorial Doctrine* (Sheffield: JSOT, 1994), esp. 288–335.

134. Davies, "Reflections," 56. Davies properly emphasizes the importance of recognizing "the stage at which John penned his Gospel in the development of Christianity in its relationship to Judaism" (ibid., 57).

that he is), Christianity's laying claim on the title "children of God" (abdicated by Jews who had rejected Jesus as the Messiah) is central to the gospel.[135] Being God's people was one of the basic beliefs of Judaism; John redefined this epithet to include anyone who believed in Jesus (cf. 1:12).[136]

Like Draper and Davies, Ekkehard Stegemann, too, believes that John's gospel presupposes the temple's destruction (see John 4:23–24).[137] According to Stegemann, the evangelist's portrayal of Jesus as the temple's substitute serves the purpose of distancing Jesus from a political construal of his messianic claims. For John, Jesus is precisely not the "king of the Jews," a messianic signs prophet, or pretender to the throne, but the Son of God and messianic "king of Israel" (1:49; 12:14–16; 20:30–31). Stegemann also notes that the temple clearing pericope establishes a direct connection between the temple's destruction and Jesus' resurrection.[138]

The contributions of these scholars, together with the works of Alexander and Goodman mentioned above, further solidify a plausible historical reconstruction behind the composition of John's gospel in which it is not the *birkat ha-minim* but the destruction of the Second Temple that provides the crucial historical context for the composition, the Christology, and the (apologetic) purpose for writing John's gospel.

2.1.2.3.3 *"Letting John Be John"*

James Dunn, in his essay "Let John Be John"—by which expression he means not "to understand John's christology *too quickly* as an expression of later orthodoxy (or later heresy) or in relation to the historical Jesus *per se*"[139]—essentially embraces J. Louis Martyn's reconstruction of the occasion of John's gospel and uses the gospel's Christology as a window onto post-AD 70 Judaism. He contends that apocalyptic and mystical strands of Judaism survived the first Jewish revolt and that John's gospel interfaces with them.[140] The Johannine Jesus is from above, he is the bringer of divine revelation, and the true Israelite is the one who fulfills the calling of Israel (according to the popular etymology of that name) to be "the one who sees God."[141] For Dunn, the two major poles of Johannine Christology are Jesus' preexistence (his heavenly origin, coupled with the descent–ascent motif) and his unity with the Father (termed by Dunn "closeness of continuity"). These, in turn, represent elaborations of the initial identification of Jesus as incarnate Wisdom.[142]

---

135. Cf. R. Alan Culpepper, "The Pivot of John's Prologue," *NTS* 27 (1980): 1–31. I essentially concur with Culpepper on the structure of the introduction to John's gospel: see my *John*, 21–22.

136. Davies, "Reflections," 59.

137. Ekkehard W. Stegemann, "Zur Tempelreinigung im Johannesevangelium," in *Die Hebräische Bibel und ihre zweifache Nachgeschichte: Festschrift für Rolf Rendtorff zum 65. Geburtstag* (ed. Erhard Blum et al.; Neukirchen-Vluyn: Neukirchener, 1990), 503–16.

138. Note that I prefer the term "temple clearing" over the more traditional "temple cleansing" (Kerr, *Temple of Jesus' Body*, 79, refers to the "temple cleaning"!).

139. Dunn, "Let John Be John," 317. One might add that between these two "extremes" (if this is what they are) there are several possible scenarios, of which Dunn's is only one. So even if, for the sake of argument, one were to agree with Dunn's diagnosis of the problem, one need not necessarily agree with him on the solution. Other scenarios are possible, if not more likely. See the critique by Motyer, *"Your Father the Devil?"* 20.

140. Dunn, "Let John Be John," 306–9.

141. Ibid., 309–11.

142. Ibid., 314–15.

Thus Dunn construes the gospel's Christology as devised "in dialogue with broader strands of apocalyptic and mystical Judaism, with the rabbis of Jabneh, and possibly with other Christians too."[143]

But is Dunn thereby "letting John be John"? Remarkably, Dunn omits any reference to the massive replacement/fulfillment theology operative in John's gospel with regard to Jesus and Jewish festivals and institutions such as the temple. Might not the center of gravity in John's apologetic be found here? One also wonders if the Jewish-Christian "dialogue" Dunn envisions belongs to a later period, so that Dunn has the fourth evangelist "responding" to developments in rabbinic Judaism that arise long after the time of the composition of John's gospel. To put it differently, how would one know whether rabbinic Judaism had arrived at the particular stage at which Dunn places it at the composition of John's gospel?

Motyer engages in substantive critique of the assessment of Jewish belief both by Dunn and particularly by Martyn. He notes that Martyn "attempts no overview of Judaism in the post–70 period, does not engage at all with the issues surrounding the destruction of the Temple and its aftermath, and leaves many contemporary Jewish sources untouched."[144] Motyer charges that Martyn's engagement of the text of John's gospel and of Jewish sources is highly selective, lamenting that while "the reconstruction has now lost its heart (the connection with the *birkat ha-minim*)," "it hangs onto life nonetheless."[145]

Motyer's own method, in which he follows, but also seeks to surpass, Dunn, is to identify "points of sensitivity" within the Johannine text, "points at which an effort is evidently being made to clarify some confusion or to counter opposing views."[146] Through dialectic between text and background and through controlled "mirror reading," Motyer hopes to improve on both Martyn and Dunn, primarily by being less selective and more holistic in dealing with the first-century evidence.[147]

2.1.2.3.4 *"Points of Sensitivity" in John's Gospel*

Motyer's first "point of sensitivity" concerns the temple and the festivals. Taking his point of departure from Raymond Brown, Motyer notes that "Yee is the only recent scholar to explore to any extent the relationship between the Johannine emphasis on the Temple and its worship, and the destruction of the Temple and the cessation of that worship in 70 AD."[148] Motyer continues, "The extent to which the relevance of these events has been ignored is quite remarkable."[149] He conjectures that this neglect may be due in part to the "tunnel-vision" resulting from an exclusive interest in the alleged history of the "Johannine community."[150] Motyer writes:

---

143. Ibid., 317. Dunn presents a similar reconstruction in *Partings of the Ways*, 220–29. See also the interaction with Dunn in the section on the Father in John's gospel below (chap. 9, sec. 19).

144. Motyer, *"Your Father the Devil?"* 25.

145. Ibid., 27, with reference to Mark W. G. Stibbe, *John as Storyteller: Narrative Criticism and the Fourth Gospel* (Cambridge: Cambridge University Press, 1992), 56–58, 61.

146. Motyer, *"Your Father the Devil?"* 33, citing Dunn, "Let John Be John," 318.

147. Compare the critique of Dunn's neglect of the destruction of the temple in his analysis above.

148. Cf. Yee, *Jewish Feasts and the Gospel of John*. Motyer adds reference to Walker's treatment of John in *Jesus and the Holy City*.

149. Motyer, *"Your Father the Devil?"* 37.

150. Ibid., 38, n. 12.

Whatever the reasons, the fact remains that no full-scale work has yet explored the thesis which seems to arise most naturally from the Johannine concentration on the Temple and its worship—namely, that the "point of sensitivity" here signalled is, *directly*, the trauma resulting from the destruction of the Temple and the cessation of its worship.[151]

Motyer points particularly to Jesus' words in John 2:19, "Destroy this temple, and I will raise it again in three days," together with the entire temple-clearing episode, as an instance that "rang with nuances and connotations fed by the readers' situation."[152] Motyer himself finds that "the reason for the prominence given to this story, and then to the festivals, is the evangelist's desire to address this trauma.... Read within a post-70 situation, there would be no difficulty for any reader, Jew or Christian, in comprehending the claim made for Jesus in 2:21f: his resurrection constitutes a rebuilding of the destroyed Temple."[153] The fourth evangelist presents Jesus as "the answer to the agonising problem of the post-70 period: how can we re-shape our lives without the Temple?"[154] John 11:47–50 and 4:21–23, too, have powerful implications when read against a post-AD 70 backdrop. Motyer concludes "that John would have been heard to address the situation faced after the destruction of the Temple in 70 AD, particularly in Judea where the loss of the Temple and its worship were felt most keenly."[155]

In a chapter devoted to assessing "Jews and Judaism after the destruction of the Temple," Motyer contends, with Neusner, that the development of the Jewish response to the loss of the Temple was "much more complex and slow-moving" than many assume, and that it was not until after AD 132–35 that "rabbinic orthodoxy" became established.[156] As Neusner notes, the temple's destruction provoked, not only physical suffering and displacement, but, more importantly, "a profound and far-reaching crisis in [the Jews'] inner and spiritual existence."[157] In a manner reminiscent of the situation prior to the destruction of the Solomonic Temple and the Babylonian exile, a presumptuous belief in the invincibility of Jerusalem preceded the disaster.[158] This presumption magnified the impact of the events of AD 66–74.[159]

---

151. Ibid., 38.
152. Ibid.
153. Ibid., 39.
154. Ibid., 41.
155. Ibid., 73. He interprets the purpose statement in John 20:30–31 evangelistically. But see the essay by Goodman on Diaspora reactions to the destruction of the temple above, which demonstrates that the effects of this event were by no means limited to Palestine.
156. Ibid., 75, with reference to Jacob Neusner, "Judaism after the Destruction of the Temple: An Overview," in *Formative Judaism: Religious, Historical and Literary Studies, Third Series: Torah, Pharisees, and Rabbis* (BJS 46; Chico, CA: Scholars Press, 1983), 83–98.
157. Neusner, "Formation of Rabbinic Judaism," 122, cited in Motyer, *"Your Father the Devil?"* 77.

158. *Sib. Or.* 3:702–13. See Lichtenberger, "Mythos," 92–107.
159. See *2 Bar.* 14:6–7, 17–19; *4 Ezra* 3:28–36; 4:23–24; 6:57. Motyer in *"Your Father the Devil?"* helpfully summarizes three basic explanations, underlying five responses. The temple's destruction is explained as: (1) God's punishment for Israel's sin (*Apoc. Ab.* 25, 27; *Sib. Or.* 4; *2 Bar.* 10:18; *4 Ezra* 7:72); (2) the work of the devil (*Sib. Or.* 5); and (3) the plan and will of God (*4 Ezra* 4:10–11; *2 and 4 Baruch*). Five responses (not necessarily mutually exclusive) are: (1) rejection of the cult (*Sib. Or.* 4:9; *T. Ab.* 12:13–18); (2) renewed emphasis on Torah (*2 Bar.* 46:4–5; 77:3–6; *4 Ezra*; *b. Ketub.* 66b); (3) resurgence of mysticism and apocalypticism; (4) quietist eschatology (*2 Baruch*; *4 Baruch*; *Sib. Or.* 5); and (5) activist eschatology and popular messianism (*Apocalypse of Abraham*). Compare Kerr, *Temple of Jesus' Body*, 50–53, who cites two explanations—chastisement for sin (e.g., *Sib. Or.* 4; *2 Baruch*) and the plan and will of God (*2 and 4 Baruch*; *4 Ezra*)—and several responses, including renewed

Following Cohen, Motyer finds that various Jewish sects defined themselves with reference to the temple. "Its destruction undermined this sectarianism and led to a rise of individualism, in which individual prophetic voices sought to make themselves heard."[160] For Motyer, John's gospel is one such voice, "seeking to bring order into the social chaos and disorientation which resulted from the disruption of the pre-70 groupings—just as, in different ways, the Rabbis, the apocalyptists, and the militants also sought to."[161] Rather than reflecting "a situation in which all contact between Jews and Christians had been severed"—as Martyn and his followers contend—John's gospel engages Jews with "a message of hope and salvation."[162] Moreover, the destruction of the temple related to messianic expectations that would have allowed John to present Jesus as the fulfillment of temple-related messianic symbolism and predictions.

2.1.2.3.5 Jewish Messianic Expectations and Jews Doing without a Temple

While exilic and postexilic prophecy could conjure up versions of an eschatological, renewed sanctuary (see esp. Ezekiel 40–48), an important alternative strand in prophecy spoke of God visiting his people directly in the person of the Messiah, the son of David (e.g., Ezekiel 34). Just as the entire OT sacrificial and priestly system is understood in the book of Hebrews as typologically anticipating the permanent high priesthood and once-for-all atoning sacrifice of Christ, the physical structures associated with the worship of God, be it the tabernacle or the original or restored temple of Solomon, could foreshadow a time when God himself would come to his people in a way that superseded and permanently replaced the local and temporary structures facilitating such worship.

The contingent nature of the temple is widespread in the OT. Solomon himself displays a clear awareness that God's presence could not be contained in a man-made Temple or house of worship (1 Kgs 8:27), an awareness Isaiah also displays (Isa 66:1–2). Jeremiah, for his part, makes clear that Israel's disobedience would result in the loss of temple and the land of promise.[163] Merely repeating, "This is the temple of the LORD, the temple of the LORD, the temple of the LORD!" (Jer 7:4) would be utterly futile when God's house had become a "den of robbers" (Jer 7:11; cf. 14–15).[164]

---

emphasis on Torah piety; Merkabah mysticism and apocalypticism; and quietist or activist eschatology. Kerr categorizes John's response under the rubric of quietist eschatology (pp. 60–62).

160. Motyer, *"Your Father the Devil?"* 103.

161. Ibid.

162. Ibid., 103–4. To this may be added the recent contribution of Kerr, *Temple of Jesus' Body*, who defends a post-AD 70 date for the gospel (pp. 19–25) and provides an effective critique of John A. T. Robinson, *Redating the New Testament* (London: SCM, 1976), esp. 275–76, who argues that "there is nothing [in John] that suggests or presupposes that the Temple is already destroyed or that Jerusalem is in ruins" (p. 275). Kerr contends that John's gospel was written in the aftermath of the destruction of the temple in order to provide the (Johannine) Christian answer to the question, "What now?" According to Kerr, the answer is essentially christological: Jesus, as the new temple, has both fulfilled and replaced the old sanctuary.

163. See Matthias Albani, "'Wo sollte ein Haus sein, das ihr mir bauen könntet?' (Jes 66,1)," in *Gemeinde ohne Tempel*, 37–56. See also Erich Zenger, "Der Psalter als Heiligtum," in ibid., 115–30, who contends that "the psalter is not particularly interested in the Temple cult but in the Temple as the sphere of YHWH's revelation" and that in quite a few psalms "the Temple functions even as a metaphor of shelter and refuge" (p. 128).

164. See Armin Lange, "Gebotsobservanz statt Opferkult: Zur Kultpolemik in Jer 7,1–8,3," in *Gemeinde ohne Tempel*, 19–35.

To this, of course, should be added God's promises that he would dwell among his people in a new temple.[165] Also relevant are prophetic notions of a new covenant, in which God would teach his people more directly and would pour out his Spirit on all of his people, making it possible for God's commandments to be written not merely on stone tablets but on people's very hearts.

Against the backdrop of previous destructions of the Jerusalem sanctuary, and of messianic expectations that in days to come God would dwell more directly and immediately with his people, apart from the temple, it is reasonable to see the destruction of the temple in AD 70 as occasioning John to think of Jesus as the fulfillment of these expectations, that is, as the permanent solution to the loss of the Jerusalem sanctuary. John may have seized on the crisis of belief resulting from the destruction of the Second Temple and formulated his Christology at least in part to commend Jesus as Messiah who fulfilled the various strands of OT messianic expectations, including those centering on God's visiting his people and dwelling with them in a more permanent way than had previously been the case.

As will be shown below, references in John's gospel—such as John 1:14, where in allusion to the OT tabernacle it is said that Jesus "lived" (more lit., "pitched his tent") among God's people, or 4:21, 23, where Jesus is quoted as saying that, "a time is coming when you will worship the Father neither on this mountain nor in Jerusalem" and that "a time is coming *and has now come* when the true worshipers will worship the Father in spirit and truth" (NIV; emphasis added)—clearly comport with this perspective.[166]

2.1.2.3.6 Conclusion

The destruction of the Second Temple in AD 70 is a most promising candidate for formative influence on John's gospel. We know it actually happened. There is general agreement that it happened not long before the composition of the gospel. The demonstrably universal impact that this destruction of the temple had on Jews, not only in Palestine but also in the Diaspora, heightens the possibility that the composition of the gospel was also marked by that impact, or rather it makes it incredible to suppose that it was not. The destruction fits into an inherited Jewish typological substructure that qualifies physical sanctuaries as merely provisional manifestations of God's presence, and cherishes expectations that the Messiah will inaugurate a fuller and more permanent manifestation of God's presence with his people. A link between the destruction of the temple and the composition of John's gospel (and in particular its Christology) would be in keeping both with previous responses to the loss of sanctuaries by God's people and with Jewish messianic expectations centered on God's coming and manifesting his presence more fully in the person of the Messiah.

---

165. E.g., Zech 2:10; Ezek 37:27; 43:7, 9. Hoskins, *Jesus as the Fulfillment of the Temple*, 118, draws attention to the verbal parallel to John 1:14b in Zech 2:14 LXX: *kataskēnōsō en mesō(i)*. Hoskins also cites Joel 3:17 and Zech 8:3.

166. See chap. 10, sec. 24.

Complementing the considerable decline in recent years of the Johannine community hypothesis, in its various permutations, has been a comparably large increase in treatments of the (undestroyed) temple in relation to Johannine theology.[167] This direction of study is certainly warranted. But the above discussion underscores the fact that it is precisely the *destroyed* temple that should occupy the attention of Johannine theologians. This contention will be validated further by a close reading of relevant portions of the gospel in the section on Jesus as the new temple in John's gospel later on in this volume (chap. 10, sec. 24). For now, it will be appropriate to turn to a treatment of the authorship and other introductory matters to John's gospel in light of the discussion above.

2.1.3 Introductory Matters
2.1.3.1 Authorship
2.1.3.1.1 Internal Evidence

John's gospel, like the Synoptics, is formally anonymous.[168] However, the author leaves tantalizing clues in his gospel, which, when examined in conjunction with the testimony of the early church fathers, points convincingly to authorship by John, the son of Zebedee and an apostle of Jesus Christ. The author identifies himself as "the disciple whom Jesus loved" (John 21:20, 24), a prominent figure in the Johannine narrative (13:23; 19:26; 20:2; 21:7, 20).[169] Although this disciple's identity is elusive, he leaves sufficient clues in the narrative to ascertain it beyond reasonable doubt.[170] The initial such clues appear in 1:14 and 2:11. The author uses the first person in 1:14, "We have seen his glory," revealing that he was an eyewitness to the accounts contained in his gospel. The "we" of 1:14 are identified in 2:11 as Jesus' disciples.[171] The writer, then, is both an apostolic eyewitness and one of Jesus' first followers.

An examination of the phrase "the disciple whom Jesus loved" later on in the gospel offers further clues to his identity.[172] The expression first appears in John 13:23 at the Last Supper, where only the Twelve were gathered, which indicates

---

167. See, e.g., Motyer, *"Your Father the Devil?"*; Kerr, *Temple of Jesus' Body*; and Mary L. Coloe, *God Dwells with Us: Temple Symbolism in the Fourth Gospel* (Collegeville, MN: Liturgical Press, 2001).

168. This discussion of introductory matters for John's gospel and letters is adapted from Andreas J. Köstenberger, L. Scott Kellum, and Charles L. Quarles, *The Cradle, the Cross, and the Crown: An Introduction to the New Testament* (Nashville: Broadman and Holman, 2009), and is used by permission.

169. Note that the label "the disciple whom Jesus loved" only occurs in the second major portion of John's gospel (first at John 13:23). This is in keeping with the marked shift in perspective in 13:1ff., where the disciples' mission is viewed from the perspective of Jesus' exaltation (Köstenberger, *Missions of Jesus and the Disciples*, 153). Hence, the casting of John in more elevated terms in chapters 13–21 is not unique in John's gospel and may be seen as indicating that the apostle, as "the disciple whom Jesus loved," has an important part to play in the post-exaltation mission of Jesus carried out through his commissioned followers. For an argument against "the disciple whom Jesus loved" as the author of the gospel, see George R. Beasley-Murray, *John* (WBC 36; Waco, TX: Word, 1987; repr. 1999), lxx–lxxv.

170. See Köstenberger, *Encountering John*, 27, for a brief treatment of the "anonymity" of John's gospel.

171. The connection between "we" and "his disciples" is clear because of the parallel between the related references to "his [Jesus'] glory" in John 1:14 and 2:11. For a discussion on John's use of "we" (21:24) and "I" (21:25), see Gerald L. Borchert, *John 1–11* (NAC 25A; Nashville: Broadman and Holman, 1996), 89–90.

172. The epithet "the disciple whom Jesus loved" is plausibly understood as an instance of authorial modesty (see Kevin J. Vanhoozer, "The Hermeneutics of I-Witness Testimony: John 21.20–24 and the 'Death' of the Author," in *Understanding Poets and Prophets: Essays in Honour of George Wishart Anderson* (ed. A. Graeme Auld; JSOTSup 152; Sheffield: JSOT, 1993], 374, who cites Augustine and Westcott, contra, C. K. Barrett, *The Gospel according to St. John* [2nd ed.; Philadelphia: Westminster, 1978], 117).

that "the disciple whom Jesus loved" must have been one of the Twelve.[173] Since the author never refers to himself by name, he cannot be any of the named disciples at the Last Supper: Judas Iscariot (13:2, 26–27), Peter (13:6–9; etc.), Thomas (14:5), Philip (14:8–9), or Judas the son of James (14:22).[174]

The writer offers more clues to his identity in the final chapter of the gospel, where he mentions "the disciple whom Jesus loved" as one of seven other apostles: "Simon Peter, Thomas (also known as Didymus ['Twin']), Nathanael from Cana in Galilee, the sons of Zebedee, and two other disciples" (John 21:2; cf. 21:7). In addition to Peter and Thomas, who have already been eliminated (see above), then, Nathanael likewise is ruled out as a possible author since, as previously noted, the author remains unnamed in John's gospel.

Thus the author must be either one of "the [two] sons of Zebedee" or one of the "two other disciples." Of the two sons of Zebedee, James and John, James can safely be excluded since he was martyred in AD 42 (see Acts 12:2). The remaining three possibilities are John the son of Zebedee and one of the "two other disciples." These latter two could be Matthew (Levi), Simon the Zealot, James the son of Alphaeus, Bartholomew, or Thaddaeus.[175] Matthew already has a gospel attributed to him.[176] Simon the Zealot, James the son of Alphaeus, Bartholomew (Nathanael?), and Thaddaeus (Judas [not Iscariot]?) are unlikely candidates. This leaves John the son of Zebedee as the most likely option.

If so, it may be asked why "the disciple whom Jesus loved" is featured only in Part II of this gospel. The most likely answer is that in John's gospel, the witness of "the disciple whom Jesus loved" is said to continue the witness of John the Baptist once it has been completed. This is indicated by the respective *inclusios* centered on these two "Johns" in this gospel:

The witness of "John" (i.e., the Baptist)	The witness of "the disciple whom Jesus loved"
1:6–8 through 10:40–41	13:23 through 21:20, 24–25

Fig. 2.1: The Witness of John the Baptist and "the Disciple Whom Jesus Loved"

"John's" (i.e., the Baptist's) witness was to Israel (John 1:31).[177] While rejected by the Jewish leadership, that witness was met with faith by a Jewish remnant,

---

173. Beasley-Murray, *John*, lxx, suggests that John's author is unclear about how many disciples are present at the Lord's Supper. However, all three Synoptic Gospels make it clear that the Last Supper was celebrated only with the Twelve (Matt 26:20; Mark 14:17; Luke 22:14).

174. Köstenberger, *Encountering John*, 22.

175. The following is a list of all the named apostles in the Gospels and Acts: Peter, his brother Andrew, James and John the sons of Zebedee, Philip, Thomas, Judas Iscariot (replaced by Matthias per Acts 1:15–26), Judas the son of James, Matthew/Levi, Simon the Zealot = Thaddaeus (?), James the son of Alphaeus, and Bartholomew = Nathanael (?) (see Matt 10:2–4; Mark 3:16; Luke 6:14; Acts 1:13). See Bauckham, *Jesus and the Eyewitnesses*, 113.

176. In addition, since Matthew's and John's style and vocabulary differ significantly, it is unlikely that the same author wrote both gospels.

177. The fourth evangelist's modesty is indicated by the fact that he cedes his own name, John, to the Baptist. Note that, similarly, Jesus' mother remains unnamed, making room for Mary Magdalene to be identified simply as "Mary."

including "the disciple whom Jesus loved" (1:35–40?). This disciple, then, continued to bear witness as the one closest to Jesus during his earthly ministry and as a member of the new messianic community that Jesus commissioned and sent out into the world. As further developed below, the *inclusios* proposed above are by no means the only ones in this gospel.[178] Complementing them is an *inclusio* that grounds the respective witness borne by "the disciple whom Jesus loved" and Peter in the ministry of Jesus:

Jesus	"The disciple whom Jesus loved"	Peter
1:18	13:23	
12:33		21:19

Fig. 2.2: The Witness of Jesus and of "the Disciple Whom Jesus Loved" and Peter

2.1.3.1.2 External Evidence

During the second half of the second century AD, Irenaeus attributed John's gospel to John the apostle: "John the disciple of the Lord, who leaned back on his breast, published the Gospel while he was a resident at Ephesus in Asia" (*Haer.* 3.1.2). Clement of Alexandria, as mentioned, followed suit: "John, last of all ... composed a spiritual gospel" (quoted by Eusebius, *Hist. eccl.* 6.14.7). From this point forward, the church unanimously attributed Johannine authorship to the apostle John for almost eighteen centuries with virtually no dissent.

Those who doubt apostolic authorship take their point of departure from a quote of Papias by Eusebius, in which the former appeared to refer to a John other than the apostle: "And if anyone chanced to come who had actually been a follower of the elders, I would enquire as to the discourses of the elders, what Andrew or what Peter said, or what Philip, or what Thomas or James, or what *John* or Matthew or any other of the Lord's disciples; and the things which Aristion and *John the Elder*, disciples of the Lord, say" (Eusebius, *Hist. eccl.* 3.39.4–5, emphasis added). If these two Johns were different people, the gospel bearing that name could have been penned by either one. Most likely, however, Papias referred to John the son of Zebedee by two different names, distinguishing between deceased eyewitnesses of Jesus' ministry and those who were still alive in his day.[179] The Papias quote wanes in importance when set in the context of other early evidence.

Reaching back further than Irenaeus, Charles Hill persuasively argued that first-century believers used John's gospel widely and authoritatively. By a scrupulous examination of the primary data, Hill was able to debunk the previous notion

---

178. See also Fig. 29.2 in chap. 12, sec. 29.

179. See D. A. Carson and Douglas J. Moo, *An Introduction to the New Testament* (2nd ed.; Grand Rapids: Zondervan, 2005), 229–54. Note also Carson and Moo's discussion of Papias's quote on pp. 233–34. For a dissenting monograph that attributes Johannine authorship to Papias's "John the elder," see Martin Hengel, *The Johannine Question* (Philadelphia: Fortress, 1989). Note that Hengel even thinks that his own "hypothesis may sound fantastic" (p. 130).

(termed "orthodox Johannophobia" by Hill) that early orthodox Christians avoided John's gospel while the early Gnostics embraced it, and that John's gospel was not regarded as orthodox until the time of Irenaeus.[180] To the contrary, Hill demonstrated that John's gospel was likely known by Polycarp, Ignatius, and the Shepherd of Hermas (all three dated to the early second century), and that the first use of John's gospel is likely found as early as 1 John (as well as possibly 2 and 3 John). One important implication of Hill's work is that the alleged nonuse of John in the first half of the second century can no longer be legitimately used as an argument against its apostolic authorship.[181]

The Synoptic and Pauline literature also provides corroborating data for Johannine authorship. The author of John consistently shows "the disciple whom Jesus loved" to be a close companion of Peter (John 13:23–24; 18:15–16; 20:2–9; 21:7), while other NT writers also note the close companionship of the apostles John and Peter (Luke 22:8; Acts 1:13; 3–4; 8:14–25; Gal 2:9). Taken by itself, this connection may be inconclusive. In conjunction with the internal and external evidence adduced above, however, it further confirms the likelihood of Johannine authorship, since as "the disciple whom Jesus loved," John is the most likely close companion of Peter and thus the author of the gospel.

In summary, therefore, a close examination of all the available internal and external evidence provides plausible grounds for the following three conclusions about Johannine authorship:[182] (1) the author is an apostle and eyewitness (John 1:14; see 2:11; 19:35); (2) he is one of the Twelve (13:23; see Matt 26:20; Mark 14:17; Luke 22:14); (3) he is John, the son of Zebedee, by far the strongest candidate on the basis of the above-adduced internal and external evidence. While the hypothesis of the apostolic authorship of John's gospel is regularly the object of derision in recent Johannine scholarship, the hypothesis has never been decisively refuted and continues to be at least as plausible as alternative explanations.[183]

2.1.3.1.3 Richard Bauckham's Challenge of Apostolic Authorship

A major challenge to the apostolic authorship of John's gospel has come from Richard Bauckham. In his work *Jesus and the Eyewitnesses*, Bauckham argued persuasively that the Gospels reflect eyewitness testimony. The ideal source in ancient Greco-Roman literature was not the dispassionate observer, but the eyewitness.[184] The written Gospels, according to Bauckham, contain oral history related to the personal transmission of eyewitness testimony, not merely oral tradition that is the

---

180. For an explication of this view, see Walter Bauer, *Orthodoxy and Heresy in Earliest Christianity* (ed. Robert Kraft and Gerhard Krodel; Philadelphia: Fortress, 1971 [1934]).
181. Hill, *Johannine Corpus in the Early Church*.
182. See Köstenberger, "John," in *NDBT*, 280.
183. See Carson, *Gospel according to John*, 68–81; Carson and Moo, *Introduction to the New Testament*, 229–54. For further information on critical and postmodern objections to the gospel's apostolic authorship, see Gail R. O'Day, "Response to 'Expulsion from the Synagogue: A Tale of a Theory' by Robert Kysar" (paper presented at the Annual Meeting of the SBL, Toronto, November 23–26, 2002), who stated that the abandonment of the apostolic authorship of John's gospel has "created space" for new readings of the gospel. Others, however, view the results of the rejection of the apostolic authorship of John's gospel in less positive terms. In any case, the derisive way in which Johannine authorship is regularly dismissed in contemporary scholarship is unjustified (Köstenberger, "Early Doubts").
184. Bauckham, *Jesus and the Eyewitnesses*, 8–11.

result of the collective and anonymous transmission of material.¹⁸⁵ "In this context," Bauckham contends, "the twelve served as 'an authoritative collegium.' "¹⁸⁶

Especially important in this regard is the phrase "from the beginning," which is found at several strategic points in the Gospels and the NT record (e.g., Luke 1:2; 1 John 1:1; see John 1:1). Several other literary devices are used to stress the Gospels' character of eyewitness testimony, such as "the *inclusio* of eyewitness testimony" (see esp. Mark 1:16–18 and 16:7 for Peter; John 1:40 and 21:24 for "the disciple whom Jesus loved"). According to Bauckham, the transmission process of the Jesus tradition resulting in our written canonical Gospels is best understood as a formal controlled tradition in which the eyewitnesses played an important, and continuing, part.¹⁸⁷

With regard to John's gospel, Bauckham contends that "the disciple whom Jesus loved" should be regarded as the author, but he identifies "John the Elder," not John the apostle, the son of Zebedee, as the author, primarily, it seems, because of his reading of patristic evidence (Papias, Polycrates, Irenaeus) and because of his understanding of the reference to the "sons of Zebedee" in John 21:2.¹⁸⁸ Regarding the latter point, Bauckham finds the anonymity of "the disciple whom Jesus loved" throughout the gospel an insurmountable obstacle to the apostolic authorship of John's gospel, since the "sons of Zebedee" are named; he believes "the disciple whom Jesus loved" is one of the two unnamed disciples in that list.

This is not impossible, but there seems to be no good reason why John the apostle (if he was the author) could not have put himself inconspicuously at the scene without lifting his anonymity as the author. Put a different way, since "the disciple whom Jesus loved" must be one of the seven disciples mentioned in John 21:2, but since he cannot be Peter, Thomas, or Nathanael, there is at least a one in four possibility that he is John the son of Zebedee, and if his brother James is ruled out (as he should be; see above), the probability rises to one in three. The argument for John the apostle as the author becomes all the more compelling when one considers the following list of concerns with Bauckham's argument:¹⁸⁹

(1) Matthew 26:20; Mark 14:17; and Luke 22:14 place the Twelve in the Upper Room with Jesus at the Last Supper. This is significant in that the number twelve was almost certainly symbolic of the twelve tribes of Israel, and Jesus' institution of a new covenant was predicated upon the presence of the Twelve as representatives of the new covenant community. Bauckham acknowledges this, writing, "The Twelve were selected for a special role of leadership in the renewed Israel,"¹⁹⁰ but he gives insufficient weight to this observation. Not commenting on Matthew, Bauckham

---

185. See esp. ibid., 36.
186. Ibid., 94 (echoing Birger Gerhardsson).
187. Ibid., 264, *et passim*.
188. But see the critique by Andreas J. Köstenberger and Stephen O. Stout, "The Disciple Jesus Loved: Witness, Author, Apostle: A Response to Richard Bauckham's *Jesus and the Eyewitnesses*," *BBR* 18 (2008): 209–32.
189. This list is reworked from Köstenberger and Swain, *Father,*

Son and Spirit, 31–33; and essentially reproduces my critique of Bauckham in "Richard Bauckham, *The Testimony of the Beloved Disciple*, D. Moody Smith, *The Fourth Gospel in Four Dimensions*, and Paul Anderson, *The Fourth Gospel and the Quest for Jesus*: Implications for History" (paper delivered at the Annual Meeting of the SBL, Boston, MA, November 23, 2008).
190. Richard Bauckham, *The Testimony of the Beloved Disciple: Narrative, History, and Theology* (Grand Rapids: Baker, 2007), 16.

contends that Mark's reference to the Twelve at the Last Supper should not be taken "overliterally"[191] and that Mark mentions the Twelve only because they were "the only disciples Mark was interested in."[192]

With regard to Luke, Bauckham argues that Luke's reference is to a broader group of disciples, stating that "Luke's Gospel in particular makes it clear that Jesus had large numbers of disciples" and that "there is no reason to suppose that no more than the Twelve were present at the Last Supper."[193] But Bauckham's attempt to broaden the Lukan reference in Luke 22:14 to a group larger than the Twelve is not supported by the six instances of the word *apostolos* in Luke's gospel. The first and foundational reference, 6:13, states explicitly that Jesus "called his disciples to him and chose twelve of them, whom he also designated apostles." In the second reference, 9:10, in the context of 9:1, again "the apostles" refers to the Twelve. The third and fourth references (11:49 and 17:5), too, most likely equate the apostles and the Twelve. The fifth reference is 22:14, the apostles celebrating the Last Supper with Jesus, and in 24:10, the sixth and final reference, in the context of 24:9, "the apostles" likewise refers to the Twelve (now the Eleven, the Twelve minus Judas).

A study of the six Lukan occurrences of *apostolos* thus shows that Luke uses *apostolos* as a technical term for the Twelve,[194] and that not only Matthew and Mark, but also Luke places the Twelve specifically with Jesus in the Upper Room. Thus a proper reading of the evidence from all the Synoptic Gospels increases the probability that "the disciple whom Jesus loved" was one of the Twelve, since the focus in all three of these gospel accounts—not just in Mark—is on the presence of the Twelve with Jesus at the occasion of his institution of a new covenant with the representatives of the new Israel.

(2) Related to this is the question of whether a disciple who was not a member of the Twelve would not only have been present at the Last Supper but is likely to have occupied a place on Jesus' side. Bauckham, following Whiteley, suggests that the beloved disciple was the host at the Last Supper and for that reason sat by Jesus' side.[195] He also contends that "the special value of the Gospel of John may be in part that it embodies a different perspective on Jesus, one from outside the circle of the Twelve."[196] However, as already mentioned, this does not sufficiently consider the importance of the Twelve as the representatives of the new Israel. Also, the named characters in John's gospel present at the Last Supper all seem to have been members of the Twelve (Peter, Judas, Thomas, Philip, and the other Judas).[197]

---

191. Ibid., 15 (with reference to Westcott).
192. Ibid., 16.
193. Ibid., 15–16.
194. See Darrell L. Bock, *Luke 9:51–24:53* (BECNT; Grand Rapids: Baker, 1996), 1719, n. 6: "Luke likes to use this term for the Twelve" (with reference to 6:13; see idem, *Luke 1:1–9:50* [BECNT; Grand Rapids: Baker, 1994], 541–42).
195. Bauckham, *The Testimony of the Beloved Disciple*, 15, citing D. E. H. Whiteley, "Was John Written by a Sadducee?" in Wolfgang Haase, ed., *Aufstieg und Niedergang der Römischen Welt* 2.25.3 (Berlin: de Gruyter, 1985), 2481–505.
196. Bauckham, *The Testimony of the Beloved Disciple*, 16.
197. See John 13:6–9, 36–38 (Peter); 13:2, 26–30 (Judas); 14:5 (Thomas); 14:8 (Philip); and 14:22 (Judas [not Iscariot]). Judas (not Iscariot) is most likely the Judas son of James mentioned in Luke 6:16 and Acts 1:13. He may be the same as the Thaddaeus referred to in Matt 10:4 and Mark 3:19 (see Bock, *Luke 1:1–9:50*, 546).

Bauckham's suggestion that John's gospel may embody an "outside perspective" on Jesus also stands in apparent conflict with Bauckham's own statement that John's gospel "puts the beloved disciple in a unique position, as a disciple uniquely close to Jesus, present at key events in the story ... the ideal witness to Jesus and his history, and therefore as the disciple ideally qualified to write a gospel."[198] An "outsider" who was "uniquely close" to Jesus, not just as the possible host of the Last Supper, but at many of the key events of Jesus' ministry? This seems unlikely, especially in light of the parallelism established in John's gospel between Jesus as uniquely close to God the Father (cf. John 1:18) and hence uniquely qualified to "tell God's story",[199] and the "beloved disciple" as closest to Jesus at the Last Supper and thus uniquely qualified to tell the story of Jesus (13:23; 21:24; cf. 21:20).[200] John hardly presents Jesus as an "outsider" who was "uniquely close" to God; if the author of John's gospel was a "uniquely close" "outsider," the above-mentioned parallelism between Jesus and the "beloved disciple"/author in 1:18 and 13:23 breaks down.

(3) Bauckham makes too little of the strong historical link between Peter and John the son of Zebedee — not "John the Elder" — in all of the available New Testament evidence (all four Gospels, the book of Acts, and Galatians).[201] This is especially significant in light of the fact that Peter and "the disciple whom Jesus loved" are indisputably and consistently linked in John's gospel.[202] The most straightforward conclusion from this consistent pattern of association between Peter and John the son of Zebedee would seem to be that "the disciple whom Jesus loved" in John's gospel (who Bauckham agrees is the author) is to be identified with John the son of Zebedee, not another John.

(4) One also wonders why the author of John's gospel omits any reference to John the son of Zebedee if "the disciple whom Jesus loved" does not refer to this John by way of a device of authorial modesty.[203] Surely it would be surprising if someone as important in the other three gospels as John the son of Zebedee were not mentioned in John's gospel at all (apart from the oblique reference in 21:2). It would seem to be considerably more likely that "the disciple whom Jesus loved" designates John the son of Zebedee.

(5) The presence of the phrase "I suppose" (*oimai*) in 21:25 ("Jesus did many other things as well. If every one of them were written down, I suppose that even the whole world would not have room for the books that would be written") as a device of authorial modesty (in keeping with the label "the disciple whom Jesus loved") supports the integrity of the entire gospel as from the same author, identified in the gospel as eyewitness at strategic points (e.g., 13:23; 19:35).[204]

---

198. Bauckham, *Testimony of the Beloved Disciple*, 16.
199. See on this Stibbe, "Telling the Father's Story," 170–93.
200. See Köstenberger, *John*, 414; Carson, *Gospel according to John*, 473; and Raymond E. Brown, *The Gospel according to John XIII–XXI* (AB 29A; New York: Doubleday, 1970), 577.
201. See, e.g., Mark 1:16–20; Acts 3–4; 8:14–25; Gal 2:9.
202. See esp. Kevin Quast, *Peter and the Beloved Disciple: Figures for a Community in Crisis* (JSNTSup 32; Sheffield: JSOT, 1989).

203. See Andreas J. Köstenberger, "'I Suppose' (οἶμαι): The Conclusion of John's Gospel in Its Literary and Historical Context," in *The New Testament in Its First Century Setting: Essays on Context and Background in Honour of B. W. Winter on His 65th Birthday* (ed. P. J. Williams, Andrew D. Clarke, Peter M. Head, and David Instone-Brewer; Grand Rapids: Eerdmans, 2004), 72–88.
204. See ibid.

(6) Methodologically, the question arises how legitimate it is to put a large amount of weight on one's reading of the patristic evidence over against the internal evidence of the Gospels themselves; it would seem that, in the end, the most plausible reading of the internal evidence ought to be given the most weight.

(7) Which other John was ever credited with the authorship of the gospel of John in the early church? Apart from the above-cited ambiguous Papias quote in Eusebius's *Ecclesiastical History* and a doubtful reference to a John mentioned in Acts 4:6 by Polycrates,[205] the answer is, "No one."

On the whole, therefore, the internal evidence adduced by Bauckham that "the disciple whom Jesus loved" in John was "John the Elder" and not the son of Zebedee does not prove compelling. It is difficult to believe that in Jesus' inner circle there was a John who was present at the Last Supper (13:23), in close proximity to Jesus (13:25), was regularly associated with the apostle Peter (13:23–25; 18:15–18; 20:1–10; 21:1–25), was given the special honor of caring for Jesus' mother (19:26–27), was one of the first to run to the tomb with Peter (20:2), and yet was not John the apostle or even one of the Twelve.

Not only does Bauckham's handling of the internal and external evidence fail to prove compelling, his rejection of apostolic authorship is surprising also since it would seem to be the most natural corollary of his overall thesis. After all, Bauckham's point is not merely that eyewitness testimony—*any* eyewitness testimony—is important for the Gospels, but that we are dealing here with *apostolic* eyewitness testimony—that is, eyewitness testimony that is credible because it comes from those who were closest to Jesus during his earthly ministry and who served as an "authoritative collegium," in Bauckham's own words. In this regard, it is hard to see how the testimony of one largely unknown "John the Elder"—not mentioned in any of the other canonical Gospels or NT writings—would satisfy Bauckham's own criterion. Apostolic authorship, by contrast, coupled with Peter's importance as a secondary witness, fits perfectly with Bauckham's overall theory and further strengthens it.

For these and other reasons I welcome and concur with Bauckham's overall thesis regarding the Gospels' eyewitness character, yet I do not find his case against the apostolic authorship of John's gospel convincing. Much more likely is the view that John's gospel, like the other three canonical gospels, is founded on apostolic eyewitness testimony, and that John's, in fact, is the gospel written by the apostle who was closest to Jesus during his earthly ministry. This claim, in turn, fits historically only with the apostle John, who, according to the unified witness of Matthew, Mark, and Luke, was one of three members of Jesus' inner circle together with Peter and John's brother James (Matt 17:1 pars.; 26:37 pars.).

2.1.3.2 Chronology of Jesus' Ministry in John's Gospel

As Tatian recognized long ago in his synopsis of the Gospels, the *Diatessaron* (c. AD 170), John's gospel follows a chronological order of Jesus' ministry. Unlike

---

205. Adduced by Bauckham, *Jesus and the Eyewitnesses*, 439.

the Synoptics, which present Jesus' movement from Galilee to Jerusalem, John evinces an oscillating pattern, with Jesus moving back and forth between Galilee and Jerusalem, where Jesus is shown to visit religious festivals throughout his ministry. The following timeline of Jesus' ministry according to John's gospel shows how selective the fourth evangelist is in choosing to include only a small fraction of events in the ministry of Jesus.

Unlike the Synoptics, John reaches all the way to the beginning of time in rooting Jesus' identity in eternity with God. This is followed, similar to the Synoptic accounts, with a presentation of the witness of John the Baptist and Jesus' calling of his first disciples. After this, the "Cana" and "Festival Cycles" trace Jesus' ministry from its inception to the rejection of Jesus by the Jews. The climactic "sign," the raising of Lazarus, is followed by the Passion Narrative and the commissioning of the Eleven, Peter, and "the disciple whom Jesus loved." Of the two major possibilities for dating Jesus' ministry, AD 26–30 or 29–33, the latter is to be preferred.[206]

Time	Location/Event	John
Origin (1:1–18)		
Eternity past	The Word was with God	1:1–18
Initial Ministry (1:19–2:12; AD 29–30)		
Summer/fall 29	John the Baptist near the Jordan	1:19–34
Subsequently	Jesus' calling of his first disciples	1:35–51
Winter/spring 30	The wedding at Cana of Galilee	2:1–12
First Passover and First Full Year of Ministry (2:13–4:54; AD 30–31)		
April 7, 30	Jesus' first Passover (Jerusalem), Temple clearing	2:13–3:21
Spring/summer 30	John the Baptist near the Jordan	3:22–36
Dec./Jan./Feb. 30/31?	Jesus' ministry in Samaria	4:1–45
Subsequently	The healing at Cana of Galilee	4:46–54
Second Year of Ministry (5:1–47; AD 31–32)		
March 27, 31	Passover not recorded in John	Matt 12:1 par.?
Oct. 21–28, 31?	The Sabbath controversy (Jerusalem)	5:1–47

---

206. See Harold W. Hoehner, *Chronological Aspects of the Life of Christ* (Grand Rapids: Zondervan, 1977); idem, "Chronology," in *Dictionary of Jesus and the Gospels* (ed. Joel B. Green, Scot McKnight, and I. Howard Marshall; Downers Grove, IL: InterVarsity Press, 1992), 118–22. See also "The Date of Jesus' Crucifixion," in *ESV Study Bible*, 1809–10. The following chronology is reproduced from Köstenberger, *John*, 11–13.

Time	Location/Event	John
Second Passover Recorded in John and Third Year of Ministry (6:1 – 11:54; AD 32 – 33)		
April 13 or 14, 32	Jesus' second Passover recorded in John (Galilee)	6:1 – 21
Subsequently	Jesus' teaching in the synagogue of Capernaum	6:22 – 71
Sept. 10 – 17, 32	Jesus at the feast of Tabernacles (Jerusalem)	7:1 – 52; 8:12 – 59
Oct./Nov. 32?	Healing of blind man, good shepherd discourse	9:1 – 10:21
Dec. 18 – 25, 32	Jesus at the feast of Dedication (Jerusalem)	10:22 – 39
Jan./Feb. 33?	Jesus' withdrawal to the area near the Jordan	10:40 – 42
March 33?	The raising of Lazarus (Bethany near Jerusalem)	11:1 – 53
March 33?	Jesus' withdrawal to Ephraim	11:54
Third Passover in John, Passion Week, Resurrection Appearances (11:55 – 21:25; AD 33)		
Friday, March 27, 33	Jesus arrives at Bethany	11:55 – 12:1
Saturday, March 28, 33	Dinner with Lazarus and his sisters	12:2 – 11
Sunday, March 29, 33	"Triumphal entry" into Jerusalem	12:12 – 50
Monday – Wednesday, March 30 – April 1, 33	Cursing of fig tree, temple clearing, temple controversy, Olivet discourse	Synoptics
Thursday, April 2, 33	Jesus' third Passover recorded in John (Jerusalem); betrayal, arrest	13:1 – 18:11
Friday, April 3, 33	Jewish and Roman trials, crucifixion, burial	18:12 – 19:42
Sunday, April 5, 33	The empty tomb, first resurrection appearance	20:1 – 25
Sunday, April 12, 33	Second resurrection appearance recorded in John	20:26 – 31
Prior to May 14, 33	Third resurrection appearance recorded in John	21:1 – 25[207]

Fig. 2.3: Chronology of Jesus' Ministry in John's Gospel

---

[207]. For the dating of the four Passovers between AD 29 and 33 mentioned above, see Colin J. Humphreys and W. G. Waddington, "The Jewish Calendar, a Lunar Eclipse, and the Date of Christ's Crucifixion," *TynBul* 43 (1992): 335.

2.1.3.3 Date, Provenance, and Destination

2.1.3.3.1 Date

When did John write his gospel? The answer to this question depends on a complex matrix of questions regarding the author, his original audience, his purpose and occasion for writing, and other factors. In the quest for the most likely date of composition, AD 70 and AD 135 serve as *termini ad quem* (the earliest and the latest plausible dates).[208] The first of these dates is established by John's reference to Peter's martyrdom (John 21:19), which occurred in AD 65 or 66, and by John's depiction of Jesus as the replacement of the temple, whose destruction took place in AD 70. The second date is determined by the twentieth-century discovery of the earliest NT papyrus manuscript to date ($\mathfrak{p}^{52}$, c. AD 135), containing John 18:31–32 and 37–38.

Within these bookends, John most likely wrote his gospel in the mid-AD 80s or early AD 90s based on the following pieces of evidence.[209] (1) Although the Synoptics and the Pauline letters refer to Jesus' divinity, John's language seems closer to the "less restrained language of Ignatius—in particular the ease and frequency with which Ignatius refers to Jesus as God."[210] In other words, it seems that sufficient time needed to elapse after Jesus' resurrection in order for John to articulate his theology in those terms.

(2) If the reconstruction of John's occasion for writing—the destruction of the temple—above is correct, the gospel was most likely written ten to twenty years after AD 70, since a certain amount of time had to pass between the temple destruction and its composition: "[It is] hard to believe that ... the date was *immediately* after AD 70 [the destruction of the temple].... The reverberations around the Empire, for both Jews and Christians, were doubtless still too powerful. A little time needed to elapse ... before a document like the Fourth Gospel could be free *not* to make an *explicit* allusion to the destruction of the Temple."[211]

(3) John lacks reference to the Sadducees.[212] Since they play such an important role in the Synoptics (written prior to John) and since they were less influential after the destruction of the temple, their omission in John makes sense if he wrote subsequent to the temple's demise.

(4) John's use of the designation "Sea of Tiberias" in clarifying the "Sea of Galilee" (6:1; 21:1) suggests a mid-AD 80/early AD 90 date of composition. Herod

---

208. Among the scholars who suggest a pre-AD 70 date for John are Robert M. Grant, *A Historical Introduction to the New Testament* (London: Collins, 1963), 152–53, 60; Leon Morris, *The Gospel according to John* (NICNT; Grand Rapids: Eerdmans, 1971), 30–35; Robinson, *Redating the New Testament*, 254–84; and Paul Barnett, "Indications of Earliness in the Gospel of John," *RTR* 64 (2005): 61–75. For a summary of arguments see Beasley-Murray, *John*, lxxvi. See the refutation in Kerr, *Temple of Jesus' Body*, 19–25; see also Carson, *Gospel according to John*, 82–86; Leon Morris, *The Gospel according to John* (rev. ed.; NICNT; Grand Rapids: Eerdmans, 1995), 25–30 (with reference to F. Lamar Cribbs, "Reassessment of the Date of Origin and the Destination of the Gospel of John," *JBL* 89 [1970]: 38–55; and C. C. Torrey, *Our Translated Gospels: Some of the Evidence* [New York: Harper, 1936], x–xi); and Wallace, "John 5,2 and the Date of the Fourth Gospel"; but see Köstenberger, *John*, 177–78.

209. See David A. Croteau, "An Analysis of the Arguments for the Dating of the Fourth Gospel," *Faith & Mission* 20/3 (2003): 47–80.

210. Carson and Moo, *Introduction to the New Testament*, 267.

211. Carson, *Gospel according to John*, 85.

212. Schlatter, *Evangelist Johannes*, 44. Note, however, Carson's caution in *Gospel according to John*, 84.

Antipas founded the city of Tiberias on the Galilean seashore around AD 17–18 (Josephus, *Ant.* 18.2.3 36). Gradually, the Galilean Sea took on the name "Sea of Tiberias." On a popular level this shift probably took place in the AD 80s or 90s.[213]

(5) If Thomas's confession of Jesus as "my Lord and my God" is intended to evoke associations of emperor worship under Domitian (AD 81–96), this would seem to require a date subsequent to AD 81.[214]

A date of composition in the mid-AD 80s or early AD 90s, then, best fits all the evidence. This date allows plenty of time for the gospel to gain the popularity needed for a copy (p^{52}) to make it to Egypt by c. AD 135.

2.1.3.3.2 Provenance

Where did John write his gospel? Early patristic testimony lends support to the notion that John wrote his gospel in Ephesus.[215] Eusebius stated that after the Jewish War (AD 66–70) dispersed the early apostles, John went to serve in Asia (*Hist. eccl.* 3.1.1), which placed him in or near Ephesus during the AD 80s and 90s. In the second century, Irenaeus wrote that "John, the disciple of the Lord ... published the gospel while living in Ephesus in Asia" (*Haer.* 3.1.2). However, some who believe that John's gospel and the book of Revelation have different authors allege that Eusebius mistakes the writer of the gospel for the author of the Apocalypse.[216]

Opponents of an Ephesian provenance of John's gospel propose three major alternatives. First, since John seems to bear affinities to Philo, some propose an Alexandrian provenance.[217] Others suggest an Antiochian origin, because they see affinities between John's gospel and Ignatius, bishop of Antioch, as well as with the *Odes of Solomon*, presumably written in Syria (of which Antioch was the capital).[218] Still others maintain that John's gospel originated in Palestine because of apparent cultural influences and John's familiarity with certain topographical details.[219]

These proposals, however, are not without problems. For example, Philo was read outside of Alexandria as well; the literary influence of Ignatius and the *Odes of Solomon* in all likelihood reached beyond Antioch; and John was probably aware of, and influenced by, Palestinian culture dating back to his role in the ministry of Jesus and thereafter.[220] Overall, then, Eusebius and Irenaeus provide the most

---

213. Köstenberger, *John*, 199.

214. Ibid., 8. Some suggested that since John is not quoted in works prior to the late second century, he probably wrote much later than AD 100 (H. Nun, *The Authorship of the Fourth Gospel* [Oxford: Alden & Blackwell, 1952], 20–32; Raymond E. Brown, *The Gospel according to John I–XII* [AB 29; Garden City, NY: Doubleday, 1966], lxxxi. But see Hill, *Johannine Corpus in the Early Church*, who demonstrated that many early second-century writers did in fact use John's gospel.

215. For a magisterial study of the life of the early Christians in Ephesus, see Paul Trebilco, *The Early Christians in Ephesus from Paul to Ignatius* (Grand Rapids: Eerdmans, 2008).

216. See Beasley-Murray, *John*, lxxix; Carson and Moo, *Introduction to the New Testament*, 254.

217. Kirsopp Lake, *An Introduction to the New Testament* (London: Christophers, 1948), 53; Sanders, *Fourth Gospel in the Early Church*, 85–86.

218. Werner G. Kümmel, *Introduction to the New Testament* (rev. ed.; trans. Howard Clark Kee; Nashville: Abingdon, 1975), 246–47.

219. Martyn, "Glimpses into the History of the Johannine Community," 151–75.

220. These critiques are offered by Carson and Moo, *Introduction to the New Testament*, 254.

reliable, albeit less than conclusive, data available.[221] Thus, John most likely wrote in Ephesus in the province of Asia Minor.

2.1.3.3.3 Destination

Where was John's audience? Since John does not explicitly identify his audience, ascertaining his intended destination is inexorably related to the above arguments regarding authorship and provenance. If Irenaeus and others are correct that John was the author of the gospel and that he wrote in Ephesus (see above), it is reasonable to assume that people living in and around Ephesus, primarily Diaspora Jews and Gentiles, were at least part of his intended readership.[222]

Beyond this, John's gospel, like the other canonical gospels, was likely written for "all Christians" rather than for readers in only one geographical location.[223] If so, John most likely wrote with Diaspora Jews and proselytes in mind without intending to limit his audience exclusively to any one group. This is also indicated by the genre of John's book: "After all, John's gospel is a *Gospel*, heralding the universal good news of salvation in Christ."[224]

2.1.3.4 Occasion and Purpose

2.1.3.4.1 Occasion

As mentioned, the destruction of the Jerusalem temple in AD 70 was a traumatic event that left Judaism in a national and religious void and caused Jews to look for ways to continue their ritual and worship.[225] It is likely that the temple's destruction served as one of the major catalysts for writing John's gospel. Its destruction threw late first-century Jews into turmoil since their faith was inextricably connected with that edifice through the sacrificial system and the priesthood. In the same way that the Babylonian exile (586 BC) precipitated a deep crisis in Jewish worship removed from the First Temple, the destruction of the Second Temple required a major reorientation of Jewish ritual. In the wake of the temple's destruction, John likely saw a window of opportunity for Jewish evangelism, seeking to encourage fellow believers to reach out to their Jewish and Gentile neighbors in the Diaspora.[226] He did so by arguing that the crucified and risen Messiah providentially replaced the temple (John 2:18–22; see 1:14; 4:21–24) and fulfilled the symbolism inherent in Jewish festivals (esp. chaps. 5–12).[227]

---

221. In addition, see the arguments for an Ephesian provenance of John's gospel from internal evidence by Ulrich B. Müller, "Die Heimat des Johannesevangeliums," *ZNW* 97 (2006): 44–63.

222. See Carson, *Gospel according to John*, 91.

223. Bauckham, *Gospels for All Christians*, 9–48.

224. Köstenberger, *Encountering John*, 26.

225. Motyer, *"Your Father the Devil?"*; Kerr, *Temple of Jesus' Body*; Walker, *Jesus and the Holy City*, 195; Draper, "Temple, Tabernacle and Mystical Experience in John," 264, 285. See esp. Alexander, "Parting of the Ways," 1–25; and Goodman, "Diaspora Reactions," 27–38; and the discussion above. For a critique of the Brown-Martyn-style "Johannine community hypothesis," see Köstenberger, *Missions of Jesus and the Disciples*, 200–210; and Carson, *Gospel according to John*, 35–36, 87–88, 369–72. The major evidence cited in support of a pre-AD 70 date of writing is the lack of reference to the destruction of the temple and the present tense verb in 5:2. But these are not determinative and are capable of alternative explanations (see, e.g., Schlatter, *Evangelist Johannes*, 23–24; Köstenberger, *John*, 177–78).

226. See Bauckham, ed., *Gospels for All Christians*.

227. Hoskins, *Jesus as the Fulfillment of the Temple*; Draper, "Temple, Tabernacle and Mystical Experience," 264–65; and discussion above.

In addition to the temple's destruction, the early Christian Gentile mission (Acts 9:16; Rom 1:13) and the emergence of early Gnostic thought likely served as part of the matrix that occasioned the writing of John's gospel. Since John wrote in the Diaspora for both Jews and Gentiles attracted to Judaism, and since he wrote fifty years after the formation of the church when the Gentile mission was well underway, it stands to reason that this mission directly affected John's writing. Gnosticism, for its part, which began to emerge in the latter half of the first century but did not come to full fruition until the second century, may provide part of the backdrop as well. Although John did not embrace or promote Gnostic teachings, like many evangelistic writings ever since he used the conceptual categories of his audience to contextualize his message (e.g., 1:1, 14). These three important factors — the temple's destruction, the Gentile mission, and Gnostic thought — likely combined as possible occasions for John's gospel.[228]

2.1.3.4.2 Purpose

Toward the end of his gospel, John states his purpose as follows: "But these [signs] are written that you may believe Jesus is the Messiah, the Son of God, and that by believing you may have life in his name" (20:31).[229] On a surface reading, "that you may believe" suggests an evangelistic purpose, that is, leading John's readers to first-time faith in Jesus as Messiah.[230]

At the same time, John's gospel seems to presuppose an audience that is already familiar with Scripture and contains detailed instructions for believers, especially in the second half of the gospel. What is more, there are only a few examples of directly evangelistic first-century documents. For reasons such as these it seems perhaps most likely that John's purpose encompassed both aspects, evangelism of unbelievers and edification of believers, and that John pursued an indirect evangelistic purpose, aiming to reach an unbelieving audience through the Christian readers of his gospel.[231]

John's purpose, then, according to 20:31, is to set forth the evidence that Jesus is the Messiah, the Son of God, so that people might believe in him and as a result have life in his name.[232] The purpose statement corresponds to the opening chapter of the gospel where John sets forth Jesus' messianic identity (e.g., 1:1–3, 14, 17, 29, 34, 41). In the body of the gospel, John presents a series of Jesus' messianic "signs"

---

228. For an examination of additional suggested factors see Borchert, *John 1–11*, 60–80.

229. Compare the purpose statement in 1 John 5:13: "I write these things to you who believe in the name of the Son of God so that you may know that you have eternal life."

230. The phrase "so that you may believe" in 20:31 is represented in textual variants as either in the present (*pisteuēte*) or the aorist subjunctive (*pisteusēte*). Some have suggested that the former would point to an edificatory purpose while the latter would suggest an evangelistic purpose, but matters are considerably more complex, and the tense of *pisteuō* in 20:31 hardly resolves the ambiguity, which may be deliberate. See the discussion in Carson and Moo, *Introduction to the New Testament*, 270.

231. Bauckham, *Gospels for All Christians*, 10. See also Klink, *Sheep of the Fold*, 250, who says John's gospel is aimed at different "types of faith" (though he does not adequately consider the possibility of John's evangelistic purpose being indirect).

232. The terms "Messiah" and "Son of God" are most likely used interchangeably (see, e.g., Acts 9:20, 22). See also the interchange between D. A. Carson, "The Purpose of the Fourth Gospel: John 20:30–31 Reconsidered," *JBL* (1987): 639–51; Gordon D. Fee, "On the Text and Meaning of John 20,30–31," in *The Four Gospels 1992: Festschrift for Frans Neirynck* (ed. F. van Segbroeck, C. M. Tuckett, G. van Belle, and J. Verheyden; BETL 100; Leuven: Leuven University Press, 1992), 3.2193–205; and D. A. Carson, "Syntactical and Text-Critical Observations on John 20:30–31: One More Round

and narrates his death, resurrection, and appearances in order to elicit in his readers' faith in Jesus as Messiah. "Believing," in John, goes beyond mere intellectual assent and involves putting one's trust in Jesus.[233] "Life" refers to eternal communion with Jesus entered into already in the here and now (e.g., 5:24; 8:12; 10:10; 17:3).

Finally, it is important not to confuse John's likely *purpose* with possible *effects* of his gospel. As Carson and Moo aptly note, "Just because John's gospel can be used to offer comfort to the bereaved in the twenty-first century does not mean that is why the evangelist wrote it."[234] John explicitly stated his purpose (20:30–31), which, against the backdrop of his provenance and occasion, is best understood as indirect evangelism. All other purposes should be seen as subordinated to this larger purpose or as effects that result from it.

2.2 The Letters

2.2.1 Authorship

2.2.1.1 Internal Evidence

B. H. Streeter's dictum is often repeated: "The three Epistles and the Gospel of John are so closely allied in diction, style, and general outlook that the burden of proof lies with the person who would deny their common authorship."[235] The similarities are so numerous and multifaceted that they dwarf any perceived differences by comparison. While admitted by all, these similarities are often attributed to a "house style" within the Johannine community or conscious imitation. So, then, it is important not simply to note the similarities but to look for those congruities that suggest a writer naturally expressing himself in ways other than conscious imitation. The following observations can be made.

(1) The same author would be expected to use similar vocabulary in similar ways. This occurs at an overwhelming rate when the letters are compared to the gospel. A small sample will give the general contours of the phenomenon.[236] The following words and phrases are significant: Jesus as the "one and only Son" (1 John 4:9; John 1:14, 18; 3:16, 18); "Word" (*logos*) referring to Jesus Christ (1 John 1:1; John 1:1, 14); "eternal life" (1 John 1:2; 2:25; 3:15; 5:11, 13, 20; John 3:15–16, 36; etc.); "the spirit of truth" (1 John 4:6; John 14:17; 16:13); "to live out the truth" (1 John 1:6; John 3:21); "from the world" (1 John 2:16; 4:5; John 8:23); "remain[ing] in him/me" (1 John 2:27; cf. 3:17; 4:13; John 15:4, 6, 7); and a host of others.[237]

---

on the Purpose of the Fourth Gospel," *JBL* 124 (2005): 693–714, which revolves around the question of whether John's purpose is to identify Jesus as the Messiah or the Messiah as Jesus.

233. See, e.g., 1:12; 3:15–16, 36; 4:50; 5:24; 6:29, 40, 47, 69; 9:38; 11:25–27; 12:44, 46; 14:1; 16:27, 30; 17:8, 20; 19:35. See David A. Croteau, "An Analysis of the Concept of Believing in the Narrative Contexts of John's Gospel" (Th.M. thesis; Wake Forest, NC: Southeastern Baptist Theological Seminary, 2002).

234. Carson and Moo, *Introduction to the New Testament*, 270.

235. B. H. Streeter, *The Four Gospels* (rev. ed.; London: Macmillan, 1930), 460.

236. Heinrich Julius Holtzmann wrote the foundational work on Johannine vocabulary: "Das Problem des ersten johanneischen Briefes in seinem Verhältnis zum Evangelium," *Jahrbuch für Protestantische Theologie* 7 (1881): 690–712; 8 (1882): 128–52, 316–42, 460–85. These were later included and adapted in English by A. E. Brooke, *A Critical and Exegetical Commentary on the Johannine Epistles* (ICC; New York: Scribner, 1912), i–xix.

237. Brooke, *Epistles*, ii–iv, listed fifty-two separate items, not including fifteen occurrences of "in this/this" followed by an explanatory clause.

Note also these marked contrasts in both documents: love and hate (1 John 3:11–15; John 3:19–21; 15:18–25); life and death (1 John 3:14; John 5:24); light and darkness (1 John 1:5; John 1:5); truth and falsehood (1 John 1:6, 8; 2:4, 21; 8:44–45); children of God and children of the devil (1 John 3:10; John 8:33–47, esp. v. 44).[238] This phenomenon is remarkable given the brevity of the letters.[239]

(2) The same author would be expected to use his stock of phrases and themes in a nimble fashion and not like an imitator. In other words, if all that were found were exact correspondences to the gospel usage, this might point to imitation. But this is not in fact the case. For example, the "helping presence" (*paraklētos*) in the gospel (the Holy Spirit) is "another helping presence" (John 14:16); Jesus is the "helping presence" in the letters (1 John 1:9).[240] The reference "God is spirit" (John 4:24; see also 3:33: "God is truthful") is similar in form to "God is love" (1 John 4:8, 16) and "God is light" (1 John 1:5). A. E. Brooke points out that the author of 1 John will frequently fill up the basic outline of a thought in John's gospel in a distinct yet closely related manner. He cites the following instances, among others: 1 John 5:10// John 3:18; 1 John 1:2//John 1:1; 1 John 3:8//John 8:41.[241] As Brooke observes, "This suggests a writer who varies his own phrases, rather than a mere copyist."[242]

(3) The same author would be expected to compose his works with a similar style. This is exactly what characterizes the letters. The relatively simple syntax is the norm for both the gospel and the letters, and the same stock of Greek words and constructions can be seen in both.[243] A peculiar example of this is the use of intersentence conjunctions. Vern Poythress has demonstrated that sentences are frequently connected by asyndeton (i.e., they are juxtaposed without coordinating conjunctions). He also noted the infrequent use of "therefore" (*oun*) and other connectors in expository discourse in both the gospel and the letters.[244]

(4) Another notable piece of evidence is the failure on the part of the proponents of the various forms of the "Johannine community hypothesis" to demonstrate Johannine style outside of the Johannine literature. If there were a "Johannine pattern" or "house style," would one not expect for it to be found also in extrabiblical literature? Indeed, there are some writings that might resemble the "house style" of the "Johannine community." The number of Papias's extant works does not allow one to draw definitive conclusions (though his extant works do not conform to

---

238. See a discussion of many of these contrasts in chap. 6, sec. 12 below.

239. Only two words are unique to 1 John and John's gospel, but these are significant: the words for "Paraclete" (*paraklētos*) and "murder" (*anthrōpoktonos*). The latter is used in John 8:44, where the devil is described as a "murderer from the beginning." It is striking that in 1 John 3:8 the word occurs in a section detailing the differences between the children of God and the children of the devil.

240. Note that throughout this book, I will be using the translation "helping presence" for the Greek word *paraklētos*.

241. Brooke, *Epistles*, v, notes that one could make the list quite long.

242. Ibid.

243. Examples include: *ekeinos* ("that one") used as a pronoun; "everyone who is -ing" (*pas ho* + participle instead of *pantes*; 1 John 3:4//John 3:16; similarly, *pan* + participle where *pantes* might be used; 1 John 5:4//John 6:37); repetition of emphatic words; *kai* + *de* combinations; *kathōs* + *kai* combinations; elliptic use of *ou kathōs* (1 John 3:11, 12//John 6:58); *hina* used like an infinitive.

244. Vern S. Poythress, "Testing for Johannine Authorship by Examining the Use of Conjunctions," *WTJ* 46 (1984): 350–69. Poythress' test has its flaws, but the general premise is well founded and still holds up to scrutiny. See L. Scott Kellum, *The Unity of the Farewell Discourse: The Literary Integrity of John 13.31–16.33* (JSNTSup 256; London/New York: T&T Clark, 2004), 113–21.

Johannine style), but there is a larger sample from John's disciple Polycarp. Yet when his *Letter to the Philippians*, for example, is examined, it does not display evidence of Johannine style.[245] Werner Kümmel's conclusion is doubtless correct: "There are no cogent reasons for assuming that I John is to be attributed to another author than J[oh]n."[246]

(5) The author's self-references indicate that he considers himself an eyewitness to Jesus (see esp. 1 John 1:1–4). There is general agreement, even among those supporting the theory of a "Johannine school," that the writer is one person rather than a community. This is evidenced by his use of the first person singular thirty-two times throughout the letters. However, what is contested is what the writer means when he uses a first person plural. While the writer does refer to himself several times in the first person plural in solidarity with his readers (1 John 1:6, 7, 8, 10; 2:1, 3, 5, 18; etc.),[247] there are at least nine instances where he refers to himself in distinction from his hearers (1 John 1:1, 2, 3, 4, 5; 4:6, 14; 3 John 10, 12). Those convinced of the presence of a "Johannine school" find support for their theory in these references.[248]

However, this is not necessarily the best way to account for this phenomenon. First, especially in the references in the introduction, the writer uses sensory language that is best understood as the speech of an eyewitness. He claims to have "heard," "seen," and "touched" with his "hands" "the Word of life" (1 John 1:1). The latter expression, using his hands to touch the Word of life, leads us to understand that "Word of life" does not refer to the *message* of life but to the Word who *is* life — Jesus Christ (see John 1:1, 14).[249] It is hard to imagine that such language would have been used by someone who was not claiming physical contact with Jesus.

(6) The author assumes an authoritative tone that is consistent with an apostle. Although he calls himself an "elder" in 2 and 3 John, this is not inconsistent with being an apostle. Peter, for example, calls himself both an "apostle" (1 Pet 1:1) and a "fellow elder" (1 Pet 5:1). The early church father Papias similarly refers to the apostles as "elders."[250] Thus there is ample reason to believe that John, likewise, could simultaneously occupy the status of both an apostle and an elder (and, in fact, as a prophet as well; see Rev 1:1–3, 9–10; 22:18–19), and in his function as an apostle write a gospel and in his role as an elder write letters to various congregations.

(7) There is also an indication that the author was advanced in years. If the letters date from the end of the first century AD, then any eyewitness would have reached old age by that time. In keeping with this, the author referred to the con-

---

245. Polycarp's letter, dated to the first decade of the second century (see above), has a decidedly non-Johannine linguistic stamp. Polycarp does not use *hina* ("in order that") in the same way as the Johannine letters; employs *oun* ("therefore") far more frequently in expository genres; does not use the word *kosmos* ("world") but features *aiōn* ("age") instead; and the very Johannine terms *ekeinos* ("that one") and *menō* ("remain") are not used at all. Yet Polycarp is thoroughly familiar with John's gospel and letters and considers them authoritative.

246. Kümmel, *Introduction to the New Testament*, 445.

247. See 1 John 3:11, 14, 16, 18, 19, 20, 21, 22, 23, 24; 4:7, 9, 10, 11, 12, 13, 16, 17, 19, 21; 5:2, 3, 9, 11, 14, 15, 18, 19, 20; 2 John 2, 4, 5, 6, 8; 3 John 8, 14.

248. See, e.g., Raymond E. Brown, *The Epistles of John* (AB 30; New York: Doubleday, 1982), 94–95; and John Painter, *1, 2, and 3 John* (SP; Collegeville, MN: Liturgical Press, 2002), 45–46.

249. Though this is by no means universally affirmed in the scholarly literature: see Marianne Meye Thompson, *1–3 John* (IVPNTC; Downers Grove, IL: InterVarsity Press, 1992), 36–37 and the other sources cited there.

250. Cited in Eusebius, *Hist. eccl.* 3.39.5–7.

gregations addressed in the letters as "dear children," including even those he calls "fathers" (1 John 2:12–14).

All the above data comports perfectly with authorship by John the son of Zebedee, who, it was argued above, also most likely wrote the gospel. As will be seen, this is further confirmed by the external evidence.

2.2.1.2 External Evidence

Early church tradition unanimously held that the author of the first letter was John, the son of Zebedee. Second and 3 John were not as strongly attested. Origen noted in the third century AD that some did not receive these letters, though he himself did.[251] In spite of the wavering of a few, 2 and 3 John were received into the canon on the strength of the conviction that John the apostle was the author.

More recently, however, confidence in the tradition has frequently been undermined by the claim that no explicit attribution to John as the author occurs until Irenaeus (c. AD 180). Statements such as the following by Raymond Brown are common: "There is no certain evidence among Christian writers of a knowledge of any of the Johannine Epistles before the middle of the second century ... the lack of early attestation makes us cautious about assuming that there was a solid tradition throughout the second century attributing them to a known figure named John."[252] This skepticism is often used to support a theory that the orthodox were initially apprehensive of the Johannine letters until their rehabilitation by Irenaeus.[253]

In response, it should be noted that these kinds of statements arise from the overly rigid demand that a text must be mentioned as "from John" before it can be used in support of Johannine authorship. However, this is an illegitimate burden imposed on the source quotation. If this is kept in mind, it becomes relevant that solid evidence of the authoritative use of the letters, likely implying the assumption and acceptance of Johannine authorship, exists well before Irenaeus.[254] Polycarp (c. AD 108),[255] Ignatius (c. AD 110), Papias (c. AD 110), the *Epistula Apostolorum* (c. AD 140), and the Epistle to Diognetus (c. AD 125–50), among others, all show at least a great appreciation for the Johannine letters prior to Irenaeus. Much of this evidence instills confidence in the Johannine origins of these letters.[256]

---

251. Cited in Eusebius, *Hist. eccl.* 6.25.10.

252. Brown, *Epistles*, 6. See also, e.g., Painter, *1, 2, and 3 John*, 40.

253. See the comments on the gospel of John above for a defense against the commonly held opinion that there was a "Johannophobia" among the orthodox (a.k.a. the OJP theory).

254. Irenaeus's quote of 2 John 7–8 comes in a context where he is referring to 1 John and citing 2 John as if it were in the same letter (*Haer.* 3.16.8). Instead of claiming that Irenaeus was mistaken, it is more commonly held that this is evidence that at least 1 and 2 John circulated together. See Brown, *Epistles*, 10.

255. Raymond E. Brown, *An Introduction to the New Testament* (ABRL; New York: Doubleday, 1997), 389, states that Polycarp's *Letter to the Philippians* must have been written prior to AD 150. However, it is possible to be more specific. In light of the fact that this letter (sent as a cover letter for the Ignatian letters) inquires about the fate of Ignatius (13.2), one can surmise that it was composed soon after his martyrdom (AD 107; Michael W. Holmes, *The Apostolic Fathers: Greek Texts and English Translations* [Grand Rapids: Baker, 2004], 203–4, places it a few months afterward). Thus many date Polycarp's *Letter to the Philippians* as early as AD 108 (e.g., Susan Lynn Peterson, *Timeline Charts of the Western Church* [Grand Rapids: Zondervan, 1999], 19). Polycarp showed not only knowledge of 1 John, but also affinities with Johannine language and thought (see esp. Polycarp, *Phil.* 9 and 10; and compare 10.1: "joined together in truth" with 3 John 8: "work together for the truth").

256. See the study by Hill, *Johannine Corpus in the Early Church*, for a thorough catalogue of early Johannine citations.

From Irenaeus's time forward, there is a steady stream of citations that continues to express the confidence evidenced in the earliest literature. A brief inventory of the more germane evidence since Irenaeus includes the following: the Muratorian Fragment (c. AD 180) refers to the letters (in the plural) as coming from John; Tertullian (late second/early third century AD) cites 1 John at least forty times as the work of John; Clement of Alexandria (end of second century AD) refers to 1 John as the "greater epistle" (*Stromata* 2.15.66); he also wrote a short commentary on 2 John. Third John is first mentioned in the extant patristic works by Origen (third century AD). Dionysius of Alexandria (Origen's successor, d. AD 265) held to the Johannine authorship of 1 John but knew that there was a "reputed" 2 and 3 John (Eusebius, *Hist. eccl.* 7.25.7–8.11).

The external data points quite early to 1 and 2 John as coming from the apostle John. The Johannine authorship of 3 John, most likely because of its brevity and a lack of extant patristic works, is supported less widely. However, since there is evidence to assume that the letters circulated together, it is not unlikely that 3 John was included as well. This would be consistent with what is known of published letter collections in antiquity.[257] So, then, the letters are cited consistently as authoritative without a single source proposing a different author. This assumption of Johannine authorship held sway until the 1800s.

2.2.1.3 Challenges to Johannine Authorship

As briefly mentioned above, in modern circles it is common to jettison the opinion of the ancient church and to propose sometimes radically different answers to the question of authorship and origins. Alternative proposals include: (1) an unknown elder in the so-called "Johannine community"; (2) a follower of the apostle John (or "the disciple whom Jesus loved"; John 13:23; etc.); or (3) the legendary "John the Elder" in Asia Minor.[258] Much of this is based on prevenient convictions pertaining to the authorship and origins of John's gospel. The prevailing theory is that a sectarian community on the fringe of orthodoxy, related to "the disciple whom Jesus loved," is responsible for the gospel. A series of events produced the gospel in stages in interaction with the "Johannine community's" parent synagogue, and later the letters were generated in response to a painful split in the community. On the assumption that the gospel and the letters come from two different hands, the theory posits that (1) the stylistic uniformity of the gospel and the letters are reflective of a "house style" but not common authorship; and (2) that the linguistic and thematic divergences suggest separate authors.

While the vast number of stylistic similarities between the gospel and the letters is undeniable, some point to several alleged divergences to support the theory

---

257. See "Appendix A: The Collection of Paul's Letters," in Donald Guthrie, *New Testament Introduction* (rev. ed.; Downers Grove, IL: InterVarsity Press, 1990), 986–1000; David Trobisch, *Paul's Letter Collection: Tracing the Origins* (Minneapolis: Fortress, 1994); and Stanley E. Porter, ed., *The Pauline Canon* (Pauline Studies 1; Leiden: Brill, 2004).

258. This was a popular decision among nineteenth-century theologians that has been reopened by Hengel, *Johannine Question*. See the discussions of Papias's statement in Eusebius, *Hist. eccl.* 3.39.4.

of separate authorship. One of the most influential early proponents of separate authorship in the first half of the twentieth century was the British scholar C. H. Dodd.[259] Dodd argued that in matters of style, the gospel has rich subtlety, "which the Epistle cannot pretend."[260] He alleged that the following linguistic phenomena pointed to a different writer: (1) a lack of Aramaic influences; (2) a high rate of *hapax legomena* (e.g., words that occur only once in the NT; 1 John has forty words that do not appear in the gospel); and (3) different language used for subjects relating to salvation. Thematically, Dodd argued that 1 John has no OT quotation and only one explicit OT reference (1 John 3:12), while the gospel is filled with OT quotes and allusions. Dodd also noted that, unlike the gospel, 1 John shows few Jewish characteristics. Instead, the letter appears to reflect Gnostic thought (e.g., "anointing" [2:20, 27]; "God's seed" [3:9]), which is foreign to the gospel.[261]

Raymond Brown, however, rightly dismissed most of Dodd's stylistic arguments as easily answered with reference to the respective genres of gospel and letter.[262] Nevertheless, Brown took up and expanded several of the thematic issues raised by Dodd, arguing against common authorship on the basis of clarity, thematic issues, and the life situation of the letters. According to Brown, the gospel writer was relatively simple and clear in his expression while the author of the letters wrote with "infuriating" obscurity.[263] Obscurity, however, is itself a subjective phenomenon; what may be obscure for some (such as Brown) may be clear to others (especially the original readers of the letters).

Specifically, Brown cited what he considered five major differences in thought between the gospel and the letters, which he found damaging to the notion of common authorship: (1) the gospel focuses on the incarnation of the Word, while 1 John testifies to the message about Jesus; (2) the gospel says Jesus was the light (John 8:12; 9:5), 1 John says the light is God (1 John 1:5); (3) the gospel says the Paraclete is the Holy Spirit, 1 John says it is Jesus (2:1); (4) the gospel's eschatology is predominantly realized, while the letters place more emphasis on Jesus' second coming (1 John 2:28–3:3); (5) the Dead Sea Scrolls parallels are closer in 1 John than in the gospel.[264]

---

259. C. H. Dodd, *The Johannine Epistles* (MNTC; New York: Harper, 1946); idem, "The First Epistle of John and the Fourth Gospel," *BJRL* 21 (1937): 129–56. This is in spite of able works countering Dodd, such as W. G. Wilson, "An Examination of the Linguistic Evidence Adduced against the Unity of Authorship of the First Epistle of John and the Fourth Gospel," *JTS* 48 (1947): 147–56; and W. F. Howard, "The Common Authorship of the Johannine Gospel and Epistles," *JTS* 48 (1947): 12–25.

260. Dodd, *Epistles*, xlix. According to Dodd, the writer of the Letters overworked certain grammatical constructions and used a smaller set of compound verbs. Moreover, he was "immoderately addicted" to conditional sentences. Following Dodd, there was a marked readiness on the part of some to disparage the author of the Letters in the effort to prove that the Gospel could not have been written by him. Kenneth Grayston, *The Johannine Epistles* (New Century Bible Commentary; Grand Rapids: Eerdmans, 1984), 7–9, for example, described a hierarchy of ability within the Johannine literature. While the gospel is the high water mark of intelligence and expression, the writer of 1 John pedantically transformed the existentialism of the Gospel into a historical expression and "thereby degraded it." Even further down the scale is the "less adept" author of 2 and 3 John, who preferred speaking to writing, simply repeated the tradition, renounced deviation, and on the whole was more limited than the writer of 1 John.

261. Dodd, *Epistles*, xlix. Dodd considered "God is love" to be Hellenistic thought hammered out on a Christian anvil. The abstract "love" would not be found in Semitic thought. John's gospel instead declares that "God is spirit" (John 4:24).

262. Brown, *Epistles*, 24, noted: "Overall, then, it seems that the variation of minute stylistic features between GJohn and 1 John is not much different from the variation that one can find if one compares one part of GJohn to another part. In particular, the Johannine Jesus speaks as the author of the Johannine Epistles writes."

263. Brown, *Epistles*, 24–25. See Painter, *1, 2, & 3 John*, 60.

264. Brown, *Introduction to the New Testament*, 389.

However, each of these arguments can be adequately accounted for on the assumption of common authorship, and none of them is conclusive evidence against such a notion. To respond to each item in turn: (1) the reference in the introduction to the gospel and to 1 John is one and the same, the person of Jesus; (2) Johannine Christology clearly would have no problem with Jesus and God being referred to interchangeably (see esp. John 10:30); (3) the reference to Jesus as "advocate" (*paraklētos*) in 1 John 2:1 has an antecedent in the reference to the Holy Spirit as "another advocate" (*paraklētos*) in John 14:16 (implying that Jesus, too, is an advocate, a *paraklētos*); (4) the gospel, likewise, has passages referring to final eschatology, including the second coming (e.g., 5:28–29; 14:3; 21:22, 24); and (5) there are parallels to the Dead Sea Scrolls in both the gospel and John's letters.[265]

Thus all of Brown's objections can be met, and, as Brown himself conceded, none of these alleged differences conclusively proves separate authorship for the gospel and the letters. In the end, what is ultimately decisive for Brown and his followers is their historical reconstruction of the "Johannine community." Brown, for his part, posits a theory that during the production of the gospel there were various struggles with outside groups. What he finds startling is that the letters, unlike the gospel, show no struggle with those outside but only with those who have arisen from the group's own ranks (1 John 2:19). He conjectures that the most likely scenario that accounts for these differences is that the gospel was written first and that the letters reflect two different kinds of interpretations of the gospel: one by a group (the "orthodox") that merged with the great church, the other by those who were funneled into the Gnostic movement.

What is more, Brown contends the issue at stake in the debate reflected in John's letters was not whether or not Jesus was the Messiah but whether or not he came in the flesh (i.e., whether or not Jesus was fully human). According to Brown, this points to a period of development and divergence within the "Johannine community." Yet it seems at least equally possible that the author of the gospel (assuming it was written first) later defended the full humanity of Jesus over against a group of proto-Gnostics who had arisen from within the church. Alternatively, the question, not only in the gospel but also in the letters, continued to be whether or not Jesus was the Messiah.[266] What is more, even if Brown's reconstruction were correct, this still would not necessarily demonstrate separate authorship.[267] If common authorship is rejected, this is often done not on the grounds of the available evidence but on a priori grounds.

---

265. See the case study by Elizabeth W. Mburu, "The *Rule of the Community* as a Valid Linguistic Resource for Understanding Truth Terminology in the Gospel of John: A Semantic Analysis" (Ph.D. dissertation; Wake Forest, NC: Southeastern Baptist Theological Seminary, 2008).

266. See Daniel R. Streett, "'They Went Out from Us': The Identity of the Opponents in First John" (Ph.D. dissertation; Wake Forest, NC: Southeastern Baptist Theological Seminary, 2008).

267. Brown, *Epistles*, 30, has himself admitted this point: "They could have been written at the same time by different men … or, and this is more probable, at a different time by either the same man (sadder and wiser as he faces a new battle, now from within the movement) or by different men."

2.2.1.4 Conclusion

In the end, therefore, none of the objections raised by Dodd, Brown, and others actually prove, or even plausibly suggest, separate authorship of John's gospel and the letters. The occasional differences in style can be accounted for by the respective genres and other factors (such as differing document lengths). The alleged thematic divergences often depend on antecedent judgments that are in themselves highly questionable or do not necessarily point to a different author. It seems reasonable to conclude that even the cumulative effect of these supposed difficulties bears insufficient weight to establish separate authorship.

In the final analysis, therefore, though there are recent objections to the Johannine authorship of the gospel and of the letters, no piece of internal or external evidence has surfaced that is inconsistent with identifying the author of the gospel with that of the letters. Coupled with the conclusions concerning the authorship of John's gospel reached above, the apostle John remains convincingly the best candidate as the author of the letters.

2.2.2 Date, Provenance, and Destination

2.2.2.1 Date

Reliable historical tradition strongly suggests that John spent his latter years in Asia Minor in and around Ephesus (e.g., Irenaeus, *Haer.* 3.1.2; cf. Eusebius, *Eccl. Hist.* 3.1.1). The apostle's move from Palestine to Asia Minor is said to have taken place sometime subsequent to the Jewish rebellion in AD 66. It was concluded in the discussion of the gospel of John that the latter was most likely written in the early to mid-AD 80s. The question concerning the date of John's letters, therefore, is: Were they written prior or subsequent to the gospel?

On balance, the latter seems more likely. While it is possible that some of the connections with the gospel in 1 John are based on a common tradition,[268] in a few places the gospel seems to be assumed. For example, 1 John 2:7–8 refers to and explicates the meaning of the new commandment of John 13:34–35 without naming it. In 1 John 5:6, reference is made to Jesus coming by "water and blood" (most likely references to the baptism and Jesus' crucifixion, respectively; note the verbal parallel with John 19:34).

Some, such as Carson and Moo, think that it is likely that the letters were written to combat heretical misinterpretations of the gospel, which would require a later date for the letters.[269] This seems entirely plausible. Yet even if the purpose for the letters were construed differently, the conclusion that they postdate the gospel still appears to be the most probable in light of the parallels mentioned above. The best date, then, given the death of John at around the turn of the century[270] and

---

268. See Brooke, *Epistles*, xix–xxii; Grayston, *Johannine Epistles*, 12–14.
269. Carson and Moo, *Introduction to the New Testament*, 676.
270. Irenaeus, *Haer.* 3.3.4 (quoted by Eusebius, *Hist. eccl.* 3.23.3–4), places John's death during the reign of Trajan (AD 98–117); Jerome, *Vir. ill.* 9, says that John died in the sixty-eighth year after Jesus' passion (i.e. AD 98 or 101).

the dating of the gospel in the early to mid-AD 80s, is somewhere in the early to mid-AD 90s.

2.2.2.2 Provenance

The ancient tradition is consistent that John spent his latter years in Ephesus in Asia Minor. Polycrates, in a letter to Victor of Rome, calls John one of the "luminaries" buried in Ephesus.[271] Irenaeus writes that John stayed in Ephesus permanently until the reign of Trajan (AD 98–117).[272] Irenaeus even includes specific statements about John's ministry in Ephesus. Without solid evidence to the contrary, most scholars assume the accuracy of the Ephesus tradition.[273]

2.2.2.3 Destination

In 1 John, John addressed various groups in the congregation as "dear children," "fathers," "young people," and "dear friends" (see, e.g., 2:12–14; 4:1, 7). These ways of addressing his audience indicate a close established relationship between John and his readers. Since 1 John does not refer to specific names and places, contains little mention of specific events, and is general in its teaching, it seems that John focused on important truths of broad relevance to address as many believers as possible. This lends credence to the view that 1 John was a circular letter sent to predominantly Gentile churches in and around Ephesus.[274]

Second and 3 John are personal letters, written to "the lady chosen by God and to her children" (2 John 1; most likely several local congregations; see discussion below) and to an individual named Gaius (3 John 1), respectively.[275]

2.2.3 Occasion

The churches to which 1 John is written are under doctrinal and emotional duress. There has been a recent departure of false teachers from the church (2:19) that was apparently both painful and unpleasant and that is still palpable in 2 John (v. 7). This is evident especially in the repeated charge against the secessionists that they do not love other believers (see, e.g., 1 John 2:9–10; 3:10; 4:7). The Christians to whom John writes in 1 John are in need of instruction, but more importantly need to be

---

271. Eusebius, *Hist. eccl.* 3.31.3; 5.24.2.

272. Irenaeus, *Haer.* 3.1.1.

273. A minority does posit other provenances. Kümmel, *Introduction to the New Testament*, 445, for example, advocates a Syrian provenance for the gospel of John on the grounds of "substantive contacts" with the *Odes of Solomon* (which presumably came from Syria) and with Ignatius of Antioch (see ibid., 247, with further bibliographic references in n. 224) and conjectures that the letters were also written there. Regarding theories that point to linguistic similarities to Gnosticism in Palestine, Rudolf Schnackenburg, *The Johannine Epistles: A Commentary* (New York: Crossroad, 1992), 40, is undoubtedly correct: "All it means is that the author was born in Palestine."

274. Augustine's ascription of the letter *ad Parthos* ("to the Parthians") is almost certainly incorrect and may be a corruption of *tou parthenou* ("of the virgin"), a possible reference to John, who was frequently regarded as celibate. See Philip Schaff, ed., *Nicene and Post-Nicene Fathers*, Vol. 7: *Augustin [sic]: Homilies on the Gospel of John, Homilies on the First Epistle of John, Soliloquies*, First Series (Peabody, MA: Hendrickson, 1994), 459, n. 1. The title of Augustine's manuscripts is "Ten Homilies on the Epistle of John to the Parthians."

275. Second and 3 John are more readily recognizable as examples of the first-century personal letter. Both are rather short (245 and 219 words, respectively) and would easily fit on one papyrus sheet (typical of first-century letters). For a helpful treatment, see the chapter on "New Testament Letters" in Carson and Moo, *Introduction to the New Testament*, 331–53, esp. 332–33 (including further bibliographic references).

reassured and comforted in light of the recent upheaval ending in the departure of the false teachers (5:13; cf. 2:19).

2.2.3.1 The Nature of the False Teaching

While there was clearly conflict among John's readers, its precise nature is difficult to determine because of the oblique nature of the references (John throughout presupposes that his readers know the issues that are at stake). Irenaeus claimed that John wrote the gospel to refute Cerinthus — an early Gnostic teacher who held that the "Christ spirit" descended on Jesus at his baptism and left him at the cross — but does not make the same claim for the letters.[276] Some, with reference to Irenaeus, claim the letters were written to combat the same opponent.[277] It is not at all certain, however, that Cerinthus was the catalyst of the secession that sparked this letter. Nascent Gnosticism of his sort, however, may have been afoot, and some form of it may have influenced the secession.[278] But wholesale identification of the Ephesian secessionists with Cerinthus's followers is unwarranted.[279]

The exact nature of the false teaching is nearly impossible to pinpoint with certainty. Rudolf Schnackenburg aptly observes, "The meager hints and the formulas used in the letter are all we have to go on."[280] As Terry Griffith has shown, these may be interpreted in different ways.[281] Nevertheless, there are some clues to help us understand the broad contours of the false teaching denounced in 1 John. The clearest indicators of the secessionists' doctrine are found in 1 John 2, where repeated reference is made to their denial that Jesus is the Messiah (2:22–23; cf. John 20:30–31).[282]

While certainty remains elusive, it is possible to identify several characteristics of the secessionists. (1) They do not truly know God, because they do not keep his commandments (1 John 2:4).

(2) They do not conduct themselves the way Jesus did, especially with regard to the commandment to love one another (1 John 2:9). In all this, their behavior

---

276. In *Haer.* 3.11.1, Irenaeus also relates a confrontation between Cerinthus and John. He notes that John refused to stay in a bath house occupied by Cerinthus and advised the people to flee, "lest even the bath house fall down." In *Haer.* 3.3.4, Irenaeus names Polycarp as the source of this tradition.

277. See, e.g., Robert Gundry, *A Survey of the New Testament* (3rd ed.; Grand Rapids: Zondervan, 1994), 448–49, who proposes that Cerinthus is the culprit. But Schnackenburg, *Epistles*, 21–23, notes several differences between the secessionists in 1 John and both Cerinthus and Ignatius's opponents mentioned below.

278. It has been pointed out that Ignatius's letter to the Smyrneans and to the Trallians (in southwest Asia Minor) both show a docetic-type heresy that denied that Christ was actually human (from Gr. *dokeō*, "seem," the teaching that Jesus only *appeared* to be human). This is also addressed in his letter to the Ephesians (Ign. *Smyrn.* 2.1, 5.2; Ign. *Trall.* 10.1; and Ign. *Eph.* 7.1). See, e.g., I. H. Marshall, *The Epistles of John* (NICNT; Grand Rapids: Eerdmans, 1978), 17–22; Paul J. Achtemeier, Joel B. Green, and Marianne Meye Thompson, *Introducing the New Testament: Its Literature and Theology* (Grand Rapids: Eerdmans, 2001), 539; and Frank Thielman, *Theology of the New Testament: A Canonical and Synthetic Approach* (Grand Rapids: Zondervan, 2005), 539–40. Since Ignatius addresses all his letters to churches in Asia Minor, it is likely that something like the docetic doctrines flourished in John's time as well.

279. So Schnackenburg, *Epistles*, 21–23.

280. Ibid., 17.

281. Terry Griffith, *Keep Yourselves from Idols: A New Look at 1 John* (JSNTSup 233; London: Sheffield Academic Press, 2002), asserts that the secessionists were reverting back to Judaism and that "in the flesh" does not refer to a docetic theology but merely represents a way of expressing the incarnation. Another nonpolemical argument is found in Judith M. Lieu, "'Authority to Become Children of God': A Study of 1 John," *NovT* 23 (1981): 210–28.

282. The statement in 1 John 2:26, "I am writing these things to you about those who are trying to lead you astray," goes back at least as far as 2:18. In 2:22, it is noted that the opponents denied

is characterized by a lack of obedience. If, then, these references were included to condemn the conduct of the secessionists, the series of contrasts in 1:6–10 probably alludes to them as well. If so, the secessionists were "walking in darkness" while claiming to be sinless and contending that sins do not impact final salvation. This lack of ethical orientation is borne out in chapter 3, where they are identified as "children of the devil" (3:10) upon an examination of their deeds.

(3) First John 4:2–3 states that the secessionists denied that Jesus came in the flesh (see also 2 John 7). This may (though need not necessarily) reflect a docetic Christology. In what follows, rather than reinforcing the humanity of Jesus, the author simply defines the denial as the failure to confess Jesus. The same pattern continues later on in the letter (see 1 John 4:15; 5:1, 5). It seems that the major emphasis lies not so much on refuting a docetic Christology but on the rejection or confession of Jesus.[283] At any rate, the underlying central denial is that Jesus is the Messiah. As to the exact reason for the denial, it is hard to be certain.[284]

(4) Another possibility is that the secessionists subscribed to a Christology that denied the atoning merit of the cross. This is hinted at in the confession found in 1 John 5:6–8, "This is the one who came by water and blood—Jesus Christ. He did not come by water only, but by water and blood." John is scrupulous to deny an understanding of Jesus that views him as having come "by water only" and not also "by blood," which seems to indicate a rejection of the sacrificial and substitutionary nature of Jesus' death for others. This, in turn, as mentioned above, may have flowed from a deficient view of the impact of sin on final salvation.

2.2.3.2 Conclusion

So what can be said about the secessionists' doctrine? First, it seems that they rejected the apostolic witness (1 John 1:1–5). They had a defective Christology that denied that Jesus was the Messiah (though the exact reason for this is unclear). Moreover, they were disobedient to the commands of God (esp. the love commandment; see 3:10b–15), evidenced particularly in their recent departure from the community. This led to a doctrine that diminished the seriousness of sin. Thus, the false teachers showed they were not truly children of God. Daniel Akin describes the false teachers well: they flaunted a new theology that "compromised the uniqueness of the person and work of Jesus Christ"; a new morality that "minimized the importance of sin; they claimed to have fellowship with God despite their unrighteous behavior"; and, finally, a new spirituality that "resulted in spiritual arrogance; consequently they did not show love to others."[285]

But there was more than secession prior to John's writing; the controversy continued. Second John 8–9 indicates the status of the controversy: "Watch out that

---

that Jesus was the Messiah (though the exact nature of this denial is not specified). The references to "deny[ing]" and "acknowledge[ing] the Son" in 2:23, likewise, are general in nature.

283. For this reason the reference to Jesus having "come in the flesh" in 1 John 4:2 may resemble the affirmation that "he appeared in a body" in 1 Tim 3:16.

284. Most are not nearly so cautious. See Achtemeier, Green, and Thompson, *Introducing the New Testament*, 539–42.

285. Daniel L. Akin, *1, 2, 3 John* (NAC 38; Nashville: Broadman and Holman, 2001), 31.

you do not lose what we have worked for, but that you may be rewarded fully. Anyone who runs ahead and does not continue in the teaching of Christ does not have God; whoever continues in the teaching has both the Father and the Son." First John 2:26 also seems to indicate that the itinerant teaching of the opponents was ongoing.[286] The situation, then, was that the secessionists were aggressively seeking to infiltrate the churches in and around Ephesus with their theology, and that the aged apostle John ("the elder"; 2 John 1; 3 John 1) took up his pen to address this situation.

2.2.4 Purpose

First John is similar to John's gospel in that the purpose statement occurs near, but not at the very end of, the book (see John 20:30–31).[287] In 1 John, the purpose statement is found at 5:13: "I write these things to you who believe in the name of the Son of God so that you may know that you have eternal life." While there are two other passages that declare John's purpose for writing (2:1 and 2:12–14), they do not carry the same global weight as 5:13. Reassurance of all genuine Christians in the churches addressed, then, is the primary purpose of the book.[288]

Nevertheless, reassurance is only part of John's purpose. The book also displays a pronounced emphasis on exhortation, which is indicated by the fact that many verbs are either formal or implied imperatives.[289] Donald Guthrie notes, "Nowhere else in the New Testament is the combination of faith and love so clearly brought out, and it seems probable that this is emphasized because the behaviour of the readers leaves much to be desired."[290] While Guthrie may have overstated his point, there is little doubt that exhortation is an important part of John's purpose for writing his first letter.[291]

2.2.5 Introductory Matters Unique to 2 and 3 John

The prescripts of 2 and 3 John differ from 1 John in that the recipients and sender are named, albeit imprecisely. The sender is identified in both letters simply as "the elder." The similarity in language and themes to 1 John makes it virtually certain they are from the same person, although this is debated.[292] The use of the term "elder" here is similar to the introduction in 1 John 1:1–4 in that the writer

---

286. The phrase "those who are trying to lead you astray" (Gr. substantive participle *tōn planōtōn*) in 1 John 2:26 is in the present tense, indicating contemporaneous action with the main verb (in this case an epistolary aorist, "I am writing"). It follows that at the time of writing of 1 John, the false teachers were still trying to infiltrate the churches with their false doctrine.

287. Thielman, *Theology of the New Testament*, 536.

288. See the discussion of Christian assurance in John's gospel and letters in chap. 12, sec. 28.5 below.

289. Robert Longacre, "Towards an Exegesis of 1 John," in *Linguistics and New Testament Interpretation* (ed. David Alan Black; Nashville: Broadman and Holman, 1992), 278–79, observes that while only about 9 percent of the verbs are imperative in form, they dominate the passages in which they occur.

290. Guthrie, *New Testament Introduction*, 867.

291. See, e.g., 1 John 2:4–5, 12–15, and the repeated exhortations to "remain/live" in Christ (1 John 2:24, 27, 28; 3:17; 4:13; 2 John 9; cf. 1 John 3:14).

292. See, e.g., Georg Strecker, *The Johannine Letters: A Commentary on 1, 2, and 3 John* (Hermeneia; trans. Linda M. Maloney; Minneapolis: Fortress, 1996), 3, who argues that both 2 and 3 John are earlier than 1 John. The usage of the term "elder" in no way lends credibility to the myth of a "John the elder" mentioned earlier.

is so well known that the simplest of ascriptions is sufficient to identify him to the readers.[293]

The designation of the recipients in 2 John as "the lady chosen by God and ... her children" (2 John 1; see also the reference to "the children of your sister, who is chosen by God" in 2 John 13) is also imprecise. These recipients have been variously interpreted as an actual woman and her offspring or as a figurative reference to a series of local congregations,[294] with the latter of these being preferable.[295] John's language is not appropriate for referring to a real person (see, e.g., 2 John 5: "And now, dear lady ... that we love one another"). The scenario underlying verses 7–11, likewise, is more appropriate to a local congregation than to a single home in it. One also notes the conspicuous absence of personal names in 2 John (compare the references to Gaius, Demetrius, and Diotrephes in 3 John), which also suggests that the intended recipient is a local congregation rather than an individual lady and her children. It is unclear why John chooses not to name the location of the church to which 2 John is addressed; the omission may be motivated by John's desire to lend his missive universal application or to protect the specific identity of the church for some other reason.[296]

The occasion of 2 John may have been the return of a delegation sent by the church to the apostle. In verse 4, John commends "some" as "walking in the truth." If related to 1 John (see esp. 1 John 2:19), the letter may intend to warn the church against welcoming the secessionists into their homes (see 2 John 8–11). Paul Achtemeier, Joel Green, and Marianne Thompson state it well: "If in 1 John we see the problem from the vantage point of the church from which the false prophets 'went out,' in 2 John we see the problem with the eyes of the church in which they may then have showed up to preach and teach."[297] If so, John wrote to encourage this local congregation to beware of these false teachers.

The third letter is specifically written "to my dear friend Gaius" (3 John 1), an otherwise unknown individual.[298] It does not specifically mention the secession or problems associated with it. Instead, it commends Gaius for receiving the brothers sent from the apostle (apparently itinerant preachers) and commends Demetrius as one of them (3 John 12). Diotrephes, however, opposed "other believers" and did not support the apostolic messengers (3 John 9–10).[299] It is safe to conclude, then, that one of the major purposes of 3 John is to provide a letter of recommendation

---

293. Schnackenburg, *Epistles*, 270.
294. Brown, *Epistles*, 652–53, notes a host of contrary opinions all revolving around a single individual: (1) a lady named "Electa"; (2) "a noble Kyria" (Alford, Bengel, de Wette, Ebrard, Lücke, and Neander); (3) "a Dear Lady" (i.e., a woman of some importance; Plummer, Ross); and (4) the universal church (Schmiedel).
295. So, e.g., Carson and Moo, *Introduction to the New Testament*, 677; Brown, *Epistles*, 655; Colin G. Kruse, *The Letters of John* (PNTC; Grand Rapids: Eerdmans, 2000), 38; Marshall, *Epistles*, 60; Brooke, *Epistles*, 167–70.
296. For a judicious treatment, see John R. W. Stott, *The Letters of John* (TNTC; rev. ed.; Grand Rapids: Eerdmans, 1988), 203–5.
297. Achtemeier, Green, and Thompson, *Introducing the New Testament*, 548.
298. As Carson and Moo, *Introduction to the New Testament*, 677, observe, this Gaius is likely neither the Gaius of Corinth (Rom 16:23; 1 Cor 1:14), nor the Gaius of Macedonia (Acts 19:29), nor the Gaius of Derbe (Acts 20:4; contra, the fourth-century AD *Apostolic Constitutions* 7.46.9).
299. Nothing is known about Demetrius or Diotrephes apart from the references to these individuals in 2 John.

for the elder's emissaries in general and for Demetrius in particular, as well as to put Diotrephes in his place prior to John's anticipated visit.

2.3 Conclusion

As mentioned at the beginning of this chapter, Biblical Theology—including Johannine theology—is properly grounded in working assumptions regarding the historical setting of a given document, including its authorship, date, provenance, destination, occasion, and purpose. For this reason it has been important to attempt a plausible reconstruction of the likely setting of John's gospel and letters.

Apostolic authorship emerged as a reasonable hypothesis in the case of both the gospel and the letters. In his gospel, John affirms that Jesus is the Messiah, possibly in light of the then-recent destruction of the Jerusalem temple. First John was most likely written to reassure believers after the departure of a group of former members of the community who denied that Jesus was the Messiah and possibly also questioned his full humanity.

After having laid the historical foundation for an investigation of John's theology, the next area of inquiry will be various matters comprising the literary foundations for a study of Johannine theology. This includes issues such as the genre of John's gospel and letters, the Johannine style and vocabulary, various literary devices, and the structure of John's gospel and letters. An investigation of these matters forms the subject of the following two chapters.

Part 2

LITERARY FOUNDATIONS FOR JOHANNINE THEOLOGY

Chapter 2

THE GENRE OF JOHN'S GOSPEL AND LETTERS

BIBLIOGRAPHY

Alexander, Loveday. "What Is a Gospel?" Pp. 13–33 in *The Cambridge Companion to the Gospels*. Ed. Stephen C. Barton. Cambridge: Cambridge University Press, 2006. **Alexander, Philip S**. "Rabbinic Biography and the Biography of Jesus: A Survey of the Evidence." Pp. 19–50 in *Synoptic Studies: The Ampleforth Conferences of 1982 and 1983*. Ed. Christopher M. Tuckett; Sheffield: JSOT, 1984. **Aune, David E**. "The Problem of the Genre of the Gospels: A Critique of C. H. Talbert's *What Is a Gospel?*" Pp. 9–60 in *Gospel Perspectives*, Vol. 2: *Studies of History and Tradition in the Four Gospels*. Ed. R. T. France and David Wenham. Sheffield: JSOT, 1981. **Bauckham, Richard**. *Jesus and the Eyewitnesses: The Gospels as Eyewitness Testimony*. Grand Rapids: Eerdmans, 2006. Idem. "Historiographical Characteristics of the Gospel of John." *NTS* 53 (2007): 17–36. **Blomberg, Craig S**. Pp. 298–303 in *The Historical Reliability of the Gospels*. 2nd ed. Downers Grove, IL: InterVarsity Press, 2007. **Brant, Jo-Ann A**. *Dialogue and Drama: Elements of Greek Tragedy in the Fourth Gospel*. Peabody, MA: Hendrickson, 2004. **Burridge, Richard**. Chap. 9 in *What Are the Gospels? A Comparison with Greco-Roman Biography*. 2nd ed. Grand Rapids: Eerdmans, 2004. **Davies, Margaret**. Chap. 3 in *Rhetoric and Reference in the Fourth Gospel*. JSNTSup 69. Sheffield: JSOT, 1992. **Guelich, Robert**. "The Gospel Genre." Pp. 183–208 in *The Gospel and the Gospels*. Ed. Peter Stuhlmacher. Grand Rapids: Eerdmans, 1991. **Gundry, Robert H**. Pp. 18–48 in *The Old Is Better: New Testament Essays in Support of Traditional Interpretations*. Tübingen: Mohr-Siebeck, 2005. **Hengel, Martin**. *The Four Gospels and the One Gospel of Jesus Christ: An Investigation of the Collection and Origin of the Canonical Gospels*. Trans. John Bowden. Harrisburg, PA: Trinity Press International, 2000. Idem. "Eye-Witness Memory and the Writing of the Gospels." Pp. 70–96 in *The Written Gospel*. Ed. Markus Bockmuehl and Donald A. Hagner. Cambridge: Cambridge University Press, 2005. **Hurtado, Larry W**. "Gospel (Genre)." Pp. 276–82 in *Dictionary of Jesus and the Gospels*. Ed. Joel B. Green, Scot McKnight, and I. Howard Marshall. Downers Grove, IL: InterVarsity Press, 1992. **Keener, Craig S**. Pp. 3–34 in *The Gospel of John: A Commentary*. 2 vols. Peabody, MA: Hendrickson, 2003. **Stamps, Dennis L**. "The Johannine Writings." Pp. 609–32 in *Handbook of Classical Rhetoric in the Hellenistic Period 330 B.C.–A.D. 400*. Ed. Stanley E. Porter. Leiden: Brill, 1997. **Stibbe, Mark W. G**.

Chap. 2 in *John as Storyteller: Narrative Criticism and the Fourth Gospel*. Cambridge: Cambridge University Press, 1992. **Swartley, Willard M**. *Israel's Scripture Traditions and the Synoptic Gospels: Story Shaping Story*. Peabody, MA: Hendrickson, 1994. **Thatcher, Tom**. "The Gospel Genre: What Are We After?" *ResQ* 36 (1994): 129–38. Idem. "John's Memory Theater: The Fourth Gospel and Ancient Mnemo-Rhetoric." *CBQ* 69 (2007): 487–505. **Votaw, C. H**. *The Gospels and Contemporary Biographies in the Greco-Roman World*. Philadelphia: Fortress, 1970 [1915]. **Watson, Francis**. "The Fourfold Gospel." Pp. 34–52 in *The Cambridge Companion to the Gospels*. Ed. Stephen C. Barton. Cambridge: Cambridge University Press, 2006. **Williams, P. J**. "Not the Prologue of John." Paper presented at the Annual Meeting of the SBL. San Diego, CA, November 17, 2007.

3 The Genre of John's Gospel
3.1 Background and History of Research
3.1.1 Introduction

The genre of John's gospel is a widely neglected area in Johannine research.[1] Of particular interest are possible parallels between the genre of John's gospel and Greco-Roman literary conventions. While there is a small specialized body of literature exploring such affinities,[2] the need remains to present these affinities in an accessible format and to assess in a balanced manner the way in which these similarities shed light on the implications of any such parallels for the interpretation of John's gospel.[3]

For this reason it will be helpful to explore similarities in genre between John's gospel and ancient Greco-Roman literature within the overall framework of John's canonical consciousness and indebtedness to Jewish, biblical historiography. As we

---

1. The discussion of genre itself is complex and beyond the scope of this chapter. The definition given in *The Oxford Classical Dictionary* (3rd ed.; ed. Simon Hornblower and Antony Spawforth; Oxford/New York: Oxford University Press, 1996), 630, will have to suffice for our present purposes: "a grouping of texts related within the system of literature by their sharing recognizably functionalized features of form and content." Similarly, Craig L. Blomberg, *The Historical Reliability of the Gospels* (2nd ed.; Downers Grove, IL: InterVarsity Press, 2007), 298, n. 7, speaks of genre "as a category of literary composition characterized by a particular style, form and content"; and Tom Thatcher, "The Gospel Genre: What Are We After?" *ResQ* 36 (1994): 137, defines genre as "a certain group of writings sharing a certain set of conventions recognizable in a certain social matrix." See also Grant R. Osborne, "Genre Criticism—Sensus Literalis," *TrinJ* NS 4 (1983): 1–27; E. D. Hirsch, *Validity in Interpretation* (New Haven: Yale University Press, 1973), chap. 3; and Robert Guelich, "The Gospel Genre," in *The Gospel and the Gospels* (ed. Peter Stuhlmacher; Grand Rapids: Eerdmans, 1991), 173–75.

2. See esp. Margaret Davies, *Rhetoric and Reference in the Fourth Gospel* (JSNTSup 69; Sheffield: JSOT, 1992), chap. 3; Craig S. Keener, *The Gospel of John: A Commentary* (2 vols.; Peabody, MA: Hendrickson, 2003), 3–34; Stibbe, *John as Storyteller*, chap. 2; Richard A. Burridge, *What Are the Gospels? A Comparison with Graeco-Roman Biography* (2nd ed.; Grand Rapids: Eerdmans, 2004), chap. 9; Jo-Ann A. Brant, *Dialogue and Drama: Elements of Greek Tragedy in the Fourth Gospel* (Peabody, MA: Hendrickson, 2004); and Richard Bauckham, "Historiographical Characteristics of the Gospel of John," *NTS* 53 (2007): 17–36.

3. The present discussion essentially reproduces my article "The Genre of the Fourth Gospel and Greco-Roman Literary Conventions," in *The New Testament in Its Hellenistic Context*, Vol. 1: *Christian Origins and Classical Culture: Social and Literary Contexts for the New Testament* (ed. Stanley E. Porter and Andrew W. Pitts; Leiden: Brill, 2009), and is used by permission. Most of the literature focuses on the genre of the gospels in general and/or on the genre of the Synoptic Gospels (see, e.g., Guelich, "Gospel Genre," 173–208; Loveday Alexander, "What Is a Gospel?" in *The Cambridge Companion to the Gospels* [ed. Stephen C. Barton; Cambridge: Cambridge University Press, 2006], 13–33).

will see, while the gospel displays surface similarities with Greco-Roman literature, these operate mostly on the level of contextualization. With regard to the theological and literary underpinnings of John's mode of presentation, John's gospel is grounded foremost in antecedent scriptural patterns.[4]

Although the first four books of the NT are commonly referred to as "gospels," this designation was not part of the original documents. None of these works carried the title *euangelion* ("gospel" or "good news"), and Mark, the only gospel that uses the expression at the outset, does so most likely not with reference to the written document.[5] The title "gospel" was attached to the accounts of Matthew, Mark, Luke, and John by the early Christian church, quite possibly when they were first collected.[6] All four Gospels focus on the earthly life and ministry of Jesus and hence share common characteristics in content, form, and general purpose. For this reason these writings are generally categorized under the same rubric of genre.[7]

At the same time, certain differences may obtain with regard to genre or sub-genre both between John and the Synoptics and among the Synoptics.[8] This raises the question of whether or not the four canonical Gospels should be classified collectively as exemplars of one and the same genre or individually as displaying similar yet distinct genre characteristics. In this regard it is important to note that John's gospel carries the traditional superscription κατὰ Ἰωάννην ("According to John"), which suggests that those who affixed this epithet considered the gospel to occupy the same literary category as the Synoptics. This construction is common to all four Gospels, indicating that the early church conceived of the gospel as one, fourfold Gospel (in the singular) rather than as four separate Gospels (in the plural).[9] Moreover, as Craig Keener points out, historically it is unlikely that John developed the gospel form independently from his Synoptic predecessors.[10]

---

4. See John 1:1; cf. Mark 1:1–3. For a thorough treatment of the use of the OT in John's gospel see Andreas J. Köstenberger, "John," in *Commentary on the New Testament Use of the Old Testament* (ed. G. K. Beale and D. A. Carson; Grand Rapids: Baker, 2007), 415–512, with further extensive bibliographic references.

5. See, e.g., William Lane, *The Gospel of Mark* (NICNT; Grand Rapids: Eerdmans, 1974), 44: "In the initial phrase of Mark's Gospel ... the word 'gospel' has not yet come to mean a written document. It refers to a living word of hope from the lips of an appointed messenger." He adds, "Not until the second century did the term 'gospel' come to designate a particular kind of document" (p. 44, n. 20). Martin Hengel, *The Four Gospels and the One Gospel of Jesus Christ: An Investigation of the Collection and Origin of the Canonical Gospels* (trans. John Bowden; Harrisburg, PA: Trinity Press International, 2000), 91, adduces the parallel opening of Hosea (LXX): "Beginning of the word of the Lord." See Hengel's entire discussion on pp. 90–96. See also Guelich, "Gospel Genre," 194–205, esp. 203–4.

6. This is the argument of Martin Hengel, *Studies in the Gospel of Mark* (Philadelphia: Fortress, 1985), 64–84; see the summary in Carson and Moo, *Introduction to the New Testament*, 140–41.

7. It is possible that the author of John's gospel was aware of the existence of at least one of the other three canonical gospels, as is argued by Richard Bauckham, "John for Readers of Mark," in *Gospels for All Christians*, 147–72 (though see the critique by Wendy E. Sproston North, "John for Readers of Mark? A Response to Richard Bauckham's Proposal," *JSNT* 25 [2003]: 449–68). See also the discussion in chap. 16, sec. 34 below.

8. Keener, *Gospel of John*, 4, points out that Willi Marxsen, *Mark the Evangelist: Studies on the Redaction History of the Gospel* (trans. James Boyce, Donald Juel, and William Poehlmann, with Roy A. Harrisville; Nashville: Abingdon, 1969), 150, objects to applying Mark's term "gospel" to Matthew and Luke, arguing that Matthew is a collection of "gospels" and sermons (p. 150, n. 106; pp. 205–6), and Luke a "life of Jesus" (p. 150, n. 106).

9. Burridge, *Gospels*, 215. See also Hengel, *Four Gospels*; Francis Watson, "The Fourfold Gospel," in *The Cambridge Companion to the Gospels* (ed. Stephen C. Barton; Cambridge: Cambridge University Press, 2006), 34–52.

10. Keener, *John*, 33. This assumes that John's was the last canonical gospel to be written, which is supported by both external and internal evidence; see Köstenberger, *John*, 6–8; and Croteau, "Dating of the Fourth Gospel."

3.1.2 History of Research

Turning to the recent history of research, as early as 1915 C. W. Votaw found similarities between the four Gospels and popular biographical literature of the Greco-Roman era.[11] He suggested that they be put in this category.[12] A few years later, Karl Ludwig Schmidt argued against this classification, suggesting instead that the Gospels should be classified as "popular or informal folk literature" (*Kleinliteratur*) rather than as "literary works" proper (*Hochliteratur*).[13] Schmidt proposed that the Gospels should not be viewed in conjunction with Greco-Roman literature but as displaying a distinct literary form and hence constituting a new literary genre. In the years following these pioneering studies, the Gospels have been variously categorized as biographies of Jesus, memoirs of the apostles, aretalogies, comedies, tragedies, Greco-Roman biography, theological biography, an allegorical two-level drama (for all or at least some of the episodes), Jewish theodicy, and christological or proclamation narrative.[14]

While Schmidt's proposal remained popular for a considerable amount of time, today the genre most commonly proposed is that of Greco-Roman biography.[15] Indeed, suggesting that Jewish Christian readers would have been familiar with Hellenistic *bioi* ("lives" of famous persons) or ancient biographies, Keener asks the question: "Since writers steeped in the OT would want to testify in historical terms concerning the one they regarded as the fulfillment of Israel's history, the nature of gospels was somewhat predetermined from the start. What form would a Gospel writer have used to describe Jesus' life even if he wished to *avoid* the genre of biography?"[16] Those who view the four Gospels as biographies attribute the differ-

---

11. C. H. Votaw, *The Gospels and Contemporary Biographies in the Greco-Roman World* (Philadelphia: Fortress, 1970 [1915]).

12. Note also that the notion of John as a drama has a long pedigree. See, e.g., F. R. M. Hitchcock, "Is the 4th Gospel a Drama?" *Theology* 7 (1923): 307–17 (repr. in *Gospel of John as Literature*, 15–24); Clayton R. Bowen, "The Fourth Gospel as Dramatic Material," *JBL* 49 (1930): 292–305; C. Milo Connick, "The Dramatic Character of the Fourth Gospel," *JBL* 67 (1948): 159–69; E. Kenneth Lee, "The Drama of the Fourth Gospel," *ExpTim* 65 (1954): 173–76; Neal Flanagan, "The Gospel of John as Drama," *Bible Today* 19 (1981): 264–70; W. R. Domeris, "The Johannine Drama," *Journal of Theology for Southern Africa* 42 (1983): 29–35.

13. Karl Ludwig Schmidt, *Der Rahmen der Geschichte Jesu* (Darmstadt: Wissenschaftliche Buchgesellschaft, 1969 [1919]).

14. See the review of the discussion by Guelich, "Gospel Genre," 175–94; the discussion by Martin Hengel, "Eye-Witness Memory and the Writing of the Gospels," in *The Written Gospel*, ed. Markus Bockmuehl and Donald A. Hagner (Cambridge: Cambridge University Press, 2005), 70–96; and the survey by Blomberg, *Historical Reliability of the Gospels*, 298–303, who lists (1) apocalypse (Mark); (2) aretalogy (accounts of the life of a "divine man"); (3) tragedy or comedy; (4) midrash; (5) OT historical narrative; (6) parable; and (7) biography. Blomberg favors the latter ("theological biographies," p. 302), over against Charles H. Talbert, *What Is a Gospel?* (Philadelphia: Fortress, 1977; see esp. the critique by David E. Aune, "The Problem of the Genre of the Gospels: A Critique of C. H. Talbert's *What Is a Gospel?*" in *Gospel Perspectives*, Vol. 2: *Studies of History and Tradition in the Four Gospels* [ed. R. T. France and David Wenham; Sheffield: JSOT, 1981], 9–60), and with reference to the work of Hengel, Hemer, and Keener. For a critique of the view by J. Louis Martyn and Raymond E. Brown that John's gospel constitutes a two-level drama, see Tobias Hägerland, "John's Gospel: A Two-Level Drama?" *JSNT* 25 (2003): 309–22; and the discussion in chap. 3, sec. 7.5 below.

15. See, e.g., Blomberg, *Historical Reliability of the Gospels*, 298–303. Burridge, *Gospels*, compares characteristics of Greco-Roman *bioi* and concludes that both the Synoptics and John fit this genre. According to him, the *bios* that is most like the canonical Gospels is Apollonius's *Life of Tyana*. However, this work was written over a century after the canonical Gospels (AD 217). See Davies, *Rhetoric and Reference*, 103.

16. Keener therefore proposes the more specific genre of *historical* biography (*John*, 30); cf. Blomberg, *Historical Reliability of the Gospels*, 302, who, as mentioned, proposes the designation "*theological* biography."

ences among the individual gospels to different ways in which the writers applied the general genre characteristics of biography.[17]

3.2 Differences between the Gospels and Greco-Roman Biographies

Similarities with Greco-Roman biographies notwithstanding, there are several important differences that have been invoked by those who suggest that the canonical Gospels constitute a unique genre of its own (*sui generis*).[18]

(1) Of the four Gospels, only Luke has a formal literary preface (Luke 1:1–4; cf. Acts 1:1–2).

(2) All four canonical Gospels, unlike their Greco-Roman counterparts, are formally anonymous.[19]

(3) The evangelists' intended audience was Christian and thus called upon to respond in faith rather than to read the document merely for enjoyment or information.

(4) The central character of the Gospels, Jesus Christ, transcends the category of "hero" in Greco-Roman literature.

(5) The Gospels lack comprehensive biographical detail regarding Jesus as well as consistent chronological order.

In this regard, it is evident that while each of the four Gospels devotes a considerable amount of space to the last few days of Jesus' life, little is known regarding the events prior to the beginning of Jesus' public ministry. However, this may not be significant in and of itself, since Greco-Roman biographies likewise did not necessarily provide complete biographical details, including only the information relevant for a given biography; nor did they always proceed in chronological order.[20] In the ultimate analysis, none of these alleged differences constitute an insurmountable obstacle to identifying John's gospel as displaying the genre of biography, yet these

---

17. See Burridge, *Gospels*, 68–69 (though a detailed exploration of the possible differences in subgenre between the Synoptics and John is beyond the scope of this chapter).

18. See the discussion in Robert H. Gundry, *The Old Is Better: New Testament Essays in Support of Traditional Interpretations* (Tübingen: Mohr-Siebeck, 2005), 18–48; and Hengel, "Eye-Witness Memory," 72.

19. Note, however, that this assumption has been challenged in recent scholarship. See especially Bauckham, *Jesus and the Eyewitnesses*, 300–302, who does not view the Gospels as anonymous for the following reasons: (1) in three cases—Matthew (emphasis on the character Matthew), Luke (Luke 1:3), and John (John 21:23–24)—the evidence of each gospel itself shows that it was not intended to be anonymous; that is, these writings were not presented as works without authors and as coming from a given community; (2) the evidence of the traditional titles of the Gospels—"According to" Matthew/Mark/Luke/John—signifies the particular version of the evangelist in question, distinct from other gospels in existence; (3) as soon as the Gospels circulated in the churches, they had the authors' names attached to them. See also Carson and Moo, *Introduction to the New Testament*, 140–50, with reference to Hengel, *Studies in the Gospel of Mark*, 64–84; and R. T. France, *Matthew—Evangelist and Teacher* (Grand Rapids: Zondervan, 1989), 50–80.

20. Only Matthew and Luke include the birth narrative (Matt 1:18–25; Luke 2:1–20); only Luke records the temple incident featuring the twelve-year-old Jesus (Luke 2:41–51); and only Matthew recounts the escape to Egypt and the subsequent return to Nazareth during Jesus' childhood (Matt 2:13–23). Apart from these accounts, little else is known of Jesus' early life, and neither Mark nor John has any additional information pertaining to Jesus' childhood or early adulthood. On this issue, see William W. Klein, Craig L. Blomberg, and Robert L. Hubbard Jr., *Introduction to Biblical Interpretation* (rev. ed.; Nashville: Nelson, 2005), 400.

concerns necessitate at least a closer look at possible alternatives. The most promising of these is Jewish historiography.

3.3 Jewish Historiography

3.3.1 Introduction

Before addressing literary conventions — whether Jewish or Greco-Roman — in greater detail, it will be helpful to pursue the implications of the fact that none of the evangelists wrote their gospel in a theological or literary vacuum. To the contrary, they demonstrably started out with a "canonical consciousness," that is, with a sense that they continued to write Scripture in continuity with antecedent Scripture.[21] In keeping with this "canonical consciousness," the evangelists imitated and took their cue not only from the theology of the Hebrew Scriptures, but also from its underlying historiographic and linguistic conventions (see, e.g., John 1:1; Mark 1:1–3; and the Septuagintalisms in Luke 1–2).

For this reason, as Hengel aptly notes, "The Gospels are simply not understood if one fails to appreciate their fundamental '*salvation-historical*' direction, which presupposes the 'promise history' of the Old Testament, equally narrative in character."[22] One obvious candidate for the genre classification of the Gospels would therefore seem to be that of historical narrative as found in Jewish works, particularly in the Hebrew Scriptures.[23] In this regard, any similarity to Greco-Roman literature on the part of the canonical Gospels (including John's gospel) may be attributable to the evangelists' desire to contextualize their message to a Greco-Roman audience. While Keener points out that the Gospels generally adhere more closely to Greco-Roman literary conventions rather than those exhibited by Palestinian Jewish writings, because they are written in Greek and have Diaspora audiences, it does not necessarily follow that the evangelists followed primarily Greco-Roman literary conventions rather than taking their cue from OT historiography.[24]

3.3.2 John's Gospel and Jewish Historiography

Indeed, similar to the historical narratives found in the Hebrew Scriptures, the canonical Gospels do not merely report historical or biographical facts. The evan-

---

21. See on this especially the important work by Willard M. Swartley, *Israel's Scripture Traditions and the Synoptic Gospels: Story Shaping Story* (Peabody, MA: Hendrickson, 1994).

22. Hengel, "Eye-Witness Memory," 71.

23. Although note Keener's comment: "The central difference between biography and history was that the former focused on a single character whereas the latter included a broad range of events (Lucian, *Vera historia* 7; also Witherington, *Sage*, 339; citing Plutarch, *Alex* 37.4; 56.1)" (*John*, 12); and Charles William Fornara's remark that "[h]istory thus contained many biographical elements but normally lacked the focus on a single person and the emphasis on characterization (*The Nature of History in Ancient Greece and Rome* [Berkeley: University of California Press, 1983], 185). See also Blomberg, *Historical Reliability of the Gospels*, 301, who registers the concern that "the Old Testament historical narratives never seem to describe the events or teachings of God's spokespersons *with an eye to focusing specifically on the nature of those prophets or leaders*, as the Gospels do with Jesus. Instead, attention is diverted beyond the individual to God's dealings with his covenant people more generally, whereas in the Gospels all the material seems constantly designed to raise the questions of Jesus' identity ... and of allegiance to him."

24. While not minimizing the Jewishness of the gospel, Keener notes that "they share more external characteristics with Diaspora or aristocratic Palestinian Jewish biographies in Greek than they do with many of the Palestinian works composed in Hebrew or Aramaic" (*John*, 25).

gelists carefully selected and arranged material that most effectively conveyed God's message of salvation, employing a Christ-centered approach that issued in a theologically grounded account of the life and work of Jesus. Similar to OT historical narrative, the Gospels focus on God's salvific activity in history and demand a faith response from the readers. In this the Gospels make use of various OT terms, motifs, and literary forms. For instance, the extended metaphor of the shepherd and the flock (John 10:1–18) draws on the shepherd imagery employed in many portions of the OT, incorporating direct quotations from and allusions to the OT, in many cases in contexts that indicate prophetic fulfillment.[25]

Mark Stibbe notes that as the narrative progresses, John develops the twin themes of Jesus as both shepherd and king, together with the portrayal of Jesus as the paschal lamb.[26] This literary style is commonly found in OT narrative. There are also biblical type-scenes that reflect the literary style of OT narratives. R. Alan Culpepper notes that the encounter between Jesus and the Samaritan woman at the well is a conventional biblical type-scene that harks back to similar scenes in the narratives featuring Abraham, Isaac, Jacob, and Moses.[27] The connection with regard to form, content, and vocabulary between John's gospel and the books of Exodus, Leviticus, Numbers, and Deuteronomy is evident as well.[28] Similarities between the portrayals of Jesus in John's gospel and Moses in the Pentateuch have likewise been noted by a considerable number of scholars.[29]

The four major modes of OT narrative—reporting of events, dramatic mode, pure description, and commentary—are all found in this gospel. The speeches and dialogues in the narrative portions provide dramatic effect and a deeper understanding of the characters involved. For instance, the conversations between Jesus and the Jewish authorities in John constitute a window into the Jewish nation's unbelief and rejection of Jesus' message and messianic claim (e.g., John 8:31–59). As in some historical narratives, especially Exodus through Deuteronomy (which narrate the exodus under Moses' leadership) and 1 and 2 Kings (where the lives of the prophets are recounted), the arrangement of material reflects the juxtaposition of events and miracles with explanatory dialogues and discourses.[30]

Rabbinic literature offers numerous anecdotes comparable to pericopae featuring Jesus in the Gospels, but no connected rabbinic biography.[31] In Jewish narrative literature, writers frequently combined historiographic and novelistic traits. While

---

25. See Köstenberger, "John," in *Commentary on the NT Use of the OT*, 461–63; idem, "Jesus the Good Shepherd Who Will Also Bring Other Sheep (John 10:16): The Old Testament Background of a Familiar Metaphor," *BBR* 12 (2002): 67–96.

26. See Stibbe, *John as Storyteller*, 115–17.

27. Culpepper, *Anatomy*, 137, citing Robert Alter, *The Art of Biblical Narrative* (New York: Basic Books, 1981), 51–58.

28. Davies, *Rhetoric and Reference*, 70, citing Howard M. Teeple, *The Mosaic Eschatological Prophet* (SBLMS 10; Philadelphia: Scholars Press, 1957); T. Francis Glasson, *Moses in the Fourth Gospel* (SBT 40; London: SCM, 1963); and Wayne A. Meeks, *The Prophet-King* (Leiden: Brill, 1967).

29. See, e.g., John 5:45; 6:25–59; 7:19. Note that some of Moses' signs in Egypt share common characteristics with the Johannine signs, such as the provision of water (Exod 15:22–23; 17; Numbers 20) and bread (Exodus 16; Numbers 11) for the Israelites in the wilderness. In fact, Davies (*Rhetoric and Reference*, 70) suggests that John's gospel be viewed as a transposition of the theological story of Moses and the Exodus (though this may be overstating the case).

30. An example of this is John 6, with the account of the feeding of the five thousand and the ensuing discourse on Jesus as the "bread of life." See Davies, *Rhetoric and Reference*, 70–71.

31. Noted by Alexander, "What Is a Gospel?" 27. See also Philip S. Alexander, "Rabbinic Biography and the Biography of Jesus: A

some Jewish writers did compose self-contained biographies, not all of them conform to Greco-Roman biographical conventions. For instance, even though Philo does display Hellenistic biographical features, his purpose in idealizing Abraham, Joseph, and Moses is to communicate his philosophical views. A Jewish collection entitled *The Lives of the Prophets*, which exhibits genre parallels to the Greek lives of poets, resembles the briefer lives.[32] Josephus's *Antiquities*, in relating the accounts of Moses, often follows Hellenistic philosophical biography and novelistic conventions, as do his treatments of Jacob, Joseph, Samson, Saul, Zedekiah, and the *Akedah* narrative.[33]

Variation in detail for literary purposes was not considered inappropriate, even when relating historical accounts, as long as one was faithful to historically accurate sources such as the OT. For instance, later storytellers often reworked biblical narratives, and these later became separate accounts (e.g., Pseudo-Philo's *Biblical Antiquities* or the *Assumption of Moses*).[34] Similar to other historical works, John's gospel features a certain number of supernatural phenomena (e.g., John 12:28; 20:12), yet it does not contain frequent imaginary appearances of heavenly beings as is common of early Jewish and Christian novels.[35] While its narrative style may be compared to Tobit or even 1 Maccabees, John's gospel more generally resembles the historical sections of the Septuagint (LXX). Like other Jewish Diaspora texts, the gospel exhibits Septuagintal stylistic and theological influences.[36]

Also, the Hebrew Bible is prone to "bio-structuring," and "much of the narrative of the Hebrew Bible is built around biographical 'story cycles' like those of Samson or Elijah, cycles in which individual tales of the hero's powers 'are so arranged to encompass his entire life, from birth to death.'"[37] These and numerous other characteristics found in OT historical narratives can be identified in John's gospel. As Larry Hurtado notes, "A writing can be associated with a particular genre only to the degree that all characteristics of the writing can be understood adequately in terms of the features of the genre."[38] Hence rather than propose that the Gospels constitute a new genre altogether or are to be identified with Greco-Roman popular biography, it may be best to understand them as belonging to the genre of OT historical narrative.

Nevertheless, because John's gospel was penned in an environment in which Jewish as well as Hellenistic ideas were prominent, both of these kinds of influence

---

Survey of the Evidence," in *Synoptic Studies: The Ampleforth Conferences of 1982 and 1983* (ed. Christopher M. Tuckett; Sheffield: JSOT, 1984), 19–50.

32. Keener, *John*, 26, citing David E. Aune, *The New Testament in Its Literary Environment* (LEC 8; Philadelphia: Westminster, 1987), 41–42.

33. Keener, *John*, 26, with additional bibliographic references.

34. Although these reworkings are not strictly midrashic or targumic, certain midrashic or haggadic principles are at times at work in their composition (Keener, *John*, 27–28). However, this variation in accuracy of detail was acceptable in both Jewish and Greco-Roman historiographic conventions (Keener, *John*, 29, citing James M. Robinson, *The Problem of History in Mark and Other Marcan Studies* [Philadelphia: Fortress, 1982], 60).

35. Keener, *John*, 34.

36. Ibid., 25, 34.

37. Alexander, "What Is a Gospel?" 27, citing Eli Yassif, *The Hebrew Folktale: History, Genre, Meaning* (Bloomington, IN: Indiana University Press, 1999), 31, and M. J. Edwards and Simon Swain, eds., *Portraits: Biographical Representation in the Greek and Latin Literature of the Roman Empire* (Oxford: Clarendon, 1997).

38. Larry Hurtado, "Gospel (Genre)," in *Dictionary of Jesus and the Gospels*, 277.

are evident. Richard Burridge points out that "the gospel belongs within the syncretistic milieu of the eastern Mediterranean towards the close of the first century AD; within such a culture, those involved in its production would have been influenced by both Jewish and Hellenistic philosophical and religious ideas—everything from Platonic thought and proto-Gnosticism to Rabbinic or 'non-conformist' Judaism—without needing actually to belong to any of these groups."[39] These include various Septuagintal, contemporary Jewish, and Greco-Roman narrative conventions.[40]

3.3.3 Conclusion

I conclude therefore with Loveday Alexander:

> It is to the biblical tradition, surely, that we should look for the origins of the "religious intensity" of the gospel narratives and their rich ideological intertextuality with the biblical themes of covenant, kingdom, prophecy and promise—all features hard to parallel in Greek biography. The evangelist's move from disjointed anecdotes and sayings to connected, theologically coherent narrative is most easily explained with reference to the narrative modes of the Hebrew Bible.[41]

Nevertheless, as Alexander points out, the writings of Philo demonstrate that "biographical narrative provided a point of cultural contact between Greek and Jew, a flexible and readily comprehensible framework that could be moulded without difficulty to reflect the ideology and cultural values of a particular ethical tradition."[42]

3.4 The Gospel and Greco-Roman Literary Conventions

In light of these observations John's gospel seems to reflect Jewish antecedents, particularly as found in OT narratives; yet owing to the influence of the Greco-Roman environment in which the evangelist found himself, and in keeping with his desire to present the life-changing message of salvation in Jesus in a way that would be perceived as relevant by his wider audience, he appears to have adapted certain Greco-Roman literary conventions. By contextualizing the good news about Jesus, John presents Christianity as a world religion with a universal scope, transcending its Jewish roots.[43]

For this reason John makes use of both Jewish and Hellenistic biographical techniques.[44] As Larry Hurtado suggests, "Similarities to other Greco-Roman

---

39. Burridge, *Gospels*, 215.
40. Keener, *John*, 30.
41. Alexander, "What Is a Gospel?" 27–28.
42. Ibid., 28. Alexander also draws attention to martyrology, such as in the case of the Maccabean martyrs (2 and 4 Maccabees), and the central message of good news through the salvation provided by Jesus (ibid., 28–30).
43. Faith in Jesus as Messiah and Son of God is presented as entrance into a personal relationship with God the Father in Christ and into the messianic community, which is no longer defined by ethnic boundaries. See Köstenberger, "John," in *NDBT*, 285.
44. Keener, *John*, 33, citing Mark W. G. Stibbe, *John's Gospel* (NT Readings; London: Routledge, 1994), 55–63.

narrative genres such as biography reflect the cultural setting in which the gospels were written.... It is likely that the evangelists consciously, and perhaps more often, unconsciously reflected features of Greco-Roman popular literature."[45] When particular literary characteristics employed in John's gospel and Greco-Roman literature are compared, numerous similarities with respect to internal and external features emerge.

3.4.1 Internal Features

3.4.1.1 Range of Topics

There is an overlap in the range of topics covered in this gospel and in Greco-Roman literature in general. This includes references to ancestry, an emphasis on the great deeds and words of the central subject, the narration of his death and its consequences, and one or several vindication scenes.

3.4.1.2 Ancestry

Certain genres of Greco-Roman literature, such as *bioi,* often include details of the subject's ancestry. This is generally traced back to an impressive ancestor, with legendary or semi-divine status. While Matthew traces Jesus' origins back to Abraham and Luke to Adam, John goes back to "the beginning," the time before creation, in eternity past. Jesus' origins are established on a cosmic scale.[46] This serves the purpose of setting Jesus' earthly ministry as narrated in the Synoptics into larger perspective. Before the reader starts reading about Jesus' earthly exploits, he is told that Jesus came to earth from heaven; that he was not a mere human but divine; and that everything he said and did served to reveal God to humans.[47]

3.4.1.3 Great Deeds and Words

Miracles and exorcisms are prominent in the Synoptics; the gospel of John likewise includes several startling feats performed by Jesus labeled "signs" by the evangelist (see, e.g., John 2:11; 4:54).[48] Notably, in comparison with the Synoptics, John downplays the miraculous character of Jesus' works. His powerful acts are presented from the vantage point of their prophetic symbolism (cf. Isa 20:3). As in the accounts of Moses and the exodus, Jesus' signs are featured as a dominant motif in John's gospel and are central to his presentation of Jesus' work.

Most likely, all the signs are narrated in the first half of John's narrative, serving the purpose of setting forth evidence for Jesus' messiahship (see esp. 12:36–40; cf. 20:30–31). Thus, in keeping with the theology of the latter portions of the book of

---

45. Hurtado, "Gospel," 282.

46. Burridge, *Gospels,* 224, with reference to Ernst Haenchen, *A Commentary on the Gospel of John* (trans. Robert W. Funk; ed. Robert W. Funk with Ulrich Busse; Hermeneia; Philadelphia: Fortress, 1984), 101, 124–25.

47. On John's portrayal of Jesus as divine in the context of first-century Jewish monotheism, see the discussion below. See also Köstenberger, *John,* 25–29, 48–50; Murray J. Harris, *Jesus as God: The New Testament Use of* Theos *in Reference to Jesus* (Grand Rapids: Baker, 1992), 51–103.

48. On the "signs" in John's gospel, see the discussion in chap. 7, sec. 15 below.

Isaiah, Jesus' signs are shown to point to a new exodus (cf. Luke 9:31),[49] and as with Moses and the later prophets, the signs' function is primarily to authenticate the one who performs them as God's true representative. While there is no universal agreement on the number and exact identity of the Johannine signs, their prominence in John's gospel is not under dispute.[50]

Not only are there important salvation-historical, intercanonical connections, on the level of contextualization, John's depiction of Jesus' startling signs doubtless resonated with the Greco-Roman *bioi*, which frequently featured records of a hero's great and mighty deeds. Dialogues and discourses magnifying the subject's "great words" also feature prominently in this gospel, just as they are found particularly in *bioi* of philosophers and teachers such as *Demonax* and *Apollonius of Tyana*, which convey the sage's lofty teachings. Satyrus' *Euripedes* also evinces this feature of dialogue.[51]

3.4.1.4 Death and Consequences

The Passion Narrative takes up one sixth of John's gospel (John 18–21) and includes accounts of Jesus' arrest, trial, crucifixion, and death, ending with his subsequent resurrection appearances. The trial scenes reflect the genre of "trial narratives" and resemble the narration of Socrates' final trial, discourses, and execution.[52] Like most *bioi*, with the exception of Isocrates' *Evagoras*, the flow in this section is chronological and focuses on the subject's death and immediate consequences at the completion of his work.[53] This mode of finishing the gospel, beginning with the Farewell Discourse and ending with the aftermath of the subject's death, is a feature typically employed in Greco-Roman *bioi*.[54]

3.4.1.5 Vindication Scene

In addition, this gospel includes a series of vindication scenes—Jesus' post-resurrection appearances—which were another common device in Greco-Roman literature.[55] The resurrection appearances (including Jesus' appearance to Mary Magdalene) and the disciples' commissioning by their risen Lord constitute the focal point of the last two chapters of John's gospel.

3.4.1.6 Emphasis and Content

There are also similarities in thematic emphasis and content between John's gospel and Greco-Roman biographies. This includes the promotion of a particular "hero," the type of material included, and the early mention of the subject's name.

---

49. Cf. David W. Pao, *Acts and the Isaianic Exodus* (WUNT 130; Tübingen: Mohr-Siebeck, 2000); Rikki E. Watts, *Isaiah's New Exodus in Mark* (BSL; Grand Rapids: Baker, 2000). See also John Dennis, "The Presence and Function of Second Exodus-Restoration Imagery in John 6," *SNTU* 30 (2005): 105–21.

50. See the discussion in chap. 7, sec. 15 below.

51. Burridge, *Gospels*, 218, 225.

52. Ibid., 225, citing John A. T. Robinson, *The Priority of John* (London: SCM, 1985), 92–93. For a study of John's presentation of Jesus' trial before Pilate, see chap. 11 below.

53. Burridge, *Gospels*, 225.

54. See Paul A. Holloway, "Left Behind: Jesus' Consolation of His Disciples in John 13,31–17,26," *ZNW* 96 (2005): 1–34, who focuses particularly on consolatory features in Greco-Roman materials.

55. Hurtado, "Gospel," 278.

3.4.1.7 Promotion of a Particular Hero

Greco-Roman historical writings treat historical figures differently from Hebrew and Aramaic Jewish texts. Rather than have the person dominate the account, in Jewish texts it is usually the events that receive the most attention. Citing the examples of Job, Ruth, Judith, Jonah, Esther, Daniel, and Tobit, all of which have books associated with them in the Greek Bible, Craig Keener notes that "only rarely is a document devoted to a person in such a way that it would be called biography ... usually the treatment of an individual is part of a larger narrative."[56] Popular Greco-Roman biographies tended to promote a particular hero or important person. Similarly, the Gospels may be said to focus on and promote a "hero." The evangelists recorded Jesus' deeds and activities and emphasized that his purpose was to save humankind.

While most believe that John's gospel evinces less interest in Jesus' activities and is mostly driven by John's theological and christological interests, an analysis of verb subjects reveals that more than half of the verbs in John's gospel are taken up with Jesus' words or deeds (55.3 percent). In fact, John gives more prominence to Jesus' activity than Matthew and Luke. This gospel, therefore, "displays the same exaggerated skew effect which is typical of Bioi in both Jesus' activity in the narrative and in the large amount of his teaching."[57] In terms of allocation of space, the last week of Jesus' life dominates this gospel (one third), as is also the case with Greco-Roman *bioi* such as *Agricola* (26 percent devoted to Mons Graupius); *Agesilaus* (37 percent to the Persian campaign); *Cato Minor* (17.3 percent to the last days); and *Apollonius of Tyana* (26.3 percent to the imprisonment dialogues, trial, death, and subsequent events).[58]

3.4.1.8 Type of Material

In terms of material included in John's gospel, one sees some similarities with political and philosophical biographies such as those featured by Cornelius Nepos and Diogenes Laertius, respectively.[59]

3.4.1.9 Early Use of Subject's Name

Bioi often use the subject's name early as a common opening feature. In the gospel of John, the opening words are, "In the beginning was the Word" (*logos*), who is later identified as Jesus Christ. While the name "Jesus Christ" does occur later on in the introductory section of John's gospel (1:17), the use of *logos* sufficiently identifies the subject of the gospel. Burridge notes, "Thus, although Jesus' actual

---

56. Keener, *John*, 26, citing Graham N. Stanton, *Jesus of Nazareth in New Testament Preaching* (SNTSMS 27; Cambridge: Cambridge University Press, 1974), 126; Aune, *Literary Environment*, 37.

57. Burridge, *Gospels*, 216–17.

58. Ibid., 217.

59. Keener, *John*, 33–34, citing Ben Witherington, *John's Wisdom: A Commentary on the Fourth Gospel* (Louisville: Westminster John Knox, 1995); Culpepper, *John, the Son of Zebedee*, 64–66. Though note the discussion in Alexander, "What Is a Gospel?" 26, who points out that "Diogenes Laertius' great collection of anecdotes about the philosophers is arranged on thematic rather than chronological lines, and there is little attempt to provide narrative coherence. And what is most obviously missing in this tradition is the *good news* aspect that is essential to the gospels."

name is not part of the immediate opening words, he is clearly identified as the subject of the introduction, and his name and messianic identity commence the text itself after the prologue."[60] An example of this feature can be observed in *Agricola*.[61]

3.4.1.10 Style

3.4.1.10.1 Narrative Style

The narrative style of John's gospel is continuous prose, unlike some noncanonical gospels that consist of a collection of sayings and discourses. John's gospel features three main types of units: (1) narratives; (2) dialogues; and (3) speeches or discourses.[62] Many scholars have noted a number of *aporias* or "literary seams" that at first glance seem to break up the narrative, such as the apparent abrupt shift from John 14:31 to 15:1 or the "conclusion" in 20:30–31 that does not in fact end the gospel but is followed by another chapter with its own conclusion.[63] These so-called "seams" or literary incongruities have been the source of numerous rearrangement theories. However, it is possible to account for the flow of these passages adequately without resorting to source or redaction-critical solutions.[64] Within this flow, there is the repetition of words, motifs, and themes, which results in a repetitive pattern.[65]

Apart from continuous prose, this gospel includes extended discourses and dialogues that frequently (though not always) explicate the inner significance of a "sign." These are usually initiated by questions from the crowd or the Jewish leaders. The largest block of discourse material in John's gospel is the Farewell Discourse (13:31–16:33), which is followed by the Johannine Passion Narrative. This style, varying continuous prose with dialogue, is common in *bioi*, particularly in philosophers such as Philostratus' *Apollonius of Tyana* and Satyrus' *Euripedes*.[66] Burridge points out that "through the *chronological narrative*, all the necessary information about Jesus' cosmic origins, earthly ministry, Passion and Resurrection is provided for the reader to realize the true identity of Jesus, while through the *discourse material* the reader comes to appreciate the teaching of Jesus and the Christian faith."[67]

3.4.1.10.2 Language

There is no consensus with regard to the nature of the language used in John's gospel. Some suggest that John's gospel has a more Hellenistic feel to it, while others emphasize its Semitic character. The sentences are generally short and connected paratactically with the characteristic Johannine intersentence connections *oun, de,*

---

60. Burridge, *Gospels*, 215.
61. Ibid.
62. Ibid., 219–20.
63. See the discussion and bibliographic references in chap. 3, sec. 7.3 below.
64. For instance, Bauckham, *Jesus and the Eyewitnesses*, 364–69, shows that this two-part conclusion is a literary device. See also Kellum, *Unity of the Farewell Discourse*.
65. Keener, *John*, 6.
66. Burridge, *Gospels*, 218.
67. Ibid., 229.

kai, or asyndeton.⁶⁸ Richard Burridge suggests that this may reflect a bi- or trilingual culture typical of the eastern Mediterranean.⁶⁹ The vocabulary is not extensive and tends to be repetitive.⁷⁰ The use of characteristic key words and dualistic contrasts that may point to Greek philosophical or Jewish religious thought fits into the social milieu of the eastern Mediterranean as well.⁷¹ This style is typical of *bioi* or treatises of Greco-Roman origin.⁷²

Another significant use of language that reflects Greco-Roman influence is the use of the " 'we' of authoritative testimony," sometimes called "the plural of majesty or authority."⁷³ Note the following conclusion to a treatise in the essay of Dionysius of Halicarnassus on *Demosthenes* (58), where the concluding three sentences read as follows:

> I would have given you examples of what I have said but for the risk of becoming a bore, especially as it is you that I am addressing. That is all *we* have to say about the style of Demosthenes, my dear Ammaeus. If god preserves us, *we* shall present you in a subsequent treatise with an even longer and more remarkable account than this of his genius in the treatment of subject-matter.⁷⁴

This use of the authoritative "we" adds force to self-reference and is sometimes used by one whose status is superior to his hearers or readers (e.g., Josephus, *Ant.* 2.68–69). James Moulton also showed evidence of this use of "we" for "I" from later Greek literature and papyrus letters.⁷⁵

There is also the use of sublimity, obscurity, and solemnity, as found in connection with religious themes in Greco-Roman rhetoric.⁷⁶ Sublimity is represented by the prolific use of asyndeton as well.⁷⁷ Obscurity, rather than rearrangement theories, may be the explanation behind some of the apparent *aporias* in John's gospel (e.g., 5:47–6:1; 14:31–15:1). Solemnity may provide the stylistic basis for the universality of language, such as at 1:3 and 4:23, and the use of symbolism and ambiguity.⁷⁸

Other stylistic features that figure prominently in John's gospel include tropes or plays on words (e.g., 3:3–5, 6–8, 14–15), the use of irony (e.g., 4:12; 7:35, 42;

---

68. Randall Buth, "Οὖν, Δέ, Καί and Asyndeton in John's Gospel," in *Linguistics and New Testament Interpretation*, 141–61.

69. Burridge, *Gospels*, 226.

70. See the discussion of Johannine vocabulary below. For a presentation of Johannine vocabulary, including statistics and frequency lists, see Andreas Köstenberger and Raymond Bouchoc, *The Book Study Concordance* (Nashville: Broadman and Holman, 2003), 479–610.

71. See the discussion of the Johannine worldview in chap. 6, sec. 12 below.

72. Burridge, *Gospels*, 226.

73. Possible instances of this use are found in John 3:11; 21:24–25; 1 John 1:1–5; 4:14; and 3 John 9–10, 12. For the use of "we" as a form of self-reference see Bauckham, *Jesus and the Eyewitnesses*, 370–83.

74. Bauckham, *Jesus and the Eyewitnesses*, 371, translation adapted from Dionysius of Halicarnassus, *The Critical Essays* (trans. S. Usher; Cambridge: Harvard University Press, 1974), 1:455 (emphasis added).

75. Bauckham, *Jesus and the Eyewitnesses*, 372, citing James Hope Moulton, *A Grammar of New Testament Greek*, Vol. 1: *Prolegomena* (3rd ed.; Edinburgh: T&T Clark, 1908), 86. See also Howard J. Jackson, "Ancient Self-Referential Conventions and Their Implications for the Authorship and Integrity of the Gospel of John," *JTS* 50 (1999): 1–34.

76. Dennis L. Stamps, "The Johannine Writings," in *Handbook of Classical Rhetoric in the Hellenistic Period 330 B.C.–A.D. 400* (ed. Stanley E. Porter; Leiden: Brill, 1997), 619.

77. E.g., John 1:40, 42, 45; 2:17; 4:6, 7; 5:12, 15; 7:32; 8:27; 9:13; 10:21, 22; 11:35, 44; 20:18.

78. Ibid., citing Thielman, "Style of the Fourth Gospel," 180–82. See also discussion in chap. 3, sec. 7.5 below.

8:22; 11:50), and metaphor (e.g., that of a flock in John 10 or of a vine in John 15).[79] Structural features such as chiasm (e.g., 1:1–18; 6:36–40; 18:28–19:16) or poetic parallelism (e.g., 3:11, 18, 20, 21; 4:36; 6:35, 55; 7:34; 8:35; 9:39; 13:16) are all demonstrable features of Johannine literary style.[80]

3.4.1.10.3 *Atmosphere*

John's gospel, unlike the Synoptics, is characterized by a meditative, contemplative style that lends the book a serious atmosphere. It has an even tone, steady mood with few variations, unlike Mark's gospel, which has an almost choppy feel to it. Burridge points out that "the attitude to the subject reflects this high estimation: Jesus is revealed as divine from the opening words of the Prologue through to Thomas' words, 'my Lord and my God,' in 20:28. There is a sense of awe which follows from this view of the subject."[81]

In addition, one detects somber, even tragic moments at critical junctures in the gospel. One such incident is when Jesus is deserted by many of his disciples (6:60–66) and Jesus asks his inner circle if they want to leave him as well. Repeated references to Judas's betrayal of Jesus cast an ominous shadow over the latter stages of Jesus' ministry (6:70–71; 13:10–11, 18–30; 15:2–3; 17:12). John's reference to Judas's departure at the Last Supper — "As soon as Judas had taken the bread, he went out. And it was night" (13:30) — reveals considerable pathos.

Tragedy is present in John's concluding reference at the end of the first part of his gospel, "Even after Jesus had performed so many signs in their presence, they still would not believe in him" (12:37). Indeed, if they did not believe in Jesus' "signs," neither will they believe when he rises from the dead (cf. Luke 16:31). The element of tragedy is also palpable when Pilate fails to recognize Jesus as the truth (John 18:38; cf. 14:6) and when the Jews disown, not merely Jesus, but their messianic hopes by telling Pilate that they have no king but Caesar (19:15).

On a structural level, the repeated references to Jesus' "time" or "hour" build suspense and accentuate the tragic element in the unfolding plot against Jesus. In perfect symmetry, three references to Jesus' "hour" having not yet come (John 2:4; 7:30; 8:20) are balanced by three passages indicating that Jesus' "hour" has now arrived (12:23; 13:1; 17:1). Jesus' ominous hiding of his presence from the Jews (8:59; 12:36b) is tragic and dramatic as well, as is the farewell of the light to the world (12:35–36) and the process of Jesus' death and resurrection (12:24; 13:1–3).[82]

---

79. Stamps, "Johannine Writings," 619, citing Paul D. Duke, *Irony in the Fourth Gospel* (Atlanta: John Knox, 1985); J. E. Botha, "The Case of Johannine Irony Reopened I: The Problematic Current Situation," *Neot* 25 (1991): 209–20; idem, "The Case of Johannine Irony Reopened II: Suggestions, Alternative Approaches," *Neot* 25 (1991): 221–32; Davies, *Rhetoric and Reference*, 162–81, 197–208; Köstenberger, *Missions of Jesus and the Disciples*, 161–67.

80. Whether this is merely a feature of good communication or a deliberate reflection of rhetorical practice remains to be seen. Stamps, "Johannine Writings," 631, contends, "The Gospel of John is a form of *bios* ... there is nothing to suggest the deliberate employment of arrangement, invention and style according to Greco-Roman rhetoric so that one can definitely specify the species of rhetoric."

81. Burridge, *Gospels*, 226.

82. See George L. Parsenios, "'No Longer in the World' (John 7:11): The Transformation of the Tragic in the Fourth Gospel," *HTR* 98 (2005): 1–21.

3.4.1.11 Characterization

The absence of character growth in all of the Gospels shows close affinities with Greco-Roman literary techniques.[83] As in the Synoptic Gospels, characterization in John's gospel is achieved indirectly through relating the subject's words and deeds.[84] In John's gospel, the signs performed by the subject are an important window into Jesus' character. The "I am" statements provide a metaphorical kind of direct characterization (e.g., 6:35, 48; 10:7, 9, 11; 15:1). In some instances, the author of the gospel reveals certain aspects of Jesus' motives (e.g., 6:15).

A protagonist's deeds and words, sayings and imputed motives, are all typical devices of characterization in Greco-Roman *bioi*.[85] Because John presents Jesus as divine from the outset of his gospel, there is a certain tension between the characterization of Jesus as both human and divine. This is further accentuated by the fact that Jesus frequently speaks in Johannine idiom seeming to convey Johannine theology. This quality of ambivalence in characterization is also found in Greco-Roman *bioi*.[86]

3.4.2 External Features

3.4.2.1 Structure

John's gospel exhibits external structural features that closely resemble those of Greco-Roman *bioi*. These include a formal preface, features related to its overall format, careful arrangement, and length.

3.4.2.1.1 Formal Preface

John's gospel begins with a preface that displays rhythmic prose or even poetic style. It serves to introduce the subject of the gospel, identified in the opening line as the *logos*. This formal opening conforms to the general style of introductions to Greco-Roman literary works.[87] P. J. Williams has recently argued, primarily on text-critical grounds, that John does not have a prologue.[88] Instead, Williams noted that the archetypical text, represented by $\mathfrak{p}^{66}$ and $\mathfrak{p}^{75}$, contained a division after John 1:5 but not after 1:18, and many early exegetes followed suit. Augustine, for example, called 1:1–5 the *capitulum primum* ("first chapter") of John.[89] Williams also notes that 1:6 involves a step into this world; 1:14 constitutes an *inclusio* with John 1:1 (*logos*) and with 2:11 (*doxa*); and 1:17 marks the climax of the naming of the previously unnamed ("Jesus Christ"). While it is thus disputed whether 1:1–5 or 1:1–18 should be regarded as the Johannine prologue (or preface), it is clear that John opens

---

83. Hurtado, "Gospel," 279.
84. On Johannine characterization, see Culpepper, *Anatomy*, 99–148.
85. Burridge, *Gospels*, 227.
86. Ibid.
87. The formal preface of Luke (Luke 1:1–4; cf. Acts 1:1) conforms even more closely to Greco-Roman introductions. See Loveday C. A. Alexander, *Acts in Its Ancient Literary Context: A Classicist Looks at the Acts of the Apostles* (LNTS 289; New York: T&T Clark, 2007).
88. P. J. Williams, "Not the Prologue of John" (paper presented at the Annual Meeting of the SBL, San Diego, CA, November, 2007).
89. Augustine, *In Evangelium Joannis tractatus centum viginti quattuor*, Tractate 2.1.

his gospel with a section that orients and introduces the reader to the identity of the gospel's main protagonist, the Word (1:1), Jesus Christ (1:17).

3.4.2.1.2 Postscript and Dual Conclusion

One striking structural feature of John's gospel is the presence of a postscript or epilogue and of two formal conclusions. The postscript, vis-à-vis the preface or introduction, provides balance and symmetry to the structure of the gospel.[90] Both units form an integral part of the theological and literary fabric of the entire narrative. Among other things, John 21 resolves the relationship between Peter and "the disciple whom Jesus loved" in terms of noncompetition and identifies the latter as the author (see 21:20–24). Beyond this, there are many other terminological links between the final chapter and the rest of the gospel.[91]

With regard to the dual conclusion, while John 20:30–31 is a statement of purpose providing closure to the gospel proper in terms of its presentation of Jesus as the Messiah and Son of God by virtue of his messianic signs, resulting in eternal life for those who believe, 21:24–25 constitutes a final affirmation of the role of the author as eyewitness and of the credibility and truthfulness of the gospel.[92] In comparison with Rev 22:18–19, the author's concern is not with the possibility that some might add or take away from the book but to assert that the gospel, while selective, is true.[93]

3.4.2.1.3 Format

Similar to Greco-Roman *bioi,* John's gospel consists of continuous prose of medium length.[94] The narrative itself, as noted above, consists of stories, dialogues, and speeches or discourses. Suggesting that proto-gospels probably existed temporarily, Craig Keener notes that "the writers of the Synoptics, like writers of most ancient historical works, probably began with a basic draft of the material in chronological order, to which a topical outline, speeches, and other rhetorical adjustments would be added later."[95]

The usual process was to check the copyist's manuscripts once the work was complete. In that way one could publish the finished product and not an unfinished form of it. The result was a polished and intricate product that was to be expected of writers in a Greco-Roman context.[96] Aristotle's recommended process, illustrated

---

90. For a discussion of John 21 see Köstenberger, *John,* 583–86, with further bibliographic references.

91. See the list in ibid., 585, n. 9.

92. R. Alan Culpepper, "John 21:24–25—The Johannine *Sphragis*" (paper presented at the Annual Meeting of the SBL, San Diego, CA, November 2007), contends that the last two verses of John's gospel serve as a *sphragis,* that is, as a "literary seal" or authenticating statement "in which the editor, speaking on behalf of the Johannine community, affirms the truthfulness of the community's gospel." Culpepper denies any element of authorial self-reference in these verses, though he does not adequately consider the first person verb *oimai* ("I suppose") in 21:25, on which see Köstenberger, "'I Suppose.'" See also Hanna Roose, "Joh 20,30f.: Ein (un)passender Schluss? Joh 9 und 11 als primäre Verweisstellen der Schlussnotiz des Johannesevangeliums," *Bib* 84 (2003): 326–43, who notes the connection between John 9 and 11 and 20:30–31.

93. See Köstenberger, *John,* 606: "John's hyperbole, however, extols neither the books people write nor the wisdom people acquire, but rather the deeds Jesus performed. Taken together with the prologue's stress on Jesus' person, the epilogue's reference to his works renders John's christological portrait not exhaustively comprehensive but sufficiently complete."

94. Burridge, *Gospels,* 223.

95. Note, however, that the old source theories concerning proto-Mark and proto-Luke are unfashionable. See Keener, *John,* 6.

96. E.g., Josephus, *Ag. Ap.* 1.47–50, Lucian, *Hist.* 16, 48; and *Demonax.* See Keener, *John,* 6, citing Burridge, *Gospels,* 203; Aune, *Literary Environment,* 82.

by the *Odyssey,* was to sketch the plot in outline, then to expand it by inserting episodes.[97] In this way, literary techniques such as foreshadowing could be achieved (Quintilian 10.1.21).

3.4.2.1.4 Careful Arrangement

Writers in the Greco-Roman context tended to arrange their material carefully, both in written form as well as in oral discourse. John's gospel is organized chronologically, most likely structured around Jesus' attendance of and participation in various Jewish festivals.[98] Burridge notes of this framework, "This is similar to the synoptic gospels, as Hengel says: 'All the gospels follow a geographical and chronological order, which contains fundamental historical features common in essentials to all the gospels, even if there are differences between the synoptic gospels and John.'"[99]

While some Greco-Roman writers preferred a continuous style and hence recommended connecting episodes to provide continuity (e.g., Lucian, *Vera historia* 55; Quintilian 7.1.1), others preferred to have disjunctions (e.g., Polybius 38.5.1–8).[100] While Mark adheres to the former continuous practice, John may be following the latter disjointed one, and this may explain certain apparent *aporias* in his narrative.[101] Alternatively, these so-called Johannine "seams" may be accounted for by various other text-critical, historical, and literary means.[102]

3.4.2.1.5 Length

With regard to length, Craig Keener notes that "Luke and Acts are roughly the same length; Matthew is within 1 percent of the length of either; John is within 1 percent of three-quarters this length and Mark is close to half."[103] Length not only indicates the author's intention to publish, but also the nature of the document's genre.[104] John's gospel, like the Synoptics, is of medium-range length (10,000–25,000 words), which conforms to that of ancient biographies. It is approximately 15,416 words, roughly the same length as *Cato Minor*.[105]

3.4.2.2 Similarities in Historiography

3.4.2.2.1 General Purpose

The general purpose of Greco-Roman *bioi* was historical rather than novelistic. Most writers aimed for historical verisimilitude rather than high probability (by modern standards; see Dio Cassius 62.11.3–4).[106] Truthfulness was expected in the

---

97. Keener, *John,* 6, citing Charles H. Talbert, *Reading John: A Literary and Theological Commentary on the Fourth Gospel and the Johannine Epistles* (New York: Crossroad, 1992), 64, with reference to Aristotle, *Poet.* 17.6–11.

98. For a detailed chronology of John's gospel see chap. 1, sect. 2.1.3.2 above.

99. Burridge, *Gospels,* 219, citing Martin Hengel, *Acts and the History of Earliest Christianity* (London: SCM, 1979), 19.

100. Keener, *John,* 6, citing Aune, *Literary Environment,* 90.

101. Keener, *John,* 6.

102. See chap. 3, sec. 7.3 below.

103. Ibid., *John,* 7, citing A. Q. Morton and G. H. C. MacGregor, *The Structure of Luke and Acts* (New York: Harper & Row, 1964), 16.

104. Keener, *John,* 7, points to Aristotle, *Poet.* 24.4, 1459b, for length in distinguishing genre.

105. Burridge, *Gospels,* 219.

106. Keener, *John,* 22; cf. Aune, *Literary Environment,* 83; Fornara, *Nature of History,* 134–36.

relating of history (e.g., Josephus, *Ag. Ap.* 1.26; Dionysius of Halicarnassus, *Thucy.* 8). If a historian was suspected of falsehood, particularly for self-serving reasons, he was harshly criticized.[107]

At least three purposes for writing history are identified by Dionysius of Halicarnassus, summed up by Craig Keener as follows: "first, that the courageous will gain 'immortal glory' that outlives them; second, that their descendants will recognize their own roots and seek to emulate their virtue; and finally, that he might show proper goodwill and gratitude toward those who provided him training and information."[108]

While specific purposes may differ from gospel to gospel, all four Gospels focus on the life of Jesus and hence to a large extent tend to be biographical. At the same time, they record historical events. John's gospel intends to present Jesus to second and subsequent generations of believers, those who did not see Jesus' signs (John 20:29) but have the gospel's written account of them (20:30–31: "these are written"). By making clear who Jesus is and what is the nature of the salvation he offers, this gospel intends to encourage and strengthen believers in their faith in Jesus as the Messiah and Son of God and equip them to share this message of good news with others.[109] As part of its hortatory function, the gospel endeavors to clarify the relationship of Jesus to Judaism by showing his superiority to the patriarchs of the Jewish faith (4:12; 6:32; 8:53–58), the replacement in his person of Jewish festivals and religious institutions (2:1–11, 19–22; 6:32–41; 7:37–39), and the relationship between the law and Moses on the one hand and Jesus Christ on the other (1:17; 5:39–40, 45–47; 7:19–23).[110]

Similarly, it was not uncommon for first-century historiography to focus on notable individuals.[111] Keener notes that the gospel's intent to promote a particular moral and religious perspective does not detract from its biographical perspective, since *bioi*, in seeking to provide role models for moral instruction, also tended to be propagandistic.[112] Jewish writers also understood the Bible's narratives as providing moral lessons (e.g., Philo, *Abraham* 4; cf. 1 Cor 10:11), and postbiblical models also served as examples of virtue (e.g., 4 Macc 1:7–8).[113] Apart from the obvious biographical purpose, some *bioi,* particularly those in political or philosophical debate, also had apologetic and polemic purposes. These can also be detected in John's gospel.[114] Since history was written differently than in modern times, these purposes, including the theological motivation of the author, did not necessarily deter from its historicity.

3.4.2.2.2 Use of Sources

While a number of scholars (such as Bultmann or Fortna) have attempted detailed source-critical analysis in the past, it is widely recognized that sources behind

---

107. Keener, *John,* 18.
108. Ibid., 15.
109. On the putative purpose of John's gospel see Köstenberger, *John,* 8, and the discussion above.
110. See Köstenberger, "John," 282.
111. Keener, *John,* 12, citing Fornara, *Nature of History,* 185.
112. Keener, John, 10.
113. Ibid., 15.
114. Burridge, *Gospels,* 229. See also Rodney A. Whitacre, *Johannine Polemic: The Role of Tradition and Theology* (SBLDS 67; Chico, CA: Scholars Press, 1982).

John's gospel are almost impossible to retrieve.[115] Recent study has shown that it is probable that the author of John's gospel was at least aware of the Synoptic tradition, if not of the Gospels themselves (particularly Mark).[116] Writers of *bioi*, particularly those concerned with philosophers and teachers, frequently altered sources in order to make them relevant in their context. At the same time, good historiography distinguished between accurate and inaccurate sources.[117] There are no sources cited explicitly by the Gospels (other than the OT) "perhaps in part because of their relatively popular level but also probably in part because they report recent events on which sources have not yet diverged greatly (like, e.g., Tacitus, who naturally does not need to cite many sources on his father-in-law *Agricola*)."[118]

Whatever the sources behind John's gospel, like ancient writers who frequently exercised their freedom to revise and alter their sources, both oral and written, this is probably true of John as well.[119] The main "source" is, of course, the testimony of "the disciple whom Jesus loved" himself (cf. 21:24), a participant at critical junctures of Jesus' ministry (e.g., 13:23; 19:35) and the gospel's author (21:24), who most likely follows the model of ancient memory techniques.[120] John's interpretive method may be said to resemble that of Josephus in his *Antiquities*, though it is far from certain whether John created new speeches in some contexts to fit the model of a Hellenistic history as did Josephus.[121] In addition, the inclusion of editorial asides for interpretive or illustrative reasons, or even for making explicit the author's point of view, was not uncommon.[122]

3.4.2.2.3 Variation in Detail

Aristotle pointed out that one distinguished a historical article from a piece of poetry not on the basis of literary style, but by whether it conveyed specific facts

---

115. The relevant works are Rudolf Bultmann, *The Gospel of John*; Robert T. Fortna, *The Gospel of Signs: A Reconstruction of the Narrative Source underlying the Fourth Gospel* (Cambridge: Cambridge University Press, 1970); idem, *The Fourth Gospel and Its Predecessor: From Narrative Source to Present Gospel* (Philadelphia: Fortress, 1988); Fortna and Thatcher, eds., *Jesus in Johannine Tradition*, 189–235. See esp. D. A. Carson, "Historical Tradition in the Fourth Gospel: After Dodd, What?" in *Gospel Perspectives*, Vol. 2: *Studies of History and Tradition in the Fourth Gospel* (ed. R. T. France and David Wenham; Sheffield: JSOT, 1981), 83–145; Eugen Ruckstuhl and Peter Dschulnigg, *Stilkritik und Verfasserfrage im Johannesevangelium: Die johanneischen Sprachmerkmale auf dem Hintergrund des Neuen Testaments und des zeitgenössischen hellenistischen Schrifttums* (NTOA 17; Göttingen: Vandenhoeck & Ruprecht, 1991); and Gilbert Van Belle, *The Signs Source in the Fourth Gospel: Historical Survey and Critical Evaluation of the Semeia Hypothesis* (BETL 116; Leuven: Leuven University Press, 1994). There are three types of Johannine source theories: (1) displacement theories; (2) theories involving multiple sources; and (3) some form of multiple edition theory. See Burridge, *Gospels*, 221.

116. See Bauckham, "John for Readers of Mark," 147–72; and the discussion in chap. 16, sec. 34 below.

117. Except when a consensus view was available; see Livy 1.1.1. See Keener, *John*, 21.

118. Ibid., 23. It is possible that they also follow some Jewish conventions on this point.

119. Burridge, *Gospels*, 222, citing Robert Kysar, *The Fourth Evangelist and His Gospel* (Minneapolis: Augsburg, 1975), 81.

120. Tom Thatcher, "John's Memory Theater: The Fourth Gospel and Ancient Mnemo-Rhetoric," *CBQ* 69 (2007): 487–505. See also *Jesus in Early Christian Memory. Essays in Honour of James D. G. Dunn* (ed. Scot McKnight and Terence C. Mournet; LNTS 349; London: T&T Clark, 2007).

121. But Josephus writes for a far more literate and Hellenized audience than John does and writes a Hellenistic history, not a biography. See Keener, *John*, 34.

122. Instances of this can be seen in Polybius 1.35.1–10; Diodorus Siculus 31.10.2; Dionysius of Halicarnussus, *Ars rhetorica* 7.65.2; Dio Cassius 1.5.4; Arrian, *Alex.* 4.10.8; and Cornelius Nepos 16 [Pelopidas], 3.1. See Keener, *John*, 14; and the discussion in chap. 3, sec. 7.1 below.

as opposed to general philosophical truths.[123] However, even with the reporting of historical fact, variation in detail was allowed and accounts could be expanded or abridged depending on the author's preference without interfering with their historical value.[124] This is explained in Theon's rhetorical exercises (*Progymn.* 4.37–42; 4.80–82). Theon's example for expanding *chreia* demonstrates how variation in detail did not detract from its basic meaning (*Progymn.* 3.224–40).[125] In some cases, poets and prose writers would sometimes add or remove material (whether essential or nonessential) for aesthetic purposes (e.g., Dionysius, *Comp.* 9). Keener adds,

> Inserting sayings from sayings-collections into narrative, or adding narratives to sayings, was considered a matter of arrangement, not a matter of fabrication.... Thus Phaedrus feels free to adapt Aesop for aesthetic reasons, meanwhile seeking to keep to the *spirit* of Aesop (Phaed. 2.prol.8). And paraphrase of sayings—attempts to rephrase them without changing their meaning—was standard rhetorical practice, as evidenced by the school exercises in which it features prominently (Theon *Progymn.* 1.93–171; cf., e.g., Epictetus *Diatr.* 1.923–25 with Oldfather's note referring to Plato *Apol.* 29C, 28E [LCL 1.70–71]).[126]

Expansion could also be attributed to the passage of time and consequent growth of tradition, though in some cases long stories ended up being shortened. Elaborations could be used for rebuttal (*Progymn.* 1.172–75) or to emphasize a point (Longinus, *Subl.* 11.1; cf. Menander Rhetor 2.3, 379.2–4).[127] However, there were limits as to how much variation in detail was permitted. Note, for example, the objections by the second-century rhetorician Lucian, directed against historical writers whose purposes were merely literary or encomiastic, or Polybius's objections to writers who amplified their accounts merely for sensationalistic purposes (15.34; 2.56.1–11; 2.57.1–2.63.6).[128]

3.4.2.2.4 Reliability of Eyewitness Testimony

Eyewitnesses and firsthand sources of the events were generally considered to provide a more reliable recounting of events (Plutarch, *Her. Mal.* 20; *Mor.* 859 B).[129] Greater credibility was attached to eyewitness testimony as opposed to hearsay, and the account was considered even more reliable if the source was a living eyewitness as he could verify the truth of the account.[130] John's gospel claims to convey eyewitness testimony of someone who refers to himself as "the disciple whom Jesus

---

123. Keener, *John*, 18; cf. Aristotle, *Poet.* 9.2, 1451b.
124. Variations in tradition and editing of sources was also not problematic in Palestinian Jewish narrative techniques, as in 2 and 4 Maccabees. See Keener, *John*, 29, citing Hugh Anderson, "Introduction to 4 Maccabees," in *Old Testament Pseudepigrapha*, Vol. 2 (ed. James H. Charlesworth; Garden City, NY: Doubleday, 1985), 555.
125. Keener, *John*, 19.
126. Ibid.
127. Ibid.
128. Ibid., 20, citing Philip L. Shuler, *A Genre for the Gospels: The Biographical Character of Matthew* (Philadelphia: Fortress, 1982), 11–12; cf. G. W. Bowersock, *Fiction as History: Nero to Julian* (Berkeley: University of California Press, 1994), 1–27. See especially Lucian, *Ver. hist.* 7–13.
129. Keener, *John*, 21.
130. Ibid., 21–22.

loved" (John 21:24–25). That this type of self-reference was not considered presumptuous can be seen in Porphyrus's *Life of Plotinus*.[131] In relating an account in which he was a participant, the writer generally referred to himself in the third person, by name (e.g., "Thucydides," "Xenophon," "Polybius," "Julius Caesar," or "Josephus").[132]

John also uses the literary device of *inclusio*, which in all likelihood enunciates the historiographic principle of eyewitness testimony from beginning to end and identifies the main eyewitness source of the gospel (1:35–40 and 21:24).[133] Since the eyewitnesses mentioned in all four Gospels had experienced the events they related, their direct experience was considered the best basis for historical accounts. This perspective is evident in Josephus's *Jewish War*, in which the author claims to be both a participant in the action and an eyewitness of the events.[134] The eyewitness terminology of John's gospel, therefore, relates to a historiographic category and constitutes "direct autopsy."[135] As Richard Bauckham contends,

> In all four Gospels we have the history of Jesus only in the form of testimony, the testimony of involved participants who responded in faith to the disclosure of God in these events. In testimony fact and interpretation are inextricable; in this testimony empirical sight and spiritual testimony are inseparable.[136]

3.5 Conclusion

In summary, John's gospel most closely resembles historical narrative as found in Jewish works, particularly in the Hebrew Scriptures. At the same time, the gospel also displays a considerable amount of surface affinities with Greco-Roman literature, both on the macro- and on the micro-level.

However, there are several important differences that suggest that rather than reflect the wholesale adoption of a particular Greco-Roman literary genre, these affinities, which relate to both internal and external features, represent John's attempt to contextualize the gospel message for a Greco-Roman audience.

As mentioned at the outset of this volume, John wrote a *theo*-drama, or even more accurately, a *Christo*- or *doxa*-drama, consisting of a *sēmeio*- and a *cruci*-drama. The gospel's beginning, middle, and end all focus on Jesus, the Word, the Messiah, the Son of God, presenting him as the incarnate, crucified, and glorified Word-made-flesh given for the life of the world.

---

131. Bauckham, *Jesus and the Eyewitnesses*, 401.

132. Ibid., 393. For additional examples, see Jackson, "Ancient Self-Referential Conventions," 28–29.

133. Bauckham, *Jesus and the Eyewitnesses*, 114–47, esp. 131.

134. Ibid., 394.

135. Ibid., 384–85. The term "direct autopsy" as well as the perspective of the importance of eyewitness testimony are from Samuel Byrskog, *Story as History—History as Story* (WUNT 123; Tübingen: Mohr-Siebeck, 2000; repr. Leiden: Brill, 2002). Bauckham notes that there is linguistic confusion surrounding the English usage of the terms "witness," "testify," and "testimony," the words comprising the *martyreō* word group. *Martyreō*, which is used of the witness of "the disciple whom Jesus loved," generally signifies a legal usage. *Autoptēs* is what translates to eyewitness. However, in John's gospel the use of *martyreō* is not only legal (see the cosmic trial motif in Lincoln, *Truth on Trial*), but also historiographic, at least in a functional sense. For this discussion see Bauckham, *Jesus and the Eyewitnesses*, 384–90.

136. Ibid., 411.

4 The Genre of John's Letters

4.1 Second and Third John

Second and Third John are prototypical examples of the first-century letter and may be some of the most situational in the NT.[137] There is an opening prescript featuring sender and recipient (in the dative) without benefit of a verb (assuming some form of "I write"); a health wish; a body; closing greeting; and a formulaic farewell. Moreover, unlike most Christian letters, and like most Greco-Roman letters, they are brief.[138] Third John may even be classified further as a letter of recommendation for one Demetrius. Thus, there is wide consensus for identifying the genre of 2 and 3 John as simple, straightforward letters.

4.2 First John

The genre of 1 John, however, is a different matter. Brown notes that "of the twenty-one NT works normally classified as epistles, 1 John is the least letterlike in format."[139] The closest parallels in the canon are Hebrews and James, both of which lack some of the formal features of a Greco-Roman letter.[140]

A wide variety of proposals have been suggested for the work. Stephen Smalley calls it "a paper."[141] Windisch suggests it is a "tractate."[142] Kenneth Grayston describes it as an "enchiridion, an instruction booklet."[143] While himself declining to settle on a specific genre designation, Raymond Brown noted that "circular epistle," "homily," and "encyclical" have all been used to describe the first letter of John, mustering only the observation that 1 John represents a "comment patterned on" the gospel of John.[144] Taking his point of departure from Raymond Brown's penchant for interpreting the letter based on the historical reconstruction of the community, Julian V. Hills suggests that it should be considered a "community rule."[145]

What is unusual regarding 1 John is that the document contains few formal characteristics that would classify it as a letter. There is no prescript, well-wish/prayer, closing, or formulaic farewell. In fact, both the opening "that which was from the beginning" and the closing "keep yourselves from idols" are highly unconventional. Between the preface and the concluding statement, the elder teaches in a somewhat cyclical manner, frequently returning to a topic he has already addressed previously only to discuss it in somewhat similar though not identical terms.[146] In this regard, 1 John is similar to Hebrews, which likewise opens with a kind of

---

137. John L. White, "Ancient Greek Letters," in *Greco-Roman Literature and the New Testament* (ed. David E. Aune; SBLSBS 21; Atlanta: Scholars Press, 1988), 100.

138. Aune, *Literary Environment*, 163–64.

139. Brown, *Epistles*, 87.

140. That is, Hebrews lacks the customary opening, while James lacks the customary ending. As will be further discussed below, 1 John lacks both.

141. Stephen S. Smalley, *1, 2, 3 John* (WBC 51; rev. ed. Nashville: Nelson, 2007), xxx.

142. Hans Windisch, *Die Katholischen Briefe* (HNT 15; 3rd rev. ed.; Tübingen: Mohr, 1951), 136, cited in Brown, *Epistles*, 87.

143. Grayston, *Johannine Epistles*, 4.

144. Brown, *Epistles*, 90, admits that this is a choice not to make a choice and instead simply to describe the contents.

145. Julian V. Hills, "A Genre for 1 John," in *The Future of Early Christianity: Essays in Honor of Helmut Koester* (ed. Birger A. Pearson, A. Thomas Kraabel, George W. E. Nickelsburg, and Norman R. Petersen; Minneapolis: Fortress, 1991), 367.

146. For example, compare 1 John 4:7–21 with 3:11–24.

preface rather than an epistolary opening, and like the letter of James, which also concludes without a formal epistolary closing. By comparison, 1 John conforms even less to the standard first-century AD epistolary format than either Hebrews or James, for the former features at least an epistolary closing and the latter an epistolary opening, while 1 John lacks both.

So, then, what is the genre of 1 John? Despite the lack of standard formal epistolary features, it is best to understand the writing in broad terms as a letter, since Greco-Roman letters exhibited a considerable degree of diversity.[147] The work is from a single authoritative source (an apostle), but the recipients are identified only in general (and figurative) terms as "dear children" (e.g., 1 John 2:1, 12, 18). There is, however, more specific information regarding the false teachers who had recently departed (2:19). It would seem, then, that the letter is designed to address a situation germane to a number of congregations in the area.

Without imposing external categories on the letter, therefore, it is probably best to understand 1 John as a kind of circular letter similar to the book of Ephesians or the letter of James. There is abundant evidence for this type of letter in antiquity, especially among the Jews. Jeremiah 29:4–13; Acts 15:23–29; and Revelation 2–3 constitute exemplars of this type of genre. If so, 1 John is a situational letter written to instruct and encourage the apostolic Christians in and around Ephesus regarding the nature of the gospel and their part in it.[148]

4.3 Conclusion

After discussing the genre of John's gospel and letters in the present chapter, we must explore several other important linguistic and literary features of these writings in the next chapter. These include Johannine vocabulary, style, and various literary devices such as narrative "asides," misunderstandings, apparent "seams," irony, and symbolism, as well as the structure of both the gospel and the letters. This will be followed by a close literary-theological reading of these writings in preparation for an investigation of the major themes in Johannine theology in Part 3 below.

---

147. See Aune, *Literary Environment,* 203.
148. See the discussion of the date, provenance, and destination of 1 John in chap. 1, sec. 2.2 above.

Chapter 3

LINGUISTIC AND LITERARY DIMENSIONS OF JOHN'S GOSPEL AND LETTERS

BIBLIOGRAPHY

Brown, Raymond E. "The Language, Text, and Format of the Gospel: Some Considerations on Style." Pp. 278–97 in *An Introduction to the Gospel of John*. Ed. Francis J. Moloney. ABRL. New York: Doubleday, 2003. **Burge, Gary M.** "The Literary Seams in the Fourth Gospel." *Covenant Quarterly* 48 (1990): 15–25. **Carson, D. A.** "Understanding Misunderstandings in the Fourth Gospel." *TynBul* 33 (1982): 59–91. **Collins, Raymond F.** "Representative Figures." Pp. 1–45 in *These Things Have Been Written: Studies on the Fourth Gospel*. Grand Rapids: Eerdmans, 1991. **Credner, Karl August**. *Einleitung in das Neue Testament*. Halle: Waisenhauses, 1837. **Culpepper, R. Alan**. *Anatomy of the Fourth Gospel: A Study in Literary Design*. Philadelphia: Fortress, 1983. **Davies, Margaret**. *Rhetoric and Reference in the Fourth Gospel*. JSNTSup 69. Sheffield: JSOT, 1992. **Duke, Paul D**. *Irony in the Fourth Gospel*. Atlanta: John Knox, 1985. **Frey, Jörg, Jan G. van der Watt, and Ruben Zimmermann**, eds. *Imagery in the Gospel of John: Terms, Forms, Themes, and Theology of Johannine Figurative Language*. WUNT 200. Tübingen: Mohr-Siebeck, 2006. **Hamid-Khani, Saeed**. *Revelation and Concealment of Christ: A Theological Inquiry into the Elusive Language of the Fourth Gospel*. WUNT 2/120. Tübingen: Mohr-Siebeck, 2000. **Jones, L. P.** *The Symbol of Water in the Gospel of John*. JSNTSup 145. Sheffield: Sheffield Academic Press, 1997. **Kellum, L. Scott**. *The Unity of the Farewell Discourse: The Literary Integrity of John 13.31–16.33*. JSNTSup 256. London/New York: T & T Clark, 2004. Idem. "On the Semantic Structure of 1 John: A Modest Proposal." *Faith & Mission* 23 (2008): 34–82. **Koester, Craig R**. *Symbolism in the Fourth Gospel: Meaning, Mystery, Community*. 2nd ed. Minneapolis: Fortress, 2003. **Köstenberger, Andreas J.** "'I Suppose' (οἶμαι): The Conclusion of John's Gospel in Its Literary and Historical Context." Pp. 77–88 in *The New Testament in Its First Century Setting: Essays on Context and Background in Honour of B. W. Winter on His 65th Birthday*. Ed. P. J. Williams, Andrew D. Clarke, Peter M. Head, and David Instone-Brewer. Grand Rapids/Cambridge: Eerdmans, 2004. **Köstenberger, Andreas, and Raymond Bouchoc**. *The Book Study Concordance*. Nashville: Broadman & Holman, 2003. **Lee, Dorothy A**. *The Symbolic Narratives of the Fourth Gospel: The Interplay of Form and Meaning*. JSNTSup 95. Sheffield: JSOT, 1994. **Leroy, Herbert**. *Rätsel und Missverständnis: Ein Beitrag zur Formgeschichte des Johannesevangeliums*. BBB. Bonn: Hanstein, 1968. **Louw, Johannes P.** "On Johannine Style." *Neot* 20 (1986):

5–12. **McRae, George W.** "Theology and Irony in the Fourth Gospel." Pp. 83–96 in *The Word and the World: Essays in Honor of Frederick L. Moriarty*. Ed. Richard J. Clifford and George W. McRae. Cambridge, MA: Weston College Press, 1973. **Morris, Leon.** "Variation: A Feature of Johannine Style." Pp. 293–319 in *Studies in the Fourth Gospel*. Grand Rapids: Eerdmans, 1969. **Moulton, James Hope.** "The Style of John." Pp. 64–79 in *A Grammar of New Testament Greek*. Vol. 4: *Style*, by Nigel Turner. Edinburgh: T&T Clark, 1976. **Ng, Wai-yee.** *Water Symbolism in John: An Eschatological Interpretation*. Studies in Biblical Literature 15. New York: Peter Lang, 2001. **O'Rourke, John J.** "Asides in the Gospel of John." *NovT* 21 (1979): 210–19. **Resseguie, James L.** *The Strange Gospel: Narrative Design and Point of View in John*. BIS 56. Leiden: Brill, 2001. **Richard, Earl J.** "Expressions of Double Meaning and Their Function in the Gospel of John." *NTS* 31 (1985): 96–112. **Ruckstuhl, Eugen.** *Die literarische Einheit des Johannesevangeliums: Der gegenwärtige Stand der einschlägigen Forschungen*. Göttingen: Vandenhoeck & Ruprecht, 1951. Idem. "Johannine Language and Style: The Question of Their Unity." Pp. 125–47 in *L'Évangile de Jean: Sources, rédaction, théologie*. Ed. Marinus de Jonge. Gembloux: J. Duculot/Leuven: Leuven University Press, 1977. **Ruckstuhl, Eugen, and Peter Dschulnigg.** *Stilkritik und Verfasserfrage im Johannesevangelium: Die johanneischen Sprachmerkmale auf dem Hintergrund des Neuen Testaments und des zeitgenössischen hellenistischen Schrifttums*. NTOA 17. Göttingen: Vandenhoeck & Ruprecht, 1991. **Rudel, P.** "Das Missverständnis im Johannesevangelium." *NKZ* 3 (1921): 351–61. **Shedd, Russell.** "Multiple Meanings in the Gospel of John." Pp. 247–58 in *Current Issues in Biblical Interpretation*. Ed. Gerald F. Hawthorne. Grand Rapids: Eerdmans, 1975. **Stamps, Dennis L.** "The Johannine Writings." Pp. 609–32 in *Handbook of Classical Rhetoric in the Hellenistic Period 330 B.C.–A.D. 400*. Ed. Stanley E. Porter. Leiden: Brill, 1997. **Tenney, Merrill C.** "The Footnotes of John's Gospel." *BSac* 117 (1960): 350–63. **Thatcher, Tom.** "A New Look at Asides in the Fourth Gospel." *BSac* 151 (1994): 428–39. **Thielman, Frank.** "The Style of the Fourth Gospel and Ancient Literary Critical Concepts of Religious Discourse." Pp. 169–83 in *Persuasive Artistry: Studies in New Testament Rhetoric in Honor of George A. Kennedy*. Ed. Duane F. Watson. JSNTSup 50. Sheffield: JSOT, 1991. **Timmins, Nicholas G.** "Variation in Style in the Johannine Literature." *JSNT* 53 (1994): 47–64. **Tovey, Derek.** *Narrative Art and Act in the Fourth Gospel*. JSNTSup 151. Sheffield: Sheffield Academic Press, 1997. **Van der Watt, Jan G.** *Family of the King: Dynamics of Metaphor in the Gospel according to John*. BIS 47. Leiden: Brill, 2000. Idem. "*Double Entendre* in the Gospel according to John." Pp. 463–81 in *Theology and Christology in the Fourth Gospel*. BETL 184. Ed. G. van Belle, J. G. van der Watt, and P. Maritz. Leuven: Leuven University Press/Peeters, 2005. **Wead, David W.** "The Johannine Double Meaning." *ResQ* 13 (1970): 106–20. Idem. *The Literary Devices in John's Gospel*. Theologische Dissertationen 4. Basel: Friedrich Reinhardt Kommissionsverlag, 1970. **Windisch, Hans.** "Der johanneische Erzählungsstil." Pp. 174–213 in *Eucharisterion: Hermann Gunkel zum 60. Geburtstage*. FRLANT N.F. 19. Ed. Hans Schmidt. Vol. 2. Göttingen: Vandenhoeck & Ruprecht, 1923.

5 Johannine Vocabulary

5.1 Survey of Johannine Vocabulary

In his gospel, John uses a total of 1,014 different words.[1] Of these, 216 words occur at least ten times, while 376 words occur only once. In 1 John, one finds 234 words, of which 41 occur at least ten times and 88 occur at least once. In 2 John, the numbers are 97, 2, and 48, respectively; in 3 John, they are 109, 3, and 70.[2] Apart from place and personal names, the following words occur in the NT only in John, and are there at least twice: *opsarion* ("fish"; 5 times); *antleō* ("draw"), *klēma* ("branch"), *psōmion* ("piece of bread"; 4 times each); *aposynagōgos* ("expelled from the synagogue"), *architriklinos* ("head steward"), *diazōnnymi* ("wrap around"), *kolymbēthra* ("pool"), *skelos* ("leg"), and *hydria* ("water jar"; 3 times each).

Other important words in terms of relative frequency in John's gospel that occur at least ten times in John include the following: *niptō* ("wash"; 76% of NT occurrences), *heortē* ("festival"; 68%), *ide* ("look!"; 54%), *alēthēs* ("true"; 53%), *phileō* ("love"; 52%), *martyreō* ("bear witness"; 43%), *kosmos* ("world"; 42%), *pisteuō* ("believe"; 41%), *theōreō* ("see, perceive"; 41%), *oun* ("therefore"; 40%), *pempō* ("send"; 40%), *hypagō* ("go"; 40%), *amēn* ("truly"; 39%), *doxazō* ("praise, glorify"; 37%), *martyria* ("testimony"; 37%), *pascha* ("Passover"; 34%), *menō* ("remain"; 33%), *patēr* ("F/father"; 32%), *phōs* ("light"; 31%), *hydōr* ("water"; 27%), *zōē* ("life"; 26%), and *agapaō* ("love"; 25%).

5.2 Major Semantic Domains in John's Gospel and Letters

Based on the above inventory of Johannine vocabulary, it is possible to compile the following list of major semantic domains represented in John's gospel and letters. The list surfaces many of the commonly recognized major themes in these writings. Theme clusters include:

- the festivals (*heortē*, *pascha*)
- love (*phileō*, *agapaō*)
- witness (*martyreō*, *martyria*)
- believing (*pisteuó*)
- truth (*alēthēs*, *amēn*; also *alēthōs*, 38%; *alēthinos*, 29%)
- God the Father (*patēr*)
- the world (*kosmos*)
- light and life (*phōs*, *zōē*)

The list lays the linguistic and conceptual groundwork for the discussion of many of the major Johannine themes in Part 3.

---

1. James Hope Moulton, *A Grammar of New Testament Greek*, Vol. 4: *Style*, by Nigel Turner (Edinburgh: T&T Clark, 1976), 76, puts the number at 1,011, and cites 112 NT *hapax legomena*.

2. For these and other data, see Köstenberger and Bouchoc, *Book Study Concordance*.

5.3 Other Observations

Another interesting vantage point on Johannine vocabulary is an investigation of major theological terms not used in John's writings. In particular, one notes the absence of terms related to repentance (*metanoia, metanoeō*) and words denoting the "good news" (*euangelion, euangelizō*) in the gospel. Words related to poverty and wealth are largely absent as well (the sole exception being the reference to Judas's objection to the anointing in John 12:5–6). Also, references to the "kingdom of God," ubiquitous in the Synoptics, are limited to one Johannine pericope (3:3, 5; cf. 18:36), with "(eternal) life" serving as an apparent functional substitute.[3] Finally, the noun *pistis* ("faith") occurs only in 1 John 5:4, though the verb *pisteuō* ("believe") occurs frequently.

6 Johannine Style

6.1 Introduction

"Style," at its most basic level, is "the author's unique mode of expression, or idiolect."[4] Any thought or concept may be communicated in a variety of ways. Thus an author's wording reflects linguistic choice from a finite set of possible modes of expression in a given language. In John's case, scholars are agreed: "One thing is certain: there is an unmistakable 'Johannine' style."[5] Normally, style is conceived as the characteristic expression of a single writer, not a community of authors. Also, similarity in style among different documents suggests common authorship. As B. H. Streeter observed, "The three Epistles and the Gospel of John are so closely allied in diction, style and general outlook that the burden of proof lies with the person who would deny their common authorship."[6]

6.2 Background and History of Research

In 1837, Karl August Credner isolated seventy-eight Johannine style characteristics.[7] Credner's list included such items as (1) *amēn, amēn* at the beginning of an utterance; (2) expression of a thought positively and then negatively; (3) frequent parentheses or asides; (4) the extensive use of the word *kosmos* ("world"); (5) the designation "prince of this world" for Satan; (6) the phrase "eternal life"; (7) vocabulary associated with judgment (*krisis, krinein*; "judgment," "to judge") and witness (*martyrein, martyria*; "testify," "testimony"); and others.

Julius Wellhausen, writing in 1908, included in his commentary a discussion of linguistic features of John's gospel.[8] He noted John's preference for simple sentences,

---

3. See Fig. 12.2 below.

4. Kellum, *Unity of the Farewell Discourse*, 91, to whom some of the following survey is indebted. See also chap. 2, sec. 3.5.10.1 above.

5. Rudolf Schnackenburg, *The Gospel according to St. John* (New York: Crossroad, 1990), 3:111. See also the classic works by Edwin A. Abbott, *Johannine Vocabulary* (London: Adam and Charles Black, 1905); idem, *Johannine Grammar* (London: Adam and Charles Black, 1906).

6. Streeter, *Four Gospels*, 460.

7. Karl August Credner, *Einleitung in das Neue Testament* (Halle: Waisenhauses, 1837), 225–30, partially reproduced in Kellum, *Unity of the Farewell Discourse*, 94–95. See also the list in Heinrich Ernst Ferdinand Guericke, *Neutestamentliche Isagogik* (3rd ed.; Leipzig: A. Winter, 1868), 223–24, n. 3.

8. Julius Wellhausen, *Das Evangelium Johannis* (Berlin: Reimer, 1908), 133–46.

penchant for parataxis and asyndeton, frequent use of historic presents, and other markers of Johannine idiolect.

Later, both W. F. Howard and Rudolf Schnackenburg observed unique Johannine expressions.[9] Howard drew attention to John's frequent use of *pas* ("all" or "every") and *hina* ("so that" or "in order that"); his extensive use of demonstrative pronouns to recall the subject; and his employment of synonyms (*aiteō, erōtaō* ["ask"]; *legō, laleō* ["say" or "speak"]; *ginōskō, oida* "[know]"). Schnackenburg noted several indicators of stylistic unity, including the phrases "prince of this world" and "Spirit of truth," and the use of an initial *pas* followed by a personal pronoun.

One of the most extensive lists of Johannine style traits was compiled in 1977 by Marie-Émile Boismard and Arnaud Lamouille, who listed as many as 416 items.[10] Among other features, they include (1) *ho pempsas me* ("the one who sent me"); (2) *martyreō peri* ("testify concerning"); (3) *menō en* ("remain in"); (4) *egō eimi* ("I am"); (5) *didōmi* ("to give"); (6) *kathōs ... kai* ("just as ... so") + pronoun; and (7) "Son of Man" plus *hypsoō* ("lift up"), *doxazō* ("glorify"), and *anabainō* ("ascend").

Eugen Ruckstuhl, aided by Peter Dschulnigg, sought to defend the unity of John's gospel against source-critical theories, identifying fifty style characteristics in a first monograph and refining and expanding his list to 153 in a sequel.[11] In identifying such traits, Ruckstuhl and Dschulnigg developed four criteria: (1) a given feature must occur in John at least three times; (2) it must appear at least twice as often as in Matthew, Mark, or Luke; (3) in relative numbers, it must not be found in the rest of the NT as often as in John; and (4) in relative numbers, it must appear in John at least as often as in a select corpus of extrabiblical Greek writings.

Vern Poythress wrote three articles developing a style test based on the use of intersentence conjunctions in John's gospel, noting John's distinctive use of *de*, *oun*, *kai*, and asyndeton.[12] In particular, Poythress observed that asyndeton is the default conjunction in John's gospel. Poythress' findings, in turn, were assessed and further developed by Stephen Levinsohn and Randall Buth.[13] Both of these scholars investigated intersentence conjunctions from the vantage point of "close connection" (an indicator of continuity) and "development" (advancing an author's purpose or argument).

---

9. W. F. Howard, *The Fourth Gospel in Recent Criticism and Interpretation* (rev. C. K. Barrett; London: Epworth, 1955), 105–7; Schnackenburg, *Gospel according to John*, 1:107–9.

10. Marie-Émile Boismard and Arnaud Lamouille, *L'évangile de Jean* (Leuven: Leuven University Press, 1979), 41–70, partially reproduced in Kellum, *Unity of the Farewell Discourse*, 97–98.

11. Eugen Ruckstuhl, *Die literarische Einheit des Johannesevangeliums: Der gegenwärtige Stand der einschlägigen Forschungen* (Göttingen: Vandenhoeck & Ruprecht, 1951); Ruckstuhl and Dschulnigg, *Stilkritik und Verfasserfrage*, partially reproduced in Kellum, *Unity of the Farewell Discourse*, 104–6. See also Eugen Ruckstuhl, "Johannine Language and Style: The Question of Their Unity," in *L'Évangile de Jean: Sources, rédaction, théologie* (ed. Marinus de Jonge; Gembloux: J. Duculot/Leuven: Leuven University Press, 1977), 127–47.

12. Vern S. Poythress, "The Use of the Intersentence Conjunctions *De, Oun, Kai*, and Asyndeton in the Gospel of John," *NovT* 26 (1984): 312–40; idem, "Testing for Johannine Authorship"; idem, "Johannine Authorship and the Use of Intersentence Conjunctions in the Book of Revelation," *WTJ* 47 (1985): 329–36. See the helpful summary in Kellum, *Unity of the Farewell Discourse*, 113–16.

13. Stephen H. Levinsohn, *Discourse Features of New Testament Greek: A Coursebook on the Information Structure of New Testament Greek* (2nd ed.; Dallas: SIL, 2000); Buth, "Οὖν, Δέ, Καί and Asyndeton in John's Gospel."

Scholars such as Oscar Cullmann have drawn attention to another interesting stylistic trait of John's gospel, the use of double entendre (double meaning).[14] This device often involves misunderstanding and taking a word's figurative meaning literally. Examples include the use of *anōthen* as denoting "again" vs. "from above" (John 3:3, 5); of *pneuma* as referring to "wind" and "spirit," respectively (3:8); of *hypsoō*, "lift up," in the sense of literal "lifting up" (crucifying) vs. figurative "lifting up" (exalting) in the Johannine "lifted up sayings" (3:14; 8:28; 12:32; cf. Isa 52:13). Verbs such as *akoloutheō* ("follow") and *menō* ("remain"), likewise, evince a progression from literal "following" and "staying" to a figurative use conveying the sense of adhering to a person's teaching (e.g., 1:37, 38, 40, 43).[15] Also, the word *typhlos* ("blind") is used with double entendre (9:39–41), pitting the literal meaning against the figurative sense of spiritual blindness.

As Earl Richard rightly notes, properly conceived, Johannine "double meaning" encompasses the notions of misunderstanding, irony, and symbolic or allusive ambiguity.[16] Ambiguities leading to misunderstanding are found in pericopae such as John 2:19–22 and 14:4–10. Other examples, such as 4:10–12; 7:34–35; and 8:21–22, involve irony as well. Symbolic expressions in John include "night," "light," "darkness," and "water."[17] Paradox attaches to the Johannine treatment of "seeing and not seeing."[18] In 15:2, *kathairō* means both "to prune" and "to purify." In 13:1 and 19:28, 30, respectively, the root *telos/teleō* implies both completion or perfection and end or death. Finally, the "signs" involve a deeper spiritual meaning beyond what meets the eye as well and thus call for spiritual perception, not mere literal seeing.[19]

Another remarkable Johannine trait is John's simplicity of style. Nigel Turner observed that John's "idiom is the very simplest and the vocabulary the poorest in the NT, relatively to the size of the book."[20] John also reflects Semitic modes of expression.[21] Thus many scholars, including C. H. Dodd, Rudolf Bultmann, and C. K. Barrett, have concluded that John thought in Aramaic but wrote in Greek. Turner posits that "John is more Semitic than the other gospels, without being a translation."[22] Hebraisms include phrases such as "to see or enter the kingdom" (John 3:3, 5), "to do the works" (5:36; 7:3, 21; 8:39, 41; 10:25, 37; 14:10, 12; 15:24; 3 John 10), "to work the works" (John 6:28; 9:4), "to come as a witness" (1:6–8), "to receive the witness" (3:11, 32–33), "to receive the words" (12:48; 17:8), and "to have the commandments" (14:21). Other examples are "look" (*ide*; e.g., 11:3, 36) and "come and see" (1:39, 46; 11:34).[23]

---

14. Oscar Cullmann, "Der johanneische Gebrauch doppeldeutiger Ausdrücke als Schlüssel zum Verständnis des vierten Evangeliums," *TZ* 4 (1948): 360–72; Earl J. Richard, "Expressions of Double Meaning and Their Function in the Gospel of John," *NTS* 31 (1985): 96–112; David W. Wead, "The Johannine Double Meaning," *ResQ* 13 (1970): 106–20; Russell Shedd, "Multiple Meanings in the Gospel of John," in *Current Issues in Biblical Interpretation* (ed. Gerald F. Hawthorne; Grand Rapids: Eerdmans, 1975), 247–58.

15. See Köstenberger, *Missions of Jesus and the Disciples*, 177–80.

16. Richard, "Expressions of Double Meaning," 97. See further the discussion below.

17. See the discussion below.

18. C. K. Barrett, "The Dialectical Theology of St John," in *New Testament Essays* (London: SPCK, 1972), 59–61.

19. See the discussion in chap. 7, sec. 15.

20. Moulton, *Grammar of New Testament Greek*, 4:64–79.

21. See esp. Ernest C. Colwell, *The Greek of the Fourth Gospel: A Study of Its Aramaisms in the Light of Hellenistic Greek* (Chicago: University of Chicago Press, 1931).

22. Moulton, *Grammar of New Testament Greek*, 4:64–79.

23. See Schlatter, *Evangelist Johannes, passim*.

6.3 Major Johannine Style Characteristics

6.3.1 Introduction

The following is a list of some of the major Johannine style characteristics.[24] The list is far from comprehensive but should provide a general orientation to the distinctiveness of John's style in comparison to the Synoptics and other biblical and extrabiblical literature.

6.3.2 Select List of Major Johannine Style Characteristics

The following twenty-two major Johannine style characteristics command broad consensus in the relevant literature.

(1) Overall simplicity of expression and use of basic terminology, including verbs of knowing and seeing, basic necessities or realities of life such as water, bread, life and death, light and darkness, etc.

(2) Overall simplicity of sentence structure and frequent juxtaposition of sentences without use of conjunctions (asyndeton)

(3) Double *amēn* introducing Jesus' pronouncements (John 1:51; 3:3, 5, 11; 5:19, 24, 25; 6:26, 32, 47, 53; 8:34, 51, 58; 10:1, 7; 12:24; 13:16, 20, 21, 38; 14:12; 16:20, 23; 21:18)

(4) Characteristic address "children" (*teknia* or *paidia*) for Jesus' followers (John 13:33; 21:5; 1 John 2:1, 12, 13, 18, 28; 3:17, 18; 4:4; 5:21)

(5) Distinctive phrase "after these things" or "after this" (*meta tauta* or *meta touto*) to indicate general time references (John 2:12; 3:22; 5:1, 14; 6:1; 7:1, 11; 11:7, 11; 13:7; 19:28, 38; 21:1)

(6) Frequent use of preposition *peri*, especially after *martyreō, legō, gongyzō, laleō*, etc. (John 1:7, 8, 15, 22, 30, 48; 2:21, 25; 5:31, 32, 36, 37, 39, 46; 7:7, 12, 13; 21:24; 1 John 2:26; 5:9, 10, 16; etc.)

(7) Frequent use of the conjunction *oun* ("so, therefore") to continue the narrative (e.g., John 6:5, 10, 13, 14, 15, 19, 21, 24, 28, 30, 32, 34, 41, 42, 43, 45, 52, 53, 60, 62, 67, 68; 11:3, 6, 12, 14, 16, 17, 20, 21, 31, 32, 33, 36, 38, 41, 45, 47, 53, 54, 56; 21:5, 6, 7, 9, 13, 15, 23)[25]

(8) Frequent use of conjunction *hina* ("in order that, so that"; e.g., John 6:5, 7, 12, 15, 28, 29, 30, 38, 39, 40, 50; 11:4, 11, 15, 16, 19, 31, 37, 42, 50, 52, 53, 55, 57; 12:1, 2, 3, 4, 11, 12, 13, 15, 21, 23, 24, 26; 1 John 1:3, 4, 9; 2:1, 19, 27, 28)

(9) Positive statement followed by converse statement (e.g., John 1:3, 6–7, 20, 48; 3:15, 17, 20; 4:42; 5:19, 24; 8:35, 45–47; 10:28; 15:5–7; 1 John 2:27)

(10) Back references to characters, sayings, or events previously mentioned in the narrative (John 4:54; 6:23, 71; 7:50; 10:40; 18:9, 14, 26; 19:39; 21:14, 20)

---

24. See esp. Credner, *Einleitung*, 1.223–30; Ruckstuhl and Dschulnigg, *Stilkritik und Verfasserfrage*, 63–162.

25. See Paul Ellingworth, "Translating *Oun* in John's Gospel," *BT* 51 (2000): 135–43.

(11) Parenthetical statements or asides by the author (John 1:39, 42, 43; 2:6, 9, 21, 24, 25; 3:19–21, 24; 4:2, 6, 9, 25, 45; etc.)[26]

(12) Frequent use of historical presents (John 1:29, 40, 42, 43, 44; 5:14; 9:13; 11:29; 13:28; 19:9; 20:6, 12, 14, 19, 26; 21:9)

(13) Frequent use of distinctive terms such as *kosmos, sarx, hamartia, thanatos, skotos, skotia, phōs, doxa, zōē aiōnios, pisteuō, menō, martyreō, martyria, krinō, krisis*, etc.[27]

(14) Frequent use of double entendre in conjunction with irony and/or misunderstanding[28]

(15) Characteristic use of *kathōs . . . kai = houtōs* ("just as . . . so"; John 6:57; 13:15, 33; 15:9; 17:18; 20:21; 1 John 2:6, 18; 4:17)

(16) Use of *ekeinos* ("he, that one") to refer to previous subject (John 1:18, 33; 5:11, 37; 6:57; 9:37; 10:1; 12:48; 14:12, 21, 26; 15:26)

(17) "The word that he had spoken" (*ho logos . . . hon eipen*; John 2:22; 4:50; 7:36; 12:38; 15:20; 18:9, 32); "of whom you say that" (*hon . . . hymeis legete hoti*; 8:54; 9:19; 10:36)

(18) "On the last day" ([*en*] *tē eschatē hēmera*; John 6:39, 40, 44, 54; 7:37; 11:24; 12:48)

(19) Frequent use of "we know that" (*oidamen hoti*; John 3:2; 4:42; 9:20, 24, 29, 31; 16:30; 21:24) or "know" (*oida*) plus indirect question (2:9; 3:8; 4:10; 5:13; 6:6, 64; 7:27, 28; 8:14 [2x]; 9:21 [2x], 25, 29, 30; 12:35; 13:18; 14:5; 15:15; 16:18; 20:2, 13)

(20) Frequent use of "believe that" (*pisteuō hoti*; John 4:21; 6:69; 8:24; 9:18; 11:27, 42; 13:19; 14:10, 11; 16:27, 30; 17:8, 21; 20:31) and "believe in" (*pisteuō eis tina*; 1:12; 2:11, 23; 3:16, 18 [2x], 36; 4:39; 6:29, 35, 40; 7:5, 31, 38, 39, 48; 8:30; 9:35, 36; 10:42; 11:25, 26, 45, 48; 12:11, 36, 37, 42, 44 [2x], 46; 14:1 [2x], 12; 16:9; 17:20)

(21) "The one who sent me" (*ho pempsas me*; John 1:22?, 33; 4:34; 5:23, 24, 30, 37; 6:38, 39, 44; 7:16, 18, 28, 33; 8:16, 18, 26, 29; 9:4; 12:44, 45, 49; 13:16, 20; 14:24; 15:21; 16:5)

(22) Use of other memorable expressions, such as "the prince of this world" (*ho archōn tou kosmou*; John 12:31; 14:30; 16:11) or "the disciple whom Jesus loved" (*ho mathētēs . . . hon ēgapa/ephilei*; 13:23; 19:26; 20:2; 21:7, 20)

6.3.3 Conclusion

The above list underscores impressively the unity of style that pervades the entire gospel and extends also to the Johannine letters and, when proper allowance is made for the differences in genre and context, even to the book of Revelation.[29] This

---

26. See sec. 7.1 below.
27. See further sec. 5 on Johannine vocabulary above.
28. See further secs. 7.2 and 7.4 below.
29. See the discussion of the authorship of John's gospel and letters in chap. 1, sec. 2 above. See also the case for the literary integrity of the Farewell Discourse and discussion of relevant issues in Kellum, *Unity of the Farewell Discourse*. The upcoming BTNT volume on the theology of Revelation will include a discussion of theological affinities between John's gospel and letters and the book of Revelation.

linguistic coherence, in turn, reflects a consistent worldview that presents Jesus and his words and works from John's vantage point in his distinctive idiom.[30] While this may not necessarily convey Jesus' message using his *ipsissima verba* (his very words), a persuasive case can be made that his *ipsissima vox* (the substance of his words, his "voice") is given eloquent and faithful expression in the unique Johannine idiolect found in the gospel of John.

7 Johannine Literary Devices

7.1 Narrative "Asides"

John uses a considerable wealth of literary devices, including "asides" or parenthetical remarks for the purpose of orienting his readers and misunderstandings that normally occur in conjunction with double entendre.[31] In addition, the following discussion will include a treatment of alleged "seams" (*aporias*) or apparent literary incongruities in John's gospel that some have taken to betray (disparate) literary sources underlying John's gospel. Also covered will be John's characteristic use of irony and some of the most significant types of symbolism featured in the gospel.

7.1.1 Introduction

While narrative "asides" are found in the other gospels as well,[32] this literary device is particularly frequent in John.[33] One of the major functions of these "asides" is that they enable the narrator to steer his readers to his desired conclusion.[34] By these parenthetical remarks, the evangelist seeks to remove ignorance on the part of his readers with regard to terminology or topography, endeavors to alleviate the possible perception of inconsistency in his presentation of events, and strives to highlight important theological motifs such as people's misunderstandings or Jesus' supernatural foreknowledge of events. The narrative "asides" thus bear witness to

---

30. See chap. 6, sec. 12 below.

31. See above. Another feature worth mentioning is John's use of virtual synonyms, such as verbs for knowing, loving, seeing, or sending. Regarding the latter, see Andreas J. Köstenberger, "The Two Johannine Verbs for Sending: A Study of John's Use of Words with Reference to General Linguistic Theory," in *Linguistics and the New Testament: Critical Junctures* (ed. Stanley E. Porter and D. A. Carson; JSNTSup 168; Studies in New Testament Greek 5; Sheffield: Sheffield Academic Press, 1999), 125–43. See also the discussion of John 21:15–19 in Köstenberger, *John*, 596, with additional bibliographic references.

32. E.g., the Gospel of Luke: see Steven M. Sheeley, *Narrative Asides in Luke–Acts* (JSNTSup 72; Sheffield: Sheffield Academic Press, 1992).

33. Bauckham, "Historiographical Characteristics," 28, reports that estimates range from 109 to 165; he notes that Luke's gospel has only eighteen "asides" (citing Sheeley, *Narrative Asides*, 98–99, 186–88).

34. See, e.g., John 6:60–71; 12:37–43; 20:30–31; 21:24–25. Helpful essays on Johannine "asides" include Tom Thatcher, "A New Look at Asides in the Fourth Gospel," *BSac* 151 (1994): 428–39; John J. O'Rourke, "Asides in the Gospel of John," *NovT* 21 (1979): 210–19; Merrill C. Tenney, "The Footnotes of John's Gospel," *BSac* 117 (1960): 350–63; Charles W. Hedrick, "Authorial Presence and Narrator in John: Commentary and Story," in *Gospel Origins and Christian Beginnings* (ed. James E. Goehring, Charles W. Hedrick, Jack T. Sanders, and Hans Dieter Betz; Sonoma, CA: Polebridge, 1990), 74–93, esp. 77–81. See also the discussion of the narrator's role in Culpepper, *Anatomy*, 34–49; the summary in Bauckham, "Historiographical Characteristics," 28–29; the list in Credner, *Einleitung*, 1.226–27; and the monograph by Gilbert van Belle, *Les parentheses dans l'évangile de Jean. Aperçu historique et classification. Texte grec de Jean* (Studiorum Novi Testamenti Auxilia 11; Leuven: Leuven University Press/Peeters, 1985).

the way in which the fourth evangelist carefully crafted his narrative with a view toward communicating his message to his first readers.[35]

7.1.2 List of Johannine "Asides"

What follows is a list of Johannine "asides" or parentheses. In some cases, this merely involves the translation of Aramaic or Hebrew terms. In other instances, the narrator explains features of Palestinian topography or Jewish customs. Other categories of "asides" are references to Jesus' supernatural insight or foreknowledge of events and references to characters or events mentioned earlier in the gospel narrative. In addition, one finds references to the fulfillment of Scripture or of Jesus' words, references to a failure to understand, clarifications of the meaning of statements made by Jesus or others, statements in relation to gospel tradition, numbering of events in the narrative, extended commentary, and other clarifying statements.[36]

7.1.2.1 Translations of Aramaic or Hebrew Terms

- "'Rabbi' (which means 'Teacher')" (1:38)
- "the Messiah (that is, the Christ)" (1:41; cf. 4:25)
- "Cephas (which, when translated, is Peter)" (1:42)
- "Siloam (this word means 'Sent')" (9:7)
- "Thomas (also known as Didymus)" (11:16; 20:24; 21:2)
- "a place known as the Stone Pavement (which in Aramaic is Gabbatha)" (19:13)[37]
- "the place of the Skull (which in Aramaic is called Golgotha)" (19:17)
- [Mary] "cried out in Aramaic, 'Rabboni!' (which means 'Teacher')" (20:16)

7.1.2.2 Explanations of Palestinian Topography

- "Now there is in Jerusalem near the Sheep Gate a pool, which in Aramaic is called Bethesda" (5:2)
- "the Sea of Galilee (that is, the Sea of Tiberias)" (6:1)
- "Bethany was less than two miles from Jerusalem" (11:18)

7.1.2.3 Explanations of Jewish Customs

- "six stone water jars, the kind used by the Jews for ceremonial washing" (2:6)
- "(For Jews do not associate with Samaritans.)" (4:9)

---

35. Cf. the self-references in John 1:14; 13:23; 18:15–16; 19:35; 20:2–9; 21:7, 20–25, which are discussed under the rubric "The Narrator and the Implied Author" in Culpepper, *Anatomy*, 43–49.

36. Bauckham, "Historiographical Characteristics," 29, notes that "asides," used for the same kinds of purposes, were also common in Greco-Roman historiography and biography (citing Sheeley, *Narrative Asides*, chap. 2), which aligns John's gospel even more closely with Greco-Roman historiography than the Synoptics (see the discussion of the genre of John's gospel in chap. 2, sect. 5 above).

37. This is actually not a translation but a different name for the same place; literally, "Gabbatha" means something like "the hill of the house."

- "Then came the Festival of Dedication at Jerusalem. It was winter" (10:22)
- "to avoid ceremonial uncleanness they did not enter the palace, because they wanted to be able to eat the Passover" (18:28)
- "This was in accordance with Jewish burial customs" (19:40)

7.1.2.4 References to Jesus' Supernatural Insight or Foreknowledge of Events or to God's Providential Ordering of Events

- "But Jesus would not entrust himself to them, for he knew all people. He did not need human testimony about them, for he knew what was in them" (2:24–25)
- "For Jesus had known from the beginning which of them did not believe and who would betray him" (6:64; cf. 6:71; 12:4)
- "At this they tried to seize him, but no one laid a hand on him, because his hour had not yet come" (7:30; cf. 2:4)
- "Yet no one seized him, because his hour had not yet come" (8:20; cf. 2:4; 7:30)
- "Jesus knew that the hour had come for him to leave this world and go to the Father.... Jesus knew that the Father had put all things under his power, and that he had come from God and was returning to God" (13:1, 3)
- "For he knew who was going to betray him, and that was why he said not every one was clean" (13:11; this could also be placed in category 8, below)
- "Jesus saw that they wanted to ask him about this" (16:19)
- "Jesus, knowing all that was going to happen to him" (18:4)
- "Later, knowing that everything had now been finished" (19:28)

7.1.2.5 References to Characters or Events Mentioned Earlier in the Narrative

- "Once more he visited Cana in Galilee, where he had turned the water into wine" (4:46; cf. 2:1–11)
- "Then some boats from Tiberias landed near the place where the people had eaten the bread after the Lord had given thanks" (6:23; cf. 6:1–15)
- "Nicodemus, who had gone to Jesus earlier and who was one of their own number" (7:50; cf. 3:1–2)
- "the man who had been blind" (9:13, 18, 24; cf. 9:1–7)
- "Then Jesus went back across the Jordan to the place where John had been baptizing in the early days" (10:40; cf. 1:28)
- "Lazarus ... whom Jesus had raised from the dead" (12:1–2, 9, 17; cf. 11:1–44)
- "Caiaphas was the one who had advised the Jewish leaders that it would be good if one man died for the people" (18:14; cf. 11:49–51)
- "One of the high priest's servants, a relative of the man whose ear Peter had cut off" (18:26; cf. 18:10)

- "He was accompanied by Nicodemus, the man who earlier had visited Jesus at night" (19:39; cf. 3:1–2)
- "Finally the other disciple, who had reached the tomb first" (20:8; cf. 20:4)
- "(This was the one who had leaned back against Jesus at the supper and had said, 'Lord, who is going to betray you?')" (21:20; cf. 13:23–25)

7.1.2.6 References to the Fulfillment of Scripture or of Jesus' Words

- "His disciples remembered that it is written: 'Zeal for your house will consume me'" (2:17)
- "This happened so that the words he had spoken would be fulfilled: 'I have not lost one of those you gave me'" (18:9; cf. 6:29; 10:28; 17:12)
- "This took place to fulfill what Jesus had said about the kind of death he was going to die" (18:32; cf. 3:14; 8:28; 12:33)
- "This happened that the scripture might be fulfilled that said, 'They divided my clothes among them and cast lots for my garment.' So this is what the soldiers did" (19:24)
- "Later ... so that Scripture would be fulfilled, Jesus said, 'I am thirsty'" (19:28)
- "These things happened so that the scripture would be fulfilled: 'Not one of his bones will be broken,' and, as another scripture says, 'They will look on the one they have pierced'" (19:36–37)

7.1.2.7 References to a Failure to Understand

- "He did not realize where it had come from, though the servants who had drawn the water knew" (2:9)
- "The man who was healed had no idea who it was, for Jesus had slipped away into the crowd that was there" (5:13)
- "For even his own brothers did not believe in him" (7:5)
- "They did not understand that he was telling them about his Father" (8:27)
- "Jesus used this figure of speech, but the Pharisees did not understand what he was telling them" (10:6)
- "Jesus had been speaking of his death, but his disciples thought he meant natural sleep" (11:13)
- "At first his disciples did not understand all this. Only after Jesus was glorified did they realize that these things had been written about him and that these things had been done to him" (12:16)
- "But no one at the meal understood why Jesus said this to him. Since Judas had charge of the money, some thought Jesus was telling him to buy what was needed for the Festival, or to give something to the poor" (13:28–29)
- "(They still did not understand from Scripture that Jesus had to rise from the dead.)" (20:9)
- "but she did not realize that it was Jesus" (20:14)
- "but the disciples did not realize that it was Jesus" (21:4)

7.1.2.8 Clarifications of the Meaning of Statements Made by Jesus or Others

- "But the temple he had spoken of was his body. After he was raised from the dead, his disciples recalled what he had said. Then they believed the scripture and the words that Jesus had spoken" (2:21–22)
- "For this reason they tried all the more to kill him; not only was he breaking the Sabbath, but he was even calling God his own Father, making himself equal with God" (5:18)
- "He asked this only to test him, for he already had in mind what he was going to do" (6:6)
- "(He meant Judas, the son of Simon Iscariot, who, though one of the Twelve, was later to betray him.)" (6:71)
- "By this he meant the Spirit, whom those who believed in him were later to receive. Up to that time the Spirit had not been given, since Jesus had not yet been glorified" (7:39)
- "His parents said this because they were afraid of the Jewish leaders, who already had decided that anyone who acknowledged that Jesus was the Messiah would be put out of the synagogue. That was why his parents said, 'He is of age; ask him'" (9:22–23)
- "Now Jesus loved Martha and her sister and Lazarus. So when he heard that Lazarus was sick, he stayed where he was two more days" (11:5–6)
- "He did not say this on his own, but as high priest that year he prophesied that Jesus would die for the Jewish nation, and not only for that nation but also for the scattered children of God, to bring them together and make them one" (11:51–52)
- "He [Judas] did not say this because he cared about the poor but because he was a thief; as keeper of the money bag, he used to help himself to what was put into it" (12:6)
- "He said this to show the kind of death he was going to die" (12:33)
- "Isaiah said this because he saw Jesus' glory and spoke about him" (12:41)
- "But because of the Pharisees they would not openly acknowledge their faith for fear they would be put out of the synagogue" (12:42)
- "Jesus said this to indicate the kind of death by which Peter would glorify God" (21:19)
- "Because of this, the rumor spread among the believers that this disciple would not die. But Jesus did not say that he would not die; he only said, 'If I want him to remain alive until I return, what is that to you?'" (21:23)

7.1.2.9 Statements in Relation to the Gospel Tradition

- "Andrew, Simon Peter's brother" (1:40; cf. 1:41)
- "(This was before John was put in prison.)" (3:24)

- "(Now Jesus himself had pointed out that prophets have no honor in their own country.)" (4:44)
- "Bethany, the village of Mary and her sister Martha. (This Mary ... was the same one who poured perfume on the Lord and wiped his feet with her hair.)" (11:1–2)

7.1.2.10 Numbering of Events in the Narrative

- "This was the second sign Jesus performed after coming from Judea to Galilee" (4:54; cf. 2:11)
- "This was now the third time Jesus appeared to his disciples after he was raised from the dead" (21:14; cf. 20:19, 26)

7.1.2.11 Extended Commentary

- "For God so loved the world that he gave his one and only Son, that whoever believes in him shall not perish but have eternal life...." (3:16–21)
- "The one who comes from above is above all; the one who is from the earth belongs to the earth, and speaks as one from the earth...." (3:31–36)

7.1.2.12 Other Clarifying or Explanatory Statements

- "although in fact it was not Jesus who baptized, but his disciples" (4:2; cf. 3:22)
- "(His disciples had gone into the town to buy food.)" (4:8)
- "For they loved human glory more than the glory of God" (12:43)
- "Judas (not Judas Iscariot)" (14:22)
- "(The servant's name was Malchus.)" (18:10)

7.1.3 Summary and Conclusion

As the above list of various categories of "asides" in John's gospel amply demonstrates, the Johannine parentheses display a considerable amount of variety. What they have in common is their function of aiding the reader in following the gospel narrative. This is done by the narrator supplying various bits and pieces of relevant information, whether in terms of translation, topographical information, and so on. On a more significant level, the narrator allows the reader to enter into Jesus' inner state of mind, providing him or her with an inside perspective of the central character of the gospel as Jesus pursues his messianic mission.

The plethora of Johannine "asides" thus fulfill an important narratological function in facilitating an informed reading of the gospel and preventing the reader from being sidelined because of missing data required for a successful decoding of the narrative. This does not remove the need for a spiritual, faith-enabled apprehension of John's message, but it greatly enhances the possibility that such can actually take place. In addition, on a literary level, several of the Johannine asides (including several back-references) enhance the cohesiveness of the narrative and constitute it as a closely interwoven textual fabric.[38]

7.2 Misunderstandings

7.2.1 Introduction

John is united with the Synoptic writers in featuring a series of "misunderstandings" on the part of those who come into contact with Jesus during the course of his earthly ministry.[39] This is paralleled by the Markan motif of "discipleship failure" (also found, albeit to a somewhat lesser extent, in Matthew and Luke). In John's case, however, the "misunderstandings" encompass a wide array of people and are frequently coupled with another distinctive Johannine literary device, that of irony.[40] R. Alan Culpepper observes that previous efforts to determine the presence of Johannine misunderstandings strictly on the basis of content or form failed to grasp the suppleness of this category in Johannine usage.[41] He correctly identifies the major issue in understanding misunderstandings as pertaining to their function and their effect on the reader.[42] The ensuing discussion will proceed from an investigation of the dynamic underlying misunderstandings to a definition and list of Johannine misunderstandings and a summary and conclusion.

7.2.2 The Dynamic Underlying Misunderstandings

The dynamic involving misunderstanding can be described as follows.[43] (1) A pronouncement is made, usually by Jesus, that involves the use of metaphor, ambiguity, or double entendre.

(2) The recipient of the statement responds in a manner that indicates that he or she has not properly understood the utterance's intended meaning. This may be indicated by a question or a protest that demonstrates that misunderstanding has occurred. Frequently, the misunderstanding hinges on a person or group taking literally what Jesus meant figuratively, resulting in a failure to comprehend the underlying spiritual message Jesus sought to impart.

(3) Typically, this is followed by an explanation by Jesus or the narrator clarifying the meaning of Jesus' statement and exposing the misunderstanding. The misunderstandings thus serve as a device for explicating the meaning of certain words of Jesus and for developing significant Johannine themes. Like other literary devices (such as drama or suspense) or forms of teaching (such as parables or illustrations),

---

38. A case in point is the fact, observed by Culpepper, *Anatomy*, 40, that the fourth evangelist introduces several significant terms related to Jesus' death in the "asides" that are subsequently taken up again in the Farewell Discourse, such as "the hour" (7:30; 8:20; 13:1; cf. 16:2, 32; 17:1); "glorify" (12:16; cf. 13:31–32; 14:13; 15:8; 16:14; 17:1, 4–5, 10); "Spirit" or "spirit" (7:39; cf. 11:33; 13:21; 14:17, 26; 15:26; 16:13); and "put out of the synagogue" (9:22; 12:42; cf. 16:2).

39. For a detailed discussion of Johannine misunderstandings, see D. A. Carson, "Understanding Misunderstandings in the Fourth Gospel," *TynBul* 33 (1982): 59–91. See also Culpepper, *Anatomy*,

152–65; Herbert Leroy, *Rätsel und Missverständnis: Ein Beitrag zur Formgeschichte des Johannesevangeliums* (BBB 30; Bonn: Peter Hanstein, 1968; but see the critique by Carson, ibid., and the critique of Carson's critique of Leroy in Culpepper, ibid., 154, n. 11).

40. See sec. 7.4 below.

41. Culpepper, *Anatomy*, 152–54, with reference to the work of Bultmann, *Gospel of John*, passim (content); and Leroy, *Rätsel und Missverständnis* (form).

42. Ibid., 155.

43. Ibid., 152.

misunderstandings allow the evangelist to highlight important teachings of Jesus, especially with regard to his otherworldly provenance and destiny.

The scope of these misunderstandings encompasses "the Jews" as well as the members of Jesus' inner circle. Importantly, it is only Jesus' crucifixion and resurrection followed by the giving of the Spirit that remove the veil preventing spiritual understanding (cf. esp. 2:22: "after he was raised from the dead"; 12:16: "only after Jesus was glorified"). As Culpepper aptly notes, not only are the misunderstandings illumined from the narrator's temporal point of view—that is, his location subsequent to the Son's "glorification" and the giving of the Spirit—they are inextricably linked to the concept of revelation.[44] Regularly, those who reject Jesus are apt to misunderstand the significance of his words or actions (including the "signs").

As such, the misunderstandings thus have an effect comparable to the Synoptic parables, serving as their Johannine functional substitute. In relation to theodicy, they confirm Jesus' opponents in their spiritual obduracy while allowing those who are open to be engaged by Jesus' words to clarify their meaning and moving them from a material to a spiritual plane (see, e.g., the dynamic unleashed in John 6:25–71; cf. Matt 13:1–23 pars.). The misunderstandings also sustain a relationship with the Johannine "signs," the difference being that while the latter are significant actions of Jesus (see the discussion in chap. 7, sec. 15 below), the former more frequently relate to Jesus' verbal utterances.[45]

Hermeneutically, it is important to note that there is a marked difference between later generations of believers and Jesus' first followers. For the NT makes clear that subsequent to the pouring out of the Spirit at Pentecost (Acts 2)—the so-called "mini-Pentecosts" in Acts 8; 10; and 19 being no real exceptions—believers receive the Spirit upon trusting in Christ (e.g., Rom 8:9; 1 Cor 12:13). Unlike the original Eleven plus Matthias and the larger circle of believers prior to Pentecost, there is no need to "wait for the gift [of the Holy Spirit" (Acts 1:4; cf. 1:8). There is therefore no direct parallel between the experience of later believers and the misunderstandings of Jesus' original followers. For living prior to Pentecost, the latter did not have the Spirit—but believers subsequent to Pentecost do.

For this reason the misunderstandings featured in John's gospel (and the Synoptics) belong inextricably to the period of Jesus' earthly ministry prior to his "glorification." The fact that John notes these misunderstandings—which hinge so palpably on the disciples' historical location prior to the crucifixion—shows that the fourth evangelist is indeed concerned not to blur the lines between the so-called "historical Jesus" and the early church's later belief in what has been called "the Christ of faith."[46] While John displays a keen interest in the implications of Jesus' earthly ministry for later believers—a concern he shares with Paul and the other NT writers—he is careful to maintain the historical boundaries between pre- and post-glorification

---

44. Ibid., 154.

45. Though not always: see, for example, the temple clearing, where misunderstanding attaches to Jesus' action of clearing the temple (2:18; though the misunderstanding is further compounded by Jesus' explication of the significance of the event; cf. 2:19–22).

46. To show this is the major burden of Carson's article "Understanding Misunderstandings."

disciples, and the device of "misunderstandings," similar to that of "signs," provides him with a suitable vehicle to maintain this distinction while drawing his readers into a deeper apprehension of various aspects of Jesus' messianic mission.

In terms of their effect on the reader, the misunderstandings keep readers' interest by presenting them with riddles they must solve in order to progress to a fuller spiritual understanding of various aspects of Jesus' mission. The misunderstandings thus serve as devices aiming to engage the reader and to convey spiritual truth, especially with regard to Jesus' death and resurrection. Similar in effect to parables, as mentioned, misunderstandings draw a line between "insiders," who understand a given spiritual truth, once explicated, and "outsiders," who do not. The transparent nature of many of the misunderstandings, such as Nicodemus's failure to grasp that Jesus spoke about spiritual rather than literal rebirth (John 3:4), further serves to draw the reader into the sphere of "insiders" by virtue of his or her superior spiritual knowledge.[47]

Understood in this manner, misunderstandings include a certain amount of hyperbole, exaggerating the degree of misunderstanding and thus accentuating it even more keenly, as well as a dimension of irony, highlighting the at times almost comical nature of a given person's incomprehension (again, Nicodemus's misunderstanding serves as a fitting example; or see 8:21–22). The misunderstandings also help the reader appreciate the spiritual nature of Jesus' words and his mission, consistently maintaining a distinction between the material and the spiritual, the earthly and the heavenly, the literal and the metaphorical. In this they are suitable for sharpening readers' perception of spiritual truth, helping them to identify the significance of Jesus' words and serving as a fitting vehicle for conveying the Johannine worldview.[48]

7.2.3 Definition and List of Johannine Misunderstandings

As mentioned, there is no consensus among commentators regarding the exact identity and number of misunderstandings in John's gospel. The reason for this lack of agreement lies in the divergent criteria used in a given scholar's method of isolating these misunderstandings, whether content, form, or some other criteria or combination thereof. In essence, I concur with Culpepper that the device of "misunderstanding" in the hands of the fourth evangelist is a rather supple vehicle for aiding the reader's comprehension that ought not to be unduly confined to any one category of statement.[49]

For purposes of identifying and providing a reasonably comprehensive list of Johannine misunderstandings, I therefore offer the following definition: "A Johannine misunderstanding is a statement, normally involving ambiguity, metaphor, or double entendre, whose intended meaning is not properly identified by the original audience of the statement, which typically leads to a subsequent explication of its proper meaning by the person making the statement (most frequently Jesus) or the

---

47. Culpepper (ibid., 164) calls this a "judgmental distance."
48. See the discussion in chap. 6, sec. 12 below.
49. Culpepper, *Anatomy*, 153–54.

narrator." On the basis of this definition, a list of Johannine misunderstandings (in narrative sequence) presents itself as follows:[50]

- The Jews believe Jesus will rebuild the temple in three literal days (2:20).
- Nicodemus thinks Jesus is talking about a literal second birth (3:4, 9).
- The Samaritan woman misconstrues Jesus' reference to "living water" (4:10–15).
- The disciples fail to grasp Jesus' mention of his "food" (4:31–34).
- The Jews are intransigent to the atonement Jesus will provide and are nonplussed as to Jesus being the "bread from heaven" and as to his being the one who gives them his "flesh" to eat (6:32–35, 52).
- People regularly display fundamental ignorance with regard to Jesus' otherworldly origin and destiny (6:42; 7:27, 33–36; 8:21–22, 27).
- People are confused concerning Jesus' Bethlehem birth (7:41–42; cf. 1:45–46; 7:52).
- The Jews take Jesus' statement regarding Abraham as pertaining to literal descent while Jesus is referring to spiritual offspring (8:31–39).
- The Jews fail to understand Jesus' statements that those who obey him will never experience death and that Abraham "saw his day" (8:51–53, 56–58).
- The Pharisees are ironically intransigent to Jesus' pronouncement regarding their own spiritual blindness (9:40–41).
- The Pharisees do not grasp the proper meaning of Jesus' parable of the shepherd and the sheep (10:6).
- The disciples misconstrue Jesus' reference to Lazarus having "fallen asleep," taking Jesus' statement literally, while Jesus had used "sleep" as a euphemism for death (11:11–13).
- Martha thinks Jesus is speaking of Lazarus's resurrection on the last day when Jesus has indicated that he intends to raise Lazarus right now (11:24).
- The crowd may hail Jesus as national deliverer, misunderstanding the true nature of Jesus' kingship (12:13).
- Only after Jesus' glorification do the disciples understand the significance of the events surrounding his triumphal entry (12:16).
- The crowd fails to understand Jesus' reference to his "lifting up" (12:32–34).
- Peter fails to understand the significance of the footwashing (13:6–11).
- The disciples in the Upper Room fail to understand the significance of Judas's leaving the meal (13:28–29).
- Peter misunderstands Jesus' point about his inability to follow him at that time (13:36–38).
- Thomas and then Philip misunderstand Jesus' reference to his being "the way" and having showed them the Father (14:5, 8).

---

50. This list is more complete than Culpepper, *Anatomy*, 161–62, who offers eighteen "misunderstandings" (see his discussion of these on pp. 155–61).

- The disciples miss Jesus' point about the "little while" (16:17–18).
- Peter, by cutting off Malchus's right ear, shows that he still fails to understand Jesus' need to "drink the cup" the Father has given him (18:11).
- Even at the empty tomb the disciples fail to understand from Scripture that Jesus must rise from the dead (20:9).
- Mary Magdalene does not realize that the man she sees is the risen Jesus, mistaking him for the gardener (20:14–15).
- The seven disciples who went fishing likewise do not realize that the one they see is their risen Lord (21:4).

7.2.4 Summary and Conclusion

As the preceding list shows, misunderstandings are virtually ubiquitous, pervading the entire gospel. As Culpepper notes, perhaps the densest distribution of misunderstandings is found in the context of Jesus' controversy with the Jews in chapters 7–8,[51] but the entire Festival Cycle (chaps. 5–10) is replete with the Jews' incomprehension of Jesus' true identity. Since they are bent on rejecting Jesus' messianic claim and thus fundamentally misconstrue the nature of his mission, it follows that they are regularly the victims of misunderstanding. As such, they regularly fail to comprehend Jesus' otherworldly provenance and destiny (6:42; 7:27, 33–36; 8:21–22, 27).

Misunderstanding is present among both of Jesus' major dialogue partners in the "Cana Cycle," Nicodemus and the Samaritan woman (3:4, 9; 4:10–15). Jesus' followers, too, are frequently prone to misunderstanding. They do not know Jesus' "food" (4:31–34), think Jesus is referring to Lazarus literally falling asleep (11:11–13), fail to understand the significance of the footwashing (13:6–11) and of Jesus' words to Judas (13:28–29), and are intransigent in the face of Jesus' imminent departure (13:36–38; 14:5, 8; 16:16–19; 18:11). Even subsequent to the resurrection, they still fail to understand (20:9, 14–15; 21:4). The most common type of misunderstanding pertains to Jesus' death and resurrection (his "glorification").[52]

7.3 Alleged "Seams" (Aporias)

7.3.1 Introduction

Ever since the famous series of articles entitled "Aporien im vierten Evangelium" by Eduard Schwartz in 1907 and 1908, if not before, there has been intense discussion of alleged "literary seams" in John's gospel that, so it is argued, reflect traces of successive stages of redaction of the Johannine material.[53] This redaction may, of course, have been performed by John on his own material in order to streamline it. Alternatively, it could have been undertaken by others after the apostle's death.

---

51. Culpepper, *Anatomy*, 162. Culpepper's entire discussion on pp. 162–65 repays careful reading.
52. See John 2:19–22; 6:51–53; 7:33–36; 8:21–22; 12:32–34; 13:36–38; 14:4–6; 16:16–19.

53. Eduard Schwartz, "Aporien im 4. Evangelium I," in *Nachrichten von der Königlichen Gesellschaft der Wissenschaften zu Göttingen* (Berlin: Weidmannsche Buchhandlung, 1907), 342–72; idem, "Aporien im 4. Evangelium II," "Aporien im 4. Evangelium III," and

What immediately raises cautions against any such proposals, however, is the fact that John's narrative is remarkably uniform, as several detailed studies performed by Eugen Ruckstuhl and his associates have shown.[54] This means that any later redactor must have performed his work rather clumsily, so that interpreters today are able to identify "seams" the redactor (unsuccessfully, it appears) attempted to patch up. Of course, to call these alleged incongruities in style "seams" is already to beg the question. It will therefore be helpful to take a brief look at some of the passages that are most commonly adduced to see whether or not they in fact reveal Johannine "seams."

7.3.2 Investigation of Alleged "Seams" in John's Gospel
7.3.2.1 Introduction

The following investigation of alleged "seams" in John's gospel will cover (1) the reference to Jesus going into the "Judean countryside" in 3:22, which allegedly overlooks the fact that Jesus had been in Judea all along; (2) the reference to a "second sign" in 4:54, apparently ignoring intervening signs in Judea (2:23; 3:2); (3) the disputed sequence in chapters 5 and 6, which has been the subject of various rearrangement theories; (4) the pericope of the adulterous woman in 7:53–8:11, which appears to break up the flow of the gospel; (5) the mention of Jesus' anointing by Mary of Bethany in 11:2 prior to the actual account of the anointing in the following chapter; (6) the "mother" of all alleged Johannine *aporias*, Jesus' statement in 14:31, "Come now; let us leave," which seems oblivious of the fact that Jesus and his followers are not explicitly said to go anywhere until 18:1; (7) Jesus' statement in 16:5, "None of you asks me, 'Where are you going?'" when Peter in 13:36, and Thomas in 14:5, had twice asked this question; and (8) the "ending" in 20:30–31, which is followed by another chapter in the gospel.

These apparent incongruities have provided ample opportunity for historical and literary critics to suggest a variety of theories in order to account for the perceived unevenness in the Johannine text at these junctures. The question arises, then: Do these "seams" betray a multiplicity of underlying sources, or are there other explanations for these apparent incongruities?

7.3.2.2 "Jesus ... Came into the Land of Judea" (3:22)

In 3:22 the text appears to be saying that Jesus "came into the land (*gēs*) of Judea" (NASB, NKJV). The apparent difficulty is that Jesus has been in Judea all along since attending a Passover festival from 2:23 to 3:21. Did it simply slip the author's (or redactor's) mind that Jesus had been in Judea in the narrative portion preceding the reference in 3:22? Apart from the unlikelihood of such a major blunder, it turns

---

"Aporien im 4. Evangelium IV," in *Nachrichten von der Königlichen Gesellschaft der Wissenschaften zu Göttingen* (Berlin: Weidmannsche Buchhandlung, 1908), 115–48, 149–88, and 497–560. See also Gary M. Burge, "The Literary Seams in the Fourth Gospel," *Covenant Quarterly* 48 (1990): 15–25; idem, chap. 3 in *Interpreting the Gospel of John*.

54. See esp. Ruckstuhl and Dschulnigg, *Stilkritik und Verfasserfrage*. See also Kellum, *Unity of the Farewell Discourse*.

out that the solution lies close at hand. It is found in an alternate meaning of *gēs*, the word translated "land." In fact, this expression can, and here most likely does, also mean "countryside." If this is correct, John would simply indicate that Jesus had now left Jerusalem and came "into the Judean countryside," as the TNIV, as already the NIV, appropriately renders this phrase (see also the ESV).

7.3.2.3 Jesus' "Second Sign" (4:54)

John 4:54 refers to a "second sign Jesus performed." But if Jesus' turning water into wine at the Cana wedding, featured in 2:1–11, was the first such sign, then what about the Jerusalem signs mentioned in 2:23 and 3:2? Again, the apparent incongruence disappears when it is realized that the phrase "second sign" is further qualified in 4:54 by the addendum "after coming from Judea to Galilee." In other words, the fourth evangelist, by way of literary *inclusio*, links the two signs performed by Jesus in Cana of Galilee in order to constitute chapters 2–4 of his gospel as a literary unit, the "Cana Cycle," with Jesus' ministry circuit beginning and ending in Cana (cf. 2:11; 4:46: "Once more he visited Cana in Galilee").

7.3.2.4 The Sequence of Chapters 5 and 6

In the present order, Jesus travels to Galilee via Samaria in John 4, is found in Jerusalem in chapter 5, and then is said at the beginning of chapter 6 to have "crossed to the far shore of the Sea of Galilee." Now it seems rather abrupt to say Jesus crossed over the Sea of Galilee when at the last occasion he was said to be in Jerusalem. Some, such as Rudolf Bultmann, have suggested that chapters 5 and 6 should be reversed in order to realign John's account.[55] In this case, it is argued, Jesus' works in Galilee are neatly combined in chapters 4 (i.e., vv. 43–54) and 6, while Jesus' feats in Judea follow in chapters 5 and 7–11.

However, there is no evidence that John's gospel ever circulated this way. What is more, there is no need to postulate that John recorded everything that took place between accounts he selected for inclusion in his gospel. Thus it may appear abrupt for Jesus to be in Jerusalem in chapter 5 and then cross the Sea of Galilee at the beginning of chapter 6, but this does not necessarily constitute evidence for an actual "seam," as is sometimes alleged. More likely, this is one of the instances in John's gospel where movement is merely implied rather than being specifically narrated.[56]

7.3.2.5 The Pericope of the Adulterous Woman (7:53–8:11)

Clearly, the pericope of the adulterous woman (7:53–8:11) interrupts the flow of the Johannine narrative. This is seen when the account is excised and 7:52 is followed

---

55. Bultmann, *Gospel of John*, 209–10.

56. See Köstenberger, *John*, 446, n. 104, with reference to Thielman, "Style of the Fourth Gospel," 180, who cites the transition from 5:47 to 6:1 as a possible instance of a "purposeful attempt at obscurity" common in ancient writers; and Kellum, *Unity of the Farewell Discourse*, 223–30, who suggests that statements implying movement in John's gospel are a function of John's economy of speech and regularly serve as ways to move along the narrative. According to Kellum, "the text implies a quick trip to Jerusalem (as the feast at 5.1 would require) and their return" (p. 225). Kellum gives numerous additional examples of implied movement in this gospel (pp. 223–29).

immediately by 8:12. Here the simple answer is that this pericope represents a floating narrative in search of a gospel home, whether Luke or John, but which was almost certainly not part of John's original gospel. This is suggested, among other things, by the presence of fourteen words not found elsewhere in the gospel; the conspicuous absence of standard Johannine vocabulary; the absence of this pericope from all pre-fifth-century AD manuscripts; its appearance in no fewer than five different places in the manuscript tradition; the lack of citation in early patristic writings up to the fourth century AD; and evidence that the pericope may have passed from its original place in the gospel according to the Hebrews to John's gospel.[57] Thus the *pericope adulterae* does not constitute a Johannine "seam" at all but was in all probability not part of the gospel John wrote.

7.3.2.6 The Reference to the Anointing of Jesus by Mary of Bethany in 11:2

In 11:2, Mary of Bethany is introduced as the woman who "poured perfume on the Lord and wiped his feet with her hair." The apparent difficulty is that this account is not found in John's gospel until the following chapter (12:1–8; see esp. v. 3).[58] But again, this may simply be an instance where John expects his readers to be familiar with basic gospel tradition. Or had Jesus not said himself, "Truly I tell you, wherever the gospel is preached throughout the world, what she has done will also be told, in memory of her" (Mark 14:9; cf. Matt 26:13)?

In this regard the passage is no different than John's introduction of Andrew as "Simon Peter's brother" in John 1:40, when Peter is mentioned only in the following verses, or John's reminder that "this was before John was put in prison" (3:24) when nothing of this sort had been mentioned previously in his gospel. This is also why John may call Bethany "the village of Mary and her sister Martha" in 11:1 without further elaboration, because Luke's gospel had provided a memorable account of these two women (cf. Luke 10:38–42).[59]

7.3.2.7 "Come Now; Let Us Leave" (14:31)

In John 14:30, Jesus tells his disciples that he will not talk to them much longer. Then he says in the following verse, "Come now; let us leave." Strikingly, however, three more chapters of material ensue (15–17). Should 14:31 perhaps be followed immediately by 18:1, where it is said that "Jesus left with his disciples and crossed the Kidron Valley"? Again, the incongruence may be merely apparent, for the plausible suggestion has been made that Jesus and his followers did indeed leave the Upper Room subsequent to 14:31 and that vineyards provided a suitable backdrop for Jesus' continued discourse in chapter 15 as he and his disciples went on their way.

---

57. See Köstenberger, *John*, 245–49.

58. See the discussion in Herman N. Ridderbos, *The Gospel of John: A Theological Commentary* (trans. John Vriend; Grand Rapids: Eerdmans, 1997), 386–87.

59. Note also Carson's observation that even if the anointing was unknown to the reader, the proleptic reference to Mary still serves as a fine literary device, urging the first-time reader onward in the narrative (*Gospel according to John*, 405).

Alternatively, Jesus may have told his disciples that it was time to leave and then added some further instruction before finally getting underway.[60] What is more, as mentioned above, Scott Kellum has shown that John characteristically implies movement rather than explicitly narrating it, which provides a plausible literary rationale for the coherence of 14:31 and the following chapters, making source-critical explanations unnecessary and underscoring the literary integrity of John's narrative as it stands.[61]

7.3.2.8 "None of You Asks Me, 'Where Are You Going?'" (16:5)

On the face of it, Jesus' statement in 16:5 seems to be in conflict with Peter's question in 13:36 and Thomas's similar query in 14:5. Some have therefore sought to place 16:5 prior to 13:36 and 14:5 in the sequence of events. But we need not approach the text so mechanically. The solution may be that Jesus chided his followers for not *really* being interested in where he was going. In other words, they were too absorbed in self-pity and their own personal situation.

Also, in John 13:36 and 14:5 the illocutionary force of the question appears to be a protest of Jesus' announced departure rather than a sincere inquiry as to his destination or the implications of his leaving.[62] If so, this would cohere perfectly with the thrust of 16:5, where Jesus is represented as expressing grief that the Eleven do not show greater interest in the salvation-historical implications of his departure (cf. 16:17).[63]

7.3.2.9 The "Ending" of 20:30–31

John 20:30–31 reads like the conclusion of the gospel. If so, then why is an additional chapter appended, with "another" ending added in 21:24–25? Again, this suggests the presence of a literary "seam" to some who argue that the fourth evangelist concluded his gospel at 20:31 while a later redactor added the final chapter.[64] This may be so, but a close look suggests that John 20 and 21 cohere quite closely. For example, the numbering system employed in 21:14 ("This was now the third time Jesus appeared to his disciples") presupposes the two previous resurrection appearances recounted in chapter 20 (vv. 19–23, 24–29).

Also, John 21 provides the climax of Peter's relationship with "the disciple whom Jesus loved," which is developed in the gospel from chapter 13 on, intensifying in chapters 18–20.[65] What is more, there is no manuscript evidence that the gospel ever circulated without chapter 21.[66] For these and other reasons it is therefore unnecessary to suppose that the transition from 20:30–31 to 21:1 constitutes a literary "seam." More likely, chapter 21, as an epilogue, corresponds structurally

---

60. See Köstenberger, *John*, 445–46.
61. See the discussion in 7.3.2.4 above. See also chap. 4 in Kellum, *Unity of the Farewell Discourse*; cf. Köstenberger, *John*, 446, n. 104.
62. See Carson, *Gospel according to John*, 470. See also the discussion and additional references in Köstenberger, *John*, 470, n. 35.
63. See Ridderbos, *Gospel of John*, 530.
64. E.g., Colin Roberts, "John 20:30–31 and 21:24–25," *JTS* 38 (1987): 409–10.
65. See John 13:23–24; 18:15–16; 20:2–9; 21:2–7, 15–23.
66. For additional reasons, see Carson, *Gospel according to John*, 667; Köstenberger, *John*, 583–86.

to John's introduction in 1:1–18 and was written by the same author as the rest of the gospel.[67]

7.3.3 Summary and Conclusion

This brief panoramic tour of some of the major alleged literary "seams" in John's gospel has yielded the result that in each instance plausible—even probable—explanations can be given in favor of the coherence of the text as it stands.[68] The solution may be text-critical (as in the case of the pericope of the adulterous woman); it may hinge on an alternative meaning of a given word (as in the instance of the term *gēs* in 3:22); or there may be other reasons why the Johannine narrative flows a certain way. At the end of the day, it is doubtful if there is even a single instance where the interpreter is driven to the conclusion that the text of John's gospel as it stands reflects a genuine literary seam, indicating incongruence in the way the Johannine narrative is told.

7.4 Irony

7.4.1 Introduction

It has been said, with appropriate hyperbole, that "in the Fourth Gospel theology *is* irony."[69] Indeed, irony is part of the warp and woof of the outlook underlying the *entire gospel*.[70] The Word became flesh (1:14); the world failed to receive the one who made it (1:10–11);[71] even God's chosen people rejected the Messiah God sent (1:11); consequently, Jesus was "lifted up" on the cross (3:14; 8:28; 12:32): his execution by the world constituted at the same time his exaltation by God, all in keeping with God's sovereign purposes (theodicy). Each of these integral planks in the Johannine narrative are saturated with deep irony.[72] As such, Johannine irony undercuts human pretense and misunderstanding and serves to expose the truth about Jesus the Messiah and Son of God, providing a compelling vehicle for leading the readers of John's gospel to faith in the Lord Jesus Christ for eternal life.

7.4.2 The Dynamic Underlying Johannine Irony

In his important work on Johannine irony, Paul Duke identifies the roots of irony in the figure of the shrewd trickster.[73] At times, irony may merely involve the clever

---

67. See the extensive discussion and additional bibliographic references in Köstenberger, *John*, 583–86. See also Köstenberger, "I Suppose," who argues that the first-person singular reference *oimai* ("I suppose") in 21:25 indicates, by way of authorial modesty, that the author of chap. 21 is the author of the entire gospel.

68. Contra, Mark Stibbe, "Magnificent but Flawed: The Breaking of Form in the Fourth Gospel," in *Anatomies of Narrative Criticism*, 150–51.

69. McRae, "Theology and Irony in the Fourth Gospel," 89.

70. See the discussion of the Johannine worldview in chap. 6, sec. 12 below. See also Duke, *Irony*, 111–15.

71. What is only implicit in Luke's statement that at Jesus' birth "there was no guest room available" for Jesus' parents (Luke 2:7) is presented in John's gospel explicitly as fraught with profound irony, creation rejecting its Creator.

72. See the discussion of the rejection, origin, identity, and death of Jesus and of discipleship in Culpepper, *Anatomy*, 169–80. See also the discussion of the cosmic trial motif in John's gospel, which involves an ironic reversal of the world's legal perspective regarding Jesus, in chap. 11 below.

73. Duke, *Irony*, 8. On irony in John's gospel, see also Culpepper, *Anatomy*, 165–80; Wead, *Literary Devices*, 47–68; George W. McRae, "Theology and Irony in the Fourth Gospel," in *The Word and the World: Essays in Honor of Frederick L. Moriarty* (ed. Richard J. Clifford and George W. McRae; Cambridge, MA: Weston College Press, 1973), 83–96; and H. Clavier, "L'ironie dans le

turn of a phrase. In other instances, it may entail a reversal of expectations. In this case, irony is close to misunderstanding. In fact, at times the categories overlap. Dramatic irony was used regularly by Greek playwrights long before John wrote his gospel. D. C. Muecke observed that irony typically (1) operates on two layers or stories; (2) posits some kind of opposition between the two levels; and (3) encompasses an element of "innocence" or lack of awareness.[74] Irony may thus be defined as the comic effect created by a character's lack of awareness of a disparity between appearance and reality.[75]

Thus irony is a "two-story" phenomenon,[76] involving two levels, "above" and "below," which are essentially incongruous or incompatible. The level "below" describes the way things appear to be on the surface. On the level "above," there is a higher, spiritual reality or significance of a given phenomenon that can be perceived only by those who possess the hermeneutical key or axiom presupposed by the author. In John's case, this key is at the heart christological, being bound up with the gospel's purpose statement in 20:30–31, which calls its readers to faith in Jesus the Messiah and Son of God. In this way the use of irony is part and parcel of the Johannine worldview or spatial dualism distinguishing between the world "above" and the world "below."[77] Jesus' challenge to his opponents applies also to the reader of John's gospel: "Stop judging by mere appearances, but instead judge correctly."[78]

In the hands of the fourth evangelist, irony invites, even entices, readers to take the leap of faith required to discern the meaning of a given utterance or action conveyed in the Johannine narrative. While "signs" are related to actions and "misunderstandings" most commonly pertain to utterances, irony is capable of being applied to both words and events.[79] The reader must first recognize the surface meaning on the level "below" as inadequate, identify alternative interpretations, and then choose a preferable meaning on the level "above" that is in keeping with the authorially intended message. This, in turn, is normally predicated upon faith in Jesus as Messiah and may interface with appropriation techniques such as typology, the use of metaphor, or other Johannine devices.[80]

Along similar lines, Wayne Booth has distinguished between *intended* and *unintended irony*.[81] Intended irony may involve the clever use of double entendre. At the same time, irony may obtain even where it is not intentionally communicated

---

quatrième evangile," in *SE* (TU 73; ed. Kurt Aland et al.; Berlin: Akademie, 1959), 261–76. Note that irony is already found in OT books such as Esther or Jonah. Another OT example of irony is 1 Sam 28:9. Regarding the figure of the trickster, see Richard D. Patterson, "The Old Testament Use of an Archetype: The Trickster," *JETS* 42 (1999): 385–94.

74. D. C. Muecke, *The Compass of Irony* (London: Methuen, 1969), 19–20.

75. Cf. ibid., 35, cited in Culpepper, *Anatomy*, 166–67. See also the statement by Haakon M. Chevalier: "The Basic Feature of Every Irony Is a Contrast between a Reality and an Appearance" (*The Ironic Temper: Anatole France and His Time* [New York/London: Oxford University Press, 1932], 42, cited by Muecke, *Compass of Irony*, 30).

76. See Culpepper, *Anatomy*, 167, with reference to the work of Muecke and Booth.

77. Culpepper, *Anatomy*, 167. See, e.g., Jesus' reference to "earthly" and "heavenly things" in John 3:12 and to the realms "below" and "above" in 8:23. See further the discussion in chap. 6, sec. 12, esp. 12.3.5, below.

78. See John 7:24. Cf. Culpepper, *Anatomy*, 167–68.

79. See further the distinction between verbal and dramatic irony below.

80. Cf. Culpepper, *Anatomy*, 167.

81. Wayne C. Booth, *A Rhetoric of Irony* (Chicago: University of Chicago Press, 1974), 5–6.

but only subsequently perceived. The important insight here is that the presence of irony does not necessarily depend on the awareness or intentionality of the person(s) involved in the original instance of irony. This opens up the possibility for a later author to exploit such instances of unintended irony, showing that a given actor or speaker uttered truth or prophesied without being aware of doing so (e.g., John 11:48–52).

In this regard, one may distinguish between *verbal* and *dramatic or situational irony*. Verbal irony involves the use of words. An example of this is sarcasm. A possible instance of sarcasm in John's gospel is Thomas's remark at the outset of the raising of Lazarus: "Let us go also, that we may die with him" (11:16).[82] As Duke explains, "While verbal irony is achieved by an intentional speaker who knows more than may be apparent, dramatic irony employs a speaker (or actant) who knows less than is apparent and whose involvement in the irony is quite unintentional."[83] While the irony was hidden from the original actor or speaker, it is quite apparent for the reader: "As its name implies, dramatic irony is preeminently the irony of theater, where spectators from good seats 'on high' view an illusory world of characters and events in which they may not interfere, but over which they exercise a kind of omniscience."[84] As Duke aptly notes, "The characters seem powerless in comparison, and the possibilities of irony-observed become endless."[85] The dynamic, therefore, is one "in which the audience shares with the author knowledge of which a character is ignorant."[86] Subcategories of dramatic irony are *irony of events* or *irony of self-betrayal*, among others.[87]

What, then, are the clues by which the reader is able to detect irony? These include: (1) straightforward explications of incongruity (e.g., 4:17–18; 11:51–52); (2) known error or misstatement of facts (e.g., 7:41–42, 52); (3) a conflict of facts presented at different junctures in the narrative (e.g., 7:48–49; 10:34; 12:19); (4) a clash of style, issuing in discrepancy, including exaggeration or understatement (e.g., 3:4); and (5) a conflict of belief between a conviction expressed by a character in the narrative and the reader's past experience or prior knowledge (e.g., 7:52).[88] In addition, irony may be indicated by a variety of "lexical intensifiers," such as "indeed," "hardly," or the like. Normally, similar to a joke told today, irony is supposed to be transparent to the reader and therefore is covert and not explicitly noted by the author.[89] Irony thus makes certain demands on the reader and involves him or her actively in discerning the irony in a given action or statement.

In terms of effects, irony may function both as a persuasive appeal and as a subtle but effective weapon.[90] It typically has a corrective function,[91] serving to unmask

---

82. This is true whether the reference is to Jesus or Lazarus (see the discussion in Köstenberger, *John*, 332). Depending on whether the presence of sarcasm is detected, commentators may interpret Thomas's statement as an instance of bravery or sarcasm (see ibid.).
83. Duke, *Irony*, 23.
84. Ibid.
85. Ibid.
86. M. H. Abrams, *A Glossary of Literary Terms* (3rd ed.; New York: Holt, Rinehart and Winston, 1971), 80.
87. Duke, *Irony*, 26–27.
88. Ibid., 32–34.
89. Culpepper, *Anatomy*, 168.
90. Duke, *Irony*, 36–41.
91. Culpepper, *Anatomy*, 168, citing Muecke, *Compass of Irony*, 23.

the fallacious beliefs, hypocritical actions, or transparent bias of a character or group of characters in the narrative and thus draw the reader to the side of the author, guiding him or her to the conclusions about the truth of a given matter intended by the narrator. Similar to misunderstandings, as mentioned, irony engages the reader and places certain demands on him or her, and a successful decoding of Johannine irony may nurture in the reader a sense of superiority of knowledge.[92] In this irony is an important literary device in an author's arsenal that can aid significantly in accomplishing his purposes.

7.4.3 Instances of Johannine Irony

As mentioned above, irony may be defined as the comic effect created by a character's lack of awareness of a disparity between appearance and reality. Following is a list of passages in John's gospel in narrative sequence that may be classified under the rubric of irony. In many instances, irony takes the form of a declaration that is punctuated as a question.[93]

- 1:10–11: "He was in the world, and though the world was made through him, the world did not recognize him. He came to that which was his own, but his own did not receive him."
- 1:46: "Nazareth! Can anything good from there?"
- 2:10: "Everyone brings out the choice wine first and then the cheaper wine after the guests have had too much to drink; but you have saved the best till now."
- 2:19: "Destroy this temple, and I will raise it again in three days."
- 3:4: "How can anyone be born when they are old?... Surely they cannot enter a second time into their mother's womb to be born!"
- 3:10: "You are Israel's teacher ... and do you not understand these things?"
- 3:13: "the Son of Man must be lifted up" (see also 8:28; 12:32, 34).[94]
- 4:7: "Will you give me a drink?"
- 4:12: "Are you greater than our father Jacob, who gave us the well...?"
- 4:17: "I have no husband," she replied. Jesus said to her, "You are right when you say you have no husband. The fact is, you have had five husbands, and the man you now have is not your husband. What you have just said is quite true."
- 4:19, 25: "Sir, I can see that you are a prophet.... I know that Messiah" (called Christ) "is coming. When he comes, he will explain everything to us."
- 5:10: "It is the Sabbath; the law forbids you to carry your mat."[95]
- 6:42: "Is this not Jesus, the son of Joseph, whose father and mother we know? How can he now say, 'I came down from heaven'?"
- 6:52: "How can this man give us his flesh to eat?"

---

92. Culpepper, *Anatomy*, 167.
93. Duke, *Irony*, 52; Culpepper, *Anatomy*, 176.
94. The "lifting up" (i.e., crucifixion as well as exaltation) of Jesus the Son of Man is one of the central ironies in John's gospel, involving double entendre and invoking Isaiah's portrayal of the suffering servant. See Köstenberger, *John*, 260, with reference to Bultmann, *John*, 350.
95. On this see the discussion in Köstenberger, *John*, 181, including the interaction on p. 181, n. 31.

- 7:3–4: "Leave Galilee and go to Judea, so that your disciples there may see the works you do. No one who wants to become a public figure acts in secret. Since you are doing these things, show yourself to the world."
- 7:15: "How did this man get such learning without having been taught?"
- 7:20: "Who is trying to kill you?"
- 7:23: "Now if a boy can be circumcised on the Sabbath so that the law of Moses may not be broken, why are you angry with me for healing a man's whole body on the Sabbath?"
- 7:26: "Have the authorities really concluded that he is the Messiah?"
- 7:27: "But we know where this man is from; when the Messiah comes, no one will know where he is from."
- 7:28: "Yes, you know me, and you know where I am from."
- 7:35–36: "The Jews said to one another, 'Where does this man intend to go that we cannot find him? Will he go where our people live scattered among the Greeks and teach the Greeks? What did he mean…?'"
- 7:41–42: "Still others asked, 'How can the Messiah come from Galilee? Does not Scripture say that the Messiah will come … from Bethlehem…?'"
- 7:48–49: "Have any of the rulers or of the Pharisees believed in him? No!" (cf. 7:50–51).
- 7:52: "Are you from Galilee, too? Look into it, and you will find that a prophet does not come out of Galilee."
- 8:22: "Will he kill himself? Is that why he says, 'Where I go, you cannot come'?"
- 8:53: "Are you greater than our father Abraham? He died, and so did the prophets. Who do you think you are?"
- 8:57: "You are not yet fifty years old … and you have seen Abraham?"
- 9:24: "Give glory to God and tell the truth.… We know this man is a sinner."[96]
- 9:27: "Why do you want to hear it again? Do you want to become his disciples too?"
- 9:29: "We know that God spoke to Moses, but as for this fellow, we don't even know where he comes from."
- 9:40: "What? Are we blind too?"
- 10:32: "I have shown you many good works from the Father. For which of these do you stone me?"
- 10:33: "We are not stoning you for any good work … but for blasphemy, because you, a mere man, claim to be God."
- 11:16: "Then Thomas … said to the rest of the disciples, 'Let us also go, that we may die with him.'"
- 11:48–50: "If we let him go on like this, everyone will believe in him, and then the Romans will come and take away both our temple and our nation."

---

96. See the discussion in ibid., 293, n. 76.

- ... "You know nothing at all! You do not realize that it is better for you that one man die for the people than that the whole nation perish."[97]
- 12:19: "See, this is getting us nowhere. Look how the whole world has gone after him!"
- 12:34: "We have heard from the Law that the Messiah will remain forever, so how can you say, 'The Son of Man must be lifted up?' Who is this 'Son of Man'?"
- 13:37–38: "Peter asked, 'Lord, why can't I follow you now? I will lay down my life for you.' ... 'Will you really lay down your life for me?'"
- 16:31: "Do you now believe?"
- 18:30: "If he were not a criminal, we would not have handed him over to you."
- 18:33, 39; 19:3, 19–22: the repeated characterization of Jesus as "the king of the Jews"
- 18:38: "What is truth?"
- 19:5: "Here is the man!"
- 19:14: "Here is your king."

7.4.4 Summary and Conclusion

Many of the above-listed ironies pertain to the origins and provenance of the Messiah, involving misunderstanding regarding Jesus' preexistence and divine nature (e.g., John 6:42; 7:27–28; 8:22, 53, 57; 9:29). Jesus' opponents and the claims on which they base their rejection of the Messiah are thoroughly exposed as fallacious. In this regard, irony is an indispensable ally in accomplishing the author's purpose of demonstrating that "Jesus is the Messiah, the Son of God" (20:31). It should also be noted that Johannine irony often operates on the *larger discourse level*, undergirding the perspective of an entire pericope.[98] Space constraints preclude the discussion of additional facets of Johannine irony, such as *ironic characterization*, *irony of identity*, and the *use of ironic imagery*.[99]

7.5 Symbolism

7.5.1 Introduction

Another distinctive feature of John's gospel is its extensive use of symbolism.[100] The crucial interpretive significance of Johannine symbolism is apparent when one considers that this feature plays a critical role in John's symbolic discourses (see esp.

---

97. See the discussion in ibid., 350–51.
98. Examples of this include Jesus' conversations with Nicodemus and the Samaritan woman in John 3 and 4 as well as Jesus' healing of the man born blind in John 9 and Jesus' trial before Pilate in John 18 and 19, the latter two instances being discussed in Duke, *Irony*, chap. 6. See also the discussions of these passages in Köstenberger, *John*, 112–32 and 141–65, and the treatment of Jesus' trial before Pilate in chap. 11 below.
99. See Duke, *Irony*, chap. 5.
100. See already the helpful treatment in C. H. Dodd, *The Interpretation of the Fourth Gospel* (Cambridge: Cambridge University Press, 1953), 133–43. More recently, see Culpepper, *Anatomy*, 180–98; and Craig R. Koester, *Symbolism in the Fourth Gospel: Meaning, Mystery, Community* (2nd ed.; Minneapolis: Fortress, 2003).

John 6; 10; and 15), the "I am" sayings, the "signs," and John's use of the OT, not to speak of the entirety of John's worldview.[101] Thus G. H. C. Macgregor's statement contains only a slight instance of hyperbole when he observes, "No understanding of the Gospel is possible without an appreciation of the part played by symbolism."[102] Günter Stemberger, in a wide-ranging study of Johannine symbolism, similarly asserts that "the ethic of John is essentially symbolic";[103] and Wayne Meeks speaks of the gospel's "symbolic universe," which renders it virtually impenetrable to outsiders who fail to grasp it.[104] These observations underscore the pervasiveness and interpretive significance of Johannine symbolism.

7.5.2 The Dynamic Underlying Johannine Symbolism
7.5.2.1 Nature and Characteristics of Symbolism

R. Alan Culpepper aptly relates symbolism to other Johannine literary devices such as irony or misunderstanding:

> The misunderstandings are a dramatic portrayal of the plight of those whose understanding is limited to the mundane. The ironies of the story, like the misunderstandings but more subtly, invite the reader to share the implied author's higher vantage point. From it the blindness of the characters around Jesus and the half-hidden truths which fill their conversations may be clearly seen. The symbols employed by the implied author and his central character open even richer and more stimulating views into the order and mystery of the world above.[105]

In the introduction to his gospel, John affirms that "no one has ever seen God, but the one and only Son ... has made him known" (John 1:18). As the Word-made-flesh (1:14), Jesus himself is the invisible-become-visible, and as the one who descended from above, he is able to convey by means of various images what God is like. As Culpepper observes, the gospel's symbols

> are often the ladder on which readers, like the angels of Jacob's dream, may ascend and descend while moving to and from the heaven opened by the story (cf. 1:51). The symbols, like the images, metaphors, motifs, and themes to which they are related, often carry the principal burden of the narrative and provide implicit commentary and directional signals for the reader.[106]

---

101. See further the discussion below. See also chap. 6, secs. 12 and 13, below.
102. G. H. C. Macgregor, *The Gospel of John* (MNTC; London: Hodder & Stoughton, 1928), xxv (cited in Culpepper, *Anatomy*, 181).
103. Günter Stemberger, *La symbolique du bien et du mal selon saint Jean* (Parole de Dieu; Paris: Editions du Seuil, 1970), 21 (cited in Culpepper, *Anatomy*, 186). Perhaps the most pronounced confirmation of Stemberger's pronouncement is the way in which the footwashing encapsulates the Johannine love ethic: see chap. 13 below.
104. Wayne A. Meeks, "The Man from Heaven in Johannine Sectarianism," *JBL* 91 (1972): 47, 49–50. Elsewhere, Meeks speaks of the "self-referring quality" of Johannine symbolism and of the "closed system of metaphors" it contains (ibid., 68–69; cited in Culpepper, *Anatomy*, 186). It is not necessary to follow Meeks in his sectarian sociological reading of the gospel to appreciate his statements regarding John's use of symbols here. For a critique of sectarian readings of John's gospel in view of the Johannine mission theme, see Köstenberger, *Missions of Jesus and the Disciples*, 203–6.
105. Culpepper, *Anatomy*, 180–81.
106. Ibid., 181.

Because of his particular cosmology and worldview, John's presentation is especially rich in symbolism. Symbols can be used to communicate matters, and in particular spiritual realities, "that cannot be adequately expressed by other means."[107] An example of this is Jesus' illustration of the difficulty to grasp the concept of a spiritual birth by the mysterious nature of the wind (John 3:6–8; exploiting the fact that the Hebrew and Greek words for "spirit" and "wind" were the same, *ruaḥ* and *pneuma*, respectively). At the same time, Johannine symbolism ought to be distinguished from an alleged sacramentarianism that unduly tends to impose later categories onto John's gospel, since Jesus, not the symbols, are the focal point in John's usage.[108]

In the most general sense, a "symbol ... is something that stands for something else."[109] Symbolism thus typically involves the use of metaphor, a procedure that may be defined as "a device which speaks of one thing (tenor) in terms which are appropriate to another (vehicle), with the vehicle serving as the source of traits to be transferred to the tenor."[110] While a metaphor thus expresses the tenor by means of a given vehicle, the symbol conveys information regarding the nature of the vehicle. In Jesus' statement "I am the bread of life" (John 6:35), for example, "I" is the tenor and "the bread of life" the vehicle, and the reader's task is to infer which features of Jesus' identity led him to use the metaphor in question.[111]

More specifically, "a symbol is an image, an action, or a person that is understood to have transcendent significance,"[112] "a connecting link between two different spheres," in keeping with the etymological root of the word "symbol" (*syn*, "together" + *ballō*, "throw"), meaning "put or throw together."[113] Symbolic language may draw on any images that "can be perceived by the senses, such as light and darkness, water, bread, a door, a shepherd, and a vine."[114] While the image itself is typically simple, straightforward, and easily recognized, complexity is introduced by the way in which the vehicle/symbol is related to the tenor.

As Culpepper notes, the tenor-vehicle relationship, and thus the meaning of a given symbol, cannot be reduced to a one-to-one correspondence and usually yields a "surplus of meaning" or "semantic energy" that derives from past associations of a given word or concept, which may evoke different nuances of meaning in various

---

107. Koester, *Symbolism*, 3.

108. See John Painter, "Johannine Symbols: A Case Study in Epistemology," *Journal of Theology for Southern Africa* 27 (1979): 26–41. See also the critique of Sandra M. Schneiders, "History and Symbolism in the Fourth Gospel," in *L'Evangile de Jean* (BETL 44; ed. Marinus de Jonge; Gembloux: Duculot / Leuven: Leuven Univ. Press, 1977), 371–76; and idem, "Symbolism and the Sacramental Principle in the Fourth Gospel," in *Segni e sacramenti nel Vangeli di Giovanni* (Studia Anselmiana 66; ed. Pius-Ramon Tragan; Rome: Editrice Anselmiana, 1977), 221–35, cited in Culpepper, *Anatomy*, 187.

109. Koester, *Symbolism*, 4.

110. Norman Friedman, *Form and Meaning in Fiction* (Athens, GA: University of Georgia Press, 1975), 289, cited in Culpepper, *Anatomy*, 181.

111. While this task may appear to be simple, in the present instance, for example, the relationship has been construed in different ways, which has given rise to momentous disputes regarding the nature of the Eucharist, in part hinging on the way in which the meaning of the word "is" has been construed, which, in turn, brings to mind similar issues that surfaced in end-of-twentieth-century American presidential politics.

112. Koester, *Symbolism*, 4.

113. Culpepper, *Anatomy*, 182, citing Harry Levin, *Contexts of Criticism* (Harvard Studies in Comparative Literature 22; Cambridge, MA: Harvard University Press, 1957), 200.

114. Koester, *Symbolism*, 4.

contexts.[115] Thus symbols provide a suitable vehicle for conveying spiritual truth, opening a window, as it were, to a world of mystery and transcendent reality and providing a place where the finite and the infinite can meet.[116] What is more, like Johannine irony, symbolism may operate not only on the level of verbal utterance but be inherent in a particular action or event. Examples of symbolic actions in John's gospel are the footwashing, and, of course, the "signs," including (I maintain) the temple clearing.[117]

Wai-yee Ng distinguishes between metaphorical symbolism (commonly found in the "I am" sayings);[118] narrative symbolism (the "signs");[119] double meaning (including ambiguous or mysterious sayings);[120] misunderstanding and irony;[121] sacramental vs. representational symbolism;[122] thematic symbolism (e.g., geographical or numerical symbolism; the descent/ascent motif);[123] and scriptural symbolism (utilizing OT imagery).[124] These categories bear testimony to the pervasiveness and great diversity of symbolic elements in John's gospel.[125]

Culpepper, summarizing William Freedman, provides a helpful discussion of how symbolism, in turn, coalesces into and operates on the level of Johannine motifs or themes. While a symbol may occur in a given narrative only once, motifs are by definition recurrent. Thus motifs can be established on the basis of (1) the frequency and recurring nature of a given symbol or group of symbols; (2) the significance of the respective contexts in which a given symbol or set of symbols occurs; (3) the consistency or coherence of the use of a given symbol throughout the course of a narrative, which may, in turn, involve a pattern of escalation[126] or an element of drama or suspense; and (4) the appropriateness of the motif in relation to the symbols employed.[127] As in the case of the other Johannine literary devices

---

115. Culpepper, *Anatomy*, 183.

116. See ibid., citing Levin, *Contexts of Criticism*, 197, drawing on Thomas Carlyle, who spoke of symbols as "a meeting point between the finite and the infinite."

117. See further the discussion in chap. 7, sec. 15 below. See also the discussion in John 13, which attests to the evocative power of the footwashing in conveying John's ethic.

118. Wai-yee Ng, *Water Symbolism in John: An Eschatological Interpretation* (Studies in Biblical Literature 15; New York: Peter Lang, 2001), 5–22.

119. See Dodd, *Interpretation of the Fourth Gospel*, 133–34; W. F. Howard, "Symbolism and Allegory," in *Fourth Gospel in Recent Criticism and Interpretation*, 185; René Kieffer, "Different Levels in Johannine Imagery," in *Aspects on the Johannine Literature* (ed. Lars Hartman and Birger Olsson; ConBNT 18; Uppsala: Almqvist & Wiksell, 1987), 74–84; Schneiders, "History and Symbolism," 371–76; and Dorothy A. Lee, *The Symbolic Narratives of the Fourth Gospel: The Interplay of Form and Meaning* (JSNTSup 95; Sheffield: JSOT, 1994).

120. David W. Wead, *The Literary Devices in John's Gospel* (Theologische Dissertationen 4; Basel: Friedrich Reinhardt Kommissionsverlag, 1970); Richard, "Expressions of Double Meaning."

121. See secs. 7.2 and 7.4, above.

122. This is a controversial subject. See the diverse viewpoints expressed by Brown, *Gospel according to John I–XII*, cxi–cxiv; Oscar Cullmann, *Early Christian Worship* (SBT 10; London: SCM, 1953), 59–117; Paul Niewalda, *Sakramentssymbolik im Johannesevangelium?* (Limburg: Lahn, 1958); James D. G. Dunn, "John VI—A Eucharistic Discourse?" *NTS* 17 (1971): 328–38 (esp. p. 330); John Painter, "John 9 and the Interpretation of the Fourth Gospel," *JSNT* 28 (1986): 31–61.

123. See Culpepper, *Anatomy*, 145–25; Wayne A. Meeks, "Galilee and Judea in the Fourth Gospel," *JBL* 85 (1966): 159–69; Godfrey Carruthers Nicholson, *Death as Departure: The Johannine Descent–Ascent Schema* (SBLDS 63; Chico, CA: Scholars Press, 1983).

124. See the discussion in chap. 10 of this volume.

125. For an alternative effort at classifying different types of symbolism in John's gospel, see Juan Leal, "El simbolismo historic del iv evangelio," *EstBib* 19 (1960): 329–48 (cited in Culpepper, *Anatomy*, 185), who distinguishes between (1) allegorical symbolism; (2) nominal symbolism; (3) biblical symbolism; (4) symbolism in action; and (5) historical symbolism.

126. As is the case in the "lifted up" sayings (John 3:14; 8:28; 12:32), which gradually develops the notion that "lifted up" means crucifixion, as is made clear by a Johannine "aside" (12:33).

127. Culpepper, *Anatomy*, 183, citing William Freedman, "The Literary Motif: A Definition and Evaluation," *Novel* 4 (1971): 124–28.

discussed above, symbolism in the form of motifs thus serves to "involve the reader more deeply in the work by weaving consistency and continuity while inviting the reader to discern patterns, implications, and levels of meaning which lie below the surface of the literary work."[128]

A distinctive feature involving symbolism in John's gospel is the presence of several symbolic discourses that develop the meaning of a given symbol in an extended fashion. Examples of this are the Bread of Life Discourse in John 6; the Good Shepherd Discourse in John 10; and the allegory of the "Vine and the Branches" in John 15 (all of which, in turn, involve "I am" statements). Jesus' words in John 10, for example, serve as a *paroimia* (10:6; cf. 16:21–25, 29), an illustration of an important set of spiritual truths: Jesus alone is the true and good shepherd, and entry into the sphere of salvation is found only in him (cf. 14:6).[129] At the same time, it must be kept in mind that the Johannine symbolic discourses are salvation-historically constrained, or else, as Ridderbos rightly cautioned, "the Fourth Gospel becomes one great cryptogram."[130]

7.5.2.2 J. Louis Martyn's "Two-Level Hermeneutic": Evaluation and Critique

Here it is in particular J. Louis Martyn's proposal of a "two-level hermeneutic" applied to John's gospel that has exerted a considerable degree of influence, most recently in D. Moody Smith's *The Fourth Gospel in Four Dimensions*.[131] Part 1 of this work ("John and Judaism") is essentially a reiteration of Smith's endorsement of Martyn's thesis, in particular his proposal that John represents a two-level drama. However, reading John's gospel following a two-level hermeneutic is problematic for several reasons.[132] First, as Richard Bauckham notes, "The most important point to make is that it [the two-level reading] has no basis in the literary genre of the Fourth Gospel," namely, Greco-Roman biography.[133] If the genre of the Gospels (including John) is that of biography, or at least some variation of it, then it follows that this gospel is primarily a story about Jesus, not John's community.

Second, again in Bauckham's words, "the Fourth Gospel itself evinces a strong sense of the pastness of the story of Jesus," "not infrequently draw[ing] explicit attention to the difference between the periods before and after the cross and resurrection

---

128. Culpepper, *Anatomy*, 184.
129. See the discussion of the genre of John 10 in Köstenberger, "Jesus the Good Shepherd," 72–75.
130. Ridderbos, *Gospel of John*, 364–65, over against the allegorical, "two-level" hermeneutic of Martyn and his followers: see Köstenberger, "Jesus the Good Shepherd," 73–74; and the discussion below.
131. D. Moody Smith, *The Fourth Gospel in Four Dimensions: Judaism and Jesus, the Gospels and Scripture* (Columbia, SC: University of South Carolina Press, 2008). See my critique in "Implications for History."

132. For a helpful critique, see Hägerland, "John's Gospel: A Two-Level Drama," who concludes that (1) there are no ancient parallels of dramas operating on two different historical levels, so that John's readers would not have been able to grasp the second level of the narrative by associating it with a well-established genre; and (2) the Johannine narrative itself shows no traces of an authorial intention to tell any other story than that of Jesus, and there is no manifest desire to present a history of a "Johannine community" (p. 321).

133. Bauckham, *Testimony of the Beloved Disciple*, 117.

of Jesus (e.g., 2:22; 7:39; 12:16; 13:7)."[134] As D. A. Carson pointed out in his article on "misunderstandings" in John's gospel long ago, John is perfectly capable of distinguishing, for example, between the original lack of comprehension of Jesus' followers and their later understanding.[135] The catalog of misunderstandings throughout John's gospel shows that John was keenly conscious of the possibility of anachronism and studiously sought to avoid it.[136]

A third difficulty of a two-level hermeneutic applied to John's gospel is that it is hard to read the entire narrative consistently as operating on two levels. Some, if not many, events in John's gospel—take the account of the Baptist's witness in 1:19–34, for example—rather transparently belong to the first level, recounting the original story of Jesus, with no apparent correspondence on a second level.[137] This means that the two-level hermeneutic can only be applied to certain parts of John's narrative, which raises the difficult methodological question as to which narratives ought to be subjected to a two-level reading and which should not. Again, Bauckham captures the essence of the difficulty:

> Moreover, the strategy cannot be applied to every part of the narrative, nor consistently to the parts of the narrative to which it is applied. Not every character in the Gospel can plausibly represent some group in the community's history and context.... Every example of the strategy in practice is riddled with arbitrariness and uncertainty. The more one realizes how complex and selective the practice of this reading strategy has to be, the less plausible it becomes.[138]

None of this is to say, as critics of a two-level hermeneutic applied to John's gospel such as Bauckham or Carson readily point out, that the circumstances prevailing at the time of John's writing were completely irrelevant to how John wrote his gospel.[139] The above-stated concerns do, however, cast doubt on the degree of specificity with which advocates of a two-level hermeneutic such as Martyn or Brown claim to be able to infer the history of the Johannine community from the text of John's gospel. For reasons such as these, to assign historical primacy to the level of the Johannine community over against Jesus represents an extreme that is unwarranted by the genre of the gospel, indications of John's consciousness of the distinction between the time of Jesus and the period subsequent to his ministry, and various other factors.

What is more, the shortcomings of the "two-level hermeneutic" critiqued above demonstrate the importance of a careful definition of symbolism in relation to history. The use of symbols does not necessarily imply that the material is unhistorical. To the contrary, John's symbolism regularly operates along typological lines that presuppose an underlying salvation-historical continuum. A case in point is Jesus'

---

134. Ibid.
135. Carson, "Understanding Misunderstandings."
136. Carson, *Gospel according to John*, 44.
137. Consider also the references to the "little while" in the Farewell Discourse, which work only on the original level of the story.
138. Bauckham, *Testimony of the Beloved Disciple*, 117.
139. Ibid.

reference to the raised-up serpent in connection with the "lifting up" of the Son of Man in 3:13–14, which works only if both the antecedent (Israel's wilderness wanderings) and future point of reference (Jesus' crucifixion) are historical rather than merely symbolic or allegorical in nature.[140]

7.5.2.3 Other Hermeneutical Observations Pertaining to Johannine Symbolism

Another important hermeneneutical observation relates to the relationship between symbolism and the Johannine "signs." At the very outset, it must be kept in mind that while all the "signs" by their very nature entail symbolism (i.e., their meaning transcends the actual act performed by Jesus), the converse does not follow: not all symbolism does therefore constitute a "sign."[141] Since the "signs" entail symbolism, since they are strategic in John's presentation of Jesus' messianic mission, and since beyond the Johannine "signs" there is a plethora of other kinds of symbolism, it can legitimately be said that symbolism makes up a large part of Jesus' revelation of God in this gospel.

It may even be said that Johannine symbolism serves as the functional substitute of Jesus' teaching in parables in the Synoptics. While parables are absent from John's gospel, symbolism is not, and, as mentioned, is particularly prominent in extended symbolic discourses concerning Jesus as the "bread of life" (John 6), the "good shepherd" (John 10), and the "vine" (John 15).[142] The failure to recognize the meaning of a given symbol in John's gospel regularly leads to misunderstanding, such as Nicodemus's interpretation of Jesus' teaching on "being born again" as a reference to a second physical birth (3:3–4; the same phenomenon is found also in the Synoptics: see, e.g., Matt 16:6–7).

One simple principle for interpreting symbolism is that, taken literally, the statement does not make sense. When Jesus claims to be "the bread of life" (John 6:35), it is patently absurd to think he asserts being a doughy mixture of flour and water. The symbolic nature of his assertion, "I am the good shepherd" (10:11), is less transparent in its symbolism, though context makes clear that Jesus' reference is not to literal shepherding of sheep but to giving spiritual oversight to people. At other times it is unclear whether or not a statement has symbolic overtones (e.g., Nicodemus's coming to Jesus "at night"; 3:2).

For the most part, while drawing on "symbols of ancestral vitality" and "symbols of cultural range" that resonate with the everyday life of the audience, Johannine symbolism tends to be *universal*, that is, not limited to the experience of first-century Palestinian Jews.[143] Examples of pervasive core symbols utilized in John's

---

140. See Köstenberger, "John," in *Commentary on the NT Use of the OT*, 434–37.

141. See the discussion of signs in chap. 7, sec. 15 below.

142. See the discussion above. On the Johannine "I am" statements, see esp. Philip B. Harner, *The "I Am" of the Fourth Gospel* (Facet Books; Philadelphia: Fortress, 1970); David M. Ball, *"I Am" in John's Gospel: Literary Function, Background and Theological Implications* (JSNTSup 124; Sheffield: Sheffield Academic Press, 1996); and Catrin H. Williams, *I Am He: The Interpretation of 'ani hu' in Jewish and Early Christian Literature* (WUNT 2/113; Tübingen: Mohr-Siebeck, 2000).

143. See Culpepper, *Anatomy*, 184, citing Philip E. Wheelwright, *Metaphor and Reality* (Bloomington, IN/London: Indiana University Press, 1962), 99–110.

gospel are "water," "bread," and "light."[144] Other symbols, which may be more localized in nature, include "shepherd" and "vine." In the latter case, in particular, reconstructing the historical-cultural background will be helpful in understanding the import of a given Johannine symbol. In the former case, the difficulty that arises is that "water" or "light" is capable of a great variety of meanings.

Before turning to a study of the major instances of symbolism in John's gospel,[145] one final important dynamic underlying Johannine symbolism should be noted. Symbolism allows a given speaker or author to lead his audience from the known to the unknown. In the present instance, the application of familiar symbols to Jesus provides both continuity while injecting at the same time an element of freshness, newness, and escalation.[146] Theologically as well as sociologically, symbolism thus becomes an important vehicle for facilitating change and transformation, especially in times of crisis or transition.[147] A potent example of this is the transfer of "temple" imagery from the literal, physical temple to Jesus, which may open up a critical window into the historical setting and occasion for John's gospel.[148]

7.5.3 Water Symbolism

7.5.3.1 Introduction

Water, together with bread, is a necessity for life, especially in an ancient Near Eastern culture such as first-century Palestine.[149] R. Alan Culpepper observes that the image of water appears in John's gospel with surprising frequency and with the most varied associations of any Johannine symbols.[150] As will be seen, on a narrative level it is interesting to observe how references to water in the first few chapters of the gospel are somewhat preliminary and gradually build to a more full-fledged explication of important Johannine theological themes such as eternal life or the Holy Spirit.

7.5.3.2 Narrative Survey

In the early chapters of the gospel, water is linked with baptism and cleansing. John the Baptist baptizes with water, conveying the notion of inner cleansing, though there is another who will baptize with the Holy Spirit (John 1:26, 31, 33). Jesus' turning of water into wine at the Cana wedding, his first "sign" (2:11), makes Jesus the focal point of water symbolism as the one who would fulfill messianic prophecy

---

144. These are the three core symbols identified by Culpepper, *Anatomy*, 190–98.

145. In what follows "water" and "bread" symbolism will be treated as case studies in Johannine symbolism. "Light" and "darkness" symbolism will be treated only briefly, since I have discussed this motif elsewhere in this volume: see chap. 2, sec. 3.3 and chap. 8, sec. 16.3. See also the discussions of the shepherd and his flock and the vine and the branches in chap. 12, secs. 29.4.1 and 2; and of "signs" in chap. 7, sec. 15.

146. Culpepper, *Anatomy*, 184.

147. Jonathan Z. Smith, "The Influence of Symbols upon Social Change: A Place on Which to Stand," *Worship* 44 (1970): 471, cited in Culpepper, *Anatomy*, 184.

148. See the discussion in chap. 1, sec. 2.1.2 and chap. 10, sec. 24.

149. For treatments of water symbolism in John's gospel see Koester, *Symbolism*, chap. 5; Ng, *Water Symbolism*; Larry Paul Jones, *The Symbol of Water in the Gospel of John* (JSNTSup 145; Sheffield: Sheffield Academic Press, 1997); and Culpepper, *Anatomy*, 92–95.

150. Culpepper, *Anatomy*, 192, noting that there are conversations about water, water pots, rivers, wells, springs, the sea, pools, basins, thirst, and drink.

and usher in end-time joy, in contrast to the barrenness of contemporary Judaism (cf. 2:6). This is further underscored by John the Baptist's reference to himself as the "friend who attends the bridegroom" in 3:29.

Water symbolism is featured again in John 3 in conjunction with Jesus' reference to a new birth "of water and the spirit" (3:5). This most likely invokes references in the latter, postexilic prophets (esp. Ezek 36:25–27) envisaging the end-time cleansing and renewal of God's people. Similar to the references to water in John 4, Jesus' reference to birth "of water and spirit" in John 3:5 involves misunderstanding as well as irony. This is followed in the Johannine narrative by further references to the baptizing activity of John the Baptist, as well as a mention of the parallel baptizing ministry of Jesus' disciples (3:22–23, 26; 4:1–2).

In John 4:7–15, Jesus' reference is to "living water," which on a literal level denotes fresh spring water in contrast to stagnant water (cf. Gen 26:19; Lev 14:6; Jer 2:13)[151] but here serves as a symbolic reference to eternal life (later tied to the Holy Spirit in John 7:37–39). Water was a fitting symbol for life, since without water people would die of thirst. This is why the abundance of water became a symbol for divine blessing and salvation (e.g., Isa 12:3). There is also an important salvation-historical connection, because water played an important role during Israel's wilderness wanderings at the exodus (Exod 17:1–7; Num 20:2–13; 21:16; cf. Ps 78:16).[152]

The healing of the lame man in John 5, another of Jesus' signs, takes place at the pool of Bethesda. Water here turns out to be an insufficient vehicle of healing. Instead, Jesus cures the man apart from resorting to natural means. This illustrates that it is not material water but Jesus who is the source of life, both in the physical and in the spiritual realms (though in the present case it appears that the man is only healed physically). The reference to Jesus walking on the water in John 6 most likely invokes the exodus motif, as the scene "portrays dramatically Jesus' power over water and his ability to use it for deliverance even when its destructive power is at its greatest."[153]

At the Festival of Tabernacles, which was associated with adequate rainfall (Zech 14:16–17) and water-pouring ceremonies,[154] Jesus invites those who are thirsty to come to him and drink (John 7:37; cf. esp. Isa 55:1). According to Jesus, "rivers of living water" will flow from believers in him (John 7:38; see esp. Neh 9:15, 19–20). The fourth evangelist explains that the reference was to the Holy Spirit (John 7:39; cf. Isa 44:3; Ezek 36:25–27; Joel 2:28). Yet the giving of the Spirit was contingent on Jesus' "glorification"; that is, it must await the Son's exaltation to the Father subsequent to the crucifixion and resurrection (cf. John 20:17, 22).

In John 9, it is the pool of Siloam that becomes the site of yet another healing. Another Johannine "sign," the healing points to the paradigmatic "Sent One," Jesus,

---

151. As Keener, *John*, 605 (citing ancient references) observes, water drawn from wells was not always "living water" (unless it was fed by an underground stream) and was therefore often thought to be less healthy than "living," that is, water drawn from a spring or from rainwater.

152. This, in turn, is picked up by Isaiah with reference to a new exodus (e.g., Isa 41:18; 43:20; 48:21; 49:10).

153. Culpepper, *Anatomy*, 194.

154. See Keener, *John*, 722–24.

as the evangelist makes clear in 9:7. In virtually allegorical fashion, the entire course of events surrounding the blind man's healing is cast as a real-life parable illustrating the spiritual blindness of the Jewish leaders in the face of Jesus' powerful display of his messianic mission (see esp. 9:39–41).

The next washing is Jesus' washing of the disciples' feet at the outset of the Farewell Discourse (John 13). Water here serves as a symbol of the cleansing power of Jesus' death and his word (cf. 15:3).

At the cross, with profound irony, it is Jesus, the giver of living water, who thirsts, and the maker of superior wine who must drink bitter vinegar (John 19:28; cf. 18:11). At 19:34, the reader learns that subsequent to the crucifixion, one of the Roman soldiers pierced Jesus' side with a spear, resulting in a "sudden flow of blood and water." In a related reference, John's first letter notes, "This is the one who came by water and blood—Jesus Christ. He did not come by water only, but by water and blood.... For there are three that testify: the Spirit, the water and the blood, and the three are in agreement" (1 John 5:6–7).

Beginning with the gospel reference, on a literal level, the spear may have pierced Jesus' heart, resulting, either directly or via chest and lung, in the flow of blood and water, which underscores that Jesus died as a fully human being.[155] Apart from an allusion to water coming out from the rock at the exodus (Exod 17:6), an allusion to Passover may be in view as well, consisting of (1) the hyssop (John 19:29); (2) the unbroken bones (19:33, 36); and (3) the mingled blood (19:34).[156] The reference in John's letter most likely marks the beginning and end of Jesus' messianic mission, that is, water baptism and crucifixion.[157]

7.5.3.3 Summary and Conclusion

In addition to the more significant instances of "water" symbolism in John 4:7–15; 7:37–39; and 19:34, water plays a part also in several other Johannine passages, including 1:26, 31, 33 (John's water baptism); 2:1, 6–10 (Jesus' turning water into wine); 3:5 (born of water and spirit); 3:23 (John's water baptism); 5:2, 7 and 9:6–11 (the healings at the pools of Bethesda and Siloam); 6:16–19 (Jesus' walking on the water); 13:4–12 (the footwashing); and 21:7 (Peter's jumping into the water at seeing Jesus).

In most of these instances, water functions primarily at the literal level, though at times it appears to symbolize cleansing (esp. in the footwashing pericope; see also John 3:5). For the most part, there seems to be a contrast between Jewish purification rites and even physical water baptism, on the one hand, and spiritual regeneration and renewal through the Holy Spirit on the other. In this, the Johannine narrative serves as an explication of the contrast made at the outset by John the Baptist at 1:32–33.

---

155. Many see here a polemic purpose of some kind, though there is no consensus as to the nature of the opponents (see references in Köstenberger, *John*, 552, n. 67).

156. For a detailed discussion and references, see Köstenberger, *John*, 552–53.

157. See esp. Streett, "They Went Out from Us," chap. 5.

The insufficiency of engaging in the rites of old Judaism is constantly reinforced, be it in the reference to Jewish ceremonial washing rites at the Cana wedding (2:6), the mention of an inconsequential argument regarding ceremonial washings (3:25), or the futility of people requiring healing lying at the pools of Bethesda or Siloam (John 5 and 9). Instead, what they need is spiritual renewal (3:5) and the new life only Jesus can give, which will issue in rivers of living water flowing from believers in the eschatological age of the Spirit (7:37–39; cf. 4:10–15).[158]

7.5.4 Bread Symbolism

In contrast to water symbolism, which is variegated and occurs intermittently throughout the gospel, bread symbolism is centered almost exclusively in the Bread of Life Discourse in John 6.[159] The setting is Passover (6:4), invoking Passover symbolism, but the location is Galilee, not Jerusalem (as in the case of Jesus' first and third Passovers narrated in John's gospel; see 2:13 and 23; 11:55 and 13:1, respectively). This places Jesus, the "elusive Christ," in possible critical distance to the Jerusalem festivities (cf. the temple clearing incident in 2:13–22; and Jesus' reluctance to go up to Jerusalem in John 7 and 11; see esp. 7:1–9 and 11:16).[160]

Despite Jesus' earlier references to food of which his followers did not know (4:8, 32), the disciples, in an instance of Johannine misunderstanding (6:7–9), again fall short of recognizing Jesus as the one who is about to perform yet another "sign" as he continues on his messianic mission. Jesus' reference to "food that spoils" in contrast to "food that endures to eternal life" in 6:27 makes clear that material bread is but the gift of the one who in his very essence is life itself and the giver not merely of physical but, more importantly, of eternal, spiritual life (cf. 11:25; 14:6). In parallel fashion, both bread and water are featured as symbols of the life that only Jesus, as God's Messiah and Son of God, is able to provide.

In the Bread of Life Discourse, which explicates the significance of the feeding of the multitude (see 6:30), Jesus proceeds to offer himself to his Jewish audience as the "bread of life," the eschatological new manna. Not only does Jesus affirm his heavenly provenance by presenting himself in continuity with, yet escalation of, the salvation-historical story of Israel, he claims to be the quintessential life-nurturing culmination point of God's salvific purposes. So profound must his audience's partaking of him be that it is best described as "eat[ing] his flesh" (not body, as in the Lord's Supper) and "drink[ing] his blood" (6:53). Together with water symbolism, the Johannine references to bread thus combine to identify Jesus as the giver of life.

---

158. See Ng, *Water Symbolism*, chap. 3: "Eschatology and the Symbolic Meaning of 'Water' in John 4."

159. For a survey of bread symbolism in John's gospel, see Culpepper, *Anatomy*, 195–97. On the broader theme of eating and drinking, see Jane S. Webster, *Ingesting Jesus: Eating and Drinking in the Gospel of John* (SBLABib 6; Atlanta: Scholars Press, 2003); and Petrus Maritz and Gilbert van Belle, "The Imagery of Eating and Drinking in John 6:35," in *Imagery in the Gospel of John: Terms, Forms, Themes, and Theology of Johannine Figurative Language* (ed. Jörg Frey, Jan G. van der Watt, and Ruben Zimmerman; WUNT 200; Tübingen: Mohr-Siebeck, 2006), 333–52 (with additional references).

160. See Culpepper, *Anatomy*, 195; on Jesus as the "elusive Christ," see Mark W. G. Stibbe, "The Elusive Christ: A New Reading of the Fourth Gospel," *JSNT* 44 (1991): 19–38.

7.5.5 Light Symbolism

"Light" is perhaps the most archetypal of all symbols used in John's gospel and letters.[161] Together with "darkness" and "life," "light" symbolism weaves a cluster of associations with God's creation "in the beginning."[162] In John's gospel "light" is thus presented as ultimately an attribute of God himself (cf. 1 John 1:5), and this attribute, in turn, is displayed by Jesus, the "light" that came into the world (John 1:9–11; cf. 1:4–5; see also 1:18; 14:9). As in the natural realm, so in the spiritual sphere of existence, light is an indispensable prerequisite for life. For this reason the coming of Jesus as "the light of the world" (8:12; 9:5) is shown to make eternal life possible for those who put their trust in him.

"Light" symbolism also has an important ethical and moral dimension in both John's gospel and letters. While "darkness" is the realm of sin and death, "light" is the sphere of moral knowledge and fellowship with God (John 3:19–21; 1 John 1:5–7; 2:8–10). The coming of the light into the world is thus shown not only to reveal the nature of God as "light"; it also has the effect of exposing the world's moral and spiritual darkness, which brings into play the Johannine themes of witness and divine judgment. In terms of salvation history, the fourth evangelist contrasts Jesus, "the light of the world," with John the Baptist, who "was a lamp that burned and gave light" (John 5:35).

In the OT, God's word is frequently said to give light (Ps 19:8; 119:105, 130; Prov 6:23). In ancient Judaism, "light" was a common symbol for the law (e.g., *2 Bar* 59:2).[163] Importantly, "light" symbolism also conveyed major messianic connotations.[164] Balaam pictured the coming of the Messiah as the rising of "a star" (Num 24:17; cf. 4QTest 9–13). Isaiah prophesied, "The people walking in darkness have seen a great light; on those living in the land of deep darkness a light has dawned" (Isa 9:2). The prophet envisions a time when the nations will walk in God's light, and the glory of the Lord will shine brightly (60:1–5; cf. 42:6–7; 49:6). Malachi spoke of "the sun of righteousness" rising "with healing in its rays" (Mal 4:2; cf. Luke 1:78–79).

Light is what God and Jesus are. Since doing in Johannine thought flows from being, Jesus the light is also the giver of light. This is illustrated at great length in one of the Johannine "signs," the healing of the man born blind in John 9, which serves as a real-life parable of seeing and blindness featuring the customary dynamic of reversal: those who think they see turn out to be blind, while the one who was blind was given sight by Jesus (9:39–41). As R. Alan Culpepper astutely notes, thus "sight becomes insight into the identity of Jesus" and "a willingness to believe."[165]

---

161. See Wheelwright, *Metaphor and Reality*, 116, cited in Culpepper, *Anatomy*, 190. On "light" symbolism in John's gospel, see, e.g., Koester, *Symbolism*, 123–54; Culpepper, *Anatomy*, 190–92; and Keener, *John*, 381–87 (with further bibliographic references).

162. See chap. 2, sec. 3.3 above and chap. 8, sec. 16.3 below. For an extensive survey of "light" imagery in biblical and extrabiblical Jewish and non-Jewish literature, see Keener, *John*, 382–87.

163. See the long list of references in Keener, *John*, 385, n. 219.

164. On "light" symbolism for the law, see Dodd, *Interpretation of the Fourth Gospel*, 201–5; Stemberger, *Symbolique*, 25–49; Painter, "Johannine Symbols." On messianic "light" symbolism, see William Horbury, *Jewish Messianism and the Cult of Christ* (London: SCM, 1998), 92–93, 99–100; Köstenberger, *John*, 31–32, 35.

165. Culpepper, *Anatomy*, 191.

Thus "light" symbolism also serves to expose the true heart condition of people in relation to the Creator and Jesus as the "signs"-working Messiah.

In addition, John also features the subordinate set of symbols of "day" and "night." While it is not always clear whether "night" is meant to convey the notion of spiritual darkness or serves merely as a time marker, several individuals or groups of people are cast in terms of "night": on the one end of the spectrum is Nicodemus, who comes to Jesus at night (John 3:2; cf. 19:39); on the other end is Judas, the traitor, who departs from the believing community and steps into the night to betray Jesus (13:30).[166] With a heightened sense of urgency, Jesus calls on people to place their trust in him while it is still "day" and before "night" comes, indicating that the days of his public ministry are rapidly drawing to a close (9:4; 11:10; 12:35–36).[167]

7.5.6 Summary and Conclusion

It has been shown that symbolism is a pervasive feature of John's narrative. As mentioned, symbolism plays a vital role in the extended symbolic discourses, the "I am sayings," the "signs," and John's use of the OT, not to speak of John's entire worldview. For this reason it is hard to overstate the interpretive significance of symbolism. It is virtually impossible to understand John's gospel without appreciating the meaning of the symbols it contains, and the gospel's "symbolic universe" renders it virtually impenetrable to outsiders who fail to grasp it. The discussions of water, bread, and light symbolism above illustrate the foundational nature played by symbolism in conveying John's theology, especially with regard to Jesus' messianic mission and the benefits it bestows on those who believe in him.

8 THE STRUCTURE OF JOHN'S GOSPEL

8.1 Overview

Another important literary matter requiring investigation is the structure of John's gospel and letters. There is wide agreement in the scholarly literature that John's gospel breaks down into an introduction (John 1:1–18); a first major unit frequently called "The Book of Signs" (1:19–12:50), which focuses on Jesus' messianic signs for the Jews; a second major unit termed "The Book of Glory" (13:1–20:31), which anticipates Jesus' exaltation with the Father subsequent to his crucifixion, burial, and resurrection; and an epilogue or postscript (21:1–25).[168]

While the divisions themselves are unobjectionable, to designate only Part 2 of John's gospel The Book of Glory is, however, of doubtful merit, since *both* the

---

166. See the discussions in Köstenberger, *John*, 120, 418.

167. Culpepper (*Anatomy*, 192) lists additional Johannine instances of "light and darkness" imagery: "The reader can also be expected to sense that torches and lanterns (18:3) are a pathetic substitute for the light of the world, and a charcoal fire (18:18) is a miserable alternative on a cold dark night and a painful reminder in the bright light of a new day (21:9). It is appropriate that Mary Magdalene goes to the empty tomb in darkness (20:1) and that the disciples find fishing at night to be futile but enclose an astonishing catch when it is early morning (21:4)."

168. See, e.g., Moloney, *Gospel of John*, v–viii.

"signs" (John 2:11; 9:3–4; 11:4) *and* the "lifting up" of the Son of Man (12:23; 17:1, 5, 24) depicted in the Passion Narrative are shown in this gospel to reveal God's glory. For this reason it is more appropriate to label Part 1 of John's gospel as The Book of Signs and Part 2 as The Book of Exaltation.

There is also considerable support for the notion that John 11–12 represent a transition or bridge from The Book of Signs to The Book of Exaltation, featuring Jesus' climactic "sign," the raising of Lazarus, which, in turn, foreshadows Jesus' own resurrection.[169] Indeed, mention of Lazarus seems to provide the glue that holds these two chapters together (11:1–44; 12:1–11, 17–19).

With regard to the structure of The Book of Signs, many believe, on the basis of literary *inclusios*, that this unit is made up of two major cycles narrating Jesus' ministry: a Cana Cycle (John 2:1–4:54; see 2:11; 4:54) and a Festival Cycle (5:1–10:42; see 1:19–34; 10:40–41).[170] In addition, some see a division between John 5–6 and John 7–10 in light of the watershed defection of many of Jesus' followers at the end of John 6.[171]

The Book of Exaltation breaks down into the Farewell Discourse (John 13–17), which can be subdivided further into a preamble (13:1–30); the Farewell Discourse proper (13:31–16:33); Jesus' final prayer (17:1–26); and the Passion Narrative (18:1–20:31), culminating in a declaration of John's purpose (20:30–31). Thus John's gospel reveals a deliberate literary plan that, in turn, reflects the evangelist's theological message.

The overarching purpose of John's entire gospel is the demonstration that Jesus, the Word, is the Messiah and Son of God (20:30–31) by weaving together several narrative strands. The introduction places the entire gospel within the framework of the eternal, preexistent Word made flesh in Jesus (1:1–18). The first half of John's narrative sets forth evidence for Jesus' messiahship in the form of seven selected signs (1:19–12:50; cf. 20:30–31).

John also includes Jesus' seven "I am" sayings and calls numerous (seven?) witnesses in support of Jesus' claims, including Moses and the Scriptures, the Baptist, the Father, Jesus and his works, the Spirit, the disciples, and the evangelist himself. Representative questions concerning Jesus' messiahship serve to lead the gospel's readers to the author's intended conclusion: Jesus is the Messiah (e.g., John 1:41; 4:25; 7:27, 31, 52; 10:24; 11:27; 12:34).

8.2 Act I: *Sēmeio*-Drama

At the heart of Act I of John's gospel drama is the demonstration of Jesus' messiahship by way of seven selected signs. While Jesus is the "Savior of the world" (John 4:42; cf. 3:16), he is emphatic that "salvation is from the Jews" (4:22). Thus Act I

---

169. Carson, *Gospel according to John*, 106–7; Ridderbos, *Gospel of John*, viii, calls John 11–12 "Prelude to the Passion Narrative"; likewise, Keener, *Gospel of John*, xvii, labels the unit "Introducing the Passion."

170. Moloney, *Gospel of John*, v–vi.

171. See, e.g., Keener, *Gospel of John*, xvi; Ridderbos, *Gospel of John*, vii; Köstenberger, *John*, 52, whose structural proposal includes both the Festival Cycle in John 5–10 and a break at a "moment of major crisis" at 6:60–71.

features a progressive display of Jesus' messianic signs directed to the Jews. Rather than lead the Jews to faith, however, the signs confirm their rejection of the Messiah (12:37–40).

John 1:19–2:11 narrates a week in Jesus' ministry.[172] This bridge section overlaps with the narration of a ministry cycle from Cana to Cana in 2:1–4:54, with an intervening appearance by Jesus in the capital city of Jerusalem (2:13–3:21). Three signs are presented in this section: the turning of water into wine in 2:1–11 (the first sign in Cana, 2:11); the temple clearing in 2:13–22 (one of Jesus' Jerusalem signs; cf. 2:23; 3:2); and the healing of the official's son (second Cana sign, 4:54).

John 5–11 (12) form the second major subsection of Act I, narrating four additional signs culminating in the raising of Lazarus.[173] Characterized by mounting controversy between Jesus and his Jewish opponents, this section is built around Jesus' participation in several Jewish festivals such as Tabernacles (John 5; 7–8), Passover (John 6), and Dedication (10:22–42). The four signs featured in this subsection include the healing of a lame man (5:1–15), the feeding of the multitudes (6:1–15), the opening of a blind man's eyes (John 9), and the raising of Lazarus (John 11).[174]

John 11–12, like 1:19–2:11, form a bridge section (note the signaling of Jesus' final week in 12:1, a possible *inclusio* with 1:19–2:11). On one level, the *inclusio* between 1:19–34 and 10:40–42 marks off 1:19–10:42 as a unit. It also sets off John 11–12 as a transition, including accounts of the raising of Lazarus (John 11) and of Jesus' anointing and triumphal entry (12:1–19). Further transitional material is found in 12:20–36 (the coming of the Greeks) and 12:37–50 (the grand tragic conclusion of Act I).

8.3 Act II: *Cruci*-Drama

Act II of John's gospel shows how Jesus ensured the continuation of his mission by preparing his new messianic community for its mission. This portion opens with Jesus' Farewell Discourse (John 13–17): the new messianic community is cleansed (by the footwashing and Judas's departure; John 13), prepared (by instructions

---

172. Charles H. Talbert, "Artistry and Theology: An Analysis of the Architecture of Jn 1,19–5,47," *CBQ* 32 (1970): 341–66, esp. 343, proposes unconvincingly that John 1:19–5:47 displays the pattern of a macro-chiasm. However, this comes at the expense of virtually ignoring the clear *inclusio* of 2:11 and 4:54, which marks this section off as a structural unit. Moreover, the very notion of a macro-chiasm is far from established. To cite but one additional weakness, at the heart of the chiasm Talbert groups 3:22–36 and 4:1–42 under the rubric "ritual and life," a hardly self-evident categorization. On the micro-level, however, Talbert's unit divisions are generally on target: 1:19–2:11; 2:13–22 (though there is no need to skip 2:12); 2:23–3:22; 3:23–36; 4:1–42; 4:43–54; 5:1–30; 5:31–47.

173. Stibbe, "Elusive Christ," has shown that John portrays Jesus as elusive both in his language (John 2–4) and in his movements (John 5–10). In John 11 and 12, "tension mounts as Jesus openly returns to the place of maximum danger and as the Sanhedrin formally plot to have Jesus killed" (p. 36). Stibbe's literary analysis further confirms the divisions sketched above into an initial Cana Cycle in John 2–4 and a Festival Cycle in John 5–10, with John 11–12 occupying a bridge function. Even the pivotal defection in John 6, followed by the narration of opposition in Jesus' family in John 7, seems to be borne out by Stibbe's study in that all but one references to the Jews seeking Jesus in order to kill him are found after this pivot (5:18; 7:1, 19, 20, 25, 30; 8:37, 40; 10:39; 11:8; see p. 22).

174. Another element in the multilayered structure of this gospel, as mentioned, is the critical mass defection of the majority of Jesus' disciples followed by Peter's confession at the end of chap. 6, which comes halfway through Act I (possibly mirroring the structure of Mark and the Synoptics).

regarding the coming Paraclete and his ministry to the disciples; John 14–16), and prayed for (John 17). The disciples are made partners in the proclamation of salvation in Christ (15:15–16), their witness being aided by the Spirit (15:26–27), and they are taken into the life of the Godhead, which is characterized by perfect love and unity (17:20–26).

The Johannine Passion Narrative (John 18–19) presents Jesus' death both as an atonement for sin (cf. 1:29, 36; 6:48–58; 10:15, 17–18), though largely without the Synoptic emphasis on shame and humiliation, and as a stage in Jesus' return to the Father (e.g., 13:1; 16:28). The resurrection appearances and the disciples' commissioning by their risen Lord constitute the focal point of the penultimate chapter (John 20), where Jesus is cast as the paradigmatic Sent One (cf. 9:7), who has now become the sender of his new messianic community (20:21–23).

The purpose statement of 20:30–31 reiterates the major motifs of the gospel: the signs, believing, (eternal) life, and the identity of Jesus as Messiah and Son of God. The epilogue portrays the relationship between Peter and "the disciple whom Jesus loved" in terms of differing yet equally legitimate roles of service within the believing community.

8.4 Proposed Structure of John's Gospel

The structure of John's entire Gospel based on Jesus' seven signs may therefore be delineated as follows:

I. Introduction: The Word Made Flesh in Jesus Christ (1:1–18)
II. The Gospel Proper: From John's to the Evangelist's Witness (1:19–20:31)
  A. Act I: The Messiah's Signs and Rejection by His Own (1:19–12:50)
   1. From John to Jesus: The Beginnings of Jesus' Ministry (1:19–50)
   2. From Cana to Cana: The Cana Cycle (2:1–4:54; Signs 1–3)
   3. From Jerusalem to Bethany: The Festival Cycle (5:1–10:42; Signs 4–6)
   4. From Bethany to Jerusalem: The Climactic Sign (11:1–12:36; Sign 7)
   5. Conclusion: The Jewish Rejection of the Messiah despite His Many Signs (12:37–50)
  B. Act II: The Messiah's Passion and Preparation of His Own (13:1–20:31)
   1. Jesus Anticipates His Exaltation: The Footwashing, the Farewell Discourse, and Jesus' Final Prayer (13:1–17:26)
   2. Jesus Completes His Earthly Mission: The Passion Narrative (18:1–20:29)
   3. Conclusion: Believe in Jesus the Messiah on Account of His Signs (20:30–31)
III. Epilogue: Jesus' Third and Final Resurrection Appearance and His Commissioning of Peter and "the Disciple Whom Jesus Loved" (21:1–25)

9 The Structure of John's Letters

9.1 Introduction

The outline of John's second and third letters is predictable and easily discernible. As typical first-century letters, both follow the simply pattern "Introduction—Body—Conclusion." The structure of 1 John, however, has generated much debate,[175] and to date no scholarly consensus has been reached. The options range from those who see an intricate macro-chiasm to those who reject any coherent structure.[176] The lack of consensus in scholarship has led several to posit various theories of a source- or redaction-critical nature.[177] Most scholars, however, dismiss such theories as unproven, unlikely, or not particularly helpful.

One reason why the structure of 1 John is rather difficult to discern is the author's subtlety. The topical transitions are virtually seamless, and the various subjects recur in cyclical intervals throughout the letter. Nevertheless, given the clear structure of the gospel and the Apocalypse, as well as the careful nuances displayed within the various paragraphs, it seems likely that the author purposefully structured his letter.[178] However, in the scholarly literature there is wide agreement only with regard to the introduction (1 John 1:1–4) and the conclusion (5:13–21).

The structural proposals for 1 John fall into three major categories: divisions into two, three, or multiple parts.[179] Among those who hold to a division into two parts, the main item of discussion is whether the break should be placed toward the end of 1 John 2 or at 3:11. Among those who hold to a three-part structure, the debate centers on whether the first major break is at 2:17, 28, or 29, and whether the second major break is at 4:1 or 4:7. Among those who see multiple divisions, one finds a plethora of proposals.[180]

---

175. For a survey of recent options see Birger Olsson, "First John: Discourse Analyses and Interpretations," in *Discourse Analysis and the New Testament: Approaches and Results* (ed. Stanley E. Porter and Jeffrey T. Reed; JSNTSup 170; Studies in New Testament Greek 4; Sheffield: Sheffield Academic Press, 1999), 369–91.

176. See, e.g., Peter J. van Staden, "The Debate on the Structure of 1 John," *Hervormde Teologiese Studies* 47 (1991): 487–502, who argues for a macro-chiasm; and Marshall, *Epistles*, 26, who suggests that there is no coherent structure. See also Kruse, *Letters of John*, 32, who writes that his analysis of the letter will not "trace any developing argument through the letter because there isn't one."

177. The most recent to propose a series of sources edited into one document is J. C. O'Neill, *The Puzzle of 1 John: A New Examination of Origins* (London: SPCK, 1966); yet Marshall, *Epistles*, 30, notes that his theory is "completely speculative, and has won no adherents." For other source theories, see Ernst von Dobschütz, "Johanneische Studien I," *ZNW* 8 (1907): 1–8; Rudolf Bultmann, *The Johannine Epistles* (Hermeneia; trans. R. Philip O'Hara et al.; Philadelphia: Fortress, 1973); and Wolfgang Nauck, *Die Tradition und der Charakter des ersten Johannesbriefes* (WUNT 3; Tübingen: Mohr, 1953). For a rearrangement theory, see K. Tomoi, "The Plan of the First Epistle of John," *ExpTim* 52 (1940–41): 117–19.

178. Schnackenburg, *Epistles*, 12–13, is doubtless correct when he says that the author "does not merely sail along without any particular plan."

179. Brown, *Epistles*, 116–29.

180. The presentation of structural proposals for 1 John below is adapted from the chart in Brown, *Epistles*, 764; see also L. Scott Kellum, "On the Semantic Structure of 1 John: A Modest Proposal," *Faith & Mission* 23 (2008): 36–38. The works cited are, in order of citation: Joseph Chaine, *Les épitres catholiques* (EBib; 2nd ed.; Paris: J. Gabalda, 1939), 97–260; Wilhelm Vrede, "Die Johannesbriefe," in *Die katholischen Briefe* (HNT 9; 4th ed.; Bonn: Hanstein, 1932), 143–92; Tomoi, "Plan"; Smalley, *1, 2, 3 John*; Longacre, "Exegesis of 1 John"; Brown, *Epistles*; Gary M. Burge, *The Letters of John* (NIVAC; Grand Rapids: Zondervan, 1996); Akin, *1, 2, 3 John*; D. Moody Smith, *First, Second, and Third John* (Interpretation; Louisville: John Knox, 1991); A. Hort, "The Divisions of the First Epistle of St. John: A Correspondence between Drs. Westcott and Hort," *The Expositor* 7/3 (1907): 481–93; Schnackenburg, *Epistles*; Horst Balz, "Die Johannesbriefe," in *Die*

9.2 Structural Proposals for 1 John
9.2.1 Division into Two Parts

Chaine, Vrede, Tomoi	Smalley, Longacre	Brown, Burge, Akin, Smith
1:5 – 2:28	1:5 – 2:29	1:5 – 3:10
2:29 – 5:12	3:1 – 5:12	3:11 – 5:12

9.2.2 Division into Three Parts

Hort, Schnackenburg	Balz, Thompson	Braun, de la Potterie
1:5 – 2:17	1:5 – 2:27	1:5 – 2:28
2:18 – 3:24	2:28 – 3:24	2:29 – 4:6
4:1 – 5:12	4:1 – 5:12	4:7 – 5:12

9.2.3 Division into Multiple Parts

D. Guthrie	Wilder	Lea/Black	Bruce	Stott	Edwards
1:5 – 2:29	1:5 – 2:17	1:5 – 2:27	1:5 – 2:2	1:5 – 2:2	1:5 – 2:11
3:1 – 24	2:18 – 27	2:28 – 4:6	2:3 – 17	2:3 – 27	2:12 – 17
4:1 – 6	2:28 – 3:24	4:7 – 5:5	2:18 – 27	2:28 – 4:6	2:18 – 27
4:7 – 21	4:1 – 6	5:6 – 17	2:28 – 3:24	4:7 – 5:5	2:28 – 3:24
5:1 – 5	4:7 – 5:12	5:18 – 21	4:1 – 6	5:6 – 17	4:1 – 6
5:6 – 12	5:13 – 21		4:7 – 21	5:18 – 21	4:7 – 5:21
5:13 – 21			5:1 – 5	5:1 – 12	
			5:6 – 12	5:13 – 21	
			5:13 – 21		

9.3 Proposed Outlines for 1, 2, and 3 John
9.3.1 Introduction

The following outline for 1 John concurs with those who see a three-part structure to the book and specifically those who suggest the following major units: 1 John 1:5 – 2:27; 2:28 – 3:24; and 4:1 – 5:12. Within this overall structure, it is possible to discern interrelated paragraphs that provide a further breakdown of the flow of the

---

"Katholischen Briefe": Die Briefe des Jakobus, Petrus, Johannes und Judas (NTD 10; 11th ed.; Göttingen: Vandenhoeck & Ruprecht, 1973); Marianne Meye Thompson, in Achtemeier, Green, and Thompson, Introducing the New Testament; François-Marie Braun, "Les épîtres de Saint Jean," in L'évangile de Saint Jean (SB; 3rd rev. ed.; Paris: Cerf, 1973), 231 – 77; Ignace de la Potterie, La vérité dans Saint Jean (2 vols.; AnBib 73 – 74; Rome: Pontifical Biblical Institute, 1977); Guthrie, New Testament Introduction; A. N. Wilder, "Introduction and Exegesis of the First, Second, and Third Epistles of John," in The Interpreter's Bible (ed. G. A. Buttrick; Nashville: Abingdon, 1957), 12:207 – 313; Thomas Lea and David Alan Black, The New Testament: Its Background and Message (2nd ed.; Nashville: Broadman & Holman, 2003); F. F. Bruce, The Epistles of John (Grand Rapids: Eerdmans, 1979); Stott, Letters of John; and Ruth B. Edwards, The Johannine Epistles (NTG; Sheffield: Sheffield Academic Press, 1996).

argument of the letter. It is best to understand 1:5–2:27 as an extended overview of the rest of the letter (especially in relation to the departure of the secessionists), with 2:28–3:24 elaborating on the meaning of true love and 4:1–5:12 on the antichrists and the love commandment.[181]

9.3.2 First John

    A. Introduction (1:1–4)
    B. The Departure of the Secessionists (1:5–2:27)
        1. True Believers Walk in the Light (1:5–2:2)
        2. True Believers Keep Jesus' Commandments (2:3–11)
        3. Grow in Christ and Do Not Love the World (2:12–17)
        4. Abiding and Departing (2:18–27)
    C. The Measure of True Love (2:28–3:24)
        1. Children of God Sanctify Themselves (2:28–3:10)
        2. Children of God Keep His Commandments (3:11–24)
    D. The Antichrists and the Love Commandment (4:1–5:12)
        1. Test the Spirits (4:1–6)
        2. The Theological Basis of Brotherly Love (4:7–12)
        3. Confidence from Correct Doctrine (4:13–21)
        4. Testimony and Proof (5:1–12)
    E. Purpose Statement and Conclusion (5:13–21)

9.3.3 Second John

    A. Introduction (1–3)
    B. Warning against Welcoming False Teachers (4–11)
        1. "Walking in the Truth" Requires Brotherly Love (4–6)
        2. "Walking in the Truth" Requires Guarding the Truth about the Son (7–11)
    C. Conclusion (12–13)

9.3.4 Third John

    A. Introduction (1–4)
    B. Commendation of Gaius and Demetrius, Condemnation of Diotrephes (5–12)
        1. Gaius's Godly Behavior toward Other Believers (5–8)
        2. The Ungodly Behavior of Diotrephes (9–10)
        3. Commendation of Demetrius (11–12)
    C. Conclusion (13–14)

---

181. For a thorough analysis of the structure of 1 John, see Kellum, "Semantic Structure of 1 John," 34–82.

9.4 Conclusion

Following the discussions of the genre of John's gospel and letters, of Johannine vocabulary, style, and literary devices, and of the structure of John's gospel and letters, it is now possible to subject these writings to close literary-theological readings. These readings, in turn, will form the basis for the discussion of major Johannine theological themes in Part 3 below.

Chapter 4

A LITERARY-THEOLOGICAL READING OF JOHN'S GOSPEL

BIBLIOGRAPHY

Beck, David R. *The Discipleship Paradigm: Readers and Anonymous Characters in the Fourth Gospel.* Biblical Interpretation Series 27. Leiden: Brill, 1997. **Bennema, Cornelis**. "A Theory of Character in the Fourth Gospel with Reference to Ancient and Modern Literature." *Biblical Interpretation* 17 (2009): 375–421. **Carter, Warren**. *John: Storyteller, Interpreter, Evangelist.* Peabody, MA: Hendrickson, 2006. **Culpepper, R. Alan**. *Anatomy of the Fourth Gospel: A Study in Literary Design.* Philadelphia: Fortress, 1983. **Hägerland, Tobias**. "John's Gospel: A Two-Level Drama?" *JSNT* 25 (2003): 309–22. **Keener, Craig S**. *The Gospel of John: A Commentary.* 2 vols. Peabody, MA: Hendrickson, 2003. **Köstenberger, Andreas J**. *John.* BECNT. Grand Rapids: Baker, 2004. **Kruse, Colin G**. *John.* TNTC. Downers Grove, IL: InterVarsity Press, 2003. **Moloney, Francis J**. *The Gospel of John.* SP. Collegeville, MN: Liturgical Press, 1998. **Ridderbos, Herman N**. *The Gospel of John: A Theological Commentary.* Grand Rapids: Eerdmans, 1997. **Stibbe, Mark W. G**. "The Elusive Christ: A New Reading of the Fourth Gospel." *JSNT* 44 (1991): 19–38. Idem. *John as Storyteller: Narrative Criticism and the Fourth Gospel.* Cambridge: Cambridge University Press, 1992. Idem. *John.* Sheffield: Sheffield Academic Press, 1993. Idem, ed. *The Gospel of John as Literature: An Anthology of Twentieth-Century Perspectives.* NT Tools & Studies 17. Leiden: Brill, 1993. **Thatcher, Tom, and Stephen D. Moore**, eds. *Anatomies of Narrative Criticism: The Past, Present, and Futures of the Fourth Gospel as Literature.* SBLRBS 55. Atlanta: SBL, 2008. **Williams, P. J**. "Not the Prologue of John." Paper presented at the Annual Meeting of the SBL. San Diego, CA, November 17, 2007.

10 A LITERARY-THEOLOGICAL READING OF JOHN'S GOSPEL

Following the discussions of important foundational literary matters in the preceding two chapters, it is now possible to embark on a literary-theological reading of John's gospel (chap. 4) and letters (chap. 5, below). By "literary-theological reading" is meant a careful reading of the gospel narrative with attention to its literary features and its various sustained and interrelated theological themes. The treatment of the structure of John's gospel above (see section 8.4) will form the framework for the following discussion.[1] In order to facilitate cross-reference with the discussion of major Johannine themes in Part 3, instances of such motifs are put in bold font. References to literary features such as irony or misunderstandings discussed in chapter 3 above are put in bold font as well.

Engaging in this close narrative reading of John's gospel and letters before attempting to present the major Johannine theological themes in Part 3 is vital, because such a literary-theological reading ensures that the presentation of John's theology is properly grounded in a contextual, narrative apprehension of the respective documents. Methodologically, Biblical Theology is inextricably wedded to a study of the writings in question in their historical and literary settings. As Adolf Schlatter observed, "In speaking of 'New Testament' theology, we are saying that it is not the interpreter's own theology or that of his church and times that is examined but rather the theology expressed by the New Testament itself."[2]

10.1 Introduction: The Word Made Flesh in Jesus Christ (1:1–18)

10.1.1 The Function of the Introduction in Relation to the Gospel as a Whole

John starts his gospel with a lengthy, exceedingly well-crafted introduction (structurally matched by a concluding section or epilogue following the purpose statement at the end of John 20).[3] What is the purpose of this introduction? Judging from the internal evidence, including the opening words, it provides a theological introduction to the gospel that (1) presents Jesus and highlights his significance within the framework of antecedent **salvation history**; and (2) clarifies the relationship between the **new messianic community** (followers of Jesus) and OT Israel. As such, the introduction sounds many of the major themes fleshed out more fully in the remainder of the gospel, similar in function to an initial orientation given to a new student or employee at the beginning of their studies or work.[4]

Specifically, this framework of antecedent salvation history into which Jesus is placed includes the following:

- **Creation** (vv. 1–5)
- John [the Baptist] (vv. 6–8, 15)
- Manifestations of God's presence and **glory** in the tabernacle and the **temple** (v. 14)
- God's giving of the law at Sinai through Moses (v. 17)

---

1. For a detailed outline, see the Table of Contents and the discussion below.

2. Schlatter, *History of the Christ*, 18.

3. P. J. Williams, "Not the Prologue of John," has argued that "Prologue" is a misnomer. His arguments are weighty. For this reason we will desist from using this nomenclature in the present volume and use the more general term "introduction."

4. Carson, *Gospel according to John*, 111, uses the illustration of a foyer. Others have called the introduction to John's gospel the "proleptic quintessence" (Harnack), a "microcosm" (Valentine), and an "adumbration" (Booser) of the entire gospel (see references in Köstenberger, *John*, 19, n. 2).

In each case, Jesus' relationship is specified by the evangelist. With regard to **creation**, Jesus was the exclusive agent (John 1:1–3). With regard to John, Jesus was the **light**, while John was only a lamp (1:6–9; 5:35) and a witness to that light (1:19–34; 3:22–36); also, Jesus, while human (1:14), was himself God (1:1, 18), while John was "a man," albeit one "sent from God" (1:6). With regard to previous manifestations of God's presence and **glory**, Jesus was the definitive, culminating manifestation of God's presence and glory (1:14, 16; esp. the "signs"). Finally, with regard to God's giving of the law and Moses' function as a mediator of divine revelation, Jesus was the One—the **Son**—who revealed the **Father** as he alone was able to do, owing to his unique relationship to God, being himself **God** (1:1, 17–18). Add to this the striking first-time reference to Jesus in the gospel, found at 1:17, as "Jesus **Christ**" (cf. 17:3), which sounds the note of Jesus' messianic identity.

With regard to the **new messianic community**, John draws on the characteristic OT expression "children of God" with reference to Israel and reapplies it to all those who believe in Jesus (1:12). In a paradoxical phrase, Israel is in the introduction still called "his own" (*hoi idioi*, 1:11), yet forfeits this epithet by rejecting Jesus as **Messiah** (as narrated in 1:19–12:50), so that when the curtain opens to Act II in the Johannine drama in John 13, it is now Jesus' followers—a faithful Jewish remnant—not Israel as a nation, who are identified as Jesus' "own" (*tous idious*, 13:1, identified as those "sent in the world" on a **mission**, cf. 17:18; 20:21).[5]

Hence there are two major special familial relationships identified in the introduction: Jesus as God's unique **Son** (1:14, 18), and those who believe in Jesus as God's children (1:12). The latter theme—that of what properly constitutes God's children—represents the subject of further explication in John 8 (the Jewish leaders are children of the devil) and 11:51–52 (Gentiles are included as well; cf. 10:16).[6]

The introduction also sounds several other important themes that will receive fuller treatment in the remainder of the gospel, such as:

- **Witness** as a major function attesting to Jesus' true identity in relation to God (vv. 6–8, 15)
- Divine **judgment** for the world's—and the Jews'—rejection of his Son, the Messiah (vv. 4–5, 10–11)
- **Revelation**, in the sense of a full disclosure of the nature and purposes of God in and through the person and mission of Jesus (v. 18)

Surprisingly, and significantly, there is no direct (or even indirect) reference to *the cross* in the introduction to John's gospel. This has suggested to some that, for John, *redemption* as a theological category has been completely swallowed up by, and subsumed under, the rubric of *revelation*.[7] If we stay strictly with the introduction,

---

5. See Pryor, *John: Evangelist of the Covenant People*, 55.
6. See R. Alan Culpepper, "The Pivot of John's Prologue," *NTS* 27 (1980): 26–31, who notes that John 1:12 mirrors 1 John 3:1–2, while John 8:31–47 finds its equivalent in 1 John 3:10.
7. E.g., Bultmann, *Theology of the New Testament*, 2:49–69, followed by J. Terence Forestell, *The Word of the Cross: Salvation as Revelation in the Fourth Gospel* (AnBib 57; Rome: Biblical Institute Press, 1974). But see the critique in Köstenberger, *Missions of Jesus and the Disciples*, 74–81.

this may be a possible inference, but as a perusal of the ensuing gospel narrative demonstrates, such a conclusion is premature. Still, it is true that revelation is the overarching category for John in describing the work of the **Son** in that even the crucifixion (redemption) is shown to serve the ultimate purpose of revealing God's **love** for the world (3:16) and his glory, consisting in the perfect obedience of Jesus the Son to the **Father**, "who sent" him (see esp. 17:1, 4 *et passim*).

Also absent from the introduction is a reference to **signs**, one of the most prominent theological themes in John's entire gospel.[8] While alluding to the *function* of the sign in the introduction by instances of the word *doxa* ("**glory**"; 1:14, 16; cf. 2:11), it is not until 2:11 that John refers to "the first [*archēn*] of the signs" performed by Jesus, adding that it is through this sign that he "revealed [*ephanerōsen*] his glory" to his disciples, who responded to him in faith.[9] Also surprisingly absent from the introduction are specific instances of the "sending" word group with reference to Jesus — though John (the Baptist) is said to be "sent from God" (*apestalmenos para theou*) in 1:6. Instead, the introduction speaks of Jesus as "the true **light**" who "was coming into the **world**" (1:9) and refers to him as the "**Word**-made-flesh" (cf. 1:14) and as "the one and only **Son**" from the **Father** (*monogenous para patros*, 1:14; cf. 1:18; 3:16, 18).[10]

These — most likely deliberate — omissions suggest that the evangelist did not intend for his introduction to touch on *everything* that was to follow in the ensuing narrative. Instead, John chose to conceal, or at least not yet mention, more specific entailments of the general framework set up in the introduction. Jesus was the unique Son of the Father; his mission was all about God's glory; his coming became the catalyst for the world's — including many of the Jews' — **unbelief**, as well as the object of **faith** for those who believed in him and thus acquired the right to become "children of God" (1:12). In all this, Jesus' coming, and the revelation he brought, cast a bright light on antecedent **salvation history**: he stood in continuity with, and yet provided fuller and definitive expression of, God's work in **creation** (1:1 – 3; cf., e.g., 5:18), previous manifestations of his presence (1:14), and his giving of the law (1:17).

10.1.2 A Thematic and Narrative Reading of the Introduction

John opens his gospel with a reference to the work of **creation** "in the beginning" through "the Word" (**1:1**). To borrow from John W. Pryor, John serves as the "evangelist of God's covenant people" here, because creation is not only a universal event, it is also part of Israel's history.[11] In fact, the message of the Genesis creation

---

8. See Andreas J. Köstenberger, "The Seventh Johannine Sign: A Study in John's Christology," *BBR* 5 (1995): 87 – 103 (essentially reproduced in chap. 7, sec. 15 below); and the following discussion.

9. Helpful studies of the "glory" motif in John's gospel include G. B. Caird, "The Glory of God in the Fourth Gospel: An Exercise in Biblical Semantics," *NTS* 15 (1968 – 69): 265 – 77; W. Robert Cook, "The 'Glory' Motif in the Johannine Corpus," *JETS* 27 (1984): 291 – 97; and Margaret Pamment, "The Meaning of *Doxa* in the Fourth Gospel," *ZNW* 74 (1973): 12 – 16. See also my essay "The Glory of God in John," in *The Glory of God* (Theology in Community 2; ed. Robert Peterson and Chris Morgan; Wheaton: Crossway, 2009).

10. "Word-made-flesh" is my own rendering. See the discussion in Köstenberger, *John*, 43 – 44.

11. Pryor, *John: Evangelist of the Covenant People*.

narrative is not so much that God created the world and later became the God of Israel, but rather that the God of Israel in the beginning created the world. Creation, in other words, is the first act of the faithful, covenant-keeping God.[12] Hence, in keeping with the message of Genesis, John reaches all the way back to creation to draw a typological connection: in the beginning the God of Israel created the world through the Word; now, in Christ, that same God took on flesh, made his residence among his people, and revealed his **glory**.

Immediately in verse 1, also, John sounds the all-important issue that will dominate much of the ensuing gospel: the **Word**'s (Jesus') relationship to **God**. John's initial words erect a certain tension that places Jesus' identity within the following matrix: the Word was at creation "with God," and the Word "was God" (with *theos*, "God," in the emphatic position in the original Greek). The former truth—that the Word was at creation with God—would have been readily conceded by everyone; the latter assertion—that the Word itself (or himself) was God—was open to question and further debate. John's argument here is that the Word, as God's creative agent, constituted an extension of God's own person, as the one through whom God's creative power became effective. Ultimately, therefore, God the Creator and the Word through which (or whom) he created are inseparable, and according to John they share the same identity while at the same time being distinct. One detects here the quarry from which later conciliar doctrines defining and describing the relationship between God the **Father** and Jesus the **Son** were hewn.[13]

To summarize: John views **creation** as the first, inaugural act of **salvation history** and bases his account of Jesus' coming into the world (i.e., the incarnation, John's equivalent of the Synoptic narrative of the virgin birth) on this primal act. By this John highlights Jesus' unparalleled relationship with God the Creator and presents him as the exclusive and unique agent of God, who is his self-expression—an extension, as it were (rightly understood), of his own identity and deity, the one through whom God's glory was eschatologically and definitively revealed to God's covenant community.

As will become evident throughout especially the first half of John's narrative (and as is intimated in the introduction; see also 3:19–21), Jesus' coming served to separate between **light** and **darkness** in a spiritual sense, just as the original creation, according to Gen 1:3–5, divided between light and darkness. The Jews' **unbelief** kept many from placing their trust in the Messiah, just as unbelief characterized Israel in the wilderness (see esp. 6:30–58 and 12:37–41). At the same time, there were those in Israel who did **believe** and continued in Jesus' teaching, and those followers became the nucleus of Jesus' **new covenant community** that was charged with spreading the message of Jesus the Messiah to the world.

After the initial reference to creation in 1:1 and the partial restatement of verse 1 in **verse 2**, John asserts in **verse 3** that everything was made through the Word, and,

---

12. Note also the reference to "grace and truth" in 1:14, which echoes the OT phrase "lovingkindness and truth" and also refers to God's covenant faithfulness (see Köstenberger, *John*, 44–45).

13. See Köstenberger and Swain, *Father, Son and Spirit*.

conversely, that nothing was made apart from the Word.[14] This seems to prepare the later point that, likewise, no one can come to God the Father apart from Jesus the Son (14:6). "In him," and only in him, "was **life**," John continues in **verse 4**, which attributes to the Word life-giving power in keeping with the OT characterization of God, and God alone, as the Life-Giver. That life also serves as people's "**light**," helping them to walk by it and exposing their moral and spiritual darkness (**v. 5**; see later 3:19–21 and 12:35–36, 46). That light also shines and is stronger than the darkness that did not overcome it (v. 5), try though it did—Satan operating through Judas and the Jewish leaders.[15]

The introduction of "a man ... whose name was John" in **verse 6** marks a transition from creation "in the beginning" (v. 1) all the way to the time immediately preceding the beginning of Jesus' ministry, leaping over all of Israel's history including the exodus, the giving of the law, the monarchy (David), the building of the temple, and other significant events in the life and history of the Jewish nation. Whatever the source-critical or literary structural issues are that have typically preoccupied scholars (often to the extent that they fail to ask biblical-theological questions at any point in their inquiry), this movement directly from creation to John (the Baptist) calls for theological exploration and explanation.[16] Whether or not the introduction to John's gospel is chiastic—among the many proposals, several suggest verse 12 as the center of a possible chiasm[17]—attention should be given to the way in which the message of the introduction unfolds as the text is read in consecutive, linear fashion.

On the one hand, verse 6 marks the introduction of a new person, a man by the name of John. Continuity is provided through the reference to God in the same verse (as well as through the references to "the light" in vv. 4–5 and vv. 7–9; see below). While being but a *man*, John was "sent from *God*" (*para theou*). This relates to the previous references in verses 1 and 2 to the Word as being "with God" (*pros ton theon*) in the beginning. The introductory word "there was" (*egeneto*) in verse 6, following up the opening expression "in the beginning" in verse 1, marks the appearance of a new, previously unmentioned, individual on the scene of the narrative. While the full identity of the Word has not yet been disclosed (and will not be disclosed until v. 17), the name of this "man sent from God" in verse 6 is immediately revealed as being "John." Readers of the Synoptics will at once know that this "John" is not the apostle or any other person by the name of John, but John the Baptist (or Baptizer), as he is called there.

---

14. Reading "that has been made" at the end of 1:3 with the preceding rather than the following clause (v. 4); see Köstenberger, *John*, 29–30. Interestingly, John says here that *"everything"* was made through the Word, avoiding reference to "the world"; in v. 10, John's wording is more specifically that *"the world* was made through him," subsequently speaking of the world's unbelief (something of which only humans are capable).

15. Assuming that the meaning of *katelaben* in v. 5 is "overcome" rather than "understood," on which see Köstenberger, *John*, 31 (see esp. n. 37).

16. Cf., e.g., Haenchen, *John*, 1.117, who believes verses 6–8 represent a rather clumsy insertion into an original hymn; and Bultmann, *Gospel of John*, 49, who holds the material is inserted to counter veneration of the Baptist. But see Ridderbos, *Gospel of John*, 42, who ardently defends the unity of the introduction to John's gospel.

17. See Köstenberger, *John*, 23, following Culpepper, "Pivot of John's Prologue."

Apart from possibly presupposing a knowledge of the Synoptics (whether by way of oral tradition or one or several of the written gospels or a combination thereof), the evangelist's identification of the Baptist merely by the name of "John" may also be a function of the fact that the other "John" looming in the background of the gospel (featured prominently in the Synoptics and mentioned also in Acts 1:13; 3–4; 8:14–25; and Gal 2:9), John the son of Zebedee (cf. John 21:2), is not explicitly named in this gospel, so that the Baptist can be identified by the name "John" without further qualification. This coheres with the lack of explicit identification by name of other significant characters in John's gospel, such as Jesus' mother.[18] Identifying the Baptist merely as "John" also serves the purpose of deemphasizing John's baptizing activity that, in this gospel, is subsumed under John's role as one of several witnesses to Jesus. Hence, for the evangelist, John "the Baptist" becomes John "the witness."

According to this gospel, then, the purpose of John's coming was ultimately not to administer baptism or even to preach repentance, but to bear **witness** to the people of Israel regarding the Messiah (see esp. 1:31: "that he might be revealed to Israel"). **Verse 7** specifies the *content* and *desired result* of John's witness: his witness is to "that light" (cf. vv. 4–5); and the desired result is that "through him [*di' autou*; the same phrase is used in v. 3 with reference to all things having been created through the Word] all might believe." Similar to verse 2 reiterating verse 1, so **verse 8** essentially reiterates (in negative terms) verse 7: John was not himself the **light**; he rather witnessed *to* the light.[19]

Some have speculated that the evangelist here sought to counter an undue allegiance to John the Baptist over against Jesus.[20] However, this is not a necessary implication from the present statement and John's self-identification later in the chapter. More plausibly, relating the Baptist's identity to that of Jesus provides an opportunity for the evangelist to clarify their respective roles and to accentuate Jesus' uniqueness in relation to John, especially since the latter was held in high esteem by many Jews in Jesus' day (Matt 14:5 pars.) and thereafter (Acts 19:1–7). What is more, as will shortly become clear, John himself, not only Jesus, fulfills an important **salvation-historical** role (see the citation of Isa 40:3 at John 1:23) and thus highlights the continuity and progressive nature of God's pursuit of his purposes for humanity centered on providing salvation through his Son, the Messiah.

Positively, there was "the true **light**" (**v. 9**) that "gives light to everyone" (though not necessarily for salvation, because the light of revelation still demands a faith response). "The true light" "was coming into the world,"[21] which now moves past

---

18. On anonymity in John's gospel, see David R. Beck, *The Discipleship Paradigm: Readers and Anonymous Characters in the Fourth Gospel* (BIS 27; Leiden: Brill, 1997).

19. For a discussion of the Johannine portrayal of the relationship between John the Baptist and Jesus in terms of *synkrisis* in ancient literature, see Christoph G. Müller, "Der Zeuge und das Licht. Joh 1,1–4,3 und das Darstellungsprinzip der *synkrisis*," *Bib* 84 (2003): 479–509. Passages discussed by this author include John 1:6–8, 15, 19–51 (esp. 1:27, 40); 3:22–43 (esp. 3:29); 5:35; and 10:40–42.

20. E.g., Bultmann, *Gospel of John*, 49.

21. For this way of reading verse 9 as a periphrastic construction see esp. Ed L. Miller, "The True Light Which Illumines Every Man," in *Good News in History, Fs. Bo Reicke* (ed. Ed L. Miller; Atlanta: Scholars Press, 1993), 63–82. Alternatively, "coming into the world" could modify "every person," but this, as a mere truism, is less likely than a reference to the *light* coming into the world, taken as an anticipatory reference to the incarnation in verse 14.

its/his role in creation to a more specific visitation that will be described even more strikingly as "[becoming] flesh" in verse 14. This characterization builds on a trajectory of OT references to the **Messiah** or Coming One in terms of light (Num 24:17; Isa 9:2 cf. 42:6–7; Mal 4:2), and "true" light also distinguishes this light from other, "false," lights that likewise made their public appearance to gain adherents.[22] Beyond this, "true" may also allude to the fulfillment of God's salvific purposes in and through Christ, which are intimated ahead of time in the form of OT typologies, predictions, and covenants and deeply embedded in Israel's various religious institutions, **festivals**, and religious observances (developed esp. in chaps. 5–10 below).

While John 1:9 speaks of the coming of the true light into the world in the past—similar to John's coming to serve as a witness in verses 6–8—**verse 10** quickly moves past this most oblique reference to the incarnation to refer globally, and in hindsight, to the "true light" having been in the world. The evangelist notes that, paradoxically, ironically, and tragically (adversative *kai*, "but"), the world made through the Word rejected that very Word and failed to recognize it/him. The world should have welcomed its Creator as a familiar friend, indeed, as a hero, Savior, and Sovereign; instead, it showed itself alien and antagonized, hostile and morally and spiritually dark, apostate and fallen.

This reference to the rejection of the Word by the **world** casts the coming of the Word, as far as its purpose for the people of Israel is concerned, largely in terms of failure (an emphasis that continues to prevail in John 6:60–66; 7:1–9; and 12:36b–41; see below). Not that the Word itself has failed; the Word, as "the light," invariably "shines in the darkness," and (better: but) "the darkness has not overcome it" (v. 5). Indeed, the light "gives light to everyone" (v. 9). No, the failure lies, not with the Word's revelation of God, but with people's lack of proper response *to* that revelation. It is this failure to respond to this revelation that renders human beings culpable and without excuse (see 15:22).

Verse 11, closely following suit on verse 10 and specifying the reference to the light's coming into the world in verse 9, states that he—the Word and true light—came, literally, "into his own things" (*ta idia*)—that is, his home (where one's possessions are kept; for this use of *ta idia* in this gospel, see 19:27). The Word came home; yet, similar to a soldier who has served in battle for a period of time and then returns home only to find it occupied by a stranger, the Word's homecoming was not a pleasant occasion for rejoicing (as it should have been), but rather highlighted the alienation between the created universe and its Creator, a result of the fall and human sin. Thus the Word's homecoming exposed a stark contrast between the world's original intended purpose of living in harmony with its Creator and its demise into a dark and inhospitable place, giving the chilliest of receptions to the One deserving of worship and eternal gratitude.

---

22. Regarding OT references to the coming of the Messiah in terms of light see esp. Horbury, *Messianism*, 92–93, 99–100. Regarding first-century messianic impostors, see, e.g., Paul W. Barnett, "The Jewish Signs Prophets—A.D. 40–70: Their Intentions and Origin," *NTS* 27 (1981): 679–97.

The second half of verse 11 then changes the grammatical gender from the Word's "own *things*" (*ta idia*; v. 11a) to "his own *people*" (*hoi idioi*; v. 11b). On one level, this need only refer to the people in the world, since "things" cannot meaningfully be said to "receive" the Word. Yet beyond this narrowing of the reference to "his own" probably looms a wordplay that includes both the world and God's chosen people, the Jews, who were uniquely God's "own," not by their own merit but by virtue of divine election. As the OT frequently notes, the people of Israel were in a special sense God's "children." Yet as **verse 12** strikingly states, now that the light has come, this special status of being God's children is bestowed only on those who "believed in his [Jesus'] name."[23]

This means that those Jews who rejected the incarnate Word's claim of being God's Messiah thereby forfeited their status of being God's children and instead proved to be one with the larger world of humanity that rejected the light owing to their alienation and moral darkness. Thus the coming of the light into the world did not merely demonstrate the world's alienation from its Creator and his truth, but also the alienation of many Jews from their covenant-keeping God, whose salvific and revelatory purposes found their ultimate fulfillment in the coming and revelation of Jesus. Jews who rejected the Messiah had thus become indistinguishable from the world, while at the same time, with faith in Jesus as Messiah constituting the sole requirement for becoming a child of God, the doors were opened for non-Jews to enter the orbit of saving grace in fulfillment of God's creative purposes that encompass "all things" (John 1:3) and his salvific purposes that include "all [people]" (v. 7; though see 12:20–36).

Reception or rejection—according to John, these are the only two stark alternatives; there is no other. As the gospel narrative will develop, secret discipleship of Jesus falls short and proves inadequate (12:42–43), and all efforts at neutrality are doomed and render a person morally culpable (e.g., Pilate). Rudolf Bultmann may have been wrong in many of his historical reconstructions of the background of John's gospel, and wrong in the particular form of existentialism he adopted and advocated, but he was surely right in saying that in and through his narrative, John calls each and every one of his readers to a decision regarding the identity of Jesus—whether or not Jesus was God—that has eternal consequences.[24]

The light has come into the world: will you and I receive it? As John's gospel makes clear and as the introduction intimates, the Jewish leaders and the nation they represented did not. But some, a Jewish remnant (the Twelve, 6:66–71; 13:1) as well as representative Samaritans and Gentiles (John 4), did. And Jesus himself envisioned a **mission** subsequent to his "glorification" through his **new messianic community** that would extend beyond the confines of ethnic Israel to all of God's children—Jews as well as Gentiles (10:16; 11:51–52). Hence the introduction in 1:12 affirms what 3:16 will later state even more emphatically—that "whoever"

---

23. For a study of the Johannine concept of authority (see the use of *exousia* ["right"] in v. 12), see Rainer Metzner, "Vollmacht im Johannesevangelium," *NovT* 45 (2003): 22–44.

24. Bultmann, *Gospel of John*, 162 *et passim*.

believes in Jesus will have eternal life, regardless of ethnicity, race, or cultural background (see 12:32; cf. Gal 3:28).

Verse 13 then strikingly elaborates on the true nature of those "children ... born of God" who become such by virtue of their faith in the name of Jesus (made explicit in v. 17). In truth, they are "born," not physically as a result of human initiative and conception, but "of God." **Born of God**! How can this be? This is precisely the question Nicodemus will ask later in John 3. In the context of his larger narrative, John here seems to speak of the spiritual regeneration that comes from faith in the Word-made-flesh, the God-sent Messiah who died and rose again, the One who is now exalted and through that same Spirit directs the mission of his followers. For John, as for Paul (2 Cor 5:17; Gal 6:15), what counts is nothing less than a new creation (the implication and imagery conjured up through the allusion at John 20:22 to the account of God's "breathing on" the first man and constituting him as a "living being" in Gen 2:7).

The reference to birth from God in John 1:13 continues to underscore the theocentric nature of the introduction. The Word, at creation, subsisted "with God" in his presence (vv. 1, 2). John was sent "from God" on a mission to testify to the Son (v. 6). And faith in the name of that Word, and that Son, allows people to enter into the privilege (adoption, as Paul called it: Rom 8:15, 23; Gal 4:5; Eph 1:5) of becoming "children of God" (John 1:12) who are "born of God" (v. 13; see also 1 John 3:9; 4:7; 5:1, 4, 18). God's presence pervades all of **salvation history**, and he is the source, both of the missions of the Word and of John (though specific "sending" terminology is not yet used with regard to Jesus in the introduction), and of the life of believers.[25] God is thus the towering, ubiquitous figure in the verses thus far considered in the introduction (John 1:1–13), and it is in his orbit that references to other agents and recipients are placed and must be understood.[26] It is in God that John and believers have their source and origin. The Word, for its part, is in a category all its own. It/He alone was with God already in the beginning and can be said to "have come into the world" in a sense that indicates prior existence.

It is the identity of this **Word** that is now the subject of further elaboration by the evangelist starting in **verse 14**. "The Word" was last mentioned explicitly in the opening verse (though it is the implicit subject of much that follows, including references to "the light"). There is not much of a transition between verses 13 and 14, and a shift of topic is clearly evident. There is also an element of repetition in that the light's "coming into the world" — the more oblique equivalent to "the Word became flesh" — has already been mentioned in verses 9 and 11. The difference between those previous references and the present one is that the former adopts a more distant vantage point while the latter operates in the mode of first-person (plural) eyewitness testimony.[27]

---

25. Contra, George R. Beasley-Murray, "The Mission of the Logos-Son," in *The Four Gospels 1992: Festschrift Frans Neirynck* (BETL 100; ed. F. van Segbroeck, C. M. Tuckett, Gilbert van Belle, and J. Verheyden; Leuven: Leuven University Press, 1992), 3:1855–68.

26. See Köstenberger and Swain, *Father, Son and Spirit*, chap. 2.

27. On eyewitness testimony in the Gospels, see Bauckham, *Jesus and the Eyewitnesses*, who seeks to reclaim the foundational significance of eyewitness testimony for interpreting the Gospels but who

The Word—the same Word that was in the beginning with God and was God; the same Word that served as the exclusive agent of God's creation—that Word was made flesh and "made his dwelling" (lit., "pitched his tent" [*skēnoō*], v. 14; elsewhere in the NT only in Rev 7:15; 12:12; 13:6; 21:3) among "us," and "we" have seen (perhaps better: perceived) his **glory**. Thus the language here shifts from the safe distance of an observer and reporter of news, as it were, to that of a participant observer whose life was affected by the Word-made-flesh.[28] Most likely, the "we" are John and his fellow apostles (cf. John 2:11; see also 13:23; 19:35; 21:24–25). The word "perceive" is *theaomai*, a stronger word in some of its Johannine occurrences than mere "seeing" (e.g., 1:32; 6:5; 11:45), indicating (spiritual) perception, discernment, and recognition of God's glory being revealed in and through the work of Jesus (as will become clear later, particularly in his signs; see esp. 2:11 but also 9:3; 11:4, 40).

This, incidentally, does not elevate perceptiveness as a human work, as if some individuals were more perceptive than others and this perceptiveness became the distinguishing characteristic between believers and nonbelievers. Nothing is said here about the *source* of this perceptiveness, though elsewhere in the gospel it is made clear that it is *God* who, through Jesus the Messiah, opens the eyes of the blind (John 9) and gives life (John 11). Nevertheless, it is true that, aided by Jesus' "signs," some perceived God's glory in Jesus while many did not, being blinded, as it were, by their (mistaken) preconceived notions of who the Messiah was going to be (gathered in 7:25–44), by their pride and sinful rebellion (8:31–59), and by other factors.

The One who was God (v. 1), thus, became a human being—"flesh" (*sarx*, v. 14; note the immediately preceding reference to *sarx* in v. 13),[29] a term more crass than "body" (*sōma*; used with reference to Jesus at 2:21; 19:31, 38, 40; 20:12) or "a human being" (*anthrōpos*; e.g., 19:5) or "a man" (*anēr*; see 1:30)—and pitched his tent among people. This, in context, refers, to be sure, to humanity at large—his home (v. 11a); but more particularly and specifically it refers to the people of Israel, the Jewish people—"his own" (v. 11b)—the descendants of the wilderness generation who had previously witnessed God's revelation in the signs and wonders of Moses (cf. 4:48); in the manna and the water from the rock; in the parting of the Red Sea and the miraculous deliverance from bondage and slavery in Egypt; in the pillar of fire; and in the tabernacle. It refers ultimately, however, to the representatives of the new messianic community, who did perceive the Word's glory—glory,

---

contends that the "disciple whom Jesus loved" (the author of John's gospel) was not one of the Twelve. This would mean that the place of honor at Jesus' side at the Last Supper was occupied by a nonmember of the Twelve (but see the critique in chap. 1, sec. 2.1.3.1.3 above; see also Köstenberger and Stout, "The Disciple Jesus Loved").

28. Cf. Bauckham, *Jesus and the Eyewitnesses*, 21–30, and his point that the ancient ideal sources for historians were considered to be oral reports of eyewitnesses and that detached observation was in no means superior to participation in the events later narrated by historians.

29. The connection between the references to *sarx* in verses 13 and 14 is obscured by the fact that many translations, including the TNIV, translate verse 14, but not verse 13, with "flesh," while rendering the first instance in verse 13 as "*human* decision" (lit. "will of the flesh"). But the connection may be significant: Jesus entered that same fleshly realm of humanity in which human birth takes place. Other instances of *sarx* in John are 3:6; 6:51, 52, 53, 54, 55, 56, 63; 8:15; and 17:2. This indicates that Jesus' instruction of Nicodemus in chap. 3 and his Bread of Life Discourse in chap. 6 are the two major pericope "fleshing out" the reference to Jesus' *sarx* in 1:14.

as John tells us, "of the one and only Son, who came from the Father, full of grace and truth" (v. 14).

Little does the unsuspecting reader of the introduction to John's gospel know, however, that the "glory" of the Son to be revealed by the Father will entail the "lifting up" of the Son of Man through crucifixion. Only gradually, the fourth evangelist reveals through the course of his narrative, and particularly in the words of Jesus, that the glory spoken of in the introduction is a *crucified* glory, a glory that shines forth initially in selected messianic "signs" of Jesus and subsequently finds its climactic expression in the exaltation of the Son at the cross, in keeping with Isaiah's vision of Jesus' glory (John 12:41). Hence the thrust of Jesus' mission in its entirety is the revelation of God's glory — from the first sign in Cana (2:11) to the cross and the raising of the new temple, Jesus' body, on the third day (12:23; 17:1; cf. 2:20–21), the perfect revelation of God's love for the world at the self-humiliation and divine exaltation of the Son (3:16; 13:1).

What started out as a relationship between God and the Word — or, perhaps better, the Word and God — in verse 1 has now become, in much more intimate and familial terms, a relationship between a one-of-a-kind **Son** and his **Father**. The former designation attests to the Word's ancient origins and to its participation already in the first act of the covenant-establishing and -keeping God and Creator; the latter introduces the more personal aspects of love as that between a unique, cherished son and his father, one who, as the heir, would be trusted by his father and entrusted with the most intimate disclosure pertaining to his purposes and plans. According to John, that Jesus is "the one and only Son" from the Father qualifies him in a unique way to reveal the inner thoughts and workings of the Father — God — to others, workings that most significantly include a substitutionary cross-death the Son would be prepared to die willingly for dark, sinful humanity (3:16).

That Son was "full of grace and truth"; that is, he proved to be a complete, perfect expression of God's covenant-keeping faithfulness (*charis* and *alētheia*, alluding to the OT expressions *ḥesed* and *ʾemet*; cf. Exod 34:6). "Grace and truth" thus continue the series of references to the salvation-historical trajectory pervading the OT of which Jesus, not only the Word but also the Son, has become the ultimate expression.

This becomes even more obvious in light of the subsequent reference to the giving of the law by Moses as a previous expression of God's grace for his people in John 1:16–17. According to John, in Jesus God exchanged (or replaced) grace by grace (understanding the preposition *anti* in the phrase *charin anti charitos* in v. 16 as denoting an exchange of "grace for grace").[30] Strikingly, the references to grace in verses 14, 16, and 17 are the only instances of the Greek word *charis* — so common in Paul — in John's gospel (like "the Word," which, as a christological designation for Jesus, likewise does not occur outside the introduction).

---

30. See Köstenberger, *John*, 46–47.

"**Truth**" (*alētheia*), on the other hand, recurs after verses 14 and 17 again numerous times in the gospel with reference to Jesus (esp. John 14:6) and later the Holy Spirit, "the Spirit of truth." This may indicate that "truth" absorbs some of the content of "grace" and that the truth brought by Jesus is a "gracious truth" that combines aspects of both fidelity to God's covenant promises and the forgiveness of sins available through the sacrificial death of God's "lamb" (1:29, 36). The "truth" theme in John, of course, is far too multifaceted to be treated in a mere paragraph. Later instances of this word group and concept will reveal a surprising variety of connotations invoked.

Nevertheless, it is remarkable to note (and this is all that needs to be said at this juncture) that in these first two instances of "truth" in John's gospel toward the end of the introduction, this term bears clear connotations of God's covenant faithfulness and loyalty. This makes the rejection of Jesus, God's "Sent One," which is narrated in the rest of the gospel (particularly in John 1:19–12:50; 18–19), a deeply personal matter—the rejection of a relationship—rather than merely a rejection of certain truth claims and the refusal of intellectual assent to them. Faith, or relational trust, is what, according to John, is called for in response to the Word's becoming flesh and pitching his tent among us and revealing God's glory (note the ninety-eight instances of the word "believe" in this Gospel, including in the purpose statement in 20:30–31).

After this reference to the Word becoming flesh in John 1:14, **verse 15** returns, perhaps surprisingly, to the topic of John (the Baptist). In the previous reference in verses 6–8, the reader was told in third-person references about John's role as a witness to the light. Now we hear from John directly in the form of direct speech (the first and only such instance in the entire introduction). Thus there is movement from the *fact* of John's being a witness to the specific *content* of John's testimony (further expanded in 1:19–34). While verses 6–8 still resonate with the previous references to creation in verses 1–5, verse 15 follows on the heels of the message conveyed in verse 14 and hence sets the stage for the immediately following narrative of John's and Jesus' ministries. The Word became flesh, and John attested that this One ranked ahead of him because he was before him (v. 15). Seniority in age (albeit by a mere six months or so) on the part of John was overruled by the enfleshed Word's preexistence. Thus John's salvation-historical function is clarified at the very outset: he was not himself the Light but a witness to it (vv. 7–8), and he attested to the origin of the Word-made-flesh in eternity.

Interestingly, verse 15 is interposed as sort of a parenthesis in the flow of the introduction, with verses 16–18 almost seamlessly continuing what was started in verse 14. Hence John, in **verse 16**, picks up where he left off in verse 14, again in the first-person language of personal testimony: "Out of his fullness we have all received" (*hēmeis . . . elabomen*, v. 16). Thus "we have seen" in verse 14 is now met with "we have all received" in verse 16. This constitutes the apostles, the representatives of the **new messianic community**, as being among those "children of God" referenced in the pivotal verse in the introduction, verse 12. The one from whose fullness the apostles and others have received is the unique Son from the Father (v. 14), and "fullness" (*plērōma*, only here in John's gospel) becomes an overall term encompassing the "grace and truth" mentioned previously in verse 14 and again in verse 17.

The reference to the giving of the law through Moses in **verse 17** is likewise surprising in the present context, but should be understood within the purview of divine revelation (rather than in terms of the law *qua lex* ["as a set of legal stipulations"]). While Moses mediated genuine divine revelation to God's covenant community Israel, Jesus — attested by John the Baptist, whose ministry focused on revealing the Messiah to Israel (1:31) — was the conveyor of divine revelation to an even greater extent; for he was the culmination of God's **salvation-historical** purposes for his people ("grace and truth," v. 17). What is more, unlike Moses, who, while being the mediator of divine revelation, had never seen God, Jesus had; and not only this, but he was in the beginning with God (v. 1) and is continually at the Father's side (**v. 18**) and is thus in a unique position to "give a full account" of him (v. 18; my paraphrase; TNIV: "has made him known").[31]

10.2 The Gospel Proper: From John's to the Evangelist's Witness (1:19–20:31)

10.2.1 Act I: The Messiah's Signs and Rejection by His Own (1:19–12:50)

10.2.1.1 From John to Jesus: The Beginnings of Jesus' Ministry (1:19–51)

10.2.1.1.1 John's Witness to Jesus (1:19–34)

The witness of John is at times today, at least on the lay level, regarded as a dispensable preamble to the story of Jesus. With his eccentric demeanor and a message narrowly focused on the Jews of his day, John seems to be a vestige of the OT era that has been rightfully transcended by the appearing of Jesus and the Christianity he founded, a Christianity that is much more broad, inclusive, and universal. There is some appeal to this argument, and even an element of truth in it, but the stubborn fact remains that all four canonical Gospels give considerable attention to John's ministry and message, which seems to call for a reassessment of the above-stated stereotypes and attitudes with regard to John the Baptist.[32]

To be sure, there is a sense in which, as Jesus himself points out later in the gospel, he needs no witness; if he is the Son of God, his words are true, and his testimony regarding himself is accurate and trustworthy (John 8:13–14). At the same time, John's ministry and testimony fulfill important OT prophecy (see below) and are in keeping with the OT principle and requirement for multiple witnesses (Deut 19:15), a requirement that is reiterated in the NT (e.g., Matt 18:16). Indeed, as the Gospels attest, considerable confusion surrounded the expectation of the forerunner

---

31. For a discussion of the important text-critical issue in verse 18 see Köstenberger, *John*, 50.

32. For a helpful treatment of John the Baptist's ministry, see Schlatter, *History of the Christ*, 25–72.

of the Messiah in the Second Temple period. Some thought Elijah would return; others thought "the Prophet" like Moses (John 1:21, 25) would make an appearance, or Jeremiah.

It is in this context that we should understand the inquiry by the "Jewish leaders in Jerusalem" by way of "priests and Levites" in **verse 19** as to John's identity.[33] John immediately denied being himself the Messiah; when asked if he was Elijah or the Prophet, he likewise answered in the negative. Positively, he identified himself as "the voice of one calling in the wilderness, 'Make straight the way for the Lord'" (**v. 23**; citing Isa 40:3).[34] This circumscribes the nature of John's witness very well in Johannine terms: he is "the voice" preparing "the way for the Lord," that is, for God's coming in the person of the Messiah to his people Israel in order to inaugurate a new exodus, as it were, through the wilderness.

Some Pharisees who were part of the delegation follow up with a question regarding John's baptism. If he is neither Elijah nor the Prophet, why does he baptize? In response, John notes that he baptizes only with water; one much greater than he is already in their midst ("the one who comes after me," *ho opisō mou erchomenos*, in **v. 27** reiterates v. 15). This is an self-deprecating response that minimizes John's water baptism and redirects attention squarely on the One who is to come, for whom John's ministry is preparatory. Implied in the narrative is that the Jerusalem delegation leaves to report back to those who sent them. A similar fact-finding mission with regard to Jesus seems to be represented by Nicodemus's coming to Jesus by night in John 3.

The next three days are clearly marked by the recurring phrase *tē epaurion* ("the next day") in **verses 29, 35, and 43**. On the first "next day," that is, the second day of the first week of Jesus' ministry, John saw Jesus coming to him and said, "Look, the Lamb of God, who takes away the sin of the world" (v. 29). **Verse 30** then reproduces almost verbatim the testimony cited in verse 15 of the introduction. Intriguingly, as noted by Schlatter, John does not limit the activity of "the Lamb of God" to Israel (cf. **v. 31**) but speaks with reference to the sin "of the world."[35] This includes both Jews and Gentiles. Contrary to Jewish prejudice, the latter were not beyond the scope of God's redemption; also contrary to the understanding of some (many?) Jews, the Jews' sacrifices did not remove their guilt, so that they, too, required more permanent atonement for sin. Hence John completely transcends the distinction drawn by the Jews in the other Gospels between "tax collectors" and other "sinners," who were in need of God's mercy and forgiveness, and themselves, who were righteous and religiously superior to non-Jews.

"Lamb of God" likely had sacrificial overtones to John's Jewish contemporaries (see on the **Passover** theme below), especially in relation to the terminology of "taking away sins." In the present context, the emphasis seems to lie on the fact that the

---

33. For a literary study of John 1:19–51, see James Muilenburg, "Literary Form in the Fourth Gospel," *JBL* 51 (1932): 40–53; repr. in Stibbe, *Gospel of John as Literature*, 65–76.

34. See Köstenberger, "John," in *Commentary on the NT Use of the OT*, 425–28.

35. Schlatter, *Evangelist Johannes*, 48–49.

Messiah is *God's* lamb, that is, the lamb provided by God himself, and on the fact (as mentioned) that the scope of the Messiah's redemptive mission extended beyond Israel to the world. Beyond this, there may also be the implication that, because the Messiah is *God's* lamb, the removal of sin would be definitive and more permanent than the Jews' current sacrificial system.

The reference to John's ignorance in **verses 31 and 33** indicates that he himself was the recipient of divine revelation in the form of the Spirit descending as a dove from heaven and remaining on Jesus (v. 32). John's reference to "the one who sent me to baptize with water" (v. 33), that is, God, reiterates the point made by the evangelist in the introduction that John was sent by God (v. 6). What remained implicit in John's earlier response to the Jerusalem delegation (vv. 26–27) now is made explicit: that Jesus would baptize "with the **Holy Spirit**." In two perfect tense verbs, indicating the permanent, settled state of John's testimony, John concludes this first day's testimony by stating that he has seen and has borne witness that Jesus is **God's Chosen One** (cf. 20:30–31).

10.2.1.1.2 Jesus' First Appearance and Gathering of First Followers (1:35–51)

On the second "next" day, that is, the third day of Jesus' ministry, John's witness is virtually identical but focused more concretely on two of his own disciples (**vv. 35–36**). As a result of John's testimony, these two disciples follow Jesus (**v. 37**). Noticing this, Jesus engages them in conversation and invites them to come and see where he is staying, and they stay with him that day (**vv. 38–39**).[36] Andrew, identified as "Simon Peter's brother" (apparently presupposing the reader's knowledge of the Synoptic Gospels or at least the gospel story from Synoptic tradition; Peter has not been mentioned by name up to this point in the narrative), is identified as one of the two disciples (**v. 40**). The other is not identified but may be "the disciple whom Jesus loved" and author of John's gospel.[37] Andrew calls Simon and tells him, "We have found the Messiah," and leads him to Jesus, who renames him Peter, "the rock"; cf. **vv. 41–42**).

On the third "next" day, that is, the fourth day of Jesus' ministry, Jesus called a third disciple, Philip (**v. 43**), who shared with Andrew and Peter the same hometown, Bethsaida in Galilee (**v. 44**). Just like Andrew told his brother Peter about Jesus (v. 41), so Philip told Nathanael (**v. 45**). This seems to provide a paradigm for the reader, encouraging him or her to bring others to Jesus once they have discovered him for themselves. Philip identified Jesus as the one of whom both Moses (in the Law) and the Prophets spoke, "Jesus of Nazareth, the son of Joseph" (v. 45). Nathanael responded, with some skepticism, whether anything good could come out of

---

36. See David A. Montgomery, "Directives in the New Testament: A Case Study of John 1:38," *JETS* 50 (2007): 275–88.

37. Bauckham, *Jesus and the Eyewitnesses*, 127–29, thinks the disciple mentioned in John 1:40 is "the disciple whom Jesus loved" and vehemently defends the notion that this disciple is the author of John's gospel (cf. 21:24–25), but he does not identify him with the apostle John (ibid., chaps. 14–17).

Nazareth (**v. 46**); this anti-Galilean prejudice will surface again later in the narrative (e.g., 7:52). Philip did not address this question himself but simply invited Nathanael to come and see for himself (v. 46; see later the Samaritan woman, 4:29).

In an encounter narrated only in John's gospel, Jesus said to the approaching Nathanael that here, truly, was an Israelite in whom there was "no deceit" (**v. 47**; an unmistakable allusion to the original "Israel," Jacob, "the trickster").[38] Nathanael, still skeptical, asked how Jesus knew him (**v. 48**). When Jesus replied that he had seen Nathanael under the fig tree before Philip called him, Nathanael was convinced: "Rabbi, you are the **Son of God**; you are the king of Israel" (**v. 49**). In response, Jesus promised Nathanael he would see greater things than these (**v. 50**). And in a weighty pronouncement (the first instance of the double *amēn* in John's gospel, **v. 51**) Jesus followed up that "you" (now in the plural, referring to the entire group of early disciples) "will see heaven open, and the angels of God ascending and descending on the Son of Man" (v. 51). Jesus, as the Danielic **Son of Man**, a human figure with a transcendent origin, will be the place where God will uniquely reveal himself in a striking and supernatural way.[39]

10.2.1.2 From Cana to Cana: The Cana Cycle: Jesus' Ministry to a Representative Jew, Samaritan, and Gentile (2:1–4:54; Signs 1–3)

10.2.1.2.1 On the Third Day: The First Sign in Cana (2:1–12)

On the "third day," that is, the final day of Jesus' first week of ministry (**v. 1**; possibly anticipating the "third day" on which Jesus rose from the dead; see the reference to the raising of Jesus' body "on the third day," cf. 1 Cor 15:4), Jesus attended a wedding in Cana of Galilee together with his mother and his first disciples (including Andrew and the unnamed disciple [John?], Peter, Philip, and Nathanael per John 1:35–51). Jesus' mother (not named, as the other characters in the pericope, with the exception of Jesus) alerted him that the wedding party had run out of wine, a major social *faux pas*, asking her son to help (**v. 3**). Jesus answered, somewhat sharply, that his mother's and his own interests diverged because his "hour" had not yet come (**v. 4**). Undaunted, his mother tells the servants to do "whatever he tells you" (**v. 5**), and Jesus' first messianic sign ensues, the turning of a large amount of water into wine (**vv. 6–11**).

The evangelist's commentary on this **sign** stresses that this was the "first" (*archēn*) of the signs; reiterates the location as Cana in Galilee (as will later become clear, to set up the outer boundaries of the "Cana Cycle," see 4:54); and notes the purpose/effect/result of the sign: the revelation of Jesus' **glory** and his disciples placing their **faith** in him (v. 11).[40] Hence this first sign constitutes the first validation of

---

38. See Patterson, "Trickster."
39. See Köstenberger, "John," in *Commentary on the NT Use of the OT*, 429–30. See also the discussions of the Son of Man in John's gospel in chap. 9, sec. 20.4 and chap. 14, sec. 31.3 below.
40. Peter-Ben Smit, "Cana-to-Cana or Galilee-to-Galilee: A Note on the Structure of the Gospel of John," *ZNW* 98 (2007): 143–49, prefers the designation "Galilee-to-Galilee" cycle, contending that the signs that "count" (i.e., bring people to faith) are performed in Cana of Galilee while the Jerusalem signs remain unnumbered because they fail to produce true faith.

the evangelist's claim in the introduction that he and his fellow disciples perceived (*theaomai*) the glory of the incarnate Word, God's one-of-a-kind Son (1:14). For Jesus' disciples, therefore, the purpose of Jesus' mission was fulfilled already at his very first sign: the revelation of God's glory in Jesus and the identification of Jesus as God's unique Son.[41]

This explicates the nature and function of the signs. We may be interested in the miracle that took place in the conversion of water into wine. John, by passing over the Greek word for "miracle" used in the Synoptics, *dynamis* ("powerful work") and instead choosing the word *sēmeion* ("sign"), pinpoints the precise purpose of this (and other) of Jesus' powerful works as signposts to Jesus' messianic claim. The "signs" are an integral part of Jesus' messianic mission and must not be separated from it. To observe a powerful work of Jesus while missing the way in which this work validates Jesus' claim of a unique relationship with God is to fail to perceive God's intended purpose of the "sign."

This, then, constitutes both the positive and the negative potential of Jesus' "signs" according to John: if people perceive in a given "sign" Jesus' glory—that is, that Jesus is the **Messiah** and **Son of God** (see the purpose statement, John 20:30–31)—"signs" are powerful signposts and an aid to **faith**. If "signs" are truncated and severed from Jesus' true identity to which they were designed to point, they fail to achieve their intended purpose and confirm people in their unbelief (see esp. 12:36b–40). Thus, as John makes clear, the "signs" are a double-edged sword, having the potential of provoking both faith and incurring judgment for the person who perceives, or fails to perceive, that to which the "signs" are designed to point. In this way John creatively, and ingeniously, transmutes the Synoptic concept of "miracle" (*dynamis*) into the Johannine concept of "sign" (*sēmeion*).[42]

As to the evangelist's narration of this first of Jesus' signs, one cannot help but notice the restraint with which he treats the sign. It is hard to imagine a more oblique way of referring to Jesus' performance of the sign. In fact, it can be said that John does not actually narrate the working of the sign at all; instead, it is left to the reader to infer from the passing reference to the master of the banquet tasting "the water that had been turned into wine" (John 2:9) that this is in fact what had taken place. This oblique way of referring to the actual turning of the water into wine further underscores the way in which John downplays the miraculous in favor of the "sign-ificance" of the feat performed by Jesus.

Other Johannine traits attached to the "sign" are **irony** and **misunderstanding**—the master of the banquet's rebuke of the bridegroom to have saved the best wine for last (John 2:10)—and the stress of the large amount of water turned into wine (120–150 gallons!), which sets a Johannine pattern of focusing on rather spectacular

---

41. This is why, as mentioned in the discussion of the structure of John's gospel in chap. 3, sec. 8, it is erroneous to designate only Part II of John's gospel as "The Book of Glory." John's *entire* gospel is a depiction of Jesus' revelation of God's glory—both in his messianic "signs" and his "lifting up" at the cross.

42. Note that the word "sign" (*sēmeion*) is used in John virtually exclusively by the evangelist; Jesus calls all his works (whether "miraculous" or not) "works" (*erga*). On the "signs" see further the discussion in chap. 7, sec. 15. See also Köstenberger, *Missions of Jesus and the Disciples*, 54–74.

or extraordinary feats of Jesus as signs. This focus on the spectacular also hints at a sign's unusual nature as a major criterion for selection among Jesus' signs as recorded in John's gospel (20:30–31 indicates that Jesus performed "many other signs"; see also 21:24–25 as well as 2:23; 3:2; and other references). Since the evangelist had such a wealth of powerful works of Jesus from which to draw, he had the luxury of choosing only the most extraordinary feats of Jesus.

10.2.1.2.2 One of Jesus' Jerusalem Signs: The Temple Clearing (2:13–22)

Linked through John 2:12 and the first words of 2:13 to the first sign in Cana, Jesus is shown to pay his first visit to Jerusalem in this gospel, one of several more to come in the chapters (and months) ahead.[43] This differs markedly from the Synoptic pattern where Jesus' early activity is concentrated in Galilee and environs and only toward the end is Jesus shown to move inexorably to Jerusalem, where rejection and crucifixion await him (see esp. Luke 9:51). Also well known is the crux of reconciling John's placement of a **temple** clearing at the *beginning* of Jesus' ministry with the similar event recorded in the Synoptics at the onset of Passion Week.

Assuming John's familiarity with the Synoptic Gospels (or at least tradition), John's placement of a temple clearing early on in his narrative should be considered deliberate rather than accidental. Also, it is hard to see how it could have escaped a writer otherwise as astute as John that there is a "conflict" between his and the Synoptic presentation of the temple clearing(s). What is therefore more likely than an actual conflict on the historical level is that John deliberately placed this pericope at this juncture.

A common "solution," of course, is to say John here traded in history for theology and that he displaced and transferred the event from its location in the Synoptics to the beginning of his gospel for theological reasons, transmuting history into theology.[44] The problem with this approach, however, is that both the Synoptics and John tie in their account of the temple clearing closely by way of historical markers and temporal references to the preceding and following narrative, so that any such displacement would seem to involve either John (by far the more common solution) or the Synoptics (rarely argued, though not completely absent from the literature) in a misrepresentation of history.

More likely in my opinion, therefore, is the hypothesis that John, rather than duplicating the Synoptic reference to the later temple clearing but in indirect acknowledgment of his awareness of the clearing recorded in the Synoptics, instead chose to feature an earlier clearing of the temple by Jesus in order to illumine the precedent for the later temple clearing early on in Jesus' ministry. This solution has the advantage of accounting more satisfactorily for the Synoptic representation of

---

43. On 2:12 as the first of several "vestigial scenes" (i.e., scenes lacking dialogue and description; cf. 3:22; 4:43, 45; 6:1–3; 10:40–42; 11:54b), see Charles W. Hedrick, "Vestigial Scenes in John: Settings without Dramatization," *NovT* 47 (2005): 354–66.

44. In an evangelical context, this procedure is defended by, among others, Keener, *John*, 518–19 (see discussion in Köstenberger, *John*, 111, esp. n. 34). I remain to be persuaded, however, that this is a legitimate option for evangelicals with an inerrant view of Scripture.

the contradictory eyewitness testimony at Jesus' Jewish trial and of involving neither the Synoptics nor John in historical misrepresentation.

This seems justified especially since John, as well as the Synoptics, has a demonstrable commitment to historical accuracy, both in his claim of eyewitness testimony in particular and in his "**witness** theme" in general.[45] Also, in his "**misunderstanding** theme" (e.g., 2:22; 7:39), John is careful to preserve the historical difference between the time period prior to and subsequent to Jesus' crucifixion.[46] In fact, John's concern for historical accuracy (not merely theological profundity) has recently seen a considerable rehabilitation in Johannine scholarship.[47]

Now that some of the debris left by the excesses of the historical-critical method has been cleared,[48] we may assess the narrative and theological function of the temple clearing pericope in John 2:13 – 22. At the outset, reference is made to the Jewish **Passover** (**v. 13**). This is the first in a whole series (crescendoing especially in the Festival Cycle in John 5 – 10) of references to **Jewish festivals** in this gospel, which has the cumulative effect of presenting Jesus as the comprehensive fulfillment of the symbolism inherent in various Jewish festivals and other institutions (such as the tabernacle or the temple) throughout the gospel.

Jesus, who is the Passover in his very own person (1 Cor 5:7), is here shown to attend the Passover in Jerusalem early on in his ministry. Similar to the reference to the "six stone water jars, the kind used by the Jews for ceremonial washing," in the preceding pericope (John 2:6), the reference to the "Jewish Passover" also has the (doubtless intended) effect of showing Jesus' coming vis-à-vis old-style Judaism that betrayed the messianic expectation nursed in the Hebrew Scriptures (culminating in the chief priests' statement in 19:15, "We have no king but Caesar"). Old-style Judaism is dead, John proclaims; Jesus is alive, and he embodies all the scriptural aspects of Jewish worship by showing how they point to him by virtue of his messianic office and identity.

Thus, the Messiah comes to God's **temple** in Jerusalem in a momentous visitation, invoking in the alert reader the mention in the introduction, "The true light that gives light to everyone was coming into the world. He was in the world, and though the world was made through him, the world did not recognize him. He came to that which was his own, but his own did not receive him" (John 1:9 – 11). Hence similar to the way in which 2:11 in the previous pericope echoes 1:14, so 2:13 – 22 echo 1:9 – 11.

The proximity between 2:13 – 22 and 1:9 – 11 may further explain John's selection of the temple clearing early on in Jesus' ministry (assuming its historicity):

---

45. See here esp. the works by Andrew T. Lincoln, *Truth on Trial: The Lawsuit Motif in the Fourth Gospel* (Peabody, MA: Hendrickson, 2000); and Bauckham, *Jesus and the Eyewitnesses*.

46. See Carson, "Understanding Misunderstandings"; cf. Eugene Lemcio, *The Past of Jesus in the Gospels* (SNTSMS 68; Cambridge: Cambridge University Press, 2005); Byrskog, *Story as History, History as Story*.

47. See esp. Blomberg, *Historical Reliability of John's Gospel*; Köstenberger, "John," in *ZIBBC*; idem, *John*; and Martin Hengel, "Das Johannesevangelium als Quelle für die Geschichte des antiken Judentums," in *Judaica, Hellenistica et Christiana: Kleine Schriften II* (WUNT 109; Tübingen: Mohr-Siebeck, 1999), 293 – 334. Contra, Casey, *Is John's Gospel True?*, who supplies a negative answer. See also the study by Morris, "History and Theology in John's Gospel," in *Studies in the Fourth Gospel*, 65 – 138.

48. See chap. 1, sec. 1 above.

Jesus' clearing of his temple and his rejection by the Jerusalem authorities serves as a perfect, paradigmatic example of the light's shining of a bright, pure ray into a corrupt temple system that was overgrown with cobwebs and in dire need of reform and renewal. Still, Jesus' agenda was not mere reform but nothing less than revolution. As the ensuing narrative makes clear, Jesus and his body are the new temple only by passing through temporary destruction and being raised again on the third day (2:20).[49]

The reference to Jesus' appearance at the temple in **2:14** should be read in light of the allusion to the tabernacle in 1:14, where John affirms that Jesus "tabernacled" or "pitched his tent" (the meaning of *skenoō*) among the new covenant community, and that "we perceived his glory." This means that temple language has already been applied to Jesus, who was said to have taken up temporary residence among his people through the incarnation. In the present pericope, it is affirmed that the Jerusalem temple, likewise, is temporary and subject to future destruction (**2:18**). By contrast, God's presence in Jesus and the manifestation of God's glory in Jesus are permanent (see esp. 1:14, 18 and below).[50]

Jesus' prediction of the "temple's" destruction subtly, yet unmistakably, echoes the reference to a similar prediction in the Synoptic Olivet Discourse (Matt 24:2 pars.). Yet in the present reference it is Jesus himself who is said to be the new, rebuilt temple that constitutes the typological fulfillment of the Jerusalem sanctuary and that represents its divinely provided replacement. It is as if Jesus' pronouncement that "new wine" be poured into "new wineskins" (Matt 9:17 pars.) provides the theological backdrop to the Johannine account of the temple clearing (see John 2:1–11), for the temple must first (proleptically) be cleared by the Messiah before God's glory can be fully manifested in the new temple, Jesus' body (2:21).

In making this connection, the evangelist leads the reader into profound theological reflection above and beyond recording Jesus' prediction of the destruction of the literal temple (and possibly its fulfillment, assuming a post-AD 70 date for John's gospel). In fact, as we have argued above, it is likely that the destruction of the literal temple provided at least one of the major stimuli for the composition of John's gospel. Now that the temple had been destroyed and the Jewish people were left stranded without a sanctuary where they could bring their sacrifices and conduct their worship, John sought to seize the day by pointing to Jesus as the new temple that had replaced the old. Thus, Jesus' words in **2:19** contained a built-in delay, as it were: while uttered at the beginning of his earthly ministry, their full relevance, historically speaking, was not revealed until the occurrence of three later

---

49. There is considerable debate as to whether "cleansing" is a proper epithet to apply to Jesus' temple action. See esp. Craig A. Evans, "Jesus' Action in the Temple: Cleansing or Portent of Destruction?" *CBQ* 51 (1989): 237–70.

50. On the Johannine temple theme, see esp. Kerr, *Temple of Jesus' Body*; Coloe, *God Dwells with Us*; Hoskins, *Jesus as the Fulfillment of the Temple*; Walker, *Jesus and the Holy City*; and the discussions in chap. 1, sec. 2 above and chap. 10, sec. 24 below. See also the more broadly conceived work by G. K. Beale, *The Temple and the Church's Mission: A Biblical Theology of the Temple* (NSBT; Downers Grove, IL: InterVarsity Press, 2004), though at times Beale's treatment seems to be unduly imaginative and lacking sufficient exegetical restraint.

events—his crucifixion (the destruction of the temple, typologically speaking; see **2:22**), his resurrection three days later, and the literal temple's destruction (AD 70; Matthew 24 pars.).

In the present pericope, then, Jesus acts as messianic prophet. He enters the temple area authoritatively and acts out symbolically the impending judgment of God's people and of the Jerusalem temple, by a prophetic "signs"-action (denouncing the commercial exploitation of the temple).[51] Just as Isaiah walked about in his underclothes to signify the coming Babylonian destruction (see, e.g., Isa 20:3), so Jesus wreaked havoc in the temple courts to signify the coming destruction of old-style Judaism, which was epitomized by the corrupt temple cult in Jesus' day. Just as Zerubbabel, a messianic figure, was consumed with zeal for God's house (see John 2:17, citing Ps 69:9), so Jesus displayed supreme zeal for God's holiness and purity.[52] In typical Synoptic-style fashion, the Jewish leaders ask Jesus for a "sign" to validate his authority in clearing the temple (John 2:18; see Matt 12:38–39; 16:1, 4; and pars.), but Jesus, characteristically, does not accede to the Jews' demand but elaborates on the significance of what he has just done, explaining that the temple clearing was the very sign the Jews were requesting.

Hence the temple clearing and the Jews' challenge provide an early opportunity for Jesus to predict his violent death ("destroy this temple," John 2:19) and his resurrection on the third day (2:19), serving as the Johannine functional equivalent to the thrice-repeated passion prediction in the Synoptics (Mark 8:31–33; 9:30–32; 10:32–34 pars.). What is more, rather than placing the first such prediction at the halfway point of the gospel as Mark did, John puts it right at the beginning of his gospel, showing compellingly that Jesus is in utter control, and completely aware, of his eventual destiny (cf. John 17:15, 17–18; see already the reference to Jesus' "hour" in 2:4). In this John shows a perfect example of 20/20 hindsight while at the same time leaving events in their original life-setting in the earthly ministry of Jesus.[53]

Later on in this volume I will defend the view that the temple clearing should in all probability be regarded as a Johannine sign.[54] To provide a brief preview of my argument, if the six undisputed Johannine signs are taken as the standard, a sign in John may be understood as (1) a public event in the ministry of Jesus that is (2) christologically significant in pointing to Jesus as Messiah in some way (John 20:30–31), and that is (3) designed explicitly as a sign in John's gospel.[55] I will argue at some length below that the temple clearing fulfills all three criteria, the dynamic

---

51. For a discussion of the rationale for Jesus' action and a comparison with the Synoptic version of the temple clearing, see Köstenberger, *John*, 106–7, with reference to C. K. Barrett, "The House of Prayer and the Den of Thieves," in *Jesus und Paulus* (ed. E. Earle Ellis and Erich Grässer; Göttingen: Vandenhoeck & Ruprecht, 1975), 13–20.

52. Note the parallel between the temple as Jesus' "Father's house" and Jesus' later reference to many rooms in his "Father's house" in 14:2. See the discussion in Köstenberger, "Destruction of the Second Temple," 94–97.

53. It reflects true humility that John acknowledges that at the time Jesus' disciples shared in the Jewish authorities' lack of understanding (though the disciples were not as antagonistic as the Jewish leaders).

54. See chap. 7, sec. 15.

55. The turning of water into wine at 2:11; the healing of the official's son at 4:54; the healing of the lame man at 7:21, 31; the feeding of the multitude at 6:14, 26, 30; the opening of the eyes of the man born blind at 9:16 (cf. 11:37); and the raising of Lazarus at 11:47 (cf. 12:18). See the chart in Köstenberger, *Missions of Jesus and the Disciples*, 60.

in 2:18 being similar to 6:31, where likewise a Jewish demand for a sign of Jesus' authority is met with an elaboration upon a sign already performed.

If so, the temple clearing constitutes one of Jesus' Jerusalem "signs" mentioned in 2:23 and 3:2 (and thus the view that the temple clearing is a Johannine sign makes excellent narrative sense), having been placed in the center of the Cana Cycle, which features "signs" in Cana at the beginning (2:11) and at the end (4:54).[56] Thus, Jesus would be shown to work signs both in Galilee and in Judea, yet it would be clear that Jesus' sign in Jerusalem (non-"miraculous" though it is) meets immediately with strong opposition by the Jewish leaders, a portent of things to come. While it would take three more years (and another 17 chapters in John's gospel) for the Jewish hostility to work itself out and lead to their rejection and crucifixion of Jesus, *in nuce*, as John shows, this Jewish rejection of the Messiah was a fait accompli from the very start.

One final observation about the temple clearing may be registered. By referring to Jesus' resurrection (proleptically) as early as in 2:22, John, similar to the effect of the introduction, robs the narrative of all suspense, showing the futility of the Jewish authorities' efforts to blunt Jesus' activity at the outset. This again seems to presuppose that John's readers (whether from reading the Synoptic Gospels or otherwise) are already familiar with the outcome of Jesus' story. By giving away the outcome of the story at the outset, it appears, John is able to shift the reader's primary attention away from the question, "What end will Jesus meet?" to exploring the spiritual dynamics that led inexorably to the end that was predetermined already both theologically and narratologically.[57] This is done in a form roughly reminiscent of a Synoptic parable. An event is shown to be imbued with symbolic potential that is explored and exploited with regard to Jesus' messianic identity and its rejection by the Jewish leaders. This is typology at its best.

The ending of the present pericope (2:22) is similar to that of the previous pericope (2:11), except that while in 2:11 the disciples are said to have perceived Jesus' glory at the time the sign was performed, in 2:22 the disciples are said to have believed and understood the full significance of the event only subsequent to the resurrection.

10.2.1.2.3 Jesus' Witness to Nicodemus (2:23–3:21)

In John 2:23, John relativizes the effectiveness of Jesus' signs, noting that many "**believed**" in Jesus—even "in his name" (compare and contrast 1:12)—on account of his signs in Jerusalem at the Passover (a back reference to, and *inclusio* with, 2:13), but that Jesus would not "entrust" (a wordplay) in these outward expressions of belief because he knew what truly was in people's hearts (**vv. 23–25**).

---

56. The symmetry in this case would be: (1) Cana Cycle: Galilee/Judea/Galilee; (2) Festival Cycle: Judea/Galilee/Judea; (3) Bridge: Judea. See Köstenberger, *Missions of Jesus and the Disciples*, 70–71.

57. See already the above comments regarding John's replacement of the Synoptic Temple clearing pericope at the end of Jesus' ministry with a corresponding temple clearing at the beginning of his ministry.

Intriguingly, none other than a Jewish Sanhedrin member, Nicodemus, "Israel's teacher" (John 3:10), serves in the ensuing narrative as the paradigmatic human being illustrating people's intransigence to Jesus' true identity. Harking back to the earlier linking of the world ("his own") and the Jews ("his own") in the introduction (1:11) over against those who truly were "his own" (cf. 1:12; see 13:1), here is a Jew who represents the world, a characterization that in Part 2 of John's gospel completely holds sway where the world and the unbelieving Jewish nation have become all but indistinguishable.[58]

Apart from the way in which Nicodemus (with thick Johannine **irony**) serves as a representative of the unbelieving world, there are several important narrative and theological links that connect the Nicodemus pericope in 2:23–3:21 with the preceding pericope narrating the temple clearing (2:12–22). Most important is the theological rationale provided for the antagonism of the Jewish leaders that leads them to challenge Jesus' authority in 2:18. As John makes clear in the Nicodemus pericope, in a commentary on the Jewish obduracy displayed at the temple clearing, as it were, the reason for the Jewish rejection of the Messiah is, at the root, the *lack of spiritual regeneration*.

This, indeed, is a profound and exceedingly perceptive theological diagnosis by the author of the "spiritual gospel." Like the Jewish leaders in 2:18, Nicodemus holds a leadership role in old-style Judaism as "a member of the Jewish ruling council," that is, the Sanhedrin (**3:1**).[59] Like them, he refers to Jesus' "**signs**" (**3:2**; see 2:18) and inquires as to their background. Unlike the Jews mentioned in 2:18, Nicodemus makes polite reference to God being with Jesus as evidenced by his powerful signs, though Jesus, illustrating the evangelist's reference to Jesus' discernment of people's hearts in the introduction to this pericope (2:23–25), is unimpressed by these opening pleasantries, cutting in his response straight to the heart of the matter: "Very truly I tell you, no one can see the kingdom of God without being born again" (**3:3**; further elaborated in **3:5**). In this sole cluster of references to the "kingdom of God" in the entire gospel, entrance into God's kingdom is predicated upon **spiritual regeneration**, a regeneration that is ultimately not merely corporate in the sense of religious national renewal (à la Ezekiel's vision of the valley of dry bones in Ezekiel 38; see the allusion to Ezekiel in John 3:5) but personal and individual in nature.

This confirms that old-style Judaism is in desperate need of spiritual, personal renewal (see John 2:6 and 2:14–18); nothing less than a **new** spiritual **birth** will suffice. But how will this new birth be accomplished?[60] In dealing with this matter, and with Nicodemus serving as representative character asking this very question,

---

58. The connection between "a man" (*anthrōpos*) of the Pharisees (3:1) and the universal human condition of unbelief (*anthrōpō*, last word in 2:23) is obscured when gender-inclusive translations omit reference to the word "man" in 3:1. For a discussion of these kinds of issues see Andreas J. Köstenberger, "Translating John's Gospel: Challenges and Opportunities," in *The Challenge of Bible Translation: Communicating God's Word to the World* (ed. Glen G. Scorgie, Mark L. Strauss, and Steven M. Voth; Grand Rapids: Zondervan, 2003), 347–64.

59. See the perceptive analysis of the pericope by Peter Cotterell and Max Turner, *Linguistics & Biblical Interpretation* (Downers Grove, IL: InterVarsity Press, 1989), 278–87.

60. On the comparison with the wind, see Karl Olav Sandnes, "Whence and Whither: A Narrative Perspective on Birth *anōthen* (John 3,3–8)," *Bib* 86 (2005): 153–73.

the reader is led to reflect on the typological significance of a past event in Israel's history: Moses' lifting up a snake in the wilderness, with the result that everyone who looked at that snake lived and did not die (**3:14**; see Num 21:9). Typologically speaking, John expounds by recounting Jesus' response. Jesus represented that snake: he was to be "lifted up" (the first, somewhat oblique but nonetheless unmistakable, reference to Jesus' crucifixion in John's gospel; later developed in John 8:28 and made explicit in 13:32–33), and, as the evangelist's commentary makes clear, "whoever believes in him shall not perish but have eternal life" (3:16).

Thus, second, just as in the two previous pericopae a "sign" was at the center encapsulating the messianic content of the passage's message (see 2:11, 18) — though, as argued, the distinction between a "sign" and typology is somewhat fluid in the case of the latter — in the present pericope it is typology that serves as the focal point of the evangelist's theological message: a message linking, and comparing and contrasting, Moses and Israel in the wilderness in the past with Jesus and believers in the present. The parallelism between Moses and Jesus is unmistakable; at the same time, there is no room in the typology for Nicodemus and the Jewish leaders, who are shut out owing to incredulity-turned-unbelief.[61]

Thus we have seen that the Messiah (Jesus) is met with a spiritually unregenerate Jewish leadership that opposes his messianic mission. At the same time, there are those in Israel — such as Nathanael, who "truly is an Israelite in whom there is no deceit" (1:47) — who follow Jesus. Spiritual, personal renewal in Israel has begun, with Jesus launching a movement that is joined by those who place their faith in the Messiah.

The extended commentary by the evangelist in **3:16–21**[62] strikingly identifies, not Israel but the *world* as the scope of God's saving activity and as the object of his love: "For God so loved the world...." *Whoever* believes in him — not just the Jews — will not perish but have eternal life. This extends the scope from (wilderness) Israel in the original historical setting to anyone who responds to the Messiah in faith (see 10:16; 11:51–52; 12:20–33). This already follows from Jesus' analogy between the "wind" that "blows wherever it pleases" (3:8) and the regenerating work of the "Spirit" (both *pneuma* in the Greek). Continuing from 3:16, the language in 3:17–21, likewise, is unmistakably that of the evangelist, as a comparison of 3:19–20 with 1:9, 5 demonstrates:

The true light that gives light to everyone	This is the verdict: Light has
was coming into the world....	come into the world,
The light shines in the darkness, and	but people loved darkness instead
the darkness has not overcome it.	of light because their deeds were evil.

---

61. The (disputed) question whether Nicodemus later became a believer is immaterial here, since everyone agrees that at least in John 3 Nicodemus shows no signs of faith. He rather represents misunderstanding (3:4) and is reduced to acknowledge his ignorance in his last recorded utterance in the pericope (3:9). See the discussion in Köstenberger, *John*, 118–20.

62. See Köstenberger, *John*, 113–14.

The darkness that was alluded to in the introduction in a creation context (where God created light to shine in the darkness, 1:5) is now typologically unpacked to signify human rebellion against God and his sent Son. What is more, the evangelist probes the depths of the mystery of human unbelief by explaining that the root cause of people's rejection of God's **love** gift of his Son is "love" of a different kind: a paradoxical "love of darkness" (cf. 3:19) and a corresponding hatred of the light (3:20), for fear that people's evil deeds will be exposed. This is contrasted with those "who live by the truth" and who come into the light so that what they have done will be shown to have been done in the sight of God (3:21).

Thus, in the discussion of the new birth in 3:3–8 and in the exploration of the sinful rejection of the light in 3:19–21, the evangelist develops themes already struck in the introduction (see 1:13 and 1:5, 9–11). The metaphor of **light** in relation to reception vs. rejection of Jesus is at the same time profound and exceedingly simple. Just as when the light is turned out, people are faced with the choice either to see themselves (including any shortcomings) in the light or to close their eyes or run away from the light into the darkness in order not to have to look at themselves in the light, so it is with the effect of Jesus'—the light's—coming into the world. Will people welcome the light's coming and exposure of their sin? Or will they, like the first man and the first woman upon recognizing their sin, run and hide from God? This is the universal human predicament and the choice every human being is called to make.

10.2.1.2.4 John's Testimony (3:22–36)

In the present section yet another element from the introduction is taken up: the testimony of John (the Baptist; see 1:6–8, 15). This provides temporary relief for the reader from the heavy-duty theological matters that have been discussed, things too deep for even "Israel's teacher" (see 3:10–12). For Jesus and his disciples, too, going into the Judean countryside after temporarily having invaded the "lion's den" of Jerusalem with the heavy scrutiny and antagonism of the Jewish leaders is welcome relief.

Supplementing the Synoptics, John provides some information here about a baptizing ministry by Jesus and his followers concurrent with the ministry of John the Baptist (**3:22**; see **v. 24**; cf. Mark 1:14). This is similar in its increased complexity to his geographical pattern, including Jesus' visits to Jerusalem throughout his ministry in the place of the Synoptic movement from Galilee to Jerusalem.

John 3:26 links the present pericope with the previous account of John's ministry in 1:19–37. The question that is raised is that of John's losing disciples to Jesus (see already 1:35–37, where John himself is shown to point his disciples to Jesus, and they desist from following John and attach themselves to Jesus instead). In human terms, this would likely provoke jealousy and a relationship of competition and rivalry; yet as the present passage elaborates, John perceived himself as the forerunner of the Messiah, referring back to his previous testimony that he was not the Messiah but sent ahead of him (**v. 28**, see 1:19–36). John was well aware of his

God-given limitations; when the bridegroom (Jesus) appeared on the scene, the best man had done his job and must fade into the background (**vv. 29–30**).[63]

Some have argued that this passage was penned by John in order to diminish the status of John the Baptist in light of a contemporary "John the Baptist movement."[64] Indeed, there is some (somewhat surprising) evidence that John the Baptist had a following in Asia Minor decades after the ascension of Jesus (Acts 19:1–7). However, in light of the care taken by John to distinguish between the past of Jesus and the present community, it is more likely that the original life-setting during Jesus' earthly ministry is primary. It is indeed highly plausible that during a period of overlap between John's and Jesus' ministry questions such as the one recounted in John 3:26 would have surfaced and that John responded the way John says he did in the present pericope.

In this the pericope coheres with and supports the earlier references to the Baptist in the introduction and in John 1:19–36, including his reference to Isa 40:3 in John 1:23. In the earlier passage, John indicated his purpose was to reveal the Messiah to Israel (1:31). Now that the Messiah had begun to work his powerful "signs," clearly the Baptist's role as a **witness** to Jesus, while of abiding value (1:15), was close to becoming obsolete. Hence also, his imprisonment (3:24) and subsequent martyrdom were no great loss to the messianic movement, for John had fulfilled his divine assignment by the time he was called from the scene. The commentary in 3:30–36, elaborating on the significance of John's witness and its implications, mirrors that appended to the Nicodemus pericope in 3:16–21.[65]

10.2.1.2.5 Jesus and the Samaritan Woman (4:1–42)

The following pericope is introduced by an interesting clarification that it was not Jesus who baptized but his disciples (**4:2**) and a reference to the fact that it was the Pharisees' hearing about Jesus' growing appeal that caused him to leave Judea entirely for Galilee. Hence, by divine necessity (**v. 4**), he came through Samaria, where he encountered a Samaritan woman at a well.[66] The scene—most notably, Jacob's well (v. 6), but also Mount Gerizim (v. 20)—is historic and invokes reminiscences of OT events and characters.

How does this pericope function in the narrative flow of John's gospel? First, there is **irony** in the implied comparison between Nicodemus's and the Samaritan's response (the juxtaposition of these accounts is almost certainly intentional).[67] The contrast could not be starker: Nicodemus is part of the establishment, a member of the Jewish Supreme Court, "Israel's teacher." The Samaritan woman lacks any such status, is part of a race shunned by the Jews, and is exposed for her immoral lifestyle in the course of her conversation with Jesus. Yet while Nicodemus is reduced to

---

63. Note also the *inclusio* between John 3:29 and 17:13, with reference to the complete "joy" experienced by John and Jesus' followers, respectively.

64. E.g., Bultmann, *Gospel of John*, 49.

65. See Köstenberger, *John*, 133.

66. For a helpful analysis of this pericope see Cotterell and Turner, *Linguistics & Biblical Interpretation*, 275–78.

67. See the comparison chart in ibid., 112.

incredulity and speechlessness by Jesus, the Samaritan emerges as a dialogue partner who continues to engage Jesus; in the end she proves seriously open to the possibility that Jesus might be the Messiah and brings her fellow townspeople to Jesus, serving as a witness and evangelist. And while Nicodemus stagnates in his spiritual perception, the Samaritan progresses from her understanding of Jesus as "a Jew" (4:9) to viewing him as "a prophet" (v. 19) to acknowledging that Jesus was "a man who told me everything I ever did," asking, "Could this be the **Messiah**?" (v. 29). This is a remarkable reversal of expectations indeed, not dissimilar to that found in the parable of the good Samaritan included in Luke's gospel (10:25–37).

Second, the pattern from "Jerusalem, and ... Judea and Samaria ... to the ends of the earth," characteristic of the early church's **mission** according to the book of Acts (Acts 1:8 *et passim*), is likely said to be reflected here already in the earthly mission of Jesus: first, to the Jew Nicodemus (John 3:1–15); then, to the Samaritan woman (4:1–42); finally, to the Gentile official (4:46–54).[68] Hence the activity of the earthly Jesus is consistent with the activity of the exalted Jesus subsequent to the ascension (see Acts 1:1: the reference to Luke's gospel recounting "all that Jesus began to do" implies that the Acts is concerned with "all that Jesus continues to do"). Thus, indirectly, this precedent in Jesus' mission would serve to validate the church's Gentile mission, which by the time of the composition of John's gospel had, of course, already proceeded for several decades. In all this one cannot help but wonder to what extent John was aware of Luke's two-volume work either directly or indirectly.

Third, as with Nicodemus, but much more explicitly, Jesus, in reaching out to the Samaritan, serves as the paradigmatic "sent one" whose activity his followers are called to emulate. This is made in the skillfully interposed section John 4:27–38, where Jesus instructs the disciples about his mission of bringing in a harvest of souls and of reaping the fruit of the labor of others. It is also implicit throughout Jesus' entire conversation with the woman as the Messiah is revealed: as the one who expresses God's love to a sinful woman (see 3:16), as the one who came to seek and save that which was lost (see Luke 19:10), and, significantly, as "the Savior," not only of the Jewish people, but "of the world" at large (John 4:42, the punch line of the entire pericope). Hence we have here the first major occurrence of the Johannine mission theme, which culminates in the commissioning scene in 20:21–22 but is proleptically foreshadowed already here and elsewhere earlier in the gospel.[69]

Fourth, the pericope is found to address adeptly the tension in Jesus' mission between his primary focus on the Jews and the wider scope of his mission. Similar to the other gospels, and in keeping with the early church's practice per the book of Acts and Paul's proclamation of the gospel, John shows Jesus affirming that his coming was first to the Jews and has him assert Jewish **salvation-historical** primacy:

---

68. Some question whether the official was a Gentile, but this is most likely. See Köstenberger, *John*, 169.

69. See the monograph-length study by Köstenberger, *Missions of Jesus and the Disciples*; and the discussion of John's trinitarian mission theology in chap. 15 below.

"Salvation is from the Jews" (John 4:22).[70] This keeps the salvation-historical pattern intact, which moves from God's chosen (OT) people Israel to the universal scope of his salvation encompassing Gentiles, of which there are already clear hints in the OT (e.g., Isa 49:6). At the same time, Jesus' ministry already provides glimpses of the eventual opening up of the scope of the effects of his mission beyond Israel, and his encounter with the Samaritan woman is the first major example in John.

This navigates a theological tension and serves as a message to the Jews that while God's Messiah came first to them, others, too, would be the beneficiaries of his mission. That this would be the case only subsequent to the crucifixion—resulting from the Jewish rejection of the Messiah—follows inexorably from the course of events already set in motion at the time Jesus addresses the Samaritan (see discussion of John 2:13–22 above). Yet by salvation-historical necessity, Jesus both "had to" pass through Samaria (4:4) and still continues to focus his mission primarily on Israel. This is apparent also in the fact that his messianic "signs" in this gospel function specifically to reveal to the Jews that he is the Messiah, albeit in vain (see esp. 12:36b–40).

Along the way, Jesus is shown to touch on several other theological concepts. He speaks of himself as "living water" that can quench people's thirst forever; if they believe in him, they will receive eternal life (4:10, 13–14; see the purpose statement in 20:30–31). This resonates with Israel's experience of God and his provision in the past in the wilderness and thus places Jesus on a trajectory subsequent to Moses. It is also part of a cluster of other references to Jesus as the living bread whom people must "eat" to live spiritually (John 6). Later in the pericope, reminiscent of the temptation narrative in Matthew 4 and Luke 4, Jesus says that it is his "food" to do the will of the one who sent him and to finish his work (John 4:34). This is put in the context of one of many Johannine **misunderstandings** when the disciples return from the village after procuring food (for a Synoptic parallel see, e.g., Mark 8:14–21).

But perhaps the climactic moment in the pericope, just preceding his (unusual) revelation of himself as the Messiah to the Samaritan in John 4:26, is Jesus' discussion of true spiritual worship—"worship in spirit and truth" (not "in the Spirit and in the truth," as the TNIV has it)[71]—in 4:21–24. This is part of the larger Johannine replacement theme, where Jesus is shown to be the new sanctuary in place of the old. Here Jesus is shown to take the opportunity, in dialogue with the Samaritan, to point out that worship is not a matter of geographical location of externals; it is a spiritual matter, just as God is spirit(ual) and thus must be worshiped spiritually.

To be sure, it will be the Holy Spirit who will help believers to worship in this way subsequent to Jesus' exaltation, but it is unlikely that, in the original historical setting, Jesus expected the Samaritan woman to understand a discussion of the role of the Holy Spirit in worship. More likely, he sought to level the playing field

---

70. See the comments on salvation history in the discussion of the introduction to John's gospel earlier in this chapter and in the section on salvation history in chap. 10, sec. 22 below.

71. See Köstenberger, *John*, 156–57.

between Jews and Samaritans—ultimately the worship of neither was up to the new standard set by Jesus. The bad news was that worship on Mount Gerizim was illegitimate (as the Jews had held all along). But, in an assertion that might have comforted the Samaritan in a conciliatory gesture, neither was Jewish worship satisfactory! For a Jew like Jesus to admit this would have been quite shocking. No, Jewish worship at the Jerusalem sanctuary must give way to true, spiritual worship of God in and through the new temple, Jesus. This is nothing really new in the context of John's narrative; John 2:13–22 said as much (see especially the reference to the temple signifying/being Jesus' body in 2:20; see also the allusion to the tabernacle in the reference to Jesus' incarnation at 1:14). But now this revelation had been made not only to the Jews but also to the Samaritans; the theme thickens into a major Johannine emphasis.[72]

One final observation remains. As mentioned, the focal point in 2:1–11 is Jesus' first messianic "**sign**." I have argued that in 2:13–22 likewise, a sign—the temple clearing—stands in the center. What is more, at the heart of this sign (if a sign it is) is the notion of divine judgment executed surrounding the rejecting of the Messiah, his "destruction," which is followed by his resurrection on the third day. While the gospel is therefore still rather implicit in Jesus' first messianic sign (though Jesus' work does reveal the glory of God), the gospel (Jesus' crucifixion and resurrection) is given much fuller expression in 2:13–22. The next pericope, 2:23–3:21, as mentioned, has as its theological focal point a typology—a close cousin to the sign—which, like 2:13–22, is centered on the crucifixion, further elaborating also on the life-giving benefit of Jesus' "lifting up" for those who believe. John 4:1–42, finally (for now), builds up to Jesus' startling declaration that he is the Messiah in 4:26: "I, the one speaking to you—I am he"—no "messianic secret" here![73] And, as mentioned, both in 2:13–22 and in 4:21–24, Jesus is shown to be the new temple on which worship, properly conceived, is to center. This will in short order be followed by another Cana sign performed in relation to a Gentile (4:46–54).

Thus, when the Cana Cycle closes at the end of John 4, John, in his "spiritual gospel," has managed to illumine several important theological points:

- the reason for the antagonism toward Jesus on the part of the Jewish leadership is their lack of spiritual regeneration
- true, God-pleasing worship must center, not on the earthly sanctuary, but on Jesus as the new temple; Jesus is the authentic manifestation of God's presence (the introduction; 1:51); to paraphrase the Synoptic Jesus: "Now one greater than the temple is here"; incidentally, holding up Jesus as the proper object of worship implies his deity[74]

---

72. See the discussion of Jesus as the new temple in chap. 10, sec. 24 below.

73. On a historical level, perhaps Jesus can afford to be less guarded here, since the Samaritan may not be as prone to nationalistic interpretations of the messianic office as her Jewish counterparts, though this remains a matter of conjecture.

74. See on this the work of Larry W. Hurtado, e.g., *Lord Jesus Christ: Devotion to Jesus in Earliest Christianity* (Grand Rapids: Eerdmans, 2003).

- at the center of Jesus' messianic mission is his cross and the resurrection; the "signs" are profoundly gospel-centered, and to the extent that they are taken or understood out of context, severing the connection between the "signs" and the gospel hinders their intended role as an aid to faith in the Messiah
- people are steeped in their traditions, be it Jews (Nicodemus), Samaritans (the Samaritan woman), or Gentiles; Jesus' revelation of God has major obstacles to overcome in the form of people's preconceived notions of how (and where) God is to be worshiped

10.2.1.2.6 The Second Sign in Cana: The Healing of the (Gentile) Official's Son (4:43–54)

The "Savior of the world" (John 4:42) now completes his intended journey back to Galilee (see 4:3), where he is "welcomed" (**v. 45**) by those who "had seen all that he had done in Jerusalem at the Passover Festival," which can only mean, in the context of the Johannine narrative, the temple clearing (see 2:13 and 23) and/or other signs done there at that time (2:23). John now leads the reader back to the scene of Jesus' "first sign," the turning of water into wine, that is, Cana in Galilee (**v. 46**).[75] A Gentile official whose son was sick some distance away at Capernaum made the trip all the way to Cana, hearing Jesus was there, in order to plead with Jesus to heal his son. This recalls similar Synoptic accounts involving Gentile officials (e.g., Matt 8:5–13; Luke 7:1–10).[76]

Jesus' performance of another **sign** is in the present instance preceded by a sharp rebuke of the people's desire (the Greek for "you" in John 4:48 is plural) to see "signs *and wonders*," that is, an unwholesome preoccupation with the miraculous. This is precisely the separation of the miraculous element of a "sign" from its messianic orientation that has been mentioned above as an improper approach to Jesus' works. Jesus thus preemptively counters a misperception of the impending healing by those who witness it. The centurion himself shows impressive **faith** on the basis of Jesus' mere word (v. 50), and his son (like that of the centurion in the Synoptics) is healed long-distance, another "hard" miracle of Jesus selected for inclusion in John's gospel.[77]

At the heart of the present pericope, then, is the correction of people's misperception of Jesus' signs as "signs *and wonders*," that is, missing their messianic significance owing to a unilateral preoccupation with the miraculous. From a narrative perspective, the "second sign" in Cana rounds out the Cana Cycle in John 2–4 by way of *inclusio*. It also completes the scope of Jesus' mission during this early stage of his ministry from Judea to Samaria to the Gentiles as narrated in John 3 and 4.

---

75. The back-reference to 2:1–11 in 4:46 is a Johannine characteristic: see, e.g., the reference to 13:23 in 21:20 or to 3:2 in 19:39; see also the discussion in chap. 3, sec. 7.1 above.

76. See also the affinity between Jesus' statement in 4:44 that "prophets have no honor in their own country" and the Synoptics (Matt 13:57; Mark 6:4; Luke 4:24).

77. See the discussion of Jesus' signs at 2:11 above.

10.2.1.2.7 Summary of the Cana Cycle

In our discussion of the first four chapters of John's gospel we have noted several ways in which the narrative picks up on themes first mentioned in the introduction: John's **witness**, the Jews' rejection of Jesus as **Messiah**, Jesus as the new **temple**, the need to be **born again**, people rejecting the **light** while preferring to continue living in **darkness**, and so on. In an incipient manner that remained to some extent implicit, John has hinted at the cross, the resurrection, and universal human sinfulness in need of divine redemption through an atoning, vicarious sacrifice.

While Jewish antagonism flared up at the temple clearing in John 2:13–22, it is not until the next unit, the Festival Cycle in John 5–10, that the conflict between Jesus and the Jerusalem authorities escalates and is characterized by an increasing degree of acrimony. In fact, as will be seen, while the *inclusio* in John 2–4 marks two messianic **signs** of Jesus in Galilee, the major *inclusio* bracketing John 5–10 is concerned with the Jews' charge of Jesus with blasphemy (5:18; 10:33).

Thus the scene has shifted from a more private, preliminary, conversational mode to a more public, advanced, and confrontational mode, which features the presentation of Jesus as the fulfillment of the meaning and substance of the major events, figures, and institutions of old-style Judaism over against the backdrop of increasing resistance of its representatives, who increasingly harden in their opposition to Jesus.

10.2.1.3 From Jerusalem to Bethany: The Festival Cycle: The Height of Jesus' Ministry to the Jews (5:1–10:42)

10.2.1.3.1 Another Jerusalem Sign: The Healing of the Lame Man (5:1–47)

Rather abruptly (see the discussion of alleged **seams** in John's gospel in chap. 3, sec. 7.3 above), John 5 places Jesus back in Jerusalem, a fact that has given rise to Rudolf Bultmann's famous displacement theory, which changes the order of chapters 5 and 6, resulting in what Bultmann considers a smoother transition. However, this "solution" is both unnecessary and completely unsupported by the available manuscript evidence.[78] "Some time later" (**v. 1**) is a vague and general time marker, and as we have noted, the *inclusio* with 2:11 in 4:54 brings an end to the previous unit, the Cana Cycle, with 5:1 starting a new literary unit in John's gospel. For this reason it is only a prevenient belief in source criticism that legitimates rearranging the Johannine narrative. What is more, as we have seen, it is characteristic for John to show Jesus engaged in an oscillating pattern from Galilee (2:1–12) to Jerusalem (2:13–3:21) and Judea (3:22–36) and back to Galilee (via Samaria; John 4), so that it should not surprise the reader that Jesus returns to Jerusalem for another (unspecified) festival.

As at the previous occasion (2:13–22; see also 2:23 and 3:2), Jesus performs a **sign** in the Jewish capital, this time on a lame man who had been afflicted for thirty-

---

78. See Köstenberger, *John*, 222, additional note on John 6:1.

eight years (**v. 5**)—another of Jesus' difficult miracles (or, better, "signs") chosen for inclusion by John.[79] Jesus engages the man, and he tells Jesus about his predicament: when the water is stirred in the Pool of Bethesda where he lay, he has no one to help him, so that by the time he gets into the pool, another has gotten there before him (v. 7). A later scribe supplied **v. 4**, probably reflecting popular superstition: "From time to time an angel of the Lord would come down and stir up the waters. The first person into the pool after each such disturbance would be cured of whatever disease they had."[80] In characteristic fashion corroborated by the Synoptic Gospels, Jesus circumvents any such theatrics and, ignoring the man's (and popular) superstition, tells him to get up, take his bed, and walk. And "immediately" the man obliged.

As it turns out, the account of this messianic "sign" by Jesus (identified as such only later in the Johannine narrative in John 6:2) constitutes but the prelude to the actual bone of contention on which the remainder of the chapter focuses: the way in which the fact that the healing took place on the Sabbath gives rise to a heated controversy between the Pharisees and Jesus, which, in turn, occasions Jesus' claim to be **Lord of the Sabbath** and thus (as the Pharisees correctly infer) equal to God (5:18). This, in turn, for the first time in John's gospel, leads to the charge of blasphemy, which in due course turns out to be the Jews' major charge against Jesus that leads to his crucifixion (see 19:7). Jesus must die because he claimed to be the Son of God; John wrote his gospel to demonstrate from Jesus' "signs" that Jesus was the Son of God (20:30–31).

It is hard to imagine a more potent clash between conflicting claims regarding Jesus than the contention of Jesus and those bearing testimony to his messianic identity (cited in 5:31–47) and his Jewish opponents. From this chapter on especially, John takes great pains to paint the contrast in the starkest terms possible (see later John 8 and 10). In doing so he makes a compelling case for why Jesus ended up on the cross. For according to OT law, Jesus was guilty of blasphemy, at least according to his opponents, and so he must—and did—die.[81]

Only after John has recounted the healing, then, does he mention that it took place on a Sabbath (**v. 9b**). The ensuing discussion, however, focuses not on the actual healing, but on the fact that, subsequent to the healing, the man, in obedience to Jesus' command, picked up his bed before walking away. This brought him in conflict, not with Scripture, but with Jewish tradition, which forbade people to

---

79. For helpful studies of Jesus' sign in John 5:1–18 see Steven M. Bryan, "Power in the Pool: The Healing of the Man at Bethesda and Jesus' Violation of the Sabbath (Jn. 5:1–18)," *TynBul* 54 (2003): 7–22; Stephen S. Kim, "The Christological and Eschatological Significance of Jesus' Miracle in John 5," *BSac* 165 (2008): 413–24; and David L. Mealand, "John 5 and the Limits of Rhetorical Criticism," in *Understanding Poets and Prophets: Essays in Honour of George Wishart Anderson* (ed. A. Graeme Auld; JSOTSup; Sheffield: JSOT, 1993), 258–72. See also Martin Asiedu-Peprah, *Johannine Sabbath Conflicts as Juridical Controversy* (WUNT 132; Tübingen: Mohr-Siebeck, 2001), esp. chaps. 3–5, who examines John 5:1–47 and 9:1–10:21 from a narrative-critical perspective. Asiedu-Peprah proposes that these pericopae be viewed as two-party juridical controversies similar to those found in the OT, with 5:1–47 serving as the initiation of the controversy and 9:1–10:21 as its resumption and conclusion. According to him, these pericopae serve to move readers "to accept the Christological credo of the narrative and so come to faith in Jesus" (p. 211).

80. On the lack of authenticity see Bruce M. Metzger, *A Textual Commentary on the New Testament* (2nd ed.; New York: United Bible Societies, 1994), 179.

81. This, incidentally, is an infinitely superior case for why Jesus had to die than that made by those who view Jesus as a teacher of wisdom, a Cynic sage, or some other benign figure.

move an object from one domain to the other on the Sabbath. By Pharisaic logic, this, in turn, made Jesus a lawbreaker, because he told the man to do something that was contrary to, and in violation of, the law (defined as Jewish tradition).

As is characteristic for them (see also John 9), the Pharisees corner the healed man and interrogate him, pressing him to reveal the identity of the one who healed him (or, rather, incriminate Jesus, of whose identity they are already aware). At first, the man is unaware of the identity of his benefactor; later, after encountering Jesus again, he wastes no time reporting him to the authorities (in marked contrast to the man similarly healed on the Sabbath in John 9; see below).[82]

So the scene shifts from the man to Jesus (**v. 17**). Jesus' response to the Jewish charge of causing the man to break the law hardly assuages his critics but, to the contrary, provokes them all the more: "My Father is always at his work to this very day, and I too am working" (v. 17). In this way Jesus effectively aligns himself and his work with that of **God the Creator** (no surprise to the reader: see 1:3–4). For now Jesus, "the elusive Christ," evades the Jews' attempt to stone him for blasphemy.[83] Here is thick Johannine **irony**: as John's readers, prepared as they are with the introduction to John's gospel, will be quick to realize, that which outrages the Jews to no end — Jesus' "calling God his own Father, making himself equal with God" (**v. 18**) — is precisely what he actually is: Jesus *is* equal to God, and he is "guilty as charged," and yet completely innocent.

The Jews' charge of blasphemy triggers the longest discourse yet (by far) in John's gospel (John 5:19–47). Uninterrupted (unlike the dialogue he engages in with Nicodemus and the Samaritan woman in John 3 and 4), Jesus provides a spirited defense of his claim of parity with the Creator (made in 5:17). This section marks perhaps the most pronounced christological high point in this gospel in terms of its sustained, and exceedingly lofty, explication of Jesus the **Son**'s unity with God the **Father**, fleshing out the initial presentation in the introduction (see 1:1–2, 14, 17–18). As the first part of Jesus' defense in **verses 19–30** makes clear, this unity and intimacy of relationship involves:

- the Son's submission to the Father (assertions of which frame the first part of the discourse: vv. 19, 30)
- the Father's **love** for the Son and his full self-disclosure to him (v. 20)
- the Father and the Son equally raising the dead and giving life (v. 21; see John 11 below)
- the Father's entrusting **judgment** to the Son (vv. 22, 27)[84]

---

82. Contra, John Christopher Thomas, "'Stop Sinning Lest Something Worse Come upon You': The Man at the Pool in John 5," *JSNT* 59 (1995): 7; Jeffrey L. Staley, "Stumbling in the Dark, Reaching for the Light: Reading Character in John 5 and 9," *Semeia* 53 (1991): 63; and a variety of other commentators who fail to perceive the implied contrast between the healed men in John 5 and 9. See the discussion in Köstenberger, *John*, 181–83, esp. p. 183, n. 41 (with further bibliographic references).

83. The epithet "elusive Christ" alludes to the article by Stibbe, "The Elusive Christ," in which Stibbe draws attention to this intriguing Johannine theme in his gospel that finds Jesus consistently slip through the fingers of his opponents.

84. See Andrew H. Trotter, Jr., "Justification in the Gospel of John," in *Right with God: Justification in the Bible and the World* (ed. D. A. Carson; Carlisle, UK: Paternoster/Grand Rapids: Baker, 1992), 126–45.

- the call on all to honor the Son just as they honor the Father, asserting Jesus' right to receive **worship** (v. 23)
- the Son's possession of **life** in himself equal to the Father (v. 26)

The second part of the discourse then moves on to adduce a series of witnesses corroborating Jesus' claim of equality with God the Father:

- John the Baptist (vv. 33–35)
- Jesus' works, including the miracles ("testimony greater than John"; cf. v. 36)
- God the Father (v. 37)
- the Scriptures (v. 39)
- Moses (v. 46)

At the outset, Jesus implicitly acknowledges that, according to the Hebrew Scriptures, a minimum of two or three **witnesses** was required to establish the truthfulness of one's claims (Deut 17:6; 19:15). Hence he supplements his testimony in John 5:19–30 regarding his unique relationship with God the Father as the Son with a list of witnesses (not without adding, however, that he needs human testimony, **v. 34**). This list (reproduced above) is weighty indeed: Jesus claims support from the Scriptures, and Moses specifically (i.e., the Pentateuch; this may pertain particularly to the messianic passages in the five books of Moses).

Jesus also invokes his works—in the Johannine context, first and foremost his messianic **signs** (such as the one just performed; John 5:1–15)—as testimony, given to him by the Father. Ultimately, it must be noted, the Father is behind all these witnesses: he is the sender of John the Baptist (see 1:6); he is the one who enables Jesus to perform his works (v. 36); and he sent Moses and inspired the Scripture he and others wrote. Hence, as the writer of Hebrews noted, God revealed himself in OT times in various ways, but in these last days he revealed himself by a son (Heb 1:1–2).

10.2.1.3.2 *The Feeding of the Multitude, the Walking on the Water, and the Bread of Life Discourse (6:1–71)*

In a rather abrupt and a bit awkward-seeming transition (**seams**), John follows up the end of Jesus' defense of his equality with God in the latter part of John 5 with a reference to Jesus "some time after this" (a vague general expression, see 5:1)[85] crossing over "to the far shore of the Sea of Galilee" in **6:1**. "I didn't even know Jesus was at the Sea of Galilee to begin with," the contemporary reader may object. Nevertheless, to resort to a displacement theory as Bultmann did is an extreme expedient that is uncalled for in the absence of manuscript support. More likely, John thinks of his various selections as vignettes that follow one another as somewhat self-contained units, connected only loosely to form a coherent sequential narrative.

---

85. See chap. 3, sec. 5 above.

Jesus' being followed by large crowds is a common sight in the Synoptics (e.g., Matt 5:1). In John, however, the present passage (**John 6:2**) is the first instance where Jesus is shown to attract a large following. This may in part reflect the fact that this is one of the few pericopae John shares with the Synoptics. In fact, the feeding of the five thousand is the only miracle story featured in all four Gospels (see Matt 14:13–21; Mark 6:30–44; Luke 9:10–17).

A comparison of these four accounts reveals several interesting points of contact with the Markan narrative,[86] though perhaps this falls short of proving that John had Mark in front of him as he wrote.[87] As in Matthew and Mark (though not Luke), the feeding pericope is followed by the account of Jesus' walking on the water (Matt 14:22–27; Mark 6:45–52), which may explain John's inclusion of it despite the fact that the walking on the water probably does not constitute a Johannine "sign"—though the event is miraculous—since, unlike in the case of the other six undisputed signs, no explicit reference is made to this event as a "sign" (*sēmeion*).[88]

Narrative continuity is provided by the reference to the reason why a large crowd is following Jesus: they had observed "the **signs** he had performed by healing the sick" (John 6:2), a clear reference to the previous chapter and the healing of the lame man in Jerusalem. This suggests that many followed Jesus all the way from Jerusalem to Galilee to hear his message. Jesus' going up on the mountain and sitting down with his disciples recall the setting for Jesus' Sermon on the Mount recorded in Matthew (see Matt 5:1). Again, we are not necessarily suggesting that John knew Matthew (nor are we suggesting that he did not), but rather that John's account of Jesus' characteristic mode of conduct coheres well with the information provided by the other gospels, underscoring the historical plausibility of John's account.

The reference to the Jewish **Passover** being near provides a helpful time marker indicating the passage of at least one year since the last Passover mentioned in the gospel (see John 2:13, 23) and continues the Passover theme in John. In the ensuing interchange leading up to the miraculous feeding Jesus involves his disciples, training them for ministry in characteristic manner portrayed in the Synoptics.[89] The sight of Jesus taking the bread, giving thanks, and distributing it to the people strikes the reader as a Eucharistic image anticipating his institution of the Lord's Supper later on in his ministry (see also the later reference to "the place where the people had eaten the bread after *the Lord had given thanks*" in 6:23, emphasis added). Intriguingly, the Lord's Supper is not explicitly narrated in John's gospel, so the present incident appears to be his functional substitute, perhaps intending to show that the Lord's Supper is grounded in the practice of Jesus during his earthly ministry.

---

86. See esp. the reference to two hundred denarii in Mark 6:37 and John 6:7; the five loaves and two fish in Mark 6:38 and John 6:9; and to the twelve baskets of leftovers in Mark 6:43 and John 6:13.

87. See Köstenberger, *John*, 196, n. 1, and the commentary on pp. 199–24.

88. Contra many commentators and popular resources that, perhaps on the assumption that there are seven signs in John, add the walking on the water on account of its miraculous nature as the seventh to the list, despite its lack of Johannine identification as a "sign." For an argument for the temple clearing in John 2 as the seventh Johannine sign, see chap. 7, sec. 15 below.

89. See Köstenberger, *Missions of Jesus and the Disciples*, with reference to Anselm Schulz, *Nachfolgen und Nachahmen: Studien über das Verhältnis der neutestamentlichen Jüngerschaft zur urchristlichen Vorbildethik* (SANT 6; München: Kösel, 1962).

Jesus' miraculous provision of more than enough food for all the people—the abundance is indicated by the fact that twelve basketfuls are left over (**vv. 12–13**)—places him in continuity with Moses' provision of manna for Israel in the wilderness and strikes the "new exodus" theme.[90] In another instance of Johannine **misunderstanding**, people promptly set out to draft him king, though, as Jesus perceives, their actions are based on entirely worldly, nationalistic, and political notions of kingship (**vv. 14–15**; note the allusion to Deut 18:15, 18 in John 6:14). Again, the "elusive Christ" evades their grasp and withdraws to a mountain by himself (v. 15). Sadly, but not unexpectedly (see v. 2), the crowds miss the true messianic significance of the "**sign**" (not identified as such until later in the narrative, see v. 26).[91]

In the flow of the Johannine narrative, the walking on the water (**vv. 16–21**), in a sense, gives the reader temporary pause ("narrative space") between the account of the feeding of the multitude (vv. 1–15) and the elaboration on its significance by Jesus in the Bread of Life Discourse (vv. 25–59). Nevertheless, the entire chapter constitutes a close-knit narrative unit that presents Jesus, who performs yet another messianic "sign," as the messianic prophet and king (see vv. 14–15), the one who, Godlike (see Job 9:8 LXX), strides majestically across the waters and identifies himself, in characteristic Johannine double entendre, by the divine name *egō eimi* (lit., "I am"; v. 20).

After Jesus' private theophany and manifestation to his disciples (in contrast to the six undisputed "signs," all of which are public in nature), the crowds eventually track Jesus down in Capernaum (his home, see John 2:12 and the Synoptics; see esp. Matt 9:1). There is no place like home—or is there? Jesus had earlier said that "prophets have no honor in their own country" (John 4:44), and this is true all the more for Jesus, who is much more (though not less) than a prophet. Notice that, somewhat imperceptibly, the scene changes throughout the ensuing Bread of Life Discourse from "the other side of the lake" (v. 25) to "the synagogue in Capernaum" (v. 59; perhaps at v. 30?). Hence this present momentous synagogue address by Jesus recorded in John 6:30–58 may represent John's functional equivalent to Jesus' synagogue address in Nazareth recorded in Luke 4:14–30.

This is now the second major discourse of Jesus in John's gospel, the first one being Jesus' disclosure of himself as equal with the Father in interaction with the Pharisees in 5:19–46. In the present Bread of Life Discourse, Jesus first challenges his interrogators simply to **believe** in him, which is the only "work" (in the singular!) God requires of them (**vv. 28–29**), rather than keeping their various traditions associated with the law (see discussion at 5:9b–18). In a familiar twist (see 2:18), Jesus' interrogators ask him for a **messianic sign**, indicating massive **misunderstanding**: had he not just fed five thousand people with a mere five barley loaves and two small

---

90. See discussion of the Bread of Life Discourse below. See also Dennis, "Presence and Function."

91. For a possible earlier instance of an unduly nationalistic interpretation of Jesus' kingship see Nathanael's reference to Jesus as "king of Israel" in John 1:49 (compare Jesus' response in 1:50–51), on which see Köstenberger, *John*, 83–84.

fish? Quite apparently, the crowds had "seen" the sign Jesus performed—what is more, they had actually eaten the bread and fish he provided and had their fill (see v. 26)—but at the same time had failed to truly "see" or perceive the way in which the "sign" pointed to Jesus as the God-sent Messiah.

This is proved by their request for a "**sign**" they had, in fact, already seen. Will Jesus perform another sign? This would serve no purpose. Instead, rather than supporting an improper disposition toward seeking "signs *and wonders*," which he previously discouraged at 4:48, what is needed is for him to explicate the significance (or, better, the *sign*-ificance) of the sign he had already performed, so that **misunderstanding** (or lack of understanding) may be turned into true spiritual perception (though, sadly, as the ensuing narrative demonstrates, this purpose remained unfulfilled, and a mass exodus ensued: 6:60–71). In this spiritual obduracy the Jews' asking Jesus for a sign in verse 30 displays the characteristics identified by John at the end of the first half of his gospel, citing a passage from the prophet Isaiah: they have blind eyes and hardened hearts, "so they can neither see with their eyes, nor understand with their hearts, nor turn—and I would heal them" (12:40; cf. Isa 6:10).

Incredibly, in thick Johannine **irony**, the crowds, by their demand for Jesus to perform a "sign" comparable to Moses' giving the Israelites "bread from heaven" in the wilderness (**vv. 30–31**), reveal that they have missed the obvious connection between Jesus' multiplication of the loaves and this antecedent event in salvation history (a typological connection akin to the one earlier adduced by Jesus in 3:13 and commented on by the evangelist in 3:16). This, in turn, gives Jesus the opportunity to unpack the messianic significance of this event in the ensuing Bread of Life Discourse, which, along the lines of an escalating typological pattern, presents Jesus as the paradigmatic "bread of God ... that comes down from heaven and gives life to the world" (**v. 33**; note the universal reference to "the world," transcending the scope of Israel; see also v. 51).

In **verse 34**, the crowds still do not understand the import of Jesus' word, asking, in a phrase reminiscent of the Samaritan woman in 4:15, "Sir ... always give us this bread," though, unlike the Samaritan, they turn out less receptive to Jesus' revelation as the Messiah. When Jesus plainly states that he is the "bread of life" and invites his hearers to believe in him (**v. 35**)—telling them that "everyone who looks to the Son and believes in him shall have eternal life" (**v. 40**), which elaborates on the similar previous reference in 3:13–16—they, like their Jewish ancestors of old, begin to grumble (**vv. 41, 43**; *gongysmos*; see later v. 61; cf. Exod 16:2, 8–9; Num 11:4–23), expressing confusion as to how to reconcile Jesus' human ancestry with his claim of heavenly origin (**v. 42**). Armed with the information provided in the introduction, the reader of John's gospel knows that the answer to this dilemma is the knowledge of Jesus' eternal preexistence with God and his incarnation at a particular moment in **salvation history** (see later the probable slur on Jesus' paternity at 8:41b).

In the end, the analogy of "eating" Jesus' flesh and of "drinking" his blood (**vv. 48–51**)—unmistakable Eucharistic allusions when read in hindsight (see comments on 6:11 and 23 above)—proves unpalatable and too much to swallow (puns intended) for Jesus' Jewish hearers (**v. 52**), though Jesus does not back down but rather reiterates even more strongly that "unless you eat the flesh of the Son of Man [Jesus] and drink his blood, you have no life in you" (**v. 53**; see also **vv. 54 – 55**). Many even of Jesus' "disciples" (*mathētai*) abandon him (**vv. 60, 61, 66**); only the Twelve remain, and even there, John notes that one of them would turn out to be a traitor (vv. 70 – 71).

Hence this first half of Act I of John's gospel ends on a profound note of failure, foreshadowing the even more pronounced and comprehensive note of failure sounded at the end of Act I in 12:36b – 40.[92] The increasing profundity of the Messiah's self-disclosure, it appears, is met and matched in the narrative by the deepening rejection of the Messiah by all but his closest followers. This illustrates the decision required from every individual regarding Jesus' true identity. In John's equivalent to the Synoptic pericope narrating Peter's confession of Jesus as the Messiah at Caesarea Philippi (Matt 16:13 – 20 pars.), Peter, speaking for the Twelve, reaffirms his allegiance to Jesus at this pivotal juncture in his ministry, acknowledging him as "the Holy One of God" (**John 6:69**). This confession provides a critical counterpoint to the virtually universal rejection of Jesus, and it is this "rock" (Matt 16:18) — or, in Johannine terms, his "own" (John 13:1; cf. 1:11; see also chap. 17) — that will serve as the foundation for the **new community** that the Messiah will establish to represent him in this world (see 20:21).[93]

10.2.1.3.3 Summary of John's Narrative up to 6:71

This, then, represents yet another messianic self-disclosure of Jesus. At the wedding in Cana, Jesus showed himself to his disciples as the messianic bridegroom (compare the Baptist's testimony at John 3:27 – 30). At the temple clearing, he acted as the authoritative prophet through the sacrifice of whose life destruction and new life would come to the nation's worship as its new temple. To Nicodemus, Jesus disclosed himself as the one who would be "lifted up" and who would become the source of eternal life upon people's believing response (3:13 – 16). To the Samaritan, he was the proclaimer of a new kind of worship "in spirit and truth," who turned out to be none other than the Messiah himself. Before the Pharisees, he asserted his claim of being on par with God himself and adduced John, his own works, God the Father, and Moses and the Scriptures as his witnesses.

Now he shows himself to be the climactic fulfillment of people's messianic expectations centered on the "prophet like [Moses]" (Deut 18:15, 18), whose coming was to be patterned after the first deliverer and lead to another "exodus" of God's people (cf. Luke 9:31, where Jesus, in conversation with Moses and Elijah, calls his impending death an "exodus" [*exodos*]). Significantly, in John 6 Jesus further elaborates on the nature of "**believing**" in him over against earlier references (e.g., 3:16). According to Jesus, this is not merely an external act (looking); rather, it involves

---

92. See the structural proposal in Köstenberger, *John*, 52.
93. For a discussion of the "representational" vs. the "incarnational" model of mission see Köstenberger, *Mission of Jesus and the Disciples*, chap. 5.

the actual taking of Jesus into one's internal being, akin to the universal human act of eating and drinking (see later, e.g., 14:23, where Jesus talks about him and the Father coming into a believer and making their residence in him). While this comparison may—and did—offend Jewish sensibilities (and later led to charges that the early Christians practiced cannibalism!)—this points to the nature of this most intimate union with Jesus entered into by the believer.[94]

By providing the reader with a glimpse inside the "Jesus movement" and showing Jesus' "little flock" (see Luke 12:32) pared down to a very small number, John illustrates that, indeed, the gate is small and the path narrow, and few are those who enter it (Matt 7:13–14). God's people were never promised they would be in the majority. To the contrary, they must brace themselves to be only a small minority in a world dominated by massive **unbelief**. This picture is at times obscured by the larger number of people (the "crowds") who are associated with the "Jesus movement" (the church) in some way but who turn out to follow Jesus only from a distance (i.e., their discipleship is shallow at best and nonexistent at worst) and who are not truly part of Jesus' inner circle of committed disciples in any meaningful sense. These insights are of perennial ecclesiological significance and continue to represent challenges for those engaged in Christian ministry.

10.2.1.3.4 Jesus at the Festival of Tabernacles (Part 1; 7:1–52)

The new unit opens with a reference to the death plot against Jesus in Judea (**v. 1**). With another **Jewish festival** approaching—this time, it is the Festival of Tabernacles (**v. 2**)—Jesus is reluctant to make another trip to the Jewish capital (note the opposition he faced there at a previous Passover, John 2:13, 23) and especially at another unspecified feast (John 5; see esp. 5:18). This already led him to remain behind and celebrate the Passover in Galilee in John 6. Similar to his mother at a previous occasion (2:4), Jesus' brothers in the present pericope prompt him to perform his works publicly (**7:4**), indicating their **unbelief** (**v. 5**). This continues on the note of unbelief that had come to a preliminary climax at the end of the previous chapter.

It is also in keeping with the Johannine **misunderstanding** theme, which here shows the members of Jesus' own family (his brothers) as misapprehending the nature of Jesus' messianic calling. It is not self-serving, as if Jesus, like a wandering salesman, were to display his wares, hoping people would find his offerings attractive. Jesus does not so much seek a following in the world as he is out to make God known (see John 1:18) for who he truly is in his own person. Everything, including the mode of Jesus' revelation, is diametrically opposed to the ways of the world. Not self-promotion, clever advertising, tactics of manipulation of popular opinion, or other dubious political or other means are the methods by which Jesus seeks to make

---

94. Compare the later images of the shepherd and his flock and the vine and the branches in John 10 and 15, respectively, on which see Köstenberger, *Missions of Jesus and the Disciples*, chap. 4.

God known. Instead, he simply calls people to believe that it is the Father who sent him (see 17:21, 23 *et passim*).

For reasons such as these Jesus initially signals that he will not attend the festival — at least, it may be presumed, not on his brothers' (and the world's) terms.[95] What he told his mother at an earlier occasion still applies: "My time is not yet here" (**vv. 6, 8**; cf. 2:4). Jesus is well aware of the world's hatred of him for no other reason than that he exposes the evil nature of people's works (**v. 7**; cf. 3:19–21 and later 15:25, citing Ps 35:19/69:4: "[They] hate me without reason"). Through the use of representative statements, John highlights the considerable diversity of opinion regarding Jesus among the visitors to the festival, ranging from "He is a good man" (**John 7:12**) to "No, he deceives the people" (**v. 12**; see also v. 47 below). He also notes the widespread fear of the Jewish authorities among the people (**v. 13**).

After the preamble concerned with the delay of Jesus' trip up to Jerusalem and the diversity of opinion among the crowds, the narrative enters a new phase in **verse 14**, marking the halfway point of the festival, at which Jesus commences his teaching activity. When people marveled at his learning (**v. 15**), Jesus affirmed his close union with God (**vv. 16–18**) and went on the counter-offensive, asking, "Why are you trying to kill me?" (**v. 19**). People deny this (though see the confirmation of Jesus' words, in contradiction to people's denial, at v. 25 below), charging Jesus with demon possession (**v. 20**).

Jesus, with a back reference to the healing of the lame man in John 5, picks up the previous controversy by making the irrefutable argument that the Jewish people themselves acknowledged certain exceptions to the Sabbath commandment by circumcising a boy if his eighth day fell on a Sabbath. This, Jesus argued with compelling logic, clearly established the principle that certain exceptions obtained to the Sabbath commandment. And arguing from the lesser to the greater, if it was appropriate under certain circumstances to circumcise a part of a person's body, why not healing an entire man? (**v. 23**). This resembles the kind of engagement of Jewish teachers of the law featured frequently in the Synoptics (e.g., Matt 19:3 pars.).

In what follows it becomes clear that inaction on the part of the Jewish authorities had begun to take a toll in that people were wondering if it represented a tacit acknowledgment that Jesus may after all be the Messiah (**John 7:26**). This indicates that the common people were looking to the leadership for guidance in adjudicating Jesus' claims. In what follows John representatively features several **messianic expectations** represented among the Jewish crowds:

- "When the Messiah comes, no one will know where he is from" (**v. 27**)
- "When the Messiah comes, will he perform more signs than this man?" (**v. 31**)

---

95. See the variants "not" (*ouk*) vs. "not yet" (*oupō*) in verse 8, which at least indicates discussion if not confusion among early copyists and a possible desire to alleviate the apparent contradiction between Jesus' statement here and his eventual going to Jerusalem (assuming the originality of *ouk*; though this reading receives only a "C" rating in UBS4, indicating "difficulty in deciding which variant to place in the text"). However, see the clarifying statement in verse 10: "not publicly, but in secret," which seems to alleviate the difficulty in either case. See the discussion in Metzger, *Textual Commentary*, 185.

- "How can the Messiah come from Galilee? Does not Scripture say that the Messiah will come from David's descendants and from Bethlehem...?" (**vv. 41–42**)

The initial view, though not necessarily scriptural, has its precedents in the notion, prevalent in certain circles in Second Temple Judaism, of a "hidden Messiah." Beyond this, Scripture (an example being Dan 7:13) did indicate that the coming of the **Son of Man** (a messianic figure) was shrouded in mystery. Hence the crowd's argument: we know where Jesus is from (cf. John 7:42), but the Messiah's origins will be unknown — thus Jesus cannot be the Messiah. In Johannine **irony**, however, rather than contradicting Jesus' claims, this statement actually confirmed those claims, since, while Jesus' *human* origins were known (though John, unlike Matthew and Luke, who include narratives of Jesus' birth, does not dwell on this), this was only *part* of the story — the *whole* truth was that Jesus was of heavenly descent (as he clearly indicated in John 6; see discussion of 6:31–59 above; see also 3:31–36).[96]

But what about people's question whether or not the Messiah will perform more "**signs**" than Jesus? This seems to be a tacit acknowledgment on their part that Jesus had indeed performed numerous such messianic signs and that they found it hard to imagine that the Messiah (if not Jesus) would perform even more such signs. In other words, most likely this represents a rhetorical question implying a negative answer: "When the Messiah comes, will he perform more signs than this man [Jesus]? We find this hard to imagine. For he certainly has performed plenty of signs" (see previous references at 2:23; 6:2, 26; and 12:28 below). Jesus therefore does seem to measure up according to the expectation that the Messiah would perform many signs (see also 6:30–31, indicating that this expectation was significantly linked with Moses' performance of many "signs and wonders" at the exodus).

What, then, about the third major messianic expectation featured in this chapter? This concerns the apparent contradiction between Jesus' known origin from Galilee and the scriptural indication that the **Messiah** would come from Bethlehem (v. 42; cf. Mic 5:2, 4 cited in Matt 2:6). Again, Johannine **irony** is apparent, for as the informed reader already knows (though Jesus' birth in Bethlehem is not actually recorded in this gospel), the apparent contradiction is resolved easily enough: Jesus had in fact been born in Bethlehem (e.g., Matt 2:1). Only later his parents had moved with the boy Jesus to Nazareth in Galilee so that he, in keeping with scriptural prediction, was "called a Nazarene" (see Matt 2:21–23).

Hence John has successfully diffused all three potential obstacles to the possibility that Jesus may indeed be the Messiah: (1) his origins, while human as to his

---

96. This is commonly referred to as part of the Johannine "dualism," though the term is perhaps not entirely fortunate (see chap. 6, sec. 12.1.1 below). John consistently holds these aspects in tension and, as was acknowledged by the later ecumenical councils, affirms both Jesus' full humanity and his deity. On Jesus' humanity, see Marianne Meye Thompson, *The Humanity of Jesus in the Fourth Gospel* (Philadelphia: Fortress, 1988), including an important critique of Käsemann. On Jesus' deity in John see Harris, *Jesus as God*, 51–129; on the Trinity and John's gospel, see Köstenberger and Swain, *Father, Son and Spirit*. See also the Johannine descent-ascent schema, on which see Nicholson, *Death as Departure*; and Köstenberger, *Missions of Jesus and the Disciples*, chap. 2.

natural earthly family, were in truth heavenly and divine; (2) his "signs" were both numerous and compelling as demonstrations of the truthfulness of his messianic claims; and (3) Jesus had indeed been born in Bethlehem as Scripture had predicted; his Galilean background presented no true obstacle. *Quod erat demonstrandum*. The defense rests its case.

The third and final stage in John's narrative in this chapter (after 7:1–13: preamble; and 7:14–36: halfway point) commences in 7:37, making "the last and greatest day of the Festival." The progression can be diagrammed as follows:

- 7:1–13: Jesus comes to the Festival, first not at all, finally "in secret" (*ou phanerōs... en kryptō*, v. 10)
- 7:14–36: Jesus begins to teach publicly at the midway point of the Festival (*edidasken*, v. 14; see later 18:20: *parrēsia... en kryptō elalēsa ouden*)
- 7:37–44: Jesus shouts out loud his invitation for people to come to him (*ekraxen*, v. 37)[97]

Shouting with a loud voice—note the accelerating boldness after his initial coming to the feast "in secret" at first (7:10; see listing above)—Jesus proclaims himself to be the dispenser of the "living water" of the Holy Spirit (see Jesus' words to the Samaritan woman in John 4 above).[98] This, in turn, is in keeping with the description of Jesus as the one who possesses the Spirit without measure at 3:34. As throughout his gospel, John carefully distinguishes between the historical perspective from the vantage point of Jesus' ministry and the period subsequent to the Son's "glorification" (cf. **7:39**, a Johannine euphemism for the cluster encompassing Jesus' crucifixion, burial, resurrection, and ascension), acknowledging that from the vantage point of Jesus in John 7, the giving of the **Holy Spirit** was yet future (see also John 14 and 16 below).[99]

The carefully scripted interchange surfacing potential obstacles to Jesus' messianic identity in popular messianic (mis)conceptions and their resolution by John issues in the spectrum of opinions listed at the end of the pericope:

- "Surely this man is the Prophet" (v. 40)
- "He is the Messiah" (!) (v. 41)
- "How can the Messiah come from Galilee?" (v. 42)

In light of the fact that the third option/objection is transparently invalid (see discussion above), this, remarkably, shows that the pendulum of public opinion is decidedly swinging in Jesus' favor. People judge him to be either "the Prophet" or even "the Messiah," a truly remarkable outcome, especially after the virtual universal

---

97. For a discussion of the connection between 7:37–38 and Isa 55:1 LXX, see Michael A. Daise, "'If Anyone Thirsts, Let That One Come to Me and Drink': The Literary Texture of John 7:37b–38a," *JBL* 122 (2003): 687–99.

98. On the exegetical questions and interpretive options presented by Jesus' statement in 7:37 see Köstenberger, *John*, 240–41. See also the discussion of thematic links between Jesus' statement and OT symbolism associated with the Festival of Tabernacles in ibid.

99. I will argue below (and have argued in Köstenberger, *John*, 574–55) that even the apparent giving of the Spirit to the Eleven at 20:22 is only proleptic of the actual giving of the Spirit at Pentecost. See the discussion at 20:22 and in chap. 9, sec. 21.3.2 below.

rejection suffered by Jesus at the end of the previous chapter and his brother's (discouraging) comment that if Jesus wanted to prove himself, he must go to Jerusalem (implying that at that point he had not yet established his messianic identity). Are people indeed ready to embrace Jesus as Messiah? The reader knows that the crowds are notoriously fickle and easily swayed. For this reason much depends on the response by the Jewish authorities—and this is precisely where the Johannine narrative turns next.

The following scene opens with the chief priests and the Pharisees asking the temple guards why they did not arrest Jesus (**v. 45**). As it turns out, even the guards who were supposed to arrest Jesus had been deeply impacted by Jesus' message (**v. 46**). In this way John underscores the profundity of Jesus' impact on the people. The identity of John's source for the pericopae that take place in the inner sanctum of the Sanhedrin is unclear (Nicodemus? Joseph of Arimathea?),[100] though from a narrative, as well as theological, standpoint, this glimpse into the inner workings of the Jewish highest council serves as a barometer of the plot against Jesus, indicating that the authorities' mind regarding Jesus has been made up a long time ago and his eventual destiny is in truth a fait accompli—the question is no longer a matter of *if* Jesus will be crucified, but merely *when* this will come to pass.

This lends the Johannine narrative a certain aura of inevitability in that John presents the events in Jesus' life and ministry as the inexorable outworking of a divine predetermined destiny. The Messiah's performance of a successive series of startling signs does not fundamentally alter the state of the Jewish leaders' heart; rather, it simply confirms them in their **obduracy** and stiffens their resolve to oppose and reject God's anointed. This, in turn, serves the Johannine purpose of **theodicy** (the vindication of God's righteousness in his dealings with humanity), showing the evil of human hearts set in sinful moral rebellion against God and redemption in Christ as the only salvation out of this universal human predicament.

Tragically, for those who, like the Jewish authorities, reject the atoning work of God's Messiah on their behalf, there is no other way: "No one comes to the Father except through me" (14:6). By rejecting Jesus, the Jews (and the unbelieving world at large, of which unbelieving Jews are a part) slam shut the only door that provides access to salvation. This outcome is truly tragic and paradoxical, as it is these very people who started out as God's chosen people, which raises profound questions concerning God's **election**, **predestination**, and the relationship between divine sovereignty and human responsibility.[101]

For now, however, Jesus' increasing appeal exacerbates the pressure on the Jewish authorities to take action to counter the growing Jesus movement. In their exasperation, the Pharisees snipe at the guards who express admiration for Jesus' words (**v. 47**), curse the ordinary people who know "nothing of the law" (**v. 49**), and main-

---

100. See Bauckham's theory in *Jesus and the Eyewitnesses*, chap. 3, that the gospel writers identify their sources by naming them in their narrative.

101. On which see further the discussion of John 12:36b–50 below.

tain that none of "the rulers or of the Pharisees" have believed in him (**v. 48**). But even this claim is put in question when Nicodemus, "who," as John duly notes, "had gone to Jesus earlier [3:1] and who *was one of their own number*" (emphasis added), challenges the propriety of their procedure of condemning Jesus without following due process; his comments indicate that even this member of the Sanhedrin may have been impacted by Jesus' message (**vv. 50–52**). Amazingly, within the course of one single chapter in John's narrative, Jesus' fortunes seem to have improved considerably, though, as will be seen, this change in fortunes is not necessarily of lasting import.

10.2.1.3.5 Jesus at the Festival of Tabernacles (Part 2; 8:12–59)

After the brief vignette from the Sanhedrin chambers (John 7:45–52), the narrative resumes with Jesus speaking to the people at the Festival of Tabernacles (so may be assumed, since no change of location is indicated).[102] Jesus' affirmation in **8:12**, "I am the **light** of the world" (to be repeated in 9:5 in the context of the next sign; note that **signs** are notably absent from John 7–8, but through 8:12 = 9:5 there is a connection between this unit and a Johannine sign nonetheless), followed by the assertion that any follower of Jesus will never walk in darkness but have the light of life, harks back to the introductory identification of the **Word**—Jesus—as the light. Not only is Jesus bread (John 6) and water (John 7), he is also light, meeting the universal human need for life—spiritual, eternal **life**.

This casts Jesus' message into even more universal terms than the Synoptic terminology of the "kingdom of God." What is more, while bread and water are essential to physical life and hence are fitting analogies for Jesus' mission to impart spiritual life to people, the "light" metaphor harks back to the beginning of time, that is, **creation**, where God created all things and separated light from darkness. This, therefore, is part of John's **"new creation" theology**, which presents Jesus' mission in continuity with the work of God at creation: like God, so Jesus too separates light from darkness by coming into the world. Yet he does so in a more overtly spiritual sense, for his mission pertains not primarily to literal separation of light and darkness but to a spiritual separation brought about by his exposure of human sinfulness and rebellion against God. Either people, like rats when light is shone into a cellar, will scurry for cover, or they will be "overcome" by the light (see John 1:5) and yield to its sovereign power. As Jesus will say at the close of his ministry to the Jews, "Put your trust in the light while you have the light, so that you may become children of light" (12:36).

All of this is strangely lost on the Pharisees, who in no way resonate with Jesus' claim but merely challenge the validity of his witness (**8:13**). This confirms their spiritual blindness (see John 9 below); they simply have not "come to the **light**" but

---

102. For the rationale for excluding the (inauthentic) pericope of Jesus and the adulterous woman in 7:53–8:11, see Köstenberger, *John*, 245–49.

dwell in **darkness** and so are unable to make out the colorful, multifaceted messianic portrait that John has painted and Jesus has revealed. For them, all is gray, if not black, and their mind is set on pressing charges against Jesus, not to "see the light" with regard to Jesus' true identity as God's Messiah. The following interchange in chapter 8 is thus essentially a rerun of John 5, revolving around the validity of Jesus' witness (see discussion at 5:31–47).

Countering the Pharisees' charge that his **witness** on his own behalf is invalid (8:13), Jesus retorts that there are in fact two witnesses confirming his identity: himself and the **Father** who sent him (**v. 18**). This leads the Pharisees to zero their investigation in on the identity of Jesus' Father (**v. 19**). Jesus, in response, affirms his oneness with the Father (see later 10:30; 14:9–10), which is met with massive misunderstanding by the Jews (**vv. 22, 25, 27**). Jesus acknowledges that it will not be until after they have "lifted up" the **Son of Man** [Jesus] that they will grasp Jesus' true identity (**v. 28**; cf. 3:13).

In what follows John sets up the reader of his narrative for a fascinating exploration of what it means to **believe**—or not to believe—in Jesus. He starts by noting that "even as he [Jesus] spoke, many put their faith in him" (**v. 30**). Then, in the next verse, he states that, "*To the Jews who had believed him*, Jesus said, 'If you *hold to my teaching*, you are really my disciples. *Then* you will know the truth, and the truth will set you free" (**vv. 31–32**, emphasis added). We have seen previously that John relativizes people's (apparent) faith in Jesus: in 2:23–25, he notes how people's faith "in his name" is met by Jesus lack of "faith" in their faith (an effort to reproduce the wordplay in the original Greek); and at 6:60, 61, 66, John notes as many as three times that it was many of Jesus' *disciples* who turned back from following him in light of his teaching that they found difficult to accept. Now Jesus makes the nature of true faith even more explicit by pointing to people's need to continue (*menō*, 8:31) in his teaching as a prerequisite for coming to know the truth (see the emphasis on "remaining" in Jesus for his disciples in John 15 below).[103]

What sets Jesus' antagonists off is not his main point—that those who would follow him must continue in his teaching—but his reference to the truth "setting" his followers "free." Those "believers" in Jesus—correctly—imply that anyone not thus liberated is thereby said by Jesus to be in bondage. But how can this be said about a people who have always been free? Or have they? Politically speaking, the Jews had for some time been subject to foreign ruling powers and were currently under Roman rule. Thus they were certainly anything but "free" as far as their national life and governance was concerned. But what about their freedom, spiritually speaking? Were they "free" in this sense?

As Jesus makes clear in his next remark, sin enslaves (**v. 34**), and, contrary to the Jews' self-understanding and self-perception, which set them in marked contrast to

---

103. For an exploration of the Johannine characterization of Jesus' disciples, including a discussion of the various instances of the term "remain" (*menō*), see chap. 12, sec. 29 below.

non-Jews by claiming a special status of spiritual enlightenment owing to their status as people chosen by God, sinfulness extends universally to all of humanity, Jews and non-Jews alike. This was affirmed already by John the Baptist, who described the mission of "the **Lamb of God**" (Jesus) as taking away "the sin of the world" (1:29). It is also argued emphatically by Paul in his letter to the Romans (Rom 1:18–3:31, esp. 3:9–24, citing a litany of OT Psalms with reference to Jews *as well as* Gentiles, rather than only Gentiles as the Jews read these psalms). Jesus, too, in the Synoptic parables, consistently made the point that a reversal was to take place through his ministry: the tax collector who knew himself to be sinful and in need of God would walk away justified rather than the self-righteous Pharisee (Luke 18:9–14); it is the sick who need a doctor rather than the healthy (Matt 9:12 pars.); and so on.

Hence Jesus exposed the Jews' defective anthropology—their view of themselves as exempt from the universal state of human sinfulness—and confronted them with their spiritual bondage that resulted from their sin and that could not be remedied until, and unless, they were prepared to acknowledge it. In Jesus' call to repentance here (see also John the Baptist's call to repentance, put in parallel with Jesus' call to repentance by Matthew: compare Matt 4:17 with Matt 3:2) enshrines a perennial need for the preacher of the gospel to lead his hearers to a recognition of their sinful state as a necessary step on the way to leading them to the acknowledgment of their need for a Savior.

Sadly, in the dispute that grows increasingly more heated, the Pharisees doggedly insist on their descent from Abraham, as if their ethnicity is able to save them. However, as Jesus makes clear, descent from Abraham, properly conceived, is not a physical, external category but, crucially, involves a spiritual dimension: following in Abraham's footsteps with regard to faith (John 8:39; for similar arguments see Galatians 3; Romans 4; and Hebrews 11). Jesus acknowledges that the Jews are Abraham's physical descendants, but he contends that Abraham would not set out to kill God's Messiah (**John 8:37**). He also, not once but twice, baits them by referring obliquely to their (true) "father" (**vv. 38, 41**).

Quite possibly, they respond by hinting at a rumor of Jesus being an illegitimate child, protesting, "We [as opposed to Jesus?] are not illegitimate children" (v. 41), claiming God—now no longer Abraham—as their only Father.[104] This, at long last, lifts the discussion fully on a spiritual plane, advancing the discussion from descent from Abraham to descent from God. Indeed, this is precisely the direction into which Jesus had intended to steer the discussion all along, and now he moves in for the kill: "You belong to your father, *the devil*" (**v. 44**, emphasis added)—for it is ultimately he who is behind the plot to kill Jesus, inciting the Jews' pride and opposition to him and eventually inciting Judas to betray him (see 13:2).

Thus, in a theological tour de force, John has managed (recounting the essence of Jesus' words, of course) to expose the true spiritual underpinnings of the opposition

---

104. For a later slur of Jesus' paternity in Jewish literature see *m. Yebam.* 4:13.

to Jesus and his messianic mission. As Paul would put it, this "struggle is not against flesh and blood, but against ... the spiritual forces of evil in the heavenly realms" (Eph 6:12), or, sharpened still further, against what John calls "the prince of this world," Satan (John 12:31; 14:30; 16:11). Thus the deadly combat between Jesus and the Pharisees that ultimately brings Jesus to the cross is presented by John as, not an internecine Jewish struggle for supremacy (as Roman officials may have surmised), but a cosmic clash between good and evil, between God and Satan, proceeding completely under **God's sovereignty** while still rendering those opposing the Messiah morally culpable and subject to judgment.

Hence Jesus concludes that the root cause of the Jews' opposition to him is that they "do not belong to God" (**v. 47**), in flat contradiction of their earlier claim (v. 41). Sound familiar? This was precisely the same point made by Jesus in his interchange with Nicodemus, the Sanhedrin member and "Israel's teacher" (see 3:3, 5). Now the point is extrapolated to old-style Judaism at large. Confronting Jewish ethnic presumption, Jesus maintained that the Jews' claim of descent from Abraham would not save them; the root problem of their sin can be remedied only by faith in the Son, who alone could set them free (v. 36). This, then, is always the problem: sin. As Paul noted, indwelling sin renders any effort of consistent law-keeping futile and ineffective. Only Jesus can save us from our wretched body that is doomed to die (see Rom 7:14–25).

The Jews, in reply, renew their charge that Jesus is demon-possessed (**John 8:48, 52**; see 7:20; 10:20; cf. the Synoptics with their reference to the Beelzebub controversy and the blasphemy of the Holy Spirit, Matt 12:24–28; Mark 3:22–29; Luke 11:14–20). If Jesus can accuse them of having the devil as their father, they, not to be outdone, can accuse him of demon-possession. Hence, in this paternity dispute, they seek to match him blow by blow.

When Jesus responds that his followers will never see death (**John 8:51**), the Jews respond that this is impossible, for even Abraham died (**v. 53**), and, surely, Jesus cannot be greater than Abraham. To which Jesus replies that Abraham eagerly anticipated his coming ("rejoiced at the thought of seeing my day," **v. 56**). This the Jews promptly misunderstand, asking how Jesus could have seen Abraham, being not even fifty years old (**v. 57**), while Jesus had claimed that Abraham had (proleptically) seen *his* day. In response, Jesus goes further still, affirming not only that Abraham had looked forward to his coming but that, in fact, Jesus preceded Abraham, implicitly claiming **preexistence** (**v. 58**; fleshing out the opening claim in the introduction: see 1:1). As they had done previously (5:18), the Jews attempted to stone Jesus on account of blasphemy, but again he eludes their grasp (**8:59**).

Hence Jesus' controversy has progressed to a point where the differences seem completely irreconcilable. In a sense, John 8 constitutes the high point (if one can call it that) of the controversy between Jesus and the Jews. After this the battle lines are drawn and the fronts harden further, but it would be hard to transcend the intensity and explicit nature of the charges that have been traded here.

10.2.1.3.6 Yet Another Jerusalem Sign: The Healing of the Man Born Blind (9:1–41)

The previous chapter in John's gospel ended with the "elusive Christ" once again evading his would-be captors. Ominously, the **glory** of God, the very presence of the divine in Jesus, had hid, departing from the **temple** (8:59). Surely, this does not bode well for the Jewish nation and its representatives. Without extended transition, chapter 9 continues the narrative by noting that, as Jesus went along, he saw a man born blind (**v. 1**). The scene is set by the disciples' query, "Rabbi, who sinned, this man or his parents, that he was born blind?" (**v. 2**). Skillfully, the evangelist also introduces the two major (sets of) characters in the ensuing narrative, the man born blind and his parents, who will take turns in being the major targets of the Jewish authorities' investigation into the healing that is about to take place.

The man's blindness presented an interesting theological problem in that it raised the question of who was responsible for the man's predicament. If sickness (including blindness) was the result of personal sin, how can this be explained in the case of someone who was *born* blind and thus could not have sinned prior to being afflicted in this way? The disciples, in their query, hint at two of the most widespread "solutions" proposed in their day: (1) prenatal sin on the part of the man born blind in his mother's womb; or (2) sin on the part of his parents that was passed on for some reason to the man at birth. Especially the first suggestion may seem fanciful to modern interpreters, but it is important to understand that once the simple formula "suffering is a result of sin" is posited, an explanation is required in each specific case of affliction in order to account for the affliction in terms of someone's sin. And if a person is already *born* blind, perhaps he sinned prior to being born?

In the case of the man born blind and the disciples' query, Jesus declares that neither solution proposed by his followers is accurate (demonstrating the danger of the disjunctive and other fallacies) but that the man's blindness occurred for the purpose of revealing God's glory (**v. 3**). In this, Jesus models an approach to suffering by Christians, both in their own lives and in the lives of others, that holds in abeyance speculation regarding the causes of a given affliction and instead, by faith, believes that this affliction came so that, somehow, God would receive glory through it. In the present case, the man's blindness is turned by Jesus into an occasion where, through his working of another messianic **sign**, God's **glory** is revealed in and through the Messiah (cf. 1:14; 2:11), who will die to transform human existence from bondage to sin to, as Paul would put it, "the glorious liberty of the children of God" (Rom 8:21, KJV).

By working this sign, Jesus will prove himself to be the "**light** of the world" (**John 9:5**), a statement that establishes a narrative link with the preceding pericope (8:12).[105] By the time John has completed telling the story, it has turned into a kind of parable contrasting the blind man's gaining of sight with the Pharisees'

---

105. See the analysis of 9:4–5 in Hisayasu Ito, "Narrative Temporality and Johannine Symbolism," *AcT* 23 (2003): 117–35.

unrepented-of spiritual blindness, which results in continued blindness (vv. 39–41). This contributes to the multiplicity of subgenres interwoven creatively by John.

It is not necessary here to follow the entire narrative of the man's healing and the aftermath.[106] A few observations relevant for our present discussion must suffice. First, the evangelist notes that the healing takes place at the Pool of Siloam, and that "Siloam" means "**Sent**" (**v. 7**). By making this connection, the evangelist implies that at the heart of the "**sign**" is the demonstration that Jesus is the God-sent **Messiah**. As mentioned, this Christocentricity of the "signs" is integral to the way in which they are portrayed in John.

Second, it is clear that John intends the reader to engage in a comparison between the healing of the lame man in John 5 and the man born blind in the present chapter (note that both are Johannine "signs," corresponding to each other as they envelope the Festival Cycle in John 5–10), similar to the way in which the pericopae featuring Nicodemus and the Samaritan woman are juxtaposed, inviting comparison between these two characters (see above). The contrast is black and white, in that the man in John 5 reported Jesus to the authorities, whereas the man in John 9 progresses (similar to the Samaritan woman) in his spiritual journey and perception of Jesus' true identity. The man born blind goes from ignorance at the beginning (**9:11**: "the man they call Jesus") to viewing Jesus as "a prophet" (**v. 17**) to acknowledging his being "from God" (v. 33; the Pharisees call him "this fellow's [Jesus'] disciple" in **v. 28**) to calling him "Lord" and falling on his knees in worship in the climactic scene of the entire pericope (**v. 38**). This process triggers Jesus' pronouncement of reversal in **verses 39–41** (so characteristic of Synoptic parables).

Thus the two men feature two possible responses to being healed by Jesus. As in the Synoptic parable where Jesus heals ten people but only one—a Samaritan—returns to give thanks, so here the one has no concern to explore the identity of the One who healed him, in his self-centeredness and sin caring only for his personal self-interest (modeling an unbelieving response to Jesus' signs), while the other is drawn by the sign, irresistibly, into a deepening personal relationship with Jesus that leads to worship of Jesus as God (modeling the response desired by God, Jesus, and the evangelist). Thus the two men turn out to be representative characters in the Johannine narrative, transcending their own personal life story and becoming for the reader figures of identification as tools in the evangelist's skillful narrative hand in order to point the way to the faith response desired by Jesus to his messianic signs.

When John thus writes in his purpose statement at the end of the gospel that "Jesus performed many other signs in the presence of his disciples, which are not recorded in this book. But these are written that you may believe that Jesus is the Messiah, the Son of God, and that by believing you may have life in his name" (20:30–31), he has already presented, in a narrative format, one such person who has modeled this believing response to Jesus' signs and thus has received life in his

---

106. For this see Köstenberger, *John*, 280–96.

name—the man born blind. The healed lame man, by contrast, stands as an illustration of an unregenerate response that left the man physically walking, but still in his sins and thus spiritually dead.

A healing by itself, therefore, unaccompanied by a believing response, is fruitless and ineffectual, for eventually the person will still die, and if his sin problem is not taken care of, his destiny is darkness and death, just as the woman would have had to come back to draw water again many times after encountering Jesus, or people's stomachs had been filled by the loaves and the fishes but they got hungry again many times. Only **faith** in Jesus, therefore, whether triggered by one of his signs or not (which is preferable; see 20:28), introduces one to the personal relationship with the Savior that alone can save and procure for the person eternal life—and, as will soon be illustrated by the raising of Lazarus, though he may die, yet he will live (11:25–26).

Third, as in the Synoptics, now that the Pharisees have proved their intransigence to Jesus' claims (see John 8), Jesus resorts to a more indirect mode of communication, a kind of enacted parable (9:39–41), though there is one more heated exchange to come in John 10, as the bookend corresponding to John 5 completing the Festival Cycle. The theme of spiritual blindness, here introduced on a literal level and then transmuted into a parable on spiritual blindness, has a central part in the evangelist's final pronouncement at the end of Act I of his gospel in 12:37–41, drawing on two passages in Isaiah.[107] This shows that in John 9 and elsewhere, even in their spiritual blindness the Pharisees fulfill scriptural prophecy and are thus, despite their sinfulness, not outside the purview of the sovereignty of God.

10.2.1.3.7 The Good Shepherd Discourse and the Festival of Dedication (10:1–42)

Strikingly, despite the beginning of a new chapter in our English versions, there is no introduction to Jesus' Good Shepherd Discourse, but his pronouncement in John 10:1–18 follows immediately on his words in 9:41.[108] This suggests that the context of Jesus' words in John 10 is the aftermath of the healing in John 9 and that John 10 constitutes Jesus' commentary on what the events narrated in John 9 reveal about the state of affairs in contemporary Judaism.

Specifically, Jesus' words seem to address the *threatened* expulsion of anyone who confessed Jesus as Messiah (9:22: "His parents said this because they were afraid of the Jewish leaders, who already had decided that anyone who acknowledged that Jesus was the Messiah would be put out of the synagogue") and the subsequent *actual* expulsion of the man born blind from the synagogue (9:34: "And they threw him out"; v. 35: "Jesus heard that they had thrown him out"). J. Louis Martyn and others following him have claimed that this is unlikely to have happened during

---

107. For a discussion of irony in John 9, see Hisayasu Ito, "Johannine Irony Demonstrated in John 9," *Neot* 34 (2000): 361–71, 373–87.

108. For a detailed analysis of John 10 and particularly its OT background see Köstenberger, "Jesus the Good Shepherd."

Jesus' ministry and reflects a later development, but it is not necessary to see this as a formalized procedure of excommunication.[109] More likely, this was more the result of an initial effort on the part of the Jewish leaders to discourage open faith in Jesus, which had not yet translated into a formally enacted, Judaism-wide policy.

Properly understood, therefore, Jesus' address is not so much about his being "the good shepherd" but, at least initially, about the "bad shepherding" of the Pharisees (note the TNIV's rendering of **10:1**: "Very truly I tell *you Pharisees*"; "Pharisees" is not in the Greek text but is probably implied, hence the TNIV's rendering; see also v. 6 [TNIV]: "*the Pharisees* did not understand").[110] In keeping with the prophecy of Ezekiel, the Jewish leaders are excoriated as illegitimate and at cross purposes with God's will. They are not the kind of shepherds he wants for his people and do not follow in the path of his beloved shepherd David. Thus they provide the dark backdrop and stark contrast to Jesus' role as "the good shepherd," who truly cares for God's people and calls them to follow him. If the Pharisees do not (or cannot) hear his voice (i.e., accept his messianic claim), the reason is that they are dull of hearing (see 12:38–40). Jesus' followers, however, hear his voice and follow him.

Most importantly, the shepherd imagery allows Jesus to make clear that, as "the good shepherd" (**10:11, 14**), he will die for his "sheep" (**vv. 15, 17–18**). Unlike the hired hand who will run when danger approaches (**vv. 12–13**), Jesus will persevere in his messianic mission to the end (cf. 13:1), even though it involves nothing less than death—not for his own sake but for the sake of others, as even the Jewish high priest acknowledges, speaking better than he knows (11:49–52). Thus Jesus will "[take] away the sin of the world" (1:29; see also 1 John 2:2: "He is the atoning sacrifice for our sins, and not only for ours but also for the sins of the whole world") while dying for his own sheep—John's way of holding in tension the fact that Jesus renders universal **atonement** while saving effectually only those who respond to him in **faith** and accept his substitutionary sacrifice on their behalf.[111]

The Jews sharply reject such teaching by renewing their charge that Jesus is demon-possessed (**10:20**; cf. 7:20; 8:48), though they are immediately countered by others who, in a characteristic Johannine back-reference, point out that a demon-possessed could hardly open the eyes of the blind (**10:21**; see John 9). This again illustrates the tension felt by those whose preset notions of the Messiah and self-interest face the growing weight of evidence, provided by Jesus' "signs," that he is the Messiah, whether or not his work and message conform to their understanding or are convenient for them personally or in support of their own position. Will they let go of their pride? Or will they harden in opposition to Jesus?

---

109. See J. Louis Martyn's work discussed in chap. 1 above and the vast literature discussing this subject, for the most part failing to support Martyn's view.

110. Emphasis added.

111. See John A. Dennis, *Jesus' Death and the Gathering of True Israel: The Johannine Appropriation of Restoration Theology in the Light of John 11.47–52* (WUNT 2/217; Tübingen: Mohr-Siebeck, 2006); Jörg Frey, "Die '*theologia crucifixi*' des Johannesevangeliums," in *Kreuzestheologie im Neuen Testament* (ed. Andreas Dettwiler and Jean Zumstein; WUNT 151; Tübingen: Mohr-Siebeck, 2002), 169–238; Rainer Metzner, *Das Verständnis der Sünde im Johannesevangelium* (WUNT 122; Tübingen: Mohr-Siebeck, 2000); Peter Stuhlmacher, "Das Lamm Gottes—eine Skizze," in *Geschichte–Tradition–Reflexion: Festschrift für Martin Hengel zum 70. Geburtstag* (ed. Hubert Cancik, Hermann Lichtenberger, and Peter Schäfer; Tübingen: Mohr-Siebeck, 1996), 3:529–42.

The next subunit suggests the latter, if John's reference that "it was winter" in **verse 22** is taken as conveying dual meaning. To be sure, the Pharisees' reception of Jesus is chilly enough. Internal coherence between 10:22–42 and 10:1–21 is provided by the reference to Jesus' "sheep" in **verses 27–30**. The unit is introduced by reference to Jesus' appearance at yet another Jewish festival, this time the Festival of Dedication, the only reference to this festival in the NT, one that postdates the OT period and celebrated the rededication of the temple in the Maccabean period.[112] This indicates that Jesus is still in Jerusalem, or in Jerusalem again, after the events and interchanges in 7:1–10:21 had transpired (also in the Jewish capital).[113]

Indeed, it is remarkable how much coverage John gives to Jesus' visits to Jerusalem at the occasion of various festivals when compared with the Synoptic Gospels. This has the effect of making the Jews' eventual rejection of Jesus much more intelligible and of showing the mounting antagonism and hostility toward Jesus on the part of the Jewish authorities. It also helpfully suggests that the final temple clearing narrated in the Synoptics, presented there as triggering the final events in Jesus' ministry issuing in his crucifixion, was only "the straw that broke the camel's back." The Jews had greeted Jesus with growing suspicion all along and had long believed he was a messianic pretender out to deceive the people, an imposter who illegitimately claimed to be on the same level as God himself and thus committed blasphemy.

It is this charge the Jews now reiterate (**v. 33**; as mentioned above, an *inclusio* with 5:18 that bookends the Festival Cycle in John 5–10): "We are not stoning you for any good work ... but for blasphemy, because you, a mere man, claim to be God." Jesus responds by a scriptural argument (**10:34–38**, citing Ps 82:6), according to which even mere human beings were occasionally called "god" in the Hebrew Scriptures, so that for him to claim to be **God's Son** (acknowledged by him in John 10:36) was not necessarily illegitimate. (For argument's sake, Jesus here accommodates himself to being "a mere man," though, of course, the gospel claims much more than that, presenting Jesus as the legitimate object of worship reserved for God alone.)[114] With his sharp eye for the truly central, John zeroes in once again in his narrative on the question that is central in his entire gospel, namely, whether Jesus is the Son of God as he claimed (see 20:30–31).

As the reader by now fully expects, another attempt to seize Jesus ensues and fails (**v. 39**; the "elusive Christ" once again), and the Festival Cycle closes with a (surprising) reference to John the Baptist, not heard from since 5:33–35, where he was cited by Jesus as one of the witnesses to him and his messianic mission. Thus, by way of a double *inclusio*, the evangelist provides closure in this chapter of Jesus' ministry

---

112. See Hengel, "Johannesevangelium als Quelle," who stresses the value of John's gospel as a historical source.

113. John C. Poirier, "Hanukkah in the Narrative Chronology of the Fourth Gospel," *NTS* 54 (2008): 465–78, argues that all of John 9 and 10, and in fact all of John 7–10, took place during the Feast of Dedication, though 7:2 specifically refers to Tabernacles,

and 10:22 more likely marks a transition to a new festival (see, e.g., the reference to it being winter).

114. For a thorough exploration of Jesus' scriptural argument here see Köstenberger, "John," in *Commentary on the NT Use of the OT*, 464–67.

(note how **10:40–41** provides the latter bookend to both 1:19–10:42[115]—wrapping up Act I—and to 5:33–35—completing the Festival Cycle). The purpose of John's ministry has been fulfilled: Jesus had been revealed to Israel (see 1:32); and even though "John never performed a sign, all that John said about this man was true" (10:41). Thus, as the introduction indicates, the effects of John's witness still resonate into the present (see the perfect tense form of the verb *kekragen*, "cries out," in 1:15).[116]

10.2.1.4 From Bethany to Jerusalem: The Climactic Sign and Final Events in Jerusalem (11:1–12:36)

10.2.1.4.1 The Climactic Sign: The Raising of Lazarus (11:1–57)

John 11 and 12 occupy a curious function in John's gospel. On the one hand, they clearly belong to Act I by concluding John's presentation of Jesus' messianic "**signs**," closing the *sēmeio*-drama of Act I with the greatest sign of all, the raising of Lazarus. This culminates and completes John's presentation of Jesus' six or seven signs addressed specifically to the Jews to move them to believe that Jesus is the Messiah. Unfortunately, as the reader has long inferred, this aspect of Jesus' messianic mission ends in failure (cf. 6:60–71) in that the signs do not accomplish their intended result and the Jews refuse to believe in Jesus (12:36b–40).

At the same time, however, John 11 and 12 are set off from John 1–10 by the *inclusio* at the end of chapter 10 (see discussion above) and thus serve a bridge function, transitioning the narrative from Jesus' ministry to the Jews—narrated in Act I—to the material in the *cruci*-drama of Act II (the Farewell Discourse and Passion Narrative, John 13–21). The mood is somewhat somber. It appears that the acrimony of Jesus' conflict with the Jews is largely past, and the die is cast. Jesus' final sign, while unparalleled in this or any of the gospels, seems not to have any serious impact on the Jewish authorities or even lead to major controversy. Instead, the raising of Lazarus is presented by John as the final trigger (comparable to the temple clearing in the Synoptics) that leads the Sanhedrin finally to act and to follow through on its murderous plot to have Jesus (and Lazarus!; see 12:10–11) killed. And, strikingly, as will be seen, Jesus does not even respond to the final messianic expectation raised by the crowd in 12:34, the question how the Messiah at the same time could be "lifted up" (i.e., killed by crucifixion) and could live forever, as was commonly believed.

Another aspect that makes John 11–12 appear as a bridge between the signs and the Passion Narrative is that the death of Jesus looms ever larger in the narrative, with Lazarus's death and raising, as well as Mary of Bethany's anointing of Jesus, foreshadowing Jesus' own death, burial, and resurrection later on in the narrative. The raising of Lazarus completely dominates 11:1–12:19 and is followed by a brief

---

115. Note the reference to Jesus going back across the Jordan "to the place where John had been baptizing in the early days" in v. 40.

116. Note also the relationship between John the Baptist's witness (marked by the *inclusio* of 1:6–8/19ff. and 10:40–41) and the fourth evangelist's witness (marked by the *inclusio* of 13:23 and 21:20, 24–25). See chap. 1, sec. 2.1.3.1.

pericope narrating the coming of Greeks to Jesus (and, for now, being turned away) and signaling the universal benefits of Jesus' death, which is now all but inevitable (see also 11:49–52). This, too, shows that from a narrative perspective, the action has moved from serious outreach to the Jews to an anticipation of Jesus' death and the fruit it will bear (note the momentous announcement by Jesus at 12:23 that now "the hour" has finally come for him "to be glorified," a Johannine euphemism for his death). Thus, chapters 11–12, like the entire narrative, reflects the solemn assurance that God (the Father) and Jesus (the Son) are in complete control of the circumstances and that the series of events marches irresistible toward its **divinely predetermined** outcome.

The account of the raising of Lazarus itself is told with great skill. The plot features an early delay—upon hearing the news that Lazarus is ill, Jesus waits two more days, at which time Lazarus dies (**11:6–7**). Also featured is an instance of Johannine **misunderstanding** (the disciples think Lazarus has merely fallen asleep rather than died; **vv. 11–13**). What is more, danger is lurking in Judea, so going to help his friend carries considerable risk for Jesus, as is acknowledged by his disciples (**vv. 8, 16**). Though not exactly as Thomas envisions, Jesus will die in Jerusalem, an instance of Johannine **irony** (cf. 13:36–38). Through forward- and back-references, John connects the narrative with what precedes and what follows (to chap. 12: **v. 2**; to chap. 9: **v. 37**).

Upon his arrival in Bethany, a small village less than two miles from Jerusalem, Jesus finds that Lazarus has been dead for as many as four days, which easily makes this the hardest of Jesus' "hard" signs (see discussion at John 2:11 above). It is truly astonishing that Jesus would raise a man from the dead who had been dead that long. In fact, as the sisters tell Jesus, Lazarus's corpse already exuded a strong stench (**11:39**). Narrative time slows through the entire buildup to the miracle as Jesus confers with the sisters and comes to the tomb, bristling at the opportunity to wrest Lazarus from death (**v. 33**) and weeping over his friend's death even though he knows he will raise him back to life (**v. 35**).

After a brief prayer of thanksgiving, Jesus tersely commands, "Lazarus, come out!" (**v. 43**), and, startlingly, the corpse come to life obliges and appears from the tomb, hands and feet still wrapped with linen strips and the facecloth still in place (**v. 44**). Jesus orders these to be removed and Lazarus let go (v. 44), and the narrative breaks off, the scene shifting to an emergency meeting of the Sanhedrin (**vv. 45–57**; similarly, 7:45–52).[117] By raising Lazarus from the dead, Jesus demonstrated publicly that he had power over death, as he had previously asserted (e.g., 10:17–18). This is a messianic, indeed, a divine, characteristic and prerogative. The

---

117. See the discussion of peaking in Cotterell and Turner, *Linguistics & Biblical Interpretation*, 244–47. The peak of the Lazarus pericope in John 11:43–44 matches the three features identified by these authors perfectly: (1) concentration of participants (all are assembled at the tomb to witness the raising of Lazarus); (2) change of pace (the pericope breaks off rather abruptly in 11:44); (3) change of location (to a meeting of the Sanhedrin in 11:47). See also Köstenberger, *John*, 347, and the references cited there. Francis J. Moloney, "Can Everyone Be Wrong? A Reading of John 11.1–12.8," *NTS* 49 (2003): 505–27, argues that all the characters in the story fail to see that Lazarus's sickness and death are designed as the means of the revelation of the glory of God and of the glorification of Jesus the Son.

proof he furnished by raising Lazarus was so strong and irrefutable that any rational argument is now rendered superfluous. The Pharisees proceed in their irrational plot to have Jesus killed.

In their deliberations, the Jews express concern that Jesus will lead a popular uprising and that then the Romans will come and destroy the **temple** and the Jewish nation (**v. 48**). Surely, if John wrote after AD 70 (as is likely), this is the ultimate instance of Johannine **irony**, since in AD 70 the Temple had indeed been utterly destroyed and Jerusalem been sacked by the Romans. The Sanhedrin's worst fears had come true—and that *despite* crucifying Jesus. And now, in a futile attempt to avoid the unavoidable, they heaped condemnation upon their own heads by putting the Messiah and the Son of God to death. What is more, in a second instance of **irony**, Caiaphas, the Jewish high priest, also predicted that Jesus would be a sort of scapegoat, sacrificed on behalf of the Jewish people (**vv. 49–52**).[118] Little did he know that Jesus would indeed die "for the people" as a **substitutionary, atoning sacrifice**, taking away the sins of the world as the "**Lamb of God**." Moreover, by crucifying Jesus, the Romans already were taking away their temple (precisely what the Sanhedrin was trying to avoid), and the ones responsible for the destruction of God's temple were the Jewish leadership itself (both in the death of Jesus and in the events of AD 70).

10.2.1.4.2 The Anointing of Jesus at Bethany and the Triumphal Entry into Jerusalem (12:1–19)

This is now the third reference to a Passover in John (11:55; 12:1; see 2:13, 23; 6:2), making Jesus' attendance of this Jewish festival, first in Jerusalem, then in Galilee, and now back (for one final time, as it turns out) in Jerusalem. The pericope of the anointing of Jesus by Mary of Bethany provides a sequel to the raising of Lazarus, though even now that, unlike in the previous chapter, Lazarus is alive, no actual words by him are reported. Not that this is needed; Lazarus's very presence at a dinner given in his honor is enough to serve as a potent reminder of the amazing messianic "sign" of Jesus that has taken place.

As a screening of the canonical Gospels reveals, John shares this anointing pericope with Matthew (Matt 26:6–13) and Mark (Mark 14:1–11; though not Luke, who features an anointing of Jesus by a "sinful woman" earlier in Jesus' ministry; see Luke 7:36–50).[119] Rather than standing alone as in the Synoptics, the anointing here follows up on the raising of Lazarus; unlike in Matthew (Matt 21:1–11) and Mark (Mark 11:1–11), where the triumphal entry precedes the anointing, John places the anointing pericope immediately prior to the triumphal entry in the flow of his narrative. Most likely, John follows the historical order here, with the

---

118. See John A. Dennis, "Conflict and Resolution: John 11.47–53 as the Ironic Fulfillment of the Main Plot-Line of the Gospel (John 1.11–12)," *SNTU* 29 (2004): 23–39.

119. For a detailed study of these anointing pericopae, including John's, with special emphasis on Greek verbal aspect theory, see Andreas J. Köstenberger, "A Comparison of the Pericopae of Jesus' Anointing," in *Studies in John and Gender*, 49–63.

anointing taking place on Saturday and the triumphal entry, as is traditionally held, on (Palm) Sunday.

A literary comparison of the Matthean, Markan, and Johannine anointing pericopae demonstrates that John's account gives proportionately more weight to Judas and his objection to Mary's act of devotion, deemphasizing the actual anointing and presenting it primarily (or at least significantly) as a place where Judas's antagonism was revealed prior to the actual betrayal (**John 12:4**; narrated in the following chapter). Hence only one verse is devoted to narrating the anointing, while five verses are given to Judas and his objection and Jesus' response to it. Also, neither Matthew (Matt 26:8: "the disciples") nor Mark (Mark 14:4: "some of those present") even identify Judas by name as the one who objected to Mary's act, while John not only names Judas but develops his part in considerable detail to the extent that his objection almost overshadows Mary's anointing.

Nevertheless, Mary's act is remarkable for several reasons. First, as Jesus points out, Mary observes the anointing in anticipation of Jesus' burial (**John 12:7**), thus seizing the moment in virtual prophetic manner.[120] Thus Mary's act is one of prophetic symbolism not all that dissimilar from Jesus' act of clearing the temple (though, of course, Mary's act is not messianic, nor is it a "sign"). It is also interesting that she anoints Jesus' body for burial ahead of time, before he has even died, preempting the later preparation for burial by Nicodemus and Joseph of Arimathea, both of whom act in secret for fear of the Jews (19:38–42; see esp. v. 38).

In a related point, second, Mary's anointing of Jesus has messianic overtones in that it is kings who were anointed in the OT. Hence Mary, whether or not she realizes the full significance of her actions, by anointing him is designating Jesus as the royal **Messiah**. Together with the triumphal entry that follows this scene, these are portents of Jesus' **death** by which he will be inaugurated as the Messiah as the Isaianic **Servant of the Lord**.

Third, John takes pain to emphasize the great value of the perfume Mary lavishly poured onto Jesus' feet to anoint him (**v. 3**) — worth a year's wages! (**v. 5**) — and this also becomes the main point of Judas's objection (v. 5). Hence this woman exemplifies unselfish and devoted discipleship to Jesus in contrast to Judas's self-seeking mode of operation — as the evangelist duly notes, Judas was a thief (**v. 6**) — and shows that even apart from the Twelve (or better, Eleven) Jesus had faithful followers, including women (cf. Luke 10:38–42 *et passim*).[121]

Fourth, in the flow of the Johannine narrative, Mary's act of love anticipates another act of love — that of Jesus himself, at the footwashing (also involving caring for another person's feet), when, "having loved his own who were in the world, he loved them to the end" (John 13:1). Hence Mary shows great Christlikeness.

---

120. Though doubtless better than she knew; the same can probably be said about Martha's confession of Jesus as the Messiah and Son of God, anticipating John's purpose statement, at 11:27 (cf. 20:30–31). On the difficult interpretive issues raised by the awkward syntax of v. 7 see the discussion in Köstenberger, *John*, 363–64.

121. See esp. chap. 14 in Margaret Elizabeth Köstenberger, *Jesus and the Feminists: Who Do They Say That He Is?* (Wheaton: Crossway, 2008).

Thus there are two parallels involving Lazarus and his family: the raising of Lazarus—in which he was entirely passive—anticipates Jesus' resurrection; and Mary's anointing—with Mary taking the initiative—prefigures the ultimate expression of Jesus' love, which is found at the footwashing only in an emblematic sense and finds its ultimate expression in Jesus' substitutionary death on the cross (see 3:16; 15:13).[122]

The anointing is followed in the Johannine narrative by Jesus' triumphal entry into Jerusalem (**12:12–19**; see discussion above). As mentioned, like the anointing, this is yet another act of deep messianic significance, fulfilling scriptural prophecy (note the citations of Ps 118:25–26 and Zech 9:9 in **John 12:13 and 15**).[123] The crowd waved palm branches as Jesus entered Jerusalem on a donkey as the humble, messianic shepherd-king, shouting, "Hosanna! Blessed is he who comes in the name of the Lord! Blessed is the king of Israel!" (v. 13). Again, the evangelist humbly notes that not even Jesus' disciples understood the significance of these events at the time; only after Jesus was glorified did they realize that they had unwittingly helped to fulfill OT prophecy (**v. 16**).

Likewise, the crowd seems not to be fully aware of the import of their actions, since, soon thereafter, they join the Jewish leaders in calling for Jesus' crucifixion. Most likely they hail Jesus as a national deliverer (cf. 6:14?, 1:49?), but as the reader knows already, this is not the kind of king Jesus is. As Jesus will tell Pilate, his kingdom is "not of this world" (18:36). At Jesus' trial, the Jewish leadership will, opportunistically, claim, "We have no king but Caesar" (19:15). The inscription on the cross read, "Jesus of Nazareth, the king of the Jews" (19:19). In Pilate's mouth, the expression seems to take on a derisive connotation, mocking the (pitiful) kind of "king" the Jews have.[124]

10.2.1.4.3 *The Coming of the Greeks (12:20–36)*

Intriguingly, the approach of some Greeks finally triggers the long-awaited pronouncement on Jesus' part that his hour is now at hand (**v. 23**). Apparently, seeing that Gentiles want to come to him evokes in Jesus the awareness that his death is now imminent, since it is only after the crucifixion that Gentiles will be able to come to him and receive salvation on the basis of his finished cross-work, which is for all, Jews and Gentiles alike (the "all" referred to in v. 32).

In another weighty pronouncement, Jesus illustrates the effects of his upcoming death by the analogy of a seed that falls into the ground and, dying, produces much fruit (**v. 24**). This models selfless sacrifice that is willing to let go of the things of this world (one's body and life), which will help preserve one's life in the world to come (eternity; **v. 25**; the saying resembles a similar statement recorded in the Synoptics: see Matt 10:39; 16:25; Mark 8:35; Luke 9:24; 17:33).

---

122. For a treatment of the footwashing as the focal point of John's ethic, see the discussion of the Johannine love ethic in chap. 13 below.

123. See the detailed discussion of these quotes in Köstenberger, "John," in *Commentary on the NT Use of the OT*, 470–74.

124. See the treatment of this passage in chap. 11 below.

Jesus' struggle described here, likewise, is reminiscent of the Synoptic account of Jesus' agony in the garden of Gethsemane (**John 12:27–28**; cf. Matt 26:38; Mark 14:34). Promptly, a divine voice comes from heaven, affirming that Jesus' **death** will be for God's **glory** (**John 12:28**). Thus there is a seamless transition in this gospel from the revelation of God's glory in Jesus' messianic signs (2:11; 9:3–4; 11:4) to the revelation of God's glory in the "lifting up" of the Son of Man (3:13; 8:28; 12:32). The crowd, in an instance of Johannine **misunderstanding**, interprets the voice as thunder or the voice of an angel (**v. 29**); Jesus, however, knows it is a harbinger of judgment on the "prince of this world," Satan, who is ultimately behind the Pharisaic plot to kill Jesus (vv. 30–31; see discussion above).

In this third and final of his "lifted up sayings" in this gospel (cf. John 3:13; 8:28), Jesus announces that, once "lifted up" (i.e., crucified as well as honored by God, a wordplay echoing Isa 52:13; see further below), he will draw all people (Jews as well as Gentiles; see above) to himself (**John 12:32**). The euphemism of "lifting up" for the crucifixion chooses to focus on the **glory** coming to the Father through the obedience of the Son rather than on the shameful rejection of the Messiah by the Jews. The phrase "he said this to show [*sēmainō*] the kind of death he was going to die" (**v. 33**) is later echoed by Jesus' prediction of Peter's martyrdom (21:19). What was left implicit in the two previous "lifted up" sayings (3:13 and 8:28) is now made explicit: Jesus' "lifting up" refers to *his kind of death*.

Jesus' statement gives occasion for one final **messianic expectation** (see discussion on John 7 above) voiced by the crowd. Sensing that Jesus was speaking of his death, how does this square with the common expectation that the Messiah would live forever (**v. 34**)? Strikingly, Jesus chooses not to respond to this question but urges them to believe in him while there is still time, and then leaves and "hid[es] himself from them" (**vv. 35–36**), another reference to Jesus' withdrawal of his presence signifying **divine judgment** (cf. esp. 8:59 and the Johannine theme of the "**elusive Christ**"). The reader, of course, already knows the proper response to the crowd's query and thus does not need the evangelist to provide them with an answer: Jesus, after being "lifted up" (crucified), will be raised on the third day (2:19), and so *both* are true: the "lifting up" *and* the Messiah living on forever.

10.2.1.5 Conclusion: The Jewish Rejection of the Messiah despite His Many Signs (12:37–50)

The note of judgment on the Jews' unbelief in **12:37** follows hard on the reference to Jesus' withdrawal in the previous verse. This now closes the book on Jesus' (failed) mission to the Jews. Not that Jesus failed in doing his part—making God known (1:18) and revealing him to Israel in keeping with the Baptist's mission (1:32). But, sadly, his mission was met with stubborn resistance by the Jewish leadership, and the crowds were mostly interested in what Jesus could do for them—fill their stomach, heal their sicknesses, or deliver them from the Romans. But this is not why Jesus came. He did not come to establish an earthly kingdom; his kingdom was "not of this world" (18:36). Instead, he came to call out a new messianic community that would spread the message of the Messiah and the eternal life he came to make available to all who were to believe in him.

Thus Act I of John's gospel ends on a note of failure as far as the primary target of Jesus' signs is concerned — the Jewish nation as represented by its leadership. But it is not on a note of *total* failure, for there remained the bright spot of the Twelve minus Judas, who stood ready to carry on Jesus' legacy once he was removed from the earth. And this will be the subject of Act II. In the meantime, the evangelist brings the *sēmeio*-drama of Act I to a close by (1) focusing one last time in Act I on the vital topic of "**signs**" in the first half of his gospel (see discussion at 2:11 above and throughout); and (2) adducing, in illumining the Jews' **unbelief**, a set of dual references from the book of Isaiah (Isa 53:1 in **John 12:38**; Isa 6:10 in **John 12:40**) that shows that the Jews' rejection of Jesus as **Messiah** fulfilled scriptural prophecy and thus occurred in keeping with the **predestination and foreknowledge of God**.

The first quote from Isa 53:1 refers, by way of a rhetorical question, to the lack of response experienced by Isaiah to his message (see 52:13 – 53:12), which was bound up with a "lifted up" Servant of the Lord who bore the sins of many (esp. 53:6, 8, 12) and was with the rich in his death (John 12:9; see esp. Isa 52:13: "See, my servant will act wisely; he will be *raised* and *lifted up* and *highly exalted*," emphasis added). Similar to Jesus' point in the (allegorical) parable of the wicked tenants in the Synoptics (see Matt 21:33 – 46; Mark 12:1 – 12; Luke 20:9 – 19), the Jews characteristically rejected the message of God's spokesmen in OT times. It is nothing new for them now to have rejected the message of the Word-made-flesh, the Lord Jesus Christ.

Second, not only *did* the Jews not **believe**, John maintains that they *could* not believe, because, as Isaiah wrote at Isa 6:10, God blinded people's eyes and hardened their hearts so they could not understand or turn and be healed (John 12:40). Just as Abraham rejoiced in the anticipation of the Messiah (8:56), so Isaiah saw Jesus' *glory* (though not Jesus) and spoke about him (**v. 41**). This shows that John's theology of the cross is grounded in Isaiah's depiction of the Suffering Servant. What is more, the appropriation of Isaiah's theology as an interpretive framework for Jesus' cross-death almost certainly goes back to Jesus himself, who made a similar point in speaking to his disciples when accounting for the Jews' opposition to his ministry (see Matt 13:14 – 15; Mark 4:12; Luke 8:10; cf. Acts 28:26 – 27).[125]

After acknowledging a group of secret "believers" even among the leaders (**John 12:42 – 43**) — hardly a commendable category in John's gospel (see v. 43) — Jesus "cried out" (*ekraxen*, **v. 44**) one last time in Act I and affirms that those who believe in him do not believe in him only but in the one who sent Jesus — God the Father; when they look at him they see the one who sent him (**v. 45**). This is how close the identification is between Jesus and the Father who sent him. Harking back to the

---

125. For a detailed discussion of the use of the OT in 12:38 – 41 see Köstenberger, "John," in *Commentary on the NT Use of the OT*, 476 – 83. On Isa 6:9 – 10, see also Craig A. Evans, *To See and Not Perceive: Isaiah 6:9 – 10 in Early Jewish and Christian Interpretation* (JSOTSup 64; Sheffield: JSOT, 1989).

introduction (see 1:4–5, 9–11), Jesus says that he came "into the world as a **light**," so that no one should "stay in **darkness**" (**12:46**).

For now Jesus judges no one (though the time will come when he will exercise judgment on God's behalf; see John 5:22–27). For Jesus' purpose for his first coming was to save the world, not to judge it (**12:47**). The basis for judging unbelievers in Jesus will be Jesus' very own words (**v. 48**), words spoken in full authorization from the Father who sent him (**vv. 49–50**). Hence all rests on the identification between Jesus the Son with God the Father and their unity in purpose, mission, and being.

10.2.2 Act II: The Messiah's Passion and Preparation of His Own (13:1–20:31)

10.2.2.1 Jesus Anticipates His Exaltation: The Footwashing, the Farewell Discourse, and Jesus' Final Prayer (13:1–17:26)

10.2.2.1.1 The Cleansing of the New Messianic Community (13:1–30)

10.2.2.1.1.1 The Literal Cleansing: The Footwashing (13:1–17) The skillfully worded preamble to the Farewell Discourse (making up John 13–17, broadly conceived, and 13:31–16:33, more narrowly conceived, if 13:1–30 is viewed as a prelude to the Farewell Discourse proper) in the Greek takes up the first four or five verses. The diction underscores the momentous nature of the events to be narrated, culminating in Jesus' death, burial, and resurrection. Turning his back on the Jews who had rejected him as Messiah (see esp. 12:37–41), Jesus now moves ahead, instructing his disciples regarding the proceedings that are about to ensue.

"It was just before the **Passover** Festival" (**13:1**) resumes the phrase "Six days before the Passover" in 12:1 (introducing the anointing; see also 11:55). The causal participate *eidōs* (having the sense "because he knew") is emphatic, stressing, at the outset of the second half of John's gospel, Jesus' supernatural knowledge that the hour for his "departure"—one of John's euphemisms for Jesus' crucifixion (also called his "glorification," 12:23)—had come and that he was about to leave this world and return to the **Father** (for further emphasis, *eidōs* recurs in 13:3).

This presents the cross as nothing but a brief stop on Jesus' return to God, a small "bump in the road," as it were, shifting the focus away from the shame and the suffering Jesus must endure on humanity's behalf and focusing instead on Jesus' return to the glory he had from eternity with God (17:24; see also 1:1–2). Hence John's **theology of the cross**, while sharing common ground with the Synoptics in that both present Jesus' work on the cross as sacrificial, substitutionary, and atoning, is distinctive as well, seeking to put the temporary nature of Jesus' suffering into eternal perspective.[126]

---

126. Similarities in thought where Jesus' and/or believers' sufferings are put into eternal perspective can be found in other NT writings, such as Rom 8:18; Heb 12:2; and 1 Pet 1:6.

At this critical juncture in Jesus' ministry, John, the "apostle of love," focuses on one final expression of Jesus' **love** for "his own" (*hoi idioi*, i.e., the Twelve; compare 1:11), namely the footwashing. Importantly, the footwashing constitutes a proleptic glimpse onto the underlying motivation for the cross: the expression of God's love for the world (see 3:16). Hence this footwashing, far from being limited to the literal sequence of events that ensues, shows that in death Jesus simply gave final expression to what characterized his earthly ministry to his disciples all along—love (see 13:1: "he loved them to the end," *eis telos ēgapēsen autous*).[127]

Jesus' supreme demonstration of his love is set in the starkest of contrasts with the action of his protagonist, the devil, who had already thrust it into the heart of Judas Iscariot to betray Jesus (**v. 2**; Jesus' foreknowledge of the betrayal is underscored in v. 11 below). Stressing the magnitude of Jesus' condescension at the footwashing, the evangelist further emphasizes Jesus' knowledge that the Father had given all things into his hands and that he had come from God and was returning to God (**v. 3**, an instance of the **descent–ascent theme**).

Knowing all this, Jesus, the disciples' Master and Teacher (**13:13**), proceeded to engage in the menial task of washing his followers' feet (**vv. 4–12**) as an emblem of the continued spiritual cleansing required for those who had already entered into spiritual allegiance with Jesus (the lesson imparted to Peter, vv. 6–10). Thus, what at first appeared to the disciples merely as an embarrassing incident—they had neglected to perceive the need to clean the feet of others or had been too proud to do so themselves—becomes a major object lesson (*hypodeigma*, "example," v. 15) that none of them would ever forget.[128]

Temporary suspense and drama is provided by Peter's **misunderstanding**, which takes up most of the narrative (vv. 6–11).[129] The spiritual condition of Peter and the rest of the Twelve (*sans* Judas)—they are essentially "clean," though in need of continual "cleansing"—is set in contrast to Judas (the betrayer), who was not "clean" and for whom temporary "cleansing" was thus not sufficient. Nevertheless, it appears (though this is not explicitly narrated) that even Judas had his feet washed by the Lord whom he was about to betray. This powerfully shows Jesus' love of his enemies, in keeping with his teaching (Matt 5:43–48).

The lesson of the footwashing, then, is believers' need for humble, loving service of one another (**John 13:14**). As Paul wrote, the followers of Christ ought to "serve one another humbly in love" (Gal 5:13) and to "carry each other's burdens, and in this way ... fulfill the law of Christ" (Gal 6:2; see also Phil 2:5–11, a passage likely inspired by the footwashing—and that even though Paul was not present at the orig-

---

127. See the treatment of the Johannine love ethic in chap. 13, sec. 30.

128. The practice seems to have become idiomatic for service of others already in the NT period (see 1 Tim 5:10: "washing the feet of the Lord's people") but has lost its original emblematic value in a day when people no longer wear sandals and walk for long distances on dusty roads on their way to dinner (though there may still be cultures where the symbol is meaningful). For an argument for footwashing as a modern-day ordinance, see John Christopher Thomas, *Footwashing in John 13 and the Johannine Community* (JSNTSup 61; Sheffield: JSOT, 1991).

129. For an insightful analysis of the dyadic dynamic underlying the footwashing narrative see Cotterell and Turner, *Linguistics & Biblical Interpretation*, 267–68.

inal event). Jesus pronounces a blessing on his disciples if they follow through on his directive (**John 13:17**), stressing the importance of action above mere words (cf. Matt 7:24–27; Jas 1:22–27: "they will be *blessed* in what they *do*," emphasis added).

10.2.2.1.1.2 The Figurative Cleansing: The Removal of the Betrayer (13:18–30)
After recounting the footwashing and the lesson Jesus sought to impart through his exemplary action (13:1–17), the evangelist zeroes in more specifically on the other important act to be revealed at this juncture: the satanically-inspired act of betrayal on the part of Judas (**vv. 18–20**). Importantly, not only did Jesus **foreknow** this event (see 6:70–71; 13:2, 10–11, 19), it also fulfilled scriptural prediction (v. 18, citing Ps 41:9; reiterated in John 17:12). Like the thrice-repeated reference to Jesus' foreknowledge earlier in the narrative (13:1, 3, 11), this underscores God's (and Jesus') utter **sovereignty** and control over the entire set of proceedings (see also 10:17–18 above and 18:4 below).

Jesus' straightforward prediction of the betrayal (**13:21**) leaves the disciples at a loss as to whom he meant (**v. 22**), so Peter motions to "the disciple whom Jesus loved" (**v. 23**) to ask Jesus as to the identity of the betrayer. In this the first reference to "the disciple whom Jesus loved" in the narrative a characteristic pattern is established, that is, this disciple's superiority over Peter in terms of access to revelation. This primacy of access is also apparent later on when Peter requires the assistance of "the disciple whom Jesus loved" to the high priest's courtyard (18:15–16) and when this same "disciple whom Jesus loved" outruns Peter to the empty tomb and is the first to believe (20:3–10). Later still, it is again "the disciple whom Jesus loved" who first recognizes the risen Jesus at the seashore and who says to Peter, "It is the Lord!" (21:7).

Finally, Peter asks Jesus to tell him about the destiny of "the disciple whom Jesus loved" but is, in essence, told to mind his own business (21:20–23). In light of the fact that it was on Peter, by virtue of his confession of Jesus as the Messiah, that Jesus had vowed to build his church (Matt 16:18), it is remarkable that such a consistent case is mounted on the part of John for the unrivalled position on the part of "the disciple whom Jesus loved" at Jesus' side. That this is intentional is further underscored by the remarkable parallelism in language between Jesus' access to the Father and the access to Jesus enjoyed by "the disciple whom Jesus loved" at the beginning of the first and at the beginning of the second half of John's gospel:

- 1:18: "... the one and only Son, who is himself God and is in closest relationship with the Father, has made him known" (*monogenēs theos ho ōn* **eis ton kolpon tou patros** *ekeinos exēgēsato*)
- 13:23: "One of them, the disciple whom Jesus loved, was reclining next to him" (*ēn anakeimenos heis ek tōn mathētōn autou* **en tō kolpō tou Iēsou** *hon ēgapa ho Iēsous*; see also 21:20)[130]

---

130. Noted, e.g., by Carson, *Gospel according to John*, 473. See also the parallel between the kind of Jesus' and Peter's death in 12:33 and 21:19, which further underscores the intentionality of the evangelist's description of both the callings of "the disciple whom Jesus loved" and of Peter in analogy to Jesus.

Against Bultmann and others, this should not be viewed as an indication that here John's community seeks to establish itself over against the Petrine segment of the church in an effort to legitimize its own existence or even superior status.[131] It is possible, however, that John mounts this case to establish the legitimacy of his undertaking of writing a gospel decades after the other canonical gospels—Matthew, Mark, and Luke—have been written. The superior access of "the disciple whom Jesus loved" to divine revelation would certainly furnish such proof that his gospel could supplement the spiritual insights presented by the already existing gospels and provide a deeper, authoritative interpretation of the by-then-familiar events of the gospel story.

Upon the inquiry by "the disciple whom Jesus loved" (**13:25**), Jesus reveals the betrayer's identity by giving a piece of bread to Judas (**v. 26**), who is promptly entered by Satan and, at Jesus' urging (**v. 27**), leaves the room and steps into the night (**v. 30**, clearly with symbolic overtones; cf. Luke 22:53) to act on his evil intentions. This concludes the preamble to the Farewell Discourse (John 13:1–30) and gives room to the Farewell Discourse proper (13:31–16:33). Now that the community has been "cleansed"—both literally (the footwashing, 13:1–17) and figuratively (the removal of the betrayer, vv. 18–30)—the path is cleared for Jesus to instruct his followers (the Eleven) for the imminent crucifixion and the events to follow.

10.2.2.1.2 The Farewell Discourse Proper (13:31–16:33)

Act I featured the revelation of Jesus to old Israel (John 12:36–41; cf. 1:31); Act II, and in particular the Farewell Discourse, is concerned with the revelation of Jesus to the new Israel, the **new messianic community** comprised of a believing Jewish remnant (see John 15). Jesus' revelation to the old covenant community was primarily based on selected messianic **signs** (see discussion above); his revelation to the new Israel is plain spoken, without signs (see 16:29–30).

Scholars have detected clear parallels between Jesus' Farewell Discourse and Moses' Farewell Discourse in the book of Deuteronomy.[132] In this the Farewell Discourse is John's answer to Matthew's Sermon on the Mount (Matthew 5–7; cf. also the Johannine fulfillment quotations, commencing at John 12:38, with the Matthean fulfillment quotations, esp. in Matthew 1–4).

The Farewell Discourse is also the functional equivalent of the Synoptic Olivet Discourse (Matthew 24; Mark 13; Luke 21), except that its focus on the "age to come" (i.e., end-time events) is transmuted in John's gospel by a focus on the mission of the exalted Jesus in the here and now through the Spirit and the new messianic community (see esp. John 14:15–27; 15:26–16:15; 17:18; 20:21–22).

This includes a pronounced focus on the role of the **Holy Spirit**, the "other helping presence" (*paraklētos*) sent by Jesus and the Father (15:26; 16:7), who empowers

---

131. Bultmann, *Gospel of John*, 483–85. See also the discussion in chap. 12, sec. 29.3.2 below.

132. See Aelred Lacomara, "Deuteronomy and the Farewell Discourse (Jn 13:31–16:33)," *CBQ* 36 (1974): 65–84; Edward J. Malatesta, *Interiority and Covenant: A Study of εἶναι ἐν and μενεῖν ἐν in the First Letter of Saint John* (AnBib 69; Rome: Biblical Institute Press, 1978); and Pryor, *John, Evangelist of the Covenant People*.

believers' witness in continuity with Jesus' earthly ministry (15:26–27) and who is the divine presence empowering the church's mission promised his followers by the resurrected Lord (Matt 28:20: "I am with you always, to the very end of the age").

Finally, the legacy of the earthly Jesus—**love** (John 13:1, 34–35; 15:9–13; 17:26), joy (15:11; 16:22–24; 17:13), peace (14:27; 16:33; 20:19, 21, 26)—is also John's answer to Paul's teaching on the "fruit of the Spirit"—love, joy, peace (Gal 5:22)—in showing that these characteristics are not original with the Spirit but are rooted already in the earthly **mission** of Jesus.[133] This is a powerful contribution to biblical and NT theology indeed.

Various proposals have been made with regard to the structure of the Farewell Discourse, including macro-chiasms (centering on John 15:1–10 or 17) or various forms of rearrangement or *relecture* theories. The latter frequently involves the conjecture that 13:31–14:31 constitutes the basic Johannine formulation (whether by the author or a "Johannine community" or "school") and John 15–16 a reworking of 13:31–14:31 by a later community.

However, in the ultimate analysis, chiastic proposals remain unconvincing, especially since the very notion of a macro-chiasm is difficult to prove, and relecture theories are likewise fraught with precarious assumptions. For this reason it seems best to read the Farewell Discourse in a linear, narrative fashion and to understand the genre as proceeding in cyclical fashion, with particular themes being recycled and further developed as the discourse progresses.

A major bone of contention in this regard has been the so-called Johannine ***aporias***, that is, "difficult passages" (the literal meaning of *aporia*), which (to some) suggest a literary seam indicating the patching together of originally separate literary sources by a later writer or redactor. However, the very label *aporia* begs the question, and any adjudication must be made on a case-by-case basis. The most notorious such *aporia* is 14:31: "Come now; let us leave." Many believe that the fact that movement is here implied but no movement is actually narrated in the gospel until 18:1 suggests that the gospel (or its precursor or source) moved originally directly from 14:31 to 18:1, and that later chapters 15–17 were inserted, leaving 14:31 as an *aporia* or somewhat awkward vestige of an inadequately redacted set of written and reworked materials.

However, as Scott Kellum has shown, a compelling case can be made for the literary unity of the gospel in its present form, without recourse to the notion of 14:31 as an *aporia*, on literary grounds. He pointed to the Johannine pattern of *implied movement* (in 14:31 and elsewhere), in which case it is left to the reader to infer that actual movement has taken place without the evangelist making this explicit in the narrative.[134]

---

133. I am not certain that John read Galatians, but I submit this is entirely possible, and, if so, it is certainly plausible that John, by featuring love, joy, and peace as the legacy bequeathed by Jesus on his followers, sought to make a connection to the initial triad in Paul's list of "the fruit of the Spirit," though this is, of course, impossible to prove.

134. See Kellum, *Unity of the Farewell Discourse*, chap. 4.

If so, 14:31 would seem to imply that, as is the traditional view, Jesus and his disciples set out for the Kidron Valley (the crossing is mentioned in 18:1) and that chapters 15–17 are delivered on the way from the Upper Room (the location of chaps. 13–14) to the site of the betrayal (18:1–14). This, then, would render *relecture* theories unnecessary and restore the legitimacy of a linear reading of the Farewell Discourse as it progresses.

10.2.2.1.2.1 The Farewell Discourse (Part 1; 13:31–14:31) The Farewell Discourse proper, then, opens in **13:31**, once again with a reference to Jesus' assertion that "now"—anticipating Judas's act of betrayal leading to Jesus' crucifixion—the **Son of Man** was "**glorified**" (cf. 12:23; 13:1). In the first of a series of references to a "little while," Jesus prepares his followers for his imminent departure (i.e., his death; **v. 33**), leaving them with "a new command": to **love** one another *as Jesus has loved them* (**vv. 34–35**; cf. 15:12).[135]

This is followed by an instance of misunderstanding, again on Peter's part (see 13:6–11 above), who pledges undying loyalty to Jesus, only to be told that he will disown Jesus three times (**vv. 36–38**; fulfilled in 18:15–18, 25–27, thus framing the Farewell Discourse on either end). Hence it is *Jesus* who must lay his life down for *Peter* and his fellow disciples, not *Peter* for *Jesus*, indicating that Jesus' witness is primary and that it is his death that enables martyrdom (cf. 21:19; note also Peter's threefold restoration in 21:15–19 corresponding to his three denials).

Jesus' next assertion, that he will go to prepare a place in his "Father's house" for his disciples (**14:2–3**), is likewise met with **misunderstanding**, with both Thomas (**v. 5**) and Philip (**v. 7**) inquiring as to "the way" Jesus is intending to take. Jesus replies that he, in his very own person, is the way, and whoever knows him also knows the way to the Father (**v. 6**). In what follows Jesus gives eloquent expression to his union with the Father (**vv. 9–14**).

Faith in Jesus will enable his followers to perform works even greater than Jesus, greater because they are later—that is, **salvation-historically** placed subsequent to Jesus' cross-work and resurrection and thus based on the fully efficacious work of Christ on behalf of sinful humanity (14:12). Also, believers are encouraged to direct believing prayer to Jesus once he has been exalted to the Father (vv. 13–14).

While **truth** will set those who continue in Jesus' teaching free (see 8:31), this liberty must not be so construed as to render obeying Jesus' commands unnecessary. To the contrary, by keeping Jesus' commands his followers will show their **love** for him (**14:15**, reiterated at 14:21 and 23). This, too, reveals Jesus' Farewell Discourse as in continuity with the parting words of Moses in the book of Deuteronomy.

With this Jesus announces the imminent arrival of "another [helping presence]," the "**Spirit** of truth," to help his followers and to be with them forever (**14:16–18**). The Spirit will come to believers per Jesus' request of the Father—striking a trinitar-

---

135. See the discussion of the footwashing and its role as the focal point of John's ethic in chap. 13. sec. 30 below.

ian note; and once the Spirit comes, it is as if Jesus himself (and the Father, 14:23) were to take residence "in" believers, analogous to his presence "among" his followers while physically present with them.[136]

This concludes 14:9–21, all of which was part of Jesus' answer to Philip's question to "show us the Father" in 14:8. In the final instance of an individual disciple's query in the Farewell Discourse (the disciples as a group are mentioned again at 16:16, 19, and 29), Judas (not the betrayer) then asks why Jesus intends to show himself to his followers but not to the world (**14:22**).

This leads Jesus to elaborate on both the closeness of his relationship with his disciples subsequent to his exaltation (esp. 15:1–17) and on the world's hatred of him and his followers (15:18–16:11). Jesus' answer, in essence, is that only those who love him will obey his teaching (**14:23**, a recurring theme: see 14:15, 21), and the **Holy Spirit** will continue Jesus' teaching ministry (**14:26**).

Just as the world hated Jesus during his earthly mission, the world will continue to hate him once he is exalted, though the focus of persecution will shift toward Jesus' followers (14:24; 15:18–25). The queries directed toward Jesus by his disciples show that they find it hard to imagine life without Jesus in their midst. For this reason, and because of the coming of the betrayer, Jesus cuts his comments short (**14:30–31**).

10.2.2.1.2.2 The Farewell Discourse (Part 2; 15:1–16:33)

10.2.2.1.2.2.1 The Illustration of the Vine and the Branches (15:1–17) Still in response to Judas's question, Jesus now elaborates on the organic unity between him and his followers that will be sustained subsequent to his exaltation with the Father in and through the **Holy Spirit** (note the trinitarian theme). To illustrate this unity Jesus uses the familiar imagery of a vineyard, the same illustration used for Israel in the OT (see esp. the Song of the Vineyard in Isa 5:1–7). This indicates that Jesus is now that vineyard, fulfilling Israel's destiny and centering God's **salvation-historical** purposes in himself. Thus it is now those related rightly to *him*, Jesus, who are proper branches of the vine.

In Jesus' allegory (or symbolic discourse), he is the true vine, God the Father is the gardener, and believers are the branches (**15:1, 5**). In keeping with the vineyard imagery, God the Father prunes the branches "in" Jesus in order to make them more fruitful (**v. 2**). The branches'—i.e., believers'—only responsibility is to remain vitally connected to the vine (Jesus), sustaining a spiritual union through the **Holy Spirit** (**v. 4**). Only if they are organically related to Jesus (the true vine) can believers bear fruit (vv. 4–8). Those not remaining in Jesus (v. 6, note the example of Judas, see 13:10) will be judged (the real-life equivalent of branches being thrown into the fire and burned, **15:6–7**).

---

136. The Greek preposition *en* can have both meanings ("in" or "among").

How do believers, then, "remain" in Jesus? By continuing in his word (15:7; cf. 8:31) and in his love (**15:9–10**) and by keeping his commands (v. 10), especially the "new command" to **love** one another as Jesus loved his followers (**vv. 12, 17**; cf. 13:34–35; see also 1 John 3:11; 4:7 *et passim*). The greatest expression of love is Jesus' death on behalf of his own (**John 15:13**). This is the kind of love that believers ought to show one another. Thus, in context, love is also the most important "fruit" disciples can bear (**vv. 8, 16**).[137]

10.2.2.1.2.2.2 The World's Hatred of Jesus' Followers (Part 1; 15:18–27) Still in response to Judas's question, "Lord, why do you intend to show yourself to us and not to the world?" (John 14:22), Jesus now turns directly to a discussion of the world and its hatred of Jesus and his followers. Essentially, Jesus says, the world loves its own but hates those who are not of it: "As it is, you do not belong to the world, but I have chosen you out of the world. That is why the world hates you" (**15:19**). Hence Jesus' answer is bound with believers' **election** (see v. 16; see also 6:37; 12:32; 17:6). This election—issuing in their new **spiritual birth** from God (1:12–13; 3:5, 7)—extricates believers from the world, as it were, and places them in a state of separation from the world and consecration in the truth (*hagiazō*; 17:17, 19; cf. 10:36). This, in turn, is a prerequisite for their effective **mission** in the world. Thus, believers are (1) born of God; (2) set apart from the world; and (3) sent back into the world with the saving message of the gospel.

Jesus proceeds to note that his disciples will be identified with him even in their suffering of persecution in the world (**15:20–21**). This, too, is part of what it means to be a follower of Jesus. This shows that Judas did not really understand this dynamic when he asked Jesus his original question. Why would Jesus not show himself to the world subsequent to the resurrection? It would have been naïve for him to do so. The world hated him and was about to put him to death. Also, the world was not going to change its opposition to God and to his Messiah after the crucifixion (or at any other time), so if the resurrected Jesus were to show himself to the world, it would still not believe in him but presumably try to kill him a second time (like those warned in Heb 6:6 against "crucifying the Son of God all over again").

But while based on **misunderstanding** (or at least inadequate understanding), Judas's question allowed Jesus to prepare his followers for the persecution that would fall on *them* once Jesus had physically been removed from the world (as evidenced in the book of Acts). It was important to be realistic about this prospect rather than to have a rosy picture that all was going to change once Jesus had been "glorified." Not so. The world's opposition was going to continue unchanged; in fact, it was going to increase and be transferred from Jesus as its primary target to his followers who remained in the world.

---

137. This is close to Paul's teaching on love as the cardinal fruit of the Spirit (Gal 5:22), if the placement of love first in the list is to be taken as an indication of love's primacy among Christian, Spirit-grown virtues (cf. 1 Corinthians 13, esp. v. 13).

Not only this, but Jesus also points out that those who hated him in reality hated God the Father who sent him (**15:23**). They are rendered culpable because they saw the works Jesus did (including his "signs"), and yet they hated both Jesus and God (**v. 24**; see 5:36; 10:32, 36–37; 14:11). Nevertheless, even this took place to fulfill Scripture, specifically, the words of the psalmist, "They hated me without reason" (**15:25**, citing Ps 35:19; 69:4; cf. John 12:37–41). This brings into play this gospel's **sending Christology**, according to which an emissary is inextricably identified with his sender, and any treatment awarded the emissary reflects a given person's stance toward his sender (the classic Jewish passage is *m. Ber.* 5:5). It also underscores the connection between a person's claims—in the present case, Jesus' claim to be the Messiah—and his works.

Jesus' repeated argument is that if people were not prepared to take him at his words and to take his claims at face value, they should at least be open to his *works* and evaluate them on their own merits. This, too, he was convinced would lead people to conclude that he was the Messiah, because he did the works of the Messiah, and these works were an important clue to his true identity. This is the function of the Johannine **signs** and of the representative characters in the narrative (esp. John 7; see above), asking questions reflecting a variety of messianic expectations, both accurate and inaccurate (reflecting **misunderstanding**).

This, in turn, serves the purpose of **theodicy**, that is, John's vindication of the righteous purposes of God: if people do not believe in Jesus, it is not because they have not been given ample opportunity to do so. They have seen his "signs" and his other works and have heard his words. They have seen the Messiah in action and have been exposed to his teaching. In light of this fullness of revelation brought by Jesus—the one who, as John noted at the outset in his introduction, "has made [God] known" (1:18)—the fault (sin and guilt) rests squarely on the intended recipients of this revelation, those who saw and heard but refused to believe. This is the clear message of 12:37–40:

> Even after Jesus had performed so many signs in their presence, they still would not believe in him. This was to fulfill the word of Isaiah the prophet:
>
> Lord, who has believed our message
> and to whom has the arm of the Lord been revealed?"
>
> For this reason they could not believe, because, as Isaiah says elsewhere,
>
> He has blinded their eyes
> and hardened their hearts,
> so they can neither see with their eyes,
> nor understand with their hearts,
> nor turn—and I would heal them."

This is also the important thrust of Jesus' words in the present passage: "If I had not come and spoken to them, they would not be guilty of sin, but now they have no excuse for their sin.... If I had not done among them the works no one else did, they would not be guilty of sin. As it is, they have seen, and yet they have hated both me and my Father" (John 15:22, 24). Hence, Jesus' followers must accept the reality of the world's rejection of Jesus. All they can realistically expect to be able to do is (as Jesus did) faithfully proclaim the gospel message to allow God to draw his elect to him and render people in the world who persist in their unbelief without an excuse. In the process, they may, like Jesus, end up on a cross; but if so, they die bearing witness to the truth (18:37) in the prospect of sharing with Jesus in his heavenly glory (14:2–3; 17:24).

The time for the disciples' testimony will come when the "other helping presence" arrives, the "**Spirit** of truth," whom Jesus will send from the Father (**15:26–27**; note the trinitarian theme). He will help the disciples fulfill their mission of bearing **witness** to Jesus, and bear witness they must, because they have been with Jesus "from the beginning" (v. 27). Just as Jesus was "in the beginning" with *God* as "the Word" (1:1–2) and hence was perfectly qualified as a witness to the God no one had ever seen (1:18), so the disciples had been with *Jesus* "from the beginning," which qualified them perfectly to bear witness to the messianic identity and divinity of Jesus.

In fact, "in the beginning" was an important phrase denoting eyewitness testimony in the ancient world (cf., e.g., Luke 1:3, who claimed to "have carefully investigated everything *from the beginning*").[138] This reference, then, is an important plank in the claim staked by John that his gospel is in itself part of this testimony Jesus envisioned would be borne after his departure. Thus the reader is told when reading the account of Jesus' crucifixion that "the man who saw it has given testimony, and his testimony is true. He knows that he tells the truth, and he testifies so that you also may believe" (John 19:35). Again, the gospel concludes with the words: "This is the disciple who testifies to these things and who wrote them down. We know that his testimony is true" (21:24).

Thus, from John (the Baptist; see John 1:6–8, 15; etc.) to John (the apostle; "the disciple whom Jesus loved"; see 19:35; 21:24–25), witness has been borne, and continues to be borne, as long as the gospel is read, having as its purpose: "But these are written that *you* [direct address to the reader] may believe that Jesus is the Messiah, the Son of God, and that by believing you may have life in his name" (20:31, emphasis added). The world and the Jews think they can put Jesus on trial and condemn him, but in truth, it is Jesus and God the Father—as well as the Spirit (see 15:26–27 and cf. 16:8–11 below)—who put an impressive list of witnesses on the witness stand. And turning the tables in a stunning reversal, it is the world that is condemned for its rejection of the Messiah despite overwhelming evidence that he is who he claimed to be. This is the **cosmic trial motif** in John's gospel (of which the "**witness motif**" is an important and integral part) that shows the universal and eternal legal repercussions of the world's rejection of Jesus.

---

138. Emphasis added. See Bauckham, *Jesus and the Eyewitnesses*, chap. 6.

10.2.2.1.2.2.3 The World's Hatred of Jesus' Followers (Part 2; 16:1–15) Jesus' purpose in preparing his followers for the persecution that lies ahead is that they "will not fall away" (**v. 1**). Jesus envisions a time when his followers will be expelled from the synagogue (**v. 2**; this had already begun to happen on a local level; see 9:22, 34) and even killed by people who think they thus render "a service to God" (16:2; Paul comes to mind as an example in his zealous persecution of Christians; see Acts 8:1–3).

Jesus then squarely addresses the grief of his disciples who have now come to realize that his departure (via the cross) is imminent (**John 16:5–15**). Counterintuitively, he argues that it is actually to his followers' advantage that he is going away, for this will enable him to send "the other helping presence" (cf. **v. 7**), and "when he comes, he will prove the world to be in the wrong about sin and righteousness and judgment" (**v. 8**), condemning the world of its sin of **unbelief** and of its unrighteousness in rejecting the Messiah, and about the judgment resulting from this rejection (**vv. 9–11**).[139]

Still on the topic of advantages of Jesus' leaving, the **Spirit** of truth will guide his followers "into all the truth," even telling them "what is yet to come," taking from what is the Son's (who in turn takes from what is the Father's, in an instance of trinitarian collaboration) and imparting it to the disciples (**vv. 13–15**). This, then, in anticipation of Jesus' passing from the (earthly) scene, ushers Jesus' followers into the next stage of salvation history, namely, the age of the Spirit. This age will underscore the continuity of the Spirit's mission with that of Jesus, who, in turn, was sent from the Father (part of the Johannine "**mission theme**"; see chap. 15, sec. 33, below).

10.2.2.1.2.2.4 The "Little While" (16:16–33) Initiating a new subject and advancing the conversation beyond the response to Judas's question (see above), Jesus now states that, "In a little while [if this was Thursday night and Jesus was crucified Friday afternoon, the "little while" was less than a day away] you will see me no more, and then after a little while [i.e., the three-day interim between his crucifixion and his resurrection] you will see me" (**v. 16**). This ought to give his disciples a clear road map for what was to follow in short order: the arrest, the Jewish and Roman trials, the crucifixion, the burial, and the resurrection and appearances (see John 18–21).

Again, however, the meaning of Jesus' statement regarding the "little whiles" is lost on his original followers (**16:17–18; misunderstanding**). Jesus responds by likening the impending grief of his disciples at the crucifixion followed by the joy at his resurrection to the emotional rollercoaster experienced by a mother at the birth of her child. The birth itself is exceedingly painful, but as soon as the mother has given birth to the child, all the pain is forgotten for joy that a new life has come into the world (**vv. 20–22**). It will be the same with the disciples: the resurrection will turn their temporary grief into abiding joy, fueling their witness to the resurrected Jesus (see John 20–21 and the book of Acts).

---

139. For an attempt at an interpretation of these difficult verses, see Köstenberger, *John*, 471–72.

This will also be the day at which believing prayer in Jesus' name will be directed to God the Father, and he will give Jesus' followers what they ask for in his name (**v. 26**). Not that Jesus will need to induce the Father to love his followers; the Father himself loves them, because they love Jesus and have believed Jesus came from God (**v. 27**).

At this the disciples, picking up on Jesus' statement at verse 25 that the time will come when he will no longer speak to them by way of illustrations (as he had done in vv. 20–22), claim they have finally seen the light: "Now you are speaking clearly and without figures of speech. Now we can see that you know all things and that you do not even need to have anyone ask you questions [as they had done throughout the Farewell Discourse; see 13:36; 14:5, 8, 22]. This makes us believe that you came from God" (**vv. 29–30**).

But, as with Peter earlier (13:36–38), the disciples are getting ahead of themselves, since it will only be subsequent to the crucifixion and resurrection and the coming of the Spirit that the spiritual veil surrounding their understanding of the significance of Jesus' death will fully be removed and they will understand in hindsight the importance of Jesus' words (see, e.g., 2:22; 12:16). Consequently, also as at previous occasions, Jesus asks, rhetorically (and with justified skepticism), "Do you now believe?... A time is coming and in fact has come when you will be scattered, each to your own home. You will leave me all alone. Yet I am not alone, for my Father is with me" (**16:31–32**).

This sets the stage perfectly for the account of Jesus' arrest in John 18 following Jesus' final prayer in John 17. Hence the Farewell Discourse concludes with the disciples prepared for what is about to follow as well as they could have been, given their persistent lack of understanding, and with a note of encouragement. While they, like Jesus, will have trouble in this world, in their Lord they will have peace. This Jesus is to say in anticipation of his victory over the world and its ruler at the cross, which will mark the "Mission accomplished!" of the obedient **Son** sent from the **Father** (**16:33**; cf. 17:4; 19:30).

10.2.2.1.3 Jesus' Final Prayer (17:1–26)

10.2.2.1.3.1 Jesus' Prayer for Himself (17:1–5) Jesus' final prayer recorded in John 17 — or his "high priestly prayer," as it is sometimes, somewhat erroneously, called — is in some ways the Johannine equivalent of Jesus' model prayer for his disciples (commonly called "the Lord's Prayer") in Matt 6:9–13 and Luke 11:2–4. In fact, this final prayer of Jesus has every right to be called "the Lord's Prayer" with at least as much legitimation as the prayer recorded in Matthew and Luke. For it is here that we are given the most extended prayer of Jesus found anywhere in the NT, strategically placed immediately prior to his arrest, which would trigger in rapid succession the various events surrounding Jesus' crucifixion. This fits the pattern, found also in the Synoptics, of Jesus' approaching God in prayer prior to important decisions or events in his earthly ministry (see, e.g., his appointment of the Twelve [Luke 6:12], and especially his prayer prior to the crucifixion in the garden of Gethsemane [Matt 26:39, 42, 44 pars.]).

At this solemn, even celebratory, occasion in John's gospel, Jesus marks the occasion of the successful accomplishment of his mission, again (in customary fashion for John's gospel) anticipating what is yet to happen. For the cross, rightly understood in a momentous Christian (Johannine) reinterpretation, represents not the world's (and Satan's) triumph over Jesus, but, contrary to what it may have initially appeared, Jesus' triumph over Satan and world, a triumph shared also by his disciples (see John 16:33). Thus, this final prayer ends the Farewell Discourse on a note markedly different from OT antecedents, which were not delivered in anticipation of a person's resurrection but in the fact of their impending death.[140]

Jesus begins his prayer by acknowledging that the hour of his death—or, in Johannine terms, of his "glory"—had now come (**v. 1**; cf. 12:23; 13:1, 31–32). As at the end of Matthew's gospel (cf. Matt 28:19), though here even prior to his crucifixion, Jesus strikes a note of universal authority ("authority over all people," **John 17:2**). Jesus has authority, delegated to him by the Father, to give eternal life to all those given him by the Father (v. 2). This shows that Jesus respected the parameters of his mission, including people's prerogative to receive or reject him as Messiah and Son of God. For he did not set out to aggressively recruit followers by overwhelming power or manipulation; rather, he humbly acknowledged that God's prevenient **elective, predestinatory choice** (his "drawing" or "giving" people to Jesus) was required for his ministry to be successful (or, better, effective).

In **John 17:3**, "eternal life" is defined as knowing "the only true **God**" (a statement reflecting Jewish monotheism) and "Jesus Christ, whom you have sent" (a third-person self-reference by Jesus, making an *inclusio* with 1:17). This shows that for Jesus Jewish monotheism was able to accommodate the notion of the Messiah being himself divine and of dispensing life together with the Life-Giver and Creator, God (cf. 5:25–26).[141]

John 17:4–5, like the entire prayer, present Jesus as a model of accountability and obedient submission to the one who sent him. In this Jesus is to serve as the example for his followers in their (future) mission (see 20:21). Verse 4 anticipates 19:30, and verse 5 speaks of the cross as part of the pathway to Jesus' preexistent **glory** with the Father (see 1:1–2 above and 17:24 below). Bringing God glory is shown to be the overarching purpose of Jesus' earthly ministry (cf. 1:14, 16), both through his messianic "signs" and ultimately through his "lifting up" at the cross. Rather than pursuing his mission as one who is self-appointed or self-serving, Jesus sets the example for his followers, who are charged with advancing the kingdom of God through their ministry rather than building a kingdom of their own (see, e.g., Mark 10:35–45 pars.).

10.2.2.1.3.2 Jesus' Prayer for His Disciples (17:6–19) Jesus now proceeds to pray for his disciples (see **v. 9**), describing his mission in terms of revelation to those God had given him out of the world, resulting in believing obedience (**v. 6**). They have

---

140. See, e.g., Genesis 49; Deuteronomy 32. For instances where farewell discourses ended with prayers, see Köstenberger, *John*, 483.

141. See chap. 9, sec. 17 below.

understood that Jesus was not self-appointed but that he came from God (**v. 7**). Likewise, the purpose of our proclamation of the gospel, properly conceived, is that people understand that our preaching is not merely what we believe on a human level, but in truth a passing on what God has revealed to us regarding his Son. For this reason it is essential for Jesus' followers to understand the role Jesus' vital connection to his sender (the Father) had in his mission, for it is this same vital connection they are called to sustain with Jesus as they embark on their own mission, which is in reality nothing but an extension of Jesus' **mission** in the power of the **Holy Spirit** (see 20:21).

Jesus' prayer for his followers is based on the fact that while he will return to the Father, they will remain in the world (**17:11**). Hence his request is for the "holy Father" to protect them by the power of his name, so that they may be one (v. 11; as Jesus and the Father were one during his earthly ministry, see 10:30, and of course beyond). While he was with them, Jesus had protected his own (except for Judas, in fulfillment of Scripture, **v. 12**), but now he is returning to the Father—hence his request that the Father continue to protect his followers after his departure.

Jesus also prays for his followers to have supernatural joy while being in a world that once was their home and natural habitat but that now hates them because they were saved out of this world in Jesus' divine rescue mission (**vv. 13–14**). Jesus does not ask God to take his disciples out of the world but to protect them from the evil one while remaining in the world (**vv. 15–16**). Jesus also prays for the disciples' continued consecration (or sanctification) in (or by) the truth as they continue in God's Word as passed on to them by Jesus (**v. 17**; cf. v. 6).

This consecration, in turn, will enable them to bear effective **witness** in the world without being drawn back into it (cf. 1 John 2:15–17). In this sense, there is a parallel between Jesus and the disciples, for just as Jesus was sent from outside the world into the world (see John 1:1, 9), so also his followers are sent (back) into the world after having been called out of it (though, of course, the analogy breaks down at one level, since believers did not share eternal preexistence with God as Jesus did).

10.2.2.1.3.3 Jesus' Prayer for Later Generations of Believers (17:20–26) Third and last in his prayer, Jesus also lifts up those who would become believers through the ministry of his immediate followers (**v. 20**). This reflects Jesus' vision of spiritual multiplication and reproduction (cf. 2 Tim 2:2). In this way his disciples would fulfill the purpose of their mission and bear fruit for the glory of the Father as Jesus had done (see John 15:8, 16). This final section in Jesus' prayer, as his final prayer in its entirety, serves as a perfect illustration of the fact that John's trinitarian teaching, rather than serving as an end in itself, contributes to its missiological thrust (see the discussion of **John's trinitarian mission theology** in chap. 15, sec. 33).

As Jesus envisions his followers embarking on their mission subsequent to his exaltation with the Father, he has one overriding concern that he presents to the Father in prayer: his disciples' unity (**17:21, 23**). For he knows that only if his followers are unified will they be able to effectively and persuasively communicate the message of Jesus' unity and oneness with his sender, the Father. In this way the unity between Son and Father will serve as the foundation and wellspring for the unity among believers; this, in turn, will make it possible for the world (or at least for those chosen from the world by God) to see through and beyond the mission of believers to the one who sent them (Jesus), just as Jesus' contemporaries were enabled to see past Jesus to the one who sent him, God the Father.

Thus lack of unity among believers is the major obstacle that Jesus asks his Father to remove "so that the world may believe that you have sent me" and "have loved them even as you have loved me" (vv. 21, 23). During the days of Jesus' earthly ministry, his followers were often anything but unified, jockeying for position in Jesus' kingdom and seeking their own interests rather than those of Christ (e.g., Matt 20:20–28; Mark 9:33–37). This, Jesus prays, should now change, with the Spirit, once given, bringing about the kind of unity among believers that will serve as a supernatural witness to the world that Jesus' claims are real and true (cf. Paul's programmatic words about the church's unity in Eph 4:1–6).

This also underscores the need for believers to love one another by way of humble service (see the discussion of John 13:1–17 above) in keeping with Jesus' "new command" (13:34–35; 15:12–13). By exemplifying the love of God in their dealings with one another, according to Jesus' vision, believers will draw yet others from the world into the circle of God's love for them in Christ, extending the circle of loving oneness beyond the triune Godhead and Jesus' first followers to future generations of believers. Jesus closes his prayer with an expression of his heart's desire that his followers will in due course see his glory in the presence of the Father (**v. 24**; cf. v. 5; 14:2–3) and with a petition of the "righteous Father" that summarizes the burden of his entire prayer (**17:25**).

10.2.2.2 Jesus Completes His Earthly Mission: The Passion Narrative and the Purpose of the Gospel (chaps. 18–20)

10.2.2.2.1 Jesus' Arrest and Peter's First Denial of Jesus (18:1–18)

After two chapters of discourse and an added chapter containing Jesus' final prayer, the narrative now, in John **18:1**, picks up where 14:31 left off, indicating movement on the part of Jesus and his disciples across the Kidron Valley and into a (walled) garden (implied by the reference to them going "into it," 18:1). The reference to Judas's familiarity with the site in **verse 2** makes clear that Jesus was not hiding from the authorities but that he followed his usual custom. This, at long last, is Judas's (and the devil's) "hour," and the betrayer comes leading a surprisingly large company of those who plan to arrest Jesus (**v. 3**). This has the **ironic** effect of pitting Jesus' lack of resistance against an overkill that would be appropriate in the case of an armed criminal but is completely out of place for Jesus, who is innocent of all the charges that will be brought against him and who has done nothing wrong (cf. Matt 26:55; Mark 14:48–49; Luke 22:52–53).

Again, as at the outset of Act II (see John 13:1–2, 11), the evangelist stresses Jesus' **divine foreknowledge** of the ensuing events and shows him as taking the initiative in his arrest (**18:4**; cf. 10:17–18). When Jesus asks the soldiers who they are looking for and they reply, "Jesus of Nazareth," Jesus, in typical Johannine **double entendre**, identifies himself by responding, "I am he" (**18:5**), which on one level means simply, "I am (the one you're looking for)," but beyond this surely has overtones of the divine name "I am" (for a similar dynamic see 6:20). This is apparent also from the effect Jesus' words have on the soldiers, who "drew back and fell to the ground," as the Scriptures indicate is customary in the case of a theophany (**18:6**).

Hence Jesus takes the initiative a second time and asks them again who it is they are looking for (**v. 7**), this time following up with a command to arrest him and let his followers go (**v. 8**). Just as the betrayal fulfilled Scripture (cf. 13:18; 17:12), so Jesus' action serve to fulfill Jesus' words just uttered in his final prayer that he had not lost any of his followers other than the betrayer (**18:9**; see 17:12; cf. 6:39).[142]

At this point in the narrative, in a dramatic gesture, Peter draws his sword and cuts off the right ear of the high priest's servant (**v. 10**).[143] This is utterly counterproductive as far as Jesus' purposes are concerned (his kingdom is not of this world, 18:36) and thus reveals a complete **misunderstanding** of the nature of Jesus' mission on Peter's part (though it is a demonstration of bravery, albeit misguided, in a futile effort to make true on Peter's pledge of loyalty at 13:36–38). It is also sure to be ineffective as there is no realistic chance Jesus and his small band will be able to overpower the large company of those who have come to arrest Jesus.

Thus, Peter's action has the potential effect of lighting a match that could easily have burned down an entire house (or forest), causing the soldiers to take severe action on Jesus and the disciples. Also, Peter's possession of a sword and his use of it to harm another person—and none other than the high priest's personal servant (a position of some significance)—renders him vulnerable to criminal prosecution in his own right, a fact that may well have contributed to his threefold denial of Jesus later on (see 18:15–18, 25–27).

In a narrative gap (found also in Matthew and Mark), John does not record Jesus' healing of the servant's ear (made explicit only by Luke; see Luke 22:51) but only Jesus' rebuke of Peter: "Put your sword away! Shall I not drink the cup the Father has given me?" (**John 18:11**). "The cup," of course, is a figurative expression denoting the need for Jesus to go to the cross. As is indicated also in the Synoptics, Peter and the other disciples did not understand that Jesus' messianic mission involved death (Matt 16:22 pars.), and as at previous occasions, Jesus had to rebuke Peter for failing to understand and for misconstruing the nature of his messianic mission (Matt 16:23 pars.).

With this the arrest proceeds and Jesus is taken into custody. He is bound (like a criminal) and brought first to Annas, the patriarch of Jewish high priests and father-in-law of Caiaphas, the current high priest (**John 18:12–14**, with customary **Johannine back-reference** to 11:49–50).

---

142. Note how Scripture and Jesus' words and their respective fulfillment are linked in 2:22.

143. Identified only here in the Gospels by his name, Malchus, an Arab name (see Köstenberger, *John*, 508–9). See Bauckham's appropriation of Theissen's concept of "protective anonymity" in *Jesus and the Eyewitnesses*, 184–87.

Peter, despite the setback he suffered at the arrest (see above), follows Jesus together with "another disciple," who most likely is none other than "the disciple whom Jesus loved" (see discussion at 13:23 above; the expressions "another disciple" and "the disciple whom Jesus loved" both refer to the same disciple at 20:2, 3, 8 and therefore likely does so here as well). In this scene, as throughout Act II, this "other disciple" "whom Jesus loved" exceeds Peter as far as access to Jesus is concerned. In the present case, this involves this disciple gaining entrance for Peter into the high priest's courtyard owing to his acquaintance with the high priest.[144]

Peter's first denial of Jesus ensues, graphically illustrated by the evangelist's reference to the fact that "it was cold" (cf. 10:22: "it was winter"; 13:30: "and it was night") and that "Peter also was standing with them, warming himself" (18:18). The latter reference shows Peter putting self-interest (keeping warm) over his allegiance to Jesus and pictures him as "standing with them," that is, those who had arrested Jesus. This is a good example of John's art of storytelling and considerable narrative acumen, as he is able, in his "spiritual gospel," to provide a highly interpretive account that nonetheless qualifies as historical narrative.[145]

10.2.2.2.2 Jesus' Hearing before Annas and Peter's Second and Third Denials of Jesus (18:19–27)

The scene, which oscillates back and forth between Jesus and Peter in this chapter, shifts now to Jesus ("meanwhile," **v. 19**), who is interrogated by Annas the high priest (cf. vv. 12–14). Jesus is asked about his disciples and his teaching (v. 19). He responds that his entire ministry was conducted in an open manner (see, e.g., John 7), so that there was no need to question him; his ministry lay before people like an open book that could be read by anyone who was interested to do so.[146] Together with the large number of soldiers sent for Jesus' arrest, the high priest's question reveals **misunderstanding** in that it misconstrues Jesus' mission as subversive and clandestine. This pattern of misunderstanding will continue when Pilate (see below) is shown to reveal an astonishing degree of ignorance with regard to Jesus and his mission.[147]

Next is an incident in which one of the officials slaps Jesus in the face and Jesus responds in a remarkably restrained fashion affirming the truthfulness of his statement (compare and contrast Paul's response to a similar provocation in Acts 23:2–5). After this Annas sends Jesus, still "bound," to Caiaphas (**v. 24**). Remarkably, these brief passing references here and at **verse 28** are all that is said here (or anywhere) about Jesus' formal Jewish trial in this gospel (just as Jesus' informal

---

144. Some have questioned whether a simple fisherman such as John the son of Zebedee (on the assumption that he was the author of the gospel) would have been personally acquainted with the high priest, but this is not an insurmountable objection to Johannine authorship; see Köstenberger, *John*, 513–14.

145. See on this point the discussion in the introduction to this volume.

146. Note that Jesus' assertion that he spoke nothing in secret does not negate his private instruction of his disciples. It merely states that generally his ministry was open to anyone and his teaching was widely known.

147. See chap. 11 below.

hearing before Annas is mentioned only in John's gospel). This suggests an effort on John's part to supplement (rather than duplicate) the Synoptic account of Jesus' Jewish and Roman trials.[148] One also notes here a focus on the Roman portion of the trial, which leads to Jesus' formal condemnation, since only the Romans had jurisdiction in capital cases in Jesus' day.[149]

10.2.2.2.3 Jesus' Trial before Pilate (18:28–19:16a)

The narrative silence regarding Jesus' formal Jewish trial between John 18:24 and 28 is filled with an account of Peter's second and third denials of Jesus (vv. 25–27), after which the evangelist informs his readers that "the Jewish leaders took Jesus from Caiaphas to the palace of the Roman governor" (v. 28; cf. v. 24). The time was now early morning (**v. 28**), which follows references to the company of those arresting Jesus carrying torches and lanterns (v. 3) and Peter warming himself at a fire during a cold night (v. 18). This, ironically, indicates that it was the Jewish leaders who tried Jesus clandestinely (see vv. 20–21) and under the cover of night.

Apparently, Roman officials commenced their work early in the morning, so when the Jewish leaders come to him, Pilate is ready to hear their charge. In another instance of Johannine **irony**, the Jews, who are about to kill their Messiah, are scrupulously concerned not to defile themselves by entering the home of a Gentile (Pilate) in order to be able to keep the traditional observance of their Passover (18:28); Pilate, remarkably, accommodates himself to their religious scruples and comes to them outside to find out the nature of their charges against Jesus (**v. 29**).

At this, the Jewish leaders assert that Jesus is a common "criminal" (more literally, "an evildoer"; **v. 30**), at which Pilate, calling their bluff, tells them to judge Jesus according their own law. This follows customary Roman procedure avoiding interference in internal Jewish religious matters (see the book of Acts, *passim*). In the present case, however, as Pilate apparently senses, because the Jews want Jesus crucified, they need the Roman governor to validate their charges and to formally pronounce the "guilty" verdict. As John notes, even this "took place to fulfill what Jesus had said about the kind of death he was going to die" (**v. 32**, a back-reference to 12:33; cf. 12:32; 3:13; 8:28), that is, his "lifting up" in keeping with Isaiah's prophecy (see 12:36–41 and the discussion there). Hence John teaches his readers to see everything in Jesus' life (and, by implication, believers' lives as well) as **sovereignly** ordained and **predetermined** by God, *especially* events surrounding Jesus' crucifixion (see also the fulfillment quotations at 19:24, 36–37 below).

As alluded to above, especially in John 18:33–38a and 19:4–15 John supplements the Synoptic account of Jesus' trial before Pilate.[150] John's account of Jesus'

---

148. As will be seen below, there is substantial overlap between the Synoptic and Johannine version of Jesus' appearance before Pilate, though even there John supplements the Synoptic portrait at certain points.

149. Köstenberger, *John*, 525–26, 533.

150. For a defense of the historicity of the account see my essay "'What Is Truth?' Pilate's Question in Its Johannine and Larger Biblical Context," in *Whatever Happened to Truth*, 21–28. The following pericope will serve as a case study in the treatment of the cosmic trial motif in chap. 11 below.

trial before Pilate, particularly in 18:33–38a, touches on several major Johannine themes. The first major motif is the **trial motif** and the perspective of the **cosmic spiritual conflict** in which Jesus and the world are engaged. Bultmann speaks of "the great trial between God and the world," which provides the larger backdrop against which Jesus' Jewish and Roman trials are conducted.[151] While Pilate is Jesus' judge according to the world's standards, the reader already knows that, in truth, it is Jesus who is the judge who decides over life and death (5:19–29).

The second major Johannine theme found in the present passage is that of Jesus' **kingship**. Jesus is acknowledged as the "king of Israel" at the outset of John's gospel by Nathanael (1:49), though, as mentioned, Nathanael's understanding of the entailments of this term may have carried nationalistic overtones, which did not accurately characterize the true nature of Jesus' kingship.[152] **Misunderstanding** is even more evident in the people's effort to make Jesus their king subsequent to the feeding of the multitude in John 6 (see esp. 6:14). While the references to Jesus as the "king of Israel" at the triumphal entry into Jerusalem in 12:13 and 15 appear to be more positive, the context there reveals that, once again, people do not truly understand the nature of Jesus' kingship. In fact, the same crowds who acclaim Jesus at that occasion less than a week later join the Jewish leaders in calling for Jesus' crucifixion.

In contrast to "king of Israel," which is essentially a positive reference, the expression "king of the Jews," as used by Pilate, seems to be somewhat derogatory (18:33, 39; 19:3, 19, 21 [2x]; cf. 19:14, 15: "your king"). This may be one reason why Jesus does not directly affirm being this figure when he is asked by Pilate, not once, but twice, whether he is the "king of the Jews" (18:33, 37). While Jesus is therefore reluctant to identify himself as *king* (cf. 6:14) — though he does enter Jerusalem on his final visit to the city in messianic fashion (12:13, 15) — he speaks openly about his *kingdom* (18:36).

Truth, in conjunction with **witness**, is a third major motif found in John's gospel. "Truth" terminology in John's gospel takes its point of departure from the references to Jesus as "full of grace and truth" in 1:14 and 17.[153] The remainder of the gospel proceeds to explicate and substantiate this claim. The reference to truth in the present passage suggests that John envisions Jesus' appearance before Pilate as a paradigmatic instance of one who is not of the world but who has been set apart and sent into the world to speak the truth, which is God's word. Jesus' witness to the truth serves as a model for his followers to emulate (cf. 17:18; 20:21).

Pilate's first of two private interrogations of Jesus narrated in John's gospel culminates in Pilate's question, "What is truth?" (**18:33–38**).[154] After Jesus has endured a severe flogging and humiliation (**19:1–6**), and after the Jewish leaders have told

---

151. Bultmann, *Gospel of John*, 655.
152. See Köstenberger, *John*, 83–84.
153. For a survey of the relevant instances of *alētheia* in John's gospel see Morris, *Gospel according to John*, 260–62.

154. John narrates Jesus' Roman trial in seven units, which display an oscillating pattern of outdoor and indoor scenes (18:29–32, 33–38a, 38b–40; 19:1–3, 4–7, 8–11, 12–15).

Pilate that the real reason why they want Jesus crucified is that he has "claimed to be the Son of God" (**19:7**), Pilate, now afraid (cf. Matt 27:19), summons Jesus one more time, asking him, "Where do you come from?" (John **19:9**). But Jesus gives him no answer. Pilate, incredulous that the prisoner would not take the opportunity to lobby the one who has authority to free him for his release, asks Jesus, "Do you refuse to speak to me? . . . Don't you realize I have power either to free you or to crucify you?" (**19:10**). But Jesus calmly points out that Pilate's authority comes "from above"—that is, from God—so that the one who delivered Jesus over to Pilate (presumably Caiaphas) is guilty of a greater sin.

10.2.2.2.4 The Crucifixion and Burial of Jesus (19:16b–42)

Once the formal verdict of crucifixion is pronounced, the action is exceedingly swift. The soldiers took charge of Jesus (**19:16b**), and, carrying his own cross (cf. the reference to Simon of Cyrene carrying Jesus' cross for part of the way per Matt 27:32 pars.), Jesus goes to the Place of the Skull (Golgotha), where he is crucified, with another man on either side of him (**John 19:17–18**). John notes that an inscription that Pilate had prepared was placed on Jesus' cross, which read, in three languages, "Jesus of Nazareth, the king of the Jews." Despite protests by the Jewish leaders, who object that Jesus only *claimed* to be "king of the Jews" (**irony**), Pilate, with newfound resoluteness, insists that the inscription stands as is (**vv. 19–22**).

This is followed by the first of several references to Scripture being fulfilled in and through various details surrounding Jesus' crucifixion. The first pertains to the fact his seamless garment is not torn but divided among the Roman soldiers guarding him, fulfilling the reference in Ps 22:18, "They divided my clothes among them and cast lots for my garment" (**John 19:24**).[155] John's comment, "So this is what the soldiers did" (v. 24), draws attention to the fact that these Roman soldiers participate in an action that fulfills Scripture completely without realizing that they thus contribute to the validation of God's Word with regard to this important salvation-historical event.

The next event in the crucifixion narrative chosen for inclusion by John is Jesus' giving charge of his mother (unnamed as elsewhere in the gospel) to "the disciple whom he loved" (**vv. 25–27**). This further underscores the trustworthy position occupied by this disciple, who was at Jesus' side at the Last Supper (13:23) and who, it turns out, is the author of the gospel (21:24) whose eyewitness testimony it reflects (see esp. 19:35; see also 1:14). Jesus' action here is historically plausible since likely none of Jesus' brothers was a believer at this point in time; only subsequent to the ascension are Jesus' brothers found among the company of believers (Acts 1:14).

Another Scripture is fulfilled when Jesus utters his second word from the cross in this gospel (cf. **19:27**), saying, "I am thirsty" (**v. 28**; cf. Exod 12:46; Num 9:12; Ps 34:20).[156] After drinking from a sponge soaked with wine vinegar (**John 19:29**),

---

155. For a thorough discussion see Köstenberger, "John," in *Commentary on the NT Use of the OT*, 500–502.

156. See ibid., 502.

Jesus says, "It is finished," bowed his head, and gave up his spirit (**v. 30**). With this somber and restrained account, the earthly mission of the Son sent from the Father in John's gospel has come to a close. The statement indicates the necessity of the work that must be done and now has been completed for the salvation of the world. It culminates the presentation of Jesus as the obedient, submissive **Son** throughout the Johannine narrative.

The unthinkable has taken place: Jesus, the preexistent **Word**, who had subsisted with God in the beginning; Jesus, the **Messiah** and **Son of God**, who was one with the **Father** and had performed many compelling **signs** as proof of his messianic identity; this Jesus has been put to death by sinful representatives of humanity—all of us—as the ultimate expression of God's **love** (3:16; 13:1; 15:13), accomplishing what only Jesus could do: take away the sins of the world as the sacrificial **Lamb** provided by God (1:29; note the **Passover** theme). At this pivotal point in **salvation history**, God's pleasure rests on his beloved Son who had come down from heaven, accomplished his mission, and had now returned to the Father who sent him (13:1, 3; 16:28). As Jesus had prayed, "I have brought you **glory** on earth *by finishing the work you gave me to do.* And now, Father, glorify me in your presence with the **glory** I had with you before the world began" (17:4–5, emphasis added; see also 12:27–28).

The Johannine narrative, however, rather than dwelling on the momentous nature of the sacrifice of "the Lamb of God," or on the preposterous putting to death of the Creator by the world made through him (1:10–11; cf. 1:3–4); rather than expounding on the paradox of the life of the Life-Giver having been taken away, or extolling, as the angels doubtless did, the unimaginable condescension of Christ to meet the need of fallen, sinful creatures—the Johannine narrative does not dwell on any of these things—instead moves on inexorably past the crucifixion to the burial of Jesus. As a proof of Jesus' full humanity (cf. 1:14), not only did Jesus truly die (see 19:34), but Jesus' dead body must now be given a proper burial.

Again (see John 18:28), Jewish tradition must be observed, and since it was the Day of Preparation, that is, the Friday of Passover Week preceding a "special Sabbath" (**19:31**), Jesus' body must be taken down prior to sunset. To expedite the death of the three crucified men, the Jewish leaders asked Pilate to have their legs broken and the bodies taken down (v. 31). After breaking the legs of the two other men, the soldiers, when coming to Jesus, notice that he is already dead and therefore do not break his legs. As in the case of the soldiers' dividing of Jesus' garment (see v. 24 above), this took place so that Scripture would be fulfilled, again involving unsuspecting soldiers in the validation of God's Word in an event surrounding Jesus' crucifixion (**v. 36**). Instead, one of the soldiers pierces Jesus' side with a spear, resulting in a flow of blood and water, again proving Jesus' full humanity (**v. 34**). "The disciple whom Jesus loved," the author of this gospel, testifies to the truthfulness of this account by affirming his own eyewitness testimony (**v. 35**). What is more, this event likewise fulfilled Scripture (**v. 37**; citing Zech 12:10; see also Rev 1:7), culminating a steady stream of scriptural fulfillment in the second half of John's gospel, and particularly in the crucifixion narrative.[157]

The cumulative effect of these references to scriptural fulfillment is designed to accomplish the task, essential for any evangelist, of accounting, for the benefit of his readers, for a crucified Messiah. This was the crowd's final question: How can you say the Son of Man must be "lifted up" when the Scriptures say the Messiah will live forever? (John 12:34). As noted earlier, at the time Jesus did not answer this question. Instead, the entire ensuing narrative—Act II of John's gospel—forms John's answer: Jesus must first be crucified and subsequently be raised, in fulfillment of Scripture, so that salvation can be provided for sinful humanity. This was both in fulfillment of sacred Scripture, properly interpreted, and in keeping with the eternal, **predestinatory** counsel of God, as is affirmed, among other things, by the heavenly voice (12:28).

In the end, it is the incredulity and rejection of this very notion of a crucified Messiah—the ultimate instance of **misunderstanding**—that constitutes the utmost of human arrogance and presumption, if we assume that the wisdom of man is superior to the **salvation-historical** plan and program of God. As Paul writes:

> For the message of the cross is foolishness to those who are perishing, but to us who are being saved it is the power of God. For it is written:
>
> "I will destroy the wisdom of the wise;
>   the intelligence of the intelligent I will frustrate."
>
> Where are the wise? Where is the teacher of the law? Where is the philosopher of this age? Has not God made foolish the wisdom of the world? For since in the wisdom of God the world through its wisdom did not know him, God was pleased through the foolishness of what was preached to save those who believe. Jews demand signs and Greeks look for wisdom, but we preach Christ crucified: a stumbling block to Jews and foolishness to Gentiles, but to those whom God has called, both Jews and Greeks, Christ the power of God and the wisdom of God. For the foolishness of God is wiser than human wisdom, and the weakness of God is stronger than human strength (1 Cor 1:18–25).

It is hard to imagine a more fitting commentary on the implications of Christ's sacrifice and the world's rejection of him.

With this Jesus is given a proper burial by two "secret disciples" of his among the members of the Sanhedrin (suggesting that its decision to put Jesus to death was less than unanimous; **John 19:38–42**). Joseph of Arimathea (not mentioned previously in this gospel, v. 38) and Nicodemus (well known to the readers, see 3:1–15; 7:50–52) bring an astonishing amount (seventy-five pounds) of material for burial

---

157. For discussions of the scriptural fulfillment narrated in vv. 36–37, see Köstenberger, "John," in *Commentary on the NT Use of the OT*, 503–6.

(**19:39**). After preparing Jesus' body for burial (v. 40), they place him in a new nearby tomb in a garden (**v. 41**). The reference to the Jewish "day of Preparation" provides a bookend of the burial narrative, which extends from verse 31 to **verse 42**.

10.2.2.2.5 The Empty Tomb and Jesus' Appearances to Mary Magdalene and the Eleven (20:1–29)

10.2.2.2.5.1 The Empty Tomb and Jesus' Appearance to Mary Magdalene (20:1–18) Just as they brought Jesus to Pilate in the "early morning" (*prōi*; 18:28), so now Mary Magdalene comes to the tomb where Jesus had been laid (cf. 19:42) "early on the first day of the week, while it was still dark," and she sees that the stone has been moved away from the tomb (**20:1**; the Synoptics include a discussion of the women on the way to the tomb as to who would roll away the stone). Characteristically, while the Synoptics feature a group of women, John singles out one, Mary Magdalene, and her encounter with Jesus (see vv. 11–18 below). In Luke the reader is told that seven demons had come out of Mary Magdalene (Luke 8:2), though John does not provide this information (note that Mary Magdalene is mentioned as the last of the women at the cross at John 19:25).

Mary ran and told Simon Peter and "the [disciple whom] Jesus loved" that the stone had been moved, and "*we* don't know where they put him" (**20:2**, emphasis added), corroborating the Synoptic information that Mary was part of a group of women at the empty tomb. The fact that Mary ran gives a sense of her excitement, and her coming to Peter and "the [disciple whom] Jesus loved" indicates her agitated state and request for help.

The sense of excitement is continued when both Peter and "the disciple whom Jesus loved" also "run" (**20:4**) to the tomb, the latter outrunning the former and arriving at the tomb first (v. 4). As at previous occasions, this establishes the "primacy" of "the disciple whom Jesus loved" over Peter (see discussion at 13:23 above). **John 20:5** establishes this disciple as an eyewitness, now not only of the crucifixion but also of the empty tomb.[158] Mary only saw that the stone had been removed from the tomb (v. 1); "the disciple whom Jesus loved" looked more closely, bending over, looking inside, and noticing the strips of linen lying there (v. 5).

Then Peter arrives, enters the tomb, and also notices the same strips of linen (**v. 6**), as well as the facecloth, the latter not lying with the strips of linen but rolled (or folded) up by itself (**v. 7**).[159] These are precious bits of early authentic eyewitness testimony, claiming that Jesus' tomb was empty early Sunday morning, the burial only having taken place Friday evening. Then the "other disciple" (the one Jesus loved) also "saw and believed" (**v. 8**; again exceeding the narrated response of Peter).

---

158. In v. 1, Mary Magdalene "saw"; now, in v. 5, it is the turn of "the disciple whom Jesus loved" to verify and authenticate Mary's witness. Note a similar pattern in Acts 8, where Peter and John are called to authenticate the coming of the Spirit on the Samaritans.

159. Notice that the vocabulary in this pericope ("strips of linen," "facecloth," etc.) is similar to that in John 11, the raising of Lazarus. To some extent, of course, this is inevitable, since both accounts deal with similar subject matter (a person's death, a tomb), though the shared terminology still highlights the (theological) connection between the raising of Lazarus as proleptic of the rising of Jesus, who is "the resurrection and the life" (11:25).

Somewhat puzzlingly, this is followed by the evangelist's comment, "They still did not understand from Scripture that Jesus had to rise from the dead" (**John 20:9; misunderstanding**). Thus "the disciple whom Jesus loved" had **faith** based on sight, but as Jesus later on tells Thomas, "Blessed are those who have not seen and yet have believed" (v. 29). Nevertheless, "seeing and believing" is certainly better than seeing and *not* believing, but it appears that the evangelist is here seeking to establish the superiority of faith based on apostolic eyewitness testimony for the benefit of later generations who will not have the opportunity to literally "see" Jesus in the flesh as he and Jesus' first followers did.

After this "the disciples" (i.e., Peter and the disciple whom Jesus loved; were others there as well?) returned home (**20:10**).

With this the narrative returns to Mary Magdalene (see vv. 1–2), who apparently had returned to the tomb (following Peter and the disciple whom Jesus loved?). Mary stood outside the tomb crying. As she wept, she bent down into the tomb (as "the disciple whom Jesus loved" had previously done; v. 5) and saw two angels in white clothes sitting, one at the head and one at the feet, where Jesus' body had lain (vv. 11–12). Appearances of angels, of course, create a heightened sense of the supernatural and often signal miraculous events in the history of God's dealings with his people, such as Gabriel's appearing to Mary to announce the virgin birth (Luke 1:26–38; cf. Gen 19:1).[160]

The angel asks Mary why she is crying. Mary responds, in words virtually identical to those in John 20:2 (though note that the first-person plural "we don't know" is replaced by the first-person singular "I don't know," which may indicate that the other women had now left), that her Lord's body has been taken away and she does not know where it has been put (**v. 13**). At this, she turns around, and, stunningly, sees Jesus, though without recognizing him just yet (**v. 14**). Jesus addresses Mary in words identical to the angel (**v. 15**; cf. v. 13), and in a combination of Johannine **irony** and **misunderstanding**, Mary, thinking Jesus is the gardener (a not unreasonable assumption, since the tomb was in a garden, and who else would be out early Sunday morning but the gardener?), tells the man that if he has taken Jesus' body, he should tell her where he has put it, so that she can get it (v. 15). This account certainly has the ring of authenticity and displays both Mary's dogged determination to recover Jesus' body and her devotion to her Lord (though not her belief in the resurrection).

At this Jesus simply calls "Mary" by name, and, turning again, she exclaims, in Aramaic, "Rabboni!" (**v. 16**). The moving recognition scene pays tribute to the evangelist's narrative art. Mary, apparently, is about to embrace Jesus, but he holds her back, saying, "Don't touch me, because I have not yet ascended to the Father." He tells her instead to go and tell his "brothers" about his ascension (**v. 17**). So Mary goes and becomes the first witness to the resurrection, testifying, "I have seen the Lord!" (**v. 18**).

---

160. See Carol Newsom, "Angels," in *ABD*, 1:248–53, esp. 249–50.

Throughout the narrative in John 20 up to this point, it is striking that neither Mary nor the disciples expect to see the risen Jesus, despite the fact that he predicted numerous times that he would rise from the dead "on the third day" (cf. 2:19; and Synoptic references). This, in turn, shows that the disciples were not the ones who created the "myth" of Jesus' resurrection but that their faith in the resurrection was the result of actually seeing the risen Jesus. Not even the empty tomb triggered in the disciples the memory of Jesus' prediction; not until they saw Jesus face-to-face did they believe that he had risen from the dead (see the appearance to Thomas below).

10.2.2.2.5.2 Jesus' Appearances to the Eleven without and with Thomas (20:19–29) Still on the evening of that first day of the week (see 20:1), Jesus appears to the disciples (the Twelve minus Judas minus Thomas (**vv. 19–23**; see v. 24). The doors are locked for fear of the Jewish authorities (cf. 9:22; perhaps the disciples remembered Jesus' words that, once he was crucified, the world's hatred would turn toward them; see 15:18–27). This, however, apparently presents no problem for the resurrected Jesus, for suddenly he appears in their midst, greeting them with the customary, "Shalom" ("Peace be with you," 20:19; cf. vv. 21, 26). When he shows the disciples his hands and his side (where the nail marks were [not explicitly mentioned in John] and the spear had pierced him [see 19:34, 37]), they rejoice, recognizing that it is "the Lord" (cf. Mary: vv. 2, 13, 18; and see 21:7 below).

At this, the crucified and risen Lord commissions the Ten as representatives of the **new messianic community** with the words, "As the **Father** has sent me, I am sending you" (**20:21**). In a momentous development, the Sent One (e.g., 9:7) has now become the Sender of his disciples, and his sending of them is predicated on the way in which the Father has sent Jesus. This brings into play the characterization of Jesus' relationship with the Father "who sent him" in the entire preceding narrative.[161]

Breathing "on" (not "into") his disciples, Jesus says, "Receive the **Holy Spirit**" (**v. 22**), which most likely refers emblematically and proleptically to the impartation of the Spirit the disciples were to receive at Pentecost not many days from the commissioning. This appears to complete, symbolically, the *inclusio* between the reference to the first creation at John 1:1–4 by indicating a **new creation**—the establishment of a **new messianic community** by the risen Jesus—through Jesus' "breathing on" his disciples (an unmistakable allusion to Gen 2:7 LXX, where the same word is used). Empowered by the Spirit, the disciples are commissioned to pronounce forgiveness of sins upon faith in Jesus and lack thereof in the case of unbelief (**John 20:23**).

In an odd twist, Thomas was not present with the disciples at Jesus' first appearance to them in 20:19–23. When the Ten tell him, echoing Mary's testimony (see v. 18), "We have seen the Lord!" he demands tangible proof that the same Jesus

---

161. See on this Köstenberger, *Missions of Jesus and the Disciples*, passim.

who was crucified had now risen (essentially, the same proof with which Jesus had supplied the Ten earlier, though Thomas phrases his demand more dramatically). In this Thomas becomes an example of one who requires "seeing" as a prerequisite for "believing," furnishing an object lesson (see at v. 29 below).

A week later, in a scene with the feel of déjà vu (except that this time Thomas is among the disciples), Jesus appears again in the disciples' midst (again, despite locked doors), and at once addresses Thomas and his objection a week earlier (thus revealing supernatural knowledge), offering the precise tangible proof Thomas demanded. Thomas' objection melts in an instant, and instead of obtaining the evidence he had sought, he exclaims in worship, "My Lord and my God!" (**v. 28**). Jesus gently rebukes him, pronouncing those blessed who believe without having (physically) seen. This, incidentally, also marks the "signs" as integrally connected to Jesus' earthly ministry, though the gospel's account of Jesus' signs is still relevant as the basis for belief in Jesus as the Messiah and Son of God (**vv. 30–31**).

10.2.2.3 Conclusion: Believe in Jesus the Messiah on Account of His Signs (20:30–31)

The readers of John's gospel, however, must believe on the basis of the apostolic testimony to these signs, no longer on the basis of seeing the **signs** themselves as did Jesus' contemporaries. With this final remark elevating "believing without seeing" over "believing on the basis of seeing," John closes the book, as it were, on his account of Jesus' signs. As at 19:35, he steps out of his narrative and, strikingly, addresses his readers directly in the second person singular: "But these are written that *you* may **believe** … and that by believing *you* may have **life** in his name" (**20:31**, emphasis added; cf. 1:12). Indeed, while the primary original recipients of Jesus' signs were the Jews, now the invitation to believe is extended to all (cf. 10:16; 11:51–52; 12:20, 32). Yet, while the story of Jesus, from his eternal subsistence with God to his incarnation, ministry, death, and resurrection, has been told, the book is not yet concluded; an epilogue follows transitioning from the story of Jesus to the mission of his followers (cf. 20:21).

10.3 The Epilogue: Jesus' Third and Final Resurrection Appearance to the Disciples and His Commissioning of Peter and of "the Disciple Whom Jesus Loved" (21:1–25)

10.3.1 Jesus' Third and Final Resurrection Appearance to the Disciples (21:1–14)

This epilogue records a third appearance of Jesus to his disciples (**v. 1**; see v. 14). John, of course, did not include all of Jesus' resurrection appearances; none of the evangelists did (a count of all of these appearances in the four canonical Gospels, the book of Acts, and 1 Cor 15:5–7 indicates at least eleven such appearances). Notably, the reference to the appearance narrated in verses 1–13 as the "third" appearance does not include Jesus' appearance to Mary Magdalene in 20:11–18, but only that to the Ten (20:19–23) and the Eleven (20:24–29).[162]

This appearance takes place at the Sea of Galilee (John 21:1) to a group of seven disciples (**v. 2**). In the list, Simon Peter, quite naturally in light of his leadership role among the disciples, is mentioned first, followed by Thomas (just mentioned in 20:24–29). Also mentioned as part of the group are Nathanael "from Cana in Galilee" (a back-reference and possible *inclusio* with John 1 and 2); the sons of Zebedee (though their first names are not given here; apparently, knowledge of them is assumed from the Synoptics), and two other unnamed disciples.[163]

In customary fashion, Peter takes a leadership role, announcing he is going out to fish, and the others follow, but as at previous occasions when unaided by Jesus, Peter and his associates catch nothing (**21:3**; cf. Luke 5:4–11). Again (see John 20:1; 18:28), it is "early in the morning" (**21:4**), and Jesus is about to appear to his disciples. As Mary before them, however, they do not yet recognize Jesus (v. 4). In the ensuing interchange, Jesus tells them where to throw their net, and they catch a large number of fish (**vv. 5–7**), 153 to be exact, though, remarkably the net does not tear (**v. 11**).

At this, "the disciple whom Jesus loved" recognizes "the Lord" (v. 7; see v. 12 below and the consistent string of references to Jesus as "the Lord" mentioned above), and Peter acts on his declaration, jumping into the water and moving toward Jesus (**vv. 7–9**). Once again, "the disciple whom Jesus loved" precedes Peter in his spiritual insight and recognition of Jesus (see discussions at 13:23; 18:15–16; and 20:3–9 above). Jesus' invitation to his disciples to have breakfast is accompanied by a certain sense of strangeness (**21:12**; see 20:17 above). It appears that while this is still the same Jesus in one sense, something has changed in his appearance and his relationship with his followers. They are no longer as free in approaching him and seem somewhat confused.[164]

Yet Jesus, in customary fashion, takes the bread and distributes it and does the same with the fish (see 6:11, 23). It is as if this gesture is designed to reassure the disciples that even in his new resurrected state, Jesus will still provide for his disciples, though he will soon ascend to his Father (see 20:17) and "come" to his disciples in the form of "another [helping presence]" (14:16). The mention of the "charcoal fire" in the present instance (*anthrakia*; 21:9) is strangely reminiscent of the "charcoal fire" (*anthrakia*) mentioned earlier during the night of Jesus' Jewish trial when Peter "warmed himself" while denying Jesus three times (cf. 18:18). That this is probably not a coincidence is suggested by the immediately following restitution of Peter to ministry in 21:15–19.

---

162. Interestingly, Jesus commissioned the Ten (without Thomas), and there is no special commissioning of Thomas afterward, unlike the special commissioning of Peter in John 21.

163. Bauckham, *Jesus and the Eyewitnesses*, 412–16, argues, primarily on the basis of the mention of the sons of Zebedee at 21:2, that John the son of Zebedee cannot be the author of the gospel since he is named here and thus must be different from the unnamed "disciple whom Jesus loved." But this is less than convincing, because John is not "named" here in the sense that his first name is given, but a mere general reference is included here to the sons of Zebedee without naming them specifically.

164. See the discussion in Köstenberger, *John*, 569.

10.3.2 The Commissioning of Peter and of "the Disciple Whom Jesus Loved" (21:15–23)

After breakfast, Jesus takes care of one item of unfinished business: reassuring Peter in a threefold recommissioning scene and thus blunting the effects of Peter's earlier threefold denials. Apparently seeking to extract from Peter a pledge of loyalty and faith, Jesus asks him if he **loves** Jesus "more than these" (**v. 15**; most likely a reference to Peter loving Jesus more than he loves his fellow disciples).[165] Three times Peter replies that he indeed loves Jesus, hurt that Jesus would repeat the question three times (**v. 17**). Three times also Jesus tells Peter to "feed his lambs" or "tend his sheep." He adds that Peter will one day give his life in martyrdom ("stretch out your hands" [cf. **v. 18**] was a customary cipher for crucifixion). In this he would resemble his Lord (**v. 19**; cf. 12:33).

The final scene has Peter inquire regarding the destiny of "the disciple whom Jesus loved" (**21:20–23**). Jesus responds, in essence, that this is not for Peter to worry about. Jesus' response apparently gave rise to the rumor that "the disciple whom Jesus loved" would not die prior to Jesus' return (v. 23), but as that disciple (who was also the author of this gospel, v. 24) makes clear, this is not what Jesus actually said, but rather that, even *if* this were Jesus' desire for that disciple, this should be of no concern to Peter. Thus John's gospel at the end dispels a rumor similar to Matthew's gospel (dealing with the rumor that the disciples stole Jesus' body; see Matt 28:11–15).

10.3.3 Conclusion: The Signature of "the Disciple Whom Jesus Loved" (21:24–25)

This gospel closes with the signature of the disciple who wrote it (in the third person singular; cf., e.g., Jesus' self-reference in the third person at John 17:3), including an affirmation of his truthfulness ("we know," most likely a first-person singular reference in the first-person plural; **21:24**) and a reference to the many other things Jesus did that are not included in this gospel (**v. 25**; cf. 20:30). This kind of ending is also attested in other Jewish and Greco-Roman literature of the time.[166] With this, we are ready to move on to a closer literary-theological reading of John's letters.

---

165. See Ilaria Ramelli, "'Simon Son of John, Do You Love *Me?*' Some Reflections on John 21:15," *NovT* 50 (2008): 332–50 (with additional bibliography).

166. See the references in Köstenberger, *John*, 606.

Chapter 5

A LITERARY-THEOLOGICAL READING OF JOHN'S LETTERS

BIBLIOGRAPHY

Akin, Daniel L. *1, 2, 3 John*. NAC 38. Nashville: Broadman & Holman, 2001. **Bray, Gerald**, ed. *James, 1–2 Peter, 1–3 John*. ACCSNT 11. Downers Grove, IL: InterVarsity Press, 2000. **Bruce, F. F.** *The Epistles of John*. Grand Rapids: Eerdmans, 1979. **Burge, Gary M.** *The Letters of John*. NIVAC. Grand Rapids: Zondervan, 1996. **Edwards, Ruth B.** *The Johannine Epistles*. NTG. Sheffield: Sheffield Academic Press, 1996. **Kruse, Colin G**. *The Letters of John*. PNTC. Grand Rapids: Eerdmans, 2000. **Marshall, I. H.** *The Epistles of John*. NICNT. Grand Rapids: Eerdmans, 1978. **Schnackenburg, Rudolf**. *The Johannine Epistles: A Commentary*. New York: Crossroad, 1992. **Smalley, Stephen S.** *1, 2, 3 John*. WBC. Waco, TX: Word, 1984. **Stott, John R. W.** *The Letters of John*. TNTC. Rev. ed. Grand Rapids: Eerdmans, 1988. **Strecker, Georg**. *The Johannine Letters: A Commentary on 1, 2, and 3 John*. Hermeneia. Trans. Linda M. Maloney. Minneapolis: Fortress, 1996. **Streett, Daniel R.** "'They Went Out from Us': The Identity of the Opponents in First John." Ph.D. diss. Wake Forest, NC: Southeastern Baptist Theological Seminary, 2008. **Thompson, Marianne Meye**. *1–3 John*. IVPNTC. Downers Grove, IL: InterVarsity Press, 1992. **Yarbrough, Robert W.** *1–3 John*. BECNT. Grand Rapids: Baker, 2008.

11 A LITERARY-THEOLOGICAL READING OF JOHN'S LETTERS

11.1 First John

11.1.1 Introduction (1:1–4)

John's first letter opens with a magnificent introduction or preface (1 John 1:1–4) that, like the gospel, speaks of "that which was from the beginning" (**v. 1**). In context, this refers to the "**Word** of life" (v. 1), that is, most likely the **preexistent**, incarnate Jesus Christ (cf. John 1:1, 14).[1] At the outset of his letter, John makes clear that this Word, which was from the beginning (and thus divine) and which entered

---

1. Beyond this, it is possible that Johannine double entendre is involved and that John's secondary reference is also to the life-giving message about Christ (see Robert W. Yarbrough, *1–3 John* [BECNT; Grand Rapids: Baker, 2008], 38, n. 24). Elsewhere later in 1 John, the reference is clearly to the message (1:10; 2:5, 7, 14), just as in John's gospel subsequent references to John 1:1, 14 are to a person's message (e.g., 2:22; 4:37, 39, 41, 50; etc.).

the world in its full humanity, was the subject of the apostolic proclamation. The Word-made-flesh presented in the gospel was a person John and his fellow apostles had heard and seen with their eyes and touched with their hands (1 John 1:1).

Quite clearly, this affirmation reasserts the opening claims of the introduction to John's gospel, which apparently had been denied by false teachers in the Johannine congregations who had since left the church (2:19). Hence it appears that the purpose of John's first letter is the defense and reaffirmation of the orthodox, apostolic proclamation of Jesus as the eternal, preexistent Word, who had been with God from the beginning, who had become flesh in recent history, and who was attested by those who had been with him "from the beginning" (John 15:27) and who therefore must testify to him.

Importantly, the desired result of this apostolic proclamation is that the readers of the letter might enjoy complete fellowship with the representatives of apostolic, mainstream Christianity, unlike those who were denying the full humanity of Jesus and thus put themselves beyond the pale of true Christian fellowship (see 1:6–7). This experience of fellowship, in turn, would make the apostles' joy complete (**1:4**; cf. 3 John 4).

The transfer of the apostolic gospel regarding the preexistent, incarnate Lord Jesus Christ that is evident in this letter marks the vital connection between the apostolic era (which was unique; cf. John 15:26–27; Eph 2:20) and subsequent generations of believers (John 17:20; 20:28). The original disciples, such as John or Thomas, were able to see that both blood and water emanated from Jesus' side at the cross (19:34) and were invited to touch even the resurrected Jesus, confirming his humanity (20:27). Now they must preserve the accuracy of this message and defend it against distortions, and others must believe on the basis of their message (cf. 17:20). This suggests that John's first letter is logically and theologically, if not chronologically, predicated upon the gospel of John.

11.1.2 The Departure of the Secessionists (1:5–2:27)

The body of John's letter starts with the phrase, "This is the message we have heard from him and declare to you" (**1:5**). The initial overview of the message comes to a close with the words, "just as it [God's anointing of believers with the Holy Spirit] has taught you, remain in him" (2:27). The major burden of this first cycle of teaching is that of reassuring the believers in the Johannine congregations subsequent to the recent departure of the false teachers (2:19). It is possible to infer the major contours of the false teaching from a close reading of the letter.

First of all, John affirms that God is **light** and there is no darkness in him at all (1:5). No doubt he learned this from Jesus, the light of all people who shone in the darkness (John 1:4–5; cf. 8:12; 9:5; 12:35–36). Hence, anyone who claimed to have fellowship with Jesus and yet "walked in darkness"—that is, habitually and characteristically engaged in immoral conduct (cf. John 3:19–21)—did not live out the truth but proved that their conduct was based on a lie, that is, erroneous, unorthodox doctrine regarding the person of the Lord Jesus Christ.

Just as in Jesus' case his divinity and his humanity must not be separated, so in believers' lives, there exists an inextricable connection between the spiritual truths they affirm and the life they live in the flesh. It is excluded for anyone to live a "dark," immoral life and yet to claim to believe in a God who is light (cf. 1 Tim 6:16; Jas 1:17). However, those who "walk in the light, as he is in the light" have fellowship with one another, and the blood of Jesus purifies them from all sin.[2] Hence it is not the claim of sinlessness that carries the day but the humble confession of the need for the cleansing blood of Christ that enables believers to continue "walking in the light" and thus to enjoy fellowship both with Jesus and with other believers.

In fact, those who claim to be sinless deceive themselves and are not in the **truth** (**1:8**). Instead, believers ought to confess their sins, trusting in the efficacious nature of the blood of Jesus, which will be the vehicle of both forgiveness and cleansing (**v. 9**). In this way God will be both "faithful and just" (v. 9), confirming the truthfulness of the gospel preached also by Paul, according to which "God presented Christ as a sacrifice of atonement . . . so as to be just and the one who justifies those who have faith in Jesus" (Rom 3:25–26). Those who deny their need for Christ's atoning sacrifice make God and Christ out to be liars and do not have their word in them (**1 John 1:10**).

Hence 1:5–10, and still **2:1–2**, addresses the false teachers' apparent denial of human sinfulness and the need of an atoning sacrifice. In 2:1–2, John continues to finely balance Christian teaching. He exhorts believers not to sin, but acknowledges that sin they will, and that in this case they have a ***paraklētos*** with the Father, "Jesus Christ, the Righteous One." This teaching presupposes the reference to the "other" *paraklētos*, the Holy Spirit, in the gospel (John 14:16).

The reference to Jesus as "the Righteous One" makes explicit the basis on which Jesus was able to provide the atoning sacrifice for believers' sins. The reference to the universal scope of **redemption** provided by Jesus ("the sins of the whole world," **1 John 2:2**) also echoes teaching in the gospel regarding Jesus as "the Lamb of God, who takes away the sin of the world" (John 1:29). In the first instance, this may widen the scope of redemption beyond the Jewish people also to Gentiles. In the case of John's first letter, it broadens the application beyond any privileged group of initiates to all who trust in Christ's atoning sacrifice. In this way, John rejects an attitude by which some in the Christian community arbitrarily sought to exclude others from the scope of salvation.

Second, not only did the false teachers deny their sin and fail to "be in the light," they also failed to keep Jesus' commandments (**1 John 2:3–11**). As Jesus challenged those who had believed in him, "If you hold to my teaching, you are really my disciples" (John 8:31), so John insists that any professions of Christian faith are vain if not accompanied by obedience. In fact, Jesus himself serves as the example for the way Christians should live (**1 John 2:6**; cf. John 13:15). This command is both old and

---

2. On "fellowship" (*koinōnia*), see William W. Combs, "The Meaning of Fellowship in 1 John," *DBSJ* 13 (2008): 3–16.

new—it is old because John's recipients had heard this message from "the beginning" (**1 John 2:7**); it is new because it is tied up with Jesus' own example and teaching (**2:8**; the allusion to Jesus' "new commandment" in John 13:34–35 is unmistakable).

Hence, a second denunciation is added to the first. Earlier, it was stated that anyone who claimed to be in the light while "walk[ing] in the darkness" (i.e., living immorally) was not a genuine believer (1:6). Now John adds to this that anyone who claims to be in the light but hates a fellow believer was likewise "still in the darkness" (i.e., not a true Christian; **2:9**). This serves the (negative) purpose of exposing, after the fact as it were (cf. 2:19), that those who had recently left the fellowship had never been, and still were not, true believers at all, despite their claims to the contrary. Their walk betrayed their talk. Their hatred for those who truly were believers betrayed the fact that they had never been converted in the first place.

After lodging these twin denunciations against the false teachers, John turns to the actual believers in the congregation who remained in order to encourage and exhort them. He divides them into three groups according to maturity: "children" (**2:12, 14a**); "fathers" (**2:13a, 14b**); and "young people" (or men; **2:13b, 14c**). Children had their sins forgiven and know the Father. Fathers "know him who is from the beginning" (i.e., Jesus; cf. 1:1). Young people (or men) are strong, have overcome the evil one, and have "the word of God" living in them. The order "children … fathers … young people" is somewhat unconventional, and the instruction to young people the most extensive. Perhaps it is the young people in the congregation who most need the assurance that they have overcome the evil one by trusting in the truthfulness of God's Word.

Overcoming the evil one (2:13b, 14c) entails not loving the world's way of thinking or getting unduly attached to material possessions (**2:15–17**). Greed, lust, and pride do not come from God, and the world in its rebellious stance of independence toward God is passing away. Ironically, it appears, while the secessionists did not love the genuine believers in the congregation, they did love the world.[3]

With this, John turns to the immediate purpose at hand, the exposure and denunciation of the false teachers who had recently departed from the congregation's midst and the reassurance of the believers who remained (**2:18–27**). Similar to Paul in his letters to Timothy (1 Tim 4:1–5; 2 Tim 3:1–5), John sets the appearance of false teachers squarely in the context of the end times that were upon the church (**1 John 2:18–19**). Because it is "the last hour," "the antichrist" is coming, which is signaled by the appearance of "many antichrists" in the here and now.[4] As John makes clear, while these individuals were at one time in the congregation, by their eventual departure they proved that they were never really part of the company of the saved to begin with, or else they would have remained (**2:19**; cf. 2 Pet 2:22). This emphasis on the need to "remain" or persevere in the faith is entirely congruent with

---

3. Cf. John 3:19–21; 12:25; 15:19; and the discussion of the "love–hate" contrast in chap. 6, sec. 12.3.7 below.

4. The "antichrist" language is pronounced in 1 John, underscoring its polemical nature (similar to Jude), and aligns the letter with the book of Revelation.

the teaching of Jesus according to John's gospel (John 8:31; 15:1–8) and other NT writers (e.g., Col 2:6–7; Heb 2:1–3).

Continuing to pursue his purpose of reassuring the believers who remained (see esp. 1 John 2:21), John reminds them that they have "an anointing" from God and that all of them "know the **truth**" (**2:20**; cf. John 8:32, where the same language is attributed to Jesus). If an incipient form of Gnosticism was already in the air (as it well may have been; cf., e.g., 1 Tim 6:21), it is as if John were telling his audience, "You are all 'gnostics' [i.e., 'those who know']," rightly understood. Children and fathers in the faith alike know the Father by believing in Jesus Christ (see 1 John 2:13a, 14). With this John identifies the nature of the antichrist—the denial that Jesus is the Messiah (**2:22**; cf. John 20:30–31). Hence it is impossible to know God apart from acknowledging the Son; "no one who denies the Son has the Father" (**1 John 2:23**).

Again, John moves from denunciation of the false teachers to exhortation of the believers, urging the latter to remain in what they have heard "from the beginning" (**2:24**; cf. 2:7). He reassures the believers that "the anointing" they received from God (most likely the Holy Spirit) remains in them (cf. John 14:17) and that they do not need anyone to teach them (**1 John 2:27**). All they need is to remain in Jesus' teaching, contrary to the claims of any contemporary would-be teachers, whether proto-gnostic or otherwise. This reiterates Jesus' own instruction to his disciples shortly prior to his departure via the cross (John 15:1–8).

11.1.3 The Measure of True Love (2:28–3:24)

Rather than turning to innovative teaching supposedly addressed to the spiritually initiated (cf. 1 John 2:2, 20; cf. 2 John 9), John's readers need to do nothing but to continue in Christ in preparation for his return (**1 John 2:28**). Since Jesus is righteous (**2:29**; cf. 2:1), it is evident that those who do what is right have been born of him. With this John celebrates the wonderful truth of believers' **spiritual rebirth** and adoption into God's family, by which they have become children of God and he their Father (**3:1**; cf. John 1:12–13; 3:3–8). In fact, the full revelation of the magnitude of this event still awaits Christ's second coming (**1 John 3:2**). In the meantime, all true children of God purify themselves (2:28–3:10).

With this John makes clear the proper foundation of biblical, Christian ethics: the new, spiritual birth, which enables believers to act righteously and to be purified when they sin. "No one who lives in him keeps on sinning" (**3:6**). Conversely, "no one who continues to sin has either seen him or known him" (3:6). In characteristic black-and-white fashion, John contends that there are only two kinds of individuals—those who are born again and those who are not. The former's life will exhibit a characteristic pattern of righteous behavior; the latter's conduct will be sinful in keeping with their unregenerate nature (cf. Titus 1:15–16).

Hence, those who characteristically act righteously prove that they are in continuity with Jesus the Righteous One, while those who live sinfully demonstrate that their true father is "the devil [who] has been sinning from the beginning" (**3:8**). The purposes of Jesus and of the devil are diametrically opposite (**3:9**). Again, John's words hark back directly to Jesus' teaching in John's gospel (John 8:31–47, esp. vv. 44–45). Underlying John's entire first letter is the premise that while appearances may be deceiving and people's true spiritual orientation may be hidden for a while, it is the underlying reality of their true spiritual paternity (whether of God or the devil) that is decisive, and this, in turn, will clarify both who the false teachers are and who believers are as well.

In all this, John makes clear that it is not spiritual perfection that is expected; such perfection awaits the second coming of Christ. Yet regeneration will inexorably produce a heart that confesses sin and continues in righteousness. Continuing in sin is an impossibility for those who are truly God's children (1 John 3:9: "cannot"). John's pronouncement in **3:10** summarizes his earlier twin denunciation of the false teachers directed against their immoral conduct and hatred toward believers (1:5–2:11). More specifically, the reference may also allude to their sin of engaging in the eschatological rebellion by denying that Jesus is the Messiah.

After the summary statement in 3:10, John continues his letter with the statement "for this is the message you heard from the beginning" (**3:11**), which is reminiscent of the opening of the body of the letter (see 1:5; see also 2:7, 24). John now elaborates on the need for true believers to love their fellow believers, returning to a subject he already addressed earlier in his letter (2:7–11; cf. 3:11–24). Those who hate their brothers and sisters are like Cain who killed Abel (**3:12**; the only reference to a human OT character in this letter).[5]

Believers are reminded that it should not surprise them if the world hates them, echoing Jesus' words to his disciples (**3:13**; cf. John 15:18–25). The phrase "passed from **death** to **life**" in **1 John 3:14** likewise echoes Jesus' words in the gospel (John 5:24). Hence John asserts that the Christian community is the company of those who **love** one another, echoing the pervasive theme of the gospel's Farewell Discourse (John 13–17). This love is congruent with eternal life (1 John 3:14; cf. 2:25), just as lack of love indicates that a person remains in a state of spiritual death. In fact, hatred is equivalent to spiritual murder, and no murderer will be granted access to God's presence in heaven (**3:15**).

How do believers know what **love** is? It is Jesus laying down his life for them (**3:16**; cf. John 10:15, 17–18; 15:13). It may be argued that Jesus' act of footwashing is presented in John's gospel as encapsulating the Johannine ethic of love demonstrated by sacrificial service, proleptically explicating the dynamic underlying the crucifixion.[6] If so, this **Johannine "love ethic"** finds its further explication and elaboration in John's first letter, which likewise presents Jesus' sacrificial love as the grounds for believers' love for other believers. This kind of practical Christianity will not close its eyes toward a brother in need but express love in action (**1 John 3:17–18**).

"This is how we know" in **3:19** reiterates the identical opening in 3:16, continuing John's exposition of those who keep his commands, which spans from 3:11 to

---

5. Like the "antichrist" language in 1 John, the reference to Cain underscores the strongly polemical character of this letter.

6. See chap. 13 below.

3:24. Even in the face of doubt, believers may know that believers are simply called to do two things: to believe in God's Son, Jesus Christ, and to love one another (**3:23**). This is how Christ and believers live in perfect union. How do we know that Jesus lives in us (**3:24**; the third time the phrase "this is how we know" is used here; cf. 3:16, 19)? We know it by the indwelling Holy Spirit (cf. 2:20, 27).

11.1.4 The Antichrists and the Love Commandment (4:1–5:12)

Harking back to the reference to the "last hour" and the "antichrists" in 1 John 2:18, John proceeds to exhort his readers to "test the spirits to see whether they are from God" (**4:1–6**). Specifically, the test is whether someone affirms that Jesus Christ "has come in the flesh" (**4:2–3**). This may refer to a failure to acknowledge the full humanity of Jesus or may merely constitute a shorthand for Jesus being the Messiah. One can only speculate as to what motivated such a denial. If the former, behind the denial may be some form of Greek dualism, which held that matter was inferior to spirit and hence that it was incompatible with the divine to be incarnated in human flesh. If the latter, there would be continuity between the purpose of John's gospel (John 20:30–31) and the false teaching combated in 1 John.

In an effort to reassure the believers, John makes clear that they have been born of God and have overcome them, that is, the false teachers as motivated by the spirit of the antichrist, while the latter are from the world, which listens to them (**1 John 4:4–5**). Those who know God listen to believers (**4:6**). Thus believers will know if anyone is from God: if they listen to their profession of Jesus as having come in the flesh, they are true believers; if not, they are from the world. The juxtaposition of the phrases "spirit of truth" and "spirit of falsehood" contrasts the underlying spiritual dynamics of the confession of Jesus and the denial of him.[7]

With this John returns to his favorite subject, Christian **love**. He notes that the proper basis of such love is God's own love expressed by his sending of his Son as an atoning sacrifice for sins (**1 John 4:10**; cf. John 3:16). Since God so loved believers, they also ought to love one another in the same way (**1 John 4:11**). No one has ever seen God (cf. John 1:18), but believers' relationship with him is given visible expression if they love one another (**1 John 4:12**). John's pronouncement in **4:13** reiterates, almost verbatim, the statement in 3:24, moving the discussion from theology to pneumatology. John's testimony that the Father has sent his Son to be the Savior of the world echoes the gospel (cf. esp. John 4:42). Also similar to the gospel, John insists that Jesus is the Son of God (1 John 3:15; later, 5:5; see also 2:22; cf. John 20:30–31).

Moving further still in his exposition of the grounds of the love command, John now states plainly that "God is **love**" (**1 John 4:16**). Believers in Jesus have nothing more to fear, including judgment, because "perfect love drives out fear" (**4:18**). John reiterates that Christians love because God first loved them in Christ (**4:19**; cf. 4:10).

---

7. Terminological parallels are found in the DSS. The TNIV capitalizes "Spirit of truth," though perhaps "spirit of truth" is preferable as in contrast with "spirit of falsehood" (cf. John 3:6–8; 4:23–24, esp. 4:24: "God is spirit").

Thus any works-righteousness or self-effort is excluded. God first loved believers in Christ, and through that experience he continues to be the grounds of their love toward himself and others. Again, John emphasizes that love of God and love of one's neighbor are inextricably intertwined (**4:19 – 21**; cf. 3:17 – 18; 4:12). This, too, is firmly grounded in Jesus' teaching (Matt 22:37 – 40 pars.).

Moving toward a conclusion, John plainly states that "everyone who believes that Jesus is the **Messiah** is **born of God**" (**1 John 5:1**; cf. 2:22). This apparently includes an affirmation of Jesus' full humanity (see esp. 4:2 – 3). It also implies that no one can acknowledge Jesus as Messiah apart from spiritual birth and divine revelation (cf., e.g., Matt 11:25 – 26; 16:17). This, in turn, implies the precedence of **divine election and predestination**, also a major theme in John's gospel (e.g., John 12:32, 37 – 41; 17:6, 9, 12). At the same time, believers are called to love God and keep his commands (**1 John 5:2 – 3**), just as Jesus taught (John 14:15).

In closing, John, returning to the issue of the false teachers' denial of Jesus' full humanity, asserts that Jesus "came by water and blood" (**1 John 5:6**).[8] This most likely alludes to the affirmation in John's gospel that a flow of "blood and water" emanated from Jesus' dead body when pierced by the soldier's spear subsequent to the crucifixion (John 19:34). Apparently, there and here, the statement serves to underscore that Jesus died in a fully human body, which was required for him to offer an atoning sacrifice for sin. A third witness to Jesus is the **Holy Spirit** (**1 John 5:6 – 7**). These three, then, satisfy the biblical requirement for two or three witnesses (e.g., Deut 17:6; 19:15; cf. John 8:17). If anyone accept this testimony God has given concerning his **Son**, they have eternal life (**1 John 5:9 – 12**; cf., e.g., John 3:16 – 17). **Life** is mediated only through the Son (cf., e.g., John 1:4; 14:6).

11.1.5 Purpose Statement and Conclusion (5:13 – 21)

In his concluding epilogue, John states his purpose for writing. His words are addressed to those who believe in Jesus the **Son of God** to reassure them that they have **eternal life** (**1 John 5:13**). Nothing, including the false teachers' claim of special revelation or insight into divine mysteries, is to shake their confidence or unsettle them. Believers can have complete confidence in their secure standing before God in Christ (**5:14**; cf. John 10:27 – 29) and in the fact that God will answer believing prayer (**1 John 5:15**; cf., e.g., John 14:13).

There is one exception to that confidence: "a sin that leads to death" (**1 John 5:16 – 17**). This is a difficult passage with no clear NT parallels.[9] Perhaps most likely is

---

8. Many editions of the NT include (usually in a text note) what is known as the "Johannine Comma," which divides the witnesses between those in heaven and those on earth: "For there are three that testify *in heaven, the Father, the Word and the Holy Spirit, and these three are One. And there are three that testify on earth:* the Spirit, the water and the blood — and these three are in agreement" (1 John 5:7 – 8; the "Johannine Comma" is in italics). This, however, is nearly universally understood to be a later addition. It appears in Erasmus's third edition of the NT (commonly known as the Textus Receptus), because a sixteenth-century Greek manuscript, the Codex Montfortianus (Britanicus), included it. This manuscript was produced for the very purpose of getting Erasmus to include it in the text (see Brown, *Epistles*, 776, 780). Most rightly reject it on the grounds that it is impossibly late.

9. There is no scholarly consensus on the exact identification of this sin. For a judicious discussion, see Stott, *Letters of John*, 189 – 93.

the position advocated by Stott, who argues that John here uses the term "brother" in a broad sense referring to another person, not necessarily a fellow Christian (cf. 2:9, 11; 3:16–17), and who identifies the "sin unto death" as "a deliberate, open-eyed rejection of known truth" akin to the "blasphemy against the Holy Spirit" committed by the Pharisees, who ascribed Jesus' miracles, done in the power of the Holy Spirit, to Satan (Matt 12:28 pars.). Other possibilities include a specific ("mortal") sin or apostasy.

Yet John ends on a positive note, affirming that anyone born of God does not continue to sin but is kept safe and cannot be harmed by the evil one (**1 John 5:18**). The position of believers is safe in God's Son Jesus Christ, who is "the true **God and eternal life**" (**5:20**), one of over a dozen or so clear affirmations of Jesus as God in the NT (cf. John 1:1, 18; 5:18; 8:58; 10:30; 20:28; also Matt 1:23; 16:16; 26:63–64; Mark 1:1; 15:39; Rom 9:5; 1 Cor 8:4–6; Phil 2:5–7; Col 2:9; Titus 2:11–13; Heb 1:3, 8; 2 Pet 1:1).[10] Somewhat surprisingly, and rather abruptly, the letter ends without a formal epistolary closing by warning the recipients to "keep [themselves] from idols" (**1 John 5:21**). Perhaps the connection is with the affirmation of the "true God" in the previous verse, so that any worship other than that of the true God (Jesus Christ) is akin to idolatry.

11.2 Second John

11.2.1 Introduction (1–3)

John's second letter is addressed to "the lady chosen by God and to her children, whom I love in the truth" (**2 John 1**), presumably a "mother" and several "daughter" churches.[11] The triple use of the word "**truth**" in the opening greeting (**vv. 1–2**) ominously signals that error is afoot and that John wants these churches to be set apart from it. "The truth, which lives in us and will be with us forever," most likely refers to the indwelling **Holy Spirit**, the "Spirit of truth" (e.g., John 14:17), who, in turn, is a representative of Jesus Christ, who is "the truth" (14:6). **Second John 3**, the opening Christian well-wish, in typically Johannine fashion refers to Jesus as "the Father's Son" and, like verse 1, balances "**truth**" and "**love**."

11.2.2 Warning against Welcoming False Teachers (4–11)

In the main body of this short letter, John develops what it means for these believers to "walk in the truth." This requires **love** for one another (**v. 5**), in keeping with the love commandment (not new, but "from the beginning," v. 5; cf. 1 John 2:7–8), which entails obedience to Jesus' commands (of which the command to "walk in love" is foremost; **2 John 6**). "Walking in the truth" also involves guarding the truth about the Son over against those who have denied that Jesus Christ came in the flesh (**vv. 7–8**; see the discussion of 1 John above).

John urges believers to continue in this teaching and instructs them not to lend hospitality or support to the false (itinerant) teachers (**2 John 9–11**). This, then,

---

10. See Harris, *Jesus as God*.   11. See the discussion in Yarbrough, *1–3 John*, 333–34.

appears to be the primary purpose of this short letter: instructing believers not to take any of the false teachers into their homes or to provide any other support for their ministry.

11.2.3 Conclusion (12–13)

In conclusion, John indicates his hope to visit his readers soon, in keeping with the standard purpose of a letter as a substitute for the writer's presence. He passes on the greeting of "the children of your sister," presumably the members of a "sister" church of the congregations to whom the letter was written.

11.3 Third John

11.3.1 Introduction (1–4)

Unlike John's second letter, his third letter is written not to an entire church but to an individual, his "dear friend" Gaius, whom he likewise "loves in the truth" (**v. 1**; cf. 2 John 1). As was the custom in ancient letters, John wishes Gaius good health in keeping with his spiritual health (**3 John 2**). He also indicates that, apparently, some members from Gaius's church have come to John and brought a report of Gaius's faithfulness to the **truth** (**v. 3**). The reference to John's joy at his "children" walking in the **truth** in **verse 4** may suggest that Gaius is one of John's spiritual children.

11.3.2 Commendation of Gaius and Demetrius, Condemnation of Diotrephes (5–12)

In the body of the letter, John commends Gaius for showing hospitality to those who have gone out for the sake of "the Name" and have received no help from the pagans (**v. 7**), and he encourages him to continue to do so (**v. 8**). In **verse 9**, John mentions a previous letter to a certain Diotrephes, "who loves to be first" and "will have nothing to do with us." John expresses his intention to confront this individual at the occasion of his planned visit (**v. 10**). Not only has Diotrephes slandered John and his associates, he also refused to welcome other believers and even put other church members out of the church who wanted to do so (v. 10).

Similar to 2 John, this letter indicates that the Johannine churches were in some degree of turmoil and required personal visits from the aged apostle, with these short letters serving as a vehicle to "troubleshoot" in the interim. Coming to the end of his brief missive, John encourages Gaius one last time to continue to do what is right, and he issues a commendation of a certain Demetrius, who may have been the carrier of the letter (**vv. 11–12**).

11.3.3 Conclusion (13–14)

The conclusion of the letter closely resembles that of 2 John, announcing a planned visit (**v. 13**) and sending greetings from "the friends here" (**v. 14**).

Part 3

Major Themes in Johannine Theology

A. Prolegomena

Chapter 6

John's Worldview and Use of Scripture

Bibliography

Ashton, John. "Dualism." Pp. 205–37 in *Understanding the Fourth Gospel*. Oxford: Clarendon, 1991. **Barrett, C. K.** "Paradox and Dualism." Pp. 98–115 in *Essays on John*. Philadelphia: Westminster, 1982. **Bauckham, Richard**. "The Qumran Community and the Gospel of John." Pp. 105–15 in *The Dead Sea Scrolls: Fifty Years after Their Discovery*. Ed. Lawrence H. Schiffman, Emmanuel Tov, James C. VanderKam, and Galen Marquis. Jerusalem: Israel Exploration Society, 2000. **Beasley-Murray, George R.** "The Eschatology of the Fourth Gospel." *EvQ* 18 (1946): 97–108. Idem. "John 12,31–32: The Eschatological Significance of the Lifting up of the Son of Man." Pp. 70–81 in *Studien zum Text und zur Ethik des Neuen Testaments: Festschrift zum 80. Geburtstag von Heinrich Greeven*. Berlin/New York: de Gruyter, 1986. **Brunson, Andrew C.** *Psalm 118 in the Gospel of John: An Intertextual Study on the New Exodus Pattern in the Theology of John*. WUNT 158. Tübingen: Mohr-Siebeck, 2003. **Bultmann, Rudolf**. "Johannine Dualism." Pp. 15–21 in *Theology of the New Testament*. Vol. 2. Trans. Kendrick Grobel. New York: Charles Scribner's Sons, 1955. **Carson, D. A**. "John and the Johannine Epistles." Pp. 245–64 in *It Is Written: Scripture Citing Scripture. Essays in Honor of Barnabas Lindars, SSF*. Ed. D. A. Carson and H. G. M. Williamson. Cambridge: Cambridge University Press, 1988. **Charlesworth, James H**. "A Study in Shared Symbolism and Language: The Qumran Community and the Johannine Community." Pp. 97–152 in *The Bible and the Dead Sea Scrolls: The Princeton Symposium on the Dead Sea Scrolls*. Vol. 3: *The Scrolls and Christian Origins*. Waco, TX: Baylor University Press, 2006. **Cook, W. Robert**. "Eschatology in John's Gospel." *CTR* 3 (1988): 79–99. **Daly-Denton, Margaret**. *David in the Fourth Gospel: The Johannine Reception of the Psalms*. AGJU 47. Leiden: Brill, 2004. **Dumbrell, William J**. "Johannine Eschatology." Pp. 235–58 in *The Search for Order: Biblical Eschatology in Focus*. Grand Rapids: Baker, 1994. **Evans, Craig A**. "On the Quotation Formulas in the Fourth Gospel." *BZ* 26 (1982): 79–83. Idem. "Obduracy and the Lord's Servant: Some Observations on the Use of the Old Testament in the Fourth Gospel." Pp. 221–36 in *Early Jewish and Christian Exegesis: Studies in Memory of William Hugh Brownlee*. Ed. Craig A. Evans and William F. Stinespring. Homage 10. Atlanta: Scholars Press, 1987. **France, R. T**. *Jesus and the Old Testament: His Application of Old Testament Passages to Himself and His Mission*. London: Tyndale, 1971. **Freed, Edwin D**. *Old Testament Quotations in the Gospel of John*. NovTSup 11. Leiden: Brill, 1965. **Frey, Jörg**. *Die johanneische Eschatologie*. 3 vols. WUNT 96, 110, 117. Tübingen: Mohr-Siebeck, 1997–2000. **Hamilton, James**. "The Influence of Isaiah on the Gospel of John." *Perichoresis* 5/2 (2007): 139–62. **Harris, W. Hall**. "Polarization in Johannine Theology" and "Eschatology in the Johannine Writings." Pp. 203–12 and 231–42 in *A Biblical Theology of the New Testament*. Ed. Roy B. Zuck. Chicago: Moody Press, 1994. **Klink, Edward W. III**. "Light of the World: Cosmology and the Johannine Literature." Pp. 74–89 in *Cosmology and New Testament Theology*. Ed. Jonathan T. Pennington and Sean M. McDonough. LNTS. London: T&T Clark, 2008. **Köstenberger, Andreas J**. "Jesus the Good Shepherd Who Will Also Bring Other Sheep (John 10:16): The Old Testament Background of a Familiar Metaphor." *BBR* 12 (2002): 67–96. Idem. "John." Pp. 415–512 in *Commentary on the New Testament Use of the Old Testament*. Ed. G. K. Beale and D. A. Carson. Grand Rapids: Baker, 2007. **Ladd, George E**. "The Johannine Dualism." Pp. 259–72 in *A Theology of the New Testament*. Rev. ed. Grand Rapids: Eerdmans, 1993. **Manning, Gary T., Jr**. *Echoes of a Prophet: The Use of Ezekiel in the Gospel of John and in Literature of the Second Temple Period*. JSNTSup 270. London/New York: T&T Clark, 2004. **Menken, Maarten J. J**. *Old Testament Quotations in the Fourth Gospel: Studies in Textual Form*. CBET 15. Kampen: Kok, 1996. **Obermann, Andreas**. *Die christologische Erfüllung der Schrift im Johannesevangelium*. WUNT 2/83. Tübingen: Mohr-Siebeck, 1996. **Reim, Günther**. *Studien zum alttestamentlichen Hintergrund des Johannesevangeliums*. SNTSMS 22. Cambridge: Cambridge University Press, 1974. **Schlatter, Adolf**. *Der Evangelist Johannes: Wie er spricht, glaubt und denkt*. 2nd ed. Stuttgart: Calwer, 1948. **Schuchard, Bruce G**. *Scripture within Scripture: The Interrelationship of Form and Function in the Explicit Old Testament Citations in the Gospel of John*. SBLDS 133. Atlanta: Scholars Press, 1992. **Smith, Robert H**. "Exodus Typology in the Fourth Gospel." *JBL* 81 (1962): 329–42. **Stählin, Gustav**. "Zum Problem der johanneischen Eschatologie." *ZNW* 33 (1934): 225–59. **Thatcher, Tom**. *Greater than Caesar: Christology and Empire in the Fourth Gospel*. Minneapolis: Fortress, 2009. **Young, Franklin W**. "A Study of the Relation of Isaiah to the Fourth Gospel." *ZNW* 46 (1955): 215–33.

12 John's Worldview

12.1. Introduction

12.1.1 Worldview, Cosmology, and the "Johannine Dualism"

In this postmodern age, worldview has been recognized as critical in interpretation.[1] Not only does every interpreter approach a given document with a set of presuppositions, every document itself reflects a worldview that underlies its message. For this reason it is important, as a prolegomenon to the exploration of major Johannine theological themes below, to discuss the Johannine "way of seeing things" (John's *Weltanschauung*). This topic has variously been called John's "cosmology" (his view of the world) or, more specifically, his "dualism" (a way of looking at the world in terms of polar opposites).[2]

In the previous century, discussions of John's "dualism" were typically controlled by a history-of-religions paradigm, which primarily studied Christianity in relation to the beliefs held by other contemporary religious systems.[3] It was frequently argued that John's "dualism" reflected the thought world of Gnosticism, which, in turn, was rooted in Greek philosophical and religious thought such as that of Plato, Plutarch, or Philo.[4] This outlook distinguished between the visible, material world, of which the human body was a part, and the invisible, immaterial sphere of existence (including the human soul), and held that the former was inferior to the latter.

Subsequent to the discovery of the Qumran documents, many have explored possible affinities between the thought worlds represented by the Dead Sea community and John's gospel.[5] In the Qumran documents, mention is made of two spirits, the "spirit of truth" and the "spirit of error," warring against each another (1QS 3:13–4:26). Both of these spirits were created by God. A cosmic battle is raging between the "children of light," who are devoted to keeping the law as interpreted by the Teacher of Righteousness, and the "children of darkness," who have corrupted proper observance of the law (1QM).

As the following discussion will show, however, while surface similarities exist,[6] any Johannine "dualism" (or, perhaps better, pairs of contrasts) differs sharply from

---

1. See, e.g., D. A. Carson, *The Gagging of God: Christianity Confronts Pluralism* (Grand Rapids: Zondervan, 1996).

2. See, e.g., C. K. Barrett, "Paradox and Dualism," in *Essays on John* (Philadelphia: Westminster, 1982), 98–115; though if "dualism" is defined as "the doctrine that there are two independent principles, one good and the other evil" (ibid., 100, with reference to the *Oxford English Dictionary*), John's thought is hardly dualistic. For a suggestive treatment of the implications of Johannine dualism for today, see Miroslav Volf, "Johannine Dualism and Contemporary Pluralism," *ModTheol* 21 (2005): 189–217.

3. See the still helpful survey of older scholarly literature on this subject by George E. Ladd, "The Johannine Dualism," in *A Theology of the New Testament* (rev. ed.; Grand Rapids: Eerdmans, 1993), 259–73, esp. his discussion of John's eschatological dualism in comparison with Greek and Qumran dualism on pp. 265–72.

4. See the classic treatment by Bultmann, *Theology of the New Testament*, 2:15–21, who contends that "John's concepts, light and darkness, truth and falsehood, freedom and bondage, life and death, come from Gnostic dualism" (p. 17; emphasis added) and that "the cosmological dualism of Gnosticism has become in John a *dualism of decision*" (p. 21; emphasis original; see also the following section, "Johannine Determinism," on pp. 21–26). But see George E. Ladd, *The Pattern of New Testament Truth* (Grand Rapids: Eerdmans, 1968), 13–31.

5. See James H. Charlesworth, ed., *John and the Dead Sea Scrolls* (Christian Origins Library; New York: Crossroad, 1990), esp. the essay by Charlesworth, "A Critical Comparison of the Dualism in 1QS 3:13–4:26 and the 'Dualism' Contained in the Gospel of John," 76–106.

6. For example, both the DSS and John's Gospel use "light and darkness" imagery with a moral, ethical connotation (see, e.g., 1QM, *passim*; John 3:19–21). On John's ethic, see chap. 13 below.

alleged Greek or Qumran parallels.[7] To begin with, as will be seen below, John's "dualism" is not merely vertical (distinguishing between the world "above" and the world "below") but also horizontal in nature (oriented toward salvation history and eschatologically focused on God's decisive intervention in human history in the person of Jesus Christ).[8] John speaks of the preexistent, divine Word being made "flesh" in Jesus (John 1:14), and Jesus' humanity is affirmed alongside his deity.[9] God and Satan are not cast as polar opposites, and Jesus' victory is never in doubt (1:5; 16:33).

More recently, John's series of contrasts has been subjected to sociological investigation, and many have argued that his outlook is sectarian.[10] John's language juxtaposing "light" and "darkness," "truth" and "falsehood," and other stark alternatives was judged to reflect an "us against them" mentality on the part of a "Johannine community" that defined itself against the world around it and loved its own members while hating those outside.[11] However, this understanding is rendered untenable by the improper application of social science models;[12] by the fact that alleged Qumran parallels are more formal than substantive and most likely reflect differing appropriations of creation language;[13] and by the pronounced emphasis on God's love for the world and John's trinitarian mission theology.[14]

Miroslav Volf, in particular, has provided a penetrating critique of the argument that John's gospel reflects a sectarian outlook.[15] While rightly noting that the classification of any document as "sectarian" is to a significant extent a matter of definition, Volf shows that John's positing of what Volf calls "oppositional dualities" has the primary intended effect of not only "affirming the positive pole of these dualities" but also of "negating the negative."[16] Volf shows, first, that a sectarian reading of John and his attitude toward outsiders (the "world") engages in a selective reading of the evidence, unduly ignoring references to God's love for the world

---

7. For this reason, it may be best to avoid the term "dualism" when applied to John's cosmology altogether. Arguably, while John uses a series of contrasts, he does not share the bipolar outlook of Greek philosophy or the Qumran sectarians.

8. So rightly Brown, *Gospel according to John I–XII*, cxvi, followed by Ladd, *Theology of the New Testament*, 268–72. See also Oscar Cullmann, *Salvation in History* (New York: Harper & Row, 1967), 268–91; the helpful discussion in Ladd, ibid., 266–68; and the discussion in chap. 10 below.

9. Thus Jesus is tired and thirsty at the well (John 4:6–7), weeps at Lazarus's tomb (11:35), and dies a genuine human death (19:34–35). See Thompson, *Humanity of Jesus*; Morris, *Jesus Is the Christ*, chap. 3: "Jesus the Man"; contra, Ernst Käsemann, *The Testament of Jesus: A Study of the Gospel of John in the Light of chap. 17* (trans. Gerhard Krodel; Philadelphia: Fortress, 1968).

10. See, e.g., Rensberger, *Overcoming the World*; Meeks, "Man from Heaven"; and Robert H. Gundry, *Jesus the Word according to John the Sectarian: A Paleofundamentalist Manifesto for Contemporary Evangelicalism, Especially Its Elites, in North America* (Grand Rapids: Eerdmans, 2001). But see the critiques in Köstenberger, *Missions of Jesus and the Disciples*, 202–5; Rudolf Schnackenburg, "Der Missionsgedanke des Johannesevangeliums im heutigen Horizont," in *Das Johannesevangelium*, Vol. 4: *Ergänzende Auslegungen und Exkurse* (HTKNT; Freiburg im Breisgau: Herder, 1984), 58–72; and Volf, "Johannine Dualism," 203–9.

11. See Bruce J. Malina and Richard L. Rohrbaugh, *Social-Science Commentary on the Gospel of John* (Minneapolis: Fortress, 1998); see, e.g., "John's Language as Antilanguage" on pp. 7–9.

12. See my review of Malina and Rohrbaugh's work in *JETS* 43 (2000): 144–45.

13. See Richard Bauckham, "The Qumran Community and the Gospel of John," in *The Dead Sea Scrolls: Fifty Years after Their Discovery* (ed. Lawrence H. Schiffman, Emmanuel Tov, James C. VanderKam, and Galen Marquis. Jerusalem: Israel Exploration Society, 2000), 105–15.

14. See chap. 15 below.

15. Volf, "Johannine Dualism," 203–9; Volf's entire study is well worth reading.

16. Ibid., 209.

(John 3:16), to Jesus' giving his life for the world (1:29; 6:51), and to Jesus' and his followers' mission *to* the world (17:18; 20:21).[17]

Second, such a reading also insufficiently appreciates the fact that God is not only the Creator but also the Redeemer of creation. This means that it is precisely the aim of God's redemptive activity to overcome "oppositional dualities"—whether darkness and light, below and above, falsehood and truth—through the incarnation of the Word (John 1:14) and the sacrifice of the Lamb of God (1:29). As a result, oppositional dualities are, at least in part, transformed into nonoppositional ones, and duality between God and the world is transformed into fellowship between Jesus and his disciples. This, in turn, sets the stage for the final consummation of human history at which the kingdom of the world will have become the kingdom of God and of his Messiah (Rev 12:10).

In the end, therefore, as Volf perceptively points out, the exact opposite dynamic of duality is shown to be powerfully at work in John's gospel, and dual opposites presuppose reconciliation on a deeper level:

> An increase in tension is exactly what we should expect, especially if redemption is to happen through the *death* of the Lamb. The apparent obliteration of good by evil is the way in which evil is overcome by the enactment of divine goodness. The very opposite of dualism is at work here. God, who is love, loves the estranged world to the point of assuming flesh in order to suffer death at the hands of the world. In this way God not only opens the road for the world's return but attracts it back. God loves first and enacts this love on the cross so that human beings may love God and God's creatures in return (cf. 1 John 3:8–10).[18]

With these broad, programmatic considerations, the ground is prepared for a closer investigation of the Johannine material.

12.1.2 The Johannine Worldview: Overview

On the most basic level, John's outlook is controlled, first, by the characteristic Jewish belief in one God, Yahweh, the God who created the world, delivered Israel from bondage in Egypt, and gave the nation the law through Moses at Sinai. Second, John believes that the Messiah predicted in the OT Scriptures was made flesh, walked the earth, and died vicariously on the cross in the person of Jesus Christ. To show this connection between the Creator God and the equally divine Messiah and Son of God-made-flesh-in-Jesus, John wrote his gospel (John 1:1, 14; 10:30; 20:30–31) because he believed that God's glory was revealed both in Jesus' signs and in his death on the cross (1:14; 2:11; 12:23, 28; 13:31–32).

John also believes in the possibility, even reality, of the supernatural—God and Jesus Christ—expressing itself in both word and deed. Consequently, he presents

---

17. Contra, Wayne A. Meeks, "The Ethics of the Fourth Evangelist," in *Exploring the Gospel of John*, 323.

18. Volf, "Johannine Dualism," 193.

Jesus' body of teachings—in form of extended revelatory discourses—and a selection of Jesus' most startling messianic manifestations—his "works," and in particular his "signs." It is John's belief that salvation is found in no one else but Jesus, who alone is the way to the Father (John 14:6), and this salvation is gained by believing that Jesus is the Messiah and Son of God (3:16; 20:31). In this way people become children of God (1:12), receive eternal life (3:16), and pass from death to life (5:24).

John also believes in universal human sinfulness (John 3:9–12; 8:34–47). He believes that Satan is "the prince of this world" (12:31; 14:30; 16:11) and that the world is in moral and spiritual darkness, from which people can escape only by coming to Jesus as "the light" (1:4–5, 7–9; 3:19–21; 8:12; 9:5; 11:9–10; 12:35–36, 46) and by becoming "children of light" (12:36). In John's worldview, there is ultimately no middle ground between the striking contrasts of light vs. darkness, life vs. death, truth vs. falsehood, love vs. hate, and trust vs. unbelief.[19] Jesus came at the climax of salvation history, eclipsing the law, being greater than all the previous servants and spokesmen of God in OT times such as Abraham (8:56, 58), Jacob (4:12), and Moses (1:17; 5:45–47). Hence John calls his readers to choose between life and death.

This, in turn, is because John also believes that God is a God of judgment and that this judgment will be executed in and through his Son, Jesus Christ (John 5:22–27, 30). John believes that Jesus, the crucified, buried, and risen one, will one day come again to bring about God's final judgment of unbelievers (5:28–29). In this way John identifies God, the Life-Giver and Judge of humankind, with Jesus as one in character and purpose (5:26; 10:30). John also believes that believers now have the privilege and responsibility to maintain spiritual union with the exalted Christ through the Spirit, who has come subsequent to Jesus' exaltation as "another [helping presence]" (14:16).

Yet John's is not an absolute dualism in which immovable boundaries are set between those who are in the light and those who live in darkness.[20] To the contrary, John's gospel is pervaded by a strong missionary thrust, driven by a desire to convey the expression of God's redeeming love in the person and work of Jesus Christ to a sinful humanity.[21] Rather than retreat into communal life, believers are therefore summoned to "go and bear fruit" (John 15:16; cf. 15:8), proclaiming the forgiveness of sins and the availability of eternal life for all who believe in God's Son (20:21–23). It remains to develop these components of the Johannine worldview in greater detail in the following discussion.[22]

---

19. This gulf can and has been bridged through Jesus, the "light" shining in the darkness (1:5; 8:12; 9:5); those who trust in him cross over from death into life (5:24; see also the following footnote).

20. Barrett, "Paradox and Dualism," 108, speaks of a dualism that is "not static but in motion" (see also p. 106). He discusses the conceptual pairs light and darkness; life and death; and above and below. See also Volf, "Johannine Dualism," 193, who states, "Even if John is not ultimately dualistic, he makes some of the most rigid oppositional dualities of any new Testament writer."

21. See Köstenberger, *Missions of Jesus and the Disciples*; and the discussion in chap. 15 below.

22. The purpose of the following sections is merely to sketch the broad contours of the Johannine worldview. Many of these aspects will be discussed in greater details later on in the present volume. For a more detailed investigation, see the helpful study by Edward W. Klink III, "Light of the World: Cosmology and the Johannine Literature," in *Cosmology and New Testament Theology* (ed. Jonathan T. Pennington and Sean M. McDonough; London: T&T Clark, 2008), 74–89, to which some of the following material is indebted.

12.2 The Cosmic Conflict between God and His Messiah vs. Satan and the World

12.2.1 Satan

The cosmic conflict between the world of light and the world of darkness is, first and foremost, a struggle between God and his Messiah on the one hand and Satan on the other.[23] In order to focus his readers' eye even more keenly on this titanic spiritual clash, John has eliminated virtually all references to demons (Jesus' opponents' charge that he is demon-possessed is no real exception; cf. John 7:20; 8:48–49, 52; 10:20–21), centering the evil supernatural on Satan (13:27), also called "the devil" (8:44; 13:2; cf. 6:70; 1 John 3:8, 10) or "the prince of this world" (John 12:31; 14:30; 16:11).

In John's gospel, Satan is said to enter Judas the betrayer at the Last Supper (John 13:27; cf. 13:2; 6:70), providing the impetus behind the inexorable movement toward Jesus' crucifixion. In 1 John, Jesus is said to have come into this world "to destroy the devil's works" (1 John 3:8; dubbed the *Christus Victor* motif). In both John's gospel and 1 John, Satan is shown to be at the root of all sin, hatred, and murder, and is the true spiritual father of those who reject Jesus as the Messiah (John 8:31–47; 1 John 3:8–15), deny their sinfulness (1 John 1:8, 10), and have no room for his atoning sacrifice (2:2; 4:10).

In John's gospel, Jesus proclaims prior to the crucifixion that he has "overcome the world" (John 16:33) and that "the prince of this world now stands condemned" (16:11). In 1 John 5:18, it is affirmed that "the evil one" cannot harm those who have been born of God, in keeping with John's teaching on Christian assurance (cf. John 10:27–30).[24] While still in control of the world, the domain of darkness (1 John 5:19), and the spiritual father of the unregenerate (e.g., 3:12), the devil is a defeated foe whose eventual doom is sure (see Rev 20:7–10). The victory belongs to Christ and his followers (1 John 5:4–5).[25]

12.2.2 The World

The word *kosmos* ("world") occurs 102 times in the Johannine corpus.[26] Seventy-eight references are found in John's gospel, compared to fourteen references in all the Synoptics combined. This underscores impressively the controlling nature of the Johannine worldview that has stamped its imprint indelibly onto its presentation of Jesus in the gospel. The term, then, in John as elsewhere in Greek writings, means first and foremost the physical, created universe, as in John 17:5, where Jesus speaks of the glory he had in God's presence "before the world began." Likewise, "the world" that could not contain the books that would need to be written if everything Jesus had said and done were recorded (21:25) is the physical universe.

---

23. See Wendy E. Sproston, "Satan in the Fourth Gospel," in *Studia Biblica 1978* (Sheffield: JSOT, 1980), 2:307–11.
24. See chap. 12, sec. 28.5 below.
25. See the discussion in Yarbrough, *1–3 John*, 275–76.
26. For an inventory of the occurrences of *kosmos* in John's gospel, see Ned H. Cassem, "A Grammatical and Contextual Inventory of the Use of *kosmos* in the Johannine Cosmic Theology," *NTS* 19 (1972): 81–91 (but see the critique in Köstenberger, *Missions of Jesus and the Disciples*, 187, n. 168). See also Stanley B. Marrow, "Κόσμος in John," *CBQ* 64 (2002): 90–102.

In addition, *kosmos* in John can also refer to humanity as the primary inhabitants of the physical universe (cf. Gen 1:26). Both uses of *kosmos* discussed thus far can be found in John 1:10, where John writes, "He was in the world [i.e., he entered the physical universe], and though the world was made through him [referring to the creation of the physical universe], the world [people, its inhabitants] did not recognize him." That the force of the third instance of *kosmos* is personal is clearly indicated by the term "recognize" in 1:10 and the parallel expressions "receive" and "believe" in 1:11 and 12.

Third, while *kosmos* may refer simply to humanity as the inhabitants of the created physical universe, the expression may in context be used with a negative connotation as referring to *sinful* humanity. As the evangelist writes, "This is the verdict: Light has come into the world, but people loved darkness instead of light because their deeds were evil" (John 3:19). Yet "God so loved the world that he gave his one and only Son, that whoever believes in him shall not perish but have eternal life. For God did not send his Son into the world to condemn the world, but to save the world through him" (3:16–17). In this context, God's love and salvation are extended to a sinful humanity subsisting in rebellion and moral darkness.

As already noted, many proponents of the "Johannine community hypothesis" have taken John's contrasts between light and darkness, life and death, and so on, to imply that the gospel reflects a sectarian outlook.[27] Yet this overlooks or unduly neglects the gospel's pronounced mission thrust. Unlike the prevailing worldview reflected in the Qumran documents, the "children of light" in John's gospel are not called to make eschatological war against the "children of darkness" (i.e., unbelievers); rather, they are "sent into the world" as messengers of God's love (John 17:18; cf. 20:21).[28] Hence, while John teaches election and predestination,[29] he does not posit determinism.

12.3 Major Contrasts in John's Worldview
12.3.1 Introduction

Within the overall framework of his depiction of the cosmic battle that rages between God and his Messiah vs. Satan and the world, John features a series of contrasts, distinguishing between light and darkness, life and death, spirit and flesh, the realms above and below, truth and falsehood, love and hate, and trust and unbelief.[30] As C. K. Barrett noted, these contrasts are not fixed or static in a deterministic sense but are rather "in motion," that is, overcome by Jesus and his victory and resurrection, by the new birth, descent–ascent, witness, and election. This is illustrated by the following survey chart:

---

27. E.g., Meeks, "Man from Heaven"; Rensberger, *Johannine Faith and Liberating Community*; Onuki, *Gemeinde und Welt*. See the overview in Köstenberger, *Missions of Jesus and the Disciples*, 203–6.

28. See further the discussion of John's mission theology in chap. 15 below.

29. See chap. 12, sec. 26.

30. See the similar survey of some of these contrasts by W. Hall Harris, "Polarization in Johannine Theology," in *A Biblical Theology of the New Testament* (ed. Roy B. Zuck; Chicago: Moody Press, 1994), 203–12, who discusses light and darkness; above and below; flesh and spirit; belief and unbelief; and love and hate. For an exploration of the Johannine love ethic, see chap. 13 below.

	Light	Life	Spirit	Above	Truth	Believe
Upper level						
Major motif	Victory	Resurrection	New birth	Descent-ascent	Witness	Election
Lower level	Darkness	Death	Flesh	Below	Falsehood	Unbelief

Fig. 12.1: Series of Johannine Contrasts and Associated Motifs

12.3.2 Light and Darkness

Both John's gospel and his first letter open with declarations regarding light and darkness.[31] John 1:5 states that "the light shines in the darkness, and [or: but, adversative *kai*] the darkness has not overcome it," while 1 John 1:5 declares that "this is the message we have heard from him and declare to you: God is light; in him there is no darkness at all." Ultimately, the language of darkness and light is clearly rooted in the biblical creation account, where God is said to have brought forth "light" as his first creative act (Gen 1:3–5). Later, God placed lights in the sky to separate light from darkness (1:14). Light, in turn, made it possible for life to exist, which was created on the fifth and sixth days of creation.

Beyond its literal use, "light" and "darkness" had figurative, moral connotations long before John wrote (see, e.g., Job 30:26).[32] In the Qumran literature, "light" and "darkness" were depicted as two forces locked in a struggle that will culminate in the eschatological war of the "children of light" against the "children of darkness" (1QM).[33] Without the same determinism, John shares with Qumran the terminology "children of light" (John 12:36). People are called not to "walk in darkness" but to come out of "darkness" by putting their trust in the light and to "walk in the light" as he is in the light (8:12; 12:35–36; 1 John 1:6–7).

Even more pronounced than in the contrast between what is "from above" and what is "from below," therefore, the juxtaposition of the polar opposites "light" and "darkness" conveys the notion of a cosmic spiritual conflict between God and Satan. Jesus, "the light," has invaded the moral darkness of the world. Neutrality is impossible; people remain in darkness and sin unless they put their trust in "the light" and thus are rescued from the domain of darkness, epitomized by Satan, the "prince of

---

31. On "light and darkness" terminology, see further the discussion of light symbolism in chap. 3, sec. 7.5.3, and of new creation theology in chap. 8, sec. 16.3 below. For a thorough treatment, see Keener, *John*, 381–87.

32. See, e.g., Elizabeth Achtemeier, "Jesus Christ, the Light of the World: The Biblical Understanding of Light and Darkness," *Int* 17 (1963): 439–49.

33. See David E. Aune, "Dualism in the Fourth Gospel and the Dead Sea Scrolls: A Reassessment of the Problem," in *Neotestamentica et Philonica: Studies in Honor of Peder Borgen* (ed. David E. Aune, Torrey Seland, and Jarl Henning Ulrichsen; NovTSup 106; Leiden: Brill, 2003), 281–303. See also James H. Charlesworth, "A Study in Shared Symbolism and Language: The Qumran Community and the Johannine Community," in *The Bible and the Dead Sea Scrolls: The Princeton Symposium on the Dead Sea Scrolls*, Vol. 3: *The Scrolls and Christian Origins* (Waco, TX: Baylor University Press, 2006), 97–152, who stresses the shared symbolism and terminology; and Bauckham, "Qumran Community and the Gospel of John," who argues for discontinuity.

this world." When Judas slipped out of the Upper Room in order to betray Jesus, "it was night" (John 13:30). This ominously foreshadowed his demise.[34]

12.3.3 Life and Death

The polarity between life and death is central to human — indeed, creaturely — existence.[35] It is one of the major great topics John addresses in his gospel. The question of life after death has occupied all the major religions and many of the world's great thinkers, past and present. The hope of bodily resurrection gradually emerges in the OT (see esp. Dan 12:2; cf. John 5:28–29) and comes to full expression in the NT in the teaching of Jesus and Paul. Greeks believed in the immortality of the soul but not in the resurrection of the body.[36] By relating Jesus to the fundamental existential question of life and death, John presents him as the answer to one of humanity's greatest problems and mysteries: the inevitability of death and the question of what will happen subsequent to the moment when a person dies. He also strikes an important salvation-historical note, as life and death are presented in God's dealings with OT Israel as the consequences of obedience or disobedience to the covenant (e.g., Deut 30:19).[37]

The core message of John's gospel regarding life is sounded at the outset in the introduction: "In him [i.e., in Jesus, the Word, through whom all things were made] was life" (John 1:4). Similarly, John opens his first letter with a reference to "the Word of life" (1 John 1:1). Jesus even affirms that "as the Father has life in himself, so he has granted the Son also to have life in himself" (John 5:26). Thus God is life, and as the life is the Life-Giver. Yet human sin has broken fellowship with God,[38] and thus Jesus came to restore this relationship and to open the way for renewed, unbroken union with God (10:10: "life ... to the full"). Consequently, John states as his purpose that his readers "may believe that Jesus is the Messiah, the Son of God, and that by believing [they] may have life in his name" (20:31). Throughout his public ministry, Jesus sought to demonstrate that he is the resurrection and the life (11:25; 14:6), seeking to lead people to put their trust in him.

This bright realm of life in Jesus is contrasted by John with the dark sphere of death and sin. John's depiction of the incompatibility of life and death, of light and darkness (a closely related set of contrasts; John 1:4–5; 1 John 1:5–7; 2:8–10), is utterly compelling. Yet, again, it should be noted that the "dualism" is modified rather than absolute: light calls out to darkness, "Embrace me!" and life woos death to "choose life." While life and death are distinct, in this life a vital choice has to be made. In fact, the Jewish leaders, Pilate, and even Judas serve as warning examples for John's readers of what happens to those who make the wrong choice, rejecting

---

34. See Köstenberger, *John*, 418.

35. See Barrett, "Paradox and Dualism," 107–8. See also the discussion of "life" in the context of John's new creation theology in chap. 8 below.

36. See Paul's presentation in 1 Corinthians 15.

37. See U. E. Simon, "Eternal Life in the Fourth Gospel," in *Studies in the Fourth Gospel* (ed. F. L. Cross; London: Mowbray, 1957), 98.

38. See the related "light/darkness" imagery in 1 John, which serves to underscore the stark contrast between living in fellowship with God and others and living in sin.

the light, in order that they might make a better, the right, choice of coming to the light and placing their faith in Jesus the Messiah and Son of God (John 20:31).

In John's eschatology, this possession of life is already a present reality.[39] "The life appeared" (1 John 1:2), "and the true light is already shining" (2:8). By believing in Jesus, people can have life—abundant life—already in the here and now (John 3:16; 10:10), having passed from death into life (5:24; 1 John 3:14). At the same time, John does not emphasize the realization of believers' hope to the extent that he denies the future consummation of this hope. To the contrary, he retains the notion that Jesus will raise the dead and give them life on the last day (John 5:28–29), which places the Johannine Jesus firmly within the realm of first-century Jewish expectation.[40] Nevertheless, as the Messiah and Son of God, Jesus emphatically shows that, in him, resurrection and life have already appeared. This is made clear by the climactic "sign" in John's gospel depicting the raising of Lazarus, emblematic of the coming of life and resurrection in the person of Jesus Christ (11:1–44).

It goes almost without saying that, in John's worldview, life transcends mere physical life and extends to spiritual, eternal life.[41] In fact, "life" and "eternal life" are used interchangeably in John's writings.[42] John's profound, penetrating thought is revealed in the fact that he substitutes the pervasive Synoptic motif of the "kingdom of God" with his emphasis on "eternal life." While ubiquitous in the Synoptics, "kingdom" occurs in John only in Jesus' interchanges with Nicodemus (John 3:3, 5) and Pilate (18:36), in the latter case affirming what Jesus' kingdom is *not*. The primary reason for this substitution may be that "kingdom" is a concept rooted in the realm of this world, harking back to kings in Israel's history, including David and Solomon, while "life" is a transcendent, universal category for all humanity, not merely Israel.[43]

What is more, the notion of Jesus' kingship is precarious in John's gospel. When Nathanael declares Jesus to be "the king of Israel" (1:49), Jesus seems ambivalent in his response. Later on, at the triumphal entry, the crowd's response has nationalistic overtones and classifies as a Johannine misunderstanding (12:13–15). Also, when the crowds come and want to make Jesus king after the feeding of the multitudes, Jesus withdraws (6:14). Pilate's repeated reference to Jesus as "king of the Jews" is pejorative as well, and Jesus maintains that any such kingship is not political in nature (18:36). Finally, the Jewish high priest expresses concern that the Romans

---

39. See the discussion in sec. 12.5 below.
40. Cf. Simon, "Eternal Life," 101.
41. See Floyd V. Filson, "The Gospel of Life: A Study of the Gospel of John," in *Current Issues in New Testament Interpretation: Essays in Honor of Otto A. Piper* (ed. William Klassen and Graydon F. Snyder; New York: Harper & Brothers, 1962), 112–13, who calls John's gospel "the Gospel of Life" and who notes that it is the term *psychē* that in John denotes physical life terminated by death (John 10:11; 12:25; 15:13; 3 John 2; so also Keener, *John*, 328).
42. See Keener, *John*, 328: "Even when not conjoined with 'eternal,' the term designates eternal life" (with one possible exception, John 4:50–51).

43. Keener (ibid.) notes that Leonhard Goppelt, *Theology of the New Testament* (trans. John E. Alsup; ed. Jürgen Roloff; 2 vols.; Grand Rapids: Eerdmans, 1981–1982), 1:45, suggested that "kingdom," as a primarily Palestinian Jewish concept, was largely unintelligible to the ears of John's Hellenistic readers, so that John chose to substitute a less frequent term from the Jesus tradition, "life." Yet Keener rightly observes that, perhaps decisively, the term "kingdom" had major political ramifications (cf. 18:36–38), which would have been particularly precarious in the context of an end-of-first-century Roman context (cf. the book of Revelation).

would take away the Jews' "place" and "nation" (11:51–52). Thomas's confession of Jesus as "my Lord and my God" (20:28) was highly countercultural at the time of writing of John's gospel, as becomes clear especially when reading the Apocalypse.

One other fruitful avenue for exploring John's substitution of "eternal life" for "kingdom of God" terminology may be bound up with the difference in historical setting between John and the Synoptics. The question arises: What happened historically between the AD 60s (the likely date of composition for the Synoptics) and the AD 80s (the probably date of composition for John's gospel) that may account for such a shift in perspective and presentation? One possible answer is the Jewish War in AD 66–73 and the destruction of the temple in AD 70 as well as increasing Roman persecution of Christians in the years following the Jewish War. By virtually omitting reference to the kingdom of God, and by qualifying Jesus' kingship as nonpolitical, John may forestall any misinterpretation of the Christian teaching on God's reign among his people.

Also, speaking about the kingdom of God may have run counter to John's realized eschatology, focusing not on a future restored kingdom for Israel (including Jesus' millennial reign) but on the way in which Jesus' first coming already introduced eternal benefits in the lives of those who put their trust in him. Thus, there may have been both theological reasons (such as realized eschatology, accentuating the universal scope of salvation in Jesus in keeping with the Gentile mission) and historical reasons (the Jewish War and the destruction of the temple) that combine to account for John's bypassing of "kingdom of God" in favor of "eternal life" terminology.[44]

The following chart illustrates the substitution of "life" for "kingdom" in John's writings:

NT Book	Instances of "Life"	Instances of "Kingdom"
Matthew	7	55
Mark	4	20
Luke	5	46
John	36	5
1–3 John	13	0
Revelation	23	9
Synoptic totals	16	121
Johannine totals	72	14

Fig. 12.2: "Life" and "Kingdom" in the Synoptics and in the Johannine Writings

---

44. Thanks are due the students in my Biblical Theology seminar at Southeastern Seminary in the Spring 2009 for sparking a helpful discussion on this subject. For a suggestive recent treatment on this topic see Tom Thatcher, *Greater than Caesar: Christology and Empire in the Fourth Gospel* (Minneapolis: Fortress, 2009), who argues that John was concerned to show that Jesus was greater than Roman imperial power and that Jesus' mission and the church's faith signified its end (though this reference should not be taken as an endorsement of the larger thesis underlying Thatcher's work).

The Word, in whom was life, was "in the beginning," before the world was made. It came into the world "from above" and thus transcends time and history. As one author explains:

> The Gospel portrays the intervention of God into human history, an event that can bring real life. It is in this way that the concept of "life" in John's gospel bears an innate narratival sense. Life in John is a living event, not an abstract concept. It is real and relational—rooted in the communion of God and humans. It is rooted in eternity; it is rooted in the one who is called "the Way, the Truth and the Life" (14:6).[45]

At the root, therefore, John's message is that in human history, life appeared in Jesus, and this life is mediated solely and exclusively in and through him.[46] Human history culminates in the realization of John's eschatological vision at Christ's return: "But we know that when Christ appears, we shall be like him, for we shall see him as he is" (1 John 3:2).

12.3.4 Flesh and Spirit

The contrast between flesh and spirit in John is yet another set of opposites conveying John's distinctive worldview. A representative passage is John 3:6: "What is born of flesh is flesh, and what is born of spirit is spirit." In this way Jesus contrasted physical birth with spiritual birth "from above" (3:3; cf. 1:12–13). Elsewhere, Jesus declared that "God is spirit, and his worshipers must worship in spirit and truth" (4:24). In 6:63, Jesus is represented as saying, "The Spirit gives life; the flesh counts for nothing. The words I have spoken to you are spirit and are life."[47]

Similar to the uses of *kosmos* as denoting the physical universe, the contrast is at the root neutral rather than negative. Unlike in Pauline usage, "flesh" does not convey the notion of sinfulness but merely of finite humanity. God is spirit, and humanity is flesh. This sets the stage for God the Word to be made flesh in the Lord Jesus Christ, uniting divinity and humanity in one person (John 1:14). He is "the man" (19:5), but he is also God (1:1, 18; 20:28), the "I am," the Son of God and Son of Man. Humanity, by contrast, is lifted up to the realm of spirit by being spiritually reborn, both individually (1:12–13; 3:3, 5) and corporately (20:22).

12.3.5 Above and Below

Perhaps the Johannine "dualism" of "above" and "below" is best encapsulated by the statement in John 3:31: "The one who comes from above is above all; the one who is from the earth belongs to the earth, and speaks as one from the earth. The one who comes from heaven is above all."[48] In this way John the Baptist, the witness to Jesus who "is from the earth" and "belongs to the earth," describes Jesus as "the one who

---

45. Klink, "Light of the World."
46. Conversely, this implies that all other promises of life apart from Jesus are false and vain.
47. The translations in this paragraph are my own.
48. See Barrett, "Paradox and Dualism," 108.

comes from above" in parallelism to calling him "the one who comes from heaven." This kind of thinking presents Jesus as the mysterious, divine-human Danielic figure of the Son of Man who came as the ultimate revelation of God (1:51; 3:13–14).[49]

Another relevant passage is John 8:23, where Jesus is represented as saying, "You are from below; I am from above. You are of this world; I am not of this world." In this way Jesus contrasts his heavenly origin with his interrogators' earthly provenance. This contrasts Jesus as the preexistent, divine Word-made-flesh with those who are finite human creatures. While appearances suggested that both Jesus and his opponents were equally human (7:27; cf. 19:5), appearances were deceiving in this case. For Jesus' origins in fact derive from another world. Thus, John contends, people must believe that Jesus is God (see 1:1, 18; 9:38; 20:28).

12.3.6 Truth and Falsehood

In John's view of the world, truth is attached to God, while falsehood is rooted in the nature of the devil. Again, there is no middle ground, and the lines of demarcation are clearly drawn. Humanity, for its part, must choose to align itself with the realm of truth by believing in Jesus as the Son of God. Otherwise, people remain in the realm of darkness (John 3:19–21), in God's wrath (3:36), and under the dominion of the devil (1 John 5:19; cf. 2:15–17).

John attributes the characteristic of truth to each of the three persons of the Godhead. God the Father is "the only true God" (John 17:3); Jesus is truth incarnate (1:17; 14:6); and the Holy Spirit is the "Spirit of truth" (14:17; 15:26; 16:13). This makes God the source of truth, Jesus the embodiment, revelation, and messenger of truth, and the Holy Spirit the one who conveys and spreads the truth about Jesus to the unbelieving world in and through believers (15:26–27; 16:8–11).

What is more, in John's gospel truth is connected to witness, because those who have the truth must witness to it.[50] This is true of John the Baptist (John 1:6–8, 15) and of a whole series of witnesses, including John the evangelist himself (21:20–25). In John's cosmic scheme, just as the light has entered the darkness in Jesus, so truth, in Jesus, has invaded the realm of falsehood, the domain controlled by the ruler of the world, the devil.

Jesus came to bring true revelation of God, a revelation resisted by the devil, who inspired Judas to betray Jesus (John 13:2, 27) and incited the Jewish leaders to have him crucified. In the dispute concerning Jesus' and the Jews' true paternity, Jesus proves that the latter ultimately do Satan's bidding. Shockingly, God's chosen people turned out to be children of the devil (8:42–47). This is apparent because they did not believe the truth that would set them free (8:31–32).

On a grand scale, therefore, John stages a trial of truly cosmic proportions, subverting the outcome of the Jewish and Roman trials of Jesus that issued in his crucifixion. This serves the purpose of vindicating Jesus and of putting the world

---

49. See the discussions of the Johannine Son of Man and the descent-ascent motif in chap. 14, sec. 31 below. See also Barrett, "Paradox and Dualism," 106–7.

50. See the discussion of truth and witness in chap. 11 below.

(including the Jews) on trial for crucifying Jesus.[51] The truth, according to John, is that the world, in its sinfulness, sought to shut out the light, preferring to continue to live in darkness. Yet in the end, truth will prevail (Revelation).

12.3.7 Love and Hate

Since love will be the subject of an entire chapter dealing with the Johannine ethic (chap. 13 below), the treatment here will be comparatively brief and be limited to a brief study of the contrast between love and hate as part of John's characteristic presentation of his theology in the form of dual opposites.[52] The first Johannine reference contrasting "love" and "hate" is found in John 3:19–21, where the sinful people in the world are said to "love darkness" and "hate the light." This involves profound paradox, because normally people would love light and hate darkness. John thus shows that sin is irrational, even absurd, and an aberration from humanity's original condition.[53]

This also roots the world's rejection of the Creator and Messiah (cf. John 1:10–11; 7:7) in its sinful condition, providing a compelling rationale for why Jesus was crucified. Just as it is irrational and self-destructive for anyone to "love darkness" and to "hate light," the world's rejection of its Savior was profoundly irrational and contrary to its own need. The initial passage contrasting "love" and "hate," while paradoxical, thus lays the foundation for the remainder of the gospel, and indeed all of the Johannine writings in this regard.

In a possible *inclusio*, the corresponding reference to "love" and "hate" in John's Book of Signs is found in John 12:25, where Jesus utters the pronouncement that "those who love their life will lose it, while those who hate their life in this world will keep it for eternal life." Again, paradox is present, and the paradox is profound: contrary to what one might expect, love of one's life in this world is not a virtue but a hindrance to experiencing eternal life, resulting in eternal loss, while "hatred" of one's life in this world will issue in possession of eternal life. The fact that this saying is attested also in the Synoptics (Matt 10:39; 16:25; Mark 8:35; Luke 9:24; 17:33) provides ample support that this is an authentic saying of Jesus.[54] In the first instance, of course, the statement is prophetic of Jesus' own sacrifice at the cross, but it quickly becomes clear that in "hating" his life in this world Jesus serves as a model for his followers to emulate (John 12:26).[55]

Significantly, nine of the twelve instances of "hate" in John's gospel are found in the Farewell Discourse. In fact, eight of these occurrences are located in the short

---

51. See esp. Lincoln, *Truth on Trial*.

52. The Johannine vocabulary for "love" and "hate" includes the *agapaō* and *phileō* word groups (virtual synonyms for "love") and, conversely, *miseō* ("hate"). John accounts for 37 of the 143 NT occurrences (25%) of *agapaō*; 13 out of 25 instances (52%) of *phileō*; and 12 out of 40 references (30%) to *miseō*. This marks "love" and "hate" as a significant Johannine theme. For complete data, see Köstenberger and Bouchoc, *Book Study Concordance*, 479–610. See also the treatment of love and hate in Harris, "Theology of John's Writings," 208–12, who rightly notes that this pair of opposites is "less obvious than some of the others but extremely important for an understanding of Johannine thought" (p. 208).

53. See the treatment of sin in chap. 12 below.

54. See also Yarbrough, *1–3 John*, 104, n. 16, who observes that "hate" understood as "not loving" reflects familiar OT usage (Deut 21:15–17; 2 Sam 19:6 [19:7 MT]; Prov 13:24; Mal 1:2–3).

55. See chap. 13 on John's love ethic below.

span of John 15:18–25. The paradox continues when Jesus tells his disciples that if they belonged to the world, the world would "love" them as its own (15:19); but because they are associated with Jesus, the world hates them just as it hates him (15:18–19; cf. 17:14). In this the principle is validated that "servants are not greater than their master" (15:20; cf. 13:16). Again, the saying is paralleled in the Synoptics (Matt 10:24; Luke 6:40).

In the context of preparation of his followers, Jesus predicts that they will be persecuted in the days subsequent to his exaltation. Again, Jesus makes clear that the root cause of the world's rejection is sin (John 15:22), and that this sin persists in rebellion against the Creator and Jesus his emissary in the face of massive revelation—Jesus' teaching and example—that Jesus is the Messiah and that his message is true. Jesus both "spoke" to the world (cf. 15:22) and did "among them the works no one else did" (15:24a). "As it is, they have seen, and yet they have hated both me and my Father" (15:24b). Like Jesus' followers, "they have seen"; but unlike them, they failed to see Jesus' *glory* in the things he said and did (cf. 1:14; 2:11).

The present reference is therefore part of John's theme of theodicy; because the world has seen and yet has rejected Jesus' message, "they have no excuse for their sin" (John 15:22). But far from obstructing God's purposes, sinful humanity in its irrational rebellion against the Creator and its illegitimate rejection of the Messiah fulfills biblical prophecy, and more specifically, Davidic typology: "But this is to fulfill what is written in their Law: 'They hated me without reason'" (15:25, citing Ps 35:19; 69:4).[56]

	3:19–21	12:25	15:18–25
Object of Love	Darkness	Life in this world	The world loving its own
Object of Hate	Light	[Eternal life]	Jesus' followers

Fig. 12.3: The Paradoxical Nature of the "Love" and "Hate" Contrasts in John's Gospel

While absent from 2 and 3 John, the word "hate" (*miseō*) occurs five times in 1 John.[57] Interestingly, all three passages make reference to hatred of believers (1 John 2:9–11; 3:13–15; 4:20). In the first instance John writes, "Those who claim to be in the light but hate a fellow believer are still in the darkness. Those who love their fellow belivers live in the light" (2:9–10).[58] Most likely, John has in mind those who had recently departed from the fellowship (2:19).[59]

---

56. See Köstenberger, "John," in *Commentary on the NT Use of the OT*, 493–95; and the discussion of Davidic typology in chap. 10, sec. 22.8 below.

57. The verb *agapaō* ("to love") is found twenty-eight times in 1 John, and the noun *agapē* ("love") occurs eighteen times. Oddly enough, the verb *phileō* ("to love") is not found in John's letters at all (compared to thirteen instances in John's gospel).

58. For an excellent discussion, see Yarbrough, *1–3 John*, 103–8, esp. 104–5. The TNIV's translation "fellow believer" in 1 John 2:9 and 4:20 is problematic in that it seems to imply that the secessionists were genuine believers, which is contradicted by the repeated statement in 1 John 2:19 that "they did not really belong to us."

59. See the discussion in chap. 1, sec. 2.2.4 above.

The second reference, "Do not be surprised, my brothers and sisters, if the world hates you" (1 John 3:13), echoes Jesus' words in John 15:18–25.[60] In the following verse, love for other believers is cited as evidence that a person has passed from death to life (1 John 3:14; cf. John 5:24). John proceeds to declare that "anyone who hates a fellow believer is a murderer" (1 John 3:15), resembling Jesus' ethic in the Synoptics (Matt 5:21–22) and similar teaching in John's gospel (John 8:44). In the latter instance, the Jewish leaders who rejected Jesus are said to be children of the devil because they plotted his death just as Satan was a quintessential murderer who brought death and sin into the world. This link between the Pharisees and the secessionists holds especially well if the latter, like the former, rejected the Christian confession that Jesus is the Messiah.[61]

The theme is reinforced in the third passage contrasting "love" and "hate" in John's first letter, where the author writes, "If we say we love God yet hate a brother or sister, we are liars. For if we do not love a fellow believer, whom we have seen, we cannot love God, whom we have not seen" (1 John 4:20). Lack of love for a believer is thus seen as evidence for the lack of regeneration and authentic possession of eternal life. Anyone who claims to love God but hates a believer is a liar.[62]

	1 John 2:9–11	3:13–15	4:19–20
Object of hate	Believers	Believers	Believers
Illustration	Light/darkness	Cain	God/believers

Fig. 12.4: Lack of Love for Believers as Evidence for Lack of Regeneration in 1 John

Thus, in 1 John, the "love" and "hate" contrast serves the dual purpose of reassuring believers of the lack of regeneration of the secessionists and of denouncing the latter as unregenerate liars whose profession of Christianity was proven false by their hatred of genuine believers.[63] The Johannine logic in 1 John, then, is one of deducing from a self-declared believers' conduct—in the present case, lack of love—his or her true spiritual heart condition. As the old adage has it, "Actions speak louder than words." The presence of love or hatred toward a believer thus serves as the quintessential Johannine criterion of whether a person is a follower of Jesus the Messiah (1 John 2:22; 4:2; 5:1). This emphasis in John's first letter constitutes a perfectly logical and compelling extension of John's "love ethic" as set forth in the Farewell Discourse of his gospel.[64]

In fact, John's "negative" criterion of lovelessness as indicator of a person's lack of authentic Christian faith and legitimate community membership constitutes the exact obverse of Jesus' "new commandment" featured in the gospel: "A new command

---

60. See the discussion in Yarbrough, *1–3 John*, 199–201.
61. See Streett, "They Went Out from Us."
62. See Yarbrough, *1–3 John*, 264–66.
63. Note also that the "love and hate" contrast interfaces with several of the other dual opposites in John's writings, such as "light and darkness" (1 John 2:9–11; cf. John 3:19–21) or "life and death" (1 John 3:14).
64. See chap. 13 below.

I give you: Love one another. As I have loved you, so you must love one another. By this everyone will know that you are my disciples, if you love one another" (John 13:34–35; cf. 1 John 1:7–8; 3:11). Thus 1 John can be seen as an application of Jesus' "love commandment" to a divisive situation in the Johannine congregations.[65] It is possible that for a while these congregations included non-messianic Jews or proselytes who sought to sway their fellow members by disputing their claim that Jesus was the Messiah while "hating" them and leaving only when such efforts proved futile.

12.3.8 Trust and Unbelief

One final polarity to be explored is that between trust and unbelief. This choice between faith or rejection of Jesus is at the heart of the great Johannine divide that separates humanity into those who put their trust in the Messiah and those who remain under God's wrath and in the realm of the world and its ruler, the devil. Indeed, for John, "believing" is primarily an act of placing one's faith in Jesus rather than a static noun of a set of convictions to be held. The verb occurs ninety-eight times in John's gospel and is found, strategically, at the pivot of the introduction (John 1:12–13) and in the purpose statement (20:30–31). Conversely, the Jews' rejection of the Messiah and failure to believe is noted in the conclusion of Act I of the Johannine drama (12:37).

Remarkably, however, the categories between faith and unbelief are not rigid in John's presentation. Rather, apparent initial belief may in due course turn out to be not genuine faith at all (see, e.g., John 2:23–25; 6:60, 66; 8:31–59). On the one end of the spectrum are the Twelve, Jesus' inner circle (a core group assumed in John's gospel; see, e.g., 6:71). Yet among them are both the evangelist, considered by many to be an "ideal disciple" and normally presented in a light superior to Peter,[66] and Judas, the paradigmatic "son of perdition" and traitor, who exemplifies the one who for a while associated with the group of disciples while never having had a regenerated heart (see esp. 13:10–11; 15:2–4).

In between, there is a group that does not fully put its trust in Jesus, including Nicodemus and Joseph of Arimathea (John 12:42–43). Then there is Pilate, whose attempt at maintaining a neutral stance toward Jesus is doomed to futility.[67] The crowds, for their part, vascillate, giving Jesus a triumphal welcome one day while joining the Jewish leaders in calling for Jesus' crucifixion only a few days later (12:12–15; 19:15).[68] Thus the reader of John's gospel must maintain a certain amount of critical distance when encountering "faith" terminology, including terms such as "believe" (*pisteuō*) or "disciple" (*mathētēs*), because in John's theology true faith, by its very nature, is faith that perseveres.[69]

---

65. See the distinctive polemical language in 1 John, including the repeated use of "antichrist" language (1 John 2:18, 22; 4:3; cf. 2 John 7) and the example of Cain killing his brother (1 John 3:12). In placing the secessionists into this kind of trajectory of evil, John is similar to the letter of Jude (see "Jude," in Köstenberger, Kellum, and Quarles, *Cradle, the Cross, and the Crown*).

66. See the discussion in chap. 12, sec. 29.3.2 below.

67. See chap. 11, sec. 25.2.2.

68. For a discussion of the crowds in John's gospel, see Köstenberger, *Missions of Jesus and the Disciples*, 145–46.

69. See esp. D. A. Carson, "Reflections on Christian Assurance," *WTJ* 54 (1992): 1–29. See also Croteau, "Analysis of the Concept of Believing."

12.4 John's Gospel as a Cosmic Drama

John's gospel does not merely use certain language that reflects its author's worldview that can be analyzed by taking inventory of certain terms such as "world" or "flesh" vs. "spirit," and so on (though this kind of terminology certainly does demonstrate John's worldview in concrete terms). His very story is shaped by his worldview, and his cosmology and dualism find expression in a particular narrative employment that presents Jesus' mission in terms consistent with John's particular outlook. For this reason it will be helpful to sketch briefly the way in which John's story is shaped by his cosmology.

In the case of the Synoptic Gospels, scholars distinguish between the life-setting in the time of Jesus (*Sitz im Leben Jesu*) and the life-setting during the time of composition (*Sitz im Leben der Kirche*). In the case of John's gospel, it is apparent that his account starts neither with Jesus nor with the virgin birth; it commences with God "in the beginning" prior to creation. John's has been described by some as a "cosmological tale" in distinction from historical and ecclesiological tales.[70] The term "tale," however, unduly suggests a nonhistorical orientation and thus is best avoided.

These cautions notwithstanding, it seems certainly appropriate to describe John as a "cosmic drama," that is, as an account of Jesus' enfleshment, salvific cross-death, and resurrection set in the context of a cosmic spiritual conflict that encompasses both heaven and earth.[71] Similar to the book of Job, this makes clear that human existence transcends the mere horizontal level and is impacted profoundly by the vertical dimension of supernatural realities. As mentioned, John's entire gospel bears a marked imprint of his cosmology, which is presented in dramatic form.

As a drama, John's gospel features several common elements, such as a focus on a hero or protagonist (Jesus Christ), conflict with his antagonists (the Pharisees), suspense (the escalating plot against Jesus), and other elements.[72] At the same time, differences obtain as well, such as the lack of coverage of Jesus' birth or boyhood or the fact that his death is not the end of the story but is followed by his resurrection and resurrection appearances.[73] Importantly, John's depiction of Jesus commences with Jesus' preexistence (John 1:1), describes Jesus by using the descent-ascent schema (e.g., John 13–14), and presents Part 2 of the gospel from the perspective of the exalted Jesus.[74]

---

70. See the discussion in Klink, "Light of the World," with reference to Adele Reinhartz, *The Word in the World: The Cosmological Tale in the Fourth Gospel* (SBLMS 45; Atlanta: Scholars Press, 1992).

71. Regarding drama, see especially the work of Vanhoozer, *Drama of Doctrine*, following von Balthasar, *Theo-Drama*. See also Fernando F. Segovia, "The Journey(s) of the Word of God: A Reading of the Plot of the Fourth Gospel," *Semeia* 53 (1991): 26–31; Brant, *Dialogue and Drama*; and Martyn, *History and Theology*, whose proposal of a two-level reading of John's gospel has, however, been subjected to a devastating critique by Carson and others.

72. See chap. 3, sec. 5.5.

73. See the discussion of the genre of John's gospel in chap. 2, sec. 3 above.

74. See the discussion of the structure of John's gospel in chap. 3, sec. 8 above. See also the discussion of the descent-ascent schema in chap. 14, sec. 31.2 below. The gospel clearly breaks down into two major parts, chaps. 1–12 and 13–21, which makes Klink's three-part proposal doubtful in dividing John as follows: (1) narrative of cosmic origins (1:1–18); (2) narrative of cosmic career (1:19–17:26); and (3) narrative of cosmic significance (18:1–21:25).

What is more, in keeping with his salvation-historical outlook, John sets the story of Jesus squarely in the context of Israel's story.[75] According to John, Jesus' story is the culmination and fulfillment of the story of Israel. This, in fact, is essential to understanding the negative characterization of the world and the Jews, both of whom opposed God's salvation-historical program by rejecting Jesus as Messiah. John places Jesus in the trajectory of Abraham (John 8:56, 58), Isaac, Jacob (4:12), Moses (1:16; 5:45–47), Elijah, and Elisha (6:8–9), while the Jews are part of the trajectory of the wilderness generation (6:41, 61), Israel's faithless shepherds (10:1–18), and the Jews failing to heed Isaiah's report (12:37–41).

In drawing on antecedents in the story of Israel, John leaves no stone unturned. Jesus is presented as the raised-up serpent (John 3:13–14) and the manna (6:31–58); he is cast as the Davidic shepherd in contrast with the Jewish leadership (10:1–18); he is depicted as the suffering Servant of Yahweh who endures humiliation and crucifixion on behalf of the people (12:37–41); he is portrayed as the vine (15:1–8), in the OT a characteristic of Israel. Believers in Jesus are called "children of God" (1:12) while those who opposed Jesus are "children of the devil" (cf. 8:44). Other characters in the gospel are skillfully employed to represent the inadequacy of human decency apart from spiritual regeneration (Nicodemus) or the futility of evading a decision regarding Jesus (Pilate).[76]

12.5 The Glory of God in Jesus

The identification of the theology of glory with the theology of the cross is at the very heart of John's gospel.[77] At the outset, John testifies that "We have seen his glory, the glory of the one and only Son, who came from the Father, full of grace and truth" (1:14), and this glory was evident both in Jesus' signs (2:11; 11:4, 40; cf. 9:3–4) and his death on the cross (12:23, 28; 13:31–32). Indeed, as mentioned, it is emphatically not only the second half of John's gospel that is a "Book of Glory"; rather, John's entire gospel was written to show that God's glory was continually on display in and through Jesus' ministry, from its inception all the way to the cross and beyond.[78] The reason for this is that Jesus' was a preexistent glory that he had with God from all eternity (17:5, 24). Within this purview of glory, the mission of the Word-made-flesh in Jesus is utterly devoted to revealing the glory of God in everything Jesus says and does (1:18), including his loving act of ultimate self-giving at the cross (13:1–3).

As with his sending Christology (cf. Isa 55:11), his use of "lifting up" terminology (cf. Isa 52:13), and his portrayal of John the Baptist (cf. Isa 40:3), John's theology of glory takes his cue from the theology of Isaiah. There the prophet "saw the Lord seated on a throne, high and exalted," and angelic creatures calling to one another, "Holy, holy, holy is the LORD Almighty; the whole earth is full of his glory" (Isa

---

75. See chap. 10, sec. 22. See also Wright, *New Testament and the People of God*.

76. See chap. 11, sec. 25.3.2.

77. For a fuller treatment of this important Johannine theme see my essay "The Glory of God in John's Gospel and the Apocalypse," in *The Glory of God* (Theology in Community 2; ed. Robert Peterson and Chris Morgan; Wheaton: Crossway, forthcoming).

78. See the discussion of the structure of John's gospel in chap. 3, sec. 8 above. See also the discussion of glory in chap. 14, below, on John's Theology of the Cross.

6:1–3). The prophet's vision of God's glory served as the point of departure for his prophetic message of judgment on an obstinate nation, Israel. The fourth evangelist, quoting from this same chapter, asserts that "Isaiah said this because he saw Jesus' glory and spoke about him" (John 12:41). Like Isaiah, therefore, John saw Jesus' glory (1:14), which led him to proclaim a message of divine judgment on unbelieving Israel, which rejected her Messiah (see esp. 12:37–40).

From the outset (see esp. John 1:14), the "glory" theme in John's gospel also invokes previous manifestations of God's presence among his people in the tabernacle and later in the temple where, according to the Hebrew Scriptures, God's glory was revealed to his people.[79] As his narrative progresses, John makes clear that the temple is now Jesus' body (2:21), which will be crucified and raised up in three days (2:19). Proper worship is to be rendered in spirit and truth (4:24), and Jesus fulfills Jewish festal symbolism (see esp. the Festival Cycle, John 5–10). Ominously, at critical junctures in the narrative, Jesus withdraws his presence in judgment on Israel (8:59; 12:36). At this culminating moment in salvation history, God's glory is thus revealed exclusively and climactically in Jesus. Just as the Father's glory is revealed in the Son, so the Father is shown to reveal his Son's glory, issuing in the sending of the Spirit. This suggests that John's "glory" theme is both trinitarian in nature and serves as an all-encompassing, paradigmatic component of the Johannine worldview.

12.6 Johannine Eschatology

12.6.1 Introduction

John's eschatology is one of the most distinctive features of his theology.[80] While in most systematic theological treatments a discussion of eschatology is put at the end, in the context of the present biblical-theological investigation the most appropriate place to begin to understand John's teaching on the end times is with the Johannine worldview or *Weltanschauung*. John's outlook, as shown, contrasts the realms above and below, light and darkness, life and death, flesh and spirit, truth and falsehood, love and hate, and belief and unbelief as part of a grand cosmic drama in which God and his Messiah are opposed by Satan, "the prince of this world," and the unbelieving world.

12.6.2 Survey of Scholarship

The study of John's eschatology in the previous century was significantly impacted by the contributions of Rudolf Bultmann and C. H. Dodd, both of whom challenged the conventional understanding of the presence of both present and future elements

---

79. See Exod 40:34–35; 1 Kgs 8:10–11; 2 Chr 5:13–14; 7:1–2; Hag 2:7; Ezek 10:4; 43:5; 44:4. See chap. 10, esp. secs. 23–24 on Jesus' Fulfillment of Festal Symbolism and Jesus as the New Temple, below.

80. For an extensive study, including a virtually exhaustive survey of a century of Johannine research, see Jörg Frey, *Die johanneische Eschatologie* (3 vols.; WUNT 96, 110, 117; Tübingen: Mohr-Siebeck, 1997–2000). See also W. Robert Cook, "Eschatology in John's Gospel," *CTR* 3 (1988): 79–99; Raymond E. Brown, "Eschatology," in *An Introduction to the Gospel of John* (ABRL; ed. Francis J. Moloney; New York: Doubleday, 2003), 234–48.

and advocated a fully realized eschatology in John's gospel.[81] Future elements (such as the references to the future resurrection in John 5:28–29 or the resurrection through Christ on "the last day" in 6:39, 40, 44, 54) were attributed by Bultmann to a later ecclesiastical redactor.[82]

According to Bultmann, this later redactor "historicized" or "demythologized" eschatology. Commenting on John's statement in John 12:31, "Now is the time for judgment on this world; now the prince of this world will be driven out," Bultmann wrote:

> The judgment of this world now takes place. The ruler of this world will now be thrown out of the domain over which he formerly held sway. The significance of the hour of decision is thus described in the cosmological terminology of the Gnostic myth. If in the evangelist's mind the myth has lost its mythological context and become historicized, his language on the other hand serves to eliminate the traditional eschatology of primitive Christianity. The turn of the ages results now ... the destiny of man has become definitive, as he believes or not. *No future in this world's history can bring anything new, and all apocalyptic pictures of the future are empty dreams.*[83]

According to Bultmann, the mention of Easter, Pentecost, and the Second Coming in close proximity to each other in the Farewell Discourse is intended to show that these events collapse and are no longer three but one: "The one event that is meant by all these is not an external occurrence, but an inner one, the victory which Jesus wins when faith arises in man by the overcoming of the offense that Jesus is to him."[84] Dodd, for his part, attributed the fourth gospel's realized eschatology to an attempt to come to terms with the delay of the *parousia* (the second coming of Christ).[85]

In subsequent scholarship, however, the thesis of a fully realized Johannine eschatology did not carry the day.[86] Bultmann's source-critical theories (including his attribution of futurist eschatology exclusively to the realm of the "ecclesiastical redactor") were questioned on the basis of the uniformity of Johannine style and other factors.[87] Jesus was widely recognized to have taught that the kingdom of God had been inaugurated in and through his earthly ministry while still awaiting

---

81. Bultmann, *Gospel of John*; idem, *Theology of the New Testament*, esp. 2:75–92 ("Faith as Eschatological Existence"); C. H. Dodd, "The Kingdom of God Has Come," *ExpTim* 48 (1936): 138–42; idem, "The Background of the Fourth Gospel," *BJRL* 19 (1935): 329–43.

82. Bultmann, *Gospel of John*, 261; idem, *Theology of the New Testament*, 2:39 (where Bultmann speaks of a "historicizing of eschatology," also citing the references to the antichrist at 1 John 2:18; 4:3). But see the critique by George R. Beasley-Murray, "The Eschatology of the Fourth Gospel," *EvQ* 18 (1946): 99, who commented that Bultmann's theory "is but an extension of that delightfully simple expedient that commentators have of dubbing all passages inimical to their interpretations as 'interpolations.'"

83. Bultmann, *Gospel of John*, 431.

84. Bultmann, *Theology of the New Testament*, 2:57.

85. C. H. Dodd, *The Coming of Christ* (Cambridge: Cambridge University Press, 1954), 6–7.

86. See esp. Gustav Stählin, "Zum Problem der johanneischen Eschatologie," *ZNW* 33 (1934): 225–59. See also George R. Beasley-Murray, *Gospel of Life: Theology in the Fourth Gospel* (Peabody, MA: Hendrickson, 1991), 1–14, esp. 5–14; and the survey by Harris, "Eschatology in the Johannine Writings," in *Biblical Theology of the New Testament*, 233–42.

87. See Ruckstuhl, *Literarische Einheit*; D. Moody Smith, *The Composition and Order of the Fourth Gospel: Bultmann's Literary Theory* (Yale Publications in Religion 10; New Haven/London: Yale University Press, 1965), esp. 230–32 (followed by Brown, *Introduction to the Gospel of John*, 241).

its final consummation at a future time.[88] With this the stage has been set for an exploration of the Johannine material below.

12.6.3 Survey of the Johannine Material

In John's presentation of Jesus, major emphasis is placed on Jesus as the preexistent Word and the descending and ascending Son of Man who, in keeping with the portrayal of God's Word in Isaiah (esp. Isa 55:11), comes into the world, accomplishes his/God's mission, and returns to the place from where he came.[89] According to John, Jesus is no mere man; he is a transcendent being who is both God and man — the Word, the Messiah, the Son of God (John 1:1, 14; 20:30 – 31).

During Jesus' incarnate life, therefore, the distinction between many of the Johannine polar opposites collapsed: the world above had descended into the world below (John 1:1, 14; 3:31); in Jesus, life had invaded the realm of death (e.g., 1:4; 11:1 – 44); light had penetrated and overcome darkness (e.g., 1:5; 3:19 – 21; 8:12; 9:5); truth had exposed falsehood (e.g., 8:42 – 47); and the impending substitutionary sacrifice of the "Lamb of God" had opened up the possibility of faith and pushed back the forces of unbelief (1:29, 36; cf. 1:12; 20:30 – 31).

As a consequence, John does not, as was common in Jewish thought, perceive eschatology as the future "age to come" replacing the "present age." Instead, for John, in Jesus the distinction between these two ages has collapsed, so that believers in Jesus are able to experience end-time blessings already in the here and now, most notably eternal, abundant life (e.g., John 3:16; 5:24; 10:10). This "inaugurated" eschatology can be detected also in Synoptic passages such as Luke 17:21 ("the kingdom of God is in your midst"), but it is John who has elevated "inaugurated" eschatology to a higher plane than the Synoptic presentation.

Yet while John clearly accentuates the inaugurated or realized aspect of eschatology, this does not mean that he reduces the end times entirely to present experience.[90] The most notable instances are John 5:28 – 29; 11:23 – 26; and 14:2 – 7 (see also 6:39 – 40, 44, 54; 12:48). As Craig Keener points out, the Pharisees and Christians agreed on futurist eschatology; what they differed on was whether "the inauguration of that hope [was] in Jesus."[91] Hence John stressed realization in Jesus to further press Jesus' messianic claims.

John likely replaced Jesus' end-time teaching found in the Synoptic Olivet Discourse (Matthew 24 pars.) and the pervasive Synoptic emphasis on the kingdom of God with an eschatology that focused on the experience of eternal life in Jesus through the Spirit already in the here and now. This cast a stark contrast between

---

88. See Darrell L. Bock, "The Kingdom of God in New Testament Theology," in *Looking into the Future: Evangelical Studies in Eschatology* (ed. David W. Baker; Grand Rapids: Baker, 2001), 32 – 33; see also Keener, *John*, 323; Köstenberger, *Encountering John*, 42.

89. For a broad presentation of John's eschatology, see Dumbrell, *Search for Order*, 235 – 58.

90. This is widely acknowledged today, though this has not always been the case. See the survey of scholarship in Keener, *John*, 320 – 23. Keener also observes that in Qumran, for example, realized and future eschatology could coexist without conscious tension (ibid., 322). For a NT example of a fully realized eschatology, denounced as heretical, see 2 Tim 2:18.

91. Ibid., 323.

those who refused to accept Jesus' messianic claims and thus persisted in projecting the Messiah's coming as still future and those who by faith had already entered into the messianic age.[92]

Notably, John's first letter has quite a few references to future eschatology. His dual mention of the "last hour" in 1 John 2:18, his discussion of the antichrist at 2:18, 22 and 4:3, his references to Jesus' coming in 2:28–3:3, his use of "lawlessness" (*anomia*) twice at 3:4, which may entail the notion of eschatological rebellion, and his reference to final judgment at 4:17, all add up to a rather full-orbed picture of eschatological expectation.[93] What is more, a motif of end-time cosmic conflict pervades John's letters, including instances of "overcoming" language.[94]

12.7 Conclusion

The Johannine worldview is as pervasive in John's gospel as it is distinctive. It provides a unique grid, or pair of glasses, through which the gospel must be read if it is to be properly understood. The components of John's view of the world include the following: (1) the cosmic conflict between God and his Messiah and Satan; (2) the world as a morally dark place in need of God's love and redemption; (3) a separation of the world into the two spheres "above" and "below"; (4) light and darkness (a function of John's new creation theology); (5) life and death (universalizing the Synoptic teaching regarding the kingdom of God); (6) flesh and spirit; (7) truth and falsehood; (8) love and hate; (9) believing and unbelief; and (10) John's gospel as grand drama of cosmic proportions, pitting God and Jesus against Satan, the "prince of this world." John also views Jesus' entire ministry, including his signs and the cross, as revealing the glory of God. John's worldview, including the resulting eschatology, thus provides a unique framework against which his theology and Christology ought to be understood. These, in turn, are significantly indebted to OT theology, which forms the next subject of investigation.

13 JOHN'S USE OF SCRIPTURE

13.1 Introduction

While the gospel of Matthew is widely known to focus on Jesus' fulfillment of OT messianic expectations, John's gospel, too, roots Jesus' mission firmly in OT conceptualities and specific texts.[95] From the very beginning and throughout the introduction, John operates within a scriptural, salvation-historical framework.[96]

---

92. See also the Johannine depiction of the Holy Spirit and his role of guiding believers into all the truth and of telling them "what is yet to come" (John 16:13).

93. For a thorough treatment of 1 John 3:4, 6, see Yarbrough, *1–3 John*, 181–85.

94. See chap. 11, sec. 25.4 below.

95. Some of the material in this section is adapted from Beale and Carson, eds., *Commentary on the NT Use of the OT*, 415–25,

and is used by permission. Note that the importance of the OT background for John's gospel was not always realized in the history of Johannine scholarship. See especially the *religionsgeschichtliche Schule* in the first half of the twentieth century that accentuated more keenly the Hellenistic background of the gospel. See the survey in Neill and Wright, *Interpretation of the New Testament*, 163–95.

96. Pryor, *John: Evangelist of the Covenant People*.

In his references to the OT, John spans the entire range from explicit quotations to verifiable allusions and thematic connections. In keeping with John's purpose statement, Jesus is identified as the Messiah and Son of God and set in relation to the major figures in Israel's history, whether Abraham, Jacob, or Moses, as well as the Prophet, by citations of, or allusions to, Scripture.

In the following discussion it will be helpful to take inventory of the explicit OT quotations in John's gospel.[97] This will include a survey of John's use of introductory formulas; a comparison between John's explicit OT citations and the rest of the NT; a survey of the alignment of John's explicit OT references with the LXX, the MT, or other texts; the attribution of OT quotations in John to specific persons, be it Jesus, the evangelist, or others; a listing of OT quotations in John's gospel in OT order (including the Psalter and author attribution, as appropriate); and a list of OT allusions and verbal parallels in John's gospel.

13.2 The Use of the Old Testament in John's Gospel: Overview

13.2.1 Explicit Old Testament Quotations in John's Gospel

There are fourteen explicit OT quotations in John's gospel, ten in Part 1 (John 1:19–12:50), four in Part 2 (John 13–21).[98] The citation format changes from Part 1 to Part 2, the latter of which features a series of "fulfillment quotations" (see chart below). Structurally, the most significant OT quotations are found at the end of Part 1 in 12:38, 40. Many of the numerous allusions and a considerable amount of the OT symbolism relate in one way or another to various Jewish religious festivals. In terms of distribution, seven quotes (or 50 percent) are from the Psalms; four from Isaiah; two from Zechariah; and one from the Pentateuch.

The overall purpose of the use of the OT in John's gospel, as evidenced by the formal quotations, is to show that both Jesus' public ministry and his cross-death fulfilled scriptural patterns and prophecies.[99] The clustering of explicit quotations around the motifs of Jewish obduracy (12:38, 40) and Jesus' passion (19:24, 28, 36–37) suggests that a major burden informing John's use of explicit OT quotations is to provide his readers with a biblical rationale for the rejection of Jesus as Messiah (cf. 20:30–31). The Suffering Servant of Isaiah 53 underlies John's portrayal of Jesus especially in John 12. Davidic typology is present in 2:17; 15:25; 19:24, 28; and several other passages.

---

97. For monograph-length studies see Edwin D. Freed, *Old Testament Quotations in the Gospel of John* (NovTSup 11; Leiden: Brill, 1965); Günther Reim, *Studien zum alttestamentlichen Hintergrund des Johannesevangeliums* (SNTSMS 22; Cambridge: Cambridge University Press, 1974); Bruce G. Schuchard, *Scripture within Scripture: The Interrelationship of Form and Function in the Explicit Old Testament Citations in the Gospel of John* (SBLDS 133; Atlanta: Scholars Press, 1992); and especially Maarten J. J. Menken, *Old Testament Quotations in the Fourth Gospel: Studies in Textual Form* (CBET 15; Kampen: Kok, 1996), who interacts extensively with these and other earlier works.

98. D. A. Carson, "John and the Johannine Epistles," in *It Is Written: Scripture Citing Scripture: Essays in Honor of Barnabas Lindas, SSF* (ed. D. A. Carson and H. G. M. Williamson; Cambridge: Cambridge University Press, 1988), 246–51.

99. Stanley E. Porter, "Can Traditional Exegesis Enlighten Literary Analysis of the Fourth Gospel? An Examination of the Old Testament Fulfilment Motif and the Passover Theme," in *The Gospels and the Scriptures of Israel* (ed. Craig A. Evans and William R. Stegner; JSNTSup 104; Sheffield: Sheffield Academic Press, 1994), 401, citing Craig A. Evans, *Word and Glory: On the Exegetical and Theolgcial Background of John's Prologue* (JSNTSup 89; Sheffield: Sheffield Academic Press, 1993), 174.

13.2.2 Introductory Formulas in John's Gospel

13.2.2.1 Survey Chart

The following is a survey of introductory formulas used for each of the explicit OT quotations in John's gospel, followed by a brief general overview.[100]

John	Introductory formula	Translation
1:23	*ephē*	he replied [said]
2:17	*hoti gegrammenon estin*	that it is written
6:31	*kathōs estin gegrammenon*	as it is written
6:45	*estin gegrammenon en tois prophētais*	it is written in the Prophets
7:38*	*kathōs eipen hē graphē*	as Scripture has said
7:42*	*ouch hē graphē eipen*	does not Scripture say
10:34	*ouk estin gegrammenon en tō nomō hymōn*	is it not written in your Law
12:13	—	—
12:14	*kathōs estin gegrammenon*	as it is written
12:38	*hina ho logos ēsaiou tou prophētou plērōthē hon eipen*	to fulfill the word of Isaiah the prophet
12:39	*hoti palin eipen ēsaias*	as Isaiah says elsewhere
13:18	*all' hina hē graphē plērōthē*	to fulfill this passage of Scripture
15:25	*all' hina plērōthē ho logos ho en tō nomō autōn gegrammenos*	to fulfill what is written in their Law
17:12*	*hina hē graphē plērōthē*	so that Scripture would be fulfilled
19:24	*hina hē graphē plērōthē [hē legousa]*	that the scripture might be fulfilled
19:28*	*hina teleiōthē hē graphē*	so that Scripture would be fulfilled
19:36	*hina hē graphē plērōthē*	so that the scripture would be fulfilled
19:37	*kai palin hetera graphē legei*	as another scripture says

Fig. 13.1: Introductory Formulas in John's Gospel

13.2.2.2 Discussion

The seven OT quotations in John 1:1–12:36a are somewhat sporadic (John 3–5; 8–9; and 11 do not feature any formal OT citations) and characterized by a certain

---

100. For more detailed discussions see the treatment of the specific quotations below. An asterisk marks passages where no OT text is cited or identifiable.

degree of variety, though the phrase *estin gegrammenon* (or *gegrammenon estin*; "it is written") constitutes a common denominator (2:17; 6:31, 45; 10:34; 12:14; the only exceptions are citations attributed to the Baptist in 1:23 and to the crowd in 12:13).

A marked shift takes place at John 12:38, the evangelist's concluding verdict on the Jews, which features the first of a string of seven fulfillment quotations (12:38; 13:18; 15:25; 17:12; 19:24, 28, 36, 37; the two follow-up quotations in 12:39 and 19:37 are no real exceptions). The phrase *hina hē graphē plērōthē* ("so that Scripture would be fulfilled") is found in 13:18; 17:12; 19:24, 36.

While the purposes of the formal OT citations in the first half of John's gospel are varied, in the second half of his gospel the evangelist consistently seeks to emphasize the fulfillment of Scripture with regard to Jesus' passion and the obduracy motif that is associated with it.[101] The closer the narrative approaches the cross, the more forcefully John stresses that even Jesus' rejection by the Jews fulfills Scripture.

13.2.3 Old Testament Quotations in John and the Rest of the New Testament

13.2.3.1 Survey Chart

The following chart, organized by type of introductory formula and listed in chronological order, provides a comparison between the explicit OT quotations in John's gospel and the OT usage found in the rest of the NT.[102]

John	OT	Rest of the NT
"It is written"		
1:23*	Isa 40:3	Matt 3:3; Mark 1:3; Luke 3:4; cf. Luke 1:76
2:17	Ps 69:9a	—
6:31	Ps 78:24b	cf. 1 Cor 10:3; Rev 2:17
6:45	Isa 54:14a	—
10:34	Ps 82:6a	—
12:13*	Ps 118:26a	Matt 21:9; Mark 11:9–10
12:15	Zech 9:9	Matt 21:5

(Continued on the next page)

---

101. Carson, "John and the Johannine Epistles," 248, with reference to Craig A. Evans, "On the Quotation Formulas in the Fourth Gospel," *BZ* 26 (1982): 79–83.

102. Again, a brief overview commentary is provided immediately following this chart. An asterisk indicates the presence of a different or no introductory formula.

(Continued)

John	OT	Rest of the NT
"So that Scripture would be fulfilled"		
12:38	Isa 53:1	Rom 10:16
12:40	Isa 6:10	Matt 13:15; Mark 4:12; Acts 28:27
13:18	Ps 41:9b	cf. Matt 26:23; Mark 14:18; Luke 22:21; John 17:12; Acts 1:16
15:25	Ps 35:19; 69:4	—
19:24	Ps 22:18	see Ps 22:1 citation in Matt 26:46; Mark 15:34; cf. Mark 9:12; Luke 24:26
19:36	Exod 12:46; Num 9:12; Ps 34:20	—
19:37	Zech 12:10	Matt 24:30; Rev 1:7

Fig. 13.2: OT Quotations in John and the Rest of the NT

13.2.3.2 Discussion

John's use of the OT, as well as Jesus' use of the OT according to John, is generally in keeping with that found in the other canonical gospels, in the book of Acts, Romans, and the book of Revelation. The Baptist's reference to Isa 40:3 is found also in the Synoptics (though only in John is the passage found on the Baptist's lips). Both references to Ps 118:25–26 and Zech 9:9 are present also in Matthew, the quotation of Psalm 118 also in Mark. The citations of Isa 53:1 and 6:10 are paralleled in Romans and Matthew, Mark, and Acts respectively. The reference to Ps 22:18 is corroborated by the specific quotations of Ps 22:1 in Matthew and Mark and possible allusions to the psalm in Mark and Luke. Finally, the citation of Zech 12:10 parallels Matt 24:30 and Rev 1:7.

Interestingly, both of Jesus' appeals to OT Scripture in the first half of this gospel (John 6:45; 10:34) are unique to John, as is Jesus' OT reference in 15:25. This may suggest that John is seeking to supplement the Synoptic Gospels and in any case attests to John's independence in writing his gospel. As Margaret Daly-Denton notes, John's use of the Psalms, too, while generally congruent with the Synoptics, evidences a certain form of independence, a feature highlighted further by John's penchant toward formal citation.[103] The same author also notes that John's use of the Psalms is spread throughout the entire gospel rather than being mainly concentrated on the Passion Narrative, as is the case in the Synoptics.

---

103. Margaret Daly-Denton, *David in the Fourth Gospel: The Johannine Reception of the Psalms* (AGJU 47; Leiden: Brill, 2004), 121.

13.2.4 Alignment of Old Testament Quotations in John's Gospel with the MT or the LXX

13.2.4.1 Survey Chart

The text form underlying the various explicit OT quotations in John's gospel has been the subject of considerable debate.[104] The following chart provides a basic survey.

John	OT	Relationship with [proto-] MT, LXX
1:23	Isa 40:3	LXX? change from *hetoimasate ... eutheias* to *euthynate*
2:17	Ps 69:9a	LXX? change from *katephagen* to *kataphagetai*
6:31	Ps 78:24b	LXX? *phagein* at end rather than beginning; *ek tou* added
6:45	Isa 54:14a	LXX? as in MT, *pantes* nom. rather than acc. (as in LXX); as in LXX, *theou* rather than *kyriou*; "your sons" omitted
10:34	Ps 82:6a	same as LXX = MT
12:13	Ps 118:26a	same as LXX = MT (adds *kai ho basileus tou Israēl*)
12:15	Zech 9:9	independent adaptation of LXX/MT: "Do not be afraid." Added (Isa 40:9?); *sou* omitted; "seated," not "mounted"; "a donkey's colt" (Gen 49:11?)
12:38	Isa 53:1	same as LXX = MT
12:40	Isa 6:10	independent adaption of LXX/MT: "hearing" omitted; concentric structure changed to parallel one; etc.
13:18	Ps 41:9b	independent of LXX, own translation from Hebrew?
15:25	Ps 35:19 or 69:4	LXX? accurately reflects both MT and LXX
19:24	Ps 22:18	same as LXX = MT
19:36	Exod 12:46/Num 9:12; Ps 34:20	? combination of Exod 12:46/Num 9:12; Ps 34:20 LXX
19:37	Zech 12:10	close to Hebrew; LXX misreads the Hebrew; *testimonium*?

Fig. 13.3: Alignment of OT Quotations in John with MT or LXX

13.2.4.2 Discussion

Overall, as the detailed discussions below will demonstrate, John seems to exhibit a pattern of closeness to the OT text in the Hebrew and as reflected in the LXX. While his default version seems to have been the Septuagint, John in no way uses it slavishly but throughout exhibits a highly intelligent and discerning mode of OT usage. In four passages, his Greek is identical to the LXX wording (John 10:34; 12:13, 38; 19:24). In several other passages, John likely adapts the LXX rendering

---

104. See especially Menken, *Old Testament Quotations in the Fourth Gospel*.

by making minor changes to suit his context (1:23; 2:17; 6:31, 45; 15:25; 19:36). In four cases, John seems to be independent of the LXX (12:15, 40; 13:18; 19:37), whereby 12:15 and 40 represent independent adaptations of the relevant texts; 13:18 may feature John's own translation from the Hebrew; and 19:37 may draw on a Christian *testimonium* (in this final case the LXX is unsuitable since it misconstrues the Hebrew).

Hence it appears that John was familiar with both the Hebrew text and the LXX (as well as with Jesus' own use and earlier Christian quotation practices) and was thus able to cite the Scriptures either in the exact or slightly adapted LXX version or to draw on the Hebrew where this suited his purposes or seemed necessary for some reason or another. Finally, in keeping with Jewish exegetical practice, John at times clusters two OT texts (John 12:13, 15; 12:38, 40; 19:36, 37) or combines interrelated texts (e.g., Zech 9:9; Isa 40:9; and Gen 49:11 LXX in John 12:15 or Exod 12:46/Num 9:12 and Ps 34:20 in John 19:36; see also 7:38).[105]

13.2.5 Attribution of Old Testament Quotes in John's Gospel and Old Testament Passages Cited

13.2.5.1 Survey Chart

Yet another way to categorize the explicit OT quotations in John's gospel is by way of attribution to specific Johannine characters. The data presents itself as follows.

John	Attribution	OT Passage
1:23	John the Baptist	Isa 40:3
2:17	disciples/evangelist	Ps 69:9a (David)
6:31	the Jews	Ps 78:24b (Asaph)
6:45	Jesus	Isa 54:14a
10:34	Jesus	Ps 82:6a (Asaph)
12:13	the crowd	Ps 118:26a (none)
12:15	evangelist	Zech 9:9
12:38	evangelist	Isa 53:1
12:40	evangelist	Isa 6:10
13:18	Jesus	Ps 41:9b (David)
15:25	Jesus	Ps 35:19 or 69:4 (David)
19:24	evangelist	Ps 22:18 (David)
19:36	evangelist	Exod 12:46/Num 9:12; Ps 34:20
19:37	evangelist	Zech 12:10

Fig. 13.4: Attribution of OT Quotations in John's Gospel

---

105. See ibid., 52–53, 159–60.

13.2.5.2 Discussion

Four OT quotations in John's gospel are attributed to Jesus (John 6:45; 10:34; 13:18; 15:25), seven to the evangelist (2:17; 12:15, 38, 40; 19:24, 36, 37), one to the Baptist (1:23), and two to the crowd (6:31; 12:13). Three of Jesus' four OT references are to the Psalms, and one is to the book of Isaiah. References to Isaiah are also attributed to the Baptist and the evangelist. Both quotations of Zechariah are the work of the evangelist. Overall, the evangelist's use of the OT is varied, featuring two references each to the book of Psalms, Isaiah, and Zechariah and one to the Pentateuch. Interestingly, references to Davidic psalms are limited to Jesus' interaction with, or perception of, the disciples (2:17; 13:18; 15:25; 19:24).

Regardless of the person to whom the respective quotes are attributed, ultimately all references have Jesus and his messianic identity in view.[106] John 1:23 defines the Baptist's role over against Jesus' as a voice preparing the way for the coming King. John 2:17 and 12:15 align Jesus' actions with those anticipated in OT messianic passages. John 6:31 and 12:13 likewise relate Jesus to messianic expectations rooted in the Hebrew Scriptures. Opposition to Jesus fulfills the pattern established in the OT (12:38–40; 13:18; 15:25), as do various details of Jesus' death (19:24, 36, 37; see also 19:28). Jesus is the Son of God (10:34), and all of God's true sons and daughters will be taught by Yahweh through him (6:45).

13.2.6 Old Testament Quotations in John's Gospel in Old Testament Order

13.2.6.1 Survey Chart

In addition to the listing of explicit OT quotations in John's gospel, it may be helpful to provide a chronological chart of these references in OT order. In the case of Psalms references, the book of the Psalter and any author attribution in the title (where available) are provided as well.[107]

OT	John
Exod 12:46/Num 9:12	19:36
Ps 22:18 (David; Book 1)	19:24
Ps 34:20 (David, Book 1)	19:36*
Ps 35:19 (David; Book 1)	15:25
Ps 41:9b (David; Book 1)	13:18
Ps 69:4 (David; Book 2)	15:25

(Continued on the next page)

---

106. See Carson, "John and the Johannine Epistles," 246.
107. An asterisk marks quotes from the Psalms proposed by Daly-Denton, *David in the Fourth Gospel*, 119–37.

(Continued)

OT	John
Ps 69:9a (David; Book 2)	2:17
Ps 69:21 (David; Book 2)	19:28*
Ps 78:15, 20 (Asaph; Book 3)	7:38*
Ps 78:24b (Asaph; Book 3)	6:31
Ps 82:6a (Asaph; Book 3)	10:34
Ps 118:26a (none; Book 5)	12:13
Isa 6:10	12:40
Isa 40:3	1:23
Isa 53:1	12:38
Isa 54:14a	6:45
Zech 9:9	12:15
Zech 12:10	19:37

Fig. 13.5: OT Quotations in John's Gospel in OT Order

13.2.6.2 Discussion

The direct OT quotations in John are concentrated on a select few portions of the canon. The OT theological center, at least as far as explicit OT quotations is concerned, is clearly the Psalter.[108] References to the Psalms are spread fairly evenly throughout the entire gospel, both through Part 1 (John 2:17; 6:31; 10:34; 12:13) and Part 2 (13:18; 15:25; 19:28; cf. 19:28, 36). Both the quantity and the consistent distribution of references to the Psalter in John's gospel are truly impressive and attest to the significance of the Psalms in John's theology and Jesus' self-understanding and to the connection between Jesus' messianic claims and identity and the person and kingship of David.[109]

The other important OT portion for John's theology is the second part of Isaiah, which, in terms of explicit quotations, is represented at the beginning (John 1:23), the middle (6:45), and the end (12:40) of Part 1 of John's gospel.[110] The Baptist, Jesus, and John, respectively, draw on passages found in the second part of Isaiah to establish (1) the identity of the Baptist as one who prepares the way for the coming of Jesus, the royal Messiah; (2) the fact that it is through Jesus' teaching ministry that God's people are taught in the eschatological age inaugurated by Jesus the

---

108. Daly-Denton, *David in the Fourth Gospel*; idem, "The Psalms in John's Gospel," in *The Psalms in the New Testament* (ed. Steven Moyise and Maarten J. J. Menken; NTSI; London: T&T Clark International, 2004), 119–37; cf. Walter R. Wifall, "David—Prototype of Israel's Future?" *BTB* 4 (1974): 94–107.

109. See Menken, *Old Testament Quotations in the Fourth Gospel*, 44.

110. Franklin W. Young, "A Study of the Relation of Isaiah to the Fourth Gospel," *ZNW* 46 (1955): 215–33; Craig A. Evans, "Obduracy and the Lord's Servant: Some Observations on the Use of the Old Testament in the Fourth Gospel," in *Early Jewish and Christian Exegesis: Studies in Memory of William Hugh Brownlee* (ed. Craig A. Evans and William F. Stinespring; Homage 10; Atlanta: Scholars Press, 1987), 221–36; Bernd Janowski and Peter Stuhlmacher, eds., *The Suffering Servant: Isaiah 53 in Jewish and Christian Scriptures* (trans. Daniel P. Bailey; Grand Rapids: Eerdmans, 2004).

Messiah; and (3) the notion that the rejection of Jesus by the Jewish nation fulfills the OT characterization of the Jews as resisting God's message as delivered through his appointed spokesmen.

Last but not least, Zechariah is represented significantly in John's gospel as well with two major references at the end of Part 1 and Part 2 respectively.[111] Both references are decidedly christological in focus: the first depicting Jerusalem's visitation by the Messiah, a humble servant-king who enters the city mounted on a donkey; the second shifting the point of application from Yahweh to Jesus as the object of people's looking "on the one they have pierced."

13.2.7 Old Testament Allusions and Verbal Parallels in John's Gospel

13.2.7.1 Survey Chart

The final survey chart lists verifiable OT allusions and verbal parallels in John's gospel. It is often precarious to identify OT allusions, especially if these are limited to those that were authorially intended. For this reason the following chart remains of necessity tentative. In order to enable a full view of OT references, explicit quotations are included in square brackets.

John	OT
1:1	Gen 1:1
1:14	Exod 34:6
1:17	Exod 34:6
1:18	Exod 33:20
1:21	Deut 18:15, 18
[1:23]	[Isa 40:3]
1:29, 36	Isa 53:6–7
1:45	Deut 18:15, 18
1:49	Ps 2:7; 2 Sam 7:14; Zeph 3:15
1:51	Gen 28:12
2:5	Gen 41:55
[2:17]	[Ps 69:9a]
3:5	Ezek 36:25–27
3:8	Eccl 11:5
3:13	Prov 30:4?
3:14	Num 21:9; Isa 52:13

(Continued on the next page)

---

111. F. F. Bruce, "The Book of Zechariah and the Passion Narrative," *BJRL* 43 (1960/61): 336–53; R. T. France, *Jesus and the Old Testament: His Application of Old Testament Passages to Himself and His Mission* (London: Tyndale, 1971), 103–10, 148–50, 208–9.

(Continued)

John	OT
3:16	Gen 22:2, 12, 16
3:28	Mal 3:1
4:5	Gen 33:19; 48:22; Exod 13:19; Josh 24:32
4:10	Num 20:8–11; cf. 21:16–18
4:14	Isa 12:3; Jer 2:13
4:20	Deut 11:29; 12:5–14; 27:12; Josh 8:33; Ps 122:1–5
4:22	Isa 2:3?
4:36	Amos 9:13?
4:37	Mic 6:15?
5:27	Dan 7:13
5:29	Dan 12:2
5:45	Deut 31:26–27
5:46	Deut 18:15, 18
6:14	Deut 18:15, 18
6:29	Mal 3:1
[6:31]	[Ps 78:24b]
[6:45]	[Isa 54:14a]
7:22	Gen 17:10–13; Lev 12:3
7:24	Lev 19:15
7:38	Neh 9:15, 19–20; cf. Num 20:11, etc.; Ps 77:16, 20 LXX; Isa 58:11; Zech 14:8
7:40	Deut 18:15, 18
7:42	2 Sam 7:12; Ps 89:3–4; Mic 5:2
7:51	Deut 1:16–17; 17:4; 19:18
8:12	Isa 9:1–2; cf. 49:6
8:15	1 Sam 16:7
8:17	Deut 17:6; 19:15
8:28	Isa 52:13
8:35	Gen 21:1–21
8:44	Gen 3:4 (cf. 2:17); Isa 14:12?
9:2	Exod 20:5; Ezek 18:20
9:5 [= 8:12]	Isa 9:1–2; cf. 49:6
9:24	Josh 7:19
9:34	Ps 51:5
10:3–4	Num 27:15–18
10:8	Jer 23:1–2; Ezek 34:2–3
10:16	Isa 56:8; Ezek 34:23; 37:24
10:33	Lev 24:16

John	OT
[10:34]	[Ps 82:6a]
12:8	Deut 15:11
[12:13]	[Ps 118:26a]
[12:15]	[Zech 9:9]
12:27	Ps 6:3; 42:5, 11
12:32	Isa 52:13
12:34	Ps 89:4, 36–37?
[12:38]	[Isa 53:1]
[12:40]	[Isa 6:10]
12:41	Isa 6:1
[13:18]	[Ps 41:9b]
15:1	Isa 5:1–7; cf. Jer 2:21
[15:25]	[Ps 35:19; 69:4]
16:22	Isa 66:14
16:32	Zech 13:7
17:12	Ps 41:9
19:7	Lev 24:16
19:18	Isa 22:16; cf. 52:13
[19:24]	[Ps 22:18]
19:28–29	Ps 69:21; cf. 22:15
19:31	Deut 21:22–23
[19:36]	[Exod 12:46; Num 9:12; Ps 34:20]
[19:37]	[Zech 12:10]
19:38	Isa 53:9
20:22	Gen 2:7
20:23	Isa 22:22?

Fig. 13.6: OT Allusions and Verbal Parallels in John's Gospel

13.2.7.2 Discussion

Apart from the fourteen direct OT quotations listed above, John's gospel features numerous OT allusions and verbal parallels with the OT.[112] The range of allusions spans virtually the entire OT. Particularly frequent are allusions to the Pentateuch, the Psalms, and OT prophetic literature, particularly Isaiah (see also Ezekiel and Zechariah).[113] In some cases, a given Johannine reference presupposes a foundational

---

112. Carson, "John and the Johannine Epistles," 251–53.
113. For John's use of Isaiah, see Young, "Study of the Relation of Isaiah to the Fourth Gospel"; Evans, "Obduracy and the Lord's Servant"; and James Hamilton, "The Influence of Isaiah on the Gospel of John," *Perichoresis* 5/2 (2007): 139–62. For John's use of Ezekiel, see Gary T. Manning Jr., *Echoes of a Prophet: The Use of Ezekiel in the Gospel of John and in Literature of the Second Temple Period* (JSNTSup 270; London/New York: T&T Clark, 2004).

passage in the OT (e.g., John 19:31 with reference to Deut 21:22–23). At times, reference is made to a particular OT event (e.g., John 3:14; 6:32; 7:22–23). In yet other instances, a given statement in John's gospel employs OT language (e.g., 16:22 with reference to Isa 66:14).

More significant still are verifiable OT allusions and verbal parallels that draw on the theology of a particular OT passage (e.g., John 10:16 with reference to Isa 56:8; Ezek 34:23; 37:24). Together with the direct OT quotations and references to broader OT themes (including the Johannine replacement motif),[114] the OT allusions found in John's gospel create a web of intertextuality that grounds the theology of John's gospel profoundly in the Hebrew Scriptures, particularly with regard to the person and teaching of Jesus.[115]

13.3 Conclusion

It is not the purpose of the present discussion to provide a full-fledged analysis of all the explicit OT quotations and verifiable allusions in John's gospel. I have attempted to do this in my contribution on John's gospel to the *Commentary on the New Testament Use of the Old Testament*. Where relevant, I will explore the OT background of John's gospel in the narrative survey in Part 2 and the treatment of major theological themes in John's gospel in Part 3 below.[116]

The importance of the OT as the primary source for Johannine theology cannot be overstated. John ties his account to OT Scripture at the outset of his gospel. His presentation of Jesus harks back to Moses and the exodus, especially with regard to Jesus' "signs." There are also allusions to the period of Elijah and Elisha, and Jesus is presented as Isaiah's Suffering Servant. Even Israel's rejection of her Messiah is shown to be consistent with a pattern of scriptural expectation and fulfillment. Davidic typology is present as well.

---

114. Carson, "John and the Johannine Epistles," 253–56.
115. Carson (ibid., 246) cites the following passages "where 'the Scripture' or some OT person or persons are said to speak or write of Jesus or of some aspect of his teaching or mission": John 1:45; 2:22; 3:10; 5:39; 5:45–46; 12:34; and 20:9.
116. See esp. chap. 10, secs. 22–24.

B. The End (Purpose; 20:30–31)

As mentioned, John's theology is conveyed first and foremost through the following three major sections in the gospel: its beginning (John 1:1–18); middle (13:1–3); and end (20:30–31). While a case can be made that first-time readers normally start reading a document from the beginning, so that an exploration of the major theological themes of John's gospel should likewise start at the beginning of John's gospel, the presentation of John's theology in the present volume is predicated on repeated readings of John's gospel. Clearly, the purpose statement is the culmination point of John's theological presentation, and it is here that he tells the reader what is central to his gospel: the Messiah and his signs.

For this reason it seems appropriate to start an investigation of John's theology with the purpose statement, especially since, remarkably, neither the signs nor the Messiah is mentioned in the introduction to the gospel (though the signs pervade the first half of John's narrative). After this, we will investigate John's gospel in light of the beginning and the middle of the Johannine drama, based on the observation that it is the major literary function of these respective introductions to Parts 1 and 2 of the gospel to sound the primary theological themes of John's *sēmeio-* and *cruci-drama* in John 1–12 and 13–21, respectively. In this way the Messiah and his signs, central to John's purpose, can set the stage for what follows.

Chapter 7

The Messiah and His Signs

Bibliography

Beale, G. K., and D. A. Carson, eds. *Commentary on the New Testament Use of the Old Testament*. Grand Rapids: Baker, 2007. **Bittner, Wolfgang J**. *Jesu Zeichen im Johannesevangelium: Die Messias-Erkenntnis im Johannesevangelium vor ihrem jüdischen Hintergrund*. WUNT 2/26. Tübingen: Mohr-Siebeck, 1987. **Brown, Raymond E**. "Appendix III: Signs and Works." Pp. 523–32 in *The Gospel According to John I–XII*. AB 29. Garden City, NY: Doubleday, 1966. **Carson, D. A**. "The Purpose of Signs and Wonders in the New Testament." Pp. 89–118 in *Power Religion*. Ed. Michael S. Horton; Chicago: Moody Press, 1992. **Charlesworth, James H**., ed. *The Messiah: Developments in Earliest Judaism and Christianity*. Minneapolis: Fortress, 1992. **Collins, John J**. *The Scepter and the Star: The Messiah of the Dead Sea Scrolls and Other Ancient Literature*. New York: Doubleday, 1995. **Davies, W. D**. "The Johannine 'Signs' of Jesus." Pp. 91–115 in *A Companion to John: Readings in Johannine*

Theology. Ed. Michael J. Taylor. New York: Alba, 1977. **De Jonge, Marinus.** "Signs and Works in the Fourth Gospel." Pp. 107–25 in *Miscellanea neotestamentica* 2. Ed. T. Baarda, A. F. J. Klijn, and W. C. van Unnik. NovTSup 48. Leiden: Brill, 1978. **France, R. T.** *Jesus and the Old Testament.* London: Tyndale, 1971. **Guthrie, Donald.** "The Importance of Signs in the Fourth Gospel." *VE* 5 (1967): 72–83. **Horbury, William.** *Jewish Messianism and the Cult of Christ.* London: SCM, 1998. **Hurtado, Larry W.** "Christ." Pp. 106–17 in *Dictionary of Jesus and the Gospels.* Ed. Joel B. Green, Scot McKnight, and I. Howard Marshall. Downers Grove: InterVarsity Press, 1992. **Lohse, Eduard.** "Miracles in the Fourth Gospel." Pp. 64–75 in *What about the New Testament? In Honor of Christopher Evans.* Ed. Morna D. Hooker and Colin J. A. Hickling. London: SCM, 1975. **Morris, Leon.** "The Relation between the Signs and the Discourses," "The Christ of God," and "The Son of God." Pp. 20–42 and 68–106 in *Jesus Is the Christ: Studies in the Theology of John.* Grand Rapids: Eerdmans, 1989. **Neusner, Jacob, William S. Green, and Ernest Frerichs,** eds. *Judaisms and Their Messiahs at the Turn of the Christian Era.* Cambridge: Cambridge University Press, 1987. **Nicol, Willem.** *The Sēmeia in the Fourth Gospel: Tradition and Redaction.* NovTSup 32. Leiden: Brill, 1972. **Porter, Stanley E.,** ed. *The Messiah in the Old and New Testaments.* McMaster NT Studies. Grand Rapids: Eerdmans, 2007. **Riga, Peter J.** "Signs of Glory: The Use of *Sēmeion* in John's Gospel." *Int* 17 (1963): 402–10. **Salier, Willis Hedley.** *The Rhetorical Impact of the Sēmeia in the Gospel of John.* WUNT 2/186. Tübingen: Mohr-Siebeck, 2004. **Schnackenburg, Rudolf.** "Excursus IV: The Johannine 'Signs.'" Pp. 515–28 in *The Gospel according to St. John.* Vol. 1. New York: Crossroad, 1992. **Thompson, Marianne Meye.** "Signs and Faith in the Fourth Gospel." *BBR* 1 (1991): 89–108. Idem. "Signs, Seeing, and Faith." Pp. 53–86 in *The Humanity of Jesus in the Fourth Gospel.* Philadelphia: Fortress, 1988. **Welck, Christian.** *Erzählte Zeichen: Die Wundergeschichten des Johannesevangeliums literarisch untersucht. Mit einem Ausblick auf Joh 21.* WUNT 2/69. Tübingen: Mohr-Siebeck, 1994. **Wilkens, Wilhelm.** *Zeichen und Werke: Ein Beitrag zur Theologie des 4. Evangeliums in Erzählungs- und Redestoff.* ATANT 55. Zurich: Zwingli, 1969.

14 The Messiah

14.1 Background and Overview

14.1.1 Terminology

"Messiah" (*mašiaḥ* in Hebrew) means "the Anointed One."[1] The Greek translation equivalent, found about forty-five times in the LXX and over five hundred times in the NT, is *Christos*, "Christ" or "Messiah" (originally an adjective, "anointed,"

---

[1]. See the magisterial study by Horbury, *Messianism.* See also Richard S. Hess, "The Image of the Messiah in the Old Testament," in *Images of Christ: Ancient and Modern* (ed. Stanley E. Porter, Michael A. Hayes, and David Tombs; Sheffield: Sheffield Academic Press, 1997), 22–33; Larry W. Hurtado, "Christ," in *Dictionary of Jesus and the Gospels*, 106–17; and Morris, "The Christ of God," in *Jesus Is the Christ*, 68–106. The discussion under the present heading is adapted from my entry "Messiah" in *The Encyclopedia of Early Christianity* (ed. George T. Kurian; Oxford: Blackwell, 2009).

from the verb *chriō*, "to smear with ointment or oil"). The transliterated form *Messias*, from the Aramaic *mešiḥa*, is found twice in John's gospel (John 1:42; 4:25), which suggests that in first-century Judaism "Messiah" had become a technical term. "Anointed" designates the special ceremony of installing an individual to an exalted position, most notably that of king or ruler (1 Sam 9:15–16; 10:1; 16:3, 12–13; 2 Sam 2:4; 5:3; 1 Kgs 1:34, 45; 5:1; 2 Kgs 9:3, 6; 11:12; 23:30).

14.1.2 The Messiah in the Old Testament and Second Temple Literature

14.1.2.1 Old Testament References to "the LORD's Anointed"

Already early in OT times, the king was called "the LORD's Anointed," "the Anointed of the God of Israel," or simply "the Anointed" (1 Sam 2:10; 24:6; 26:16; 2 Sam 1:14, 16; 23:2; cf. Dan 9:25–26). Even the patriarchs are occasionally called God's "anointed" (e.g., Abraham, Isaac, and Jacob; Ps 105:15). Considerably less common are references to the anointing of prophets or priests (Exod 28:41; Lev 4:3–5; Num 3:3; 1 Kgs 19:16; cf. 1QM 11:8). An alternate messianic title in the OT is "Son of God." Thus in Psalm 2, it is said of the Messiah that Yahweh said to him, "You are my son, today I have begotten you" (Ps 2:2; cf. Acts 4:25–26; 13:33; Heb 1:5; 5:5; 4Q174).[2]

The presence of "royal" or "enthronement psalms" in the OT Psalter attests to the presence of the messianic hope in Israel (e.g., Psalms 2; 72; 89; 110; 132), as do messianic passages in many of the OT prophetic books, which center around the Davidic dynasty (cf. 4Q174) or a coming descendant of David (most notable passages in Isaiah, Jeremiah, Ezekiel, Hosea, Amos, Zechariah).[3] Zerubbabel is the object of messianic prophecy as well (Hag 2:20–23; Zech 3:8; 4:6–10; 6:12). Hence, the messianic hope finds expression in all the major sections of the Hebrew Bible—the Pentateuch, the Psalms, and the Prophets.

14.1.2.2 The Old Testament Messianic Hope

Yet the messianic hope that finds expression throughout the OT is considerably broader than references to "the LORD's Anointed."[4] Moses is one of the earliest prototypes of the Messiah as the miracle-working deliverer and less commonly as a prophet or even king (e.g., Deut 33:5; Isa 63:11). David is portrayed in various passages as a suffering yet ultimately victorious king (e.g., Psalms 21; 22) who received promises regarding his dynasty (2 Sam 7:14; cf. Jer 30:9; Ezek 34:23; 37:25; Hos

---

2. On the Johannine characterization of Jesus as "the Son," including "the Son of God," see chap. 9, sec. 20 below.

3. See also the reference to a "ruler" from Judah in Gen 49:10 (cf. 4Q252) and the "proto-evangelion" in Gen 3:15, envisaging a future "offspring" of the woman who will crush Satan's head.

4. See Philip E. Satterthwaite, Richard S. Hess, and Gordon J. Wenham, eds., *The Lord's Anointed: Interpretation of Old Testament Messianic Texts* (Grand Rapids: Baker, 1995); Antti Laato, *A Star Is Rising: The Historical Development of the Old Testament Royal Ideology and the Rise of the Jewish Messianic Expectations* (Atlanta: Scholars Press, 1997); Horbury, *Messianism*; Tremper Longman, "The Messiah: Explorations in the Law and Writings" and Mark J. Boda, "Figuring the Future: The Prophets and Messiah," in *The Messiah in the Old and New Testaments* (McMaster NT Studies; ed. Stanley E. Porter; Grand Rapids: Eerdmans, 2007), 13–34 and 35–74, respectively.

3:5). A related figure is the Suffering Servant of Yahweh (see esp. Isaiah 53). Also relevant are the smitten shepherd of Zech 13:7, who is part of a cluster of messianic references in Zechariah, and the Son of Man mentioned in Dan 7:13 (cf. *1 Enoch*).

14.1.2.3 The Second Temple Period

At least from the Hellenistic period (after 331 BC), and certainly from the second century BC onward, the absolute designation "the Anointed" was broadly understood to refer to a coming figure who embodied the hopes of Israel and would serve as a God-sent deliverer. The Qumran scrolls likewise attest to the presence of the messianic hope in the Second Temple period, referring variously to a "messiah of Aaron and Israel" (4Q266; 1QSa=1Q28 2:12: "the messiah") or to two separate messiahs, both royal and priestly (1QS 9:10–11; CD 12:22–23), as do numerous other passages in Second Temple literature, such as the late-first century BC *Psalms of Solomon* (*Pss. Sol.* 17:32; 18:7).[5]

While some form of messianic expectations was thus common, however, there was no consensus regarding the exact figure whose coming was expected or the circumstances surrounding his arrival, and first-century Judaism displayed a variety of messianic expectations.[6] Some understood the Messiah in terms of the Davidic king, while others looked to the Prophet like Moses or some other figure (cf., e.g., Matt 16:14; John 6:14). Hence the NT usage of "Messiah" or "Christ" with reference to Jesus taps into this already existing usage and provides the background for the Christian understanding that Jesus was in fact "the LORD's Anointed," the king, ruler, and deliverer predicted in the OT.

14.1.3 The Messiah in the New Testament

14.1.3.1 Overview

In the NT, the term "Messiah" or "Christ" is frequently linked with the expression "Son of God," which may suggest belief in the divinity of Jesus the Messiah (e.g., Matt 16:16; John 20:30–31).[7] The term "Christ," often as part of the designation "Jesus Christ," "Christ Jesus," or "Lord Jesus Christ," and sometimes absolutely as "Christ" (e.g., Rom 9:5), is virtually ubiquitous in Paul's writings (almost 400 of the 500 NT references). It is comparatively less frequent in the four Gospels.[8]

---

5. Al Wolters, "The Messiah in the Qumran Documents," in *Messiah in the Old and New Testaments*, 77–80, with reference to John J. Collins, *The Scepter and the Star: The Messiah of the Dead Sea Scrolls and Other Ancient Literature* (New York: Doubleday, 1995), speaks of four messianic paradigms: (1) the Davidic king; (2) the eschatological priest; (3) the prophet or teacher; and (4) the heavenly Messiah. See also James H. Charlesworth, Hermann Lichtenberger, and Gerbern S. Oegema, eds., *Qumran-Messianism: Studies on the Messianic Expectations in the Dead Sea Scrolls* (Tübingen: Mohr-Siebeck, 1998); and Craig A. Evans, "The Messiah in the Dead Sea Scrolls," in *The Scrolls and the Scriptures: Qumran Fifty Years After* (ed. Stanley E. Porter and Craig A. Evans; Sheffield: Sheffield Academic Press, 1997), 183–97.

6. See Jacob Neusner, William S. Green, and Ernest Frerichs, eds., *Judaisms and Their Messiahs at the Turn of the Christian Era* (Cambridge: Cambridge University Press, 1987).

7. For a survey, see Craig L. Blomberg, "Messiah in the New Testament," in Hess and Carroll R., *Israel's Messiah*, 111–41.

8. The expression is found sixteen times in Matthew; seven times in Mark; twelve times in Luke; nineteen times in John; and twenty-five times in Acts.

14.1.3.2 The Four Gospels

The references to Jesus as the Messiah in Matthew's and Mark's gospels are closely aligned (though generally more explicit in Matthew).[9] In Matthew, Jesus is referred to at the outset as "Jesus the Messiah the son of David" (Matt 1:1; cf. 2:1–4). In both Matthew and Mark, Peter confesses Jesus as "the Messiah" at a watershed juncture in Jesus' ministry (Matt 16:16; Mark 8:29), though at that time Jesus did not want this fact openly proclaimed, presumably owing to the likelihood that his messianic nature would be misconstrued in political or nationalistic terms. Later, Jesus is asked directly by the Jewish high priest whether he is the Messiah, and he responds in the affirmative (Matt 26:63–64; Mark 14:61–62; cf. Dan 7:13).

In Luke, likewise, early reference is made to the coming of "a Savior," who is "the Messiah, the Lord" (Luke 2:11; cf. Acts 2:36). Simeon prophetically links Jesus' coming to "the Lord's Messiah" (Luke 2:26). References to Jesus as the Messiah in the body of Luke's gospel closely parallel those in the other Synoptic Gospels, except for the programmatic statement in Luke 4:16–30 (citing Isa 61:1–2 and 58:6), which presents Jesus as God's anointed prophet.[10] Distinctive Lucan references to Jesus as the Messiah predicted in the Hebrew Scriptures are found at the end of his gospel (Luke 24:26–27, 44–47). The references to "Jesus Christ," "Christ Jesus," and "the Lord Jesus Christ" in Acts largely parallel Pauline usage.

Similar to the Synoptics, John identifies Jesus as the Messiah in keeping with Jewish messianic expectations. In keeping with the purpose statement (John 20:30–31; cf. 11:27), Jesus' messianic identity is revealed in his encounters with his first followers (1:41; cf. 1:49), a Samaritan woman (4:25, 29), and the crowds (7:25–44; 12:34). This includes the Messiah's uncertain provenance (7:27), his performance of signs (7:31; cf. 20:30–31), his birth in Bethlehem (7:40–44), and his crucifixion and subsequent exaltation (his "lifting up"; cf. 3:14; 8:28; 12:34). Already in 9:22, confession of Jesus as the Christ leads to synagogue expulsion. When asked directly whether or not he is the Messiah, Jesus responds with an indirect affirmation (10:34–39). The identification of the heaven-sent Son of Man with Jesus the Messiah and Son of God is at the center of John's gospel.[11]

14.1.4 Conclusion

While the crucifixion of Jesus constituted a major obstacle for the Christian proclamation of Jesus as Messiah, the belief that Jesus is the Messiah in keeping with Jewish messianic hopes is foundational to Christianity. According to all four Gospels, the Jewish rejection of Jesus is tantamount to the rejection of their Messiah. Not only does the identification of Jesus with the Messiah root Christianity in Israel's

---

9. See I. Howard Marshall, "Jesus as Messiah in Mark and Matthew," in *Messiah in the Old and New Testaments*, 117–43, who observes that in Matthew Jesus' filial relation to God, his role as a teacher, and his superior authority are emphasized more keenly than in Mark.

10. See Stanley E. Porter, "The Messiah in Luke and Acts: Forgiveness for the Captives," in *Messiah in the Old and New Testaments*, 144–64.

11. See further the discussion and narrative survey below.

hopes, but Christian devotion of Jesus transcends OT messianism, making explicit Jesus' divine nature and directing worship to Jesus as God on a par with Yahweh himself.

14.2 Preliminary Considerations in the Study of John's Christology

14.2.1 The Centrality of Christology in John's Gospel and Letters

Christology is at the front and center of John's gospel. It is at the very beginning. The opening is not, as in Genesis, "In the beginning *God*," but, "In the beginning *the Word*" (John 1:1). This is not to pit theology against Christology, as if one were necessarily more important for John than the other. In fact, for John theology and Christology are inseparable. For God the Father is everywhere called "the one who sent" Jesus and who stands behind his filial mission. Yet from the introduction (1:1–18) to the purpose statement (20:30–31) the Johannine narrative focuses on Jesus and his identity as the Word, the Messiah, and the Son of God.

One primary reason for this is that the identity of *God* was not in dispute among first-century Jews; the identity of *Jesus* was. All Jews believed that there was one God; they were monotheists. Yet it was precisely because they believed there was one, and only one, God that Jesus' claim to deity seemed to conflict with their monotheism. John, then, squarely chose to address this quandary: How does Jesus' claim to be God cohere with the Jewish belief, and the affirmation of the Hebrew Scriptures, that "the Lord our God, the Lord is one" (Deut 6:4)?[12]

14.2.2 The Limitations of a "Titles of Christ" Approach

In the history of Johannine scholarship, the Christology of John's gospel has often suffered from a certain degree of compartmentalization resulting from a "titles of Christ" type of approach. Too often the underlying paradigm in exploring Johannine themes, including Christology, whether explicitly or implicitly, has been some variation of a history-of-religions model, a form of the historical-critical method, or a strictly literary, narrative paradigm. What is needed, however, is a literary-theological paradigm that does not cut off historical questions but takes its point of departure from the final text in its entirety and seeks to understand its theology globally and holistically. This, of course, runs counter to the prevailing practice in contemporary scholarship in which scholars are engaged in their own narrow areas of research and approaches but rarely interact with anyone outside of their own field.[13]

Consequently, scholars have provided detailed discussions of the various individual titles applied to Jesus throughout John's gospel — Son of Man, Son of God,

---

12. See on this the discussion in chap. 9, sec. 17 below.

13. Kevin Vanhoozer, in *Drama of Doctrine*, has called for "theological interpretation," by which he means, among other things, that these barriers impeding a full-orbed understanding of the biblical text must be broken down. This is indeed an urgent *desideratum*. See my faculty lecture published as "Of Professors and Madmen: Currents in Contemporary New Testament Scholarship," *Faith & Mission* 23/2 (Spring 2006): 3–18.

Messiah, king of Israel, Prophet like Moses, and so on. In each case, they sought to determine the content and likely OT, Second Temple, or Hellenistic background. In the end, they put these individual investigations together in order to construct a composite picture from their investigations that, they claimed, was an accurate representation of John's Christology. This procedure, however, is inadequate, for it does not do sufficient justice to the narrative christological fabric of John's gospel in its entirety. I hope to show that John is considerably more holistic in his understanding of Jesus' identity.

14.2.3 Toward a Holistic Approach: Climactic Fulfillment in Jesus

In light of the considerations registered under the previous heading, therefore, the question is not so much whether Jesus was the Son of Man, or the Prophet like Moses, or the Messiah, and so on, and, if so, exactly what this meant for John; but rather that for John, as for Jesus, in Jesus *all of these figures* found their culmination. He fulfilled the entire fabric of scriptural messianic material: he was the Son of Man (John 3:13; 5:27; cf. Dan 7:13); he was the Prophet like Moses (John 6:14; cf. Deut 18:18); he was the Suffering Servant who was at the heart of Isaiah's message (John 12:38–40; cf. Isa 52:13–53:12); and he was the Messiah, the Son of God (John 20:30–31 *et passim*; 1 John 5:1; cf. 2 Sam 7:14; Ps 2:2).

Thus, it is John's message that in Jesus, all the various scriptural messianic predictions and typology converged, not only in his life but most signally in his death (John 19:24, 27, 28). Thus it misses the point to argue that one messianic figure is more central in John's portrayal of Jesus' identity than another.[14] In a very important sense, John's message is that in Jesus *all* of salvation history finds its climactic fulfillment.

14.3 Major Aspects of John's Portrayal of Jesus as Messiah

14.3.1 The Word, the Light

Keeping in mind the cautions registered above, it will now be helpful to study the way in which John develops his Christology in the unfolding narrative of his gospel. The introduction provides the reader with the major heading under which John's Christology is to be subsumed: "the Word," a designation that, in turn, is developed in terms of "light" and "life." "In him was life" (John 1:4), John's readers are told, and he was also "the true light" that came into the world (1:9). Being "life" puts Jesus on par with God, who alone is the Life-Giver; and being the "light" has both messianic overtones and sets Jesus against the dark moral backdrop of a reprobate, rebellious world that has rejected God's rule and his law and therefore will also reject his Messiah.[15]

---

14. Cf. John Lierman, *The New Testament Moses: Christian Conceptions of Moses and Israel in the Setting of Jewish Religion* (WUNT 137; Tübingen: Mohr-Siebeck, 2004).

15. See the discussion of "light" symbolism in chap. 3, sec. 7.5.4 above.

14.3.2 Messiah, Elijah, the Prophet

The second christological installment, like the first (John the Baptist's denial of being the light, John 1:7–8), is given in negative form, indicating what John is not: the Messiah, Elijah, and the Prophet (1:21–23). By implication, it appears, John intends to say through these denials that precisely what John is *not*, Jesus *is*: the Messiah, "Elijah," and the Prophet. For in Jesus, as mentioned, all scriptural messianic expectations converge and find their climactic fulfillment. Jesus is the Messiah, the "Anointed One."

While, unlike the Synoptics, the fourth evangelist does not record Jesus' baptism and the voice from heaven, he does seize upon the essence of the heavenly testimony to Jesus the Son: he is the "Anointed One," the one begotten of the Father (cf. Ps 2:2). Properly understood, Jesus fulfills, in escalating fashion, the miraculous ministry performed in the era of Elijah/Elisha (cf. 2 Kings 4:42–44). And he is the Prophet like Moses, working "signs" as Moses did at the exodus. In fact, he does not merely *give* people bread from heaven to eat; he *is* this heavenly bread (John 6).[16]

14.3.3 Lamb of God, King of Israel

In addition, John gathers a series of additional christological designations in the remainder of John 1, including "Lamb of God" (1:29, 36), "king of Israel" (1:49), and others—designations whose deeper significance he will unpack more fully in the unfolding narrative. By the time John has told his story, his reader will know that Jesus took away the sin of the world by his atoning sacrifice on the cross and that he truly is the messianic king of Israel. In fine Johannine irony, this is a fact that escaped Pilate, who mockingly referred to him as "the king of the Jews" but who spoke better than he knew. While not a king in a political, nationalistic sense, Jesus was the messianic king (18:36–37), and only those who believed in him and were spiritually born again would get to enter his kingdom (3:3, 5).[17]

14.3.4 Popular Messianic Expectations

Also, the fourth evangelist gathers various messianic expectations current in Jesus' day in John 7 and provides various correctives in order to clarify who Jesus was over against common misconceptions or partial conceptions of the Messiah in first-century Judaism. As the Messiah, Jesus performed numerous "signs" (John 7:31). Jesus the Messiah hailed indeed from Bethlehem, not Galilee (7:41–42). What is more, in a climactic clarification, John shows that while Jesus the Son of Man will remain forever, as the Suffering Servant he must die and be raised back to life (12:32–34). Rightly understood, Jesus was indeed the Prophet like Moses and Israel's king, but he was not "the king of the Jews" in a political, nationalistic

---

16. See the discussion of "bread" symbolism in chap. 3, sec. 7.5.3 above.

17. See the discussion of the cosmic trial motif in chap. 11 and of the new birth in chap. 12 below.

sense (hence he withdraws as the "elusive Christ"; cf. 6:15). He came to teach God's people in these last days, and was called "rabbi" by his disciples, and yet he did so as the Messiah, the Son of God, who was so much more than a mere religious teacher.[18]

14.3.5 Signs

Perhaps the most critical move in this regard by John is that of shifting the emphasis away from "miracles" as striking displays of divine power to "signs," which reveal beyond the external act the way in which God's glory was revealed in and through Jesus.[19] Together with Jesus' "signs" (called mere "works" by Jesus himself; e.g., John 9:3–4; 10:25, 32) John also features Jesus' words in extended discourses, in some cases further explicating the "sign-ificance" of Jesus' "signs," in other cases explicating aspects of his own messianic identity (such as his self-reference as the "Son of Man" in 3:13–14 or his various "I am sayings"). Hence both "signs" and "discourses," both works and words, combine to paint a full-orbed portrait of the way in which Jesus, as John's purpose statement asserts, is "the Messiah, the Son of God" (20:30–31; cf. 11:27).

14.3.6 The Coming One

Finally, Jesus is progressively identified as the Messiah in the Johannine narrative by a series of references to him as "the Coming One," indicating his fulfillment of OT messianic expectations.[20] In fact, the terms "the Coming One" and "Messiah" are often found side by side (see John 4:25; 7:27, 31, 41, 42; 11:27).[21] One or both of these expressions are used in the following passages: *Iēsous Christos* in 1:17 and 17:3; *Messias* in 1:41 and 4:25; and *Christos*, apart from these passages, in 4:29; 7:26, 27, 31, 41, 42; 9:22; 10:24; 11:27; 12:34; and 20:31; "the Prophet who is to come into the world" in 6:14; and references to the shepherd-king quoting the OT in 12:13 and 15. A study of these relevant passages reveals that John uses the utterances of representative characters to guide his readers in their own investigation as to whether or not Jesus is in fact the Messiah.[22]

---

18. See my essay "Jesus as Rabbi in the Fourth Gospel," *BBR* 8 (1998): 97–128.
19. See the discussion below.
20. See also Edwin D. Freed, "*Egō eimi* in John 8,24 in the Light of Its Context and Jewish Messianic Belief," *JTS* 33 (1982): 163–67, who argues that the expression *egō eimi* in John 8:24 reflects a messianic claim on the part of Jesus, referring to the expectation that the Messiah would reprove sinners to *Pss. Sol.* 17:25; 2 Esdr 12:32; 13:13–38; and 4QpIsa on Isa 11:1–5. Commenting on the possible connection between John 8:18 and Isa 43:10 Freed contends, "It would be easy for John to make the transition from servant to Messiah, since for him Jesus surely fulfilled both roles. It was a foregone conclusion in all Jewish Messianic belief that the Messiah would be chosen and sent by God to be his special agent" (p. 167).
21. See also Eduardo Arens, *The Elthon-Sayings in the Synoptic Tradition: A Historico-Critical Investigation* (OBO 10; Freiburg: Universitätsverlag/Göttingen: Vandenhoeck & Ruprecht, 1976), 288–300.
22. Note that the term "representative characters" does not imply a negative evaluation of the historicity of the gospel's characters. Contra, Marinus de Jonge, "Jewish Expectations about the 'Messiah' according to the Fourth Gospel," *NTS* 19 (1973): 246–70; Raymond F. Collins, "Representative Figures," in *These Things Have Been Written* (Grand Rapids: Eerdmans, 1991), 1–45.

14.4 The Narrative Unfolding of John's Presentation of Jesus as Messiah

It remains to trace the development of references to Jesus as the Messiah within the unfolding narrative framework of John's gospel.

14.4.1 *The Introduction and the Cana Cycle: Could This Be the Messiah?*

The first person in the Johannine narrative to identify Jesus as the Messiah is Peter's brother Andrew, professing confidently, "We have found the Messiah" (John 1:41). Andrew's confession, and his subsequent recruitment of Peter, is the initial impetus in a movement during which several others are shown to follow Jesus in rapid succession.

Jesus is not as welcome in Jerusalem, where he clears the temple and his authority is promptly challenged by the Jewish leadership (2:18), a fact that conspicuously points to Jesus' eventual crucifixion and resurrection (2:19–21). Nicodemus, "Israel's teacher" (3:10), while politely referring to Jesus as "a teacher who has come from God" (3:2, with reference to his "signs"), lacks spiritual understanding and is instructed as to the necessity of spiritual regeneration and of the "lifting up" of the Son of Man (3:3–15).

The Samaritan woman is more receptive toward Jesus' self-disclosure, and returning to her village after conversing with Jesus, asks her fellow villagers, "Could this be the Messiah?" (4:29). Her witness is successful, and many conclude that Jesus is indeed the "Savior of the world" (4:42).

Thus the Cana Cycle closes with the Johannine narrative having recorded the confident claim of Jesus' followers that they have found the Messiah and with even a Samaritan seriously contemplating the possibility that Jesus may be the Messiah. By contrast, the Jewish leadership is portrayed as either sharply antagonistic (the Pharisees) or spiritually intransigent (Nicodemus).

14.4.2 *The Festival Cycle: Popular Messianic Expectations and Misconceptions*

The Festival Cycle features increasing references to Jesus as Messiah. At the Festival of Tabernacles some of the people in Jerusalem deliberate, "Have the authorities really concluded that he is the Messiah?" (John 7:26). By way of representative characters, the fourth evangelist deals with several popular expectations or misconceptions regarding the Messiah, including his origin (7:27) and his authenticating signs (7:31).[23]

These treatments, in turn, anticipate the purpose statement of 20:30–31, where Jesus the Messiah is identified also as "the Son of God" and where Jesus' signs are

---

23. On the issue of "more signs" in 7:31, see Wolfgang J. Bittner, *Jesu Zeichen im Johannesevangelium: Die Messias-Erkenntnis im Johannesevangelium vor ihrem jüdischen Hintergrund* (WUNT 2/26; Tübingen: Mohr-Siebeck, 1987), "Exkurs: Messias und Fülle," 114–15.

given as proof of his messiahship. Shortly thereafter in the narrative some maintain, "He [Jesus] is the Messiah" (7:41). With characteristic irony, the evangelist records their query as to whether the Messiah could come from Galilee (7:52).

As the Johannine drama escalates, readers are informed that anyone who acknowledged Jesus as Messiah was expelled from the synagogue (9:22).[24] The obduracy of the Jewish leaders is revealed by their demand, "If you are the Messiah, tell us plainly" (10:24). Throughout the gospel, the reader has witnessed their refusal to draw the proper conclusion from Jesus' teaching and messianic signs: he is the Messiah who came from God.[25]

14.4.3 The Transition from the Book of Signs to the Book of Exaltation

Martha, on the other hand, becomes an identification figure for those readers who come to the conclusion desired by the evangelist: "I believe that you are the Messiah, the Son of God, who was to come into the world" (John 11:27). Finally, one last, and perhaps the greatest, possible objection to Jesus' messiahship is dealt with: How could the Messiah be "lifted up," that is, be crucified, when the Scriptures say he is to live forever (cf. 12:34)?[26]

As in 3:14–15, this involves a reference to the "lifting up" of Jesus the Son of Man, only that now the fourth evangelist makes explicit that this refers to the kind of death Jesus was going to die (12:33). As the dying seed, Jesus' crucified body would produce "many seeds" (12:24), and subsequent to Jesus' exaltation, he would draw all people, Gentiles as well as Jews, to himself (12:32).

14.4.4 The Purpose Statement

All these utterances take on their full meaning in the light of the purpose statement in John 20:31: "But these [signs] are written that you may believe that Jesus is the Messiah, the Son of God, and that by believing you may have life in his name." This purpose statement needs to be given full weight in understanding the structure of John's gospel: the record of the messianic signs,[27] the references to Jesus' divine nature and origin,[28] and one of the major purposes of his mission, the giving of life, represent the organizing principles of John's gospel.

---

24. Whether this is an anachronistic reference reflecting a situation in John's day toward the end of the first century, whether this is a historical reminiscence, or whether it is both is disputed. Cf. Martyn, *History and Theology*, 2nd ed., 37–62.

25. See Severino Pancaro, *The Law in the Fourth Gospel: The Torah and the Gospel, Moses and Jesus, Judaism and Christianity according to John* (NovTSup 42; Leiden: Brill, 1975), *passim*.

26. The source of this reference may be Ps 61:6–7. As Gillian Bampfylde, "More Light on John 12,34," *JSNT* 17 (1983): 87–89, points out, this passage alone contains all three elements also found in John 12:34: (1) the Christ (Psalm 61 is a Davidic psalm; reference is made not to the "line" or seed of the king as in Ps 89:36 but to the king himself); (2) "remains" (LXX: *diamenei*); and (3) "forever."

27. On the Messiah and signs, cf. Bittner, *Jesu Zeichen*, "Exkurs 1: Messias und Wunder," 136–50. Cf. Isa 11:2; 42:1–9; 61:1–2; Matt 11:2–6; Luke 7:18–23.

28. The term "Son of God" is probably added to give precision to the term "Messiah." Cf. Bittner, *Zeichen Jesu*, 213–16; cf. Brown, *Gospel according to John XIII–XXI*, 1059–61. Brown notes on p. 1060, "Throughout the Gospel John demands not only belief that Jesus is the Messiah predicted by the prophets, but also belief that Jesus came forth from the Father as His special representative in the world (xi 42, xvi 27, 30, xvii 8), that Jesus and the Father share a special presence to one another (xiv 11), and that Jesus bears the divine name 'I AM' (viii 24, xiii 19)," referring also to Thomas's confession of Jesus as "my Lord and my *God*" in 20:28 (emphasis added).

The occurrences of "Messiah" (*Christos*) in John's gospel are designed to guide the reader gradually but inevitably in his or her own determination as to whether or not Jesus is the Messiah and Son of God. In fact, the characters featured in the gospel as well as the gospel's readers are judged on the basis of their decision regarding the messiahship of Jesus.[29] In this regard, it is particularly the signs that invite such judgment, in keeping with John's purpose statement (20:30–31).

14.4.5 First, Second, and Third John

The term *Christos* occurs in 1 John several times as part of the title "Jesus Christ," whether as part of the phrase "his Son, Jesus Christ" (1 John 1:3; 3:23; 5:20) or with reference to "Jesus Christ, the Righteous One" (2:1) or "the one who came by water and blood—Jesus Christ" (5:6). Jesus' filial relationship with God the Father is developed at great length in the gospel; the reference to Jesus as "an advocate with the Father" in 1 John 2:1 picks up on what is implicit in the designation of the Holy Spirit as "another advocate" in John 14:16; and the reference to Jesus as having come by water and blood most likely circumscribes Jesus' earthly ministry by its beginning and end points—water baptism and death by crucifixion, respectively.

In the three important remaining instances, the term *Christos* is part of a confessional statement: (1) "Who is the liar? It is whoever denies that Jesus is the Messiah" (1 John 2:22); (2) "This is how you can recognize the Spirit of God: Every spirit that acknowledges that Jesus [is the] Christ [or: Messiah] has come in the flesh is from God, but every spirit that does not acknowledge Jesus is not from God" (4:2–3); and (3) "Everyone who believes that Jesus is the Messiah is born of God" (5:1).

Especially if the second instance, "Jesus is the Messiah come in the flesh," is a variation of the first and third declaration that "Jesus is the Messiah," the resemblance with the purpose statement of John's gospel is palpable (John 20:31).[30] Possibly, the opponents targeted by John in his first letter therefore failed to acknowledge Jesus as Messiah. Thus, apparently, for a certain amount of time messianic and nonmessianic Jews and proselytes were both members of these Johannine congregations until the nonmessianic contingent departed, leaving the Johannine Christians behind (1 John 2:19).

John's second letter contains three instances of *Christos*: (1) the greetings, "Grace, mercy and peace from God the Father and from Jesus Christ, the Father's Son" (2 John 3); (2) "Many deceivers, who do not acknowledge Jesus [as the] Christ [or: Messiah] as coming in the flesh, have gone out into the world. Any such person is the deceiver and the antichrist" (2 John 7; cf. 1 John 4:2); and (3) "Anyone who

---

29. Cf. de Jonge, "Jewish Expectations," 248, who emphasizes the literary character of the Jewish messianic expectations referred to in John's gospel: "Representative people ... express representative beliefs and raise representative objections." De Jonge considers John's gospel as a source for "Jewish beliefs concerning the Messiah *at the time the Fourth Gospel was written*" (p. 247; emphasis added). However, there seems no good reason to doubt that the gospel presents actual Jewish messianic expectations prevalent at the time of Jesus' earthly ministry.

30. See Streett, "They Went Out from Us."

runs ahead and does not continue in the teaching of Christ does not have God; whoever continues in the teaching has both the Father and the Son" (2 John 9). The second of these passages, which bears a close resemblance to 1 John 4:2, is the most important of these, referring either to the confession of Jesus as Messiah or to a denial of the full humanity of Christ. There are no references to *Christos* in John's third letter.

15 The Signs

15.1 Introduction

Studies on the "signs" in John's gospel are legion.[31] It is therefore surprising that there is no treatment of the exact number and identity of the Johannine signs. Such a study, however, is needed for several reasons. (1) As will be seen, while six Johannine signs are commonly acknowledged, there is no agreement regarding possible other signs in John's gospel. Indeed, some even question whether one should look for further signs in John at all. By a thorough exploration of the alternative proposals, perhaps greater clarity, if not consensus, could be achieved.

(2) If a seventh or even other signs could be identified with a significant degree of plausibility, a closer investigation may aid in our apprehension of the characteristics of the Johannine signs in general.

(3) Such a study is important since the signs occupy a central place in John's Christology (cf. 20:30–31).[32] Clarity regarding the number and identity of the Johannine signs would therefore result in a refined understanding of the christological presentation of John's gospel as a whole.

(4) Since the Johannine signs function as an important structural component, a precise delineation of the signs may also help clarify the structure of the gospel.

---

31. The following discussion represents an adaptation of my article "The Seventh Johannine Sign: A Study in John's Christology," *BBR* 5 (1995): 87–103, and is used by permission. On signs in John's gospel, cf. Jürgen Becker, "Wunder und Christologie: Zum literarkritischen und christologischen Problem der Wunder im Johannesevangelium," *NTS* 16 (1969/70): 130–48; Otto Betz, "Das Problem des Wunders bei Flavius Josephus im Vergleich zum Wunderproblem bei den Rabbinen und im Johannesevangelium," in *Jesus: Der Messias Israels. Aufsätze zur biblischen Theologie* (WUNT 42; Tübingen: Mohr-Siebeck, 1987), 409–19; Bittner, *Jesu Zeichen*; Raymond E. Brown, "Appendix III: Signs and Works," in *Gospel according to John I–XII*, 525–32; D. A. Carson, "The Purpose of Signs and Wonders in the New Testament," in *Power Religion* (ed. Michael S. Horton; Chicago: Moody Press, 1992), 89–118; W. D. Davies, "The Johannine 'Signs' of Jesus," in *A Companion to John: Readings in Johannine Theology* (ed. Michael J. Taylor; New York: Alba, 1977), 91–115; Fortna, *Gospel of Signs*; Donald Guthrie, "The Importance of Signs in the Fourth Gospel," *VE* 5 (1967): 72–83; Marinus de Jonge, "Signs and Works in the Fourth Gospel," in *Miscellanea neotestamentica* 2 (ed. T. Baarda, A. F. J. Klijn, and W. C. van Unnik; NovTSup 48; Leiden: Brill, 1978), 107–25; Mark Kiley, "The Exegesis of God: Jesus' Signs in John 1–11," in *SBL Seminar Papers* 27 (Atlanta, GA: Scholars Press, 1988), 555–69; Eduard Lohse, "Miracles in the Fourth Gospel," in *What about the New Testament? In Honor of Christopher Evans* (ed. Morna D. Hooker and Colin J. A. Hickling; London: SCM, 1975), 64–75; Morris, *Jesus Is the Christ*, 20–42; Willem Nicol, *The Semeia in the Fourth Gospel: Tradition and Redaction* (NovTSup 32; Leiden: Brill, 1972); Peter J. Riga, "Signs of Glory: The Use of Sēmeion in John's Gospel," *Int* 17 (1963): 402–10; Schnackenburg, *Gospel according to St. John*, 1:515–28; Udo Schnelle, *Antidocetic Christology in the Gospel of John: An Investigation of the Place of the Fourth Gospel in the Johannine School* (trans. Linda M. Maloney; Minneapolis: Fortress, 1992), 74–175; Marianne Meye Thompson, "Signs and Faith in the Fourth Gospel," *BBR* 1 (1991): 89–108; idem, "Signs, Seeing, and Faith," in *Humanity of Jesus*, 53–86; and Wilhelm Wilkens, *Zeichen und Werke: Ein Beitrag zur Theologie des 4. Evangeliums in Erzählungs- und Redestoff* (ATANT 55; Zurich: Zwingli, 1969). See also the bibliography in Brown, *Gospel according to John I–XII*, 531–32, with reference to some helpful older treatments on signs in John's gospel.

32. Though not surprising, there are no instances of *sēmeion* in John's letters.

15.2 The Six Commonly Acknowledged Signs in John's Gospel

How many signs are there in John's gospel, and what are they? John's gospel explicitly identifies, and commentators generally acknowledge, the following six signs:[33]

(1) the changing of water into wine (2:1–11)
(2) the healing of the nobleman's son (4:46–54)
(3) the healing of the lame man (5:1–15)
(4) the feeding of the multitude (6:1–15)
(5) the healing of the blind man (9:1–41)
(6) the raising of Lazarus (11:1–57)[34]

Whether any other work of Jesus is referred to as a "sign," however, is disputed.

Why should one look further? Should one not rest content with six Johannine signs, regarding the *number* of signs in John as merely incidental and irrelevant or possibly finding in the number six evidence for John's view that Jesus' signs are of necessity imperfect and incomplete, thus accentuating the uniqueness and significance of Jesus' resurrection?[35] Indeed, care should be taken not to press one's search for a seventh, or even other, Johannine signs unduly. Nevertheless, the number seven appears to have some importance for John in the case of the seven "I am" sayings of Jesus (cf. 6:35, 51; 8:12=9:5; 10:7, 9; 10:11, 14; 11:25; 14:6; and 15:1, 5).

But regardless of whether the number seven is significant for John or not, and whether any symbolism is to be attached to the numbers six *or* seven, it is important to identify properly all the signs in John's gospel. They are too crucial a part of John's christological presentation — and, indeed, of the purpose of his entire gospel — for ambiguity regarding the number and identity of the Johannine signs to be allowed to prevail.

---

33. There are seventeen occurrences of the term *sēmeion* in John's gospel: 2:11, 18, 23; 3:2; 4:48, 54; 6:2, 14, 26, 30; 7:31; 9:16; 10:41; 11:48; 12:18, 37; and 20:30. John 2:11 refers to Jesus' changing water into wine; 2:18 to the Temple clearing; 2:23 and 3:2 make general reference to "the signs" Jesus is doing; in 4:48, Jesus chastises people for their insistence on "signs and wonders" in order to believe; 4:54 refers to Jesus' healing of the nobleman's son; 6:2 talks about signs Jesus is doing upon the sick; 6:14 relates to Jesus' feeding of the multitudes; 6:30 records the Jews' request for yet another sign; 7:31 asks, in the context of discussion over Jesus' healing of the lame man (cf. 5:1–15), whether the Christ will do more signs than Jesus; 9:16 makes reference to Jesus' opening the eyes of a blind man; 10:41 says that John the Baptist did not do any signs; 11:47 and 12:18 refer to Jesus' raising of Lazarus; 12:37 concludes that even though Jesus did all these signs, the Jews still did not believe in him; and 20:30 notes that Jesus did many other signs, but that the evangelist selected certain signs to lead his readers to faith in Jesus. Some commentators, while acknowledging the six signs listed below, may also include additional signs. These will be treated as possible signs below.

34. Cf. Morris, *Jesus Is the Christ*, 21; Stephen S. Smalley, *John: Evangelist and Interpreter: History and Interpretation in the Fourth Gospel* (Greenwood, SC: Attic, 1978), 86–87; and Dodd, *Interpretation of the Fourth Gospel*, 438; Fortna (*Gospel of Signs*, 100–101) concludes that John's source originally comprised seven signs. Fortna combines the feeding and walking on the sea miracles of chapter 6 as one sign and includes the catch of fish in chapter 21 as the seventh sign. Some have organized these *sēmeia* in various ways, such as two groupings of three, each incorporating a nature and two healing miracles (cf. J. N. Sanders, *A Commentary on the Gospel according to St. John* [London: Adam & Charles Black, 1968], 5) or as three signs occurring in Galilee and three in Jerusalem and vicinity). It should be noted that until the issue of possible further signs in John is settled, such classifications remain preliminary. Since it is possible to group the Johannine signs in a number of plausible ways, the question remains which, if any, of these classifications reflects Johannine intent.

35. Cf. Sanders, *St. John*, 5, who holds that John has six signs, not seven, and that the number six, being one less than the perfect number, points to the great sign of the resurrection.

Before seeking to identify the characteristics of a Johannine sign, it seems advisable to investigate briefly the conceptual background. John did not operate in a vacuum in formulating his theology. While there is no consensus regarding the most likely general background for John's thought or that of his various sources, it is apparent that John is deeply rooted in OT symbolism.[36] The case cannot be fully argued here, nor is it necessary to do so. I will merely take a brief look at the OT in an effort to trace the development of the "signs" concept. This survey, in turn, will provide a general backdrop for the study of the Johannine signs below.

15.3 Signs in the Old Testament

Of the roughly 120 references to "signs" in the OT and the Apocrypha, the vast majority are clustered around two events or types of ministries: the exodus, where frequent reference is made to the "signs *and wonders*" performed by God through Moses, and the "signs" forming part of the activity of the OT prophets.[37] The common element between these two clusters of references is that in both cases the signs function to authenticate the divine messengers, whether Moses during the exodus or later OT prophets.[38] While the emphasis regarding the signs performed during the exodus, however, is usually on their miraculous nature, this miraculous element later retreats into the background.[39]

There is little that is "miraculous," for example, in Isaiah's walking stripped and barefoot for three years as a sign of judgment against Egypt and Cush (cf. Isa 20:3; see also Ezek 4:1–3). The emphasis rather lies on the authentication of Isaiah's prophecy, and ultimately of God's sovereign power. While such prophecies were usually given on a merely verbal level, occasionally God chose to communicate by way of a visual aid, that is, a "sign." In the case of prophetic signs, there are thus two important elements: the prophetic component and the inherent symbolism. Both aspects combine to provide a way of revelation that, once the sign has been realized, proves the prophet to be authentic and brings glory to God.

A look at the explicitly identified Johannine signs reveals that John's "signs" concept fits well within the general development from an emphasis on the miraculous to a focus on the prophetic-symbolic dimension of a "sign."[40] The "miraculous"

---

36. Regarding the OT background to John in general, see especially Pryor, *John: Evangelist of the Covenant People.* Cf. Carson, "John and the Johannine Epistles," 245–64; and Evans, *Word and Glory,* 146–86.

37. In the vast majority of instances, *sēmeion* translates the Hebrew *ʾôt.* For references to signs (and wonders) during the exodus, see Exod 4:8, 9, 17, 28, 30; 7:3, 8–9; 8:23; 10:1–2; 11:9, 10; 12:13; 13:9, 16; Num 14:22; 21:8 (bronze serpent); Deut 4:34; 6:22; 7:19; 11:3; 13:1–2; 26:8; 29:2, 3; 34:10–12; Josh 24:5; Neh 9:10; Ps 78:43; 105:27; 135:9; Jer 32:20, 21; Bar 2:11). For signs in the ministry of the OT prophets, cf. 1 Sam 2:34; 2 Kgs 19:29; 20:8, 9; 2 Chr 32:24; Ps 74:9; Isa 7:11, 14; 20:3; 38:7, 22; 44:24–25; 66:18–19; Ezek 4:3; 9:4, 6; 20:12, 20; Sir 36:6. Almost all of the remaining references can be grouped under either general category. For example, Esth 10:3 (LXX) refers to God's working of "signs and wonders" in the events commemorated in the feast of Purim. Occasionally, the term "sign" is applied to the sun, moon, and stars in the heavens (e.g., Gen 1:14).

38. Cf. Davies, "Johannine 'Signs,'" 92, who refers to the turning of a rod into a serpent in Exod 4:1–9: "but it is not only called a wonder, but a sign [*ʾôt*], because it points beyond itself to the power of Moses' God."

39. Cf. Bittner, *Jesu Zeichen,* 24–27, who also points to the scholarly neglect of the question why the term "sign" gains central importance for John's Christology while it is avoided by the Synoptics. See also Fritz Stolz, "Zeichen und Wunder: Die prophetische Legitimation und ihre Geschichte," *ZKT* 69 (1972): 125–44.

40. This is inadequately recognized by Karl Heinrich Rengstorf, who claims that the Johannine signs are "theologically and fundamentally the same kind as the classical σημεῖα of the OT, the signs

element is certainly not missing in the signs of John's gospel. It appears, however, that this is not where John's emphasis lies. This seems to be suggested by the fact that the phrase "signs and wonders," which is characteristic for the types of signs performed during the exodus, occurs only once in John's gospel, and there on the lips of Jesus with a strongly negative connotation (cf. 4:48). In all the other cases, the thrust of a *sēmeion* reference appears to be prophetic-symbolic: the sign's symbolism is developed and the prophetic component is emphasized—in the case of John's gospel the authentication of Jesus' messianic claims.[41]

Whether one agrees with every detail of this reconstruction or not, the most significant insight for the purposes of the present study is that not all of the events called "signs" in the OT were miraculous. On the one hand, if John can be shown to fall within this general conceptual framework, one should not therefore require an event to be miraculous for it to qualify as a Johannine sign. On the other hand, one may expect a possible sign to display a combination of prophetic and symbolic elements. The event thus points to a future where the symbol will become a reality, at which time God's messenger will be proved authentic and God will receive glory.

15.4 Signs in John's Gospel

As one surveys the six explicitly identified and commonly acknowledged Johannine signs in an effort to identify their common characteristics, the following observations can be made.

(1) *Signs are public works of Jesus.* In each case, the term *sēmeion* in John's gospel is linked with the term *poiein* ("do"; cf. 2:11, 23; 3:2; 4:54; 6:2, 14, 30; 7:31; 9:16; 10:41; 11:47; 12:18; 12:37; 20:30), *idein* ("see"; 4:48; 6:26), or *deiknymi* ("show"; 2:18); the verb *akouein* is never used. This pattern of usage indicates that a "sign" is something Jesus *does* (or, in the case of 10:41, John the Baptizer has not done), not merely something he says, and it is something people can *see*, not merely hear. "Signs" in John are therefore *works* of Jesus, not mere words. They are events, not mere utterances.[42]

---

in Egypt in the time of Moses" ("σημεῖον, et al.," *TDNT*, 7:256). See also Brown, *Gospel according to John I–XII*, 528–29, who considers the exodus narrative to be the primary background for both signs and works terminology in John's gospel; and Robert H. Smith, "Exodus Typology in the Fourth Gospel," *JBL* 81 (1962): 329–42.

41. As C. K. Barrett maintains, a *sēmeion* is "a special part of the prophetic activity; no mere illustration, but a symbolic anticipation or showing forth of a greater reality of which the *sēmeion* is nevertheless itself a part" (*Gospel according to St. John*, 76). He contends that, seen against their most probable background, the Johannine signs are therefore *sēmeia* "in the Old Testament sense, special demonstrations of the character and power of God, and partial but effective realizations of his salvation." See also Schnackenburg, who refers to the symbolic actions of the prophets, where the symbol was "a creative prefiguration of the future" and a "revelatory sign" (*Gospel according to St. John*, 1:527). Schnackenburg believes that John developed his notion of signs "in the course of his meditation on

the Gospel tradition," while Barrett thinks that John the evangelist himself chose the term σημεῖον. Others, such as Bultmann or Fortna, conjecture that John's signs terminology stems from his use of a *sēmeia*-source. However, the answer to this question does not materially affect the conclusion below.

42. It is improper to equate completely Jesus' works and words in John's gospel, as Bultmann does when he asserts, "The works of Jesus are his words"; see Bultmann, *Theology of the New Testament*, 2:60; see also the critique by de Jonge, "Signs and Works in the Fourth Gospel," 125. Note also that Jesus habitually refers to things he does in John's gospel as mere "works" (the only disparaging references made to "signs" by Jesus are found in John 4:48 and 6:26), while it is John or other characters in the gospel that use the terms "sign" or "signs" (John: 2:11, 23; 4:54; 6:14; 12:18, 37; 20:30; Nicodemus, the Jews, or people in the crowds: 2:18; 3:2; 6:30; 7:31; 9:16; 11:47). Cf. Guthrie, "what Jesus meant by works was identical with what John meant by signs" ("Importance of Signs in the Fourth

Moreover, all six commonly recognized Johannine signs are works done by Jesus not merely before his disciples but before an unbelieving world.[43] The changing of water into wine, the feeding of the multitude, and the various healings (including the raising of Lazarus from the dead) all share in common that they have as their audience people other than merely Jesus' followers. All these signs are collectively referred to by John's summary statement at the end of Part 1 of his gospel: "Even after Jesus had performed so many signs *in their presence,* they [i.e. 'the Jews'] still would not believe in him" (John 12:37, emphasis added). The signs in John's gospel are therefore confined to the period of Jesus' public ministry (i.e., John 1–12).

(2) *Signs are explicitly identified as such in John's gospel.* All six commonly acknowledged Johannine signs are called "signs": the changing of water into wine (cf. 2:1–11) in 2:11; the healing of the nobleman's son (cf. 4:46–54) in 4:54; the healing of the lame man (cf. 5:1–15) is included in the reference to *pleiona sēmeia* ("more signs") in 7:31 (cf. 7:21); the feeding of the multitude (cf. 6:1–15) is called a "sign" in 6:14, 26, 30; the healing of the blind man (cf. John 9) in 9:16; and the raising of Lazarus (cf. John 11) in 11:47 (cf. 12:18). Ultimately, the only way a "sign" can be identified as such in John's gospel is by explicit reference to an event in Jesus' public ministry as a "sign."[44]

(3) *Signs, with their concomitant symbolism, point to God's glory displayed in Jesus, thus revealing Jesus as God's authentic representative.* The prominence of the signs in the two major summary sections of John's gospel underscores their centrality in John's Christology. Within the framework of this sending Christology, the signs are shown to authenticate Jesus as the true representative of God, revealing God's glory in Jesus. Thus people's acceptance of the genuineness of Jesus' signs should lead to their acceptance of Jesus' messianic mission. This is true both for Jesus' original audience and for the readers of John's gospel, to whom testimony regarding Jesus' signs is supplied.

That the signs are works of Jesus that reflect God's glory can already be seen in John's account of the first sign: "What Jesus did here in Cana of Galilee was the first of the signs through which he revealed his glory; and his disciples put their faith in him" (2:11). The reader of John's gospel is almost certainly expected to draw the connection between this statement and the earlier assertion found in the introduction to the gospel: "The Word became flesh and made his dwelling among us. We have seen his glory, the glory of the one and only Son, who came from the Father,

---

Gospel," 79). Thus it appears that the term "sign" in John's gospel reflects the perspective of the audience of Jesus' works, pointing to the perceived attesting function or symbolic content of the deeds done by Jesus.

43. Cf. John 12:37 (emphasis added): "Even after Jesus had performed so many signs *in their presence,*" that is, "the Jews." In 20:30 (emphasis added), reference is made to "many other signs" Jesus performed "*in the presence of his disciples.*" The latter passage probably points to the disciples as the primary witnesses of Jesus' signs in relation to the gospel's readers and should not be taken to negate the fact that Jesus' signs had a wider audience than merely the disciples. Cf. Barrett, *Gospel according to St. John,* 575: "The stress on signs done by Jesus and beheld by his disciples is important and illuminates the structure and method of the gospel as a whole; there is no disparagement of the role of eye-witnesses."

44. Of course, this does not mean that there may not be some ambiguity regarding the referent of a given *sēmeion* passage in John's gospel. See the discussion below.

full of grace and truth" (1:14). John thus presents Jesus' signs as the vehicles through which God's glory is revealed in Jesus (see also 9:3–4; 11:4). While the word "glory" is not always used in conjunction with Jesus' working of signs, all of Jesus' signs are presented as evidence that Jesus is God's authentic representative (cf. 5:17–47; 6:25–59; 7:14–24; 9:3–5, 35–41; 11:25–27, 40). John's gospel also reflects Jewish expectations that both the coming Prophet and the Messiah would perform signs to prove their divine commission (cf. 6:14; 7:31).[45]

But what kind of works are Jesus' signs according to John? Great care must be taken not to import an understanding of the term "miracle" into John's gospel that is foreign to it.[46] As has been argued above, the most likely background for the Johannine signs are the signs of the OT prophets, where the symbolic-prophetic element generally predominated over the miraculous. I agree therefore with C. H. Dodd when he maintains, "to the evangelist a *sēmeion* is not, in essence, a miraculous act, but a significant act, one which, for the seeing eye and the understanding mind, symbolizes eternal realities."[47] Indeed, the signs in John "are not mere displays of power but are symbol-laden events rich in meaning for those with eyes to see."[48]

In the light of these observations, a tentative definition of a "sign" in John's gospel can be constructed as follows: "A sign is a symbol-laden, but not necessarily 'miraculous,' public work of Jesus selected and explicitly identified as such by John for the reason that it displays God's glory in Jesus who is thus shown to be God's true representative (cf. 20:30–31)."[49]

In screening the options suggested for additional signs in John's gospel, the following criteria may therefore be used:

(1) Is a given work performed by Jesus as part of his public ministry?
(2) Is an event explicitly identified as a "sign" in John's gospel?
(3) Does the event, with its concomitant symbolism, point to God's glory displayed in Jesus, thus revealing Jesus as God's true representative?

If it can be shown that one or more events in John's gospel fit these criteria, these should take their proper place alongside the commonly recognized six signs. If, however, no such event(s) can be identified, it would be likely that there are merely six signs in John.

---

45. See the discussion of the OT background of the Johannine signs above.

46. Contra, translations such as the NIV, which render *sēmeion* in John's gospel regularly as "miraculous sign."

47. Dodd, *Interpretation of the Fourth Gospel*, 90. Contra, Schnackenburg, who understands the gospel's "signs" as Jesus' major miracles: "The signs are important works of Jesus, performed in the sight of his disciples, miracles, in fact, which of their nature should lead to faith in 'Jesus the Messiah, the Son of God'" (*Gospel according to St. John*, 1:515); and Morris, who defines a sign simply as "a miraculous happening that points to some spiritual truth" (*Jesus Is the Christ*, 22).

48. Carson, "Purpose of Signs and Wonders," 93.

49. This definition is not unlike that by Thompson, who describes a Johannine sign as "a manifestation, through the person of Jesus, of God's work in the world" ("Signs and Faith in the Fourth Gospel," 93–94). Cf. Beasley-Murray, *John*, 387: "The 'signs' of the first twelve chapters are specifically actions of Jesus, generally miraculous, which find their exposition in discourses." Note also the possible connection between the term *sēmeion* and the expression *logos* in John's gospel, an intriguing interrelation that cannot be further explored here. Likewise, it might be worthwhile to investigate further the relationship between the Johannine signs and the "I am" sayings, which are sometimes, but not always, linked.

15.5 Possible Additional Signs in John's Gospel

The suggestions for additional signs in John's gospel include the following:[50]

(1) Jesus' clearing of the temple (cf. 2:14–17)[51]
(2) Jesus' word regarding the serpent in the wilderness (cf. 3:14–15)[52]
(3) Jesus' walking on the water (cf. 6:16–21)[53]
(4) the anointing of Jesus (12:1–8)[54]
(5) the triumphal entry (12:12–16)[55]
(6) the footwashing (13:1–11)[56]
(7) Jesus' crucifixion and resurrection (18:1–19:42)[57]
(8) his resurrection appearances (20:1–21:25)[58]
(9) the miraculous catch of fish (21:1–14)[59]

Which of the above alternatives, if any, fits the general characteristics outlined in the above definition?

(1) *Is a given work performed by Jesus as part of his public ministry?* All six commonly recognized Johannine signs occur during the course of Jesus' public ministry (John 1–12). Of the suggested additional signs, only three fall into this category: the temple clearing, the anointing of Jesus, and the triumphal entry. Jesus' word regarding the serpent in the wilderness is not an event at all but merely a word of Jesus and should therefore be ruled out from consideration.[60] The walking on the

---

50. While not exhaustive, the following alternatives represent the most frequently made suggestions. It should be noted that some writers define the concept of a Johannine "sign" so broadly as to include virtually everything Jesus did or said in John's gospel. Davies, for example, also includes the signs of "new birth" (John 3), "new worship" (John 4), the "light of the world" (John 7–8), and "signs that Jesus brings life through death" (11:55–12:36), including the anointing, the triumphal entry, and the grain of wheat saying ("Johannine Signs," 95–112). However, this terminology demonstrably departs from the Johannine usage. Dodd's concept of "signs" in John, too, appears to be unduly broad when he writes, "The works of Christ are all 'signs' of his finished work" (*Interpretation of the Fourth Gospel*, 383). On one level that may be true, but clearly John selects certain events in Jesus' ministry by designating them as "signs" and by exposing their symbolic significance. All signs contain symbolic elements, but not every symbolic element in John's gospel is therefore a sign. To subsume various allusions to the OT as well as instances of Johannine irony and double meaning under the category of "Johannine sign" fails to observe this distinction between symbolism and "signs."

51. Beasley-Murray, *John*, 42; Carson, *Gospel according to John*, 181; Dodd, *Interpretation of the Fourth Gospel*, 300–303, 370.

52. Brown, *Gospel according to John I–XII*, 528.

53. Morris, *Jesus Is the Christ*, 21. Cf. also Davies, "Johannine 'Signs,'" 93, calling this the traditional view.

54. Dodd, *Interpretation of the Fourth Gospel*, 438.

55. Ibid.

56. Mary L. Coloe, "Welcome into the Household of God: The Footwashing in John 13," *CBQ* 66 (2004): 400–415, who claims that the footwashing in its entirety is a Johannine *sēmeion* whose significance is explicated in the remainder of the Farewell Discourse.

57. Betz, "Problem des Wunders," 412–13; Carson, *Gospel according to John*, 661: "the greatest sign of them all is the death, resurrection and exaltation of the incarnate Word"; Dodd, *Interpretation of the Fourth Gospel*, 379: "The death of Christ by crucifixion ... is a *sēmeion* of the reality which is the exaltation and the glory of Christ" (see also pp. 438–40); Forestell, *Word of the Cross*, 71, who refers to "the supreme sign of the entire gospel, the exaltation and glorification of the Son of Man"; Bruce H. Grigsby, "The Cross as a Expiatory Sacrifice in the Fourth Gospel," *JSNT* 15 (1982): 64, n. 6: "it does not seem to be speculative to discuss the Johannine cross as a 'sign'"; Lucius Nereparampil, *Destroy This Temple. An Exegetico-Theological Study on the Meaning of Jesus' Temple-Logion in Jn 2:19* (Bangalore: Dharmaram Publications, 1978), 92–97; Nicol, *Sēmeia in the Fourth Gospel*, 115: "John never directly says the resurrection is also a *sēmeion*, but it is significant that when the Jews ask Jesus for a *sēmeion* in 2:18, he answers by referring to his resurrection"; and Wilhelm Thüsing, *Die Erhöhung und Verherrlichung Jesu im Johannesevangelium* (NTAbh 21; Münster: Aschendorff, 1979), 289 *et passim*, who repeatedly refers to Jesus' exaltation at the cross as a "Glaubenszeichen."

58. Bultmann, *Theology of the New Testament*, 2:56; Beasley-Murray, *John*, 387.

59. Smalley, *John: Evangelist and Interpreter*, 87; idem, "The Sign in John XXI," *NTS* 20 (1974): 275–88; Fortna, *Gospel of Signs*, 87–98.

60. Dodd, *Interpretation of the Fourth Gospel*, 300: "for John a 'sign' is something that actually happens."

water, while being something Jesus *does,* is not a part of Jesus' public ministry but occurs privately before Jesus' disciples; thus, it should also be excluded. The remaining suggestions — that is, Jesus' crucifixion and the resurrection, his resurrection appearances, and the miraculous catch of fish — are not a part of Jesus' ministry narrated in chapters 1–12 and can therefore not be considered "signs" in the Johannine sense of the word. These considerations are further clarified by dealing with the second characteristic of a Johannine "sign."

(2) *Is an event explicitly identified as a "sign" in John's gospel?* Of the three events identified above that fit the first criterion (i.e., being works performed by Jesus as part of his public ministry), only the temple clearing also appears to meet the second qualification, since neither the anointing of Jesus nor the triumphal entry is called a "sign" in John's gospel. Even in the case of the temple clearing, the designation is somewhat indirect. When Jesus, immediately after cleansing the temple, is asked to perform a sign, he explains the significance of what he has just done, thus apparently implying that the temple clearing itself already constituted the sign people were asking for.[61] As one commentator has it, "Indeed, if the authorities had eyes to see, the cleansing of the temple was already a 'sign' they should have thought through and deciphered in terms of Old Testament scripture."[62]

That this is a legitimate inference is suggested by the parallel in 6:30, where after Jesus' feeding of the multitude, the Jews similarly demand a sign; yet in response Jesus offers an interpretation of what has already happened, inviting his questioners to see in the actual occurrence of the feeding of the multitude the *sēmeion* they desired.[63]

Apart from the fact that the other suggested possibilities already failed to meet the first criterion, they also appear to fall short of standing the second test. None of these alternatives is called a "sign" in John's gospel. It may be objected that Jesus' crucifixion and resurrection, and perhaps even the resurrection appearances, should be included in the purview of the Johannine "signs" by virtue of being covered by the statement in 20:30.[64] This suggestion, however, while possible, should probably be ruled out for the following reasons.

(a) Jesus' crucifixion and resurrection are the reality to which the signs point. Rather than symbolizing anything, they are significant in and of themselves. As Rudolf Schnackenburg asserts, "An extension of the concept of 'sign' to take in the

---

61. Nereparampil, *Destroy This Temple,* 92–97, objects to an inclusion of the temple clearing under the Johannine signs by arguing that the temple clearing cannot be a sign since it is not "miraculous." He sees the resurrection as the sign and the temple logion as the promise of a sign, maintaining that the resurrection represents "the supreme 'sign' in the full sense of the Johannine concept of *semeion.*" But Nereparampil's objection loses its force in the light of the fact that a "miraculous" element is not a necessary component of the Johannine conception of a "sign." Moreover, Jesus' resurrection is not a part of Jesus' public work and relates to the Johannine signs as reality does to symbol rather than serving as a symbol of a reality other than itself.

62. Carson, *Gospel according to John,* 181.

63. Dodd, *Interpretation of the Fourth Gospel,* 301. Dodd also notes the implication of the quote of Ps 69:10 in John 2:17, that is, "that, just as the Righteous Sufferer of the Psalm paid the price of his loyalty to the Temple, so the action of Jesus in cleansing the Temple will bring him to grief." The connection is also noted by Clavier, "L'ironie," 272.

64. Cf., e.g., Carson, *Gospel according to John,* 661, who comments, somewhat tentatively, "It is possible that *miraculous signs* refers only to the miracles reported in chs. 2–12.... But ... the greatest sign of them all is the death, resurrection and exaltation of the incarnate Word.... But however far *miraculous signs* extends...."

cross of Jesus cannot be justified."[65] The reason for this is, according to C. K. Barrett, that "in the death and resurrection of Jesus, sign and its meaning coincide."[66] W. D. Davies agrees: "The sign is not essential to the truth to which it points, but only illustrative. But the death of Jesus is not simply an illustration or a sign; it is an actual death.... The cross—not as a symbol or an idea, but as an actual act of self-giving—is, for John, the point where God's glory is actually seen. Not the sign, not the intent, but the deed is the manifestation of the glory."[67]

(b) The "signs" in John's gospel are preliminary in nature. This temporary function is intrinsic to John's conception of a "sign." Once the reality to which Jesus' "signs" point has come, no further signs are needed, nor can the crucifixion and resurrection that accomplish that reality *themselves* be called "signs." As de Jonge notes, Jesus' "death and resurrection ... are *not* explicitly called signs.... This may be because from the Evangelist's post-resurrectional viewpoint, the signs bear a preliminary character, whereas death and resurrection mark the beginning of a new period."[68] Raymond Brown writes:

> Thus, the miracle is a sign, not only qualitatively (a material action pointing toward a spiritual reality), but also temporally (what happens before *the hour* prophesying what will happen after the hour has come). That is why, as we have explained, the signs of Jesus are found only in the first half of the Gospel (chs. i–xii).[69]

(b) While the "signs" reference in 20:30 allows for the possible inference that Jesus' crucifixion and resurrection should be numbered among the Johannine "signs," this inference falls short of making the connection explicit. Other explanations are possible. As passages such as 2:22 (cf. also 12:16) indicate, even the disciples' understanding of events in Jesus' ministry was predicated upon the actual occurrences of Jesus' crucifixion and resurrection. Their reception of the Holy Spirit and their commissioning by Jesus were not possible until *after* these events. Thus John may choose to mention Jesus' "signs" once more, not because he wants to include Jesus' crucifixion and resurrection in their purview, but because the disciples are now fit to witness to the true significance of the "signs" Jesus had performed during his public ministry.

It had been necessary for Jesus' crucifixion and resurrection, the reality to which those "signs" pointed, to occur in order for the disciples to be able to function as eyewitnesses in the power of the Spirit (cf. 15:26–27). Indeed, what the Farewell Discourse expounds is not so much the significance of Jesus' death (which had already been foreshadowed by word and deed in John 1–12) as the *implications* of Jesus' death for the mission of his followers.[70]

---

65. Schnackenburg, *Gospel according to St. John*, 1:520, n. 7.
66. Barrett, *Gospel according to St. John*, 78.
67. Davies, "Johannine 'Signs,'" 113–14.
68. De Jonge, "Signs and Works in the Fourth Gospel," 111 and 117, n. 24.
69. Brown, *Gospel according to John I–XII*, 530.
70. Contra, Carson, *Gospel according to John*, 661: "But to place this conclusion here suggests that the greatest sign of them all is the death, resurrection and exaltation of the incarnate Word, the significance of which has been carefully set forth in the farewell discourse."

(d) It probably would have appeared rather inappropriate (if not blasphemous) to Jesus' own disciples, and to the author of John's gospel, to place Jesus' crucifixion and resurrection into the same category as the commonly acknowledged six Johannine signs. The inclusion of Jesus' crucifixion and resurrection among the "signs" appears to run counter to John's consistent emphasis on Jesus' salvation-historical and personal uniqueness (cf., e.g., 1:14, 18; 3:16). The book of Acts finds the early church preaching, not Jesus' signs, but his resurrection.

For these reasons Jesus' crucifixion, resurrection, and appearances should not be considered Johannine "signs." They do not fit the criteria laid out above in that they are neither a "public work" of Jesus nor called "signs" in John. In line with the OT background sketched earlier in this essay, the Johannine "signs" point symbolically to God's future intervention. Jesus' crucifixion and resurrection, however, represent the very reality to which the earlier signs had referred. If the raising of Lazarus is a "sign," it may be asked, and if its symbolic significance is that Jesus is "the resurrection and the life," how can Jesus' resurrection *itself* also be a sign? This seems to be logically inconsistent.

Finally, the miraculous catch of fish in John 21, too, should be ruled out from consideration, since it is neither a part of Jesus' public ministry nor explicitly identified as a "sign" in John.

(3) Does the event, with its concomitant symbolism, point to God's glory displayed in Jesus, thus revealing Jesus as God's true representative? To some extent, this criterion is met not merely by the six commonly acknowledged Johannine "signs" but also by the various suggestions for additional "signs." In a sense, everything Jesus does and says points to God's glory and reveals Jesus as God's true representative. Not everything Jesus does or says, however, is selected by John as a "sign." It has already been suggested that the temple clearing alone meets the first two criteria; all that remains to be done is to discuss whether this event is presented in John's gospel as an incident that reveals God's glory in Jesus and that reveals him as God's authentic representative.

It has already been argued that Jesus' response to the Jews' demand for a "sign" consisted in his explication of the significance of the temple clearing he had just performed so that the temple clearing itself is presented as a Johannine "sign" (cf. 2:18–21).[71] It is not necessary here to discuss in detail all the implications of Jesus' temple logion in 2:19. Suffice it to say that Jesus' words were uttered in explicit response to the Jews' challenge of his authority (cf. 2:18). In Jesus' eyes, the temple

---

71. Note also the connection between the changing of water into wine and the temple clearing. What the first sign indicates, namely, that Jesus replaces Judaism in its various features, is applied in the case of the temple clearing to the Jewish temple. Cf. Dodd, *Interpretation of the Fourth Gospel*, 303: "it seems clear that both the Miracle of Cana and the Cleansing of the Temple are *sēmeia* which signify the same foundational truth: that Christ has come to inaugurate a new order in religion." Cf. Nereparampil, *Destroy This Temple*, 89; and Pryor, *John: Evangelist of the Covenant People*, 17, who likewise emphasizes the close connection between Jesus' first sign at the wedding in Cana and the temple clearing: "the two pericopae form an impressive and united introduction to the ministry of Jesus. Both point to the passing away of the old religion (signified by water and temple), and its replacement by the newness and superiority of Christ. He is the wine of the new age, he is its temple, the focus of worship and devotion." On the Johannine replacement motif, see especially Carson, "John and the Johannine Epistles," 254–56.

clearing was symbolic of the crucifixion and resurrection of his body, which, in turn, would replace the temple's significance in the life and worship of the Jewish nation (cf. 4:21–24; cf. *eskēnōsen* in 1:14). Indeed, Jesus had the authority to lay down his life and to take it up again (cf. 10:18). In this, Jesus is confirmed to be God's authentic representative.

If the temple clearing is indeed the seventh sign of John's gospel, the question arises why interpreters have generally failed to identify it as such. A few possible reasons come to mind. Scholarship on the temple clearing in John has frequently focused on its placement at the beginning of Jesus' public ministry in John's gospel in contrast with the Synoptic placement at the end of Jesus' work. Moreover, the temple clearing is not a "healing miracle," as are four of the other Johannine signs, nor is it a "nature miracle," as are two other signs in John. Therefore the temple clearing does not seem to fit the common stereotype of a Johannine sign.

Indeed, signs in John have often been understood in terms of the miraculous in line with the Synoptic portraits of Jesus' miracles. The six commonly acknowledged Johannine signs appear to fit the stereotype of a Synoptic-style miracle very well: they are amazing feats, displays of Jesus' power over nature, indeed, even over sickness and death. The temple clearing, on the other hand, if measured by those characteristics, appears to fall short.

While providing a number of possible explanations for the failure of some to identify the temple clearing as the seventh Johannine sign, however, none of these obstacles is insurmountable.[72] Once one substitutes the Johannine concept of "signs" for the Synoptic framework of "miracles," the temple clearing fits the category of "Johannine sign" very well indeed. As has been argued, what John considers a "sign" is not primarily an amazing feat of power but an event in Jesus' public ministry that has special symbolic significance in attesting to Jesus as God's authentic representative. Not the so-called "miraculous" element but the christological symbolism and Jesus' messianic authority are significant for John.

Ultimately, all signs point to *Jesus* as the true messenger of God, the giver of life, a reality that finds its fullest expression in Jesus' resurrection from the dead, but a reality that is already given preliminary expression in the signs performed during Jesus' public ministry. According to John, the "signs," including the temple clearing, are revelatory pictures of Jesus' true identity: he is the Christ, the Son of God (cf. 20:30–31).

15.6 Implications for the Structure of John's Gospel

The identification of the temple clearing as an additional Johannine sign would have significant implications for one's understanding of the structure of John's gospel. The inclusion of the temple clearing has two important effects on the structure of John's gospel: first, it makes the raising of Lazarus the seventh climactic sign,

---

72. Note also that there have been a significant minority of scholars, including C. H. Dodd, D. A. Carson, and George R. Beasley-Murray, who have identified the temple clearing as a Johannine sign.

providing the ultimate sign of Jesus' own resurrection; second, it reveals the probable division of the first six Johannine signs into two categories: three inaugural signs, and three further signs characterized by mounting controversy.

Jesus' raising of Lazarus, of course, is linked with Jesus' saying, "I am the resurrection and the life" (11:25), and shortly followed by the conclusion of John that "even after Jesus had performed so many signs in their presence, they still would not believe in him" (12:37). It appears that after Jesus' raising of Lazarus no greater sign could be given. The Jews' unbelief in the face of such evidence for Jesus' messianic identity made it clear that they would not believe Jesus' own resurrection either. The number seven, indicating completeness and perfection, shows that Jesus' performance of a resurrection provides a climax in the number of the Johannine signs.

John himself gives some clues that signs 1 and 3, and then signs 4 and 6, form the outer parameters of two groupings of three signs each. In the case of signs 1 and 3, John numbers them as having both been performed in Cana of Galilee (4:54). The two healings in chapters 5 and 9 contain numerous textual connections. The sequence of locations for the six signs reflect Jesus' continued movement from Galilee to Judea and back again in John's gospel. The progression would be as follows: Galilee/Judea/Galilee; Judea/Galilee/Judea. The climactic sign, finally, occurs in Judea.

With all seven signs taking place during Jesus' public ministry in John 1–12, the references to Jesus' signs in the concluding sections of Parts 1 and 2 of John's gospel appear to relate to one another in the following way. The conclusion in 12:37 shows that Jesus' messianic signs had been rejected by the old covenant community. The conclusion in 20:30 indicates that Jesus' messianic signs would be witnessed to by the new covenant community. Between these two conclusions, one finds sections on the implications of Jesus' exaltation for the new covenant community (John 13–17); on the reality to which the signs point, that is, Jesus' crucifixion and resurrection (John 18–19); and on the resurrection appearances and commissioning of the new covenant community (John 20–21).

On a different note, it is crucial to view the signs in John's gospel, not in an isolated fashion, but in their interrelationships with one another. All Johannine signs *jointly* point to various aspects of Jesus' messianic identity, authority, and mission. Any one sign may only reveal a *part* of this mission. Taken together, the signs provide a complete picture of the Christ, who is Jesus.

Finally, why are the messianic signs of Jesus emphasized in John's gospel? One reason may be John's expectation that a focus on Jesus' messianic signs would add persuasiveness to the portrait of a crucified and risen Messiah, especially if Jews were at least part of his envisioned audience.[73] The added emphasis on the earthly ministry of Jesus points also to the abiding value of Jesus' works, demonstrating that

---

73. This, of course, is hotly disputed. The point cannot be argued here, but in the light of the internal clues provided in John's gospel itself, there appears no good reason why Jews (Diaspora Jews as well as proselytes) could not have been the intended audience of John's gospel. See the discussion in Köstenberger, *Missions of Jesus and the Disciples*, 200–206.

Jesus' works are reflections of who he is. Thus for John, Christology is not limited to soteriology, and Jesus' crucifixion and resurrection are shown to be in continuity with his earthly ministry.

15.7 Conclusion

It appears that the temple clearing, and it alone, meets all the criteria for inclusion in the Johannine signs. It is a work performed by Jesus as part of his public ministry, it is identified as a "sign" in John's gospel, and it symbolically points to God's glory displayed in Jesus, thus revealing Jesus as God's true representative.[74] Jesus' crucifixion and resurrection, by contrast, should not be considered as signs, since they relate to the seven signs featured in John 1–12 as reality does to symbol.

If the thesis argued here is correct, greater clarity regarding one's understanding of the signs in John's gospel will be achieved. The discussion of the OT background and the investigation of the characteristics of a Johannine sign have illuminated not only John's concept of a sign but also his entire christological presentation. The identification of the temple clearing as an additional sign has also provided a proposed clarified structure for John's gospel. Nevertheless, the thesis remains tentative and awaits further scholarly discussion.

---

74. If the temple clearing were a Johannine sign, this would also provide an antecedent sign, notably in Jerusalem, for references to "the signs" Jesus was doing shortly thereafter in the gospel narrative (cf. 2:23; 3:2). It appears that the reference to "the second sign" in 4:54 merely pertains to Jesus' working of signs *in Galilee*, though this is disputed.

C. The Beginning (Introduction; 1:1–18)

Chapter 8

The Word: Creation and New Creation

Bibliography

Barrosse, Thomas. "The Seven Days of the New Creation in St. John's Gospel." *CBQ* 21 (1959): 507–16. **Beale, G. K.** "The New Testament and New Creation." Pp. 159–73 in *Biblical Theology: Retrospect and Prospect*. Ed. Scott J. Hafemann. Downers Grove, IL: InterVarsity Press, 2002. **Brown, Jeannine K**. "Creation's Renewal in the Gospel of John." *CBQ* (forthcoming). **Carmichael, Calum M.** *The Story of Creation: Its Origin and Its Interpretation in Philo and the Fourth Gospel*. Ithaca, NY: Cornell University Press, 1996. **DuRand, Jan A.** "The Creation Motif in the Fourth Gospel: Perspectives on Its Narratological Function within a Judaistic Background." Pp. 21–46 in *Theology and Christology in the Fourth Gospel: Essays by the Members of the SNTS Johannine Writings Seminar*. Ed. G. Van Belle, J. G. Van der Watt, and P. Maritz. Leuven: Leuven University Press, 2005. **Endo, Masanobu**. *Creation and Christology: A Study on the Johannine Prologue in the Light of Early Jewish Creation Accounts*. WUNT 2/145. Tübingen: Mohr-Siebeck, 2002. **Humphrey, Edith M.** "New Creation." Pp. 536–37 in *Dictionary for Theological Interpretation of the Bible*. Ed. Kevin J. Vanhoozer. Grand Rapids: Baker, 2005. **Koester, Craig R., and Reimund Bieringer**, eds. *The Resurrection of Jesus in the Gospel of John*. WUNT 222. Tübingen: Mohr-Siebeck, 2008. **Painter, John**. "Earth Made Whole: John's Rereading of Genesis." Pp. 65–84 in *Word, Theology, and Community in John*. Edited by John Painter, R. Alan Culpepper, and Fernando F. Segovia. St. Louis, MO: Chalice, 2002. **Phillips, Thomas E.** "'The Third Fifth Day?' John 2:1 in Context," *ExpTim* 115 (2004): 328–31. **Phythian-Adams, W. J.** "The New Creation in St. John." *Church Quarterly Review* 144 (1947): 52–75. **Suggit, John**. "Jesus the Gardener: The Atonement in the Fourth Gospel as Re-Creation." *Neot* 33 (1999): 161–68. **Tidball, Derek**. "Completing the Circle: The Resurrection according to John." *ERT* 30 (2006): 169–83. **Witherington, Ben III**. "New Creation or New Birth? Conversion in the Johannine and Pauline Literature." Pp. 119–42 in *Conversion in the Wesleyan Tradition*. Ed. Kenneth J. Collins and John H. Tyson. Nashville: Abingdon, 2001. **Wright, N. T.** *John for Everyone*.

Louisville: Westminster John Knox, 2004. Idem. Pp. 662–82 in *The Resurrection of the Son of God*. Christian Origins and the Question of God 3. Minneapolis: Fortress, 2003. **Wyatt, Nicolas**. "'Supposing Him to Be the Gardener' (John 20,15): A Study of the Paradise Motif in John." *ZNW* 81 (1990): 21–38.

16 New Creation: The Word, Life, and Light

16.1 Introduction

Paul's writings include several explicit references to new creation.[1] It is less clear whether John conceived of Jesus' coming in terms of a new creation, since, unlike Paul, he never uses the term. Nevertheless, it is highly probable that John, too, espoused a "new creation" theology.[2] This is most apparent in the introduction to the gospel, which casts the Word's coming into the world in terms reminiscent of creation, most notably by way of references to "life" and "light," both of which constitute creation terminology. Also, John's presentation of Jesus' early ministry as encompassing a week in keeping with the week of creation is suggestive of a new creation.[3]

The themes of "life" and "light" in Jesus are sustained, albeit somewhat unevenly, throughout John's gospel.[4] The Johannine Passion Narrative, perhaps suggestively, is set in a garden (18:1; 19:41), and Jesus is, albeit mistakenly, identified by Mary as a gardener (20:15). Also, Pilate calls Jesus "the man" (a possible allusion to Adam), and the risen Jesus' breathing the Spirit on his followers likewise invokes new creation theology (20:22).[5] While not as explicit as Revelation 21–22, John's gospel thus may likewise be found to espouse a "(new) creation" theology that presents Jesus' coming and mission as God's eschatological renewal of his original creation.[6]

---

1. See 2 Cor 5:17; Gal 6:15; see also Rom 8:18–22. See Douglas J. Moo, "Creation and New Creation," paper presented at the Annual Meeting of the Institute of Biblical Research, Boston, MA, November 22, 2008. See also Moyer V. Hubbard, *New Creation in Paul's Letters and Thought* (Cambridge: Cambridge University Press, 2002); W. Hulitt Gloer, *An Exegetical and Theological Study of Paul's Understanding of New Creation and Reconciliation in 2 Cor. 5:14–21* (Mellen Biblical Press Series 42; Lewiston, NY: Mellen, 1996).

2. See esp. Jeannine K. Brown, "Creation's Renewal in the Gospel of John," *CBQ* (forthcoming), with further bibliographic references. See also Jan A. DuRand, "The Creation Motif in the Fourth Gospel: Perspectives on Its Narratological Function within a Judaistic Background," in *Theology and Christology in the Fourth Gospel: Essays by the Members of the SNTS Johannine Writings Seminar* (ed. G. Van Belle, J. G. Van der Watt, and P. Maritz; Leuven: Leuven University Press, 2005), 21–46.

3. See Köstenberger, *John*, 56. See Thomas E. Phillips, "'The Third Fifth Day?' John 2:1 in Context," *ExpTim* 115 (2004): 328–31, who discusses the seeming alteration of temporal framework between chap. 1 with its references to "the next day" in 1:29, 35, 43 and John 2 with its reference to "the third day." According to Phillips, this strategy is designed to draw attention to the days of creation in Genesis.

4. "Life" (*zōē*) occurs 36 times in John's gospel (1:4; 3:15, 16, 36; 4:14, 36; 5:24, 26, 29, 39, 40; 6:27, 33, 35, 40, 47, 48, 53, 54, 63, 68; 8:12; 10:10, 28; 11:25; 12:25, 50; 14:6; 17:2, 3; 20:31; in several of these verses, the term occurs more than once; see also the three instances of "give life," *zōopoieō* in 5:21 and 6:63) and 13 times in 1 John (1:1, 2; 2:25; 3:14, 15; 5:11, 12, 13, 16, 20). "Light" (*phōs*) is found 23 times in John's gospel (1:4, 5, 7, 8, 9; 3:19, 20, 21; 5:35; 8:12; 9:5; 11:9, 10; 12:35, 36, 46; see also "give light," *phōtizō*, in 1:9) and 6 times in 1 John (1 John 1:5, 7; 2:8, 9, 10). See further the discussions in chap. 3, sec. 7.5.4 and chap. 6, secs. 12.3.2 and 3 above; and in sec. 16.3 below.

5. In addition, 1 John may supplement the gospel by emphasizing both the eschatological aspect of the light's dawning as well as the moral aspects of the light for believers. Walking in the light—in the reality of the dawning new creation—is what believers do by definition. I am indebted for this insight to Daniel R. Streett.

6. First John 3:2 is a key passage as well for the idea of new/renewed humanity, which comes by a renewal of God's presence with humans, that is, when we eschatologically see God/Jesus. It is

16.2 Creation through the Word and the Word Made Flesh

At the outset, John refers to creation.[7] The phrase "in the beginning" echoes the opening phrase of the Hebrew Bible (Gen 1:1) and establishes a canonical link between the first words of the OT Scriptures and John's gospel.[8] "Beginning" points to a time prior to creation.[9] Yet while John's readers would have expected the phrase "In the beginning *God*," the evangelist instead spoke of "the Word." The focus of this verse is to show the Word's preexistence, preparing for the later reference to a new "beginning," the incarnation of the Word (cf. John 1:14).

The designation "Word"—used in a christological sense only in the introduction (John 1:1, 14)—conveys the notion of divine self-expression or speech (cf. Ps 19:1–4). The Genesis creation account establishes the effectiveness of God's word: he speaks, and things come to pass (Gen 1:3, 9; cf. 1:11, 15, 24, 30). Psalmists and prophets alike portray God's word in close-to-personal terms (Ps 33:6; 107:20; 147:15, 18; Isa 55:10–11). Yet only John claims that this Word has appeared as an actual person, Jesus Christ (cf. 1 John 1:1; Rev 19:13).

As a comprehensive christological designation, the expression "the Word" encompasses Jesus' entire ministry, placing all of Jesus' works and words within the framework of both his eternal being and existence and God's self-revelation in salvation history. The term "Word" appears to have been used by the evangelist at least in part in order to contextualize the gospel message among his Hellenistic audience.[10] Yet John's theology of the "Word" is steeped in the OT depiction of the word of God. This is suggested by:

(1) the evangelist's deliberate effort to echo the opening words of the Hebrew Scriptures by the phrase "in the beginning"

(2) the reappearance of several significant terms from Genesis 1 in John 1 ("light," "darkness," "life")

(3) the introductory OT allusions to Israel's wilderness wanderings (John 1:14: "pitched his tent") and to the giving of the law (1:17–18)

(4) perhaps most decisively, the evangelist's adaptation of Isa 55:9–11 for his basic christological framework[11]

---

also worth noting that "life" terminology is also juxtaposed with the term "believe" both in the introduction to the gospel (John 1:4–5, 12) and in the gospel's purpose statement (20:30–31). These references to life through faith in the Messiah thus envelop the entire gospel, accentuating the eschatological dimension of Jesus' coming. As Brown ("New Creation," 3) notes, "It is curious that this connection between 'life' and new creation theology is discussed infrequently in Johannine dialogue. Part of the reason may be the tendency to hear 'eternal life' as primarily an abstract or privatized concept rather than as a notion concretized in its Jewish context as creational (i.e., historical) and communal as well as eschatological."

7. The discussion under the present heading includes adaptations of several paragraphs from Köstenberger, *John*, 25–41.

8. For an interesting (though not necessarily compelling) study of John's "rereading" and "rewriting" of Genesis, see John Painter, "Earth Made Whole: John's Rereading of Genesis," in *Word, Theology, and Community in John* (ed. John Painter, R. Alan Culpepper, and Fernando F. Segovia; St. Louis, MO: Chalice, 2002), 65–84.

9. Apart from "beginning," the Greek term *archē* can also mean "first cause." It is possible that John here seeks to convey both meanings, "in the beginning of history" and "at the root of the universe" (Morris, *Gospel according to John*, 65).

10. For a discussion of the background to John's theology of "the Word," see Köstenberger, *John*, 26–27.

11. See esp. Benedict T. Viviano, "The Structure of the Prologue of John (1:1–18): A Note," *RB* 105 (1998): 182: "this passage of Isaiah [Isa. 55:10–11] almost certainly had *the* decisive effect on John 1:1–18" (emphasis his).

The Word: Creation and New Creation

Since the Word existed in the beginning, one might think either that the Word *was* God or that the Word was *with* God. John affirmed both: not only was the Word *with* God (1:1), the Word itself *was* God (1:2).[12] Clearly, calling Jesus "God" stretched the boundaries of first-century Jewish monotheism.[13] The affirmation that all things were made through *wisdom* or even through God's *word* would have been in keeping with Jewish belief. Yet John contends that everything—i.e., the *kosmos* (world) of 1:10—came into being through "him," that is, *Jesus*, God-made-flesh.[14]

After affirming the Word's participation in creation, the evangelist continues to elaborate on the Word's involvement in creation in John 1:4–5 in terms of both "life" and "light." At creation, calling forth "light" was God's first creative act (Gen 1:3–5). Later, God placed lights in the sky to separate between light and darkness (1:14–18). Light, in turn, makes it possible for life to exist. Thus on the fifth and sixth days of creation, God made animate life to populate both the waters and dry land, culminating in his creation of humankind (1:20–31; 2:7; 3:20).

John next asserts that life was "in him," Jesus. *He* is the source of life, both physical and eternal. Only those who possess spiritual, eternal life have the capacity to "walk in the light," that is, to make moral decisions that are in accordance with God's revealed will. Conversely, "darkness" in John's gospel is the world alienated from God, spiritually ignorant and blind, fallen and sinful, dominated by Satan. The evangelist announces at the outset that the darkness has not overcome the light (John 1:5).[15] For John, light and darkness are no equally matched duality, but Jesus, "the light," is the overwhelming victor.

Once again, John contextualizes. While drawing on OT concepts, he employs these terms to engage adherents of other religions and worldviews.[16] For some, light was wisdom (or wisdom was even superior to light; cf. Wis 7:26–30). For others, light was given by the Mosaic law (*2 Bar* 59:2) or Scripture (Ps 19:8; 119:105, 130; Prov 6:23). Still others looked for enlightenment in philosophy, morality, or a simple lifestyle. In this religiously pluralistic context, John proclaims Jesus as the supreme light, who is both eternal and universal and yet personal.

---

12. For a brief survey of the divinity and uniqueness of Jesus, particularly claims of Jesus' preexistence, see Köstenberger, *Missions of Jesus and the Disciples*, 46–47 (see relevant bibliography in nn. 7–8).

13. See chap. 9, sec. 17 below.

14. Though note that Jesus is not explicitly mentioned until 1:17. While startling, the substance of the present assertion is in no way unique to John; it pervades much of the NT (cf. 1 Cor 8:6; Col 1:16; Heb 1:2).

15. This reading is suggested, among other things, by 12:35, the closest parallel in John's gospel (see also 16:33). The major translations divide more or less evenly between "understood" or "overcome," usually mentioning the one not chosen in a footnote: (1) NIV: "understood"; NASB, NKJV: "comprehend"; (2) NLT: "extinguish"; NET: "mastered"; ISV: "put out"; HCSB, ESV, NRSV: "overcome." Notably, the TNIV changed the NIV's "understood" to "overcome."

16. Some believe that John is here alluding to the Greek dualism between light and darkness. Rather than affirming belief in a personal God who is sovereign, all-powerful, and good, the Greeks viewed reality in terms of polar opposites, such as light and darkness or good and evil. John, however, refutes this kind of thinking in his first letter, where he states emphatically, "God is light; in him there is no darkness at all" (1 John 1:5). Another kind of light/darkness dualism is found in the Dead Sea Scrolls, particularly the "War Scroll" (1QM) depicting the battle between the "sons of light" and the "sons of darkness." But because of the sectarian nature of the Qumran community, light is never offered to those who live in darkness (cf. 1QS 3:21; 4:9–14). In John, however, Jesus urges his listeners to "put your trust in the light while you have the light, so that you may become children of light" (12:36; cf. 8:12; 9:5).

In John 1:9–14, the categories of 1:1–5 are developed in terms of Jesus' coming into the world. "The true light ... was coming into the world" is a subtle way of conveying the gospel to Hellenistic ears.[17] The phrase "come into the world," with its corollary "return to the Father," is used to depict Jesus as the one who enters the world from the outside and returns to his place of departure, that is, to the presence of God the Father (see 13:1, 3; 14:12, 28; 16:28; 18:37). As elaborated in 3:19, the light was not received but rejected, resulting in judgment (cf. 9:39; 12:46–47).

The contrast between light and darkness is also found in a significant cluster of OT passages.[18] Isaiah depicts the coming Messiah as a light entering the darkness, writing that "the people walking in darkness have seen a great light; on those living in the land of deep darkness a light has dawned" (Isa 9:2), and he envisions a time when the nations will walk in God's light and the glory of the Lord will shine brightly (60:1–5; cf. 42:6–7; 49:6). By affirming that Jesus is the "true light" — just as he is the "true bread from heaven" (John 6:32) and the "true vine" (15:1) — John indicates that Jesus is the fulfillment of OT hopes and expectations.[19] As the "true light," Jesus is here presented as the source of spiritual light,[20] a light that enlightens every person, whether Jew or non-Jew (see 1:12–13; 3:16; 10:16; 12:32; cf. 1:10; 3:19–21).

He — the Word who was the light — "was" in the world: not just paying a fleeting visit, but, as John goes on to elaborate in 1:14, "dwelling among us" (or, more literally still, "pitching his tent among us," an allusion to the tabernacle). Even though the world was created through the Word (echoing 1:3), it did not recognize that Word because it was estranged from him. The first half of John's gospel documents how not only the pagan world, but even Israel — "his own" — failed to recognize Jesus as Messiah and rejected the light, including all demonstrations of Jesus' deity and messiahship (his "signs"; cf. 12:37–43 citing Isa 53:1).

Whether or not there is a progression in the evangelist's use of the term *kosmos*,[21] the evangelist highlights the irony — even tragedy — of the world's rejecting the one

---

17. John uses the term *kosmos* (world) seventy-eight times in his gospel (as compared to eight instances in Matthew and three each in Mark and Luke). The expression can mean "physical universe" (John 1:9, 10) or "a large number of people" (12:19). Most characteristically, however, the term refers to sinful humanity (e.g., 3:16). See the discussion of the Johannine worldview above.

18. See esp. Horbury, *Messianism*, 92–93, 99–100, who also discusses rabbinic interpretations. Important OT references include Num 24:17 (cf. 4Q175 = 4QTest 9–13); Isa 9:2 (cf. 42:6–7); and Mal 4:2 (cf. Luke 1:78–79).

19. The term *alēthinon* ("true") here and elsewhere in John conveys the notion of genuineness in conjunction with typology: Moses gave the manna, Jesus *is* the true bread from heaven — he gives life in an ultimate sense. Israel was God's vineyard; Jesus is God's vineyard — typified by fruitfulness — par excellence. Moreover, *alēthinon* here also conveys a sense of ultimacy: in Jesus, God has revealed himself in an escalated, eschatological sense.

20. Later in John's gospel, Jesus calls himself "the light of the world" (John 8:12; 9:5). See also the depiction of Jesus in the book of Revelation (Rev 1:14, 16; 2:18; 19:12; 21:23; 22:5, 16; cf. Matt 17:2 par.; Heb 1:3; 2 Pet 1:19). The contrast conveyed by the expression "true light" is primarily between previous OT manifestations of God and God's final, definitive revelation through Jesus Christ.

21. Barrett, *Gospel according to St. John*, 162, says there is only one sense of *kosmos* in this verse. Morris, *Gospel according to John*, 85 contends that the first two instances refer to everyone, while the third reference is to those who came in contact with Jesus. Beasley-Murray, *John*, 12, sees a progression from "the world inhabited by humankind" in 1:10a to "the world including human beings" in 1:10b to "humanity, fallen and in darkness" in 1:10c. Carson, *Gospel according to John*, 123, demonstrates that the word *kosmos* never has a positive usage and only a few neutral ones.

through whom it was made. The thrice-repeated term *kosmos* contributes to the solemnity and emphatic nature of the reference. The general statement in John 1:10 is developed with reference to God's chosen people Israel—"his own [people]"—in 1:11. Not only was Jesus not received by a world made through him, he was also rejected by God's chosen people Israel (cf. Exod 19:5).[22] Consequently, the entire gospel is taken up with the narration of the ever-escalating confrontation between "the Jews" and Jesus, culminating in Jesus' crucifixion.[23]

By way of *inclusio*, John returns in John 1:14 to the preexistent Word (cf. 1:1–2).[24] The major burden of 1:14–18 is to identify the Word explicitly with Jesus. Rather than using the words *anthrōpos* (man) or *sōma* (body), John here employs the almost crude term *sarx* (flesh; cf. Rom 8:3). The powerful Word of God has been born in the form of frail humanity. The affirmation that "the Word was made flesh" takes the opening statement in 1:1 one step further: that same glorious, divine, preexistent Word has now been born as a frail, "fleshly" human being and taken up physical residence among God's people.[25]

John's message was that the incarnation represents an event every bit as momentous as creation (if not more so). Since the world—including God's chosen people (John 1:10–11)—was dark, fallen, and sinful, humanity's need was for spiritual rebirth (1:13; cf. 3:3, 5), available only through the preexistent, enfleshed Word (cf. 1:29, 36). This, in turn, went counter to Gnostic thought, which denied not only Jesus' incarnation but also human sinfulness (1 John 1:8, 10) and need for atonement (2:2; 4:10) and hence denied that Jesus had truly "come in the flesh" (4:1–3; 2 John 7). Before moving on to a discussion of new creation theology in the Passion Narrative, we will briefly explore the relationship between life and light in the remainder of John's gospel.

16.3 Life and Light

16.3.1 Introduction

From the introduction onward, "life" and "light" are important Johannine themes, ones that are closely related to John's creation theology.[26] For this reason it is appropriate to study these motifs in their own right before turning to other creation

---

22. According to Culpepper, *Anatomy*, 169, the "foundational irony of the gospel is that the Jews rejected the Messiah they eagerly expected." A similar conclusion is reached by Duke, *Irony*, 117, who suggests that John 1:9–12 represents a summary of the dominant irony in John's gospel and notes how this primary irony (Jesus' rejection by the Jews) is played out in the narrative in chapter 9.

23. Culpepper, *Anatomy*, 125–32, has a helpful discussion of the evangelist's characterization of "the Jews." For a critique of Culpepper's methodology of characterization and an alternate proposal see Stibbe, *John as Storyteller*, 24–25.

24. The second-century church father Irenaeus considered John 1:14 to be a "summary" of 1:1–13 (cited in John Behr, "The Word of God in the Second Century," *Pro Ecclesia* 9 [2000]: 102).

25. While John does not elaborate on the precise way in which Jesus was made flesh, his contention that deity assumed human nature in Jesus would have been anathema for Greeks who held to a spirit-matter dualism and could hardly have imagined that immaterial Reason could become a physical being. The idea of gods appearing in human form was not uncommon to the ancients. But John makes clear that the Word did not merely manifest itself as an apparition—as was alleged by the Docetists (from *dokeō*, "seem")—but that it literally was made flesh.

26. On the possible background to "life" and "light" imagery, see Keener, *John*, 381–87.

terminology in the Book of Signs and in the Passion Narrative. I will first look at references to "life" in John's gospel and then survey references to "light." This will be followed by an overview discussion and a list of pertinent observations from a study of "life" and "light" terminology in John's gospel.

16.3.1.1 References to Life in John's Gospel and Letters

There are sixteen major clusters of references to "life" in John's gospel, spanning from the introduction (John 1:4) to the purpose statement (20:31), and six such clusters in 1 John. "Eternal life" is the subject of conversation in Jesus' interchange with Nicodemus in John 3 and with the Samaritan woman in chapter 4. The topic features prominently in the "Sabbath controversy" in chapter 5 and in the "bread of life" discourse in chapter 6. All told, "life" is the subject in virtually every chapter in the first half of John's gospel. The references in the second half of the gospel thin out somewhat, but "life" features significantly in Jesus' pronouncements in 14:6 and 17:2–3.[27]

"Life" is also a major theme in John's first letter. It opens with a reference to the apostolic message regarding the "Word of life" and its incarnation (1 John 1:1–2). The letter also speaks of passing from death to life similar to the gospel (3:14; cf. John 5:24) and connects the possession of life to love (1 John 3:14–15). The purpose statement at the end of 1 John mentions "life" five times in the short span of three verses, striking a note of reassurance. All in all, this letter features thirteen instances of "life" (*zōē*) and one occurrence of the verb "to live" (*zaō*; 4:9).

A list of major references to "life" in John's gospel and letters presents itself as follows:

- John 1:4: "In him was life, and that life was the light of all people."
- John 3:15–16, 36: "'Just as Moses lifted up the snake in the wilderness, so the Son of Man must be lifted up, that everyone who believes may have eternal life in him.' For God so loved the world that he gave his one and only Son, that whoever believes in him shall not perish but have eternal life.... Whoever believes in the Son has eternal life, but whoever rejects the Son will not see life, for God's wrath remains on them."
- John 4:10, 14: "If you knew the gift of God and who it is that asks you for a drink, you would have asked him and he would have given you living water ... the water I give them will become in them a spring of water welling up to eternal life."
- John 4:36: "Even now those who reap draw their wages, even now they harvest the crop for eternal life."
- John 5:21, 24–26, 28–29: "For just as the Father raises the dead and gives them life, even so the Son gives life to whom he is pleased to give it....

---

27. For a similar survey, see Filson, "Gospel of Life," 119; see also the study by Jan G. van der Watt, "Everlasting Life in John and the Permanence of Salvation. Life Metaphor in John's Gospel," posted at http://jcsm.org/EternalSecurity/JanGabrielvanderWatt.htm.

Very truly I tell you, whoever hears my word and believes him who sent me has eternal life and will not be judged but has crossed over from death to life. Very truly I tell you, a time is coming and has now come when the dead will hear the voice of the Son of God and those who hear will live. For as the Father has life in himself, so he has granted the Son also to have life in himself... a time is coming when all who are in their graves will hear his voice and come out—those who have done what is good will rise to live."

- John 6:27, 33, 35, 40, 47, 48, 51, 53, 54, 57–58: "Do not work for food that spoils, but for food that endures to eternal life, which the Son of Man will give you.... For the bread of God is the bread that comes down from heaven and gives life to the world.... I am the bread of life.... For my Father's will is that everyone who looks to the Son and believes in him shall have eternal life, and I will raise them up at the last day.... Very truly I tell you, whoever believes has eternal life. I am the bread of life.... This bread is my flesh, which I will give for the life of the world.... Very truly I tell you, unless you eat the flesh of the Son of Man and drink his blood, you have no life in you. Whoever eats my flesh and drinks my blood has eternal life, and I will raise them up at the last day.... Just as the living Father sent me and I live because of the Father, so the one who feeds on me will live because of me.... Your ancestors ate manna and died, but whoever feeds on this bread will live forever."
- John 6:63, 68: "'The Spirit gives life; the flesh counts for nothing. The words I have spoken to you—they are full of the Spirit and life.'... 'Lord, to whom shall we go? You have the words of eternal life.'"
- John 7:38: "Whoever believes in me ... rivers of living water will flow from within them."
- John 8:12: "I am the light of the world. Whoever follows me will never walk in darkness, but will have the light of life."
- John 10:10, 28: "I have come that they may have life, and have it to the full.... I give them eternal life, and they shall never perish."
- John 11:25–26: "I am the resurrection and the life. Anyone who believes in me will live, even though they die; and whoever lives by believing in me will never die."
- John 12:25: "Those who love their life will lose it, while those who hate their life in this world will keep it for eternal life."
- John 12:50: "I know that his command leads to eternal life."
- John 14:6, 19: "I am the way and the truth and the life.... Because I live, you also will live."
- John 17:2–3: "For you granted him authority over all people that he might give eternal life to all those you have given him. Now this is eternal life: that they know you, the only true God, and Jesus Christ, whom you have sent."

- John 20:31: "But these are written that you may believe that Jesus is the Messiah, the Son of God, and that by believing you may have life in his name."
- 1 John 1:1–2: "... this we proclaim concerning the Word of life. The life appeared; we have seen it and testify to it, and we proclaim to you the eternal life."
- 1 John 2:25: "And this is what he promised us—eternal life."
- 1 John 3:14–15: "We know that we have passed from death to life, because we love each other.... Anyone who hates a fellow believer is a murderer, and you know that no murderers have eternal life in them."
- 1 John 5:11–13: "And this is the testimony: God has given us eternal life, and this life is in his Son. Whoever has the Son has life; whoever does not have the Son of God does not have life. I have written these things to you who believe in the name of the Son of God so that you may know that you have eternal life."
- 1 John 5:16: "If you see any brother or sister commit a sin that does not lead to death, you should pray and God will give them life."
- 1 John 5:20: "And we are in him who is true by being in his Son Jesus Christ. He is the true God and eternal life."

16.3.1.2 References to Light in John's Gospel and Letters

While references to "life," though more prominent in Act I of the Johannine drama, pervade the entire gospel, references to "light" occur only in Act I. "Light" and "life" are juxtaposed in John 1:4 and 8:12. References to "light" frame Act I by being four in 1:4–5, 7–9 and in 12:35–36, 46. They are featured in the context of "I am sayings" (8:12) and of Jesus' "signs" (9:4–5; 11:9–10). "Light" is thus part of John's creation theology and intersects with several other Johannine themes. In John's first letter, "light" and "darkness" serve as ciphers for fellowship and living in sin or immorality, respectively.

A list of major clusters of instances of "light" terminology in John's gospel and letters presents itself as follows:

- John 1:4–5, 7–9: "In him was life, and that life was the light of all people. The light shines in the darkness, and the darkness has not overcome it.... He [John the Baptist] came as a witness to testify concerning that light.... He himself was not the light; he came only as a witness to the light. The true light that gives light to everyone was coming into the world."
- John 3:19–21: "Light has come into the world, but people loved darkness instead of light.... All those who do evil hate the light, and will not come into the light for fear that their deeds will be exposed. But those who live by the truth come into the light, so that it may be seen plainly that what they have done has been done in the sight of God."

- John 5:35: "John was a lamp that burned and gave light, and you chose for a time to enjoy his light."
- John 8:12: "I am the light of the world. Whoever follows me will never walk in darkness, but will have the light of life."
- John 9:4–5: "As long as it is day, we must do the works of him who sent me. Night is coming, when no one can work. While I am in the world, I am the light of the world."
- John 11:9–10: "Are there not twelve hours of daylight? Those who walk in the daytime will not stumble, for they see by this world's light. It is when people walk at night that they stumble, for they have no light."
- John 12:35–36, 46: "You are going to have the light just a little while longer. Walk while you have the light, before darkness overtakes you. Those who walk in the dark do not know where they are going. Put your trust in the light while you have light, so that you may become children of light.... I have come into the world as a light, so that no one who believes in me should stay in darkness."
- 1 John 1:5, 7: "This is the message we have heard from him and declare to you: God is light; in him there is no darkness at all.... But if we walk in the light, as he is in the light, we have fellowship with one another."
- 1 John 2:8–10: "The darkness is passing and the true light is already shining. Those who claim to be in the light but hate a fellow believer are still in the darkness. Those who love their fellow believers live in the light, and there is nothing in them to make them stumble."

16.3.1.3 Observations Regarding the Use of Life and Light Terminology in John's Gospel and Letters

The following observations flow from a close study and comparison of all the references to life and light in John's gospel.

- The themes of life and light are explicitly interwined and juxtaposed in the introduction to both John's gospel (John 1:4–5) and first letter (1 John 1:1–2, 5, 7) and in the body of John's gospel (John 8:12).
- Life and light terminology is used by the evangelist (John 1:4–5, 7–9; 3:16, 19–21, 36; 20:31) and is found particularly in Jesus' discourses (3:15; 4:10–11, 14, 36; 5:21, 24–26, 29, 39–40; etc.); Johannine idiom blends Jesus' and the evangelist's terminology.
- Life terminology is more pervasive and encompassing than light terminology (16 vs. 7 clusters of references), suggesting that life is the more basic category of the two (see esp. John 1:4; 20:31; see also 14:6, 19; 17:2–3).
- The obverse of life is death (including the dimensions of perishing, the flesh, sin, the world, judgment; e.g.. John 3:16; 5:24; 6:63), the obverse of light is darkness, a contrast made explicit in virtually every instance of "light" terminology in John's gospel (1:4–5; 3:19–21; 8:12; 9:4–5; 11:9–10; 12:35–36, 46).

- Life and eternal life are used interchangeably in John's gospel, with the latter, fuller expression predominating (16 times in John's gospel) and the term "life" typically serving as a shorthand for eternal life (e.g., John 1:4; 20:31); "eternal" focuses on the aspect of life received in Christ that transcends existence in this world.
- Both themes intersect with Jesus' "I am" sayings: "life" in three different instances (John 6:35, 48; 11:25; 14:6) and "light" in one (8:12; 9:5).
- Both are connected with creation; life is connected with OT types, particularly in relation to God's provision for Israel in the wilderness (John 3:14–16; 6:31–58).
- References to light are limited to the first half of John's gospel (last at 12:46); references to life likewise are primarily found in John 1–12, with the exception of 14:6, 19; 17:2–3; and 20:31.
- Life is mentioned in the gospel's purpose statement (John 20:31), providing an *inclusio* with 1:4 and underscoring the importance of the theme of life in the gospel.
- Life and light are tied to believing in Jesus (John 3:15–16, 36; 5:24; 6:40, 47; 17:2–3), the one through whom everything was created and the one who is both life and light (e.g., 11:25; 14:6).
- The possession of life and light is a divine prerogative shared by God the Father and Jesus the Son (e.g., John 5:21, 26).
- It is also shared by the Holy Spirit, who is presented under the emblem of living water (John 4:10–11, 14; 7:38).
- The possession of life is both a present reality (realized eschatology; John 5:24; 10:10) and a future expectation (awaiting consummation at the second coming; 5:39–40; 6:54).
- Jesus' word is also said to be "life" in the sense that believing acceptance of it gives life to those who hear it with faith (John 6:63, 68).
- The church's mission will be infused with the life of the Holy Spirit (John 7:38; cf. 20:21–22) and result in a harvest for eternal life (4:36).
- Eternal life is contrasted with life in this world (John 12:25) and is given by the Spirit (6:63; cf. 1:13; 3:6); restored spiritual life is thus the result of a new creation (7:38; 20:22).
- John's use of the universal motifs of life and light highlights the universal nature of the gospel transcending ethnic boundaries; rooting the Christian message in creation through Christ and new creation in Christ, John lifts the gospel to a higher plane than the Mosaic law or the kingdom motif.
- John the Baptist relates to Jesus as a lamp relates to the light (John 5:35; cf. 1:7–9).
- Light in John has a moral dimension; in the light, people's sins are exposed (John 3:19–21); in the context of Jesus' ministry to the Jews, the period of "the light" is the time of Jesus' earthly ministry in their midst. Once Jesus has departed, the Jews' opportunity to receive the light has passed; this is

why references to "light" (similar to references to Jesus' "signs") are found only in chapters 1–12 of John's gospel (see esp. 12:35–36, 46).

16.3.1.4 The Old Testament Backdrop for the Life and Light Motifs in John's Gospel and Letters

"In him was *life*, and that *life* was the *light* of all people" (John 1:4, emphasis added). This statement toward the beginning of John's gospel links the two important Johannine terms "life" and "light."[28] What is the likely background for these twin motifs in John's gospel?[29] In the first instance, the foundational passage is the Genesis narrative of God's creation of the world. As his first creative act by his word, God called forth light (Gen 1:3–5). Later he placed lights in the sky to separate between light and darkness (1:14–18). This light, in turn, made it possible for life to exist. Thus God called forth living creatures in the water and on the land (1:20–31), culminating in his creation of man (2:7; 3:20). The tree of life and the tree of the knowledge of good and evil were set in the garden, linking life with obedience to God (2:9).

In the remainder of the OT, it becomes clear that life is more than merely "physical existence sustained by material bread; it rests upon the word and act of God" (cf. Deut 8:3).[30] God is the living God (Ps 42:2) and the fountain of life (36:9). Perhaps most importantly, "life" is an integral part of covenant language in the OT and thus has an important salvation-historical dimension. The Deuteronomic covenant presented Israel with a choice between "life and prosperity, death and destruction," and people were commanded "to love the LORD your God, to walk in obedience to him, and to keep his commands, decrees and laws" (Deut 30:15–16). Many of these theme clusters are present in John's gospel with reference to Jesus' new covenant community, especially in the Farewell Discourse.[31]

In John's creation theology that explicitly links that which was "in the beginning" (John 1:1; cf. Gen 1:1) with the incarnation of Christ (John 1:14), the above-painted scenario forms the backdrop against which Jesus' coming is more readily understood. Humanity's sin had issued in the loss of life, resulting in physical death, and plunged humanity into moral darkness, rendering it incapable of living life the way it had been intended by the Creator. The crying need was for human beings to be restored to life, "eternal life," and to be brought back into the light, that is, moral insight unclouded by the pervasive presence and power of sin.

---

28. On the "light/darkness" motif as part of the Johannine worldview, see already the discussion in chap. 2, sec. 3.4 above. On "life," see Filson, "Gospel of Life"; Simon, "Eternal Life"; Rudolf Schnackenburg, "The Idea of Life in the Fourth Gospel," in *Gospel according to St. John*, 2:352–61; Charles F. D. Moule, "The Meaning of 'Life' in the Gospel and Epistles of St. John," *Theology* 78 (1975): 114–25; J. C. Coetzee, "Life (Eternal Life) in John's Writings and the Qumran Scrolls," *Neot* 6 (1972): 48–66; George Barker Stevens, *Johannine Theology: A Study of the Doctrinal Contents of the Gospel and Epistles of the Apostle John* (rev. ed.; New York: Charles Scribner's Sons, 1908), 312–27; and Keener, *John*, 328–29 and 385–86 (with further primary and secondary references). On "light," see Keener, *John*, 382–85, 386–87, 739–40, 742, 920, 1178, and 1189 (with additional references).

29. See also Keener, *John*, 381–87.

30. See Filson, "Gospel of Life," 116.

31. See the discussion in chap. 12, sec. 29; see also Pryor, *John: Evangelist of the Covenant People*, 54–72, 157–80, *et passim*; Lacomara, "Deuteronomy and the Farewell Discourse."

In this regard, it is instructive to compare John's gospel to the other canonical gospels. What the Synoptic writers, especially Matthew and Luke, present in terms of God's kingdom, John grounds in creation realities that were perverted through the fall but had now been restored through Jesus the Messiah.[32] While "kingdom" language dominates in the Synoptics, references to "life" are not absent in their portrayal of Jesus (see Matt 25:46 [= the kingdom in v. 34]; Mark 7:14; 9:43, 45 [= the kingdom in v. 47]; 10:17 [cf. 10:15, 23]; Luke 10:25).

In John's gospel, the "kingdom of God" and "eternal life" are the subject of his conversation with Nicodemus (John 3:1–15). There Jesus makes clear that no one can enter the kingdom of God apart from personal regeneration as envisioned in prophetic passages such as in the book of Ezekiel (e.g., Ezek 36:25–27; 37). Yet, importantly, this life is not merely to be experienced in the age to come; it can be entered into already in the here and now (e.g., John 3:16; 5:24; 10:10).[33]

Also relevant for an understanding of Johannine "light" and "life" terminology may be passages in the Psalms, such as the following:

> They feast on the abundance of your house;
>   you give them drink from your river of delights.
> For with you is the fountain of life;
>   in your light we see light. (Ps 36:8–9)[34]

Passages such as these provide a fertile soil for Jesus' promise of living water (John 4:10–15), of rivers of living water emanating from people's innermost being (7:38), and of the blessing of abundant life brought by Jesus' coming for believers (10:10). As Jeremiah had lamented, people had forsaken God, "the spring of living water," and had "dug their own cisterns" (Jer 2:13; cf. 17:13); they must return to the Lord.

The terms "light" and "life" were also associated in the common phrase "the light of life," which is found in John's gospel as well (John 8:12; cf. Job 3:20; 33:30; Ps 49:19; 56:13; Isa 53:11). In the Johannine writings, the vision of restored, abundant life in God's presence is given final expression at the end of the book of Revelation (Rev 22:1–2), echoing similar visions in the latter, postexilic prophets (e.g., Ezek 47:12).

16.3.1.5 Conclusion

The themes of "life" and "light" are inextricably wedded in John's theology. Both attest to the blessing resulting from Jesus' coming into the world: new, eternal life

---

32. See the discussion of life and death in chap. 2, sec. 3.4.2 above.

33. Simon, "Eternal Life," 98. The roots of "eternal life" terminology in Jesus' usage may well lie in the occurrence of the expression "everlasting life" in Dan 12:2 in the context of future eschatological resurrection: "Multitudes who sleep in the dust of the earth will awake: some to everlasting life, others to shame and everlasting contempt" (see ibid., 97).

34. For extrabiblical Jewish references to "life," see Keener, *John*, 328–29, with reference to Ladd, *Theology of the New Testament*, 255, *et al.*, citing Tob 12:9–10; *Pss. Sol.* 14:7; 2 Macc 7:9–14; *4 Ezra* 7:137; 14:22. As Keener notes, however, John's gospel "employs the term somewhat differently from contemporary Jewish sources and the Synoptics. Linking it with present-tense verbs, the Fourth Gospel declares that the life of the kingdom era is available to those living in the present through faith in Christ. His resurrection has already inaugurated the resurrection era that the rest of Judaism still awaited in the future. This motif thus provides a major contribution to the realized eschatology of the Fourth Gospel" (ibid., 329).

made available through his substitutionary death to "everyone who believes," issuing in believers' crossing over from death into life and from darkness into light. Jesus thus renews creation on both a cosmic and a personal scale. He satisfies the psalmist's longings, makes possible the prophets' highest aspirations, and paves the way for the fulfillment of the apocalyptist's vision of abundant, eternal life in God's presence.

16.4 Creation and New Creation Theology in the Book of Signs

16.4.1 The First Week of Jesus' Ministry

Introduction (1:1–18)	The Book of Signs (1:19–12:50)	The Book of Exaltation (13:1–21:25)
Creation through the Word	Jesus' first week of ministry (1:29–2:11)	Garden (18:1, 26; 19:41; 20:15)
"In the beginning" (1:1–5)	The new birth (3:3, 5)	Jesus' resurrection (20:1–31)
The new birth (1:12–13)	Jesus Lord of the Sabbath (5:1–47; 9:1–41)	Creation of community (20:22)

Fig. 16.1: Creation and New Creation Theology in John's Gospel

In analogy with the first week of creation (see Genesis 1), John presents the first week of Jesus' ministry in a way that may suggest an intentional parallelism.[35] Starting in John 1:29, the fourth evangelist links his narrative sequence with the expression "the next day." Starting with John the Baptist's testimony in 1:19–28, it is possible to reconstruct an entire week of ministry:

Day 1: John's testimony regarding Jesus (1:19–28)
Day 2: John's encounter with Jesus (1:29–34: "the next day")
Day 3: John's referral of two disciples to Jesus (1:35–39; "the next day")
Day 4: Andrew's introduction of his brother Peter to Jesus (1:40–42)
Day 5: Philip and Nathanael follow Jesus (1:43–51; "the next day")
Day 7: Wedding at Cana (2:1–11: "on the third day")[36]

If this seven-day pattern is intended to invoke the memory of the first week of creation in Genesis 1, this would continue the "creation" motif struck in the introduction to the gospel and provide a bridge to the possible instance of "creation" theology in John 5.[37]

---

35. See Köstenberger, *John*, 56; Carson, *Gospel according to John*, 167–68; Marie-Emile Boismard, *Du baptême à Cana (Jean 1,19–2,11)* (Paris: Cerf, 1956), 288–89; Thomas Barrosse, "The Seven Days of the New Creation in St. John's Gospel," *CBQ* 21 (1959): 507–16.

36. See Phillips, "Third Fifth Day."

37. See the discussion below. Note also the reference to the resurrection of Jesus' body within three days in 2:20–21, which anticipates the account of Jesus' resurrection in John 20.

16.4.2 The New Birth

Another possible instance of the creation motif in the first half of John's gospel is the reference to being "born again" "of water and the Spirit" (John 3:3, 5; cf. 1:12–13).[38] This new birth, required for entrance into God's kingdom and reception of eternal life, invokes the prophetic vision of a decisive inner transformation in the end times (e.g., Jer 31:33–34; Ezek 11:19–20; 36:25–27).[39] Perhaps the closest parallel is Ezek 36:25–27, which presages God's cleansing of human hearts with water and their inner transformation by his Spirit (see also Isa 44:3–5; *Jub.* 1:23–25). As in Ezekiel's vision of the valley of dry bones (Ezekiel 37), the end times will witness national restoration under one king, with important personal ramifications as well.

16.4.3 The Sabbath Controversy

The next occurrence of the "creation" motif is found in the context of the "Sabbath controversy" in John 5. When charged with causing the healed lame man to work on the Sabbath by telling him to pick up his mat, Jesus retorted in self-defense, "My Father is always at his work to this very day, and I too am working" (5:17). Jesus' Jewish opponents have no difficulty recognizing in Jesus' statement an implicit claim to deity, made explicit by the fourth evangelist (5:18). The primary OT background is Gen 2:2–3, where it is said that, "By the seventh day God had finished the work he had been doing; so on the seventh day he rested [*šābat*] from all his work. Then God blessed the seventh day and made it holy, because on it he rested from all the work of creating that he had done."[40]

If, then, God the Creator rested on the seventh day, none other than the Creator had the authority to determine whether engaging in a particular activity on the day of rest was appropriate. By asserting that he had such authority, Jesus in effect identified himself as the Creator and thus, in the eyes of his opponents, violated not only the Sabbath commandment, but, more grievously, committed blasphemy, punishable by death. In fact, of course, it was first-century Jews who had engaged in petty casuistry, seeking to stipulate which kinds of activity were or were not permissible on the Sabbath.[41] Yet rather than objecting to this casuistry, Jesus claimed equality

---

38. See John A. Dennis, "Begotten by the Spirit: Johannine Eternal Life in Biblical-Theological Perspective" (paper presented at the Annual Meeting of the ETS; Providence, RI, November 19, 2008). See also the discussions in Köstenberger, *John*, 121–25; Carson, *Gospel according to John*, 191–96, esp. 194–95; and Robert V. McCabe, "The Meaning of 'Born of Water and the Spirit' in John 3:5," *DBSJ* 4 (1999): 85–107.

39. See in more detail chap. 12, sec. 28.2 below.

40. While Gen 2:2–3 teaches that God rested (*šābat*) on the seventh day of creation, Jewish rabbis were agreed that God indeed works constantly, yet without breaking the Sabbath (*Exod. Rab.* 30:9; cf. *Gen. Rab.* 11:10), on the grounds that the whole world is God's domain (Isa 6:3) and that he fills the entire universe (Jer 23:24). Thus Jesus places his mission in continuity with the Creator's ongoing work (John 5:17; cf. 4:34).

41. Although the Jewish leaders may have thought of passages such as Exod 31:12–17; Jer 17:21–27; or Neh 13:15, 19, the man did not actually break any *biblical* Sabbath regulations. According to Jewish *tradition*, however, he was violating a code that prohibited the carrying of an object "from one domain into another" (*m. Šabb.* 7:2), in the present instance, his mat. Apparently, it was permissible to carry a bed *with a person lying on it*, but not one that was empty (*m. Šabb.* 10:5). Thus Jesus is accused, not of violating the law himself, but of enticing another person to sin by issuing a command that would have caused that person to break the law.

with the Creator.[42] This significantly advances the "creation theology" sounded in the introduction to the gospel and presents the Creator in terms of "Father" and "Son."[43]

The "Sabbath controversy" erupts again in John 9, where Jesus, in another Johannine "sign," heals the man born blind, again on the Sabbath (9:14). Again, the Pharisees object that Jesus had violated the Sabbath command by making mud in the process of healing the man (9:15–16). In this instance, Jesus does not duplicate his extended self-defense but transforms the healing and the Pharisees' opposition into a real-life parable on the subject of blindness and seeing. With thick irony, Jesus states, "For judgment I have come into this world, so that the blind will see and those who see will become blind" (9:39). When the Pharisees ask whether Jesus thinks they too are blind, Jesus replies, "If you were blind, you would not be guilty of sin, but now that you claim you can see, your guilt remains" (9:41).

Thus the Word, Creator and now made flesh in Jesus, asserts his authority over the Sabbath and, in two Johannine "signs" designed to elicit faith among the Jews, heals a lame man and a man born blind, both on the Sabbath—in the second instance using language of "coming into the world" (reminiscent of the reference to light coming into the world in the introduction) and invoking imagery of seeing and blindness. This shows the Creator and that Word-made-flesh engage in his messianic activity of making the lame walk and making the blind see (and subsequently raising the dead), in powerful extension and escalation of creation and new creation theology. As the Creator, Jesus is the Giver and Restorer of life, and the one who has authority over the Sabbath.

16.5 Creation and New Creation Theology in the Passion Narrative

16.5.1 Introduction

As mentioned above, the introduction opens the gospel with an unmistakable reference to God's original creation and the Word's participation in it. This serves to convey to John's readers the entire framework of creation theology in which to place the coming of Jesus as the incarnate Word. It also shows that Jesus' coming has implications far beyond merely the Jewish people, extending to the entire cosmos (the "world"). As the "universal" gospel, John transcends predominantly Jewish categories such as "kingdom" and replaces these with expressions such as "life," "light," and "world." Thus John seeks to demonstrate that Jesus' coming encompasses all of human history, both temporally and spatially.

---

42. With regard to healing on the Sabbath, Jesus maintained that the one who made the Sabbath had authority over it, determining its purpose, use, and limitations. What is more, as Jesus was careful to point out, even the Jews made exceptions to the rule of refraining from work on the Sabbath, most notably in the case of circumcision (see John 7:23; cf. *m. Šabb.* 18:3; 19:2–3). If God is therefore above Sabbath regulations, so is Jesus (cf. Matt 12:1–14 pars.). See Brown, *Gospel according to John I–XII*, 217; Barrett, *Gospel according to St. John*, 256; and Carson, *Gospel according to John*, 247–49.

43. This is developed in the first major sustained discourse in John's gospel in 5:18–47 (esp. vv. 18–20). On the interpretation of 5:18–20, see Köstenberger, *John*, 184–87.

What is more, as mentioned, the initial creation setting in John's gospel is carried forward by the presentation of the first week of Jesus' ministry in possible analogy to the first week of creation and the discussion of the new birth in Jesus' conversation with Nicodemus (in further development of John 1:12–13). While the initial references to creation in the introduction pertain primarily to God's original creation in and through Jesus "the Word," the Passion Narrative toward the end of the gospel builds on these references and sets Jesus' crucifixion and resurrection within the context of a new creation.

16.5.2 Possible Instances of the New Creation Motif in the Passion Narrative

As mentioned, there are several possible indications for the presence of such "new creation theology" in the Passion Narrative, including the following:

- the setting of the Passion Narrative in a garden (*kēpos*; 18:1, 26; 19:41; note that this is a unique Johannine feature not present in the other gospels)
- Pilate's identification of Jesus as "the man" (19:5), which may identify Jesus as the "new Adam," a possible instance of double entendre and Johannine irony
- the possible presentation of Jesus' resurrection as the beginning of a new creation (20:1; cf. 1:3)[44]
- the (albeit mistaken) identification of Jesus as "the gardener" (*kēpouros*) by Mary (20:15), reflecting misunderstanding and possibly irony as well
- Jesus' bodily resurrection and appearances to his followers in keeping with repeated predictions earlier in the Johannine narrative (chap. 20; cf. 2:20–21; 10:17–19)
- Jesus' breathing on his disciples and giving of the Spirit in the final commissioning scene (20:22), invoking the creation of Adam in Gen 2:7 (cf. Ezek 37:9)[45]

From the first verse of the Passion Narrative (18:1) to the final chapter, therefore, this section reverberates with "new creation" theology, harking back to the opening references to the original creation in the introduction to the gospel. By this the fourth evangelist seeks to imply that salvation through faith in Jesus as Messiah anticipates the consummation of human history in the new creation. This further means that John's gospel is the gospel equivalent to the Johannine Apocalypse, which likewise ends with the eschatological consummation of what began in the garden of Eden in the New Jerusalem.

In this regard, as mentioned, it is also significant that the entire gospel is pervaded by references to life—"eternal life," which those who believe in Jesus will receive—as well as "light" and "darkness" symbolism. Also, the anticipation of

---

44. See Derek Tidball, "Completing the Circle: The Resurrection according to John," *ERT* 30 (2006): 169–83.

45. See DuRand, "Creation Motif in the Fourth Gospel," 21–46, esp. 43–46.

the giving of the Spirit finds expression several times in the gospel, from sporadic initial references (John 3:34; 7:39) to the crescendoing promise of his coming subsequent to Jesus' exaltation in chapters 14–16 and his (symbolic?) impartation in 20:22. Hence John makes clear throughout his narrative that life in the Spirit will characterize the eschatological experience of believers in Jesus the Messiah once he has been exalted to the Father.

Jeannine Brown mentions yet another possible instance of "new creation theology" in John's gospel, namely the reference to "the first day of the week" in 20:1 and 19 and to the phrase "a week later" in 20:26 in conjunction with references to Jesus completing his work in 19:28, 30 (cf. 17:4, which forms an *inclusio* with 4:34).[46] It is clear from John's gospel that Jesus came to complete his Father's work (see esp. 5:17). In fact, as noted, Jesus did several of his "signs" on the Sabbath (e.g., 5:9b, 17; 9:3–4, 14). While according to Gen 2:2, God rested from all his work (*erga*; LXX) on the seventh day, now Jesus, on the eighth day, resumed and completed God's work. Thus, subsequent to the cross, God's eternal Sabbath can begin (19:31; 20:1).

16.5.3 The Climax of New Creation Theology in Jesus' Resurrection

But perhaps most importantly, the new creation theology of John's gospel climaxes in the resurrection of the Word-made-flesh, the lifted-up Son of Man, and the Suffering Servant, who, as Creator and Sender, breathes life into his new messianic community and commissions his followers to proclaim the message of forgiveness and eternal life through believing in Jesus (20:22). Thus the Johannine narrative builds inexorably from creation to new creation, spanning the entire range from preexistent, glorious Word to the enfleshed Word's return to its preexistent glory subsequent to its death, burial, and resurrection. Thus the Isaianic pattern of the divine Word's mission has been fulfilled in Jesus, the Messiah and Son of God (Isa 55:11). In the logic of the Johannine narrative, the resurrection of Jesus constitutes the central plank.[47]

16.6 Conclusion

New creation theology in John's gospel is not at odds with salvation history but provides the larger framework for it. While setting the universal stage for the salvation-historical drama pitting the Christ against Satan and the unbelieving world against a cosmic backdrop, John shows that Jesus epitomized true Israel and fulfilled the symbolism underlying the nation's religious observances. This includes the law

---

46. Brown ("Creation's Renewal") also contends that the resurrection is the eighth Johannine "sign," also forming a part in John's "new creation theology." This is one of the few unpersuasive elements of Brown's paper, since the resurrection does not seem to fit the Johannine conception of a "sign." Instead, it is the reality to which the "signs" point and cannot therefore itself be a sign as well. See Köstenberger, "Seventh Johannine Sign."

47. For a collection of essays on various aspects of Jesus' resurrection in John's gospel, see *The Resurrection of Jesus in the Gospel of John* (ed. Craig R. Koester and Reimund Bieringer; WUNT 222; Tübingen: Mohr-Siebeck, 2008).

(including the Sabbath), the temple, and festivals such as Passover, Tabernacles, and Dedication.[48] Jesus is the new and true Israel (the "vine," 15:1), and his "own" are the believing remnant who place their faith in him as Messiah (13:1; cf. 1:11). Thus the Johannine drama of the Christ plays out in true cosmic proportions while at the same time encompassing the salvation-historical dimension of the Messiah coming to Israel, whose rejection of Christ, in turn, opens the way for believing Gentiles to be incorporated into the new messianic community, Jesus' "flock."[49]

Introduction (1:1–18)	**Book of Signs (1:19–12:50)**	**Farewell (13:1–17:26)**	**Passion Narrative (18:1–21:25)**
Creation, new creation, and the children of God	The Messiah, his signs, and the world's rejection	The Messiah and the believing remnant	Completion of the Son's mission, new creation and commission

Fig. 16.2: New Creation Theology and Salvation History in John's Gospel

---

48. See chap. 10, below.

49. See chap. 12, sec. 29.

Chapter 9

GOD: FATHER, SON, AND SPIRIT

BIBLIOGRAPHY

Ball, David M. *The "I Am" in John's Gospel: Literary Function, Background and Theological Implications*. JSNTSup 124. Sheffield: Sheffield Academic Press, 1996. **Bauckham, Richard**. *God Crucified: Monotheism and Christology in the New Testament*. Grand Rapids: Eerdmans, 1998. Idem. "Biblical Theology and the Problems of Monotheism." Pp. 187–232 in *Out of Egypt: Biblical Theology and Biblical Interpretation*. Ed. Craig G. Bartholomew, Mary Healy, Karl Moller, and Robin Parry. Carlisle, UK: Paternoster/Grand Rapids: Zondervan, 2004. Idem. "Monotheism and Christology in the Gospel of John." Pp. 153–63 in *Contours of Christology in the New Testament*. Ed. Richard N. Longenecker. Grand Rapids: Eerdmans, 2005. **Burkett, Delbert**. *The Son of Man in the Gospel of John*. JSNTSup 56. Sheffield: JSOT, 1991. **Fisher, Matthew C**. "God the Father in the Fourth Gospel: A Biblical Patrology." Ph.D. diss. Southeastern Baptist Theological Seminary, 2003. **Harner, Philip B**. *The "I Am" of the Fourth Gospel*. Facet Books. Philadelphia: Fortress, 1970. **Harris, Murray J**. *Jesus as God: The New Testament Use of* Theos *in Reference to Jesus*. Grand Rapids: Baker, 1992. **Hurtado, Larry W**. *Lord Jesus Christ: Devotion to Jesus in Earliest Christianity*. Grand Rapids: Eerdmans, 2003. **Koester, Craig R**. "God." Pp. 25–52 in *The Word of Life: A Theology of John's Gospel*. Grand Rapids: Eerdmans, 2008. **Köstenberger, Andreas J**. "Jesus as Rabbi in the Fourth Gospel." *BBR* 8 (1998): 97–128. **Köstenberger, Andreas J., and Scott R. Swain**. *Father, Son and Spirit: The Trinity and John's Gospel*. NSBT 24. Leicester, UK/Downers Grove, IL: InterVarsity Press, 2008. **Lee, Aquila H. I**. *From Messiah to Preexistent Son: Jesus' Self-Consciousness and Early Christian Exegesis of Messianic Psalms*. WUNT 2/192. Tübingen: Mohr-Siebeck, 2005. **Loader, William**. *The Christology of the Fourth Gospel*. BBET 23. Frankfurt am Main: Peter Lang, 1992. **Meyer, Paul W**. "'The Father': The Presentation of God in the Fourth Gospel." Pp. 255–73 in *Exploring the Gospel of John: In Honor of D. Moody Smith*. Ed. R. Alan Culpepper and C. Clifton Black. Louisville: Westminster John Knox, 1996. **Moloney, Francis J**. *The Johannine Son of Man*. Biblioteca di Scienze Religiose 14. 2nd ed. Rome: Libreria Ateneo Salesiano, 1978. **Morris, Leon**. Pp. 43–169 in *Jesus Is the Christ: Studies in the Theology of John*. Grand Rapids: Eerdmans, 1989. **Nicholson, Godfrey Carruthers**. *Death as Departure: The Johannine Descent-Ascent Schema*. SBLDS 63. Chico, CA: Scholars Press, 1983. **Pollard, T. E**. *Johannine Christology and the Early Church*. SNTSMS 13. Cambridge: Cambridge University Press, 1970. **Stibbe, Mark W. G**. "Telling the Father's Story: The Gospel of John as Narrative

Theology." Pp. 170–93 in *Challenging Perspectives on the Gospel of John*. Ed. John Lierman. WUNT 2/219. Tübingen: Mohr-Siebeck, 2006. **Thompson, Marianne Meye**. *The Humanity of Jesus in the Fourth Gospel*. Philadelphia: Fortress, 1988. Idem. *The Promise of the Father*. Louisville: Westminster John Knox, 2000. Idem. *The God of the Gospel of John*. Grand Rapids: Eerdmans, 2001. **Tolmie, Donald François**. "The Characterization of God in the Fourth Gospel." *JSNT* 69 (1998): 57–75. **Williams, Catrin H**. *I Am He: The Interpretation of 'ani hu' in Jewish and Early Christian Literature*. Tübingen: Mohr-Siebeck, 2000. **Wright, Christopher J. H**. *The Mission of God: Unlocking the Bible's Grand Narrative*. Downers Grove, IL: InterVarsity Press, 2006.

17 JOHN, JESUS, AND JEWISH MONOTHEISM

17.1 John's Portrayal of Jesus in the Context of Jewish Monotheism

The Jews' belief in one God was firmly grounded in the Shema: "Hear, O Israel: The LORD our God, the LORD is one" (Deut 6:4).[1] The Decalogue, likewise, in the first two commandments forbids Israelites to have (monotheism) or worship (monolatry) any gods other than Yahweh (Exod 20:2–6; Deut 5:6–10). Everywhere in the Hebrew Scriptures, it is this one God who manifests his character and acts in human history both redemptively and in terms of revelation.[2] This includes seminal events such as the exodus (Exod 20:2; Deut 4:32–39; Isa 43:15–17), the giving of the law, and the Assyrian and Babylonian exiles. This God is the Creator and sole and sovereign Ruler of all things.[3]

Not only is God recognized as the one and only God, he alone is worshiped. As Bauckham notes, "Judaism was unique among the religions of the Roman world in demanding the exclusive worship of its God.... Jewish monotheism was defined by its adherence to the first and second commandments."[4] This sharp distinction between God as being God alone and worthy of worship stood in distinct contrast to Hellenistic conceptions, which held that worship was a matter of degree because divinity, likewise, was a matter of degree. Thus worship was to be rendered to the

---

1. Section 17 represents a partial adaptation of chap. 1 of Köstenberger and Swain, *Father, Son and Spirit*, specifically pp. 34–37 and 43–44 (used by permission).

2. See esp. Peter Machinist, "The Question of Distinctiveness in Ancient Israel," in *Essential Papers on Israel and the Ancient Near East* (ed. F. E. Greenspan; New York: New York University Press, 1991), 420–42, who notes that affirmations of the uniqueness of Israel's God are found in every genre and at every stage of OT literature; similarly, Ronald E. Clements, "Monotheism and the Canonical Process," *Theology* 87 (1984): 336–44; and the chart in Christopher J. H. Wright, *The Mission of God: Unlocking the Bible's Grand Narrative* (Downers Grove, IL: InterVarsity Press, 2006), 104.

3. See esp. Isa 43:11; 44:6; 45:5–6, 14, 18, 21–22; 46:9; Bauckham, *God Crucified*, 10–11.

4. Richard Bauckham, "Worship of Jesus," *ABD*, 3:816. See also Robert K. Gnuse, *No Other Gods: Emergent Monotheism in Israel* (JSOTSup 241; Sheffield: Sheffield Academic Press, 1997); Nathan MacDonald, *Deuteronomy and the Meaning of "Monotheism"* (FAT 2/1; Tübingen: Mohr-Siebeck, 2003); idem, "Whose Monotheism? Which Rationality?" in *The Old Testament in Its World* (ed. Robert P. Gordon and Johannes Cornelis de Moor; Leiden: Brill, 2005), 45–67; Richard Bauckham, "Biblical Theology and the Problems of Monotheism," in *Out of Egypt: Biblical Theology and Biblical Interpretation* (ed. Craig G. Bartholomew, Mary Healy, Karl Moller, and Robin Parry; Carlisle, UK: Paternoster; Grand Rapids: Zondervan, 2004), 187–232 (including a critique of Gnuse); and Wright, *Mission of God*, 73–74.

extent appropriate to its object. Judaism, however, viewed God as unique and thus uniquely worthy of worship.[5]

The belief in, and worship of, one and only one God set Israel apart from the polytheistic beliefs and practices of its pagan neighbors, including the Greco-Roman pantheon, which was made up of dozens of gods. While the Jews had lapsed into the worship of other deities in the period prior to the exiles,[6] postexilic Judaism, including that of the first century AD, was committed to monotheism and monolatry.[7] In fact, this became an important distinguishing characteristic of Jewish religion in a polytheistic environment and was recognized as a hallmark of Jewish faith by Greco-Roman historians such as Tacitus, who wrote, "The Jews conceive of one God only" (*Hist.* 5.5).

As Christopher Wright observes, faith in the one and only God anchored "the theocentric, monotheistic worldview of first-century Jews" and constituted "the assumptive bedrock of Jesus and all his first followers."[8] "This God," Wright continues, "was acknowledged now by Israel, his covenant people. But the God of Israel was also the universal God to whom all nations, kings, and even emperors must finally submit."[9] As the NT attests, strikingly, Jesus claimed—and his followers believed—that he shared the identity of YHWH, the one and only God of Israel and of the nations, indicated by the application of *maranatha* (Aram. "O Lord, come") to Jesus (1 Cor 16:22; Rev 22:20) and the appellation of Jesus as *kyrios* ("Lord") in the Christian confession *kyrios Iēsous* ("Jesus is Lord").[10]

In light of the Jewish context of John's gospel noted above and the Jewish belief in monotheism, it is apparent that any claims to deity by an individual such as Jesus would have been fiercely opposed by pious first-century Jews. Numerous passages in John's gospel suggest that this is in fact what occurred when Jesus' Jewish contemporaries repeatedly attempted to stone Jesus on account of blasphemy (e.g., John 5:18; 8:59; 10:31–33; cf. 11:8). Also, at Jesus' trial before Pilate, the Jews, after initially insinuating Jesus was a political threat to Roman imperial power, eventually insist that Jesus "must die, because he claimed to be the Son of God" (19:7). Hence Jesus died first and foremost because he claimed to be God (cf. Matt 26:65).

Some believe that Second Temple Judaism held to a strict monotheism that rendered it impossible to attribute divinity to anyone other than God. In this case, only a radical break with Judaism would have allowed his followers to attribute divinity

---

5. Bauckham, *God Crucified*, 15. Cf. Hurtado, *Lord Jesus Christ*, 31, who notes, "For devout Jews, the core requirement of Judaism was the exclusive worship of Israel's God." Hurtado also points out that none of the "divine agents" of God were "treated as rightful recipients of cultic worship in any known Jewish circles of the time" (ibid.).

6. See Bernhard Lang, *Der einzige Gott: Die Geburt des biblischen Monotheismus* (Munich: Kösel, 1981); idem, *Monotheism and the Prophetic Minority* (Sheffield: Almond, 1983); Saul M. Olyan, *Asherah and the Cult of Yahweh in Israel* (SBLMS 34; Atlanta: Scholars Press, 1988); and Mark S. Smith, *The Early History of God: Yahweh and the Other Deities in Ancient Israel* (San Francisco: Harper & Row, 1990), cited in Hurtado, *Lord Jesus Christ*, 29–30, n. 5.

7. See esp. Larry W. Hurtado, "First-Century Jewish Monotheism," *JSNT* 71 (1998): 3–26.

8. Wright, *Mission of God*, 105.

9. Ibid.

10. See esp. Acts 2:36; Rom 10:9; 1 Cor 12:3; Phil 2:11 cf. Isa 45:22–23. See chap. 4 in ibid., esp. pp. 106–9.

to Jesus. Hence Maurice Casey contends that "the deity of Jesus is ... *inherently unJewish*. The witness of Jewish texts is unvarying: belief that a second being is God involves departure from the Jewish community."[11] Others favor the view that Second Temple Judaism was more flexible, pointing to various intermediary figures such as angels, exalted humans, or personified divine attributes, claiming that these provide Jewish precedents for identifying Jesus as divine.[12]

Indeed, the OT and Second Temple literature feature several passages where beings other than God are called "god." Philo refers to Moses as "god" (*Mos.* 1.155–158; *Prob.* 42–44; cf. Exod 7:1).[13] Human judges are called "gods" in the LXX (Exod 22:27), as are angels (Ps 8:6; 82:1, 6; 97:6; 138:1) and the mysterious figure of Melchizedek (11QMelch 2:24–25).[14] Yet intermediary figures such as these were clearly understood as creatures, and the line between God and created beings was clearly drawn (cf. Ezek 28:2; Hos 11:9). Instead of blurring divine-human distinctions, in passages such as these beings who are not God are shown to exercise divine prerogatives.[15] Hence these instances cannot serve as genuine precedents.

Rather than pointing to Jewish intermediary figures, therefore, it is most plausible that the early Christians identified "Jesus directly with the one God of Israel" and included "Jesus in the unique identity of this one God."[16] If correct, this view has revolutionary implications for understanding the Christology of the NT. In Bauckham's words:

> The highest possible Christology, the inclusion of Jesus in the unique divine identity, was central to the faith of the early church even before any of the New Testament writings were written.... Although there was development in understanding this inclusion of Jesus in the identity of God, the decisive step of so including him was made at the beginning.[17]

What is more, this high Christology was entirely possible within strict Jewish monotheism. This explains why neither John nor the other NT writers evidence any consciousness of tension between the attribution of deity to Jesus and their

---

11. Maurice Casey, *From Jewish Prophet to Gentile God: The Origins and Development of New Testament Christology* (Louisville: Westminster John Knox, 1991), 176, cited in Marianne Meye Thompson, *The God of the Gospel of John* (Grand Rapids: Eerdmans, 2001), 28. See the critique of Casey's work in Hurtado, *Lord Jesus Christ*, 43–44; and James D. G. Dunn, "The Making of Christology—Evolution or Unfolding?" in *Jesus of Nazareth: Lord and Christ. Essays on the Historical Jesus and New Testament Christology* (ed. Joel B. Green and Max Turner; Grand Rapids: Eerdmans, 1994), 437–52.

12. See Larry W. Hurtado, *One God, One Lord: Early Christian Devotion and Ancient Jewish Monotheism* (Edinburgh: T&T Clark, 1988); and idem, *Lord Jesus Christ*. See, however, the important clarification in Hurtado, *Lord Jesus Christ*, 29, n. 3, where Hurtado notes that he believes Jewish "divine agency" traditions "were *not* by themselves sufficient to explain the emergence or distinctive character of devotion to Jesus."

13. Philo also calls the Logos "a second god" (*QG* 2.62; cf. Justin Martyr, *1 Apol.* 63.15; *Dial.* 56.4).

14. See Jesus' citation of Ps 82:6 in John 10:34, discussed in 10.2.1.3.7; 18.3.2; and 20.3.3.

15. So rightly Thompson, *God of the Gospel of John*, 45.

16. Bauckham, *God Crucified*, 4.

17. Ibid., 27. Bauckham's findings stand in sharp contrast to those of James D. G. Dunn, *Christology in the Making: A New Testament Inquiry into the Origins of the Doctrine of the Incarnation* (2nd ed.; Grand Rapids: Eerdmans, 1996). See also the critique by D. A. Carson, "Unity and Diversity in the New Testament: The Possibility of Systematic Theology," in *Scripture and Truth* (ed. D. A. Carson and John D. Woodbridge; Grand Rapids: Zondervan, 1983), 71–79.

Jewish monotheistic beliefs. Jesus' inclusion in the unique deity was novel, but it did not compromise Jewish monotheism. John's gospel also shows Jesus appropriating the divine name *ʾanî hûʾ* (LXX: *egō eimi*).[18] At times, the expression is used simply meaning "I am" without indicating a claim to deity on Jesus' part. At other times, especially in [the seven absolute "I am" sayings,] Jesus' deity is clearly implied.[19]

In keeping with Isaiah's vision of a new exodus for God's people, the four Gospels provide a new narrative of God's acts.[20] Just as Israel knew God as the one who delivered the nation out of Egypt and told the story of that God, the NT writers identify God as the God of Jesus Christ and tell the story of Jesus as the account of the deliverance of God's people from sin.[21] This new story is consistent with the OT account of God and his acts on behalf of his people, yet it is new in the way God now has revealed himself and provided redemption in a final and universal way (John 1:18; cf. Heb 1:1–3). In Jesus, the Creator and Ruler of the world has become its universal Savior (John 4:42; cf. Luke 2:1).

Jesus' inclusion in the identity of God means that God must be conceived in relational terms, uniting God as Father, Son, and Holy Spirit. God thus transcends one-dimensional conceptions of human identity. This entails an element of novelty: "Nothing in the Second Temple Jewish understanding of divine identity contradicts the possibility of interpersonal relationship within the divine identity, but on the other hand there is little, if anything, that anticipates it."[22] Jesus is now "God with us" (Matt 1:23) and "will be with" his people (cf. 28:20).[23] "The Father, the Son, and the Holy Spirit" names the newly disclosed identity of God revealed in the Gospels' account of Jesus (e.g., 28:19).[24]

Thus the present discussion has come full circle. It was noted at the outset that Israel's belief in one God was grounded in the Shema of Deut 6:4. As passages such as 1 Cor 8:4–6 show, Paul and the early church, as well as John, included Jesus within the identity of the one God confessed in the Shema and believed that Jesus shared in the identity of YHWH, in keeping with Jesus' own claim that he and the Father were one.[25] Contrary to the Jewish charge that Jesus' claim constituted a breach of their monotheistic beliefs (e.g., John 10:31–33), Jesus' followers understood that Jesus' claim did not imply that he was a second God alongside, and in addition to, God the Father (ditheism), but that his deity was to be accommodated within the framework of Jewish monotheism in such a way that the one and only

---

18. Harner, *"I Am" of the Fourth Gospel*; Ball, *"I Am" in John's Gospel*; Williams, *I Am He*; Richard Bauckham, "Monotheism and Christology in the Gospel of John," in *Contours of Christology in the New Testament* (ed. Richard N. Longenecker; Grand Rapids: Eerdmans, 2005), 153–63.

19. John 4:26; 6:20; 8:24, 28; 13:19; 18:5, 6, 8. Both Isaiah 40–66 and John's gospel feature a total of nine (**seven plus two**) references to God or Jesus as "I am."

20. Bauckham, *God Crucified*, 71; and idem, *Jesus and the Eyewitnesses*, 277. See also Vanhoozer, *Drama of Doctrine*.

21. See esp. John 1:14–18 with its repeated allusions to Exodus 33–34, esp. 33:18 and 34:6.

22. Bauckham, *God Crucified*, 75.

23. See the important monograph-length treatment by David D. Kupp, *Matthew's Emmanuel: Divine Presence and God's People in the First Gospel* (SNTSMS 90; Cambridge: Cambridge University Press, 1996).

24. Bauckham, *God Crucified*, 76.

25. See Paul's application of Deut 6:4 to Jesus in 1 Cor 8:4–6, on which see Bauckham, "Biblical Theology and the Problems of Monotheism," 224 (cited in Wright, *Mission of God*, 111–12); and Hurtado, *Lord Jesus Christ*, 123–26.

God affirmed in the Shema could be subsumed under the notion of Father, Son, and Spirit—three in one—being God.[26]

17.2 Implications for John's Gospel

The understanding of the Jewish monotheistic framework for the characterization of Jesus in John's gospel is relevant for a proper reading of the introduction to John's gospel and for understanding the portrayal of Jesus throughout the gospel as the Son of the Father, as one with the Father, and as the "I am." The depiction of the Word in John 1:1 and of its instrumentality in creation in 1:3 makes clear that the Word, rather than being a creature, belongs to God's own unique, uncreated identity and thus has life in itself (1:4; cf. 5:26). John's christological retelling of Genesis has several Second Temple precedents, though it is of course unique in its reference to Jesus as the Word.[27]

According to John, the Word, while distinct from God, is at the same time intrinsic to his own identity—it existed with God "in the beginning" (1:1).[28] In the gospel proper, however, the designation of Jesus as the Word is, naturally, superseded by Jesus' own way of speaking of himself as the Son of the Father. In its portrayal of Jesus as distinct from God and yet intrinsic to his identity, John's gospel does not compromise Jewish monotheism, since, while being "with God," the Word "was God" in its own right, and hence one with God (1:1–2; cf. 10:30; see also 5:26). Jesus was not a second God, that is, a divine entity apart from the one and only God revealed in Scripture as the Creator and Ruler of all things.

Implicit in Jesus' inclusion in the identity of God is his right to receiving worship (5:23; cf. 9:38; 20:28). His inclusion in the divine identity is also indicated by the possible allusion to the Shema of Deut 6:4 in John 10:30 (cf. 1 Cor 8:6).[29] As Bauckham writes, "Without contradicting or rejecting any of the existing features of Jewish monotheism, the Fourth Gospel, therefore, redefines Jewish monotheism as christological monotheism. Christological monotheism is a form of monotheism in which the relationship of Jesus the Son to his Father is integral to the definition of who the one true God is."[30] With this, we are ready to embark on our study of John's characterization of God, the Father, the Son, and the Spirit.[31]

---

26. For a discussion of the background of John's portrayal of Jesus' preexistence, as well as Christ-devotion and exclusivist Jewish monotheism, see Köstenberger and Swain, *Father, Son and Spirit*, 39–44, with reference to Aquila H. I. Lee, *From Messiah to Preexistent Son: Jesus' Self-Consciousness and Early Christian Exegesis of Messianic Psalms* (WUNT 2/192; Tübingen: Mohr-Siebeck, 2005); Hurtado, *Lord Jesus Christ*; Bauckham, *God Crucified*, 29–31; and idem, "Monotheism and Christology," 148–66.

27. Bauckham, "Monotheism and Christology," 150.

28. Note in this regard Bauckham's thesis in *Jesus and the Eyewitnesses* that the four canonical Gospels, including John, constitute eyewitness testimony and his proposal that John, like Mark and Luke, features an *inclusio* of eyewitness testimony, in 1:40 and 21:24. This may be so, but, more importantly, it seems that 1:1, in conjunction with 1:18, indicates that Jesus himself, who was "in the beginning" with God, serves as the ultimate eyewitness (cf. 18:37), whose testimony is foundational for that of "the disciple whom Jesus loved" (compare Jesus' position *eis ton kolpon* per 1:19 with the position of "the disciple whom Jesus loved" *en tō kolpō* of Jesus per 13:23 [reiterated in slightly different terms at 21:20]).

29. The change from masculine to neuter "one" is a necessary adaptation of language (Bauckham, "Monotheism and Christology in the Gospel of John," 163).

30. Ibid., 165.

31. Sections 18–21, below, cover the same material as chaps. 2–5 in Köstenberger and Swain, *Father, Son and Spirit*. While a certain degree of overlap is unavoidable, the material has been reworked as much as possible.

18 GOD

18.1 Introduction

God never appears in John's gospel as a character, and the only words he speaks are (lit.) "and I have glorified it, and will glorify it again" (12:28).[32] Thus God is characterized not directly by what he says or does but by what Jesus, his authorized emissary, says about him.[33] Accordingly, in his introduction the fourth evangelist sets the stage for the ensuing narrative as follows: "No one has ever seen God, but the one and only Son, who is himself God and is in closest relationship with the Father, has made him known" (1:18).[34]

It follows that the gospel is not so much about the evangelist telling *Jesus'* story but about *Jesus* telling the story of *God*, with the evangelist receding into the background so as to allow Jesus to tell his story.[35] According to John's gospel, therefore, God is characterized by Jesus, and once one has understood the gospel's characterization of Jesus, one has understood its characterization of God.[36] Nevertheless, Jesus and God — the Father — are separate and so must be considered individually.[37]

18.2 The Introduction to John's Gospel

The introduction to John's gospel serves to provide the reader with the proper lens through which to interpret the subsequent narrative.[38] Two major issues are addressed: (1) the relationship between God and the Word (Jesus); and (2) the possibility of a close relationship between God and human beings.[39]

---

32. Culpepper, *Anatomy*, 113. But see Stibbe, "Telling the Father's Story," 177, who notes that "it is precisely through this lack of disclosure that John manages to preserve a sense of the Father's [God's] transcendence." Later in his discussion, Stibbe (ibid., 184–86, citing Marianne Meye Thompson, "'God's Voice You Have Never Heard, God's Form You Have Never Seen': The Characterization of God in the Gospel of John," *Semeia* 63 [1993]: 198) relates 12:27–28 to 12:32 and ties Jesus' glorification of the name of the Father in with Gentiles as well as Jews coming to Jesus subsequent to his glorification.

33. Culpepper, *Anatomy*, 113. Similarly, Paul W. Meyer, "'The Father': The Presentation of God in the Fourth Gospel," in *Exploring the Gospel of John* (ed. R. Alan Culpepper and Clifton C. Black; Louisville: Westminster John Knox, 1996), 255: "The only 'presentation of God' in the Fourth Gospel is the self-presentation of Christ in its narratives and discourses." For some literary-critical comments on the characterization of God in John's gospel see Thompson, "Characterization of God," 177–87.

34. Cf. Moloney, *Gospel of John*, 47.

35. See esp. Stibbe, "Telling the Father's Story," 170, who makes the point that John's gospel is not so much a "life" (*bios*) of Jesus as it is a "life of God" (*bios theou*) or, better still, a "life" of God the Father (*bios patros*). See also Birger Olsson, "*Deus Semper Maior*? On God in the Johannine Writings," in *New Readings in John: Literary and Theological Perspectives* (ed. Johannes Nissen and Sigfred Pedersen; JSNTSup 182; Sheffield: Sheffield Academic Press, 1999), 143, who writes, "The Gospel of John is in form a narrative about Jesus, but its contents are in fact a narrative about what God has done and continues to do through Jesus."

36. Meyer, "The Father," 256, also makes the converse point: "everything in the Gospel's presentation of Christ is also a 'presentation of God.'" Meyer is rightly critical of both Bultmann's reductionistic reading of Jesus as revealing nothing but that he is the Revealer, and of Käsemann's famous characterization of the Johannine Jesus as God striding across the earth. Neither does theology collapse into Christology (Bultmann, *Theology of the New Testament*, 2:66), nor does Christology collapse into theology (Käsemann, *Testament of Jesus*, 9 et passim; cf. Meyer, "The Father," 255–56). The Father-Son relationship retains a distinction in persons, and John's "very Christocentricity is theocentric" (p. 256, with reference to the influential essay by C. K. Barrett, "Christocentric or Theocentric? Observations on the Theological Method of the Fourth Gospel," in *Essays on John* [Philadelphia: Westminster, 1982], 1–18).

37. As Thompson, "Characterization of God," 188, puts it, citing Culpepper, "the Gospel does not confuse or conflate Father and Son." Yet Thompson agrees that "it is the words and deeds of Jesus that serve as a characterization of God."

38. Cf. Donald François Tolmie, "The Characterization of God in the Fourth Gospel," *JSNT* 69 (1998): 61: "The primary purpose of the prologue is to serve as a comprehensive introduction that will enable the implied reader to gain a firm hold on the basic ideological perspective presented in the Gospel."

39. Ibid., 62–63.

The introduction includes eight references to *theos*. Of these, six refer to God the Father and two to the Word or Jesus Christ.[40] In 1:1a, the "beginning" of the story, God is set in relation to the Word,[41] who subsisted as an eternal being prior to creation.[42] In 1:1b, the Word, too, is referred to as *theos*.[43] Not only was the Word *with* God, he was himself God.[44]

In 1:2, the Word's eternal subsistence with God "in the beginning" is reiterated.[45] The next verse moves from preexistence to creation, and the Word is presented as God's agent. By implication, God is the Creator, and the Word is his agent in creating "all things." The emphatic way in which this is stated, and the converse denied, underscores the Word as *exclusive* agency.

In 1:6, God is said to be the sender of John (the Baptist).[46] Hence God is shown to take the initiative not only in creation but also in redemptive history.

In the likely pivot of the introduction to John's gospel (1:12),[47] believers are referred to as children of God.[48] In the following verse, they are said to be "born from God." This implies that God is the spiritual Father of believers.[49] John's presentation of God has moved from portraying God as Creator (1:3) to casting him as Savior (1:12) through sending John the Baptist (1:6–8) and "the light" coming into the world (1:9–11).

The final mention of God in 1:18 makes reference to his invisibility (cf. 5:37; 6:46), an attribute that necessitated revelation through the *monogenēs theos*, Jesus Christ (1:17–18; cf. 1:14). The closeness of relationship between Jesus and the Father made possible the full account given by Jesus of God the Father (1:18).[50] This

---

40. See John 1:1, 2, 6, 12, 13, 18; and 1:1, 18, respectively. John's favorite expression for God in his gospel is "Father" of Jesus (cf. 1:14, 18). On "God" and "Father" in the gospel of John, see the monographs by Marianne Meye Thompson, *The Promise of the Father* (Louisville: Westminster John Knox, 2000); idem, *God of the Gospel of John*. On the characterization of God in John's gospel, see also Tolmie, "Characterization of God," 57–75; on God the Father, see Meyer, "The Father," 255–73; and Matthew C. Fisher, "God the Father in the Fourth Gospel: A Biblical Patrology" (Ph.D. dissertation; Wake Forest, NC: Southeastern Baptist Theological Seminary, 2003).

41. As Stibbe, "Telling the Father's Story," 175, rightly notes, it is the Word, rather than God (who "is introduced here as an indeterminate figure"), who is placed in the foreground in 1:1. This pattern continues throughout the remainder of the introduction to John's gospel (see, e.g., 1:6: "sent from God"; 1:12: "children of God").

42. Note the four instances of *ēn*, "was," in 1:1–2.

43. Stibbe, "Telling the Father's Story," 175, aptly observes that the dynamic of the introduction to John's gospel significantly revolves around the progressive characterization of the God/Word relationship in terms of a Father/Son relationship. On the complex grammatical and theological issues involved in the interpretation of John 1:1 see Harris, *Jesus as God*, 57–71, 301–13; Millard J. Erickson, *God in Three Persons: A Contemporary Interpretation of the Trinity* (Grand Rapids: Baker, 1995), 198–201; and Köstenberger, *John*, 25–29.

44. Calling the Word—Jesus—God stretched the boundaries of Jewish monotheism: see the discussion in sec. 17 above. See Richard Bauckham, *God Crucified: Monotheism and Christology in the New Testament* (Grand Rapids: Eerdmans, 1998); idem, *Jesus and the God of Israel: God Crucified and Other Studies on the New Testament's Christology of Divine Identity* (Grand Rapids: Eerdmans, 2008); Hurtado, *One God, One Lord*; idem, *Lord Jesus Christ*. For an exegetical discussion of 1:1, see Köstenberger, *John*, 25–29; see also Daniel B. Wallace, *Greek Grammar beyond the Basics* (Grand Rapids: Zondervan, 1996), 256–70.

45. "In the beginning" appears to serve the dual purpose of anchoring John's creation theology (cf. 20:22) and salvation-historical presentation (cf. 1:6–8, 17) and of rooting the gospel's eyewitness testimony to Jesus in Jesus' own preexistent witness from "the beginning." This insight builds on, yet transcends, the proposal by Bauckham, *Jesus and the Eyewitnesses*.

46. This is implied in the divine passive of *apestalmenos* ("sent") and explicit in the phrase "from God."

47. Köstenberger, *John*, 19–23, 38–39.

48. As Stibbe, "Telling the Fathers' Story," 176, observes, believers are called "children" rather than "sons" or "daughters," perhaps because at this early point in the gospel the evangelist is still trying to establish the uniqueness of the relationship between the Logos and God as Son and Father; for the same reason they are also called "children of God" rather than "children of the Father."

49. So rightly Stibbe, "Telling the Father's Story," 175: "The words 'children' and 'born' set up a picture of God as a parent."

50. Cf. Moloney, *Gospel of John*, 47, who notes that the verb *exēgeisthai* has the basic meaning "to tell at length," "to relate in

reference comes on the heel of allusions to God manifesting his presence at previous junctures in salvation history: in the Tent of Meeting (1:14) and in his giving of the law through Moses (1:17). Yet it was only in and through Jesus Christ that the fullness of God's grace and truth were revealed (1:14, 16–17).

To sum up, God is presented in the introduction to John's gospel as eternal (1:1–2; cf. 1:18), as the Creator (1:3), as the sender of John the Baptist (1:6), as the source of believers' spiritual rebirth (1:12–13), as the Father of Jesus the one and only Son (1:14, 18), and as invisible (1:18). This sets the stage for the gospel, which proceeds to narrate Jesus' telling of the story of God.[51]

18.3 The Book of Signs

Most of the instances of *theos* in John's gospel are found in the Book of Signs (1:19–12:50). While references to God are not found or are rare in certain chapters (John 2; 4; 7; 12), others feature entire clusters of references (chaps. 3; 5; 6; 8; 9; 10).[52]

The remaining references in the rest of chapter 1 are in the genitive, placing God in relation to Jesus as "the Lamb of God" (1:29, 36) and as the "Chosen One" or "Son of God" (1:34, 49), and to the "angels of God" (1:51). John the Baptist uses both christological titles "Lamb of God" (1:29, 36) and "Chosen One of God" (cf. 1:34).[53]

Thus the Son's redemptive mission is firmly grounded in God at the very outset of John's gospel. John's baptizing ministry, in turn, is shown to focus on the revelation of Jesus, "the Lamb of God," to Israel. Later in the chapter, Jesus is confessed by Nathanael as "Son of God" (1:49). The reference to "angels of God" in 1:51 mentions messengers of God other than God's Son.

18.3.1 The Cana Cycle

After a hiatus in chapter 2, references to *theos* resume in Jesus' interchange with Nicodemus. The latter calls Jesus a "teacher come from God," for unless God were with him, he could not perform his "signs" (3:2). Jesus retorts that in order for anyone to enter the kingdom of God, that person must be born again (3:3, 5; cf. 1:12–13).

The remaining references to God in chapter 3 are supplied by the evangelist (3:16–21, 31–36).[54] He first elaborates on Jesus' reference to the lifting up of the

---

full," "to recount a narrative"; and Stibbe, "Telling the Father's Story."

51. See Stibbe, "Telling the Father's Story," 175. Stibbe's entire essay warrants careful reading. One weakness, however, is that Stibbe does not distinguish rigorously enough between the terms *theos* and *patēr* in John's gospel.

52. See 3:2–5, 16–18, 33–36; 5:18; 6:27–29; 8:40–42, 47; 9:29–33; and 10:33–36.

53. On the text-critical issue associated with the reading

"Chosen One of God" in 1:34, see Köstenberger, *John*, 88. See also Charlesworth, "Shared Symbolism," 113, who notes the reference to the "Elect of God" (בחיר אלהא; *bḥir ʾlhʾ*) in the *Elect of God Text* (4Q534 = 4QMess) at Qumran.

54. See Köstenberger, *John*, 113–14, 133, 138. The presence of *monogenēs* only in the introduction to John's gospel and the present section constitutes strong evidence that 3:16–21 are by the evangelist. See Carson, *Gospel according to John*, 203.

Son of Man (3:13–14; called Son of God in 3:18) by grounding this event in God's love for the world (3:16–17). The unit closes with a reference to works "done in the sight of God" (3:21).

Second, in 3:31–36, "the one who comes from above" (Jesus; cf. 3:13) is contrasted with "the one who is from the earth" (John the Baptist). The latter testifies to what he has seen and heard (though his witness is largely rejected); the former utters the words of God (3:32, 34; cf. 12:47–48; 14:10). God most likely also is the implied Giver of the Spirit (3:34),[55] and his wrath is said to rest, and to continue to rest, on those who refuse to believe in his Son (3:36).

The ensuing interchange between Jesus and the Samaritan woman contains two additional references to God. In 4:10, Jesus refers somewhat obliquely to "the gift of God," that is, "living water" (later identified as the Spirit; 7:37–39). In 4:24, Jesus maintains that because God is spirit, those who would worship him must do so in spirit and truth (cf. 1:1–2, 18).[56]

18.3.2 The Festival Cycle

The controversy surrounding the characterization of God as Jesus' Father erupts in full force in 5:17–47.[57] Thus in 5:18, the Jewish leaders take strong exception to Jesus' claim that God is his Father. By making himself equal to God, they charge, Jesus is committing blasphemy. In the ensuing interchange Jesus elaborates on the nature of his relationship with God the Father in considerable detail (5:19–30), in the process calling himself "the Son of God" (5:25; cf. 1:49).

Later, Jesus, for his part, charges that his opponents reject him because they do not have love for God in their hearts and do not seek the glory that comes from "the only God" (5:42, 44). Intriguingly, at the very occasion where Jesus is charged with violating Jewish monotheism by claiming to be the Son of God, he affirms such by speaking of "the only God."

Continuing his interchange with the Jewish leaders in the aftermath of his feeding of the multitudes, Jesus asserts that God—the Father—has put his seal on him, the Son of Man (6:27). When they ask what are "the works God requires," they are urged to perform the one and only "work of God" necessary for salvation—to believe in the one God has sent (6:28–29).

Jesus proceeds to call himself "the bread of God" who has come down from heaven and gives life to the world (6:35). He thus claims to be the end-time fulfillment of God's provision through Moses during the exodus (see 6:31). In the same context, he also claims to be the end-time fulfillment of Isaiah's prophecy that all will be taught by God (6:45, citing Isa 54:13; see John 7:17).

---

55. So Tolmie, "Characterization of God," 65, who notes the effect of the ambiguity in this verse on the reader.

56. Similarly, in OT times the Israelites were not to make idols "in the form of anything" as did the surrounding nations (Exod 20:4). The phrase "God is spirit" does not refer to the Holy Spirit (contra, TNIV), much less to the human spirit, but identifies God as a spiritual rather than material being. The reference is qualitative, "stressing the nature or essence of God" (so Wallace, *Greek Grammar beyond the Basics*, 270); see the similar phrase in 3:6. On the broader theological issues see Davies, *Gospel and the Land*, 288–335, esp. 298–302.

57. Tolmie, "Characterization of God," 65.

Following the mass defection of Jesus by many of his followers, Peter, speaking for the Twelve, confesses Jesus as "the Holy One of God" (John 6:69; cf. 1:34).[58] Through the device of "internal focalization," Peter becomes the lens through which the portrayal of Jesus as "the Holy One of God" in John's gospel is refracted for its readers.[59]

The only reference to *theos* in John 7 designates God as the source of Jesus' teaching. In 7:17, anyone who is prepared to do God's will is promised that he will know whether Jesus' teaching is of human or divine origin.

God features prominently in the paternity dispute between Jesus and the Jewish leaders (8:40–54; cf. 5:18–47; 6:31–58). In 8:40, Jesus points to God as the source from which he heard the truth. In response to Jesus' insinuation that their father may be someone other than God, the Jews insist that their only father is God (8:41). Jesus retorts that if God truly were their Father, they would love him, because he had come from God (8:42; cf. 3:2; 5:42). Jesus' logic is compelling: "Anyone who is from God listens to God's words. This is why *you* don't listen—because you're not from God!" (cf. 8:47).[60] Finally, 8:54 harks back to the Jews' earlier claim that God is their Father (cf. 8:41). To the contrary, Jesus insists that they do not in fact know God, though he himself does.[61]

In John 9, the existence and character of God as revealed in the Hebrew Scriptures are everywhere assumed. The question is, "Who is Jesus in relation to this God?" In 9:3, Jesus affirms that not human sin, but "the works of God" are the ultimate purpose of the blind man's condition. In 9:16, the Pharisees contend that Jesus is not from God because he does not keep the Sabbath. "Give glory to God" (9:24) is a customary exhortation to truthfulness.[62] In 9:29, the Pharisees affirm that God spoke to Moses but question that he spoke to Jesus—because the latter is clearly a "sinner" since he does not keep the Sabbath commandment. The healed man, on the other hand, contends that God does not listen to sinners but only to those who fear him and do his will (9:31). Thus if Jesus were not from God, he could do nothing (9:33).

In John 10:33, in an *inclusio* with 5:18, Jesus' opponents renew their charge that Jesus, whom they consider to be a mere man, makes himself out to be God (cf. 10:30). In self-defense, citing Ps 82:6, Jesus contends that if Scripture can call the recipients of God's word "gods," he can legitimately claim to be the "Son of God" (cf. 10:34–36).[63]

---

58. This is part of Peter's characterization throughout John's gospel: see 13:6–10; 20:2–10; 21:7, 15–19 (cf. Matt 14:28–33; Luke 5:8; 22:33). Note in this regard Bauckham's (*Jesus and the Eyewitnesses*, 165–72, 180) well-taken challenge and proposed corrective to the common notion that Peter typically serves as a spokesman for the Twelve throughout the Gospels. See also Bauckham's characterization of Peter in ibid., 177.

59. The term is Bauckham's, who defines "internal focalization" as a literary device that "enables readers to view the scene from the vantage point ... of a character within the story" (ibid., 162–63).

60. My translation. Cf. 1:12–13.

61. Note in this regard the way in which 1 John picks up on the language and themes in John 8 (see esp. 1 John 3:7–15), on which see Streett, "They Went Out from Us."

62. See Josh 7:19; 2 Chr 30:8; Jer 13:16.

63. As he does in John 5:25, another *inclusio*. See also 11:4 below. See Köstenberger, "John," in *Commentary on the NT Use of the OT*, 464–67. For the charge of blasphemy against Jesus see Larry W. Hurtado, "Pre-70 C.E. Jewish Opposition to Christ-Devotion," *JTS* 50 (1999): 35–58, esp. 36–37.

18.3.3 Transition from the Book of Signs to the Book of Exaltation

In 11:4, Jesus responds to the news of Lazarus's illness by claiming its purpose is the glory of God and of the Son of God (11:4; cf. 9:3). In 11:22, Martha affirms her belief that God will give Jesus whatever he asks of him (cf. 9:31) and subsequently calls Jesus "the Messiah, the Son of God" (11:27; cf. 20:30–31).[64] Immediately prior to raising Lazarus, Jesus again identifies the glory of God as the purpose of his work (11:40).

Later in the same chapter the evangelist makes reference to the gathering of God's children even beyond Israel as the purpose of Jesus' impending death (11:52; cf. 1:12–13; 8:34–47). The final reference to God in the Book of Signs indicts secret believers in Jesus among the Jewish leaders as seeking human rather than God's glory (12:43; cf. 5:44), in obvious contrast to Jesus (cf. 9:3; 11:4, 40).

18.4 The Book of Exaltation

18.4.1 The Farewell Discourse

References to God in the Book of Exaltation are considerably less frequent than in the Book of Signs.[65] At the outset, the evangelist makes programmatic reference to Jesus' knowledge that he had come from God and was returning to God (13:3). Immediately after Judas leaves the Upper Room, Jesus exclaims that now the Son of Man is glorified and God is glorified in him, an obvious reference to the impending crucifixion (13:31–32). These verses continue the string of references in the Book of Signs to God's glory as the purpose of Jesus' mission (e.g., 9:3; 11:4, 40).

At the onset of the dark hour of his arrest and passion, Jesus' encouragement to his followers is that they believe in both God and himself (14:1). Except for the incidental reference that those who kill the disciples will believe they are offering a service to God (16:2), virtually the entire Farewell Discourse is lacking any explicit reference to God (14:2–16:26). Only in 16:27 and 30 does one find references to the disciples having believed that Jesus came from God.[66]

In his final prayer, Jesus refers once again to God as the "only true God" (17:3; cf. 5:44), as previously in conjunction with himself ("and Jesus Christ, whom you have sent"; cf. 13:31–32; 14:1).

18.4.2 The Passion Narrative

After this, the pattern of fairly sparse references to God in the second half of John's gospel continues; there is no explicit reference to God in 17:4–20:16 except for

---

64. Martha's witness to Jesus in 11:27 in terms virtually identical to the purpose statement makes her christological confession at least the virtual equivalent to Peter's confession of Jesus as "the Holy One of God" in 6:68–69 and beyond this renders hers the anticipatory confession of Jesus as the Christ and Son of God in John's gospel. Like her sister, Mary, who anticipates Jesus' burial by anointing him (12:3; cf. 12:7), Martha captures (albeit not fully) the essence of Jesus' identity. See also Fig. 29.2 below.

65. There are a total of sixteen references in John 13–21, compared with sixty-seven in John 1–12, a ratio of about 1:4.

66. A possible *inclusio* with 13:3.

the Jewish leaders' charge before Pilate that Jesus deserved to die because he made himself the Son of God (19:7; cf. 5:18; 10:33).

The final references to God in John's gospel are Jesus' reference to his return to "my God and your God" after his resurrection (20:17), the confession of Jesus as "my Lord and my God" by Thomas (20:28; cf. 1:1, 18),[67] the identification of Jesus as the Messiah and Son of God in the purpose statement (20:31), and the prediction of Peter's God-glorifying martyrdom (21:19).

18.5 First, Second, and Third John

There are sixty-two references to *theos* in 1 John, a large number; 2 and 3 John features two and three references to *theos*, respectively. In 1 John, references to God gradually increase in number, with one reference in chapter 1; three in chapter 2; ten in chapter 3; twenty-nine in chapter 4; and nineteen in chapter 5. In 1 John 1:5, John writes that "God is light; in him there is no darkness at all." Those who claim to have fellowship with him while living in darkness do not live out the truth (1:6). In 2:5, God is said to be the object of complete love by the one who obeys his word. In 2:14, John writes that the young people are strong, and God's word lives in them, and they have overcome the evil one; in 2:17 he adds that whoever does the will of God lives forever.

First John 3 opens with a reflection on the privileges of being God's children (vv. 1, 2). First John 3:8–10 states the purpose of the Son of God's coming as the destruction of the devil's work (v. 8); the author asserts that those who are born of God will not continue to sin because God's seed (the Holy Spirit?) remains in them (v. 9; cf. 5:18), and he lists as the distinguishing marks between God's and the devil's children that the latter neither do what is right nor love their brothers and sisters (v. 10). Later in the chapter, John asks how the love of God can be in someone who sees a brother or sister in need and has the means to help them but does not do so (v. 17). Because God is greater than our hearts, we can have confidence before him, because we keep his commands and do what pleases him (vv. 20–21; cf. 5:14).

References to God are found in fifteen of twenty-one verses in 1 John 4. Believers are enjoined to test the spirits to see whether they are from God; they can recognize the Spirit of God by the confession that Jesus Christ [or Jesus is the Messiah who] has come in the flesh (4:1–3). John assures his readers that they are from God, and that those who are from God listen to them (vv. 4–6). Love is held up as incontrovertible proof that a person comes from God, has been born of God, and knows God (vv. 6–8).

God has proved his love for believers in that he "sent his one and only Son into the world that we might live through him" (1 John 4:9; cf. John 3:16). Love is not believers loving God but God loving believers and sending his Son as an atoning sacrifice for their sins (1 John 4:10). Yet since God so loved them, they also ought to

---

67. Harris, *Jesus as God*, 128, identifies John 1:1, 18 and 20:28 as literary *inclusios*, commenting, "The Prologue ends (1:18) as it begins (1:1), and the Gospel ends (20:28) as it begins (1:1), with an assertion of the deity of Jesus."

love one another (v. 11). No one has ever seen God (v. 12; cf. John 1:18), but if believers love one another, God lives in them. In fact, God lives in those who acknowledge that Jesus is the Son of God (1 John 4:15; cf. 5:5; John 20:31). John's message in this section is best summed up in the statement that "God is love. Whoever lives in love lives in God, and God in them" (1 John 4:16b). Anyone who claims to love God but hates a brother or sister is a liar; those who love God must also love one another (vv. 20–21).

First John 5 features references to God in thirteen out of its twenty verses. Everyone who believes that Jesus is the Messiah is born of God (v. 1); God's children are known by loving God and obeying his commands (vv. 2–3). Everyone born of God overcomes the world through his or her faith in Jesus as the Son of God (vv. 4–5). Through his Spirit, God has given testimony concerning his Son, testimony even greater than water and blood (vv. 9–10): "And this is the testimony: God has given us eternal life, and this life is in his Son" (v. 11). This also is John's purpose for writing: to assure his readers that by believing in the name of the Son of God they have eternal life (v. 13).

In closing, John reiterates believers' status as God's children and that anyone born of God will not continue to sin. He assures believers that they are in him who is true (God) by being in his Son Jesus Christ, who "is the true God and eternal life" (1 John 5:20). If, as is likely, "true God and eternal life" in 5:20 indeed have Jesus as their referent, John ends his first letter with a major exclamation point. Having referred to Jesus throughout his letter as the "Son" or as the "Son of God," with every single instance of *theos* having God the Father as its referent, in his final reference involving *theos*, John transfers this epithet from Father to Son. *Jesus* is the true God; anyone who fails to confess him as such is guilty of idol worship (5:21).

In 2 John, John wishes his readers "grace, mercy and peace from God the Father and from Jesus Christ, the Father's Son" (v. 3) and maintains that anyone who "does not continue in the teaching of Christ does not have God" (v. 9).

In 3 John, Gaius is enjoined to send off believers in a manner worthy of God (v. 6) and is reminded that anyone who does what is good is from God (v. 11).

18.6 Summary

Jesus is responsible for almost half of the instances of *theos* in John's gospel.[68] The fourth evangelist provides a quarter of the references;[69] and another nine come from the Jewish leaders.[70] The remaining fourteen references are supplied by the Baptist (1:29, 34, 36), Nicodemus (3:2), and various of Jesus' disciples.[71] Many of these references focus on the question of Jesus' identity in relation to God. The Jewish

---

68. The specific number is 39 out of 83 times: John 1:51; 3:3, 5; 4:10, 24; 5:25, 42, 44; 6:27, 29, 33, 45 [OT], 46; 7:17; 8:40, 42 (2x), 47 (3x), 54; 9:3; 10:34 [OT], 35 (2x), 36; 11:4 (2x), 40; 12:43; 13:31, 32 (2x); 14:1; 16:2, 27; 17:3; 20:17 (2x).

69. There are twenty-one instances: John 1:1 (2x), 2, 6, 12, 13, 18 (2x); 3:16, 17, 18, 21, 23, 34 (2x); 36; 11:52; 13:3 (2x); 20:31; 21:19.

70. Nine references: John 5:18 (2x); 6:28; 8:41; 9:16, 24, 29; 10:33; 19:7.

71. This includes Nathanael (John 1:49); Peter (6:69); the formerly blind man (9:31, 33); Martha (11:22 [2x], 27); the disciples as a group (16:30); and Thomas (20:28).

leaders consistently dispute Jesus' divine provenance[72] while Jesus affirms it,[73] as do his followers.[74] Jesus, for his part, disputes the Jews' claim of knowing God[75] while asserting the same for himself (7:29; 10:15).

Jesus is the overt referent of *theos* in John 1:1, 18, and 20:28. He is also repeatedly called "Son of God."[76] In addition, Jesus is called "the Lamb of God" (1:29, 36), the "Chosen [or] Holy One of God" (cf. 1:34 variant; 6:69), and the "bread of God" (6:33).

By way of survey, God is characterized in John's gospel and letters as follows. He is eternal (John 1:1, 2), the source of the new birth (1:13; 1 John 2:29; 3:9; 4:7; 5:1, 4, 18), a being who is invisible and spiritual (John 1:18; 4:24), and the source of Jesus' coming (3:2; 6:46; 8:42, 47; 9:33; 13:3; 16:27, 30; 1 John 4:10, 14). He loves the world (John 3:16; 1 John 4:14; cf. 1 John 2:2), is the only true God (John 3:33; 5:44; 17:3; 1 John 5:20), sends the Son (John 3:17, 34; etc.; 1 John 4:10, 14), and approves of Jesus (John 6:27; 1 John 5:9–11). He is the Father (John 6:27; etc.) and the source of Jesus' teaching and of truth (7:17; 8:40). He is the Jews' alleged (but not real) father (8:41, 42, 47, 54), the one who spoke to Moses (9:29), the one who hears righteous prayer (9:31; 11:22), the destination of Jesus after his resurrection (13:3), and the God of Jesus and his followers (20:17).[77]

On the whole, as mentioned, God as a character remains in the background.[78] In semantic, though not ontological contrast, the Father is characterized in more active terms than when the reference is generically to God.[79] While John maintains God's transcendence, he portrays him at the same time as a loving Father who gives and draws people to Jesus.[80] There are also several references to God's nature or essential attributes: God is eternal (John 1:1–2) and invisible and spiritual (1:18; 4:24), and he is the only true God (3:33; 5:44; 17:3; 1 John 5:20).[81] These attributes accentuate God's uniqueness and otherness.[82]

In the controversy surrounding Jesus, which pervades the entire gospel, God is the one whose support is invoked by both sides in the escalating debate.[83] The identity of Jesus is directly tied to the question of his relationship to God. While Jesus

---

72. John 5:18; 9:16; 10:33; 19:7.
73. John 5:25; 6:27, 33, 46; 7:17; 8:42, 47; 10:34–36; 11:4, 27; 13:31–32; 14:1; 16:27; 17:3; 20:17.
74. John 1:20, 34, 36, 49; 6:69; 9:31, 33; 11:22, 27; 20:28.
75. John 7:28; 8:19, 54–55; cf. 15:21; 16:3; 17:25.
76. John 1:49; 3:18; 5:25; 10:36; 11:4, 27; 20:31; and possibly 1:34; his claim is disputed in 19:7.
77. Beyond this *theos* occurs in the following genitival constructions: children of God (John 1:12; 11:52; 1 John 3:1, 2, 10; 5:2, 19); angels of God (John 1:51); kingdom of God (3:3, 5); work(s) of God, or in God (3:21; 6:28, 29; 9:3); words of God (3:34; 8:47), or Word of God (10:35); wrath of God (3:36); and gift of God (4:10). God is also presented as the object of glory (9:24; 11:4, 40; 12:43; 13:31–32; 21:19; or as the one who glorifies, 13:32), love (5:42), faith (14:1), and worship (16:2). The Baptist is sent by God (1:6), and his people are taught by God (6:45). A similar list is found in Culpepper, *Anatomy*, 113–14.
78. Cf. Culpepper (ibid., 113): "God is the reality beyond the transcendent presence." References to God's actions are limited to his loving the world (3:16) and sending (3:17) and approving of his Son (6:27); to his hearing righteous prayer (9:31; 11:22); and to his glorifying the Son (13:32).
79. See the list in ibid.
80. So rightly ibid.
81. Culpepper (ibid.) also includes "God is light" (John 3:21), but this does not reflect a direct statement but an inference. In 1 John, the author writes that God is both light (1 John 1:5) and love (4:8, 16) and that "he is the true God and eternal life" (5:20).
82. Culpepper, *Anatomy*, 114.
83. As Nils A. Dahl, "The Neglected Factor in New Testament Theology," in *Jesus Is the Christ: The Historical Origins of Christological Doctrine* (ed. Donald H. Juel; Minneapolis: Fortress, 1991), 58–60, has noted, the NT writers regularly presuppose or make only indirect reference to contemporary beliefs about God. See Meyer, "The Father," 257 (also citing Jouette M. Bassler, "God in the NT," *ABD*, 2:1049).

consistently claims to be the Messiah and Son of God, his opponents vehemently deny this claim, considering it blasphemous. Most striking in the gospel are opening and closing references to Jesus as God that serve as bookends for the entire narrative (John 1:1, 18; 20:28). In these passages, the expression *theos*, which everywhere else in the gospel has the God of the Hebrew Scriptures as its referent, is redirected toward Jesus, in a striking expansion of rigid notions of Jewish monotheism including Jesus in the identity of Yahweh.[84]

In the opening verse of the gospel, both God and the Word are called *theos*, a striking affirmation calling for explication of the exact nature of this relationship of two divine persons to each other, an explication that it takes for the remainder of the gospel to provide (cf. 1:18). The movement of the Johannine plot is thus from Jesus the Word (1:1) to Jesus the Messiah and Son of God (20:31), from the Word being made flesh (1:14) to the Son of Man being lifted up and thus glorified (3:14; 8:28; 12:32; cf. 19:30). As the Creator and as the one who in his love for the world sent his one and only Son, God's presence looms large throughout the entirety of John's narrative, not least in his role as the Father and sender of his Son, which constitutes the subject of the next two sections below.

Matters are somewhat different in John's first letter. While John's gospel, as mentioned, is Christocentric in nature,[85] 1 John includes an overwhelming number of references to God. God is clearly in the center of the entire discourse, especially in 1 John 3–5, while Jesus' identity appears to be somewhat under siege and is defended with reference to God's testimony regarding him as the Son of God. Perhaps because of the recent departure of the secessionists (2:19), great emphasis is placed on God as being the source of love for believers, who are called in turn to love one another. This is the same love that led God to send his Son as an atoning sacrifice for believers' sins (4:10). The closing reference to Jesus as "the true God and eternal life" in 5:20, if Jesus is in fact the referent, would be striking indeed.

19 THE FATHER

19.1 Introduction

The notion of God as Father is rather infrequent in the OT.[86] Where the term does occur, it is applied to God as Father of Israel as a nation rather than of individual Jews.[87] The situation is very different in John's gospel, where references to God as *patēr* are pervasive.[88] While pervasive, however, they are not evenly spread. In many

---

84. See sec. 17 above.

85. See chap. 7, sec. 15.

86. Morris, *Jesus Is the Christ*, 129. As Stibbe, "Telling the Father's Story," 171, observes, until not too long ago, it would have been possible to speak of "the forgotten Father" in Johannine research. As Tord Larsson, *God in the Fourth Gospel: A Hermeneutical Study of the History of Interpretation* (Stockholm: Almquist & Wiksell International, 2001), 14, notes, "Despite the fact that some have realized that a main theme of the FG is theology and not only Christology, we must conclude that there is no satisfactory treatment of God in the FG in twentieth-century NT scholarship." Recently, Marianne Meye Thompson, Paul Meyer, Francis Tolmie, and Mark Stibbe, among others, in the works cited above, have sought to fill this lacuna and provided perceptive explorations of the Father in John's gospel.

87. See the discussion in Fisher, "God the Father," 55–96.

88. There are 136 instances of *patēr*, of which 120 have God as a referent. Morris, *Jesus Is the Christ*, 130, finds 122 references to God as Father in John's gospel (he also notes that the only other

chapters, the expression is not or is rarely found (chaps. 1–3; 7; 9; 11; 13; 18–19; 21).⁸⁹ Major clusters occur in the Festival Cycle (John 5; 6; 8; 10) and the Farewell Discourse (John 14–16). Virtually all references are in discourse rather than narrative portions,⁹⁰ which suggests that "Father" language in John's gospel harks back to the terminology of Jesus himself.⁹¹ The emphasis on the Father as the one who sent Jesus and who testifies to him casts him as the one who authorizes and authenticates Jesus' messianic mission.⁹²

19.2 The Introduction to John's Gospel

The introduction to John's gospel contains two strategic references to God as Father by the evangelist. In John 1:14, Jesus is called the *monogenēs* from the Father.⁹³ Analogous to the human phenomenon of a father cherishing his only son, this description conveys a special relationship of love and trust. Jesus, the Father's "one and only Son," is said to be, literally, in the Father's "lap" (1:18; cf. Prov 8:30; Luke 16:22), a relationship that enabled him to tell the Father's story.⁹⁴ The Word that was with God "in the beginning" thus renders the primary witness (John 18:37), which, in turn, results in witness being borne by those who have been with Jesus "from the beginning" (15:27), especially "the disciple whom Jesus loved" (21:20–25; cf. 13:23; 19:35).

NT writer who comes even close to the pervasiveness of this motif is Matthew, with 45 references to God as the heavenly Father). Culpepper, *Anatomy*, 113, following Merrill C. Tenney, "Topics from the Gospel of John. Part I: The Person of the Father," *BSac* 132 (1975): 38, puts the number at 118 for John, as does Meyer, "The Father," 269, n. 27. Gottlob Schrenk, "πατήρ," *TDNT*, 5:996, counts 115 instances, and Thompson, "Characterization of God," 196, n. 17, puts the number at 131. Occasionally, *patēr* refers to Jacob (4:12) or Abraham (8:39, 53, 56), the father of the servant healed by Jesus (4:53), or (in the plural) to the Jewish ancestors (e.g., 4:20; 6:31, 49, 58; 7:22). In 8:44, the repeated referent of *patēr* is the Devil.

89. The absence of the term "Father" in John 7 is noted, among others, by John Ashton, *Understanding the Fourth Gospel* (Oxford: Clarendon, 1991), 318, cited in Meyer, "The Father," 262, who does, however, draw the hardly defensible conclusion that "nowhere in this chapter is there the slightest hint that Jesus regarded himself as the Son of God."

90. This is noted by Meyer, "The Father," 264; Thompson, "Characterization of God," 196, who provides a careful and sensitive study of the characterization of God (including that of "Father") in John's gospel, using Robert Alter's scale of characterization moving from his actions to his appearance, his direct speech, his inward speech, and finally statements by the narrator (pp. 187–204); and Stibbe, "Telling the Father's Story," 175: "we learn most about the Father not from narrated material but rather from discourse or spoken material."

91. The historicity of Jesus' calling God "Father" seems secure (but see the important remarks by Cornelius Plantinga, "The Fourth Gospel as Trinitarian Source Then and Now," in *Biblical Hermeneutics in Historical Perspective* [ed. Mark S. Burrows and Paul Rorem; Grand Rapids: Eerdmans, 1991], 307); space does not permit a defense of Jesus' use of this term. See the references in Meyer, "The Father," 267, n. 17, and his listing of Synoptic instances of Jesus' use of "Father" on p. 267, n. 20. Meyer notes that, on the assumption of Markan priority, the earliest canonical gospel contains the fewest references to God as Father while the last (John) features the most (though Meyer's fairly extensive list of Synoptic references to God as Father hardly justifies his judgment that such references are "surprisingly scarce in the pre-Johannine gospel tradition," p. 258). Nor does Meyer's verdict appear on target that the "Father" language in John's gospel "has its roots in post-Easter theological development and is part of the community's confessional language." To say that an "appeal to Jesus' own religious usage at this point only stands in the way of examining carefully how this language functions in the evangelist's text" seems to considerably overstate one's point.

92. Cf. Meyer, "The Father," 265, who calls the Father "the Vindicator and Authorizer of Jesus."

93. Cf. Stibbe, "Telling the Father's Story," 176, who notes that the narrator starts at the "beginning" of the story, i.e., the Word's eternal preexistence prior to creation (1:1), and then moves to the "middle" of the story, the Word's incarnation in then-recent history. As Stibbe observes, remarkably, the "end" of the story is left open (ibid.), though Meyer's remark that "what is distinctively Johannine about this presentation of God as Father is that ... eschatology has been replaced by protology" ("The Father," 265, cited in Stibbe, "Telling the Father's Story," 176) and speaking of "replacement" takes matters too far.

94. See Köstenberger, *John*, 49–50.

19.3 The Book of Signs
19.3.1 *The Cana Cycle*

The next reference to the Father comes from Jesus himself, who when clearing the temple calls it his "Father's house" (John 2:16).[95] The temple clearing represents a prophetic sign of Jesus' messianic authority to cleanse Israel from corrupt worship and to restore the true worship of God.[96] As Jesus' pronouncements make clear, this would involve his crucifixion, followed in three days' time by resurrection.

In another unit supplied by the evangelist,[97] mention is made of the Father's love for the Son (3:35). The Father has entrusted all things to the Son. This passage, together with 1:14 and 18, suggests that "Father and Son" is the evangelist's preferred way of conveying the nature of Jesus' relationship with God.

In his interchange with the Samaritan woman, Jesus repeatedly refers to God as his Father when addressing the question of the proper worship of God (4:21–23).[98] While *patēr* is used in parallelism with *theos* (cf. 4:24), *patēr* is more personal, conveying the notion of an intimate personal family relationship between God and Jesus (cf. 1:18). Thus Jesus is able to reveal God as he truly is. In the present instance, Jesus explains to the Samaritan woman that God is spirit, so that people must worship him in spirit and truth. The Father is said to actively "seek" such kinds of worshipers, and Jesus is shown on a mission "recruiting" these individuals, not merely among Jews, but also among Samaritans.

It is noteworthy that both of Jesus' references to the Father in the Cana Cycle involve the question of worship (2:16; 4:21–23). At the temple in Jerusalem, Jesus decries the corruption of Jewish worship and acts to restore proper worship. At the foot of Mount Gerizim in Samaria, Jesus instructs the Samaritan woman that true, spiritual worship is rendered to God regardless of physical location. As the evangelist makes clear in a narrative aside, Jesus himself, in a major paradigm shift, becomes the new sanctuary that is to be the proper sphere of worship (2:20).[99]

19.3.2 *The Festival Cycle*

A considerable number of references to God as Father are clustered in 5:17–47, the aftermath of the so-called "Sabbath controversy" between Jesus and the Jewish leaders. Jesus' pronouncement that his Father is at work until now and that Jesus, too, is working draws fierce opposition from the Jewish leaders because of Jesus' implicit claim of equality with God (5:17–18). Jesus' address for God as "my Father" in 5:17

---

95. The fact that the same expression is found on Jesus' lips in Luke 2:49 is a strong indication of authenticity. As Stibbe ("Telling the Father's Story," 179), proposes, citing warnings against abstracting "from the Gospel some detached doctrine of God" (Meyer, "The Father," 256; cf. Gail R. O'Day, "'Show Us the Father, and We Will Be Satisfied' (John 14:8)," *Semeia* 85 [1999]: 11, 16), "we will therefore look at the references to God as Father as they appear in the landscape of the unfolding story."

96. See the section on signs in chap. 7, sec. 15 above.

97. So, e.g., Mark W. G. Stibbe, *John* (Sheffield: Sheffield Academic Press, 1993), 61. Surprisingly, in his narrative study of the Father in John's gospel ("Telling the Father's Story," 179–84), Stibbe does not discuss 3:35.

98. See the discussion of John 4:24, above.

99. On the temple motif in John's gospel, see esp. Kerr, *Temple of Jesus' Body*; Coloe, *God Dwells with Us*; Walker, *Jesus and the Holy City*; and Köstenberger, "Destruction of the Temple." See already Davies, *Gospel and the Land*, 289–302.

and elsewhere has few OT precedents (though see Jer 3:4, 19; cf. Ps 89:26). The Jews were committed monotheists, believing in only one God (see Num 15:37–41; Deut 6:4; 11:13–21).[100]

Indeed, the Hebrew Scriptures make clear that God is incomparable and without equal (e.g., Isa 40:18, 25) and that those who "make themselves" like God, such as Pharaoh (Ezek 29:3), Joash (2 Chr 24:24), Hiram (Ezek 28:2), or Nebuchadnezzar (Isa 14:14; Daniel 4), are subject to severe judgment. The Jewish belief in only one God became an important distinguishing characteristic of Jewish religion in a polytheistic environment (Tacitus, *Hist.* 5.5).[101] Jesus' claim of a unique relationship with God seemed to compromise this belief by elevating Jesus to the same level as the Creator as a second God (5:18; 8:58–59; 10:30–31; 19:7).

In what follows, Jesus elaborates on the Father-Son relationship. Just as sons, including Jesus, customarily followed in their fathers' footsteps by learning their trade, Jesus claims to take his cue from his Father (5:20; cf. 1:18).[102] Not only does the Father love the Son, he has shown him everything he does (cf. 15:15), including the ability to give life (5:21; cf. 5:26). He also delegated all judgment to the Son (5:22; cf. 5:27). Thus whoever fails to honor the Son dishonors the Father who sent him (5:23).

Later on, Jesus cites his works as evidence that the Father sent him (5:36; cf. 5:19–20). What is more, the Father himself bears witness to Jesus (5:37; cf. 12:28). Yet while Jesus has come in his Father's name, people reject him (5:41). Nevertheless, it is not Jesus who will accuse them before the Father, but Moses, for he wrote about Jesus (5:45–46).

Another cluster of references to God as Father is set in the wake of Jesus' feeding of the multitudes, where Jesus repeatedly refers to his close relationship with the Father (6:27–65). The Son's mission is totally dependent on the Father, who "gives" or "draws" people to Jesus (6:37, 44–45, 65),[103] so that all who believe in him have eternal life (6:40). Jesus alone has seen the Father (cf. 1:18), and "the living Father" sent him (6:57).

In the aftermath to Jesus' appearance at the Festival of Tabernacles in Jerusalem, he once again affirms his close association with the Father who sent him and who testifies concerning him (8:16, 18; cf. 5:37). When Jesus is challenged by some who ask, in effect, "Where is your father?" he retorts that his interrogators do not know the Father or they would acknowledge him (8:19; cf. 6:42). Thus Jesus asserts that the Father is known through him and him alone (cf. 10:7–9; 14:6).

The following instance of Johannine misunderstanding anticipates the ensuing paternity dispute (8:27; cf. 6:42; 8:19).[104] While the Father is the source of Jesus'

---

100. Emil Schürer, *The History of the Jewish People in the Age of Jesus Christ (175 B.C.–A.D. 135* [rev. and ed. Geza Vermes, Fergus Millar, and Matthew Black; Edinburgh: T&T Clark, 1979]), 2:454–55; Hurtado, *One God, One Lord*.

101. See S. S. Cohon, "The Unity of God: A Study in Hellenistic and Rabbinic Theology," *HUCA* 26 (1955): 425–79.

102. Jesus' statement in 5:20 echoes that of the evangelist in 3:35, except that *agapaō* is replaced by *phileō*.

103. On divine election in John's gospel see, e.g., Robert W. Yarbrough, "Divine Election in the Gospel of John," in *The Grace of God, the Bondage of the Will* (ed. Thomas R. Schreiner and Bruce A. Ware; Grand Rapids: Baker, 1995), 1:47–62. More broadly, see D. A. Carson, *Divine Sovereignty and Human Responsibility: Biblical Perspectives in Tension* (Atlanta: John Knox, 1981).

104. See Stibbe, *John*, 97, cited by Tolmie, "Characterization of God," 66.

teaching, his opponents' real father is the devil. To be sure, ethnically speaking, Abraham is their father (8:39). Yet spiritually speaking, their hatred of Jesus proves that their true spiritual father is in fact the devil (8:44). When charged with demon-possession by his opponents, Jesus maintains that he knows his Father and his opponents dishonor him (8:49).[105] Not that he seeks glory for himself; the Father — the very one whom the Jews claim as their God — is glorifying him (8:54). The pericope ends on a note of increased hostility and conflict.[106]

After a hiatus in John 9, another cluster of references to God as Father is found in the aftermath of Jesus' Good Shepherd Discourse, where the trusting and caring relationship between a shepherd and his sheep serves to illustrate Jesus' relationship with the Father (10:15–38). Just as Jesus and the Father know each other, Jesus knows his own and they know him (10:15).[107] The Father loves Jesus, because he is prepared to sacrifice his life for those who need salvation (10:17–18). Once again, Jesus points to the witness of his works performed in his Father's name (10:25; an *inclusio* with 5:36). In keeping with previous assertions, Jesus affirms that no one can snatch those the Father has given him out of his hand, for the Father is greater than all (10:29; cf. esp. 6:37, 44).

Jesus proceeds to affirm his unity of purpose and mission with the Father: "I and the Father are one" (10:30; cf. 5:17–18).[108] The statement echoes the basic confession of Judaism, "Hear, O Israel: The LORD our God, the LORD is one" (Deut 6:4).[109] For Jesus to be one with the Father yet distinct from him amounts to a claim to deity (cf. John 1:1–2).[110] While the present emphasis is on the unity of their works,[111] an ontological unity is presupposed.[112] Clearly, more is in view than a mere oneness of will between Jesus and the Father. The Jews, perceiving blasphemy, promptly pick up stones in a renewed attempt to kill Jesus.[113]

In the following interchange Jesus points to his "many good works from the Father" and asks for which of these his opponents want to stone him (10:32). They answer that Jesus' offense is not good works but blasphemy. Rather than retract his claim, Jesus proceeds to assert that the Father set him — the Son of God — apart and sent him into the world (10:36), again offering "the works of [his] Father" as

---

105. Cf. the discussion of the children of the Devil and the children of God in 1 John (esp. 3:7–15), which reinforces the point that paternity is determined by confession/faith.

106. On Jesus and the Jews in John's gospel, see especially Motyer, *Your Father the Devil*; and Lars Kierspel, *The Jews and the World in the Fourth Gospel: Parallelism, Function, and Context* (WUNT 2/220; Tübingen: Mohr-Siebeck, 2007). On the alleged anti-Semitism of John's gospel, see Reimund Bieringer, Didier Pollefeyt, and Frederique Vandecasteele-Vanneuville, eds., *Anti-Judaism and the Fourth Gospel* (Louisville: Westminster John Knox, 2001), and *Anti-Judaism and the Fourth Gospel: Papers of the Leuven Colloquium, 2000* (Assen, the Netherlands: Royal van Gorcum, 2001).

107. On the OT background of John 10, see Köstenberger, "Jesus the Good Shepherd," 67–96; idem, "John," in *Commentary on the NT Use of the OT*, 461–64.

108. "One," *hen*, is neuter singular, indicating that Jesus and the Father are one "entity," not one person. See also the following note.

109. Note the variance from Deut. 6:4, where *heis* (masculine) is used.

110. See the discussion in sec. 17 above.

111. Ridderbos, *Gospel of John*, 371.

112. See esp. Carson, *Gospel according to John*, 394–95.

113. Jesus' assertion of oneness with the Father challenged narrow Jewish notions of monotheism, even though the Hebrew Scriptures already hint at a plurality within the Godhead, as Jesus observed at other occasions (e.g., Matt 22:41–46 par.). His unity with the Father later serves as the basis on which Jesus prays for the unity of his followers (17:11, 22; note again the neuter *hen*).

evidence that the Father is in him and he in the Father (10:37–38). Again, the Jews attempt to stone him, but he eludes their grasp.

Throughout the Festival Cycle, God is consistently characterized as Jesus' Father, who has sent Jesus on his earthly mission and who bears continual testimony to him, especially in and through his works.[114] The Festival Cycle ends as it began: with Jesus' unequivocal alignment of himself with God's purposes and the Jews' fierce opposition to him. The "signs," for their part, rather than serving their intended purpose of eliciting faith from those who witness them, only harden the Jews' opposition. When the Festival Cycle closes with the *inclusio* pertaining to the ministry of John the Baptist, the battle lines are drawn even more firmly than when the Sabbath controversy first erupted. With this the stage is set for what is about to follow.

19.3.3 Transition from the Book of Signs to the Book of Exaltation

The term *patēr* is absent from chapter 11, with the exception of Jesus' customary address of God as "Father" in his prayer at Lazarus's tomb.[115] The portrayal of Jesus as one whose prayers are heard identifies him as a righteous man who does God's will (cf. 9:31; 11:22). The prayer is uttered, not for Jesus himself, but for the sake of the crowds standing at Lazarus's gravesite, seeking to elicit faith in the one whom God sent. The fact that Jesus prays prior to raising Lazarus from the dead is part of the gospel's pervasive emphasis on Jesus' total dependence on God the Father in carrying out his mission. As the following events make clear, the Father, as always, hears and answers Jesus' prayer.

Later, when instructing his followers on the nature of true discipleship, Jesus promises that the Father will honor anyone who serves him (12:26). In a struggle reminiscent of the Synoptic account of Gethsemane, Jesus poses the rhetorical question of whether he should ask the Father to rescue him from the hour of death, only to immediately discard the notion: "No . . . Father, glorify your name!" (12:27–28).[116] His prayer is promptly answered by a voice from heaven, the only direct utterance of God in this gospel (12:27–28). This shows that the closeness of relationship between Jesus and the Father continues unabated even with the crucifixion rapidly approaching (cf. 12:24).

The Book of Signs concludes with Jesus' emphatic assertion that his teaching is in keeping with that of his Father who sent him and that the purpose of his Father's command is eternal life.

19.4 The Book of Exaltation

In the Farewell Discourse, the vantage point of the narrative shifts from Jesus' earthly ministry to the Jews—which ends in rejection—to the anticipation of his

---

114. Tolmie, "Characterization of God," 67.
115. See 11:41; cf. 12:27–28; 17:1, 5, 11, 21, 24, 25.
116. For this rendering, and a discussion of alternative interpretations, see Köstenberger, *John*, 380–81.

glorious exaltation with the Father.[117] At the outset of the Book of Exaltation, the evangelist makes clear that Jesus faces the prospect of his imminent demise fully cognizant that the Father has given everything into his hands and that he has come from God and is returning to God (13:1–3).[118]

19.4.1 The Farewell Discourse

The Farewell Discourse continues the pattern of portraying Jesus' relationship with God by way of frequent references to God as Father, which serves to convey the intimate nature of Jesus' disclosure of his messianic mission in these final hours of his earthly ministry.[119] The characterization of God as Father in the Farewell Discourse underscores the intricate connection between the Father and Jesus and explicates the implications of their relationship for believers in Jesus.[120]

With regard to Jesus, the Father: (1) has handed all things over to him (13:3; 17:2); (2) has sent him (13:3, 20; 15:21; 16:5, 28, 30; 17:3, 8, 18, 25); (3) will glorify him (13:31, 32; 17:1, 5, 22); (4) reveals himself through him (14:6–11; 17:6, 11, 14, 26); (5) is in him (14:10–11, 20); (6) tells him what to say and do (14:10, 24, 31; 15:10, 15); (7) grants his requests (14:16); (8) is greater than he (14:28); (9) loves him (15:9; 17:23, 26); (10) gives people to him (17:6, 9); and (11) is one with him (17:10, 11, 21–22).

With regard to believers, the Father: (1) has adequate space for them in his "house" (14:2); (2) will send the *paraklētos* to them (14:16, 26; 15:26); (3) will love them (14:21, 23; 16:27); (4) will come and stay with them (14:23); (5) will prune them in order that they may bear more fruit (15:2); (6) will grant their requests (15:16; 16:23); (7) will protect them from the evil one (17:15); and (8) will enable them to be one (17:21–22).[121]

After Judas the betrayer has left the Upper Room and Jesus has predicted Peter's three-time denial, Jesus tells his followers that he will prepare a place for them in his "Father's house" (14:2).[122] In the ensuing interchange with first Thomas and then Philip, Jesus couches his relationship with God pervasively in terms of "Father" and "Son."[123] When Thomas asks Jesus to show his disciples the way, Jesus responds that he *is* the way and that no one can come to the Father except through him (14:5–6). Philip follows up, asking Jesus to show them the Father, to which Jesus replies that

---

117. See Köstenberger, *Missions of Jesus and the Disciples*, 149–53 et passim.

118. Note the clear verbal echo of 3:35, also by the evangelist.

119. There are a total of forty-four references to God as Father in the Farewell Discourse proper (John 13:31–16:33) and six in Jesus' final prayer in John 17. Tolmie, "Characterization of God," 71, points out that the events narrated in chaps. 13–17 are set in an intimate atmosphere. He notes the marked change in the way in which the relationship between God and people is portrayed (moving from possibility to reality) and observes that there are no new traits of God revealed in these chapters (p. 72).

120. Ibid., 72, though note that Tolmie does not distinguish between references to *theos* and *patēr*.

121. See the discussion in Stibbe, "Telling the Father's Story," 187–88, who also cites Meyer's ("The Father," 264) list of active verbs used in conjunction with the word *patēr* when applied to God.

122. This is the same expression as in 2:16 (though note that the Greek term for "house" in 14:2 is *oikia*, while in 2:16 it is *oikos*), which is why some have suggested that here, too, the temple is in view. However, owing to the lack of contextual indicators in the present passage, heaven is a more likely referent (Köstenberger, "John," in *ZIBBC*, 2:137; idem, *John*, 425–27).

123. The densest concentration of references to God as Father is found in 14:6–13, where twelve references occur in a span of eight verses.

having seen *him* is having seen the Father (14:7, 9), an amazing assertion in light of the fact that no one can or has ever seen God (1:18). Jesus "the Son" has made the invisible God, "the Father," visible.

After this, Jesus continues to elaborate on the closeness of his relationship with the Father, explaining that he is "in" the Father and the Father is "in" him (14:10–11). Clearly, this conveys the notion of an exceedingly intimate familial relationship. Rather than suggesting a "mystical" relationship between Jesus and the Father,[124] the "in" language characterizes Jesus' relationship with God the Father as one of great intimacy, love, and trust. Thus Jesus explains that his words truly come from the Father, who does his works in him (14:11).

Rather than constituting a tragic loss, Jesus' return to the Father will enable his followers to do greater works even than Jesus did during his earthly ministry.[125] This promise of "greater works" (NASB; TNIV: "greater things") is predicated on Jesus' exaltation with the Father (14:12c).[126] Once exalted, Jesus will answer the disciples' prayer offered in his name so that the Father will be glorified in the Son and his followers' mission will be accomplished (14:13). At Jesus' bidding, the Father will also send the Spirit (14:16). Once Jesus has risen, the disciples will know that he is in the Father (14:20), and those who obey Jesus will be loved by the Father as well (14:21).

Indeed, Jesus and the Father will come and make their home in believers (14:23). Since the Spirit is likewise said to indwell believers (14:17), this means that in a sense the entire triune Godhead will be present in believers, though perhaps more precisely it is the indwelling Spirit who is sent by the Father in Jesus' name and who serves as their representative (cf. 14:16, 26). Jesus' message is not his own but the Father's (14:24). In what follows, the promise of the Father's sending of the Spirit in Jesus' name is reiterated (14:26). As Jesus came in the Father's name, so the Spirit will come in Jesus' name.

Jesus proceeds to encourage his followers that his return to the Father, rather than being a source of mourning, ought to be cause for rejoicing, because the Father is greater than he (14:28). The contradiction with his previous affirmation, "I and the Father are one" (10:30), is only apparent. There the point was Jesus' and the Father's unity of purpose; here the reference is to the Son's subordination to the Father, which is consistently affirmed in the gospel: the Father sends Jesus; Jesus obeys and depends on the Father; he comes from and returns to the Father; and the Father does his work and speaks his words through him.[127] Thus Jesus concludes

---

124. As has been argued by some of the proponents of the history-of-religions school, who have evoked parallels with first- and second-century mystery religions.

125. See Köstenberger, *Missions of Jesus and the Disciples*, 71–75.

126. See the introduction to this section (19.3) above.

127. This subordination is nonreversible: the Son does not send the Father; the Father does not depend on the Son; etc. Contra, Stanley J. Grenz, *Women in the Church* (Downers Grove, IL: InterVarsity Press, 1995), 514 (with reference to Pannenberg), according to whom the persons of the Trinity are mutually dependent, so that the "Father is dependent on the Son," not merely for his Fatherhood but even "for his deity." See my "Review of *Women in the Church* by Stanley J. Grenz," *JETS* 41 (1998): 517–18. See also Christopher Cowan, "The Father and Son in the Fourth Gospel: Johannine Subordination Revisited," *JETS* 49 (2006): 115–35.

Part 1 of the Farewell Discourse by affirming his commitment to obey the Father in order for the world to know that he loves him (14:31).

At this Jesus illustrates the spiritual union he desires with his followers subsequent to his exaltation with the Father by way of the allegory of the vine and the branches. The entire allegory is told by Jesus in personal terms, his Father being the vinedresser and Jesus himself being the vine (15:1).[128] The Father is glorified by Jesus' followers' bearing much fruit (15:8).[129] And so the chain continues: just as the Father has loved Jesus, so he loves the disciples (15:9); and just as Jesus has obeyed the Father, so his followers ought to obey him as well (15:10).[130]

No longer does Jesus call his disciples his "servants" (13:16; cf. 12:26). Rather, they are his "friends," because he has made known to them all the things he has heard from the Father (15:15; cf. 5:19–20). Hence Jesus' followers are included in his close familial relationship with the Father. And once again, the disciples are enjoined to petition the Father in Jesus' name (15:16; cf. 14:13–14). Conversely, whoever hates Jesus also hates the Father (15:23–24), and the disciples as well (15:18–25).[131] Once more, Jesus promises the coming of the Spirit, this time by stating that he himself will send the Spirit "from" the Father (15:26). The world, for its part, will persecute Jesus' followers, because it knows neither the Father nor Jesus (16:3).

The closeness of relationship between Father, Son, and Spirit is apparent in that the Spirit will take from what is Jesus' and reveal it to the disciples, just as all things that are the Father's are Jesus' as well (16:14–15). At that time, however, the disciples do not yet understand what Jesus meant when he spoke of his return to the Father (16:17). In what follows Jesus once again raises the specter of answered prayer to the Father in his name (16:23; cf. 14:13–14; 15:16). Yet Jesus' disciples still fail to grasp the meaning of his words; only later, following Jesus' departure and return to the Father, they will understand (16:25–28). As the Farewell Discourse draws to a close, Jesus predicts his disciples' wholesale defection while expressing his assurance that the Father is always with him (16:32; cf. 1:18).

19.4.2 *The Final Prayer*

Jesus' final prayer in John's gospel contains repeated addresses of God as Jesus' "Father."[132] At the outset, Jesus asks the Father to glorify the Son, so that the Son may glorify him (17:1; see also v. 5). He asks that the "holy Father" keep the disciples, who will remain in the world subsequent to Jesus' departure, one in his name, just as he and the Father are one (17:11). This, in turn, will serve the purpose of helping the world believe that the Father sent Jesus (17:21). As he concludes his prayer, Jesus asks the Father to show his followers the glory he had with him before the world

---

128. Note the frequent reference to the Father as "my" Father in this chapter (15:1, 10, 15, 23–24).

129. Note the verbal allusion to Jesus' bearing of fruit in 12:24.

130. See further the discussion of 20:21 in sec. 21 below.

131. Cf., e.g., 5:19; 13:16, 20; 14:9.

132. There are a total of six such instances of "Father" in John 17. On prayer in John's gospel, see the discussion of the Johannine mission theme in chap. 15 below.

was made (17:24; cf. 17:5). The prayer closes with a reference to God as "righteous Father" (17:25).

19.4.3 The Passion Narrative

The sole reference to the Father in John 18–19 is found in Jesus' affirmation of his resolve to drink the "cup" the Father has given him (18:11). This shows that Jesus embraced the cross as part of the Father's will for his life and mission. Following the resurrection, Jesus spoke of his imminent departure to "my Father and your Father, to my God and your God" (20:17). Here Jesus maintains a distinction between the way in which God is Jesus' Father and the way in which he is the Father of believers.[133] The final reference to God as Father in the gospel is found in the commissioning scene, where Jesus is shown to send his followers as the Father had sent him (20:21).[134]

19.5 First, Second, and Third John

John's first letter features ten references to "the Father," with 2 John containing four references and 3 John none. On the whole, there is little (if any) discernible difference between the portrayal of the Father-Son relationship in John's gospel and John's letters. Interestingly, in 1 John, "God" (*theos*), not "Father," is the dominant designation for God the Father. References to the Father in John's first letter are found in 1 John 1:2, 3; 2:1, 15, 16, 22, 23, 24; 3:1; and 4:14. It is noteworthy that after a cluster of references to the Father toward the end of chapter 2, and the opening mention in chapter 3, there is only one more instance of "Father" in the last two chapters (4:14). This may be because God is presented as the source of believers' love, apart from his relationship to Jesus the Son as his Father.

19.6 Summary

Father-Son is the dominant, controlling metaphor used for Jesus' relationship with God in John's gospel and letters. The persons of God the Father and the Son are thoroughly and inextricably intertwined.[135] Jesus derives his mission from the Father and is fully dependent on him in carrying it out. The imagery of "father" and "son" plainly draws on Jewish cultural mores pertaining to father-son relationships, especially those pertaining to only sons.[136]

The vast majority of instances of *patēr* in John's gospel is found in discourse material. Emphatically, it is Jesus himself who refers to God as "the" Father and in close

---

133. Tolmie, "Characterization of God," 74, speaks of 20:17 as the "conclusion, and indeed climax" of the characterization of God in John's gospel, since it is only here that God is characterized not only as Father of Jesus, but also as Father of believers. This is clearly an important point, but we will argue below that 20:21 is a more likely climax.

134. On the theological and missiological implications of this verse see Köstenberger, *Missions of Jesus and the Disciples*; and the discussion in chap. 15 below.

135. See esp. the "just as" statements relating the Father and the Son in this gospel (e.g., 5:21, 23, 26; 6:57; 8:28; 10:15; 12:50; 17:18; 20:21) and references to Jesus being "in" the Father and the Father being "in" him (e.g., 10:38; 14:11, 20).

136. See Köstenberger, *Missions of Jesus and the Disciples*, 115–21, in interaction with the relevant literature.

to twenty instances even as "his" Father.[137] "The Father" is Jesus' natural—almost unselfconscious—way of referring to God. Particularly prominent are references to the Father sending Jesus.[138] One also notes the absence of the terms *theos* and *patēr* in the pericope of the adulterous woman (7:53–8:11).[139]

20 THE SON

20.1 Introduction

The term "Son" occupies a central role in the Christology of John's gospel and letters.[140] While the term *logos* ("the Word") is limited to the introduction and Jesus is occasionally addressed in the Gospel as *kyrios* ("sir" or "Lord") or *rabbi* ("teacher"),[141] it is the term *huios* ("Son") that pervades the gospel, both by itself and in conjunction with other titles.[142] Twice Jesus is called the "son of Joseph." Five times he is called the "one and only Son" (*monogenēs*). "Son of God" is applied to Jesus eight times in the gospel and seven times in 1 John. Thirteen times Jesus refers to himself as the "Son of Man."[143] Finally, there are eighteen references each to Jesus as "the Son" in the gospel and the letters, virtually always vis-à-vis God the Father.[144]

Jesus as the Son	Passage in John's gospel or letters
son of Joseph (2)	John 1:45; 6:42
one and only [Son] (5)	John 1:14, 18; 3:16, 18; 1 John 4:9
Son of God (15)	John 1:49; 3:18; 5:25; 10:36; 11:4, 27; 19:7; 20:31; 1 John 3:8; 4:15; 5:5, 10, 12, 13, 20
Son of Man (13)	John 1:51; 3:13, 14; 5:27; 6:27, 53, 62; 8:28; 9:35; 12:23, 34 (2x); 13:31
the Son (34)	John 3:16, 17, 35, 36 (2x); 5:19 (2x), 20, 21, 22, 23 (2x), 26; 6:40; 8:36; 14:13; 17:1 (2x); 1 John 1:3, 7; 2:22, 23, 24; 3:23; 4:9, 10, 14; 5:9, 10, 11, 12, 20; 2 John 3, 9

Fig. 20.1: Jesus as the Son in John's Gospel and Letters

---

137. John 2:16; 5:17, 43; 6:32, 40; 8:19 (2x), 49; 10:18, 25, 29, 37; 14:2, 7, 20, 21, 23; 15:1, 8, 10, 15, 23, 24; 20:17. Several times the term "Father" is used by the evangelist (1:14, 18; 3:35; 13:1, 3). In 8:41, Jesus' Jewish opponents claim they have one Father—God.

138. John 5:23, 36, 37; 6:44, 57; 8:16, 18; 12:49; 14:24; 20:21. The same close connectedness between Father and Son also pervades 1 John (and, according to 1 John 3:1–3, will be extended to believers as well).

139. See Köstenberger, *John*, 245–49. The terms *huios* and *pneuma* are absent from this pericope as well.

140. References to God as Father in John's gospel are considerably more frequent than references to Jesus as the Son, suggesting that Jesus speaks more frequently about the Father than he does about himself.

141. *Kyrios*: 4:11, 15, 49; 5:7; 11:34, 39; *rabbi*: 1:38, 49; 3:2; 4:31; 6:25; 9:2; 11:8; 13:13–14; cf. 20:16.

142. The term *huios* is found fifty-five times in John's gospel, of which forty-one refer to Jesus. If the four references to Jesus as the "one and only Son" (*monogenēs*) are included, this makes a total of forty-five references to Jesus as "Son" in John's gospel (forty-three if references to Jesus as *monogenēs huios* are only counted once) and twenty-four references in the letters (twenty-three if 1 John 4:9 is only counted once), for a total of seventy-one (see the chart below).

143. Since "Son of Man" was Jesus' chosen self-designation, it is not surprising that John's letters do not contain any references to Jesus as the "Son of Man."

144. The first five references to Jesus as the Son are by the evangelist (John 3:16, 17, 35, 36 [2x]). All other instances of "the Son"

20.2 One and Only Son

As mentioned, five times in John's gospel and letters Jesus is called God's "one and only Son" (*monogenēs*; John 1:14, 18; 3:16, 18; 1 John 4:9). While the precise term is found only in John's gospel, the expression may hark back to the Synoptic designation of Jesus as God's "beloved Son" (*huios agapētos*), applied to Jesus at his baptism (Mark 1:11 par. Matt 3:17; Luke 3:22) and transfiguration (Mark 9:7 par. Matt 17:5; Luke 9:35) and implied also in the parable of the tenants (Mark 12:6 par. Matt 21:38; Luke 20:13).

The introduction to John's gospel refers to Jesus as the *monogenēs* or "one and only Son" from the Father (John 1:14) and stresses his unique relationship with him (1:18).[145] The predominant OT usage of *monogenēs* is "only child."[146] Being an only child makes a child particularly special to its parents.[147] Hence the LXX often uses *agapētos* instead of *monogenēs*.[148] In Gen 22:2, 12, and 16, Isaac is called Abraham's "one and only son" (Heb. *yaḥid*),[149] despite the fact that the patriarch had earlier fathered Ishmael.[150] *Monogenēs*, therefore, means in all likelihood, not "only begotten," but "one-of-a-kind" son.[151]

In both the Hebrew Scriptures and Second Temple literature, the Son of David and Israel are called God's "firstborn" or "only" son.[152] In John's writings, Jesus is called God's "one and only" Son par excellence. In light of its affinity with the Isaac narrative and the parable of the tenants, the term *monogenēs* in John has significant soteriological implications, especially in the affirmation in 3:16 that "God so loved the world that he sent his one and only Son."[153]

By way of *inclusio*, the phrase "the one and only Son, who is himself God," in John 1:18 serves as a commentary on what is meant in 1:1c where it is said that "the Word was God."[154] The Word was God, and so Jesus is "unique and divine, though

---

are self-references by Jesus: 5:19 (2x), 20, 21, 22, 23 (2x), 26; 6:40; 8:36; 14:13; and 17:1 (2x). The reference in 3:17 to *God* (rather than "the Father") sending the Son is noteworthy.

145. On Jesus as God's "one-of-a-kind Son," see Köstenberger, *John*, 42–44, 49 and the literature cited there.

146. Judg 11:34; Prov 4:3; Amos 8:10; Jer 6:26; Zech 12:10.

147. Cf. Luke 7:12; 8:42; 9:38. See Gerard Pendrick, "*Monogenēs*," *NTS* 41 (1995): 593–94.

148. Gen 22:2, 12, 16; Amos 8:10; Jer 6:26; Zech 12:10; cf. Prov 4:3; in Judg 11:34 both are used.

149. Note the probable allusion to this text in 3:16.

150. Genesis 16; cf. Heb 11:17; Josephus, *Ant.* 1.22. Joseph A. Fitzmyer, "μόνος," *EDNT*, 2:440; Paul Winter, "Μονογενὴς παρὰ Πατρός," *ZRGG* 5 (1953): 337–40; and Dale Moody, "God's Only Son: The Translation of John 3:16 in the Revised Standard Version," *JBL* 72 (1953): 213–19, esp. 217.

151. In Isaac's case, "son of promise." For an argument that the notion of Jesus as the "only begotten" of the Father is foreign to Johannine thought and was read into the gospel only later during the patristic period, see Pendrick, "*Monogenēs*," 587–600. Among other pieces of evidence, Pendrick cites ancient references where *monogenēs* is applied to an only child who was not the only begotten, "for the father might have begotten other children who died young and so the preservation of his name rests on the only surviving son" (p. 590). In light of the high infant mortality rate in the ancient world, Pendrick notes that "there must have been many only children who were not the only ones begotten by their parents" (p. 590, n. 23). See also Moody, "God's Only Son," 213–19; W. O. Walker Jr., "John 1.43–51 and 'the Son of Man' in the Fourth Gospel," *JSNT* 56 (1994): 41, n. 37.

152. Cf. Ps 89:27; *4 Ezra* 6:58; *Pss. Sol.* 18:4; *Jub.* 18:2, 11, 15.

153. The designation also likely provides the basis for Jesus' claim that no one can come to the Father apart from him (14:6).

154. There is some question as to whether the original reading here is *monogenēs huios* ("one and only Son") or *monogenēs theos* ("one and only Son, who is himself God"). With the acquisition of p66 and p75, both of which read *monogenēs theos*, the preponderance of the evidence now leans in the direction of the latter reading. Harris, *Jesus as God*, 78–80, expresses a "strong preference" for *monogenēs theos*, for at least four reasons: (1) its superior manuscript support; (2) it represents the more difficult reading; (3) the phrase serves as a more proper climax to the entire introduction to John's gospel, attributing deity to the Son by way of *inclusio* with 1:1 and 14; (4) this reading seems best to account for the other variants. Most likely, then, *monogenēs huios* represents a scribal assimilation to 3:16 and 18.

flesh."[155] The phrase "one and only Son, who is himself God" is both striking and unusual.[156] The Jews believed there was only one God (Deut 6:4). Jesus' claim to deity brought him into increasing conflict with the Jewish leaders, and the primary charge leading to his crucifixion was blasphemy (John 19:7; cf. 10:33).

The phrase "in closest relationship with the Father" (*eis ton kolpon*, John 1:18) conveys Jesus' unmatched familiarity with the Father, which enabled him to reveal him in an unprecedented manner.[157] The expression serves as an idiom for greatest possible intimacy,[158] showing how close the evangelist considered Jesus' relationship with the Father to be.[159] While no one, including Moses, had ever seen God,[160] Jesus made him known in a unique, climactic, and definitive way.[161]

The references to Jesus as God's "one and only Son" in the introduction are fleshed out more fully in John 3:16 and 18. In the former passage, the emphasis is on the greatness of God's gift and the intensity of his love.[162] The word "gave" draws attention to the sacrifice involved in God the Father's sending his Son.[163] In the latter passage, Jesus is called "God's one and only Son" in the context of the world's condemnation for failing to believe in his name. This indicates the severity of guilt incurred by those who take lightly God's sacrifice of his most precious Son.

20.3 Son of God

20.3.1 Introduction

John's gospel features eight references to Jesus as the Son of God, of which seven are positive.[164] The evangelist develops these references to Jesus as the Son of God strategically as his narrative progresses. The initial reference to Jesus as Son of God by Nathanael is part of a series of early elevated christological references to Jesus by his first followers (John 1:49). The evangelist's reference to Jesus as Son of God in 3:18 is mirrored by the concluding reference to Jesus as Son of God at the end of the gospel (20:31).

At the heart of the gospel's characterization of Jesus as Son of God are three self-references of Jesus as Son of God in 5:25; 10:36 (toward the beginning and the

---

155. Rather than functioning attributively ("the one and only God"), *monogenēs* probably is to be understood as a substantive in its own right as in 1:1 ("the one and only Son"), with *theos* in apposition ("who is himself God"). See also Henry Mowvley, "John 1,14–18 in the Light of Exodus 33,7–34,35," *ExpTim* 95 (1984): 37.

156. Note the equally clear ascriptions of deity to Jesus in 1:1 and 20:28.

157. Wallace, *Greek Grammar beyond the Basics*, 360. Cf. the contrast with Moses in 1:17; Brown, *Gospel according to John I–XII*, 36.

158. Cf. Prov 8:30. See Otfried Hofius, "'Der in des Vaters Schoss ist,' Joh 1,18," *ZNW* 80 (1989): 163–71. This is the way the term is used in the OT, where it portrays the devoted care of a parent or caregiver (Num 11:12; Ruth 4:16; 2 Sam 12:3; 1 Kgs 3:20; 17:19; Lam 2:12; cf. *b. Yebam.* 77a; Hofius, ibid., 166, nn. 19–21). Greek parallels include Aristotle, *Mir.* 846b.27 and Demosthenes, *Orat.* 47.58. The most pertinent NT parallel is the reference to "Abraham's side" (TNIV) in Luke 16:22.

159. The evangelist later uses the same expression with regard to himself, "the disciple whom Jesus loved," indicating that his closeness to Jesus during his earthly ministry made him the perfect person to write this gospel (13:23; see Fig. 2.2). On the character of the Gospels as eyewitness testimony see Bauckham, *Jesus and the Eyewitnesses*, though Bauckham falls short of appreciating the full nature of John's gospel as *apostolic* eyewitness testimony.

160. Morris, *Gospel according to John*, 100.

161. The term *exēgeomai* is found only in 1:18 in John's gospel and typically refers to giving a full account of a matter (cf. Luke 24:35; Acts 10:8; 15:12, 14; 21:19).

162. Carson, *Gospel according to John*, 204.

163. See Genesis 22; 1 John 4:9. See also Witherington, *John's Wisdom*, 101.

164. The eighth reference to Jesus as Son of God is uttered by Jesus' hostile Jewish opponents before Pilate (19:7).

end of the Festival Cycle, a likely *inclusio*); and 11:4 (at the outset of the climactic seventh sign of Jesus narrated in the gospel, the raising of Lazarus anticipating Jesus' own resurrection). Jesus' self-reference in 11:4 is echoed later in the same narrative by Martha (11:27), whose confession, in turn, anticipates the purpose statement in 20:31.

At first, seven or eight references to Jesus as Son of God may seem to be a small number.[165] Yet the Synoptics do not feature a single instance of Jesus calling himself "Son of God."[166] In John, by contrast, Jesus establishes such a claim as early as 5:25, and again later in 10:36 and 11:4.[167] This helpfully illumines how the high priest at Jesus' trial in the Synoptics can arrive at the charge of blasphemy after interrogating Jesus even though Jesus has not overtly claimed to be the Son of God previously in the Synoptics.[168]

John	Content
1:49	Nathanael declares Jesus to be the Son of God and king of Israel.
3:18	Evangelist states that failure to believe in Jesus as the Son of God will incur certain judgment.
5:25	First self-reference by Jesus: The dead will hear the voice of the Son of God and live.
10:36	Second self-reference by Jesus: Jesus legitimately claims to be the Son of God (cites OT).
11:4	Third self-reference by Jesus: Lazarus's death will bring glory to the Son of God (cf. 5:25).
11:27	Martha confesses Jesus as the Messiah and Son of God (anticipating 20:31).
19:7	Jewish leaders deny before Pilate that Jesus is the Son of God.
20:31	Evangelist's purpose is to lead readers to faith in Jesus as Messiah and Son of God.

Fig. 20.2: References to Jesus as the Son of God in John's Gospel

20.3.2 Jesus' Calling of His First Disciples and the Cana Cycle

Nathanael fires the opening salvo when he exclaims, "Rabbi, you are the Son of God; you are the king of Israel" (John 1:49). These two epithets, "Son of God" and

---

165. Though note the possible numerical symbolism entailed by the number seven.

166. He comes closest to doing so when answering the high priest's question at his Jewish trial whether or not he is the Son of God in the affirmative (Matt 26:63 par. Luke 22:70). Otherwise, it is Satan or his demons (Matt 4:3, 6 par. Luke 4:3, 9; Mark 3:11; Luke 4:41; Matt 8:29 par. Mark 5:7 and Luke 8:28); the angel Gabriel (Luke 1:35); the Twelve (Matt 14:33) or Peter (16:16); the centurion (27:54 par. Mark 15:37); or those who mock his messianic claims (Matt 27:40, 43) who refer to Jesus as the "Son of God" in the Synoptics.

167. As noted, the first two instances bracket the Festival Cycle, which begins and ends with the Jews trying to stone Jesus for blasphemy.

168. Cf. John 19:7. This should be set within the context of the "interlocking patterns" between John and the Synoptics (see Carson, *Gospel according to John*, 52–58, esp. 53, in further development of Morris, *Studies in the Fourth Gospel*, 40–63).

"king of Israel," bear a certain affinity to one another in that both are messianic designations.[169] By calling Jesus "Son of God," Nathanael identifies him at the outset of the gospel as the Messiah predicted in the OT.[170] Nevertheless, Jesus' words in 1:50–51 may provide a corrective, as he was clearly leery of any unwelcome political or nationalistic overtones such titles may convey (cf. 6:15; 12:16; 18:36).

The evangelist's references to Jesus as Son of God in 3:16–18 and 20:31 both speak of believing and having life in the "name" of Jesus the Son of God, giving further definition to the reference to "those who believed in his name" in the introduction to the gospel (cf. 1:12). The reference in 3:16–18 also harks back to the reference to many who "saw the signs he was performing and believed in his name" in 2:23–25 and to the references to Jesus as the "one and only Son" in 1:14–18.[171]

In 3:18, the major point is that faith in Jesus "God's one and only Son" will enable people to evade divine judgment while unbelief will incur it. The fact that 3:16–21 comes on the heels of Jesus' interchange with Nicodemus, the "teacher of Israel," indicates that the Jewish people are not exempt from the need to place their faith in the sacrifice provided by the lifted-up Son of Man (cf. 3:13–14). Thus Jesus' encounter with Nicodemus serves as a paradigmatic encounter which, in turn, forms the basis for the concluding purpose statement (20:30–31).

20.3.3 The Festival Cycle

In Jesus' self-reference in 5:25, "Son of God" is parallel to "the Son" (5:26) and "the Son of Man" (5:27). As in 3:16–18, the focus is on Jesus being the catalyst for divine judgment, depending on whether or not one believes in him as God's Son (cf. 1 John 5:11–12). Jesus' words in John 5:25, "Very truly I tell you, a time is coming *and has now come* when the dead will hear the voice of the Son of God and those who hear will live" (emphasis added), are realized when Jesus raises Lazarus from the dead in the climactic seventh sign of the gospel (see esp. 11:4 and 27).[172]

Jesus' self-reference in 10:36 harks back to 5:25 but makes the Jewish charge of blasphemy more explicit (cf. 10:31–33), coming on the heels of Jesus' claim that he and the Father are one (10:30). Jesus' public ministry to the Jews has all but come to a close. Jewish obduracy is sealed, and their rejection of Jesus a virtual certainty (12:37–41; 19:7). Like Jesus' first sign in Cana (2:11), the raising of Lazarus is thus performed to reveal Jesus' glory to his own (11:4), and Martha's confession stands in striking contrast with the Jews' rejection of Jesus.

---

169. Cf. Barrett, *Gospel according to St. John*, 186; cf. Ridderbos, *Gospel of John*, 91. "Messiah" and "king of Israel" are juxtaposed in Matt 27:42/Mark 15:32, though note that "king of Israel" may have nationalistic overtones (Morris, *Gospel according to John*, 147, n. 115). Nathanael's judgment is vindicated, and his expectation apparently fulfilled, when Jesus is hailed as "king of Israel" at the triumphal entry in John 12:13 (where "king of Israel" is added by the evangelist to his quotation of Ps 118:25–26).

170. See 2 Sam 7:14; Ps 2:7; cf. 1 Sam 26:17, 21, 25. The term "Son [of God]" was also a current messianic title in Jesus' day (cf. 1QSa 2:11–12; *4 Ezra* 7:28–29). On the reference to "Son of God" and "Son of the Most High" in 4Q246, see the discussion in Charlesworth, "Shared Symbolism," 113–14, with further bibliographic references. Elsewhere in Jewish literature the Davidic king is also described as God's son (see also 4QFlor 1:6–7; *1 En.* 105:2; *4 Ezra* 13:52; 14:9; cf. Carson, *Gospel according to John*, 162).

171. Notably, "one and only Son," "Son," and "Son of God" are used virtually interchangeably in 3:16–18.

172. The statement in 5:25 is reminiscent of Ezekiel's vision of the valley of dry bones in Ezekiel 37. Cf. Rom 4:17; Eph 2:1–5.

Jesus' pronouncement in 10:36 constitutes the first major climax in John's gospel.[173] The Jews' charge against Jesus in 10:33 appears to be based on Lev 24:16, which says that "anyone who blasphemes the name of the LORD is to be be put to death. The entire assembly must stone him."[174] As mentioned, 10:36 constitutes an *inclusio* with 5:18, which, together with 7:25, 8:59, and 10:36, punctuates the escalating pattern of controversy between Jesus and the Jews in the Festival Cycle.

Jesus' rebuttal in John 10:34–38 involves a quotation of Ps 82:6. The quotation, following on the heels of the Good Shepherd Discourse (John 10:1–18, 25–30), occurs in the context of a trial scene that focuses, in turn, on the dual question of whether Jesus is the Messiah (10:24) and Son of God (10:33). In both cases, the Jews mount an initial charge (10:24, 33), which is rebutted by Jesus (10:25–30, 34–38) but rejected by the Jews, who unsuccessfully attempt to stone or arrest him (10:31, 39).[175]

Defending himself against the charge of blasphemy, therefore, Jesus retorts: "Is it not written in your Law, 'I have said you are gods'? If [it][176] called them 'gods,' to whom the word of God came ... what about the one whom the Father set apart as his very own and sent into the world?" (10:34–36). The reference in "the Law" cited by Jesus is Ps 82:6, which reads, "I said, 'You are "gods"; you are all sons of the Most High.'" In essence, Jesus is saying that there is OT precedent for humans being referred to as "gods."[177]

Jesus then proceeds to adduce his works as evidence for his claim of divine sonship (10:37–39). If people see the kinds of works he does, works that stand in continuity with the works done by God the Father, they will recognize that Jesus is one with the Father and therefore rightfully claims to be the Son of God. In this the passage harks back to John 5, where Jesus, when accused of breaking the Sabbath in the process of healing the lame man, responded that he had done his work in continuity with that of God the Father (cf. 5:17).

20.3.4 Transition from the Book of Signs to the Book of Exaltation

Finally, Jesus' statement at the inception of the Lazarus narrative, "It is for God's glory so that God's Son may be glorified through it" (John 11:4), parallels his earlier verdict regarding the man's blindness from birth.[178] Here as elsewhere in the gospel,

---

173. Carson, *Gospel according to John*, 395. The second, no less important climax is Jesus' cry, "It is finished," on the cross (19:30). See Hengel, "Johannesevangelium als Quelle," 319.

174. See also Num 15:30–31; Deut 21:22.

175. The contrast with Martha's confession is clear (11:27; cf. 20:30–31; Daly-Denton, *David in the Fourth Gospel*, 123). A similar line of investigation is found in the Synoptic accounts of Jesus' Jewish trial before the Sanhedrin (Mark 14:62; Luke 22:67, 70). However, in contrast to the Synoptics, who locate Jesus' trial at the end of his ministry, John's gospel has Jesus on trial throughout his entire ministry. What is more, John's "trial motif" turns the notion of trial on its head by focusing, not on Jesus' guilt, but on the Jews' culpability in rejecting their Messiah despite ample evidence to the contrary (see esp. 12:37–41). See Lincoln, *Truth on Trial*; Daly-Denton, *David in the Fourth Gospel*, 124; and chap. 11 below.

176. That is, the Law (more likely than "he" as in the TNIV). See Köstenberger, *John*, 314.

177. See the treatment of the OT quote in John 10:34 in Köstenberger, "John," in *Commentary on the NT Use of the OT*, 464–67.

178. See John 9:3; see also the possible *inclusio* with 2:11. As Carson, *Gospel according to John*, 406 (cf. Barrett, *Gospel according to St. John*, 390), observes, it is not that the sickness occurred *in order* for God to be glorified, but rather that it constituted an occasion for God's glory to be revealed.

God's self-disclosure takes place preeminently in his Son (13:31; 14:13; 17:4).[179] As mentioned, Martha's almost creedlike confession of Jesus as "the Messiah, the Son of God, who was to come into the world" (11:27),[180] strikingly anticipates the purpose statement at the end of the gospel (20:30–31).[181]

20.3.5 Conclusion

References to Jesus as the Son of God thus pervade John's gospel to a much more significant degree than the Synoptics. The opening confession of Nathanael, the evangelist's identification of Jesus as the Son of God, and Jesus' first self-reference in 5:25 set the stage for the christological controversy that dominates the entire first half of the gospel, focused on the question of whether Jesus is the Messiah and Son of God (cf. 10:36; 11:4, 27). While the Jews deny this (19:7), the purpose statement answers the question in the affirmative (20:31).

20.3.6 First John

In addition to the references to Jesus as the "Son of God" in John's gospel discussed above, 1 John features an astonishingly large number of references to Jesus as "Son of God" as well. In this relatively short letter, Jesus is referred to as "Son of God" seven times (1 John 3:8; 4:15; 5:5, 10, 12, 13, 20). He came to destroy the devil's work (3:8). Jesus must be acknowledged as Son of God for God to live in believers (4:15). Overcoming faith is possessed only by those who believe that Jesus is the Son of God (5:5). Those who believe in Jesus as the Son of God accept God's testimony regarding him (5:10); those, and only those, who have the Son of God have eternal life (5:12–13). The Son of God has come and has revealed the one and only true God to us (5:20). In conjunction with the references to Jesus as Messiah (esp. 2:22; 4:2; 5:1), as in John's gospel, the expression "Son of God" serves as a messianic title.

20.4 Son of Man

20.4.1 Introduction

Jesus' references to himself as "Son of Man" pervade the entire first half of John's gospel, spanning from John 1:51 to 13:31 (the outset of the Farewell Discourse).[182] Remarkably, they are otherwise absent from the Farewell Discourse proper and the Passion Narrative. Almost half of the Johannine instances of "Son of Man" form part of a cluster of references commonly called "the lifted-up sayings," involving the term *hypsoō* in the passive voice ("to be lifted up"), a euphemism for Jesus' crucifixion (see 3:13–14; 8:28; 12:32–34). Otherwise, the references to Jesus as the "Son of Man" in John's gospel bear a fairly close resemblance to those in the Synoptics.

---

179. Carson, *Gospel according to John*, 406; Ridderbos, *Gospel of John*, 387.

180. My translation.

181. See the discussion in Ridderbos, *Gospel of John*, 399–400; Morris, *Gospel according to John*, 489–90; and Köstenberger, *John*, 336, n. 72.

182. John 1:51; 3:13, 14; 5:27; 6:27, 53, 62; 8:28; 9:35; 12:23, 34 (2x); 13:31. There are no references to Jesus as the "Son of Man" in John's letters.

Passage in John's gospel	Content
1:51	The Son of Man as the locus of new divine revelation
3:13–14	First "lifted up" saying
5:27	The Son of Man's authority to judge
6:27, 53, 62	The Son of Man's descent as the "Bread of Life"
8:28	Second "lifted up" saying
9:35	Jesus' self-reference to the formerly blind man
12:23	Now is the Son of Man glorified
12:34	Third "lifted up" saying (cf. 12:32)
13:31	Now is the Son of Man glorified

Fig. 20.3: References to the Son of Man in John's Gospel

20.4.2 Jesus' Calling of His First Disciples

In the initial reference to Jesus as the Son of Man in the gospel, Jesus identifies himself as the Danielic figure of "one like a son of man" (1:51; cf. Dan 7:13). This mysterious figure, with its transcendent origins, has come as a human being to complete his mission and will return to earth in the last days to serve as the final judge. Jesus thus claims to be that Son of Man, the one who has seen God and given a full account of him (cf. John 1:18), was "lifted up" at the cross (cf. 3:14; 8:28; 12:32), and will return in all his glory at the end of time (cf. Matt 26:64).

The picture invoked in 1:51 is drawn from Jacob's vision of a stairway "resting on the earth, with its top reaching to heaven, and the angels of God ... ascending and descending on it" (Gen 28:12). As the angels ascended and descended on Jacob (later renamed "Israel")—a sign of God's faithfulness to his promises made to Abraham—the disciples are promised further divine confirmation of Jesus' messianic identity. In fact, Jesus will be the locus of much greater divine revelation than that given at previous occasions to Abraham, Jacob, Moses, and Isaiah.

Thus Jesus is the "new Bethel," the place where God is revealed and where heaven and earth, God and humanity meet. In fact, he is the culmination of all of God's revelatory expressions—the Word (1:1; cf. 1:14, 18)—providing a fullness of divine self-disclosure of which even Jacob/Israel could only dream. Jesus' followers, who as of yet knew little of what awaited them, would soon witness revelation that far exceeded that received by any Israelite in previous salvation history.

20.4.3 The Cana Cycle

The second and third references to Jesus as the Son of Man come at the end of Jesus' interaction with Nicodemus (3:13). In this instance, Jesus contrasts himself with other human figures who allegedly entered heaven, including Enoch, Elijah,

Moses, Isaiah, or Ezekiel.[183] While all these figures entered heaven, only Jesus first descended *from* heaven, because he was the heaven-sent Son of Man. Elsewhere in the gospel, those who are said to have descended from heaven are the Spirit (1:32–33), angels (1:51), and the divine bread (6:33, 38, 41, 42, 50, 51, 58).[184]

Not only has this Son of Man descended from heaven and will ascend back into heaven, he will also be "lifted up" (3:14). The expression "lifted up" (*hypsoō*) almost certainly echoes Isaianic language regarding the Servant of Yahweh, who "will be raised and lifted up and highly exalted" (Isa 52:13: *hypsōthēsetai kai doxasthēsetai*, LXX). There is great irony in the fact that the Jews, by having Jesus crucified, are actually "lifting" him up. John is the only NT writer to use this term in a dual sense with reference both to Jesus' crucifixion and his exaltation.

20.4.4 *The Festival Cycle*

The fourth reference to Jesus as the Son of Man occurs in the context of the aftermath of the Sabbath controversy at the beginning of the Festival Cycle (5:27).[185] In this passage, Jesus claims to possess the authority to judge, a divine prerogative (cf., e.g., Gen 18:25; 1 Sam 2:10; Ps 9:8; 82:8; 94:2). The assertion comes on the heels of the claim that Jesus was granted by God to have life in himself, also a divine attribute (5:26). As mentioned above, exercising divine judgment is part of the function of the Danielic figure of the "son of man."

The next three references to Jesus as the Son of Man are found in the Bread of Life Discourse (6:27, 53, 62), the common point of reference being the giving of manna to wilderness Israel. Like the manna, Jesus claims to have descended from heaven. Unlike the manna, Jesus will ascend to heaven again in the future (see esp. 6:62). This suggests that Jesus' crucifixion — his giving of his flesh and blood for the life of the world (6:51) — will not constitute Jesus' demise but be followed by divine vindication (cf. 1:51; 3:13–14).

The eighth reference to the Son of Man in John's gospel comes at the outset of the paternity dispute between Jesus and the Jewish leaders, where Jesus refers for a second time to the "lifting up" of the Son of Man (see John 8:28; cf. 3:14). The theme of the "lifting up" of the Son of Man is continued in 12:32, where it is said that, once "lifted up," Jesus will draw "all people" — that is, all *kinds* of people, Gentiles as well as Jews — to himself.[186] At that point the evangelist also makes it plain that Jesus' "lifting up" is his crucifixion (12:33).

Thus the crucifixion is presented as the central plank in Jesus' universal mission to all of humanity, including non-Jews. Jesus' sacrificial cross-death is required

---

183. Enoch: Gen 5:24; cf. Heb 11:5; Elijah: 2 Kgs 2:1–12; cf. 2 Chr 21:12–15; Moses: Exod 24:9–11; 34:29–30; Isaiah: Isa 6:1–3; Ezekiel: Ezek 1:10.

184. That is, Jesus himself in fulfillment of manna symbolism.

185. The reference is unique in that the phrase reads more literally "he is Son of Man," the only instance of this christological title without articles before both "Son" and "Man" in the entire NT. This may indicate an allusion to Dan 7:13 LXX, where the expression "son of man" likewise does not feature the article (cf. Rev 1:13; 14:14).

186. For this interpretation and the text-critical issue involved, see Köstenberger, *John*, 384, 388; see also Carson, *Gospel according to John*, 444; and Morris, *Gospel according to John*, 531–32 (citing Calvin).

for Jesus to be able to draw all people to himself. This is an exceedingly important truth that is at the heart of the message of the entire gospel (see esp. 1:12; 3:16; 20:30–31). No longer does the Jews' salvation-historical privilege obtain, but faith in Jesus' name has now become the sole prerequisite for inclusion among God's new covenant people.

The ninth reference to Jesus as Son of Man in this gospel occurs when Jesus identifies himself to the healed man born blind after he has been expelled from the synagogue by the Jewish leaders and calls him to believe in him (9:35). In a striking development, the man, upon Jesus' self-identification, says, "Lord, I believe," and worships him (9:38). In this the man becomes a figure of identification for those who in John's day may have experienced similar ostracism by the hands of Jewish synagogue authorities (cf. 16:2).

20.4.5 Transition from the Book of Signs to the Book of Exaltation

The tenth reference to Jesus as the Son of Man announces, strikingly, that now "the hour has come for the Son of Man to be glorified" (12:23). This follows repeated references earlier in the gospel to the hour of Jesus as not yet having come (2:4; 7:30; 8:20). But now the coming of some Greeks to Jesus signals the imminent demise of the Son of Man (12:20). The glorification of the Son of Man will involve his dying and loss of life (12:23–24), yet by so dying, the Son of Man will produce many seeds (12:24).

The same occasion features the penultimate instances of "Son of Man" language in John's gospel (12:34). In this instance of messianic misunderstanding, the crowds interrogate Jesus, "We have heard from the Law that the Messiah will remain forever, so how can you say, 'The Son of Man must be lifted up'? Who is this 'Son of Man'?" (12:34).[187] As mentioned in the discussion of 8:28 above, Jesus is here identified as the Isaianic Suffering Servant who through his vicarious death "will be raised and lifted up and highly exalted."

20.4.6 The Farewell Discourse

Similar to Jesus' statement at 12:23, in the final instance of "Son of Man" language in John's gospel Jesus exclaims immediately after Judas the betrayer has gone out into the night that it is "now" that "the Son of Man [is] glorified and God is glorified in him" (13:31). The new messianic community has been cleansed and is about to be prepared for its future mission. With this culminating reference to Jesus as the Son of Man, there is no more need for further instances of such terminology.

---

187. Interestingly, Jesus' words in 12:32 do not feature the term "Son of Man." It is possible that John did not record Jesus' words in their entirety or that he paraphrased them. It is also possible that the crowd is referring to Jesus' similar words (which do include the expression "Son of Man") at 8:28.

20.5 The Son

20.5.1 Introduction

There are eighteen references to Jesus as "the Son" in John's gospel, all but the first five are self-references by Jesus. The references to Jesus as the Son are not as pervasive as might be expected. Eight instances are in 5:19–26; two additional references occur later in the Festival Cycle (6:40; 8:36); and the remaining three references are found in the Farewell Discourse (14:13; 17:1 [2x]). Nevertheless, in light of the fact that the frequent references to God as Jesus' Father clearly imply his sonship, and in conjunction with the above-discussed christological titles "Son of God" and "Son of Man," "Son" language proves to be the predominant christological designation for Jesus in John's gospel.[188]

20.5.2 The Cana Cycle

The first major cluster of "Son" references is supplied by the fourth evangelist in John 3:16–18. Interestingly, in these verses the evangelist refers to Jesus twice as the "one and only Son" (*monogenēs huios*; 3:16, 18) and once as "his [God's] Son" (3:17). This shows the close relationship between these terms. While God is the one who "gave" or "sent" his Son, the Son is unique and the Son of God; in fact, he himself is God as well (see 1:1, 18; cf. 20:28).

The second major cluster of "Son" references, structurally corresponding to the first such cluster in 3:16–18, is found in 3:35–36, where Jesus is identified as "the Son" three times. The Baptist testifies concerning Jesus that the Father gave all things to the Son because of his love for him. The important implication from this is that unless people believe in the Son (resulting in eternal life), God's wrath will continue to rest on them (3:36; cf. 1 John 5:9–13).

20.5.3 The Festival Cycle

The third and perhaps most significant major cluster of "Son" references is found in John 5:19–26 where, as mentioned, Jesus is referred to as the "Son" eight times.[189] In response to the Jewish leaders' charge of blasphemy, Jesus avers that, while equal to God, he is subordinate to him as a son is to his father.[190] Rather than assert his independence, Jesus is dependent on the Father, being at once coeternal with and subordinate to him.[191]

---

188. References to Jesus as "the Son" are not unique to John's gospel. Most striking is the so-called "Johannine thunderbolt" found in Matt 11:27 = Luke 10:22: "All things have been committed to me by my Father. No one knows the Son except the Father, and no one knows the Father except the Son and those to whom the Son chooses to reveal him." Another Synoptic instance of "Son" language is Matt 24:36 = Mark 13:32: "About that day or hour no one knows, not even the angels in heaven, nor the Son, but only the Father." In Matt 28:19, reference is made to baptism "in the name of the Father and of the Son and of the Holy Spirit." While "Son" language is thus more pronounced in John, it is not entirely absent from the other gospels.

189. In addition, he is also called "Son of God" (5:25) and "Son of Man" (5:27).

190. Morris, *Gospel according to John*, 277; Carson, *Gospel according to John*, 250–51.

191. Craig S. Keener, "Is Subordination within the Trinity Really Heresy? A Study of John 5:18 in Context," *TrinJ* 20 NS (1999): 39–51. The illustration in 5:19–20 may reflect Jesus' own experience with his adoptive father, Joseph, from whom he learned the craftsman's

The latter part of 5:19 features the first of four consecutive *gar*-clauses ("for"), asserting that "it is impossible for the Son to take independent, self-determined action that would set him over against the Father as another God."[192] The second *gar*-clause states the basis for the Son's dependence: the Father's love for him (5:20). The third and fourth clauses refer to the Son's delegated authority to raise the dead and to exercise judgment (5:21, 22).

The Father's love for the Son expresses itself in his free self-disclosure to the Son; the Son's love for the Father in his obedient submission to the Father's will, including death on the cross.[193] The "greater works" the Father will show the Son are raising the dead and exercising judgment (5:21–23).[194] This finds proleptic fulfillment in Jesus' raising of Lazarus, the climactic "sign" performed by Jesus in this gospel.

The Son gives life to whom he is pleased to give it, just as the Father raises the dead and gives them life.[195] Because the OT and Second Temple literature concur that raising the dead and giving life are divine prerogatives,[196] Jesus' contemporaries did not believe that the Messiah would be given authority to raise the dead.[197] This renders Jesus' claim of being able to raise the dead and to give them life at will all the more startling.

Not only is the Son able to give life as he pleases, he also has been entrusted with all judgment (5:22). Again, the OT teaches that judgment is the exclusive prerogative of God (e.g., Gen 18:25; cf. Judg 11:27).[198] The Messiah very much remains in the background with regard to judgment in the Second Temple literature, apart from carrying out God's judgment on his enemies in keeping with Jewish nationalistic expectations (e.g., *Pss. Sol.* 17:21–27).[199]

The purpose of the Father's delegation of authority to give life and to render judgment to the Son is that people might honor the Son as they do the Father.[200] Conversely, whoever fails to honor the Son also fails to honor the Father who sent him. In the OT, Moses and the prophets were considered to be God's agents and mouthpieces who acted and spoke on God's behalf. The Jewish maxim regarding a messenger was that "a man's agent is like the man himself."[201]

Jesus' role as the sent Son thus highlights both his equality with the Father and his obedience to him in carrying out his mission: "it is a legal presumption that an agent will carry out his mission" (*b. 'Erub.* 31b–32a; cf. *b. Ketub.* 99b).[202] According

---

trade (cf. Matt 13:55; Mark 6:3). On Joseph's and Jesus' trade being that of craftsmen rather than that of carpenters, see Ken M. Campbell, "What Was Jesus' Occupation?," *JETS* 48 (2005): 501–19.

192. Carson, *Gospel according to John*, 251.
193. Ibid.
194. Morris, *Gospel according to John*, 278. The matching statement in John 13–21 may be the reference to believers' "greater works" in 14:12.
195. This makes Jesus' claim more startling than Elijah's ability to raise the dead.
196. See Deut 32:39; 1 Sam 2:6; 2 Kgs 5:7; Tob 13:2; Wis 16:13.
197. Cf. *b. Ta'an.* 2a (attributed to Rabbi Yohanan, c. AD 70) and the *Shemoneh 'Esreh* (c. AD 70–100, cited in Schürer, *History of the Jewish People*, 2:455–63).

198. Though see the association of "the LORD" with "his anointed [one]" in rule and judgment in Ps 2:2.
199. The singular exception is the Son of Man (or "Chosen One") in the *Similitudes of Enoch* (*1 En.* 37–71; esp. 49:4; 61:9; 62:2–6; 63:11).
200. In effect, this establishes Jesus' right to be worshiped (Carson, *Gospel according to John*, 255) and amounts to a claim to deity (Morris, *Gospel according to John*, 279).
201. E.g., *m. Ber.* 5:5. See Karl Heinrich Rengstorf, "ἀποστέλλω, κτλ.," *TDNT*, 1:414–20.
202. Contra, Kevin J. Giles, *Jesus and the Father: Modern Evangelicals Reinvent the Doctrine of the Trinity* (Downers Grove, IL: InterVarsity Press, 2006), 117–24.

to John, this is precisely what Jesus did: he was made flesh, accomplished the mission entrusted to him by the Father, and returned to the one who sent him (John 4:34; 17:4; 19:30; cf. 1:1, 14; Isa 55:11–12).

Jesus proceeds to assert that, just as the Father has life in himself, he has given the Son to have life in himself (John 5:26; cf. v. 21). The OT states repeatedly that God grants life to others.[203] But here Jesus claims that God granted him life *in himself,* a divine attribute.[204] The remaining two references to Jesus as "the Son" come in 6:40 in conjunction with references to Jesus as the Son of Man and in 8:36 where "the Son" claims to bring true liberation from the slavery of sin.

20.5.4 The Farewell Discourse

Jesus is referred to as the Son in two passages in the Farewell Discourse. In 14:13, he promises to answer prayer offered in his name "that the Father may be glorified in the Son." Similarly, in his final prayer Jesus asks the Father to glorify his Son that his Son may glorify him (17:1). Thus the Father-Son motif in John's gospel culminates in the Son's "glorification" at the cross, which, in turn, becomes the basis for Jesus' commissioning of his followers (20:21).[205]

20.5.5 First, Second, and Third John

Like John's gospel, his letters feature eighteen references to Jesus as "the Son," all but two being found in 1 John.[206] There is little that is distinctive in John's characterization of Jesus as "the Son" in these letters. On the whole, the references continue the familiar pattern of John's depiction of the Father-Son relationship between Jesus and God the Father. For this reason it will not be necessary to provide a detailed discussion of each of these references here.

20.6 Summary

Apart from the fourth evangelist (1:14, 18; 3:16–18), Jesus' first followers (1:45, 49), and John the Baptist (3:35–36), it is primarily Jesus who speaks of himself as "the Son," variously referring to himself as "the Son," "the Son of Man," or even "the Son of God" (though not as *monogenēs*). The focal point of "Son" language in John's gospel is Jesus' defense against the charge of blasphemy in 5:19–26, which features a total of ten instances of "Son" language.

The study of the characterization of God (*theos*), the Father (*patēr*), and the Son (*huios*) in the previous three sections has shown that the Word made flesh in the Son and God the Father are both equally God; thus Jesus can say, "I and the Father are one" (10:30). At the same time, Jesus, while himself God, sustains a relationship

---

203. See Gen 2:7; Job 10:12; 33:4; Ps 36:9.
204. The verse relates to the "eternal generation of the Son" (Carson, *Gospel according to John*, 257).
205. See the discussion of John's trinitarian mission theology in chap. 15 below.
206. See 1 John 1:3, 7; 2:22, 23, 24; 3:23; 4:9, 10, 14; 5:9, 10, 11, 12, 20; 2 John 3, 9.

with God (Yahweh) that can be described as that of a Son (who is "sent") to a Father ("the one who sent").

21 THE SPIRIT

21.1 Introduction

Anyone seeking to explore the role of the Spirit in John's gospel is initially struck with the way in which the Son-Father relationship between the Word made flesh and God the Father completely predominates in the first half of John's gospel. This is not to say that the Spirit is completely absent; yet it is not until the second half of the gospel, with the Son's departure to the Father being imminent, that the Spirit moves into the foreground.

There is no reference to the Spirit in John's introduction, and Act I of the Johannine drama features a mere four passages in which reference to the Spirit is made, all of which relate to his role in Jesus' ministry. The Spirit rests on Jesus (John 1:32–33), and does so to an unlimited degree (3:34). Jesus' words give life and are spirit (6:63; *contra* the TNIV's "full of the Spirit"), and the Spirit will be given only subsequent to Jesus' glorification (7:39).

References to the Spirit in the second half of the gospel increase dramatically in both number and prominence in keeping with the Spirit's pivotal role in the disciples' mission subsequent to Jesus' departure and return to God the Father. The three names for the Spirit are "the Spirit of truth" (14:17; 15:26; 16:13); "the Holy Spirit" (14:26; 20:22; cf. 1:33); and *paraklētos* or "helping presence" (cf. 14:16, 26; 15:26; 16:7).

21.2 The Book of Signs

21.2.1 John's and Jesus' Early Ministry

The initial references to the Spirit are in connection with Jesus' baptism by John the Baptist (John 1:32–33). The Baptist testifies that he saw the Spirit descend from heaven as a dove and remain on Jesus. He had been told by God that the person so designated would be the one who would baptize, not with water as John did, but with the Holy Spirit (1:33).[207] Thus the Spirit's first appearance in the gospel serves to confirm Jesus as the God-sent future dispenser of the Spirit.

21.2.2 The Cana Cycle

The next possible cluster of references is found in Jesus' interchange with Nicodemus. Jesus' reference to being "born again" (3:3) is explicated as "born of water and spirit" (3:5),[208] most likely conveying the notion of spiritual birth effecting cleansing

---

207. Cf. Matt 3:11; Mark 1:8; Luke 3:16; Acts 1:5; see also John 14:26; 20:22.

208. My translation. This rendering is preferable to the TNIV's "born of water and the Spirit."

and renewal. Most likely, however, the reference is not to the Holy Spirit but to the spiritual nature of the birth required for entering God's kingdom.[209] The same is true for the analogy between wind and spirit (3:8).

Thus having ruled out 3:5–8 as containing likely references to the Spirit, the next mention of the Spirit after 1:32–33 is found in 3:34. In a section explicating the significance of the Baptist's testimony for John's readers, the evangelist comments that "he" (most likely God; made explicit by the TNIV)[210] gives the Spirit without measure (i.e., to an unlimited extent; cf. 1:33).

As in 3:5–8, the instances of *pneuma* in 4:23–24 do not have the Spirit as their referent.[211] Instead, the emphasis is on the kind of worship to be rendered by those who would please God, worship that is spiritual rather than focused on physical location of worship. A reference to the Spirit would have hardly been intelligible to the Samaritan woman. What is more, the reference to God as *pneuma*, "spirit," in 4:24 is almost certainly not a reference to the Holy Spirit.

21.2.3 The Festival Cycle

The first of several instances where Jesus refers to the Spirit in this gospel is found in the context of Jesus' instruction of the Twelve subsequent to a mass defection by Jesus' other followers (6:63). Jesus affirms that the Spirit gives life and that Jesus' words are spirit and life. The latter reference should probably be taken to mean that Jesus' words are life-giving because they are infused by the Spirit, who rests on Jesus (1:33) to an unlimited degree (3:34).

The next reference to the Spirit is part of an aside by the evangelist who explains a given utterance of Jesus with reference to the Spirit (7:39). The context is Jesus' invitation, uttered on the final day of the Festival of Tabernacles, for people to come to him and drink (7:37).[212] The festival was celebrated in hopes of Israel's joyful restoration and the ingathering of the nations. Jesus here presents himself as God's agent in bringing about these end-time events.

The Scripture adduced in Jesus' saying, "Whoever believes in me, as Scripture has said, rivers of living water will flow from within them" (John 7:38), is likely common prophetic teaching.[213] "From within them" probably refers to believers in Jesus rather than to Jesus himself, with the first clause, "Whoever believes in me," serving as a pendent subject.[214] The evangelist adds that Jesus' reference is to the future giving of the Spirit (7:39; cf. 1:33).[215]

---

209. See the following verse: "That which is born of flesh is flesh, and that which is born of spirit is spirit" (3:6; my translation).

210. Köstenberger, *John*, 155–58.

211. Note the similarity between the references to "spirit and truth" in 4:23 and to "water and spirit" in 3:5.

212. This passage harks back to Jesus' interchange with the Samaritan woman in 4:7–15.

213. Suggestions of specific passages include Ps 77:16, 20 LXX (with the epithet "living" coming from Zech 14:8) or Isa 58:11 (cf. Prov 4:23; 5:15). See Carson, *Gospel according to John*, 325–28.

214. So a majority of commentators, including Ridderbos, *Gospel of John*, 273; Carson, *Gospel according to John*, 323–25; and others. Less likely, Jesus is presented as the source of "streams of living water." Other examples of pendent subjects in this gospel include 1:12; 6:39; 15:2; and 17:2. See the discussion and references in Köstenberger, *John*, 240–41, esp. n. 59.

215. This reflects hindsight and represents an effort by the evangelist to preserve the historical perspective prior to Jesus' "glorification," a Johannine euphemism for the cluster of events centering in the crucifixion. See Carson, "Understanding Misunderstandings"; and

21.3 The Book of Exaltation

The Spirit rises to considerable prominence in the Farewell Discourse, whose major thrust is the preparation of Jesus' followers for the time subsequent to his departure. Once Jesus has been exalted, the Spirit will play a pivotal role in the mission of his followers. This is evident by the multiple references to the Spirit as "Spirit of truth,"[216] as the "Holy Spirit,"[217] and as the *paraklētos* or "helping presence."[218]

Passage in John	Content
1:32–33	The Spirit descends on Jesus; Jesus will baptize with the Spirit.
3:34	God gives the Spirit without measure.
6:63	The Spirit gives life.
7:39	The Spirit will be given subsequent to Jesus' glorification.
14:17; 15:26; 16:13	The "Spirit of truth"
14:26; 20:22	The "Holy Spirit"
14:16, 26; 15:26; 16:7	The "other helping presence"

Fig. 21.1: References to the Spirit in John's Gospel

21.3.1 The Farewell Discourse

References to the Spirit are plentiful in John 14:15–24, where Jesus envisions the giving of the Spirit subsequent to his exaltation.[219] Jesus' identification with the Spirit, the "other *paraklētos*," is so strong that Jesus can say that he *himself* will return to his followers in the person of the Spirit (14:18).[220] While "yet a little while" (my translation) in 14:19 and "on that day" in 14:20 may at first appear to refer to Jesus' resurrection appearances, his promise not to leave his followers as orphans (14:18) is hardly satisfied by these appearances, which were temporary in nature. More likely, the reference is to the coming of the Spirit.[221]

Contrary to the disciples' sentiments at the time, Jesus' departure will be beneficial for them in several ways. Most importantly, Jesus will petition the Father to send "another helping presence" like Jesus. As the evangelist has made clear earlier in the gospel, this giving of the Spirit will be possible only subsequent to Jesus' glorification (7:39). With this glorification now imminent (cf. 12:23; 13:1), Jesus spends his final hours before the crucifixion preparing his followers for life in the age of the Spirit.

Lemcio, *Past of Jesus*. Since the reference in 11:33 is to *Jesus'* spirit (as also in 13:21 and 19:30), not the Holy Spirit, this concludes the fairly sparse list of references to the Spirit in the first half of the gospel.

216. John 14:17; 15:26; and 16:13. The phrase "of truth" most likely is an objective genitive, conveying the sense of the Spirit *conveying* truth.

217. John 14:26 and 20:22 (cf. 1:33).

218. John 14:16, 26; 15:26; and 16:7.

219. The remainder of this section on the Spirit closely follows pp. 96–103 in chap. 5 of my book *Father, Son and Spirit* and is used by permission.

220. For this interpretation and a discussion of the issues involved see Köstenberger, *John*, 439; and the discussion further below.

221. This is suggested also by Jesus' response to Judas's (not Iscariot's) question in 14:22 with reference to Jesus and the Father making their dwelling in believers.

In the first half of the gospel, the fourth evangelist's treatment of the Spirit largely resembled that of the Synoptics. Like them, he featured John the Baptist's reference to Jesus as the one who would baptize with the Holy Spirit (John 1:32–33; cf. Matt 3:11 par.) and stressed that the Spirit in all his fullness rested on Jesus during his earthly ministry (John 1:32; 3:34; cf. Luke 4:18). He also noted the Spirit's role in the giving of life (John 6:63). But as in his portrayal of Jesus' followers,[222] the adoption of a postexaltation vantage point leads to a vastly enhanced portrait of the Spirit in the Farewell Discourse, where the Spirit is featured primarily as "the *paraklētos*" and "the Spirit of truth," two closely related terms.[223]

Unsatisfactory approaches to resolving the meaning of the term *paraklētos* in John's gospel are legion.[224] The expression does not occur in the LXX[225] and elsewhere in the NT only in 1 John 2:1, there with reference to Jesus as our "advocate" with God the Father.[226] Jesus' reference to the Spirit as "another *paraklētos*" in 14:16 indicates that the Spirit's presence with the disciples will replace Jesus' encouraging and strengthening presence with them while on earth (cf. 14:17). When the Spirit comes to indwell believers, it will be as if Jesus himself were taking up residence in

---

222. See the discussion in chap. 12, sec. 29 below.

223. See 15:26. For a treatment of the Spirit-Paraclete in the context of the references to the Spirit in the entire gospel narrative see Davies, *Rhetoric and Reference*, 139–53. For a comparison of the treatments of the Spirit in John and the Synoptics see Köstenberger, *Encountering John*, 156. On the translation of the term see Köstenberger, *John*, 436, n. 70.

224. Otto Betz, *Der Paraklet: Fürsprecher im häretischen Spätjudentum, im Johannes-Evangelium und in neu gefundenen gnostischen Schriften* (Leiden: Brill, 1963) unconvincingly argues for a Qumran background (the archangel Michael; cf. A. Shafaat, "Geber of the Qumran Scrolls and the Spirit-Paraclete of the Gospel of John," *NTS* 27 [1980–81]: 263–69, who likewise adduces DSS parallels; A. R. C. Leaney, "The Johannine Paraclete and the Qumran Scrolls," in *John and Qumran* [ed. James H. Charlesworth; London: G. Chapman, 1972], 38–61, who says the Paraclete is God himself). Hans Windisch, *The Spirit-Paraclete in the Fourth Gospel* (Philadelphia: Fortress, 1968) advances the hardly more plausible hypothesis that the Paraclete is "a kind of angel…in human form," be it a prophet or teacher. George Johnston, *The Spirit-Paraclete in the Gospel of John* (SNTSMS 12; Cambridge: Cambridge University Press, 1970) unsuccessfully proposes that the *paraklētos* is an active divine power that has become embodied in certain leaders of the apostolic church, such as John (see the critiques by Raymond E. Brown, "The Paraclete in the Fourth Gospel," *NTS* 13 [1967]: 126; idem, "The Spirit-Paraclete in the Gospel of John," *CBQ* 33 [1971]: 268–70, for whom the Paraclete is the "alter ego of Jesus" ["Paraclete," 132, cited in Stephen S. Smalley, "'The Paraclete': Pneumatology in the Johannine Gospel and Apocalypse," in *Exploring the Gospel of John*, 297]; cf. Gary M. Burge, *The Anointed Community* [Grand Rapids: Eerdmans, 1987]). Bultmann, *Gospel of John*, 566–72, views the concept as a Johannine appropriation of his gnostic source's figure of "helper." Harald Riesenfeld, "A Probable Background to the Johannine Paraclete," in *Ex Orbe Religionum. Studia Geo Widengren* (SHR 21; ed. Claas J. Bleeker et al.; Leiden: Brill, 1972), 1:266–74, postulates a sapiential provenance, which is equally unlikely. M. Eugene Boring, "The Influence of Christian Prophecy on the Johannine Portrayal of the Paraclete and Jesus," *NTS* 25 (1978): 113–23, claims the Paraclete is an angel demythologized as the "spirit of prophecy"! Antony Billington, "The Paraclete and Mission in the Fourth Gospel," in *Mission and Meaning: Essays Presented to Peter Cotterell* (ed. Antony Billington, Tony Lane, and Max Turner; Carlisle, UK: Paternoster, 1995), 90–115, appropriately stresses the Paraclete's role in mission. If the disciples are to witness to Jesus, they must understand the significance of his coming; witness to Jesus and the Paraclete's ministry are thus inseparable (John 15:26–27; 16:8–11; 20:21–23). For a helpful discussion of the Paraclete as part of the gospel's lawsuit motif, esp. in 15:26–16:15, see Lincoln, *Truth on Trial*, 110–23, esp. 113–14.

225. But see Aquila's and Theodotion's use of a related noun form in Job 16:2.

226. For a survey of all known examples from the fourth century BC to the third century AD, see Kenneth Grayston, "The Meaning of *paraklētos*," *JSNT* 13 (1981): 67–82, who concludes that *paraklētos* was a more general term that was sometimes (but not always) used in legal contexts, meaning supporter or sponsor. The closest contemporaneous usage is found in Philo, who uses the expression to convey the notion of rendering of general help, be it by giving advice or support (with the latter meaning being the more common). In later rabbinic usage the term in its transliterated form is used alongside the transliterated term for a Greek expression meaning "advocate" (*synēgoros*). Patristic references include *Did.* 5:2; *2 Clem.* 6:9; and Clement of Alexandria, *The Rich Man's Salvation* 25:7. For a study of the Johannine Paraclete in the church fathers, see Anthony Casurella, *The Johannine Paraclete in the Church Fathers: A Study in the History of Exegesis* (Tübingen: Mohr-Siebeck, 1983).

them.²²⁷ Thus Jesus can refer to the Spirit's coming by saying, "*I* will come to you" (14:18, emphasis added).²²⁸

This realization relieves a primary concern for Jesus' first followers in the original setting of the Farewell Discourse: Jesus' departure will not leave them as orphans (cf. 14:18); just as God was present with them through Jesus, he will continue to be with them through his Spirit.²²⁹ The Spirit thus ensures continuity between Jesus' pre- and post-glorification ministry. What is more, the Spirit's coming will actually constitute an advance in God's work with and through the disciples (16:7; cf. 14:12).

The initial reference to the Spirit as *paraklētos* in 14:17 is the first of five Paraclete sayings in the Farewell Discourse, in each case with reference to the Holy Spirit (cf. 14:26; 15:26; 16:7–11, 12–15).²³⁰ As Jesus' emissary, the Spirit will have a variety of functions in believers' lives: (1) he will bring to remembrance all that Jesus taught his disciples (14:26); (2) he will testify regarding Jesus together with his followers (15:26); (3) he will convict the world of sin, (un)righteousness, and judgment (16:8–11); and (4) he will guide Jesus' disciples in all truth and disclose what is to come (16:13). Historically, this included the formation of the NT canon as apostolic testimony to Jesus.

While initially focused on the eleven (cf. John 15:26), the Spirit, in a secondary sense, fulfills similar roles in believers today. He illumines the spiritual meaning of Jesus' words and works both to believers and, through believers, also to the unbelieving world. In all of these functions, the ministry of the Spirit remains closely linked with the person of Jesus. Just as Jesus is everywhere in John's gospel portrayed as the Sent One who is fully dependent on and obedient to the Father, the Spirit is said to be "sent" by both the Father and Jesus (14:26; 15:26) and to focus his teaching on the illumination of the spiritual significance of God's work in Jesus (14:26; 15:26; 16:9).

The Spirit is also called "the Spirit of truth" (cf. 15:26; 16:13). In the context of the present chapter, Jesus has just been characterized as "the truth" (14:6) in keeping with statements already made in the introduction (1:14, 17). The concept of truth in John's gospel encompasses several aspects:

(1) truthfulness as opposed to falsehood: "to speak the truth" means to make a true rather than false statement, that is, to represent the facts as they actually are (cf. 8:40, 45, 46; 16:7; "to witness to the truth": 5:33; 18:37)

---

227. "The Spirit is the divine presence when Jesus' physical presence is taken away from his followers" (Morris, *Jesus is the Christ*, 159).

228. Though, as Moloney, *Gospel of John*, 407, points out, there are differences between Jesus and the Spirit as well: the latter neither becomes flesh nor dies for our sins. Alternatively, the statement refers to Jesus' postresurrection appearances to his followers (so Ridderbos, *Gospel of John*, 505; Carson, *Gospel according to John*, 501; Morris, *Gospel according to John*, 578–79; Beasley-Murray, *John*, 258; Gerald L. Borchert, *John 12–21* [NAC 25B; Nashville: Broadman & Holman, 2002], 126). Barrett, *Gospel according to St. John*, 464, says the passage refers neither to Jesus' coming in the person of the Holy Spirit nor the *parousia*; rather, Jesus is using language appropriate to both the resurrection and *parousia* to refer to both.

229. As Brown, *Gospel according to John XIII–XXI*, 642, points out, the promise of the divine presence with Jesus' followers in John 14:15–24 includes the Spirit (14:15–17), Jesus (14:18–21), and the Father (14:22–24), hence involving all three persons of the Godhead in the indwelling of believers.

230. In 1 John, the term refers to the exalted Jesus (1 John 2:1). In secular Greek, *paraklētos* refers primarily to a "legal assistant" or "advocate" (though the word never became a technical term such as its Lat. equivalent *advocatus*). In John's gospel, legal overtones are most pronounced in 16:7–11.

(2) truth in its finality as compared to previous, preliminary expressions: this is its *eschatological* dimension (cf. esp. 1:17: "the law was given through Moses; grace and truth came through Jesus Christ")

(3) truth is an identifiable body of knowledge with actual propositional content (e.g., 8:32: "you will know the truth"; 16:13: "he will guide you into all truth")

(4) truth as a sphere of operation, such as in sanctification (17:17, 19)

(5) truth as relational fidelity (1:17; 14:6)[231]

The Spirit is involved in all five aspects: he accurately represents the truth regarding Jesus; he is the eschatological gift of God; he imparts true knowledge of God; he is operative in both worship and sanctification; and he points people to the person of Jesus.

The expression "spirit of truth" was current in Judaism (e.g., *T. Jud.* 20:1–5). Similarly, Qumran literature affirms that God placed within man "two spirits so that he would walk with them until the moment of his visitation; they are the spirits of truth and of deceit" (1QS 3:18; cf. 4:23–26). Yet these parallels are in all likelihood merely those of language, not of thought.[232] For while these expressions are part of an ethical dualism in Second Temple literature (including Qumran), John's gospel does not feature a "spirit of error" corresponding to the Spirit of truth.[233] Rather, the Spirit of truth is the "other helping presence" who takes the place of Jesus while he was on earth with his disciples. This "other helping presence," the "Spirit of truth," the world cannot accept,[234] because it neither sees nor knows him. Yet Jesus' followers do, because "he resides with you and will be in you" (see 1 John 3:24; 4:13).[235]

On the other side, John acknowledges the presence of "the devil" (13:2), "Satan" (13:27), the "prince of this world" (12:31), or the "evil one" (17:15), though references to demon exorcism are notably absent in John.[236] This suggests that, in John, Satan is pitted against Jesus and the Spirit whom he would send subsequent to his departure, but not in the sense of two equally matched dualities of good and evil, but in the sense that Satan opposes the triune God's salvation-historical purposes centered in Jesus' God-glorifying cross-death, his "lifting up." This, we submit, is

---

231. For the first four categories see Scott R. Swain, "Truth in the Gospel of John" (Th.M. thesis; Wake Forest, NC: Southeastern Baptist Theological Seminary, 1998). For a recent treatment of Pilate's question, "What is truth?" in John 18:38, in its Johannine context, see Köstenberger, "What Is Truth?" On the larger issue of truth in theological, philosophical, and hermeneutical perspective, see the essays in the same volume by R. Albert Mohler, J. P. Moreland, and Kevin J. Vanhoozer (in *Whatever Happened to Truth?*).

232. See James H. Charlesworth, "A Critical Comparison of the Dualism in 1QS iii,13–iv,26 and the 'Dualism' Contained in the Fourth Gospel," *NTS* 15 (1969): 389–418.

233. But see 1 John 4:6, where "the Spirit [or spirit] of truth and the spirit of falsehood" occur together. For a comparative study of truth terminology in the Community Rule (1QS) and John's gospel, see Mburu, "Truth Terminology in the Gospel of John."

234. See at John 1:10; cf. 10:26; 12:39; see also 1 Cor 2:14.

235. D. Moody Smith, *John* (ANTC; Nashville: Abingdon, 1999), 274–75, notes that "you" here is plural, which leads him to infer that the statement does not necessarily refer to personal indwelling. In principle, this is true. The Spirit indwells the community of Jesus Christ *as* a community (cf. 1 Cor 3:16). But the statement certainly does not rule out the Spirit's indwelling of individual believers (note, e.g., the singular pronoun *kakeinos* in John 14:12, and compare the Pauline teaching on the Spirit's indwelling of individual believers in 1 Cor 6:19).

236. This pattern continues in 1 John; see esp. 3:7–15, and here esp. vv. 8–10.

quite different from the Qumran theology of the two spirits, the spirit of truth and the spirit of falsehood.[237]

21.3.2 The Commissioning Scene

The final reference to the Spirit is found in the context of Jesus' commissioning statement, "As the Father has sent me, I am sending you" (20:21),[238] which climaxes the characterization of Jesus as the sent Son.[239] The disciples are drawn into the unity and mission of Father and Son.[240] Succession is important both in the OT and in Second Temple literature. In the present gospel, Jesus succeeds the Baptist and is followed by both the Spirit and the Twelve (minus Judas), who serve as representatives of the new messianic community. OT narratives involving succession feature Joshua (following Moses) and Elisha (succeeding Elijah).

The reference to Jesus' breathing on his disciples while saying, "Receive the Holy Spirit,"[241] probably represents a symbolic promise of the soon-to-be-given gift of the Spirit, not the actual giving of it fifty days later at Pentecost.[242] Against many commentators, the present pericope does not constitute the Johannine equivalent to Pentecost,[243] nor is the proposal satisfactory that at John 20:22 the disciples "were only sprinkled with His grace and not [as at Pentecost] saturated with full power."[244] The present event does not mark the actual fulfillment of these promises other than by way of anticipatory sign.[245]

On any other view of the present passage, it is hard to see how John would not be found to stand in actual conflict with Luke's Pentecost narrative in Acts 2, not

---

237. See the discussion in Charlesworth, "Shared Symbolism," 132, and especially 136–37, where the author strenuously seeks to maintain John's direct dependence on Qumran pneumatology, against Bauckham, "Qumran Community and the Gospel of John," whose caution is in our view well taken, however.

238. Cf. Matt 28:18–20; Luke 24:46–49. The statement harks back to John 17:18, albeit without reference to the sphere of the disciples' commission (i.e., the world), indicating the emphasis in the present passage is on the disciples' authorization rather on the realm of their activity (Ridderbos, *Gospel of John*, 643). Compare also the general statement in 13:20, which suggests that the present passage extends beyond the original disciples also to later generations of believers (Morris, *Gospel according to John*, 746, n. 55 et al.).

239. Köstenberger, *Missions of Jesus and the Disciples*, esp. 96–121, 180–98. The vast majority of the instances of "sending" in John's gospel relate to Jesus' having been sent by the Father. "Sending" terminology also occurs with regard to God's sending of the Baptist, the Father's and the Son's sending of the Spirit, and Jesus' sending of his disciples. The present passage features two sending verbs, *pempō* and *apostellō*, with no apparent difference in meaning (as is the virtual consensus among major commentators, including Ridderbos, Morris, Carson, Barrett, Schnackenburg, and Raymond Brown); see also Köstenberger, "Two Johannine Verbs for Sending." Morris, *Gospel according to John*, 746, n. 56, notes that this is already suggested by the use of *kathōs* linking the two verbs.

240. Cf. John 17:21–26; Ridderbos, *Gospel of John*, 642.

241. The absence of the article in the expression "Holy Spirit"

may indicate a focus on "the quality of the gift of the Holy Spirit rather than on the individuality of the Spirit" (Morris, *Gospel according to John*, 747, n. 59).

242. See Acts 2; Carson, *Gospel according to John*, 649–55; cf. Witherington, *John's Wisdom*, 340–41. The critique by Thomas R. Hatina, "John 20,22 in Its Eschatological Context: Promise or Fulfillment?" *Bib* 74 (1993): 196–219, who says the reference is to the indwelling Paraclete, fails to convince.

243. So Brown, *Gospel according to John XIII–XXI*, 1038; Barrett, *Gospel according to St. John*, 570, who says the present passage cannot be harmonized with Acts 2; Bultmann, *Gospel of John*, 691; et al.

244. So John Calvin, *The Gospel according to St. John* (trans. T. H. L. Parker; Edinburgh: Oliver & Boyd, 1959), 1:205. Beasley-Murray, *John*, 382, followed by Borchert, *John 12–21*, 307–8, believes John telescoped the giving of the Spirit without concern for chronology (citing the reference to the ascension in 20:17 as a parallel). Max Turner, "The Concept of Receiving the Spirit in John's Gospel," *VE* 19 (1977): 24–42, thinks the reference is not to the Spirit at all, but to Jesus' message as Spirit and life. Schnackenburg, *Gospel according to St. John*, 3.325, surprisingly contends that the Johannine instance involves all believers while the events in Acts 2 pertain to the apostles. If anything, one might have expected the opposite kind of reasoning, with John's account anticipating the general outpouring narrated in Acts 2.

245. Contra, Gary M. Burge, *John* (NIVAC; Grand Rapids: Zondervan, 2002), 558; cf. idem, *Anointed Community*, 148–49.

to mention his own disclaimers earlier in the narrative that the Spirit would only be given subsequent to Jesus' glorification, which entailed his return to the Father.[246] The disciples' behavior subsequent to the present incident would also be rather puzzling had they already received the Spirit.[247] The present gesture is made to the group in its entirety rather than to the separate individuals constituting it, just as the authority to forgive or retain sins is given to the church as a whole.[248]

The Greek verb *enephysēsen* means "breathed *on*" (TNIV) rather than "breathed *into*." The theological antecedent is plainly Gen 2:7, where the exact same form is used in the LXX.[249] There God breathes his Spirit into Adam at creation, which constitutes him as a "living being." Here, at the occasion of the commissioning of his disciples, Jesus constitutes them as the new messianic community, in anticipation of the outpouring of the Spirit subsequent to his ascension.[250] Hence the circle closes, from creation in John 1:1 to new creation in 20:22.[251]

21.4 First John

Beyond the gospel, 1 John makes a significant contribution to Johannine pneumatology. One important aspect is John's use of "anointing" language. Immediately following the reference to the departure of the schismatics in 1 John 2:19, John writes, "But you have an anointing from the Holy One, and all of you know the truth" (2:20). Together with the reference to the Father and the Son in 2:22, this passage contains clear trinitarian teaching, with the three persons of the Godhead working in tandem, the Spirit teaching believers about the Father's having sent the Son. This impression is reinforced by the second reference to an "anointing" in 2:27: "As for you, the anointing you received from him remains in you, and you do not need anyone to teach you. But as his anointing teaches you about all things and as that anointing is real, not counterfeit—just as it has taught you, remain in him."

These are the only instances of the rare term "anointing" (*chrisma*) in the entire NT, though the verb "to anoint" (*chriō*) occurs in a handful of significant NT passages. In Luke 4:18, Jesus, quoting Isa 61:1, says of himself, "The Spirit of the Lord is on me, because he has anointed me...." In Acts 4:27, the believers in the early church, in prayer, speak of the conspiracy against "your holy servant Jesus, whom

---

246. E.g., 7:39; 14:12, 16–18, 25–26; 16:12–15; cf. 20:17. Luke's account of Pentecost hardly reads as if Acts 2 represents merely "one of several additional empowerings of the Spirit" as Hatina, "John 20,22," 201, alleges. Talbert, *Reading John*, 252, concludes from 20:22 that Jesus must have ascended by then or, according to 7:39, he could not yet have given the Spirit. But this presupposes that the Spirit was in fact imparted at 20:22. If not, there is no need to suppose that Jesus had already ascended.

247. In 20:26, the doors are still locked (as prior to 20:22 in 20:19), presumably still "for fear of the Jewish leaders"; in 21:3, Peter decides to go fishing and is joined by six others, but they catch nothing. The argument by Hatina, "John 20,22," 200, that the latter may have been "an atypical circumstance," fails to convince, as does his claim that Peter's threefold confession of love suggests reception of the Spirit (cf. Peter's earlier offer in 13:37 to lay down his life for Jesus).

248. Morris, *Gospel according to John*, 747, 749.

249. See also 1 Kgs 17:21; Ezek 37:9; Wis 15:11; cf. Philo, *Op.* 135.

250. This "new creation" theme is noted by several commentators, including Morris, *Gospel according to John*, 747, n. 58 (who also cites Ezek 37:9); Barrett, *Gospel according to St. John*, 570; Brown, *Gospel according to John XIII–XXI*, 1035, 1037; and Witherington, *John's Wisdom*, 342; see also the discussion in chap. 8, esp. sec. 16.5) Rodney A. Whitacre, *John* (IVPNTC 4; Downers Grove, IL: InterVarsity Press, 1999), 482, speaks of the present event as the church's "conception," and of Pentecost as its "birth." See also Wright, *New Testament and the People of God*, 416–17 (though I do not agree with all of Wright's conclusions there, such as some of the wisdom parallels he adduces).

251. See chap. 8 above.

you anointed." And in Acts 10:38, Peter mentions "how God anointed Jesus of Nazareth with the Holy Spirit and power, and how he went around doing good and healing all who were under the power of the devil, because God was with him." In 2 Cor 1:21–22, Paul writes, "He [God] anointed us, set his seal of ownership on us, and put his Spirit in our hearts as a deposit, guaranteeing what is to come." The final NT reference is found in Heb 1:9, a citation of Ps 45:6–7.

What becomes clear, then, is that the anointing of Jesus with the Holy Spirit at his baptism, which marks the beginning of his messianic mission, serves as the paradigm for believers' reception (or "anointing with") the Holy Spirit at conversion. This marks them as "little anointed ones," followers of Jesus the Messiah, who, like he, have the Holy Spirit rest on them. This "anointing," in turn, provides them with accurate teaching regarding Jesus and marks them as belonging to God as a seal of his ownership of them. In this context, too, the reference to the Spirit as one of the three witnesses to Jesus together with water and blood (1 John 5:6–7) is fitting, especially if, as argued, "water" refers to Jesus' baptism. There may also be a connection between true believers affirming that Jesus is the Messiah (*Christos*) and themselves receiving an anointing (*chrisma*), while those who reject Jesus' messianic claim are instead infused by the "spirit of the antichrist" (*antichristos*; 2:18, 22; 4:3).

Another interesting contribution of John's first letter to Johannine pneumatology is the explicit contrast between the "spirit of truth" and the "spirit of falsehood" in 1 John 4:6, a contrast also found in the DSS (1QS 3:18; cf. 1QS 4:23–26; see also 1 John 1:8).[252] The treatment in 4:1–6 is also significant in its teaching that the spirits must be tested to determine whether or not they are "of God."[253] The cardinal test, as in the gospel, is whether such spirits confess Jesus as Messiah (4:2–3).[254] The lack of proper christological confession divides between truth and error, as the then-recent departure of the schismatics had made clear (2:19).

Also significant is John's teaching regarding the Spirit's external witness through water and the blood (i.e., Jesus' baptism and crucifixion, marking the beginning and end points of his ministry) in 1 John 5:6–8, and regarding the Spirit's internal witness in 5:10. The latter aspect of the Spirit's testimony is predicated upon his external witness as it is confirmed in the believer's heart (*en heautō*, "within himself"; cf. Rom 8:16; 9:1).[255] Those who believe that Jesus is the Christ and Son of God

---

252. The TNIV (as well as the NLT and the ESV) here capitalizes "Spirit" and reads, "the Spirit of truth, and the spirit of falsehood," though it is probably best here to understand the reference as generic and read "spirit of truth" (so, e.g., the NASB, KJV, NKJV, NRSV; see also text note in TNIV). See the discussion in Yarbrough, *1–3 John*, 229.

253. The rendering "of God" (*ek theou*) is preferable to the TNIV's "from God," because the latter could convey a more direct descent from God and in Johannine terminology "from God" corresponds to *apo theou* (see Yarbrough, *1–3 John*, 221, n. 4).

254. See Streett, "They Went Out from Us," who contends, contra the conventional consensus (represented, e.g., by Yarbrough, *1–3 John*, 223–24, who speaks of a reference to "Jesus' full human-ity as well as his full divinity," p. 223), that the reference in 1 John 4:2 ("that Jesus Christ has come in the flesh") is a simple shorthand for acknowledging Jesus' messiahship (see the parallel in 1 John 4:3: "does not acknowledge Jesus"; the same expression is found at 2 John 7).

255. The internal witness of the Holy Spirit is recognized by translations such as the NIV and NRSV (cf. RSV, ESV, HCSB) but not supported in the TNIV, NLT, and CEV. See also Marshall, *Epistles*, 241; Schnackenburg, *Johannine Epistles*, 239–40; and Kruse, *Letters of John*, 181. But see the discussion in Yarbrough, *1–3 John*, 287, who writes, "It is hard to see how better to render ἐν ἑαυτῷ, which seems largely otiose, and it is hard to explain why John wrote it at all."

receive God's "anointing" (1 John 2:20, 27), are cleansed from sin (1:7, 9), and have the Holy Spirit indwell and teach them all things regarding Christ (John 14:17–18; 16:13–15; 1 John 4:15).

21.5 Summary

In the few references to the Spirit in the first half of John's gospel, Jesus is associated with the Spirit in his present ministry and as the future dispenser of the Spirit subsequent to his exaltation to the Father. References to the Spirit increase dramatically in the second half of the gospel, which is taken up with the anticipation of the disciples' mission subsequent to Jesus' crucifixion, resurrection, and ascension (his "glorification").

It is that Spirit—the "Spirit of truth," the "Holy Spirit," the "helping presence" sent by Jesus from the Father—who will continue Jesus' ministry and empower the disciples' mission in the unbelieving world. As in the case of the Father-Son relationship, the references to the Spirit in John's gospel culminate in the commissioning passage in John 20:21–22, a (proleptic) reference to the disciples' reception of the Spirit for the purpose of their mission of extending forgiveness of sins upon people's belief in Jesus.

John's first letter adds to Johannine pneumatology references to the "anointing" of believers with the Holy Spirit; enjoins Christ's followers to test the spirits to see whether or not they are of God; and distinguishes between the Spirit's external and internal witness, that is, between his public and private testimony regarding Christ in the messianic mission of Jesus and the believer's heart, respectively.

In this, John's first letter further develops the teaching on the Spirit in the gospel by showing various communal applications, especially in conjunction with the departure of the schismatics. Thus while in John's gospel the primary thrust of the Holy Spirit is related to mission, that is, believers' Spirit-aided witness to the world (e.g., John 15:26–27; 16:8–11; 20:21–23), in 1 John the primary application is to the testing of spirits in conjunction with the separation of those who failed to confess Jesus as Messiah from the community.[256]

---

256. See Andreas J. Köstenberger, "The Contribution of the General Epistles and Revelation to a Biblical Theology of Religions," in *Christianity and the Religions: A Biblical Theology of World Religions* (ed. Edward Rommen and Harold Netland; EMS Series 2; Pasadena, CA: William Carey Library, 1995), 124–27.

Chapter 10

Salvation History: Jesus' Fulfillment of Festal Symbolism

Bibliography

Coloe, Mary L. *God Dwells with Us: Temple Symbolism in the Fourth Gospel*. Collegeville, MN: Liturgical Press, 2001. **Davies, W. D**. *The Gospel and the Land: Early Christianity and Jewish Territorial Doctrine*. Sheffield: JSOT, 1994. **Ego, Beate, Armin Lange, and Peter Pilhofer**, eds. *Gemeinde ohne Tempel: Zur Substituierung und Transformation des Jerusalemer Tempels und seines Kults im Alten Testament, antiken Judentum und frühen Christentum*. WUNT 118. Tübingen: Mohr-Siebeck, 1999. **Hahn, Johannes**, ed. *Zerstörungen des Jerusalemer Tempels. Geschehen–Wahrnehmung–Bewältigung*. WUNT 147. Tübingen: Mohr-Siebeck, 2002. **Hoskins, Paul M**. *Jesus as the Fulfillment of the Temple in the Gospel of John*. Paternoster Biblical Monographs. Carlisle, UK: Paternoster, 2007. **Kerr, Alan R**. *The Temple of Jesus' Body: The Temple Theme in the Gospel of John*. JSNTSup 220. Sheffield: Sheffield Academic Press, 2002. **Porter, Stanley E**. "Can Traditional Exegesis Enlighten Literary Analysis of the Fourth Gospel? An Examination of the Old Testament Fulfilment Motif and the Passover Theme." Pp. 396–428 in *The Gospels and the Scriptures of Israel*. Ed. Craig A. Evans and William R. Stegner. JSNTSup 104. Sheffield: Sheffield Academic Press, 1994. **Pryor, John W**. *John: Evangelist of the Covenant People*. Downers Grove, IL: InterVarsity Press, 1992. **Schlund, Christine**. "*Kein Knochen soll gebrochen warden*": *Studien zu Bedeutung und Funktion des Pesachfests in Texten des frühen Judentums und im Johannesevangelium*. WMANT 107. Neukirchen-Vluyn: Neukirchener, 2005. **Walker, Peter W**. *Jesus and the Holy City: New Testament Perspectives on Jerusalem*. Grand Rapids: Eerdmans, 1996. **Yarbrough, Robert W**. *The Salvation Historical Fallacy? Reassessing the History of New Testament Theology*. History of Biblical Interpretation Series. Leiden: Deo, 2004. **Yee, Gale A**. *Jewish Feasts and the Gospel of John*. Wilmington, DE: Michael Glazier, 1989.

22 Salvation History

22.1 Introduction

It is widely acknowledged that a salvation-historical perspective is held by Luke in his two-volume work Luke–Acts. In Johannine studies, however, the notion that the fourth evangelist embraced a salvation-historical perspective is at best a minority position. In the first three quarters of the past century, it was the hegemony of the history-of-religions school (*religionsgeschichtliche Schule*) that diminished such a notion, with John's gospel being viewed largely along Hellenistic lines, whether mystery religions or various types of Gnosticism.[1]

In the last quarter of the past century, it was the rise of the "Johannine community hypothesis" that cast the gospel largely in a sectarian mold, again minimizing the extent to which John was to be read as part of the canonical mainstream, including the Hebrew Scriptures and the other canonical gospels.[2] As will be seen below, this neglect of the salvation-historical perspective is rather surprising, because the gospel itself furnishes ample evidence for such a connection.[3] Perhaps the time has come for the tide of Johannine scholarship to turn.

According to John Pryor, John is the "Evangelist of the Covenant People." Pryor detects two primary concerns in John's gospel, one christological and the other ecclesiological: "His presentation of Christ sets him eternally in the presence of God, and is the backdrop against which the whole drama of the ensuing chapters must be understood. But the prologue also focuses the person of the Logos in relation to Israel, as one rejected by his people, but also as one who both fulfils and is superior to all that has come before in the faith of Israel."[4]

Pryor continues, "Ecclesiologically, the Johannine community is also defined. Filling the void created by Israel's rejection of the Logos, a new community of God's children is established, brought into the family of God by faith in Jesus. In their experiences of the incarnate Logos (v. 14) is fulfilled all that was foreshadowed in Israel's redemptive experience."[5] I believe that Pryor has put his finger on a crucial dimension of John's outlook that has unfortunately been neglected in recent years as a result of the ascendancy of the "Johannine community hypothesis."

Why does John start his gospel with creation? It is because creation is both a universal event and yet also the first chapter in the history of Israel. In this way, similar to Luke, John is able to root the ministry of Jesus both in world history and in the history of God's people. What is more, Israel's divine election is shown to be followed by her rejection of God's Messiah, despite the "signs," which presents the crucifixion, redemption, and resurrection as planks in the divine salvation-historical program with universal ramifications.

Along these lines, John connects Jesus' coming with every major aspect of Israel's history: creation, the exodus, the giving of the law, the manifestation of God's presence in the tabernacle and the temple, Davidic typology, and the exile. This salvation-historical pattern is seen in the introduction to the gospel. It is evident also in the two-part structure that focuses in Part 1 on the Messiah's "signs" for Israel (God's chosen people) and in Part 2 on Jesus' preparation of the new messianic community (now "his own") for their mission to the world.

---

1. To this day, there are many skeptics who disparage a salvation-historical perspective as an imposition onto the biblical data. For a judicious assessment, see Robert W. Yarbrough, *The Salvation Historical Fallacy? Reassessing the History of New Testament Theology* (History of Biblical Interpretation Series; Leiden: Deo, 2004).

2. See the critique in chap. 1, sec. 2.1.2.1 above.

3. For a thorough treatment of the use of the OT in John's gospel see Köstenberger, "John," in *Commentary on the NT Use of the OT*. See also Schlatter, *Evangelist Johannes*.

4. Pryor, *John: Evangelist of the Covenant People*, 115.

5. Ibid.

Salvation History: Jesus' Fulfillment of Festal Symbolism

The major themes associated with salvation history in John's gospel are diagrammed below. Note how John found in creation, the exodus, the exile, and various Jewish festivals and institutions the quarry from which he developed his theological presentation of Jesus. With regard to his twin themes of revelation and redemption in Jesus, for example, John's theology harks back to the "signs" (revelation) and the Passover (redemption). Particularly pronounced is John's indebtedness to Genesis, Exodus, Isaiah, Ezekiel, and Daniel.[6]

Creation	New Creation
Original creation	New birth
Sabbath	Jesus Lord over the Sabbath
Exodus	New Exodus
"The signs"	Jesus' messianic signs (calling for faith)
Passover	Jesus the Passover (redemption)
The law	Jesus the Word of God (revelation)
Jewish Festivals and Institutions	Fulfillment and Replacement
Tabernacles	Jesus the light of the world
The temple	Jesus the new temple
Exile	Restoration
Faithless shepherds	Jesus the good shepherd
A fruitless vineyard	Jesus the true vine
Jewish obduracy	Jesus the Suffering Servant
Need for redemption	Jesus the Son of Man

Fig. 22.1: Jesus and Salvation History in John's Gospel

22.2 Creation as the Beginning of the Covenant

The gospel's opening words, "In the beginning was the Word" (John 1:1), echo the opening phrase of the Hebrew Bible, "In the beginning God created the heavens and the earth" (Gen 1:1), and, in an effect similar to Luke's use of septuagintal language in the first two chapters of his gospel, establish a canonical link between the first words of the OT Scriptures and John's gospel.[7] Yet instead of "In the beginning God created," John has "In the beginning [i.e., prior to creation] was the Word." This locates Jesus' existence in eternity past with God and sets the stage for John's lofty Christology, which is unmatched by any of the other canonical gospels.

---

6. See Table 4.4 in Köstenberger, *Encountering John*, 52. See also idem, "Jesus the Good Shepherd."

7. Some of the remainder of sec. 22 and sec. 23 adapt and incorporate various smaller portions of material from my writings *John* and "John," in *Commentary on the NT Use of the OT*.

In this regard, it is also significant that John does not use the term "wisdom" as it appears in passages such as Proverbs 8 and in Second Temple literature but instead draws directly on creation terminology. This seems to suggest that it was John's purpose to convey a greater sense of directness of access and intimacy of relationship between the Word and God than is intimated by "wisdom" terminology and conceptuality. In this way John cuts through centuries of "wisdom" speculation and harks back directly to the beginning of God's relationship with the world he has made.

In the following verses of the introduction to the gospel, the evangelist, after explicitly referring to the Word's instrumentality in creation (1:3), continues to draw on Genesis motifs, particularly the contrast between light and darkness (1:4–5, 7–9; cf. Gen 1:3–5, 14–18) and the notion of life (John 1:4; cf. Gen 1:20–31; 2:7; 3:20). Significantly, "light" symbolism is also found in later OT prophetic, including messianic, passages.[8] John's choice to open his gospel with a reference to creation provides a dual perspective on Jesus' coming from the vantage points of both the world and Israel.[9]

22.3 God's Manifestation through the Law, the Tabernacle, and the Temple

Later in the introduction to his gospel, John alludes to God's presence among Israel during the exodus (John 1:14: *skenoō*, "pitched his tent")[10] and to God's giving of his law through Moses (1:17; cf. Exod 31:18; 34:28). In both cases, John's purpose of adducing these OT antecedent passages is to locate Jesus at the climactic end of the spectrum of God's self-disclosure to his people. In the past, God was present among his people in the tabernacle (e.g., Exod 33:9; 40:34–35) and the temple (e.g., 1 Kgs 8:10–11).[11] Now he has taken up residence among his people in the person of Jesus Christ (John 1:14). In the past, God made himself known through the law given by Moses. Now he has revealed himself definitively in and through Jesus Christ (1:16–17).[12]

The reference to Jesus' taking up residence among God's people resulting in the revelation of God's glory in 1:14 (the first occurrence of the term *doxa* in this gospel) also harks back to OT references to the manifestation of the presence and glory (*kābôd*) of God, whether in theophanies, the tabernacle, or the temple (e.g., Exod 33:22; Num 14:10; Deut 5:22; Ps 26:8; 102:16; Jer 17:12; Ezek 10:4). While the Second Temple period was marked by the relative paucity of God's revelation due to Israel's apostasy, John makes clear that, now, in Jesus, God's glory has taken up residence in the midst of his people once again. This indeed marked a momentous event in salvation history.

---

8. E.g., Isa 9:2; 42:6–7; 49:6; 60:1–5; Mal 4:2; cf. Luke 1:78–79; see already Num 24:18; cf. 4QTest 9–13 (4Q175).

9. See further the discussion of John's "new creation theology" in chap. 8 above.

10. Cf. Exod 25:8–9; 33:7; 2 Sam 7:6; Ps 15:2; 26:8; 27:4–6; 43:3; 74:7; 84:1; Ezek 37:27–28.

11. For a discussion of God's "dwelling" (*šākan*) among his people in the OT, see Carson, *Gospel according to John*, 127–28.

12. For the interpretive issues surrounding the phrase "grace [in return for] grace" in John 1:16 and the explication of this phrase in 1:17, see Köstenberger, *John*, 46–48.

22.4 The Coming of "A Voice Crying in the Wilderness"

All four Gospels identify the Baptist as the forerunner of Jesus. Luke in particular provides a thorough account of John's origins, including the unusual circumstances surrounding his birth (Luke 1–2). Whereas the Synoptics portray John's ministry as more multifaceted, John depicts him as the paradigmatic, though by no means only, witness to Jesus.[13] Like Luke (1:1–4), John stresses the accuracy of the facts set forth in his gospel. In keeping with this concern, the fourth evangelist focuses on the Baptist's role as a witness to Jesus (John 1:7–8, 15, 19, 32–34; 3:26; 5:33–36; cf. 10:40–41). This makes the Baptist the first, though not the weightiest (5:36), among a whole series of witnesses to Jesus presented in this gospel.[14]

After first indicating who John is *not*—the Messiah (John 1:20; cf. 1:8, 15), Elijah (1:21a), or the Prophet (1:21b; cf. 6:14; 7:40; Deut 18:15, 18)—the fourth evangelist then identifies John as "the voice of one crying out in the wilderness, 'Make straight the way for the Lord'" (John 1:23; featured in Isa 40:3).[15] In this characterization of John, the evangelist coheres fully with the Synoptic portrayal of the Baptist (cf. Matt 3:3; Mark 1:3; Luke 3:4). According to the evangelist, John's witness centered on Jesus' role in the divine plan of salvation as the "Lamb of God, who takes away the sin of the world" (John 1:29, 36). At its very heart, the purpose of John's baptism and ministry is described as being bound up with revealing Jesus' true identity to Israel (1:32).

In the original Isaianic context, the message delivered by the "voice of the one crying in the wilderness" to God's people is that they are to prepare Yahweh's way in the wilderness and make straight in the desert a highway for their God. This was in keeping with normal procedure preparing for a visiting dignitary.[16] The prophet Ezekiel had depicted Yahweh as abandoning Jerusalem (Ezekiel 9–11); now Yahweh will return to take up residence in his city once again, which calls for major preparation (see Isa 35:8–10; cf. 35:1). How are God's people to prepare the way for his return? In one word: "repentance." If Yahweh is to return, his people must repent of their sins that caused them to be led into exile. This is borne out clearly by the Baptist's message: "Produce fruit in keeping with repentance" (Matt 3:8). As Isa 40:1–2 makes clear, God's ultimate purpose for his people is not judgment but salvation, life not death (cf. John 3:17–18; 12:47).

---

13. See esp. Lincoln, *Truth on Trial*, 58–73. As Lincoln notes (p. 21), not only does the lawsuit motif (see Isaiah 40–55, esp. 42:18–25; 43:22–28; 50:1–3) occur in each of the five main sections of John's narrative (prologue; John 1:19–12:50; 13–17; 18–20; epilogue), but it does so in highly significant ways, forming the narrative framework of the gospel (p. 141). According to Lincoln, just as there are seven signs and seven discourses in John's gospel, there are seven witnesses: John the Baptist, Jesus himself, Jesus' works, God the Father, the Scriptures, the Samaritan woman, and the crowd (more likely, the fourth evangelist).

14. See the fuller treatment of the embeddedness of the treatment of John the Baptist in the "witness" motif in John's gospel in Köstenberger, *John*, 32–34.

15. Interestingly, the Qumran community applied the same passage in Isaiah to itself, specifically to the role of the community council and the Interpreter in the study of the law of Moses. Both 1QS 8:14 and 4Q259 3:4–5 envision a time when the community is "to be segregated from the dwelling of the men of sin to walk to the desert in order to prepare the path of truth," citing Isa 40:3 (see also 4Q176 frag. 1–2 col. 6–7). Yet while these covenanters understood the passage as a call to dwell in the desert and to devote themselves to the study of God's Word, the Baptist recognized it as a call to prepare the people of Israel for the coming Messiah (Morris, *Gospel of John*, 121).

16. J. A. Motyer, *The Prophecy of Isaiah: An Introduction and Commentary* (Downers Grove, IL: InterVarsity Press, 1993), 300.

Yet comfort for God's people comes not from anything they do, but solely from "the activity of the Lord, his coming into the sphere of human activity ... the revelation of him in human sight."[17] The purpose for these preparations is the revelation of God's glory (one of the "ruling concepts" of Isaiah),[18] not merely to Israel and Judah, but to all of humanity (Isa 40:5; cf. 60:1–3). This, in turn, harks back to the exodus, where God's glory was revealed at a previous juncture of salvation history (Exod 16:10; 24:16–18; 33:18; 40:34). That all humanity will witness Yahweh's triumphant return to his lowly people is part of the prophetic defiance of political realities (cf. Isa 49:26; 66:16, 23–24).[19]

Later on, Isaiah also speaks of the coming "Servant" (esp. Isa 52:13–53:12), who will provide an even greater deliverance, to be consummated in the new heaven and new earth (Isaiah 65–66). Similar to other OT prophetic writings, Isaiah's vision draws heavily on exodus typology.[20] The Messiah and his redemption will bring about a new exodus at which God's glory will be revealed. As Isa 40:3, in the context of Isaiah as a whole, makes clear, God's people, conceived more broadly than OT Israel, would be called to prepare for Yahweh's coming by a prophetic voice. According to John the Baptist and the fourth evangelist, the Baptist is that voice.

Several elements of the original context of Isa 40:3 resonate with the passage's use in John 1:23: (1) the wilderness as the site of prophetic activity; (2) the focus away from the messenger to the message; (3) the coming revelation of God's glory through his visible coming and bringing of salvation, not merely to Israel, but to all humanity; and (4) the need for repentance to prepare the way. Isaiah 40:3, in turn, invokes the larger exodus motif, which also entails the themes of salvation and God's glory. The use of Isa 40:3 in John 1:23 suggests, therefore, that the Baptist's salvation-historical role is that of "the herald of a new exodus, announcing that God is about to redeem his people from captivity, as he had in the days of Moses,"[21] and to do so through the instrumentality of John the Baptist, who served as the Isaianic "voice in the wilderness." In accordance with Isaiah's prophecy, the Baptist calls God's people to repentance in preparation for the coming Servant.[22]

22.5 The Manifestation of God's Glory, Grace, and Covenant-Keeping Faithfulness in Christ

To bring glory to God is said to be Jesus' overriding purpose in John's gospel (1:14, 16). As he brings glory to God, glory also comes to Jesus. This continues what was true of Jesus already prior to his coming. For glory characterized Jesus' eternal relationship with God (17:5) as well as his preincarnate state (12:41). During his earthly ministry, Jesus' glory is revealed to his first followers primarily through his "signs" (cf. 2:11; 9:3; 11:4, 40). As the obedient, dependent Son, Jesus brings glory to God

---

17. John N. Oswalt, *The Book of Isaiah* (2 vols.; NICOT; Grand Rapids: Eerdmans, 1998), 2.50.
18. Ibid., 52.
19. Joseph Blenkinsopp, *Isaiah 40–55* (AB 19A; New York: Doubleday, 2002), 183.
20. E.g., Jer 2:6–7; 7:22, 25; 11:4, 7; Hos 2:16–17; 11:1; 12:10, 14; 13:4–5; Amos 2:9–10; 3:1–2; 9:7; Mic 6:4; see also Isa 10:24, 26; 11:16–18.
21. Keener, *John*, 266.
22. Carson, *Gospel according to John*, 144.

the Father in everything he says and does. But he does so supremely by submitting to the cross, which for John is the place of God's—and Jesus'—ultimate glorification (cf. 12:23–33; 13:31–32; 14:13; 17:1, 4–5).

A significant OT allusion that underscores God's manifestation of his glory, grace, and covenant-keeping faithfulness in the Messiah is the depiction of Jesus as "full of grace and truth" (1:14, 17) in John's introduction. In all probability, the expression harks back to the phrase "love and faithfulness" in Exod 34:6 (cf. 33:18–19; Ps 25:10; 26:3; 40:10; Prov 16:6; cf. Ps 83:12 LXX = Ps 84:11). In its original context, this expression referred to God's covenant faithfulness to his people Israel. John's message is that this covenant faithfulness found ultimate expression in the sending of God's one and only Son (John 1:14, 18).

In presenting Jesus as the manifestation of God's glory, grace, and covenant-keeping faithfulness, John relates God's giving of the law through Moses (cf. Exod 31:18; 34:28) to the appearing of grace and truth in and through Jesus Christ (1:16–17). John's message is that true grace—final, eschatological grace—came through Jesus Christ.[23] Rather than drawing a sharp contrast between the giving of the law through Moses and the grace and truth brought by Jesus,[24] John presents Jesus as the climactic eschatological revelation of God's covenant love and faithfulness. As the following narrative will develop in greater detail, Jesus is superior to Moses (5:46–47; cf. 9:28), just as he is superior to Jacob (4:12) and Abraham (8:53).

22.6 The Offering of Isaac and God's "One and Only Son"

John, distinctively and uniquely, calls Jesus God's "one and only Son."[25] A closer look reveals that this designation, too, has OT and salvation-historical underpinnings. The predominant OT sense of the term *monogenēs* is "only child" (Judg 11:34; Amos 8:10; Jer 6:26; Zech 12:10; cf. Prov 4:3). The seminal event in OT history in this regard is Abraham's offering of Isaac (the *Aqedah*), who in Gen 22:2, 12, 16 is called Abraham's "one and only son" (Heb. *yāḥîd*), even though the patriarch had earlier fathered Ishmael (cf. Heb 11:17; Josephus, *Ant*. 1.22). *Monogenēs* means therefore, not "only begotten," but "one-of-a-kind" son (in Isaac's case, son of promise).

In both OT and Second Temple literature, the Son of David and Israel are called God's "firstborn" or even "only" son (cf. Ps 89:27; 4 Ezra 6:58; *Pss. Sol.* 18:4; *Jub.* 18:2, 11, 15). In a decisive step further, John applies the designation *monogenēs* to God's "one and only Son" par excellence, Jesus (John 1:14, 18; 3:16, 18; 1 John 4:9). This is similar to the designation of Jesus as God's "beloved son," which surfaces in the Synoptics in the voice from heaven at Jesus' baptism and transfiguration and in the parable of the tenants (see esp. Mark 1:11; 9:7; 12:6; cf. Luke 20:13).

---

23. Köstenberger, *John*, 47.
24. Note the absence of the word "but" between the two phrases in v. 17 in the original Greek.
25. For a fuller discussion see chap. 9, sec. 20.2, portions of which are here reproduced for convenience's sake.

In keeping with the Isaac narrative and the parable of the tenants, the term *monogenēs* in John's gospel thus contains a significant soteriological dimension, culminating in John's assertion in 3:16 that "God so loved the world that he sent his one and only Son" (cf. John 3:18). This designation also provides the basis for Jesus' claim that no one can come to the Father except through him (14:6). Thus what is perhaps the best-known verse in John's gospel and in the entire Bible, John 3:16, in all probability harks back to the OT narrative of Abraham offering Isaac and presents Jesus along the continuum of the biblical "one and only son" typology.

22.7 The Message of Isaiah and Jewish Unbelief

Act I of the Johannine *Christo*-drama concludes with the indictment, "Even after Jesus had performed so many signs in their presence, they still would not believe in him" (12:37).[26] The failure of the Jews to believe in Jesus' day is reminiscent of the unbelief of the wilderness generation, which had witnessed God's mighty acts of power displayed through Moses at the exodus (Deut 29:2–4).[27] No greater sign than the raising of Lazarus—the seventh climactic sign in John—could be given. The Jews' continued opposition to Jesus confirms them in their obduracy. However, as John makes clear, rather than thwart God's purposes, the Jews' rejection of their Messiah actually fulfilled Scripture.

The first passage cited in John 12:38 is Isa 53:1 (LXX; cf. Rom 10:16). In its original context, the prophet refers to the Servant of the Lord who was rejected by the people but exalted by God (cf. Isa 52:13–15). In John, the verse is applied to Jesus the Messiah, who is that promised Servant, and to the rejection of his message and signs ("arm of the Lord") by the Jews. Hence the Jewish rejection of God's messengers is far from unprecedented in salvation history—just as Isaiah's message had been rejected, so was Jesus'.[28] John's statement, "For this reason they could not believe" (John 12:39; cf. 10:26), is unambiguously predestinarian yet compatibilist, including both elements of divine sovereignty and human responsibility.[29]

In the scriptural quote of Isa 6:10 in John 12:40, faith and the divine activity are connected, indicating that "even unbelief has some place in the purpose of God."[30] John here accounts for the fact—surprising for some—that the Jews, God's chosen old covenant people, failed to accept their Messiah. His answer, far from implying that they are not responsible for their refusal to believe (19:11–12, 15), points to the ultimate purpose as God's judicial hardening of the Jewish people (similar to

---

26. Croteau, "Analysis of the Concept of Believing," 63, plausibly contends that the antecedents of the reference to people's unbelief in 12:37 include all previous instances of unbelief in the narrative, including 2:23; 4:45–48; 6:14; 7:31; 8:30–31; 11:47; and 12:11 (viewed negatively by Croteau).

27. Carson, *Gospel according to John*, 447; Ridderbos, *Gospel of John*, 444; Brown, *Gospel according to John I–XII*, 485.

28. See Ridderbos, *Gospel of John*, 444.

29. Carson, *Gospel according to John*, 447; Barrett, *Gospel according to St. John*, 431. The balancing emphasis is provided by Ridderbos (*Gospel of John*, 444–45), who notes that "unbelief is not thereby blamed on God in a predestinarian sense, but is rather described as a punishment from God...." Carson (*Gospel according to John*, 448–49), too, engages in theodicy when he writes that "God's judicial hardening is not presented as the capricious manipulation of an arbitrary potentate ... but as a holy condemnation of a guilty people who are condemned to do and be what they themselves have chosen." See also the discussion in chap. 12, sec. 26.

30. Morris, *Gospel of John*, 536.

Pharaoh; cf. Rom 9:17). John's appropriation of the cited passage, found frequently in the NT (Isa 6:10; cf. Matt 13:13–15 par.; Acts 28:26–27), indicates that he is well within the mainstream of early Christian tradition.[31]

The evangelist concludes that "Isaiah ... saw Jesus' [lit. "his"] glory" (John 12:41; cf. 8:56). In light of the preceding quotation of Isa 6:10, some believe that the background for John's statement is the call narrative in Isaiah 6. Yet while *autou* ("his") probably refers to Jesus, John does not actually *say* that Isaiah saw *Jesus*, but that he saw his *glory*. Thus it is not necessary to surmise that the evangelist believed Isaiah saw "the preexistent Christ"[32] or Jesus "in some preincarnate fashion."[33] Rather, Isaiah foresaw that God was pleased with a *suffering* Servant who would be "raised and lifted up and highly exalted" (Isa 52:13), yet was "pierced for our transgressions" and "bore the sin of many" (53:5, 12).[34] Isaiah knew that God's glory would be revealed through a suffering Messiah (cf. John 12:34). Like Abraham, Isaiah saw Jesus' "day" (8:58).

22.8 Davidic Typology

Another major salvation-historical pattern appropriated by John in his gospel is Davidic typology (see esp. 2:17; 15:25; 19:24, 26). The fact that Jesus is in the inaugural scenes of the gospel referred to as the "Messiah" (1:41), the "Son of God" (1:49; cf. 2 Sam 7:14; Ps 2:7; cf. Ps 89:26–29), and the "king of Israel" (John 1:49) makes it plausible that observing Jesus' clearing of the temple invoked in his followers the memory of David's words in Ps 69:9. This, in turn, is in keeping with Jewish expectations, current in the first century, that the Messiah would purge and reconstitute the temple (*Pss. Sol.* 17:21–22, 36; cf. Mark 14:61).[35] Such an action would follow, and transcend, the pattern of great national deliverance last experienced by the Jews when Judas Maccabeus rededicated the temple in December, 165 BC, after it had been desecrated by Antiochus Epiphanes IV (cf. John 10:22–39; see also 8:31–38).

Psalm 69 (cited in John 2:17 and 15:25; see also 19:28) and Psalm 22 (cited in John 19:24) share in common Davidic typology and the theme of the righteous sufferer.[36] The use of these Davidic passages, in turn, is part of a larger pattern, both in Jesus' understanding and in the fourth evangelist's presentation, of aligning Jesus and his ministry with the experience of a king and/or prophet who is zealous for God and as a result suffers humiliation by God's own people, a pattern that encompasses the use of Psalm 69 both in John 2:17 and in 15:25 and extends also

---

31. See esp. Evans, *To See and Not Perceive*.
32. Schnackenburg, *Gospel according to John* 2:416; cf. Talbert, *Reading John*, 180; Smith, *John*, 244.
33. Carson, *Gospel according to John*, 449. Though it is, of course, the case that the notion of a preexistent Christ who was present and active in the history of Israel is found elsewhere in the NT (1 Cor 10:4), and Jewish interpreters after Isaiah speculated that the prophet looked into the future and saw "what was to occur to the end of time and the hidden things before they happened" (Sir 48:24–25). Note that elsewhere the evangelist affirms the impossibility of a direct vision of God (John 1:18; 5:37; 6:46).
34. See esp. Evans, "Obduracy and the Lord's Servant."
35. Daly-Denton, "Psalms in John's Gospel," 123.
36. Marvin E. Tate, *Psalms 51–100* (WBC 20; Dallas: Word, 1990), 196.

to the use of Psalm 22 in John 19:24 and the possible allusion to Ps 69:21 in John 19:28–30.[37]

Jesus' appropriation of the phrase "they hated me without reason" in Ps 69:4 or 35:19 in the face of his imminent cross-death (John 15:25) evokes the type of the righteous sufferer, possibly including various entailments supplied by the context of the original passage such as: (1) the large number of the sufferer's enemies; (2) their great power; (3) the false charges leveled by the enemies; and (4) the righteous sufferer's prayerful trust in God. In his final instructions to his followers, Jesus points out that the hatred of his opponents directed against him is "without reason," that is, not based on rational argument or legitimate charges, but fueled by improper motives and a sinful disposition. The Johannine account of Jesus' mission to the Jews in 1:19–12:50 and chapters 18–19 provides ample documentation of this groundless hatred that motivated those who brought charges against Jesus and had him nailed to a cross.

As in 2:17, Jesus' and the evangelist's use of an OT psalm reflecting the experience of the righteous sufferer taps into the typological pattern of one who is zealous for God and his cause but is persecuted by his enemies as a result. Yet while the OT psalmist expected deliverance from his enemies and salvation from their wrath, God allowed his wrath to fall on Jesus for the sake of humanity's salvation. Jesus found a precedent for this in the adversity and antagonism encountered by David, which in the ultimate analysis were no "strange misfortune" but David's "own predestined lot."[38] Davidic typology in John's gospel climaxes in the events of the crucifixion, again involving allusions to the life of David (see esp. 19:24, 28).

22.9 Conclusion

The above discussion amply documents the prevalence of a salvation-historical perspective in John's gospel. John's *Christo*-drama places Jesus' story squarely within the context of Israel's story. In so doing, the evangelist draws richly on antecedent theology in the Hebrew Scriptures, including creation, the exodus, the revelation of God's glorious presence in the tabernacle and the temple (which furnishes material for both John's *sēmeio-* and *cruci-*drama), the exile, and Davidic typology.

That this is so is apparent from the opening verse of the gospel and follows clearly from a close reading of the introduction, which, in turn, provides the blueprint for the remainder of the narrative. In the following two sections, an attempt will be made to flesh out the demonstration of John's salvation-historical perspective even more. This will involve a discussion of his portrayal of Jesus' fulfillment of the symbolism inherent in Jewish religious festivals and institutions, including John's portrayal of Jesus as the new temple.

---

37. Jesus' expression of anguish in 12:27 (cf. 11:33; 13:21; 14:1, 27) may invoke Davidic psalms such as Ps 6:3 or Ps 42:5, 11. This depiction of Jesus in Davidic terms, too, involves Davidic typology and adds to the presentation of Jesus in terms thoroughly prepared by OT messianic passages.

38. Derek Kidner, *Psalms 1–72* (TOTC; London: Inter-Varsity Press, 1973), 144.

23 Jesus' Fulfillment of Festal Symbolism

23.1 Introduction

Throughout his gospel, John highlights Jesus' fulfillment of symbolism inherent in Jewish religious festivals and institutions. Under the present heading, I will discuss Jesus' fulfillment of festal symbolism related to Passover and Tabernacles. Topics will include Jesus as the "Lamb of God," the new temple (as far as it involves Passover symbolism), and the "bread of life"; the prophecy of Jesus' vicarious death and his anointing for burial; Jesus' celebration of Passover with the representatives of his new messianic community; and Jesus as the Passover sacrifice.[39]

Jesus' fulfillment of the symbolism inherent in several major Jewish festivals constitutes a major structural and theological plank in John's gospel, particularly in the Festival Cycle, which spans from John 5–10 and extends also to the transitional chapters 11 and 12. A list of references to major Jewish festivals in John's gospel will provide the framework for the discussion of Jesus' fulfillment and replacement of Jewish festivals below. It will also demonstrate that Jesus' attendance of Jewish festivals is a significant aspect of John's structure.

Name of Festival	Reference in John
Passover	2:13, 23
"One of the Jewish festivals"	5:1
Passover	6:4
Tabernacles (Booths)	7:2
Dedication (Hanukkah)	10:22
Passover	11:55; 12:1; 13:1

Fig. 23.1: References to Jewish Festivals in John's Gospel

While the Synoptics present Jesus' ministry as proceeding geographically from Galilee to Jerusalem, climaxing in Jesus' death (possibly following the Markan framework, with Luke featuring his distinctive "travel narrative"), John shows Jesus' pilgrimage to Jerusalem throughout his ministry and features a total of three Passovers, which suggests that Jesus' ministry spanned at least two, and most likely three, years.[40]

As D. A. Carson observes, "What is perhaps most noteworthy is not how many of the themes and institutions converge on Jesus, but how they are so presented

---

39. A fuller investigation of John's presentation of Jesus as the new temple will be provided in sec. 24.

40. See the chronology in chap. 1, sec. 2.1.3.2 above. Michael A. Daise, *Feasts in John: Jewish Festivals and Jesus' "Hour" in the Fourth Gospel* (WUNT 2/229; Tübingen: Mohr-Siebeck, 2007), sets forth the unusual theory that the feasts of John's entire gospel unfold within a single liturgical year, marking the progress toward Jesus' "hour." However, Daise's theory is predicated on the doubtful premise that the Passover mentioned in John 6:4 is not a regular Passover but the "second Passover" of Num 9:9–14. Also, to accommodate his theory, Daise has to invert chapters 5 and 6, which, likewise, is rather implausible.

as to make Jesus 'fulfill' them and actually *replace* them."[41] While the Synoptics only mention Passover, John's gospel also refers to Tabernacles and Dedication, and "these are presented in contexts where Jesus' activity or utterance shows where the true significance of that feast now lies."[42] Nevertheless, Passover symbolism in John's gospel is particularly rich, which is why it will form the backbone of discussion in the remainder of this section below.

23.2 Jesus' Fulfillment of Passover Symbolism

As Mark Stibbe observes, "there is evidence in John's story of a rich Passover symbolism. The whole of the Gospel could be described as a *Passover plot* in that it moves through the three Passover festivals in 2.13, 6.4 and 13.1."[43] In commenting on John's portrayal of Jesus' death, Stibbe notes several symbolic details that combine to create "an implicit commentary on the death of Jesus as the perfect paschal sacrifice."[44]

In fact, as Stanley Porter notes, the evidence of a Passover theme in John's gospel is stronger than many recognize: "The Passover theme essentially states that Jesus is seen by the author of the Fourth Gospel as the suitable and in fact ideal or perfect Passover victim. Since the animal sacrificed at Passover symbolized deliverance from the angel of death as well as redemption from the oppression of Egypt, which leads to the exodus and, eventually, entrance into Canaan,"[45] the Moses typology in John's gospel, including the "signs," the references to the Passover, both direct and indirect, and various other motifs combine to a consistent strand of Passover references in the gospel.

23.2.1 Jesus the "Lamb of God"

The Baptist's reference to Jesus as "the Lamb of God, who takes away the sin of the world" in John 1:29 (cf. v. 36) likely involves multiple levels of meaning. Perhaps the Baptist here speaks better than he knows, thinking primarily of the lamb led to the slaughter referred to in Isa 53:7,[46] which contemporary Judaism interpreted not with reference to a dying Messiah, but as conveying the notion of substitutionary suffering for sin that fell short of actual death (cf. Matt 11:2–3; Luke 7:18–20).

It is also possible that the Baptist may have proclaimed Jesus as the apocalyptic warrior lamb who would bring judgment.[47] Some who hold this view also say that the evangelist thinks that the Baptist is speaking better than he knows (much as Caiaphas does in 11:49–52).[48] If so, this would mean that while the Baptist believes

---

41. Carson, "John and the Johannine Epistles," 254.
42. Ibid., 255.
43. Stibbe, *John*, 36. Cited in Porter, "Traditional Exegesis," 405–6. See also Gerald L. Borchert, "The Passover and the Narrative Cycles in John," in *Perspectives on John: Method and Interpretation in the Fourth Gospel* (ed. Robert B. Sloan and Mikeal C. Parsons; Lewiston, NY: Mellen, 1993), 303–16.
44. Stibbe, *John*, 196.
45. Porter, "Traditional Exegesis," 406.
46. LXX: *amnos*; elsewhere in the NT only in Acts 8:32 (citing Isa 53:7 LXX) and 1 Pet 1:19 (cf. 2:21–25).
47. Cf., e.g., *1 En.* 90:9–12; *T. Jos.* 19:8; *T. Benj.* 3:8; Rev 5:6, 12; 7:17. Cf. Brown, *Gospel according to John I–XII*, 59, citing esp. Luke 3:17; Carson, *Gospel according to John*, 150; and Beasley-Murray, *John*, 24–25; Schlatter, *Evangelist Johannes*, 46–47, refers to both; for the Baptist's message of judgment, see esp. Matt 3:7–12; Luke 3:7–17; Carson (*Gospel according to John*, 149) also notes the doubts expressed by the Baptist in Matt 11:2–3.
48. Carson, *Gospel according to John*, 150–51.

Jesus "takes away" the sin of the world in his capacity as the warrior lamb, the evangelist knows that, whatever truth there is in this perspective, he also "takes away" the sin of the world by means of the cross.[49]

Another possible association that may be in the purview of the Baptist's reference to Jesus as the "Lamb of God" is the lamb provided by God for Abraham when he was ready to offer up his "one and only son," Isaac, in obedience to the divine command.[50] This is especially suggestive since John probably alludes to this scene in 3:16, except that God actually did what Abraham was spared from doing at the last minute, giving up his one and only Son (cf. Rom 8:32).[51]

The evangelist, for his part, places the Baptist's declaration into the wider context of his Passion Narrative, where Jesus is shown to be the ultimate fulfillment of the annual Passover lamb, whose bones must not be broken.[52] This "Lamb of God" will *take away sin*, presumably by means of a sacrificial, substitutionary death.[53] According to the pattern set by the OT sacrificial system, the shed blood of the substitute covered the sins of others and appeased the divine wrath by way of atonement (cf. 1 John 2:2; 4:10).[54]

Moreover, as the "Lamb of God," Jesus takes upon himself the sin, not merely of Israel, but of *the entire world* (cf. John 1:10). The idea that the Messiah would suffer for the sins of *the world* (rather than merely for Israel) was foreign to Jewish first-century ears; but John makes clear that Jesus came to save the entire world (3:17; 1 John 2:2) and that he is the Savior of the world, not merely Israel (John 4:42; 1 John 4:14). The NT's depiction of Jesus as "the Lamb of God" culminates in Revelation, where Jesus is the "Lamb who was slain" and returns in universal triumph.[55]

John's teaching on Jesus' substitutionary atonement builds on his earlier reference to Jesus' incarnation. For it is in the flesh that Jesus suffered vicariously; his humanity was an indispensable prerequisite for his cross-work on behalf of others. In fact, the atonement theme, far from being absent, is part of the warp and woof of John's gospel: Jesus is the "bread of life" who gives his flesh for the life of the world; he is the "good shepherd" who lays down his life for his sheep; and his sacrifice fulfills Passover symbolism (e.g., 19:14, 31).[56]

---

49. See the melding together of the Lamb who was slain and of the triumphant Lion of Judah in Rev 5:5–6, 12–13.

50. See Gen 22:8, 13, 14. For a discussion of additional alternatives, see Morris, *Gospel of John*, 127–29; cf. Barrett, *Gospel according to St. John*, 176; Ridderbos, *Gospel of John*, 73–74.

51. Involving bulls and goats, not lambs: see Leviticus 14; Numbers 6. Less likely options are the gentle lamb of Jer 11:19 (no overtones of bearing sin); the scapegoat that symbolically bore the sins of the people and was banished to the desert (a goat, not a lamb; Leviticus 16); and the guilt offering sacrificed to deal with sin.

52. See John 19:36; cf. Exod 12:46; Num 9:12; Ps 34:20. See also John 19:14; cf. 1 Cor 5:7. See Burge, *John*, 73–74; Barrett, *Gospel according to St. John*, 176.

53. Morris, *Gospel of John*, 130.

54. As the book of Hebrews makes clear, however, the entire OT sacrificial system was merely provisional until the coming of Christ.

55. See Rev 5:6, 9, 12; 7:17; 12:11; 13:8; 17:14; 19:7, 9; 21:22–23; 22:1–3.

56. "Bread of life": 6:48; cf. 6:32–33, 51, 53–58; "good shepherd": 10:14; cf. 10:17–18. See Porter, "Traditional Exegesis," 407–11. Porter discusses the following instances of Passover symbolism in John's gospel: 1:29–36; 2:13–25; 6:1–14, 22–71; 11:47–12:8; 13:1–17:26; and 19:13–42 (esp. vv. 14, 29, 31, 36–37). Paul M. Hoskins, "Deliverance from Death by the True Passover Lamb: A Significant Aspect of the Fulfillment of the Passover in the Gospel of John," *JETS* 52 (2008): 285–99 also adduces 8:31–47.

23.2.2 Jesus the New Temple

Because of the significance of the "temple" theme in John's gospel, an entire section will be devoted to this topic below. In the present context, it is necessary only to probe implications from John's account of Jesus' clearing of the temple (John 2:13–22) for the possible presence of Passover symbolism.[57] The reference to Passover in both 2:13 and 23, a likely *inclusio*, sets Jesus' clearing of the temple squarely within the framework of the celebration of the Jewish Passover. For this reason it is likely, as Stanley Porter contends, in interaction with Mark Stibbe, that the references to Passover in 2:13 and 23 constitute more than mere literary plot markers but instead reveal an important theological point made by the fourth evangelist.[58]

In essence, Jesus is shown to institute a new Passover with himself rather than the temple as its focus. He drives out the sacrificial animals from the temple, indicating the corrupt nature of the present system, and speaks of the temple's impending destruction and reconstitution in his own body (2:19; cf. 2:20–21). Thus "a New Order had arrived. The 'Holy Place' is to be displaced by a new reality, a rebuilt 'temple' (*naos*), which John refers to as 'the temple of his body,'"[59] In conjunction with the reference to Jesus as "the Lamb of God" in 1:29 and 36 and the depiction of Jesus as the new manna and the Passover sacrifice, the temple clearing thickens the thematic plot of this important Johannine theme.

23.2.3 Jesus the Bread of Life

D. A. Carson well connects the depiction of Jesus as the "bread of life" in John 6 to previous and subsequent instances of the Passover motif in John's gospel: "The connections become complex: the sacrifice of the lamb anticipates Jesus' death, the Old Testament manna is superseded by the real bread of life, the exodus typologically sets forth the eternal life that delivers us from sin and destruction, the Passover feast is taken over by the eucharist (both of which point to Jesus and his redemptive cross-work)."[60]

Jesus' feeding of the multitude (John 6:1–15), one of the Johannine "signs" (6:26, 30), presents Jesus as the new and greater Moses (6:14; cf. Deut 18:15, 18), fulfilling Passover symbolism.[61] The bountiful meal evokes OT messianic prophecy.[62] The divine provision of manna for wilderness Israel is celebrated in later OT passages (see esp. Ps 78:24; 105:40; Neh 9:15). The Second Temple literature, likewise, looked forward to a time when God would again provide manna for his people.[63]

---

57. See Porter, "Traditional Exegesis," 411–13.
58. Ibid., 412, with reference to Stibbe, *John*, 49.
59. Davies, *Gospel and the Land*, 289–90 (cited in Porter, "Traditional Exegesis," 413).
60. Carson, *Gospel according to John*, 268–69 (cited in Porter, "Traditional Exegesis," 414–15, n. 3). He quotes Edwyn Hoskyns and F. N. Davey, *The Fourth Gospel* (2 vols.; London: Faber & Faber, 1940), 1:281, who remark, "The movement from the miracle to the discourse, from Moses to Jesus (*vv.* 32–5, *cf.* i.17), and, above all, from *bread* to *flesh*, is almost unintelligible unless the reference in *v.* 4 to the Passover picks up i.29, 36, anticipates xix.36 (Exod. xii.46; Num. ix.12), and governs the whole narrative."
61. See the reference to the Passover at John 6:4.
62. See Isa 25:6–8; 49:9–11; cf. Matt 22:1–14; Luke 22:15–30; Ridderbos, *Gospel according to John*, 213.
63. Wis 16:20; cf. Philo, *Leg.* 3.169–76; *Det.* 118; *Her.* 79, 191; *Mut.* 259–60.

Three factors, then, link John 6 with the exodus account: (1) the Passover motif; (2) Jesus as the prophet like Moses and other exodus allusions; and (3) the expectation that God would again provide manna in the messianic age.[64] The implicit contrast is between Moses and Jesus.[65] As in 3:14, an event during Israel's wilderness wanderings during the exodus is shown to anticipate typologically God's provision of salvation in and through Jesus.[66] Also as in 3:14, the typology entails an element of escalation.[67]

While the manna was heaven-sent as well as life-nurturing and sustaining, it was unable to impart life that is eternal: those in the wilderness who ate the manna still died (6:49–50). By contrast, anyone who believes in Jesus will live forever. Jesus' assertion that the bread is his flesh, which he will "give for the life of the world,"[68] evokes the memory of the Suffering Servant, who "poured out his life unto death" and "bore the sins of many."[69] Just as the scope of the Servant is universal (Isa 49:6), so Jesus will give his life not merely for Israel, but for the world.

23.2.4 The Prophecy of Jesus' Vicarious Death and His Anointing for Burial

In 11:50, the Jewish high priest Caiaphas is represented as saying that "it is better ... that one man die for the people than that the whole nation perish." The fourth evangelist, in one of the many parenthetical "asides" in the gospel, editorializes that Caiaphas "did not say this on his own, but as high priest that year he prophesied that Jesus would die for the Jewish nation, and not only for that nation but also for the scattered children of God, to bring them together and make them one" (11:51–52).

While Caiaphas, like possibly John the Baptist in 1:29, 36, was speaking better than he knew, this unwitting prophecy presents Jesus as the vicarious sacrifice for the nation of Israel, and, by Johannine extension, also for the "scattered children of God" (i.e., the Gentiles; cf. 12:20–33). The immediate reference to the Jewish Passover in 11:55, and the reference to the Passover at the outset of Jesus' anointing for burial by Mary of Bethany in 12:1, mark Jesus as the Passover sacrifice being prepared to render vicarious atonement for God's people.[70]

23.2.5 Jesus' Celebration of the Passover with the Representatives of His New Messianic Community

The reference to the Passover Festival in John 13:1, like similar instances (2:13, 23; 6:4; 11:55; 12:1), signals to the reader of John's gospel that the following narrative is to be understood in terms of Jesus' fulfillment of Passover symbolism.

---

64. Ridderbos, *Gospel of John*, 226; Morris, *Gospel of John*, 321; Beasley-Murray, *John*, 91.

65. Ridderbos, *Gospel of John*, 226–27.

66. See Barrett, *Gospel according to St. John*, 290.

67. While the manna in the wilderness had Israel as its recipient, God's gift of Jesus is universal in scope and extends beyond believing Israelites also to believing Gentiles (e.g., 10:16; 11:51–52; 12:32). See Carson, *Gospel according to John*, 287.

68. John 6:51; cf. 1:29, 36; paralleled later in 10:11, 15; cf. 11:51–52; 15:13; 17:19; 18:14.

69. See Isa 53:12; cf. 52:13–53:12; see also the citation of Isa 54:13 in John 6:45.

70. See Porter, "Traditional Exegesis," 415–16.

These repeated references to the Passover in the gospel narrative, together with other Johannine features such as references to Jesus' "hour," create an unmistakable crescendo building toward the actual sacrifice of Jesus the Passover, which is narrated in the Johannine Passion Narrative in John 18 and 19.[71]

The series of ensuing events in John 13–17 almost certainly commences with a Passover meal celebrated by Jesus and the representatives of his new messianic community.[72] While some question whether John's chronology regarding the Last Supper can be aligned with the one found in the Synoptics, a strong case can be made that, as in the Synoptics, Jesus is depicted in John as celebrating a Passover meal with his closest followers shortly prior to his crucifixion, which, in turn, is shown in terms reminiscent of the offering of the Passover sacrifice.[73]

Especially if 13:1 serves as the heading for the entire Farewell Discourse in chapters 13–17,[74] Jesus' celebration of the Passover meal (13:1, 4) with the Twelve is presented from the vantage point of Passover symbolism in a number of ways. (1) Jesus' use of "vine" imagery in 15:1–10 may be predicated upon his and the disciples' partaking of wine just prior to his use of this imagery at the Passover meal.[75]

(2) The "bearing" and "taking away" language in John 15–17 may hark back to similar terminology in the reference to Jesus as the "Lamb of God" in 1:29.

(3) "Glory" language binds together a cluster of motifs that center on Jesus' crucifixion as his glorification, a theology that is significantly indebted to Isaiah's depiction of the Suffering Servant, who would be "lifted up and highly exalted" (Isa 52:13) and who would "sprinkle many nations" (52:15). That Servant "bore our suffering" and "was pierced for our transgressions" (53:4–5); "the punishment that brought us peace was on him, and by his wounds we are healed" (53:5); "he was led like a lamb to the slaughter" (53:7); yet "after he has suffered, he will see the light of life" (53:11).[76]

The concept of the crucifixion as the supreme occasion for the glorification of the Son envelops the entire Farewell Discourse (see esp. John 12:23, 28; 17:5). As Stanley Porter aptly notes, "In Jesus' prayer, as the meal draws to a close, it is perhaps not too much to see Jesus offering a new prayer of blessing and consecration for the Passover feast—one that he himself is about to re-enact as its victim."[77] In

---

71. See the discussion under the next heading below.

72. See the discussion in chap. 12, esp. sec. 29.2, below. Note that all three Synoptic Gospels represent the Twelve as celebrating the Passover with Jesus (Matt 26:20; Mark 14:17; Luke 22:14: "his apostles"). See my essay "The Last Supper as a Passover Meal," in a forthcoming publication edited by Thomas R. Schreiner.

73. Some propose that *paraskeuē* in John 19:14 refers to the day preceding Passover, that is, the day on which preparations for Passover were made (in the present case, Thursday morning). If so, John says Jesus is executed at the time at which Passover lambs are slaughtered in the temple. The Synoptics, however, clearly have Jesus and his disciples celebrate Passover on the night prior to the crucifixion, and use *paraskeuē* as referring to the day preceding the Sabbath (Matt 27:62; Mark 15:42; Luke 23:54; cf. Josephus, *Ant.* 16.6.2 163–64). Thus the term most likely refers to the day of preparation for the Sabbath (i.e., Friday; cf. *Did.* 8:1; *Mart. Pol.* 7:1), and *tou pascha* in John 19:14 means not "of the Passover," but "of Passover week" (NIV). Thus, all four canonical Gospels concur that Jesus' Last Supper was a Passover meal eaten on Thursday evening (by Jewish reckoning, the onset of Friday). See esp. Joachim Jeremias, *The Eucharistic Words of Jesus* (NTL; trans. Norman Perrin; London: SCM, 1966), 56–82. See also Köstenberger, *John*, 401–2, 524, 529–30, 537–38, 551; Blomberg, *Historical Reliability of the Gospels*, 221–29; Carson, *Gospel according to John*, 603–4.

74. So Porter, "Traditional Exegesis," 417.

75. J. K. Howard, "Passover and Eucharist in the Fourth Gospel," *SJT* 20 (1967): 335.

76. Cf. 8:12 (so the DSS; see also LXX; not in the MT).

77. Porter, "Traditional Exegesis," 417–18.

the inexorable progression of John's narrative, the references to Jesus as the "Lamb of God" (1:29), the new temple (2:13–22), the "bread of life" (John 6), and the vicarious sacrifice prepared for burial (11:50–12:8), and to Jesus' celebration of the Passover with the Twelve in anticipation of his own impending vicarious, sacrificial death all set the stage for Jesus' self-giving in fulfillment of Passover symbolism.

23.2.6 Jesus the Passover Sacrifice

The final two OT "fulfillment" quotations in John's gospel, both of which are associated with Jesus' crucifixion, culminate and complete the Passover theme in John's gospel.[78] As Stanley Porter notes, "Thus, in the death of Jesus, as climactically defined by the Old Testament quotations, the Old Testament fulfillment motif and the Passover theme converge."[79] When the soldiers came to Jesus and saw he was already dead, they did not break his legs, but one of the soldiers pierced his side with a spear, and at once blood and water came out (John 19:34).

The flow of blood and water indicates that Jesus died as a fully human being.[80] An allusion to the Passover may also be in view (*m. Pesaḥ.* 5:5–8; cf. *m. ʾOhal.* 3:5), consisting of (1) the hyssop (19:29); (2) the unbroken bones (John 19:33, 36); and (3) the mingled blood (19:34).[81] If so, John may witness to all three events that portray Jesus as the Passover lamb. After 19:24 and 28, the OT reference in 19:36 is the third scriptural proof adduced by John that Jesus' death fulfills OT Scripture.

After Jesus had breathed his last, his legs were not broken in fulfillment of OT Passover symbolism.[82] Moreover, not only did Jesus escape the breaking of his legs (unlike those crucified with him), his body was pierced by a spear, again without sustaining bone damage. Two sets of Scripture converge: (1) Ps 34:20, depicting God's care for the righteous man; and (2) Exod 12:46 and Num 9:12, specifying that no bone of the Passover lamb may be broken.[83] Apparently, the Jews viewed disfiguration as an obstacle to resurrection, which may further explain why John takes pains to stress that no bone was broken.[84]

By this series of fulfillment citations the evangelist underscores the pattern of scriptural fulfillment in Jesus' death. This authenticates Jesus' claim of his messianic identity. In particular, a powerful link is established between Jesus' sacrificial death and the Jewish Passover, which commemorated the deliverance of the Israelites from

---

78. See 19:36, 37; cf. 19:24. OT allusions are found in 19:18, 28–29, 31, and 38.

79. Porter, "Traditional Exegesis," 401.

80. See *Rab. Lev.* 15:2 on Lev 13:2; cf. 1 John 5:6–8. John may also be alluding esp. to Exod 17:6: "Strike the rock, and water will come out of it for the people to drink" (cf. Num 20:11; see Carson, *Gospel according to John*, 624).

81. Barrett, *Gospel according to St. John*, 557; Burge, *John*, 532.

82. See Christine Schlund, *"Kein Knochen soll gebrochen warden": Studien zu Bedeutung und Funktion des Pesachfests in Texten des frühen Judentums und im Johannesevangelium* (WMANT 107; Neukirchen-Vluyn: Neukirchener, 2005); Porter, "Traditional Exegesis," 418–21.

83. Applied to Jesus in 1 Cor 5:7 and 1 Pet 1:19. See Brown, *Gospel according to John XIII–XXI*, 952–53; Moloney, *Gospel of John*, 509. The reference to bones not being broken in Exod 12:46 comes in the context of requirements for Passover observance. No bone of the sacrificial animal must be broken, among other reasons, as a symbol of the unity of the worshiping family and of the entire covenant community. This passage forms the conclusion of the exodus narrative, which began with references to people's bondage in Egypt and Moses' call in chapters 1–4.

84. David Daube, *The New Testament and Rabbinic Judaism* (London: Athlone, 1956), 325–29; cf. Alexander Scheiber, "'Ihr sollt kein Bein dran zerbrechen,'" *VT* 13 (1963): 95–97.

their bondage in Egypt (Exod 12:46; Num 9:12). This marks out Jesus as the "Lamb of God, who takes away the sin of the world" (John 1:29, 36) in keeping with the Baptist's witness. This pattern of typology is also part and parcel of the Johannine replacement theme, according to which Jesus fulfills the symbolism inherent in a variety of Jewish festivals and institutions.

Also, in keeping with Davidic typology, Jesus is presented as a righteous man who is preserved by God in keeping with the assurance expressed by God's servants in the past (Ps 34:20). According to the fourth evangelist, just as God brought about deliverance from bondage for OT Israel through the exodus, he provided redemption from sin through the vicarious death of Jesus. This Passover symbolism, in turn, is applied to God's preservation of the righteous sufferer, signaling that both motifs converge in Jesus, who was both God's perfect Passover lamb and the paradigmatic Davidic righteous sufferer.

23.3 Jesus' Fulfillment of Tabernacles Symbolism

John 7 and 8 do not include any "sign" of Jesus, featuring instead two cycles of Jesus' teaching at the Festival of Tabernacles (7:1–52; 8:12–59).[85] This is now the third (and as it turns out, final) trip of Jesus to Jerusalem (cf. 2:13; 5:1), which finds Jesus spending two months in the Jewish capital from the Festival of Tabernacles to the Festival of Dedication (10:22). At this stage of Jesus' ministry, he is increasingly viewed within the matrix of messianic expectations. Was the Coming One to emerge from secret, mysterious beginnings (7:4, 10, 27), or was he a known figure of Davidic descent (7:41–42)? Did Jesus' miracles identify him as Messiah (7:21, 31)?

In John 7 and 8, the evangelist addresses these issues by (1) showing Jesus' fulfillment of symbolism pertaining to the Festival of Tabernacles, and (2) dealing with representative questions regarding Jesus' identity. The narrative depicting Jesus' first teaching cycle in chapter 7 builds toward the climax of 7:37b–38, where Jesus issues the invitation to all who are thirsty to come to him and drink, so that believers would, once the Spirit had been given, become sources of "streams of living water." Thus, in keeping with the theme of Tabernacles, "with joy you will draw water from the wells of salvation" (Isa 12:3), the prophetic vision of 58:11 would be fulfilled.

Tabernacles was celebrated from 15–21 Tishri, which fell in September or October, after the grape harvest and two months prior to Dedication.[86] The feast followed shortly after the Day of Atonement and marked the conclusion of the annual cycle of religious festivals that began with Passover and Unleavened Bread six months earlier. Originally a harvest festival, Tabernacles (also called the Festival of Booths) recalled God's provision for his people during the wilderness wanderings (Lev 23:42–43; cf. Matt 17:4 pars.). Festivities lasted seven days, culminating in an eighth day of special celebration and festive assembly. Because of the daily solemn outpouring of water during the festival (Num 28:7; Isa 12:3), Tabernacles came to

---

85. The discussion under the present heading is adapted from Köstenberger, *John*, 226, 229, 239–40, and 250.

86. Lev 23:33–43; Num 29:12–39; Neh 8:13–18; Hos 12:9; Zech 14:16–19; *m. Sukkah* 5:2–4.

be associated with eschatological hopes (Zech 14:16–19). Immensely popular, it was simply called "the Festival" by the Jews.[87] Josephus (*Ant.* 8.4.1) called it "the greatest and holiest feast of the Jews."

John 7:37–39 finds Jesus at the last and greatest day of the festival. Every day during Tabernacles, priests would march in solemn procession from the Pool of Siloam to the temple and pour out water at the base of the altar. The seventh day of the festival, the last day proper (Lev 23:34, 41–42), was marked by a special water-pouring rite and lights ceremony (*m. Sukkah* 4:1, 9–10). This was to be followed by a sacred assembly on the eighth day, which was set apart for sacrifices, the joyful dismantling of the booths, and repeated singing of the *Hallel* (Psalms 113–118; cf. Lev 23:36; Num 29:35; Neh 8:18). Hence, by the first century, many Jews had come to think of the Feast as an eight-day event (Josephus, *Ant.* 13.245; *b. Sukkah* 48b; *m. Sukkah* 5:6; 2 Macc 10:6).

Whether Jesus' words in 7:37–38 and 8:12 were uttered on the climactic seventh day with its waterpouring and torchlighting ceremonies or on the eighth day of joyful assembly and celebration, they would have had a tremendous impact on the pilgrims.[88] Just when the events of the Festival, and their attendant symbolism, were beginning to sink into people's memories, Jesus' words promised a continuous supply of water and light, perhaps also alluding to the supply of water from the rock in the wilderness.

Jesus' invitation in 7:37, "Let anyone who is thirsty come to me and drink," harks back to OT prophetic passages such as Isa 55:1.[89] Tabernacles was associated with adequate rainfall (cf. Zech 14:16–17, a passage that was read on the first day of the feast, according to the liturgy in *b. Meg.* 31a). Another OT passage associated with this feast was Isa 12:3: "With joy you will draw water from the wells of salvation." This water rite, though not prescribed in the OT, was nonetheless firmly in place well before the first century AD.[90] The festival seems to speak of the joyful restoration of Israel and the ingathering of the nations. Here Jesus presents himself as God's agent to make these end-time events a reality.

The following reference to Scripture by Jesus creates difficulty in that it does not seem to conform precisely to any one OT passage: "Whoever believes in me, as Scripture has said, rivers of living water will flow from within them" (7:38). Possible scriptural allusions include those promising spiritual blessings (Isa 58:11; cf. Prov 4:23; 5:15; Zech 14:8), including the blessing of the Spirit (Isa 12:3; 44:3; 49:10; Ezek 36:25–27; 47:1; Joel 3:18; Amos 9:11–15; Zech 13:1), in line with the Festival itself.[91] Clearly, however, it is not any one of those passages by itself, but the entire matrix of scriptural expectations associated with the eschatological abundance presaged by the Festival of Tabernacles that is in view, as reflected in the references to

---

87. E.g., 1 Kgs 8:2, 65; 12:32; 2 Chr 5:3; 7:8; Neh 8:14, 18; Ps 81:3; Ezek 45:25.

88. On the water-drawing ceremony, see Keener, *John*, 722–24.

89. Cf. Ps 42–43; Matt 5:6; John 4:10–14; 6:35; Rev 22:1–2, 17; Sir 24:19–21; 51:23–24.

90. See perhaps 1 Sam 7:6; rabbinic sources that may or may not reach back to the first century are *Pesiq. Rab.* 52:3–6; *t. Sukkah* 3:3–12.

91. Neh 9:15, 19–20; cf. Exod 17:6; Ps 105:41; Prov 18:4; Isa 43:19–20; 48:21; 55:1; Jer 2:13; 17:13; cf. 1QH 16:4–40.

the Festival in Nehemiah 9 and this chapter's references to the provision of water from the rock during Israel's wilderness wanderings.[92]

John 8:12–59 records the second teaching cycle of Jesus at the Festival of Tabernacles. In 8:12, Jesus launches a major discourse, commencing with the startling claim, "I am the light of the world." The term "light" spans the entire first half of John's gospel, from the prologue (1:4, 5, 7, 8, 9) to the concluding section (12:35, 36, 46). The motif of light and darkness ties in several thematic strands in the gospel: (1) the Word's participation in creation (1:3), (2) the moral contrast between spiritual life and spiritual death (12:35–36), (3) Jesus' fulfillment of Tabernacles symbolism (chap. 7; 8:12), and (4) Jesus' healing of the man born blind (9:4–5), which becomes a parable of the Pharisees' spiritual blindness in contrast to the man's new-found vision. The evangelist returns to the light motif at the raising of Lazarus (11:9–10) and Jesus' final indictment of Jewish unbelief (12:37–50).

23.4 Conclusion

Throughout his gospel, John taps deeply into the matrix of OT traditions in his effort to show Jesus as the fulfillment and replacement of the major institutions of Judaism. This includes holy days such as the Sabbath as well as festivals like Passover and Tabernacles. As the Johannine *Christo*-drama unfolds, it sets Jesus' story plainly within the framework of Israel's story, showing how Jesus' coming constitutes the climax and fulfillment of the messianic hopes of Israel.[93]

As Jesus is shown in Matthew's gospel to bring out the deeper meaning in the Mosaic law in the Sermon on the Mount, therefore, John demonstrates that Jesus represents the very essence conveyed by the symbolism inherent in the traditions of Judaism. For this reason it is believers in Jesus who are true to the aspirations of Judaism, while those who reject Jesus turn a deaf ear and a blind eye to God's revelation of the true meaning of these institutions in the person and work of Jesus.

24 Jesus as the New Temple

24.1 The Johannine Temple Motif and the Historical Setting of John's Gospel

As argued in the historical section of the present volume above (Part 1, chap. 1, sec. 2.1.2), the destruction of the Second Temple in AD 70 represents a plausible historical datum impacting the composition of John's gospel. It remains to validate this contention by a close reading of relevant portions of the gospel itself.[94] As will be seen, the insights generated from such a reading of this gospel in light of the

---

92. See the magisterial, detailed treatment in Carson, *Gospel according to John*, 326–28.
93. See Wright, *The New Testament and the People of God*, passim.
94. The discussion below is adapted from Köstenberger, "Destruction of the Second Temple," 104–8 (used by permission).

In addition to the sources cited in chap. 1, sec. 2.1.2 above, see also T. Desmond Alexander and Simon Gathercole, eds., *Heaven on Earth: The Temple in Biblical Theology* (Carlisle, UK: Paternoster, 2004). The essay on John's gospel was contributed by Bill Salier, "The Temple in the Gospel according to John" (pp. 121–34), who

then-recent destruction of the temple strongly underscores the plausibility of the thesis that the destruction of the Second Temple constitutes an important part of the matrix that occasioned the composition of this document. Such a study will also contribute to a better apprehension of the salvation-historical substructure of John's gospel, including the Johannine replacement theme.

The discussion below will trace the emerging Johannine motif of Jesus as the fulfillment of Jewish religious symbolism related both to religious institutions such as the tabernacle or the temple (1:14, 51; 2:14–22; 4:19–24) and to various religious festivals such as Tabernacles or Dedication (7:1–8:59; 10:22–39). This includes the recognition that physical locations of worship are inadequate (4:19–24) and that Jesus now is the proper focus of worship (9:38; 20:28). While the temple is acknowledged as an important symbol of Jewish religious identity in Jesus' day (11:48–52), John's gospel conveys the recognition that there needed to be a permanent substitute for the temple in the life and worship of God's people in keeping with OT messianic expectations, whereby the silence regarding the temple in John 13–17 points to Jesus as the temple's permanent replacement.

Before dealing with the internal evidence concerning the destruction of the Second Temple in John's gospel, a preliminary adjudication must be made as to which passages are relevant to this subject. Unfortunately, the literature does not yield a clear consensus. R. J. McKelvey, in his important work *The New Temple*, includes 1:14; 1:51; 2:13–22; 4:20–26; 10:16; 11:52; and 12:20ff. The last three passages deal with the gathering of people as the new temple.[95]

Peter Walker, in his survey of the temple theme in the NT, discusses 1:14; 2:20–21; 4:21–24; 7:14–8:59; 10:22–39; and 11:48–53. Under a separate heading, Walker deals with "the Temple of believers," treating 14:2, 23, and other passages. Walker acknowledges that this theme "has been noted less frequently."[96]

Mary Coloe, in her revised thesis *God Dwells with Us*, treats 1:1–18; 2:13–25; 4:1–45; 7:1–8:59; 10:22–42; 14:1–31; and 18:1–19:42. While Coloe favors a replacement motif in these passages, she gives little consideration to historical issues.[97] This is true also of another recent dissertation by Paul Hoskins, who first (owing to the passage's primary importance) discusses 2:18–22 and then proceeds to deal with 1:14, 51 and 4:20–24.[98] In a separate chapter, Hoskins covers Jesus' fulfillment of the Jewish festivals Passover, Tabernacles, and Dedication.[99]

---

notes that "John portrays Jesus as not only revealing the divine presence in the midst of the Temple, but also replacing the Temple as the locus of divine presence" (p. 125).

95. R. J. McKelvey, *The New Temple: The Church in the New Testament* (Oxford Theological Monographs; Oxford: Oxford University Press, 1969), 75–84. Cf. the survey by Kerr, *Temple of Jesus' Body*, 2–8.

96. Walker, *Jesus and the Holy City*, 170.

97. Coloe, *God Dwells with Us*. See also Kinzer, "Temple Christology in the Gospel of John," 447–64, who points to John 1:14; 1:51; 2:20; 4:20–24; chaps. 7–10; and 14:2–3 and notes links with wisdom Christology; Jesus as the bearer of the divine name and glory; the vision of God; heaven; and pneumatology, and contends that "the Gospel of John may tell us as much about first-century Jewish Temple mysticism as it does about the first-century Jesus movement" (p. 464).

98. Hoskins, *Jesus as the Fulfillment of the Temple*, chap. 3.

99. Ibid., chap. 4. Studies of individual Johannine passages include those by Nereparampil, *Destroy this Temple*; James McCaffrey, *The House with Many Rooms: The Temple Theme of Jn 14,2–3* (Rome: Biblical Institute Press, 1988). Judith Lieu, "Temple and Synagogue in John," *NTS* 45 (1999): 51–69, esp. 66–67, contends that Jesus neither replaces nor fulfills the Jerusalem temple.

Accepting these findings as representative, I will treat John 1:14, 51; 2:14–22; 4:19–24; 7:1–8:59; 10:22–39; 11:48–52; and will add 9:38 and 20:28.[100] The reason for exclusion of 10:16 and 12:20ff is that these passages contain no demonstrable direct temple references (though the OT background is rich).[101] Alleged temple references in 13:1–17 are likewise doubtful and rest on parallels that can hardly establish links between the footwashing or the Father's house and the temple.[102] Finally, 18:20 simply refers to the public nature of Jesus' teaching "in synagogue and temple" and should not be overtheologized.[103] The reasons for including 9:38 and 20:28 should become clear in discussion of those texts.

It would seem, then, that all temple references relevant to this discussion appear in the first eleven chapters of the gospel.[104] In these chapters, the temple, as the center of Jewish national and religious identity, serves as the setting for Jesus' interaction with "the Jews." As will be seen below, in these chapters are several passages that suggest that Jesus will replace the temple in the life and worship of the new messianic community. The question remains whether the second half of John's gospel (John 13–21) conjures up notions of temple theology with reference to Jesus (as McCaffrey, Kerr, and others have argued) or whether subsequent to Jesus' exaltation there is no substitute for the temple other than Jesus himself (my view).[105] Rather than starting with 2:18–22 (as Hoskins does), it seems best for the most part to follow the narrative sequence, which also happens to sort the passages almost perfectly by thematic context.

The following discussion will trace the Johannine motif of Jesus as the fulfillment (and thus replacement) of Jewish religious symbolism, including sites of worship such as the tabernacle or the temple (1:14, 51; 2:14–22; 4:19–24) and various religious festivals such as Tabernacles or Dedication (7:1–8:59; 10:22–39).[106] This fulfillment Christology entails the recognition that physical locations of worship are inadequate (esp. 4:19–24) and leads to the conclusion that Jesus is now the proper

---

100. There will be an inevitable overlap with the previous section, where Jesus' fulfillment of symbolism related to Jewish festivals and holy days was the subject of discussion. In the present section the focus is on Jesus as the new temple.

101. On John 10:16, see Köstenberger, "Jesus the Good Shepherd."

102. See, e.g., Kerr, *Temple of Jesus' Body*, 268–313, who essentially follows and further develops McCaffrey, *House with Many Rooms*, though by his own admission temple parallels in 13:1–14:3 are "less clear" and "in effect [the] argument is cumulative" (p. 7). Kerr argues that, by cleansing them, Jesus prepares his followers for entry in the new temple, just as priests needed to be cleansed in order to be ceremonially clean prior to entering the OT sanctuary. He also maintains that the "Father's house" in 14:2, taken in connection with 2:21, is Jesus himself (p. 292). However, these conclusions are hardly self-evident. Rather, the emphasis in the Farewell Discourse seems to be on the lack of need on the part of Jesus' followers for any mediatorial device once Jesus is exalted to the Father (see below). Cf. the critique of McCaffrey's proposal in Hoskins, *Jesus as the Fulfillment of the Temple*, 12–15. See also Salier, "Temple," 133 (also contra, McCaffrey), who "wonders if this is not overreading the motif in a Gospel that remains very much Christoloigcally centred."

He continues, "Certainly the language of intimacy and relationship abounds throughout the farewell discourse, but it does not appear to draw in the imagery of the Temple such that the disciples replace the Temple in any sense through their association with Jesus. This is language for other voices in the New Testament." As Salier notes, the "Temple's" presence will continue "through the ministry of the Spirit and the word."

103. Contra, Lieu, "Temple and Synagogue," 51–69, esp. 66–67, who contends that in John the temple is not placed under judgment and hence Jesus does not replace the temple. However, this hardly squares with both the action performed and the words spoken by Jesus at the temple clearing in 2:14–22 (see the similar criticism in Kerr, *Temple of Jesus' Body*, 5, n. 25).

104. Cf. Kinzer, "Temple Christology in the Gospel of John," 450: "The key texts for Temple Christology in John are found primarily in the prologue and 'The Book of Signs' (Jn 1–12)."

105. If so, this would be in harmony with Rev 21:22: "I did not see a temple in the city, because the Lord God Almighty and the Lamb are its temple" (cf. v. 3). See further below.

106. In this regard there will be a certain amount of inevitable overlap between the treatment below and the discussion in the preceding section (23).

focus of worship (9:38; 20:28). As the proper focus of worship, Jesus replaces any temple, implying that the Jerusalem temple is obsolete (11:48–52; 13–21). The silence regarding the temple in John 13–21 is a rhetorical device pointing to Jesus as its permanent replacement.

This discussion will serve both to elucidate theological concerns John entertains in light of the loss of the temple and to yield evidence from the gospel itself to confirm our supposition that the destroyed temple indeed preoccupied John.

24.2 Jesus as Fulfillment of Temple and Related Symbolism

Oscar Cullmann expresses well how comprehensively Jesus replaces the temple in John's gospel:

> Opposition to the Temple worship, or rather, the spiritualization of the Temple worship is an essential idea for the Fourth Gospel. The divine Presence, which had until now been bound to the Temple of Jerusalem, is from now on visible in the Person of Jesus Christ, in the Word made flesh. The Evangelist sees the idea that Christ takes the place of the Temple to be realized *in the events of the life of Jesus.*

Cullmann continues:

> He [the evangelist] tries to show through the life of the incarnate Jesus that from now on the question of worship must be asked differently.... The Divine glory, in Hebrew *shekinah*, previously limited to the Temple is visible in Jesus Christ.... For every Jew the *shekinah*, the Divine glory, is limited to the Temple. But from now on it is separated from the Temple, because it is bound to the *Logos* become flesh.[107]

Following Cullmann, Jesus' replacement of the Temple constitutes a fundamental axiom of Johannine Christology, an axiom given concrete expression in various specific pericopae of the Johannine narrative.[108]

The first four chapters of John's gospel develop a Christology of Jesus as the fulfillment of the symbolism of Jewish religious institutions such as the tabernacle (1:14), Bethel (where Jacob saw the ladder of angels), which means "the house of God" (1:51), the temple (2:14–22), and Jerusalem (4:19–24).

24.2.1 The Word Made Flesh: The New Tabernacle

Not only does John's gospel acknowledge the Temple's central significance in the life of the Jewish nation even as it points to the inadequacy of physical locations of worship, it presents the manifestation of God's presence in Jesus as the climax of

---

107. Oscar Cullmann, "A New Approach to the Interpretation of the Fourth Gospel," *ExpTim* 71 (1959): 12, 41–42, cited in Walker, *Jesus and the Holy City*, 170.

108. Apart from fulfilling Temple symbolism, Jesus is also presented as fulfilling symbolism related to a variety of Jewish religious festivals, including Passover (1:29, 36; 6:4), the Sabbath (5:1–15; chap. 9), Tabernacles (7:14–8:59), and Dedication (10:36; see further below). On the Johannine replacement motif, see especially Carson, *Gospel according to John*, 399; Brown, *Gospel according to John I–XII*, lxx; and Davies, *Gospel and the Land*, 296 (the latter two cited in Walker, *Jesus and the Holy City*, 170).

previous, provisional manifestations of God in the history of God's people. This is evident in the programmatic, salvation-historical references to Jesus in the opening verses of the Gospel.

John's introduction provides significant data for our present purposes in at least two ways. To begin with, by presenting Jesus as God's agent in creation, who came to his own but suffered rejection (1:3–4, 10–11), the introduction provides a pattern taken up in the narrative of Jesus' visitation of the temple in 2:14–22. As Peter Walker aptly notes, "When it becomes clear that this God is the God of Israel and that Jesus is himself a Jew, the question is inevitably raised: What will happen when Jesus comes to Jerusalem?"[109]

A second way in which the introduction prepares the reader for the temple clearing is the reference to the Word being made flesh and "dwelling among us" (*skenoō*, 1:14), which links Jesus with God's presence among his people in the tabernacle and later the temple (Exodus 26–27; 1 Kgs 6:13).[110] Hence Jesus is here shown to appropriate the temple's theological status and to fulfill God's promise to dwell among his people in a new temple.[111] What contemporary Judaism claimed for Jerusalem and the Torah, namely, that they were the focal points of the entire cosmos, John claims for Jesus.[112]

Particularly important here is the linkage between the notion of the Word being made flesh in Jesus and the notion of the presence of divine glory, since glory is frequently in the OT related to God's self-manifestation in the tabernacle and Solomon's Temple.[113] Moreover, the Second Temple period witnessed the growing expectation that God would manifest his glory at some future time.[114] Against the backdrop of Exod 33:18–23, where Moses asked for, but did not receive, a (full) revelation of God's glory, but was instead promised the divine name, Jesus is shown to reveal God's glory, and people are called to believe in his "name" and become children of God.[115]

In a further development of the thinking in 1:14, the fourth evangelist makes clear in 1:16–17 that, while the law constitutes an earlier instance of God's gracious provision for his people, the fullness of his grace was given in and through Jesus Christ. The thought of 1:14–17 culminates in 1:18 where Jesus is shown to surpass

---

109. Ibid., 163–64, who goes on to suggest that "as with the other Gospels, the prophecy in Mal. 3:1 (of the 'Lord coming to his Temple') may not be far from the evangelist's mind" (ibid., 164, n. 11).

110. See the thorough discussion of possible links between the introduction to John's gospel and the temple in Kerr, *Temple of Jesus' Body*, 102–25. On 1:14 in relation to Jesus' replacement of the temple in John, see Hoskins, *Jesus as the Fulfillment of the Temple*, 116–24. See also the treatment of 1:14–17 in Salier, "Temple," 126–28.

111. See the discussion of messianic expectations above. On the connection between NT "filling" references with the OT Temple, see Andreas J. Köstenberger, "What Does It Mean To Be Filled with the Spirit?" *JETS* 40 (1997): 229–40, esp. 230.

112. Walker, *Jesus and the Holy City*, 165, n. 14, citing Wright, *New Testament and the People of God*. As Walker (ibid., 165, citing Koester, *Dwelling of God*, 115) notes, the tabernacle and the temple could rightly be seen "as God's preparation of his people for the eventual coming of Jesus."

113. For references see Hoskins, *Jesus as the Fulfillment of the Temple*, 119, n. 54. See also Gordon McConville, "God's 'Name' and God's 'Glory,'" *TynBul* 30 (1979): 149–68.

114. Cf. Sir 36:19; 2 Macc 2:7–8; 4QFlor [4Q174] 1:5.

115. See Salier, "Temple," 127, who observes, "Glory seems to connote the divine majesty of God that is somehow dangerous and therefore unapproachable, while the name connotes 'accessibility, availability, and approachability in worship'" (citing William J. Dumbrell, *The Search for Order: Biblical Eschatology in Focus* [Grand Rapids: Baker, 1994], 239).

all previous revelations of God, including those to Moses and those expressed in the law, the tabernacle, and the temple.

24.2.2 Jesus and the Open Heaven: The New House of God

While the interpretation of John 1:51 is disputed, on any of the major readings the implication of this passage is that it is in and through the Son of Man that God now speaks to his people.[116] As the recipient of God's word, like Jacob, Jesus conveys God's message to others. Similar to Jacob's ladder, Jesus is also the means by which God communicates. Thus Jesus constitutes the typological fulfillment of the pattern both initiated and anticipated by Bethel, the first "house of God."

The Son of Man will be "lifted up" (a double entendre, meaning "crucified" as well as "honored"; John 3:14; 8:28; 12:32), which focuses God's revelation in his Son particularly in the Son's crucifixion and resurrection (joined in John's gospel under the rubric of "glorification," 12:23; 17:1). The Son of Man of 1:51 is the incarnate Word of 1:14, and both titles anticipate 2:14–22 and 4:19–24, where the Johannine christological motif of Jesus' replacement and/or fulfillment of sacred space emerges.[117]

24.2.3 Clearing the Sanctuary: The New Temple

Perhaps the primary expression of the replacement/fulfillment motif is the account of Jesus' clearing of the temple in 2:14–22.[118] I have argued elsewhere that the temple clearing is properly to be considered a Johannine sign.[119] While not "miraculous" in the sense of natural laws being suspended, the event, as an act of predictive-prophetic symbolism, closely resembles the OT *sēmeion* (e.g., Isa 20:3). This is affirmed by Walker, among others, who suggests "that Jesus' cleansing of the Temple was an enacted parable, a sign of its forthcoming destruction."[120] Interpreted this way, the temple clearing takes on pivotal significance for John's portrayal of Jesus' messianic mission. As one of Jesus' early Jerusalem signs (see John 2:23; 3:2), the temple clearing signals Jesus' zeal to restore pure worship of God in the central sanctuary of the Jewish capital (echoing OT prophetic concerns: cf. Zech 14:21; Mal 3:1, 3).[121] What is more, Jesus' "ironic imperative" in John 2:19 portends that "the Temple would be profoundly affected by the coming of Jesus, and especially by his death."[122]

---

116. Though note Kerr, *Temple of Jesus' Body*, 136–66, who devotes an entire chapter to an investigation of 1:51 and concludes that there is in that passage no reference to Jacob's ladder or to the house of God, Bethel, nor is there any pre-Christian evidence linking Bethel with the temple (contra, Davies, *Gospel and the Land*, 296–97; A. T. Hanson, *The Prophetic Gospel* [Edinburgh: T&T Clark, 1991], 73; and McKelvey, *New Temple*, 77).

117. Hoskins, *Jesus as the Fulfillment of the Temple*, 135.

118. See Hoskins (ibid., 108–16), who discusses 2:18–22 first.

119. See the treatment of the Johannine "signs," chap. 4, sec. 10.2.1.2.2 and chap. 7, sec. 15 above. On the NT characterization of the Jerusalem temple, see esp. Walker, *Jesus and the Holy City*, 162, who notes that 80 percent of the Johannine narrative is located in Jerusalem compared with 30 percent in Matthew.

120. Walker, *Jesus and the Holy City*, 165.

121. See ibid., 177–80; Morris, *Gospel according to John*, 166–69. For the present purposes, it is sufficient to suppose that the clearing recorded in John is historical rather than merely theologically motivated. This is suggested, among other things, by the fairly tight chronological embeddedness of the pericope in the Johannine narrative and by the fact that John's gospel as a whole seems to follow a chronological format of presentation (see esp. the chart in Köstenberger, *Encountering John*, 67, and the more detailed chart in idem, "John," in *ZIBBC*, 2:23).

122. Walker, *Jesus and the Holy City*, 166.

The season in which the temple clearing occurs, Passover (2:13, 23), lends further significance to the event and is part of the fourth evangelist's portrayal of Jesus in terms of Passover fulfillment and replacement.[123] At the heart of the temple clearing is judgment symbolism. Jesus hints at the future destruction of the temple ("destroy this temple," 2:19), an event probably lying in the recent past for the readers of John's gospel, and the evangelist identifies the "temple" as Jesus' body (2:21). It is not that the physical structure of the temple will be "raised" (i.e., restored after destruction); rather, Jesus' body will be raised from the dead after having been crucified. The need for renewal of the Jerusalem sanctuary thus gives way to an expectation of its replacement.

The Jews, for their part, are incredulous that something as enduring as the temple (note the reference to the forty-six years in 2:20[124]) would be destroyed, forgetting that similar judgment fell on the sanctuary at the time of the Babylonian exile. They are even more incredulous that it could be restored in just three days. Yet what to them sounded like the utterances of one who had quite literally lost his mind came to pass in the years to come: Jesus was raised, and the temple was destroyed (cf. Matt 24:1–2 par.). While Jerusalem lost its central place of worship, with Jesus a new center of worship arose, one that commanded widespread faith and acceptance.

The interim between Jesus' resurrection and the destruction of the temple still veiled the revolutionary implications of these events for Judaism. Yet when the temple was finally destroyed, Jewish worship, already condemned by Jesus as corrupt and defiled, suffered a fatal blow, which left worship of Jesus (understood as temple) without an operative (temple) alternative. It is my contention that it is this vacuum that John sought to exploit by writing his gospel. This is why the second Johannine sign still possessed relevance for his audience: the recent destruction of the temple transparently vindicated Jesus' act of clearing the temple as a precursor of the complete divine judgment, which demonstrated the truth of the prophetic symbolism in his actions.

The Jews in Jesus' original audience do not understand the symbolism; having witnessed the temple clearing, Jesus' prophetic sign of the Jerusalem sanctuary's destruction, they still ask for a sign (2:18). Jesus provides none; instead, he discourses on the significance of the sign he has just performed. What is more, as the evangelist frankly acknowledges, Jesus' followers likewise failed to understand the sign. Only when their memory is triggered by the resurrection itself do they make the connection (2:22).

The fourth gospel's intended readers had the benefit of being able to read the temple clearing pericope in the light not only of Easter, but also of the events of AD 70. John's first readers were in a position to understand the temple clearing as a sign

---

123. See the previous section.

124. On the interpretation of the reference to the forty-six years in 2:20, see Köstenberger, "John," in *ZIBBC*, 2.33. Contra, Brown, *Gospel according to John I–XII*, 115, who starts counting from the start (rather than completion) of construction in 20/19 BC and thus reaches a date of AD 27/28 (rather than 29/30), and then puzzlingly says the fifteenth year of Tiberius referred to in Luke 3:1 is AD 27/28 according to the Syrian calendar with antedating (more likely, with Tiberius's reign commencing in AD 14, the 15th year is AD 29).

indicating the inner meaning of Jesus' crucifixion and bodily resurrection, a sign that presented Jesus as both the fulfillment and the replacement of the symbolic meaning of the temple, the new and true center of worship for his new messianic community. Indeed, "Jesus himself, in his own body, was a new 'Temple' ... [who] embodied in himself the meaning of the Temple and all that it had previously signified."[125]

24.2.4 The Inadequacy of Physical Locations of Worship: The New Worship

The motif of Jesus' replacement of sacred space emerges with increasing clarity as the Johannine narrative progresses, as allusions in 1:14 and 51 give way to more overt references in 2:14–22 and the present passage (4:19–24).[126] While Jesus is identified already as the "new temple" at the temple clearing, his interchange with the Samaritan woman in 4:19–24 crystallizes the thrust of this identification yet further. In response to the Samaritan's question of whether proper worship was to be rendered on Mount Gerizim or in Jerusalem, Jesus transcends the dichotomy by suggesting that acceptability of worship to God is not contingent on physical location but that acceptable worship is a matter of spirit and truth. The clear implication of Jesus' words is that, while Jewish worship is clearly superior to Samaritan worship in that it is based, not on ignorance, but on knowledge (4:22), even the Jerusalem temple is not the final word on the subject.

Just as the Samaritan temple had been destroyed 150 years prior to Jesus' conversation with the Samaritan (Josephus, *Ant.* 13.255–56), so the Jerusalem sanctuary did not represent the permanent standard for worship of God.[127] Rather, such worship must be rendered "in spirit and in truth" (John 4:23 NIV). This follows from the fact that God himself is spirit (4:24). As Walker notes, "even though the events of AD 70 took place forty years later, the manifestation of Jesus meant that in principle the time had already come when 'Jerusalem' (4:21) would lose its distinctive status: 'the time is coming and *has now come*' (4:23)."[128] Later in the Johannine narrative, the formerly blind man becomes an example of true worship (9:38). Perhaps significantly, this worship is rendered after the man's expulsion from the synagogue (9:22).[129]

Worship in spirit and truth, then, is superior to worship at physical locations such as the temple for a number of reasons. (1) Such spiritual worship is commensurate to God's nature as spirit. (2) Worship in spirit rather than tied to a physical location is in keeping with faith as the universal requirement for inclusion in the people of God, which transcends belonging to an ethnic group as a distinctive (cf. John 1:12; 3:16). (3) Such worship is "in truth," that is, focused on Jesus as "the truth" (14:6) and based on his final, definitive revelation of the Father (14:9–11; cf. 1:18; 10:30). Such worship is part of the discipleship desired by Jesus, which

---

125. Walker, *Jesus and the Holy City*, 163.
126. See Hoskins, *Jesus as the Fulfillment of the Temple*, 135; and the same author's examination of 4:20–24 in light of its context in John's gospel as well as the OT and extrabiblical Jewish parallels on pp. 135–45.
127. See Walker, *Jesus and the Holy City*, 166.
128. Ibid., 197; similarly, 166.
129. See ibid., 169. On 9:38, see the discussion below.

involves holding to his teaching, which in turn results in liberation by and for truth (8:31–32). (4) There also seems to be an implicit connection between worship "in spirit and truth" and the "Spirit of truth" (14:17; 15:26; 16:12), whom Jesus' followers were about to receive.

While the first four chapters of John's gospel feature the emerging motif of Jesus' replacement of Jewish religious institutions such as the tabernacle (1:14), Bethel the "house of God" (1:51), the temple (2:14–22), or Jerusalem itself (4:19–24), the second major portion of the first half of John's gospel (i.e., John 5–12) further develops this motif in terms of Jesus' fulfillment/replacement of the symbolism of various Jewish religious festivals such as Tabernacles or Dedication.[130]

24.2.5 Jesus at the Festival of Tabernacles: The New Provision

Subsequent to the temple clearing of John 2:14–22, Jesus several times returns to Jerusalem and the temple at the occasions of religious festivals, such as Tabernacles (7:1–8:59) or Dedication (10:22–39). As Walker correctly points out, the placement of the temple clearing early in John's gospel has the effect of placing Jesus' subsequent involvement with the temple "under a cloud."[131] The readers are aware that Jesus' appearances at the temple must not be construed as his endorsement of that institution; the temple simply served as the natural site for Jesus' instruction of his followers in Jerusalem (cf. 18:20). At the same time, Jesus' return visits to the temple are necessitated by his identity as the temple's substitute, the "new temple." It is impossible for him to claim to be such at a distance; this claim must be asserted on site.

Jesus does so in several ways. (1) He relates his coming to symbolism contained in the Festival of Tabernacles—which looked back to Moses' producing water by striking the rock in the wilderness (Exod 17:1–7; Num 20:8–13) and looked forward to a day when water would flow from Jerusalem and the temple (Ezek 47:1–12; Zech 14:8)—by issuing the statement that "rivers of living water" would flow from the innermost being of believers in the Messiah (John 7:37–38).[132] Thus, prophetic symbolism is not only fulfilled but superseded: water would flow, not from Jerusalem and the temple, but from believers nurtured by their messianic faith.

(2) Jesus claims to be "the light of the world" (not merely Jerusalem, John 8:12; cf. 9:5), once again fulfilling yet transcending Jewish categories. This statement not only engages in Tabernacles symbolism, it also involves a claim on Jesus' part regarding the "I am," the divine name. Replacement theology is inherent in Jesus' self-designation "I am," which comes to the fore in the series of "I am statements" featured in John's gospel. Prior to Jesus' coming, the temple constituted the locus of the divine name. Now John presents us with "a new *locus*—not a place but a person.... The time of fulfillment has come: the Temple is to be replaced—by a person."[133] Notably, the

---

130. Other examples include the Sabbath (John 5) and Passover (John 6).
131. See Walker, *Jesus and the Holy City*, 167.
132. This presupposes a traditional (rather than narrowly christological) reading of the present passage (see, e.g., Barrett, *Gospel according to St. John*, 327). See already the discussion of Jesus' fulfillment of Tabernacles symbolism in the previous section above.
133. Walker, *Jesus and the Holy City*, 168.

conflict surrounding Jesus issues in his departure from the temple, an act of judgment akin to the withdrawal of the divine presence (8:59; cf. Matt 23:38–24:1).

24.2.6 Jesus at the Festival of Dedication: The New Liberation

Jesus returns to the temple in 10:22–39, though "compared to the extended episode in 7:14–8:59, this is but a brief return, and Jesus' location 'in Solomon's Colonnade' indicates his comparative 'disengagement' from the festival proceedings."[134] The visit turns out to be the final visit to the temple recorded in John's gospel. There is but one more mention of Jesus' presence at the temple in the subsequent narrative in 18:20, where reference is made to his preceding public teaching ministry. In the Johannine context, this can only refer to the previous instances recorded in 2:14–22; 7:14–8:59; and 10:22–39.[135]

24.3 Jesus as the Proper Focus of Worship

24.3.1 Giving Sight to the Blind: A New Way of Seeing

The first major reference to an individual's worship of Jesus in John's gospel is the account of the man born blind in 9:38. In light of the opening references to Jesus Christ as the preexistent, divine Word, not to mention other references to Jesus' preexistence in this gospel (e.g., 8:58; 17:25), this scene of worship (together with other references, such as 20:28; see below) clearly identifies Jesus as both divine and the proper object of worship. While it has often been alleged that the high Christology of John's gospel (including its reference to Jesus as the object of worship) is a late development and unhistorical, such skepticism seems unfounded.

On the one hand, not only John but also the Synoptics make clear that the major charge against Jesus leading to his crucifixion was that of blasphemy.[136] Hence even his opponents acknowledged not only that Jesus performed remarkable miracles, but that he claimed divinity for himself. If this is so, however, there seems to be no good reason to dispute that Jesus' followers directed worship toward Jesus. Clearly Jesus was no ordinary rabbi; he taught with unparalleled authority and supported his messianic claims with tangible demonstrations of his identity (the "signs").[137]

24.3.2 Eliciting Faith from the Skeptic: Seeing and Believing

Thomas's confession of Jesus as "my Lord and my God" in 20:28 constitutes an *inclusio* with 1:1 and represents the most overt instance of worship of Jesus as God in any of the Gospels. Earlier in this gospel, Thomas emerged as a sharp yet skeptical member of the Twelve (11:16). The present instance follows on the heels of Jesus' resurrection appearance to the Twelve-minus-Judas-minus-Thomas. When Jesus

---

134. Ibid., 169. As mentioned at 12.2.1.3.7 above, Poirier, "Hanukkah," contends that John 7–10 in their entirety take place at the Feast of Dedication, though this is doubtful in light of the reference to Tabernacles at 7:2 and the wording of 10:22.

135. So rightly Walker, *Jesus and the Holy City*, 169, n. 32.

136. See Darrell L. Bock, *Blasphemy and Exaltation in Judaism and the Final Examination of Jesus* (WUNT 2/106; Tübingen: Mohr-Siebeck, 1998).

137. See my essay "Jesus as a Rabbi"; on Jesus' signs, see the discussion in chap. 7, sec. 15 above.

appears again to the same group, this time with Thomas present, the latter becomes the foil for Jesus' lesson that believing apart from seeing is superior to believing on the basis of physical sight.

For the gospel's readers, this constitutes an encouragement to believe the apostolic testimony enshrined in the present gospel rather than expecting or demanding "signs" akin to the one Jesus had performed during the course of his earthly ministry with the Jews.[138] As in the case of the formerly blind man in 9:38, Thomas's believing confession climaxes the narrative. What is more, Thomas's confession climaxes the entire gospel, making the decisive point that the only proper response to the revelation in John's gospel that Jesus is the fulfillment of Jewish religious symbolism is that of worship.

24.4 And What of the Temple?

24.4.1 The Destruction of the Temple as a Symbol of Jewish Religious Identity

Placed toward the end of the first half of the gospel, 11:48–52 is one of several passages which show the importance of the temple as a symbol of Jewish religious identity in Jesus' day. In this irony-laden passage, the Jewish high priest, Caiaphas, justifies the Sanhedrin's decision to have Jesus crucified by saying this is necessary in order to avert the threat of the Roman destruction of "our temple and our nation" (11:48). Hence, the temple is viewed as central to the nation's ethos.

As the reader is perfectly aware, of course, Caiaphas's strategy turned out to be a miscalculation of colossal proportions. Not only did Jesus rise (thus thwarting the Jewish leadership's attempt to silence him), but the temple was destroyed by the Romans all the same. This means that Jesus, not the Jewish leadership, stands vindicated by the divine verdict rendered in favor of Jesus and against the representatives of old-style Judaism, which centered on the temple and the external trappings of Jewish worship.

Ironically, therefore, Jesus would still "be involved mysteriously in the Temple's destruction—though not in the way the Sanhedrin feared."[139] As Peter Walker asks:

> Was there ... any organic connection between the eventual fate of the Temple and the way Jesus, who had already been presented as a new "Temple" (2:22), was sacrificed so that that "old" Temple might be preserved? John does not make this connection explicit; yet his readers have been given some clear encouragement to develop their thoughts along these lines.[140]

In its acknowledgment of the temple as a central Jewish religious symbol, John's gospel is firmly in keeping with historical evidence that the temple did indeed

---

138. The same dynamic is at work in the "three witnesses" text in 1 John 5:6–10, where a second generation of believers is assured in their faith by the historical acts of Jesus (water and blood)—knowledge of which is mediated through the apostolic testimony—but more immediately by the Holy Spirit's presence in the community and individuals. See Streett, "They Went Out from Us."
139. Walker, *Jesus and the Holy City*, 166–67.
140. Ibid., 196.

have such a function in Jewish life in Jesus' day. This explains why Jesus squarely addressed the function of the temple in contemporary Judaism and related his own coming as Jewish Messiah to the temple's significance. The reference to the temple in 11:48–52 comes at an important juncture in John's gospel, where old-style Judaism is shown to cling vainly to its national symbol.

24.4.2 A Telling Silence: The Setting Aside of the Temple

Notably, the fourth evangelist is silent on the temple in the second half of his gospel. As Bill Salier observes, "By the end of chapter 10 the Temple has been set aside within John's narrative."[141] This highlights the fulfillment and replacement of the temple in the person of Jesus. In the same vein, Peter Walker notes, "The subsequent setting aside of the Temple within John's narrative indicates how it has also been set aside within the purposes of God. The Temple has been eclipsed."[142]

Walker contends that for John believers share in Jesus' status as the new temple, pointing especially to the reference to the "Father's house" in 14:2. However, it is far from clear that this reference is to be construed in terms of temple imagery.[143] Moreover, Walker's contention seems to conflict with the observation that John is silent regarding the temple in the second half of his gospel. To be sure, other NT writers (such as Paul and Peter) apply temple symbolism to believers; it is not clear that the fourth evangelist does this.

More promising, however, is the emphasis on Jesus as the one who provides direct access to the Father in the Farewell Discourse (e.g., 14:6–11; 16:26–27). No longer must worshipers come to God by sacrificing in the temple; they can simply approach God through prayer in Jesus' name. It is consistent with a section that everywhere anticipates Jesus' exaltation with the Father that the temple is all but gone, since Jesus' presence with the Father will render any other mediatorial edifice unnecessary.[144] As Jesus predicted in the sign of the temple clearing and in his statement to the Samaritan woman, and as the fourth evangelist explained, Jesus himself in his body is the temple through whom worshipers in the future must offer worship acceptable to the Father.

24.4.3 The Temple for the Nations

What is more, as Bill Salier perceptively notes, "the theme of the Temple is also connected to the wider perspective evinced by the Gospel. As Jesus replaces the Temple for Israel there are also hints that he will fulfill the role of the Temple with respect to the nations."[145] The Johannine narrative provides several indications of

---

141. Salier, "Temple," 131.
142. Ibid., 169.
143. Cf. Köstenberger, "John," in *ZIBBC*, 2.137. For a contrasting perspective, see Steven M. Bryan, "The Eschatological Temple in John 14," *BBR* 15 (2005): 187–98.
144. See also 1 John, with its emphasis on the cultic nature of Christ's work (blood atonement and present priestly intercession; 2:1–2), as well as the idea that God dwells in/among his people (4:4). And note that in Revelation 21, John notes that there in the new heaven and the new earth there is no longer any need for a temple.
145. Salier, "Temple," 131. For a treatment of the nations in the context of biblical theology, see Andreas J. Köstenberger, "Nations," in *NDBT*, 676–78 (with additional bibliographic references on p. 678).

this enlarged framework. (1) The introduction to John's gospel casts Jesus' coming into the world against the backdrop of creation (1:1–5, 10–11).

(2) As early as in the Cana Cycle, the fourth evangelist injects the universal scope of the "world" as the sphere of God's and Jesus' activity even at what may seem to be unlikely places, such as Jesus' conversations with a Jew (Nicodemus; 3:16) or a Samaritan woman (4:42). Importantly, no longer will it be the Jerusalem temple or any other physical locations of worship, but worship "in spirit and in truth" that will be the mark of true worshipers.[146]

(3) The reference to living water, alluding to OT prophetic passages such as Zechariah 14 and Ezekiel 37, invokes the image of water flowing from the temple that "extends beyond the borders of Israel for the benefit of the nations."[147] As Salier observes, "this picks up some of the thought of the Old Testament prophets who depicted the eschatological hope of the restored Temple as the centre of the nations."[148]

(4) Even more explicitly, in the transitional section John 10–12, there are several indications that the scope of Jesus' redemptive work exceeds the confines of Israel (10:16; 11:51–52; 12:20–34). At the coming of the Greeks, Jesus makes clear that his death on the cross will produce "many seeds" (12:24), and explains that "I, when I am lifted up from the earth, will draw all people to myself" (12:32) — which most likely means "all people, both Jews and Gentiles."[149]

(5) This, in turn, is coupled with the pronouncement of the Jews' rejection of their Messiah at the conclusion of Part I of the Johannine drama (12:36b–41). In keeping with Jesus' prediction and the fourth evangelist's explanatory "aside" in 2:19–21, the temple of Jesus' body will thus be destroyed, that is, be subjected to crucifixion, and after three days be raised. Jesus, then, the fulfillment and replacement of the temple, will become the center of new worship, not only for Israel, but for all the nations.

24.5 Conclusion

Reading the gospel against the backdrop of the then-recent destruction of the temple results in recovering an important aspect of John's message, highly relevant for John's first readers. Now that the temple had been destroyed, the resurrected Jesus was without peer or rival as the new tabernacle, the new temple, and the new center of worship for a new nation that encompasses all who are united by faith in Jesus as Messiah. Walker crystallizes the issue well:

> As a result, if any of his readers felt bereft of the Temple and of the spiritual focus provided by Jerusalem, John would have encouraged them not to mourn

---

146. In light of the statement that "God is spirit" in John 4:24 and the contrast between physical and spiritual locations of worship pervading the passage, the rendering "worship in spirit and in truth" is preferable to the TNIV's "worship in the Spirit and in truth." This does not deny the reality that this kind of worship must be Spirit-aided, but it takes into account the fact that a reference to the Holy Spirit at this juncture in Jesus' ministry, with the Samaritan woman as his audience, would have been rather unlikely (see chap. 9, sec. 21, esp. 21.2, above).

147. Salier, "Temple," 132.

148. Ibid., with reference to Isa 2:2–4; Mic 4:1–3; and Jer 3:17; see also McKelvey, *New Temple*, Appendix A, pp. 188–92.

149. See Köstenberger, *John*, 384–85.

the loss of the city, but rather to see what God had done for them in Jesus.... The Evangelist, writing after the Temple's destruction, does not bemoan its loss.... The presence of God has not been withdrawn, for Jesus has taken the place of the Temple. Jesus gives more than the Temple had ever given.... Jesus stands in the place of everything that Israel has lost.[150]

In fact, "everything previously associated with Jerusalem was now available in the person of Jesus, mediated by the Spirit." He was the new temple, the true vine; "in Jesus these Jewish beliefs were all affirmed."[151] Now a new allegiance was required, and "a preparedness to say good-bye to the old." Contrary to what his audience may have felt, there was indeed "life after the destruction of the Temple," life "without Jerusalem."[152] The old order had given way to the new.

> From the moment Jesus first appeared in the city, the role of Jerusalem and its temple were destined to undergo a dramatic change. These entities would no longer be necessary for any sense of proximity to God.... God was now found in Jesus, and Jesus through the Spirit....
>
> To urge his (predominantly) Jewish readers to take this farewell to the old, and to step out into the adventure of a new life now and forever in communion with Jesus the Messiah, John wrote his Gospel.[153]

What is more, John's presentation of Jesus as the new temple is part and parcel of his depiction of Jesus' coming within the framework of salvation-history, Israel's story, which had now become the story of the followers of Jesus. Because all the various strands of OT symbolism were shown to point to, and were fulfilled in, Jesus, faith in Jesus the Word, the Messiah, the Son of God provided entrance into the rich heritage and legacy of the Hebrew scriptural material regarding the one who was to come, who would fulfill the destiny and satisfy the longings, hopes, and dreams of Judaism. At the same time, the Jewish nation, represented by its leaders (who had rejected Jesus as Messiah), is shown to be unregenerate and thus disqualified from entrance into the kingdom of God—a topic that will form the subject of further investigation in the following chapter.

---

150. Walker, *Jesus and the Holy City*, 197, citing Hoskyns and Davey, *Fourth Gospel*, 1:144; and Stephen Motyer, "John 8:31–59 and the Rhetoric of Persuasion in the Fourth Gospel" (Ph.D. thesis; King's College, London, 1992), 3. See also Pryor, *John: Evangelist of the Covenant People*, 115.

151. Walker, *Jesus and the Holy City*, 198.

152. Ibid., 199.

153. This is true despite Walker's comment that "John's reflection upon Jerusalem might not be simply a response to the great events of AD 66–70; it could be an explication of things which long before that date he had discerned to be implicit in the essential gospel message about Jesus" (*Jesus and the Holy City*, 199).

Chapter 11

THE COSMIC TRIAL MOTIF: THE WORLD, THE JEWS, AND THE WITNESSES TO JESUS

BIBLIOGRAPHY

Aalen, S. "'Truth,' a Key Word in St. John's Gospel." Pp. 3–24 in *SE* 2. Ed. Frank L. Cross. Berlin: Akademie, 1964. **Asiedu-Peprah, Martin.** *Johannine Sabbath Conflicts as Juridical Controversy.* WUNT 132. Tübingen: Mohr-Siebeck, 2001. **Bennema, Cornelis**. "The Identity and Composition of ΟΙ ΙΟΥΔΑΙΟΙ in the Gospel of John." *TynBul* 60 (2009): forthcoming. **Bieringer, Reimund, Didier Pollefeyt, and Frederique Vandecasteele-Vanneuville**, eds. *Anti-Judaism and the Fourth Gospel.* Louisville: Westminster John Knox, 2001. Idem. *Anti-Judaism and the Fourth Gospel: Papers of the Leuven Colloquium, 2000.* Assen, the Netherlands: Royal van Gorcum, 2001. **Cassem, Ned H**. "A Grammatical and Contextual Inventory of the Use of *kosmos* in the Johannine Cosmic Theology." *NTS* 19 (1972): 81–91. **Hawkin, David J**. "The Johannine Concept of Truth." *EvQ* 59 (1987): 3–13. **Kierspel, Lars**. *The Jews and the World in the Fourth Gospel: Parallelism, Function, and Context.* WUNT 2/220. Tübingen: Mohr-Siebeck, 2007. **Köstenberger, Andreas J.**, ed. *Whatever Happened to Truth?* Wheaton: Crossway, 2005. **Lincoln, Andrew T**. *Truth on Trial: The Lawsuit Motif in the Fourth Gospel.* Peabody, MA: Hendrickson, 2000. **Lindsay, Dennis R**. "What Is Truth? *Alētheia* in the Gospel of John." *ResQ* 35 (1993): 129–45. **Marrow, Stanley B**. "Κόσμος in John." *CBQ* 64 (2002): 90–102. **Söding, Thomas**. "Die Macht der Wahrheit und das Reich der Freiheit: Zur johanneischen Deutung des Pilatus-Prozesses (Joh 18,28–19,16)." *ZTK* 93 (1996): 35–58. **Swain, Scott R**. "Truth in the Gospel of John." Th.M. thesis. Southeastern Baptist Theological Seminary, 1998. **Thiselton, Anthony C**. "Truth." Pp. 874–902 in Vol. 3, *NIDNTT*. **Trites, Allison A**. *The New Testament Concept of Witness.* SNTSMS 31. Cambridge: Cambridge University Press, 1977. **Volf, Miroslav**. *Exclusion and Embrace: A Theological Exploration of Identity, Otherness, and Reconciliation.* Nashville: Abingdon, 1996. Idem. "Johannine Dualism and Contemporary Pluralism." *Modern Theology* 21 (2005): 189–217. **Woodbridge, Paul**. "'The World' in the Fourth Gospel." Pp. 1–31 in *Witness to the World: Papers from the Second Oak Hill College Annual School of Theology.* Ed. David Peterson. Carlisle, UK: Paternoster, 1999.

25 THE COSMIC TRIAL MOTIF

25.1 Introduction

Ti estin alētheia?[1] "What is truth?"[2] Pilate asks Jesus, and without waiting for an answer, turns on his heels and goes outside to report to the Jewish leaders the results of his investigation. Ironically, with Truth Incarnate before his very eyes, the Roman governor glibly dismisses, if not the possibility, at least the relevance of truth in trying Truth itself. Yet, as did the Jewish high priest Caiaphas before him (John 11:49–50; cf. 18:14), Pilate spoke better than he knew. In its Johannine context, therefore, the meaning of Pilate's question is by no means exhausted by the meaning intended by Pilate himself. The way in which he falls short of understanding the true significance of the events in which he is involved parallels the ignorance and obliviousness of many other characters in John's gospel and illustrates the pervasive human hardening toward God's revelation in his Son, which encompasses Jew (Caiaphas) and Gentile (Pilate) alike.

25.2 Truth and the Cosmic Trial Motif in John's Gospel

The term *alētheia* had currency in Greek philosophy, Roman thought, and the Hebrew Bible (including its many uses in the LXX).[3] In Greek philosophy, one of the senses of *alētheia* involved an accurate perspective on reality (e.g., Marcus Aurelius 9.1.2).[4] The Romans similarly spoke of *veritas* as a factual representation of events (e.g., Cicero, *Inv.* 2.53.161).[5] In the Hebrew Scriptures, "truth" (*ʾemet, ʾemunah*) primarily conveyed the notion of God's faithfulness to his covenant. This faithfulness had been revealed throughout the history of Israel and, according to John, found supreme expression in the life, ministry, and substitutionary death of Jesus (John 1:14; 14:6).[6]

In John's gospel, where the importance of "truth" is underscored by forty-eight instances of the *alēth-* word group in comparison with a combined total of ten for the Synoptics,[7] the notion of truth is inextricably related to God and to Jesus' relationship with God.[8] Is Jesus the Son of God, or is he guilty of blasphemy (see esp.

---

1. There is a good possibility that Pilate and Jesus discoursed in Greek, the *lingua franca* of the day, which would have provided common ground between Pilate, who spoke Latin, and Jesus, who spoke Aramaic. See Keener, *John*, 1113. Most of the material in this section is adapted from "'What Is Truth?' Pilate's Question to Jesus in Its Johannine and Larger Biblical Context," *JETS* 48 (2005): 33–62, also published in *Whatever Happened to Truth?* and is used by permission.

2. Or, perhaps, with Beasley-Murray, *John*, 332: "Truth—what is *that*?!"

3. E.g., Gen 24:27, 48; 32:10; 47:29; Exod 28:26; Deut 22:20; 33:8; Josh 2:14; Jdg 9:15; etc. Keener, *John*, 418, notes that 99 percent of the instances of *alētheia* in the LXX translate the Hebrew *ʾemet* and concludes that "'truth' often includes the sense of 'covenant faithfulness' in the Fourth Gospel."

4. See the discussion in Keener, *John*, 417–19.

5. A possible parallel to the present passage is Cicero, *Nat. d.* 1.67: *sed ubi est veritas?* ("But where is truth?"). Cited in *Neuer Wettstein: Texte zum Neuen Testament aus Griechentum und Hellenismus*, Band I/2: *Texte zum Johannesevangelium* (ed. Udo Schnelle; Berlin/New York: Walter de Gruyter, 2001), 795.

6. When Jesus spoke to Pilate about a "kingdom" of truth, Pilate most likely would have thought of a kingdom of philosophers (e.g., Epictetus, *Diatr.* 3.22.49; Plutarch, *Flatterer* 16; *Mor.* 58E), who hardly ever challenged the security of the state. See Keener, *John*, 418.

7. The breakdown is as follows: *alētheia*: 25 times in John, 7 times in the Synoptics; *alēthēs*: 14 times in John, 2 times in the Synoptics; *alēthinos*: 9 times in John, once in the Synoptics.

8. For a helpful study on truth in John's gospel, see Swain, "Truth in the Gospel of John." See also the fine study by Dennis R. Lindsay, "What is Truth? Ἀλήθεια in the Gospel of John," *ResQ* 35 (1993):

Matt 26:59–66; Mark 14:55–64; Luke 22:66–71)?[9] Jesus claims he is the Son of God, and John's purpose for writing his gospel is tied up with demonstrating the veracity of Jesus' claim (John 20:30–31). The Jewish leaders, by contrast, consider Jesus a blasphemer (5:18; 8:59; 10:33–36; 19:7). In John's gospel, then, truth is first and foremost a theological, and perhaps even more accurately, a christological concept.[10]

Rather than merely connoting correspondence with reality, as in Greek philosophy, or factual accuracy, as in Roman thought, truth, for John, is a *personal, relational* concept that has its roots and origin in none other than God himself. As the psalmist (Ps 31:5) and the prophet (Isa 65:16) call God "the God of truth,"[11] so John's gospel proclaims that God is truth and that hence his Word is truth.[12] Jesus, then, is the truth, because he has been sent from God and has come to reveal the Father and to carry out his salvation-historical purposes.[13] For this reason, too, the only way for us to know the truth is to know God through Jesus Christ (John 8:31; 14:6; 17:3).

John's account of Jesus' trial before Pilate, particularly in 18:33–38a, forms an integral part of several major Johannine themes. The first major Johannine theme interfacing with this passage is the trial motif and the perspective of the cosmic spiritual conflict in which Jesus and the world are engaged. Rudolf Bultmann speaks of "the great trial between God and the world" that provides the larger backdrop against which Jesus' Jewish and Roman trials are conducted. While Pilate is Jesus' judge according to the world's standards, the reader already knows that, in truth, it is Jesus who is the judge who decides over life and death (5:19–29). Melba Maggay points out that political dynamics are transcended by spiritual realities and that history witnesses the clash of two kingdoms, the kingdom of God and the kingdom of darkness.[14]

129–45; as well as S. Aalen, " 'Truth,' a Key Word in St. John's Gospel," in *SE II* (TU 87; ed. F. L. Cross; Berlin: Akademie, 1964), 3–24; D. M. Crump, "Truth," *Dictionary of Jesus and the Gospels*, 859–62; Lester J. Kuyper, "Grace and Truth: An Old Testament Description of God, and Its Use in the Johannine Gospel," *Int* 18 (1964): 3–19; Ignace de la Potterie, "The Truth in Saint John," in *The Interpretation of John* (ed. and trans. John Ashton; IRT 9; 2nd ed.; Philadelphia: Fortress/London: SPCK, 1986), 67–82; David J. Hawkin, "The Johannine Concept of Truth," *EvQ* 59 (1987): 3–13; Anthony C. Thiselton, "Truth," *NIDNTT*, 3:874–902, esp. 879–80, 889–94; Jean Giblet, "Aspects of the Truth in the New Testament," in *Truth and Certainty* (ed. Edward Schillebeeckx and Bas van Iersel; New York: Herder & Herder, 1973), 35–42; and Geerhardus Vos, " 'True' and 'Truth' in the Johannine Writings," *BRev* 12 (1927): 507–20. See also James Barr, *The Semantics of Biblical Language* (London: SCM, 1961), 187–205; Roger Nicole, "The Biblical Concept of Truth," in *Scripture and Truth* (ed. D. A. Carson and John D. Woodbridge; Grand Rapids: Baker, 1992), 287–98; and L. Russ Bush III, "Knowing the Truth," *Faith & Mission* 11/2 (1994): 3–13.

9. On the charge of blasphemy against Jesus and a defense of its historicity, see especially Bock, *Blasphemy and Exaltation*.

10. Cf., e.g., Thomas Söding, "Die Macht der Wahrheit und das Reich der Freiheit: Zur johanneischen Deutung des Pilatus-Prozesses (Joh 18,28–19,16)," *ZTK* 93 (1996): 48–49.

11. The TNIV renders the phrases in these two passages "my faithful God" and "the one true God," respectively.

12. This belief is also reflected in later Jewish writings, such as *y. Sanh.* 18a: "The seal of God is truth. What is truth? that he is the living God and the King eternal" (Beasley-Murray, *John*, 332, citing Schlatter, *Evangelist Johannes*, 341; cf. Westcott, *Gospel according to St. John*, 261, with reference to Lightfoot).

13. Cf. Beasley-Murray, *John*, 331: "Jesus is not speaking of truth in an abstract, or even general way, but specifically in relation to his ministry." Moreover, as Barrett, *Gospel according to St. John*, 538, notes, in John truth is "truth in motion," entering and addressing the world and liberating those who are capable of hearing it (John 8:32). Its ultimate point of reference is not a world of timeless forms but God's plan of salvation. Morris, *Gospel according to John*, 260, notes the association of truth with God (and Jesus' ministry in fulfillment of God's covenant promises) in Paul's letter to the Romans (Rom 1:25; 3:7; 15:8).

14. Melba Maggay, "Jesus and Pilate: An Exposition of John 18:28–40," *Transformation* 8 (1991): 33.

A. T. Lincoln has argued that the "witness" and "judgment" word groups are part of a "cosmic trial" or "lawsuit motif" in John's gospel, "in which Jesus as God's uniquely authorized agent acts as both witness and judge."[15] According to Lincoln, the lawsuits between God and the nations as well as God and Israel in the Septuagint of Isaiah 40–55 form the background for the Johannine "lawsuit motif." In the context of the lawsuit, truth stands for the whole process of judging, culminating in the verdict. At the heart of John's gospel is the question of whether the crucified Jesus is the Messiah (John 20:31) and whether he rightly claims to be one with God. "Truth" is in essence an affirmative answer to these questions. The reason why John does not record a Jewish trial is because his entire ministry is a trial (John 1–12).

Truth, in conjunction with witness, is another major motif found in John's gospel.[16] While truth and witness are part of the larger Johannine trial theme, it is important to look specifically at "truth" terminology in John's gospel.[17] The first two relevant references to *alētheia* are found in the introduction to the gospel, where the evangelist writes that Jesus is full of grace and truth (John 1:14) and that grace and truth came through Jesus Christ (1:17).

In light of the numerous parallels between John 1:14–17 and Exodus 33–34, most likely the phrase "grace and truth" (*charis kai alētheia*) in John's introduction harks back to the phrase "[steadfast] love and faithfulness" (*ḥesed weʾemet*) in Exod 34:6.[18] While Moses was unable to see God (33:20–23), the one and only Son of the Father has made him known (John 1:18); and while Moses was the mediator of the law (Exodus 34), the fullness of God's grace and truth came through Jesus Christ (John 1:17).[19] The subsequent gospel proceeds to explicate and substantiate this claim.[20]

---

15. Andrew T. Lincoln, "Reading John: The Fourth Gospel under Modern and Postmodern Interrogation," in *Reading the Gospels Today* (McMaster NT Studies; ed. Stanley E. Porter; Grand Rapids: Eerdmans, 2004), 128, summarizing his thesis in *Truth on Trial*; see the review in *TrinJ* 22 NS (2001): 269–72.

16. As mentioned, John's gospel features 46 uses of the *alēth*-word group compared to a combined total of 10 for the Synoptics; the Johannine letters contain 27 further instances. What is more, as Schnackenburg (*Gospel according to St. John*, 2.225) points out, "truth" in the Synoptic texts is largely without theological significance (cf. Matt 22:16 = Mark 12:14 = Luke 20:21; Mark 5:33; 12:32; Luke 4:25; 22:59; the same is true for the book of Acts: see Acts 4:27; 10:34; 26:25). A fuller exploration of the semantic field of "truth" in John's gospel would, apart from instances of the noun *alētheia*, also include an analysis of the related adjectives and adverbs *alēthēs*, *alēthinos*, and *alēthōs*, as well as other terms such as the double *amēn* (on which see the excursus in Swain, "Truth in the Gospel of John," 68–75; Crump, "Truth," in *Dictionary of Jesus and the Gospels*, 860; and Brown, *Gospel according to John I–XII*, 499–501). However, it is sufficient here to limit the scope of the study to the passages that feature the noun *alētheia*. For a brief history of the study of truth in John's gospel in the twentieth century spanning the spectrum from Hellenism to a Jewish background see the excursus "The Johannine Concept of Truth" in Schnackenburg (*Gospel according to St. John*, 2:225–26), discussing works by Büchsel (Hellenistic syncretism),

Bultmann ("divine reality" in line with an existential interpretation of John's Gospel), Dodd (Hermetic literature), Becker (relationship between John and Qumran), and de la Potterie (Jewish background). Schnackenburg also provides a helpful survey of the Johannine usage and semantic categories as well as of the comparative and historical background (ibid., 2:227–37). See also the survey of recent scholarship on truth in the gospel of John in Swain, "Truth in the Gospel of John," 4–10.

17. For a survey of the relevant instances of *alētheia* in John's gospel see Morris, *Gospel according to John*, 260–62.

18. There are twenty-seven instances in the Hebrew Scriptures where the terms *ḥesed* and *ʾemet* are juxtaposed, half of which are in the Psalms: Gen 24:27, 49; 32:11; 47:29; Exod 34:6; Josh 2:12, 14; 2 Sam 2:6; 15:20; Ps 25:10; 40:11, 12; 57:4, 11; 61:8; 69:14; 85:11; 86:15; 89:15; 115:1; 117:2; 138:2; Prov 3:3; 14:22; 16:6; 20:28.

19. Cf. Lindsay, "Truth in John," 131–33, with reference to Adolf Schlatter, *Der Glaube im Neuen Testament* (6th ed.; Stuttgart: Calwer, 1982 = 1927), 552 (see also ibid., 145, n. 68). As George Ernest Wright notes, "the 'grace and truth' of Jesus Christ (John 1.14) are not abstract virtues but the active *ḥesed* and *ʾemet*, rooted in the covenant conception" (*God Who Acts: Biblical Theology as Recital* (London: SCM, 1954), 114, cited in Morris, *Gospel according to John*, 261, n. 126; similarly, Schnackenburg, *Gospel according to St. John*, 1:272–73; 2:228).

20. See the comments on John 18:36–38 below.

Tracing the instances of "truth" in John's gospel sequentially, we read in John 4:23–24 that worship of God must be rendered in spirit and truth (perhaps harking back to the phrase "in sincerity and truth" in Josh 24:14)[21] and that John the Baptist came as a witness to the truth (John 5:33, a passage that parallels and anticipates Jesus' self-reference in 18:37).[22] The climactic (seven) references to truth in the first half of John's gospel occur in John 8, where Jesus exhorts those who had "believed him" to continue in his teaching, so that they may know the truth, which will set them free (implying that his teaching is truth; 8:32).[23]

In John 8:40, Jesus identifies himself as "a man who has told you the truth" (cf. Jer 9:5; Zech 8:16; and esp. 2 Chr 18:15; see also John 8:45, 46), in contrast to the devil, who does not stand in the truth and in whom there is no truth (8:44; cf. Gen 3:4–5).[24] As far as the Johannine narrative is concerned, this is the end of truth in the first half of the gospel, which is concerned with Jesus' public ministry to the Jewish people.

The next set of references to truth is found in the Farewell Discourse. Importantly, truth takes on a trinitarian dimension[25] when, in 14:6, Jesus is identified as the way, the truth, and the life (cf. 1:14, 17; see also 1QH 4:40: "for you [O God] are truth");[26] the Holy Spirit is called "the Spirit of truth" in John 14:17; 15:26; and 16:13 (cf. 1 John 4:6; 5:6; 1QS 3:18–19; 4:23), who will guide believers in all truth (John 16:13; cf. Ps 25:5); and God's (the Father's) Word is described as truth (John 17:17; cf. Ps 119:160; Jer 10:10; see also 2 Sam 7:28; 1 Kgs 17:24; Ps 119:142, 151), in which believers are to be consecrated (John 17:19; cf. 1QS 4:20–21).[27]

The immediately preceding passage where truth is mentioned in John's gospel (17:17–19) is also the major passage other than 18:37 where "truth" and "world" are juxtaposed. The term *kosmos* occurs as many as eight times in the span of 17:14–19, and *alētheia* is found three times. This suggests that John envisions Jesus' appearance before Pilate as a paradigmatic instance of one who was not of the world but who was set apart and sent into the world to speak the truth, which is God's word.

---

21. TNIV: "with all faithfulness." So Lindsay, "Truth in John," 135–37, with reference to Otto Betz, "'To Worship God in Spirit and in Truth': Reflections on John 4,20–26," in *Standing before God: Studies on Prayer in Scriptures and in Tradition. In Honor of John M. Oesterreicher* (trans. Nora Quigley; New York: Ktav, 1981), 58–61, who also cites Qumran parallels. Dodd, *Interpretation of the Fourth Gospel*, 174–75, adduces Ps 145:18 as a potential parallel.

22. The close verbal parallel between the Baptist and Jesus "bearing witness to the truth" in John 5:33 and 18:37 (noted, e.g., by Brown, *Gospel according to John XIII–XXI*, 854) follows a pattern linking Jesus' mission with that of selected followers such as Peter (12:33; 18:32; 21:19) and "the disciple whom Jesus loved" (1:18; 13:23; 21:20). Brown, *Gospel according to John I–XII*, 224, cites the parallel wording in 1QS 8:6: "witnesses to the truth."

23. On the politically charged interchange between Jesus and "the Jews" in John 8, see Lincoln, "Reading John," 138–43; Motyer, *Your Father the Devil*.

24. See the discussion of John 8:30–47 in Lindsay, "Truth in John," 138–40.

25. See Lincoln, "Reading John," 147–48, who notes that the "truth witnessed to by the Fourth Gospel involves the triune God," citing esp. 15:26.

26. See Lindsay, "Truth in John," 140–41.

27. See ibid., 140–43. Thiselton, "Truth," 892, notes that the Greek phrase in John 17:17 is identical with the LXX form of Ps 119:142 as found in Codex Sinaiticus (though not the MT and other LXX mss., which read "your law is truth"). The relevance of the references to truth in the Farewell Discourse for John 18:33–38a is affirmed, among others, by Thomas L. Brodie, *The Gospel according to John: A Literary and Theological Commentary* (New York/Oxford: Oxford University Press, 1993), 534, who notes that in 17:17–19, as in 18:37–38a, there is a triple use of "truth." Brodie also alludes to the trinitarian dimension of truth in John's gospel when he writes that for John, truth, "in practice," means "the revelation of the mystery of salvation in Jesus, the Son of the Father" and "the possibility of becoming Spirit-led children of God" (p. 535, citing de la Potterie).

Jesus' witness to the truth served as a model for his followers to emulate (cf. 17:18; 20:21).

This sets the stage for Jesus' interchange with Pilate in 18:37–38, which includes the final three references to truth in John's gospel. This, then, provides some closure to the presentation of truth in the Johannine narrative. Jesus' mission is summed up as bearing "witness to the truth" (cf. 3:11, 32; 7:7; 8:14);[28] everyone who is of the truth listens to Jesus; and Pilate is dismissive of, or at least indifferent to, the truth. Likely, the three references to truth in 18:36–38 constitute an *inclusio* with the three references to grace and truth, grace, and grace and truth in 1:14, 16–17.

If so, rather than repeating the allusion to God's covenant faithfulness struck in the introduction, the present passage indicates progression in that, according to John, truth now has come before Pilate, the Roman (i.e., Gentile) governor, which is in keeping with the universal message of the gospel. As in Luke–Acts, there is therefore a movement from Jew to Gentile.[29] In the context of the entire Johannine narrative (similar to the ending of Luke–Acts), Pilate's question, "What is truth?" remains open-ended and still rings through the ages, calling for an answer from every reader of the gospel.[30]

25.3 Jesus' Witness to the Truth: His Trial before Pilate

While it may appear that the two major characters in John's account of Jesus' trial before Pilate are Jesus and Pilate, a third group of people looms large in the background: the Jewish leaders. It is they who have charged Jesus with sedition, and it is they whom Pilate is trying to appease in the way he deals with Jesus. For this reason, a literary investigation of Pilate's trial before Jesus must properly commence with a study of the Jewish leaders.[31]

25.3.1 The Jewish leaders

The Jewish leaders' hostility toward Jesus grows steadily in John's gospel, particularly during the second half of Jesus' public ministry narrated in John 5–12. The entire first half of this gospel narrates a total of seven signs, directed specifically toward the Jewish people to convince them that Jesus is in fact the long-expected

---

28. See 1 Tim 6:13, which calls this interchange Jesus' "good confession" before Pilate.

29. See John 3–4; 11:49–52; 12:20–50, esp. vv. 32, 37–40; cf. Acts 1:8; 13:46–48; 28:17–31; Rom 1:14–16. Note in this context the interesting suggestion made by Kuyper, "Grace and Truth," 14, that the reason why, in the phrase "grace and truth" in John 1:14 and 17, the word "truth" continues to be used while the word "grace" is not, is that the evangelist "intends to let the word truth carry the full import of the concept within the expression, grace and truth." In Pilate's case, of course, grace was available, but it was not effective because of the governor's unbelief (18:37–38).

30. In another sense, while John "records no answer in words," Morris (*Gospel according to John*, 682) is surely correct that "the whole of the following narrative of the death and resurrection of Jesus is John's answer in action. On the cross and at the empty tomb we may learn what God's truth is." Morris makes the same point on pp. 260–61, where he also refers to Alf Corell, *Consummatum Est: Eschatology and Church in the Gospel of St. John* (London: SPCK, 1958), 161.

31. For a perceptive, albeit brief, study of the characterization of Jesus, Pilate, and the Jews in John 18:28–19:16a, plus a list of ironies in this unit, see Stibbe, *John*, 186–92. Stibbe notes that while Pilate evokes our sympathy, the Jewish leaders evoke the reader's antipathy. They are guilty of hypocrisy (18:28), choose Barabbas over Jesus (18:40), and, according to Stibbe, misquote a Passover hymn when they shout in 19:15, "We have no king but Caesar!" (p. 189). For a defense of the historicity of John's account of Jesus' trial before Pilate, see Köstenberger, "What Is Truth," 21–28.

Messiah.³² Jesus had turned water into wine at the Cana wedding (2:1–12), cleared the Jerusalem temple in a startling display of his messianic authority (2:14–22), healed the centurion's son long-distance (4:45–54), healed the lame man (5:1–15), fed the multitudes (6:1–15), opened the eyes of the man born blind (9:1–41), and raised Lazarus from the dead (11:1–57). Yet at the end of this long string of striking displays of Jesus' messianic identity, the Jewish leaders have become more hardened toward Jesus' claims than ever before and are ever more determined to kill the one who claimed to be the Son of God but whom they considered to be a mere messianic pretender, deceiver, and blasphemer.

The evangelist's closing indictment of the Jewish nation as represented by its leaders is therefore severe: "Even after Jesus had performed so many signs in their presence, they still would not believe in him" (12:37). As the evangelist proceeds to note, however, in God's sovereign providence, the Jewish leaders' hardening toward God's salvific purposes in and through Jesus Christ fulfilled Scripture, particularly Isaiah's words in Isa 53:1 and 6:10 (John 12:38, 40). What is more, as the evangelist makes clear, by its rejection of Jesus as Messiah, the Jewish nation joined the world at large in its sinful rejection of the truth. Hence the Jews had forfeited their divine election as God's chosen instrument to display his nature and carry his message to the world.

The second major unit of John's gospel (John 13–21) is consequently devoted to the Messiah's formation and instruction of a new messianic community made up of those who believe in him. While the Twelve, Jesus' inner circle, were Jewish, it was not their Jewishness that commended these followers but their faith in Jesus as Messiah. What is already implicit in the evangelist's closing verdict in chapter 12 of John's gospel plays itself out in the Passion Narrative in chapters 18–19, where the Jewish leaders intimidate the Roman procurator to accede to their wishes and to give his consent to have Jesus crucified.

In his narration of Jesus' passion, John seems to presuppose the Synoptic Passion Narratives. He does not cover Jesus' formal Sanhedrin trial before Caiaphas (skipping over it in 18:24 and 28), which is recounted in some detail in the Synoptics. At the same time, he recounts Jesus' interrogation by Pilate in considerably more detail. Why this shift in perspective? It is hard to be certain, but it is possible that the evangelist feels he has already demonstrated the hardening of the Jewish leaders in the first half of his gospel, culminating in Caiaphas's statement in 11:49–50 and in the negative verdict of 12:37. Thus, he focuses his trial narrative on Pilate's complicity in the world's rejection of the Messiah, which, as mentioned above, also includes Jesus' rejection by his own people, the Jews.

In lodging charges against Jesus, the Jewish leaders display a shrewd yet deceptive progression from presenting Jesus to the Roman governor initially as a common criminal (18:30).³³ Only later, when Pilate appears inclined to free Jesus, do they

---

32. See the discussion of the Johannine "signs" in chap. 7, sec. 15 above.

33. The word *houtos* (lit., "this man") likely has a derogatory connotation.

reveal the real reason why they wanted Jesus dead: "We have a law, and according to that law he must die, because he claimed to be the Son of God" (19:7).

A second tactic employed by the Jewish leaders is that of manipulation and intimidation. When their lobbying for Jesus' death seems to fall on deaf ears, they tell Pilate, "If you let this man go, you are no friend of Caesar. Anyone who claims to be a king opposes Caesar" (19:12). Here they frame in political terms—Jesus' kingship—what they in fact perceived as a religious claim, Jesus' divine sonship, fully aware that this rendered Pilate vulnerable with his Roman superiors. In the end, the Jewish leaders prevail and get their wish when Pilate delivers Jesus over to be crucified (19:16)—but not before disavowing their own messianic hopes and professing before Pilate to "have no king but Caesar" (19:15) in a massive and eminently culpable betrayal of their own religious heritage (cf. Jdg 8:23; 1 Sam 8:7; Isa 26:13 where God is said to be Israel's only king).[34]

Hence, according to John, the Jewish leaders are the driving force behind the crucifixion of Jesus. Pilate turns out to be a comparatively minor character who is too weak, unconcerned, and unprincipled to resist the Jewish leaders. Jesus, for his part, allows the arrest, trial, and crucifixion to proceed, knowing that God will vindicate him in resurrection and trusting that God's purposes for humanity will be accomplished in and through his crucifixion.

On one level, the Jewish leaders emerge as the temporary victors from the present incident. In the end, they get their way, and Jesus is handed over to them by Pilate to be crucified. Yet their victory is pyrrhic on several counts. (1) In order to gain Pilate's concession, they first have to renounce their own messianic hope and to pledge sole allegiance to the Roman emperor (19:15). Thus Pilate's cooperation is secured at a high cost, namely, that of a betrayal of the Jews' own religious heritage and national identity. (2) Prevailing upon Pilate to condemn Jesus to die implicates the Jews in crucifying not only an innocent man, but the God-sent Messiah. By this they incur great guilt (cf. Matt 27:25) and unwittingly collaborate with Satan in opposing the purposes of God.[35]

In contrast to Pilate, who, as will be seen, lacks spiritual insight to comprehend the true nature of the Jewish case against Jesus and the spiritual dimension of his kingdom, the Jewish leaders are fully aware of the import of Jesus' claim of being the Messiah.[36] While Pilate thus is part of the Johannine "misunderstanding" theme (witness Pilate's repeated ignorant references to Jesus as "the king of the Jews"), the

---

34. Cf. Darrell L. Bock, *Jesus according to Scripture: Restoring the Portrait from the Gospels* (Downers Grove, IL: InterVarsity Press, 2002), 535, n. 65, who also cites the Jewish national prayer, *Shemoneh Esreh*, benediction 11, which reads in an address to God, "May you be our King, you alone," and notes that "at the Passover, the Jews would have affirmed the unique sovereignty of God" (*m. Roš Haš.* 1:2).

35. At a higher level, of course, God uses the Jewish rejection of the Messiah to fulfill Scripture and to accomplish his salvation-historical purposes, but this is not to excuse the Jewish leaders' actions.

36. Cf. Reimund Bieringer, "'My Kingship Is Not of This World' (John 18,36): The Kingship of Jesus and Politics," in *The Myriad Christ: Plurality and the Quest for Unity in Contemporary Christology* (BETL 152; ed. T. Merrigan and J. Haers; Leuven: Leuven University Press/Peeters, 2000), 171: "For a brief moment it seems as if Pilate was going to understand that Jesus claims a *basileia* different from that of the Jews. But, as the inscription 'King of the Jews' which Pilate has put on the cross (19,19) demonstrates, Pilate ultimately remains closed to the religious dimension of Jesus' person and message."

Jewish leaders are shown to reject Jesus in the full knowledge of his actions (the "signs") and affirmations of oneness with God (e.g., 10:30). By his characterization of the Jewish leaders throughout his gospel, John places the primary responsibility for Jesus' crucifixion squarely on them.

25.3.2 Pilate

In his dealings with the Jewish leaders, Pilate displays the customary reluctance of Roman government officials to get involved in what he perceives to be inner-Jewish religious affairs (e.g., Gallio in Acts 18:14–15). However, in the ensuing interrogation, nothing seems to go as Pilate has planned, and things increasingly spin out of control.[37] Pilate's first attempt to extricate himself from the situation has him tell the Jewish leaders, "Take him yourselves and judge him by your own law" (John 18:31).[38] Yet because only the Romans had jurisdiction to put a man to death and because it was death that the Jewish leaders wanted for Jesus, Pilate's first attempt to avoid dealing with Jesus, coupled with the Jewish leaders' resolve to have Jesus crucified, fails.

This is followed by Pilate's first of two private interrogations of Jesus narrated in John's gospel, which culminates in Pilate's question, "What is truth?" (18:33–38).[39] The narrative does not explain why Pilate, having been told that Jesus was a "criminal" (lit., "evildoer," 18:30), asks Jesus whether or not he is the "king of the Jews" (18:33). The answer is, however, intimated in Jesus' counter-question in 18:34, "Is that your own idea ... or did others talk to you about me?" The Jewish leaders had likely implicated Jesus as a political threat to Roman imperial rule in Palestine, and it is this charge that Pilate sets out to investigate.[40]

Pilate's answer to Jesus reveals both a possible anti-Semitic streak ("Am I a Jew?" 18:35)[41] and a hint of impatience: "Your own people and the chief priests handed you over to me. What is it you have done?" (18:35, *Ti epoiēsas;* echoing *kakon poiōn* in 18:30; see also Matt 27:23: "What crime has he committed?").[42] Beyond this, Pilate may also be offended at what he may consider Jesus' insinuation that he is merely parroting the charge leveled against him by the Jewish leaders. If so, Pilate here asserts his own independent judgment. He is not a puppet but is conducting

---

37. Among the errors of judgment committed by Pilate (as listed by Stibbe, *John,* 188–89) are the following: he calls Jesus "the king of the Jews" (John 18:39), which further provokes the Jewish leaders; he ends up having to free Barabbas, which is hardly what Pilate had intended in the first place; he calls Jesus "the man" (19:5), which may have unwelcome connotations to the ears of the Jews; and he finally brings Jesus out and says, "Here is your king" (19:14). Most likely, these errors of judgment reveal Pilate's ignorance and ineptitude rather than constituting intentional provocations of the Jews.

38. The pronouns "yourselves" (*hymeis*) and "your own" (*hymōn*) in 18:31 are emphatic.

39. John narrates Jesus' Roman trial in seven units, which display an oscillating pattern of outdoor and indoor scenes (John 18:29–32, 33–38a, 38b–40; 19:1–3, 4–7, 8–11, 12–15). Culpepper, *Anatomy,* 142, traces the identification of the seven scenes to R. H. Strachan, *The Fourth Gospel: Its Significance and Environment* (3rd ed.; London, SCM, 1941), 310. Stibbe, *John,* 187, and Keener, *John,* 1097, propose a chiastic structure, with 19:1–3 in the center. Pilate's question, "What is truth?" in 18:38a is part of the second scene of the Johannine account of Jesus' Roman trial.

40. See the discussion of the Synoptic Gospels above.

41. Cf. Charles Homer Giblin, "John's Narration of the Hearing before Pilate (John 18,28–19,16a)," *Bib* 67 (1986): 227, n. 18; Helen K. Bond, *Pontius Pilate in History and Interpretation* (Cambridge: Cambridge University Press, 1998), 177. Hoehner, *Chronological Aspects,* 105, notes that Pilate's mentor Sejanus "was a dedicated anti-Semite who wanted to exterminate the Jewish race," citing Philo, *Flacc.* 1; *Leg.* 159–61.

42. Alfred Plummer, *The Gospel according to St. John* (Thornapple Commentaries; Grand Rapids: Baker, 1981), 319, and Westcott, *Gospel according to St. John,* 261, detect impatience in Pilate's question in 18:38a, "What is truth?"

his own investigation. Ironically, however, Pilate's verdict does not reflect his own independent judgment (i.e., that Jesus is innocent) but falls in line with the verdict already reached by the Jewish leaders. Hence Jesus' insinuation proves correct: this is not a true fact-finding mission but a hasty affair in which truth is not served.

Pilate's interaction with Jesus also reveals that he does not know much (if anything) about Jesus and his claims and actions as they have been narrated in the first half of the gospel and demands an answer from his prisoner that will enable him to adjudicate the matter (cf. Luke 23:5–7). Clearly, his assumption is that Jesus must have done something to draw the intense hatred and opposition of the Jewish leaders, and he expects him to confess what it is he has done to attract such antagonism.

Jesus' answer, however, does nothing of the sort. Rather than confess his wrong, Jesus corrects the impression Pilate has been given by the Jewish leaders regarding the nature of Jesus' kingship. Jesus' kingdom is not of this world. Jesus has indeed a kingdom, and he is indeed a king, but his kingdom and kingship are tied up, not with political exploits, but with truth.[43] And it is to this truth that Jesus has come to witness. As Pilate's question, "What is truth?" makes clear, he is not the least interested in this kind of kingdom.[44]

Pilate did not even want to take up Jesus' case to begin with; he is even less interested in listening to Jesus' elaboration on the nature of his kingdom or on the more precise substance of the truth to which he came to witness. If Jesus does not present a political threat, he ought to be released. In what follows Pilate never wavers from his conviction that Jesus ought to be released and caves in only to persistent Jewish demands to have him executed (John 18:38b–19:16a).

In some sense, then, similar to the Jewish leaders discussed above, Pilate seems to come out on top of both of the other protagonists, Jesus and the Jewish leaders.[45] Pilate does not give in to the Jews' demands until they have denied their own religious heritage and pledged allegiance to Rome and until Jesus is removed as a potential threat to Roman authority in Palestine. Yet, as R. Alan Culpepper points out, Pilate's, too, is a hollow victory. In fact, it is no victory at all. All of his actions can be summed up under the rubric of avoiding to make a decision regarding Jesus. In the end, this strategy failed; the Jewish leaders forced Pilate's hand, and he made his decision, against Jesus. Again, Culpepper is correct in noting that everything that follows—the inscription on the cross, the permission to haste death by having Jesus' legs broken, and the approval of a proper burial—constitutes attempts by

---

43. For an exploration of the Johannine presentation of Jesus' kingship, see Köstenberger, "What Is Truth," 28–29.

44. Cf. Bultmann, *Gospel of John*, 656.

45. Friedrich Nietzsche, *Twilight of the Idols and the Anti-Christ* (trans. R. J. Hollingdale; London: Penguin, 1990), 174, even credited Pilate with enriching the NT "with the only expression which possesses value—which is its criticism, its *annihilation* even: 'What is truth?'" (cited in Miroslav Volf, *Exclusion and Embrace: A Theological Exploration of Identity, Otherness, and Reconciliation* [Nashville: Abingdon, 1996], 270). For Nietzsche, disregard for truth went hand in hand with disregard for human (especially Jewish) life, as when he attributes to Pilate the thought, "One Jew more or less [i.e., Jesus]—what does it matter?" (*Twilight*, 174, cited in Volf, *Exclusion and Embrace*, 271). According to Nietzsche, any belief in truth enslaves; only when one jettisons the very notion of truth is one truly free (*The Birth of Tragedy and The Genealogy of Morals* [trans. Francis Golffing; Garden City, NY: Doubleday, 1956], 287, cited in Volf, *Exclusion and Embrace*, 270).

Pilate to atone for condemning a man to die who he sensed was innocent. Culpepper's conclusion regarding Pilate is worth quoting in full:

> Like other characters caught between the Jews and Jesus (principally Nicodemus, the lame man, and the blind man), Pilate is a study in the impossibility of compromise, the inevitability of decision, and the consequences of each alternative. In the end, although he seems to glimpse the truth, a decision in Jesus' favor proves too costly for him. In this maneuver to force the reader to a decision regarding Jesus, the evangelist exposes the consequences of attempting to avoid a decision. Pilate represents the futility of attempted compromise. The reader who tries to temporize or escape through the gate of indecision will find Pilate as his companion along that path.[46]

The parallelism with Nicodemus is particularly evident.[47] Nicodemus, the Jewish rabbi, does not understand the entrance requirement into the kingdom of God, that is, spiritual regeneration. Pilate, the Roman governor, does not understand the nature of Jesus' kingdom, namely, truth. In both cases, their conversation with Jesus ends on an abrupt note with an exasperated question on their part. "How can this be?" Nicodemus asks, which reveals his lack of understanding of spiritual realities. "What is truth?" is Pilate's question, which displays his lack of understanding of the true truth that can be comprehended only by those who first embrace the Truth sent from God and are guided by the Spirit of truth.[48]

In the end, therefore, Pilate is a tragic figure who fails to realize the momentous significance of the present encounter. His curt dismissal of the larger question of truth will have eternal personal consequences, and he can ill afford to brush aside the issue as glibly as he does. In contrast to Jesus' great humility (evidenced, among other things, by his mere self-reference as one who came to "testify to the truth"), Pilate displays considerable arrogance in the way he deals with the one charged with wrongdoing who stands before him. In this Pilate serves as a representative character of all those who fail to recognize that they are called to render a verdict regarding Jesus and who deem themselves to be in the judgment seat regarding Jesus while in fact it is they who will be judged on the basis of their decision concerning Jesus.

In an act that has fatal supernatural consequences, Pilate, in Rudolf Bultmann's words, "shuts the door on the claim of the revelation, and in so doing he shows that he is not of the truth—he is of the lie."[49] But, as Bultmann points out, Pilate is

---

46. Culpepper, *Anatomy*, 143; cf. R. H. Lightfoot, *St. John's Gospel: A Commentary* (London: Oxford University Press, 1956), 311, who states that "the position now reached ... is that he will take the side neither of accusers [18³⁵] nor of Accused [18³⁸], and that he seeks, as before, to avoid the responsibility of a decision." The parallel to Nicodemus is also adduced by Barrett, *Gospel according to St. John*, 538, who writes (citing Haenchen) that, "like Nicodemus (7.50f.), Pilate for all his fair play and open-mindedness is not of the truth; he is of this world." For an assessment of Nicodemus as a character in John's gospel see also Köstenberger, *John*, 117–20.

47. Cf., e.g., Bond, *Pontius Pilate*, 178, who notes that Pilate understands neither the nature of Jesus' kingship nor his reference to truth. Bond also notes that in a sense, Pilate shows that he is "a Jew" (cf. 18:35) in that he joins the unbelieving world—epitomized by the Jewish leaders—in their rejection of Jesus (ibid., 179).

48. Cf. Thiselton, "Truth," 893, who points out that "Pilate remains baffled because there are certain questions about truth which can be answered only when a man is fully open to hear the witness of Jesus. This brings us back to the claim of Jn. 14:6, that Jesus Christ not only states the truth; he *is* the truth."

49. Bultmann, *Gospel of John*, 656.

different from the Jewish leaders who are bent on killing Jesus and on perpetrating a lie in keeping with the intentions of their true spiritual father, the devil (8:44). Pilate is not a Jew at all, so that for him it is not envy (Matt 27:18; Mark 15:10) or religious prejudice that might cause him to condemn a fellow countryman. Rather, he is called upon to judge Jesus as one on the outside, both ethnically and religiously. Can Pilate retain his neutrality?

Because Jesus' kingdom is not merely "an isolated sphere of pure inwardness" or "a private area for the cultivation of religious needs, which could not come into conflict with the world," but rather a word of judgment challenging the world's sin, he cannot. A neutral stance toward Jesus is a decision against Jesus, and in the end Pilate "does not have the strength to maintain the standpoint which he had taken," but casts his lot with the Jewish leaders and the world because he cannot take his stand on the side of Jesus.[50]

25.3.3 Jesus

John's primary goal in his characterization of Jesus throughout the Passion Narrative, including his Roman trial, is the demonstration of his innocence of all the charges brought against him by the Jewish leaders, including the central charge of blasphemy (19:7). If Jesus is innocent—that is, negatively, he is "not guilty" as charged—it logically follows that, positively, he is who he claimed to be and who John believes him to be, namely, the Christ, the Son of God (20:30–31). This is how, on a larger scale, Jesus' trial before Pilate fits in with the purpose statement of John's gospel. While Pilate in the present instance yields to the Jewish leaders, he, as the representative of Roman law, considers Jesus innocent (18:38; 19:4, 6), a fact that retains its significance despite the fact that Jesus ends up at the cross.

The Passion Narrative begins in 18:1. Jesus is betrayed by Judas (18:1–11), denied three times by Peter (18:15–18, 25–27), and interrogated by Annas the high priest (18:12–14, 19–24) and by Caiaphas (18:24, 28). Throughout the proceedings against him, Jesus is shown to maintain a calm demeanor. When those who would arrest him enter the garden, he steps forward and identifies himself as the one they have come to take into custody (18:4–5). When they hesitate, he identifies himself a second time in order to shield his followers from arrest (18:8–9). When Peter draws his sword and cuts off Malchus's ear, Jesus rebukes Peter and expresses his resolve to "drink the cup" the "Father has given" him (18:11).

When interrogated by Annas about his disciples and his teaching, Jesus responds that he always taught openly in synagogues and in the temple; his teaching was no secret (18:20–21). At this, one of the officers standing by strikes Jesus with his hand, saying, "Is this the way you answer the high priest?" (18:22). Again, Jesus retains his calm demeanor, responding only, "If I said something wrong … testify as to what is

---

50. Ibid., 657. For a critique of Bultmann's interpretation of Pilate as a representative of the state, see Giblin, "John's Narration of the Hearing Before Pilate," 226–27, with further bibliographic references on p. 226, n. 16. Giblin notes that, unlike Matthew and Luke, John never refers to Pilate as governor.

wrong. But if I spoke the truth, why did you strike me?" (18:23). Jesus has testified to the truth, and the truth is its own best defense. Neither hearing before Annas or Caiaphas leads to any charges being conclusively proven against Jesus, and with this Jesus is transferred to Pilate.

Now inside the governor's palace alone with Pilate, Jesus is asked by the governor whether or not he is "the king of the Jews"[51] (18:33). Jesus is fully aware that the epithet "king of the Jews" is capable of more than one definition, especially given the different cultural, political, and religious backgrounds of Jews and Romans. As Darrell Bock points out, "If Pilate is asking from his own Roman interests, 'Do you have zealot-like designs against Caesar in an alternative political kingship?' then Jesus' reply would be negative. If he is asking from a Jewish perspective, 'Are you the promised Messiah?' then Jesus would respond positively."[52]

Hence, Jesus cannot simply answer Pilate's question; he must first define the sense in which he is and is not a king. Thus, with full composure, Jesus replies with a counter-question: "Is that your own idea ... or did others talk to you about me?" (John 18:34).[53] Jesus, of course, knows the answer (it was the latter), but he apparently poses the question nonetheless in order to elicit Pilate's response to the Jewish leaders' charge before answering the governor's question himself. Pilate brusquely retorts, "Am *I* a Jew?" (adding the emphatic pronoun *egō*), making it clear that it was the Jewish leaders who had presented Jesus to Pilate as a messianic pretender and political threat to Rome.

Then Jesus answers Pilate's question, yet he does so not in terms of his *kingship*, but his *kingdom*.[54] Jesus' use of the term "kingdom" harks back both to Israel's monarchy under David and his successors and to the OT prophetic tradition, most notably Daniel (e.g., Daniel 2 and 7).[55] On a literary level in John's gospel, Jesus' reference to his kingdom marks a critical shift from 3:3, 5: the kingdom of God has now become the kingdom *of Jesus*![56] Jesus' kingdom is not of this world—that is, it does not have its origin or derive its authorization from the world; rather, it transcends the political and material sphere of this world.[57]

---

51. This is the first reference to Jesus as "the king of the Jews" in this gospel (cf. 18:39; 19:3, 19, 21 [2x]; see also 18:37 [2x]; 19:12, 14, 15 [2x]). Earlier, Jesus had eluded efforts by the people to make him their king (6:15). Jesus is acknowledged as the "king of Israel" by Nathanael in 1:49 and hailed as such at the triumphal entry (12:13, 15, with reference to the messianic passages Ps 118:25–26 [though "king of Israel" is the evangelist's epexegetical addition] and Zech 9:9).

52. Bock, *Jesus according to Scripture*, 531.

53. The intense personal nature of the interchange and Jesus' standing his ground before Pilate is revealed in that both in 18:33, 34 and in 18:37, Jesus reciprocates to an emphatic "you" (*sy*) by Pilate with an emphatic "you" of his own: Pilate: "Are *you* the king of the Jews?" Jesus: "Is that *your own* idea ...?" (18:33–34); Pilate: "*You* are a king, then!" Jesus: "*You* say that I am a king" (18:37; emphasis added in all cases).

54. Bultmann, *Gospel of John*, 654; Brown, *Gospel according to John XIII–XXI*, 868; cited in Beasley-Murray, *John*, 330; Bieringer,

"My Kingship Is Not of This World," 170.

55. See also Amos 9:11–12 (cited by James in Acts 15:16–18). Acts 1:3 records that Jesus spoke to his followers about the kingdom of God at some length prior to his ascension. Yet they still do not understand the time frame and progression involved in the establishment of Jesus' kingdom and hence ask him, "Lord, are you at this time going to restore the kingdom to Israel?" (Acts 1:6). In Acts 3:19, Peter speaks about future "times of refreshing" and restoration.

56. In the book of Revelation, the loud voices raised in heaven anticipate the consummation of this development: "The kingdom of the world has become the kingdom of our Lord and of his Messiah, and he will reign for ever and ever" (Rev 11:15). Bieringer, "My Kingship Is Not of This World," 171, sees a parallel between the reference to God's kingdom presupposing a birth "from above" (alternate meaning for *anōthen*) in John 3:3, 5 and Jesus' kingdom being "not of this world" in 18:36.

57. As Beasley-Murray, *John*, 331, rightly notes, the fact that

When Pilate probes further, "So you are a king?" (18:37; cf. 18:33), Jesus again does not provide a direct answer.[58] Instead, he responds, *"You say* that I am a king" (18:37, emphasis added).[59] While not denying that he is a king, Jesus again does not focus on his own kingship but on the larger purpose for which he has come into the world: to bear witness to the truth (18:37).[60] The reader knows that Jesus is much more than a mere witness to the truth; he is the truth in his very own person. Yet, before Pilate, Jesus is humbly content to speak of his coming as a *witness to* the truth; to establish the reign of the truth and to witness to it, this is the purpose for which Jesus was born and has come into the world (18:37).

This truth, in turn, calls for a personal response: "Everyone on the side of truth listens to me" (18:37).[61] Within the framework of the gospel, this statement echoes Jesus' words in his Good Shepherd Discourse in 10:3, 16, and especially 27 (see also 3:3, 21). In the context of the Johannine narrative, this echo may invoke the notion of Jesus as messianic shepherd who describes the nature of his kingship to the Roman governor.[62] While it is Jesus who is ostensibly the one being tried here, Jesus' words put the spotlight, at least momentarily, on Pilate: Will he respond to the truth and listen to Jesus? Or will he listen to his accusers?[63]

In principle, it would be possible for him to respond to Jesus. But doing so now would mean a radical break with his past, so radical that it is virtually unthinkable. Pilate's past enslaves him, and his present is too cluttered with political expediency and compromise to allow the truth to break through.[64] Like the Jewish leaders (10:26), Pilate is not among Jesus' "sheep." So, disappointingly but not surprisingly, after no more than perhaps a moment's hesitation, Pilate dismissively retorts, "What

---

Jesus' kingdom is not of this world does not imply that it is "not *active* in this world," nor that it "*has nothing to do with* this world" (italics his). Jesus' kingdom *affects* this world, but it does not *belong* to it; Brown, *Gospel according to John XIII–XXI*, 869; Bultmann, *Gospel of John*, 657, both cited in Beasley-Murray, *John*, 331). Maggay, "Jesus and Pilate," 31, makes the important point that "while, on the one hand, it is wrong to politicize Jesus' Kingship ... it is also just as inappropriate to spiritualize Jesus' Kingship and see it as entirely future." He refers to Mary's *Magnificat*, which makes clear that "the coming of the King and of his kingdom will mean a concrete historical reversal: the mighty will be overthrown and the humble and lowly lifted up." Hence the power of God becomes visible in the political struggles of our time.

58. This is in keeping with the Johannine motif of the "elusive Christ" (the term is Stibbe's: see Stibbe, "Elusive Christ," 20–39, alluded to also in idem, *John*, 187) and is an instance of what A. D. Nuttall calls "discontinuous dialogue," which is caused by Jesus' "technique of deliberate transcendence," creates suspense, and ironically contributes to his own condemnation (see A. D. Nuttall, *Overheard by God: Fiction and Prayer in Herbert, Milton, Dante and St John* [London: Methuen, 1980], 129, cited in Stibbe, *John*, 188).

59. Commentators (e.g., John Henry Bernard, *A Critical and Exegetical Commentary on the Gospel according to St. John* [ICC; 2 vols. Edinburgh: T&T Clark, 1928], 611; Heinrich August Wilhelm Meyer, *Critical and Exegetical Hand-Book to the Gospel of John*

[trans. William Urwick; New York: Funk & Wagnalls, 1884], 494) regularly note the incredulous if not contemptuous nature of Pilate's question, "You are a king, then!" in 18:37, which is underscored by the fact that the personal pronoun "you" (*sy*) is put last in the sentence.

60. Note the two references to "my kingdom" in 18:36, which forms an *inclusio* and contrasts with the two references to "kingdom of God" in 3:3, 5.

61. Though not quite in the way in which Rudolf Bultmann, "ἀλήθεια, κτλ.," *TDNT* 1:246, conceives of it. Bultmann is at his existential best when he writes that John 18:37 "shows again that *alētheia* is the self-revealing divine reality, and that its comprehension is not a free act of existence, but is grounded in the determination of existence by divine reality."

62. See especially the echoes of Ezekiel 34 and other OT messianic passages in John 10, on which see Köstenberger, "Jesus the Good Shepherd." See also the discussion of the nature of Jesus' kingship in the context of his appearance before Pilate in Bond, *Pontius Pilate*, 169–71.

63. Colin G. Kruse, *John* (TNTC; Downers Grove, IL: InterVarsity Press, 2003), 360.

64. As Ulrich Wilckens, *Das Evangelium nach Johannes* (NTD 4; Göttingen: Vandenhoeck & Ruprecht, 1998), 282, writes, Pilate "wants to remain judge rather than becoming a disciple" (my translation).

is truth?" and brusquely breaks off the interrogation, returning outside to render his verdict regarding Jesus to the Jewish leaders.[65]

After Jesus has endured a severe flogging and humiliation (19:1–6), and after the Jewish leaders have told Pilate that the real reason why they wanted Jesus crucified was that he had "claimed to be the Son of God" (19:7), Pilate, now afraid (cf. Matt 27:19), summons Jesus one more time, asking him, "Where do you come from?" (19:9). But Jesus gives him no answer.[66] The reader of the gospel, of course, knows the answer — Jesus is the eternal, preexistent Word of God (1:1) — but this truth would be lost on Pilate.[67]

Pilate, incredulous that the prisoner would not take the opportunity to lobby the one who had authority to free him for his release, asks Jesus, "Do you refuse to speak to me?... Don't you realize I have power either to free you or to crucify you?" (John 19:10). But Jesus calmly points out that Pilate's authority came "from above" — that is, from God (cf. Rom 13:1) — so that the one who delivered Jesus over to Pilate (presumably Caiaphas) was guilty of a greater sin.[68]

Hence throughout the entire proceedings against Jesus, while Judas and Peter are hard-pressed and face inner turmoil, while the Jewish leaders change their story and seek to cajole and intimidate Pilate to render a "guilty" verdict concerning Jesus, and while Pilate is quite literally torn between Jesus and the Jewish leaders, Jesus stays calm, "knowing all that was going to happen to him" (18:4), resolved to "drink the cup the Father has given" him (18:11). In fact, the Jewish leaders' seeking his death by crucifixion is shown "to fulfill what Jesus had said about the kind of death he was going to die" (18:32). In all of his suffering and humiliation, Jesus respects the authority of Pilate and the Jewish leaders and entrusts himself to God the Father.

As we assess the outcome and implications of Jesus' trial before Pilate for Jesus, it is important to realize at the outset that, in many ways, the present encounter is merely a culmination of preceding developments and dynamics. When Pilate interrogates Jesus, he had behind him a life replete with political ruthlessness and compromise. His is a hardened conscience and a willful rejection of truth in just about every possible sense. The Jewish leaders, too, have shown in their response to Jesus' signs and teaching that they will not listen to God's Messiah. The road that Jesus walked prior to his appearance before Pilate, by contrast, was one of love, ministry

---

65. Cf. William Barclay, *The Gospel of John* (DSB; rev. ed.; Louisville: Westminster John Knox, 1975), 2.243, who notes that Pilate had "not the courage to defy the world in spite of his past, and to take his stand with Christ and a future which was glorious." See also Beasley-Murray, *John*, 332, who notes that Jesus' statement "implicitly conveys an invitation," placing "Pilate in a situation of decision": "Jesus the prisoner sets his judge in the dock!

66. As Bock, *Jesus according to Scripture*, 533, notes, Jesus had already said that his kingdom was not of this world and that he "came into the world" (John 18:36–37).

67. In 16:28, Jesus had told the Eleven, "I came from the Father and entered the world, now I am leaving the world and going back to the Father." In 12:46, Jesus had said, "I have come into the world as a light, so that no one who believes in me should stay in darkness."

68. See the Jewish leaders' self-reference as having "handed ... over" (*paredōkamen*) Jesus to Pilate in 18:30 and Pilate's reference to Jesus' "own people and chief priests" having "handed" him over (*paredōkan*) to him in 18:35. See also Jesus' comment that if his kingdom were of this world, his servants would fight to prevent his arrest by the Jewish leaders (18:36; so rightly the NIV, TNIV, and the NLT, though almost all other translations incorrectly render the phrase *paradothō tois Ioudaiois* "handed over *to* the Jews"; e.g., KJV; NKJV; NASB; NRSV; ESV; HCSB).

to others, and uncompromising obedience to the one who sent him. In many ways, these three characters merely act out their part in a way that is consistent with the character they previously displayed.

How does Jesus fare in comparison to the Jewish leaders and Pilate? As mentioned above, both the Jewish leaders and Pilate temporarily emerge from the proceedings against Jesus in some sense victorious and yet fatally wounded. The Jews' victory over Pilate and Jesus comes at the high cost of betraying their religious hope and incurs immeasurable guilt, and Pilate agrees to condemn a man to die who he senses is innocent. Jesus, by contrast, the one who appears to be the major loser and victim of the Jewish leaders' and Pilate's "unprincipled alliance,"[69] has in fact not yielded anything, has ultimately lost nothing, and gained everything.

First, Jesus stayed true to his mission of testifying to the truth. He respected those whom God had put in authority over him (cf. Rom 13:1) and entrusted himself in faith to God the Father.

Second, Jesus fulfilled both the revelatory and the redemptive mission he had set out to accomplish (1:18; 4:34; 17:4; 19:31). On the cross, Jesus revealed God's love for humankind (3:16) and as the "Lamb of God" made atonement for sin (1:29, 36). Hence, according to Johannine theology, the cross, far from being a place of shame, became for Jesus a place of glory, the place where his perfect submission and obedience to the will of the Father were manifested, which included the provision of redemption for humankind.

Third, as John 20 and 21 make clear, Jesus rose from the dead on the third day, which marks the overruling of the Jewish plot to kill Jesus and Pilate's decision to condemn Jesus to die. Hence, in typical Johannine fashion, Jesus in the Farewell Discourse does not dwell on the imminent crucifixion but euphemistically subsumes it under his "return to the Father." The way John tells it, "Jesus knew that the hour had come for him to leave this world and go to the Father. Having loved his own who were in the world, he loved them to the end" (13:1). The cross merely marks Jesus' departure out of this world to the Father. Or as Jesus says in 14:12, believers will perform even greater works than he did subsequent to his departure, "because I am going to the Father." Listening to Jesus, it is as simple as that: "I came from the Father and entered the world; now I am leaving the world and going back to the Father" (16:28) — barely a mention of the cross as a station on the way back to Jesus' place of glory with the Father (cf. 17:5, 24).[70]

In this way, then, Jesus, though apparently the loser in the Jewish and Roman trials against him, emerges as the ultimate victor in the gospel, eliciting from Pilate the acknowledgment that he was either indifferent to the truth or incapable of determining what it was (18:37–38a), plotting his strategy to spread his message of salvation (John 13–17), commissioning his followers as the Father had sent him (20:21), and calling Peter and the other disciples to follow him until he returns (21:19, 22). Pilate, however, as is known from subsequent history, continues to clash

---

69. The term is from Ridderbos (*Gospel of John*, 587).   70. See chap. 14 below.

with his Jewish subjects and is recalled to Rome three short years after pronouncing the death sentence on Jesus.

25.3.4 Conclusion

Commentators regularly note the irony of Pilate's question, "What is truth?" in light of the fact that Truth incarnate, "the way and the truth and the life" (14:6), is standing right in front of him.[71] While this is doubtless apt, an even more striking irony may be at work here. As Miroslav Volf aptly notes:

> Trials are supposed to be about finding out what happened and meting out justice. In Jesus' trial, neither the accusers nor the judge cared for the truth.... The judge scorns the very notion of truth: "What is truth?" he asks, and uninterested in any answer, he leaves the scene of dialogue.... For both the accusers and the judge, the truth is irrelevant because it works at cross-purposes to their hold on power. The only truth they will recognize is "the truth of power." It was the accused who raised the issue of truth by subtly reminding the judge of his highest obligation—find out the truth.[72]

In the context of the trial narrative, Pilate, as the one called to judge concerning the truth regarding Jesus, here dismisses the entire question of truth. If the judge cares nothing about the truth, what does that say about the value of Jesus' trial and the verdict that is reached regarding Jesus? The message is obvious: the question of truth was dismissed as glibly as Pilate's question dismissed Jesus' claim that he came to witness to the truth.

A second observation pertains to the parallelism maintained by John regarding Caiaphas and Pilate, the Jewish high priest and the Roman governor. Both speak better than they know, Caiaphas unwittingly arguing for the necessity of Jesus' provision of substitutionary atonement (11:49–50; 18:14), Pilate unwittingly acknowledging Jesus as the truth (18:37). Both also share in their complicity in Jesus' death—Caiaphas as the one who handed Jesus over to Pilate (19:11), and Pilate in handing Jesus over to the Jews to have him crucified (19:16). In this momentous hour of salvation history, the evangelist therefore shows how these two characters are unequally yoked in the rejection of Jesus as the Messiah and "king of the Jews."

Caiaphas's action, representing the Jewish nation, and Pilate's action, representing the non-Jewish world, include Jew as well as non-Jew in the sin of crucifying the Truth. Whether by actively pursuing Jesus' death (the Jewish leaders) or by passively acquiescing to pressure (Pilate), the religious and political authorities in charge at the time of Jesus' trial conspired together against the Lord's anointed, as Psalm 2 envisages (Ps 2:1–2; cf. Acts 4:25–26). This is evidence of the pervasive sinfulness engulfing a world that lies in darkness apart from the light that has come in Jesus.

---

71. Cf. Keener, *John*, 1114, citing Duke, *Irony*, 130; Witherington, *John's Wisdom*, 292.

72. Volf, *Exclusion and Embrace*, 266. Volf's entire discussion of Jesus' trial before Pilate (entitled "Jesus before Pilate: Truth against Power," 264–71) repays careful reading.

Third, christologically and salvation-historically, truth is inextricably linked to the cross. In Jesus, the truth is crucified.[73] This does not mean the death of truth, for truth cannot be permanently kept down. Yet truth is intensely personal. It is Jesus who represents the truth in his very own person, and it is he who calls people to respond to him in faith. People's rejection of the truth, likewise, manifests itself in their rejection, not of a set of abstract propositions, but of Jesus. To employ the kind of reasoning John repeatedly employs in his first letter, if anyone claims to love the truth and yet rejects Jesus, who is the Truth, how can that person's claim to love the truth be valid?

In a world that often refers to God but rarely mentions Jesus, the fact that it is specifically in Jesus, rather than generically in God, that Truth is found is profoundly significant and intensely relevant. Not only this, but in this world, the Truth, like Jesus, will always be called to suffer. The cross therefore ought to serve as a perennial reminder that, in this world, the only truth is a crucified truth. In this world, Jesus could not be the truth without ending up being called to die for the truth and as the truth. It will be the same for his followers.

Fourth, if the above analysis is on target, the two major characters or groups in the Johannine trial narrative are the Jewish leaders and Jesus, while Pilate turns out to be a comparatively minor character. As a character, Pilate only surfaces in John chapters 18 and 19, and even there, he is continually shown to be torn in the clashing claims between the Jewish leaders and Jesus, as a spider caught in its own net. By contrast, in the context of the Johannine narrative, both Jesus and the Jewish leaders pervade the story from beginning to end. The first clash between Jesus and the Jewish authorities occurs at the temple clearing in 2:14–22. It reaches its first major climax in chapter 5 (esp. 5:18) and continues to escalate especially in chapters 8 and 10. Hence, even in chapters 18 and 19, while Pilate is temporarily in the foreground of the narrative, it is the Jewish leaders who have handed Jesus over to Pilate (18:30, 35, 36) and who receive him back from Pilate to have him crucified (19:16).

The implication of this is that the Jews cannot blame Pilate for putting Jesus on the cross. The truth, certainly according to John's gospel, is that they not only asked Pilate to render a "guilty" verdict regarding Jesus, but they exerted extensive pressure on Pilate to coerce him into compliance. This is not the place to defend John and his gospel against the charge of anti-Semitism, nor does John need to be defended in this regard, since such charges are anachronistic impositions of modern concerns onto the Gospel.[74] In the end, Jew and non-Jew alike stand guilty before God in their complicity of rejecting the Messiah and the Truth, and every person stands in need to respond to Jesus' vicarious death for humankind in personal faith.[75]

---

73. Cf. Lincoln, "Reading John," 145, who speaks of "crucifying the truth."

74. I am aware that calling Pilate a "comparatively minor" character in the Johannine trial narrative is potentially explosive and open to misrepresentation, but in the spirit of Luther, as an interpreter of the Johannine narrative, "Here I stand, I can do no other." On the alleged anti-Semitism of John's Gospel, see Bieringer, Pollefeyt, and Vandecasteele-Vanneuville, *Anti-Judaism and the Fourth Gospel* and the fuller volume with the same title published by Royal Van Gorcum in 2001. See my review of this work in *Them* 28/2 (2003): 71–73.

75. Cf. Whitacre, *John*, 443: "So now both Jew and Gentile have been given a chance to respond to the one come from God."

Finally, Jesus' Roman trial speaks to the relationship between power and truth. If I may be allowed this anachronism, the view of a lone, helpless prisoner before the representative of imperial Roman power is not unlike the much more recent image, broadcast all around the world, of the Chinese student defying a tank at the demonstrations in Tiananmen Square. Truth is pitted against power, and "the truth of power" is pitted against "the power of truth."[76] Jesus' example shows that the power of truth does not depend on power, and in his willingness to die for the truth and for others and in his refusal to resort to violence, he models "the power of self-giving love."[77] Contrary to the claims of postmodernism, it is not true that the only truth there is is power.[78] In this Jesus gives hope to all those who stand for truth and as a result are oppressed by those in power.

25.4 The Cosmic Trial Motif in John's Letters

Like the gospel, John's first letter claims to represent eyewitness testimony. The author bears witness concerning "the Word of life ... which was with the Father and has appeared to us" (1 John 1:1–2) and testifies "that the Father has sent his Son to be the Savior of the world" (4:14). Ten of the twelve instances of "witness" terminology in 1 John (*martyreō*, "testify"; *martyria*, "testimony") appear in 5:6–11, the passage concerning the three witnesses regarding Jesus: the Spirit, the water, and the blood.[79] Most likely, "water" refers to Jesus' baptism and "blood" to the crucifixion, the beginning and end points of his public ministry.[80] If people believe in Jesus the Son of God, they have life, eternal life; apart from him, there is no life.

The "world" (*kosmos*) is mentioned in 1 John first at 2:2, where it is said that Jesus' atoning sacrifice was sufficient "for the sins of the whole world." The term is used in a different sense in its six instances in 2:15–17, where the readers are warned not to "love the world or anything in the world." The threefold reference to "the cravings of sinful people, the lust of their eyes and their boasting about what they have and do" (2:26) echoes the scenario at the fall (see also the reference to Cain at 3:12) and affirms the world's sinfulness, which unbelievers in Jesus the Son treated lightly (1:5–2:2). As such, the world is antagonistic, in fact, hateful toward believers in Jesus (3:1, 13).

---

76. The phrase is Volf's (*Exclusion and Embrace*, 266), to whose suggestive treatment on pp. 264–71 this paragraph is partially indebted. See the references to Volf's work above.

77. The phrase is Lincoln's ("Reading John," 145), to whose treatment on pp. 143–46 this paragraph is partially indebted.

78. Cf. Lincoln, "Reading John," 143, who sums up postmodernism's own "grand narrative" as holding that "power produces what passes for truth and this truth then becomes the means by which the powerful wield more power." As Lincoln rightly points out, there is "a cost to leaving open the question of truth," because "the person who treats the question about truth with contempt has no compelling reason not to treat human life with contempt." Lincoln aptly notes that "we need to be alert not only to the dangers but also to the potential for human wellbeing bound up with claims to truth, including that of the Fourth Gospel, which sees truth embodied in Jesus" (ibid., 144).

79. This may be in keeping with the "two or three witness" requirement in Deut 17:6; 19:15 also upheld by Jesus (Matt 18:16) and Paul (2 Cor 13:1). There may also be a link with the Trinity—Father, Son, and Spirit.

80. So rightly Yarbrough, *1–3 John*, 282–83, and the majority of commentators. Yarbrough cites the following NT passages as associating Jesus' atoning death with "blood": Matt 26:28; Acts 20:28; Rom 3:25; 5:9; Eph 1:7; Col 1:20; Heb 9:12; 13:12. Less likely is a reference to John 19:34 or to the sacraments of baptism and the Eucharist (ibid., 282, n. 5).

The world is also the sphere of operation of many false prophets (1 John 4:1), deceivers exhibiting the "spirit of the antichrist" (4:3; cf. 2:18, 22; 2 John 7). Yet the Holy Spirit, the "Spirit of truth" (1 John 4:6; cf. John 14:17; 15:26; 16:13), who indwells believers, is greater than "the one who is in the world" (1 John 4:4), "the spirit of falsehood" (4:6; cf. 1QS 3:18; see also 1QS 4:23–26).[81] This sinful world was also the place where God sent his Son as an atoning sacrifice for sins (1 John 4:9–10; cf. 2:2; John 1:29, 36; 3:16–17) to be the Savior of the world (1 John 4:14; cf. John 4:42).

John observes that "in this world we are like Jesus" (1 John 4:17), "for everyone born of God overcomes the world" (5:4–5; cf. John 1:5; 16:33): "the victory that has overcome the world" is "our faith" (the only instance of the noun "faith," *pistis*, in John's gospel and letters) in Jesus as the Son of God (1 John 5:4–5). The last reference to the world in 1 John is found in 5:19: "We know that we are children of God, and that the whole world is under the control of the evil one." This again underscores the necessity of a new, spiritual birth and asserts that the world is controlled by "the evil one," the devil or Satan (see the references to the "prince of this world" in John 12:31; 14:30; 16:11).

In addition, John makes reference to his expectation of a future "day of judgment" (1 John 4:17; cf. John 12:48). As John's gospel makes clear, this judgment (*krisis*) has already confronted people in the person and work of Christ (John 3:19). It can be averted by believing in the Son (5:24). Yet those who reject the Son will be subject to divine judgment executed by the Son himself (5:22, 27, 29).[82]

"World" and "witness" terminology thus shows that the world is a place under the dominion of Satan, inhabited by the "children of the devil," who are haters of the things of God, especially his Christ, and also the people of God. Yet Jesus gave himself up as an atoning sacrifice for the whole world, and it is incumbent upon believers, the "children of God," to bear witness to Jesus the Son of God.

The presence of Satan in this world is also felt through the spirit of the antichrist, which pervades it in the persons of the "many false prophets" who "have gone out into the world" (1 John 4:1; cf. 2 John 7). Hence, believers are thrust into the intense spiritual warfare of the cosmic conflict that came to a head when Jesus and Satan squared off at the cross. Though Satan had intended to be Jesus' demise, God had determined before time for the cross to be the place of glorification for the obedient Son at the completion of his mission of love.

This cosmic conflict, in turn, is in essence a battle concerning truth.[83] According to John, no one who denies his own sin lives in truth. With such denial of sin also comes a disregard for God's remedy for sin, the atoning sacrifice of the Lord Jesus Christ (1 John 1:5–10). Another sign of lacking the truth is disobedience to God's commands (2:4–6). Believers, for their part, "know the truth," which is

---

81. See Köstenberger, *John*, 437–38.
82. See the survey in Yarbrough, *1–3 John*, 258.
83. John's first letter exhibits a rich "truth" vocabulary, including the noun "truth" (*alētheia*; 1 John 1:6, 8; 2:4, 21 [2x]; 3:18, 19; 4:6; 5:6); the adjectives "true" or "real," *alēthes* (2:8, 27) and *alēthinos* (2:8; 5:20 [3x]); and the adverb "truly" (*alēthōs*; 2:5).

essentially bound up in the affirmation that "Jesus is the Messiah" (2:22). In this John's letters and the gospel concur. The "Spirit of truth" who stands in opposition to the "spirit of falsehood" (4:6) testifies because "the Spirit is the truth" (5:6).

John's letters, therefore, contain all the same ingredients of the cosmic trial motif as does the gospel. One finds terminology related to witness, the world, truth, and references to the battle between God's Christ and Satan. While focused on Jesus, who has "overcome the world" (John 16:33) and destroyed "the devil's work" (1 John 3:8), this cosmic conflict has also engulfed believers, who have the victory by their faith in the victorious Son of God, who has broken the power of the evil one. Thus John's opening words in the gospel are proven true: "The light shines in the darkness, and the darkness has not overcome it."

Chapter 12

THE NEW MESSIANIC COMMUNITY: DIVINE SOVEREIGNTY AND HUMAN RESPONSIBILITY

BIBLIOGRAPHY

Bass, Christopher D. *That You May Know: Assurance of Salvation in 1 John*. NAC Studies in Bible & Theology. Nashville: Broadman & Holman, 2008. **Brown, Raymond E.** "Roles of Women in the Fourth Gospel." *TS* 36 (1975): 688–99. Idem. "Crucial Questions in Johannine Theology." Pp. 220–77 in *An Introduction to the Gospel of John*. ABRL. Ed. Francis J. Moloney. New York: Doubleday, 2003. **Carson, D. A**. *Divine Sovereignty and Human Responsibility: Biblical Perspectives in Tension*. Atlanta: John Knox, 1981. Idem. "Reflections on Christian Assurance." *WTJ* 54 (1992): 1–29. **Chennattu, Rekha M.** *Johannine Discipleship as a Covenant Relationship*. Peabody, MA: Hendrickson, 2006. **Conway, Colleen M**. *Men and Women in the Fourth Gospel: Gender and Johannine Characterization*. SBLDS 167. Atlanta: SBL, 1999. **Croteau, David A**. "An Analysis of the Concept of Believing in the Narrative Contexts of John's Gospel." Th.M. thesis. Southeastern Baptist Theological Seminary, 2002. **Ferreira, Johan**. *Johannine Ecclesiology*. JSNTSup 160. Sheffield: Sheffield Academic Press, 1998. **Hasitschka, Martin**. *Befreiung von Sünde nach dem Johannesevangelium: Eine bibeltheologische Untersuchung*. Innsbruck: Tyrolia, 1989. **Marrow, Stanley B.** "Johannine Ecclesiology." *CS* 37 (1998): 27–46. **Metzner, Rainer**. *Das Verständnis der Sünde im Johannesevangelium*. WUNT 122. Tübingen: Mohr-Siebeck, 2000. **Owings, T. L.** "The Concept of Sin in the Fourth Gospel." Ph.D. diss. Louisville, KY: SBTS, 1983. **Quast, Kevin**. *Peter and the Beloved Disciple: Figures for a Community in Crisis*. JSNTSup 32. Sheffield: JSOT, 1989. **Schnackenburg, Rudolf**. "Is There a Johannine Ecclesiology?" Pp. 247–56 in *A Companion to John: Readings in Johannine Theology*. Ed. Michael J. Taylor: New York: Alba, 1977. Idem. "The Notion of Faith in the Fourth Gospel." Pp. 558–75 in *The Gospel according to St. John*. Vol. 1. New York: Crossroad, 1990. **Schnelle, Udo**. "Johanneische Ekklesiologie." *NTS* 37 (1991): 37–50. **Seim, Turid K.** "Roles of Women in the Gospel of John." Pp. 56–73 in *Aspects on the Johannine Literature*. Ed. Lars Hartman and Birger Olsson. ConBNT 17. Stockholm: Alqvist & Wiksell International, 1987. **Yarbrough, Robert W**. "Divine Election in the Gospel of John." Pp. 47–62 in *The Grace of God, the Bondage of the Will*. Vol. 1. Ed. Thomas R. Schreiner and Bruce A. Ware. Grand Rapids: Baker, 1995.

26 Divine Election and Predestination

26.1 Introduction

In the present chapter, I set out to explore a variety of complex and related teachings found in John's gospel and letters: divine election and predestination, sin and divine judgment, faith and the new birth, and the new messianic community. All of these motifs are part of the Johannine teaching on how a person comes to faith in Christ and is incorporated into the new messianic community.

On the divine side of the equation, John teaches that, ultimately, a person's coming to faith is preceded by divine election and predestination. This means that human sin never has the final word. To the contrary, in Johannine theology, even human sin fulfills Scripture and is ultimately part of God's sovereign purposes.

On the human side, there is the reality of pervasive sinfulness and need for salvation and the necessity of faith in Jesus the Messiah. This, again, invokes dimensions related to the divine work. Sin incurs divine judgment, while faith is shown to result in the new birth, spiritual regeneration.

In the first instance, John makes clear that both sin and faith are ultimately personal in nature. At the same time, individual faith ensues in the incorporation of a believer into the new messianic community summoned by the Christ to discipleship and sent out by him to its mission to the world. In this chapter, then, it is my purpose to explore the Johannine teaching regarding these various aspects in relation to one another.

26.2 Divine Sovereignty and Human Responsibility

John's gospel affirms both divine sovereignty and human responsibility.[1] At the heart of John's call to human responsibility is his emphasis on people's need to "believe" in Jesus, a topic discussed under the next heading. While faith is a major theme in Johannine theology, however, John makes clear that humans require divine enablement to believe. Thus Jesus says, "And I, when I am lifted up from the earth, will draw all people to myself" (12:32; cf. 6:44, 65). In his final prayer, Jesus speaks of "those whom God has given him" out of the world (cf. 17:2, 6, 24; cf. 6:37; 10:29). These passages indicate God's prevenient action prior to people's coming to faith.

More specifically, John can describe this action in terms of divine "choosing" or election. This election may be attributed to God the Father or be said to be effected through Jesus Christ as his agent. When many abandon Jesus at a critical juncture of his ministry, Jesus, at Peter's confession of him as "the Holy One of God," replies, "Have I not chosen you, the Twelve? Yet one of you is a devil!" (speaking of Judas the betrayer; 6:70; cf. 13:18; 17:12).[2] Later, Jesus affirms regarding his disciples,

---

[1]. See Carson, *Divine Sovereignty & Human Responsibility*, whose book is subtitled "Biblical Perspectives in Tension."

[2]. Jesus' choice of Judas as one of the Twelve raises a knotty theological problem, since in his case at least, election proved ineffectual. It should be noted, however, that Judas was neither saved nor regenerated (cf. 13:10–11; 15:2). While this does not alleviate the difficulty entirely, John makes clear that Judas's betrayal served to fulfill OT prophecy (17:12) and that Jesus' choice of Judas took place in full cognizance (foreknowledge) of Judas' true nature (6:70–71). See also Carson, *Divine Sovereignty and Human Responsibility*, 130–32.

"You did not choose me, but I chose you and appointed you so that you might go and bear fruit—fruit that will last" (15:16; cf. 15:19).

It is clear that this divine election is necessitated by the fact that the disciples, like all humans, were prior to that election part of the world and in bondage to sin and moral darkness.[3] With regard to humanity in general, this is taught by the evangelist in 3:19–21, where he speaks of people clinging to darkness and fleeing the light. With regard to the Jews, Jesus affirms that "everyone who sins is a slave to sin" and that only "if the Son sets you free, you will be free indeed" (8:34, 36). With regard to the disciples, by speaking of them as having been given to Jesus "out of the world," Jesus makes clear that human sinfulness requires divine election.[4]

What is more, John stresses that *apart* from divine election, it is impossible for anyone to be saved and receive eternal life. This shows that prior to the human choice to believe, resulting in salvation and eternal life, is the divine choice of election, enabling some, but mysteriously not others, to believe and place their trust in Christ. On a human level, this may be counterintuitive and hard to understand, if not appear to militate against human notions of fairness. Yet this reality is clearly taught in several Johannine passages, most notably Jesus' pronouncements in 8:47; 10:26; and 14:17 and in the evangelist's words at the end of the Book of Signs.

Consider the following statements:

- 8:47: "Whoever belongs to God hears what God says. *The reason you do not hear is that you do not belong to God.*"
- 10:25b–26: "The works I do in my Father's name testify about me, but *you do not believe because you are not my sheep.*"
- 12:37–40: "Even after Jesus had performed so many signs in their presence, they still would not believe in him. This was to fulfill the word of Isaiah the prophet: 'Lord, who has believed our message and to whom has the arm of the Lord been revealed?' For this reason they *could not believe*, because, as Isaiah says elsewhere: 'He has blinded their eyes and hardened their hearts, so they can neither see with their eyes, nor understand with their hearts, nor turn—and I would heal them.'"
- 14:17: "The world *cannot accept him*, because it neither sees him nor knows him. But you know him...."[5]

In these passages, the logic typically moves from lack of divine election to failure to believe. People do not belong to God; that is why they do not listen to Jesus (8:47). People are not Jesus' sheep; that is why they do not believe (10:25b–26). God blinded people's eyes and hardened their hearts; that is why they cannot believe (12:40). This kind of reasoning places human unbelief ultimately within the sphere of God's sovereignty, and more specifically his (positive or negative) elective purposes. While

---

3. See Carson, *Divine Sovereignty and Human Responsibility*, 163–67.

4. See also the unique reference in 16:7–11 to the Spirit's convicting work of people in the world, presumably through the gospel preaching of the church, which exposes sin and speaks of righteousness and judgment, as a prevenient divine work leading unbelievers to faith in Christ.

5. Emphasis added in all cases.

not rendering people free from responsibility, their unbelief is ultimately shown to be grounded not in human choice but in divine hardening.

Perhaps the statement in 12:39 is the most striking, where the evangelist writes that people "could not believe" because God had blinded their eyes and hardened their hearts.[6] On a human level, one may indeed ask how God, if it was he who caused a human heart to harden, can still fault that person for failing to believe. But John clearly does not condone this kind of reasoning and has no problem affirming both divine sovereignty and human responsibility in proper proportion to one another, with divine sovereignty serving as the comprehensive framework within which human agents are called to make responsible choices—most importantly, believing in Jesus as Messiah.

26.3 The Introduction to John's Gospel

The larger theme of divine sovereignty runs through the entire gospel.[7] In the introduction to his gospel, John speaks of the Word's presence with God in the beginning and of his activity in creation (1:1–5). He also introduces the Baptist as "a man sent from God," indicating divine initiative (1:6). Hence both in creation and in salvation, God's sovereign plan is presented as foundational. God the Father's sending of "the light," that is, the Lord Jesus Christ, is likewise shown to be a function of God's sovereign initiative, completely apart from human prompting (1:9–11).[8] The new birth following faith, likewise, is said to be a result, not of human choice, but of God's doing (1:13).[9]

In what follows, John indicates that the Word was made flesh and took up residence on this earth as part of God's redemptive program for humanity (1:14). Divine initiative in redemption is necessitated by human sinfulness ("darkness"); divine initiative in revelation is required by the fact that "no one has ever seen God" (1:18). Because God is spirit and hence invisible, humans can know God only if he takes the first step in revealing himself to them, and this he did in and through the incarnation and earthly ministry of the Lord Jesus Christ, "the one and only Son, who is himself God and is in closest relationship with the Father" (1:18).

What is more, in Jesus humans have received "grace" from the one who was "full of grace and truth" (1:14). This emphasis on "grace" in 1:14–17 (where all four of the word's occurrences in this gospel are found) puts people in the place of recipients of divine action on their behalf, just as the reference to people "receiving" and "believing" in Jesus in 1:12 casts humans as respondents to God's provision of eternal life in Christ. Thus, in its consistent emphasis on God's initiative in creation, redemption,

---

6. See the discussion under the heading "Reprobation" in Carson, *Divine Sovereignty and Human Responsibility*, 195–97.

7. See especially references to Jesus' foreknowledge (12:23; 13:1, 3; 18:4) and the Johannine fulfillment quotations (12:38; 19:24, 28, 36–37) focusing on the underlying rationale for Jesus' crucifixion (on the latter, see the discussion of Johannine Theology and the OT above). Other instances include 1:42, 48; 2:4, 19, 24–25; 4:17–18; 6:64, 70; 11:4, 11–14; 13:10–11, 33, 38; 14:2–3, 16, 29; 16:2, 4,

8, 20, 32; and 21:18–19. See also references to Jesus' preservation of his own (e.g., 10:28–29; 17:12; see Carson, *Divine Sovereignty and Human Responsibility*, 192–95).

8. Note also the salvation-historical reference to God's people Israel, "his own" (*hoi idioi*), in 1:11, which implies the election of Israel as God's "chosen people." See further the discussion below.

9. See further the discussion under the next heading below.

and revelation, the introduction to the gospel sets the stage for John's teaching on God's sovereignty and on divine election in the remainder of the gospel.

26.4 The Book of Signs and the Book of Exaltation

As John's gospel illustrates, election does not merely have a doctrinal dimension; the concept is deeply grounded in salvation-historical realities.[10] As mentioned, the reference to God's people Israel, "his own" (*hoi idioi*), in 1:11 implies Israel's election as God's "chosen people." What Israel's case makes clear, however, is that God's corporate election of Israel as a nation was not necessarily met by faith in every individual case, or even by the Jewish leadership (see Paul's exposition of this topic in Romans 9–11). The same dynamic is present in Jesus' ministry as presented in John's gospel. Even though Jesus furnishes many startling proofs of his messianic identity (the "signs"), the Jewish people, represented by their leaders, rejected him (12:37), in fulfillment of Scripture (12:38–41). Hence 1:19–12:50 serves as the narrative explication of 1:11.

The thought of the Father "giving" individuals to Jesus is a repeated theme in the gospel (see 6:39; 10:29; 17:2, 6; 18:9). Thus Jesus takes no credit for attracting people to himself by his own oratory or miraculous power. As the Father's sent Son, he receives those who come to him because of the Father's prevenient work.[11] John 6:37 is significantly elaborated on in 6:44, where Jesus states that no one can come to him "unless the Father who sent me draws them." Despite the rejection mentioned in 6:36, Jesus is confident that certain ones will come to him.[12] This seems to indicate the notion of divine predestination (cf. 6:39),[13] which culminates in chapter 12.

John 6:37 encapsulates the gospel's "universalism" (better: its "universal scope"), "individualism," and "predestinarianism."[14] On the basis of the Father's prevenient work, Jesus will receive the ones who come to him. What he will *not* do is fail to recognize these individuals as his own and eject them from his fellowship;[15] what he *will* do is keep and preserve them.[16] This motif culminates in the Good Shepherd Discourse (esp. 10:28–29)[17] and continues through Jesus' final prayer (esp. 17:6, 9, 11–12; cf. 18:9) and his concluding commissioning of Peter and "the disciple Jesus loved" (chap. 21).[18]

---

10. See Yarbrough, "Divine Election," 53–54, who notes that Jesus himself is the product of divine election (e.g., 1:29, 34; 3:35; 5:20; 7:27, 46; 10:36) and that predictive prophecy is likewise part of the "salvation-historical infrastructure chosen and implemented by God" (p. 53). Yarbrough also notes "giving" (esp. *didōmi*) terminology and the Johannine "signs" (*sēmeion*). On the latter aspect, see also Carson, *Divine Sovereignty and Human Responsibility*, 186–88.

11. Ridderbos, *Gospel of John*, 230.

12. Ibid. See also Carson, *Gospel according to John*, 290.

13. Carson, *Gospel according to John*, 290; contra, Witherington, *John's Wisdom*, 158.

14. Barrett, *Gospel according to St. John*, 294.

15. Ridderbos, *Gospel of John*, 231, n. 123. "Everything" in 6:37 and 39 is neuter, used in a qualitative, collective sense (Brown, *Gospel according to John I–XII*, 270; Barrett, *Gospel according to St. John*, 294; Borchert, *John 1–11*, 265), though ultimately people (not things) are in mind (BDF § 138 1., pp. 76–77, with specific reference to John 6:67; cf. Morris, *Gospel according to John*, 325; Moloney, *Gospel of John*, 216).

16. Carson, *Gospel according to John*, 290; Burge, *John*, 200. As Carson (ibid.) notes, the present figure of speech is a *litotes*, a stylistic device declaring a certain truth by nullifying its corollary.

17. Schnackenburg, *Gospel according to St. John*, 2.47.

18. The idea of accepting someone called by God into the community and not rejecting him is also found in the Qumran literature (e.g., 1QS 6:16, 19, 22; 9:15–16; 11:13–14).

Jesus' welcoming attitude is contrasted with the Pharisees' casting the formerly blind man out of the synagogue (9:34–35). While the focus in 6:37 seems to be on the Father's work of "giving" people to Jesus and on his receptive attitude, it is nonetheless true that persons must "come" to him. This underscores the need for a positive human response to the divine initiative.[19] Still, there is no indication here or elsewhere in this gospel that God's predestinatory purposes ever fail.[20]

In 6:44, Jesus proceeds to underscore the human inability to gain salvation apart from divine assistance. People can come to him only if the Father who sent Jesus draws them. Ultimately, therefore, salvation depends not on humans believing, but on the "drawing" action of the Father (presumably by the Holy Spirit), by which God moves a person to faith in Christ (cf. 12:32; see also Jer 31:3; Hos 11:4).[21] The reference to the Father "drawing" is balanced by people "coming" to Jesus.

Jesus' point here is not merely general but specific and salvation-historical. Because the Jews are refusing to come to God in his prescribed manner—through faith in the Messiah—they cannot receive eternal life. Jewish obduracy constitutes the focus of the "paternity dispute" in chapter 8, the healing of the blind man in chapter 9, the Good Shepherd Discourse in chapter 10, and the events surrounding the raising of Lazarus in chapters 11–12. The Pharisee-led plot against Jesus that surfaces intermittently in the narrative (esp. during the Festival Cycle in chaps. 5–10) is due to the Jews' unwillingness to come to God on his terms.

Then, in 13:1, the Twelve are called Jesus' "own" (*idioi*), indicating that Jesus' new messianic community has now taken Israel's place.[22] These references, in turn, are integrally related to expressions such as "children of God," a designation that likewise had Israel in view in the OT Scriptures. John, for his part, however, recasts and, in fact, reverses the conventional understanding of which people were God's children. To begin with, he makes clear that being a child of God means one has been "born of God" (1:13; cf. 3:3–5). Also, becoming a child of God is predicated on "receiving him," that is, believing in Jesus as the Messiah and Son of God (1:12). By implication, this means that those who rejected Jesus' messianic claims, including the Jewish leaders, thereby forfeited their status of being counted among God's children.

This reality is underscored by Jesus in his interchange with "the Jews who had [initially] believed him" (John 8:31) but who did not finally accept his claim and consequently turned out to be "children of the devil" (cf. 8:31–59; see esp. 8:42–47). Just as 1:12 is pivotal in the introduction to the gospel, so 8:31–59 constitutes the culminating demonstration of what constitutes the true nature of a child of God

---

19. Borchert, *John 1–11*, 265.
20. Contra, Witherington, *John's Wisdom*, 158.
21. Ridderbos, *Gospel of John*, 232. Rabbinic sources use the expression "to bring near to the Torah" with reference to conversion (*m. ʾAbot* 1:12 [Hillel; first cent. AD]; Moloney, *Gospel of John*, 220). There is a certain affinity between John's teaching on predestination and the Qumran doctrine of the "two spirits" (1QS 3:14–4:6). The rabbinic view is summed up by the saying attributed to Rabbi Akiba (c. AD 135): "All is foreseen, but freedom of choice is given" (*m. ʾAbot* 3:19). Cf. Josephus, *Ant.* 18.13, 16, 18; *J.W.* 2.162–65; and the excursus in Schnackenburg, *Gospel according to St. John*, 2:265–70.

22. See John W. Pryor, "Jesus and Israel in the Fourth Gospel—John 1:1," *NovT* 32 (1990): 201–18. See also the references to Jesus' followers as "my children" (*teknia*; 13:33); "brothers" (20:17); and "friends" (or "children"; *paidia*; 21:4–5).

in the Johannine narrative. Then, after John has redefined and narrowed the scope of "children of God"—including contrasting the term with "children of the devil" and subsuming unbelieving Jews under "the [unbelieving] world"—he broadens the concept to include not only Jewish believers in Jesus, but also "the scattered children of God," that is, Gentiles, whom Jesus' followers would gather together and make one (11:53; cf. 1 John 2:2).[23]

The monumental insight conveyed by John is therefore that God's elective purposes encompass not merely Israel but all who believe in Jesus as Messiah, whether Jews or non-Jews. Hence faith in Jesus has replaced ethnic membership of Israel as the major constitutive principle of belonging to the people of God. As Paul makes clear in Romans 9–11, properly understood, this principle already obtained in OT times. While, for the most part, the OT foreshadows the universal nature of God's people in an incipient or anticipatory form by showing the inclusion of individual Gentiles or the exclusion of individual Israelites, the NT witnesses to the fulfillment of the prophetic vision in a paradigm shift that moves the constitutive principle of inclusion in God's community from primarily ethnic to primarily spiritual.

This salvation-historical turn of events is marked in the Johannine narrative by the coming of the Greeks to Jesus in 12:20, resulting in Jesus' pronouncement that, once exalted, he will "draw all people" to himself—"all people" being all *kinds of* people, Gentiles as well as Jews—in the post-Pentecost period through the church's Spirit-empowered witness.[24] If, as is likely, John wrote several decades after the launch of the church's Gentile mission, this means that in his gospel, he seeks to furnish demonstration that Jesus' vision, uttered during the days of his earthly ministry, had by the time of writing become a reality, thus further vindicating and validating Jesus' messianic claims for those with ears to hear and eyes to see. Indeed, it was not too late for Jews to conclude that the nation's leaders had been wrong and that Jesus was in fact the Messiah he had claimed to be.[25]

26.5 Conclusion

It follows from the survey of the major relevant passages in John's gospel above that the fourth evangelist presents Jesus' entire ministry from the vantage point of God's sovereignty, including his foreknowledge, election, and predestination.[26] According to John, the ability to believe in Jesus is given by God, who "gives" people to Jesus, "draws" them to him, and enables them to have spiritual eyes to see that Jesus is the Messiah and Son of God. This does not completely remove the mystery surrounding

---

23. This is already hinted at in 10:16, where Jesus asserts, "I have other sheep that are not of this sheep pen. I must bring them also ... and there shall be one flock and one shepherd." See Köstenberger, "Jesus the Good Shepherd."

24. See John 15:26–27; and cf. Acts 2–28; cf. 1:1, 4–5, 7–8. See the discussion in Yarbrough, "Divine Election," 52; contra, Grant R. Osborne, "Soteriology in the Gospel of John," in *The Grace of God, the Will of Man: A Case for Arminianism* (ed. Clark H. Pinnock; Grand Rapids: Zondervan, 1989), 249.

25. This is especially true if John wrote subsequent to the destruction of the temple in AD 70, a monumental event shaking the foundations of Judaism, which would have created an opportunity for renewed Jewish evangelism. See the discussion in chap. 1, sec. 2 and of Jesus as the new temple in chap. 10, sec. 24 above.

26. See the conclusion by Carson, *Divine Sovereignty and Human Responsibility*, 198: "God's gracious sovereignty, mediated by Christ, is the exclusive ultimate ground of any man's salvation."

the question why some believe and others do not, but it does assign theological priority squarely to where it is properly placed: with God and Jesus his Messiah.[27]

27 SIN AND JUDGMENT

27.1 Sin

27.1.1 The Gospel of John

Sin seems to be a somewhat underserved theme in Johannine theology,[28] yet one that, especially in conjunction with the motif of divine judgment, is exceedingly important, as it lays the foundation for the human need of redemption and the necessity of faith and the new birth. The significance of this motif is underscored by the fact that the noun *hamartia* ("sin") occurs seventeen times in John's gospel[29] compared to seven instances in Matthew, six in Mark, and eleven in Luke. In addition, the adjective *hamartōlos* is found four times (9:16, 24, 25, 31) and the verb *hamartanō* once (5:14). To this should be added the fact that "sin" terminology in 1 John is even more frequent than in John's gospel.[30]

27.1.1.1 The Book of Signs

27.1.1.1.1 Jesus the "Lamb of God"

At the outset of John's gospel, Jesus is identified by John the Baptist as the "Lamb of God, who takes away the sin of the world" (1:29). The reader has already been told that "the world did not recognize" Jesus as Messiah (1:10) in its moral darkness. Reference has also been made to the possibility of "receiving" Jesus by faith, resulting in a new spiritual birth (1:12–13). In essence, the world's sin consists of its rejection of Jesus as Messiah, which, in turn, is evidence of its spiritual rebellion against the Creator. However, Jesus, as the "Lamb of God," "takes away" the world's sin as the sacrificial lamb provided by God.[31]

27.1.1.1.2 The Cana Cycle

In the Cana Cycle, it becomes evident that the Jewish leaders in particular and the Jewish people at large are part of the world's rejection of Jesus as Messiah and thus included in the world's sin. The Jewish leaders challenge Jesus' authority at the temple clearing (John 2:13–22), and one of their leaders, Nicodemus, lacks spiritual regeneration (3:3–9) and thus requires faith in Jesus, the crucified, lifted-up

---

27. For a helpful discussion see Carson (ibid., 125–98). See also Yarbrough, "Divine Election," 56–60, critiquing Osborne, "Soteriology in the Gospel of John."

28. But see Stevens, "chap. VI: The Doctrine of Sin," in *Johannine Theology*, 127–55; T. L. Owing, "The Concept of Sin in the Fourth Gospel" (Ph.D. dissertation; Louisville, KY: SBTS, 1983); Martin Hasitschka, *Befreiung von Sünde nach dem Johannesevangelium: Eine bibeltheologische Untersuchung* (Innsbruck: Tyrolia, 1989); and Rainer Metzner, *Das Verständnis der Sünde im Johannesevangelium* (WUNT 122; Tübingen: Mohr-Siebeck, 2000).

29. John 1:29; 8:21, 24 (2x), 34 (2x), 46; 9:34, 41 (2x); 15:22 (2x), 24; 16:8, 9; 19:11; 20:23.

30. See below (though there are no references to "sin" in 2 and 3 John).

31. On the Passover motif, see chap. 10, sec. 23, esp. 23.2.1.

Son of Man (3:13–14). As the evangelist editorializes, "For God so loved the world that he gave his one and only Son, that whoever believes in him shall not perish but have eternal life" (3:16).[32] God's purpose for the world is not judgment but salvation (3:17).

27.1.1.1.3 The Festival Cycle

With the beginning of the Festival Cycle in John 5, the clash between Jesus and the Jewish authorities escalates, and Jewish obduracy becomes more and more apparent (see esp. 5:18). The failure of Jesus' earthly mission to the Jews is signaled by the defection of Jesus by even many of his disciples at the end of chapter 6 and the unbelief of Jesus' brothers at the beginning of chapter 7. At the end of chapter 7, the reader is told that the hearts of many on the Jewish ruling council, the Sanhedrin, are irrevocably hardened.

The climactic passage dealing with the issue of sin in John's gospel is clearly John 8:21–47, which features six of the seventeen references to *hamartia* in the gospel. The passage opens with Jesus' pronouncement that the Jews who reject him will "die in [their] sins" (8:21; twice reiterated in 8:24). This draws the ire of Jesus' Jewish antagonists, because, in keeping with the Synoptic portrayal of the Jewish leaders, only non-Jews were considered sinful while Jews were generally regarded as righteous if they observed the Mosaic law as interpreted and supplemented by the various additional rabbinic stipulations.

In the ensuing interchange, Jesus asserts that "everyone who sins is a slave to sin" (8:34; cf. 8:46, where Jesus claims to be free from sin). According to Jesus, the Jews are not Abraham's children but children of the devil, who is a murderer from the beginning. This explains the Jews' desire to kill Jesus, who has done nothing wrong. Thus sin is at the root of the Jews' and the world's rejection of Jesus. No one can believe, be saved, and be born again unless he or she first acknowledges their own sinfulness. Conversely, those who deny their own sinfulness hold to a defective anthropology and as a result deny the foundational reality of their existence that requires redemption. Paradoxically, and tragically, the very sinfulness that requires salvation keeps people from acknowledging their sin and need for redemption in the first place.

The Jews' definition of sinfulness vs. righteousness as depending on observance of the Mosaic law is made clear in the following pericope where Jesus heals the man born blind on the Sabbath, which involves the man's picking up his mat, a matter forbidden by rabbinic tradition (though not by the law itself). As a result, the Jews repeatedly accuse Jesus of being a "sinner" (9:24; cf. 9:16, 25, 31). They are also shown to hold to a strict "suffering is the result of sin" theology (9:34), held even by Jesus' own disciples (cf. 9:2–3; but see 5:14). As Jesus notes in the conclusion to this pericope, however, it is precisely the Pharisees' failure to acknowledge their sin

---

32. See Andreas J. Köstenberger, "Study Notes on John," in *ESV Study Bible* (Wheaton: Crossway, 2008), 2025.

that puts them beyond the pale of divine salvation (9:41). Thus the entire chapter is turned into a parable depicting the Pharisees' spiritual blindness, which keeps them from acknowledging their own sinfulness. This ironically reverses the destiny of the man born blind (whom they consider a "sinner" but who walks away healed) and themselves (who deny their own sinfulness and thus remain in their sin).

27.1.1.2 The Book of Exaltation
27.1.1.2.1 The Farewell Discourse

This verdict is reiterated by Jesus in the subsequent instruction of his followers, where he also points to the Jews' culpable rejection of his works as evidence for his messianic identity (15:22–24). This reinforces the notion of theodicy in that the Jews' rejection of Jesus as Messiah is clearly stated to be a function, not of lacking evidence, but of Jewish obduracy (see 12:36b–41, where it is also made clear that the Jewish rejection of Jesus took place in order to fulfill scriptural prophecy).

Later in the Farewell Discourse, Jesus notes that the sole function of the Holy Spirit with regard to the world is bound up with "prov[ing] the world to be in the wrong about sin and righteousness and judgment: about sin, because people do not believe in me" (16:8–9). This reiterates the notion that the ultimate sin according to John is the world's unbelief with regard to Jesus. Jesus came to "take away" the sin of the world, but the offer of salvation in Jesus becomes effectual only when those whom God has given to Jesus out of the world put their trust in Jesus (e.g., 17:6; the motif of divine election in John; see the discussion below).

Thus there is a level playing field: the world at large and the Jews alike are sinners and must believe in Jesus for salvation. As long as they persist in their unbelief, the Jews are no better than the world; in fact, they are part of it. Paul's words ring true: "There is no difference between Jew and Gentile, for all have sinned and fall short of the glory of God, and all are justified freely by his grace through the redemption that came by Christ Jesus. God presented Christ as a sacrifice of atonement, through the shedding of his blood—to be received by faith" (Rom 3:22–25). In this cluster of assertions Johannine and Pauline theology are in perfect harmony.

27.1.1.2.2 The Passion Narrative

The final reference to sin in this gospel is found as part of the concluding commissioning statement. There the disciples are charged with forgiving or retaining people's sins, presumably based on their acceptance or rejection of the message regarding Jesus (20:22; cf. Matt 16:19; Luke 24:47).

27.1.2 First John

Remarkably, words related to sin are even more frequent in John's first letter, which features seventeen instances of *hamartia* (1 John 1:7, 8, 9 [2x]; 2:2, 12; 3:4 [2x], 5 [2x], 8, 9; 4:10; 5:16 [2x], 17 [2x]) and ten occurrences of *hamartanō* (1:10; 2:1 [2x]; 3:6 [2x], 8, 9; 5:16 [2x], 18). John makes clear that only "the blood of Jesus ... purifies us from all sin" (1:7). Only those who confess their sins are purified; those who claim to be without sin and maintain that they have not sinned make God out to be a liar and do not have God's Word in them (1:8–10). Jesus Christ, the Righteous One, is the advocate with the Father; he is "the atoning sacrifice for our sins, and not only for ours but also for the sins of the whole world" (2:1–2; cf. 4:10). It appears that what is behind John's teaching and admonition in these verses is precisely the same situation addressed in chapters 8 and 9 of his gospel—the Jewish denial of their sinfulness resulting in their rejection of Jesus as Messiah.[33]

The densest concentration of "sin" terminology in John's first letter is found in 3:4–9, which features as many as ten occurrences of *hamartanō* or *hamartia*, and in addition two instances of *anomia*, "lawlessness" (3:4). The various affirmations strung together in this unit reiterate teaching found in the Gospel:

- Jesus appeared to take away our sins (1 John 3:5; cf. John 1:29)
- In him is no sin (1 John 3:5; cf. John 8:46)
- The one who is sinful is of the devil, because the devil has been sinning from the beginning (1 John 3:8; cf. John 8:44)

In addition, however, John's main point in the letter, reiterated several times in this unit alone, is this: "No one who lives in him keeps on sinning" and, conversely, "No one who continues to sin has either seen him or known him" (1 John 3:6). In this regard, John asserts the decisive difference made by spiritual rebirth: "Those who are born of God *will not continue* to sin, because God's seed remains in them; they *cannot go on sinning*, because they have been born of God" (3:9, emphasis added; cf. 5:18). In this, John is seeking to reassure the recipients of his letter subsequent to the departure of the false teachers from the congregation (cf. 2:19).[34]

Tracing sin to its salvation-historical roots, Cain is cited as the epitome of one "who belonged to the evil one and murdered his brother" (1 John 3:11). In the typology of evil,[35] Cain, and ultimately Satan, are the spiritual ancestors of those who persist in sin and do not believe in the Son of God and the atoning sacrifice he has provided. In his fratricide, Cain exemplified the sin and hatred of others that stands in stark contrast with the love that is characteristic of the followers of Jesus (3:23; 4:7, 11, 12; 2 John 5). As Yarbrough notes, "Cain's behavior and underlying attitude were the utter antithesis of love."[36] Sin, then, is the root cause of lovelessness.

Finally, an *inclusio* related to sin is provided by the instances of *adikia* in 1 John 1:9 and 5:17, The former speaks of purification from all unrighteousness upon confession of sin; the latter is connected to the "sin leading to death," affirming that "all wrongdoing is sin." The reference to a "sin that leads to death" in 5:16–17 has no clear NT parallels.[37] Most likely is the interpretation that the "sin unto death" is

---

33. On the continuity of purpose between John's gospel and 1 John, see especially Streett, "They Went Out from Us."

34. The remaining references involving "sin" terminology in 1 John pertain to the "sin that leads to death" (5:16–18), which is briefly addressed in chap. 5 above.

35. See Yarbrough, *1–3 John*, 198, who calls John's reference to Cain "narratival or even typological."

36. Ibid. For discussions of references to Cain in extrabiblical literature, see ibid., 198–99; and Kruse, *Letters of John*, 235–42.

37. See the brief discussion in chap. 5, sec. 11.1.5 above.

"a deliberate, open-eyed rejection of known truth" akin to the "blasphemy against the Holy Spirit" committed by the Pharisees (Matt 12:28 pars.). Other possibilities include a specific ("mortal") sin or apostasy.[38]

27.1.3 Conclusion

John's teaching regarding sin is of perennial relevance. Unless a person acknowledges that he or she is a sinner, they will not be able to receive forgiveness and salvation through the only means available—the atoning sacrifice of the Lord Jesus Christ (John 1:29; 1 John 2:1–2; 4:10). The reality of universal human sinfulness undercuts any possibility of "merit theology" or works-righteousness (cf., e.g., Rom 10:3). Those who fail to come to terms with their own sinfulness remain under God's wrath (John 3:36) and bring judgment on themselves on account of their unbelief (3:18).

27.2 Divine Judgment

In his seminal two-volume *Theology of the New Testament*, Rudolf Bultmann elevated the notion of *krisis* to a level of utmost importance in understanding the theology of John's gospel.[39] According to him, Jesus' coming into this world threw the entire *kosmos* into *krisis*.[40] Jesus came to reveal God's glory, though "it turns out in the end that Jesus as the Revealer of God *reveals nothing but that he is the Revealer.*"[41] Commenting on John 3:18 in his equally famous John commentary, Bultmann writes, "Thus the judgment is not a specially contrived sequel to the coming and the departure of the Son. It is not a dramatic cosmic event which is yet to come and which we must still await. Rather the mission of the son, complete as it is in his descent and exaltation, *is* the judgment."[42]

It is now commonly recognized that Bultmann's interpretive grid, viewing John's gospel against the backdrop of second-century Gnosticism, skewed his apprehension of John's teaching. Clearly, Jesus' work is presented in John's gospel in terms of revelation (e.g., 1:18), but it is equally shown to encompass the work of redemption (e.g., 1:29).[43] In fact, the two aspects of Jesus' work merge when it is said that Jesus' redemptive cross-work was at the same time the revelation of God's love for the world (3:16). Likewise, saying that there is no future judgment, as Bultmann did, does not square with Johannine passages such as 5:28–29 (not to speak of the book of Revelation; see also 1 John 4:17).

Nevertheless, Bultmann grasped an important aspect of Johannine theology bound up with his teaching on divine judgment. As will be seen, within the framework of his realized (or at least inaugurated) eschatology John makes clear that, in

---

38. See also the discussion by Yarbrough, *1–3 John*, 510–13, who suggests that to "sin unto death" is "to have a heart unchanged by God's love in Christ and so to persist in convictions and acts and commitments like those John and his readers know to exist among ostensibly Christian people of their acquaintance, some of whom have now left those whom John addresses" (p. 311), and who proves various reasons why John prohibited prayer for such persons.

39. Bultmann, *Theology of the New Testament*, 2:33.
40. Ibid. See the title of chap. III: "The 'Krisis' of the World."
41. Ibid., 66 (emphasis original).
42. Bultmann, *Gospel of John*, 155 (emphasis original). See also Bultmann's comments on p. 157.
43. See on this chap. 14, sec. 32 below.

an important sense, God's judgment was already brought about by the light's coming into the world in the incarnation of the Son (1:14).[44] This coming of the light into the world, in turn, confronts people everywhere with the decision of whether to embrace the light or to go into hiding and persist in darkness. In this, John's teaching on judgment and faith serves as a theological reworking of Jesus' question to his followers: "But who do you say that I am?"

In the preceding unit, I have surveyed John's teaching on sin. The theme of divine judgment for sin is a natural corollary in John's gospel.[45] The noun *krisis* occurs eleven times (3:19; 5:22, 24, 27, 29, 30; 7:24; 8:16; 12:31; 16:8, 11); the related noun *krima* occurs once (9:39); and the verb *krinō* is found nineteen times (3:17, 18 [2x]; 5:22, 30; 7:24 [2x], 51; 8:15 [2x], 16, 26, 50; 12:47 [2x], 48 [2x]; 16:11; 18:31). This compares with eighteen instances of *krinō* or *krisis* in Matthew, one in Mark, and ten in Luke. The sole reference involving *krisis* word group in John's letters is 1 John 4:17 ("the day of judgment").

In keeping with the above-discussed notion that sin is ultimately bound up with rejection of Jesus, John correspondingly makes clear that it is this same rejection of Jesus that incurs divine judgment (John 3:17–19). According to John, God's purpose for sinful humanity is salvation, not condemnation (cf. 12:47), and those who prefer to continue in moral darkness rather than light ultimately pronounce judgment on themselves (3:19–21). In this sense, Jesus, the "light," is merely the catalyst for this judgment to take place (9:39; cf. 12:48). The basis of God's judgment is therefore whether people acknowledge their sinfulness and need of salvation and whether they believe in God's provision of that salvation in the atoning sacrifice rendered by the Lord Jesus Christ (3:13–16).

The most sustained treatment of divine judgment in John's gospel is found in 5:22–30, which features seven instances of "judgment" terminology.[46] There it is taught that God the Father has entrusted all judgment to Jesus, "the Son of Man" (5:22, 27).[47] Since the judgment of the world was considered by the Jews to be the exclusive prerogative of God (e.g., Gen 18:25; cf. Judg 11:27; though see Ps 2:2), this presents Jesus as sharing in a divine function (cf. John 12:48).[48] By believing in Jesus, people escape judgment already in the here and now (5:24), though the final judgment awaits the end of time (5:28–29). In this way realized and final eschatology are shown to be congruent.

In paradoxical fashion, the world's judgment of Jesus is in fact shown by John to be the judgment of the world and Satan, "the prince of this world" (John 12:31;

---

44. See esp. the evangelist's extended commentary in 3:16–21.

45. In addition, the judgment theme is also part of the cosmic trial motif in John's gospel, on which see chap. 11 above.

46. The affirmation in 5:22 stands in apparent tension with 3:17, which is resolved by the semantic range of *krinō*, which in 3:17 refers to "outright condemnation," while in 5:22 it talks about the judicial "principle of discrimination" (Carson, *Gospel according to John*, 254). Also, 3:17 has as its subject the purpose for the Son's coming into the world, whereas 5:22 addresses the issue of the distinctiveness of the Father's and Son's respective roles (Carson, ibid.).

47. Compare the references to the "Son of Man" (or "Chosen One") in the *Similitudes of Enoch* (*1 Enoch* 37–71; esp. 49:4; 61:9; 62:2–6; 63:11).

48. By contrast, in Second Temple literature the Messiah remains very much in the background as far as judgment is concerned, apart from carrying out God's judgment on his enemies, in keeping with Jewish nationalistic expectations (e.g., *Pss. Sol.* 17:21–27). Rabbinic writings likewise ascribe judging the world to God alone.

cf. 16:8, 11).[49] This makes clear that the ultimate agent promoting unbelief and rebellion against God the Creator and his Messiah, the Lord Jesus Christ, is Satan, the devil, who inspired Judas to betray his Master (13:2, 27). The final judgment of Satan is the subject of the fifth and final book in the Johannine corpus, the book of Revelation (Rev 20:7–10).

28 BELIEVING AND THE NEW BIRTH

28.1 Introduction

Apart from "Jesus" (241 times) and "Father" (136 times), there is no theologically significant word that occurs more frequently in John's gospel than the word "believe" (*pisteuō*). The ninety-eight instances of this term in John's gospel compare to eleven in Mark, fourteen in Matthew, and nine in Luke.[50] Thus it seems justified for Merrill Tenney to call John "the Gospel of belief." Interestingly, while John used the *verb* "to believe" almost one hundred times, the corresponding *noun* (*pistis*, "faith") is absent from his gospel (though see 1 John 5:4). It appears, therefore, that John's primary purpose was to engender in his readers the *act* of believing, of placing their trust in Jesus Christ.

The term "to believe" is prominent in John's purpose statement: "Jesus performed many other miraculous signs in the presence of his disciples, which are not recorded in this book. But *these are written that you may believe* that Jesus is the Christ, the Son of God, and *that by believing you may have life in his name*" (John 20:30–31, emphasis added). The central verse of John's introduction, too, includes a reference to believing: "Yet to all who did receive him, to those who *believed in his name*, he gave the right to become children of God" (1:12, emphasis added). John's summary indictment of the Jews at the end of the Book of Signs is that "even after Jesus had performed so many signs in their presence, *they still would not believe in him*" (12:37, emphasis added).

Thus, in a sense, John divides all of humanity into two classes of people: those who believe that Jesus is the Messiah, the Son of God, and those who do not. Those who believe have eternal life; those who do not will be condemned at the final judgment. Those who believe walk in the light; those who fail to believe walk in darkness. To adapt Shakespeare's words, John's message is this: "*To believe or not to believe — that's* the question." In what follows I will provide a brief survey of the references to believing in John's gospel.[51] As the survey of these passages will show, the struggle between believing and not believing provides the entire narrative with its inner dynamic, suspense, and drama, and many of the gospel's characters serve as examplars of different kinds of belief or unbelief.

---

49. See chap. 11 above.
50. To this should be added nine instances in 1 John (3:23; 4:1, 16; 5:1, 5, 10 [3x], and 13).

51. For a more detailed study see Croteau, "Analysis of the Concept of Believing."

A careful study of the instances of *pisteuō* reveals that the word "believe" (similar to the term "disciple," *mathētēs*) in John does not necessarily refer to "saving faith." Context must decide. Thus the Jews who had "believed" Jesus in 8:31 turn out in the ensuing interchange to be "children of the devil," just as "many of his [Jesus'] *disciples*" had earlier deserted Jesus (6:60–61, 66). Likewise, when many "believed in Jesus' name" on account of his signs in Jerusalem, Jesus did not "entrust himself" (a play on words) to them (2:23–25)—that is, he did not necessarily trust the genuineness of their "conversion." Thus there are secret believers in Jesus, such as Joseph of Arimathea (19:38), or sincere inquirers, such as Nicodemus (3:1–10; 7:50–52; 19:39–42; cf. 12:42–43). There is also "doubting Thomas" (11:16; 20:24–29). This makes clear that the term "believe" in John's gospel does not necessarily refer to saving faith; the term is more fluid. Occasionally, initial faith turns out to be spurious, while at other times it must be confirmed by a more definitive commitment.[52]

28.2 References to Believing and the New Birth in the Introduction to John's Gospel

28.2.1 Believing

John 1:12–13 is possibly the climactic statement of the introduction to John's gospel, and by way of *inclusio* epitomizes the purpose for which the gospel was written: for people to "believe" and have life "in his name" (cf. 20:31).[53] The present statement sharply contrasts those who received him and believed with those who did not, marking out believers as those who "went against the current, who broke with the general pattern by which the world thinks, lives, and acts."[54] John 1:12–13 also protects 1:5, 10, and 11 from being misunderstood.

The term *elabon* ("did receive"), a cognate of *parelabon* ("received") in John 1:12, is parallel to *pisteuō* ("believe"; cf. 5:43–44). "Receiving him" means to entrust oneself to Jesus, to acknowledge his claims, and to confess him before others.[55] John 1:12–13 strikes the balance between human responsibility ("to receive, believe") and divine sovereignty ("born of God").[56] In 1:7, "believing" has already been

---

52. The same is true in 1 John, which especially emphasizes that one's confession of faith is spurious if one does not keep the commandments and love the brothers. First John also continues the gospel's emphasis on believers' need to "abide" in Christ for final salvation. Relevant passages with regard to perseverance in 1 John are 2:10; 3:9; and 5:18; as well as the reference to the "sin that leads to death" in 5:16–17.

53. See Witherington, *John's Wisdom*, 56. For a helpful chart summarizing people's belief or lack thereof in the remainder of the gospel see Croteau, "Analysis of the Concept of Believing," 120 (on believing in John's gospel, see also J. Gaffney. "Believing and Knowing in the Fourth Gospel," *TS* 26 (1965): 215–42; Richard R. Melick, "A Study in the Concept of Belief: A Comparison of the Giospel of John and the Epistle to the Romans" (Th.D. dissertation; Fort Worth, TX: Southwestern Baptist Theological Seminary,

1976); and Craig R. Koester, "Hearing, Seeing, and Believing in the Gospel of John," *Bib* 70 (1989): 327–48. In the first half of the narrative, negative responses predominate; the few instances of believing in the second half are all positive. This seems to support the notion, defended in the present commentary, that Jesus' mission in John 1–12 is predominantly (though not exclusively) one of failure owing to people's lack of believing response, while John 13–21 are taken up with Jesus' focus on the nucleus of the new messianic community. Hence 1:12, as the pivot of the introduction to John's gospel, serves to encapsulate the entire scope of John's presentation of people's responses to the Messiah in terms of reception or rejection with the result of eternal life or judgment.

54. Ridderbos, *Gospel of John*, 45.

55. Carson, *Gospel according to John*, 125–26.

56. See the discussion above.

identified as the purpose of John's testimony to Jesus as "the light." Now believing is said to be "in his [Jesus'] name," which may place particular emphasis on the fact that in order to believe in Jesus, one must believe that he bears the divine name. For John, then, believing in Jesus entails accepting him "to the full extent of his self-revelation."[57]

Being a child of God is not a quality possessed by all, nor is it an exclusive prerogative for Israelites. Rather, it is an entitlement for those who believe in the Word made flesh in Jesus.[58] The expression translated "right" in 1:12 (*exousia*; cf. 5:27; 10:18; 17:2; and 19:10) refers to the authorization or legitimate claim of becoming God's children, a privilege that has now been made available to all who believe in Jesus as Messiah. This assumes that in one sense sinful people are not God's children—even though they are created by God—unless and until they believe in Jesus Christ.[59] The privilege of *being* God's children is extolled in 1 John 3:1–2; here the focus is on "becoming" God's children, indicating a change of status. The Word's ability to give this right is proof of his exclusive and unique relationship with God.

28.2.2 Born of God

The opposite of being born of God spiritually is natural procreation, mentioned by the evangelist in three different expressions. Spiritual birth is not the result of human initiative but of supernatural origin.[60] "Natural descent" in 1:13 renders the phrase "bloods," that is, a blood relationship, on the basis of the belief that natural procreation entails the intermingling of bloods (cf. Ezek 16:6; Wis 7:1–2). Descent from the patriarchs was vital in the Jews' understanding of their divine sonship (cf. esp. John 8:31–41). John's point here is that being a child of God is not a result of blood relations, as if a Jew, for instance, could simply presume upon his descent from Abraham or Moses. Spiritual birth must rather be sought and received from God on the basis of faith (specifically, faith in Jesus as Messiah).[61]

The phrase "of human decision" in 1:13 renders the literal "will of flesh," whereby "flesh" does not denote what is sinful (as so often in Paul's writings) but

---

57. Schnackenburg, *Gospel according to St. John*, 1.263.

58. Ridderbos, *Gospel of John*, 46. Calvin, *Gospel according to St. John 1–10*, 17, understands *exousia* in 1:12 as "honor"; Schlatter, *Evangelist Johannes*, 19, glosses the word as "authorization" (*Ermächtigung*).

59. In the OT, the Hebrews are called God's children (Deut 14:1), even God's son and firstborn (Exod 4:22). Yet OT believers did not call God "Father" or "Abba."

60. Schnackenburg, *Gospel according to St. John*, 1.263. Some identify "children of God," not "those who believe" as the antecedent of the relative clause beginning 1:13, in order not to make faith follow regeneration (Bultmann, *Gospel of John*, 59, nn. 4, 5). However, this is both syntactically awkward and implausible and theologically unnecessary. For "those who believe" immediately precedes the relative clause and is thus most naturally taken as the antecedent, and the relationship between faith and rebirth is not easily reduced to a set sequential formula. The statement in 1 John 5:1, "Everyone who believes that Jesus is the Messiah is born of God," allows one to deduce from a person's belief that person's regenerate state; regeneration (being "born of God") and saving faith thus go together and cannot be separated. Spiritual rebirth takes place at God's initiative; people are called to faith based on God's revelation in Christ. John nowhere elaborates on the precise temporal relationship of these two aspects. Here and elsewhere in his gospel (6:44–45; 10:26; 12:37–40), he jointly affirms divine sovereignty and human responsibility, and as interpreters we must do no less (see Carson, *Divine Sovereignty and Human Responsibility*).

61. See Borchert, *John 1–11*, 118, who says that spiritual birth is not the result of blood-line relations. Witherington (*John's Wisdom*, 56) paraphrases this as "ethnic origins," Carson (*Gospel according to John*, 126) as "natural descent."

merely relates to what is natural as opposed to what is supernatural. The reference to "a husband's will" implies the OT concept of male headship, in the present context perhaps with reference to the initiative usually taken by the husband in sexual intercourse resulting in procreation. Alternatively, the reference could more generally be to parental determination or will.[62] The expression "born of God" is reminiscent of OT passages in which God is said to have given birth to his people Israel (Deut 32:18).

28.2.3 Conclusion

Thus John 1:12–13, placed at the very heart of the introduction to John's gospel, put believing in Jesus and the new birth at the center of John's teaching with regard to an individual's responsibility and the implications from the preexistent Word's coming into this world. The rest of the gospel will flesh out the imperative nature of faith in Jesus as Messiah, which, as mentioned, requires an acknowledgment of one's own sinfulness and of the reality and righteousness of God's judgment on human sin. John does not endeavor to resolve the theological tension between divine election and predestination on one hand and the necessity for humans to believe on the other. Both are affirmed in this gospel and exist side by side.[63]

28.3 References to Believing and the New Birth in the Book of Signs and the Book of Exaltation

28.3.1 The Book of Signs

28.3.1.1 The Cana Cycle

28.3.1.1.1 Believing

Significantly, the evangelist notes that Jesus' first "sign" in this gospel, the turning of water into wine at the wedding in Cana, was met by Jesus' disciples with faith (2:11). This identifies the disciples as those who saw Jesus' glory (1:14) in his "signs" (2:11). At the same time, the disciples were able to understand certain of Jesus' sayings only subsequent to the resurrection (2:22). Intriguingly, John contrasts the faith of Jesus' disciples with that of the crowds in Jerusalem, who likewise witnessed demonstrations of Jesus' messianic nature (his "signs"; 2:23) and who even "believed in his name" (2:23), but whose faith was viewed by Jesus with suspicion. In fact, it is likely that Nicodemus serves as an example of this group, who witnessed Jesus' "signs" (3:2) and showed some surface evidence of believing but at closer scrutiny fell short of actual saving faith (see also 3:12).[64]

As is made clear in 3:15–16, such faith must affirm that Jesus was the lifted-up Son of Man, that is, the crucified sacrifical Lamb of God, who provided atonement for the sin of the world (3:14; see 1:29, 36). Only such christological, cross-centered

---

62. Borchert, *John 1–11*, 118.
63. See the discussion above.
64. See Köstenberger, *John*, 117–20.

faith is true faith in the Johannine—and biblical—sense (the converse is stated in 3:18; see also 3:36). It is important to note that virtually all these early references to "believing" belong to the evangelist, who guides the reader of his gospel in discerning the nature of true faith (1:7, 12; 2:11, 23–24; 3:16, 18, 36). In 4:41–42, it is made apparent that the inhabitants of a Samaritan village initially believed on account of the Samaritan woman's witness but that they subsequently came to believe through their firsthand encounter with Jesus himself. In 4:48, Jesus denounces belief based on "signs and wonders." By contrast, the royal official believes Jesus' word (4:50, 53) and receives his son back healed (the "second sign" in Cana).

28.3.1.1.2 Born from Above/Again

The reference to being "born again/from above" in 3:3, 5 harks back to the reference to being "born of God" in the introduction (1:13). The notion of a new beginning and a decisive inner transformation of a person's life is reminiscent of certain OT prophetic passages (e.g., Jer 31:33–34; Ezek 11:19–20; 36:25–27). This concept of a new spiritual birth is not dissimilar to that of a "new creation" (cf. 2 Cor 5:17; Gal 6:15).[65] The term *anōthen* (translated "again" in the TNIV in 3:3, 7) can mean either "from above," be it figuratively (3:31; 19:11; Jas 1:17; cf. 3:15, 17) or literally ("from top to bottom": Matt 27:51=Mark 15:38; John 19:23), or "from the beginning" (Luke 1:3; Acts 26:4: "for a long time"; Gal 4:9: "all over again": with *palin*, "again"). This potential ambiguity opens up the possibility of misunderstanding.[66] Nicodemus thought the phrase meant literally "again," yet as John indicates, he misunderstood Jesus' true message, which pointed to the rabbi's need to be born "from above," that is, born spiritually.[67]

"Born again/from above" in John 3:3 is further explained as "born of water and the spirit" in 3:5.[68] Rather than referring to water and spirit baptism,[69] two kinds

---

65. See the discussion of John's new creation theology in chap. 8 above.

66. Brown, *Gospel according to John I–XII*, 130; Ridderbos, *Gospel of John*, 127; Barrett, *Gospel according to St. John*, 208; Carson, *Gospel according to John*, 190; Morris, *Gospel according to John*, 190. The remark by Peter Cotterell, "The Nicodemus Conversation: A Fresh Approach," *ExpTim* 96 (1985): 240, that there was no double meaning in Aramaic is unduly dismissive, because it disregards the fact that John's gospel has come to us in Greek, where misunderstanding is not only possible, but almost certainly intended by the evangelist. Frank Thielman, "Style of the Fourth Gospel," 179, n. 1, points to the frequency of double meanings in the present pericope (see 3:3, 7, 8), "which give the reader pause and serve to 'emphasize' the point at hand."

67. Beasley-Murray, *John*, 45, n. b. Morris, *Gospel according to John*, 190, proposes that rather than being obtuse, Nicodemus may have been wistful, choosing not to understand because he was unwilling to accept the implications of Jesus' pronouncement.

68. Johannes P. Louw, "On Johannine Style," *Neot* 20 (1986):

9–10. Carson, *Gospel according to John*, 195, rightly contends that the NIV's "water and the Spirit" is misleading (retained in the TNIV); "water and spirit" is preferable (see 3:6–8). Also contra, the proposal by Talbert, *Reading John*, 99, who renders the phrase "of water which is Spirit."

69. Note the single preposition governing both nouns (Ridderbos, *Gospel of John*, 127). Some have suggested that "born of water" refers to water baptism, be it John the Baptist's or Christian baptism or both (Schnackenburg, *Gospel according to St. John*, 1:369; Barrett, *Gospel according to St. John*, 203, 208–9; Brown, *Gospel according to John I–XII*, 141–42; Ridderbos, *Gospel of John*, 127–28; Beasley-Murray, *John*, 49; J. Ramsey Michaels, *John* [NIBC; Peabody, MA: Hendrickson, 1989], 57). But it would hardly have been meaningful for Jesus to inform Nicodemus that he must get baptized to go to heaven. Nothing in the context indicates that this is the case, and it is unlikely that Jesus would have expected Nicodemus already to have known this. Moreover, the emphasis here is on the Spirit's activity, not on human ritual observance (Morris, *Gospel of John*, 193).

of birth,[70] or a variety of other possibilities,[71] the phrase probably denotes one, spiritual birth.[72] This is suggested by the fact that "born of water and the spirit" in 3:5 further develops "born again/from above" in 3:3, the use of one preposition (*ek*) to govern both phrases in 3:5, and antecedent OT (prophetic) theology. The closest OT parallel is Ezek 36:25–27, which presages God's cleansing of human hearts with water and their inner transformation by his Spirit (see also Isa 44:3–5; *Jub.* 1:23–25).[73]

In John 3:6, Jesus here seeks to move Nicodemus from a woodenly literal to a spiritual understanding of what it means to be "born again/from above." In response to Nicodemus's question (3:4), Jesus maintains that even if it were possible for a person to be literally born a second time, such a "second birth" would accomplish nothing: for it would still be only a *physical* birth. However, what is needed is a *spiritual* birth (cf. 1:12–13; see also Gal 4:29). "Born of flesh" refers to natural birth (cf. 1:13), "flesh" to "a person in his or her natural existence as begotten by a father and given birth to by a mother";[74] "spirit" represents "the principle of divine power and life operating in the human sphere."[75] Although the OT does not literally refer to God's Spirit "giving birth" to spirit (cf. 6:63), it does hold out the vision that God, who is spirit (4:24), will "put a new spirit" in his people (Ezek 36:26; cf. 37:5, 14).

Jesus here tells his rabbinic counterpart to "stop being surprised" (cf. John 3:7; the force of the phrase in the original). For Jesus' teaching on the necessity of a spiritual birth was not in fact a new doctrine. Rather, it reiterated a vision clearly laid out in OT prophetic literature. In the phrase "you must be born from above," "you" is in the plural, which shows that this requirement does not extend solely to Nicodemus but to the entire group he represents (cf. "someone" in 3:3, 5; "we" in 3:2, 11). This includes the Pharisees and the Sanhedrin—and thus the Jewish religious leadership—but ultimately the entire nation. Part of Nicodemus's dismay may in fact stem not from actual ignorance of the OT, but from the fact that it is he and his Pharisaic colleagues who are said to be in need of spiritual regeneration (see 3:17).

Jesus illustrates his saying with an analogy between the wind and the person born of spirit. "Wind"—a common image for the Spirit—and "spirit" translate the same Greek and Hebrew words (*pneuma*; Heb. *ruah*).[76] In the present instance, the

---

70. Contra, those who say "born of water" refers to physical birth and "born of the Spirit" to spiritual birth (e.g., Witherington, *John's Wisdom*, 97, referring to 1 John 5:6–8; and Laney, *John*, 78; but see Carson, *Gospel according to John*, 191.

71. For a listing of options and discussion see Carson, *Gospel according to John*, 191–95.

72. Ibid., 194.

73. See already Schlatter, *Evangelist Johannes*, 89. For helpful discussions see Carson, *Gospel according to John*, 191–96, esp. 194–95; and Robert V. McCabe, "The Meaning of 'Born of Water and the Spirit' in John 3:5," *Detroit Baptist Seminary Journal* 4 (1999): 85–107. See also Cotterell, "Nicodemus Conversation," 241; and W. L. Kynes, "New Birth," in *Dictionary of Jesus and the Gospels*, 574–76, esp. 575. The terminology may also be reminiscent of first-century proselyte baptism where the Gentile convert to Judaism was compared to a newborn child. Thus R. Yose ben Halafta (c. A.D. 130–160) said, "One who has become a proselyte is like a child newly born" (*b. Yebam.* 48b; cf. 22a; 62a; 97b; *b. Bek.* 47a).

74. Ridderbos, *Gospel of John*, 128; cf. Morris, *Gospel according to John*, 194; the Pauline connotation of sinfulness is absent here; contra, Calvin, *Gospel according to John*, 66.

75. Brown, *Gospel according to John I–XII*, 131.

76. Both OT and Jewish literature contain numerous references to the mystery of the wind's origin (cf. Eccl 8:8; 11:5; *1 En.* 41:3; 60:12; *2 Bar.* 48:3–4).

point of Jesus' analogy is that both wind and spiritual birth are mysterious in origin and movement—wind goes sovereignly where it pleases; yet while the wind's origin is invisible, its effects can be observed; it is the same with the Spirit.[77] Despite its inscrutability, spiritual birth is nonetheless real, as real as the mysterious movements of the wind.[78] Moreover, just as the wind blows "where it pleases," so the Spirit's operation is not subject to human control, eluding all efforts at manipulation.[79]

Similar to Ezekiel's vision of the valley of dry bones (Ezekiel 37), Jesus' pronouncement that Nicodemus ("you" in the singular) and his fellow Sanhedrin members ("you" in the plural) must be spiritually reborn speaks of the necessity of cleansing and renewal and inner transformation in the life of Judaism. This is similar in import as the turning of water into wine at the Cana wedding (note the reference to Jewish purification rites in 2:6) and the thrust of the temple clearing (2:13–22).

What is more, not only does Jesus' pronouncement have corporate implications for Israel as a whole, it is personal in orientation. Nicodemus, "Israel's teacher," must exercise repentance and put his trust in Jesus' death on the cross for his sins (see 3:13–14) to experience this new, spiritual birth and enter God's kingdom for eternal life. This was at the same time in keeping with OT prophetic expectation and came to decisive fulfillment in the life and ministry of the Lord Jesus Christ to the Jewish nation.

28.3.1.2 The Festival Cycle

Several references to "believing" in John 5 revolve around the Jews' need to believe that Jesus is the Messiah sent from God the Father (5:24, 38, 44, 46, 47). Their unbelief is directed not only at Jesus but also fails to give credence to Moses and the Scriptures. When Jesus, in 6:29, identifies believing in him as God's Sent One as the key requirement of God, the Jews, characteristically, request a "sign," which reflects their unbelief (6:30; cf. 2:18; 4:48). After several references to "believing" in Jesus' Bread of Life Discourse (6:35, 36, 40, 47), John notes that Jesus knew from the beginning who would—or would not—believe in him, including Judas the betrayer (cf. 2:23–25).

The departure of "many of his disciples" at this juncture of Jesus' ministry marks a major watershed in his ministry (John 6:60), a crisis that is further accentuated by similar unbelief among his own brothers (7:5). Again, it is the evangelist who helps his readers explore the inadequate depth of the belief of some (6:60) and the lack of faith among others, even those close to Jesus (7:5). Neither superficial faith nor outright unbelief is adequate.

John proceeds to note that some in the crowd believed (7:31), though by now the reader is rightly suspicious that this reflects more than temporary allegiance.

---

77. Ridderbos, *Gospel of John*, 129; Carson, *Gospel according to John*, 197.
78. Cf. Paul's statement in 1 Cor 15:50 that "flesh and blood cannot inherit the kingdom of God."
79. Moloney, *Gospel of John*, 93.

In 7:38–39, the readers are told that true believers in Jesus are promised the Spirit subsequent to the glorification of Jesus. In 7:48, it is made clear that the Jewish authorities did not believe in Jesus, and in 8:24, Jesus warns that anyone who does not believe in him will die in his sins.

This is followed by yet another Johannine vignette regarding a group who "believed" for a season but turned out to possess only fleeting faith. Thus "the Jews who had believed him" (8:31; cf. 8:30) are excoriated by Jesus for their unbelief (8:45–46) and called children of the devil. Later, the healed blind man is challenged by Jesus to believe, and he falls down in worship (9:36–38). Once again, in 10:25–26 Jesus denounces his opponents for their unbelief. As in 8:37, the Johannine Jesus probes the motivation for people's unbelief by noting that the reason why they do not believe is that they are not among Jesus' "sheep" (10:26). This makes clear that divine election properly precedes faith but that people are nonetheless held responsible for their lack of faith.[80]

At the end of the Festival Cycle, Jesus urges people to believe in him at least on account of his works (10:38), and, indeed, many are said to believe in Jesus at that time (10:42), though by this time the reader may be forgiven for being suspicious about the lasting nature of these people's faith (cf. 2:23–25; 8:30–31).

28.3.1.3 The Transition between the Book of Signs and the Book of Exaltation

In 11:15, at the outset of the Lazarus miracle, Jesus declares that the purpose of this "sign" is "so that you may believe" (cf. 11:42). In 11:25–27, Jesus challenges Martha to believe, and she utters a confession that bears a remarkable resemblance to the gospel's purpose statement (20:30–31). Yet doubtless the reader who has read past the Passion Narrative knows more fully what it means for Jesus to be the Messiah and Son of God than Martha can be expected to have known at this juncture of the narrative (note the renewed subsequent challenge in 11:40).

John 11:45 features yet another reference to "many" who believed in Jesus, in the present instance on account of his raising of Lazarus. By this time, Jesus' appeal is such that the Pharisees fear that soon "everyone will believe in him" (11:48), resulting in their own demise by the hands of the Romans. The Pharisees' worst fears seem to be realized when the evangelist notes (in 12:11) that on account of the raising of Lazarus "many of the Jews" put their faith in Jesus. The concluding appeal by Jesus is for people to "put your trust in the light" before darkness comes (12:36; a veiled reference to the crucifixion).

The Johannine account of Jesus' mission to the Jews ends on a profound note of unbelief (12:37–39), which closes the Book of Signs with the verdict that Jesus' "signs" were largely met with Jewish unbelief, in keeping with scriptural prophecy. Nevertheless, the evangelist notes that "many even among the leaders believed in

---

80. See the discussion of divine election in the previous unit. Note also that 1 John applies the same rhetoric to the antichrists as that used in John's gospel to Jesus' opponents in John 8.

him" (12:42), yet not openly for fear of being expelled from the synagogue. Transparently, this kind of "faith" is inadequate. In closing out the Book of Signs, Jesus makes clear that faith in him is ultimately faith in the one who sent Jesus, that is, God the Father (12:44; cf. 14:1).

28.3.2 The Book of Exaltation
28.3.2.1 The Farewell Discourse

The sole reference to believing in 13:19 pertains to Jesus' prediction of Judas's betraying him, which is said to serve once again the purpose of inspiring faith in Jesus' followers. The references to believing in chapter 14 all revolve around the disciples' need to understand Jesus' close connection with the Father (14:10–12; cf. 14:5). John 14:29 echoes 13:19, predicting Jesus' departure to God the Father.

Interestingly, references to "believing" are absent from chapter 15, which instead discusses the disciples' need to "remain" (*menō*) in Jesus. References to the disciples' faith in 16:27 and 30 are quickly blunted by Jesus' prediction that they will shortly be scattered (16:31). Jesus' final prayer includes references to the belief of his followers (17:8) and of those who would believe on account of their testimony (17:20), and even to the belief of the world (17:21).

28.3.2.2 The Passion Narrative

Remarkably, no reference to believing is found from 18:1 to 19:34, which narrates Jesus' arrest, trials, and crucifixion. In 19:35, the evangelist's testimony to the crucifixion is said to have as its purpose the faith of his readers. In 20:8, it is the same evangelist, as a part of the narrative, who is said to "believe" at the empty tomb (on the basis of "seeing"). Thomas's unbelief (20:25) sets up Jesus' concluding pronouncement of blessing on those who believe apart from seeing (20:29). The final reference to believing occurs in the context of the purpose statement, which states that Jesus' "signs" recorded in this gospel have as their purpose to lead its readers to "believe that Jesus is the Messiah, the Son of God" (20:30–31).

28.3.3 Conclusion

"To believe or not to believe, that is the question" for John and his readers. Remarkably, twice the fourth evangelist steps out of his third person narrator role and addresses his readers directly. In both cases, he appeals to them to believe:

- "The man who saw it has given testimony, and his testimony is true. He knows that he tells the truth, and he testifies so that *you also may believe.*" (19:35, emphasis added)
- "Jesus performed many other signs in the presence of his disciples, which are not recorded in this book. But these are written that *you may believe* that Jesus is the Messiah, the Son of God, and that *by believing you may have life* in his name." (20:30–31, emphasis added)

The fourth evangelist claims to have been at Jesus' side at the most critical junctures of his earthly ministry: at the institution of the Lord's Supper in the Upper Room (13:23) and at the foot of the cross (19:35). As he writes in his first letter:

> That which was from the beginning, which we have heard, which we have seen with our eyes, which we have looked at and our hands have touched—this we proclaim concerning the Word of life. The life appeared; we have seen it and testify to it, and we proclaim to you the eternal life, which was with the Father and has appeared to us. We proclaim to you what we have seen and heard...." (1 John 1:1–3)

As an eyewitness of Jesus' ministry and of his sufferings and glorious resurrection, John appeals to his readers to believe—not just in anything, but specifically that Jesus is the Messiah, the Son of God (John 20:31). Eternal life is found only by those who believe *in his name* (20:31). Have you believed? Will you believe that Jesus is the Messiah, the Son of God?

28.4 References to Believing and the New Birth in 1 John

First John features nine instances of the verb *pisteuō* ("to believe"; 1 John 3:23; 4:1, 16; 5:1, 5, 10 [3x], 13) and one occurrence of the noun *pistis* ("faith"; 5:4). Perhaps surprisingly, the first instance of *pisteuō* in 1 John is not found until 3:23 in the following characteristic summary of John's message: "And this is his command: to believe in the name of his Son, Jesus Christ, and to love one another as he commanded us." It is notable how here believing and loving are intertwined. As in James's letter, this is to say that confession and conduct must go hand in hand.

The themes of believing and of the new birth are juxtaposed in 1 John 5:1, where John maintains that "everyone who believes that Jesus is the Messiah is born of God." Proper confession of Jesus is thus cited as evidence for a person's regenerate condition. In 5:5, it is said that the one who believes that Jesus is the Son of God overcomes the world. Proper faith is thus shown as the path to victory over the domain of darkness controlled by the devil (cf. 5:19). Above all, people are enjoined to believe in God's testimony regarding his Son (5:10). Those who believe in Jesus as the Son of God have eternal life (5:13). In this the message of 1 John is entirely consistent with that of John's gospel (see John 3:16; 20:30–31).

First John also has six references to believers being "born of God" (cf. 2:29; 3:9; 4:7; 5:1, 4, 18). Because Jesus is righteous, we can know that "everyone who does what is right has been born of him" (2:29). Also, those who are born of God will not continue to sin because of the indwelling Holy Spirit (3:9; 5:18). What is more, "Everyone who loves has been born of God and knows God" (4:7); "everyone who believes that Jesus is the Messiah is born of God" (5:1); and "everyone born of God overcomes the world" (5:4). Thus, in building on the teaching of John's gospel (see esp. John 1:12–13; 3:3–8), John here provides a series of categorical statements citing various indicators of the new birth in people's lives. This can be demonstrated by the following survey chart:

Categorical Statement	Passage in 1 John
"Everyone who does what is right has been born of him"	2:29
"Those who are born of God will not continue to sin"	3:9; cf. 5:18
"Everyone who loves has been born of God and knows God"	4:7
"Everyone who believes that Jesus is the Messiah is born of God"	5:1
"Everyone born of God overcomes the world"	5:4
"Anyone born of God does not continue to sin"	5:18; cf. 3:9

Fig. 28.1: Evidence for a Person's Having Been "Born of God" in 1 John

28.5 Christian Assurance in John's Gospel and Letters

Not only does John teach that an individual's salvation is ultimately the result of divine election and predestination, and not only does he teach the necessity of faith and a new, spiritual birth, he also makes clear that the objects of divine election, and the subjects of faith and recipients of the new birth, are eternally secure.[81] This is already apparent from the reference to the "right to become children of God—children born not of natural descent ... but born of God" in the introduction to the gospel (John 1:12). If anyone has become God's child and been born of God, it is inconceivable that these divine acts can or will be undone. Nor is it likely that God's enablement of people to come to Jesus (6:65) as well as Jesus' own drawing of people to himself (12:32) and the Father's "giving" people to Jesus (17:2, 6) are rendered ineffectual.

What is more, Jesus' power is actively at work on behalf of those who have come to him. He is united with them in personal relationship through his Word, in which they are called to abide (8:31; 15:7; 17:17), and through the indwelling Holy Spirit (14:17). Because Jesus has given his followers eternal life, they shall never perish, and no one will snatch them out of his hand (10:28). "My Father, who has given them to me, is greater than all; no one can snatch them out of my Father's hand. I and the Father are one" (10:29). The reason why no one can snatch believers in Jesus out of his or the Father's hand is because it is the Father who has given believers to Jesus. The same power that drew people to Jesus and effected their spiritual birth is also the power that keeps people safely in Jesus' and the Father's hand.

Christian assurance is an even more prominent theme in John's first letter.[82] In fact, the grounds for assurance given in John's letters are so prominent that some have seen these letters as supplying "tests of life."[83] However, construing 1 John in

---

81. For a study of Christian assurance in 1 John, see Christopher D. Bass, *That You May Know: Assurance of Salvation in 1 John* (NAC Studies in Bible & Theology; Nashville: Broadman & Holman, 2008).

82. For an excellent treatment of this topic in 1 John and the rest of the NT, see D. A. Carson, "Reflections on Christian Assurance."

83. See Robert Law, *The Tests of Life: A Study of the First Epistle of St. John* (3rd ed.; Edinburgh: T&T Clark, 1914; repr. Grand Rapids: Baker, 1979).

terms of "tests" fails to understand the primary nature of the letter as reassuring believers that they were genuinely saved after the congregation had recently been shaken by the defection of individuals who, it turned out, had never truly been part of the community (1 John 2:19). Thus it is preferable to read 1 John in terms of reassurance rather than "tests." Thus John writes to his audience, "But you have an anointing from the Holy One, and all of you know the truth. I do not write to you because you do not know the truth, but because you do know it, and because no lie comes from the truth" (2:20–21). In fact, John's very purpose for writing is bound up with providing assurance for his readers: "I write these things to you who believe in the name of the Son of God so that you may know that you have eternal life" (5:13).

The point of 1 John, then, is to instill confidence in true believers that their salvation is assured. At the same time, John in his first letter, similar to Jesus in John's gospel, couples these words of assurance with exhortations to persevere (e.g., 1 John 2:5–6). True believers must keep God's commandments, above all the command to love one another, not merely in word but also in deed (3:11–24; 4:7–21). John does not deny that believers will still sin; yet when they do, they simply need to confess their sin, knowing that they have an Advocate with God the Father, Jesus Christ (1:8–2:2).

Everyone who is truly born of God is assured that "the One who was born of God keeps them safe, and the evil one cannot harm them" (1 John 5:18). Thus 1 John, in further development of Jesus' words of reassurance and exhortation in the gospel, serves as a manifesto of Christian assurance, which paints a realistic, yet supremely hopeful picture of Christian discipleship and perseverance, which is ultimately undergirded, not by human effort, but by the power of God.

29 THE NEW MESSIANIC COMMUNITY

29.1 Johannine Ecclesiology

It is frequently observed that the term *ekklēsia* is not used in the fourth gospel.[84] It should be noted, however, that the expression is likewise absent in Mark and Luke while occurring only twice in Matthew (Matt 16:19; 18:17). Moreover, it appears that the absence of *ekklēsia* in John's gospel can be explained by the fact that the gospel purports to set forth primarily the life and passion of Jesus rather than dealing directly with issues in the later church.

John's gospel contains a number of corporate metaphors for Jesus' messianic community, such as "the flock" (John 10) or "the vine" (John 15). These metaphors transfer descriptions of OT Israel to the group of Jesus' followers, thus marking an important salvation-historical development. Attention needs also be given to the

---

84. Some of the material in this section is adapted from my *Missions of Jesus and the Disciples*, chap. 4 (used by permission).

Johannine characterization of the disciples as a group and of individual disciples such as Peter or "the disciple whom Jesus loved."

Recent scholarship has increasingly viewed the fourth gospel's disciples as figures representing the "Johannine school,"[85] "circle,"[86] or "community."[87] Within such a framework, the gospel's disciples become vehicles of the history of the "Johannine community."[88] In these treatments, the focus tends to shift from the historical level in the life of Jesus to the time of writing.[89] John's representation of the disciples is consequently viewed as an expression of the "Johannine community's" self-understanding in the light of its faith in Jesus.[90] This "Johannine community," it is maintained, should be understood as a "sect," defining itself in contrast to the surrounding world, a mindset that some trace to a possible dependence on Gnostic thought.[91]

While often insightful, these studies nevertheless appear to make too little of the care taken by the evangelist to preserve the distinction between the understanding of the disciples during the time before and after Jesus' resurrection. Also, many of these studies appear to focus on John's literary art to the extent that historical matters are neglected.[92] However, the possibility that John retains historical points of reference while engaging in more sophisticated literary strategies of characterization should not be ruled out.

29.2 The Characterization of Jesus' Followers in John's Gospel

There is a significant number of studies on the Johannine characterization of the disciples.[93] The difficult hermeneutical issue of the relationship between the disciples and later generations of believers in John's gospel, however, is rarely discussed. An investigation of this issue properly begins with a survey of the instances where the term *mathētēs* is used to designate the followers of Jesus during his earthly ministry (i.e., "the Twelve" as well as a broader, less clearly defined circle of followers).

---

85. R. Alan Culpepper, *The Johannine School* (SBLDS 26; Missoula, MT: Scholars Press, 1975).

86. Cullmann, *Johannine Circle*.

87. Brown, *Community of the Beloved Disciple*. See the discussion in chap. 1, sec. 2.1 above.

88. Martyn, *History and Theology*; idem, "Glimpses," 149–75; Rensberger, *Overcoming the World*; Onuki, *Gemeinde und Welt*; Brown, *Community of the Beloved Disciple*; idem, "Other Sheep," 5–22.

89. This is the sense in which the term "history" is used in J. Louis Martyn's *History and Theology in the Fourth Gospel*. Martyn advocates a reading of John's gospel on two levels, namely, the purported life-setting in Jesus' day and the setting contemporary to the writing of the gospel.

90. Thus Günther Baumbach, "Gemeinde und Welt im Johannesevangelium," *Kairos* 14 (1972): 128, for example, sees the figure of "the disciple whom Jesus loved" in John's gospel as an expression of the Johannine community's self-understanding.

91. In addition to the works of Martyn, Meeks, Brown, Onuki, and Rensberger, see also Baumbach, "Gemeinde und Welt im Johannesevangelium"; and Andreas Lindemann, "Gemeinde und Welt im Johannesevangelium," in *Kirche: Festschrift für Günther Bornkamm zum 75. Geburtstag* (ed. Dieter Lührmann and Georg Strecker; Tübingen: Mohr-Siebeck, 1980), 133–61.

92. See Collins, "Representative Figures"; de Jonge, "Messianic Expectations"; Baumbach, "Gemeinde und Welt," 128.

93. From the growing body of literature on the church and the disciples in John's gospel, see especially Rudolf Schnackenburg, "Jünger, Gemeinde, Kirche im Johannesevangelium," in *Das Johannesevangelium (Kap. 13–21)* (HTKNT III; 2nd ed.; Freiburg–Basel–Wien: Herder, 1976), 231–45; and the more recent treatment by Culpepper, *Anatomy*, 99–148, esp. 115–23, 132–44. See also Baumbach, "Gemeinde und Welt"; Henri van den Bussche, "Die Kirche im vierten Evangelium," in *Vom Christus zur Kirche: Charisma und Amt im Urchristentum* (Wien: Herder, 1966), 79–107; Corell, *Consummatum Est*; Nils Alstrup Dahl, "The Johannine Church and History," in *Current Issues in New Testament Interpretation: Festschrift für Otto A. Piper* (ed. William Klassen and

As in the other gospels, the disciples in John are part of a story line that is inextricably tied to the events surrounding Jesus' earthly ministry.[94] Nevertheless, as will be seen, especially as the gospel progresses, there is an increasing widening of the designation "disciples" that transcends the original followers of Jesus to include later, post-resurrection believers. There are also instances where given disciples, or the disciples as a group, function as representative figures and figures of identification for John's readers.

29.2.1 The Term Mathētēs Designating the First Followers of Jesus in John's Gospel

The term *mathētēs* ("disciple") occurs seventy-eight times in John's gospel.[95] Most of these references are to the followers of Jesus, usually with the pronoun *autou* ("his").[96] As do the other gospels, John features the disciples as significant characters. After their call (John 1:37–43), they accompany Jesus (2:2, 11, 17), begin to participate in Jesus' work (4:2, 8, 27, 31, 33, 38), and gradually step into the foreground (cf. 6:3, 8, 12, 16, 22, 24, 60–71). The loyalty of Jesus' inner circle is contrasted with the unbelief of Jesus' own brothers (7:2–5).

Discipleship is also discussed in a number of discourses (John 8:12, 31; 9:27–29; 10). The disciples play an important role on the way to Jerusalem (9:2; 11:7–16, 54; 12:16, 21–22) and during their time of preparation and instruction in Jesus' Farewell Discourse (chaps. 13–17). Judas, one of Jesus' disciples, betrays him (6:70–71; 12:4–8; 13:21–30; 17:12). Finally, the risen Jesus appears to his disciples and commissions them (chaps. 20–21; esp. 20:19–23).

The way John distinguishes between Jesus' close followers and those who follow him from a distance can be illumined by his use of the term *ochlos* ("crowd"). One writer identifies the following characteristics of this term in John, all of which entail a somewhat distant relationship to Jesus: (1) the crowd follows Jesus only externally (6:2, 5, 22, 24); (2) it is only impressed by Jesus' miracles (7:31; 12:9, 12, 17–18);

Graydon F. Snyder; New York: Harper & Brothers, 1962), 124–42 and 284–88; Ernst Gaugler, "Die Bedeutung der Kirche in den johanneischen Schriften," *IKZ* 14 (1924): 97–117, 181–219; 15 (1925): 27–42; Herbert Giesbrecht, "The Evangelist John's Conception of the Church as Delineated in His Gospel," *EvQ* 58 (1986): 101–19; Klaus Haacker, "Jesus und die Kirche nach Johannes," *TZ* 29 (1973): 179–201; Severino Pancaro, "'People of God' in St John's Gospel?" *NTS* 16 (1970): 114–29; idem, "The Relationship of the Church to Israel in the Gospel of John," *NTS* 21 (1975): 396–405; John W. Pryor, "Covenant and Community in John's Gospel," *RTR* 47 (1988): 44–51; idem, *John: Evangelist of the Covenant People*, 157–80; Rudolf Schnackenburg, "Is There a Johannine Ecclesiology?" in *A Companion to John: Readings in Johannine Theology* (ed. Michael J. Taylor; New York: Alba, 1977), 247–56; Udo Schnelle, "Johanneische Ekklesiologie," *NTS* 37 (1991): 37–50; Eduard Schweizer, "Der Kirchenbegriff im Evangelium und den Briefen des Johannes," in *SE* (TU 73; ed. Kurt Aland et al.; Berlin: Akademie, 1959), 363–81; Jeffrey S. Siker-Gieseler, "Disciples and Discipleship in the Fourth Gospel: A Canonical Approach," *SBT* 10 (1980): 199–227; Adela Yarbro Collins, "Crisis and Community in John's Gospel," *CurTM* 7 (1980): 196–204.

94. See Karl Heinrich Rengstorf, "μανθάνω, κτλ.," *TDNT*, 4:390–461.

95. The term *mathētai* (pl.) is applied to followers of Jesus in the following passages: 2:2, 11, 17, 22; 3:22; 4:1, 2, 8, 27, 31, 33; 6:3, 8, 12, 16, 22 (2x), 24, 60, 61, 66; 7:3; 8:31; 9:2, 27, 28; 11:7, 8, 12, 54; 12:4, 16; 13:5, 22, 23, 35; 15:8; 16:17, 29; 18:1 (2x), 2, 17, 19, 25; 20:8, 10, 18, 19, 20, 25, 26, 30; 21:1, 2, 4, 8, 12, 14. The term *mathētēs* (sg.) occurs in 18:15 (2x), 16; 19:26, 27 (2x), 38; 20:2, 3, 4, 8; 21:7, 20, 23, 24. All the references in the singular refer to "the disciple whom Jesus loved," who is simply called "another disciple" when appearing with Peter.

96. See the designation of Jesus as teacher (*rabbi*, *didaskalos*) and Lord (*kyrios*) in John's gospel. Jesus is called *rabbi* by Andrew, Nicodemus, the disciples, and Mary Magdalene (John 1:38, 49; 3:2; 4:31; 6:25; 9:2; 11:8; 20:16). In Matthew, only Judas calls Jesus *rabbi* (Matt 26:25, 49), in Mark also Peter (Mark 9:5; 11:21). Luke never uses *rabbi*; he always employs the Greek equivalent *didaskalos*, a

(3) otherwise its opinion is divided (7:12, 40–43); (4) the crowd is without understanding (cf. 11:42; 12:29, 43).[97]

The predominant characteristic of the crowds in John's gospel is unbelief, which is all the more striking since they witness a number of messianic signs performed by Jesus. Crowds are at hand when Jesus heals a man on the Sabbath (5:13). Multitudes are fed by Jesus (6:2, 5, 22, 24, 26). Crowds are also present at various feasts in Jerusalem (7:12, 20, 31, 32, 40, 43, 49; 12:12, 17, 18, 29, 34) and at the raising of Lazarus (11:42; 12:9). While Jesus wanted people to believe (7:31; 11:42), John notes that, despite Jesus' many signs, the crowds would still not place their faith in him (12:36b–41).

At times, the crowds in John's gospel express messianic expectations. They wonder whether the Messiah will perform more signs than Jesus (7:31) and marvel at Jesus' statement that the Son of Man must be "lifted up" (12:34–35).[98] In those instances, the crowds' reluctance to believe becomes prominent. Generally, the crowds seem to function in Johannine characterization as an example of "following Jesus" that falls short of actual discipleship, or, as in the case of 8:31, of discipleship that proves spurious.

Overall, John's characterization of the disciples is consistent with the way these figures are cast in the Synoptics. As Anselm Schulz comments:

> The use of the term *mathētēs* in the Fourth Gospel provides an impressive corroboration of this document's historical and theological accuracy. To begin with, the expression designates in John in the vast majority of cases the disciple of Rabbi Jesus, in agreement with the Synoptic tradition (cf. 2:2, 11, 12, 17, 22; 3:22; 4:2, 8, 27, 31, 33; 6:3, 8, 16; etc.). The disciple's most salient characteristic is captured by the term *akolouthein*, i.e. the close relationship with his Messianic teacher.... The disciples live together with their teacher (cf. 2:2, 11; 6:3, 60, 66; 11:7, 54; 13:1; 18:2). They accompany him on his travels (cf. 2:12; 3:22; 11:7; 12:16; 18:1). They carry out various services for their teacher (cf. 4:8, 27, 31, 33; 6:10, 12). Finally, they witness his teachings and address their questions to him (cf. 6:60; 9:2).[99]

The disciples also share in their teacher's sufferings (13:16; 15:20).

The extent of the group referred to by the term *mathētēs* in John's gospel is ambiguous. The designation "disciples" may be taken to refer in John, as in Luke, to Jesus' inner circle, that is, the Twelve,[100] or it may extend to a larger group of

---

term also used by John in 1:38; 3:2, 10; 11:28; 13:13, 14; 20:16. See Köstenberger, "Jesus as Rabbi."

97. See Schnackenburg, *Johannesevangelium*, 3:236, n. 5. The *mathētai* of 6:60–61, 66 are probably those who had identified themselves more closely with Jesus. The same kinds of people are probably also referred to in 7:3.

98. Other terms referring to (otherwise unidentified) characters in the Fourth Gospel include *polloi* (15 times; 8 times with *pisteuō*: 2:23; 4:39; 7:31; 8:30; 10:42; 11:45; 12:11, 42); *tines* (used absolutely six times; often describing elements hostile to Jesus: 6:64; 7:25, 44; 9:16; 11:37, 46); *alloi* (12 times: 7:12, 41; 9:9 [2x], 16; 10:21; 12:29); and *houtoi* (4 times). All of these terms refer to persons of varying degrees of interest in or hostility toward Jesus while falling short of being actual *mathētai*.

99. See Schulz, *Nachfolgen*, 137, 143. See also Hans-Dieter Betz, *Nachfolge und Nachahmung Jesu Christi im Neuen Testament* (BHT 37; Tübingen: Mohr-Siebeck, 1967), esp. 36–40.

100. John 6:22, 24; 9:2; 11:7, 8, 12, 16, 54; 12:4, 16; 13:5, 22, 23; 16:17, 29; 18:1, 2; 20:18, 19, 25, 26.

Jesus' followers.[101] At times it is difficult to know which exact group is referred to.[102] While thus the lines between a narrow and a broader circle of Jesus' followers are often fluid, the distinction that is more significant is that between the first disciples, wide or narrow, and later believers. In this regard, the question arises whether or not what is predicated about the disciples in John's gospel necessarily extends to post-resurrection disciples. This issue will be the subject of discussion below.

29.2.2 The Twelve

There are only two pericopae in the entire gospel where reference to "the Twelve" is made.[103] The first, 6:67–71, is set in a context where many of Jesus' disciples desert him owing to his "hard teaching" (6:60). Peter, however, speaking for "the Twelve," pledges loyalty to Jesus and acknowledges him as "the Holy One of God" (6:69). The designation "the Twelve" may be used at this point in the narrative to point to the symbolism inherent in the number twelve, relating the twelve tribes of OT Israel to "the Twelve" as the representatives of Jesus' new messianic community. In the second occurrence of the term, Thomas is almost incidentally identified as "one of the Twelve" (20:24), similarly to Judas in 6:71.

The fact that the expression "the Twelve" is used in only one significant pericope in the entire gospel, apart from the incidental reference in 20:24, suggests that the Twelve are not viewed by John as the only ones who are sent or participate in Jesus' mission. The gospel does, however, emphasizes that, at a critical juncture, the Twelve followed Jesus while "disciples" with inadequate faith fell away (cf. Matt 16:13–16; Mark 8:27–30; Luke 9:18–20). This becomes especially significant in light of the references to discipleship in later chapters of John's gospel, where many of "the Jews" fail to arrive at full faith in Jesus (John 8:31–59; 9:1–41; 10:1–39; 12:39–50).

The inclusion of these passages in John's gospel indicates that the evangelist recognized the historical configuration of twelve disciples who were especially chosen by Jesus (cf. 6:70). Nevertheless, in light of the scarcity of the expression in this gospel, care should be taken not to place an undue emphasis on the Johannine characterization of the Twelve. Rather, it appears that John's gospel, being a gospel and having been written subsequent to the other canonical gospels, assumed this important part of tradition and referred to it incidentally without pursuing any elaborate literary strategies of characterization.

But this has not prevented some scholars from trying. Wolfgang Bauder, for example, finds a theological distinction between "the disciples" and "the Twelve" in John's gospel:

> *Hoi mathētai* are not simply the equivalent of *hoi dōdeka*, the Twelve.... The circle of the Twelve was both a symbolic representation of the twelve tribes of

---

101. John 4:1; 6:60, 61, 66; 7:3; 9:27, 28; 18:17, 19, 25; 19:38.
102. John 18:15, 17, 25; 19:26; 20:2, 3, 4, 30. See Schulz, *Nachfolgen*, 137–38; Schnackenburg, *Johannesevangelium*, 3:235–36; Quast, *Peter and the Beloved Disciple*, 23.

103. Note that under the present heading only corporate references to "the Twelve" in the gospel are treated. A discussion of individual named members of the Twelve is found under a separate heading below.

Israel, and thus of the whole people of God, and also a section of the larger circle of disciples which Jesus summoned to discipleship from a still wider group of adherents.... The disciples would have been a circle of immediate followers who were commissioned to particular service.[104]

Raymond Collins holds that the Twelve of the fourth gospel actually "represent a group among Jewish Christians."[105] He interprets John's portrayal of "the Twelve" as negative, especially in comparison with the Synoptics: "Simon Peter's confession does not earn the response of Jesus' self-revelation. Rather Jesus responds by speaking about his betrayal. The response indicates that the faith of those for whom Peter serves as spokesperson is not all that it ought to be. From the standpoint of the Fourth Gospel, the corporate faith of the twelve is somehow inadequate."[106] However, as noted, the Twelve do pledge allegiance to Jesus at a critical juncture in the Johannine narrative (see John 6:69).[107]

It may be concluded that John portrays the Twelve rather positively. John appears to view them as the core group of Jesus' messianic community, an entity that is also discussed in terms of the corporate metaphors of a "flock" or a "vine" later in the gospel.[108] Indeed, the group of the Twelve extends beyond the historical followers of Jesus, fulfilling an important representative function in the gospel. In this, John does not differ significantly from the other gospels. Instead of reflecting sophisticated literary strategies on John's part, the references to the Twelve in John's gospel should probably be viewed as hints to the tradition common to all four Gospels, which John assumes and which at times surfaces almost incidentally.

29.2.3 The Widening of the Term Mathētēs in John's Gospel

A characteristic and significant feature of John's portrayal of Jesus' followers is his widening of the term *mathētēs* during the course of his gospel. This movement, from the concept of a mere physical following of Jesus to an adherence to Jesus with a more explicitly spiritual connotation, facilitates the transition from the disciples of the historical Jesus to later believers. Thus one can discern a development in John's gospel from a physical remaining with Jesus (1:37–43) to a spiritual remaining in Jesus' word (8:31) and a remaining "in Jesus" beyond the time of his earthly ministry (15:4–7). Gradually, the designation "disciple" is released from a following of the historical Jesus to a spiritual "following" that is not constrained by boundaries of time and space (e.g., 8:31; 13:35; 15:8; 17).[109]

---

104. See Bauder, "Disciple," *NIDNTT*, 1:489.
105. See Collins, *These Things Have Been Written*, 81.
106. Ibid., 83.
107. Note also that one may infer from the Synoptics that it was the Twelve who were the primary audience of the farewell discourses (cf. Mark 14:17). Although this is not explicitly mentioned in John's gospel, it may be suggested by the parallel between the sayings "I know those I have chosen," plus a reference to Judas the betrayer (13:18), and "Have I not chosen you, the Twelve? Yet one of you is a devil!" (6:70). However, even if this is so, the Twelve would still function as representatives of later followers of Jesus, so that the teachings of the discourse would extend to subsequent generations of believers as well.
108. See the discussion of corporate metaphors below.
109. See Schulz, *Nachfolgen*, 139.

Indeed, the activity of the disciples will transcend that of Jesus' earthly ministry, since it is no longer limited to the spatial-temporal form of the incarnate Word but is transformed into the work of the exalted Lord through his disciples and thus lifted out of its historical boundaries (cf. 14:12b).[110] According to John, the believing response of the first disciples to Jesus functions as a model for the discipleship of later generations of believers. In the case of subsequent followers of Jesus, their lives of discipleship are no longer rooted in personal eyewitness experience or a call of Jesus. In fact, the faith of such believers is not based on any direct personal experience of Jesus but on the obedient reception of another's testimony to Jesus.[111] "Following Jesus," no longer limited to people who leave their profession for the sake of attaching themselves to their Lord, becomes in Johannine theology the spiritual exodus from a world alienated from God that is motivated by faith in the one sent from God, who bestows on his followers the salvific blessings of eternal life.[112]

This widening of the concept of discipleship in John's gospel, however, does not entail a complete obliteration of the function and figures of Jesus' first disciples. As Schnackenburg maintains,

> Disciples are initially the close followers of Jesus, subsequently also his committed adherents, finally all of those who believe in him. This "widening" is grounded in theological reflection and deliberate formulation.... While the fourth evangelist is certainly aware of the historical followers of Jesus, later believers are incorporated into discipleship. This is a development of ecclesial significance.[113]

Inherent in the gradual widening of John's concept of discipleship is a certain degree of ambiguity. If the exact delineation of the group of Jesus' followers occasionally appears unclear and imprecise, the reason is most likely that the concept of "disciple" is already opening up, widening, and preparing for a new point of reference.[114] This becomes apparent in passages where discipleship is spoken of in a way that does not limit it to Jesus' historical audience, as is the case, for example, in 8:31. Originally and in context, this statement is addressed to Jews who turned out to be spurious believers. Since the statement is phrased in general terms, however, it is relevant for every potential follower of Jesus (see also 8:12, 51). Thus the concept of discipleship is transferred to any person who would believe in Jesus.

It may be asked whether the general Johannine practice of widening the term *mathētēs necessarily* extends to postresurrection disciples.[115] In John 15:26–27, the disciples' witnessing activity in conjunction with the Spirit is predicated on their

---

110. See ibid., 141.
111. Ibid., 142.
112. Ibid., 175.
113. See Schnackenburg, *Johannesevangelium*, 3:237 (my translation).
114. Ibid., 3:236.
115. See Siker-Gieseler, "Disciples and Discipleship." This author contends that the gospel's *disciples* are largely negative models while persons embodying *discipleship*, such as the Samaritan woman or the man born blind, are positive reflections of what it will mean to follow Jesus after his departure. However, this distinction can hardly be sustained. Certainly the concept of *discipleship* in John's gospel is also related to the gospel's *disciples*. After all, only the characters designated "disciples" are traced in the fourth gospel from their "coming" to Jesus to their "following" Jesus to their being "sent" by Jesus. It would be better to distinguish between pre- and postglorification disciples.

having been with Jesus "from the beginning," a possible allusion to the Twelve. In the context of John's gospel, this points to those disciples who had been called by Jesus at the beginning of his public ministry (1:37–43) and had persevered in following him (6:60–71). But does this mean that John's gospel presents the task of witnessing as limited to the Twelve or to those who followed Jesus during his earthly ministry? At first glance, this seems to be the case, since witnessing in this gospel usually relates to the earthly Jesus (1:7, 8, 15, 32, 34; 3:11, 26, 28, 32; 15:26–27; 19:35; 21:24) and since the term "witness" (*martyreō*) is frequently in the Johannine writings tied to "seeing" (cf. 3:11, 32; 19:35; 1 John 1:1–3; 4:14).

However, as argued, the Twelve, as well as the *mathētai* in John's gospel in general, apart from retaining their historical point of reference, also function as representatives of Jesus' messianic community. Thus the responsibility of witnessing, while given primarily to Jesus' first disciples, derivatively also extends to later generations of believers.[116] Nevertheless, it is only on the basis of the word of the first disciples that later believers are able to bear witness (see 17:20). This line drawn between first and later generations of believers drawn in John's gospel also serves the function of authorizing the witness of the first disciples, including that of the fourth evangelist.

Stott keeps those dimensions in proper balance when he distinguishes between the "primary witness" of the apostles and the "secondary" and "subordinate" witness of later believers:

> We have no liberty to preach Jesus Christ according to our own fantasy, or even according to our own experience. Our personal witness does indeed corroborate the witness of the biblical authors, especially that of the apostles. *But theirs is the primary witness*, for they were "with Jesus" and knew him, and they have borne witness to what they heard with their ears and saw with their eyes. Our witness is always secondary and subordinate to theirs.[117]

Indeed, the original disciples are to witness to what they have heard and seen. Yet, as may be inferred from 20:29, faith in Jesus after his ascension will be based on hearing the apostolic message regarding Jesus rather than on seeing Jesus. And such hearing, too, must result in witnessing to what one has heard.[118] In characteristic Johannine dual reference, the healed blind man's statement, "I was blind but now I see!" (9:25), too, has overtones of spiritual "seeing" (cf. 9:39–41). Thus physical seeing by those who had been with Jesus from the beginning is not a necessary prerequisite for witnessing.

Similarly, Jesus' statement to his disciples that the coming *paraklētos* would teach them all things and bring to their remembrance all that Jesus had told them

---

116. See Carson, *Gospel according to John*, 529; Matthew Vellanickal, "Evangelization in the Johannine Writings," in *Good News and Witness* (ed. Lucien Legrand, J. Pathrapankal, and Matthew Vellanickal; Bangalore: Theological Publications in India, 1973), 142–46.

117. See John R. W. Stott, *Christian Mission in the Modern World* (Downers Grove, IL: InterVarsity Press, 1975), 48.

118. The importance of trusting in Jesus' *word* already related to "the Twelve" (cf. 6:68). It is again noted in 17:20, where the original disciples have become the bearers of Jesus' word to others.

(14:26; cf. 16:12–15), while originally referring to the first disciples, in all probability extends derivatively also to later believers. These later believers will, through the instrumentality of the original disciples, be taught all things and be "reminded" of all Jesus had said.[119]

Do the privileges and responsibilities conferred upon the first followers of Jesus therefore extend also to postresurrection disciples? On the one hand, John's gospel preserves the original disciples' historical function as witnesses to the earthly Jesus. The notion is retained that they alone followed Jesus during his earthly ministry, including his crucifixion and resurrection (see 18:19; 19:35; 20:30). This historic specificity also extends to the references in the Farewell Discourse regarding "the little while" during which Jesus would be absent and "the little while" for which he would be reunited with his disciples (see 7:33; 12:35; 13:33; 14:19; 16:16–19), or even to the fourth evangelist himself (see 21:24). Thus, the general references in John's gospel to believers should not be taken to imply that all boundary lines between the first and later disciples are removed. On the other hand, the original disciples, while primary, also function in John's gospel as representatives and models for later generations of believers. Thus, what is *primarily* true for Jesus' original followers extends *derivatively* also to later believers.

These observations have important implications for the study of John's teaching on mission. For example, the major "sending" passages in John's gospel (4:38; 17:18; 20:21), while originally referring to the first followers of Jesus, extend as a result of this group's representative function also to later believers. Indeed, all who believe in Jesus will form the newly created messianic community; the eleven postresurrection disciples are merely its first historic representatives. Therefore all believers, likewise, are sent into the world to bear witness to Jesus (see 17:18, 20). Moreover, all believers are to pattern their relationship with Jesus, *their* sender, after Jesus' relationship to *his* sender, the Father (see 20:21).

The reference to the "greater works" also pertains to every believer regardless of his or her position before or after Jesus' crucifixion and resurrection (see 14:12). Moreover, numerous benefits are extended indiscriminately to every believer. For example, every believer has the privilege of becoming a child of God (1:12) and of receiving the gift of eternal life (3:16; 20:31). Likewise, many responsibilities are given to every believer alike. Thus all of Jesus' disciples share the duty of serving one another (13:14–17), of loving one another (13:35), of obeying Jesus' commandments (15:14), and of living with one another in unity (17:20–25).

In the original historical setting, the important question arose what it meant to "follow" Jesus after his physical departure. The answer was that following Jesus would be possible by the Spirit whom Jesus would send. This Spirit would continue many of the same functions Jesus had fulfilled while physically with his disciples (see 14:16–17). The Johannine widening of the term "disciple" to include later believers

---

119. Carson, *Gospel according to John*, 505, may draw the line a bit too sharply when he writes, "The promise of v. 26 has in view the Spirit's role to the first generation of disciples, not to all subsequent Christians."

together with Jesus' original followers is an important device John uses in order to facilitate the transition from the followers of the historical Jesus to those disciples who would depend on the witness of the original disciples. The relationship of later disciples to their glorified Lord, already anticipated in 14:12 and chapter 15, is thus shown to be mediated by the first disciples. Both original and later disciples, in turn, are united in their believing, dependent relationship with their glorified Lord by the Spirit.

John also asserts the primacy of Jesus' first followers by exercising his own witnessing role while at the same time pointing out the important connection between original and later disciples. Perhaps the insistence in 1:37–43 that even the original disciples came to believe in Jesus through the witness of another can be seen in this context. The word of the risen Lord in 20:29, "Blessed are those who have not seen and yet have believed," functions as a further indication that having been a follower of the historical Jesus does not guarantee faith in him. Jesus elevates "believing" over mere "seeing," rebuking Thomas's unbelief. The superiority of believing over merely seeing was doubtless of great importance for the first and subsequent readers of the gospel.

Moreover, there seems to be a progression in the characterization of the disciples from the first to the second part of the gospel. While the disciples are in chapters 1–12 set in relation to the earthly Jesus, chapters 13–21 find them as participants with the Father, the exalted Jesus, and the Spirit in their mission. Their love for one another, as well as their mission to the world, is shown to be grounded in the Father-Son relationship between Jesus and his sender (see 13:35; 17:18; 20:21). This transformation of followers and disciples of the earthly Jesus into representatives of the exalted Jesus (see 13:16, 20; 15:20) is made possible by Jesus' "glorification" and takes place subsequent to Jesus' return to the Father.

The second part of John's gospel also shows a change from a teacher-disciple relationship between Jesus and his followers to a more intimate relationship, as is indicated by the more endearing terms used by Jesus for his followers (*idioi* in 13:1; *teknia* in 13:33; *philoi* in 15:15; *tois anthrōpois hous edōkas moi* in 17:6 and *ta ema* in 17:10; *adelphoi* in 20:17; and *paidia* in 21:4–5).[120] However, even at the end of the gospel, Jesus' disciples are still called to "follow" Jesus (see 21:19, 22).

29.3 The Johannine Characterization of Individual Disciples

Two more aspects of Johannine characterization remain to be discussed: the characterization of individual disciples in John's gospel and corporate metaphors. A study of the Johannine characterization of individual disciples, especially that of Peter and of "the disciple whom Jesus loved," is important since such an investigation will

---

120. Regarding *idioi*, see 1:11, where reference is made to Jesus' "own" who "did not receive him." As Pryor, *John: Evangelist of the Covenant People*, 55, contends, the probable reference to Israel in 1:11 may be set in antithesis to 13:1, where *idioi* refers to Jesus' disciples. Moreover, Jesus' use of *idioi* for his own disciples in the second part of the gospel is already foreshadowed by the reference to Jesus' "own sheep" (*ta idia* or *ta idia probata*; 10:3, 4, 12) in contrast to "the Jews," who do not belong to Jesus' "sheep."

help clarify whether passages regarding the mission of individual disciples in John's gospel should be restricted to these individuals or whether these disciples should be regarded as having a representative function for later believers as well.

29.3.1 General Observations

Johannine characterization is a subject that has attracted considerable attention in recent years. Collins seeks to show that John's gospel was originally a series of homilies highlighting the faith response of certain individuals, with the goal of strengthening the faith of the "Johannine community."[121] He contends that each original homily selected a particular individual as a type of faith or lack of faith in Jesus. However, of the fifteen figures Collins identifies, not all appear to fit this pattern.[122] Does only Philip represent "the disciple who misunderstands" in John's gospel?[123] Is it accurate to consider Mary as the one who "symbolizes the one who faithfully awaits the messianic times"?[124] On a larger scale, Collins' work appears to be aimed at shifting the emphasis from the Christology of John's gospel to patterns of reader response.

Nevertheless, there does appear to be a number of characters in John's gospel who, besides representing historical persons, are used by John to show the issues involved in a person's becoming a disciple of Jesus or growing into such discipleship. One writer identifies the Samaritan woman (from questioning Jesus to leading others to Jesus); the Capernaum official (the issue of giving priority to faith in Jesus as a person over "signs"); the man born blind (progressive understanding and faith); and Martha (right confession but not necessarily an adequate grasp of who Jesus is) as figures fulfilling this function.[125] Thus, persons other than Jesus' disciples (*mathētai*) may be used by John to teach about "discipleship."

29.3.2 Peter and "the Disciple Whom Jesus Loved"

Perhaps the most important aspect of Johannine characterization is the development of the characters of Peter and "the disciple whom Jesus loved."[126] This

---

121. See Collins, "Representative Figures," in *These Things Have Been Written*, 1–45. See also idem, *John and His Witness* (Zacchaeus Studies: New Testament; Collegeville, MN: Liturgical Press, 1991), 56–78.

122. The figures Collins identifies are: John the Baptist, Nathanael, Mary (the mother of Jesus), Nicodemus, the Samaritan woman, the royal official, the lame man, Philip, the man born blind, Lazarus, Judas, Mary Magdalene, Thomas, Peter, and "the disciple whom Jesus loved." Each of the homilies, according to Collins, highlights one core characteristic in these persons' faith. Thus John the Baptist is a type of the witness to Jesus; Nathanael is the true, Scripture-literate Israelite (in contrast to "the Jews"); Nicodemus is a type of the (Jewish) unbeliever (see also Collins' separate article, "Jesus' Conversation with Nicodemus"); the Samaritan woman is a type of the Christian messenger who brings others to faith in Jesus; etc.

123. Ibid., 25.

124. Ibid., 32–33.

125. See Siker-Gieseler, "Disciples and Discipleship," 215–20. To Siker-Gieseler's list other figures such as Nicodemus or disciples like Thomas may be added. On Nicodemus, see Jouette M. Bassler, "Mixed Signals: Nicodemus in the Fourth Gospel," *JBL* 108 (1989): 635–46.

126. See also the interesting suggestion by J. S. Billings, "Judas Iscariot in the Fourth Gospel," *ExpTim* 51 (1939–40): 156–57, who argues that the fourth gospel's characterization of Judas as *ho huios tēs apōleias* indicates that John saw the antichrist (referred to by the same term used in 2 Thess 2:3) as already incarnate in Judas in the light of his realized eschatology (see also John 6:70, where Judas is called *diabolos*; 12:4, where he is called a robber; and 13:11, where he is called "unclean"). Another possible representative type of characterization is the emphasis on one disciple's leading another person to Jesus in chap. 1 (cf. Culpepper, *Anatomy*, 115–16). It is especially Andrew who is cast as leading others to Jesus: his own brother (1:41), a boy (6:8), and the "Greeks" (12:22). On Andrew in

development is sustained throughout the gospel, culminating in the concluding pericope (21:15–23).[127] This consistent characterization of Peter in relation to "the disciple whom Jesus loved" appears to point to the gospel's coherent perspective, which would have remained incomplete had the final chapter not been included.[128] The primary question at issue is whether the characterization of these two figures involves their function as representative characters for the readers of John's gospel. If this were in fact the case, it would be highly relevant for John's teaching on mission, since Peter and "the disciple whom Jesus loved" would be invested with a message transcending their historical significance.

Generally, it appears that John probably wanted to convey a particular understanding of the relationship between Peter and "the disciple whom Jesus loved," since the latter is in all but one occurrence closely identified with Peter.[129] The question remains, however, what kind of relationship John's gospel ascribes to Peter and "the disciple whom Jesus loved." This relationship has been variably described as one of rivalry, differentiated roles, or as essentially unrelated.

One of the proponents of the view that Peter and "the disciple whom Jesus loved" are cast in terms of rivalry speaks of the strong "anti-Petrinism" of John's gospel. This writer argues that "the figure of the Beloved Disciple, as one more authoritative than the other disciples, especially those later designated as apostles, is an absolute necessity to the structure of the Gospel of John."[130] M. B. Moreton maintains that "the figure of the beloved disciple in the Fourth Gospel is basically a device, intended to correct a growing reverence for Peter."[131]

Savas Agourides, too, contends "that its [the fourth gospel's] author or editors were trying to combat the prestige and authority of Peter among the readers to whom the Gospel was addressed, on the basis of the superior position of this 'beloved disciple' of Jesus."[132] According to Agourides, "one of the aims of the Evangelist was to correct certain false impressions in the Church concerning the position of Peter, interpretations based perhaps on texts of the synoptic tradition such as Matt.

---

the fourth gospel, see Peter M. Peterson, *Andrew, Brother of Simon Peter* (NovTSup 1; Leiden: Brill, 1963), 4–5. Other figures include Nathanael, the "true Israelite" (see Paul L. Trudinger, "An Israelite in Whom There Is No Guile: An Interpretative Note on John 1,45–51," *EvQ* 54 [1982]: 117–20), and Thomas, a disciple who demands tangible evidence for believing (cf. Culpepper, *Anatomy*, 123–24).

127. Quast, *Peter and the Beloved Disciple*. See also the helpful study by Thorwald Lorenzen, *Der Lieblingsjünger im Johannesevangelium: Eine redaktionsgeschichtliche Studie* (SBS 55; Stuttgart: KBW, 1970); Collins, "Discipleship in John's Gospel," in *These Things Have Been Written*, 46–55; and William S. Kurz, "The Beloved Disciple and Implied Readers: A Socio-Narratological Approach," *BTB* 19 (1989): 100–107.

128. Cf. Culpepper, *Anatomy*, 96; Paul S. Minear, "The Original Functions of John 21," *JBL* 201 (1983): 85–98; Willem S. Vorster, "The Growth and Making of John 21," in *The Four Gospels 1992: Festschrift Frans Neirynck* (BETL 100; ed. F. van Segbroeck, C. M. Tuckett, G. van Belle, and J. Verheyden; Leuven: Leuven University Press, 1992), 3:2207–21. Minear argues that only John 21 provides a sense of closure regarding the relationship between Peter and "the disciple whom Jesus loved" (pp. 91–93), and that chap. 21 clarifies the relationship between the fourth evangelist and "the disciple whom Jesus loved" (p. 95).

129. See 1:37–42; 6:68–70; 13:6–10, 23–25, 36–38; 18:15–18, 25–27; 19:26–27, 35; 20:2–10; 21:7–24. The references to "another disciple" in 18:15–16 and 20:2–8 should probably be taken as referring to "the disciple whom Jesus loved," since 20:2 combines both expressions (*ton allon mathētēn hon ephilei ho Iēsous*). Moreover, Peter and "the disciple whom Jesus loved"/"other disciple" are consistently featured jointly in John's gospel.

130. See Graydon F. Snyder, "John 13.16 and the Anti-Petrinism of the Johannine Tradition," *BR* 16 (1971): 14.

131. See M. B. Moreton, "The Beloved Disciple Again," in *Studia Biblica 1978. II. Papers on The Gospels* (JSNTSup 2; ed. E. A. Livingstone; Sheffield: JSOT, 1980), 218.

132. See Savas Agourides, "Peter and John in the Fourth Gospel," *SE IV* (ed. F. L. Cross; Berlin: Akademie, 1968), 3.

16, 18."[133] Raymond Brown suggests that the portrayal of "the disciple whom Jesus loved" in John's gospel seeks to counteract the dominance of "the Twelve" in the developing church.[134]

Many see Peter and "the disciple whom Jesus loved" as assuming the same basic function in their respective communities. Rudolf Bultmann interprets "the disciple whom Jesus loved" as an ideal figure representative of Gentile Christianity and Peter of Jewish Christianity, an interpretation that is integral to his basic understanding of the gospel.[135] William Watty views the portrayal of the anonymous "disciple whom Jesus loved" as the "response to a pastoral situation which seems to have necessitated a corrective to a developing Petrine tradition."[136] Similarly, a group of interpreters believes "the [Johannine] community secured its own position by placing the Beloved Disciple alongside Simon Peter.... Chapter 21 is not an attack on the pastoral authority of Peter; it is a demand for the recognition of another type of discipleship, just as authentic as that of the original apostles."[137]

John Gunther understands the superiority of "the disciple whom Jesus loved" in the Johannine tradition in terms of spiritual insight, perception, and interpretation of the events of the life of Jesus.[138] Kevin Quast, taking his cue from 1 John 2:19, hypothesizes that the schism of Johannine community led to its absorption either into the apostolic churches or Gnosticism. The death of "the disciple whom Jesus loved," according to Quast, led the final editors, representatives of the Johannine community, to look at Peter as a potential figure for identification.[139] Thus, according to Quast, John's gospel "confronts an exclusivist attitude within the Johannine community" and constitutes an effort to bring apostolic and Johannine Christians together (see especially John 21).[140]

Others see the relationship between Peter and "the disciple whom Jesus loved" in John's gospel as one of differentiated roles. As Patrick Hartin notes, the relationship is not one "of rivalry, nor of opposition," but rather "each has a distinctive function to perform."[141] Alv Kragerud sees "the disciple whom Jesus loved" as the representative of a pneumatic circle (*Geist*), while Peter functions as the holder of an ecclesiastical office (*Amt*).[142] Barnabas Lindars distinguishes between the "prophetic ministry" of "the disciple whom Jesus loved" and the local "pastoral ministry" of Peter.[143] Thus the "rivalry" is not in terms of competition but in terms of differentiation of

---

133. Ibid.
134. Brown is, of course, supposing that "the disciple whom Jesus loved" was not a member of "the Twelve." See Brown, *Community of the Beloved Disciple*, 191.
135. See Bultmann, *Gospel of John*, 673, followed by Margaret Pamment, "The Fourth Gospel's Beloved Disciple," *ExpTim* 94 (1983): 363–67.
136. See William W. Watty, "The Significance of Anonymity in the Fourth Gospel," *ExpTim* 90 (1979): 209–12.
137. See Raymond E. Brown, Karl P. Donfried, and John Reumann, ed., *Peter in the New Testament* (Minneapolis: Augsburg, 1973), 147.
138. See John J. Gunther, "The Relation of the Beloved Disciple to the Twelve," *TZ* 37 (1981): 135.
139. See Quast, *Peter and the Beloved Disciple*, 165–70.
140. See ibid., 170. However, Quast appears to move too easily from the rhetoric of the text to a supposed situation in the life of the community.
141. See Patrick J. Hartin, "The Role of Peter in the Fourth Gospel," *Neot* 24 (1990): 58.
142. Alv Kragerud, *Der Lieblingsjünger im Johannesevangelium: Ein exegetischer Versuch* (Hamburg: Grosshaus Wegner, 1959), 65–67.
143. See Barnabas Lindars, *The Gospel of John* (NCBC; Grand Rapids: Eerdmans, 1981), 602.

functions. Peter's ecclesiastical authority contrasts with the didactic authority of "the disciple whom Jesus loved."

Yet others do not detect any rivalry at all between Peter and "the disciple whom Jesus loved" in John's gospel. These scholars argue that "the disciple whom Jesus loved" may be symbolically significant while not being in direct relationship with Peter.[144] R. Alan Culpepper views "the disciple whom Jesus loved" as "the ideal disciple, the paradigm of discipleship."[145] François-Marie Braun maintains that "the disciple whom Jesus loved" is not a rival to Peter, but the image of the believer in his love, faith, and attachment to Jesus.[146] Peter serves as a subordinate spokesman, representing the Twelve in the common tradition. Oscar Cullmann asserts that John's gospel "nowhere attempts to deny directly the special role of Peter within the group of disciples. It only has the tendency to lessen this role, in so far as it seeks to show that beside the unique position of Peter there is the somewhat different special role of the 'Beloved Disciple.'"[147]

Indeed, a discussion of the relationship between Peter and "the disciple whom Jesus loved" merely in terms of "rivalry" or "contrast" may be too simplistic. On the one hand, it appears likely that the fourth evangelist conceived of "the disciple whom Jesus loved," as of Peter, as a historical figure. This can be seen, for example, in the Passion Narrative, where both figures function side by side. It is difficult to imagine a procedure that would have inserted "the disciple whom Jesus loved" as an ideal figure alongside Peter, a historical figure. At the same time, John appears to invest these two figures also with representative roles.[148]

This can be seen especially in those passages where explicit parallels or analogies are established between Jesus on the one hand and Peter or "the disciple whom Jesus loved" on the other. Regarding "the disciple whom Jesus loved," the major analogy is that of his closeness to Jesus (see 13:23: *en tō kolpō tou Iēsou*), similar to Jesus' closeness to the Father (see 1:18: *ho ōn eis ton kolpon tou patros*). This analogy, an unmistakable allusion, is accentuated by the fact that both of these references occur at the respective openings of the two parts of the gospel and by the fact that "the disciple whom Jesus loved" is introduced by that designation only in the second part of the gospel (13:23).

Jesus' closeness to the Father is presented in 1:18 as providing the perfect qualification and legitimization for Jesus to "narrate" (*exēgeisthai*) the Father. "The disciple whom Jesus loved," on the surface level of the narrative, is simply physically closer to Jesus and thus in a position to pass on another's inquiry to his Master. But in the

---

144. See Schnackenburg, who sees a relationship of coordination and mutual recognition between the "disciple whom Jesus loved" and Peter. The association of the anonymous "disciple whom Jesus loved" with Peter would increase the former's prestige. See "Der Jünger, den Jesus liebte," in *Evangelisch-Katholischer Kommentar zum Neuen Testament: Vorarbeiten* (Zürich: Neukirchener, 1970), 2:105–7.

145. See Culpepper, *Anatomy*, 121. He observes, "He ['the disciple whom Jesus loved'] has no misunderstandings." "The disciple whom Jesus loved" could, however, be viewed as included in the misunderstandings of the gospel's disciples (see 2:22; 4:33; 11:12; 12:16; 16:17–18; 20:9; cf. 13:22).

146. See Braun, *Jean le théologien*, 1:302–3, 327.

147. See Oscar Cullmann, *Peter: Disciple, Apostle, Martyr* (trans. Floyd V. Filson; London: SCM, 1976), 27.

148. See Brown, *Community of the Beloved Disciple*, 83: "The Beloved Disciple was no less a real human being than was Simon Peter, but the Fourth Gospel uses each of them in a paradigmatic capacity."

light of Johannine multilayered language, it is hard to escape the notion that 13:23, in allusion to 1:18, also presents "the disciple whom Jesus loved," who is later identified as the gospel's author (21:24), as in a position of proximity to Jesus that enables him to provide a close-up account of the life and mission of the Messiah.[149]

The major analogy between Jesus and Peter concerns the kinds of deaths Jesus and Peter were to die. The fourth evangelist's comment on Jesus' death is worded thus: *touto de elegen sēmainōn poiō thanatō ēmellen apothnēskein* (12:33). Peter's death is spoken of in almost identical terms: *touto de eipen sēmainōn poiō thanatō doxasei ton theon* (21:19). In the context of 21:15–23, this kind of death is seen within the scope of yet another analogy between Jesus and Peter, namely their role as "shepherds." Jesus is presented as the "good shepherd" in John 10, while Peter is commissioned by Jesus in 21:15–17 to "tend" Jesus' "sheep" (21:16). Thus the disciple's calling extends to dying the same kind of death Jesus died—though in Peter's case without any atoning significance[150]—as well as to "shepherding" Jesus' "flock." In one sense, Peter's salvation-historical role as the one first commissioned by Jesus and the one leading the early church is distinct. Yet he also functions as a representative for subsequent believers whom Jesus likewise calls to "shepherd" his people.

Another passage where "the disciple whom Jesus loved" and Peter are featured together in John's gospel is 21:15–23. While scholars may differ on the question whether this material was part of the original gospel, it is still necessary to account for the theological reason why the person responsible for the final text included this pericope. At the culmination of John's consistent characterization of Peter and "the disciple whom Jesus loved" in relation to one another, this passage characterizes their roles with the accompanying exhortation that each should fulfill the role assigned him by his Lord while not questioning that of the other.

As a part of his overall presentation of mission, John here shows that the two disciples, and the callings they represent, have different, complementary roles within the messianic community. The role of "the disciple whom Jesus loved" is that of bearing faithful witness to Jesus, a role he discharged, among other things, by writing his gospel. Peter's ministry, likewise, has as a component the faithful bearing of witness to Jesus. His role is one of loving, faithful "shepherding" of Jesus' "flock"[151]

---

149. See Schnackenburg's comment, quoted in Lorenzen, *Lieblingsjünger*, 100, n. 11: "He ['the disciple whom Jesus loved'] was viewed as a reliable tradent of tradition, what is more, as the Spirit-illumined proclaimer and interpreter of Jesus' message" (translation mine). Note, however, that the term used for Jesus is "made known" (John 1:18), while the expression used for the "disciple whom Jesus loved" is "testify" (19:35; 21:24–25). But in 18:37 it is also said of Jesus that he came to "witness to the truth." There may also be a relationship between the roles of "John" (i.e., the Baptist) and of "the disciple whom Jesus loved," both of whose functions it is to witness to Jesus. John 1–12 may be considered as presenting Jesus as witnessed to by John (the Baptist), while John 13–21 may be seen as portraying Jesus as witnessed to by "the disciple whom Jesus loved." Note also that both John and "the disciple whom Jesus loved" were aided in this witnessing role by the Spirit (1:32–33; 15:26–27). John's role was "to baptize with water" for the purpose "that he [Jesus] might be revealed to Israel." Perhaps this is still the (primary) purpose of "the disciple whom Jesus loved" in his writing of the gospel.

150. On the issue of whether Peter's death was "for the community" or not, see Theofried Baumeister, "Der Tod Jesu und die Leidensnachfolge des Jüngers nach dem Johannesevangelium und dem ersten Johannesbrief," *Wissenschaft und Weisheit* 40 (1977): 96, n. 50.

151. The emphasis is not on Peter's representative rule but on his obligation to love and care for Jesus' "flock." See the Johannine characterization of Jesus as the shepherd who gives his life for his sheep (10:11, 15–18), who protects his own (10:28–29; see also 17:12), and who cares for those entrusted to him even beyond his physical presence with them (cf., e.g., the provision of care of Jesus

and of bold, courageous witness ending in a violent, Christlike (though not atoning), God-glorifying death.[152] Peter's role as a shepherd should probably not be seen as merely pastoral in the sense of nurturing believers only. Rather, as in the case of Jesus, the role of a shepherd also entails his bringing to the flock yet other dispersed sheep (see 10:16). Thus 21:15–23 transcends mere nurture of believers to include outreach to unbelievers.[153]

In light of the above observations, it may be concluded that both Peter and "the disciple whom Jesus loved," in addition to having their historical and specific identities, also appear to fulfill a representative role in John's gospel. Thus their respective roles serve as models for subsequent believers.[154] As one surveys the gospel, it appears that some duties are shown to pertain to every disciple of Jesus, such as the duty to obey Jesus and to love one's fellow disciples, while other callings are specific to the individual disciple, such as certain kinds of witness, be it by pastoring or other forms of representing Jesus. This becomes apparent in John's characterization of individual disciples, especially of Peter and of the "disciple whom Jesus loved."[155]

In both cases, John is careful to highlight an analogous element between Jesus and "the disciple whom Jesus loved" or Peter and yet to include hints regarding the limitations of this analogy.[156] Jesus, who is described in John's gospel as the unique Son, shares with "the disciple whom Jesus loved" a proximity to the person they "narrate" or bear witness to. However, only Jesus is witnessed *to*. Jesus, the eschatological Shepherd-teacher, and Peter both fulfill a shepherding role and die violent deaths. Yet only Jesus' death is of atoning significance.[157]

---

for his own mother, of the Spirit for the disciples, of salvation for the world, and of Peter for his "flock"). See also the emphasis in 1 Pet 5:2–3 on shepherding not by lording over the "flock" but by example, and the charge in Acts 20:28 for the elders to "watch over" their "flock" (i.e., provide spiritual protection; both passages share with John 21:15–17 the use of *poimainō* or variants). See Beasley-Murray, *John*, 406–7.

152. See Lindars, *Gospel of John*, 637, who observes, "Peter's death is to reproduce the act by which Jesus most fully revealed God's glory ... it reflects the meaning of Jesus' death, on the principle that true discipleship continues Jesus' mission (17.10)." As Carson, *Gospel according to John*, 678–79, contends, Peter is neither given founding preeminence nor comparative authority. His is a reinstatement to service, not an elevation to primacy. The three pledges of loyalty to Jesus correspond to the three denials (Barrett, *Gospel according to St. John*, 583). See also Beasley-Murray, *John*, 405, who refers to the fact that Peter's "re-establishment [was] commensurable with the seriousness of the defection." Bultmann, *Gospel of John*, 714, notes that 21:19 echoes 13:36.

153. See Beasley-Murray, *John*, 405, who refers to Jesus' preparation of Peter "for responsible leadership among the people of the Kingdom and for the mission to Israel and the nations," and who, commenting on 21:15–23, draws attention to "the aspect of the Shepherd's calling to seek the lost sheep and gather them into the flock, hence the aspect of *mission*." Beasley-Murray concedes, however, that this is not the primary emphasis of John 21:15–17 (ibid.,

407, emphasis his). See also Barrett, *Gospel according to St. John*, 583, who contends: "The interest here lies not in the mission of the church (as in 20.21) but in leadership and pastoral care within it (Bultmann)." See also Luke 21:32 and Peter's activities narrated in Acts 3 and 4.

154. Cf. Bradford B. Blaine, Jr., *Peter in the Gospel of John: The Making of an Authentic Disciple* (SBL Academic Biblica 27; Atlanta/Leiden: SBL/Brill, 2008), who argues that Peter represents praxis while John represents faith.

155. It is more difficult to know *why* the fourth evangelist characterizes Peter and "the disciple whom Jesus loved" the way he does, and *why* he seeks to impart the lessons described here. Did the fourth evangelist seek to correct an undue regard for Peter among his readers? It is true that this was part of the Corinthian problem (see the reference to a "Cephas party" in 1 Cor 1:12). Certainty is elusive. But the lessons transcend any one historical setting, so that it may be best to emphasize the timeless lessons over a speculative *Sitz im Leben*.

156. See also Fig. 2.2 in chap. 1, sec. 2.1.3.1.1. Another analogy drawn between Jesus and the disciples—that is, of the way in which they are "sent" (17:18; 20:21)—is likewise not without its boundaries.

157. Perhaps the term "glorify," too, is deliberately used to focus on the revelatory rather than the atoning function of Peter's death. On this, see Baumeister, "Tod Jesu und Leidensnachfolge," 97, n. 55.

29.3.3 Minor Characters

Compared to the prominence awarded "the disciple whom Jesus loved" and Peter in John's gospel, the characterization of other followers of Jesus recedes into the background.[158] Andrew appears in three pericopae: at the beginning of the gospel, he introduces his brother Simon Peter to Jesus (1:40, 44); later on at the occasion of the feeding of the five thousand, identified as "Simon Peter's brother," he alerts Jesus to the presence of a boy with five barley loaves and two fish (6:8); and at the end of the first half of John's gospel, Andrew is enlisted by Philip to go to Jesus when Philip is approached by Greeks who want to see Jesus (12:22). In each instance, Andrew introduces people to Jesus: his brother, the boy, and the Greeks.[159]

Interestingly, Philip and Andrew appear jointly in three pericopae (1:43–44; 6:5–9; 12:21–22), both hailing from the town of Bethsaida. The first of these is the account narrating Philip's call to follow Jesus and his bringing of Nathanael to Jesus. The second and third occasions have already been noted in the discussion of the characterization of Andrew above. In addition, Philip also appears in the Farewell Discourse, requesting that Jesus show his disciples the Father, a request for which he is promptly rebuked by Jesus (14:8–9). As R. Alan Culpepper notes, while starting well by bringing Nathanael to Jesus (1:44), Philip fails both his "bread" and his "Greek" test (6:7–8; 12:21–22). He also fails to see the Father revealed in Jesus (14:8).[160]

Thomas, the "Twin" (11:16; 21:2), another member of the Twelve, is featured in four pericopae: at the outset of Jesus' raising of Lazarus, he ventures the—possibly sarcastic—opinion that the disciples should go with Jesus "that we may die with him" (11:16); in the Upper Room, he asks Jesus to show them the way where he is about to go (14:5), revealing misunderstanding; in the climactic pericope of the gospel proper, Thomas demands to see tangible proofs of Jesus' resurrection as a precondition to faith, but when brought face to face with Jesus, confesses him as "my Lord and my God" (20:28); in 21:2, finally, he is mentioned as one among seven members of the Twelve who go fishing. As Culpepper notes, Thomas "understands Jesus' flesh but not his glory," embracing the earthly Jesus while failing to recognize the risen Christ.[161]

Another disciple venturing to ask Jesus a question in the Upper Room is Judas (not Iscariot; 14:22). This disciple is most likely the Thaddaeus mentioned in the Synoptic lists (e.g., Matt 10:3).[162]

Nathanael was already mentioned above as the one who was brought to Jesus by Philip (1:44).[163] Similar to Thomas, Nathanael expresses skepticism, asking whether anything good can come from Nazareth, Jesus' hometown (1:46). Jesus, for his part,

---

158. For a study of various "minor characters" in John's gospel, see Culpepper, *Anatomy*, 132–44. Culpepper discusses John the Baptist, Jesus' mother, Nicodemus, the Samaritan woman, the royal official, the lame man, the brothers of Jesus, the blind man, Mary, Martha, and Lazarus, Pilate, and Mary Magdalene. Minor characters among Jesus' disciples are discussed on pp. 119–25.

159. Culpepper, *Anatomy*, 119–20. For a monograph-length study of Andrew, see Peterson, *Andrew, Brother of Simon Peter*.

160. Culpepper, *Anatomy*, 120.

161. Ibid., 123–24, with reference to Eva Krafft, "Die Personen des Johannesevangeliums," *EvT* 16 (1956): 27.

162. Bauckham, *Jesus and the Eyewitnesses*, 99–101.

163. For a brief sketch of the Johannine characterization of Nathanael, see Culpepper, *Anatomy*, 123.

calls Nathanael "an Israelite in whom there is no deceit" (1:47), a likely allusion to Isaac's son Jacob, who used deceit to take the birthright away from Esau (Genesis 27, esp. v. 35).[164] When confronted by Jesus, Nathanael recognizes him as the Son of God and the king of Israel (1:49). At the end of the gospel, in an apparent *inclusio*, Nathanael is mentioned as "from Cana in Galilee" as one of the group of seven going fishing (21:2). Nathanael may be the same individual as the Bartholomew mentioned in the Synoptic lists (e.g., Matt 10:3).

This just-mentioned group going fishing is also said to have included "the sons of Zebedee" (21:2), known from the other gospels as John and James. Bauckham believes that this reference precludes the possibility that John the son of Zebedee was the author of the Gospel, though there seems to be no good reason why John, if the author, could not have referred to the "sons of Zebedee" in the third person in the present narrative, remaining inconspicuously in the background.[165] This would be in keeping with his use of the epithet "the disciple whom Jesus loved," which is properly identified as a literary device conveying authorial modesty.[166]

Apart from Peter and "the disciple whom Jesus loved," the member of the Twelve that is featured most prominently in John's gospel is Judas, the betrayer.[167] At the midway point of the first half of John's gospel, the reader is made aware that Judas, though one of the Twelve, would betray Jesus (6:70–71). The account of the anointing of Jesus in chapter 12 serves mainly the purpose of revealing more fully Judas's antagonism toward Jesus, which would shortly lead to his betrayal of Jesus (12:1–8).[168] At the Last Supper, Judas is identified as the betrayer, and Satan is shown to enter him the moment he is unmasked by Jesus (13:2, 26–27). Judas betrays Jesus following the Farewell Discourse, at the outset of the Passion Narrative (18:2–3).

In terms of Johannine characterization, Judas represents a member of the messianic community who was one only outwardly and only for a season (13:10–11). For this reason he was eventually cut off from the vine (15:2–4). As such, Judas is similar to other "disciples" who "believed in Jesus' name" or "followed" Jesus for a period of time but who later fell away (2:23–25; 6:60–61, 66; 8:31–58). Culpepper calls him "the representative defector."[169] Others, such as Joseph of Arimathea, failed to confess Jesus publicly out of fear of the Jewish authorities (12:42–43; 19:38).

To sum up, of the Twelve, nine are mentioned in this gospel: Peter, Andrew, Philip, Thomas, Nathanael, Judas, and Judas (not Iscariot), as well as the sons of Zebedee (most likely including "the disciple whom Jesus loved"; the same figure may also be the second disciple besides Andrew who is mentioned in 1:35–40). Compared with the Synoptic lists, it appears that only Matthew/Levi, James the

---

164. See J. Ramsey Michaels, "Nathanael Under the Fig Tree," *ExpTim* 78 (1967): 182–83.

165. See the discussion of the authorship of John's gospel in chap. 1 above.

166. See Köstenberger, "I Suppose."

167. Culpepper, *Anatomy*, 124–25. See also Billings, "Judas Iscariot."

168. See Köstenberger, "Anointing Pericopae."

169. Culpepper, *Anatomy*, 125. Culpepper's comment, however, that "his loss, therefore, is Jesus' failure ... Jesus was not able to make him clean ... or alter his course by the gesture of love" (ibid.) seems to be off target in light of the repeated predestinarian statements in John's gospel regarding Judas (see esp. 17:12).

son of Alphaeus, and Simon the Zealot are not named. This places John's gospel in rather close affinity with the Synoptics in its coverage of the Twelve.

29.3.4 Women in John's Gospel

John also features several women in his gospel: Jesus' mother, the Samaritan woman, Mary and Martha, and Mary Magdalene.[170]

Passage in John	Woman Characters	Description
2:1–12; 19:25–27	Jesus' mother	Cana wedding, Capernaum; at the cross with the Beloved Disciple
4:1–42	A Samaritan woman	Encounter at a well in Samaria
11:1–37; 12:1–8	Mary and Martha	Raising of Lazarus, anointing of Jesus
20:1–18	Mary Magdalene	Recognition scene at the empty tomb

Fig. 29.1: Significant Women Characters in John's Gospel

Jesus' mother is mentioned at the beginning and at the end of John's gospel (a possible *inclusio*; 2:1–12; 19:25–27). She remains unnamed, possibly because there are two other women named Mary mentioned in the gospel (Mary of Bethany and Mary Magdalene) and also because John probably assumes his reader's familiarity with the gospel story (including the name of Jesus' mother).[171] On the whole, the gospel presents Jesus' relationship with his mother as respectful, loving, and caring, but at the same time Jesus is shown to subordinate this relationship to the larger purposes of his messianic mission.

The Samaritan woman serves to provide a contrast with Nicodemus, the Jewish member of the Sanhedrin, who is shown in chapter 3 to lack spiritual regeneration.[172] The conversion of the Samaritans in chapter 4 is also a plank in John's presentation of Jesus' mission as unfolding along the familiar pattern of Jerusalem and Judea/Samaria/Gentiles in chapters 3 and 4. Like Jesus' mother, the Samaritan woman remains unnamed. She progresses in her understanding, from calling Jesus a prophet (4:19; cf. 4:29, 39) to serving, albeit somewhat ambivalently, as a witness (4:27–30).[173]

The sisters Mary and Martha are an integral part of the story of Jesus' raising of Lazarus (11:1–37). Apparently John assumes his readers' familiarity with Mary

---

170. See Colleen M. Conway, *Men and Women in the Fourth Gospel: Gender and Johannine Characterization* (SBLDS 167; Atlanta: SBL, 1999); Robert G. Maccini, *Her Testimony Is True: Women as Witnesses according to John* (JSNTSup 125; Sheffield: Sheffield Academic Press, 1996); and chap. 14 in Köstenberger, *Jesus and the Feminists*. See also the shorter studies by Raymond E. Brown, "Roles of Women in the Fourth Gospel," *TS* 36 (1975): 688–99; Jane Kopas, "Jesus and Women: John's Gospel," *ThTo* 41 (1984): 201–5; and Sandra M. Schneiders, "Women in the Fourth Gospel and the Role of the Women in the Contemporary Church," *BTB* 12 (1982): 35–45.

171. See Troy W. Martin, "Assessing the Johannine Epithet 'the Mother of Jesus,'" *CBQ* 60 (1998): 63–73. See also Beck, *Discipleship Paradigm*, 54–62; Köstenberger, *John*, 92–96 and 548–49.

172. See Okure, *Johannine Approach to Mission*.

173. See Craig L. Blomberg, "The Globalization of Biblical Interpretation: A Test Case—John 3–4," *BBR* 5 (1995): 11. See the analysis in Köstenberger, *John*, 141–43.

(most likely from the Synoptic witness; see 11:2; cf. Matt 26:13; Mark 14:9; see also Luke 10:38–42). John selected the raising of Lazarus as the climactic messianic "sign" of Jesus. The subsequent anointing pericope (12:1–8) serves in this gospel to reveal the antagonism of Judas the betrayer prior to the Last Supper and Jesus' arrest (13:18–30; 18:1–5), while the actual anointing is somewhat downplayed by comparison to the Synoptics.[174]

Perhaps most significant is the fact that Martha's confession in 11:27 ("*I believe that you are the Messiah, the Son of God*, who was to come into the world") anticipates the gospel's purpose statement in 20:31 ("But these are written that *you may believe that Jesus is the Messiah, the Son of God*," emphasis added in both cases). It is remarkable that John would choose to record a woman's utterance of this confession as proleptic of the confession desired by all believers in Jesus. In this John's characterization of Martha parallels his presentation of the witness of "the disciple whom Jesus loved" and Peter in relation to Jesus:

Martha	**11:27**	**Purpose statement**	**20:31**
Jesus	1:18	"The disciple whom Jesus loved"	13:23
Jesus	12:32	Peter	21:19

Fig. 29.2: Inclusios regarding Specific Individuals in John's Gospel

The final major female character in John's gospel is Mary Magdalene. She is mentioned as one of the women at the cross in 19:25 and then becomes the focus of the resurrection narrative in chapter 20.[175] While the Synoptists feature several woman on the way to the tomb, John focuses exclusively on Mary Magdalene (20:1–2, 11–18). Mary is awarded the privilege of being the first person to see Jesus subsequent to the resurrection. In a moving recognition scene, Mary attempts to embrace Jesus, but he responds that he must ascend to the Father. Notably, the appearance is not numbered among Jesus' resurrection appearances to his disciples in 21:14 (cf. 20:19–21:13).

29.4 Corporate Metaphors

John uses two major metaphors for the new messianic community: that of a flock and that of branches of a vine.

29.4.1 *The Shepherd and His Flock*

The metaphor of a "flock" is commonly found in the OT as a designation for God's people Israel.[176] This is the controlling image of chapter 10, where Jesus identifies himself as "the good shepherd" and his followers as "sheep" who hear his voice. The

---

174. For an analysis of the anointing pericope, with special attention to Greek verbal aspect theory, see Köstenberger, "Anointing Pericopae."

175. See the analysis in Köstenberger, *John*, 560–70.

176. Cf., e.g., Ps 77:20; 78:52; 97:7; Isa 40:11; Jer 23:1; Ezek 34:11.

term "flock" occurs in 10:16 in the context of Jesus' vision of uniting his sheep with yet "other sheep" so that there will be "one flock and one shepherd" (an allusion to Ezek 34:23). The reference to the imminent "scattering" of Jesus' disciples and the passages in John 17 regarding Jesus' protection of his own (e.g., 17:12) also may imply the imagery of a flock. Finally, in 21:15–17 Jesus gives Peter charge over his "flock."

At the outset, John's use of corporate metaphors appears to function as a device to balance the gospel's emphasis on the individual with the communal dimension of a believer's life.[177] Moreover, as John Pryor observes, the gospel's corporate metaphors may be part of a larger framework that casts the believing community as God's new covenant people.[178] This can be illustrated by the following examples:

- the use of *idioi* in 1:11 with reference to Israel and in 13:1 with regard to Jesus' followers
- the insistence of 15:1 that Jesus is the "true vine" embodying the true Israel
- the "creation" of the new messianic community by breathing on it the Spirit (20:22)
- the gospel's portrayal of Jesus as the Mosaic prophet (even though Jesus exceeds both Moses and Abraham categories: see 1:17; 8:58; 13–17 patterned after the book of Deuteronomy)[179]
- the implication of 1:51 that Jesus replaces Israel as the locus of the revelation of God's glory
- the use of "shepherd" and "flock" imagery for the relationship between Jesus and a community that transcends Jewish ethnic lines (John 10)
- the claim that Jesus' glory "made his dwelling among us" (the messianic community), in allusion to God's dwelling among his old covenant people, Israel (1:14)
- the insistence that Jesus' sonship is unique (see the term *monogenēs* in 1:14, 18; 3:16, 18)
- John's adaptation of the covenantal terminology and patterns found in the primary texts of Judaism, that is, Exodus and Deuteronomy[180]

It is highly instructive to understand the relationship of John 10 to its OT antecedents in Ezek 34:23–24 and Zech 13:7–9. Jesus is the fulfillment of the messianic promise, the messianic shepherd in contrast to the failing leaders of the

---

177. See Schnackenburg, *Gospel according to John*, 3:209; Dan O. Via, "Darkness, Christ and Church in the Fourth Gospel," *SJT* 14 (1961): 172–93. Contra, Charles F. D. Moule, "The Individualism of the Fourth Gospel," in *Essays in New Testament Interpretation* (Cambridge: Cambridge University Press, 1982), 91–109, who views the Johannine corporate metaphors in the light of John's emphasis on the individual.

178. Pryor, *John: Evangelist of the Covenant People*. The points taken below are from ibid., 55, 64, 89, 119–20, 126, 130–31, 158, 160, 166, *et passim*.

179. See also Lacomara, "Deuteronomy and the Farewell Discourse." But see Carson, *Gospel according to John*, 480, who notes that, unlike Moses, Jesus fully expected to return shortly, so that the title Farewell Discourse only partially captures the occasion in John 14–16. Thus there is a point where the analogy between Jesus' and Moses' "farewell discourses" breaks down.

180. Pryor, *John: Evangelist of the Covenant People*, 216, n. 8, notes that the first major verb themes of 14:15–24 (to love, obey, live, know, and see) have their basis in the covenant theology of Exodus 33–34 and Deuteronomy. See also Malatesta, *Interiority and Covenant*, 42–77.

Jewish people.[181] Remarkably, the impact of the messianic shepherd transcends the boundaries of ethnic Israel, even to the extent that ethnic Jews can be said not to be of Jesus' sheep (John 10:26; cf. 8:31–59). In continuity with, even escalation of, the OT theme of the failure of Israel's leadership, the Jewish leaders do not believe in Jesus because they do not belong to his sheep. Those who do believe know themselves to be a new community belonging to the messianic eschatological shepherd.

However, these believers, though originally almost all Jewish, no longer define themselves by their ethnic identity, but rather by their characteristic as *believers*, which opens up the possibility of membership in the messianic community to a universal and diverse group of people. Indeed, most take the "other sheep" in 10:16 to refer to Gentiles. This gives expression to Jesus' vision of one messianic community composed of believing Jews and Gentiles.[182]

Thus, in terms of individual discipleship as well as belonging to this messianic community, criteria for membership in this new entity have been extended beyond ethnic boundaries to assume universal dimensions. One may view the entire gospel as an unfolding presentation of the movement from old definitions of discipleship and belonging to the people of God to a new understanding of such categories. Judaism is viewed as a system that has been transcended by the appearance of the Messiah, which left Judaism an empty shell and exposed its futile adherence to customs now obsolete as well as its clinging to power that would soon be gone. Even the figures Judaism claimed as its own founding fathers, Abraham and Moses, Jesus denied to them by claiming that they pointed toward himself and were preparatory for him.[183]

29.4.2 The Vine and the Branches

The second significant corporate metaphor in John is that of the "vine" and the "branches" (John 15). The barely concealed reference to Israel[184] casts Jesus as the true vine, the representative of Israel, and his disciples as the branches, participants

---

181. See Schnackenburg, *Gospel according to St. John*, 3:210.
182. See Schnackenburg, "Johannine Ecclesiology," 251. The reference to "other sheep" in 10:16 refers back to 10:1–5, where Jesus speaks of "sheep" following him out of the "sheep pen" of Judaism. Thus, as Carson, *Gospel according to John*, 390, contends, the category presupposed by "other sheep" is Gentiles. Contra, John A. T. Robinson, *Twelve New Testament Studies* (SBT 34; London: SCM, 1962), 114–15. J. Louis Martyn's thesis that the "other sheep" are Christians in other Christian communities who have been scattered by the persecution of the AD 80s is needlessly anachronistic (*The Gospel of John in Christian History: Essays for Interpreters* [New York: Paulist, 1978], 115–21). Brown, "Other Sheep," 5–22, developing Martyn's thesis further, claims to be able to "read off" six different groups from John's gospel: the synagogue of "the Jews," crypto-Christians, Jewish Christians, Christians of apostolic churches, Johannine Christians, and secessionist Johannine Christians. He identifies the "other sheep" of 10:16 with Christians of apostolic churches with which the Johannine Christians hoped to be reconciled and ecclesiastically united. However, this hypothesis, too, is unduly speculative.

183. Thus Klaus Haacker, *Die Stiftung des Heils: Untersuchungen zur Struktur der johanneischen Theologie* (Stuttgart: Calwer, 1972), properly draws attention to the "founder motif" in John's gospel. It seems unwarranted, however, to characterize Jesus and Moses exclusively in these terms. John's gospel presents Jesus not just as the antitype of the Moses typology but also as the true heir of Abraham and as the fulfillment of many Jewish institutions and festivals. On Moses and exodus typology in John's gospel, see Jacob J. Enz, "The Book of Exodus as a Literary Type for the Gospel of John," *JBL* 76 (1957): 208–15; Glasson, *Moses in the Fourth Gospel*; Marinus de Jonge, "Jesus as Prophet and King in the Fourth Gospel," *ETL* 49 (1973): 160–77; Meeks, *Prophet-King*; Rudolf Schnackenburg, "Die Erwartung des 'Propheten' nach dem Neuen Testament und den Qumran-Texten," in *SE* (TU 73; ed. F. L. Cross; Berlin: Akademie, 1959), 622–39; and Smith, "Exodus Typology in the Fourth Gospel."

184. See Ps 80:8–16; Isa 5:1–7; 27:2–6; Jer 2:21; Ezek 15; 19:10–14; Hos 10:1.

in Jesus, the "new" Israel.[185] Notably, it is not the messianic community that replaces Israel, but Jesus himself. The Father is the "vinedresser" as well as the one to whose glory the disciples are to "bear fruit." The metaphor of the vine illustrates even more vividly than that of the shepherd and his flock the organic unity between Jesus and his disciples.[186] John emphasizes that Jesus is not merely the person in whom the faith of his followers is rooted but that he should also be the continuing source of nurture and strength in the life of individual believers and of the community.[187]

Thus both the "flock" and the "vine" metaphors accentuate elements of unity between Jesus and his followers. Another common element between these metaphors is that both occur in reference to Jesus' death.[188] This points to the centrality of Jesus' death for the community's birth and subsequent life.[189] Moreover, both corporate metaphors are also significant for the concept of mission. The shepherd motif of chapter 10 is applied to Peter in 21:15–17. The vine metaphor of chapter 15 is linked with references to the disciples' "going" and bearing of fruit (cf. 15:8, 16). These two connections clearly indicate that the circle begun with Jesus' death is not closed until his redeemed community goes and accomplishes its mission.

The primary significance of the corporate metaphors for mission in John's gospel lies neither in the imagery itself nor in its OT antecedents. It rather consists of the new referents of these metaphors in contrast to their conventional references, that is, believers in Jesus the Messiah regardless of their ethnic, racial, or gender identity rather than OT Israel. By establishing one sole criterion for belonging to what is described by various corporate metaphors—that is, believing in Jesus the Messiah—and by pointing to the *world* as the destination where both Jesus and the disciples are sent (cf. 3:16; 17:18; 20:21), John reveals the universal scope of Jesus' mission and work, yet without sacrificing its historical particularity.

The message for Jews and proselytes reading his gospel is clear: a reversal has taken place, necessitating a rethinking of categories. The issue is no longer one of others joining *Jews* in *their* special and privileged position with God, but for Jews to join the universal messianic community inaugurated by the mission of the Messiah, the Son of God, that is, *Jesus*. "The Jews" had rejected the Messiah, but God had raised him from the dead. The effects of Jesus' death extend to the world *through*

---

185. See Pryor, "Covenant and Community," 49; contra, Rainer Borig, *Der wahre Weinstock: Untersuchungen zu Jo 15,1–10* (SANT 16; Munich: Kösel, 1967). Pryor's view that 15:1–17 sees "the JohCom ... in Israel categories" is doubtful, however; it seems more likely that the community of believers in general is in view.

186. Some have seen this passage as the Johannine equivalent to the Pauline "body of Christ" metaphor in the way it expresses the organic unity between Christ and his disciples (cf. Schweizer, "Kirchenbegriff," 368–70; Haacker, "Jesus und die Kirche," 183). However, in contrast to Paul, who develops the "body" metaphor primarily in terms of the relationship of the various members to one another (but see Eph 5:21–33, which also develops the body's relationship to the "head," Jesus Christ), John focuses on the necessary connection of each individual to Jesus. Nevertheless, there are similarities between the Pauline metaphor and Johannine imagery. Both presuppose that the earthly, historical Jesus has become the exalted, glorified Christ, who will continue to extend his work through his followers.

187. See Schnackenburg, *Gospel according to St. John*, 3:212. See also Pryor, "Covenant and Community," 49–50, who draws attention to the term *menō* in John 15 and other places in John's gospel. Following Malatesta, *Interiority and Covenant*, he argues that this term (as well as *einai en*) suggests the presence of new covenant theology in John. See also Pryor, *John: Evangelist of the Covenant People*, 63–65.

188. See 10:11, 15, 17, 18; 15:13.

189. See Corell, *Consummatum Est*, 25–26.

the disciples who are sent into the world to do greater works than even those Jesus did during his earthly ministry, in the power of his Spirit. The eschatological time of harvest had dawned; and the readers of this gospel, too, should believe that the Messiah is Jesus (cf. 20:30–31).[190]

29.5 The Disciples' Task

While Jesus' task is referred to in John's gospel in terms of "works" (*erga*) and "signs" (*sēmeia*), the range for describing his followers' task is much more limited. The disciples do not perform any "signs" in John's gospel. There is no mention of their "work" (in the singular). Even reference to the disciples' "works" is limited to one, albeit significant, instance (14:12). Other passages speak of their task in terms of a harvest they are sent to reap (4:38), or an appointment to go and bear fruit (15:16). Jesus' followers are to testify to him in conjunction with the Spirit (15:26–27) and to forgive others their sins as Jesus' representatives (20:23).

One notes that the disciples' participation in Jesus' mission is almost exclusively discussed in the second part of the gospel, except for the proleptic reference in 4:38 and the possible implications drawn from 10:16 and 12:20–32. The disciples' participation in the mission of the earthly Jesus in chapters 1–12 is limited to the ordinary tasks of disciples, such as buying food (cf. 4:8) or helping Jesus to distribute food and gathering leftovers (cf. 6:5–13). By contrast, the disciples' participation in the exalted Jesus' mission is much more significant (chaps. 13–21): the disciples will do even "greater works" than their Master did during his own earthly mission (14:12).

29.5.1 The "Greater Works"

In 14:12, John relates Jesus' prediction that believers will do the works he has been doing and "even greater things than these." What is the meaning of this startling saying? Surely Jesus is not saying that his followers will work greater miracles than the raising of Lazarus or the walking on the water? Many have taken this statement to refer to the great missionary successes of the early church narrated in the book of Acts. Is this John's point of reference? In context, one finds the explanation that these "greater works" will be possible because Jesus is about to "go to the Father" (14:12c). In this new era of salvation history, where Jesus becomes the object of believers' prayer and grants them their requests from his exalted heavenly position, Jesus' followers will be able to do "greater works" even than Jesus during the time of his earthly ministry.[191]

Thus the primary point of reference appears to be an eschatological one. The disciples will be able to do "greater works" owing to their later placement in the history of salvation. Their work will be based on Jesus' finished work of salvation. They

---

190. Carson, "Purpose of the Fourth Gospel: Jn 20:31 Reconsidered."

191. See Matt 11:11; cf. John 1:50; 5:20. If John knew the Synoptics, since Luke and Acts form a two-volume work, most likely John also knew Acts—in which case the mission of the early church as narrated in Acts may indeed be in view here.

will be able to apply the full benefits of forgiveness and life to those who receive their message regarding the Messiah (20:23). As C. K. Barrett notes, "The death and exaltation of Jesus are the condition of the church's mission.... The work of the disciples [is] greater not because they themselves are greater but because Jesus' work is now complete."[192] The results of believers' mission include a broader stream of God's life-giving powers (17:2), the gathering together of the dispersed children of God (11:52), and the judgment of the unbelieving world (16:8–11).

In a sense, the reference in 14:12 elevates the future works of believers above Jesus' "signs" of chapters 1–12. It also reveals Jesus' perspective of his own work in relation to that of the disciples *after* the accomplishment of his earthly mission.[193] Jesus' death and resurrection are thus set in the context of not just *salvation* but *mission*. Jesus is the sower of the eschatological harvest (4:34–38) as well as the grain of wheat that falls into the ground and dies, *bearing much fruit* (12:24). Yet, in eschatological perspective, it is only the age of the Spirit that will see the disciples help gather the eschatological harvest and thus do "greater works" even than Jesus. As one writer sums up 14:12–14, "The disciples go forth in their mission and seek the Lord's aid therein, and in response to their prayers *he* will do through them 'greater things' than in the days of his flesh, 'that the Father may be glorified in the Son' — in the powerful mission that *he* continues!"[194]

The acknowledgment of the disciples' misunderstandings before the giving of the Spirit in John's gospel underscores the fact that it is the *Spirit* who accounts for the disciples' later understanding and ability. It is he who continues the revelation and work of Jesus who is now exalted. This keeps Jesus the Messiah from being merely a past chapter of history that fades forever from living memory. Rather, the Spirit is a living Presence[195] who applies Jesus' work to the world through his representatives: by teaching and reminding them of Jesus' words (14:26; 16:13–14), by bearing witness to Jesus (15:26), and by convicting the world of its unbelief (16:8–11). Closing the gap between AD 30 and 90, John's gospel portrays the works of the messianic community as the continued work of the exalted Messiah, "greater works" even than the signs performed during Jesus' earthly ministry. In a real sense, these "greater works" are works *of the exalted Christ* through believers.

29.5.2 Following and Being Sent

A central term regarding the disciples' mission, never applied to Jesus and spanning from 1:37–43 to 21:19–21, is that of "following." Notably, not all *keep* following Jesus (cf., e.g., 6:60–71 or 8:31–33). Before his passion, Jesus predicts that even his close disciples will be scattered and that all will leave him (16:32).

---

192. Barrett, *Gospel according to St. John*, 460.
193. Contra, Christian Dietzfelbinger, "Die grösseren Werke (Joh 14.12f.)," *NTS* 35 (1989): 27–47, who views the "greater works" logion merely as a later reflection on the part of the community rather than being rooted in the teaching of the historical Jesus. But it is unlikely that the later community would construe such a saying that appears to elevate it above its own Lord.
194. Beasley-Murray, *John*, 380.
195. *Paraklētos*: 14:16, 26; 15:26; 16:7; cf. 7:37–39.

Only later, by the "reminding" ministry of the Spirit (14:26), will Jesus' disciples remember Jesus' words and understand their significance (2:22; 12:16). Thus, according to John, faithful following of Jesus is only possible *after* the cross and Jesus' glorification.

In his use of the term "following," John moves from literal to figurative "following."[196] While the opening call narrative still entails the disciples' literal following of Jesus, 8:12 asserts that those who "follow" Jesus will not "walk in darkness" but will have "the light of life" (i.e., salvation; cf. 10:9–10). The literal and figurative meanings of "following" are used side by side in 13:36–38. There is also a widening from the "following" of Jesus' original disciples to that of every believer.[197] This is especially evident in chapter 10, where Jesus elaborates on the kind of trust relationship that characterizes his relationship with believers individually and corporately. John 12:26 adds to this the notion that following Jesus involves "death" to self-interest (cf. 21:15–23; Synoptics). In life and death, in humiliation and glory, Jesus' disciple is to be with his Master (cf. 14:3; 17:24).

The context of 12:24–26 is one of (Gentile) mission.[198] The Greeks address themselves to the disciples. Indeed, it is the disciples who will mediate access to Jesus—but not now. First comes the "hour" of Jesus' glorification (cf. 12:23). Jesus will be "lifted up" and draw "all people" to himself (12:32–33; cf. 12:24). Thus 12:32 can be taken as an indirect answer to the Greeks' question in 12:21. Paradoxically, it is through his *exaltation* that Jesus will become accessible to the Greeks. Read in connection with 14:12 and 15:16, it may be concluded that the "following" of 12:26 includes the disciples' participation in Jesus' drawing of all people to himself after Jesus has been exalted. John 10:16, too, may imply the disciples' participation in Jesus' future mission to "other sheep" (i.e., Gentiles).

In another lesson on "following," John uses Peter to illustrate the impossibility of an adequate following of Jesus before Jesus' glorification (cf. 13:36–38). Moreover, the final pericope featuring Peter and "the disciple whom Jesus loved" indicates that there are different ways of following the crucified and risen Messiah, and that following Jesus does not *necessarily* entail *physical* death, though it entails "death" to self (12:26).

The other significant term regarding the disciples' mission is that of being "sent." Unlike the term "following," this expression overlaps with Jesus' mission (cf. esp. 17:18; 20:21). In 17:18 ("sent ... into the world"), the point of comparison between the missions of Jesus and his followers appears to be the way they were sent: they were set apart (cf. 10:36), equipped with the Spirit (cf. 1:34–36; 3:34) and sent out. The disciples' mission is set in relation to the world: the disciples are set apart from it (cf. 13:8–14; 15:3), equipped for service, and then sent back into it.

The disciples share with Jesus an otherworldly orientation and the resulting suffering of rejection in the world (cf. esp. 15:18–27). As a dark place alienated from

---

196. See 1:37, 40, 43 and 8:12; cf. 13:13–38.
197. See 1:37–43; 8:12; 10.
198. See 12:20–21; cf. 10:6; 11:49–52.

God,[199] the world nonetheless remains an object of his love (cf. 3:16).[200] While believers must love each other (13:34; 15:12) and be unified (17:11, 22–23), these qualities are presented, not as ends in themselves, but as prerequisites for the believer's mission in the world. Moreover, the "destination" of the church's mission is not primarily defined in geographical but in spiritual terms.

In 20:21, the point seems to be that the mission of Jesus' followers is to be guided by the same kinds of parameters that determined the sender-sent relationship between Jesus and the Father. Also, Jesus is shown to invest the disciples with authority and legitimacy. The more general reference to "sending" ties the disciples' mission to the characteristics of Jesus' relationship to his own sender, the Father. At this stage, Jesus, the paradigmatic "Sent" One (9:7), turns sender. Now Jesus' followers are to embody the qualities characteristic of their Lord during his earthly mission. As Jesus did his Father's will, they have to do *Jesus'*. As Jesus did his Father's works, they have to do *Jesus'*. As Jesus spoke the words of his Father, they have to speak *Jesus'*. Their relationship to their sender, Jesus, is to reflect his relationship with *his* sender.

This highlights the underlying continuity between Jesus and his representatives. The Son's mission does not end with his exaltation to the Father. While the form of fulfillment is to be changed, the mission will continue and be effective. The disciples are commissioned to carry on Christ's work rather than to begin a new one. The Spirit, too, provides a crucial element of continuity between the missions of Jesus and of the disciples: "The risen Lord, in associating his disciples with his continuing mission in the world, bestows the Spirit, through whom his own ministry in the flesh was carried out in the power of God."[201] Finally, Jesus' commission to his followers to forgive or retain sins should probably be seen in the context of people's reception or rejection of Jesus as the Christ, that is, in the context of belief or unbelief in Jesus.[202]

29.6 Conclusion

As the study of the theme of the "new messianic community" in this chapter has shown, the Johannine ecclesiology, when compared with the other canonical gospels, is distinct, even unique. The subject of discussion was the characterization of Jesus' followers: his first followers, the disciples (*mathētai*); the "Twelve"; the widening of the term *mathētēs* to include later followers of Jesus; and the characterization of individual disciples, most notably "the disciple whom Jesus loved" and Peter.

While the term *ekklēsia* ("church" or "community") is not found in John's gospel (but note that it is absent from Mark's and Luke's gospels as well; though see Matt 16:18; 18:17), John represents Jesus as drawing on OT depictions of God's

---

199. Cf. 8:23–24, 34–37; 9:39–41; 15:22; 16:8–11.
200. See the helpful survey by Paul Woodbridge, "'The World' in the Fourth Gospel," in *Witness to the World: Papers from the Second Oak Hill College Annual School of Theology* (ed. David Peterson; Carlisle, UK: Paternoster, 1999), 1–31.
201. Beasley-Murray, *John*, 380.
202. Carson, *Gospel according to John*, 655.

relationship with Israel to characterize his relationship with his followers: the shepherd and his flock (John 10), and the vine and its branches (John 15).

While in the first half of John's gospel Jesus' followers are presented in pedestrian terms akin to the Synoptics, the second half of John's gospel elevates them to responsible agents charged with representing the message of salvation in Jesus the Messiah to the unbelieving world as aided by the Spirit (e.g., 17:18; 20:21). Subsequent to Jesus' return to the Father, they will perform "greater works" (14:12) as they are sent into the world by Jesus in the manner in which Jesus was sent into the world by the Father.

Thus, as I will develop more fully in John 15, Jesus' followers are taken into the mission of the triune God and serve as his divinely commissioned representatives. Initially, Jesus' new messianic community consisted of the Twelve: those who persisted with Jesus when many other disciples fell away (6:70), those who were with him at the Last Supper and in his final hours and were the recipients of his parting instructions (John 13–17), and those who witnessed three resurrection appearances and were commissioned by the risen Jesus (20:19–21:14; though in each case Judas is not a true member of the Twelve, in fulfillment of Scripture; 17:12).

Beyond this, the Twelve served as representatives of the new messianic community, which would also include others who would come to believe in Jesus on account of their message (17:20). Thus, ultimately, the new messianic community is comprised of all who have placed their faith in Jesus on the basis of the apostolic witness, Jew and Gentile alike. This new messianic community is united by faith in Jesus as Messiah, the true and new Israel, the good shepherd and the vine, the one who fulfilled Israel's calling and purpose and, as the Jewish high priest unwittingly prophesied, died for the sins of his people (11:48–51).

D. The Middle (Preamble to Part Two; 13:1–3)

Chapter 13

The Johannine Love Ethic

Bibliography

Balz, Horst. "Johanneische Theologie und Ethik im Licht der 'letzten Stunde.'" Pp. 35–56 in *Studien zum Text und zur Ethik des Neuen Testaments: Festschrift zum 80. Geburtstag von Heinrich Greeven*. Berlin/New York: de Gruyter, 1986. **Burridge, Richard A**. Pp. 285–346 in *Imitating Jesus: An Inclusive Approach to New Testament Ethics*. Grand Rapids: Eerdmans, 2007. **Coloe, Mary L**. "Welcome into the Household of God: The Footwashing in John 13." *CBQ* 66 (2004): 400–15. **Culpepper, R. Alan**. *Anatomy of the Fourth Gospel: A Study in Literary Design*. Philadelphia: Fortress, 1983. **Hays, Richard B**. *The Moral Vision of the New Testament*. San Francisco: Harper, 1996. **Meeks, Wayne A**. "The Man from Heaven in Johannine Sectarianism." *JBL* 92 (1972): 44–72. Idem. "The Ethics of the Fourth Evangelist." Pp. 317–26 in *Exploring the Gospel of John: In Honor of D. Moody Smith*. Edited by R. Alan Culpepper and C. Clifton Black. Louisville: Westminster John Knox, 1996. **Morris, Leon**. "Love in the Fourth Gospel." Pp. 27–43 in *Saved by Hope: Festschrift R. C. Oudersluys*. Grand Rapids: Eerdmans, 1978. **Popkes, Enno Edzard**. *Die Theologie der Liebe Gottes in den johanneischen Schriften*. WUNT 2/197. Tübingen: Mohr-Siebeck, 2005. **Segovia, Fernando F**. *Love Relationships in the Johannine Tradition. Agapē/Agapan in 1 John and the Fourth Gospel*. SBLDS 58. Chico, CA: Scholars Press, 1982. **Smith, D. Moody**. "Ethics and the Interpretation of the Fourth Gospel." Pp. 109–22 in *Word, Theology, and Community in John*. Edited by John Painter, R. Alan Culpepper, and Fernando F. Segovia. St. Louis, MO: Chalice, 2002. **Spicq, Ceslas**. *Agapē in the New Testament*. Vol. 3: *Agapē in the Gospel, Epistles, and Apocalypse of John*. Trans. Marie A. McNamara and Mary H. Richter. St. Louis/London: Herder, 1966. **Stemberger, Günter**. *La symbolique du bien et du mal selon saint Jean*. Parole de Dieu. Paris: Editions du Seuil, 1970. **Van der Watt, Jan G**. "Ethics and Ethos in the Gospel according to John." *ZNW* 97 (2006): 147–76. Idem. "Ethics Alive in Imagery." Pp. 421–48 in *Imagery in the Gospel of John: Terms, Forms, Themes, and Theology of Johannine Figurative Language*. Ed. Jörg Frey, Jan G. van der Watt, and Ruben Zimmerman. WUNT 200.

Tübingen: Mohr-Siebeck, 2006. **Volf, Miroslav.** "Johannine Dualism and Contemporary Pluralism." *Modern Theology* 21 (2005): 189–217.

30 John's Moral Vision

30.1 Introduction: Does John Have an Ethic, and, If So, What Is "Wrong" with It?

What is John's moral vision?[1] Some have difficulty identifying John's ethic or allege a limited interest in moral conduct on John's part.[2] Others, such as Wayne Meeks, go one step further, arguing not only that John's gospel contains no moral system but that what can be gleaned from it "not ... many of us would happily call 'Christian' in a normative sense."[3] In fact, according to Meeks, there are a lot of things that are "wrong" with the fourth gospel as a vehicle of moral formation. (1) John's moral instruction lacks specificity. His only rule is "love one another," and that rule is "both vague in application and narrowly circumscribed, being limited solely to those who are firmly within the Johannine circle."[4]

(2) The Johannine narrative "does not provide a plausible and universalizable [*sic*] model for behavior."[5] Neither Jesus nor his followers are imitable. The disciples "play an almost entirely passive role," while the Johannine Jesus "is too alien to human weakness to provide a convincing model, too much 'the god striding over the face of the earth.'"[6] John does not depict Jesus as living a normal human life or as dying a normal human death. Instead, he shows the victory of Jesus over Satan and the glorification of the Son at the cross as one who is equal to God the Father.

(3) Not only are there no specific rules for behavior or credible models to emulate, John's "narrative is profoundly troubling to rational kinds of moral discourse."[7] In its essence, John's approach to life is "antirational," defying ordinary rationality,

---

1. The material in this section (though not the interaction with Meeks) essentially reproduces my "The Moral Vision of John," *Midwestern Journal of Theology* 4/2 (Spring 2006): 3–23, by permission. The choice of the term "moral vision" is indebted to the title of Richard B. Hays' book, *The Moral Vision of the New Testament* (San Francisco: Harper, 1996). For other treatments of John's ethic, see Jan G. van der Watt, "Ethics and Ethos in the Gospel according to John," *ZNW* 97 (2006): 147–76; János Bolyki, "Ethics in the Gospel of John," *Acta Antiqua* 44 (2004): 99–107; and the work of Meeks referred to later in this paragraph.

2. Frank Matera, *New Testament Ethics: The Legacies of Jesus and Paul* (Louisville: Westminster John Knox, 1996), 92; Wolfgang Schrage, *The Ethics of the New Testament* (Edinburgh: T&T Clark, 1996), 297; Michael Theobald, *Herrenworte im Johannesevangelium* (HBS 34; Freiburg im Breisgau: Herder, 2002), 565; and others cited in Jan G. van der Watt, "Ethics and Ethos," 147, nn. 4 and 5. See also Brian K. Blount, *Then the Whisper Put on Flesh: New Testament Ethics in an African American Context* (Nashville: Abingdon, 2001), 93, who states that "John does not do ethics. Or so it seems."

3. Wayne A. Meeks, "Ethics of the Fourth Evangelist," 317. See the interaction with Meeks in D. Moody Smith, "Ethics and the Interpretation of the Fourth Gospel," in *Word, Theology, and Community in John* (ed. John Painter, R. Alan Culpepper, and Fernando F. Segovia; St. Louis, MO: Chalice, 2002), 109–13; and in Volf, "Johannine Dualism."

4. Meeks, "Ethics of the Fourth Evangelist," 318, citing D. Moody Smith, *Johannine Christianity: Essays on its Setting, Sources, and Theology* (Columbia, SC: University of South Carolina Press, 1984), 178.

5. Meeks, "Ethics of the Fourth Evangelist," 318.

6. Ibid., alluding to a famous characterization of the depiction of Jesus in John's Gospel by Käsemann, *Testament of Jesus* (but see Thompson, *Humanity of Jesus*). See on this point the critique by Volf, "Johannine Dualism," 215, n. 48, who notes that even if Jesus *were* unilaterally presented as divine in John's gospel, the imitation of divinity is a common religious motif, referring to Linda Zagzebski, "The Virtues of God and the Foundation of Ethics," *Faith and Philosophy* 15 (1998): 538–53. What is more, John's depiction of Jesus as a model of self-giving love does not differ substantially (if at all) from the way he is portrayed in the other NT writings.

7. Meeks, "Ethics of the Fourth Evangelist," 319.

teaching subversion in its many forms of metaphor, irony, and double entendre. Subversion, however, cannot be the foundation of ethics.

(4) The dividing line between those on the inside and those on the outside is "shrouded in mystery."[8] Divine election and predestination are inimical to "a morally free decision," which is the essential ingredient of any human ethic. Thus, "whether we will enter ... depends entirely on the choice we make, but the basis of the choice seems entirely arbitrary and beyond our finding out."[9]

(5) John's characterization of "the Jews" carries a strong negative stereotype and stigmatizes them as "children of the devil." While not holding John responsible for gas chambers and the Holocaust, postmodern readers cannot forget the untold horrors associated with such a characterization, and such a gospel can hardly serve as a model of moral discourse. The "voice of the fourth evangelist ... becomes perhaps the most foreign of any in the New Testament," a voice that "is sharply sectarian" and knows nothing about love for one's enemies, and his sectarian stance may at best serve as a challenge to "the world's oppressive orders."[10] "Still," Meeks concludes, "for the shaping of moral sensibilities, this is not the Gospel for all seasons."[11] For models of moral instruction, we must look elsewhere in the NT.

What are we to say in response to Meeks' charge that John does not present an ethic and that what moral instruction is found in his gospel is not only unusable but wrong? (1) While Meeks' point that John does not present a full-fledged ethical system in the sense of a systematic ethical presentation doubtless contains an element of truth, his critique of John's gospel as containing but one rule—that of love—and that this one rule is unduly vague misses the mark. To the contrary, John's "love ethic," as it may be called, reflects careful theological thought on the part of the fourth evangelist and is the product of John's deliberate focalization of all of Jesus' ethical demands in the command to love. In fact, it may be argued that in this John essentially reproduces the OT commandment to love God and one's neighbor, which, in turn, formed the backbone of Jesus' ethical instruction (Matt 22:37–40 pars.; cf. Deut 6:5; Lev 19:18).

Thus, far from being sectarian, John taps into the mainstream of Judaism and Jesus' moral teaching as portrayed in the other canonical gospels. What is more, not only is John's "love ethic" not limited to the sphere of the community; rather, the Johannine "mission" motif strongly suggests that love of enemies is part of the compass of a gospel that speaks of God's love for the world (John 3:16) and calls on its readers to embark on a mission to the world (17:18; 20:21).[12] Thus, John's moral instruction is sufficiently specific and properly in keeping with the ethical core of the OT and of Jesus' teaching.[13]

---

8. Ibid.
9. Ibid., 320.
10. Ibid., 324–25.
11. Ibid., 325.
12. This is unduly minimized by Meeks, "Ethics of the Fourth Evangelist," 322, when he remarks, "While we cannot plausibly speak of this group's having a sense of 'mission' to the world in the aggressive and optimistic sense in which modern Christianity has used that word, it does see itself as presenting, by its own very existence and its own countercultural form of life, 'testimony' to the world." See the critique of Meeks in Volf, "Johannine Dualism," 215, n. 47, who points out that the whole gospel is structured around the affirmation of God's love for the world and the "enactment of divine self-giving love."

13. See Richard Burridge, "Imitating Jesus: An Inclusive Approach to the Ethics of the Historical Jesus and John's Gospel"

(2) Regarding Meeks' objection that the Johannine narrative does not provide a plausible and universalizable model for behavior, it will be argued at length below that the account of Jesus' washing of his disciples' feet provides just such a model that the fourth evangelist calls his readers to emulate. In this regard, Meeks exaggerates the degree to which Jesus is unilaterally presented as divine in John's gospel and unduly neglects his genuine humanity. Meeks also disregards the explicit exhortation by the Johannine Jesus, "I have set you an example that you should do as I have done for you.... Now that you know these things, you will be blessed if you do them" (John 13:15, 17). This clearly constitutes an instance—in fact, as will be argued, the paradigmatic instance—of normative ethical instruction in John's gospel and serves as the focal point of John's love ethic, which is centered on the cross as the supreme display of God's love for the world (3:16), not just the community, though it is, of course, true that Jesus' "own" were the special objects of his love (13:1).

(3) For this reason, it is inaccurate for Meeks to allege that John's moral instruction is merely subversive; it contains a strong positive ethic of love, which the reader is specifically enjoined to emulate. In fact, love is the glue that holds the ethic of this gospel together, and the various literary devices in the Johannine narrative merely serve to underscore the paradoxical nature of various aspects of the drama surrounding Jesus—his "lifting up," which amounted to his exaltation; the trial of Jesus, which constituted in truth the trial of the world; and so on.[14] Far from being merely subversive, John's moral teaching is therefore profoundly constructive.

(4) Meeks is to be commended for his intellectual honesty in recognizing the strong Johannine teaching on divine election and predestination.[15] Indeed, people are said in John's gospel to enter God's kingdom not primarily on the basis of a free human moral choice but on the basis of, to use Johannine parlance, the Father "drawing" people and "giving" them to Jesus. However, the Johannine teaching of the necessity of a prevenient work of God enabling human faith is hardly without parallels in NT teaching (see, e.g., Eph 2:8–9). And while one can appreciate Meeks' difficulty with such a teaching in that it seems to preclude the notion of a "free" human choice for Jesus, there are models that intelligibly explain the existence of divine election and human agency side by side.[16]

(5) Finally, with regard to the negative characterization of "the Jews" in John's gospel, again one can understand Meeks' misgivings. Yet a plausible case can be

---

(paper presented at the Annual Meeting of the SBL; San Diego, CA, November 17, 2007), who writes, "Therefore, while John may not have all the parables and teachings of the kingdom as in the Synoptics, this does not mean that his biographical account 'offers no moral instruction,' to use Meeks' words. The whole portrait of the divine love bringing us truth is full of ethical implications in both words and deeds if we want to know that truth and live in that love. John's ethical challenge is for us to imitate Jesus' self-sacrificial example of the divine love." See more fully Richard Burridge, *Imitating Jesus: An Inclusive Approach to New Testament Ethics* (Grand Rapids: Eerdmans, 2007).

14. See the discussion of irony in chap. 3, sec. 7.4, and of the cosmic trial motif in chap. 11 above.

15. See chap. 12, sec. 26 above for a discussion of these Johannine themes.

16. E.g., Carson, *Divine Sovereignty and Human Responsibility*, who speaks of "compatibilism."

made that John's characterization of "the Jews" in his gospel does not disqualify him from making an important contribution to NT and biblical ethics.[17] While this may be a difficult case to make in the highly sensitized contemporary political climate, on a biblical-theological level John's designation "the Jews" arguably serves as an identification marker for Jesus' opponents, who rejected his messianic claim and who, on a salvation-historical level, fulfilled the rejection of OT Jews and by their rejection opened up the way to believing Gentiles (see esp. 12:37–41).[18]

What Meeks fails to appreciate, therefore, is that for John, "the Jews" is not primarily an ethnic label but a salvation-historical entity.[19] This is brought out well by John Pryor in his important study *John: Evangelist of the Covenant People*. Over against Meeks' earlier article, "The Man from Heaven in Johannine Sectarianism," Pryor notes the prevalence of the mission motif in John's gospel and contends that the Farewell Discourse, for its part, does "not aim to reinforce an isolationist worldview, but to encourage the covenant relation of the community to its Lord."[20]

Miroslav Volf, in particular, provides a powerful rebuttal of Meeks' charges at this point.[21] He notes, first, that Jesus' negative characterization of the Jews in John's gospel is predicated regularly on their charge of Jesus as demon-possessed (John 7:20; 8:48, 52; 10:20) and their effort to kill him (5:18; 7:1, 19, 25, 30; 8:37, 40; 11:53). He notes that there are no negative designations of the Jews prior to the "Sabbath controversy" in chapter 5. Second, when cast in a negative light, "the Jews" in John's narrative are demonstrably not the Jewish people in their entirety but primarily the Jewish authorities. Without exception, "the Jews" refers to concrete persons who are in conflict with Jesus. Third, there are also positive statements regarding Jews in John's gospel, including the characterization of Nicodemus or Jesus' statement that "salvation comes from the Jews" (4:22). Fourth, John's gospel shows that Jesus died for the very Jews who had him crucified, in keeping with the high priest's prophecy (11:49–50). Thus the Jews, as part of the unbelieving world, are shown to be the object of God's love in Christ. It is hard to imagine a more powerful demonstration of an ethic that preaches love for one's enemies.[22]

On the whole, therefore, Meeks is mistaken to suggest that John's voice is "sharply sectarian" and his moral instruction unusable if not erroneous.[23] John's

---

17. See the interaction in Volf, "Johannine Dualism," 213, nn. 29 and 31; and 216, n. 54.

18. See chap. 10 and chap. 11 above (esp. sec. 25.3.1). See also chap. 12, sec. 29.

19. There is a movement among some scholars to translate the Greek word *Ioudaios* by the English word "Judean" rather than "Jew." For a discussion of this issue, see Andreas J. Köstenberger, "Translating John's Gospel: Challenges and Opportunities," in *The Challenge of Bible Translation: Communicating God's Word to the World* (ed. Glen G. Scorgie, Mark L. Strauss, and Steven M. Voth; Grand Rapids: Zondervan, 2003), 353–55.

20. Pryor, *John: Evangelist of the Covenant People*, 165–66; see Pryor's entire discussion, "Sectarianism?" on pp. 164–67. See also Pryor's treatment of the question "An Anti-Semitic Gospel?" on pp. 181–84.

21. Volf, "Johannine Dualism," 198–200.

22. Indeed, as argued in chap. 2, sec. 3.1, John's "dualism" is not static but rather "in motion," allowing for those in darkness to come to the light, for those who are dead to cross over to life, and for those who are children of the devil to become children of God.

23. On the question of whether or not John reflects a "sectarian outlook" see the remarks by Volf, "Johannine Dualism," 212, n. 17, *et passim*.

single-minded focus on love lends his ethic a strong continuity with the teaching of the OT and of Jesus and powerfully connects it with his theology of the cross and other important Johannine themes. John's moral instruction is sufficiently specific; it is profoundly constructive and applicable; and it is cross-centered and has an important missiological thrust. For these reasons we are justified in embarking on a close study of John's "love ethic" below.

30.2 John's Ethic of Love: Introduction

A thorough study of John's gospel in search for the apostle's — and Jesus' — ethic reveals that the best way to encapsulate John's moral vision is by the phrase "the power of love."[24] God, in his love, sent his Son to die so that everyone who believes in him has eternal life (John 3:16–17). Jesus expressed this love for people, and especially believers, to the fullest extent (13:1). Believers, in turn, are to emulate Jesus' example, loving one another so that the world may know God's love through them and believe that God sent Jesus to die for them (13:34–35; 15:10–17; 17:20–25).

This, in a nutshell, is John's moral vision. The following treatment will seek to demonstrate and flesh out this understanding of John's ethic by looking at the interface of two major motifs, love and mission, in John's gospel, with a special focus on the Farewell Discourse, where, as will be seen, John's ethic finds its fullest and climactic expression. My thesis regarding John's moral vision, as developed by an inductive study of John's gospel, is essentially this: at the heart of John's ethic is a call to evangelistic mission that is grounded in God's love for the world and undergirded by communal love and unity.[25]

Before turning to a demonstration of this thesis, however, it is necessary to address and adjudicate several important preliminary matters. First, what is meant by the term "John's" moral vision? In recent years it has been increasingly suggested that behind John's gospel stands a community that traces its origins to the apostle but that is engaged in its own struggle against a nonmessianic Jewish synagogue. This community, which is responsible for John's gospel, it is alleged, was expelled from the synagogue on account of its conviction that Jesus was in fact the Messiah.[26] If the "Johannine community hypothesis" were true, we should speak no longer of *John's* moral vision — except perhaps in a fairly distant sense — but of the moral

---

24. Or, in Hays' words, "living in the present in a way that authentically manifests the love of God in Christ" (*Moral Vision*, 153). For a study of John's love ethic, including the footwashing, in the context of a familial ethos, see van der Watt, "Ethics and Ethos," 158–75.

25. See the brief reflections under the heading "Foundations for the Disciples' Mission: Love and Unity," in Köstenberger, *Missions of Jesus and the Disciples*, 189–90; and the section on "Love within the Community" in Hays, *Moral Vision*, 144–46.

26. The classic expression of this thesis is found in Martyn, *History and Theology*. See also Brown, *Community of the Beloved Disciple*. Unfortunately, Hays' treatment in *Moral Vision*, esp. 146–47, presupposes the Martyn-Brown version of the "Johannine community hypothesis" (see ibid., 157, n. 15), identifying as the life-setting of John's Gospel — and ethics — the "communal crisis of identity" precipitated by the community's expulsion from the synagogue (which, according to Hays, is "referred to three times in the course of the Gospel"). This perspective makes the gospel's "exhortations for love within the community sound less exclusionary and more like an urgent appeal for unity within an oppressed minority community." See also Hays' comments on p. 154.

vision of the *Johannine community* in light of its recent experience of synagogue expulsion. Moreover, the connection with *Jesus'* moral vision would be significantly more remote than if the apostle John were the gospel's author.

This is not the place to engage in a full-fledged critique of the "Johannine community hypothesis."[27] As has been shown at the outset of this volume, this view rests on a precarious foundation and is not able to bear the weight that is put on it by its adherents. Problems associated with the "Johannine community hypothesis" in its various expressions are numerous. They include, first, the illegitimate "mirror-reading," "two-level" hermeneutic practiced by many of its proponents;[28] and, second, the false dichotomy posed between the Synoptics as interested in history and John as concerned with theology.[29] Once these obstacles are removed, it is possible to proceed in the confidence that by looking at John's gospel one will discover not only *John's* ethic, but also a reliable representation of *Jesus'* ethic, albeit refracted through the lenses of John's own perception and theological thought.

Another relevant consideration relates to John's relationship with the Synoptics. It is sometimes claimed that John's ethic differs significantly from that of the other gospel writers. John, it is argued, similar to the Qumran community, stressed the need for mutual love among Jesus' followers, but did not instruct believers to love their neighbor, more broadly defined, as does Luke, or even their enemies, as in the gospel of Matthew.[30] John's vision was sectarian, while that of the other evangelists transcended narrow intracommunitarian concerns.[31]

The problem with this portrayal that is most immediately obvious, however, is the strong emphasis on mission in John's gospel. While not denying the existence of a strong dualism between believers and the world in John, the gospel does not urge hostility or retreat, but rather evangelistic outreach in keeping with Jesus' own practice and in obedience to his parting commission. Hence John famously refers to God's love for the world prompting the sending of his one-of-a-kind Son, and when he tells his fellow believers not to love the world, this relates merely to the allures and temptations emanating from it rather than shutting down the believing community's mission in and to the world.[32] While John's moral vision may therefore be said to be unique and distinctive, it complements that of the other evangelists rather than standing in actual conflict with it.

---

27. See Köstenberger, *John*, 3; and the discussion in chap. 1 above.

28. The original use of this term in found in the writings of J. Louis Martyn, esp. the second edition of *History and Theology in the Fourth Gospel* (1979). Then, as noted above, the method is unfortunately also embraced by Hays, *Moral Vision*, 153–54.

29. See Bauckham, "John for Readers of Mark," in *Gospels for All Christians*, 147–71; Köstenberger, "Jesus as a Rabbi"; and Morris, *Studies in the Fourth Gospel*; and the discussion in chap. 1 above.

30. Hays, *Moral Vision*, 139, cites as examples Käsemann, *Testament of Jesus*, 59; J. L. Houlden, *Ethics and the New Testament* (New York: Oxford University Press, 1973), 36; and Jack T. Sanders, *Ethics in the New Testament* (Philadelphia: Fortress, 1975), 100. See also the discussion in Hays, ibid., 145.

31. Traces of this illegitimate stereotype are found in Hays' speaking of the "strongly sectarian character of the Johannine [moral] vision" (*Moral Vision*, 139) and of conceding that "the sectarian character of this material is undeniable" (p. 140).

32. Having said this, it is clear that John's definition of mission is not that mission is "everything the church is sent into the world to do," as Stott famously wrote in *Christian Mission in the Modern World*, 30, but Spirit-led, evangelistic outreach that preaches forgiveness of sins on account of Jesus' vicarious cross-death. See David J. Hesselgrave, *Paradigms in Conflict: 10 Key Questions in Mission Today* (Grand Rapids: Kregel, 2006).

30.3 The Contours of John's Moral Vision

30.3.1 Problems with an "Incarnational Angle" on John's Moral Vision

As mentioned, an inductive study of John's moral vision yields the result that at the heart of John's ethic is a call to evangelistic mission that is grounded in God's love for the world and undergirded by communal love and unity, a vision that finds its fullest expression in the Johannine Farewell Discourse. Some may argue that a better approach may be to see how the stories John has included demonstrate or embody moral examples that the reader is expected to emulate (what may be called the "incarnational angle" of John's moral vision). After all, it is a literary principle that writers embody or incarnate their meanings, in the present instance ethical meanings, in concrete forms.

While certainly sound in principle, however, in John's case this approach encounters several major obstacles. First, Jesus' "signs" and major discourses in John's gospel are messianic in nature and are designed to support the claim that Jesus is the Son of God sent by the Father. It is therefore unclear how the "signs," which form the backbone of John's presentation of Jesus' earthly ministry to the Jews, can be said to provide a pattern of ethical behavior to be emulated by Jesus' followers. As Richard Hays notes:

> The difficulty, however, is how this formal assertion of Jesus as ethical pattern is to be unpacked in terms of specific behaviors. Jesus in the Fourth Gospel does not actually do much of anything except make grandiloquent revelatory speeches. The actions that he does perform are primarily of a miraculous character: changing water into wine, healing the blind and lame, and raising Lazarus from the dead. Can these serve as patterns for the community's action?[33]

The fact that the term *sēmeion* ("sign") is never used in John's gospel with reference to Jesus' followers (the reference to believers' "greater [works]" than Jesus in John 14:12 notwithstanding) seems to suggest that founding John's ethic on Jesus' "signs" in John's gospel would be mistaken and misguided.[34]

Second, not only the "signs" but also Jesus' major dialogues with individuals in John's gospel are devoted, not primarily to ethical instruction, but to messianic revelation and the impartation of major spiritual truths. In Jesus' conversation with Nicodemus, for example, it is precisely not Nicodemus's moral pedigree or righteousness or lack thereof that Jesus challenges but rather his lack of spiritual rebirth (John 3:3). And while Jesus' conversation with the Samaritan woman contains a moral dimension—his call for her to get her husband, knowing she had engaged in a series of illicit relationships—the climax of the pericope is decidedly not some ethical command or demonstration of moral conduct, but Jesus' messianic self-revelation, "I, the one speaking to you—I am he" (i.e., the Messiah; 4:26).

---

33. Hays, *Moral Vision*, 143.
34. On Jesus' "signs" in John's gospel, see the discussion in chap. 7, sec. 15 above.

For these reasons a focus on the "incarnational angle" in John's stories about Jesus seems to be ill suited for the actual material with which we are confronted in John's gospel. As I have argued at some length in my John commentary, the first twelve chapters of John's gospel are primarily devoted to one end: the demonstration of the failure of Jesus' messianic mission to the Jews owing to massive Jewish obduracy, which, in turn, sets up Jesus' cleansing and instruction of his new messianic community in John 13–17 in anticipation of his exaltation subsequent to his crucifixion. It stands to reason, therefore, that chapters 13–17 may be expected to provide the primary body of material for John's, and Jesus', moral vision as well, and this is in fact what we find.

Nevertheless, we will briefly look at the pericope narrating Jesus' encounters with Nicodemus and the Samaritan woman in John 2:23–3:21 and 4:1–42 to see what, if anything, studying these narratives may add to our understanding of the Johannine ethic. John's narration of the Nicodemus incident spans 2:23–3:15. The conversation is framed with reference to Jesus' performance of signs (3:2). Jesus' own emphasis in his response is on the necessity of spiritual regeneration, which takes up essentially the entire interchange with Nicodemus (3:3–9). Throughout the narrative, there is also an emphasis on Nicodemus's—and, by implication, the Sanhedrin's—ignorance and unbelief. This is indicated by the repeated use of verbs of knowing (3:2, 8, 10, 11) and believing (3:11, 12, 15), mostly in a negative form (cf., similarly, 4:39, 41, 42).

The Nicodemus narrative in 2:23–3:15 is followed by the evangelist's own commentary in 3:16–21. What is most remarkable is that while references to "love" are entirely absent from the actual narrative in 2:23–3:15, the evangelist frames the incident from the outset in terms of "love": "For God so loved the world..." (3:16). A second instance of "love" terminology is found in 3:19, where, in a contrasting reference, people in the world are said to "love" darkness rather than light. Hence what at first appears as a "battle of knowledge" between two Jewish teachers—Nicodemus, "Israel's teacher" (3:10), and Jesus, who is called "rabbi" by Nicodemus (3:2)—is interpreted by the evangelist in terms of the substitutionary atonement provided by a God who "so loved the world" that he sent his one-of-a-kind Son (3:16).

The second narrative, Jesus' encounter with the Samaritan woman in 4:1–42, focuses squarely on the progressive revelation of Jesus' true identity. Jesus is not bothered by Jewish-Samaritan animosity (4:9); he supernaturally knows the woman's past (4:16); and he teaches on the proper way of worship (4:21–24). The climax is found in 4:25–26, where Jesus identifies himself to the woman as the Messiah. While it could doubtless be said that Jesus' actions toward the woman were prompted by love, this is not in fact the point made by John. The pericope does not contain a single instance of "love" terminology. Rather, the emphasis seems to be on truth: those who want to worship God must worship him in spirit and truth (4:23–24), and the Samaritans know that Jesus is "truly" the Savior of the world (4:42).

What do we learn from our study of the Johannine narratives depicting Jesus' encounters with Nicodemus and the Samaritan woman? (1) On the assumption that John's ethic centers on love, this emphasis cannot be easily gleaned from the narratives in John 3 and 4, though the evangelist's commentary on the Nicodemus narrative in 3:16 provides confirmation for our thesis.

(2) This shows the wisdom of a hermeneutic that discerns doctrine on the basis of didactic passages (such as the Farewell Discourse) rather than narrative passages (such as John 3 and 4). On a secondary level, a study of narrative passages may corroborate findings attained by an analysis of didactic material, but it seems problematic to derive one's understanding of John's ethic primarily from narrative material.

(3) The narratives in John 3 and 4 both convey a theocentric or christocentric rather than an anthropocentric perspective. Birth from God, God's love in giving his Son, true worship of God, and Jesus' self-revelation as Messiah frame the Johannine presentation, while human responsibility is circumscribed primarily as "knowing" and "believing." Belief must be based on proper knowledge, and the revelation of this knowledge is found in Jesus, the Son of God and Son of Man.

30.3.2 John's Love Ethic in the Farewell Discourse

The second half of John's gospel opens as follows: "It was just before the Passover Festival. Jesus knew that the hour had come for him to leave this world and go to the Father. Having loved his own who were in the world, he loved them to the end" (13:1). With this preamble the evangelist sets the stage for the footwashing as a paradigmatic—or "hypodeigmatic": the Greek word for "example" in 13:15 is *hypodeigma*—demonstration of Jesus' love for his followers.[35] Hence, before Jesus asks his disciples to do anything, he first performs on them a humble act of service, which, as the evangelist tells us, was prompted and motivated by love.[36]

In the logic of the ensuing narrative, Jesus' act of love, and his teaching that this act was to serve as a model for his followers in their conduct toward one another, constitutes the foundation of his "new commandment" in John 13:34–35: "A new command I give you: Love one another. As I have loved you, so you must love one another. By this everyone will know that you are my disciples, if you love one another." In John's first letter, fulfilling this commandment is elevated as proof that a given person is in fact a believer (1 John 2:7–11; cf. 3:23; 4:19–21; 5:2–3). While the commandment itself is not new, Jesus' point of reference is this: his followers' love for one another is to be grounded in none other than Jesus' own example. Remarkably, this kind of love will serve as the unique mark of Jesus' disciples (13:35). What is more, Jesus washes his disciples' feet *before* Judas's departure, exhibiting love for his enemies (cf. Matt 5:44).

---

35. Hays, *Moral Vision*, 144, calls the footwashing an "enacted parable."

36. For a sensitive reading of the footwashing pericope, see Coloe, "Welcome into the Household of God." Taking her cue from Jan G. van der Watt, *Family of the King: Dynamics of Metaphor in the Gospel according to John* (BIS 47; Leiden: Brill, 2000), Coloe argues that John's narrative unfolds in five stages, portraying Jesus as sharing a meal with the representatives of God's household, in keeping with the tradition of the Greco-Roman banquet or symposium (see Dennis E. Smith, *From Symposium to Eucharist: The Banquet in the Early Christian World* [Minneapolis: Fortress, 2003], 222; see also Holloway, "Left Behind"). The difficulty with this proposal is the implied movement at 14:31 and the "vineyard" discourse in chap. 15, which to many suggests that the meal scene is broken up at this point and the prayer is no longer uttered in the Upper Room.

Later in the Farewell Discourse, Jesus' "love commandment" is reiterated and expanded in 15:9–17, which together with 15:1–8 forms the literary "peak" of the Farewell Discourse: "As the Father has loved me, so have I loved you. Now remain in my love. If you keep my commands, you will remain in my love, just as I have kept my Father's commands and remain in his love.... My command is this: Love each other as I have loved you. Greater love has no one than this: to lay down one's life for one's friends.... This is my command: Love each other." Several observations flow from a study of this unit.

(1) Before Jesus sent his disciples on a mission, he showed them his love. Note the formal parallel between 15:9, "As the Father has loved me, so have I loved you," with the Johannine commissioning passage in 20:21: "As the Father has sent me, I am sending you," which in turn represents the fulfillment of Jesus' final prayer in 17:18. Knowing God's love in his Son precedes the call to Christian service and mission.

(2) The disciples are taken into the loving relationship between God the Father and Jesus the Son. They are the objects of God's love as expressed in Jesus, the Word-become-flesh, who has given full expression to the Father (1:1, 14, 18). Mission will involve proclaiming God's love for the world as expressed in Jesus and inviting people to believe and to be taken into the circle of this loving relationship between Father and Son, which also encompasses all true believers as children of God (1:12).

(3) Believers are called to remain in Jesus' love. They will do so as they "obey his commands," that is, to abide by his teaching and follow his instructions (cf. 8:31; 1 John 2:3–8). Jesus' body of teaching thus becomes a "new law" for believers in keeping with, and yet transcending, the pattern set with the regulations found in the Mosaic law, indicating the fulfillment of Jeremiah's vision that God will write his law on people's hearts in the days of the new covenant (Jer 31:31–34). As Hays writes, "The Law of Moses plays no explicit role in John's moral vision; it is read as prefiguring Jesus, and its meaning is seemingly absorbed into his person."[37] He continues, "Nowhere in John do we find any appeal to the Law as prescriptive of moral conduct; it cannot be assumed that the Torah implicitly remains normative for John's community."[38]

(4) The love of Jesus, which found its expression in the footwashing, is further elaborated in Jesus' statement in 15:13: "Greater love has no one than this: to lay down one's life for one's friends" (cf. 1 John 3:16). Hence the love of the Son expressed at the cross, which, in turn, is an expression of God's love for the world (3:16), is at once the culminating act of the mission of the obedient Son (19:30) and the fullest possible expression of God's love, encapsulated in the following principle: "laying down one's life for one's friends."[39]

This statement broadens the scope of reference beyond the crucifixion to the principle of "laying down one's life" in the sense of self-denying, others-oriented service, in keeping with Jesus' earlier statement in 12:24–26:

---

37. Hays, *Moral Vision*, 138.
38. Ibid., 139.

39. See ibid., 144–45. Hays writes that "Jesus' death is depicted by John ... as an act of self-sacrificial love that establishes the

> Very truly I tell you, unless a kernel of wheat falls to the ground and dies [a veiled reference to the crucifixion], it remains only a single seed. But if it dies, it produces many seeds. Those who love their life will lose it, while those who hate their life in this world will keep it for eternal life. Whoever serves me must follow me; and where I am, my servant also will be. My Father will honor the one who serves me.

While "laying down one's life" for others is therefore not limited to martyrdom, it does include it, which underscores the costly nature of serving others in the community of believers as required by Jesus.[40]

Also, the immediate scope of "laying down one's life," according to Jesus, is "one's friends," that is, his followers, or in the case of believers, other believers. That this is not to be interpreted primarily with regard to the extent of the atonement is made clear by John's statement in 1 John 2:2: "He [i.e., Jesus Christ] is the atoning sacrifice for our sins, and not only for ours but also for the sins of the whole world" (see also John 1:29; 3:16). Rather, Jesus' pronouncement is based on the recognition that the members of his new messianic community are united by a special bond—their shared knowledge of the love of God for them in Jesus (witness the author's self-designation as "the disciple whom Jesus loved"; 13:23 *et passim*)—and that the successful accomplishment of their mission is predicated on their practice of this love within their own community. If they fail to do so, they fail to undergird their verbal witness to Jesus by the visual demonstration of the reality of Jesus' love in the lives of his followers, which undercuts their mission and renders it ineffective. As will be seen further below, loving one another is putting first things first, without reducing believers' obligations exclusively to reciprocal love.

This aspect of Jesus' love commandment is further elaborated in the final major cluster of references to love in the Farewell Discourse (17:20–26), the conclusion of Jesus' final prayer in which he prays for his disciples' future mission to the world. We observe that in 17:23 Jesus includes the world in the scope of his reach when he draws a line from the Father's love for the Son and for believers, to believers' unity, to the world coming to know the Father's love for them through the Son as represented by the community of believers.

It is evident that (1) unity here serves as a virtual synonym for love: if and to the extent that believers love one another, they are unified; when John writes in his first letter that "we know that we have passed from death to life because we love each other" (1 John 3:14), he does so against the dark backdrop of a recent schism in the congregation (2:19) that set off those who failed to love and preserve unity and thereby proved that they were never truly part of the community in the first place.[41] (2) A unified mission presupposes a unified community; conversely, a unified com-

---

cruciform life as the norm for discipleship" (p. 145). See also David Gibson, "The Johannine Footwashing and the Death of Jesus: A Dialogue with Scholarship," *SBET* 25 (2007): 50–60.

40. So rightly Hays, *Moral Vision*, 145. Hays also mentions the "pragmatic spin" given the love commandment in 1 John 3:11, 16–18, where application is made to the issue of economic justice.

41. See Hays, *Moral Vision*, 150.

munity will embark on a unified mission. (3) Just as the Son is a critical link between the Father and the disciples and the world, owing to his obedience and dependence on the Father and his expression of the Father's love to the disciples and the world, so Jesus' followers are a critical link between the Father and the Son on the one hand and the world on the other; yet they are able to fulfill this critical function only if and to the extent that they are unified and engaging in reciprocal, Christlike love. This, in turn, everywhere presupposes the work of the Holy Spirit in believers' lives as the "other helping presence" sent by Jesus from the Father (14:26; 15:26).

So far the focus has been primarily on the presence of "love" language in the Farewell Discourse. A brief screening of "love" terminology in the rest of the gospel will reveal that this relative neglect of other portions of John's gospel has not been a major loss. In fact, the first twelve chapters of John include only three theologically significant instances of the *agap-* word group: 3:16 (by the evangelist), with its reference to God's love for the world, to which repeated reference has been made; and the virtually identical affirmations of the Father's love for the Son in 3:35 (also by the evangelist) and 10:17 (by Jesus). The only remaining instances of the *agap-* word group in John's gospel pertain to Jesus' love for Lazarus (11:5) and for "the disciple whom Jesus loved" (13:23; 19:26; 21:7, 20), and to Jesus' interchange with Peter in the last chapter of the gospel (21:15, 16).[42]

The occurrences of the other major Johannine word for "love," *phileō*, corroborate this pattern of usage but add little to the overall semantic profile.[43] This confirms and convincingly demonstrates that the epicenter of John's moral vision, focusing on love, is found in the Johannine Farewell Discourse. We turn now to a brief study of the integration of John's love ethic with other themes in the Farewell Discourse and the gospel as a whole, and in particular of the interface of John's love ethic with the gospel's mission theme.

30.3.3 *John's Love Ethic in Its Larger Context*

As mentioned, John's love ethic takes its departure from the footwashing at the outset of John 13. This is followed by the strongly contrasting negative example of Judas, who rejects Jesus' love and removes himself from the loving circle of fellowship surrounding Jesus and his disciples. Unlike the other members of the Twelve, Judas did not "remain" in Jesus' love (15:9; cf. 15:2, 6; 13:10–11). The evangelist had hinted at this at the first major juncture indicating the failure of Jesus' mission at the end of chapter 6 (cf. 6:70–71).

Judas's antagonism became even more explicit in his objection to Mary's act of devotion in 12:4–8.[44] Judas's departure is the signal to begin the Farewell Discourse

---

42. Negative references involving "love" are found in 3:19; 5:42; 8:42; and 12:43.

43. The use of *phileō* in 5:20 corresponds to the use of *agapaō* in 3:35. For the references involving *phileō* in 11:3, 36, see the use of *agapaō* in 11:5. With regard to 20:2, see 13:23; 19:26; 21:7, 20. Concerning the use of *phileō* in 21:15–17, cf. the use of *agapaō* in 21:15–16. For the negative references involving *phileō* in 12:25 and 15:19, cf. 3:19; 5:42; 8:42; and 12:43. The references to the Father's love for believers and to believers' love for Jesus involving *phileō* in 16:27 correspond to the references involving *agapaō* in the Farewell Discourse discussed above.

44. For a comparative analysis of John's account of the anointing in relation to the Synoptics see Köstenberger, "Pericopae of Jesus' Anointing."

proper, as is indicated by the prominent transition of 13:30–31: "and it was night." Judas goes out of the "light" into the "darkness," illustrating the rejection of the love ethic (but see 1:5). Subsequent to Judas's departure, Peter's misguided pledge of loyalty furnishes an example of the insufficient nature of human loyalty not undergirded by the Spirit's enablement (13:36–38).

The unit elaborating on Jesus' "new commandment" in 13:34–35, that is, 15:9–17, is preceded by 15:1–8, a section that underscores the importance of sustaining a vital spiritual union with the exalted Christ via the Holy Spirit and forms the literary "peak" of the entire Farewell Discourse. Hence believers' love toward one another, too, must be so empowered.

Finally, the unit following 15:9–17, that is, 15:18–16:4a, contrasts Jesus' command for believers to love one another with the world's hatred toward them. Love among believers will therefore provide a starkly contrasting witness to the world's spiritual darkness. It will also provide a community of support and encouragement as believers together face the world's rejection and hostility. This theme is developed further in John's first letter and particularly in the book of Revelation.

One of the most paradoxical truths held together in John's gospel are the facts, both equally true, that the world hates believers and yet believers are called to and sent on a mission to that same world. God's love-inspired action, mentioned in 3:16, of sending his Son into the world, the very world steeped in darkness and rebellion (cf. 3:19–21), forms the paradigm on which the Christian mission to the world is based. Such love is inexplicable, because not only is it not contingent on the lovability of its object, it acts and persists in the face of abject rejection, even rebellion, of its advances and overtures. As Jesus said elsewhere, "The Son of Man came to seek and to save what was lost" (Luke 19:10). Not only did God in Jesus come to pursue rebellious sinners out of love, he did so in the most sacrificial way imaginable. This attitude of self-humbling and commitment to others-centered service is the message of the footwashing and seeks to be implanted, by the Holy Spirit, also in every believer's heart as a follower of Christ (cf. 12:24–27; 15:18–16:4a).

30.3.4 The Interface between Love and Mission

In the first half of John's gospel, the Father is continually affirmed as the one who sent Jesus, and Jesus as the obedient, dependent sent Son of the Father.[45] But it is in the second half of John's gospel that this portrait of Jesus as the sent Son is made the paradigm for the disciples' mission and predicated on their mutual love and unity. In programmatic passages in 13:16, 20 and 15:20–21, Jesus makes clear that the disciples will serve as his representatives and that in keeping with the *šaliaḥ* principle — "servants are not greater than their master" — people's response to Jesus will be evidenced in their response to Jesus' followers.

---

45. See the uses of *apostellō* and *pempō* in 3:34; 4:34, 38; 5:23, 24, 30, 36, 37; 6:29, 38, 39, 44, 57; 6:16, 18, 28, 29, 33; 8:16, 18, 26, 29, 42; 9:4, 7; 10:36; 11:42. On the Johannine verbs for "sending," see Köstenberger, "Two Johannine Verbs for Sending."

The Johannine mission theme unites the three persons of the Godhead when the Father is said to send the Spirit in Jesus' name (14:26) and the Son is said to send the Spirit from the Father (15:26; cf. 16:7) to aid the disciples in their mission (15:26–27).[46] The convergence between Jesus' sending from the Father and his sending of his followers finds its anticipatory expression in Jesus' final prayer (17:3, 8, 18, 21, 23, 25; see esp. 17:18) and culminates in the Johannine commissioning passage, 20:21–22, which features the three persons of the Godhead once again united in mission: as the Father sent the Son, so the Son now sends his followers; and he does so by giving them his Spirit. As they remain in him and his love by abiding by his teaching, and as they love one another and are united in purpose, Jesus' disciples are sent on a mission to the world.[47]

30.4 Conclusion

John's moral vision is simple yet profound. Knowing the world's spiritual and moral darkness apart from the light, Jesus Christ, John holds out no hope for those without Christ. He does not discuss keeping the law; he does not explicitly address the issue of righteousness other than to urge rejection of sin (1 John 3:6; cf. 3:4–10);[48] he does not engage the issue of works, other than to report Jesus' answer to those who asked him what they must do to perform the works required by God: "The work of God is this: to believe in the one he has sent" (John 6:29).

John's moral vision is simply this: believers must recognize that they are deeply loved by God and must believe in the one God has sent; by believing, they enter into the circle of love existing between the persons of the Godhead, and they also enter in the triune God's purpose and mission: to spread the message of God's love for the world in his Son in the face of opposition and hostility.

Nevertheless, believing oneself loved by God and entering into the triune circle of love is not devoid of moral moorings, which is indicated by John's (and Jesus') use of OT language and particularly the repeated reference to Jesus' "commandments":

- "Whoever has my commands and keeps them is the one who loves me" (14:21)
- "If you keep my commands, you will remain in my love" (15:10)
- "We know that we have come to know him if we keep his commands. Those who say, 'I know him,' but do not do what he commands are liars, and the truth is not in them. But if anyone obeys his word, love for God is truly made complete in them" (1 John 2:3–5)

---

46. See the discussion of John's trinitarian mission theology in chap. 15 below.

47. This is even clearer in 17:18 than it is in 20:21. The natural way to read 20:21–23 is with reference to an evangelistic mission.

48. "Righteous" (*dikaios*) in John's gospel is only the Father (17:25; cf. 1 John 1:9; Rev 15:3; 16:5, 7; 19:2), and the only two instances of the term "righteousness" (*dikaiosynē*) in John's gospel probably have Jesus as a referent (16:8, 10; cf. 1 John 2:1, 29; Rev 19:11; alternatively, reference is made to the world's lack of righteousness; see the discussion in Köstenberger, *John*, 472). The sole exceptions in the Johannine corpus where the *dikaio-* word group refers to righteous actions by believers are found in 1 John 3:7 (positive reference), 10 (negative reference), 12 (Abel); and Rev 22:11.

This may not be in keeping with our definition of morality or ethics.[49] But what does that tell us? It may be an indication that our definition of these matters privileges certain biblical writers—Paul, Matthew—while neglecting others (John). Yet at the core, John's moral vision is at least as valid, and perhaps even more profound, than that of other NT voices. In his simple manner of presentation, John cuts to the heart of a given issue, practicing what one may call a "sanctified reductionism." Nonessentials are stripped away, leaving what is most essential.

In the present case, what is most essential is God's love for a lost world, his sending of his Son to die for humanity on the cross, and people's need to believe in the one God has sent. For those who do, however, the story does not end there. In fact, by believing they embark on a most amazing venture: joining the divine triune mission to the world by being taken into the sphere of the Godhead's love and mission. There is no dichotomy between Jesus being Savior and Lord, no dichotomy between discipleship and evangelism, no dichotomy between salvation and sanctification. All there is is Jesus' commission of his followers to serve as his representatives and proclaim the good news of salvation and forgiveness in Christ and to "go and bear fruit—fruit that will last" (John 15:16).

What is more, with its emphasis on intracommunitarian love and mission to the world, John's gospel also highlights the clearly defined parameters of the community of Jesus' followers on the one hand and of those who do not believe in Jesus on the other. One need not affirm the "Johannine community hypothesis" to realize that this has important social implications as well. Conversion, while spiritual in nature and entailing regeneration (3:3, 5), must be accompanied by confession of Jesus and a transfer of allegiance from one's previous faith community to the new messianic community.

"Secret discipleship" is strongly disparaged (cf. 9:18–23; 12:42–43), and indecision not an option.[50] Evasion of the world's hatred by failing to identify oneself clearly with Jesus and his followers is inconsistent with Christian discipleship and places one outside the pale of the community of believers. Hence, following John's moral vision entails not merely obedience but also courage: a willingness to emulate the example of Jesus, who was prepared to lose, and in fact did lose, his life for the sake of others, only to enter eternal life, which by virtue of our identification with Jesus is ours already in the here and now and will be ours for all eternity.[51]

---

49. Cf. Hays, *Moral Vision*, 146, who comments regarding 1 John 4:20–21, "This may not be the last word to be said about Christian ethics, but it is not a bad place to begin."

50. See Köstenberger, "What Is Truth?" Cf. Hays, *Moral Vision*, 148, 155–56.

51. On John's eschatology, see Hays, *Moral Vision*, 148–50, 152–53.

Chapter 14

JOHN'S THEOLOGY OF THE CROSS

BIBLIOGRAPHY

De Boer, Martinus C. *Johannine Perspectives on the Death of Jesus.* CBET 17. Kampen: Kok, 1996. **Dennis, John A.** *Jesus' Death and the Gathering of True Israel: The Johannine Appropriation of Restoration Theology in the Light of John 11.47–52.* WUNT 2/217. Tübingen: Mohr-Siebeck, 2006. **Frey, Jörg.** "Die 'theologia crucifixi' des Johannesevangeliums." Pp. 169–238 in *Kreuzestheologie im Neuen Testament.* Ed. Andreas Dettwiler and Jean Zumstein. WUNT 151. Tübingen: Mohr-Siebeck, 2002. **Frey, Jörg, and Jens Schröter**, eds. *Deutungen des Todes Jesu im Neuen Testament.* WUNT 181. Tübingen: Mohr-Siebeck, 2005. **Grigsby, Bruce H.** "The Cross as an Expiatory Sacrifice in the Fourth Gospel." *JSNT* 15 (1982): 51–80. **Knöppler, Thomas**. *Sühne im Neuen Testament: Studien zum urchristlichen Verständnis der Heilsbedeutung des Todes Jesu.* WMANT 88. Neukirchen-Vluyn: Neukirchener, 2001. **Koester, Craig R.** "Why Was the Messiah Crucified? A Study of God, Jesus, Satan, and Human Agency in Johannine Theology." Pp. 163–80 in *The Death of Jesus in the Gospel of John.* Ed. Gilbert van Belle. BETL 200. Leuven: Leuven University Press/Peeters, 2007. Idem. "Crucifixion and Resurrection." Pp. 108–33 in *The Word of Life: A Theology of John's Gospel.* Grand Rapids: Eerdmans, 2008. **Matera, Frank J.** "'On Behalf of Others,' 'Cleansing,' 'Return': Johannine Images for Jesus' Death." *LS* 13 (1988): 161–78. **Metzner, Rainer.** *Das Verständnis der Sünde im Johannesevangelium.* WUNT 122. Tübingen: Mohr-Siebeck, 2000. **Morris, Leon.** "The Atonement in John's Gospel." *CTR* 3 (1988): 49–64. **Müller, Ulrich B.** "Die Bedeutung des Kreuzestodes Jesu im Johannesevangelium: Erwägungen zur Kreuzestheologie im Neuen Testament." *KD* 21 (1975): 48–71. **Nicholson, Godfrey Carruthers.** *Death as Departure: The Johannine Descent-Ascent Schema.* SBLDS 63. Chico, CA: Scholars Press, 1983. **Osten-Sacken, Peter von der.** "Leistung und Grenze der johanneischen Kreuzestheologie." *EvT* 36 (1976): 154–76. **Schlund, Christine.** *"Kein Knochen soll gebrochen warden." Studien zu Bedeutung und Funktion des Pesachfests in Texten des frühen Judentums und im Johannesevangelium.* WMANT 107. Neukirchen-Vluyn: Neukirchener, 2005. **Smith, Robert H.** "Exodus Typology in the Fourth Gospel." *JBL* 81 (1962): 329–42. **Söding, Thomas.** "Kreuzerhöhung: Zur Deutung des Todes Jesu nach Johannes." *ZTK* 103 (2006): 2–25. **Stuhlmacher, Peter.** "Das Lamm Gottes—eine Skizze," Pp. 529–42 in *Geschichte–Tradition–Reflexion: Festschrift für Martin Hengel zum 70. Geburtstag.* Vol. 3. Ed. Hubert Cancik, Hermann Lichtenberger, and Peter Schäfer. Tübingen: Mohr-Siebeck, 1996. **Thüsing, Wilhelm.** *Die Erhöhung und Verherrlichung Jesu* *im Johannesevangelium*. NTAbh 21. Münster: W. Aschendorff, 1979. **Turner, Max**. "Atonement and the Death of Jesus in John: Some Questions to Bultmann and Forestell." *EvQ* 62 (1990): 99–122. **Van Belle, Gilbert**. *The Death of Jesus in the Fourth Gospel*. BETL 200. Leuven: Leuven University Press/Peeters, 2007.

31 The Nature of Jesus' Coming

31.1 Introduction

The discussion of John's *theologia crucis* will take its point of departure from a treatment of John's portrayal of Jesus as the one who came into the world and returned to the Father.[1] As will be seen, "going back to the Father" is the major Johannine euphemism for the crucifixion, showing that the cross was not the end but only a station on Jesus' "return trip" back to heaven, where the Father exalted and glorified him after completing his mission as the obedient Son.[2] Metaphorically, this "coming and going" (messianic language in the OT) is depicted as the Son of Man's descent and ascent, which requires special consideration of the Johannine theology surrounding the "Son of Man" as part of our quest to delineate the Johannine theology of the cross.

31.2 Coming and Going and Descent–Ascent

The terminology of coming and going is consistently used throughout John's gospel.[3] Occasionally, descent–ascent language is interspersed. The latter terminology should therefore be viewed as supplementary to the broader conceptuality of coming and returning.[4] While sending terminology focuses more on the human side of Jesus' mission, coming and going terminology appears to emphasize Jesus' divine provenance and destination.

The first reference to Jesus' coming into the world is found in the introduction to the Gospel: "the true light ... was coming into the world" (John 1:9). The statement is reiterated in 3:19: "Light has come into the world." In both cases, the evangelist links this assertion with the fact that the light was not received but rejected (cf. 1:5, 9, 11; 3:19). This theme of rejection, with resulting judgment, is also expressed in 9:39, where Jesus indicts those who, due to spiritual pride, fail to receive him: "For judgment I have come into this world, so that the blind will see and those who see will become blind." Jesus' healing of a blind man thus becomes an acted parable of salvation as well as of judgment.

---

1. The material in this section adapts some of the material from chap. 3 of my *Missions of Jesus and the Disciples*, and is used by permission. For a survey of the history of scholarship, see John A. Dennis, "Jesus' Death in John's Gospel: A Survey of Research from Bultmann to the Present with Special Reference to the Johannine Hyper-Texts," *CurBR* 4 (2006): 331–63 (by "hyper-texts," Dennis means 6:51; 10:11, 15; 11:50–52; and 15:13). See also Gilbert van Belle, "The Death of Jesus in the Fourth Gospel. Colloquium Biblicum Lovaniense LIV (2005)," *ETL* 81 (2005): 567–79.

2. See, e.g., Thomas Söding, "Kreuzerhöhung: Zur Deutung des Todes Jesu nach Johannes," *ZTK* 103 (2006): 2–25.

3. See Köstenberger, *Missions of Jesus and the Disciples*, 90–92.

4. For this reason Nicholson's terminology, "descent–ascent schema," which for Nicholson comprises all of the references to Jesus' coming and going as well as descent–ascent language in John's gospel, appears to be inadequate (*Death as Departure*, *passim*).

Again, 12:46–47, in the concluding section of the Book of Signs, links Jesus' coming into the world with the concept of light: "I have come into the world as a light, so that no one who believes in me should stay in darkness.... For I did not come to judge the world, but to save the world." Other references to Jesus' "coming into the world" are found in 16:28, where Jesus summarizes his mission as follows: "I came from the Father and entered the world; now I am leaving the world and going back to the Father"; and in 18:37, where Jesus asserts before Pilate: "In fact, the reason I was born and came into the world is to testify to the truth."[5]

Apart from these occurrences of "coming into the world" terminology, there are also numerous references to Jesus' "coming" and "going." In his introduction to the Farewell Discourse the evangelist writes, "Jesus knew that the hour had come for him to leave this world and go to the Father.... Jesus knew that the Father had put all things under his power, and that he had come from God and was returning to God" (13:1, 3). The remainder of the Farewell Discourse includes a number of references to Jesus' return ("going") to the Father (see 14:4, 5, 12, 28; 16:5, 7, 10, 17, 28; 17:11, 13; cf. 7:35–36; 8:14, 20–21).[6] There are also references to a brief temporary return of Jesus (his resurrection appearances: 14:18, 28; 20–21), and to Jesus' "coming again" (14:3; 21:22) after ascending to the Father (cf. 20:17).[7]

The different kinds of references to Jesus' coming and going in John's gospel may be grouped thematically as follows.[8] First, there are references to Jesus' "coming into the world" (1:9; 3:19; 9:39; 12:46; 16:28; 18:37). Second, sometimes the term "come" occurs absolutely (10:10; 12:47; 15:22). In both kinds of uses one finds occasionally an attached purpose statement (cf. 9:39; 10:10; 12:46, 47; 18:37). The fact that instances of both phrases at times carry a purpose statement, as well as the use of "coming into the world" in 12:46 and "come" in 12:47 in parallel fashion, suggests that these two groups are equivalent. The emphasis seems to lie in Jesus' coming from another sphere (i.e., heaven; cf., e.g., 3:31) into the world to accomplish a purpose.

Third, there are instances where "come" is used parallel to sending (cf. 5:43; 7:28). In those cases, the context indicates that the contrast is between one's coming in one's own authority or on one's own initiative and one's having been sent. Thus these instances of "come" do not allude to an otherworldly provenance as such.

---

5. John 18:37 would certainly not fail to provide great reassurance to Jesus' followers at the time John's gospel was written and began to circulate in their own struggle to testify to the truth in a world just as hostile to them as it was to Jesus (cf. 15:18–27).

6. See Ulrich B. Müller's thesis that 7:31–35 and 8:21–24 represent an "Entrückungstheologie," which draws on OT Enoch (cf. Gen 5:24) as a precedent of one who was pleasing to God and who was therefore taken up to be with God ("Die Bedeutung des Kreuzestodes Jesu im Johannesevangelium: Erwägungen zur Kreuzestheologie im Neuen Testament," *KD* 21 [1975]: 48–71). But there are many obvious differences between Enoch and John's presentation of Jesus. See also Roland Mörchen, "'Weggehen.' Beobachtungen zu Joh 12,36b," *BZ* 28 (1984): 240–42, who argues that *aperchomai* in 12:36b, besides referring to Jesus' literal leaving, also carries connotations of the completion of Jesus' public ministry, so that 12:36b

should be located on two different levels of meaning (p. 241).

7. Contra, Moule, "Individualism of the Fourth Gospel."

8. For a classification of Jesus' *ēlthon*-sayings in John, see Arens, *Elthon-Sayings*, 303–7. Arens notes that there are twelve *ēlthon*-sayings in John, six in the aorist (8:14; 9:39; 10:10b; 12:27, 47; 15:22) and six in the perfect (5:43; 7:28; 8:42; 12:46; 16:28; 18:37). The purposes of Jesus' coming are addressed (with *ēlthon*) in the aorist in 9:39; 10:10b; 12:47 (salvation/judgment); in the perfect in 12:46 (cf. 1:9; 3:19; 8:12; light); and 18:37 (witness to truth). Of these purpose sayings, 9:39; 12:46; and 18:37 include the phrase "into the world." The following sayings relate to the origin of Jesus: 5:43; 7:26b–29; 8:14b; 16:27b–28a. References to Jesus' coming that are not in the first person singular include 1:9, 11; 3:2, 19; 7:27, 31, 41, 42. Note also the chart on pp. 321–22 comparing the meaning of *erchesthai* and *apostellō/pempō*.

Fourth, there are references where coming and going occur together or one term is used while implying the other (cf. 7:35; 8:14, 21–22; 13:33; 14:2, 3, 12, 28; 16:7, 28; 17:11, 13). The emphasis of this kind of usage appears to be on the cyclical dimension of Jesus' mission, that is, his return to the place from where he came. What this category has in common with the first two is a reference to Jesus' otherworldly provenance.[9]

It seems best to understand the varied terminology as composing one conglomerate picture of a coming and returning, descending and ascending Messiah whose purpose on earth is the accomplishment of a task. While the emphasis of John's sending terminology appears to be on Jesus' relationship with his sender as well as on the fulfillment of OT expectations,[10] "coming and going" language may be viewed as accentuating Jesus' heavenly origin. The divine purpose embodied in Jesus' coming, Jesus' accomplishment of his divine mission, and his return to heavenly glory with the Father are primarily in view.

Jesus' coming and going as well his descent and ascent may be viewed as part of an overarching "journey theme" in John's gospel.[11] After three trips "up" to Jerusalem, Jesus' fourth trip to Jerusalem is presented by John as indeed a journey back to the Father by way of the cross.[12] The cross is thus in John's gospel viewed as part of a journey, a "way" (cf. 14:6).[13] This way, first travelled by Jesus, is also to be followed by his disciples (cf. 12:26). According to John, the cross is a station along the way to Jesus' return to the Father's glory rather than a place of shame and humiliation. By presenting the cross as a station along the way to the Father's glory and as the culmination of the Son's obedience to the Father, John maintains a thoroughly theocentric focus. It is not human need that is the ultimate reference point of Jesus' mission, but rather the Father's will.

Apart from "coming and going" terminology, John's gospel also uses the word pair "descend" and "ascend" to characterize Jesus' mission.[14] However, unlike "coming and going," the terms "descend" and "ascend" are used infrequently in John's gospel and should therefore be seen as subordinate to the portrait of Jesus the Messiah as coming into the world and returning to the Father. The use of descent–ascent language clusters around two characterizations of Jesus: the Son of Man (3:13; 6:62; cf. 20:17?), and the bread of life (6:33, 38, 41, 42, 50, 51, 58).[15]

---

9. For a critique of studies of John's portrayal of Jesus as coming and going or of his descent and ascent, see Köstenberger, *Missions of Jesus and the Disciples*, 123–25.

10. The exception to this is the technical term "the Coming One," on which see the discussion of the Messiah and his signs in chap. 7 above.

11. Nicholson, *Death as Departure*.

12. See ibid., 145.

13. See also Margaret Pamment, "Path and Residence Metaphors in the Fourth Gospel," *Theology* 88 (1985): 118–24; Mathias Rissi, "Der Aufbau des vierten Evangeliums," *NTS* 29 (1983): 48–54.

14. These terms are also used for the Spirit in 1:33 and 34, and for angels in 1:51. On descent–ascent, cf. W. Groussow, "La glorification du Christ dans le quatrième évangile," in *L'Évangile de Jean: Études et problèmes* (ed. Marie-Émile Boismard et al.; RechBib 3; Bruges: Desclée de Brouwer, 1958), 131–45; Martin McNamara, "The Ascension and Exaltation of Christ in the Fourth Gospel," *Scr* 19 (1967): 65–73; Nicholson, *Death as Departure*; Ernest M. Sidebottom, "The Ascent and Descent of the Son of Man in the Gospel of St. John," *AThR* 39 (1957): 115–22; Charles H. Talbert, "The Myth of a Descending-Ascending Redeemer in Mediterranean Antiquity," *NTS* 22 (1976): 418–40; idem, "Appendix: Descending-Ascending Redeemer Figures," 265–84; Thüsing, *Erhöhung und Verherrlichung Jesu*.

15. In light of this limited use of descent–ascent terminology and the distinct Jewish flavor of both contexts in which this

31.3 The Son of Man

The term "Son of Man," with its intriguing conflation of the concepts of humanity and its possible Danielic apocalyptic overtones, holds in tension the divine and human aspects in Jesus' person and mission.[16] It is not necessary to agree with Rudolf Bultmann or Charles Talbert who point to the Gnostic descending–ascending revealer myth as the background for the Johannine descent–ascent motif. The Son of Man in John's gospel fulfills the following roles: he is the gate of heaven of Jacob's vision (1:51); he alone descended and ascended (3:13; cf. 6:62); he is to be lifted up and glorified (3:14; 8:28; 12:34); he is judge (5:27); and he provides the "bread of life," that is, his flesh (6:27, 53).[17] This considerable range in the gospel's description of the Son of Man appears too broad to be easily accomodated by the kind of generalization postulated by Bultmann and Talbert.

Writers disagree in their general assessment of the emphasis in the gospel's "Son of Man" concept. Francis Moloney finds the humanity of Jesus accentuated: "The Johannine Son of Man is the human Jesus, the incarnate Logos, he has come to reveal God with a unique and ultimate authority and in the acceptance or refusal of this revelation the world judges itself."[18] George Mlakuzhyil regards the Johannine "Son of Man" as fulfilling a bridge function between the titles "Messiah" and "Son (of God)": "Because 'the Son of Man' has a mysterious heavenly origin (3,13; 6,62), this Christological title may be considered a theological bridge between the Messianic title 'the Christ' and the divine title 'the Son' (of God)."[19]

Most helpful is the discussion by Delbert Burkett, who provides a separate treatment for those passages in John's gospel where "Son of Man" terminology is linked with descent–ascent language. According to Burkett, there is not just one single source for the idea of the descending and ascending Son of Man in John's gospel but rather three different OT passages: for John 1:51, Gen 28:12; for John 3:13, Prov 30:4; and for John 6:26–65, Num 11:9 and Isa 55:10–11.[20] Burkett also notes that part of the OT passages underlying John 3:13 and 6:26–65 are associations with the word of Yahweh and with God himself.[21] If Burkett is correct, at least in general, one should avoid the tendency of forcing the various Johannine references

---

terminology is used, the suggestion that Gnostic conceptualities constitute the background for this terminology appears improbable. Schnackenburg, *Johannesevangelium*, 4:119–31, in the search for a possible background of the term "bread of life" investigates Jewish mysticism, Qumran-Essenism, Pharisaic rabbinism, and Jewish Diaspora Hellenism. Noting that there appears no instance of the term "bread of life" in rabbinic writings, Schnackenburg finds the sole parallel in terminology in the Jewish-Hellenistic work *Joseph and Aseneth*. He conjectures that the writer of this work and John may both have drawn on the Jewish concept that the manna gives a part in the heavenly life and that it promises the life to come (cf. 3:16, 36; 5:24, 26; 6:63, 68; 8:12; 10:10; 11:25; 14:6; cf. *2 Bar.* 29:8). Cf. Peder Borgen, *Bread from Heaven: An Exegetical Study of the Concept of Manna in the Gospel of John and the Writings of Philo* (NovTSup 10; Leiden: Brill, 1965), who sets forth the thesis that the passage represents a midrash on Ps 78:24 as quoted in John 6:31.

16. See already the discussion of the Son of Man in chap. 9, sec. 20.4 above.

17. See Sidebottom, "Ascent and Descent."

18. See Francis J. Moloney, *The Johannine Son of Man* (Biblioteca di Scienze Religiose 14; 2nd ed.; Rome: Libreria Ateneo Salesiano, 1978), 220.

19. See George Mlakuzhyil, *The Christocentric Literary Structure of the Fourth Gospel* (AnBib 117; Rome: Pontifical Bible Institute, 1987), 270–71.

20. See Delbert Burkett, *The Son of Man in the Gospel of John* (JSNTSup 56; Sheffield: JSOT, 1991), 38; but see the review by Douglas R. A. Hare in *JBL* 112 (1993): 158–60.

21. Ibid., 48.

to a descending and ascending Son of Man into one explanatory grid. In fact, it may be best to treat these instances separately from designations of Jesus as "Son" or "Son of God."

As Wayne Meeks observes, the *pattern* of descent and ascent is already introduced in John's gospel in 1:51, albeit of angels, as is the term Son of Man. Both of these concepts recur in 3:13 with reference to Jesus.[22] The Son of Man who descends (*ho katabas*) is in turn presupposed in chapter 6.[23] It appears, therefore, that John wants the readers of his gospel to understand the pericope regarding the descending bread of life in the context of the descending and ascending Son of Man. Indeed, the purposes of both figures are identical: the giving of life (cf., e.g., 3:15; 6:33). Notably, the bread of life pericope is framed by references to the Son of Man in 6:27 and 62. These two passages, 3:13 and 6:30–59, also develop the concept of the Son of Man's "exaltation": he will be "lifted up" (3:13), giving his "flesh" "for the life of the world" (6:51; cf. 6:52–58). In 6:53, reference is even made to "the flesh of *the Son of Man*" and to "his blood."

In connection with the recurrence of the term "lifted up" (*hypsoun*) in 8:28 and 12:32, 34 (in both contexts also with "Son of Man" language), one is further able to trace John's gradual development of the theme of the lifted-up Son of Man for the purpose of giving life.[24] The "lifting up" of the Son of Man on the cross combines two elements of Jesus' mission. As Barnabas Lindars observes, John "adopts an unusual word for 'lifted up,' which normally refers to exaltation in an honorific sense, and thereby contrives to combine the two notions of crucifixion and exaltation in a single ambiguous word."[25] Thus the "lifting up" of Jesus is not to be understood merely in terms of Jesus' exaltation but also as the completion of the obedient, dependent mission of the Son sent by the Father.[26]

---

22. See Meeks, "Man from Heaven," 51; cf. Meeks' treatment of John 3:13 on pp. 52–57.

23. See ibid., 57.

24. See especially Thüsing, *Erhöhung und Verherrlichung*, 3–40. Thüsing sees Jesus' mission in John's gospel proceed along two stages: his being "lifted up" and his being "glorified" (see esp. pp. 311–15). For a generally competent treatment of the Johannine "lifted up sayings," see Nicholson, *Death as Departure*, 75–144, and especially the summary on pp. 141–44. Nicholson argues that "since all allusions to the crucifixion contained in the LUS [i.e., 'lifted-up sayings'] are embedded in sections which deal with the return of Jesus to the Father, they emphasize that the crucifixion of Jesus is to be understood in terms of exaltation/ascent/return.... Thus, what might appear to have been an ignominious death, was in reality a return to glory" (pp. 142 and 144). Nicholson's final point is doubtless true; however, regarding his contention that the crucifixion of Jesus is to be understood in terms of exaltation, one may ask if John in fact drains Jesus' death *completely* of notions of atonement and suffering. The exaltation of the Son of Man in John's gospel is also discussed by Antoine Vergote, "L'exaltation du Christ en croix selon le quatrième évangile," *ETL* 28 (1952): 5–23, who argues that Jesus' crucifixion and resurrection are merged in John's gospel. See also Burkett, *Son of Man in John*, 120–28; Bampfylde, "More Light on John 12,34"; George R. Beasley-Murray, "John 21,32–34: The Eschatological Significance of the Lifting Up of the Son of Man," in *Studien zum Text und zur Ethik des Neuen Testaments: Festschrift zum 80. Geburtstag von H. Greeven* (ed. Wolfgang Schrage; Berlin/New York: de Gruyter, 1986), 70–81.

25. See Barnabas Lindars, *Jesus Son of Man: A Fresh Examination of the Son of Man Sayings in the Gospels in the Light of Recent Research* (Grand Rapids: Eerdmans, 1983), 146.

26. This is insufficiently recognized by some who talk of "lifting up" in John exclusively in terms of exaltation. See, e.g., Nicholson, *Death as Departure*. Forestell, *Word of the Cross*, 81, is balanced here: "The cross is ... the way by which Jesus returns to the Father.... On the cross Jesus fulfills the mission for which he was sent into the world." It should also be noted that the bread of life discourse is precipitated in John's gospel by people's failure to understand the sign Jesus had done in feeding the multitude. Indeed, the "food that endures to eternal life, which the Son of Man will give you" (6:27), is the bread of life (cf. 6:35, 48), that is, Jesus, who is also the Son of Man. One also notes the interweaving of sending terminology with references to the bread of life's descent (cf. 6:29, 38–39, 57).

Wayne Meeks finds in the descent–ascent pattern a "cipher for Jesus' unique self-knowledge as well as for his foreignness to the men of this world" (cf. 3:8; 7:23–29, 37–52; 8:14; 9:29; 19:9).[27] He states categorically, "in every instance the motif points to contrast, foreignness, division, judgment," maintaining that "the descent and ascent of the Son of Man thus becomes not only the key to his identity and identification, but the primary content of his esoteric knowledge which *distinguishes* him from the men who belong to 'this world.'"[28] Indeed, "in this manner the descent, as a 'coming into the world,' is clearly identified as the judgment of the world (9:39, but adumbrated already in 3:14–21)."[29] As Eugen Ruckstuhl contends, however, chapters 3 and 6 should be viewed in the light of assurances in John's gospel that everyone can come to Jesus and is welcome (cf. 3:16; 6:37; 12:32; etc.).[30]

31.4 Conclusion

Since sending terminology is a feature pervading the entire fourth gospel while the theme of the descent of the bread of life is only found in chapter 6, one should seek to understand the descent motif in the larger context of the gospel's sending terminology. The Son of Man's descent and ascent as well as the bread of life's descent are to be seen in the context of the obedient, dependent Sent One, who came into the world for the purposes outlined above. Yet the opposite is true as well. As Meeks observes, "Ch. 17 as a whole is only intelligible within the descent/ascent framework, for it is the summary 'de-briefing' of the messenger who … has accomplished his work in the lower regions and is returning."[31] The descent–ascent motif should therefore be allowed to make its own contribution to the mission theology of John's gospel and not be totally subsumed under sending terminology.

Finally, the question arises whether the crucifixion and resurrection are linked in John's gospel with sending language or with coming and going/descending and ascending terminology. While these events may be included in the "work" of the obedient Sent One (cf. 4:34; 17:4), it appears that the connections of the crucifixion and resurrection with descent–ascent language by way of *hypsoun* are more pronounced. In light of these observations, it is possible to conclude that perhaps the most central feature of the Johannine mission concept (i.e., the sending of the Son) is put into perspective by other mission terminology such as "coming into the world" or descent/ascent language.[32] Moreover, it is apparent that these terms emphasize the eschatological character of Jesus' coming. John blends sending language with

---

27. Meeks, "Man from Heaven," 60. In general, Meeks' analysis of the Johannine descent–ascent pattern provides many helpful insights (pp. 46–66). But when Meeks launches into his own sociological application of the gospel's textual data, his treatment becomes increasingly speculative (pp. 67–72).

28. Ibid., 67 and 60–61.

29. Ibid., 61.

30. See Eugen Ruckstuhl, "Abstieg und Erhöhung des johanneischen Menschensohnes," in *Jesus und der Menschensohn: Für Anton Vögtle* (ed. Rudolf Pesch and Rudolf Schnackenburg; Freiburg im Breisgau: Herder, 1975), 339, in response to Meeks.

31. See Meeks, "Man from Heaven," 66.

32. On the relationship between coming and returning terminology and descent–ascent language, see Meeks, "Man from Heaven," 63: "the identity of Jesus … in … the ascent/descent motif … is bound up with the pattern of his coming from heaven and going back there."

"coming and going" terminology, also developing the latter metaphorically by way of descent and ascent language.

32 The Nature of Jesus' Work

32.1 Introduction

The question regarding the nature of Jesus' work according to John's gospel becomes significant in the light of the link between the works of Jesus and of his followers established in 14:12. The first issue of importance is whether the work of Jesus according to John includes both revelatory and redemptive aspects. The second matter requiring clarification is whether this aspect or these aspects are tied to unique christological characterizations or tasks in John's gospel, such as the working of signs or the incarnation for Jesus' work of revelation or his life-giving cross-death for Jesus' redemptive work. If the elements of Jesus' work are indeed tied to unique christological designations, the contribution of the disciples should be seen not as participation in Jesus' revelatory and redemptive work in a primary sense of the term, but rather as a witness to the work already accomplished by Jesus. Thus the task of the disciples would be perceived more humbly, and a line would be drawn between the original contribution of Jesus and the subordinate function of the disciples.

In other words, the question needs to be answered whether John is concerned to reserve for Jesus an ontological uniqueness. If so, it may still be said in a *secondary* sense that the disciples participate in Jesus' revelatory and redemptive work, but they should be considered as doing so only on the basis of Jesus' unique and complete work and mission. The relation between the missions of Jesus and of his followers, while involving elements of continuity, would then have to be seen in the light of this fundamental dissimilarity in person, role, and function.

Once again, however, it is possible that the line between Jesus' work and the works of his followers is not drawn so absolutely. The following discussion will first address the issue whether Jesus' work in John's gospel is comprised of elements of revelation *and* redemption or whether it is solely revelatory in nature. Then the question will be asked whether these aspects of Jesus' work are in John's gospel tied to certain christological formulations.

32.2 Narrative Survey

The subject of the nature of Jesus' work is directly addressed in 3:17: "For God did not send his Son into the world to condemn the world, but to save the world through him" (cf. 12:47). It probably is the evangelist himself who describes the purpose of Jesus' mission as follows: "that whoever believes in him shall not perish but have eternal life" (3:16). The giving of life by Jesus may be the most consistently stated purpose of Jesus' mission in John's gospel.[33] This terminology, besides in 3:16,

---

33. Cf. James McPolin, "Mission in the Fourth Gospel," *ITQ* 36 (1969): 118: "the primary purpose, to which all others are subordinated, is to confer life" (cf. 3:16–17 and 10:9–10: salvation; 8:12: light; 14:6: truth).

is also found in 6:57; 10:10; and 17:2 (cf. 5:24). In different settings, such as the Bread of Life Discourse (6:57–58), the Good Shepherd Discourse (10:7–10), and the Farewell Discourse (17:2–4), the purpose for Jesus' mission is equally said to be the giving of life.

It is remarkable that in all these passages (3:16–17; 6:57–58; 10:7–10; 17:2–3), reference is made in the immediate context to Jesus' giving of his own life for the salvation of others (cf. 14:6). The "giving" of God's Son in 3:16, a possible allusion to the *Aqedah* of Genesis 22, follows hard on Jesus' reference to the serpent in the wilderness: "Just as Moses lifted up the snake in the desert, so the Son of Man must be lifted up, that everyone who believes may have eternal life in him" (3:14–15). This "lifting up" of the Son of Man, while still somewhat enigmatic in John 3, is later made more explicit: it refers to Jesus' death on the cross (cf. 12:32–33). The statement in 6:57–58 regarding the "bread [of life] that came down from heaven" is preceded by a reference to the flesh and blood of the Son of Man (6:53–56). Both of these passages (3:13–17 and 6:53–58) feature descending/ascending terminology.

Both passages are also developing OT themes regarding Israel's wilderness wanderings and God's gracious provision. One thinks of the introduction to the gospel, where the grace given through God by Moses is related to the grace given through God by Jesus (cf. 1:17). One also is reminded of the introduction's Logos Christology and one of its possible theological antecedents, Isa 55:11.[34] The third passage speaking of Jesus' giving of his life, John 10:7–10, speaks of Jesus' giving of his own life for others in terms of the "good shepherd," who lays down his life for the sheep (10:11–18; cf. Ezekiel 34; Zechariah 9–14; and Isaiah 53; cf. John 15:13).[35] Finally, Jesus' farewell prayer is preceded by Jesus' prediction that "a time is coming and in fact has come when you will be scattered, each to your own home. You will leave me all alone. Yet I am not alone, for my Father is with me" (16:32).

The glorification of the Son mentioned in 17:1–5 harks back to statements made in 12:23–33. There the "lifting up" of the Son of Man, mentioned before in 3:14 and 8:28, is finally explicitly identified with the kind of death Jesus was going to die. The pericope's introductory statement, 12:23, also bears a resemblance to the language of 17:1–5: "The hour has come for the Son of Man to be glorified." The passage is immediately followed by Jesus' prediction: "Very truly I tell you, unless a kernel of wheat falls to the ground and dies, it remains only a single seed. But if it dies, it produces many seeds" (12:24).[36]

---

34. Note further Wis 16:20: "Instead of these things you gave your people food of angels, and without their toil you supplied them from heaven with bread ready to eat, providing every pleasure and suited to every taste."

35. Cf. France, *Jesus and the Old Testament*, building on Paul Lamarche, *Zacharie IX–XIV: Structure litteraire et messianisme* (Paris: Librairie Lecoffre, J. Gabalda, 1961). See also Johannes Beutler, "Der alttestamentlich-jüdische Hintergrund der Hirtenrede in Johannes 10," in *The Shepherd Discourse of John 10 and Its Context* (ed. Johannes Beutler and Robert T. Fortna; SNTSMS 67; Cambridge: Cambridge University Press, 1991), 18–32.

36. On Jesus' death on the cross in John's gospel, see esp. Theophil Müller, *Das Heilsgeschehen im Johannes-Evangelium: Eine exegetische Studie, zugleich der Versuch einer Antwort zu Rudolf Bultmann* (Zürich/Frankfurt am Main: Gotthelf, 1961); Müller, "Bedeutung des Kreuzestodes Jesu"; Peter von der Osten-Sacken, "Leistung und Grenze der johanneischen Kreuzestheologie," *EvT* 36 (1976): 154–76; Johannes Riedl, *Das Heilswerk Jesu nach Johannes* (Freiburger Theologische Studien 93; Freiburg im Breisgau: Herder, 1973).

Overall, Jesus' mission is presented in John's gospel as one of "giving life" by giving his own life for others. Mission terminology is found prominently in all four passages: "descending and ascending" in 3:13; "sending" in 3:17 and "coming into the world" in 3:19; "sending," "descending and ascending" in 6:29–62; "coming" in 10:10; and "sending" in 17:3. The larger contexts of chapters 10 and 17 reveal further instances of mission terminology: that is, in the case of chapter 10, "bringing" (10:16) and "following"; in the case of chapter 17, "coming" and further instances of "sending." This shows that the Son's "giving of his life" for the sins of the world is at the heart of the mission of God, which in John's gospel is shown to have a trinitarian dimension and which, in turn, becomes the basis for the mission of the new messianic community to the world (17:18; 20:21).[37]

32.3 Revelation and/or Salvation

One's assessment of John's presentation of Jesus' work seems to depend to a significant extent on one's view of the gospel's presentation of the person of Jesus.[38] If one finds that in John's presentation of Jesus, Jesus' *divinity* predominates, one will likely conclude that Jesus' work of *revelation* is tantamount. If one notes in John a significant strand of presenting Jesus as human as well as divine, one is more likely to detect also references to Jesus' work of *salvation*.[39]

Rudolf Bultmann contends, "The thought of Jesus' death as an atonement for sin has no place in John."[40] He argues that for John, the plight of human beings is alienation from God and existence in unbelief, darkness, and ignorance of God. Humanity does not need an appeasing sacrifice but a revealer, light, and the knowledge of God. Jesus provides for these needs, not through the cross but through a ministry ranging from incarnation to glorification. The cross is simply a transition to glory. The one "work" Jesus has come to do is to *reveal*.[41] This work is accom-

---

37. See chap. 15 below.

38. On the nature of Jesus' work in John's gospel, see Max Turner, "Atonement and the Death of Jesus in John: Some Questions to Bultmann and Forestell," *EvQ* 62 (1990): 99–122. See also the relevant contributions by Rudolf Schnackenburg, "Ist der Gedanke des Sühnetodes Jesu der einzige Zugang zum Verständnis unserer Erlösung durch Jesus Christus?" in *Der Tod Jesu: Deutungen im Neuen Testament* (QD 74; ed. Karl Kartelge; Freiburg im Breisgau: Herder, 1976), 205–30; Johannes Beutler, "Die Heilsbedeutung des Todes Jesu im Johannesevangelium nach Joh 13:1–20," in *Der Tod Jesu*, 188–204; Grigsby, "Cross as an Expiatory Sacrifice"; Leon Morris, "The Atonement in John's Gospel," *CTR* 3 (1988): 49–64; Müller, "Bedeutung des Kreuzestodes Jesu"; Georg Richter, "Die Deutung des Kreuzestodes Jesu in der Leidensgeschichte des Johannesevangeliums (Jo 13–19)," *BibLeb* 9 (1968): 121–36; and Jean Zumstein, "L'interprétation johannique de la mort du Christ," in *The Four Gospels 1992: Festschrift Frans Neirynck* (BETL 100; ed. F. van Segbroeck, C. M. Tuckett, G. van Belle, and J. Verheyden; Leuven: Leuven University Press, 1992), 2119–38.

39. Bultmann, further developed by Forestell, who view the Johannine Jesus as revealer, and Käsemann, who believes to find in John a docetic Jesus, both deny that John considers Jesus' work also as redemptive. Cf. Bultmann, *Gospel of John*, 1971; idem, *Theology of the New Testament*, 2:49–69; idem, "Die Bedeutung der neuerschlossenen mandäischen und manichäischen Quellen für das Verständnis des Johannesevangeliums," in *Johannes und sein Evangelium* (WF 82; ed. Karl Heinrich Rengstorf; Darmstadt: Wissenschaftliche Buchgesellschaft, 1973 [1925]), 402–64; Forestell, *Word of the Cross*; Käsemann, *Testament of Jesus*. For a critique of Bultmann and Käsemann, see Thompson, *Humanity of Jesus*; Leon Morris, "The Jesus of Saint John," in *Unity and Diversity in New Testament Theology: Essays in Honor of George E. Ladd* (ed. Robert A. Guelich; Grand Rapids: Eerdmans, 1978), 37–53.

40. See Bultmann, *Theology of New Testament*, 2:54.

41. Note, however, that revelation does not appear to be as major a theme in John's gospel as is Jesus' "giving of life." The words *phōtizō* (1:9), *phainō* (1:5), *apokalyptō* (12:38), and even the rather mundane word *deiknymi* (2:18; 5:20; 10:32; 14:8, 9; 20:20) are used rather infrequently. The word *horaō* occurs more often (1:18, 34, 39, 50; 3:11, 32, 36; 4:45; 5:37; 6:2, 36, 46; 8:38, 57; 9:37; 11:40; 14:7, 9; 15:24; 16:16, 17, 19, 22; 19:35, 37; 20:18, 25, 29).

plished by signs and discourses that interpret them. The Johannine sin, according to Bultmann, is ignorance; the Johannine salvation is revelation of the knowledge of God.

Terence Forestell, seeking to modify Bultmann's thesis, states the aim of his work plainly, namely, "to show that the proper Johannine theology of salvation does not consider the death of Jesus to be a vicarious and expiatory sacrifice for sin."[42] He begins by attempting to establish the Bultmannian thesis that redemptive revelation is the central theme of Johannine theology. But while Bultmann claims that Jesus effectively only revealed that he is the revealer, Forestell understands revelation as the apocalyptic disclosure of salvation in Jesus.[43] What is more important, while Bultmann sees the cross in John's gospel simply as a stepping stone on Jesus' way to glory, Forestell views it as the focal point of the revelation of God's love for humankind. He points to the three Johannine references to the "lifting up" of Jesus (cf. 3:14–15; 8:28–29; 12:32) and to the movement of the Johannine narrative toward the "hour" of Jesus' glorification.

Forestell denies that Jesus' cross-death is presented as sacrificial in passages such as 6:51 or 10:15, arguing that "Jesus' death is a revelation to men that God loves them with the self-devotion of the good shepherd."[44] In sum, for Forestell, the cross is central to John as revelation, not as an objective event of atonement. The reference to forgiveness in 20:23 Forestell considers a later addition, and the assertion in 1:29 that Jesus is "the Lamb of God" is understood by him as a mere cultic metaphor.[45]

For these reasons Forestell concludes that Theophil Müller was right in criticizing Bultmann's view that the death of Jesus has no salvific meaning for John, but wrong to give it the character of a vicarious expiation for sin. Rather, according to Forestell, "the evangelist understands the cross as the culminating act of a revelatory process in which God manifests himself to men and bestows upon them his own divine life."[46]

On the other side of the issue, Bruce Grigsby contends that "through the use of 'Akedah' [1:29; 3:16; 19:17], Paschal [1:29; 19:14, 29, 36], and 'living water' [19:34; cf. 4:10–15; 7:37; 13:10] themes, the Evangelist has clearly endorsed the cultic rationale wherein sin is cleansed by either the outpoured blood of the sacrificial victim or the cultic washing with 'living water.'"[47] He goes on to argue:

> However, alongside the obvious revelatory themes just noted, the casual reader of the Fourth Gospel must also recognize that the Evangelist conceived of an expiatory rationale, however "johannized," behind Christ's death. Salvation in

---

42. See Forestell, *Word of the Cross*, 2; see also Fortna, *Fourth Gospel and Its Predecessor*, 227, who maintains that the soteriological dimension of Jesus' death is entirely missing from John's gospel.

43. Forestell, *Word of the Cross*, 42.

44. Ibid., 76.

45. See ibid., 149, 161–62, 165–66, 194–95. See also the assessment by William Loader, *The Christology of the Fourth Gospel* (BBET 23; Frankfurt am Main: Peter Lang, 1992), 13, 93–146; and Nicholson, *Death as Departure*, 2–9.

46. See Forestell, *Word of the Cross*, 191.

47. See Grigsby, "Cross as Expiatory Sacrifice," 62.

the Fourth Gospel is presented not only as the bestowal of eternal life, but also as a state of existence wherein sin is eliminated and judgment is escaped; and though an expiatory rationale between Christ's death and sin's removal is not as explicitly spelled out as in the Pauline literature, there are sufficient hints throughout the Gospel to suppose that the Evangelist endorsed such a rationale.[48]

George Carey, too, argues that far from being an isolated statement, John 1:29 introduces a theme that recurs frequently in John's gospel (i.e., in John 3; 4; 6; 10; and in 12:24).[49] Jesus is the Lamb of God, God's Son sent to accomplish his Father's will and to redeem humankind, the expiation of the sins of the whole world.[50] As Carey contends, "In this breathtaking notion that Jesus is sinbearer of the world the evangelist announces a full-blooded concept of the atonement which is of importance to our interpretation of the cross."[51]

Max Turner criticizes Forestell for casting salvation by revelation and salvation by sacrificial atonement as mutually exclusive rather than embracing François-Marie Braun's view that "salvation by faith in the Word and salvation by the sacrifice of the Lamb (or by the blood) are two stages in the process of salvation."[52] Pointing to 1 John 2:2, Turner demonstrates that in Johannine thought, sin broke fellowship with God and required an atoning sacrifice (*hilasmos*). In fact, Turner argues that a combination of the two views — namely, the cross as an objective atoning event *and* as such the high point of redemptive revelation — provides a more coherent explanation of the place of the cross in John than Forestell's position does.[53]

Turner asks, "If the cross is merely a revelation of God's love, and not a sacrifice of atonement, *why is it that salvation*, for John (on Forestell's understanding), *can only be bestowed after the cross?*"[54] This author maintains, "The view Forestell opposes (namely that Jesus must effect objective redemption for sins at the cross before there can be redemption mediated by revelation and received subjectively in faith) could at least explain *why*, for John, Jesus' redemptive revelation can only become effective *after* the 'glorification.'"[55]

But the sharpest question is this one: "If the cross does not accomplish something objectively for us, *how* is it Jesus' giving of his life 'for us'; and *how* is it a revelation of *God's love for us?*"[56] Why was Jesus' *death* chosen as the focal point of the revela-

---

48. See ibid., 52. Reference is made to Müller, "Bedeutung des Kreuzestodes Jesu"; Beutler, "Heilsbedeutung," 188–205; and Siegfried Schulz, *Das Evangelium nach Johannes* (13th ed.; Göttingen: Vandenhoeck & Ruprecht, 1975), 237–38.

49. See George L. Carey, "The Lamb of God and Atonement Theories," *TynBul* 32 (1981): 97–122.

50. Ibid., 112 and 114. Carey notes that Schnackenburg interprets 1:29 in terms of a vicarious sacrifice while Dodd, Barrett, and Brown do not (pp. 117, 120). See also the excellent treatment of 1:29 by Carson, *Gospel according to John*, 148–51.

51. See Carey, "Lamb of God," 121. See further Frank J. Matera, "'On Behalf of Others,' 'Cleansing,' 'Return': Johannine Images for Jesus' Death," *LS* 13 (1988): 161–78. Matera deals with the gospel's use of the preposition *hyper* with reference to Jesus' death (pp. 164–70), the footwashing (pp. 170–72), and Jesus' exaltation and return (pp. 173–77). While Matera's discussion is helpful at many points, he concedes too much when he concludes, "The Fourth Evangelist may not explain Jesus' death as an expiatory sacrifice for sin, but he does view this death as a genuine self-sacrifice on behalf of others" (p. 177).

52. See Turner, "Atonement and Death of Jesus," 113; quoting Braun, *Jean le théologien*, Vol. 4: *Sa théologie: Le mystère de Jésus-Christ* (Paris: J. Gabalda, 1966), 172.

53. See Turner, "Atonement and Death of Jesus," 115.

54. Ibid.

55. Ibid., 116.

56. Ibid.

tion of God's love for humankind? Following Forestell's line of reasoning, one may well consider this mode of revelation arbitrary. Certainly it may seem capricious that God would choose as mode for his revelation a death as cruel as Jesus' if other modes of revelation would have equally served God's purpose (i.e., revealing his love).

As Turner rightly observes, Forestell, by excluding sacrificial atonement as a possible explanation for Jesus' death, creates an interpretational vacuum that he is unable to fill. While Forestell rightly focuses on the cross as central to Johannine soteriology, and while he correctly views the cross as a supreme revelation of God's love in John's gospel, he errs in ruling out an objective atonement accomplished by Jesus' cross-work. The Baptist's references to the "Lamb of God" and the references to Jesus' giving of his life for his sheep in the Good Shepherd Discourse are best explained by viewing the cross as achieving atonement for sin.[57] As Turner concludes, "John's ... emphasis on the cross as salvific revelation was intended to be understood as complementary to the traditional objective explanations rather than as a denial of them."[58]

32.4 Implications

The history of the debate of the nature of Jesus' work in John's gospel has often been one of extremes and reaction.[59] While it seems inappropriate to deny that John's gospel is entirely free from the notion of salvation through sacrificial atonement, it is apparent that this aspect of Jesus' work is not focused upon as much as in other NT writings.[60] One should therefore be careful not to overstate one's case for the presence of atonement motifs in John's gospel.[61] Generally, John seems to assume and presuppose the notion of substitutionary sacrifice and atonement rather than elaborating on these elements as much as the other evangelists. Especially if John knew (of) the Synoptic Gospels and wrote to supplement rather than to duplicate them, it seems reasonable to expect him to build on their tradition rather than simply to repeat it.[62]

John appears to regard the nature of Jesus' work as unique and set apart from the activity of Jesus' followers.[63] According to John, Jesus' cross-death was part of the accomplished mission of the Son who was sent by the Father, as well as a station

---

57. See Dennis, *Jesus' Death and the Gathering of True Israel*; Stuhlmacher, "Lamm Gottes"; Frey, "*Theologia crucifixi*," 169–238, esp. 197–98, 201; Metzner, *Verständnis der Sünde*, 131; and Thomas Knöppler, *Sühne im Neuen Testament: Studien zum urchristlichen Verständnis der Heilsbedeutung des Todes Jesu* (WMANT 88; Neukirchen: Neukirchener, 2001), 49.

58. See Turner, "Atonement and Death of Jesus," 122. See also the use of "blood" language in 1 John 1:7; 5:6, 8. Many see the emphasis on atonement in 2:2; 4:10 as a response to those who hold the view that Forestell finds in John's gospel.

59. See, e.g., Morris, "Atonement in John," for an example of a reaction to Bultmann (Morris does not refer to Forestell). While Morris helpfully summarizes John's teachings on sin, judgment, and Jesus' death, he does not fully acknowledge the distinctiveness of the gospel's presentation of Jesus' death and its significance. Morris's essay thus has the effect of seeking to approximate John's treatment to that of the Synoptics while perhaps not fully appreciating the distinctiveness of John's perspective on the cross.

60. See Grant R. Osborne, "Redactional Trajectories in the Crucifixion Narrative," *EvQ* 51 (1979): 92, who points out that John has removed the details that suggest the horror of the crucifixion: the wine mixed with myrrh, the cry of dereliction and the Elijah account, the darkness, and the taunts of the bystanders.

61. See Müller, "Bedeutung des Kreuzestodes Jesu," 63.

62. See the discussion in chap. 16, sec. 34 below.

63. See Baumeister, "Tod Jesu und die Leidensnachfolge," 84, who writes, "The uniqueness of Jesus in his work and in his death is the main theme of the entire gospel" (my translation).

on Jesus' return to the one who had sent him.[64] It is also the Son's exaltation and the return to his preexistent glory (cf. 12:23; 17:1, 5, 24). Finally, John's theology of the cross may be particularly designed to illumine for his readers the notion of a crucified Messiah. Doubtless this was a serious obstacle to faith for Jesus' own contemporaries, and the cross remained a major stumbling block for potential Jewish converts in John's day. With regard to the work of Jesus' followers, both the revelatory and redemptive aspects of Jesus' work in John's gospel are tied to the unique personal characteristics of Jesus to such an extent that his followers can be said to participate in these only in a secondary sense.[65]

32.5 Conclusion

Working from the "middle" of the Johannine narrative toward the end, I have attempted in the present chapter, following a treatment of the Johannine love ethic in the previous chapter, to discuss the Johannine theology of the cross. We have seen that John's *theologia crucis* is predicated upon his portrayal of Jesus as the preexistent one who came into this world, accomplished his mission, and returned to his sender, God the Father. A parallel conceptuality was shown to be that of the descending and ascending Son of Man. While John presents Jesus' work significantly in terms of revelation, he also makes clear that Jesus came to provide redemption. Thus both aspects of Jesus' work ought to be held together.

The preamble to Part 2 of the Johannine drama makes clear that for Jesus, the crucifixion was but a station on his return to the Father (13:1). It was also the supreme occasion at which God's love for the world was revealed (13:1), the footwashing serving as a proleptic expression of this perfect love God has for his own. Hence Part 2 of John's gospel, including the Passion Narrative, presents Jesus already from the vantage point of his impending exaltation with the Father, depicting the crucifixion as the Son's glorification. The Jews' opposition is anticipated to be a thing of the past, their unbelief having been absorbed in the world's rejection of its Creator. Thus the Johannine exalted Jesus braces for his mission to the world as he equips his followers to bear witness in the power of the Holy Spirit.

---

64. On the Johannine "departure theme," see Nicholson, *Death as Departure*.

65. See the discussion of John's trinitarian mission theology in chap. 15 below.

Chapter 15

JOHN'S TRINITARIAN MISSION THEOLOGY

BIBLIOGRAPHY

Bosch, David J. *Transforming Mission: Paradigm Shifts in Theology of Mission.* Maryknoll, NY: Orbis, 1991. **Erdmann, Martin.** "Mission in John's Gospel and Letters." Pp. 207–26 in *Mission in the New Testament: An Evangelical Approach.* Ed. William J. Larkin Jr. and Joel F. Williams. Maryknoll, NY: Orbis, 1998. **Hesselgrave, David J.** *Paradigms in Conflict: 10 Key Questions in Mission Today.* Grand Rapids: Kregel, 2006. **Köstenberger, Andreas J.** "The Contribution of the General Epistles and Revelation to a Biblical Theology of Religions." Pp. 113–40 in *Christianity and the Religions: A Biblical Theology of World Religions.* EMSS 2. Ed. Edward Rommen and Harold Netland. Pasadena, CA: William Carey Library, 1995. Idem. *The Missions of Jesus and the Disciples according to the Fourth Gospel.* Grand Rapids: Eerdmans, 1998. **Köstenberger, Andreas J., and Peter T. O'Brien.** *Salvation to the Ends of the Earth: A Biblical Theology of Mission.* NSBT 11. Downers Grove, IL: InterVarsity Press, 2001. **McPolin, James.** "Mission in the Fourth Gospel." *ITQ* 36 (1969): 113–22. **Okure, Teresa.** *The Johannine Approach to Mission.* WUNT 2/31. Tübingen: Mohr-Siebeck, 1988. **Schnabel, Eckhard J.** *Early Christian Mission.* 2 vols. Downers Grove, IL: InterVarsity Press, 2004. **Wright, Christopher J. H.** *The Mission of God: Unlocking the Bible's Grand Narrative.* Downers Grove, IL: InterVarsity Press, 2006.

33 JOHN AND MISSION

33.1 Introduction

"For God so loved the world that he gave his one and only Son, that whoever believes in him shall not perish but have eternal life" (3:16).[1] John's entire gospel is pervaded by this divine mission: God, the Father, in his love sending Jesus, his Son, to save all those who believe in him, for eternal life.[2] The Spirit, too, is shown to play an important part in Jesus' mission as well as in the mission of his followers, jointly

---

1. This section builds on chap. 8 in Andreas J. Köstenberger and Peter T. O'Brien, *Salvation to the Ends of the Earth: A Biblical Theology of Mission* (NSBT 11; Downers Grove, IL: InterVarsity Press, 2001). See also "John's Trinitarian Mission Theology," *SBJT* 9/4 (2005): 14–33; and chap. 9 in *Father, Son and Spirit*, portions of which (pp. 149, 151–58) are used by permission.

2. John's letters contribute little to the mission theme in that they deal primarily with the departure of the secessionists (1 John) and other local matters (2–3 John). However, this does not mean that these documents are sectarian. In 1 John, for example, John writes that Jesus "is the atoning sacrifice ... for the sins of the whole world" (1 John 2:2) and that "the Father has sent his Son to be the Savior of the world" (4:14).

witnessing with them (15:26–27) and empowering the community's proclamation of forgiveness and salvation in Jesus (20:22–23).

The discussion here seeks to demonstrate the following dual thesis: (1) John's mission theology is an integral part of his presentation of Father, Son, and Spirit; and (2) rather than John's mission theology being a function of his trinitarian theology, the converse is in fact the case: John's presentation of Father, Son, and Spirit is a function of his mission theology. After a brief summary of John's presentations of Father, Son, and Spirit, with particular attention to their role in mission,[3] we will discuss the way in which John's trinitarian theology culminates in several strategic references to mission involving the persons of the triune Godhead toward the end of the gospel. Father, Son, and Spirit all contribute to God's mission to the world.

33.2 The Father

While the notion of God as Father is not common in the Hebrew Scriptures, in John's gospel "Father-Son" is the dominant, controlling metaphor for Jesus' relationship with God. The two persons of God the Father and the Son are thoroughly and inextricably intertwined. Jesus derives his mission from the Father and is fully dependent on him in carrying it out. The imagery of "father" and "son" plainly draws on Jewish cultural expectations related to father-son relationships, especially those pertaining to only sons.[4]

The emphasis on the Father as the one who sent Jesus and who witnesses to him portrays him as the Authorizer and Authenticator of Jesus. Emphatically, it is Jesus himself who refers to God as "the" Father and in close to twenty instances even as "his" Father. "The Father" is Jesus' natural—almost unselfconscious—way of referring to God. The climactic reference to the Father in the context of John's trinitarian mission theology is found in the context of the commissioning scene, where Jesus affirms, "As the Father has sent me, I am sending you" (20:21).

33.3 The Son

As developed at length elsewhere,[5] John represents Jesus' mission in three distinct yet related ways: (1) Jesus as the sent Son; (2) Jesus as the eschatological shepherd-teacher; (3) Jesus as the one who comes into the world and returns to the Father (descent–ascent). Jesus' work in John's gospel is described in terms of "signs" performed as part of his ministry to "the Jews" (John 1–12) and of "works" performed "from the Father." Everything Jesus says and does is presented under the rubric of the revelation of God and of his glory, including even the cross.

With regard to the first aspect of his mission, Jesus' mission as the sent Son significantly entails the gathering of the new messianic community and its commissioning for its mission to the world (20:21). As mentioned, in this respect Jesus' union with the Father forms the basis for believers' union in their mission, which places the Father-Son

---

3. See chap. 9 above.
4. See especially Köstenberger, *Missions of Jesus and the Disciples*, 96–121.

5. Ibid., *passim*.

relationship under the rubric of mission as well. Especially in the Farewell Discourse, it becomes clear that the disciples are taken into the love and unity of the persons of the Godhead as responsible agents and representatives of Jesus the sent Son.

One way in which Jesus' dependence on the Father is expressed in John's gospel is through prayer directed to the Father by the Son. When feeding the multitudes, Jesus is shown to give thanks (6:11; cf. 6:23, where the phrase "the Lord" reveals hindsight). When about to raise Lazarus, Jesus directs a short prayer of thanksgiving to the Father (11:41–42). When about to be arrested and crucified, Jesus petitioned the Father not to take him out of this situation, but to glorify his name (12:27–28). Finally, at the end of the Farewell Discourse, Jesus offered a lengthy prayer to the Father, reporting to him that he had accomplished his mission on earth and that he was ready to return to him (chap. 17). As a result, his followers would be able to direct believing prayer to Jesus, once he was in his exalted position (14:13–14, 16; 15:7, 16; 16:23–27; cf. 1 John 3:21–23; 5:14–15).[6]

With regard to the second aspect of Jesus' mission, Jesus as the eschatological shepherd-teacher, this accentuates his role as the messianic shepherd and teacher who gathers the new messianic community, cleanses it (i.e., the footwashing and the removal of Judas the betrayer in 13:1–30), and prepares it for its mission. This aspect is evident especially in Jesus' Good Shepherd Discourse (chap. 10) and in his commissioning of Peter at the end of the gospel (chap. 21). Against the backdrop of an entire set of OT messianic images and expectations, Jesus' mission is presented as part of an eschatological framework that shows him as inaugurating the messianic age in which "all" will "be taught by God" (6:45; cf. Isa 54:13). Jesus' mission of gathering God's children "into one" community (11:52) continues after his ascension as the new messianic community, indwelt by Father, Son, and Holy Spirit, is formed into a community whose love is a magnetic force to a watching world (13:35; 17:20–23).

With regard to the third aspect of Jesus' mission, Jesus as the one who comes into the world and returns to the Father (descent–ascent), this marks out Jesus as uniquely being the Word coming into the world (the incarnation, 1:14) and being sent by God on a mission, accomplishing this earthly mission, and as returning to his sender (e.g., 13:3; 16:28; 17:4; cf. Isa. 55:11–12). While the first aspect, the mission of the sent Son, focuses more on the horizontal dimension, the third, Jesus as coming into the world and as returning to the Father, lays more stress on the vertical dimension of Jesus' descent and ascent.[7]

There is no need to trace the narrative outworking of these motifs here. Since "Father" and "Son" language are inextricably intertwined in John's gospel, this has already been done in the respective chapters on the "Father" and the "Son" above. Suffice it to say that Father, Son, and Spirit are shown to be united in the messianic mission of the Son, distinct in personhood yet one in purpose, actively collaborating

---

6. For a study of prayer in the Johannine writings, see Michael Bryant, "A Study of Prayer in the Johannine Writings" (Ph.D. dissertation; Wake Forest, NC: Southeastern Baptist Theological Seminary, 2008). See also W. Bingham Hunter, "The Prayers of Jesus in the Gospel of John" (Ph.D. dissertation; Aberdeen, Scotland: University of Aberdeen, 1979).

7. See, e.g., the Bread of Life Discourse in chapter 6 or the "Son of Man" in the "lifted-up sayings" (3:13; 8:28; 12:32).

to bring about the new people of God, whose identity is centered on faith in Jesus as Messiah and Son of God. This new people of God, in turn, on the basis of their identification with Jesus and their commission from him, are sent on a mission to the world overseen by the exalted Jesus and empowered by the Spirit.

33.4 The Spirit

Undisputed references to the Spirit in the first half of John's gospel are few.[8] In every case where the Spirit is clearly in view, the reference relates to the Spirit's role in Jesus' ministry (1:32–33; 3:34; 6:63; 7:39). This sets up the pattern of the Spirit's remaining on Jesus, which in the second half of the gospel is transferred to believers in Jesus. While John's treatment of the Spirit in the first half of the gospel largely resembles that of the Synoptics, his adoption of a postexaltation vantage point leads to a vastly enhanced portrayal of the Spirit in the Farewell Discourse. As noted, references to the Spirit in the second half of John's gospel increase dramatically, both in number and prominence, in keeping with the Spirit's pivotal role in the disciples' mission subsequent to Jesus' departure and return to God the Father. Specifically, the Spirit is referred to as the Spirit of truth (14:17; 15:26; 16:13) and as the Holy Spirit (14:26; 20:22; cf. 1:33) as well as by the adumbration *paraklētos* or "helping presence" (cf. 14:16, 26; 15:26; 16:7).

Significantly, reference to the Spirit is repeatedly part of a trinitarian pattern that presents God the Father, Jesus, and the Spirit jointly (or in relationship to one another) at work in the lives of believers. Jesus' reference to the Spirit as "another *paraklētos*" in 14:16, for example, indicates that the Spirit's presence with the disciples will replace Jesus' encouraging and strengthening presence with them while on earth (cf. 14:17). When the Spirit comes to dwell in believers, it is as if Jesus himself takes up residence in them (14:18). This relieves a primary concern for Jesus' first followers in the original setting of the Farewell Discourse: Jesus' departure will not leave them as orphans; just as God was with them through Jesus, he will continue to be with them through the Spirit. The Spirit's role thus ensures continuity between Jesus' pre- and postglorification ministry.

As Jesus' emissary, the Spirit will have a variety of functions in believers' lives: he will bring to remembrance all that Jesus taught his disciples (14:26); he will testify regarding Jesus together with his followers (15:26); he will convict the world of sin, (un)righteousness, and judgment (16:8–11); and he will guide Jesus' disciples in(to) all truth and disclose what is to come (16:13). In all of these functions, the ministry of the Spirit remains closely linked with the person of Jesus. Just as Jesus is the Sent One who is fully dependent on and obedient to the Father, the Spirit is sent by both the Father and Jesus (14:26; 15:26) and focuses his teaching on the spiritual significance of God's work in Jesus (14:26; 15:26; 16:9).

Particularly significant for John's trinitarian mission theology is the final reference to the Spirit at Jesus' commissioning of his followers (20:21; cf. Matt 28:18–20;

---

8. See chap. 9 above.

Luke 24:46–49), which climaxes the characterization of Jesus as the sent Son. Here the disciples are shown to be drawn into the unity and mission of Father and Son. In a clear allusion to Gen 2:7, where God breathes his Spirit into Adam at creation, constituting him as a living being, at the commissioning of his disciples Jesus constitutes them as the new messianic community in anticipation of the outpouring of the Spirit subsequent to his ascension (20:22). As mentioned above, the references to the Spirit in 1 John are primarily directed toward reassuring believers and enabling them to deal with heterodox confessions.[9]

33.5 Father, Son, and Spirit: The Three Persons of the Godhead United in One Mission

The relationships between the Father, the Son, and the Spirit are presented in John's gospel within a clearly defined relational as well as salvation-historical framework. In relational terms, it is the Father who sends the Son, not the Son the Father. Likewise, it is the Father and the Son who send the Spirit rather than vice versa. In salvation-historical terms, God the Father sends the Son as the incarnate Word to mark an event of comparable import as creation. This intersects with John the Baptist's ministry, whose purpose it is to reveal the Christ to Israel. John sees the Spirit descend and rest on Jesus. At the same time, Jesus is said to live in constant intimate fellowship with God the Father throughout his earthly ministry.

As he goes about his work, the Son consistently affirms his unity with the Father in both his works and his words. In the context of the Sabbath controversy, Jesus affirms that the Father is still working and so is he. Later in the gospel, Jesus states even more plainly that he and the Father are one (not one person, but one God).[10] At the same time, Jesus can affirm that the Father is greater than he. Jesus is everywhere in John's gospel presented as equal yet obedient to God the Father. The Spirit, in turn, is sent by the Father and Jesus, yet is set in continuity to their salvific and revelatory work. Throughout the gospel it is made clear that the Spirit will be sent only subsequent to the Son's exaltation as the next salvation-historical milestone to follow.

In John's presentation of the interface between Father, Son, and Spirit, the programmatic division of the gospel in two major parts of equal length features significantly. The first half deals with Jesus' ministry to the Jews and presents Jesus' claims in the context of a pattern of escalating controversy between him and his opponents. Jesus' repeated claims of a unique relationship with God — including calling himself the Son of God — constitute the major bone of contention between him and his opponents, which in due course issues in the main charge leading to his crucifixion. The pattern of rejection is evident both at the midway point of the first half of John's gospel (end of John 6) and at the end of the first major unit (end of chap. 12).

In the second half, particularly in the Farewell Discourse, both the evangelist and Jesus adopt a vantage point subsequent to Jesus' exaltation with the Father (his

---

9. See chap. 9, sec. 21.4 above.
10. Bauckham, "Monotheism and Christology in the Gospel of John," 163.

"glorification"). This has two important consequences. First, the unity between Father, Son, and Spirit emerges all the more clearly, since Jesus' exaltation—which is now imminent—marks the point at which the Spirit will be sent by him and the Father. Jesus' followers are told about a soon-coming era during which their mission will be directed by the exalted Jesus and enabled by the indwelling Holy Spirit. Second, the disciples themselves are taken into the unity and love of the Father, Son, and Spirit as they carry out their mission.

Thus, not only is the ministry of the Son grounded in the love and commission of the Father, the ministry of Jesus' followers is grounded in the love and commission of Jesus. What is more, by virtue of Jesus' close relationship with both the Father on the one hand and the Spirit on the other, believers' ministry is rooted also in the unity of Father, Son, and Spirit among one another. This does not obliterate all distinctions of role or authority. Just as Jesus is the Son who does the bidding of the Father who sent him, so his followers are to pursue their mission in total dependence on the Son and under the direction of the Holy Spirit. In the end, Father, Son, and Spirit provide redemption and revelation to a community that is itself sent on a redemptive and revelatory mission.

On the receiving end of this mission of unity, love, and redemption is a dark and dying world. Satan, the ruler of this world, inspires the Jewish nation in particular and the world at large to unite in their rejection of the Christ. Repeatedly in the course of the gospel narrative Father, Son, and Spirit are mentioned together.[11] In 1:33–34, the Baptist says that "the one who sent" him (i.e., the Father) told him that the Spirit would mark the one who was to come as the Son of God. The collocation of references to Father, Son, and Spirit is particularly pronounced in the Farewell Discourse, especially in passages pertaining to the Spirit's sending by the Father or the Son—or both (14:26; 15:26).

This joint characterization culminates in the commissioning reference in 20:21–22, where Jesus sends his followers as the Father sent him and (proleptically?) equips them with the Spirit.[12] Hence mission proves to be the major thrust of John's depiction of Father, Son, and Spirit. In one way or another, all three persons are intimately involved in the mission of believers:[13] just as the Son represented the Father, so Jesus' followers are to represent the Son as they are indwelt and enabled by the Spirit. This unity of mission in no way overrides personal distinctions between Father, Son, and Spirit. Neither does it compromise the ontological distinction between Father, Son, and Spirit on the one hand and believers in the Messiah on the other.

33.6 Conclusion

The study of the portrayal of the Father, the Son, and the Spirit in John's gospel has demonstrated that the three persons of the Godhead are involved in one great mission—the revelation of God to humanity and the redemption of humanity for

---

11. See Erickson, *God in Three Persons*, 7.
12. Cf. 15:26–27; 16:7–11; see also 14:16–24.
13. Erickson, *God in Three Persons*, 207.

God. Not only are the three persons of the Godhead united in this mission, the presentation of Father, Son, and Spirit in John's gospel—John's trinitarian theology—is clearly missiologically constrained. Rather than being one of several aspects or implications of John's trinitarian theology, mission was shown to be the nexus and focal point of his presentation of the Father, the Son, and the Spirit, individually and in relation to one another. Hence it can truly be said, not only that John's mission theology is trinitarian (which in and of itself is a significant statement), but that his trinitarian teaching is part of his mission theology—a truly revolutionary insight.

The insight is revolutionary because, if heeded, it calls the church to focus its major energies on *acting on and acting out her Lord's commission*, "As the Father has sent me, I am sending you" (20:21), in the power of the Spirit, rather than merely engaging in the study of God or cultivating personal holiness (as important as this may be within the larger framework presented here). The insight is revolutionary also because a proper understanding of John's trinitarian mission theology ought to lead the church to *understand its mission in trinitarian terms*—that is, as originating in and initiated by the Father (the "one who sent" Jesus), as redemptively grounded and divinely mediated by Jesus the Son (the "Sent One" turned sender, 20:21), and as continued and empowered by the Spirit, the "other helping presence," the Spirit of truth.

What is more, not only is John's mission theology trinitarian in nature, it is universal in scope. A comparison with Luke's two-volume work, the gospel of Luke and the book of Acts, may prove instructive at this point. In essence, Luke, in his first volume, provides an account of the saving mission of Jesus culminating in his substitutionary cross-death and his resurrection. Yet, as Luke is careful to show, this is only the beginning. In his second volume, Luke narrates the coming of the Spirit (in fulfillment of Jesus' promise; cf. Luke 24:48–49; Acts 1:4–5) and the church's Spirit-empowered witness "to the ends of the earth" (Acts 1:8).[14]

It is our contention that John's salvation-historical outlook is much the same as Luke's, except that John accomplishes in one volume what Luke achieves in two.[15] This lends John's gospel a virtually unparalleled theological compactness and coherence. In John's presentation, the Son is the focal point of the *missio Dei* in that he is the sent Son from God the Father, himself God, who also, together with the Father, becomes the sender of the Holy Spirit, who thus empowers Jesus' followers for their universal witness. The universal scope of this witness is underscored by several means:

(1) Believing in Jesus is made the sole requirement for inclusion in Jesus' new messianic community (1:12; 3:16; 20:30–31 *et passim*).[16]

---

14. Helpful works on Luke-Acts that are sensitive to these dynamics include Bock, *Luke*; idem, *Acts* (BECNT; Grand Rapids: Baker, 2007); William J. Larkin Jr., *Acts* (IVPNTC; Downers Grove, IL: InterVarsity Press, 1995); and I. Howard Marshall and David Peterson, eds., *Witness to the Gospel: The Theology of Acts* (Grand Rapids: Eerdmans, 1998).

15. Though note the elegant and skillful way in which Luke uses the ascension as a unifying theological and literary element between his two volumes: Luke 9:51; 24:50–51; Acts 1:9–11. See also the Lukan witness theme (e.g., Luke 24:48; Acts 1:8), which is also given expression by the "two" theme in Luke's corpus predicated upon the Jewish requirement of a minimum of two witnesses in Deut 19:15 (including the fact that Luke writes a two-volume work; the pairing of Simeon and Anna in Luke 2 and the witness of Peter and Paul in Acts; two disciples on the road to Emmaus in Luke 24:13; two angels at the ascension in Acts 1:10; etc.).

16. See Croteau, "Analysis of the Concept of Believing."

(2) The pattern of Jesus' mission is shown to anticipate the (through Acts) familiar pattern of the early church's mission, from Jerusalem and Judea (John 3) to Samaria (John 4:1–42) to the Gentile world (John 4:43–54).[17]

(3) John's gospel divides into major halves, John 1–12 narrating Jesus' earthly mission to the Jews and John 13–21 presenting the exalted Jesus' mission to the world through his followers. While the events of John 13–21 still take place during the final days of Jesus' earthly mission, he is shown to anticipate the time subsequent to his "departure" (one of the Johannine euphemisms for the crucifixion) in the Farewell Discourse and at the commissioning toward the end of the book.

(4) Israel's OT salvation-historical privilege (still acknowledged in 4:22) is transcended, extending the salvific scope of Jesus' mission to the Gentiles (cf., e.g., 4:34–38; 10:16; 11:51–52; 12:20–36; 15:8). By being the "true vine" representing Israel (15:1), Jesus becomes the center of God's salvific purposes and the channel through which salvation, subsequent to the cross and the resurrection, can be freely extended to "whoever" believes in Jesus, the Christ, the Son of God, whether Jew or Gentile.

(5) In this way John manages to be true to the historical vantage point of his gospel prior to Jesus' crucifixion, resurrection, and ascension while at the same time showing the seeds and anticipatory signs of the universalization of the *missio Dei* in and through Jesus, which would ensue subsequent to the cross and the sending of the Spirit. This, of course, is something that had long taken place by the time of the writing of John's gospel.

Coupled with the emphatic presentation of Jesus as sharing the identity of Yahweh, the one and only true God, the compelling message of John's gospel is that there is no other god besides the one who is "the way and the truth and the life," the one who unequivocally stated that "no one comes to the Father except through me" (14:6). John's gospel thus follows Isaiah's teaching that because there is only one God, there can be only one Savior (Isa 43:11; 45:21). Anyone, therefore, who has not believed in Jesus the Christ and Son of God must urgently be implored to place his or her faith in Jesus, for there is no other way of salvation, and God's wrath continues to rest on those who refuse to believe (John 3:36) and prefer their own moral darkness over the "light [that] has come into the world" (3:19–21). John (the Baptist's) witness still rings true today: "Whoever believes in the Son has eternal life, but whoever rejects the Son will not see life, for God's wrath remains on them" (3:36; cf. 3:26–30; 1:15).[18]

---

17. Köstenberger, *John*, 141.

18. For a discussion of the implications for the church's mission from a study of John's mission theology, see Köstenberger and Swain, *Father, Son and Spirit*, 158–64. See also Köstenberger, "Contribution of the General Epistles and Revelation," 124–27.

Part 4

Johannine Theology and the Canon of Scripture

Chapter 16

THE THEOLOGY OF JOHN AND OTHER NEW TESTAMENT VOICES

BIBLIOGRAPHY

Barrett, C. K. "John and the Synoptic Gospels." *ExpTim* 85 (1974): 228–33. **Bauckham, Richard.** "John for Readers of Mark." Pp. 147–71 in *The Gospels for All Christians: Rethinking the Gospel Audiences.* Ed. Richard Bauckham. Grand Rapids: Eerdmans, 1998. Idem. *Jesus and the Eyewitnesses: The Gospels as Eyewitness Testimony.* Grand Rapids: Eerdmans, 2006. **Blomberg, Craig L.** "Problems in the Gospel of John." Pp. 196–240 in *The Historical Reliability of the Gospels.* 2nd ed. Downers Grove, IL: InterVarsity Press, 2007. **Brown, Raymond E.** "The Relation between the Fourth Gospel and the Synoptic Gospels." Pp. 143–216 in *New Testament Essays.* Milwaukee: Bruce Chapman, 1965. **Bultmann, Rudolf.** *Theology of the New Testament.* 2 vols. Trans. Kendrick Grobel. New York: Charles Scribner's Sons, 1951, 1955. **Burge, Gary M.** "History of Interpretation." Pp. 15–35 in *Interpreting the Gospel of John.* GNTE. Grand Rapids: Baker, 1992. **Carson, D. A.** "The Relation between the Fourth Gospel and the Synoptics." Pp. 49–58 in *The Gospel according to John.* PNTC. Grand Rapids: Eerdmans, 1991. **Denaux, Adelbert**, ed. *John and the Synoptics.* BETL 101. Leuven: Leuven University Press/Peeters, 1992. **Dvořák, James D.** "The Relationship between John and the Synoptic Gospels." *JETS* 41 (1998): 201–13. **Köstenberger, Andreas J.** "Diversity and Unity in the New Testament." Pp. 144–58 in *Biblical Theology: Retrospect & Prospect.* Ed. Scott J. Hafemann. Downers Grove, IL: InterVarsity Press, 2002. **Ladd, George E.** *A Theology of the New Testament.* Rev. ed. Grand Rapids: Eerdmans, 1993. **Morris, Leon.** "The Relationship of the Fourth Gospel to the Synoptics." Pp. 15–64 in *Studies in the Fourth Gospel.* Grand Rapids: Eerdmans, 1969. **Schlatter, Adolf.** *New Testament Theology: The History of the Christ* and *The Theology of the Apostles.* Trans. Andreas J. Köstenberger. Grand Rapids: Baker, 1997, 1999. **Schnackenburg, Rudolf.** "Relationship to the Synoptics." Pp. 26–43 in *The Gospel according to John.* Vol. 1. New York: Crossroad, 1992. **Smith, D. Moody.** *John among the Gospels: The Relationship in Twentieth-Century Research.* Philadelphia: Fortress, 1992. Idem. "The Love Command: John and Paul?" Pp. 207–17 in *Theology and Ethics in Paul and His Interpreters: Essays in Honor of Victor Paul Furnish.* Nashville: Abingdon, 1996. **Stanton, Graham N.** "The Fourfold Gospel." *NTS* 43 (1997): 317–46. **Trotter, Andrew H. Jr.** "Justification in the Gospel of John." Pp. 126–45 in *Right with God: Justification in the Bible and the World.* Ed. D. A. Carson. Carlisle, UK: Paternoster/Grand

Rapids: Baker, 1992. **Windisch, Hans**. *Johannes und die Synoptiker: Wollte der vierte Evangelist die älteren Evangelien ergänzen oder ersetzen?* Leipzig: J. C. Hinrichs'sche Buchhandlung, 1926.

34 THE THEOLOGY OF JOHN COMPARED TO THE SYNOPTICS

34.1 Introduction

The relationship between John and the Synoptic Gospels has been the subject of extensive debate over the centuries.[1] Traditionally, it was held that John wrote to supplement the other canonical gospels (*Ergänzungstheorie*).[2] Only at the turn of the nineteenth century, scholars began to propagate the view that John wrote to correct or replace Matthew, Mark, and Luke (*Verdrängungstheorie*). The theory that increasingly gained ground in recent decades is that John wrote independently of the Synoptics (*Unabhängigkeitstheorie*).[3]

Space does not permit a full rehearsal of this exceedingly complex topic. Nor does it seem likely that consensus on these matters is forthcoming anytime soon. In keeping with the hermeneutical triad mentioned at the outset of this study, the discussion below will, first, take up the matter of history and ask the question, What is the historical value of John's gospel in relation to the Synoptics? After this, I will focus my attention on a second question: What is the literary relationship (if any) between John and the other canonical Gospels?

34.2 The Historical Value of John's Gospel in Relation to the Synoptics

34.2.1 Introduction: Enlightenment Doubts

What is the historical value of John's gospel? At least since the end of the eighteenth century, critics have alleged that the Synoptics and John stand in irreconcilable conflict.[4] The solution, adopted by the vast majority of commentators, has been that the Synoptics are more interested in history, while John is primarily concerned with theology.[5] After all, did not Clement of Alexandria call John's a "spiritual

---

1. For surveys of research, see D. Moody Smith, *John among the Gospels: The Relationship in Twentieth-Century Research* (Philadelphia: Fortress, 1992); Adelbert Denaux, ed. *John and the Synoptics* (BETL 101; Leuven: Leuven University Press/Peeters, 1992). See also the survey by James D. Dvořák, "The Relationship between John and the Synoptic Gospels," *JETS* 41 (1998): 201–13.

2. Dvořák, "Relationship," 201, calls this "the dominant view" until about World War II. The nomenclature and taxonomy in this paragraph follows Hans Windisch, *Johannes und die Synoptiker: Wollte der vierte Evangelist die älteren Evangelien ergänzen oder ersetzen?* (Leipzig: J. C. Hinrichs'sche Buchhandlung, 1926), 1.

3. See further the discussion of the contribution of Gardner-Smith and Robinson's "new look" below.

4. See Burge, *Interpreting the Gospel of John*, 15–35; Andreas J. Köstenberger, "Diversity and Unity in the New Testament," in *Biblical Theology: Retrospect & Prospect* (ed. Scott J. Hafemann; Downers Grove, IL: InterVarsity Press, 2002), 146–49.

5. Cf. Smith, *Fourth Gospel in Four Dimensions*, who regularly presupposes that either John or the Synoptics are inaccurate, though he argues that more often than is recognized, it is John who provides accurate historical information rather than the Synoptics. Paul N. Anderson, *The Fourth Gospel and the Quest for Jesus: Modern Foundations Reconsidered* (New York: T&T Clark, 2006), proposes a complex and highly conjectural model that strives to break free from the historical-critical "quest" mentality but remains caught in many of its internal contradictions. See my review of both of these works in "Implications for History."

Gospel"?[6] After initial doubts arose in the 1790s, it was particularly Karl Gottlieb Bretschneider (1820) and later David Friedrich Strauss (1835) who, respectively, discredited John's historical reliability and proposed that the gospel deals with "myth," not historical narrative.[7] As Gary Burge sums up Johannine research during this period, "the Synoptics, rather than John, are viewed as the primary evidence for the life of Jesus. The reasoning confines John's interest to theology, not history. The Fourth Gospel presents an 'idea' of Jesus (a myth, Strauss called it) and cannot be seen as an historical account."[8] Thus in 1910, William Sanday diagnosed a serious prejudice against John, describing the scholarly mood as being characterized by "an uncompromising rejection" of John's gospel.[9]

34.2.2 The Rehabilitation of John's Historical Reliability in Recent Scholarship

In recent years, however, the historical reliability of John's gospel has witnessed a remarkable rehabilitation.[10] It is now widely recognized that the above-sketched appraisal of the relationship between the Synoptics and John is not only unduly simplistic but in fact inaccurate.[11] There are several reasons for this. (1) There are a notable number of what some have called "interlocking connections" between John and the Synoptics, that is, instances where John's gospel fills in a detail or connection in the Synoptic Gospels.[12] This includes, in particular, instances where John seems to presuppose his readers' familiarity with the Synoptic tradition and possibly one or several of the written gospels (e.g., 1:40; 3:24; 4:44; 6:67, 71; 11:1–2).[13] This suggests that the Synoptics and John are not in conflict but sustain a complementary relationship.

(2) It has been shown that many historical, geographical, and topographical details in John's gospel are in fact historically accurate; that is, they can be corroborated by archaeology and extant extrabiblical sources.[14] Archaeological discoveries such as artifacts related to Caiaphas and the high priestly family or the location of the pool of Siloam are cases in point.[15] No less a historian than Martin Hengel considers John's gospel to be an important source for first-century Judaism, crediting its author with an excellent knowledge of Palestinian topography and the Jewish calendar.[16] Hengel also points out that several pieces of information are found in John's gospel for the first time, such as the Samaritan village named Sychar (4:5); *ta*

---

6. Cited in Eusebius, *Hist. eccl.* 6.14. See the discussion in chap. 1, sec. 1.2 above.
7. See Köstenberger, "Early Doubts." The references are to Bretschneider's *Probabilia* and Strauss' *Life of Jesus*.
8. Burge, *Interpreting the Gospel of John*, 19.
9. William Sanday, *The Criticism of the Fourth Gospel* (Morse Foundation Lectures for 1904, Union Theological Seminary; New York: Scribner's Sons, 1905), cited in Burge, *Interpreting the Gospel of John*, 20.
10. See esp. Blomberg, *Historical Reliability of John's Gospel*; Köstenberger, "John," in *ZIBBC*.
11. See Marianne Meye Thompson, "The Historical Jesus and the Johannine Christ," in *Exploring the Gospel of John*, 21–42.
12. Leon Morris, "The Relationship of the Fourth Gospel to the Synoptics," in *Studies in the Fourth Gospel*, 15–63; Carson, *Gospel according to John*, 49–58, esp. 52–55; Blomberg, *Historical Reliability of the Gospels*, 203–4.
13. See Bauckham, "John for Readers of Mark"; Köstenberger, *Encountering John*, 36–37.
14. Köstenberger, "John," in *ZIBBC*, and the literature cited there.
15. Urban C. von Wahlde, "Archaeology and John's Gospel," in James H. Charlesworth, ed., *Jesus and Archaeology* (Grand Rapids: Eerdmans, 2006), 523–86.
16. Hengel, "Johannesevangelium als Quelle," 295, 322.

enkainia as a designation for the Festival of Tabernacles (10:22); and the characterization of Annas as Caiaphas's father-in-law (18:13).[17] And John's portrayal of Annas and Caiaphas earns Hengel's highest praise.[18]

In cases where John's gospel overlaps with the Synoptics, John frequently supplies additional information.[19] He mentions a boy with five barley loaves and two small fish as well as Jesus' interchange with Philip and Andrew, two of his disciples, at the occasion of the feeding of the multitudes (6:5–9). John makes reference to the fragrance of the perfume and identifies Judas as the one who objected to Mary of Bethany's anointing of Jesus' feet prior to the crucifixion (12:3–8; Matt 26:8 globally refers to "the disciples," Mark 14:4 to "some of those present"). He specifies Malchus as the name of the servant whose ear Peter cut off at Gethsemane (18:10).[20]

Perhaps the most commonly noted difficulty in reconciling John's account with the Synoptic one is related to the dating of Jesus' final Passover with his disciples.[21] On account of the reference to "the day of Preparation of the Passover" in John 19:14, some have seen John as placing the Last Supper on Wednesday night, with the crucifixion taking place on Thursday afternoon when the Passover lambs would have been slaughtered in preparation for Passover later that evening. However, a closer look reveals that both John and the Synoptics present Jesus as having eaten a final meal with his disciples, a Passover meal, on Thursday night, with the crucifixion having taken place on Friday afternoon.

The resolution is found in 19:14, where we are told that Jesus' crucifixion took place on "the day of Preparation," with the next day being a "special Sabbath," that is, the Sabbath of Passover week. Thus, even in John the crucifixion takes place on Friday, with "the day of Preparation" in John, as in Mark and Luke, referring not to the day of preparation for the Passover but for the Sabbath (Mark 15:42; Luke 23:54; see Josephus, *Ant.* 16.163–64). Moreover, since Passover lasted an entire week (in conjunction with the associated Festival of Unleavened Bread; see Luke 22:1), it was customary to speak of the day of preparation for the Sabbath as "the day of Preparation *of Passover week*" (NIV), though not of the Passover in a more narrow sense, as a better rendering of the phrase in John 19:14.

Further apparent discrepancies between John and the Synoptics are likewise capable of resolution.[22] John's more extended discourses in comparison with the shorter aphorisms in the Synoptics may simply represent an effort on John's part to provide more thorough expositions of fewer selected topics.[23] The different mode of presentation need not constitute a discrepancy but may reflect a theological transposition of the Synoptic tradition onto a higher scale.[24] The Johannine signs

---

17. Ibid., 296, 322 (in general); p. 301 (Sychar), p. 317 (Tabernacles), p. 323 (Annas).
18. Ibid., 322–33, esp. p. 333.
19. Köstenberger, *John*, 17–18, and the references cited there.
20. See in this regard Bauckham's appropriation of Theissen's theory of "protective anonymity" (*Jesus and the Eyewitnesses*, 184–87; contra, those who argue that greater detail and specificity typically occur in a folk-traditioning process as the story is embellished by each new tradent).
21. Köstenberger, "Diversity and Unity," 147–48, and the literature cited there.
22. See ibid., 148–49; and the further discussion below.
23. See chap. 5 in Blomberg, *Historical Reliability of the Gospels*.
24. For a brief survey, see Köstenberger, *Encountering John*, 198–200.

deemphasize the miraculous in Jesus' works in order to focus on their christological symbolism. The Synoptic exorcisms are replaced by repeated references to Satan as Jesus' chief protagonist. Jesus' attendance at several Jewish festivals in Jerusalem is shown to fulfill their inherent symbolism. There is thus good reason to conclude that John and the Synoptics provide mutually complementing theologies.

(3) The dichotomy between the Synoptics' alleged primary interest in history and John's focus on theology is itself highly suspect, as Marianne Meye Thompson and others have shown.[25] As mentioned, many aspects of the historical reliability of John's gospel have been demonstrated by archaeological and extrabiblical sources. Also, scholars have increasingly come to realize that the Synoptics, too, are interested in theology, in the sense that they reveal the respective theological interests and emphases of the evangelists. Thus Luke has a special interest in those with low status in society, such as the poor, Gentiles, women, and children, and deals extensively with issues related to wealth and poverty; Matthew presents Jesus' teaching in the form of five extended discourses after the pattern of Moses and the Pentateuch. Such examples could be multiplied.

Hence the conclusion seems warranted that *both* the Synoptics *and* John are interested in *both* history *and* theology. This is also confirmed by the strong emphasis on eyewitness testimony in John's gospel (e.g., 1:7–8, 15; 5:31–47).[26] It is hard to imagine why a gospel that explicitly and repeatedly stresses the importance of eyewitness testimony would at the same time display a low view of historicity. As mentioned, the author claims to be an eyewitness of the Last Supper (13:23) and the crucifixion (19:35)—in fact, of the events recorded in the entire gospel narrative (21:24–25). For these reasons the distinction between history and theology in describing the relationship between the Synoptics and John is false and should be abandoned.

34.3 The Literary Relationship between John's Gospel and the Synoptics

34.3.1 Survey of Scholarship

What is the literary relationship (if any) between John and the other canonical gospels? At the turn of the twentieth century, it was still widely assumed that since John wrote a generation after the other canonical gospels, he knew and used the Synoptics.[27] Yet the question arose why, if John knew the other gospels, he made so little use of them. In fact, while 93 percent of Mark is found in Matthew and Luke, only 8 percent of John parallels the Synoptics, and 92 percent is unique.[28] What is more, even in the 8 percent of overlapping material, John rarely (if ever) is

---

25. Thompson, "Historical Jesus and the Johannine Christ"; Morris, "History and Theology in the Fourth Gospel," in *Studies in the Fourth Gospel*, 65–138.

26. Morris, "Was the Author of the Fourth Gospel an Eyewitness?" in *Studies in the Fourth Gospel*, 139–214. See also Bauckham, *Jesus and the Eyewitnesses*.

27. See Streeter, *Four Gospels*.

28. See Burge, *Interpreting the Gospel of John*, 23, with reference to Westcott.

close enough in wording to justify the conclusion that he had one or several of the Synoptics in front of him as he wrote.[29]

In a little, yet highly influential book published in 1938, Percival Gardner-Smith drew what seemed to be the most logical conclusion: What if John in fact drew on his own independent traditions that *antedated* the Synoptics?[30] If so, it could no longer be assumed that where John had no Synoptic parallels, or where John and the Synoptics seemed to disagree, the latter were accurate and John was in error. Instead, the possibility presented itself that the Johannine and the Synoptic traditions were independent and both contained an actual historical core. In Gardner-Smith's own words, "If in the Fourth Gospel we have a survival of the type of first century Christianity which owed nothing to synoptic developments, and which originated in quite a different intellectual atmosphere, its historical value may be very great indeed."[31]

In 1957, therefore, John A. T. Robinson contrasted the "old look" with a "new look" on the fourth gospel.[32] The "old look" held that (1) John was dependent on the Synoptics; (2) John's background was Greek, most likely Gnostic; (3) John is not a reliable witness to the historical Jesus; (4) John's theology reflects developments prevalent at the end of the first century AD; and (5) the author was neither the apostle John nor an eyewitness. In contrast, the "new look" maintained that (1) John drew on a tradition independent from the Synoptics; (2) John's background was predominantly Jewish; and (3) there is a genuine connection between Johannine tradition and the historical Jesus. In addition, Robinson proposed that John may have written his gospel in the AD 60s because he is conspicuously silent about the destruction of the temple in AD 70.[33] However, while this resulted in a partial reversal of the low esteem for the historical value of John's gospel, it did not completely turn back the clock to the traditional view that the apostle John wrote the gospel and that he knew and used the other canonical gospels.[34]

The last few decades of the twentieth century saw a variety of developments in adjudicating the literary relationship between John and the other canonical gospels.[35] One such effort was the source-critical proposal of Robert Fortna, who, in part on the basis of "literary seams," sought to reconstruct the underlying literary sources of John's gospel.[36] However, Fortna's proposals have not won the day.[37] Others, such as Raymond Brown and J. Louis Martyn, have applied redaction-critical methodology in order to delineate the history of the "Johannine community."[38] While their

---

29. For a representative comparative study, see Paul W. Barnett, "The Feeding of the Multitude in Mark 6/John 6," in *Gospel Perspectives* (ed. David Wenham and Craig Blomberg; Sheffield: JSOT, 1986), 6:273–93, who concludes that the two accounts were essentially independent, "with each resting in all probability on independent eyewitness recollection" (p. 289). See also Barnabas Lindars, "John and the Synoptic Gospels: A Test Case," *NTS* 27 (1981): 287–94.
30. Percival Gardner-Smith, *Saint John and the Synoptic Gospels* (Cambridge: Cambridge University Press, 1938).
31. Ibid., 96.
32. Robinson, "New Look."
33. Robinson, *Redating the New Testament*; idem, *Priority of John*.
34. A case in point is the work of C. H. Dodd, who on the one hand could conclude that John was "better informed than the tradition behind the Synoptics" but at the same time rejected the "symbolic" use of place names in John's gospel. See his *Historical Tradition in the Fourth Gospel*, 120; appendix. See the critique by D. A. Carson, "Historical Tradition."
35. See the analysis by Tom Thatcher, "Anatomies of the Fourth Gospel," in *Anatomies of Narrative Criticism*, 6–8, who discusses the history of Johannine scholarship of this period under the headings "In the Shadow of the Sources" and "In the Shadow of the Community."
36. Fortna, *Gospel of Signs*; idem, *Fourth Gospel and Its Predecessor*.
37. See van Belle, *Signs Source*.
38. Brown, *Community of the Beloved Disciple*; Martyn, *History and Theology*.

proposal reached virtual paradigmatic status in the early 1990s, the "Johannine community hypothesis" has now peaked and is fast receding in influence.[39] Others, such as R. Alan Culpepper, have engaged in a close literary reading of the Johannine narrative while laying aside questions of historicity.[40]

More recently, James Dunn proposed that the four Gospels represent "Jesus remembered" and that oral tradition had a more significant part in the transmission of Jesus material than is recognized by purely literary theories of gospel relationships.[41] Dunn, in turn, became the target of a major critique by Richard Bauckham, who in his *Jesus and the Eyewitnesses* made a massive, and largely compelling, case for the Gospels as eyewitness testimony in keeping with ancient historiographic conventions.[42] This truly turned back the clock beyond even the "new look," questioning the nebulous notion of "traditions" and contending that the material in the Gospels, including John, was rooted in apostolic eyewitness testimony.[43] Others have similarly urged additional study in the way memory works.[44]

Bauckham's work, then, has radically recast the landscape in gospel and Johannine studies. No longer is John merely dependent on the Synoptics. No longer is he simply drawing on independent early traditions. John is an eyewitness in his own right, as seems to be affirmed at critical junctures in the gospel (1:14; 13:23; 19:35; 21:24–25). At the same time, John, like the other canonical gospels, was aimed at a general audience rather than representing a sectarian document.[45] In this scholarly climate, it seems entirely reasonable to reopen also the question whether John, while an eyewitness and while apparently not following the Synoptic Gospels in wording or even general literary plan, knew and worked from the Synoptics in some way as he conceived his own distinct and unique account.

34.3.2 *John's Effort to Interpret, Develop, and Supplement the Synoptic Pattern*

34.3.2.1 Introduction

Space does not permit a detailed defense of this position; however, there are various strands of evidence that converge to suggest that John wrote to interpret, develop, and supplement the Synoptic treatment and that he did so in a most strategic and deliberate manner (to coin a term in keeping with the three theories mentioned in the introduction to this section, one might call this a *Transpositionstheorie*).[46] While, as mentioned, it is widely acknowledged that John did not use the Synoptics

---

39. See the discussion in chap. 1, esp. sec. 2.1.2.1, above.
40. Culpepper, *Anatomy*.
41. James D. G. Dunn, *Jesus Remembered* (Christianity in the Making 1; Grand Rapids: Eerdmans, 2003).
42. Bauckham, *Jesus and the Eyewitnesses*.
43. Note, however, that Bauckham does not affirm the apostolic authorship of John's gospel, on which see the discussion in chap. 1, sec. 2.1.3.1 above.
44. Tom Thatcher, ed., *Jesus, the Voice, and the Text: Beyond the Oral and the Written Gospel* (Waco, TX: Baylor University Press, 2008); Bockmuehl, *Seeing the Word*, esp. chap. 6: "Living Memory and Apostolic History"; McKnight and Mournet, *Jesus in Early Christian Memory*; cf. Bauckham, *Jesus and the Eyewitnesses*, chap. 13: "Eyewitness Memory" (with additional bibliographical references).
45. See Bauckham, *Gospels for All Christians*.
46. Among those who continued to affirm that John was familiar with one or several of the Synoptic Gospels is Barrett, *Gospel according to St. John*; idem, "John and the Synoptic Gospels," *ExpTim* 85 (1974): 228–33; see also Lightfoot, *St. John's Gospel*; and

literally in the way they did each other (depending on one's "solution" to the Synoptic "problem"), there is sufficient implicit evidence that suggests that John was aware of what one might call the Synoptic "pattern" of presentation.[47] To begin with, as mentioned, at several junctures of the Johannine narrative information provided by the Synoptics but not previously (or at all) in John seems assumed.[48]

34.3.2.2 List of Johannine Transpositions of the Synoptic Accounts

The following observations regarding the way in which John develops the Synoptic pattern of presentation combine to make a cumulative case for John's attempt to interpret, develop, and supplement the Synoptic treatment.[49] I will first list and then discuss a possible scenario as to how John might have gone about transposing the Synoptic accounts. The list is intended to be representative and suggestive rather than exhaustive. This will be followed by a brief discussion of the significance of these observations in interaction with previous scholarship on the subject.

Synoptics/Acts	John
1. Temple cleansing at end of Jesus' ministry	Raising of Lazarus as climactic "sign"
2. Temple cleansing at end of Jesus' ministry	Temple clearing at inception of Jesus' ministry
3. Church's mission to Jerusalem, Judea/Samaria/Gentiles	Jesus' mission in Jerusalem, Judea/Samaria/Gentiles
4. Peter's confession at Caesarea Philippi	Peter's confession after Bread of Life Discourse
5. Eschatological Olivet Discourse	Thoroughgoing realized/inaugurated eschatology
6. Reference to future destruction of Jerusalem Temple	Reference to "destruction" and rebuilding of the new temple, Jesus' body

---

the comment by D. Moody Smith, "John and the Synoptics: Some Dimensions of the Problem," *NTS* 27 (1980): 443: "I am beginning to be able to conceive of a scenario in which John knew, or knew of, the synoptics and yet produced so dissimilar a gospel as the one which now follows them in the New Testament." More recently, see Bauckham, "John for Readers of Mark." In an oral discussion at the Annual Meeting of the SBL in Boston, MA on November 23, 2008, Bauckham cited the difference between John's gospel and the Synoptics as a (for him) insurmountable obstacle for accepting the apostolic authorship of John's gospel, since it seems to him inconceivable that from the same circle of the Twelve originated two so very different accounts as Matthew's (cf. Mark, Luke) and John's. Yet later in the discussion, Bauckham himself suggested other possible reasons for the difference between Mark and John: Mark's reporting vs. John's reflective mode, and John's selectivity and greater narrative development of fewer miracles.

47. Cf. Dvořák, "Relationship," 201–2, who sketches three distinct positions: (1) John is literarily dependent on one or more of the Synoptics; (2) John is literarily independent of the Synoptics and similarities between them are due to common traditions; (3) John is literarily independent of the Synoptics but was aware of them and their traditions.

48. See, e.g., the references to Andrew as "Simon Peter's brother" in 1:40; to John the Baptist's imprisonment in 3:24; to "the Twelve" in 6:67, 70–71; and to Mary of Bethany as "the same one who poured perfume on the Lord and wiped his feet with her hair" in 11:2.

49. See the survey of the "mediating view" in Dvořák, "Relationship," 211–13, who cites especially Morris' proposal in *Studies in the Fourth Gospel*, later reinforced by Carson, of "interlocking traditions" between John and the Synoptics.

Synoptics/Acts	John
7. Institution of new covenant at Last Supper	Jesus' reference to "eating his flesh" and "drinking his blood" in the Bread of Life Discourse
8. Virgin birth of Jesus	Jesus' preexistence with God
9. Synoptic miracles displaying Jesus' power over nature, sickness, death, and the evil supernatural	Selected messianic "signs" focusing on messianic symbolism
10. Jesus as friend of sinners and tax collectors	Virtually nothing on economic issues; eternal life
11. Jesus' legal disputes with the teachers of the law	The incarnation as the coming of grace and truth
12. Large number of parables (esp. on kingdom of God)	Real-life "parables," symbolic discourses
13. Demon exorcisms	Satan as chief antagonist
14. Basic information about major characters and events in the gospel story	Assumption of readers' familiarity with basic gospel information
15. Large number of actions and sayings of Jesus	Selected "signs" and extended discourses
16. Jesus' painful suffering on the cross for our sins	The cross as part of Jesus' "glorification" and as a station on the way of Jesus' return to the Father
17. Emphasis on Jesus' Jewish trial	Emphasis on Jesus' Roman trial; cosmic trial motif
18. References to Isa 6:9–10 on Jewish obduracy	Ending to Part I (12:40), quoting same text
19. Ministry of earthly and exalted Jesus in Luke-Acts	Book of Signs and Book of Exaltation (cf. 13:1–3)
20. Institution of Lord's Supper	Extensive Farewell Discourse (13:1–17:26)

Fig. 34.1: Comparison between John's Gospel and the Synoptic Pattern

34.3.2.3 Discussion of Transpositions

The following discussion provides a succinct description of a possible scenario in which John transposes various aspects of the Synoptic accounts in what might be a logical sequence (though this is only a minor part of my proposal). Subsequent to the discussion below I will explore the significance of this proposal in the context of previous scholarship on the relationship between John and the Synoptics.

(1) John selected the raising of Lazarus (11:1–44) as the culmination point of Jesus' ministry to the Jews, since it corresponded to and anticipated Jesus' resurrection and was thus judged to be the perfect climax of John's Book of Signs. This meant that the temple clearing recorded at the end of Jesus' ministry in the Synoptics must give way to the Lazarus narrative. While in the Synoptics it is Jesus'

clearing of the temple that serves as the final impetus for the crucifixion, in John it is the raising of Lazarus. In his selection of the Lazarus narrative, John supplemented the Synoptic account of the anointing of Jesus by Mary of Bethany, Lazarus's sister (Matt 26:6–13; Mark 14:1–9).[50]

(2) This, in turn, led John to select another temple clearing, performed at the beginning of Jesus' ministry, for inclusion (2:13–22). In John's gospel, this temple clearing serves as an incipient prophetic sign of judgment predicting the destruction of the Jewish nation. It also serves to signal prophetically Jesus' resurrection three days after the crucifixion (2:19–21).

(3) In chapters 3 and 4, John endeavors to validate, in the mission of the earthly Jesus, the early church's pattern of mission "from Jerusalem and Judea and Samaria to the Gentiles" (Acts 1:8 *et passim*). Hence John shows that Jesus engaged in outreach to Jews (Nicodemus; 3:1–21), Samaritans (the Samaritan woman; 4:1–42), and Gentiles (the Roman centurion; 4:43–54). What is more, John stresses the universal scope of the *missio Dei*. Nicodemus becomes a representative of sinful humanity (2:23–3:1), and the Samaritan evinces common human misunderstandings as to locations of worship (4:19–24). At the end of the respective pericopae the evangelist emphasizes God's love *for the world* (3:16) and the fact that Jesus is the Savior *of the world* (4:42). Not ethnicity or gender or social status matter; what matters is universal human sinfulness, the need for a Savior, and trusting in Jesus the Messiah, the lifted-up Son of Man (cf. Gal 3:28).

(4) In the Synoptic presentation of Jesus' ministry, the pivotal confession of Jesus as the Christ by Peter at Caesarea Philippi with just the Twelve (Matt 16:13–20; Mark 8:27–30; Luke 9:18–20) serves as the major turning point; in John's gospel this is replaced by Peter's equivalent confession of Jesus as "the Holy One of God" (6:69). In a major watershed moment, Jesus is left by all but the Twelve (eventually the Eleven, minus Judas).

(5) John replaces the Synoptic Olivet Discourse (Matthew 24; Mark 13; Luke 21:5–38) with a thoroughgoing presentation of realized eschatology. Without entirely eliminating references to the second coming, John places a major emphasis on the spiritual reality that those who believe in Jesus for eternal life experience this kind of life already in the here and now.

(6) In a related move, John replaces Jesus' reference to the future destruction of the literal Jerusalem temple in the Olivet Discourse with a reference to the destruction of the figurative "temple," Jesus' body (2:19–21). Especially if written subsequent to the actual destruction of the Jerusalem sanctuary, this allows John to present Jesus as the substitute for the temple.

(7) John interweaves references to Jesus' "flesh and blood" in the Bread of Life Discourse (6:31–59) instead of recording Jesus' institution of the new covenant at

---

50. See also Luke 10:38–42. The anointing of Jesus by a sinful woman featured in Luke 7:36–50 most likely refers to a different occasion (see Köstenberger, "Pericopae of Jesus' Anointing").

the Last Supper (cf. 13:1–30). In this he provides an important theological background for the practice of the Last Supper from Jesus' teaching during his earthly ministry.

(8) Instead of recording the virgin birth (cf. Matt 1:18–25; Luke 1:34–35), John roots Jesus' origin ultimately in his eternal preexistence with God (1:1).

(9) John interprets the significance of the Synoptic miracles (*dynameis*), which display Jesus' power over nature, sickness, death, and the evil supernatural, by selecting particularly spectacular events or "hard" miracles performed by Jesus and by drawing out the messianic significance of these "signs" (2:11, 23; 3:2; 4:54; etc.)

(10) John focuses on eternal life (e.g., 3:16; 20:31) and other spiritual realities while virtually ignoring socioeconomic issues so prominent in Luke. This means, for example, that he has no room for a presentation of Jesus as a friend of tax collectors (e.g., Matt 9:10). There is also no mention of the poor (other than in 12:5, 8) or of the dangers of wealth in John's gospel.

(11) The Synoptics frequently show Jesus as embroiled in legal disputes with the teachers of the law (e.g., Matt 19:1–12). In John's gospel, the role of the law with regard to Jesus is addressed globally in 1:17, where Jesus' coming is described as the advent of "grace and truth." However, John does choose to retain the "Sabbath controversy," showing Jesus to be Lord of the Sabbath (see the references to the Sabbath in 5:9; 9:14 and the controversies that ensue). This enables John to reinforce Jesus' alignment with the Creator (5:18) and to demonstrate the spiritual blindness inherent in a rejection of Jesus owing to his alleged lack of observance of the law (9:39–41).

(12) John does not include any of the Synoptic parables, featuring instead several symbolic discourses (see esp. chaps. 10 and 15). John 9 comes perhaps closest in character to a Synoptic parable, but here it is an actual series of events that is given a parabolic interpretation by Jesus at the end (9:39–41). It is as if John were making the point that one need not resort to recounting Jesus' parables—made-up, true-to-life stories; there is plenty of parabolic-type material to be gleaned from real-life events in Jesus' ministry.

(13) John does not record any demon exorcisms but instead focuses all of his attention on Satan, the major supernatural antagonist in the gospel (see esp. 13:2, 27 and the references to the "prince of this world" at 12:31; 14:30; 16:11).[51]

(14) Repeatedly in the Johannine narrative, the perceptive reader finds clues that John assumed basic familiarity with the gospel story on the part of his readers. This includes information pertaining to the identity of Peter (1:40), Mary the mother of Jesus (2:1), the imprisonment of John the Baptist (3:24), the Twelve (6:67, 70–71), and Mary of Bethany (11;1–2).

---

51. For discussions see Ronald A. Piper, "Satan, Demons and the Absence of Exorcisms in the Fourth Gospel," in *Christology, Controversy and Community: New Testament Essays in Honour of David R. Catchpole* (ed. David G. Horrell and Christopher M. Tuckett; NovTSup 99; Leiden: Brill, 2000), 253–78; Eric Plumer, "The Absence of Exorcisms in the Fourth Gospel," *Bib* 78 (1997): 350–68. See also Graham H. Twelftree, *In the Name of Jesus: Exorcism among Early Christians* (Grand Rapids: Baker, 2007), chap. 9, who suggests that in John's gospel the entire ministry of Jesus is characterized as a battle with Satan, whereby the demonic is overcome by truth rather than by the power encounter of an exorcism.

(15) John is selective in both the number of "signs" and the number of discourses he records (cf. 20:30–31).[52] In both cases, this enabled him to feature these events and speeches at considerably greater length. This, in turn, affords him the opportunity to provide the reader with a more detailed presentation of Jesus' works and words.

The "signs" have already been discussed above; a list of Jesus' discourses in John presents itself as follows:[53]

5:19–47	Jesus' unique relationship with the Father
6:32–58	Jesus' Bread of Life Discourse
10:1–18	Jesus' Good Shepherd Discourse
13:31–17:25	Jesus' Farewell Discourse and final prayer

Fig. 34.2: The Major Discourses of Jesus in John's Gospel

It is apparent that these discourses are found primarily in the Festival Cycle (John 5–10) and in the opening section of Act II of John's gospel drama. Commentators regularly note that the discourses are couched in Johannine idiom; that is, the language is virtually indistinguishable from the narrative sections in the rest of the gospel. This is regularly taken as evidence that John either created these speeches or at least that he significantly embellished what Jesus actually said. However, if, as Richard Bauckham has argued, each gospel (including John) represents eyewitness testimony, John would have heard Jesus teach and could have reproduced these discourses from memory. It is also possible that Jesus' language impacted John's idiom rather than John imposing his diction on Jesus.

(16) As mentioned in the discussion of John's theology of the cross in chapter 14 above, while the Synoptics present Jesus' suffering primarily from the vantage point of Jesus' enduring of painful agony and separation from God on behalf of sinful humanity, John transforms the cross into a place where Jesus the Son is exalted ("lifted up") and glorified, in likely adaptation of Isaianic terminology.

(17) The Synoptics, in presenting Jesus first and foremost as the Jewish Messiah, focus on Jesus' Jewish trial before the Sanhedrin and Caiaphas. John, in building on the Synoptics and yet in emphasizing the universal nature of Jesus' rejection and the universal scope of his mission, focuses on Jesus' trial before Pilate, the Roman governor. In addition, John transforms the entire notion of a trial and presents Jesus' ministry *in its entirety* as a trial, yet not one where *Jesus* is on trial but one where

---

52. Bauckham, "Historiographical Characteristics," 36, speaks of "John's extreme selectivity."

53. For a discussion of the Johannine discourses in comparison with Greco-Roman literature, see the discussion in Bauckham, "Historiographical Characteristics," 30–36. Bauckham notes particularly the generative function of the "Amen, Amen, I say to you" formula (pp. 33–34). He also maintains that "what is typical of many of the distinctive characteristics of Jesus' speech in John is that, in many cases, John adopts a usage that is rare in the Synoptic tradition and makes more extensive use of it," citing as examples "Father" and "Son" language (Matt 11:27; Mark 13:32; cf. Matt 28:19) and references to "life" in parallelism to "kingdom" terminology (p. 35; see discussion in chap. 2, sec. 3.4 above).

those who rejected him, Jew and Gentile alike, are put on trial and found guilty by a series of weighty witnesses to Jesus' messianic identity.

(18) John takes the Synoptics' references to Jewish obduracy in Isa 6:9–10 (cf. Matt 13:14–15; Mark 4:12; and esp. Acts 28:26–27) and gives the passage more weight, placing it strategically at the end of his Book of Signs (12:40). In this way, and in conjunction with a citation of Isa 53:1 (12:38), John provides an Isaianic rationale for the Jews' rejection of the Messiah, aligning Jesus with Isaiah and the Jews with those who rejected the prophet's message in his day.

(19) Luke–Acts presents in two volumes the ministry of the earthly and the exalted Jesus (see esp. Acts 1:1). John accomplishes the equivalent in one work, his gospel, by juxtaposing two "books," the Book of Signs and the Book of Exaltation, presenting the ministry of the earthly and the exalted Jesus. In this way he is able to maintain both the historical orientation of Jesus' mission first to the Jews and at the same time to affirm the universal scope of Jesus' mission also to the Gentiles.[54]

(20) Going beyond the Synoptic account of the institution of the Lord's Supper, John includes an extensive account of Jesus' final instructions to his disciples in the Johannine Farewell Discourse (John 13–17). This capitalizes on the fact that John, as "the disciple whom Jesus loved" (13:23), is an eyewitness at this occasion and can thus draw on his personal recollection of Jesus' instruction while at the same time patterning this section of his gospel after the model of Moses' farewell discourse in Deuteronomy.

34.3.2.4 Significance of Transposition-by-an-Eyewitness Proposal

In the past, the study of the relationship between John and the Synoptics has frequently been hindered by scholars asking the wrong questions and employing inadequate methods. In particular, the rejection of the eyewitness nature of the Gospels (including John) has led to the prevalence of literary paradigms or discussions merely in terms of common "traditions." When John's literary dependence on the Synoptics could not be established in light of the available evidence, the pendulum swung to the other extreme, that is, John's independence from the Synoptics. It due course, it became clear that the notion of Johannine independence from the Synoptic Gospels, likewise, fails to do full justice to the relationship between John and the Synoptics. Various efforts at mediating positions were only partially successful in addressing the issues involved.

In this context, Richard Bauckham's recent work, *Jesus and the Eyewitnesses*, has opened up a fruitful new avenue in the field of the study of the Gospels.[55] Not that the idea of John's gospel constituting eyewitness testimony is entirely new, but Bauckham provided massive ancient evidence to buttress his case, which lent the theory an unprecedented degree of plausibility. It remains, however, to draw the necessary implications from Bauckham's work for the relationship between John and

---

54. See, e.g., 10:16; 11:51–52; 12:20–32; and the pattern of Jesus' mission in chaps. 3–4; see point (3) above.

55. See the discussion of Bauckham's contribution in chap. 1, sec. 2.1.3.1.3 above.

the Synoptics. If the author of John's gospel was an eyewitness, a solution that is considerably less complicated than many other theories on the subject lies close at hand: John was *both* an eyewitness *and* knew the Synoptics. As an eyewitness, he was free to draw on his own memory of events in Jesus' ministry (a possible example being the Farewell Discourse). As one familiar with the Synoptic Gospels, he reflected on their deeper theological significance while writing his own unique account.

If the above-sketched scenario is even approximately on target, then neither literary dependence nor Johannine independence adequately describes the relationship between John and the Synoptics, nor does the proposal of "interlocking traditions" sufficiently address all the pertinent issues. Literary dependence theories fail because John and the Synoptics are too different to render such a hypothesis plausible. Independence is historically implausible if John wrote a generation after the Synoptics. It also does not give sufficient consideration to the possibility that John transposed the pattern of the Synoptic accounts in the way I have attempted to describe above. The notion of interlocking traditions helps alleviate the charge of historical discrepancies between John and the Synoptics, but it does so on the premise that these are, at least in part, undesigned coincidences.[56] By contrast, I have suggested that John's transposition of various aspects of the Synoptic accounts was both conscious and deliberate.

Richard Bauckham, in oral remarks made at the 2008 annual meeting of the Society of Biblical Literature, arguing against Johannine authorship, maintained that it is virtually inconceivable for two members of the Twelve, such as Matthew and John, to produce such drastically differing accounts.[57] However, the obstacle is not nearly as insurmountable as Bauckham considers it to be. First, there is the major time gap between the times of composition, which allowed for sustained theological reflection. Second, there are the different temperaments and theological insights of the respective evangelists. Third, there is the vital intervening datum of the destruction of the temple.[58] On the whole, there is no reason why John, as a creative theological thinker and eyewitness, could not have written the kind of gospel that has come down to us in the form of John's gospel.

On the one hand, as an apostolic eyewitness, he would have had the confidence, and the historical distance, not to follow the Synoptic accounts slavishly. On the other hand, there was also no need for John to operate in a vacuum. He took the Synoptic pattern of presentation and transformed it in the ways described above, producing an original work that is yet not entirely novel but builds on the work of his predecessors and does so with great theological sophistication and creative imagination. Rigid source or redaction-critical models are inadequate to capture this process, nor is it adequate to describe John's procedure merely on the basis of common underlying traditions. Even pointing to the presence of "interlocking

---

56. To borrow a term from F. F. Bruce, "Is the Paul of Acts the Real Paul?" *BJRL* 58 (1976): 282–305 (describing the relationship between the Paul of Acts and the Paul depicted in the apostle's own letters).

57. Bauckham is also ambivalent regarding Matthean authorship; see his treatment in *Jesus and the Eyewitnesses*.

58. See the discussion in chap. 1, sec. 2 above.

traditions" only takes matters so far. A model of conscious Johannine transposition of the Synoptic pattern best explains the available evidence.

At the end of the day, this kind of *Transpositionstheorie* combines the strengths and avoids the weaknesses of both the dependence and the independence models. It affirms Johannine dependence in the sense that it acknowledges that John knew the Synoptics and in a sense "used" them (yet without making their pattern the pattern of his presentation). It also acknowledges Johannine independence in the sense that John forged his own path in writing his gospel, yet without taking this notion to the extreme of maintaining that John was unaware of the existence of the Synoptic Gospels. Rightly understood, then, John was *both* dependent *and* independent of the Synoptics. A theory of conscious Johannine transposition of the Synoptic pattern capitalizes on the legitimate aspects of the various other available models while advancing a mediating position that is bolder than the mere affirmation of common or interlocking traditions.[59]

34.3.3 Conclusion

Indeed, the strategic decisions made by John in relation to the Synoptic pattern are bold.[60] They represent a conscious and theologically sophisticated effort to interpret for the reader the significance of Jesus' coming and ministry in a way that builds on and is compatible with the Synoptic portrait, but yet advances beyond it and thus is able to deepen the reader's understanding of Jesus' mission in many ways. Not only was John in all probability an apostolic eyewitness, but as the above sketch suggests, he was in all likelihood aware of the Synoptic pattern of presentation. In fact, it is hard to imagine John's gospel apart from the Synoptic pattern, which looms large and remains discernible in the way in which John has chosen to interpret, develop, and supplement it. On a larger canonical level, therefore, once prepared by the Synoptic witness, the readers are readied to climb the Johannine peak.

35 Johannine and Pauline Theology and the Theology of the Other New Testament Writings

35.1 Relationship with the Pauline Writings

John's gospel and Paul's letters reflect different but not contradictory perspectives.[61] Both emphasize love (John 13:13–14; 1 Corinthians 13),[62] consider the world to be in darkness and its wisdom futile, and use the phrase "in Christ" or "in him." They also depict Israel's destiny using similar imagery, whether branches of a vine

---

59. It is also superior to Paul Anderson's highly complex and conjectural theory of "interfluentiality" between various aspects of Johannine and Synoptic tradition (*Fourth Gospel and the Quest for Jesus*).

60. For a humorous treatment, see Bob Hudson, "Dear John the Evangelist," *CT* 42/8 (July 13, 1998): 60–61.

61. Of necessity, my remarks on the relationship between John's theology and the theology of Paul and the other NT writers must be considerably more succinct than the exploration of the relationship between John and the Synoptics above.

62. D. Moody Smith, "The Love Command: John and Paul?" in *Theology and Ethics in Paul and His Interpreters: Essays in Honor of Victor Paul Furnish* (Nashville: Abingdon, 1996), 207–17.

(John 15) or of an olive tree (Romans 11). Both subordinate the law to faith in Jesus (John 1:17; Romans and Galatians), and both depict God as "the Father," with John stressing the Father's role in believers' conception ("born of God") and Paul emphasizing his role in adoption (e.g., Gal 4:4–6). For both writers the gospel is centered on Jesus Christ crucified, buried, and risen (John 18–20; 1 Cor 15:1–4), and they both teach divine sovereignty and predestination in the context of theodicy (John 12:37–40; Romans 9–11).

There is also remarkable affinity in John's presentation of Nicodemus and the Samaritan woman as sinful human beings needing salvation irrespective of ethnicity, gender, or social status (John 3–4; see discussion above) and Paul's affirmation that "there is neither Jew nor Gentile, neither slave nor free, neither male nor female, for you are all one in Christ Jesus" (Gal 3:28). Even Paul's subsequent statement, "If you belong to Christ, then you are Abraham's seed, and heirs according to the promise" (Gal 3:29), is essentially replicated in John's gospel in Jesus' challenge of the Jews' claim of Abrahamic descent in John 8 (see esp. 8:33–47).

At the same time, John and Paul differ in many respects. Unlike Paul, John nowhere elaborates on the relationship between sin and the law; thus John lacks an equivalent to the Pauline antithesis between works and faith (though see John 6:28–29). The Pauline term "flesh" in contrast to the Spirit is without parallel in John (3:6 is no real exception). Likewise, John has no explicit doctrine of justification;[63] nor does he feature full-fledged versions of the Pauline corollaries to justification, such as reconciliation, calling, and sanctification (see, e.g., Rom 8:28–30). This, of course, should surprise no one, as it was left to Paul to flesh out these things in greater detail.

35.2 Relationship with the Other New Testament Writings

John shares with Hebrews a high Christology, particularly in the introductory sections. Both books stress that Jesus is the locus of God's final revelation (John 1:18; Heb 1:2), and both set God's redemptive work through Christ in parallel to his work of creation (John 1:1; Heb 1:3). Both also stress that Jesus is the last in a long series of divine emissaries and bearers of revelation (John 4:34; Heb 1:2). Both emphasize faith (John throughout; Hebrews 11) and portray Jesus as exalted subsequent to his suffering. But John's eschatology is mostly realized while Hebrews accentuates hope (though the eschatology in 1 John may be more futuristic than the gospel's); Johannine "in Christ" language is absent from Hebrews; and Hebrews portrays the Christian life more in terms of struggle, owing to the readers' weariness and reluctance to suffer.

The affinities between James and John are limited, most likely because the issues they sought to address differed considerably. Important topics in James include wisdom, the law, and dealing with the rich. References to Jesus Christ are rare (though

---

63. Though see Trotter, "Justification in the Gospel of John"; Scott Celsor, "The Human Response in the Creation and Formation of Faith: A Narrative Analysis of John 12:20–50 and Its Application to the Doctrine of Justification," *HBT* 30 (2008): 115–35.

there are allusions to Jesus' teaching), and the letter is largely devoted to the giving of practical advice to the congregation to which his letter is addressed. John, by contrast, squarely focuses on the question of Jesus' identity, while wisdom, the law, and issues related to wealth and poverty are at the periphery at best.

John and Peter are associated in ministry in the early portions of the book of Acts. It is therefore not surprising that they have similar perspectives on a number of issues.[64] Both emphasize that the fall of Judaism is part of God's plan (John 12:37; 1 Pet 2:8). Both present Jesus simultaneously as Lamb and as shepherd (John 1:29, 36; 10:12; 21:15–19; 1 Pet 1:19; 2:25; 5:2–4). Both portray believers as those who are "in Christ" (1 John 2:5–6; 1 Pet 5:14) and who believe in Jesus although they do not now see him (John 20:29; 1 Pet 1:8). Both emphasize mutual love (John 13:34; 15:9, 12, 17; 17:26; 1 Pet 1:22; 2:17; 4:8), regard Jesus' death as the norm for Christian conduct (15:13; 1 Pet 2:21–25; 3:17–18), challenge the church to suffer joyfully for Christ (John 15:18–25; 1 Pet 2:13–4:2), and acknowledge the Spirit as the witness to Jesus (John 15:26; 1 Pet 1:11–12) and the life-giver (6:63; 1 Pet 3:18). Finally, neither discusses the law or the constitution of the church.

A brief comment on the relationship between John's gospel and the letters may be appropriate in conclusion. Daniel Streett has recently made a strong case for the possibility that John's gospel and 1 John share in common the basic concern to defend the notion that Jesus is the Messiah.[65] Similar to Bauckham's work, this has the potential of opening up new avenues of research and to move the field past the current consensus that John primarily wrote to address some form of early Gnosticism. Indeed, it is entirely plausible and historically conceivable that John in his first letter sought to defend the main thesis of his gospel. If so, ironically, the situation would have been the precise opposite of the Brown-Martyn version of the "Johannine community hypothesis." Rather than the Johannine Christians having been expelled from their Jewish parent synagogue on account of their confession of Jesus as Messiah, it would have been nonmessianic Jews who departed from the Johannine congregation(s) who affirmed Jesus' messianic identity (though the exact circumstances of their departure are impossible to reconstruct with certainty).

As to the relationship between John's gospel and the book of Revelation, it is not necessary here to explore in detail the theological affinities between the gospel and letters on the one hand and Revelation on the other, since an entire separate volume in the BTNT series will cover the theology of the book of Revelation in detail. A treatment of the rather complex questions related to the possible common authorship of these respective documents and the conceptual relationship between them will therefore have to await the projected volume on the theology of Revelation. With this, the time has come for me to conclude, for now, this journey through the Johannine theological landscape.

---

64. See Merrill C. Tenney, "Some Possible Parallels between 1 Peter and John," in *New Dimensions in New Testament Study* (ed. Richard N. Longenecker and Merrill C. Tenney; Grand Rapids: Zondervan, 1974), 370–77.

65. Streett, "They Went Out from Us."

Conclusion

It has been my purpose in this volume to explore the various major aspects of Johannine theology by using a sound methodological biblical theology approach. This involved, first, a proper grounding of our study in an appraisal of the relevant historical and introductory matters related to John's gospel and letters. It also entailed, second, a laying of the literary foundations for Johannine theology, including an assessment of the genre of John's gospel and letters, a study of Johannine vocabulary, style, literary devices, and the structure of John's gospel and letters, and a sustained literary-theological reading of these documents. This was done in the conviction that any responsible and fully adequate treatment of major themes in Johannine theology must be properly grounded in a close reading of John's narrative and letters themselves.

The bulk of the volume, then, explored the contours and substance of Johannine theology. After a consideration of the Johannine worldview and John's use of Scripture, major Johannine themes were explored from the vantage point of the end (purpose statement), beginning (the introduction), and middle (the preamble to Part 2) of John's gospel. John's purpose was shown to be bound up inextricably with the Messiah and his signs, which formed the first topics of investigation. This was followed by a study of John's "new creation theology"; a discussion of God as Father, Son, and Spirit; a consideration of salvation history (including such themes as Jesus' fulfillment of festal symbolism and Jesus as the new temple); the cosmic trial theme (including the world, the Jews, and witnesses to Jesus); and a cluster of related theological themes surrounding a person's coming to faith in the sphere of God's sovereignty (including divine election and predestination, sin and divine judgment, faith and the new birth, and the new messianic community). This was followed by a series of studies of topics that started most pronouncedly in the middle of John's narrative: the Johannine love ethic, John's theology of the cross, and his trinitarian mission theology.

I concluded the volume with a brief consideration of Johannine theology in its larger NT and biblical-theological canonical contexts. This section included a discussion of John's theology in comparison with the Synoptics and a study of theological affinities with the other NT documents. With regard to John's relationship to the Synoptics, I advanced the possibility that John's approach might best be described as that of a "conscious transposition" of the Synoptic pattern by an eyewitness, combining elements of both dependence and independence models on the foundational premise that the author of John's gospel was an apostolic eyewitness.

No one can claim to have exhausted the depths of biblical revelation, including the theology of John. God's revelation is so rich, so inexhaustible, that there will invariably be many loose ends remaining to be tied together at the end of this kind of investigation. Perhaps it is fitting, therefore, to close this book with a paraphrase of the concluding statement in John's gospel: "John wrote about many other things as well; if every one of them were written down, I suppose that even the whole world would not have room for the books that would be written" (cf. 21:25).

The writing of books on John's gospel will no doubt continue. In the end, any book *about* John's gospel and letters is a poor substitute for continual reading of these writings themselves. If the present volume can serve as a small aid to a better understanding of these magnificent contributions to the NT canon, the labors of this writer will be amply rewarded. I love the gospel of John, and I hope that this book will ignite a similar passion for this wonderful gospel in you. Thank you for joining me on this journey, embarked on not primarily by a scholar seeking to master the gospel but by a worshiper and disciple longing to be mastered by it. *Soli Deo gloria*.

Bibliography

Aalen, S. "'Truth,' a Key Word in St. John's Gospel." Pp. 3–24 in *Studia Evangelica II*. Texte und Untersuchungen 87. Edited by F. L. Cross. Berlin: Akademie, 1964.

Abbott, Edwin A. *Johannine Vocabulary*. London: Adam and Charles Black, 1905.

———. *Johannine Grammar*. London: Adam and Charles Black, 1906.

Abrams, M. H. *A Glossary of Literary Terms*. 3rd ed. New York: Holt, Rinehart and Winston, 1971.

Achtemeier, Elizabeth. "Jesus Christ, the Light of the World: The Biblical Understanding of Light and Darkness." *Interpretation* 17 (1963): 439–49.

Achtemeier, Paul J., Joel B. Green, and Marianne Meye Thompson. *Introducing the New Testament: Its Literature and Theology*. Grand Rapids: Eerdmans, 2001.

Agourides, Savas. "Peter and John in the Fourth Gospel." Pp. 3–7 in *Studia Evangelica IV*. Edited by F. L. Cross. Berlin: Akademie, 1968.

Akin, Daniel L. *1, 2, 3 John*. New American Commentary 38. Nashville: Broadman & Holman, 2001.

Albani, Matthias. "'Wo sollte ein Haus sein, das ihr mir bauen könntet?' (Jes 66,1)." Pp. 37–56 in *Gemeinde ohne Tempel: Zur Substituierung und Transformation des Jerusalemer Tempels und seines Kults im Alten Testament, antiken Judentum und frühen Christentum*. Wissenschaftliche Untersuchungen zum Neuen Testament 118. Edited by Beate Ego, Armin Lange, and Peter Pilhofer. Tübingen: Mohr-Siebeck, 1999.

Albertz, Rainer. "Die Zerstörung des Jerusalemer Tempels 587 v. Chr.: Historische Einordnung und religionspolitische Bedeutung." Pp. 23–39 in *Zerstörungen des Jerusalemer Tempels: Geschehen–Wahrnehmung–Bewältigung*. Edited by Johannes Hahn. Wissenschaftliche Untersuchungen zum Neuen Testament 147. Tübingen: Mohr-Siebeck, 2002.

Alexander, Loveday C. A. "What Is a Gospel?" Pp. 13–33 in *The Cambridge Companion to the Gospels*. Edited by Stephen C. Barton. Cambridge: Cambridge University Press, 2006.

———. *Acts in Its Ancient Literary Context: A Classicist Looks at the Acts of the Apostles*. Journal for the Study of the New Testament Supplement 276. Edinburgh: T&T Clark, 2007.

Alexander, Philip S. "Rabbinic Biography and the Biography of Jesus: A Survey of the Evidence." Pp. 19–50 in *Synoptic Studies: The Ampleforth Conferences of 1982 and 1983*. Edited by Christopher M. Tuckett. Sheffield: JSOT, 1984.

———. "'The Parting of the Ways' from the Perspective of Rabbinic Judaism." Pp. 1–25 in *Jews and Christians: The Parting of the Ways A.D. 70 to 135*. Edited by James D. G. Dunn. Tübingen: Mohr-Siebeck, 1992.

Alexander, T. Desmond, and Brian S. Rosner, eds. *New Dictionary of Biblical Theology: Exploring the Unity & Diversity of Scripture*. Leicester, UK: Inter-Varsity Press, 2000.

Alexander, T. Desmond, and Simon Gathercole, eds. *Heaven on Earth: The Temple in Biblical Theology*. Carlisle, UK: Paternoster, 2004.

Alter, Robert. *The Art of Biblical Narrative*. New York: Basic Books, 1981.

Anderson, Hugh. "Introduction to 4 Maccabees." Pp. 531–43 in *Old Testament Pseudepigrapha*. Vol. 2. Edited by James H. Charlesworth. Garden City, NY: Doubleday, 1985.

Anderson, Paul N. *The Fourth Gospel and the Quest for Jesus: Modern Foundations Reconsidered.* New York: T&T Clark, 2006.

Arens, Eduardo. *The Elthon-Sayings in the Synoptic Tradition: A Historico-Critical Investigation.* Orbis biblicus et orientalis 10. Freiburg: Universitätsverlag/Göttingen: Vandenhoeck & Ruprecht, 1976.

Ashton, John. *Understanding the Fourth Gospel.* Oxford: Clarendon, 1991.

Attridge, Harold W. "Response to 'The De-historicizing of the Gospel of John' by Robert Kysar." Paper presented at the Annual Meeting of the Society of Biblical Literature. Toronto, November 23–26, 2002.

Aune, David E. "The Problem of the Genre of the Gospels: A Critique of C. H. Talbert's *What Is a Gospel?*" Pp. 9–60 in *Gospel Perspectives.* Vol. 2: *Studies of History and Tradition in the Four Gospels.* Edited by R. T. France and David Wenham. Sheffield: JSOT, 1981.

———. *The New Testament in Its Literary Environment.* Library of Early Christianity 8. Philadelphia: Westminster, 1987.

———. "Dualism in the Fourth Gospel and the Dead Sea Scrolls: A Reassessment of the Problem." Pp. 281–303 in *Neotestamentica et Philonica: Studies in Honor of Peder Borgen.* Edited by David E. Aune, Torrey Seland, and Jarl Henning Ulrichsen. Novum Testamentum Supplement 106. Leiden: Brill, 2003.

Avemarie, Friedrich. "Ist die Johannestaufe ein Ausdruck von Tempelkritik? Skizze eines methodischen Problems." Pp. 395–410 in *Gemeinde ohne Tempel: Zur Substituierung und Transformation des Jerusalemer Tempels und seines Kults im Alten Testament, antiken Judentum und frühen Christentum.* Wissenschaftliche Untersuchungen zum Neuen Testament 118. Edited by Beate Ego, Armin Lange, and Peter Pilhofer. Tübingen: Mohr-Siebeck, 1999.

Baird, William. *History of New Testament Research.* 2 vols. Minneapolis: Fortress, 1992, 2003.

Ball, David M. *The "I Am" in John's Gospel: Literary Function, Background and Theological Implications.* Journal for the Study of the New Testament Supplement 124. Sheffield: Sheffield Academic Press, 1996.

Balthasar, Hans Urs von. *Theo-Drama: Theological Dramatic Theory.* 4 vols. Translated by G. Harrison. San Francisco: Ignatius, 1988, 1990, 1992, 1994.

Balz, Horst. "Johanneische Theologie und Ethik im Licht der 'letzten Stunde.'" Pp. 35–56 in *Studien zum Text und zur Ethik des Neuen Testaments: Festschrift zum 80. Geburtstag von Heinrich Greeven.* Berlin/New York: de Gruyter, 1986.

———. "Die Johannesbriefe." In *Die "Katholischen Briefe": Die Briefe des Jakobus, Petrus, Johannes und Judas.* Das Neue Testament Deutsch 10. 11th ed. Göttingen: Vandenhoeck & Ruprecht, 1973.

Bampfylde, Gillian. "More Light on John 12,34." *Journal for the Study of the New Testament* 17 (1983): 87–89.

Barclay, William. *The Gospel of John.* Daily Study Bible. 2 vols. Rev. ed. Louisville: Westminster John Knox, 1975.

Barnett, Paul W. "The Jewish Signs Prophets—A.D. 40–70: Their Intentions and Origin." *New Testament Studies* 27 (1981): 679–97.

———. "The Feeding of the Multitude in Mark 6/John 6." Pp. 273–93 in *Gospel Perspectives.* Volume 6: *The Miracles of Jesus.* Edited by David Wenham and Craig Blomberg. Sheffield: JSOT, 1986.

———. "Indications of Earliness in the Gospel of John." *Reformed Theological Review* 64 (2005): 61–75.
Barr, James. *The Semantics of Biblical Language*. London: SCM, 1961.
Barrett, C. K. "The Dialectical Theology of St John." Pp. 49–69 in *New Testament Essays*. London: SPCK, 1972.
———. "John and the Synoptic Gospels." *Expository Times* 85 (1974): 228–33.
———. "The House of Prayer and the Den of Thieves." Pp. 13–20 in *Jesus und Paulus*. Edited by E. Earle Ellis and Erich Grässer. Göttingen: Vandenhoeck & Ruprecht, 1975.
———. *The Gospel according to St. John*. 2nd ed. Philadelphia: Westminster, 1978.
———. "Christocentric or Theocentric? Observations on the Theological Method of the Fourth Gospel." Pp. 1–18 in *Essays on John*. Philadelphia: Westminster, 1982.
———. "Paradox and Dualism." Pp. 98–115 in *Essays on John*. Philadelphia: Westminster, 1982.
Barrosse, Thomas. "The Seven Days of the New Creation in St. John's Gospel." *Catholic Biblical Quarterly* 21 (1959): 507–16.
Bass, Christopher D. *That You May Know: Assurance of Salvation in 1 John*. NAC Studies in Bible & Theology. Nashville: Broadman & Holman, 2008.
Bassler, Jouette M. "Mixed Signals: Nicodemus in the Fourth Gospel." *Journal of Biblical Literature* 108 (1989): 635–46.
———. "God in the NT." Pp. 1049–55 in *The Anchor Bible Dictionary*. Vol. 2. Edited by David Noel Freedman. New York: Doubleday, 1992.
Bauckham, Richard. "Worship of Jesus." Pp. 812–19 in *The Anchor Bible Dictionary*. Vol. 3. Edited by David Noel Freedman. New York: Doubleday, 1992.
———. "John for Readers of Mark." Pp. 147–72 in *The Gospels for All Christians: Rethinking the Gospel Audiences*. Edited by Richard Bauckham. Grand Rapids: Eerdmans, 1998.
———. *God Crucified: Monotheism and Christology in the New Testament*. Grand Rapids: Eerdmans, 1998.
———. "The Qumran Community and the Gospel of John." Pp. 105–15 in *The Dead Sea Scrolls: Fifty Years after Their Discovery*. Edited by Lawrence H. Schiffman, Emmanuel Tov, James C. VanderKam, and Galen Marquis. Jerusalem: Israel Exploration Society, 2000.
———. "Biblical Theology and the Problems of Monotheism." Pp. 187–232 in *Out of Egypt: Biblical Theology and Biblical Interpretation*. Edited by Craig G. Bartholomew, Mary Healy, Karl Möller, and Robin Parry. Carlisle, UK: Paternoster/Grand Rapids: Zondervan, 2004.
———. "Monotheism and Christology in the Gospel of John." Pp. 153–63 in *Contours of Christology in the New Testament*. Edited by Richard N. Longenecker. Grand Rapids: Eerdmans, 2005.
———. *Jesus and the Eyewitnesses: The Gospels as Eyewitness Testimony*. Grand Rapids: Eerdmans, 2006.
———. *The Testimony of the Beloved Disciple: Narrative, History, and Theology in the Gospel of John*. Grand Rapids: Baker, 2007.
———. "Historiographical Characteristics of the Gospel of John." *New Testament Studies* 53 (2007): 17–36.
Bauckham, Richard, ed. *The Gospels for All Christians: Rethinking the Gospel Audiences*. Grand Rapids: Eerdmans, 1998.

———. *Jesus and the God of Israel: God Crucified and Other Studies on the New Testament's Christology of Divine Identity.* Grand Rapids: Eerdmans, 2008.

Bauder, Wolfgang. "Disciple." Pp. 480–94 in *New International Dictionary of New Testament Theology.* Vol. 1. Edited by Colin Brown. Grand Rapids: Zondervan, 1986.

Bauer, Walter. *Orthodoxy and Heresy in Earliest Christianity.* Edited by Robert Kraft and Gerhard Krodel. Philadelphia: Fortress, 1971 [1934].

Baumbach, Günther. "Gemeinde und Welt im Johannesevangelium." *Kairos* 14 (1972): 121–36.

Baumeister, Theofried. "Der Tod Jesu und die Leidensnachfolge des Jüngers nach dem Johannesevangelium und dem ersten Johannesbrief." *Wissenschaft und Weisheit* 40 (1977): 81–99.

Beale, G. K. "The New Testament and New Creation." Pp. 159–73 in *Biblical Theology: Retrospect and Prospect.* Edited by Scott J. Hafemann. Downers Grove, IL: InterVarsity Press, 2002.

———. *The Temple and the Church's Mission: A Biblical Theology of the Temple.* New Studies in Biblical Theology. Downers Grove, IL: InterVarsity Press, 2004.

Beasley-Murray, George R. "The Eschatology of the Fourth Gospel." *Evangelical Quarterly* 18 (1946): 97–108.

———. "John 21,32–34. The Eschatological Significance of the Lifting Up of the Son of Man." Pp. 70–81 in *Studien zum Text und zur Ethik des Neuen Testaments: Festschrift zum 80. Geburtstag von H. Greeven.* Edited by Wolfgang Schrage. Berlin/New York: de Gruyter, 1986.

———. *John.* Word Biblical Commentary 36. Waco, TX: Word, 1987.

———. *Gospel of Life: Theology in the Fourth Gospel.* Peabody, MA: Hendrickson, 1991.

———. "The Mission of the Logos-Son." Pp. 1855–68 in *The Four Gospels 1992: Festschrift Frans Neirynck.* Bibliotheca ephemeridum theologicarum lovaniensium 100. Vol. 3. Edited by F. van Segbroeck, C. M. Tuckett, G. van Belle, and J. Verheyden. Leuven: Leuven University Press, 1992.

Beck, David R. *The Discipleship Paradigm: Readers and Anonymous Characters in the Fourth Gospel.* Biblical Interpretation Series 27. Leiden: Brill, 1997.

Becker, Jürgen. "Wunder und Christologie: Zum literarkritischen und christologischen Problem der Wunder im Johannesevangelium." *New Testament Studies* 16 (1969/70): 130–48.

Behr, John. "The Word of God in the Second Century." *Pro Ecclesia* 9 (2000): 85–107.

Bennema, Cornelis. "A Theory of Character in the Fourth Gospel with Reference to Ancient and Modern Literature." *Biblical Interpretation* 17 (2009): 375–421.

———. "The Identity and Composition of ΟΙ ΙΟΥΔΑΙΟΙ in the Gospel of John." *TynBul* 60 (2009): forthcoming.

Bernard, John Henry. *A Critical and Exegetical Commentary on the Gospel according to St. John.* International Critical Commentary. 2 vols. Edinburgh: T&T Clark, 1928.

Betz, Otto. *Der Paraklet: Fürsprecher im häretischen Spätjudentum, im Johannes-Evangelium und in neu gefundenen gnostischen Schriften.* Leiden: Brill, 1963.

———. *Nachfolge und Nachahmung Jesu Christi im Neuen Testament.* Beiträge zur historischen Theologie 37. Tübingen: Mohr-Siebeck, 1967.

———. "'To Worship God in Spirit and in Truth': Reflections on John 4,20–26." Pp. 53–72 in *Standing before God: Studies on Prayer in Scriptures and in Tradition. In Honor of John M. Oesterreicher.* Translated by Nora Quigley. New York: KTAV, 1981.

———. "Das Problem des Wunders bei Flavius Josephus im Vergleich zum Wunderproblem bei den Rabbinen und im Johannesevangelium." Pp. 409–19 in *Jesus: Der Messias Israels. Aufsätze zur biblischen Theologie*. Wissenschaftliche Untersuchungen zum Neuen Testament 42. Tübingen: Mohr-Siebeck, 1987.

Beutler, Johannes. "Die Heilsbedeutung des Todes Jesu im Johannesevangelium nach Joh 13:1–20." Pp. 188–204 in *Der Tod Jesu: Deutungen im Neuen Testament*. Quaestiones Disputatae 74. Edited by Karl Kartelge. Freiburg im Breisgau: Herder, 1976.

———. "Der alttestamentlich-jüdische Hintergrund der Hirtenrede in Johannes 10." Pp. 18–32 in *The Shepherd Discourse of John 10 and its Context*. Edited by Johannes Beutler and Robert T. Fortna. Society for New Testament Studies Monograph Series 67. Cambridge: Cambridge University Press, 1991.

Bieringer, Reimund. "'My Kingship Is Not of This World' (John 18,36): The Kingship of Jesus and Politics." Pp. 159–75 in *The Myriad Christ: Plurality and the Quest for Unity in Contemporary Christology*. Bibliotheca ephemeridum theologicarum lovaniensium 152. Edited by T. Merrigan and J. Haers. Leuven: Leuven University Press/Peeters, 2000.

Bieringer, Reimund, Didier Pollefeyt, and Frederique Vandecasteele-Vanneuville, eds. *Anti-Judaism and the Fourth Gospel*. Louisville: Westminster John Knox, 2001.

———. *Anti-Judaism and the Fourth Gospel: Papers of the Leuven Colloquium, 2000*. Assen, the Netherlands: Royal van Gorcum, 2001.

Billings, J. S. "Judas Iscariot in the Fourth Gospel." *Expository Times* 51 (1939–40): 156–57.

Billington, Antony. "The Paraclete and Mission in the Fourth Gospel." Pp. 90–115 in *Mission and Meaning: Essays Presented to Peter Cotterell*. Edited by Antony Billington, Tony Lane, and Max Turner. Carlisle, UK: Paternoster, 1995.

Bittner, Wolfgang J. *Jesu Zeichen im Johannesevangelium: Die Messias-Erkenntnis im Johannesevangelium vor ihrem jüdischen Hintergrund*. Wissenschaftliche Untersuchungen zum Neuen Testament 2/26. Tübingen: Mohr-Siebeck, 1987.

Blaine, Bradford B. Jr. *Peter in the Gospel of John: The Making of an Authentic Disciple*. Society of Biblical Literature Academia Biblica 27. Atlanta: Society of Biblical Literature/Leiden: Brill, 2008.

Blenkinsopp, Joseph. *Isaiah 40–55*. Anchor Bible 19A. New York: Doubleday, 2002.

Blomberg, Craig L. "To What Extent Is John Historically Reliable?" Pp. 27–56 in *Perspectives on John: Method and Interpretation in the Fourth Gospel*. Edited by Robert B. Sloan and Michael C. Parsons. NABPR Special Studies Series. Lewiston, NY: Mellen, 1993.

———. "The Globalization of Biblical Interpretation: A Test Case—John 3–4." *Bulletin of Biblical Research* 5 (1995): 1–15.

———. "The Historical Reliability of John: Rushing in Where Angels Fear to Tread?" Pp. 71–82 in *Jesus and Johannine Tradition*. Edited by Robert T. Fortna and Tom Thatcher. Louisville: Westminster John Knox, 2001.

———. *The Historical Reliability of John's Gospel*. Leicester, UK: Inter-Varsity Press, 2002.

———. "Messiah in the New Testament." Pp. 111–41 in *Israel's Messiah in the Bible and the Dead Sea Scrolls*. Edited by Richard S. Hess and M. Daniel Carroll R. Grand Rapids: Baker, 2003.

———. *The Historical Reliability of the Gospels*. 2nd ed. Downers Grove, IL: InterVarsity Press, 2007.

Blount, Brian K. *Then the Whisper Put on Flesh: New Testament Ethics in an African American Context*. Nashville: Abingdon, 2001.

Bock, Darrell L. *Luke.* Baker Exegetical Commentary on the New Testament. 2 vols. Grand Rapids: Baker, 1994, 1996.

———. *Blasphemy and Exaltation in Judaism and the Final Examination of Jesus.* Wissenschaftliche Untersuchungen zum Neuen Testament 2/106. Tübingen: Mohr-Siebeck, 1998.

———. "The Kingdom of God in New Testament Theology." Pp. 28–60 in *Looking into the Future: Evangelical Studies in Eschatology.* Edited by David W. Baker. Grand Rapids: Baker, 2001.

———. *Jesus according to Scripture: Restoring the Portrait from the Gospels.* Downers Grove, IL: InterVarsity Press, 2002.

———. *Acts.* Baker Exegetical Commentary on the New Testament. Grand Rapids: Baker, 2007.

Bockmuehl, Markus N. A. *Seeing the Word: Refocusing New Testament Study.* Studies in Theological Interpretation. Grand Rapids: Baker, 2006.

Boda, Mark J. "Figuring the Future: The Prophets and Messiah." Pp. 35–74 in *The Messiah in the Old and New Testaments.* McMaster New Testament Studies. Edited by Stanley E. Porter. Grand Rapids: Eerdmans, 2007.

Boismard, Marie-Émile. *Du baptême à Cana (Jean 1,19–2,11).* Paris: Cerf, 1956.

Boismard, Marie-Émile, and Arnaud Lamouille. *L'évangile de Jean.* Leuven: Leuven University Press, 1979.

Bolyki, János. "Ethics in the Gospel of John." *Acta Antiqua* 44 (2004): 99–107.

Bond, Helen K. *Pontius Pilate in History and Interpretation.* Cambridge: Cambridge University Press, 1998.

Booth, Wayne C. *A Rhetoric of Irony.* Chicago: University of Chicago Press, 1974.

Borchert, Gerald L. "The Passover and the Narrative Cycles in John." Pp. 303–16 in *Perspectives on John: Method and Interpretation in the Fourth Gospel.* Edited by Robert B. Sloan and Mikeal C. Parsons. Lewiston, NY: Mellen, 1993.

———. *John 1–11.* New American Commentary 25A. Nashville: Broadman & Holman, 1996.

———. *John 12–21.* New American Commentary 25B. Nashville: Broadman & Holman, 2002.

Borgen, Peder. *Bread from Heaven: An Exegetical Study of the Concept of Manna in the Gospel of John and the Writings of Philo.* Novum Testamentum Supplement 10. Leiden: Brill, 1965.

Borig, Rainer. *Der wahre Weinstock: Untersuchungen zu Jo 15,1–10.* Studien zum Alten und Neuen Testament 16. Munich: Kösel, 1967.

Boring, M. Eugene. "The Influence of Christian Prophecy on the Johannine Portrayal of the Paraclete and Jesus." *New Testament Studies* 25 (1978): 113–23.

Bosch, David J. *Transforming Mission: Paradigm Shifts in Theology of Mission.* Maryknoll, NY: Orbis, 1991.

Botha, J. E. "The Case of Johannine Irony Reopened I: The Problematic Current Situation." *Neotestamentica* 25 (1991): 209–20.

———. "The Case of Johannine Irony Reopened II: Suggestions, Alternative Approaches." *Neotestamentica* 25 (1991): 221–32.

Bowen, Clayton R. "The Fourth Gospel as Dramatic Material." *Journal of Biblical Literature* 49 (1930): 292–305.

Bowersock, G. W. *Fiction as History: Nero to Julian.* Berkeley: University of California Press, 1994.

Brant, Jo-Ann A. *Dialogue and Drama: Elements of Greek Tragedy in the Fourth Gospel.* Peabody, MA: Hendrickson, 2004.

Braun, François-Marie. *Jean le théologien.* Vol. 1: *Jean le théologien et son évangile dans l'église ancienne.* Paris: J. Gabalda, 1959.

———. *Jean le théologien.* Vol. 4: *Sa théologie: Le mystère de Jésus-Christ.* Paris: J. Gabalda, 1966.

———. "Les Epîtres de Saint Jean." Pp. 231–77 in *L'Evangile de Saint Jean.* In *La Sainte Bible de Jérusalem.* 3rd rev. ed. Paris: Cerf, 1973.

Bray, Gerald, ed. *James, 1–2 Peter, 1–3 John.* Ancient Christian Commentary on Scripture, New Testament 11. Downers Grove, IL: InterVarsity Press, 2000.

Bretschneider, Karl Gottlieb. *Probabilia de evangelii et epistolarum Joannis, apostolic, indole et origine eruditorum judiciis modeste subjecit.* Leipzig: A. Barth, 1820.

Brodie, Thomas L. *The Gospel according to John: A Literary and Theological Commentary.* New York/Oxford: Oxford University Press, 1993.

Brooke, A. E. *A Critical and Exegetical Commentary on the Johannine Epistles.* International Critical Commentary. New York: Scribner, 1912.

Brooke, George J. "Miqdash Adam, Eden, and the Qumran Community." Pp. 285–301 in *Gemeinde ohne Tempel: Zur Substituierung und Transformation des Jerusalemer Tempels und seines Kults im Alten Testament, antiken Judentum und frühen Christentum.* Wissenschaftliche Untersuchungen zum Neuen Testament 118. Edited by Beate Ego, Armin Lange, and Peter Pilhofer. Tübingen: Mohr-Siebeck, 1999.

Brown, Jeannine K. "Creation's Renewal in the Gospel of John." *Catholic Biblical Quarterly* (forthcoming).

Brown, Raymond E. "The Relation Between the Fourth Gospel and the Synoptic Gospels." Pp. 143–216 in *New Testament Essays.* Milwaukee: Bruce Chapman, 1965.

———. *The Gospel according to John.* Anchor Bible 29. 2 vols. Garden City, NY: Doubleday, 1966, 1970.

———. "The Paraclete in the Fourth Gospel." *New Testament Studies* 13 (1967): 113–32.

———. "The Spirit-Paraclete in the Gospel of John." *Catholic Biblical Quarterly* 33 (1971): 268–70.

———. "Roles of Women in the Fourth Gospel." *Theological Studies* 36 (1975): 688–99.

———. "'Other Sheep Not of This Fold': The Johannine Perspective on Christian Diversity in the Late First Century." *Journal of Biblical Literature* 97 (1978): 5–22.

———. *The Community of the Beloved Disciple.* New York: Paulist, 1979.

———. *The Epistles of John.* Anchor Bible 30. New York: Doubleday, 1982.

———. *An Introduction to the New Testament.* Anchor Bible Reference Library. New York: Doubleday, 1997.

———. *An Introduction to the Gospel of John.* Anchor Bible Reference Library. Edited by Francis J. Moloney. New York: Doubleday, 2003.

Brown, Raymond E., Karl P. Donfried, and John Reumann, eds. *Peter in the New Testament.* Minneapolis: Augsburg, 1973.

Bruce, F. F. "The Book of Zechariah and the Passion Narrative." *Bulletin of the John Rylands Library* 43 (1960): 336–53.

———. "Is the Paul of Acts the Real Paul?" *Bulletin of the John Rylands Library* 58 (1976): 282–305.

———. *The Epistles of John.* Grand Rapids: Eerdmans, 1979.

Brunson, Andrew C. *Psalm 118 in the Gospel of John: An Intertextual Study on the New Exodus Pattern in the Theology of John*. Wissenschaftliche Untersuchungen zum Neuen Testament 158. Tübingen: Mohr-Siebeck, 2003.

Bryan, Steven M. "Power in the Pool: The Healing of the Man at Bethesda and Jesus' Violation of the Sabbath (Jn. 5:1–18)." *Tyndale Bulletin* 54 (2003): 7–22.

———. "The Eschatological Temple in John 14." *Bulletin of Biblical Research* 15 (2005): 187–98.

Bryant, Michael. "A Study of Prayer in the Johannine Writings." Ph.D. dissertation. Wake Forest, NC: Southeastern Baptist Theological Seminary, 2008.

Bultmann, Rudolf. *Theology of the New Testament*. 2 vols. Translated by Kendrick Grobel. New York: Charles Scribner's Sons, 1951, 1955.

———. *The History of the Synoptic Tradition*. Translated by John Marsh. New York: Harper & Row, 1963 [1957].

———. "ἀλήθεια, κτλ." Pp. 232–51 in *Theological Dictionary of the New Testament*. Vol. 1. Edited by Gerhard Kittel. Translated by Geoffrey W. Bromiley. Grand Rapids: Eerdmans, 1964.

———. *The Gospel of John*. Translated by George R. Beasley-Murray. Philadelphia: Westminster, 1971.

———. *The Johannine Epistles*. Hermeneia. Translated by R. Philip O'Hara et al. Philadelphia: Fortress, 1973.

———. "Die Bedeutung der neuerschlossenen mandäischen und manichäischen Quellen für das Verständnis des Johannesevangeliums." Pp. 402–64 in *Johannes und sein Evangelium*. Wege der Forschung 82. Edited by Karl Heinrich Rengstorf. Darmstadt: Wissenschaftliche Buchgesellschaft, 1973 [1925].

Burge, Gary M. *The Anointed Community*. Grand Rapids: Eerdmans, 1987.

———. "The Literary Seams in the Fourth Gospel." *Covenant Quarterly* 48 (1990): 15–25.

———. *Interpreting the Gospel of John*. Guides to New Testament Exegesis. Grand Rapids: Baker, 1992.

———. *The Letters of John*. NIV Application Commentary. Grand Rapids: Zondervan, 1996.

———. *John*. NIV Application Commentary. Grand Rapids: Zondervan, 2000.

———. "Interpreting the Gospel of John." Pp. 357–90 in *Interpreting the New Testament: Essays on Methods and Issues*. Edited by David Alan Black and David S. Dockery. Nashville: Broadman & Holman, 2001.

———. "Situating John's Gospel in History." Pp. 35–46 in *Jesus in Johannine Tradition*. Edited by Robert T. Fortna and Tom Thatcher. Louisville: Westminster John Knox, 2001.

Burkett, Delbert. *The Son of Man in the Gospel of John*. Journal for the Study of the New Testament Supplement 56. Sheffield: JSOT, 1991.

Burridge, Richard. *What Are the Gospels? A Comparison with Greco-Roman Biography*. 2nd ed. Grand Rapids: Eerdmans, 2004.

———. *Imitating Jesus: An Inclusive Approach to New Testament Ethics*. Grand Rapids: Eerdmans, 2007.

———. "Imitating Jesus: An Inclusive Approach to the Ethics of the Historical Jesus and John's Gospel." Paper presented at the Annual Meeting of the Society of Biblical Literature, San Diego, CA, November 17, 2008.

Bush, L. Russ III. "Knowing the Truth." *Faith & Mission* 11/2 (1994): 3–13.

Buth, Randall. "Οὖν, Δέ,, Καί and Asyndeton in John's Gospel." Pp. 141–61 in *Linguistics and New Testament Interpretation: Essays on Discourse Analysis.* Edited by David Alan Black. Nashville: Broadman & Holman, 1992.

Byrskog, Samuel. *Story as History—History as Story.* Wissenschaftliche Untersuchungen zum Neuen Testament 123. Tübingen: Mohr-Siebeck, 2000. Reprint Leiden: Brill, 2002.

Caird, G. B. *New Testament Theology.* Completed and edited by L. D. Hurst. Oxford: Clarendon, 1995.

———. "The Glory of God in the Fourth Gospel: An Exercise in Biblical Semantics." *New Testament Studies* 15 (1969): 265–77.

Calvin, John. *The Gospel according to St. John.* 2 vols. Translated by T. H. L. Parker. Edinburgh: Oliver & Boyd, 1959.

Campbell, Ken M. "What Was Jesus' Occupation?" *Journal of the Evangelical Theological Society* 48 (2005): 501–19.

Carey, George L. "The Lamb of God and Atonement Theories." *Tyndale Bulletin* 32 (1981): 97–122.

Carmichael, Calum M. *The Story of Creation: Its Origin and Its Interpretation in Philo and the Fourth Gospel.* Ithaca, NY: Cornell University Press, 1996.

Carson, D. A. *Divine Sovereignty and Human Responsibility: Biblical Perspectives in Tension.* Atlanta: John Knox, 1981.

———. "Historical Tradition in the Fourth Gospel: After Dodd, What?" Pp. 83–145 in *Gospel Perspectives: Studies of History and Tradition in the Four Gospels.* Edited by R. T. France and David Wenham. Sheffield: JSOT, 1981.

———. "Understanding Misunderstandings in the Fourth Gospel." *Tyndale Bulletin* 33 (1982): 59–91.

———. "Unity and Diversity in the New Testament: The Possibility of Systematic Theology." Pp. 61–95 in *Scripture and Truth.* Edited by D. A. Carson and John D. Woodbridge. Grand Rapids: Zondervan, 1983.

———. "The Purpose of the Fourth Gospel: Jn 20:31 Reconsidered." *Journal of Biblical Literature* 106 (1987): 639–51.

———. "John and the Johannine Epistles." Pp. 245–64 in *It Is Written: Scripture Citing Scripture. Essays in Honor of Barnabas Lindars, SSF.* Edited by D. A. Carson and H. G. M. Williamson. Cambridge: Cambridge University Press, 1988.

———. "The Role of Exegesis in Systematic Theology." Pp. 39–76 in *Doing Theology in Today's World.* Edited by John D. Woodbridge and Thomas E. McComiskey. Grand Rapids: Zondervan, 1991.

———. *The Gospel according to John.* Pillar New Testament Commentary. Grand Rapids: Eerdmans, 1991.

———. "The Purpose of Signs and Wonders in the New Testament." Pp. 89–118 in *Power Religion.* Edited by Michael S. Horton. Chicago: Moody Press, 1992.

———. "Reflections on Christian Assurance." *Westminster Theological Journal* 54 (1992): 1–29.

———. *The Gagging of God: Christianity Confronts Pluralism.* Grand Rapids: Zondervan, 1996.

———. "Syntactical and Text-Critical Observations on John 20:30–31: One More Round on the Purpose of the Fourth Gospel." *Journal of Biblical Literature* 124 (2005): 693–714.

———. "The Challenge of the Balkanization of Johannine Studies." Pp. 133–59 in *John, Jesus, and History*. Vol. 1: *Critical Appraisals of Critical Views*. Edited by Paul N. Anderson, Felix Just, S.J., and Tom Thatcher. SBL Semeia Studies 44. Atlanta: Society of Biblical Literature, 2007.

———. "Reflections upon a Johannine Pilgrimage." Pp. 87–104 in *What We Have Heard from the Beginning: The Past, Present, and Future of Johannine Studies*. Edited by Tom Thatcher. Waco, TX: Baylor University Press, 2007.

Carson, D. A., and Douglas J. Moo. *An Introduction to the New Testament*. 2nd ed. Grand Rapids: Zondervan, 2005.

Carter, Warren. *John and Empire: Initial Explorations*. London: T&T Clark, 2008.

Casey, Maurice. *From Jewish Prophet to Gentile God: The Origins and Development of New Testament Christology*. Louisville: Westminster John Knox, 1991.

———. *Is John's Gospel True?* London/New York: Routledge, 1996.

Cassem, Ned H. "A Grammatical and Contextual Inventory of the Use of κόσμος in the Johannine Cosmic Theology." *New Testament Studies* 19 (1972): 81–91.

Casurella, Anthony. *The Johannine Paraclete in the Church Fathers: A Study in the History of Exegesis*. Tübingen: Mohr-Siebeck, 1983.

Celsor, Scott. "The Human Response in the Creation and Formation of Faith: A Narrative Analysis of John 12:20–50 and Its Application to the Doctrine of Justification." *Horizons in Biblical Theology* 30 (2008): 115–35.

Chaine, Joseph. Pp. 97–260 in *Les epîtres catholiques*. Études biblique. 2nd ed. Paris: J. Gabalda, 1939.

Charlesworth, James H. "A Critical Comparison of the Dualism in 1QS iii,13–iv,26 and the 'Dualism' Contained in the Fourth Gospel." *New Testament Studies* 15 (1969): 389–418.

———. "A Study in Shared Symbolism and Language: The Qumran Community and the Johannine Community." Pp. 97–152 in *The Bible and the Dead Sea Scrolls: The Princeton Symposium on the Dead Sea Scrolls*. Vol. 3: *The Scrolls and Christian Origins*. Waco, TX: Baylor University Press, 2006.

Charlesworth, James H., ed. *John and the Dead Sea Scrolls*. Christian Origins Library. New York: Crossroad, 1990.

———. *The Messiah: Developments in Earliest Judaism and Christianity*. Minneapolis: Fortress, 1992.

Charlesworth, James H., Hermann Lichtenberger, and Gerbern S. Oegema, eds. *Qumran-Messianism: Studies on the Messianic Expectations in the Dead Sea Scrolls*. Tübingen: Mohr-Siebeck, 1998.

Chennattu, Rekha M. *Johannine Discipleship as a Covenant Relationship*. Peabody, MA: Hendrickson, 2006.

Chevalier, Haakon M. *The Ironic Temper: Anatole France and His Time*. New York/London: Oxford University Press, 1932.

Clavier, H. "L'ironie dans le quatrième Evangile." Pp. 261–76 in *Studia Evangelica*. Texte und Untersuchungen 73. Edited by Kurt Aland, F. L. Cross, Jean Danielou, Harald Riesenfeld, and W. C. Van Unnik. Berlin: Akademie, 1959.

Clements, Ronald E. "Monotheism and the Canonical Process." *Theology* 87 (1984): 336–44.

Coetzee, J. C. "Life (Eternal Life) in John's Writings and the Qumran Scrolls." *Neotestamentica* 6 (1972): 48–66.

Cohen, Shaye J. D. "Yavneh Revisited: Pharisees, Rabbis, and the End of Jewish Sectarianism." Pp. 45–61 in *Society of Biblical Literature 1982 Seminar Papers*. SBL Seminar Papers Series 21. Edited by Kent H. Richards. Chico, CA: Scholars Press, 1982.

Cohon, S. S. "The Unity of God: A Study in Hellenistic and Rabbinic Theology." *Hebrew Union College Annual* 26 (1955): 425–79.

Collins, Adela Yarbro. "Crisis and Community in John's Gospel." *Currents in Theology and Mission* 7 (1980): 196–204.

Collins, John J. *The Scepter and the Star: The Messiah of the Dead Sea Scrolls and Other Ancient Literature*. New York: Doubleday, 1995.

Collins, Raymond F. *John and His Witness*. Zacchaeus Studies: New Testament. Collegeville, MN: Liturgical Press, 1991.

———. "Representative Figures." Pp. 1–45 in *These Things Have Been Written. Studies on the Fourth Gospel*. Grand Rapids: Eerdmans, 1991.

Coloe, Mary L. *God Dwells with Us: Temple Symbolism in the Fourth Gospel*. Collegeville, MN: Liturgical Press, 2001.

———. "Welcome into the Household of God: The Footwashing in John 13." *Catholic Biblical Quarterly* 66 (2004): 400–15.

Colwell, Ernest C. *The Greek of the Fourth Gospel: A Study of Its Aramaisms in the Light of Hellenistic Greek*. Chicago: University of Chicago Press, 1931.

Combs, William W. "The Meaning of Fellowship in 1 John." *Detroit Baptist Seminary Journal* 13 (2008): 3–16.

Connick, C. Milo. "The Dramatic Character of the Fourth Gospel." *Journal of Biblical Literature* 67 (1948): 159–69.

Conway, Colleen M. *Men and Women in the Fourth Gospel: Gender and Johannine Characterization*. SBL Dissertation Series 167. Atlanta: Society of Biblical Literature, 1999.

Cook, W. Robert. *The Theology of John*. Chicago: Moody Press, 1979.

———. "The 'Glory' Motif in the Johannine Corpus." *Journal of the Evangelical Theological Society* 27 (1984): 291–97.

———. "Eschatology in John's Gospel." *Criswell Theological Review* 3 (1988): 79–99.

Corell, Alf. *Consummatum Est: Eschatology and Church in the Gospel of St. John*. London: SPCK, 1958.

Cotterell, Peter. "The Nicodemus Conversation: A Fresh Approach." *Expository Times* 96 (1985): 237–42.

Cotterell, Peter, and Max Turner. *Linguistics & Biblical Interpretation*. Downers Grove, IL: InterVarsity Press, 1989.

Cowan, Christopher. "The Father and Son in the Fourth Gospel: Johannine Subordination Revisited." *Journal of the Evangelical Theological Society* 49 (2006): 115–35.

Credner, Karl August. *Einleitung in das Neue Testament*. Halle: Waisenhauses, 1837.

Cribbs, F. Lamar. "Reassessment of the Date of Origin and the Destination of the Gospel of John." *Journal of Biblical Literature* 89 (1970): 38–55.

Croteau, David A. "An Analysis of the Concept of Believing in the Narrative Contexts of John's Gospel." Th.M. thesis. Wake Forest, NC: Southeastern Baptist Theological Seminary, 2002.

———. "An Analysis of the Arguments for the Dating of the Fourth Gospel." *Faith & Mission* 20/3 (2003): 47–80.

Crump, D. M. "Truth." Pp. 859–62 in *Dictionary of Jesus and the Gospels*. Edited by Joel B. Green, Scot McKnight, and I. Howard Marshall. Downers Grove, IL: InterVarsity Press, 1992.

Cullmann, Oscar. "Der johanneische Gebrauch doppeldeutiger Ausdrücke als Schlüssel zum Verständnis des vierten Evangeliums." *Theologische Zeitschrift* 4 (1948): 360–72.

———. *Early Christian Worship*. Studies in Biblical Theology 10. Translated by A. Stewart Todd and James B. Torrance. London: SCM, 1953.

———. "A New Approach to the Interpretation of the Fourth Gospel." *Expository Times* 71 (1959): 39–43.

———. *Salvation in History*. New York: Harper & Row, 1967.

———. *The Johannine Circle*. Translated by John Bowden. London: SCM, 1976.

———. *Peter: Disciple, Apostle, Martyr*. Translated by Floyd V. Filson. London: SCM, 1976.

Culpepper, R. Alan. *The Johannine School*. SBL Dissertation Series 26. Missoula, MT: Scholars Press, 1975.

———. "The Pivot of John's Prologue." *New Testament Studies* 27 (1980): 1–31.

———. *Anatomy of the Fourth Gospel: A Study in Literary Design*. Philadelphia: Fortress, 1983.

———. *John, the Son of Zebedee: The Life of a Legend*. Columbia: University of South Carolina Press, 1994. Reprint Minneapolis: Fortress, 2000.

———. "John 21:24–25—The Johannine *Sphragis*." Paper presented at the Annual Meeting of the Society of Biblical Literature. San Diego, CA, November 2007.

Dahl, Nils A. "The Johannine Church and History." Pp. 124–42 and 284–88 in *Current Issues in New Testament Interpretation: Essays in Honor of Otto A. Piper*. Edited by William Klassen and Graydon F. Snyder. New York: Harper & Brothers, 1962.

———. "The Neglected Factor in New Testament Theology." *Reflection* 73/1 (1975): 5–8. Reprinted pp. 58–60 in *Jesus Is the Christ: The Historical Origins of Christological Doctrine*. Edited by Donald H. Juel. Minneapolis: Fortress, 1991.

Daise, Michael A. "'If Anyone Thirsts, Let That One Come to Me and Drink': The Literary Texture of John 7:37b–38a." *Journal of Biblical Literature* 122 (2003): 687–99.

———. *Feasts in John: Jewish Festivals and Jesus' "Hour" in the Fourth Gospel*. Wissenschaftliche Untersuchungen zum Neuen Testament 2/229. Tübingen: Mohr-Siebeck, 2007.

Daly-Denton, Margaret. *David in the Fourth Gospel: The Johannine Reception of the Psalms*. Arbeiten zur Geschichte des antiken Judentums und des Urchristentums 47. Leiden: Brill, 2004.

———. "The Psalms in John's Gospel." Pp. 119–37 in *The Psalms in the New Testament*. The New Testament and the Scriptures of Israel. Edited by Steven Moyise and Maarten J. J. Menken. London: T&T Clark International, 2004.

Daube, David. *The New Testament and Rabbinic Judaism*. London: Athlone, 1956.

Davies, Margaret. *Rhetoric and Reference in the Fourth Gospel*. Journal for the Study of the New Testament Supplement 69. Sheffield: JSOT, 1992.

Davies, W. D. "The Johannine 'Signs' of Jesus." Pp. 91–115 in *A Companion to John: Readings in Johannine Theology*. Edited by Michael J. Taylor. New York: Alba, 1977.

———. *The Gospel and the Land: Early Christianity and Jewish Territorial Doctrine*. Sheffield: JSOT, 1994.

———. "Reflections on Aspects of the Jewish Background of the Gospel of John." Pp. 43–64 in *Exploring the Gospel of John: In Honor of D. Moody Smith*. Edited by R. Alan Culpepper and C. Clifton Black. Louisville: Westminster John Knox, 1996.

Day, Gail R. "Response to 'Expulsion from the Synagogue: A Tale of a Theory' by Robert Kysar." Paper presented at the Annual Meeting of the Society of Biblical Literature. Toronto, November 23–26, 2002.

De Boer, Martinus C. *Johannine Perspectives on the Death of Jesus*. Contributions to Biblical Exegesis and Theology 17. Kampen: Kok, 1996.

Denaux, Adelbert, ed. *John and the Synoptics*. Bibliotheca ephemeridum theologicarum lovaniensium 101. Leuven: Leuven University Press/Peeters, 1992.

Dennis, John A. "Conflict and Resolution: John 11.47–53 as the Ironic Fulfillment of the Main Plot-Line of the Gospel (John 1.11–12)." *Studien zur neutestamentlichen Umwelt* 29 (2004): 23–39.

———. "The Presence and Function of Second Exodus-Restoration Imagery in John 6." *Studien zur neutestamentlichen Umwelt* 30 (2005): 105–21.

———. "Restoration in John 11,47–52. Reading the Key Motifs in Their Jewish Context." *Ephemerides theologicae lovanienses* 81 (2005): 57–86.

———. "Jesus' Death in John's Gospel: A Survey of Research from Bultmann to the Present with Special Reference to the Johannine Hyper-Texts." *Currents in Biblical Research* 4 (2006): 331–63.

———. *Jesus' Death and the Gathering of True Israel: The Johannine Appropriation of Restoration Theology in the Light of John 11.47–52*. Wissenschaftliche Untersuchungen zum Neuen Testament 2/217. Tübingen: Mohr-Siebeck, 2006.

———. "Begotten by the Spirit: Johannine Eternal Life in Biblical-Theological Perspective." Paper presented at the Annual Meeting of the Evangelical Theological Society. Providence, RI, November 19, 2008.

Dietzfelbinger, Christian. "Die grösseren Werke (Joh 14.12f.)." *New Testament Studies* 35 (1989): 27–47.

Dobschütz, Ernst von. "Johanneische Studien I." *Zeitschrift für die neutestamentliche Wissenschaft* 8 (1907): 1–8.

Dodd, C. H. "The Background of the Fourth Gospel." *Bulletin of the John Rylands Library* 19 (1935): 329–43.

———. "The Kingdom of God Has Come." *Expository Times* 48 (1936): 138–42.

———. "The First Epistle of John and the Fourth Gospel." *Bulletin of the John Rylands Library* 21 (1937): 129–56.

———. *The Johannine Epistles*. Moffatt New Testament Commentary. New York: Harper, 1946.

———. *The Interpretation of the Fourth Gospel*. Cambridge: Cambridge University Press, 1953.

———. *The Coming of Christ*. Cambridge: Cambridge University Press, 1954.

Domeris, W. R. "The Johannine Drama." *Journal of Theology for Southern Africa* 42 (1983): 29–35.

Draper, J. A. "Temple, Tabernacle and Mystical Experience in John." *Neotestamentica* 31 (1997): 263–88.

Duke, Paul D. *Irony in the Fourth Gospel*. Atlanta: John Knox, 1985.

Dumbrell, William J. *The Search for Order: Biblical Eschatology in Focus*. Grand Rapids: Baker, 1994.

Dunn, James D. G. "John VI—A Eucharistic Discourse?" *New Testament Studies* 17 (1971): 328–38.

———. "Let John Be John: A Gospel for Its Time." Pp. 293–322 in *The Gospel and the Gospels*. Edited by Peter Stuhlmacher. Grand Rapids/Cambridge: Eerdmans, 1991.

———. *The Partings of the Ways between Christianity and Judaism and their Significance for the Character of Christianity.* London: SCM/Philadelphia: Trinity International, 1991.

———. "The Making of Christology—Evolution or Unfolding?" Pp. 437–52 in *Jesus of Nazareth: Lord and Christ. Essays on the Historical Jesus and New Testament Christology.* Edited by Joel B. Green and Max Turner. Grand Rapids: Eerdmans, 1994.

———. *Christology in the Making: A New Testament Inquiry into the Origins of the Doctrine of the Incarnation.* 2nd ed. Grand Rapids: Eerdmans, 1996.

———. *The Theology of Paul the Apostle.* Grand Rapids: Eerdmans, 1997.

———. *Jesus Remembered.* Christianity in the Making 1. Grand Rapids: Eerdmans, 2003.

DuRand, Jan A. "The Creation Motif in the Fourth Gospel: Perspectives on Its Narratological Function within a Judaistic Background." Pp. 21–46 in *Theology and Christology in the Fourth Gospel: Essays by the Members of the SNTS Johannine Writings Seminar.* Edited by G. Van Belle, J. G. Van der Watt, and P. Maritz. Leuven: Leuven University Press, 2005.

Dvořák, James D. "The Relationship between John and the Synoptic Gospels." *Journal of the Evangelical Theological Society* 41 (1998): 201–13.

Edwards, M. J., and Simon Swain, eds. *Portraits: Biographical Representation in the Greek and Latin Literature of the Roman Empire.* Oxford: Clarendon, 1997.

Edwards, Ruth B. *The Johannine Epistles.* New Testament Guides. Sheffield: Sheffield Academic Press, 1996.

Ellingworth, Paul. "Translating *Oun* in John's Gospel." *Bible Translator* 51 (2000): 135–43.

Enz, Jacob J. "The Book of Exodus as a Literary Type for the Gospel of John." *Journal of Biblical Literature* 76 (1957): 208–15.

Erdmann, Martin. "Mission in John's Gospel and Letters." Pp. 207–26 in *Mission in the New Testament: An Evangelical Approach.* Edited by William J. Larkin Jr. and Joel F. Williams. Maryknoll, NY: Orbis, 1998.

Erickson, Millard J. *God in Three Persons: A Contemporary Interpretation of the Trinity.* Grand Rapids: Baker, 1995.

Eshel, Esther. "Prayer in Qumran and the Synagogue." Pp. 323–34 in *Gemeinde ohne Tempel: Zur Substituierung und Transformation des Jerusalemer Tempels und seines Kults im Alten Testament, antiken Judentum und frühen Christentum.* Wissenschaftliche Untersuchungen zum Neuen Testament 118. Edited by Beate Ego, Armin Lange, and Peter Pilhofer. Tübingen: Mohr-Siebeck, 1999.

Eshel, Hanan. "Josephus' View on Judaism without the Temple in Light of the Discoveries at Masada and Murabba'at." Pp. 229–38 in *Gemeinde ohne Tempel: Zur Substituierung und Transformation des Jerusalemer Tempels und seines Kults im Alten Testament, antiken Judentum und frühen Christentum.* Wissenschaftliche Untersuchungen zum Neuen Testament 118. Edited by Beate Ego, Armin Lange, and Peter Pilhofer. Tübingen: Mohr-Siebeck, 1999.

Evans, Craig A. "On the Quotation Formulas in the Fourth Gospel." *Biblische Zeitschrift* 26 (1982): 79–83.

———. "Obduracy and the Lord's Servant: Some Observations on the Use of the Old Testament in the Fourth Gospel." Pp. 221–36 in *Early Jewish and Christian Exegesis: Studies in Memory of William Hugh Brownlee.* Homage 10. Edited by Craig A. Evans and William F. Stinespring. Atlanta: Scholars Press, 1987.

———. "Jesus' Action in the Temple: Cleansing or Portent of Destruction?" *Catholic Biblical Quarterly* 51 (1989): 237–70.

———. *To See and Not Perceive: Isaiah 6:9–10 in Early Jewish and Christian Interpretation*. Journal for the Study of the Old Testament Supplement 64. Sheffield: JSOT, 1989.

———. *Word and Glory: On the Exegetical and Theological Background of John's Prologue*. Journal for the Study of the New Testament Supplement 89. Sheffield: Sheffield Academic Press, 1993.

———. "The Messiah in the Dead Sea Scrolls." Pp. 183–97 in *The Scrolls and the Scriptures: Qumran Fifty Years After*. Edited by Stanley E. Porter and Craig A. Evans. Sheffield: Sheffield Academic Press, 1997.

Evanson, Edward. *The Dissonance of the Four Generally Received Evangelists and the Evidence of Their Authenticity Examined*. Ipswich, 1792.

Fee, Gordon D. "On the Text and Meaning of John 20,30–31." Pp. 2193–205 in *The Four Gospels 1992: Fs. Frans Neirynck*. Bibliotheca ephemeridum theologicarum lovaniensium 100. Vol. 3. Ed. F. van Segbroeck, C. M. Tuckett, G. van Belle, and J. Verheyden. Leuven: Leuven University Press, 1992.

Filson, Floyd V. "The Gospel of Life: A Study of the Gospel of John." Pp. 111–23 in *Current Issues in New Testament Interpretation: Essays in Honor of Otto A. Piper*. Edited by William Klassen and Graydon F. Snyder. New York: Harper & Brothers, 1962.

Fisher, Matthew C. "God the Father in the Fourth Gospel: A Biblical Patrology." Ph.D. dissertation. Wake Forest, NC: Southeastern Baptist Theological Seminary, 2003.

Fitzmyer, Joseph A. "μονός." Pp. 440–42 in *Exegetical Dictionary of the New Testament*. Vol. 2. Edited by Horst Balz and Gerhard Schneider. 3 vols. Grand Rapids: Eerdmans, 1991.

Flanagan, Neal. "The Gospel of John as Drama." *Bible Today* 19 (1981): 264–70.

Forestell, J. Terence. *The Word of the Cross: Salvation as Revelation in the Fourth Gospel*. Analecta biblica 57. Rome: Biblical Institute Press, 1974.

Fornara, Charles William. *The Nature of History in Ancient Greece and Rome*. Berkeley: University of California Press, 1983.

Fortna, Robert T. *The Gospel of Signs: A Reconstruction of the Narrative Source Underlying the Fourth Gospel*. Cambridge: Cambridge University Press, 1970.

———. *The Fourth Gospel and Its Predecessor: From Narrative Source to Present Gospel*. Philadelphia: Fortress, 1988.

France, R. T. *Jesus and the Old Testament: His Application of Old Testament Passages to Himself and His Mission*. London: Tyndale, 1971.

———. *Matthew—Evangelist and Teacher*. Grand Rapids: Zondervan, 1989.

Freed, Edwin D. *Old Testament Quotations in the Gospel of John*. Novum Testamentum Supplement 11. Leiden: Brill, 1965.

———. "*Egō eimi* in John 8,24 in the Light of its Context and Jewish Messianic Belief." *Journal of Theological Studies* 33 (1982): 163–67.

Freedman, William. "The Literary Motif: A Definition and Evaluation." *Novel* 4 (1971): 123–31.

Frei, Hans W. *The Eclipse of Biblical Narrative*. New Haven/London: Yale University Press, 1974.

Frey, Jörg. "Temple and Rival Temple—The Cases of Elephantine, Mt. Gerizim, and Leontopolis." Pp. 171–203 in *Gemeinde ohne Tempel: Zur Substituierung und Transformation des Jerusalemer Tempels und seines Kults im Alten Testament, antiken Judentum und frühen*

Christentum. Wissenschaftliche Untersuchungen zum Neuen Testament 118. Edited by Beate Ego, Armin Lange, and Peter Pilhofer. Tübingen: Mohr-Siebeck, 1999.

———. *Die johanneische Eschatologie*. 3 vols. Wissenschaftliche Untersuchungen zum Neuen Testament 96, 110, 117. Tübingen: Mohr-Siebeck, 1997–2000.

———. "Die '*theologia crucifixi*' des Johannesevangeliums." Pp. 169–238 in *Kreuzestheologie im Neuen Testament*. Wissenschaftliche Untersuchungen zum Neuen Testament 151. Edited by Andreas Dettwiler and Jean Zumstein. Tübingen: Mohr-Siebeck, 2002.

Frey, Jörg, and Jens Schröter, eds. *Deutungen des Todes Jesu im Neuen Testament*. Wissenschaftliche Untersuchungen zum Neuen Testament 181. Tübingen: Mohr-Siebeck, 2005.

Frey, Jörg, Jan G. van der Watt, and Ruben Zimmermann, eds. *Imagery in the Gospel of John: Terms, Forms, Themes, and Theology of Johannine Figurative Language*. Wissenschaftliche Untersuchungen zum Neuen Testament 200. Tübingen: Mohr-Siebeck, 2006.

Friedman, Norman. *Form and Meaning in Fiction*. Athens, GA: University of Georgia Press, 1975.

Gaffney, J. "Believing and Knowing in the Fourth Gospel." *Theological Studies* 26 (1965): 215–42.

Gardner-Smith, Percival. *Saint John and the Synoptic Gospels*. Cambridge: Cambridge University Press, 1938.

Gaugler, Ernst. "Die Bedeutung der Kirche in den johanneischen Schriften." *Internationale Kirchliche Zeitschrift* 14 (1924): 97–117, 181–219; 15 (1925): 27–42.

Giblet, Jean. "Aspects of the Truth in the New Testament." Pp. 35–42 in *Truth and Certainty*. Edited by Edward Schillebeeckx and Bas van Iersel. New York: Herder & Herder, 1973.

Giblin, Charles Homer. "John's Narration of the Hearing Before Pilate (John 18,28–19,16a)." *Biblica* 67 (1986): 221–39.

Gibson, David. "The Johannine Footwashing and the Death of Jesus: A Dialogue with Scholarship." *Scottish Bulletin of Evangelical Theology* 25 (2007): 50–60.

Giesbrecht, Herbert. "The Evangelist John's Conception of the Church as delineated in his Gospel." *Evangelical Quarterly* 58 (1986): 101–19.

Giles, Kevin J. *Jesus and the Father: Modern Evangelicals Reinvent the Doctrine of the Trinity*. Downers Grove, IL: InterVarsity Press, 2006.

Glasson, T. Francis. *Moses in the Fourth Gospel*. Studies in Biblical Theology 40. London: SCM, 1963.

Gloer, W. Hulitt. *An Exegetical and Theological Study of Paul's Understanding of New Creation and Reconciliation in 2 Cor. 5:14–21*. Mellen Biblical Press Series 42. Lewiston, NY: Mellen, 1996.

Gnuse, Robert K. *No Other Gods: Emergent Monotheism in Israel*. Journal for the Study of the Old Testament Supplement 241. Sheffield: Sheffield Academic Press, 1997.

Goodman, Martin. *The Ruling Class of Judaea: The Origins of the Jewish Revolt against Rome, A.D. 66–70*. Cambridge: Cambridge University Press, 1987.

———. "Diaspora Reactions to the Destruction of the Temple." Pp. 27–38 in *Jews and Christians: The Parting of the Ways A.D. 70 to 135*. Edited by James D. G. Dunn. Tübingen: Mohr-Siebeck, 1992.

Goppelt, Leonhard. *Theology of the New Testament*. Translated by John E. Alsup. Edited by Jürgen Roloff. 2 vols. Grand Rapids: Eerdmans, 1981–1982.

Grant, Robert M. *A Historical Introduction to the New Testament*. London: Collins, 1963.

Grayston, Kenneth. "The Meaning of *Paraklētos*." *Journal for the Study of the New Testament* 13 (1981): 67–82.

———. *The Johannine Epistles.* New Century Bible Commentary. Grand Rapids: Eerdmans, 1984.

Green, Joel B., Scot McKnight, and I. Howard Marshall, eds. *Dictionary of Jesus and the Gospels.* Downers Grove, IL: InterVarsity Press, 1992.

Grenz, Stanley J. *Women in the Church.* Downers Grove, IL: InterVarsity Press, 1995.

Griffith, Terry. *Keep Yourselves from Idols: A New Look at 1 John.* Journal for the Study of the New Testament Supplement 233. London: Sheffield Academic Press, 2002.

Grigsby, Bruce H. "The Cross as a Expiatory Sacrifice in the Fourth Gospel." *Journal for the Study of the New Testament* 15 (1982): 51–80.

Grillmeier, Alois. *Christ in Christian Tradition.* Vol. 1: *From the Apostolic Age to Chalcedon (431).* Translated by John Bowden. 2nd rev. ed. Atlanta: John Knox, 1975.

Groussow, W. "La glorification du Christ dans le quatrième évangile." Pp. 131–45 in *L'Évangile de Jean: Études et problèmes.* Recherches bibliques 3. Edited by Marie-Émile Boismard et al. Bruges: Desclée de Brouwer, 1958.

Guelich, Robert. "The Gospel Genre." Pp. 183–208 in *The Gospel and the Gospels.* Edited by Peter Stuhlmacher. Grand Rapids: Eerdmans, 1991.

Guericke, Heinrich Ernst Ferdinand. *Neutestamentliche Isagogik.* 3rd ed. Leipzig: A. Winter, 1908.

Gundry, Robert. *A Survey of the New Testament.* 3rd ed. Grand Rapids: Zondervan, 1994.

———. *Jesus the Word according to John the Sectarian: A Paleofundamentalist Manifesto for Contemporary Evangelicalism, Especially Its Elites, in North America.* Grand Rapids: Eerdmans, 2002.

———. *The Old Is Better: New Testament Essays in Support of Traditional Interpretations.* Tübingen: Mohr-Siebeck, 2005.

Gunther, John J. "The Relation of the Beloved Disciple to the Twelve." *Theologische Zeitschrift* 37 (1981): 129–48.

Guthrie, Donald. "The Importance of Signs in the Fourth Gospel." *Vox Evangelica* 5 (1967): 72–83.

———. *New Testament Introduction.* Rev. ed. Downers Grove, IL: InterVarsity Press, 1990.

Guthrie, George H. "Boats in the Bay: Reflections on the Use of Linguistics and Literary Analysis in Biblical Studies." Pp. 23–35 in *Linguistics and the New Testament: Critical Junctures.* Journal for the Study of the New Testament Supplement 168. Studies in New Testament Greek 5. Edited by Stanley E. Porter and D. A. Carson. Sheffield: Sheffield Academic Press, 1999.

Haacker, Klaus. *Die Stiftung des Heils: Untersuchungen zur Struktur der johanneischen Theologie.* Stuttgart: Calwer, 1972.

———. "Jesus und die Kirche nach Johannes." *Theologische Zeitschrift* 29 (1973): 179–201.

Haenchen, Ernst. *A Commentary on the Gospel of John.* Hermeneia. Translated by Robert W. Funk. Edited by Robert W. Funk with Ulrich Busse. Philadelphia: Fortress, 1984.

Hägerland, Tobias. "John's Gospel: A Two-Level Drama?" *Journal for the Study of the New Testament* 25 (2003): 309–22.

Hahn, Johannes, ed. *Zerstörungen des Jerusalemer Tempels: Geschehen–Wahrnehmung–Bewältigung.* Wissenschaftliche Untersuchungen zum Neuen Testament 147. Edited by Johannes Hahn. Tübingen: Mohr-Siebeck, 2002.

Hamid-Khani, Saeed. *Revelation and Concealment of Christ: A Theological Inquiry into the Elusive Language of the Fourth Gospel*. Wissenschaftliche Untersuchungen zum Neuen Testament 2/120. Tübingen: Mohr-Siebeck, 2000.

Hamilton, James. "The Influence of Isaiah on the Gospel of John." *Perichoresis* 5/2 (2007): 139–62.

Hanson, A. T. *The Prophetic Gospel*. Edinburgh: T&T Clark, 1991.

Hare, Douglas R. A. "Review of *The Son of Man in the Gospel of John* by Delbert Burkett." *Journal of Biblical Literature* 112 (1993): 158–60.

Harner, Philip B. *The "I Am" of the Fourth Gospel*. Facet Books. Philadelphia: Fortress, 1970.

Harris, Murray J. *Jesus as God: The New Testament Use of* Theos *in Reference to Jesus*. Grand Rapids: Baker, 1992.

Harris, W. Hall. "A Theology of John's Writings." Pp. 167–242 in *A Biblical Theology of the New Testament*. Edited by Roy B. Zuck and Darrell L. Bock. Chicago: Moody Press, 1994.

Hartin, Patrick J. "The Role of Peter in the Fourth Gospel." *Neotestamentica* 24 (1990): 49–61.

Hasitschka, Martin. *Befreiung von Sünde nach dem Johannesevangelium: Eine bibeltheologische Untersuchung*. Innsbruck: Tyrolia, 1989.

Hatina, Thomas R. "John 20,22 in Its Eschatological Context: Promise or Fulfillment?" *Biblica* 74 (1993): 196–219.

Hawkin, David J. "The Johannine Concept of Truth." *Evangelical Quarterly* 59 (1987): 3–13.

Hays, Richard B. *The Moral Vision of the New Testament*. San Francisco: Harper, 1996.

Hedrick, Charles W. "Authorial Presence and Narrator in John: Commentary and Story." Pp. 74–93 in *Gospel Origins and Christian Beginnings*. Edited by James E. Goehring, Charles W. Hedrick, Jack T. Sanders, and Hans Dieter Betz. Sonoma, CA: Polebridge, 1990.

———. "Vestigial Scenes in John: Settings without Dramatization." *Novum Testamentum* 47 (2005): 354–66.

Hengel, Martin. *Acts and the History of Earliest Christianity*. London: SCM, 1979.

———. *Studies in the Gospel of Mark*. Philadelphia: Fortress, 1985.

———. *The Johannine Question*. Philadelphia: Fortress, 1989.

———. *Die johanneische Frage*. Wissenschaftliche Untersuchungen zum Neuen Testament 67. Tübingen: Mohr-Siebeck, 1993.

———. "Das Johannesevangelium als Quelle für die Geschichte des antiken Judentums." Pp. 293–334 in *Judaica, Hellenistica et Christiana: Kleine Schriften II*. Wissenschaftliche Untersuchungen zum Neuen Testament 109. Tübingen: Mohr-Siebeck, 1999.

———. *The Four Gospels and the One Gospel of Jesus Christ: An Investigation of the Collection and Origin of the Canonical Gospels*. Translated by John Bowden. Harrisburg, PA: Trinity Press International, 2000.

———. "Eye-Witness Memory and the Writing of the Gospels." Pp. 70–96 in *The Written Gospel*. Edited by Markus Bockmuehl and Donald A. Hagner. Cambridge: Cambridge University Press, 2001.

Hess, Richard S. "The Image of the Messiah in the Old Testament." Pp. 22–33 in *Images of Christ: Ancient and Modern*. Edited by Stanley E. Porter, Michael A. Hayes, and David Tombs. Sheffield: Sheffield Academic Press, 1997.

Hesselgrave, David J. *Paradigms in Conflict: 10 Key Questions in Mission Today.* Grand Rapids: Kregel, 2006.

Hill, Charles E. *The Johannine Corpus in the Early Church.* Oxford/New York: Oxford University Press, 2004.

Hills, Julian V. "A Genre for 1 John." Pp. 367–77 in *The Future of Early Christianity: Essays in Honor of Helmut Koester.* Edited by Birger A. Pearson, A. Thomas Kraabel, George W. E. Nickelsburg, and Norman R. Petersen. Minneapolis: Fortress, 1991.

Hirsch, E. D. *Validity in Interpretation.* New Haven, CT: Yale University Press, 1973.

Hitchcock, F. R. M. "Is the 4th Gospel a Drama?" *Theology* 7 (1923): 307–17. Reprinted pp. 15–24 in *The Gospel of John as Literature: An Anthology of Twentieth-Century Perspectives.* NT Tools & Studies 17. Edited by Mark W. G. Stibbe. Leiden: Brill, 1993.

Hoehner, Harold W. *Chronological Aspects of the Life of Christ.* Grand Rapids: Zondervan, 1977.

———. "Chronology." Pp. 118–22 in *Dictionary of Jesus and the Gospels.* Edited by Joel B. Green, Scot McKnight, and I. Howard Marshall. Downers Grove, IL: InterVarsity Press, 1992.

Hofius, Otfried. "'Der in des Vaters Schoss ist,' Joh 1,18." *Zeitschrift für die neutestamentliche Wissenschaft* 80 (1989): 163–71.

Holloway, Paul A. "Left Behind: Jesus' Consolation of His Disciples in John 13,31–17,26." *Zeitschrift für die neutestamentliche Wissenschaft* 96 (2005): 1–34.

Holmes, Michael W. *The Apostolic Fathers: Greek Texts and English Translations.* 3rd ed. Grand Rapids: Baker, 2004.

Holtzmann, Heinrich Julius. "Das Problem des ersten johanneischen Briefes in seinem Verhältnis zum Evangelium." *Jahrbuch für Protestantische Theologie* 7 (1881): 690–712; 8 (1882): 128–52, 316–42, 460–86.

Horbury, William. "The Benediction of the *Minim* and Early Jewish-Christian Controversy." *Journal of Theological Studies* 33 (1982): 19–61.

———. *Jewish Messianism and the Cult of Christ.* London: SCM, 1998.

Hornblower, Simon, and Antony Spawforth, eds. *The Oxford Classical Dictionary.* 3rd ed. Oxford/New York: Oxford University Press, 1996.

Hoskins, Paul M. *Jesus as the Fulfillment of the Temple in the Gospel of John.* Paternoster Biblical Monographs. Carlisle, UK: Paternoster, 2007.

———. "Deliverance from Death by the True Passover Lamb: A Significant Aspect of the Fulfillment of the Passover in the Gospel of John." *Journal of the Evangelical Theological Society* 52 (2009): 285–99.

Hoskyns, Edwyn, and F. N. Davey. *The Fourth Gospel.* 2 vols. London: Faber & Faber, 1940.

Houlden, J. L. *Ethics and the New Testament.* New York: Oxford University Press, 1973.

Howard, J. K. "Passover and Eucharist in the Fourth Gospel," *Scottish Journal of Theology* 20 (1967): 329–37.

Howard, W. F. "The Common Authorship of the Johannine Gospel and Epistles." *Journal of Theological Studies* 48 (1947): 12–25.

———. *The Fourth Gospel in Recent Criticism and Interpretation.* Revised by C. K. Barrett. London: Epworth, 1955.

Hubbard, Moyer V. *New Creation in Paul's Letters and Thought.* Cambridge: Cambridge University Press, 2002.

Hudson, Bob. "Dear John the Evangelist." *Christianity Today* 42/8 (July 13, 1998): 60–61.

Humphrey, Edith M. "New Creation." Pp. 536–37 in *Dictionary for Theological Interpretation of the Bible.* Edited by Kevin J. Vanhoozer. Grand Rapids: Baker, 2005.

Humphreys, Colin J., and W. G. Waddington. "The Jewish Calendar, a Lunar Eclipse, and the Date of Christ's Crucifixion." *Tyndale Bulletin* 43 (1992): 331–51.

Hunter, W. Bingham. "The Prayers of Jesus in the Gospel of John." Ph.D. dissertation. Aberdeen, Scotland: University of Aberdeen, 1979.

Hurtado, Larry W. *One God, One Lord: Early Christian Devotion and Ancient Jewish Monotheism.* Edinburgh: T&T Clark, 1988.

———. "Christ." Pp. 106–17 in *Dictionary of Jesus and the Gospels.* Edited by Joel B. Green, Scot McKnight, and I. Howard Marshall. Downers Grove: InterVarsity Press, 1992.

———. "Gospel (Genre)." Pp. 276–82 in *Dictionary of Jesus and the Gospels.* Edited by Joel B. Green, Scot McKnight, and I. Howard Marshall. Downers Grove, IL: InterVarsity Press, 1992.

———. "First-Century Jewish Monotheism." *Journal for the Study of the New Testament* 71 (1998): 3–26.

———. "Pre–70 C.E. Jewish Opposition to Christ-Devotion." *Journal of Theological Studies* 50 (1999): 35–58.

———. *Lord Jesus Christ: Devotion to Jesus in Earliest Christianity.* Grand Rapids: Eerdmans, 2003.

Hüttenmeister, Frowald G. "Die Synagoge: Ihre Entwicklung von einer multifunktionalen Einrichtung zum reinen Kultbau." Pp. 357–69 in *Gemeinde ohne Tempel: Zur Substituierung und Transformation des Jerusalemer Tempels und seines Kults im Alten Testament, antiken Judentum und frühen Christentum.* Wissenschaftliche Untersuchungen zum Neuen Testament 118. Edited by Beate Ego, Armin Lange, and Peter Pilhofer. Tübingen: Mohr-Siebeck, 1999.

Ito, Hisayasu. "Johannine Irony Demonstrated in John 9." *Neotestamentica* 34 (2000): 361–71, 373–87.

———. "Narrative Temporality and Johannine Symbolism." *Acta Theologica* 23 (2003): 117–35.

Jackson, Howard M. "Ancient Self-Referential Conventions and Their Implications for the Authorship and Integrity of the Gospel of John." *Journal of Theological Studies* 50 (1999): 1–34.

Janowski, Bernd, and Peter Stuhlmacher, eds. *The Suffering Servant: Isaiah 53 in Jewish and Christian Scriptures.* Translated by Daniel P. Bailey. Grand Rapids: Eerdmans, 2004.

Jeremias, Joachim. *The Eucharistic Words of Jesus.* Translated by Norman Perrin. London: SCM, 1966.

Johnson, S. Lewis Jr. *The Old Testament in the New: An Argument for Biblical Inspiration.* Grand Rapids: Zondervan, 1980.

Johnston, George. *The Spirit-Paraclete in the Gospel of John.* Society for New Testament Studies Monograph Series 12. Cambridge: Cambridge University Press, 1970.

Jones, Larry Paul. *The Symbol of Water in the Gospel of John.* Journal for the Study of the New Testament Supplement 145. Sheffield: Sheffield Academic Press, 1997.

Jonge, Marinus de. "Jesus as Prophet and King in the Fourth Gospel." *Ephemerides theologicae lovanienses* 49 (1973): 160–77.

———. "Jewish Expectations about the 'Messiah' according to the Fourth Gospel." *New Testament Studies* 19 (1973): 246–70.

———. "Signs and Works in the Fourth Gospel." Pp. 107–25 in *Miscellanea neotestamentica* 2. Novum Testamentum Supplement 48. Edited by T. Baarda, A. F. J. Klijn, and W. C. van Unnik. Leiden: Brill, 1978.

Käsemann, Ernst. *The Testament of Jesus.* Translated by Gerhard Krodel. Philadelphia: Fortress, 1968.

Katz, Steven T. "Issues in the Separation of Judaism and Christianity after 70 C.E.: A Reconsideration." *Journal of Biblical Literature* 103 (1984): 43–76.

Kealy, Seán P. *John's Gospel and the History of Biblical Interpretation.* 2 vols. Mellen Biblical Press Series 60a–b. Lewiston, NY: Mellen, 2002.

Keener, Craig S. "Is Subordination within the Trinity Really Heresy? A Study of John 5:18 in Context." *Trinity Journal* 20 NS (1999): 39–51.

———. *The Gospel of John*: *A Commentary.* 2 vols. Peabody, MA: Hendrickson, 2003.

Kellum, L. Scott. *The Unity of the Farewell Discourse: The Literary Integrity of John 13.31–16.33.* Journal for the Study of the New Testament Supplement 256. London/ New York: T&T Clark, 2004.

———. "On the Semantic Structure of 1 John: A Modest Proposal." *Faith & Mission* 23 (2008): 34–82.

Kerr, Alan R. *The Temple of Jesus' Body: The Temple Theme in the Gospel of John.* Journal for the Study of the New Testament Supplement 220. Sheffield: Sheffield Academic Press, 2002.

Kidner, Derek. *Psalms 1–72.* Tyndale Old Testament Commentary. London: Inter-Varsity Press, 1973.

Kieffer, René. "Different Levels in Johannine Imagery." Pp. 74–84 in *Aspects on the Johannine Literature.* Coniectanea Biblica, New Testament Series 18. Edited by Lars Hartman and Birger Olsson. Uppsala: Almqvist & Wiksell, 1987.

Kierspel, Lars. *The Jews and the World in the Fourth Gospel: Parallelism, Function, and Context.* Wissenschaftliche Untersuchungen zum Neuen Testament 2/220. Tübingen: Mohr-Siebeck, 2007.

Kiley, Mark. "The Exegesis of God: Jesus' Signs in John 1–11." Pp. 555–69 in *SBL 1998 Seminar Papers Part One.* SBL Seminar Papers 37. Atlanta, GA: Scholars Press, 1988.

Kim, Stephen S. "The Christological and Eschatological Significance of Jesus' Miracle in John 5." *Bibliotheca Sacra* 165 (2008): 413–24.

Kimelman, Reuven. "*Birkat Ha-Minim* and the Lack of Evidence for an Anti-Christian Jewish Prayer in Late Antiquity." Pp. 226–44 in *Jewish and Christian Self-Definition.* Volume Two: *Aspects of Judaism in the Graeco-Roman Period.* Edited by E. P. Sanders. London: SCM, 1981.

Klein, William W., Craig L. Blomberg, and Robert L. Hubbard, Jr. *Introduction to Biblical Interpretation,* Rev. ed. Nashville: Nelson, 2005.

Klink, Edward W. III. *The Sheep of the Fold: The Audience and Origin of the Gospel of John.* Society for New Testament Studies Monograph 141. Cambridge: Cambridge University Press, 2007.

———. "Light of the World: Cosmology and the Johannine Literature." Pp. 74–89 in *Cosmology and New Testament Theology.* Library of New Testament Studies. Edited by Jonathan T. Pennington and Sean M. McDonough. London: T&T Clark, 2008.

Knöppler, Thomas. *Sühne im Neuen Testament: Studien zum urchristlichen Verständnis der Heilsbedeutung des Todes Jesu.* Wissenschaftliche Monographien zum Alten und Neuen Testament 88. Neukirchen-Vluyn: Neukirchener, 2001.

Koester, Craig R. *The Dwelling of God: The Tabernacle in the Old Testament, Intertestamental Jewish Literature, and the New Testament.* Catholic Biblical Quarterly Monograph Series 22. Washington, DC: Catholic Biblical Association of America, 1989.

———. "Hearing, Seeing, and Believing in the Gospel of John." *Biblica* 70 (1989): 327–48.

———. *Symbolism in the Fourth Gospel: Meaning, Mystery, Community.* 2nd ed. Minneapolis: Fortress, 2003.

———. "Why Was the Messiah Crucified? A Study of God, Jesus, Satan, and Human Agency in Johannine Theology." Pp. 163–80 in *The Death of Jesus in the Gospel of John.* Bibliotheca ephemeridum theologicarum lovaniensium 200. Edited by Gilbert van Belle. Leuven: Leuven University Press/Peeters, 2007.

———. *Word of Life: A Theology of John's Gospel.* Grand Rapids: Eerdmans, 2008.

Koester, Craig R., and Reimund Bieringer, eds. *The Resurrection of Jesus in the Gospel of John.* Wissenschaftliche Untersuchungen zum Neuen Testament 222. Tübingen: Mohr-Siebeck, 2008.

Kopas, Jane. "Jesus and Women: John's Gospel." *Theology Today* 41 (1984): 201–5.

Köstenberger, Andreas J. "The Seventh Johannine Sign: A Study in John's Christology." *Bulletin of Biblical Research* 5 (1995): 87–103.

———. "The Contribution of the General Epistles and Revelation to a Biblical Theology of Religions." Pp. 113–40 in *Christianity and the Religions: A Biblical Theology of World Religions.* Evangelical Missiological Society Series 2. Edited by Edward Rommen and Harold Netland. Pasadena, CA: William Carey Library, 1995.

———. "Review of *Die johanneische Frage* by Martin Hengel." *Journal of the Evangelical Theological Society* 39 (1996): 154–55.

———. "What Does It Mean To Be Filled with the Spirit?" *Journal of the Evangelical Theological Society* 40 (1997): 229–40.

———. *The Missions of Jesus and the Disciples according to the Fourth Gospel.* Grand Rapids: Eerdmans, 1998.

———. "Jesus as Rabbi in the Fourth Gospel." *Bulletin of Biblical Research* 8 (1998): 97–128.

———. "Review of *Women in the Church* by Stanley J. Grenz." *Journal of the Evangelical Theological Society* 41 (1998): 517–18.

———. "Aesthetic Theology: Blessing or Curse? An Assessment of Narrative Hermeneutics." *Faith & Mission* 15/2 (1998): 27–44.

———. *Encountering John: The Gospel in Historical, Literary, and Theological Perspective.* Encountering Biblical Studies. Grand Rapids: Baker, 1999.

———. "The Two Johannine Verbs for Sending: A Study of John's Use of Words with Reference to General Linguistic Theory." Pp. 125–43 in *Linguistics and the New Testament: Critical Junctures.* Journal for the Study of the New Testament Supplement 168. Studies in New Testament Greek 5. Edited by Stanley E. Porter and D. A. Carson. Sheffield: Sheffield Academic Press, 1999.

———. "John." Pp. 280–85 in *New Dictionary of Biblical Theology.* Edited by T. Desmond Alexander and Brian S. Rosner. Leicester, UK: Inter-Varsity Press, 2000.

———. "Nations." Pp. 676–78 in *New Dictionary of Biblical Theology.* Edited by T. Desmond Alexander and Brian S. Rosner. Leicester, UK: Inter-Varsity Press, 2000.

———. "Review of Bruce Malina and Richard Rohrbaugh, *Social-Science Commentary on the Gospel of John.*" *Journal of the Evangelical Theological Society* 43 (2000): 144–45.

———. "Early Doubts of the Apostolic Authorship of the Fourth Gospel in the History of Modern Biblical Criticism." Pp. 17–47 in *Studies in John and Gender: A Decade of Scholarship*. Studies in Biblical Literature 38. New York: Peter Lang, 2001.

———. "A Comparison of the Pericopae of Jesus' Anointing." Pp. 49–63 in *Studies in John and Gender: A Decade of Scholarship*. Studies in Biblical Literature 38. New York: Peter Lang, 2001.

———. "John." Pp. 1–216 in *Zondervan Illustrated Bible Backgrounds Commentary*. Edited by Clinton E. Arnold. Vol. 2: *John–Acts*. Grand Rapids: Zondervan, 2002.

———. "Jesus the Good Shepherd Who Will Also Bring Other Sheep (John 10:16): The Old Testament Background of a Familiar Metaphor." *Bulletin of Biblical Research* 12 (2002): 67–96.

———. "Diversity and Unity in the New Testament." Pp. 144–58 in *Biblical Theology: Retrospect & Prospect*. Edited by Scott J. Hafemann. Downers Grove, IL: InterVarsity Press, 2002.

———. "Translating John's Gospel: Challenges and Opportunities." Pp. 347–64 in *The Challenge of Bible Translation: Communicating God's Word to the World*. Edited by Glen G. Scorgie, Mark L. Strauss, and Steven M. Voth. Grand Rapids: Zondervan, 2003.

———. *John*. Baker Exegetical Commentary on the New Testament. Grand Rapids: Baker, 2004.

———. "'I Suppose' (οἶμαι): The Conclusion of John's Gospel in Its Literary and Historical Context." Pp. 77–88 in *The New Testament in Its First Century Setting: Essays on Context and Background in Honour of B. W. Winter on His 65th Birthday*. Edited by P. J. Williams, Andrew D. Clarke, Peter M. Head, and David Instone-Brewer. Grand Rapids/Cambridge: Eerdmans, 2004.

———. "'What Is Truth?' Pilate's Question in Its Johannine and Larger Biblical Context." Pp. 19–51 in *Whatever Happened to Truth?* Edited by Andreas J. Köstenberger. Wheaton: Crossway, 2005.

———. "John's Trinitarian Mission Theology." *Southern Baptist Journal of Theology* 9/4 (2005): 14–33.

———. "The Destruction of the Second Temple and the Composition of the Fourth Gospel." *Trinity Journal* 26 NS (2005): 205–42. = Pp. 69–108 in *Challenging Perspectives on the Gospel of John*. Wissenschaftliche Untersuchungen zum Neuen Testament 2/219. Edited by John Lierman. Tübingen: Mohr-Siebeck, 2006.

———. "Of Professors and Madmen: Currents in Contemporary New Testament Scholarship." *Faith & Mission* 23/2 (Spring 2006): 3–18.

———. "John." Pp. 415–512 in *Commentary on the New Testament Use of the Old Testament*. Edited by G. K. Beale and D. A. Carson. Grand Rapids: Baker, 2007.

———. "Progress and Regress in Recent Johannine Scholarship—Reflections upon the Road Ahead." Pp. 105–7 in *What We Have Heard from the Beginning: The Past, Present, and Future of Johannine Studies*. Edited by Tom Thatcher. Waco, TX: Baylor University Press, 2007.

———. "Review of Edward W. Klink III, *The Sheep of the Fold: The Audience and Origin of the Gospel of John*." *Journal of the Evangelical Theological Society* 51 (2008): 654–56.

———. "Richard Bauckham, *The Testimony of the Beloved Disciple*, D. Moody Smith, *The Fourth Gospel in Four Dimensions*, and Paul Anderson, *The Fourth Gospel and the Quest for Jesus*: Implications for History." Paper delivered at the Annual Meeting of the Society of Biblical Literature. Boston, MA, November 23, 2008.

———. "Study Notes on John." Pp. 2015–72 in *ESV Study Bible*. Wheaton: Crossway, 2008.

———. "Messiah." In *Encyclopedia of Christian Civilization*. Edited by George T. Kurian. Oxford: Blackwell, forthcoming.

———. "The Genre of the Fourth Gospel and Greco-Roman Literary Conventions." In *The New Testament in Its Hellenistic Context*. Vol. 1: *Christian Origins and Classical Culture: Social and Literary Contexts for the New Testament*. Edited by Stanley E. Porter and Andrew W. Pitts. Leiden: Brill, 2009.

———. "The Glory of God in John's Gospel and the Apocalypse." In *The Glory of God*. Theology in Community 2. Edited by Robert Peterson and Chris Morgan. Wheaton: Crossway, forthcoming.

———. "The Last Supper as a Passover Meal." In publication edited by Thomas R. Schreiner. Nashville: Broadman & Holman, forthcoming.

Köstenberger, Andreas J., ed. *Whatever Happened to Truth?* Wheaton: Crossway, 2005.

Köstenberger, Andreas, and Raymond Bouchoc. *The Book Study Concordance*. Nashville: Broadman & Holman, 2003.

Köstenberger, Andreas J., and Peter T. O'Brien. *Salvation to the Ends of the Earth: A Biblical Theology of Mission*. New Studies in Biblical Theology 11. Downers Grove, IL: InterVarsity Press, 2001.

Köstenberger, Andreas J., and Richard D. Patterson. *Invitation to Biblical Interpretation*. Grand Rapids: Kregel, forthcoming.

Köstenberger, Andreas J., L. Scott Kellum, and Charles L. Quarles. *The Cradle, the Cross, and the Crown: An Introduction to the New Testament*. Nashville: Broadman & Holman, 2009.

Köstenberger, Andreas J., and Scott R. Swain. *Father, Son and Spirit: The Trinity and John's Gospel*. New Studies in Biblical Theology 24. Leicester, UK/Downers Grove, IL: InterVarsity Press, 2008.

Köstenberger, Andreas J., and Stephen O. Stout. "The Disciple Jesus Loved: Witness, Author, Apostle: A Response to Richard Bauckham's *Jesus and the Eyewitnesses*." *Bulletin of Biblical Research* 18 (2008): 209–32.

Köstenberger, Margaret Elizabeth. *Jesus and the Feminists: Who Do They Say That He Is?* Wheaton: Crossway, 2008.

Krafft, Eva. "Die Personen des Johannesevangeliums." *Evangelische Theologie* 16 (1956): 18–32.

Kragerud, Alv. *Der Lieblingsjünger im Johannesevangelium: Ein exegetischer Versuch*. Hamburg: Grosshaus Wegner, 1959.

Kruse, Colin G. *The Letters of John*. Pillar New Testament Commentary. Grand Rapids: Eerdmans, 2000.

———. *John*. Tyndale New Testament Commentary. Downers Grove, IL: InterVarsity Press, 2003.

Kümmel, Werner G. *Introduction to the New Testament*. Rev. ed. Translated by Howard Clark Kee. Nashville: Abingdon, 1975.

Kupp, David D. *Matthew's Emmanuel: Divine Presence and God's People in the First Gospel*. Society for New Testament Studies Monograph Series 90. Cambridge: Cambridge University Press, 1996.

Kurz, William S. "The Beloved Disciple and Implied Readers: A Socio-Narratological Approach." *Biblical Theology Bulletin* 19 (1989): 100–107.

Kuyper, Lester J. "Grace and Truth: An Old Testament Description of God and Its Use in the Johannine Gospel." *Interpretation* 18 (1964): 3–19.

Kynes, W. L. "New Birth." Pp. 574–76 in *Dictionary of Jesus and the Gospels*. Edited by Joel B. Green, Scot McKnight, and I. Howard Marshall. Downers Grove, IL: InterVarsity Press, 1992.

Kysar, Robert. *The Fourth Evangelist and His Gospel*. Minneapolis: Augsburg, 1975.

———. "The Expulsion from the Synagogue: The Tale of a Theory." Chapter 15 in *Voyages with John*. Waco, TX: Baylor University Press, 2005.

———. "The Dehistoricizing of the Gospel of John." Pp. 75–101 in *John, Jesus, and History*. Vol. 1: *Critical Appraisals of Critical Views*. SBL Semeia Studies 44. Edited by Paul N. Anderson, Felix Just, S.J., and Tom Thatcher. Atlanta: Society of Biblical Literature, 2007.

Laato, Antti. *A Star Is Rising: The Historical Development of the Old Testament Royal Ideology and the Rise of the Jewish Messianic Expectations*. Atlanta: Scholars Press, 1997.

Lacomara, Aelred. "Deuteronomy and the Farewell Discourse (Jn 13:31–16:33)." *Catholic Biblical Quarterly* 36 (1974): 65–84.

Ladd, George E. *The Pattern of New Testament Truth*. Grand Rapids: Eerdmans, 1968.

———. *A Theology of the New Testament*. Rev. ed. Grand Rapids: Eerdmans, 1993.

Lake, Kirsopp. *An Introduction to the New Testament*. London: Christophers, 1948.

Lamarche, Paul. *Zacharie IX–XIV: Structure litteraire et messianisme*. Paris: Librairie Lecoffre, J. Gabalda, 1961.

Lane, William. *The Gospel of Mark*. New International Commentary on the New Testament. Grand Rapids: Eerdmans, 1974.

Laney, Carl. *John*. Moody Gospel Commentary. Chicago: Moody Press, 1992.

Lang, Bernhard. *Der einzige Gott: Die Geburt des biblischen Monotheismus*. Munich: Kösel, 1981.

———. *Monotheism and the Prophetic Minority*. Sheffield: Almond, 1983.

Lange, Armin. "Gebotsobservanz statt Opferkult: Zur Kultpolemik in Jer 7,1–8,3." Pp. 19–35 in *Gemeinde ohne Tempel: Zur Substituierung und Transformation des Jerusalemer Tempels und seines Kults im Alten Testament, antiken Judentum und frühen Christentum*. Wissenschaftliche Untersuchungen zum Neuen Testament 118. Edited by Beate Ego, Armin Lange, and Peter Pilhofer. Tübingen: Mohr-Siebeck, 1999.

Larkin, William J. Jr. *Acts*. IVP New Testament Commentary. Downers Grove, IL: InterVarsity Press, 1995.

Larsson, Tord. *God in the Fourth Gospel: A Hermeneutical Study of the History of Interpretation*. Stockholm: Almquist & Wiksell International, 2001.

Law, Robert. *The Tests of Life: A Study of the First Epistle of St. John*. 3rd ed. Edinburgh: T&T Clark, 1914. Reprint Grand Rapids: Baker, 1979.

Lea, Thomas D., and David Alan Black. *The New Testament: Its Background and Message*. 2nd ed. Nashville: Broadman & Holman, 2003.

Leal, Juan. "El simbolismo historic del iv evangelio." *Estudios bíblicos* 19 (1960): 329–48.

Leaney, A. R. C. "The Johannine Paraclete and the Qumran Scrolls." Pp. 38–61 in *John and Qumran*. Edited by James H. Charlesworth. London: G. Chapman, 1972.

Lee, Aquila H. I. *From Messiah to Preexistent Son: Jesus' Self-Consciousness and Early Christian Exegesis of Messianic Psalms*. Wissenschaftliche Untersuchungen zum Neuen Testament 2/192. Tübingen: Mohr-Siebeck, 2005.

Lee, Dorothy A. *The Symbolic Narratives of the Fourth Gospel: The Interplay of Form and Meaning*. Journal for the Study of the New Testament Supplement 95. Sheffield: JSOT, 1994.

Lee, E. Kenneth. "The Drama of the Fourth Gospel." *Expository Times* 65 (1954): 173–76.

Lemcio, Eugene. *The Past of Jesus in the Gospels*. Society for New Testament Studies Monograph 68. Cambridge: Cambridge University Press, 2005.

Leroy, Herbert. *Rätsel und Missverständnis: Ein Beitrag zur Formgeschichte des Johannesevangeliums*. Bonner biblische Beiträge. Bonn: Hanstein, 1968.

Levin, Harry. *Contexts of Criticism*. Harvard Studies in Comparative Literature 22. Cambridge, MA: Harvard University Press, 1957.

Levinsohn, Stephen H. *Discourse Features of New Testament Greek: A Coursebook on the Information Structure of New Testament Greek*. 2nd ed. Dallas: Summer Institute of Linguistics, 2000.

Lichtenberger, Hermann. "Zion and the Destruction of the Temple in 4 Ezra 9–10." Pp. 239–49 in *Gemeinde ohne Tempel: Zur Substituierung und Transformation des Jerusalemer Tempels und seines Kults im Alten Testament, antiken Judentum und frühen Christentum*. Wissenschaftliche Untersuchungen zum Neuen Testament 118. Edited by Beate Ego, Armin Lange, and Peter Pilhofer. Tübingen: Mohr-Siebeck, 1999.

———. "Der Mythos von der Unzerstörbarkeit des Tempels." Pp. 92–107 in *Zerstörungen des Jerusalemer Tempels: Geschehen–Wahrnehmung–Bewältigung*. Wissenschaftliche Untersuchungen zum Neuen Testament 147. Edited by Johannes Hahn. Tübingen: Mohr-Siebeck, 2002.

Lierman, John. *The New Testament Moses: Christian Conceptions of Moses and Israel in the Setting of Jewish Religion*. Wissenschaftliche Untersuchungen zum Neuen Testament 137. Tübingen: Mohr-Siebeck, 2004.

Lieu, Judith M. "'Authority to Become Children of God': A Study of 1 John." *Novum Testamentum* 23 (1981): 210–28.

———. "Temple and Synagogue in John." *New Testament Studies* 45 (1999): 51–69.

Lightfoot, R. H. *St. John's Gospel: A Commentary*. London: Oxford University Press, 1956.

Lincoln, Andrew T. *Truth on Trial: The Lawsuit Motif in the Fourth Gospel*. Peabody, MA: Hendrickson, 2000.

———. "Reading John: The Fourth Gospel under Modern and Postmodern Interrogation." Pp. 127–49 in *Reading the Gospels Today*. McMaster New Testament Studies. Edited by Stanley E. Porter. Grand Rapids: Eerdmans, 2004.

Lindars, Barnabas. *The Gospel of John*. New Century Bible Commentary. Grand Rapids: Eerdmans, 1981 [1972].

———. "John and the Synoptic Gospels: A Test Case." *New Testament Studies* 27 (1981): 287–94.

———. *Jesus Son of Man: A Fresh Examination of the Son of Man Sayings in the Gospels in the Light of Recent Research*. Grand Rapids: Eerdmans, 1983.

Lindemann, Andreas. "Gemeinde und Welt im Johannesevangelium." Pp. 133–61 in *Kirche: Festschrift für Günther Bornkamm zum 75. Geburtstag*. Edited by Dieter Lührmann and Georg Strecker. Tübingen: Mohr-Siebeck, 1980.

Lindsay, Dennis R. "'What Is Truth? Ἀλήθεια in the Gospel of John." *Restoration Quarterly* 35 (1993): 129–45.

Loader, William. *The Christology of the Fourth Gospel.* Beiträge zur biblischen Exegese und Theologie 23. Frankfurt am Main: Peter Lang, 1992.

Lohse, Eduard. "Miracles in the Fourth Gospel." Pp. 64–75 in *What about the New Testament? In Honor of Christopher Evans.* Edited by Morna D. Hooker and Colin J. A. Hickling. London: SCM, 1975.

Longacre, Robert. "Towards an Exegesis of 1 John Based on the Discourse Analysis of the Greek Text." Pp. 271–86 in *Linguistics and New Testament Interpretation.* Edited by David Alan Black. Nashville: Broadman & Holman, 1992.

Longman, Tremper. "The Messiah: Explorations in the Law and Writings." Pp. 13–34 in *The Messiah in the Old and New Testaments.* McMaster New Testament Studies. Edited by Stanley E. Porter. Grand Rapids: Eerdmans, 2007.

Lorenzen, Thorwald. *Der Lieblingsjünger im Johannesevangelium: Eine redaktionsgeschichtliche Studie.* Stuttgarter Bibelstudien 55. Stuttgart: Katholisches Bibelwerk, 1971.

Louw, Johannes P. "On Johannine Style." *Neotestamentica* 20 (1986): 5–12.

Lücking, Stefan. "Die Zerstörung des Tempels 70 n. Chr. als Krisenerfahrung der frühen Christen." Pp. 140–65 in *Zerstörungen des Jerusalemer Tempels: Geschehen–Wahrnehmung–Bewältigung.* Wissenschaftliche Untersuchungen zum Neuen Testament 147. Edited by Johannes Hahn. Tübingen: Mohr-Siebeck, 2002.

Maccini, Robert G. *Her Testimony Is True: Women as Witnesses according to John.* Journal for the Study of the New Testament Supplement 125. Sheffield: Sheffield Academic Press, 1996.

MacDonald, Nathan. *Deuteronomy and the Meaning of "Monotheism."* Forschungen zum Alten Testament 2/1. Tübingen: Mohr-Siebeck, 2003.

———. "Whose Monotheism? Which Rationality?" Pp. 45–67 in *The Old Testament in Its World.* Edited by Robert P. Gordon and Johannes Cornelis de Moor. Leiden: Brill, 2005.

MacGregor, G. H. C. *The Gospel of John.* Moffatt New Testament Commentary. London: Hodder and Stoughton, 1928.

Machinist, Peter. "The Question of Distinctiveness in Ancient Israel." Pp. 420–42 in *Essential Papers on Israel and the Ancient Near East.* Edited by F. E. Greenspan. New York: New York University Press, 1991.

Maggay, Melba P. "Jesus and Pilate: An Exposition of John 18:28–40." *Transformation* 8 (1991): 31, 33.

Malatesta, Edward J. *St. John's Gospel 1920–1965.* Analecta biblica 32. Rome: Pontifical Biblical Institute, 1967.

———. *Interiority and Covenant: A Study of εἶναι ἐν and μενεῖν ἐν in the First Letter of Saint John.* Analecta biblica 69. Rome: Biblical Institute Press, 1978.

Malina, Bruce J., and Richard L. Rohrbaugh. *Social-Science Commentary on the Gospel of John.* Minneapolis: Fortress, 1998.

Manning, Gary T. Jr. *Echoes of a Prophet: The Use of Ezekiel in the Gospel of John and in Literature of the Second Temple Period.* Journal for the Study of the New Testament Supplement 270. London/New York: T&T Clark, 2004.

Maritz, Petrus and Gilbert van Belle. "The Imagery of Eating and Drinking in John 6:35." Pp. 333–52 in *Imagery in the Gospel of John: Terms, Forms, Themes, and Theology of Johannine Figurative Language.* Wissenschaftliche Untersuchungen zum Neuen Testament 200. Edited by Jörg Frey, Jan G. van der Watt, and Ruben Zimmerman. Tübingen: Mohr-Siebeck, 2006.

Marrow, Stanley B. "Johannine Ecclesiology." *Chicago Studies* 37 (1998): 27–46.

———. "Κοσμός in John." *Catholic Biblical Quarterly* 64 (2002): 90–102.

Marshall, I. Howard. *The Epistles of John*. New International Commentary on the New Testament. Grand Rapids: Eerdmans, 1978.

———. "Jesus as Messiah in Mark and Matthew." Pp. 144–64 in *The Messiah in the Old and New Testaments*. McMaster New Testament Studies. Edited by Stanley E. Porter. Grand Rapids: Eerdmans, 2007.

Marshall, I. Howard, and David Peterson, eds. *Witness to the Gospel: The Theology of Acts*. Grand Rapids: Eerdmans, 1998.

Martin, Troy W. "Assessing the Johannine Epithet 'the Mother of Jesus.'" *Catholic Biblical Quarterly* 60 (1998): 63–73.

Martínez, Florentino García. "Priestly Functions in a Community without Temple." Pp. 303–19 in *Gemeinde ohne Tempel: Zur Substituierung und Transformation des Jerusalemer Tempels und seines Kults im Alten Testament, antiken Judentum und frühen Christentum*. Wissenschaftliche Untersuchungen zum Neuen Testament 118. Edited by Beate Ego, Armin Lange, and Peter Pilhofer. Tübingen: Mohr-Siebeck, 1999.

Martyn, J. Louis. *History and Theology in the Fourth Gospel*. 1st ed. New York: Harper & Row, 1968. 2nd ed. Nashville: Abingdon, 1979. 3rd ed. New Testament Library. Louisville: Westminster John Knox, 2003.

———. "Glimpses into the History of the Johannine Community." Pp. 149–75 in *L'Évangile de Jean: Sources, rédaction, théologie*. Bibliotheca ephemeridum theologicarum lovaniensium 44. Edited by Marinus de Jonge. Gembloux: Duculot, 1977.

———. *The Gospel of John in Christian History: Essays for Interpreters*. New York: Paulist, 1978.

Marxsen, Willi. *Mark the Evangelist: Studies on the Redaction History of the Gospel*. Translated James Boyce, Donald Juel, and William Poehlmann, with Roy A. Harrisville. Nashville: Abingdon, 1969.

Matera, Frank J. "'On Behalf of Others,' 'Cleansing,' 'Return': Johannine Images for Jesus' Death." *Louvain Studies* 13 (1988): 161–78.

———. *New Testament Ethics: The Legacies of Jesus and Paul*. Louisville: Westminster John Knox, 1996.

Mburu, Elizabeth W. "The *Rule of the Community* as a Valid Linguistic Resource for Understanding Truth Terminology in the Gospel of John: A Semantic Analysis." Ph.D. dissertation. Wake Forest, NC: Southeastern Baptist Theological Seminary, 2008.

McCabe, Robert V. "The Meaning of 'Born of Water and the Spirit' in John 3:5." *Detroit Baptist Seminary Journal* 4 (1999): 85–107.

McCaffrey, James. *The House with Many Rooms: The Temple Theme of Jn 14,2–3*. Rome: Biblical Institute Press, 1988.

McConville, J. Gordon. "God's 'Name' and God's 'Glory.'" *Tyndale Bulletin* 30 (1979): 149–68.

McKelvey, Robert J. *The New Temple: The Church in the New Testament*. Oxford Theological Monographs. Oxford: Oxford University Press, 1969.

McKnight, Scot, and Terence C. Mournet, eds. *Jesus in Early Christian Memory: Essays in Honour of James D. G. Dunn*. Library of New Testament Studies 349. London: T&T Clark, 2007.

McNamara, Martin. "The Ascension and Exaltation of Christ in the Fourth Gospel." *Scripture* 19 (1967): 65–73.

McPolin, James. "Mission in the Fourth Gospel." *Irish Theological Quarterly* 36 (1969): 113–22.

McRae, George W. "Theology and Irony in the Fourth Gospel." Pp. 83–96 in *The Word and the World: Essays in Honor of Frederick L. Moriarty.* Edited by Richard J. Clifford and George W. McRae. Cambridge, MA: Weston College Press, 1973.

Mealand, David L. "John 5 and the Limits of Rhetorical Criticism." Pp. 258–72 in *Understanding Poets and Prophets: Essays in Honour of George Wishart Anderson.* JSOT Supplement Series. Edited by A. Graeme Auld. Sheffield: JSOT, 1993.

Meeks, Wayne A. "Galilee and Judea in the Fourth Gospel." *Journal of Biblical Literature* 85 (1966): 159–69.

———. *The Prophet-King.* Leiden: Brill, 1967.

———. "The Man from Heaven in Johannine Sectarianism." *Journal of Biblical Literature* 91 (1972): 44–72.

———. "Breaking Away: Three New Testament Pictures of Christianity's Separation from the Jewish Communities." Pp. 93–115 in *"To See Ourselves as Others See Us": Christians, Jews, "Others" in Late Antiquity.* Chico, CA: Scholars Press, 1985.

———. "The Ethics of the Fourth Evangelist." Pp. 317–26 in *Exploring the Gospel of John: In Honor of D. Moody Smith.* Edited by R. Alan Culpepper and C. Clifton Black. Louisville: Westminster John Knox, 1996.

Melick, Richard R. "A Study in the Concept of Belief: A Comparison of the Gospel of John and the Epistle to the Romans." Th.D. dissertation. Fort Worth, TX: Southwestern Baptist Theological Seminary, 1976.

Menken, Maarten J. J. *Old Testament Quotations in the Fourth Gospel: Studies in Textual Form.* Contributions to Biblical Exegesis and Theology 15. Kampen: Kok, 1996.

Metzger, Bruce M. *A Textual Commentary on the New Testament.* 2nd ed. New York: United Bible Societies, 1994.

Metzner, Rainer. *Das Verständnis der Sünde im Johannesevangelium.* Wissenschaftliche Untersuchungen zum Neuen Testament 122. Tübingen: Mohr-Siebeck, 2000.

———. "Vollmacht im Johannesevangelium." *Novum Testamentum* 45 (2003): 22–44.

Meyer, Heinrich August Wilhelm. *Critical and Exegetical Hand-Book to the Gospel of John.* Translated by William Urwick. New York: Funk & Wagnalls, 1884.

Meyer, Paul W. "'The Father': The Presentation of God in the Fourth Gospel." Pp. 255–73 in *Exploring the Gospel of John: In Honor of D. Moody Smith.* Edited by R. Alan Culpepper and C. Clifton Black. Louisville: Westminster John Knox, 1996.

Michaels, J. Ramsey. "Nathanael under the Fig Tree." *Expository Times* 67 (1967): 182–83.

———. *John.* New International Biblical Commentary. Peabody, MA: Hendrickson, 1989.

Middlemas, Jill. *The Templeless Age: An Introduction to the History, Literature, and Theology of the "Exile."* Louisville: Westminster John Knox, 2007.

Miller, Ed L. "The True Light Which Illumines Every Man." Pp. 63–82 in *Good News in History: Fs. Bo Reicke.* Edited by Ed L. Miller. Atlanta: Scholars Press, 1993.

Minear, Paul S. "The Original Functions of John 21." *Journal of Biblical Literature* 102 (1983): 85–98.

Mlakuzhyil, George. *The Christocentric Literary Structure of the Fourth Gospel.* Analecta biblica 117. Rome: Pontifical Bible Institute, 1987.

Moloney, Francis J. *The Johannine Son of Man.* Biblioteca di Scienze Religiose 14. 2nd ed. Rome: Libreria Ateneo Salesiano, 1978.

———. *The Gospel of John.* Sacra Pagina. Collegeville, MN: Liturgical Press, 1998.

———. "Can Everyone Be Wrong? A Reading of John 11.1–12.8." *New Testament Studies* 49 (2003): 505–27.

Montgomery, David A. "Directives in the New Testament: A Case Study of John 1:38." *Journal of the Evangelical Theological Society* 50 (2007): 275–88.

Moo, Douglas J. "Creation and New Creation." Paper presented at the Annual Meeting of the Institute of Biblical Research. Boston, MA, November 22, 2008.

Moody, Dale. "God's Only Son: The Translation of John 3:16 in the Revised Standard Version." *Journal of Biblical Literature* 72 (1953): 213–19.

Mörchen, Roland. "'Weggehen.' Beobachtungen zu Joh 12,36b." *Biblische Zeitschrift* 28 (1984): 240–42.

Moreton, M. B. "The Beloved Disciple Again." Pp. 215–18 in *Studia Biblica 1978. II. Papers on the Gospels.* Journal for the Study of the New Testament Supplement 2. Edited by E. A. Livingstone. Sheffield: JSOT, 1980.

Morris, Leon. *Studies in the Fourth Gospel.* Grand Rapids: Eerdmans, 1969.

———. *The Gospel according to John.* New International Commentary on the New Testament. Grand Rapids: Eerdmans, 1971.

———. "The Jesus of Saint John." Pp. 37–53 in *Unity and Diversity in New Testament Theology: Essays in Honor of George E. Ladd.* Edited by Robert A. Guelich. Grand Rapids: Eerdmans, 1978.

———. "Love in the Fourth Gospel." Pp. 27–43 in *Saved by Hope: Festschrift R. C. Oudersluys.* Grand Rapids: Eerdmans, 1978.

———. "The Atonement in John's Gospel." *Criswell Theological Review* 3 (1988): 49–64.

———. *The Gospel according to John.* New International Commentary on the New Testament. Rev. ed. Grand Rapids: Eerdmans, 1995.

Morton, A. Q., and G. H. C. MacGregor. *The Structure of Luke and Acts.* New York: Harper & Row, 1964.

Motyer, J. A. *The Prophecy of Isaiah: An Introduction and Commentary.* Downers Grove, IL: InterVarsity Press, 1993.

Motyer, Stephen. "John 8:31–59 and the Rhetoric of Persuasion in the Fourth Gospel." Ph.D. thesis. King's College, London, 1992.

———. *'Your Father the Devil'? A New Approach to John and 'the Jews.'* Carlisle, UK: Paternoster, 1997.

Moule, Charles F. D. "The Meaning of 'Life' in the Gospel and Epistles of St. John." *Theology* 78 (1975): 114–25.

———. "The Individualism of the Fourth Gospel." *Novum Testamentum* 5 (1962): 171–90. Reprinted pp. 91–109 in *Essays in New Testament Interpretation.* Cambridge: Cambridge University Press, 1982.

Moulton, James Hope. *A Grammar of New Testament Greek.* Vol. 1: *Prolegomena.* 3rd ed. Edinburgh: T&T Clark, 1908.

———. *A Grammar of New Testament Greek.* Vol. 4: *Style.* By Nigel Turner. Edinburgh: T&T Clark, 1976.

Mowvley, Henry. "John 1,14–18 in the Light of Exodus 33,7–34,35." *Expository Times* 95 (1984): 135–37.

Muecke, D. C. *The Compass of Irony.* London: Methuen, 1969.

Muilenburg, James. "Literary Form in the Fourth Gospel." *Journal of Biblical Literature* 51 (1932): 40–53. Repr. pp. 65–76 in *The Gospel of John as Literature: An Anthology of*

Twentieth-Century Perspectives. New Testament Tools and Studies 17. Edited by Mark W. G. Stibbe. Leiden: Brill, 1993.

Müller, Christoph G. "Der Zeuge und das Licht: Joh 1,1–4,3 und das Darstellungsprinzip der σύγκρισις." *Biblica* 84 (2003): 479–509.

Müller, Theophil. *Das Heilsgeschehen im Johannes-Evangelium: Eine exegetische Studie, zugleich der Versuch einer Antwort zu Rudolf Bultmann.* Zürich/Frankfurt am Main: Gotthelf, 1961.

Müller, Ulrich B. "Die Bedeutung des Kreuzestodes Jesu im Johannesevangelium: Erwägungen zur Kreuzestheologie im Neuen Testament." *Kerygma und Dogma* 21 (1975): 48–71.

———. "Die Heimat des Johannesevangeliums." *Zeitschrift für die neutestamentliche Wissenschaft* 97 (2006): 44–63.

Nauck, Wolfgang. *Die Tradition und der Charakter des ersten Johannesbriefes.* Wissenschaftliche Untersuchungen zum Neuen Testament 3. Tübingen: Mohr, 1953.

Neill, Stephen, and Tom Wright. *The Interpretation of the New Testament 1861–1986.* 2nd ed. Oxford: Oxford University Press, 1988.

Nereparampil, Lucius. *Destroy This Temple: An Exegetico-Theological Study on the Meaning of Jesus' Temple-Logion in Jn 2:19.* Bangalore: Dharmaram, 1978.

Neusner, Jacob. "Judaism in a Time of Crisis: Four Responses to the Destruction of the Second Temple." *Judaism* 21 (1972): 313–27.

———. "The Formation of Rabbinic Judaism: Methodological Issues and Substantive Theses." Pp. 99–144 in *Formative Judaism: Religious, Historical and Literary Studies, Third Series: Torah, Pharisees, and Rabbis.* Brown Judaic Studies 46. Chico, CA: Scholars Press, 1983.

———. "Judaism after the Destruction of the Temple: An Overview." Pp. 83–98 in *Formative Judaism: Religious, Historical and Literary Studies, Third Series: Torah, Pharisees, and Rabbis.* Brown Judaic Studies 46. Chico, CA: Scholars Press, 1983.

Neusner, Jacob, William S. Green, and Ernest Frerichs, eds. *Judaisms and Their Messiahs at the Turn of the Christian Era.* Cambridge: Cambridge University Press, 1987.

Newsom, Carol. "Angels." Pp. 248–53 in *Anchor Bible Dictionary.* Vol. 1. Edited by David Noel Freedman. New York: Doubleday, 1992.

Ng, Wai-yee. *Water Symbolism in John: An Eschatological Interpretation.* Studies in Biblical Literature 15. New York: Peter Lang, 2001.

Nicholson, Godfrey Carruthers. *Death as Departure: The Johannine Descent-Ascent Schema.* SBL Dissertation Series 63. Chico, CA: Scholars Press, 1983.

Nicol, Willem. *The Semeia in the Fourth Gospel. Tradition and Redaction.* Novum Testamentum Supplement 32. Leiden: Brill, 1972.

Nicole, Roger. "The Biblical Concept of Truth." Pp. 287–98 in *Scripture and Truth.* Edited by D. A. Carson and John D. Woodbridge. Grand Rapids: Baker, 1992.

Nietzsche, Friedrich. *The Birth of Tragedy and The Genealogy of Morals.* Translated by Francis Golffing. Garden City, NY: Doubleday, 1956.

———. *Twilight of the Idols and the Anti-Christ.* Translated by R. J. Hollingdale. London: Penguin, 1990.

Niewalda, Paul. *Sakramentssymbolik im Johannesevangelium?* Limburg: Lahn, 1958.

Nun, H. *The Authorship of the Fourth Gospel.* Oxford: Alden & Blackwell, 1952.

Nuttall, A. D. *Overheard by God: Fiction and Prayer in Herbert, Milton, Dante and St John.* London: Methuen, 1980.

Obermann, Andreas. *Die christologische Erfüllung der Schrift im Johannesevangelium.* Wissenschaftliche Untersuchungen zum Neuen Testament 2/83. Tübingen: Mohr-Siebeck, 1996.

O'Day, Gail R. "'Show Us the Father, and We Will Be Satisfied' (John 14:8)." *Semeia* 85 (1999): 11–17.

———. "Response to 'Expulsion from the Synagogue: A Tale of a Theory' by Robert Kysar." Paper presented at the Annual Meeting of the Society of Biblical Literature. Toronto, November 23–26, 2002.

Okure, Teresa. *The Johannine Approach to Mission.* Wissenschaftliche Untersuchungen zum Neuen Testament 2/31. Tübingen: Mohr-Siebeck, 1988.

Olsson, Birger. "*Deus Semper Maior*? On God in the Johannine Writings." Pp. 143–71 in *New Readings in John: Literary and Theological Perspectives.* Journal for the Study of the New Testament Supplement 182. Edited by Johannes Nissen and Sigfred Pedersen. Sheffield: Sheffield Academic Press, 1999.

———. "First John: Discourse Analysis and Interpretations." Pp. 369–91 in *Discourse Analysis and the New Testament: Approaches and Results.* Journal for the Study of the New Testament Supplement 170. Studies in New Testament Greek 4. Edited by Stanley E. Porter and Jeffrey T. Reed. Sheffield: Sheffield Academic Press, 1999.

Olyan, Saul M. *Asherah and the Cult of Yahweh in Israel.* SBL Monograph Series 34. Atlanta: Scholars Press, 1988.

O'Neill, J. C. *The Puzzle of 1 John: A New Examination of Origins.* London: SPCK, 1966.

Onuki, Takashi. *Gemeinde und Welt im Johannesevangelium.* Wissenschaftliche Monographien zum Alten und Neuen Testament 56. Neukirchen-Vluyn: Neukirchener, 1984.

O'Rourke, John. "Asides in the Gospel of John." *Novum Testamentum* 21 (1979): 210–19.

Osborne, Grant R. "Redactional Trajectories in the Crucifixion Narrative." *Evangelical Quarterly* 51 (1979): 80–96.

———. "Genre Criticism—Sensus Literalis." *Trinity Journal* NS 4 (1983): 1–27.

———. "Soteriology in the Gospel of John." Pp. 243–60 in *The Grace of God, the Will of Man: A Case for Arminianism.* Edited by Clark H. Pinnock. Grand Rapids: Zondervan, 1989.

Osten-Sacken, Peter von der. "Leistung und Grenze der johanneischen Kreuzestheologie." *Evangelische Theologie* 36 (1976): 154–76.

Oswalt, John N. *The Book of Isaiah.* 2 vols. New International Commentary on the Old Testament. Grand Rapids: Eerdmans, 1998.

Owing, T. L. "The Concept of Sin in the Fourth Gospel." Ph.D. dissertation. Louisville, KY: Southern Baptist Theological Seminary, 1983.

Painter, John. "Johannine Symbols: A Case Study in Epistemology." *Journal of Theology for Southern Africa* 27 (1979): 26–41.

———. "John 9 and the Interpretation of the Fourth Gospel." *Journal for the Study of the New Testament* 28 (1986): 31–61.

———. *1, 2, and 3 John.* Sacra Pagina. Collegeville, MN: Liturgical Press, 2002.

———. "Earth Made Whole: John's Rereading of Genesis." Pp. 65–84 in *Word, Theology, and Community in John.* Edited by John Painter, R. Alan Culpepper, and Fernando F. Segovia. St. Louis, MO: Chalice, 2002.

Pamment, Margaret. "The Meaning of *Doxa* in the Fourth Gospel," *Zeitschrift für die neutestamentliche Wissenschaft* 74 (1973): 12–16.

———. "The Fourth Gospel's Beloved Disciple." *Expository Times* 94 (1983): 363–67.

———. "Path and Residence Metaphors in the Fourth Gospel." *Theology* 88 (1985): 118–24.

Pancaro, Severino. "'People of God' in St John's Gospel?" *New Testament Studies* 16 (1970): 114–29.

———. *The Law in the Fourth Gospel: The Torah and the Gospel, Moses and Jesus, Judaism and Christianity according to John*. Novum Testamentum Supplement 42. Leiden: Brill, 1975.

———. "The Relationship of the Church to Israel in the Gospel of St. John." *New Testament Studies* 21 (1975): 396–405.

Panzram, Sabine. "Der Jerusalemer Tempel und das Rom der Flavier." Pp. 166–82 in *Zerstörungen des Jerusalemer Tempels: Geschehen–Wahrnehmung–Bewältigung*. Wissenschaftliche Untersuchungen zum Neuen Testament 147. Edited by Johannes Hahn. Tübingen: Mohr-Siebeck, 2002.

Pao, David W. *Acts and the Isaianic Exodus*. Wissenschaftliche Untersuchungen zum Neuen Testament 130. Tübingen: Mohr-Siebeck, 2000.

Parsenios, George L. "'No Longer in the World' (John 7:11): The Transformation of the Tragic in the Fourth Gospel." *Harvard Theological Review* 98 (2005): 1–21.

Patterson, Richard D. "The Old Testament Use of an Archetype: The Trickster." *Journal of the Evangelical Theological Society* 42 (1999): 385–94.

Pendrick, Gerard. "*Monogenēs*." *New Testament Studies* 41 (1995): 587–600.

Peterson, Peter M. *Andrew, Brother of Simon Peter: His History and His Legends*. Novum Testamentum Supplement 1. Leiden: Brill, 1963.

Peterson, Susan Lynn. *Timeline Charts of the Western Church*. Grand Rapids: Zondervan, 1999.

Phillips, Thomas E. "'The Third Fifth Day?' John 2:1 in Context." *Expository Times* 115 (2004): 328–31.

Phythian-Adams, W. J. "The New Creation in St. John." *Church Quarterly Review* 144 (1947): 52–75.

Piper, Ronald A. "Satan, Demons and the Absence of Exorcisms in the Fourth Gospel." Pp. 253–78 in *Christology, Controversy and Community: New Testament Essays in Honour of David R. Catchpole*. Novum Testamentum Supplement 99. Edited by David G. Horrell and Christopher M. Tuckett. Leiden: Brill, 2000.

Plantinga, Cornelius. "The Fourth Gospel as Trinitarian Source Then and Now." Pp. 303–21 in *Biblical Hermeneutics in Historical Perspective*. Edited by Mark S. Burrows and Paul Rorem. Grand Rapids: Eerdmans, 1991.

Plumer, Eric. "The Absence of Exorcisms in the Fourth Gospel," *Biblica* 78 (1997): 350–68.

Plummer, Alfred. *The Gospel according to St. John*. Thornapple Commentaries. Grand Rapids: Baker, 1981.

Pohlmann, Karl-Friedrich. "Religion in der Krise—Krise einer Religion: Die Zerstörung des Jerusalemer Tempels 587 v. Chr." Pp. 40–60 in *Zerstörungen des Jerusalemer Tempels: Geschehen–Wahrnehmung–Bewältigung*. Wissenschaftliche Untersuchungen zum Neuen Testament 147. Edited by Johannes Hahn. Tübingen: Mohr-Siebeck, 2002.

Poirier, John C. "Hanukkah in the Narrative Chronology of the Fourth Gospel." *New Testament Studies* 54 (2008): 465–78.

Pollard, T. E. *Johannine Christology and the Early Church*. Society for New Testament Studies Monograph 13. Cambridge: Cambridge University Press, 1970.

Popkes, Enno Edzard. *Die Theologie der Liebe Gottes in den johanneischen Schriften: Studien zur Semantik der Liebe und zum Motivkreis des Dualismus.* Wissenschaftliche Untersuchungen zum Neuen Testament 2/197. Tübingen: Mohr-Siebeck, 2005.

Porter, Stanley E. "Can Traditional Exegesis Enlighten Literary Analysis of the Fourth Gospel? An Examination of the Old Testament Fulfilment Motif and the Passover Theme." Pp. 396–428 in *The Gospels and the Scriptures of Israel.* Journal for the Study of the New Testament Supplement 104. Edited by Craig A. Evans and William R. Stegner. Sheffield: Sheffield Academic Press, 1994.

———. "The Messiah in Luke and Acts: Forgiveness for the Captives." Pp. 144–64 in *The Messiah in the Old and New Testaments.* McMaster New Testament Studies. Edited by Stanley E. Porter. Grand Rapids: Eerdmans, 2007.

Porter, Stanley E., ed. *The Pauline Canon.* Pauline Studies 1. Leiden: Brill, 2004.

———. *The Messiah in the Old and New Testaments.* McMaster New Testament Studies. Grand Rapids: Eerdmans, 2007.

Potterie, Ignace de la. *La vérité dans Saint Jean.* 2 vols. Analecta biblica 73–74. Rome: Pontifical Biblical Institute, 1977.

———. "The Truth in Saint John." Pp. 67–82 in *The Interpretation of John.* Issues in Religion and Theology 9. 2nd ed. Edited and translated by John Ashton. Philadelphia: Fortress/London: SPCK, 1986.

Poythress, Vern S. "Testing for Johannine Authorship by Examining the Use of Conjunctions." *Westminster Theological Journal* 46 (1984): 350–69.

———. "The Use of the Intersentence Conjunctions *De, Oun, Kai,* and Asyndeton in the Gospel of John." *Novum Testamentum* 26 (1984): 312–40.

———. "Johannine Authorship and the Use of Intersentence Conjunctions in the Book of Revelation." *Westminster Theological Journal* 47 (1985): 329–36.

Pryor, John W. "Covenant and Community in John's Gospel." *Reformed Theological Review* 47 (1988): 44–51.

———. "Jesus and Israel in the Fourth Gospel—John 1:1." *Novum Testamentum* 32 (1990): 201–18.

———. *John: Evangelist of the Covenant People.* Downers Grove, IL: InterVarsity Press, 1992.

Quast, Kevin. *Peter and the Beloved Disciple: Figures for a Community in Crisis.* Journal for the Study of the New Testament Supplement 32. Sheffield: JSOT, 1989.

Ramelli, Ilaria. "'Simon Son of John, Do You Love *Me*?' Some Reflections on John 21:15." *Novum Testamentum* 50 (2008): 332–50.

Reim, Günther. *Studien zum alttestamentlichen Hintergrund des Johannesevangeliums.* Society for New Testament Studies Monograph 22. Cambridge: Cambridge University Press, 1974.

Reinhartz, Adele. *The Word in the World: The Cosmological Tale in the Fourth Gospel.* SBL Monograph Series 45. Atlanta: Scholars Press, 1992.

———. "'And the Word Was Begotten': Divine Epigenesis in the Gospel of John." *Semeia* 85 (1999): 83–103.

Rengstorf, Karl Heinrich. "ἀποστέλλω, κτλ." Pp. 398–447 in *Theological Dictionary of the New Testament.* Vol. 1. Edited by Gerhard Kittel. Translated by Geoffrey W. Bromiley. Grand Rapids: Eerdmans, 1964.

———. "μανθάνω, κτλ.." Pp. 390–461 in *Theological Dictionary of the New Testament.* Vol. 4. Edited by Gerhard Kittel. Translated by Geoffrey W. Bromiley. Grand Rapids: Eerdmans, 1967.

———. "σημεῖον, κτλ." Pp. 200–69 in *Theological Dictionary of the New Testament*. Vol. 7. Edited by Gerhard Kittel and Gerhard Friedrich. Translated by Geoffrey W. Bromiley. Grand Rapids: Eerdmans, 1971.

Rensberger, David. *Johannine Faith and Liberating Community*. Philadelphia: Westminster, 1988.

———. *Overcoming the World: Politics and Community in the Gospel of John*. London: SPCK, 1988.

Resseguie, James L. *The Strange Gospel: Narrative Design and Point of View in John*. Biblical Interpretation Series 56. Leiden: Brill, 2001.

Richard, Earl J. "Expressions of Double Meaning and Their Function in the Gospel of John." *New Testament Studies* 31 (1985): 96–112.

Richter, Georg. "Die Deutung des Kreuzestodes Jesu in der Leidensgeschichte des Johannesevangeliums (Jo 13–19)." *Bibel und Leben* 9 (1968): 121–36.

Ridderbos, Herman N. *The Gospel of John: A Theological Commentary*. Translated by John Vriend. Grand Rapids: Eerdmans, 1997.

Riedl, Johannes. *Das Heilswerk Jesu nach Johannes*. Freiburger Theologische Studien 93. Freiburg im Breisgau: Herder, 1973.

Riesenfeld, Harald. "A Probable Background to the Johannine Paraclete." Pp. 266–74 in *Ex Orbe Religionum. Studia Geo Widengren*. Studies in the History of Religions 21. Edited by Claas J. Bleeker et al. Vol. 1. Leiden: Brill, 1972.

Riga, Peter J. "Signs of Glory: The Use of *Semeion* in John's Gospel." *Interpretation* 17 (1963): 402–10.

Rissi, Mathias. "Der Aufbau des vierten Evangeliums." *New Testament Studies* 29 (1983): 48–54.

Roberts, Colin. "John 20:30–31 and 21:24–25." *Journal of Theological Studies* 38 (1987): 409–10.

Robinson, James M. *The Problem of History in Mark and Other Marcan Studies*. Philadelphia: Fortress, 1982.

Robinson, John A. T. "The New Look on the Fourth Gospel." Pp. 338–50 in *Studia Evangelica*. Texte und Untersuchungen 73. Edited by Kurt Aland et al. Berlin: Akademie, 1959. Reprinted pp. 94–106 in *Twelve New Testament Studies*. Studies in Biblical Theology 34. London: SCM, 1962.

———. *Redating the New Testament*. London: SCM, 1976.

———. *The Priority of John*. London: SCM, 1985.

Roose, Hanna. "Joh 20,30f.: Ein (un)passender Schluss? Joh 9 und 11 als primäre Verweisstellen der Schlussnotiz des Johannesevangeliums." *Biblica* 84 (2003): 326–43.

Ruckstuhl, Eugen. *Die literarische Einheit des Johannesevangeliums: Der gegenwärtige Stand der einschlägigen Forschungen*. Göttingen: Vandenhoeck & Ruprecht, 1951.

———. "Abstieg und Erhöhung des johanneischen Menschensohnes." Pp. 314–41 in *Jesus und der Menschensohn: Für Anton Vögtle*. Edited by Rudolf Pesch and Rudolf Schnackenburg. Freiburg im Breisgau: Herder, 1975.

———. "Johannine Language and Style: The Question of Their Unity." Pp. 125–47 in *L'évangile de Jean: Sources, rédaction, théologie*. Edited by Marinus de Jonge. Gembloux: J. Duculot/Leuven: Leuven University Press, 1977.

Ruckstuhl, Eugen, and Peter Dschulnigg. *Stilkritik und Verfasserfrage im Johannesevangelium: Die johanneischen Sprachmerkmale auf dem Hintergrund des Neuen Testaments und des zeitgenössischen hellenistischen Schrifttums*. Novum Testamentum et Orbis Antiquus 17. Göttingen: Vandenhoeck & Ruprecht, 1991.

Rudel, P. "Das Missverständnis im Johannesevangelium." *Neue Kirchliche Zeitschrift* 3 (1921): 351–61.

Ruwe, Andreas. "Die Veränderung tempeltheologischer Konzepte in Ezechiel 8–11." Pp. 3–18 in *Gemeinde ohne Tempel: Zur Substituierung und Transformation des Jerusalemer Tempels und seines Kults im Alten Testament, antiken Judentum und frühen Christentum*. Wissenschaftliche Untersuchungen zum Neuen Testament 118. Edited by Beate Ego, Armin Lange, and Peter Pilhofer. Tübingen: Mohr-Siebeck, 1999.

Salier, Bill. "The Temple in the Gospel according to John." Pp. 121–34 in *Heaven on Earth: The Temple in Biblical Theology*. Edited by T. Desmond Alexander and Simon Gathercole. Carlisle, UK: Paternoster, 2004.

Salier, Willis Hedley. *The Rhetorical Impact of the Sēmeia in the Gospel of John*. Wissenschaftliche Untersuchungen zum Neuen Testament 2/186. Tübingen: Mohr-Siebeck, 2004.

Sanday, William. *The Criticism of the Fourth Gospel*. Morse Foundation Lectures for 1904, Union Theological Seminary. New York: Scribner's Sons, 1905.

Sanders, J. N. *The Fourth Gospel in the Early Church: Its Origin and Influence on Christian Theology up to Irenaeus*. Cambridge: Cambridge University Press, 1943.

———. *A Commentary on the Gospel according to St. John*. London: Adam & Charles Black, 1968.

Sanders, Jack T. *Ethics in the New Testament*. Philadelphia: Fortress, 1975.

Sandnes, Karl Olav. "Whence and Whither: A Narrative Perspective on Birth *anōthen* (John 3,3–8)." *Biblica* 86 (2005): 153–73.

Satterthwaite, Philip E., Richard S. Hess, and Gordon J. Wenham, eds. *The Lord's Anointed: Interpretation of Old Testament Messianic Texts*. Grand Rapids: Baker, 1995.

Schäfer, Peter. "Die sogenannte Synode von Jabne. Zur Trennung von Juden und Christen im ersten/zweiten Jh. n. Chr." *Judaica* 31 (1975): 54–64, 116–24.

Schaff, Philip, ed. *Nicene and Post-Nicene Fathers*. Vol. 7: *Augustin [sic]: Homilies on the Gospel of John, Homilies on the First Epistle of John, Soliloquies*. First Series. Peabody, MA: Hendrickson, 1994.

Scheiber, Alexander. "Ihr sollt kein Bein dran zerbrechen." *Vetus Testamentum* 13 (1963): 95–97.

Schiffman, Lawrence H. "At the Crossroads: Tannaitic Perspectives on the Jewish-Christian Schism." Pp. 115–56 in *Jewish and Christian Self-Definition. Volume Two: Aspects of Judaism in the Graeco-Roman Period*. Edited by E. P. Sanders. London: SCM, 1981.

———. "Community without Temple: The Qumran Community's Withdrawal from the Jerusalem Temple." Pp. 267–84 in *Gemeinde ohne Tempel: Zur Substituierung und Transformation des Jerusalemer Tempels und seines Kults im Alten Testament, antiken Judentum und frühen Christentum*. Wissenschaftliche Untersuchungen zum Neuen Testament 118. Edited by Beate Ego, Armin Lange, and Peter Pilhofer. Tübingen: Mohr-Siebeck, 1999.

Schlatter, Adolf. *Der Evangelist Johannes: Wie er spricht, glaubt und denkt*. 2nd ed. Stuttgart: Calwer, 1948.

———. *Der Glaube im Neuen Testament*. 6th ed. Stuttgart: Calwer, 1982.

———. *New Testament Theology: The History of the Christ* and *The Theology of the Apostles*. Translated by Andreas J. Köstenberger. Grand Rapids: Baker, 1997, 1999.

———. "Atheistic Methods in Theology." Pp. 211–25 in *Adolf Schlatter: A Biography of Germany's Premier Biblical Theologian*. By Werner Neuer. Translated by Robert W. Yarbrough. Grand Rapids: Baker, 1996 [1905].

Schlund, Christine. *"Kein Knochen soll gebrochen werden": Studien zu Bedeutung und Funktion des Pesachfests in Texten des frühen Judentums und im Johannesevangelium*. Wissenschaftliche Monographien zum Alten und Neuen Testament 107. Neukirchen-Vluyn: Neukirchener, 2005.

Schmidt, Karl Ludwig. *Der Rahmen der Geschichte Jesu*. Darmstadt: Wissenschaftliche Buchgesellschaft, 1969 [1919].

Schnabel, Eckhard J. *Early Christian Mission*. 2 vols. Downers Grove, IL: InterVarsity Press, 2004.

Schnackenburg, Rudolf. "Die Erwartung des 'Propheten' nach dem Neuen Testament und den Qumran-Texten." Pp. 622–39 in *Studia Evangelica I*. Texte und Untersuchungen 73. Edited by F. L. Cross. Berlin: Akademie, 1959.

———. "Der Jünger, den Jesus liebte." Pp. 105–7 in *Evangelisch-Katholischer Kommentar zum Neuen Testament: Vorarbeiten*. Vol. 2. Zürich: Neukirchener, 1970.

———. "Ist der Gedanke des Sühnetodes Jesu der einzige Zugang zum Verständnis unserer Erlösung durch Jesus Christus?" Pp. 205–30 in *Der Tod Jesu: Deutungen im Neuen Testament*. Quaestiones Disputatae 74. Edited by Karl Kartelge. Freiburg im Breisgau: Herder, 1976.

———. "Is There a Johannine Ecclesiology?" Pp. 247–56 in *A Companion to John: Readings in Johannine Theology*. Edited by Michael J. Taylor: New York: Alba, 1977.

———. "Der Missionsgedanke des Johannesevangeliums im heutigen Horizont." Pp. 58–72 in *Das Johannesevangelium*. Vol. 4: *Ergänzende Auslegungen und Exkurse*. Herders Theologischer Kommentar zum Neuen Testament. Freiburg im Breisgau: Herder, 1984.

———. *The Gospel according to St. John*. 3 vols. New York: Crossroad, 1990.

———. *The Johannine Epistles: A Commentary*. New York: Crossroad, 1992.

Schneiders, Sandra M. "History and Symbolism in the Fourth Gospel." Pp. 371–76 in *L'évangile de Jean: Sources, rédaction, théologie*. Bibliotheca ephemeridum theologicarum lovaniensium 44. Edited by Marinus de Jonge. Gembloux: Duculot/Leuven: Leuven University Press, 1977.

———. "Symbolism and the Sacramental Principle in the Fourth Gospel." Pp. 221–35 in *Segni e sacramenti nel Vangeli di Giovanni*. Studia Anselmiana 66. Edited by Pius-Ramon Tragan. Rome: Editrice Anselmiana, 1977.

———. "Women in the Fourth Gospel and the Role of the Women in the Contemporary Church." *Biblical Theology Bulletin* 12 (1982): 35–45.

Schnelle, Udo. "Johanneische Ekklesiologie." *New Testament Studies* 37 (1991): 37–50.

———. *Antidocetic Christology in the Gospel of John. An Investigation of the Place of the Fourth Gospel in the Johannine School*. Translated by Linda M. Maloney. Minneapolis: Fortress, 1992.

Schnelle, Udo, ed. *Neuer Wettstein: Texte zum Neuen Testament aus Griechentum und Hellenismus*. Band I/2: *Texte zum Johannesevangelium*. Berlin/New York: de Gruyter, 2001.

Schrage, Wolfgang. *The Ethics of the New Testament*. Edinburgh: T&T Clark, 1996.

Schreiner, Thomas R. *Paul, Apostle of God's Glory in Christ: A Pauline Theology*. Downers Grove, IL: InterVarsity Press, 2001.

Schrenk, Gottlob. "πατήρ, κτλ." Pp. 945–1022 in *Theological Dictionary of the New Testament*. Vol. 5. Edited by Gerhard Kittel and Gerhard Friedrich. Translated by Geoffrey W. Bromiley. Grand Rapids: Eerdmans, 1967.

Schuchard, Bruce G. *Scripture within Scripture: The Interrelationship of Form and Function in the Explicit Old Testament Citations in the Gospel of John.* SBL Dissertation Series 133. Atlanta: Scholars Press, 1992.

Schulz, Anselm. *Nachfolgen und Nachahmen: Studien über das Verhältnis der neutestamentlichen Jüngerschaft zur urchristlichen Vorbildethik.* Studien zum Alten und Neuen Testament 6. München: Kösel, 1962.

Schulz, Siegfried. *Das Evangelium nach Johannes.* 13th ed. Göttingen: Vandenhoeck & Ruprecht, 1975.

Schürer, Emil. *The History of the Jewish People in the Age of Jesus Christ (175 B.C.–A.D. 135).* 4 vols. Revised and edited by Geza Vermes, Fergus Millar, and Matthew Black. Edinburgh: T&T Clark, 1979.

Schwartz, Eduard. "Aporien im 4. Evangelium I." Pp. 342–72 in *Nachrichten von der königlichen Gesellschaft der Wissenschaften zu Göttingen.* Berlin: Weidmannsche Buchhandlung, 1907.

———. "Aporien im 4. Evangelium II," "Aporien im 4. Evangelium III," and "Aporien im 4. Evangelium IV." Pp. 115–48, 149–88, and 497–560 in *Nachrichten von der königlichen Gesellschaft der Wissenschaften zu Göttingen.* Berlin: Weidmannsche Buchhandlung, 1908.

Schweizer, Eduard. "Der Kirchenbegriff im Evangelium und den Briefen des Johannes." Pp. 363–81 in *Studia Evangelica I.* Texte und Untersuchungen 73. Edited by Kurt Aland et al. Berlin: Akademie, 1959.

Scobie, Charles H. H. *The Ways of Our God: An Approach to Biblical Theology.* Grand Rapids: Eerdmans, 2003.

Segovia, Fernando F. *Love Relationships in the Johannine Tradition: Agapē/Agapan in 1 John and the Fourth Gospel.* SBL Dissertation Series 58. Chico, CA: Scholars Press, 1982.

———. "The Journey(s) of the Word of God: A Reading of the Plot of the Fourth Gospel." *Semeia* 53 (1991): 26–31.

Seim, Turid K. "Roles of Women in the Gospel of John." Pp. 56–73 in *Aspects on the Johannine Literature.* Coniectanea Biblica, New Testament Series 17. Ed. Lars Hartman and Birger Olsson. Stockholm: Alqvist & Wiksell International, 1987.

Shafaat, A. "Geber of the Qumran Scrolls and the Spirit-Paraclete of the Gospel of John." *New Testament Studies* 27 (1981): 263–69.

Shedd, Russell. "Multiple Meanings in the Gospel of John." Pp. 247–58 in *Current Issues in Biblical Interpretation.* Edited by Gerald F. Hawthorne. Grand Rapids: Eerdmans, 1975.

Sheeley, Steven M. *Narrative Asides in Luke–Acts.* Journal for the Study of the New Testament Supplement 72. Sheffield: Sheffield Academic Press, 1992.

Shuler, Philip L. *A Genre for the Gospels: The Biographical Character of Matthew.* Philadelphia: Fortress, 1982.

Sidebottom, Ernest M. "The Ascent and Descent of the Son of Man in the Gospel of St. John." *Anglican Theological Review* 39 (1957): 115–22.

Siegert, Folker. "'Zerstört diesen Tempel ...!' Jesus als 'Tempel' in den Passionsüberlieferungen." Pp. 108–39 in *Zerstörungen des Jerusalemer Tempels: Geschehen–Wahrnehmung–Bewältigung.* Wissenschaftliche Untersuchungen zum Neuen Testament 147. Edited by Johannes Hahn. Tübingen: Mohr-Siebeck, 2002.

Siker-Gieseler, Jeffrey S. "Disciples and Discipleship in the Fourth Gospel: A Canonical Approach." *Studia Biblica et Theologica* 10 (1980): 199–227.

Simon, U. E. "Eternal Life in the Fourth Gospel." Pp. 97–109 in *Studies in the Fourth Gospel*. Edited by F. L. Cross. London: Mowbray, 1957.

Smalley, Stephen S. "The Sign in John XXI." *New Testament Studies* 20 (1974): 275–88.

———. *John: Evangelist and Interpreter. History and Interpretation in the Fourth Gospel.* Cambridge: Cambridge University Press, 1978.

———. *1, 2, 3 John.* Word Biblical Commentary 51. Waco, TX: Word, 1984.

———. "'The Paraclete': Pneumatology in the Johannine Gospel and Apocalypse." Pp. 289–300 in *Exploring the Gospel of John: In Honor of D. Moody Smith*. Edited by R. Alan Culpepper and C. Clifton Black. Louisville: Westminster John Knox, 1996.

Smit, Peter-Ben. "Cana-to-Cana or Galilee-to-Galilee: A Note on the Structure of the Gospel of John." *Zeitschrift für die neutestamentliche Wissenschaft* 98 (2007): 143–49.

Smith, D. Moody. *The Composition and Order of the Fourth Gospel: Bultmann's Literary Theory.* Yale Publications in Religion 10. New Haven, CT/London: Yale University Press, 1965.

———. "John and the Synoptics: Some Dimensions of the Problem." *New Testament Studies* 27 (1980): 425–44.

———. *Johannine Christianity: Essays on its Setting, Sources, and Theology.* Columbia, SC: University of South Carolina Press, 1984.

———. "The Contribution of J. Louis Martyn to the Understanding of the Gospel of John." Pp. 275–94 in *The Conversation Continues: Studies in Paul and John in Honor of J. Louis Martyn*. Edited by Robert T. Fortna and Beverly R. Gaventa. Nashville: Abingdon, 1990.

———. *First, Second, and Third John.* Interpretation. Louisville: John Knox, 1991.

———. *John among the Gospels: The Relationship in Twentieth-Century Research.* Philadelphia: Fortress, 1992.

———. "The Love Command: John and Paul?" Pp. 207–17 in *Theology and Ethics in Paul and His Interpreters: Essays in Honor of Victor Paul Furnish*. Nashville: Abingdon, 1996.

———. *John.* Abingdon New Testament Commentaries. Nashville: Abingdon, 1999.

———. "Ethics and the Interpretation of the Fourth Gospel." Pp. 109–22 in *Word, Theology, and Community in John*. Edited by John Painter, R. Alan Culpepper, and Fernando F. Segovia. St. Louis, MO: Chalice, 2002.

———. "John—Historian or Theologian?" *Bible Review* 20 (2004): 22–31, 45.

———. *The Fourth Gospel in Four Dimensions: Judaism and Jesus, the Gospels and Scripture.* Columbia, SC: University of South Carolina Press, 2008.

Smith, Dennis E. *From Symposium to Eucharist: The Banquet in the Early Christian World.* Minneapolis: Fortress, 2003.

Smith, Jonathan Z. "The Influence of Symbols upon Social Change: A Place on Which to Stand." *Worship* 44 (1970): 457–74.

Smith, Mark S. *The Early History of God: Yahweh and the Other Deities in Ancient Israel.* San Francisco: Harper & Row, 1990.

Smith, Robert H. "Exodus Typology in the Fourth Gospel." *Journal of Biblical Literature* 81 (1962): 329–42.

Snyder, Graydon F. "John 13,16 and the Anti-Petrinism of the Johannine Tradition." *Biblical Research* 16 (1971): 5–15.

Söding, Thomas. "Die Macht der Wahrheit und das Reich der Freiheit: Zur johanneischen Deutung des Pilatus-Prozesses (Joh 18,28–19,16)." *Zeitschrift für Theologie und Kirche* 93 (1996): 35–58.

———. "Kreuzerhöhung. Zur Deutung des Todes Jesu nach Johannes." *Zeitschrift für Theologie und Kirche* 103 (2006): 2–25.

Spicq, Ceslas. *Agapē in the New Testament.* Vol. III: *Agapē in the Gospel, Epistles, and Apocalypse of John.* Translated by Marie Aquinas McNamara and Mary Honoria Richter. St. Louis/London: Herder, 1966.

Sproston North, Wendy E. "John for Readers of Mark? A Response to Richard Bauckham's Proposal." *Journal for the Study of the New Testament* 25 (2003): 449–68.

Sproston, Wendy E. "Satan in the Fourth Gospel." Pp. 307–11 in *Studia Biblica 1978.* Volume II: *Papers on The Gospels.* Journal for the Study of the New Testament Supplement Series 2. Edited by E. A. Livingstone. Sheffield: JSOT, 1980.

Stählin, Gustav. "Zum Problem der johanneischen Eschatologie." *Zeitschrift für die neutestamentliche Wissenschaft* 33 (1934): 225–59.

Staley, Jeffrey L. "Stumbling in the Dark, Reaching for the Light: Reading Character in John 5 and 9." *Semeia* 53 (1991): 55–80.

Stamps, Dennis L. "The Johannine Writings." Pp. 609–32 in *Handbook of Classical Rhetoric in the Hellenistic Period 330 B.C.–A.D. 400.* Edited by Stanley E. Porter. Leiden: Brill, 1997.

Stanton, Graham N. *Jesus of Nazareth in New Testament Preaching.* Society for New Testament Studies Monograph Series 27. Cambridge: Cambridge University Press, 1974.

———. *A Gospel for a New People: Studies in Matthew.* Edinburgh: T&T Clark, 1992.

———. "The Fourfold Gospel." *New Testament Studies* 43 (1997): 317–46.

Stegemann, Ekkehard W. "Zur Tempelreinigung im Johannesevangelium." Pp. 503–16 in *Die Hebräische Bibel und ihre zweifache Nachgeschichte: Festschrift für Rolf Rendtorff zum 65. Geburtstag.* Edited by Erhard Blum et al. Neukirchen-Vluyn: Neukirchener, 1990.

Steinmetz, David. "The Superiority of Pre-critical Exegesis." *Theology Today* 37 (1980): 27–38. Reprint pp. 26–38 in *The Theological Interpretation of Scripture: Classic and Contemporary Readings.* Blackwell Readings in Modern Theology. Edited by Stephen E. Fowl. Oxford: Blackwell, 1997.

Stemberger, Günter. *La symbolique du bien et du mal selon saint Jean.* Parole de Dieu. Paris: Editions du Seuil, 1970.

Stevens, George Barker. *The Johannine Theology: A Study of the Doctrinal Contents of the Gospel and Epistles of the Apostle John.* Rev. ed. New York: Scribner's Sons, 1908 [1894].

Stibbe, Mark W. G. "The Elusive Christ: A New Reading of the Fourth Gospel." *Journal for the Study of the New Testament* 44 (1991): 19–38.

———. *John as Storyteller: Narrative Criticism and the Fourth Gospel.* Cambridge: Cambridge University Press, 1992.

———. *John.* Sheffield: Sheffield Academic Press, 1993.

———. *John's Gospel.* New Testament Readings. London: Routledge, 1994.

———. "Telling the Father's Story: The Gospel of John as Narrative Theology." Pp. 170–93 in *Challenging Perspectives on the Gospel of John.* Wissenschaftliche Untersuchungen zum Neuen Testament 2/219. Edited by John Lierman. Tübingen: Mohr-Siebeck, 2006.

———. "Magnificent but Flawed: The Breaking of Form in the Fourth Gospel." Pp. 149–66 in *Anatomies of Narrative Criticism: The Past, Present, and Futures of the Fourth Gospel as Literature.* Edited by Tom Thatcher and Stephen D. Moore. Waco, TX: Baylor University Press, 2008.

Stibbe, Mark W. G., ed. *The Gospel of John as Literature: An Anthology of Twentieth-Century Perspectives.* New Testament Tools and Studies 17. Leiden: Brill, 1993.

Stolz, Fritz. "Zeichen und Wunder: Die prophetische Legitimation und ihre Geschichte." *Zeitschrift für Theologie und Kirche* 69 (1972): 125–44.

Stott, John R. W. *Christian Mission in the Modern World*. Downers Grove, IL: InterVarsity Press, 1975.

———. *The Letters of John*. Tyndale New Testament Commentaries. Rev. ed. Grand Rapids: Eerdmans, 1988.

Strachan, R. H. *The Fourth Gospel: Its Significance and Environment*. 3rd ed. London: SCM, 1941.

Strauss, David Friedrich. *The Christ of Faith and the Jesus of History*. Translated and edited by Leander E. Keck. Philadelphia: Fortress, 1977 [1865].

Strecker, Georg. *The Johannine Letters: A Commentary on 1, 2, and 3 John*. Hermeneia. Translated by Linda M. Maloney. Minneapolis: Fortress, 1996.

Streeter, B. H. *The Four Gospels*. Rev. ed. London: Macmillan, 1930.

Streett, Daniel R. "'They Went Out from Us': The Identity of the Opponents in First John." Ph.D. dissertation. Wake Forest, NC: Southeastern Baptist Theological Seminary, 2008.

Stuhlmacher, Peter. "Das Lamm Gottes—eine Skizze." Pp. 529–42 in *Geschichte–Tradition–Reflexion: Festschrift für Martin Hengel zum 70. Geburtstag*. Vol. 3. Edited by Hubert Cancik, Hermann Lichtenberger, and Peter Schäfer. Tübingen: Mohr-Siebeck, 1996.

Suggit, John. "Jesus the Gardener: The Atonement in the Fourth Gospel as Re-Creation." *Neotestamentica* 33 (1999): 161–68.

Swain, Scott R. "Truth in the Gospel of John." Th.M. thesis. Wake Forest, NC: Southeastern Baptist Theological Seminary, 1998.

Swartley, Willard M. *Israel's Scripture Traditions and the Synoptic Gospels: Story Shaping Story*. Peabody, MA: Hendrickson, 1994.

Talbert, Charles H. "Artistry and Theology: An Analysis of the Architecture of Jn 1,19–5,47." *Catholic Biblical Quarterly* 32 (1970): 341–66.

———. "The Myth of a Descending-Ascending Redeemer in Mediterranean Antiquity." *New Testament Studies* 22 (1976): 418–40.

———. *What Is a Gospel?* Philadelphia: Fortress, 1977.

———. *Reading John: A Literary and Theological Commentary on the Fourth Gospel and the Johannine Epistles*. New York: Crossroad, 1992.

Tate, Marvin E. *Psalms 51–100*. Word Biblical Commentary 20. Dallas: Word, 1990.

Taylor, Michael J., ed. *A Companion to John: Readings in Johannine Theology (John's Gospel and Epistles)*. New York: Alba House, 1977.

Teeple, Howard M. *The Mosaic Eschatological Prophet*. SBL Monograph Series 10. Philadelphia: Scholars Press, 1957.

Tenney, Merrill C. "The Footnotes of John's Gospel." *Bibliotheca Sacra* 117 (1960): 350–63.

———. "Some Possible Parallels between 1 Peter and John." Pp. 370–77 in *New Dimensions in New Testament Study*. Edited by Richard N. Longenecker and Merrill C. Tenney. Grand Rapids: Zondervan, 1974.

———. "Topics from the Gospel of John. Part I: The Person of the Father." *Bibliotheca Sacra* 132 (1975): 37–46.

Teppler, Yaakov Y. *Birkat haMinim*. Texts and Studies in Ancient Judaism 120. Translated by Susan Weingarten. Tübingen: Mohr-Siebeck, 2007.

Thatcher, Tom. "The Gospel Genre: What Are We After?" *Restoration Quarterly* 36 (1994): 129–38.

———. "A New Look at Asides in the Fourth Gospel." *Bibliotheca Sacra* 151 (1994): 428–39.

———. "John's Memory Theater: The Fourth Gospel and Ancient Mnemo-Rhetoric." *Catholic Biblical Quarterly* 69 (2007): 487–505.

———. *Greater than Caesar: Christology and Empire in the Fourth Gospel*. Minneapolis: Fortress, 2009.

Thatcher, Tom, ed. *What We Have Heard from the Beginning: The Past, Present, and Future of Johannine Studies*. Waco, TX: Baylor University Press, 2007.

———. *Jesus, the Voice, and the Text: Beyond the Oral and the Written Gospel*. Waco, TX: Baylor University Press, 2008.

Thatcher, Tom, and Stephen D. Moore, eds. *Anatomies of Narrative Criticism: The Past, Present, and Futures of the Fourth Gospel as Literature*. Society of Biblical Literature Resources for Biblical Study 55. Atlanta: Society of Biblical Literature, 2008.

Theobald, Michael. *Herrenworte im Johannesevangelium*. Herders Biblische Studien 34. Freiburg im Breisgau: Herder, 2002.

Thielman, Frank. "The Style of the Fourth Gospel and Ancient Literary Critical Concepts of Religious Discourse." Pp. 169–83 in *Persuasive Artistry: Studies in New Testament Rhetoric in Honor of George A. Kennedy*. Journal for the Study of the New Testament Supplement 50. Edited by Duane F. Watson. Sheffield: JSOT, 1991.

———. *Theology of the New Testament: A Canonical and Synthetic Approach*. Grand Rapids: Zondervan, 2005.

Thiselton, Anthony C. "Truth." Pp. 874–902 in *New International Dictionary of New Testament Theology*. Vol. 3. Edited by Colin Brown. Grand Rapids: Zondervan, 1986.

Thomas, John Christopher. *Footwashing in John 13 and the Johannine Community*. Journal for the Study of New Testament Supplement 61. Sheffield: JSOT, 1991.

———. "'Stop Sinning Lest Something Worse Come upon You': The Man at the Pool in John 5." *Journal for the Study of the New Testament* 59 (1995): 3–20.

Thompson, L. A. "Domitian and the Jewish Tax." *Historia* 31 (1982): 329–42.

Thompson, Marianne Meye. *The Humanity of Jesus in the Fourth Gospel*. Philadelphia: Fortress, 1988.

———. "Signs and Faith in the Fourth Gospel." *Bulletin of Biblical Research* 1 (1991): 89–108.

———. *1–3 John*. IVP New Testament Commentary. Downers Grove, IL: InterVarsity Press, 1992.

———. "'God's Voice You Have Never Heard, God's Form You Have Never Seen': The Characterization of God in the Gospel of John." *Semeia* 63 (1993): 177–204.

———. "The Historical Jesus and the Johannine Christ." Pp. 21–42 in *Exploring the Gospel of John: In Honor of D. Moody Smith*. Edited by R. Alan Culpepper and C. Clifton Black. Louisville, KY: Westminster John Knox, 1996.

———. *The Promise of the Father*. Louisville: Westminster John Knox, 2000.

———. *The God of the Gospel of John*. Grand Rapids: Eerdmans, 2001.

———. "The 'Spiritual Gospel': How John the Theologian Writes History." Pp. 103–7 in *John, Jesus, and History*. Vol. 1: *Critical Appraisals of Critical Views*. SBL Semeia Series 44. Edited by Paul N. Anderson, Felix Just, and Tom Thatcher. Atlanta: Society of Biblical Literature, 2007.

Thüsing, Wilhelm. *Die Erhöhung und Verherrlichung Jesu im Johannesevangelium.* Neutestamentliche Abhandlungen 21. Münster: W. Aschendorff, 1979.

Tidball, Derek. "Completing the Circle: The Resurrection according to John." *Evangelical Review of Theology* 30 (2006): 169–83.

Timmins, Nicholas G. "Variation in Style in the Johannine Literature." *Journal for the Study of the New Testament* 53 (1994): 47–64.

Tolmie, Donald François. "The Characterization of God in the Fourth Gospel." *Journal for the Study of the New Testament* 69 (1998): 57–75.

Tomoi, K. "The Plan of the First Epistle of John." *Expository Times* 52 (1940–41): 117–19.

Torrey, C. C. *Our Translated Gospels: Some of the Evidence.* New York: Harper, 1936.

Tovey, Derek. *Narrative Art and Act in the Fourth Gospel.* Journal for the Study of the New Testament Supplement 151. Sheffield: Sheffield Academic Press, 1997.

Trebilco, Paul. *The Early Christians in Ephesus from Paul to Ignatius.* Grand Rapids: Eerdmans, 2008.

Trites, Allison A. *The New Testament Concept of Witness.* Society for New Testament Studies Monograph Series 31. Cambridge: Cambridge University Press, 1977.

Trobisch, David. *Paul's Letter Collection: Tracing the Origins.* Minneapolis: Fortress, 1994.

Trotter, Andrew H. "Justification in the Gospel of John." Pp. 126–45 in *Right with God: Justification in the Bible and the World.* Edited by D. A. Carson. Grand Rapids: Baker, 1992.

Trudinger, Paul. "'An Israelite in Whom There Is No Guile': An Interpretive Note on John 1,45–51." *Evangelical Quarterly* 54 (1982): 117–20.

Turner, George Allen. "The Date and Purpose of the Gospel of John." *Bulletin of the Evangelical Theological Society* 6 (1963): 82–85.

Turner, Max. "The Concept of Receiving the Spirit in John's Gospel." *Vox Evangelica* 19 (1977): 24–42.

———. "Atonement and the Death of Jesus in John: Some Questions to Bultmann and Forestell." *Evangelical Quarterly* 62 (1990): 99–122.

Twelftree, Graham H. *In the Name of Jesus: Exorcism among Early Christians.* Grand Rapids: Baker, 2007.

Van Belle, Gilbert. *Les parentheses dans l'évangile de Jean: Aperçu historique et classification. Texte grec de Jean.* Studiorum Novi Testamenti Auxilia 11. Leuven: Leuven University Press/Peeters, 1985.

———. *Johannine Bibliography 1966–1985: A Cumulative Bibliography on the Fourth Gospel.* Bibliotheca ephemeridum theologicarum lovaniensium 132. Leuven: Leuven University Press/Peeters, 1988.

———. *The Signs Source in the Fourth Gospel: Historical Survey and Critical Evaluation of the Semeia Hypothesis.* Bibliotheca ephemeridum theologicarum lovaniensium 116. Leuven: Leuven University Press/Peeters, 1994.

———. "The Death of Jesus in the Fourth Gospel: Colloquium Biblicum Lovaniense LIV (2005)." *Ephemerides theologicae lovanienses* 81 (2005): 567–79.

———. *The Death of Jesus in the Fourth Gospel.* Bibliotheca ephemeridum theologicarum lovaniensium 200. Leuven: Leuven University Press/Peeters, 2007.

Van den Bussche, Henri. "Die Kirche im vierten Evangelium." Pp. 79–107 in *Vom Christus zur Kirche: Charisma und Amt im Urchristentum.* Wien: Herder, 1966.

Van der Watt, Jan G. *Family of the King: Dynamics of Metaphor in the Gospel according to John.* Biblical Interpretation Series 47. Leiden: Brill, 2000.

———. "*Double entendre* in the Gospel according to John." Pp. 463–81 in *Theology and Christology in the Fourth Gospel*. Bibliotheca ephemeridum theologicarum lovaniensium 184. Edited by G. van Belle, J. G. van der Watt, and P. Maritz. Leuven: Leuven University Press/Peeters, 2005.

———. "Ethics and Ethos in the Gospel according to John." *Zeitschrift für die neutestamentliche Wissenschaft* 97 (2006): 147–76.

———. "Ethics Alive in Imagery." Pp. 421–48 in *Imagery in the Gospel of John: Terms, Forms, Themes, and Theology of Johannine Figurative Language*. Wissenschaftliche Untersuchungen zum Neuen Testament 200. Edited by Jörg Frey, Jan G. van der Watt, and Ruben Zimmerman. Tübingen: Mohr-Siebeck, 2006.

———. "Everlasting Life in John and the Permanence of Salvation: Life Metaphor in John's Gospel." Posted at http://jcsm.org/EternalSecurity/JanGabrielvanderWatt.htm.

Van Staden, Peter J. "The Debate on the Structure of 1 John." *Hervormde Teologiese Studies* 47 (1991): 487–502.

Vanhoozer, Kevin J. "A Lamp in the Labyrinth: The Hermeneutics of 'Aesthetic Theology.'" *Trinity Journal* 8 NS (1987): 25–56.

———. "The Hermeneutics of I-Witness Testimony: John 21.20–24 and the 'Death' of the Author." Pp. 366–87 in *Understanding Poets and Prophets: Essays in Honour of George Wishart Anderson*. Journal for the Study of the Old Testament Supplement 152. Edited by A. Graeme Auld. Sheffield: JSOT, 1993.

———. *The Drama of Doctrine: A Canonical-Linguistic Approach to Christian Theology*. Louisville: Westminster John Knox, 2005.

Vellanickal, Matthew. "Evangelization in the Johannine Writings." Pp. 121–68 in *Good News and Witness*. Edited by Lucien Legrand, J. Pathrapankal, and Matthew Vellanickal. Bangalore: Theological Publications in India, 1973.

Vergote, Antoine. "L'exaltation du Christ en croix selon le quatrième évangile." *Ephemerides theologicae lovanienses* 28 (1952): 5–23.

Via, Dan O. "Darkness, Christ and Church in the Fourth Gospel." *Scottish Journal of Theology* 14 (1961): 172–93.

Viviano, Benedict T. "The Structure of the Prologue of John (1:1–18): A Note." *Revue biblique* 105 (1998): 176–84.

Vogel, Manuel. "Tempel und Tempelkult in Pseudo-Philos Liber Antiquitatum Biblicarum." Pp. 251–63 in *Gemeinde ohne Tempel: Zur Substituierung und Transformation des Jerusalemer Tempels und seines Kults im Alten Testament, antiken Judentum und frühen Christentum*. Wissenschaftliche Untersuchungen zum Neuen Testament 118. Edited by Beate Ego, Armin Lange, and Peter Pilhofer. Tübingen: Mohr-Siebeck, 1999.

Volf, Miroslav. *Exclusion and Embrace: A Theological Exploration of Identity, Otherness, and Reconciliation*. Nashville: Abingdon, 1996.

———. "Johannine Dualism and Contemporary Pluralism." *Modern Theology* 21 (2005): 189–217.

Volfing, Annette. *John the Evangelist in Medieval German Writing: Imitating the Inimitable*. Oxford: Oxford University Press, 2001.

Vorster, Willem S. "The Growth and Making of John 21." Pp. 2207–21 in *The Four Gospels 1992: Festschrift Frans Neirynck*. Bibliotheca ephemeridum theologicarum lovaniensium 100. Vol. 3. Edited by F. van Segbroeck, C. M. Tuckett, G. van Belle, and J. Verheyden. Leuven: Leuven University Press, 1992.

Vos, Geerhardus. "'True' and 'Truth' in the Johannine Writings." *Biblical Review* 12 (1927): 507–20.

Votaw, C. H. *The Gospels and Contemporary Biographies in the Greco-Roman World.* Philadelphia: Fortress, 1970 [1915].

Vrede, Wilhelm. "Die Johannesbriefe." Pp. 143–92 in *Die Katholischen Briefe.* Die Heilige Schrift des Neuen Testaments 9. 4th ed. Bonn: Hanstein, 1932.

Wahlde, Urban C. von. "Archaeology and John's Gospel." Pp. 523–86 in *Jesus and Archaeology.* Edited by James H. Charlesworth. Grand Rapids: Eerdmans, 2006.

Walker, Peter W. *Jesus and the Holy City: New Testament Perspectives on Jerusalem.* Grand Rapids: Eerdmans, 1996.

Walker, W. O. Jr. "John 1.43–51 and 'the Son of Man' in the Fourth Gospel." *Journal for the Study of the New Testament* 56 (1994): 31–42.

Wallace, Daniel B. "John 5,2 and the Date of the Fourth Gospel." *Biblica* 71 (1990): 177–205.

———. *Greek Grammar beyond the Basics.* Grand Rapids: Zondervan, 1996.

Watson, Francis. "The Fourfold Gospel." Pp. 34–52 in *The Cambridge Companion to the Gospels.* Edited by Stephen C. Barton. Cambridge: Cambridge University Press, 2006.

Watts, Rikki E. *Isaiah's New Exodus in Mark.* Biblical Studies Library. Grand Rapids: Baker, 2000.

Watty, William W. "The Significance of Anonymity in the Fourth Gospel." *Expository Times* 90 (1979): 209–12.

Wead, David W. "The Johannine Double Meaning." *Restoration Quarterly* 13 (1970): 106–20.

———. *The Literary Devices in John's Gospel.* Theologische Dissertationen 4. Basel: Friedrich Reinhardt Kommissionsverlag, 1970.

Webster, Jane S. *Ingesting Jesus: Eating and Drinking in the Gospel of John.* Society of Biblical Literature Academia Biblica 6. Atlanta: Society of Biblical Literature, 2003.

Wellhausen, Julius. *Das Evangelium Johannis.* Berlin: Reimer, 1908.

Westcott, A. "The Divisions of the First Epistle of St. John: A Correspondence between Drs. Westcott and Hort." *The Expositor* 7/3 (1907): 481–93.

Westcott, B. F. *Commentary on the Gospel according to St. John.* Grand Rapids: Eerdmans, 1975 [1908].

Wheelwright, Philip E. *Metaphor and Reality.* Bloomington, IN/London: Indiana University Press, 1962.

Whitacre, Rodney A. *Johannine Polemic: The Role of Tradition and Theology.* SBL Dissertation Series 67. Chico, CA: Scholars Press, 1982.

———. *John.* IVP New Testament Commentary 4. Downers Grove, IL: InterVarsity Press, 1999.

White, John L. "Ancient Greek Letters." Pp. 85–105 in *Greco-Roman Literature and the New Testament.* SBL Sources for Biblical Studies 21. Edited by David E. Aune. Atlanta: Scholars Press, 1988.

Whiteley, D. E. H. "Was John Written by a Sadducee?" Pp. 2481–2505 in *Aufstieg und Niedergang der Römischen Welt* 2.25.3. Edited by Wolfgang Haase. Berlin: Walter de Gruyter, 1985.

Wifall, Walter R. "David—Prototype of Israel's Future?" *Biblical Theology Bulletin* 4 (1974): 94–107.

Wilckens, Ulrich. *Das Evangelium nach Johannes.* Das Neue Testament Deutsch 4. Göttingen: Vandenhoeck & Ruprecht, 1998.

Wilder, A. N. "Introduction and Exegesis of the First, Second, and Third Epistles of John." Pp. 207–313 in *The Interpreter's Bible.* Vol. 12. Edited by G. A. Buttrick. Nashville: Abingdon, 1957.

Wilkens, Wilhelm. *Zeichen und Werke: Ein Beitrag zur Theologie des 4. Evangeliums in Erzählungs- und Redestoff.* Abhandlungen zur Theologie des Alten und Neuen Testaments 55. Zurich: Zwingli, 1969.

Willi-Plein, Ina. "Warum musste der Zweite Tempel gebaut werden?" Pp. 57–73 in *Gemeinde ohne Tempel: Zur Substituierung und Transformation des Jerusalemer Tempels und seines Kults im Alten Testament, antiken Judentum und frühen Christentum.* Wissenschaftliche Untersuchungen zum Neuen Testament 118. Edited by Beate Ego, Armin Lange, and Peter Pilhofer. Tübingen: Mohr-Siebeck, 1999.

Williams, Catrin H. *I am He: The Interpretation of 'ani hu' in Jewish and Early Christian Literature.* Wissenschaftliche Untersuchungen zum Neuen Testament 2/113. Tübingen: Mohr-Siebeck, 2000.

Williams, P. J. "Not the Prologue of John." Paper presented at the Annual Meeting of the Society of Biblical Literature. San Diego, CA, November 17, 2007.

Wilson, W. G. "An Examination of the Linguistic Evidence Adduced against the Unity of Authorship of the First Epistle of John and the Fourth Gospel." *Journal of Theological Studies* 49 (1947): 147–56.

Windisch, Hans. "Der johanneische Erzählungsstil." Pp. 174–213 in *Eucharisterion: Hermann Gunkel zum 60. Geburtstage.* Forschungen zur Religion und Literatur des Alten und Neuen Testaments N. F. 19. Edited by Hans Schmidt. Vol. 2. Göttingen: Vandenhoeck & Ruprecht, 1923.

———. *Johannes und die Synoptiker: Wollte der vierte Evangelist die älteren Evangelien ergänzen oder ersetzen?* Leipzig: J. C. Hinrichs'sche Buchhandlung, 1926.

———. *Die Katholischen Briefe.* Handbuch zum Neuen Testament 15. 3rd rev. ed. Tübingen: Mohr, 1951.

———. *The Spirit-Paraclete in the Fourth Gospel.* Philadelphia: Fortress, 1968.

Winter, Paul. "Μονογενὴς παρὰ πατρός." *Zeitschrift für Religions- und Geistesgeschichte* 5 (1953): 337–40.

Witherington, Ben III. *John's Wisdom: A Commentary on the Fourth Gospel.* Louisville: Westminster John Knox, 1995.

———. "New Creation or New Birth? Conversion in the Johannine and Pauline Literature." Pp. 119–42 in *Conversion in the Wesleyan Tradition.* Edited by Kenneth J. Collins and John H. Tyson. Nashville: Abingdon, 2001.

Wolters, Al. "The Messiah in the Qumran Documents." Pp. 75–89 in *The Messiah in the Old and New Testaments.* McMaster New Testament Studies. Edited by Stanley E. Porter. Grand Rapids: Eerdmans, 2007.

Woodbridge, Paul. "'The World' in the Fourth Gospel." Pp. 1–31 in *Witness to the World: Papers from the Second Oak Hill College Annual School of Theology.* Edited by David Peterson. Carlisle, UK: Paternoster, 1999.

Wright, Christopher J. H. *The Mission of God: Unlocking the Bible's Grand Narrative.* Downers Grove, IL: InterVarsity Press, 2006.

Wright, George Ernest. *God Who Acts: Biblical Theology as Recital.* London: SCM, 1954.

Wright, N. T. *The New Testament and the People of God.* Christian Origins and the Question of God 1. Minneapolis: Fortress, 1992.

———. *The Resurrection of the Son of God.* Christian Origins and the Question of God 3. Minneapolis: Fortress, 2003.

———. *John for Everyone.* Louisville: Westminster John Knox, 2004.

Wyatt, Nicolas. "'Supposing Him to Be the Gardener' (John 20,15): A Study of the Paradise Motif in John." *Zeitschrift für die neutestamentliche Wissenschaft* 81 (1990): 21–38.

Yarbrough, Robert W. "Divine Election in the Gospel of John." Pp. 47–62 in *The Grace of God, the Bondage of the Will.* Vol. 1. Edited by Thomas R. Schreiner and Bruce A. Ware. Grand Rapids: Baker, 1995.

———. *The Salvation Historical Fallacy? Reassessing the History of New Testament Theology.* History of Biblical Interpretation Series. Leiden: Deo, 2004.

———. *1–3 John.* Baker Exegetical Commentary on the New Testament. Grand Rapids: Baker, 2008.

Yassif, Eli. *The Hebrew Folktale: History, Genre, Meaning.* Bloomington, IN: Indiana University Press, 1999.

Yee, Gale A. *Jewish Feasts and the Gospel of John.* Wilmington, DE: Michael Glazier, 1989.

Young, Franklin W. "A Study of the Relation of Isaiah to the Fourth Gospel." *Zeitschrift für die neutestamentliche Wissenschaft* 46 (1955): 215–33.

Zagzebski, Linda. "The Virtues of God and the Foundation of Ethics." *Faith and Philosophy* 15 (1998): 538–53.

Zenger, Erich. "Der Psalter als Heiligtum." Pp. 115–30 in *Gemeinde ohne Tempel: Zur Substituierung und Transformation des Jerusalemer Tempels und seines Kults im Alten Testament, antiken Judentum und frühen Christentum.* Wissenschaftliche Untersuchungen zum Neuen Testament 118. Edited by Beate Ego, Armin Lange, and Peter Pilhofer. Tübingen: Mohr-Siebeck, 1999.

Zumstein, Jean. "L'interprétation johannique de la mort du Christ." Pp. 2119–38 in *The Four Gospels 1992: Festschrift Frans Neirynck.* Bibliotheca ephemeridum theologicarum lovaniensium 100. Edited by F. van Segbroeck, C. M. Tuckett, G. van Belle, and J. Verheyden. Leuven: University Press, 1992.

Scripture Index

Genesis
1. . . . . 338, 349
1:1 . . . . 307, 347, 405
1:3–5. . . . . . . 179, 283, 339, 347, 406
1:3, 9 338
1:11 338
1:14–18 . . . . 339, 347, 406
1:14 . . . . 283, 325
1:15 338
1:20–31 . . . . 339, 347, 406
1:24 338
1:26 282
1:30 338
2:2–3 350
2:2 353
2:7 . . . . 184, 259, 309, 339, 347,
          352, 392, 400, 406, 543
2:9 347
2:17 308
3:4–5. 440
3:4 308
3:15 313
3:20 . . . . 339, 347, 406
5:24 . . . . 388, 527
16 381
17:10–13 308
18:25 . . . . 388, 391, 469
19:1 258
21:1–21 308
22 . . . . 382, 533
22:2 . . . . 308, 381, 409
22:8 415
22:12 . . . . 308, 381, 409
22:13 415
22:14 415
22:16 . . . . 308, 381, 409
24:27 . . . . 437, 439
24:48 437
24:49 439
26:19 163
27 498
27:35 498
28:12 . . . . 307, 387, 529
32:10 437
32:11 439
33:19 308
41:55 307
47:29 . . . . 437, 439
48:22 308
49 247
49:10 313
49:11 304

Exodus
1–4 419
4:1–9 325
4:8 325
4:9 325
4:17 325
4:22 472
4:28 325
4:30 325
7:1 358
7:3, 8–9 325
8:23 325
10:1–2 325
11:9, 10 325
12:13 325
12:46 . . . . 254, 302–5, 309, 415,
          419–20
13:9, 16 325
13:19 308
15:22–23 109
16 109
16:2, 8–9 212
16:10 408
17 109
17:1–7 . . . . 163, 430
17:6 . . . . 164, 419, 421
19:5 341
20:2–6 356
20:2 356
20:4 364
20:5 308
22:27 358
24:9–11 388
24:16–18 408
25:8–9 406
26–27 426
28:26 437
28:41 313
31:12–17 350
31:18 . . . . 406, 409
33–34 . . . . 359, 439, 501
33:7 406
33:9 406
33:18–23 426
33:18–19 409
33:18 . . . . 359, 408
33:20–23 439
33:20 307
33:22 406
34 439
34:6 . . . . 186, 307, 359, 409, 439
34:28 . . . . 406, 409
34:29–30 388
40:34–35 . . . . 295, 406
40:34 408

Leviticus
4:3–5 313
12:3 308
13:2 419
14 415
14:6 163
16 415
19:15 308
19:18 511
23:33–43 420
23:34 421
23:36 421
23:41–42 421
23:42–43 420
24:16 . . . . 308, 309, 385

Numbers
3:3 313
6 415

9:9–14. 413
9:12 . . . . . 254, 302–5, 309, 415–16, 419–20
11. 109
11:4–23. 212
11:9 .529
11:12 382
14:10 406
14:22 .325
15:30–31. 385
15:37–41. 373
20 109
20:2–13 163
20:8–13 430
20:8–11 308
20:11 . . . . .308, 419
21:8 325
21:9 . . . . .199, 307
21:16–18 308
21:16 .163
21:22 .385
24:17 . . . . 166, 182, 340
24:18 406
27:15–18 308
28:7 420
29:12–39. 420
29:35 .421

Deuteronomy

1:16–17 308
4:32–39. 356
4:34 325
5:6–10. 356
5:22 406
6:4 . . . . . 316, 356, 359–60, 373–74, 382
6:5 511
6:22 325
7:19 325
8:3 347
11:3 325
11:13–21 373
11:29 308
12:5–14. 308
13:1–2 325
14:1 472
15:11 .309
17:4 308
17:6 . . . . .209, 270, 308, 454
18:15 . . . . .211, 213, 307–8, 407, 416
18:18 . . . . 211, 213, 307–8, 317, 407, 416
19:15 . . . . . . 188, 209, 270, 308, 454, 545
19:18 308
21:15–17 289
21:22–23. 309–10
22:20 437
26:8 325
27:12 308
29:2–4. 410
29:2, 3. 325
30:15–16. 347
30:19 284
31:26–27. 308
32. 247
32:18 .473
32:39 .391
33:5 313
33:8 437
34:10–12. 325

Joshua

2:12 439
2:14 . . . . .437, 439
7:19 . . . . 308, 365
8:33 308
11:27 469
24:5 325
24:14 440
24:32 308

Judges

8:23 443
9:15 437
11:27 .391
11:34 . . . . .381, 409

Ruth

4:16 382

1 Samuel

2:6 391
2:10 . . . . .313, 388
2:34 .325
3:10 44
7:6 421
8:7 443
9:15–16 313
10:1 313
16:3 313
16:7 308
16:12–13. 313
24:6 313
26:16 .313
26:17, 21, 25. 384
28:9 151

2 Samuel

1:14, 16 313
2:4 313
2:6 439
5:3 313
7:6 406
7:12 308
7:14 . . . . 307, 313, 316, 384, 411
7:28 440
12:3 382
15:20 439
19:6 289
23:2 313

1 Kings

1:34, 45 313
3:20 382
5:1 313
6:13 426
8:2 421
8:10–11 . . . . 295, 406
8:27 70
8:65 421
12:32 .421
17:19 382
17:21 400
17:24 440
19:16 .313

2 Kings

2:1–12. 388
4:42–44 318
5:7 391
9:3, 6 .313
11:12 .313
19:29 .325
20:8, 9 325
23:30 .313

2 Chronicles

5:3 421
5:13–14 295

7:1–2 295
7:8 421
18:15 440
21:12–15 388
24:24 373
30:8 365
32:24 325

Nehemiah
3:15 350
8:13–18 420
8:14 421
8:18 421
9. 422
9:10 325
9:15, 19–20 . . . . . .163, 308, 416, 421

Esther
10:3 325

Job
3:20 348
9:8 211
10:12 392
16:2 396
30:26 283
33:4 392
33:30 348

Psalms
2. .313, 452
2:1–2 452
2:2 . . . . .313, 317–18, 391, 469
2:7 . . . . .307, 384, 411
6:3 .309, 412
8:6 358
9:8 388
15:2 406
19:1–4 .338
19:8 . . . . .166, 339
21. 313
22 . . . . 313, 411–12
22:1 302
22:15 309
22:18 . . . . 254, 302–5, 309
25:5 440
25:10 . . . . 409, 439
26:3 409
26:8 406
27:4–6 406
31:5 438
33:6 338
34:20 . . . . .254, 302–5, 309, 415, 419–20
35:19 . . . . .215, 243, 290, 302–5, 309, 412
36:8–9 348
36:9 . . . . .347, 392
40:10 409
40:11, 12 439
41:9 . . . . 237, 302–5, 309
42–43 421
42:2 347
42:5, 11 . . . . .309, 412
43:3 406
45:6–7 .401
49:19 348
51:5 308
56:13 348
57:4, 11 439
61:6–7 .321
61:8 439
69. 411
69:4 . . . . .215, 243, 290, 302–5, 309, 412
69:9 . . . . 196, 301, 303–4, 306–7, 411
69:10 330
69:14 439
69:21 . . . . 306, 309, 412
72. 313
74:7 406
74:9 325
77:16 . . . . 308, 394
77:20 . . . . 308, 394, 500
78:15 306
78:16 163
78:20 306
78:24 . . .301, 303–4, 306, 308, 416, 529
78:43 325
78:52 500
80:8–16 502
81:3 421
82:1 358
82:6 . . . . .227, 301, 303–4, 306, 309, 358, 365, 385
82:8 388
84:1 406
84:11 409
85:11 439
86:15 439
89. 313
89:3–4 308
89:4 309
89:15 439
89:26–29 411
89:26 373
89:27 409
89:36–37 309
94:2 388
97:6 358
97:7 500
102:16 406
105:15 .313
105:27 .325
105:40 .416
105:41 .421
107:20 .338
110. 313
113–118 421
115:1 439
117:2 439
118. 302
118:25–26 . . . . . . 232, 302, 384, 448
118:26 . . . . 301, 303–4, 306, 309
119:105, 130 . . . . .166, 339
119:142, 151 440
119:160 440
122:1–5 308
132. 313
135:9 325
138:1 358
138:2 439
147:15, 18 338

Proverbs
3:3 439
4:3 .381, 409
4:23 . . . . .394, 421
5:15 . . . . .394, 421
6:23 . . . . .166, 339
8:30 . . . . .371, 382
13:24 289
14:22 439
16:6 . . . . 409, 439
18:4 421
20:28 439
30:4 . . . . .307, 529

Ecclesiastes
8:8 475
11:5 .307, 475

Isaiah
2:2–4 434
2:3 308
5:1–7 . . . . .241, 309, 502
6 411
6:1–3 . . . . 294–95, 388
6:1 309
6:3 350
6:9–10 . . . . .234, 561
6:10 . . . . 212, 234, 302–4, 306, 309,
410–11, 442
7:11, 14 325
9:1–2 308
9:2 . . . . 166, 182, 340, 406
10:24, 26 408
11:2 321
11:16–18 408
12:3 . . . . 163, 308, 420, 421
14:12 308
14:14 373
20:3 . . . . .112, 196, 325, 427
22:16 309
22:22 309
25:6–8 416
26:13 443
27:2–6 502
35:1 407
35:8–10 407
38:7, 22 .325
40–66 359
40–55 . . . . .407, 439
40:1–2 407
40:3 . . . . . 181, 189, 201, 294, 301–4,
306–7, 407–8
40:5 408
40:9 304
40:11 500
40:18, 25 373
41:18 163
42:1–9 321
42:6–7 . . . . 166, 182, 340, 406
42:18–25 407
43:11 . . . . 356, 546
43:15–17 356
43:19–20 421
43:20 163
43:22–28 407
44:3–5 .475
44:3 . . . . 163, 421
44:6 356
44:24–25 325
45:5–6, 14, 18, 21–22 356
45:21 546
45:22–23 357
46:9 356
48:21 . . . . .163, 421
49:6 . . . . . . 166, 203, 308, 340, 406
49:9–11 .416
49:10 . . . . .163, 421
49:26 408
50:1–3 407
52:13–53:12 . . . . . 234, 317, 408, 417
52:13–15 410
52:13 . . . . 132, 233–34, 294, 307–9,
388, 411, 418
52:15 418
53 . . . . .299, 314, 533
53:1 . . . . 234, 302–4, 306, 309, 340,
410, 442, 561
53:4–5 418
53:5 . . . . 411, 418
53:6–7 307
53:6 234
53:7 . . . . 414, 418
53:8 234
53:9 309
53:11 . . . . .348, 418
53:12 . . . . 234, 411, 417
54:13 . . . . 364, 541
54:14 . . . . 301, 303–4, 306, 308
55:1 .163, 421
55:9–11 .338
55:10–11 . . . . .338, 529
55:11–12 . . . . 392, 541
55:11 . . . . 294, 297, 353, 533
56:8 310
58:6 315
58:11 . . . . 308, 394, 420–21
60:1–5 . . . . 166, 340, 406
60:1–3 408
61:1–2 . . . . 315, 321
61:1 400
63:11 313
65–66 408
65:16 438
66:1–2 70
66:14 309–10
66:16 408
66:18–19 325
66:23–24 408

Jeremiah
2:6–7 408
2:13 . . . . 163, 308, 348, 421
2:21 . . . . 309, 502
3:4 373
3:17 434
3:19 373
6:26 . . . . .381, 409
7:4 70
7:11 70
7:22, 25 408
9:5 440
10:10 440
11:4, 7 408
11:19 415
13:16 365
14–15 70
17:12 406
17:13 . . . . .348, 421
17:21–27 350
23:1–2 308
23:1 500
23:24 350
29:4–13 126
30:9 313
31:3 462
31:31–34 519
31:33–34 . . . . .350, 474
32:20, 21 325

Lamentations
2:12 382

Ezekiel
1:10 388
4:1–3 325
4:3 325
9–11 407
9:4, 6 325
10:4 . . . . 295, 406
11:16 63
11:19–20 . . . . .350, 474
15 502

Scripture Index

16:6 472
18:20 308
19:10–14 502
20:12, 20 325
28:2 . . . . .358, 373
29:3 373
34 . . . . .70, 449, 533
34:11 500
34:23–24 501
34:23 . . . . 308, 310, 313, 501
36:25–27. . . 163, 307, 348, 350, 421, 474–75
36:26 .475
37 . . . . 348, 350, 384, 434, 476
37:5 475
37:9 . . . . 352, 400
37:14 .475
37:24 . . . . .308, 310
37:25 .313
37:27–28 406
37:27 71
38 198
40–48 .70
43:5 295
43:7, 9 .71
44:4 295
45:25 .421
47:1–12 430
47:1 421
47:12 348

Daniel

2 448
4 373
7 448
7:13 . . . . 216, 308, 314–15, 317, 387–88
9:25–26. 313
12:2 . . . . 284, 308, 348

Hosea

2:16–17 408
3:5 313–14
10:1 502
11:1 408
11:4 462
11:9 358
12:9 420
12:10, 14 408
13:4–5. 408

Joel

2:28 163
3:17 71
3:18 421

Amos

2:9–10 408
3:1–2 408
8:10 . . . . .381, 409
9:7 408
9:11–15 421
9:11–12 448
9:13 308

Micah

4:1–3 434
5:2 . . . . .216, 308
5:4 216
6:4 408
6:15 308

Zephaniah

3:15 307

Haggai

2:7 295
2:20–23 313

Zechariah

2:10 71
2:14 71
3:8 313
4:6–10 313
6:12 313
8:3 71
8:16 440
9–14 533
9:9 . . . . . . 232, 301–4, 306, 309, 448
12:10 . . . . 255, 302–4, 306, 309, 381, 409
13:1 421
13:7–9 501
13:7 . . . . .309, 314
14 434
14:8 . . . . 308, 394, 421, 430
14:16–19 420–21
14:16–17 . . . . .163, 421
14:21 427

Malachi

1:2–3 289
3:1 . . . . .308, 426–27
3:3 427
4:2 . . . . 166, 182, 340, 406

Matthew

1–4 238
1:1 315
1:18–25 . . . . .107, 559
1:23 . . . . .271, 359
2:1–4 .315
2:1 216
2:6 216
2:13–23 107
2:21–23 216
3:2 221
3:3 . . . . .301, 407
3:7–12 414
3:8 407
3:11 . . . . .393, 396
3:17 381
4 203
4:3, 6 .383
4:17 221
5–7 238
5:1 210
5:6 421
5:21–22 291
5:43–48 236
5:44 518
6:9–13 246
7:13–14 214
7:24–27 237
8:5–13 205
8:29 383
9:1 211
9:10 559
9:12 221
9:17 195
10:2–4 73
10:3 497–98
10:4 77
10:24 290
10:39 . . . . .232, 289
11:2–6 321
11:2–3 414
11:11 504
11:25–26 270

11:27 . . . . 390, 560	24:2 . . . . 61, 195	4:12 . . . . 234, 302, 561
12:1–14. .351	24:30 302	5:7 383
12:1 80	24:36 390	5:33 439
12:24–28. 222	25:34 348	6:3 391
12:28 . . . . .271, 468	25:46 348	6:4 205
12:38–39. 196	26:6–13 . . . . .230, 558	6:30–44 .210
13:1–23. .142	26:8 .231, 552	6:37 210
13:13–15 .411	26:13 . . . . 148, 500	6:38 210
13:14–15 . . . . .234, 561	26:20 . . . . 73, 75–76, 418	6:43 210
13:15 302	26:23 302	6:45–52. .210
13:55 391	26:25 483	7:14 348
13:57 205	26:28 454	8:14–21 203
14:5 181	26:37 79	8:27–30 . . . . .485, 558
14:13–21 .210	26:38 233	8:29 315
14:22–27 .210	26:39, 42, 44 246	8:31–33. .196
14:28–33. 365	26:46 302	8:35 . . . . 232, 289
14:33 383	26:49 483	9:5 483
16:1, 4 196	26:55 249	9:7 . . . . 380, 409
16:6–7. 161	26:59–66. 438	9:12 302
16:13–20 . . . . .213, 558	26:63–64 . . . . .271, 315	9:30–32. .196
16:13–16 485	26:63 383	9:33–37 249
16:14 314	26:64 387	9:43, 45 348
16:16 . . . . 271, 314–15, 383	27:19 . . . . .254, 450	9:47 348
16:17 270	27:23 444	10:15 348
16:18 . . . . 213, 237, 492–93, 507	27:25 443	10:17 348
16:19 . . . . 466, 481	27:32 254	10:23 348
16:22 250	27:40 383	10:32–34. 196
16:23 250	27:42 384	10:35–45 .247
16:25 . . . . 232, 289	27:43 383	10:38–42. 148
17:1 79	27:51 474	11:1–11 230
17:2 340	27:54 383	11:9–10. .301
17:4 420	27:62 418	11:21 483
17:5 381	28:11–15. 262	12:1–12. 234
18:16 . . . . .188, 454	28:18–20. . . . . 399, 542	12:6 . . . . 380, 409
18:17 . . . . .481, 507	28:19 . . . . 247, 359, 390, 560	12:14 439
19:1–12. .559	28:20 . . . . .239, 359	12:32 439
19:3 215		13. .238, 558
20:20–28 249	**Mark**	13:32 . . . . 390, 560
21:1–11. 230	1:1–3. . . . . .105, 108	14:1–11 230
21:5 301	1:1 271	14:1–9. 558
21:9 301	1:3 .301, 407	14:4 .231, 552
21:33–46. 234	1:8 393	14:9 . . . . 148, 500
21:38 381	1:11 .381, 409	14:17 . . . . 73, 75–76, 418, 486
22:1–14. .416	1:14 200	14:18 302
22:16 439	1:16–20. 78	14:34 233
22:37–40 . . . . .270, 511	1:16–18. .76	14:48–49. 249
22:41–46. 374	3:11 383	14:55–64. 438
23:38–24:1 431	3:16 73	14:61–62 .315
24. . . . . 196, 238, 297, 558	3:19 77	14:61 411
24:1–21 428	3:22–29 222	14:62 385

15:32 384	7:36–50. . . . . .230, 558	23:54 . . . . .418, 552
15:34 302	8:2 257	24:9 77
15:37 383	8:10 234	24:10 77
15:38 474	8:28 383	24:13 545
15:39 271	8:42 381	24:26–27 315
15:42 . . . . .418, 552	9:1 77	24:26 302
16:7 76	9:10–17 210	24:35 382
	9:10 77	24:44–47 315
Luke	9:18–20 558	24:46–49. . . . . 399, 543
1–2 . . . . 108, 407	9:24 . . . . 232, 289	24:47 466
1:1–4. . . . . 107, 118, 407	9:31 . . . . 113, 213	24:48–49. 545
1:2 76	9:35 381	24:48 545
1:3 . . . . 107, 244, 474	9:38 381	24:50–51 545
1:26–38. 258	9:51 . . . . .193, 545	
1:34–35. 559	10:22 390	**John**
1:35 383	10:25 348	1–12 . . . . 293, 311, 327, 329–31,
1:76 301	10:38–42. . . . . .231, 500, 558	334–35, 346–47, 366, 424,
1:78–79. . . . . 166, 340, 406	11:2–4. 246	439, 471, 490, 495, 504–5,
2. 545	11:14–20 222	540, 546
2:1–20. 107	11:49 77	1–10 229
2:1 359	12:32 214	1–3 371
2:7 150	16:22 . . . . .371, 382	1. . . . . 261, 337–38, 363, 491
2:11 315	16:31 117	1:1–12:36 300
2:26 315	17:5 77	1:1–18 . . . . .80, 117, 118, 150,
2:41–51. 107	17:21 297	167, 170, 293, 311, 316,
3:1 428	17:33 . . . . 232, 289	336, 338, 349, 354, 423
3:4 .301, 407	18:9–14. 221	1:1–13. . . . . .184, 341
3:7–17. 414	19:10 . . . . 202, 522	1:1–5. . . . . .118, 176, 187, 340, 349,
3:16 393	19:18–20. 485	434, 460
3:17 414	20:9–19. 234	1:1–4. .259
3:22 381	20:13 . . . . .381, 409	1:1–3. . . . . 84, 177, 178
4. 203	20:21 439	1:1–2. . . . . . 208, 235, 244, 247, 341,
4:3, 9 383	21 238	360, 362–64, 369, 374
4:14–30. 211	21:5–38. 558	1:1 . . . . .49, 76, 86–88, 105, 108,
4:16–30. 315	21:32 496	118–19, 177–81, 184–85,
4:18 . . . . 396, 400	22:1 552	188, 222, 248, 263, 271,
4:24 205	22:8 75	279, 287–88, 293, 297,
4:25 439	22:14 . . . . 73, 75–77, 418	307, 316, 338–39, 341, 347,
4:41 383	22:15–30 416	360, 362, 367–71, 381–82,
5:4–11. 261	22:21 302	387, 390, 392, 405, 431,
5:8 365	22:33 365	450, 519, 559, 564
6:12 246	22:51 250	1:2 . . . . 179–81, 184, 339, 362,
6:13 77	22:52–53. 249	368–69
6:14 73	22:53 238	1:3–4. . . . . 208, 255, 426
6:16 77	22:59 439	1:3 . . . . 116, 133, 179–80, 183,
6:40 290	22:66–71 438	340, 352, 360, 362–63,
7:1–10. 205	22:67 385	406, 422
7:12 381	22:70 . . . . .383, 385	1:4–5. . . . . . 166, 177, 180–81, 235,
7:18–23. 321	23:5–7. 445	264, 280, 284, 338–39,
7:18–20. 414	23:28–31. 61	344–45, 406

1:4 . . . . 180, 270, 284, 297, 317, 337, 342, 344–47, 360, 406, 422
1:5 . . . . 87, 118, 180, 182, 200, 219, 278, 280, 297, 337, 339, 422, 455, 471, 522, 526, 534
1:6–9. 177
1:6–8. . . . . 39, 73, 132, 176–77, 180–82, 187, 200, 228, 244, 288, 362
1:6–7. 133
1:6 . . . . 118, 177–78, 180, 184, 190, 209, 362, 368–69, 460
1:7–9. . . . . . 180, 280, 344–46, 406
1:7–8. . . . . 187, 318, 407, 553
1:7 . . . . .133, 181, 183, 337, 422, 471, 474, 488
1:8 . . . . . 133, 181, 337, 407, 422, 488
1:9–14. 340
1:9–12. 341
1:9–11. . . . . 166, 194, 200, 235, 362, 460
1:9 . . . . 178, 181–82, 184, 248, 337, 340, 422, 526–27, 534
1:10–11 . . 49, 150, 153, 177, 255, 289, 341, 426, 434
1:10 . . . . 180, 182, 282, 339–41, 398, 415, 464, 471
1:11 . . . . 150, 177, 182–85, 198, 213, 236, 282, 341, 354, 460–61, 471, 490, 501, 526–27
1:12–13. . . . . 242, 267, 287, 292, 340, 349, 350, 352, 363, 365, 366, 464, 471, 473, 475, 479
1:12 . . . . 49, 66–67, 86, 134, 177–78, 180, 183–84, 187, 197–98, 260, 280, 282, 294, 297, 362, 368–69, 384, 389, 394, 429, 460, 462, 470, 472, 474, 480, 489, 519, 545
1:13 . . . . .184–85, 200, 341, 346, 362, 368–69, 460, 462, 472, 474–75
1:14–18. . . . . .49, 341, 359, 384
1:14–17. . . . . 426, 439, 460
1:14 . . . . . 39, 49, 71–72, 75, 84–86, 88, 118, 136, 150, 156, 176–79, 181–82, 184–88, 194–95, 204, 208, 223, 247, 253–55, 263, 278–79, 287, 290, 294–95, 297, 307, 328, 332–33, 338, 341, 347, 362–63, 370–72, 380–81, 387, 392, 397, 404, 406, 409, 423–27, 429–30, 437, 439, 440–41, 460, 469, 473, 501, 519, 555
1:15 . . . . .39, 133, 176–77, 181, 187, 189, 200–201, 228, 244, 288, 407, 488, 546, 553
1:16–18. .187
1:16–17. . . . 186, 363, 406, 409, 426, 441
1:16 . . . . .177–78, 186–87, 247, 294, 406
1:17–18. . . . . .177, 208, 338, 362
1:1 . . . . 39, 48, 85, 114, 118–19, 121, 176, 178, 180, 184, 186–88, 247, 253, 280, 288, 307, 319, 362–63, 397–98, 406, 409, 416, 439–41, 501, 533, 564
1:18 . . . . 48, 74, 78, 86, 118, 134, 156, 166, 177–78, 188, 195, 214, 233, 237, 243–44, 269, 271, 287–88, 307, 332, 359–64, 367–73, 377–78, 380–82, 387, 390, 392, 409, 411, 426, 429, 439–40, 451, 460, 468, 494–95, 500–501, 519, 534, 564
1:19–20:31 . . . . .58, 170, 188
1:19–17:26 293
1:19–12:50 . . . . . . 167–68, 170, 177, 187–88, 299, 354, 363, 407, 412, 461
1:19–10:42 . . . . .169, 228
1:19–5:47 169
1:19–2:11 169
1:19–51 . . . . 181, 188–89
1:19–50. 170
1:19–37. 200
1:19–36. . . . . 200, 201
1:19–34. . . . . .80, 160, 168–69, 177, 186, 188
1:19–28. 349
1:19 . . . . .189, 360, 407
1:20 . . . . .48, 133, 369, 407
1:21–23. 318
1:21 . . . . .189, 307, 407
1:22 133–34
1:23 . . . . . . 181, 189, 201, 300–301, 303–7, 407–8
1:25 189
1:26–27. 190
1:26 .162, 164
1:27 .181, 189
1:28 137
1:29–2:11 349
1:29–36. 415
1:29–34. 349
1:29 . . . . 50, 85, 134, 170, 187, 189, 221, 226, 255, 265, 279, 297, 307, 318, 337, 341, 349, 363, 368–69, 407, 414, 416–20, 425, 451, 455, 461, 464, 467–68, 473, 520, 535–36, 565
1:30 . . . . .133, 185, 189
1:31 . . . . .73, 162, 164, 181, 188–90, 238
1:32–34. 407
1:32–33. . . . .164, 388, 393–96, 495, 542
1:32 . . . . 185, 190, 228, 233, 396, 407, 488
1:33–34. 544
1:33 . . . . 134, 162, 164, 190, 393–95, 528, 542
1:34–36. 506
1:34 . . . . .85, 363, 365, 368–69, 461, 488, 528, 534
1:35–51 . . . . .80, 190–91
1:35–40. 498
1:35–39. 349
1:35–37. 200
1:35–36. 190
1:35 .189, 337
1:36 . . . . .170, 187, 297, 307, 318, 341, 363, 368–69, 407, 414, 416–17, 420, 425, 451, 455, 473, 565
1:37–43. . . . 483, 486, 488, 490, 492, 505–6
1:37 . . . . .132, 190, 506

1:38–39 190
1:38 . . . . 132, 136, 380, 483–84
1:39 . . . . 132, 134, 534
1:40–42 349
1:40 . . . . 76, 116, 132, 134, 139, 148,
   181, 190, 360, 497, 506,
   551, 556, 559
1:41–42. .190
1:41 . . . . 85, 134, 136, 139, 168, 315,
   319, 411, 491
1:42 . . . . 116, 134, 136, 313, 460
1:43–51. 349
1:43–44 497
1:43 . . . . 132, 134, 189–90, 337, 506
1:44 . . . . .134, 190, 497
1:45–46. 144
1:45 . . . . 116, 190, 307, 310, 380, 392
1:46 . . . . 132, 153, 191, 497
1:47 . . . . 191, 199, 498
1:48 . . . . .133, 191, 460
1:49 . . . . 67, 191, 211, 232, 253,
   285, 307, 315, 318, 363–64,
   368–69, 380, 382–83, 392,
   411, 448, 483, 498
1:50–51. . . . . .211, 384
1:50 . . . . .191, 504, 534
1:51–13:31 386
1:51 . . . . 133, 156, 191, 204, 288,
   307, 368–69, 380, 386–87,
   423–25, 427, 429–30, 501,
   528–30
2–12 330
2–4 . . . . 147, 169, 205–6
2:1–4:54 . . . . 168–70, 191
2. . . . . 210, 261, 337, 363
2:1–12. . . . . . 80, 191, 206, 442, 499
2:1–11. . . . . . 121, 137, 147, 169, 195,
   204–5, 324, 327, 349
2:1 . . . . 164, 191, 559
2:2 483–84
2:3 191
2:4 . . . . . . 117, 137, 191, 196, 214–15,
   389, 460
2:5 . . . . .191, 307
2:6–11. 191
2:6–10. 164–65
2:6 . . . . 134, 136, 163, 194, 198, 476
2:9 . . . . .134, 138, 192
2:10 .153, 192

2:11 . . . . 49, 72, 75, 112, 118,
   134, 140, 147, 162, 168–69,
   178, 185–86, 191, 194,
   196–97, 199, 205–6, 223,
   229, 233–34, 279, 290,
   294, 324, 326–27, 384–85,
   408, 473–74, 483–84, 559
2:12–22. 198
2:12 . . . . 133, 169, 193, 211, 484
2:13–3:21 . . . . .80, 169, 206
2:13–25. . . . . .415, 423
2:13–22. . . . . 165, 169, 193–94,
   203–4, 206, 416, 419, 423,
   464, 476, 558
2:13 . . . . 165, 193–94, 197, 205, 210,
   214, 230, 413–14, 416–17,
   420, 428
2:14–22. . . . . . . 423–24, 426–27,
   429–31, 442, 453
2:14–18. 198
2:14–17. 329
2:14 195
2:16 . . . . 372, 376, 380
2:17 . . . . 116, 138, 196, 299,
   300–301, 303–7, 330,
   411–12, 483–84
2:18–22. . . . . 84, 423, 427
2:18–21. 332
2:18 . . . . 142, 195–99, 211,
   320, 324, 326, 332, 428,
   476, 534
2:19–22. . . . . 121, 132, 142, 145
2:19–21. . . . . .320, 434, 558
2:19 . . . . . 69, 153, 195–96, 233, 259,
   332, 416, 427–28, 460
2:20–21. . . . .186, 349, 352, 416, 423
2:20 . . . . . . 144, 195, 204, 372, 423,
   428
2:21–22. . . . . .69, 139
2:21 . . . . 133–34, 185, 195, 295,
   424, 428
2:22 . . . . 134, 142, 160, 194,
   196–97, 246, 250, 263,
   310, 331, 428, 432, 473,
   483, 484, 494, 506
2:23–3:22 169
2:23–3:21 . . . 146, 197–98, 204, 517
2:23–3:15 517
2:23–3:1 558

2:23–25. . . . 197–98, 220, 292, 384,
   471, 476–77, 498
2:23–24 .474
2:23 . . . . 134, 146–47, 165, 169, 193,
   197–98, 205–6, 210, 214,
   216, 230, 324, 326, 335,
   410, 413, 416–17, 427–28,
   473, 484, 559
2:24–25. . . . . .137, 460
2:24 134
2:25 133–34
3–5 300
3–4 . . . . 441, 564
3. . . . . 155, 184–85, 189, 199,
   205–6, 208, 329, 342, 363,
   499, 518, 533, 536, 546,
   558
3:1–21. .558
3:1–15. . . . . 202, 256, 348
3:1–10. .471
3:1–2. . . . . .137, 138
3:1 . . . . .198, 219
3:2–5. 363
3:2 . . . . 134, 146–47, 161, 167,
   169, 193, 197–98, 205–6,
   320, 324, 326, 335, 363,
   365, 368–69, 380, 427, 473,
   475, 483–84, 517, 527, 559
3:3–15. 320
3:3–9. . . . . .464, 517
3:3–8. . . . . .200, 267, 479
3:3–5. . . . . .116, 462
3:3–4. 161
3:3 . . . . 130, 132–33, 198,
   222, 285, 287, 318, 341,
   349, 350, 363, 368–69,
   393, 448–49, 474–75,
   516, 524
3:4 . . . . . .143–45, 152–53, 164, 199,
   475
3:5–8. 394
3:5 . . . . .130, 132–33, 163,
   165, 198, 222, 242, 285,
   287, 307, 318, 341, 349–50,
   363, 368–69, 393–94,
   448–49, 474–75, 524
3:6–8 . . . . 116, 157, 269, 474
3:6 . . . . 185, 287, 346, 364, 394,
   475, 564

3:7 . . . . 242, 474–75
3:8 . . . . 132, 134, 199, 307, 394, 474, 517, 531
3:9–12. 280
3:9 . . . . 144–45, 199
3:10–12. 200
3:10 . . . . 153, 198, 310, 320, 484, 517
3:11 . . . . .116–17, 132–33, 441, 475, 488, 517, 534
3:12 . . . . 151, 473, 517
3:13–17. .533
3:13–16. . . . . 212–13, 469
3:13–14. . . . 161, 288, 294, 319, 364, 384, 386–88, 465, 476
3:13 . . . . 153, 212, 220, 233, 252, 307, 317, 364, 380, 386–87, 528–30, 534, 541
3:14–21. .531
3:14–16. 346
3:14–15 . . . . . 116, 321, 329, 533, 535
3:14 . . . . 50, 132, 138, 150, 158, 199, 307, 310, 315, 370, 380, 386–88, 417, 427, 473, 529, 533
3:15–16 . . . . 86, 342, 346, 473
3:15 . . . . 133, 337, 345, 517, 530
3:16–21 . . . . 140, 199, 201, 363, 384, 469, 517
3:16–18 . . . . . 363, 383–84, 390, 392
3:16–17 . . . . 270, 282, 364, 455, 514, 532–33
3:16 . . . . .50, 58, 86–87, 134, 168, 178, 183, 186, 199, 202, 212–13, 232, 236, 255, 269, 279–80, 285, 297, 308, 332, 337, 340, 345, 348, 368–69, 380–82, 389–90, 409–10, 415, 429, 434, 451, 465, 468, 474, 479, 489, 501, 503, 507, 511–12, 517–22, 529, 531–33, 535, 539, 545, 558–59
3:17–21. .199
3:17–19. 469
3:17–18. 407
3:17 . . . . .133, 368–69, 380–81, 390, 415, 465, 469, 475, 532, 534

3:18 . . . . 86–87, 117, 134, 178, 364, 368–69, 380–84, 390, 409–10, 468–69, 474, 501
3:19–21 . . . . . 87, 134, 166, 179–80, 200, 215, 264, 266, 277, 280, 288–91, 297, 340, 344–46, 459, 469, 522, 546
3:19–20. .199
3:19 . . . . 200, 282, 337, 340, 455, 469, 517, 521, 526–27, 534
3:20 . . . . 117, 133, 200, 337
3:21 . . . . 86, 117, 200, 337, 364, 368–69, 449
3:22–43 .181
3:22–36 . . . . .80, 169, 177, 200, 206
3:22–23 .163
3:22 . . . . . 133, 140, 146, 150, 193, 200, 483–84
3:23–36 .169
3:23 . . . . 164, 368
3:24 . . . . . . .134, 139, 148, 200–201, 551, 556, 559
3:25 165
3:26–30 546
3:26 . . . . 163, 200–201, 407, 488
3:27–30 .213
3:28 . . . . 200, 308, 488
3:29–30 .201
3:29 . . . . 163, 181, 201
3:30–36 .201
3:31–36. . . . . 140, 216, 363–64
3:31 . . . . 287, 297, 474, 527
3:32–33. .132
3:32 . . . . 364, 441, 488, 534
3:33–36 363
3:33 .87, 369
3:34 . . . . . . 217, 353, 364, 368–69, 393–96, 506, 522, 542
3:35–36. . . . . 390, 392
3:35 . . . . 372–73, 376, 380, 461, 521
3:36 . . . . .86, 134, 288, 337, 342, 345–46, 364, 368–69, 380, 390, 468, 474, 529, 534, 546
4. . . . . .147, 155, 163, 183, 204–6, 208, 217, 329, 342, 363, 499, 518, 536, 558
4:1–45. . . . . 80, 423
4:1–42. . . 169, 201–2, 204, 499, 517, 546, 558

4:1–2. 163
4:1 .483, 485
4:2 . . . . 134, 140, 201, 483–84
4:3 205
4:4 .201, 203
4:5 .308, 551
4:6–7 278
4:6 . . . . .116, 134, 201
4:7–15 . . . . 163–64, 394
4:7 . . . . 116, 153
4:8 . . . . 140, 165, 483–84, 504
4:9 . . . . .134, 136, 202, 517
4:10–15. . . . . 144–45, 165, 348, 535
4:10–14. .421
4:10–12. .132
4:10–11 345–46
4:10 . . . . . .134, 203, 308, 342, 364, 368–69
4:11 380
4:12 . . . . . . 116, 121, 153, 280, 294, 371, 409
4:13–14. 203
4:14 . . . . 308, 337, 342, 345–46
4:15 . . . . 212, 380
4:16 517
4:17–18. . . . . .152, 460
4:17 153
4:19–24. .423–25, 427, 429–30, 558
4:19 . . . . .153, 202, 499
4:20–26 423
4:20–24 . . . . 423, 429
4:20 . . . . .201, 308, 371
4:21–24. . . 84, 203–4, 333, 423, 517
4:21–23. . . . . .69, 372
4:21 . . . . .71, 134, 429
4:22 . . . .168, 203, 308, 429, 513, 546
4:23–24 . . . . . 67, 269, 394, 440, 517
4:23 . . . . .71, 116, 394, 429
4:24 . . . . .87, 91, 269, 287, 295, 364, 368–69, 372, 394, 429, 434, 475
4:25–26 .517
4:25 . . . . . . 134, 136, 153, 168, 313, 315, 319
4:26 . . . . 203–4, 359, 516
4:27–38 202
4:27–30 499
4:27 .483–84
4:29 . . . . .191, 202, 315, 319–20, 499
4:31–34. 144–45

4:31 . . . . 380, 483–84	5:1 . . . . 133, 206, 209, 413, 420	5:26 . . . . 209, 212, 280,
4:32 165	5:2 . . . . 60, 84, 136, 164	284, 337, 346, 360, 373,
4:33 . . . . 483–84, 494	5:4 207	379–81, 384, 388, 392, 529
4:34–38 . . . . 505, 546	5:5 207	5:27 . . . . 208, 308, 317, 373,
4:34 . . . . . . 134, 203, 350, 353, 392,	5:7 . . . . 164, 207, 380	380, 384, 386–88, 390,
451, 522, 531, 564	5:9–18 211	455, 469, 472, 529
4:36 . . . . 117, 308, 337, 342, 345–46	5:9 . . . . 207, 353, 559	5:28–29 . . . . . 92, 211, 280, 284–85,
4:37 . . . . 263, 308	5:10 153	296–97, 342, 468–69
4:38 . . . . 483, 489, 504, 522	5:11 134	5:29 . . . . 308, 337, 345, 455, 469
4:39 . . . . 134, 263, 484, 499, 517	5:12 116	5:30 . . . . . . 134, 208, 280, 469, 522
4:41–42 474	5:13 . . . . 134, 138, 484	5:31–47 . . . . 169, 207, 220, 553
4:41 . . . . 263, 517	5:14 . . . . 133–34, 464–65	5:31 133
4:42 133–34,	5:15 116	5:32 133
168, 202, 205, 269, 320,	5:17–47 . . . . 328, 364, 372	5:33–36 407
359, 415, 434, 455, 517, 558	5:17–18 . . . . 372, 374	5:33–35 . . . . 209, 227–28
4:43–54 . . . . 147, 169, 205, 546, 558	5:17 . . . . 208, 350, 353, 372,	5:33 . . . . 397, 440
4:43 193	380, 385	5:34 209
4:44 . . . . 140, 205, 211, 551	5:18–47 . . . . 351, 365	5:35 . . . . . 166, 177, 181, 337, 345–46
4:45–54 442	5:18–20 351	5:36 . . . . 132–33, 209, 243, 373–74,
4:45–48 410	5:18 . . . . 139, 169, 178, 206–8,	380, 407, 522
4:45 . . . . 134, 193, 205, 534	214, 222, 227, 271, 350,	5:37 . . . . 133–34, 209, 362, 373,
4:46–54 . . . . 80, 202, 204, 324, 327	357, 363–65, 367–69, 373,	380, 411, 522, 534
4:46 . . . . 137, 147, 205	438, 453, 465, 513, 559	5:38 476
4:48 . . . . . . 185, 205, 212, 324, 326,	5:19–47 . . . . 208, 560	5:39–40 . . . . 121, 345–46
474, 476	5:19–46 211	5:39 . . . . 133, 209, 310, 337
4:49 380	5:19–30 . . . . 208–9, 364	5:40 337
4:50–51 285	5:19–29 . . . . 253, 438	5:41 373
4:50 . . . . 86, 134, 205, 263, 474	5:19–26 . . . . 390, 392	5:42 . . . . 364–65, 368–69, 521
4:53 . . . . 371, 474	5:19–20 . . . . 373, 378, 390	5:43–44 471
4:54 . . . . 112, 133, 140, 146–47,	5:19 . . . . 133, 208, 378, 380–81, 391	5:43 . . . . 380, 527
168–69, 191, 196–97, 206,	5:20 . . . . 208, 373, 380–81, 391,	5:44 . . . . 364, 366, 368–69, 476
324, 326–27, 334–35, 559	461, 504, 521, 534	5:45–47 . . . . 121, 280, 294
5–12 . . . . 84, 169, 430, 441	5:21–23 391	5:45–46 . . . . 310, 373
5–11 169	5:21 . . . . . . 208, 337, 342, 345–46,	5:45 . . . . 109, 308
5–10 . . . . 145, 168–69, 182,	373, 379, 380–81, 391–92	5:46–47 409
194, 206, 224, 227, 295,	5:22–30 469	5:46 . . . . 133, 209, 308, 476
413, 462, 560	5:22–27 . . . . 235, 280	5:47–6:1 116
5:1–10:42 . . . . 168, 170, 206	5:22 . . . . . . 208, 373, 380–81, 391,	5:47 . . . . 147, 476
5–6 168	455, 469	6 . . . . 109, 146–47, 156, 159,
5 . . . . 146–47, 165, 169, 206,	5:23 . . . . 134, 209, 360, 373,	161, 165, 168–69, 185, 203,
208–9, 214–15, 220,	379–81, 522	206, 213–14, 219, 253, 318,
224–25, 334, 342, 349–50,	5:24–26 . . . . 342, 345	324, 342, 363, 371, 413,
363, 371, 385, 413, 430,	5:24 . . . . 86–87, 133–34,	416, 419, 430, 465, 521,
453, 465, 476, 513	268, 280, 285, 291, 297,	530, 531, 536, 543
5:1–47 . . . . 80, 206–7, 349	337, 342, 345–46, 348,	6:1–71 209
5:1–30 169	455, 469, 476, 522, 529, 533	6:1–21 81
5:1–18 207	5:25–26 247	6:1–15 . . 137, 169, 211, 324, 327, 416,
5:1–15 . . . . . 169, 209, 324, 327, 425,	5:25 . . . . 133, 364–65, 368–69, 380,	442
442	382–84, 386, 390	6:1–14 415

6:1–3...................193
6:1.........82, 133, 136, 147, 209
6:2.....207, 210–11, 216, 230, 324, 326, 483–84, 534
6:3........................483–84
6:4......165, 413–14, 416–17, 425
6:5–13.....................504
6:5–9...................497, 552
6:5............133, 185, 483–84
6:6......................134, 139
6:7–9.......................165
6:7–8.......................497
6:7.....................133, 210
6:8–9.......................294
6:8..........483–84, 491, 497
6:9.........................210
6:10....................133, 484
6:11..............212, 261, 541
6:12–13....................211
6:12...................133, 483–84
6:13...................133, 210
6:14–15....................211
6:14.......133, 196, 211, 232, 253, 285, 308, 314, 317, 324, 326–28, 407, 410, 416
6:15.....118, 133, 211, 319, 384, 448
6:16–21................211, 329
6:16–19.....................164
6:16..................483–84
6:19..........................133
6:20..............211, 250, 359
6:21..........................133
6:22–71.................81, 415
6:22......................483–84
6:23....133, 137, 210, 212, 261, 541
6:24..................133, 483–84
6:25–71....................142
6:25–59.........109, 211, 328
6:25.................211, 380, 483
6:26–65....................529
6:26.......133, 196, 211, 216, 324, 326–27, 484
6:27–65....................373
6:27–29....................363
6:27..........165, 337, 343, 364, 368–69, 380, 386–88, 529–30
6:28–29................364, 564
6:28...........132–33, 368–69

6:29–62.....................534
6:29........86, 133–34, 138, 308, 368–69, 476, 522–23, 530
6:30–59....................530
6:30–58...............179, 211
6:30–31...............212, 216
6:30........133, 165, 196, 211–12, 324, 326–27, 330, 476
6:31–59...............216, 558
6:31–58...........294, 346, 365
6:31.......197, 300–301, 303–6, 308, 364, 371, 529
6:32–58.....................560
6:32–41.....................121
6:32–35................144, 416
6:32–33.....................415
6:32........121, 133, 310, 340, 380
6:33........212, 337, 343, 368–69, 388, 528, 530
6:34....................133, 212
6:35.....117–18, 134, 157, 161, 212, 324, 337, 343, 346, 364, 421, 476, 530
6:36–40.....................117
6:36................461, 476, 534
6:37........87, 242, 373–74, 458, 461–62, 531
6:38–39.....................530
6:38.........133–34, 388, 522, 528
6:39–40.....................297
6:39.......133–34, 250, 296, 394, 461, 522
6:40...........86, 133–34, 212, 296, 337, 343, 346, 373, 380–81, 390, 392, 476
6:41.........133, 212 294, 388, 528
6:42.....133, 144–45, 153, 155, 212, 373, 380, 388, 528
6:43....................133, 212
6:44–45................373, 472
6:44.......134, 296–97, 374, 380, 458, 461–62, 522
6:45......133, 300–306, 308, 364, 368–69, 417, 541
6:46.......362, 368–69, 411, 534
6:47.....86, 133, 337, 343, 346, 476
6:48–58.....................170
6:48–51.....................212
6:48....118, 337, 343, 346, 415, 530

6:49–50.....................417
6:49..........................371
6:50................133, 388, 528
6:51–53.....................145
6:51..........185, 212, 279, 324, 343, 388, 415, 417, 526, 528, 530, 535
6:52–58.....................530
6:52........133, 144, 153, 185, 213
6:53–58................415, 533
6:53–56.....................533
6:53.......133, 165, 185, 213, 337, 343, 380, 386–88, 529–30
6:54–55.....................213
6:54........134, 185, 296–97, 337, 343, 346
6:55.....................117, 185
6:56..........................185
6:57–58................343, 533
6:57........134, 373, 379–80, 522, 530, 533
6:58..............87, 371, 388, 528
6:59..........................211
6:60–71...135, 168, 212, 228, 483, 487, 505
6:60–66................117, 182
6:60–61..........471, 484, 498
6:60........133, 213, 220, 292, 476, 483–85
6:61....212, 213, 220, 294, 483, 485
6:62....133, 380, 386–88, 528–30
6:63..................185, 287, 337, 343, 345–46, 393–96, 529, 542, 565
6:64................134, 137, 460, 484
6:65....................373, 458
6:66–71.....................183
6:66..........213, 220, 292, 471, 483–85, 498
6:67–71.....................485
6:67........133, 461, 551, 556, 559
6:68–70.....................492
6:68–69.....................366
6:68....133, 337, 343, 346, 488, 529
6:69......86, 134, 213, 365, 368–69, 485–86, 558
6:70–71.....117, 213, 237, 458, 483, 498, 521, 556, 559
6:70........281, 458, 460, 485–86, 491, 508

6:71 . . . . .133, 137, 139, 213, 292, 485, 551	7:27–28. 155	7:50 .133, 137
7–11 147	7:27 . . . . .134, 144–45, 154, 168, 215, 288, 315, 319–20, 420, 461, 527	7:51 . . . . 308, 469
7–10 . . . . .168, 227, 423, 431		7:52 . . . . .144, 147, 152, 154, 168, 191, 321
7:1–10:21 227	7:28 . . . . .134, 154, 369, 522, 527	7:53–8:11 . . . . 146–47, 219, 380
7–8 . . . . 145, 169, 219, 329	7:29 522	8–9 300
7:1–8:59 . . . . .423–24, 430	7:30 . . . . .117, 137, 141, 169, 389, 513	8. . . . . 177, 207, 220, 222, 225, 363, 365, 371, 420, 440, 453, 462, 467, 477, 564
7. . . . . 165, 169, 217, 219, 233, 243, 251, 318, 363, 365, 371, 420, 422, 465	7:31–35 527	
	7:31 . . . . . . .134, 168, 196, 215, 315, 318–20, 324, 326–28, 410, 420, 476, 483–84, 527	8:12–59. . . . . .81, 219, 420, 422
7:1–52. . . . . .81, 214, 420		8:12 . . . . 86, 91, 148, 166, 219, 223, 264, 280, 283, 297, 308, 324, 337, 339, 340, 343–46, 348, 418, 421–22, 430, 483, 487, 506, 527, 529, 532
7:1–13. .217	7:32 . . . . .116, 484	
7:1–9. . . . . .165, 182	7:33–36. 144–45	
7:1 . . . . 133, 169, 214, 513	7:33 . . . . .134, 489, 522	
7:2–5. 483	7:34–35. 132	
7:2 . . . . 214, 227, 413, 431	7:34 117	
7:3–4. 154	7:35–36. . . . . .154, 527	8:13–14 .188
7:3 . . . . 132, 483–85	7:35 . . . . .116, 528	8:13 219–20
7:4 .214, 420	7:36 134	8:14 . . . . 134, 441, 527–28, 531
7:5 . . . . .134, 138, 214, 476	7:37–52. 531	8:15 . . . . .185, 308, 469
7:6 215	7:37–44. 217	8:16 . . . . . . .134, 373, 380, 469, 522
7:7 . . . . .133, 289, 441	7:37–39. . . . . 121, 163–65, 364, 421, 505	8:17 . . . . 270, 308
7:8 215		8:18 . . . . 134, 220, 373, 380, 522
7:10 . . . . .217, 420	7:37–38. . . . . . . 217, 420–21, 430	8:19 . . . . .220, 369, 373, 380
7:11 133	7:37 . . . . 134, 163, 217, 394, 421, 535	8:20–21. 527
7:12 . . . . .133, 215, 484	7:38–39. 477	8:20 . . . . 117, 137, 141, 389
7:13 . . . . 133, 215	7:38 . . . . . . .134, 163, 300, 304, 306, 308, 343, 346, 348, 394, 421	8:21–47. 465
7:14–8:59 . . . . .423, 425, 431		8:21–24. 527
7:14–36. 217	7:39 . . . . . .134, 139, 141, 160, 163, 194, 217, 353, 393–95, 400, 542	8:21–22. . . . . 132, 143, 144–45, 528
7:14–24. 328		8:21 464–65
7:14 . . . . 215, 217		8:22 . . . . .117, 154–55, 220
7:15 . . . . .154, 215	7:40–44. 315	8:23–24 507
7:16–18. 215	7:40–43. 484	8:23 . . . . .86, 151, 288
7:16 . . . . 134, 522	7:40 . . . . 217, 308, 407, 484	8:24 . . . . 134, 321, 359, 464–65, 477
7:17 . . . . 364–65, 368–69	7:41–42. . . . . . 144, 152, 154, 216, 318, 420	8:25 220
7:18 . . . . .134, 522		8:26 . . . . .134, 469, 522
7:19–23. 121	7:41 . . . . 217, 319, 321, 484, 527	8:27 . . . . 116, 138, 144–45, 220, 373
7:19 . . . . 109, 169, 215, 513	7:42 . . . . 116, 216–17, 300, 308, 319, 527	8:28–29 535
7:20 . . . . . . 154, 169, 215, 222, 226, 281, 484, 513		8:28 . . . . 50, 132, 138, 150, 158, 199, 220, 233, 252, 308, 315, 359, 370, 379–80, 386–89, 427, 529–30, 533, 541
	7:43 484	
7:21 . . . . .132, 196, 327, 420	7:44 484	
7:22–23. 310	7:45–52. . . . . .219, 229	
7:22 . . . . 308, 371	7:45 218	8:29 . . . . 134, 522
7:23–29. 531	7:46 . . . . .218, 461	8:30–47. 440
7:23 . . . . 154, 215, 351	7:47 . . . . .215, 218	8:30–31. . . . . .410, 477
7:24 . . . . .151, 308, 469	7:48–49. . . . . .152, 154	8:30 . . . . .134, 220, 477, 484
7:25–44. . . . . .185, 315	7:48 . . . . .134, 219, 477	8:31–59. . . . . . 109, 185, 292, 462, 485, 502
7:25 . . . . 169, 215, 385, 484, 513	7:49 . . . . .218, 484	
7:26–29. 527	7:50–52. . . . . .219, 256, 471	8:31–58. 498
7:26 . . . . .154, 215, 319–20	7:50–51. 446	8:31–47. . . . . . . 177, 268, 281, 415

8:31–41..............472	8:58......133, 222, 271, 280, 294, 411, 431, 501	9:29–33...............363
8:31–39..............144		9:29..........134, 154–55, 365, 368–69, 531
8:31–38..............411	8:59....117, 222–23, 233, 357, 385, 431, 438	
8:31–33..............505		9:30................134
8:31–32.........220, 288, 430	9..........119, 155, 165–66, 169, 185, 208, 223–27, 229, 327, 334, 341, 351, 363, 365, 371, 374, 425, 462, 467, 559	9:31....134, 365–66, 368–69, 375, 464–65
8:31......220, 240, 242, 265, 267, 438, 462, 471, 477, 480, 483–84, 486–87, 519		9:33...........224, 365, 368–69
		9:34–35..............462
	9:1–10:21...........81, 207	9:34....225, 245, 308, 389, 464–65
8:32..........267, 398, 438, 440	9:1–41....223, 324, 349, 442, 485	9:35–41..............328
8:33–47............87, 564	9:1–7................137	9:35........134, 225, 380, 386–87
8:34–47...........280, 366	9:1................223	9:36–38..............477
8:34–37............507	9:2–3................465	9:36................134
8:34.......133, 220, 459, 464–65	9:2........223, 308, 380, 483–84	9:37.............134, 534
8:35.............117, 133, 308	9:3–5................328	9:38........86, 224, 288, 360, 389, 423–25, 429, 431–32
8:36....222, 380–81, 390, 392, 459	9:3–4......49, 168, 233, 294, 319, 328, 353	
8:37............169, 221, 477, 513		9:39–41.....132, 164, 166, 224–25, 488, 507, 559
8:38................221, 534	9:3....185, 223, 365–66, 368–69, 385, 408	
8:39............132, 221, 371, 374		9:39.....117, 351, 469, 526–27, 531
8:40–54..............365	9:4–5.........223, 344, 345, 422	9:40–41...............144
8:40–42............363	9:4..........132, 134, 167, 522	9:40................154
8:40........169, 365, 368–69, 397, 440, 513	9:5..........91, 166, 219, 223, 264, 280, 297, 308, 324, 337, 339–40, 346, 430	9:41......225, 351, 464, 466
		10–12..............434
8:41.....87, 132, 212, 221–22, 365, 368–69, 380		10..............117, 156, 159, 161, 207, 214, 225, 227–28, 363, 371, 374, 433, 449, 453, 462, 481, 483, 495, 500–501, 503, 506, 508, 534, 536, 541, 559
	9:6–11................164	
8:42–47.........288, 297, 462	9:7......136, 164, 170, 224, 259, 507, 522	
8:42.....365, 368–69, 521–22, 527		
8:44–45............87, 268	9:9................484	
8:44....87, 221, 281, 291, 294, 308, 371, 374, 440, 467	9:11................224	
	9:13............116, 134, 137	10:1–42..............225
8:45–47..............133	9:14............351, 353, 559	10:1–39..............485
8:45–46............477	9:15–16..............351	10:1–21..............227
8:45................397, 440	9:16......196, 324, 326–27, 365, 368–69, 464–65, 484	10:1–18.....109, 225, 294, 385, 560
8:46.........397, 440, 464–65, 467		10:1.............133–34, 226
8:47....222, 363, 365, 368–69, 459	9:17................224	10:3–4..............308
8:48–49..............281	9:18–23..............524	10:3................449, 490
8:48..........222, 226, 513	9:18............134, 137	10:4................490
8:49..............374, 380	9:19................134	10:6.......138, 144, 159, 226, 506
8:50................469	9:20................134	10:7–10..............533
8:51–53..............144	9:21................134	10:7–9..............373
8:51.............133, 222, 487	9:22–23..............139	10:7................118, 133, 324
8:52.............222, 281, 513	9:22....52, 141, 225, 245, 259, 315, 319, 321, 429	10:8................308
8:53–58..............121		10:9–10..............506, 532
8:53......154–55, 222, 371, 409	9:24......134, 137, 154, 308, 365, 368–69, 464–65	10:9................118, 324
8:54–55..............369		10:10...86, 284–85, 297, 337, 343, 346, 348, 527, 529, 533–34
8:54........134, 365, 368–69, 374	9:25..........134, 464, 465, 488	
8:56–58..............144	9:27–29..............483	10:11–18..............533
8:56......222, 234, 280, 294, 371, 411	9:27..............154, 483, 485	10:11......118, 161, 226, 285, 324, 417, 495, 503, 526
	9:28..........224, 409, 483, 485	
8:57............154–55, 222, 534		
8:58–59..............373		

10:12–13 226
10:12 . . . . .490, 565
10:14 . . . . .226, 324, 415
10:15–38. 374
10:15–18. 495
10:15 . . . . . 170, 226, 268, 374, 379, 417, 503, 526, 535
10:16 . . . . . 177, 183, 199, 260, 308, 310, 340, 417, 423–24, 434, 449, 463, 496, 501–2, 504, 506, 534, 546, 561
10:17–19. 352
10:17–18. . . 170, 226, 229, 237, 249, 268, 374, 415
10:17 . . . . .503, 521
10:18 . . . . .333, 380, 472, 503
10:20–21. 281
10:20 . . . . 222, 226, 513
10:21 . . . . .116, 226, 484
10:22–42 423
10:22–39. . . . . . . 411, 423, 430–31
10:22 . . . . . . 116, 137, 227, 251, 413, 420, 431
10:22–42 . . . . .169, 227
10:22–39. . . . . .81, 424
10:24 . . . . 168, 319, 321, 385
10:25–37. 202
10:25–30. 385
10:25–26. . . . . .439, 477
10:25 . . . . .132, 319, 374, 380
10:26 . . . . . . 398, 410, 449, 459, 472, 477, 502
10:27–30. . . . . .227, 281
10:27–29. 270
10:27 449
10:28–29. . . . . 460–61, 495
10:28 . . . . . . .133, 138, 337, 343, 480
10:29 . . . . . .374, 380, 458, 461, 480
10:30–31. 373
10:30 . . . 92, 220, 248, 271, 279–80, 360, 365, 374, 377, 384, 392, 429, 444
10:31–33. . . . . 357, 359, 384
10:31 385
10:32 . . . . 154, 243, 319, 374, 534
10:33–36. . . . . 363, 438
10:33 . . . . . 154, 206, 227, 308, 365, 367–69, 382, 385
10:34–39. 315

10:34–38. . . . . .227, 385
10:34–36. . . . . .365, 369, 385
10:34 . . . . 152, 300–306, 309, 358, 368, 385
10:35 .368–69
10:36–37. 243
10:36 . . . . .134, 242, 368–69, 374, 380, 383–86, 425, 461, 506, 522
10:37–39. 385
10:37–38. 375
10:37 . . . . 132, 380
10:38 . . . . .379, 477
10:39 . . . . .169, 227, 385
10:40–42 . . . .
. . . . 81, 169, 181, 193
10:40–41. . . . . . . 73, 168, 228, 407
10:40 . . . . .133, 137, 228
10:41 . . . . 228, 324, 326
10:42 . . . . .134, 477, 484
11–12 . . . . . .168–69, 228–29, 462
11:1–12:36 . . . . .170, 228
11:1–12:19. 228
11 . . . . .119, 165, 169, 185, 208, 228, 257, 300, 327, 371, 375, 413
11:1–57. . . . . 228, 324, 442
11:1–53. 81
11:1–44. . . . . 137, 168, 285, 297, 557
11:1–37. 499
11:1–2. . . . . 140, 551, 559
11:1 148
11:2 . . . . .146, 148, 229, 500, 556
11:3 . . . . 132–33, 521
11:4 . . . . 49, 133, 168, 185, 233, 294, 328, 365–66, 368–69, 380, 383–86, 408, 460
11:5–6. 139
11:5 521
11:6–7. 229
11:6 133
11:7–16. 483
11:7 . . . . 133, 483–84
11:8 . . . . 169, 229, 357, 380, 483–84
11:9–10. . . . . 280, 344–45, 422
11:9 337
11:10 . . . . 167, 337
11:11–14 460
11:11–13. . . . . 144–45, 229

11:11 133
11:12 . . . . 133, 483–84, 494
11:13 138
11:14 133
11:15 . . . . .133, 477
11:16 . . . . .133, 136, 152, 154, 165, 229, 431, 471, 484, 497
11:17 133
11:18 136
11:19 133
11:20 133
11:21 133
11:22 . . . . 366, 368–69, 375
11:23–26. 297
11:24 . . . . .134, 144
11:25–27. . . . . 86, 328, 477
11:25–26. . . . . 225, 343
11:25 . . . . . . 134, 165, 257, 284, 324, 334, 337, 346, 529
11:26 134
11:27 . . . . 134, 168, 231, 315, 319, 321, 366, 368–69, 380, 383–86, 500
11:28 484
11:29 134
11:31 133
11:32 133
11:33 . . . . . . 133, 141, 229, 395, 412
11:34 . . . . 132, 380
11:35 . . . . .116, 229, 278
11:36 . . . . 132–33, 382, 521
11:37 . . . . .133, 196, 229, 484
11:38 133
11:39 . . . . .229, 380
11:40 . . . . 185, 294, 328, 366, 368–69, 408, 477, 534
11:41–42. 541
11:41 . . . . .133, 375
11:42 . . . 133–34, 321, 477, 484, 522
11:43–44. 229
11:43 229
11:44 . . . . .116, 229
11:45–57. 229
11:45 . . . . 133–34, 185, 477, 484
11:46 484
11:47–12:8 415
11:47–50. 69
11:47 . . . .133, 196, 229, 326–27, 410
11:48–53. 423

11:48–52.....152, 423–25, 432–33
11:48–51....................508
11:48–50......................154
11:48......134, 230, 324, 432, 477
11:49–52.......226, 229–30, 414, 441, 506
11:49–51.....................137
11:49–50....250, 437, 442, 452, 513
11:50–12:8....................419
11:50–52.....................526
11:50............117, 133, 417
11:51–52....139, 152, 177, 183, 199, 260, 286, 417, 434, 546, 561
11:52......133, 366, 368–69, 423, 505, 541
11:53...............133, 463, 513
11:54........81, 133, 193, 483–84
11:55–12:36..................329
11:55–12:1....................81
11:55...133, 165, 230, 235, 413, 417
11:56.......................133
11:57.......................133
12.......50, 228–29, 299, 363, 413, 442, 461, 498, 543
12:1–19...................169, 230
12:1–11......................168
12:1–8......148, 329, 498–99, 500
12:1–2......................137
12:1....133, 169, 230, 235, 413, 417
12:2–11.....................81
12:2........................133
12:3–8......................552
12:3.............133, 148, 231, 366
12:4–8..................483, 521
12:4.....133, 137, 231, 483–84, 491
12:5–6......................130
12:5....................231, 559
12:6...................139, 231
12:7...................231, 366
12:8...................309, 559
12:9...........137, 234, 483–84
12:10–11....................228
12:11......133–34, 410, 477, 484
12:12–50.....................81
12:12–19....................232
12:12–16....................329
12:12–15....................292
12:12..................133, 483–84
12:13–15....................285

12:13..........133, 144, 232, 253, 300–301, 303–6, 309, 319, 384, 448
12:14–16.....................67
12:14...................300–301
12:15....133, 232, 253, 301, 303–6, 309, 319, 448
12:16..........138, 141–42, 144, 160, 232, 246, 331, 384, 483–84, 494, 506
12:17–19....................168
12:17–18....................483
12:17..................137, 484
12:18......196, 324, 326, 328, 484
12:19...............152, 155, 340
12:20ff.....................423–24
12:20–50....................441
12:20–36......169, 183, 232, 546
12:20–34....................434
12:20–33...............199, 417
12:20–32................504, 561
12:20–21....................506
12:20............260, 389, 463
12:21–22...............483, 497
12:21..................133, 506
12:22...................491, 497
12:23–33...............409, 533
12:23–24....................389
12:23.............49, 117, 133, 168, 186, 229, 232, 235, 240, 247, 279, 294, 380, 386–87, 389, 395, 418, 427, 460, 506, 533, 538
12:24–27.....................522
12:24–26...............506, 519
12:24..........117, 133, 232, 321, 375, 378, 389, 434, 505–6, 533, 536
12:25......232, 266, 285, 289–90, 337, 343, 346, 521
12:26...133, 289, 375, 378, 506, 528
12:27–28....233, 255, 361, 375, 541
12:27..................309, 412, 527
12:28....49, 110, 216, 233, 256, 279, 294, 361, 373, 418
12:29...................233, 484
12:30–31.....................233
12:31......134, 222, 280–81, 296, 398, 455, 469, 559

12:32–34........144–45, 318, 386
12:32–33..............199, 506, 533
12:32..........50, 132, 150, 158, 184, 233, 242, 252, 260, 270, 309, 321, 340, 361, 370, 387–88, 417, 427, 434, 441, 458, 462, 480, 500, 506, 530–31, 535, 541
12:33............74, 138–39, 158, 233, 237, 252, 262, 321, 388, 440, 495
12:34–35....................484
12:34...........155, 168, 228, 233, 256, 309–10, 315, 319, 321, 380, 386–87, 389, 411, 484, 529–30
12:35–36....117, 167, 180, 233, 264, 280, 283, 344–45, 347
12:35......134, 337, 339, 422, 489
12:36–50....................218
12:36–41......182, 238, 252, 434, 466, 484
12:36–40......49, 112, 192, 203, 213, 228
12:36......117, 134, 219, 280, 283, 295, 337, 339, 422, 477, 527
12:37–50........169–70, 233, 422
12:37–43..................135, 340
12:37–41...179, 225, 235, 243, 270, 294, 384–85, 513
12:37–40...169, 243, 295, 441, 459, 472, 564
12:37–39....................477
12:37...........117, 134, 233, 292, 324, 326–27, 334, 410, 442, 461, 470, 565
12:38–41...............234, 461
12:38–40..............226, 305, 317
12:38..........134, 234, 238, 299, 300–306, 309, 410, 442, 460, 534, 561
12:39–50....................485
12:39......300–301, 398, 410, 460
12:40...212, 234, 299, 302–6, 309, 410, 442, 459, 561
12:41......139, 186, 234, 295, 309, 408, 411
12:42–43..........183, 234, 292, 471, 498, 524

12:42 . . . . 134, 139, 141, 478, 484
12:43 . . . . . . 140, 234, 366, 368–69, 484, 521
12:44 . . . . 86, 134, 234, 478
12:45 . . . . 134, 234
12:46–47 . . . . 340, 527
12:46 . . . 86, 134, 180, 235, 280, 337, 344–47, 422, 450, 527
12:47–48 364
12:47 . . . . . . 235, 407, 469, 527, 532
12:48 . . . . 132, 134, 235, 297, 455, 469
12:49–50 235
12:49 . . . . 134, 380
12:50 . . . . 337, 343, 379
13–21 . . . . . . 72, 228, 293, 299, 311, 366, 391, 424–25, 442, 471, 490, 495, 504, 546
13:1–20:31 . . . . 167, 170, 235
13:1–18:11 81
13–17 . . . . 168–69, 235, 268, 334, 376, 407, 418, 423, 451, 483, 501, 508, 517, 561
13:1–17:26 . . . . . 170, 235, 354, 415
13–14 . . . . 240, 293
13:1–14:3 424
13 . . . . 50, 149, 164, 169, 177, 371, 521
13:1–30 . . . . . 168, 235, 238, 541, 559
13:1–17 . . . . . 235, 237–38, 249, 424
13:1–11 329
13:1–3 . . . . . . 117, 294, 311, 376, 509
13:1–2 249
13:1 . . . . 49, 117, 132, 137, 141, 165, 170, 177, 183, 186, 198, 213, 226, 231, 235–36, 239–40, 247, 255, 340, 354, 380, 389, 395, 413–14, 417–18, 451, 460, 462, 484, 490, 501, 512, 514, 518, 527, 538
13:2 . . . . . . 73, 77, 221, 236–37, 281, 288, 398, 470, 498, 559
13:3 . . . . 137, 235–37, 255, 340, 366, 368–69, 376, 380, 460, 527, 541
13:4–12 . . . . 164, 236
13:4 418
13:5 483–84
13:6–11 . . . . 144–45, 236, 240

13:6–10 . . . . 236, 365, 492
13:6–9 . . . . 73, 77
13:7 . . . . 133, 160
13:8–14 506
13:10–11 . . . . 117, 237, 292, 458, 460, 498, 521
13:10 . . . . 241, 535
13:11 . . . . 137, 236–37, 249, 491
13:12 134
13:13–38 506
13:13–14 . . . . 380, 563
13:13 . . . . 236, 484
13:14–17 489
13:14 . . . . 236, 484
13:15 . . . . . . 134, 236, 265, 512, 518
13:16 . . . . . . 117, 133–34, 290, 378, 484, 490, 522
13:17 . . . . 237, 512
13:18–30 . . . . 117, 237–38, 500
13:18–20 237
13:18 . . . . . 134, 237, 250, 300–305, 309, 458, 486
13:19 . . . . . . 134, 237, 321, 359, 478
13:20 . . . . 133–34, 376, 378, 399, 490, 522
13:21–30 483
13:21 . . . . . . 133, 141, 237, 395, 412
13:22 . . . . 237, 483–84, 494
13:23–25 . . . . 79, 138, 492
13:23–24 . . . . 75, 149
13:23 . . . . 72–75, 78–79, 90, 122, 136, 185, 205, 228, 237, 251, 254, 257, 261, 360, 371, 382, 440, 479, 483–84, 494–95, 500, 520–21, 553, 555, 561
13:25 . . . . 79, 238
13:26–30 77
13:26–27 . . . . 73, 498
13:26 238
13:27 . . . . 238, 281, 288, 398, 470, 559
13:28–29 . . . . 138, 144–45
13:28 134
13:30–31 522
13:30 . . . . . . 117, 167, 238, 251, 284
13:31–17:25 560
13:31–16:33 . . . . 115, 168, 235, 238, 376
13:31–14:31 239–40

13:31–32 . . . 141, 247, 279, 294, 366, 369, 409
13:31 . . . . 240, 368, 376, 380, 386–87
13:32 . . . . 368–69, 376
13:33 . . . . . . 133–34, 240, 460, 462, 489–90, 528
13:34–35 . . . . 93, 239–40, 242, 249, 266, 292, 514, 518, 522
13:34 . . . . 507, 565
13:35 . . . 483, 486, 489–90, 518, 541
13:36–38 . . . . . 77, 144–45, 229, 240, 246, 250, 492, 506, 522
13:36 . . . . 146, 149, 246, 496
13:37–38 155
13:37 400
13:38 . . . . 133, 460
14–17 190
14–16 . . . . 170, 353, 371, 501
14 . . . . 217, 560
14:1–31 423
14:1 . . . . 86, 134, 366, 368–69, 412, 478
14:2–16:26 366
14:2–7 297
14:2–3 . . . . . 240, 244, 249, 423, 460
14:2 . . . . 196, 376, 380, 423–24, 433, 528
14:3 . . . . 92, 506, 527–28
14:4–10 132
14:4–6 145
14:4 527
14:5–6 376
14:5 . . . . . 73, 77, 134, 144–46, 149, 240, 246, 478, 497, 527
14:6–13 376
14:6–11 . . . . 376, 433
14:6 . . . . 117, 165, 180, 187, 218, 240, 270–71, 280, 284, 287–88, 324, 337, 343, 345–46, 373, 381, 397–98, 410, 429, 437–38, 440, 446, 452, 528–29, 532–33, 546
14:7 . . . . 240, 377, 380, 534
14:8–9 . . . . 73, 497
14:8 . . . . . 77, 144, 145, 241, 246, 497, 534
14:9–21 241
14:9–14 240
14:9–11 429

14:9–10 220
14:9 . . . . 166, 377–78, 534
14:10–12 478
14:10–11 376–77
14:10 . . . . 132, 134, 364, 376
14:11 . . . . . . 134, 243, 321, 377, 379
14:12–14 505
14:12 . . . . 132–34, 240, 340,
    377, 391, 397–98, 400,
    451, 487, 489–90, 504–6,
    508, 516, 527–28, 532
14:13–14 . . . . 240, 378, 541
14:13 . . . . 141, 270, 377, 380–81,
    386, 390, 392, 409
14:15–27 238
14:15–24 . . . . 395, 397, 501
14:15–17 397
14:15 . . . . 240–41, 270
14:16–24 544
14:16–18 . . . . 240, 400
14:16–17 489
14:16 . . . . 87, 92, 261, 265, 280, 322,
    376–77, 393, 395–96, 460,
    505, 541–42
14:17–18 402
14:17 . . . .86, 141, 267, 271, 288, 377,
    393, 395–97, 430, 440,
    455, 459, 480, 542
14:18–21 397
14:18 . . . . 395, 397, 527, 542
14:19 . . . . . . 343, 345–46, 395, 489
14:20 . . . . 376–77, 379–80, 395
14:21 . . . 132, 134, 240–41, 376–77,
    380, 523
14:22–24 397
14:22 . . . . .73, 77, 140, 241–42,
    246, 497
14:23 . . . 214, 240–41, 376–77, 380,
    395, 423
14:24 . . . . . . 134, 241, 376–77, 380
14:25–26 400
14:26 . . . . 134, 141, 241,
    376–77, 393, 395, 397, 489,
    505–6, 521, 523, 542, 544
14:27 . . . . .239, 412
14:28 . . . . .340, 376–77, 527–28
14:29 . . . . 460, 478
14:30–31 .241
14:30 . . .134, 148, 222, 280–81,
    455, 559

14:31–15:1 116
14:31 . . . 115, 146, 148–49, 239–40,
    249, 376, 378, 518
15–17 . . . . 148, 239–40, 418
15–16 239
15:1–16:33 241
15 . . . . . 117, 148, 156, 159, 161, 214,
    220, 238, 478, 481, 490,
    502–3, 508, 518, 559, 564
15:1–17 . . . . 239, 241, 503
15:1–10 . . . . .239, 418
15:1–8 . . . . 267, 294, 519, 522
15:1 . . . . .115, 118, 241, 309,
    324, 340, 354, 378, 380,
    501, 546
15:2–4 . . . . 292, 498
15:2–3 117
15:2 . . . 132, 241, 376, 394, 458, 521
15:3 . . . . 164, 506
15:4–8 241
15:4–7 486
15:4 . . . . 86, 241
15:5–7 133
15:5 .241, 324
15:6–7 241
15:6 . . . . .86, 241, 521
15:7 . . . . 86, 242, 480, 541
15:8 . . . . 141, 242, 248, 280, 378,
    380, 483, 486, 503, 546
15:9–17 . . . . .519, 522
15:9–13 239
15:9–10 242
15:9 . . . . 134, 376, 378, 519, 521, 565
15:10–17 514
15:10 . . . . . . 242, 376, 378, 380, 523
15:11 239
15:12–13 249
15:12 . . . . .240, 242, 507, 565
15:13 . . . . 50, 232, 242, 255,
    268, 285, 417, 503, 519,
    526, 533, 565
15:14 489
15:15–16 170
15:15 . . . . . . 134, 373, 376, 378, 380,
    490
15:16 . . . . . .242, 248, 280, 376, 378,
    459, 503–4, 506, 524, 541
15:17 . . . . 242, 565
15:18–16:11 241
15:18–16:4 522

15:18–27 . . . . .242, 259, 506, 527
15:18–25 . . . . . 87, 241, 268, 290–91,
    378, 565
15:18–19 290
15:19 . . . . . . .242, 266, 290, 459, 521
15:20–21 . . . . 242, 522
15:20 . . . . 134, 290, 484, 490
15:21 . . . . .134, 369, 376
15:22–24 .465
15:22 . . .182, 244, 290, 464, 507, 527
15:23–24 .378
15:23 . . . . 243, 380
15:24 . . . . . . 132, 243–44, 290, 380,
    464, 534
15:25 . . . . . . .215, 243, 290, 299–305,
    309, 411–12
15:26–16:15 . . . . 238, 396
15:26–27 . . . . 170, 239,
    244, 264, 288, 331, 396,
    402, 463, 487–88, 495,
    504, 523, 540, 544
15:26 . . . . 134, 141, 238, 288,
    376, 378, 393, 395–97,
    430, 440, 455, 489, 505,
    521, 523, 542, 544, 565
15:27 . . . . 244, 264, 371
16 217
16:1–15 245
16:1 245
16:2 . . . . .141, 245, 366, 368–69,
    389, 460
16:3 . . . . .369, 378
16:4 460
16:5–15 245
16:5 . . . . .134, 146, 149, 376, 527
16:7–11 . . . . .397, 459, 544
16:7 . . . . . 238, 245, 393, 395, 505,
    523, 527–28, 542
16:8–11 . . . . 244, 288, 396–97, 402,
    505, 507, 542
16:8–9 466
16:8 . . . . 245, 460, 464, 469–70, 523
16:9–11 245
16:9 . . . . 134, 397, 464, 542
16:10 . . . . .523, 527
16:11 . . . . . . .134, 222, 280–81, 455,
    469–70, 559
16:12–15 . . . . .397, 400, 489
16:12 430
16:13–15 . . . . .245, 402

16:13–14 505
16:13 . . . 86, 141, 288, 298, 393, 395,
    397–98, 440, 455, 542
16:14–15 .378
16:14 141
16:16–33 .245
16:16–19 . . . . .145, 489
16:16 . . . . .241, 245, 534
16:17–18 . . . . 145, 245, 494
16:17 . . . 149, 378, 483–84, 527, 534
16:18 134
16:19 . . . . .137, 241, 534
16:20–22 245–46
16:20 . . . . 133, 460
16:21–25 .159
16:22–24 239
16:22 . . . . 309–10, 534
16:23–27 .541
16:23 . . . . .133, 376, 378
16:25–28 .378
16:25 246
16:26–27 433
16:26 246
16:27–28 .527
16:27 . . . . . . 86, 134, 246, 321, 366,
    368–69, 376, 478, 521
16:28 . . . . 170, 255, 340, 376,
    450–51, 527–28, 541
16:29–30 . . . . 238, 246
16:29 . . . . 159, 241, 483–84
16:30 . . . 86, 134, 321, 366, 368–69,
    376, 478
16:31–32 246
16:31 . . . . .155, 478
16:32 . . . . 141, 309, 378, 460,
    505, 533
16:33 . . . . . . 239, 246–47, 278, 281,
    339, 455, 456
17 . . . . 170, 213, 246, 376, 378,
    486, 501, 531, 534, 541
17:1–26 . . . . 168, 246
17:1–5 . . . . 246, 533
17:1 . . . . . 49, 117, 141, 168, 178, 186,
    247, 375–76, 378, 380–81,
    390, 392, 409, 427, 538
17:2–4 533
17:2–3 . . . . . . 342–43, 345–46, 533
17:2 . . . . .185, 247, 337, 376,
    394, 458, 461, 472, 480,
    505, 533

17:3 . . . . 86, 177, 247, 262, 288,
    319, 337, 366, 368–69, 376,
    438, 523, 534
17:4–20:16 366
17:4–5 . . . . . . 49, 141, 247, 255, 409
17:4 . . . . . . 178, 246–47, 353, 386,
    392, 451, 531, 541
17:5 . . . . 168, 247, 249,
    294, 375–76, 378–79, 408,
    418, 451, 538
17:6–19 247
17:6 . . . . . . 242, 247–48, 270, 376,
    458, 461, 466, 480, 490
17:7 248
17:8 . . . . . . 86, 132, 134, 321, 376,
    478, 523
17:9 . . . . 247, 270, 376, 461
17:10 . . . . 141, 376, 490, 496
17:11–12 .461
17:11 . . . . . . 248, 374–76, 378, 507,
    527–28
17:12 . . . . .117, 138, 237,
    248, 250, 270, 300–302,
    309, 458, 460, 483, 495,
    498, 501, 508
17:13–14 248
17:13 . . . . 201, 239, 527, 528
17:14–19 440
17:14 . . . . .290, 376
17:15–16 248
17:15 . . . . .196, 376, 398
17:17–19 440
17:17–18 .196
17:17 . . . . . . 242, 248, 398, 440, 480
17:18 . . . . . . 50, 58, 134, 177, 238,
    253, 279, 282, 376, 379,
    399, 441, 489–90, 496, 503,
    506, 508, 511, 519, 523, 534
17:19 . . . . .242, 398, 417, 440
17:20–26 . . . . .170, 248, 520
17:20–25 . . . . .489, 514
17:20–23 .541
17:20 . . . . . . 86, 134, 248, 264, 478,
    488–89, 508
17:21–26 399
17:21–22 .376
17:21 . . . . . . 134, 215, 248, 249, 375,
    378, 478, 523
17:22–23 5–7
17:22 . . . . .374, 376

17:23 . . . 215, 248–49, 376, 520, 523
17:24 . . . . 168, 235,
    244, 247, 249, 294, 375,
    379, 451, 458, 506, 538
17:25 . . . . 249, 369, 375–76, 379,
    431, 523
17:26 . . . . .239, 376, 565
18–21 . . . . 113, 245
18:1–21:25 . . . . .293, 354
18–20 . . . . 149, 249, 407, 564
18:1–20:31 168
18:1–20:29 170
18–19 . . . . . . 155, 170, 187, 334, 371,
    379, 412, 442
18:1–19:42 . . . . .329, 423
18:1–19:34 478
18 . . . . .246, 418, 453
18:1–18 249
18:1–14 240
18:1–11 447
18:1–5 500
18:1 . . . . . . .146, 148, 239–40, 249,
    337, 349, 352, 447, 483–84
18:2–3 498
18:2 . . . . 249, 483–84
18:3 . . . . 167, 249, 252
18:4–5 447
18:4 . . . . 137, 237, 249, 450, 460
18:5 . . . . .250, 359
18:6 . . . . .250, 359
18:7 250
18:8–9 447
18:8 .250, 359
18:9 . . . . 133–34, 138, 250, 461
18:10 . . . . .134, 140, 250, 552
18:11 . . . 145, 164, 250, 379, 447, 450
18:12–19:42 81
18:12–14 . . . . 250–51, 447
18:13 552
18:14 . . . . . . 133, 137, 417, 437, 452
18:15–18 . . . . .79, 240, 250, 447, 492
18:15–16 . . . . . . 75, 136, 149, 237, 261
18:15 . . . . .483, 485
18:16 483
18:17 . . . . .483, 485
18:18 . . . . .167, 251–52, 261
18:19–27 .251
18:19–24 447
18:19 . . . . .251, 483, 485, 489
18:20–21 . . . . .252, 447

18:20 . . . . 217, 424, 430–31
18:22 447
18:23 448
18:24 . . . . 251–52, 442, 447
18:25–27 . . . . 240, 250, 252, 447, 492
18:25 . . . . .483, 485
18:26 . . . . 133, 137, 349, 352
18:28–19:16 . . . . 117, 252, 441
18:28 . . . 137, 251–52, 255, 257, 261,
        441–42, 447
18:29–32 . . . . 253, 444
18:29 252
18:30 . . . 155, 252, 442, 444, 450, 453
18:31–32 82
18:31 . . . . 444, 469
18:32 . . . . . . 134, 138, 252, 440, 450
18:33–38 . . . . 252–53, 438, 440, 444
18:33–34 448
18:33 . . . . . . 155, 253, 444, 448–49
18:34 448
18:35 . . . . 444, 446, 450, 453
18:36–38 . . . . .285, 439, 441
18:36–37 . . . . .318, 450
18:36 . . . . . . 130, 232–33, 250, 253,
        285, 384, 448–50, 453
18:37–38 . . . . 82, 440–41, 451
18:37 . . . . . 244, 253, 340, 360, 397,
        440, 448–49, 452, 495, 527
18:38–19:16 445
18:38–40 . . . . 253, 444
18:38 . . . . 117, 155, 444, 446–47
18:39 . . . . 155, 253, 444, 448
18:40 441
19 . . . . .418, 453
19:1–6 . . . . .253, 450
19:1–3 . . . . 253, 444
19:3 . . . . 155, 253, 448
19:4–15 .252
19:4–7 . . . . 253, 444
19:4 447
19:5 . . . . 155, 185, 287–88, 352, 444
19:6 447
19:7 . . . . 207, 254, 309,
        367–69, 373, 380, 382–84,
        386, 438, 443, 447, 450
19:8–11 . . . . 253, 444
19:9 . . . . .134, 254, 450, 531
19:10 . . . . .254, 450, 472
19:11–12 410
19:11 . . . . .452, 464, 474

19:12–15 . . . . 253, 444
19:12 . . . . 443, 448
19:13–42 415
19:13 136
19:14 . . . . . . .155, 253, 415, 418, 444,
        448, 535, 552
19:15 . . . . . . .117, 194, 232, 253, 292,
        410, 441, 443, 448
19:16–42 254
19:16 . . . . .254, 443, 452
19:17–18 254
19:17 . . . . .136, 535
19:18 . . . . .309, 419
19:19–22 . . . . 155, 254
19:19 . . . . 232, 253, 448
19:21 . . . . 253, 448
19:23 474
19:24 . . . . 138, 252, 254–55,
        299, 300–305, 309, 317,
        411–12, 419, 460
19:25–27 . . . . 254, 499
19:25 . . . . .257, 500
19:26–27 . . . . .79, 492
19:26 . . . 72, 134, 411, 483, 485, 521
19:27 . . . . 182, 254, 317, 483
19:28–30 412
19:28–29 . . . . .309, 419
19:28 . . . . 132–33, 137, 138,
        164, 254, 299–301, 305–6,
        317, 353, 411–12, 419, 460
19:29 . . . . 164, 254, 415, 419, 535
19:30 . . . . . . 132, 246–47, 255, 353,
        370, 385, 392, 395, 519
19:31 . . . 185, 255, 257, 309–10, 353,
        415, 419, 451
19:33 . . . . .164, 419
19:34–35 278
19:34 . . . 93, 164, 255, 259, 264, 270,
        419, 454, 535
19:35 . . . . . . 53, 75, 78, 86, 122, 136,
        185, 244, 254–55, 260,
        371, 478–79, 488–89, 492,
        495, 534, 553, 555
19:36–37 . . . . 138, 252, 256, 299,
        415, 460
19:36 . . . . . 164, 255, 300–306, 309,
        415–16, 419, 535
19:37 . . . . .255, 259, 300–306, 309,
        419, 534
19:38–42 . . . . .231, 256

19:38 . . . . . . 133, 185, 231, 256, 309,
        419, 471, 483, 485, 498
19:39–42 471
19:39 . . . . .133, 138, 167, 205, 257
19:40 . . . . .137, 185
19:41 . . . . 257, 337, 349, 352
19:42 257
20–21 . . . . .245, 334, 483, 527
20:1–21:25 329
20 . . . . . . .149, 170, 176, 259, 349,
        352, 451, 500
20:1–31 349
20:1–29 257
20:1–25 .81
20:1–18 . . . . .257, 499
20:1–10 79
20:1–2 . . . . 258, 500
20:1 . . . . 167, 257, 259, 261, 352–53
20:2–10 . . . . .365, 492
20:2–9 . . . . .75, 136, 149
20:2 . . . . . 72, 79, 134, 251, 257–59,
        483, 485, 521
20:3–10 237
20:3–9 .261
20:3 . . . . .251, 483, 485
20:4 . . . . 138, 257, 483, 485
20:5 257–58
20:6 . . . . .134, 257
20:7 257
20:8 . . . . 138, 251, 257, 478, 483
20:9 . . . . 138, 145, 258, 310, 494
20:10 . . . . .258, 483
20:11–18 . . . . .257, 261, 500
20:11–12 258
20:12 . . . . 110, 134, 185
20:13 . . . . .134, 258, 259
20:14–15 145
20:14 . . . . .134, 138, 258
20:15 . . . . 258, 337, 349, 352
20:16 . . . . 136, 258, 380, 483–84
20:17 . . . . 163, 258, 261, 367–69,
        379–80, 399–400, 462,
        490, 527–28
20:18 . . . . 116, 258–59, 483–84, 534
20:19–21:14 508
20:19–21:13 500
20:19–29 259
20:19–23 . . . . 149, 259, 261, 483
20:19 . . . . . . 134, 140, 239, 259, 353,
        400, 483–84

20:20 . . . . 483, 534
20:21–23 . . . . 170, 280, 396, 402, 523
20:21–22 . . . . 50, 202, 238, 346, 402, 523, 544
20:21 . . . . 58, 134, 177, 213, 239, 247–48, 253, 259–60, 279, 282, 378–80, 392, 399, 441, 451, 489–90, 496, 503, 506–8, 511, 519, 534, 540, 542, 545
20:22–23 540
20:22 . . . . 163, 184, 217, 259, 287, 309, 346, 349, 352–53, 362, 393, 395, 399–400, 466, 501, 542–43
20:23 . . . . 259, 309, 464, 504–5, 535
20:24–29 . . . . 149, 261, 471
20:24 . . . . 136, 259, 485
20:25 . . . . 478, 483–84, 534
20:26–31 81
20:26 . . . . . . 134, 140, 239, 259, 353, 400, 483–84
20:27 264
20:28 . . . . . . 117, 225, 260, 264, 271, 286–88, 321, 360, 367–70, 382, 390, 423–25, 431, 497
20:29 . . . . . . 121, 258, 260, 478–88, 490, 534, 565
20:30–31 . . . . 48, 67, 69, 86, 95, 97, 112, 115, 119, 121, 135, 146, 149, 151, 168, 170, 187, 190, 192–93, 196, 203, 207, 224, 227, 231, 260, 267, 269, 279, 292, 297, 299, 311, 314–17, 319–20, 322–23, 328, 333, 338, 366, 384–86, 389, 438, 447, 470, 477–79, 504, 545, 560
20:30 . . . 262, 324, 326–27, 330–31, 334, 483, 485, 489
20:31 . . . . 49, 85, 134, 149, 155, 244, 260, 280, 284–85, 319, 321–22, 337, 342, 344–45, 367–70, 380, 382–84, 386, 439, 471, 479, 489, 500, 559
21 . . . . 119, 149–50, 261, 324, 332, 346, 371, 407, 451, 461, 492–93, 541

21:1–25 . . . . 79, 81, 167, 170, 260
21:1–14 . . . . 260, 329
21:1–13 260
21:1 . . . . . 82, 133, 149, 260–61, 483
21:2–7 149
21:2 . . . . . . 73, 76, 78, 136, 181, 261, 483, 497–98
21:3 . . . . 261, 400
21:4–5 . . . . 462, 490
21:4 . . . . 138, 145, 167, 261, 483
21:5–7 261
21:5 133
21:6 133
21:7–24 492
21:7–9 261
21:7 . . . . 72–73, 75, 133–34, 136, 164, 237, 259, 261, 365, 483, 521
21:8 483
21:9 . . . . 133–34, 167, 261
21:11 261
21:12 . . . . 261, 483
21:13 133
21:14 . . . 133, 140, 149, 260, 483, 500
21:15–23 . . . . 149, 262, 492, 495–96, 506
21:15–19 . . . . 135, 240, 261, 365, 565
21:15–17 . . . . 495–96, 501, 503, 521
21:15–16 521
21:15 . . . . 133, 262, 521
21:16 . . . . 495, 521
21:17 262
21:18–19 460
21:18 . . . . 133, 262
21:19–21 505
21:19 . . . . 74, 82, 139, 233, 237, 240, 262, 367–69, 440, 451, 490, 495–96, 500
21:20–25 . . . . 136, 288, 371
21:20–24 119
21:20–23 . . . . 237, 262
21:20 . . . . 72–73, 78, 133–34, 138, 205, 228, 237, 360, 440, 483, 521
21:22 . . . . 92, 451, 490, 527
21:23–24 107
21:23 . . . . 133, 139, 262, 483
21:24–25 . . . . . 73, 116, 119, 124, 135, 149, 185, 190, 193, 228, 244, 262, 495, 553, 555

21:24 . . . . 53, 72, 76, 78, 92, 122, 133–34, 244, 254, 262, 360, 483, 488–89, 495
21:25 . . . . 72, 78, 119, 150, 262, 281, 567

Acts

1:1–2 107
1:1 . . . . 118, 463, 561
1:3 448
1:4–5 . . . . 463, 545
1:4 142
1:5 393
1:6 448
1:7–8 463
1:8 . . . . 142, 202, 441, 545, 558
1:9–11 545
1:10 545
1:13 . . . . 73, 75, 77, 181
1:14 254
1:15–26 73
1:16 302
2–28 463
2 . . . . 142, 399–400
2:36 . . . . 39, 315, 357
3–4 . . . . 75, 78, 181
3 496
3:19 448
4 496
4:25–26 . . . . 313, 452
4:27 . . . . 400, 439
7:14–25 222
8 . . . . 142, 257
8:1–3 245
8:14–25 . . . . 75, 78, 181
8:32 414
9:16 85
10 142
10:8 382
10:34 439
10:38 401
12:2 73
13:33 313
13:46–48 441
15:12, 14 382
15:16–18 448
15:23–29 126
18:14–15 444
19 142
19:1–7 . . . . 181, 201

19:29 98	1:18–25 256	**Philippians**
20:4 98	2:14 398	2:5–11 236
20:28 . . . . .454, 496	3:16 398	2:5–7 271
21:19 382	5:7 . . . . 194, 415, 419	2:11 357
23:2–5 251	6:19 398	
26:4 474	8:4–6 . . . . .271, 359	**Colossians**
26:25 439	8:6 . . . . .339, 360	1:16 339
28:17–31 441	10:4 411	1:20 454
28:26–27 . . . . 234, 411, 561	10:11 121	2:6–7 267
28:27 302	12:3 357	2:9 271
	12:13 142	
Romans	13 242	**2 Thessalonians**
1:13 85	13:13 242	2:3 491
1:14–16 441	15 284	
1:18–3:31 221	15:1–4 564	**1 Timothy**
1:25 438	15:4 191	3:16 96
3:7 438	15:5–7 260	4:1–5 266
3:9–24 221	15:12–20 39	5:10 236
3:22–25 466	15:50 .476	6:13 441
3:25–26 265	16:22 .357	6:16 265
3:25 454		6:21 267
4 221	**2 Corinthians**	
4:17 384	1:21–22 400	**2 Timothy**
5:9 454	5:17 . . . . 184, 337, 474	2:2 248
8:3 341	13:1 454	2:18 297
8:9 142		3:1–5 266
8:15 184	**Galatians**	
8:16 401	2 53	**Titus**
8:18–22 337	2:9 . . . . .75, 78, 181	1:15–16 267
8:18 235	3 221	2:11–13 271
8:21 223	3:28 . . . . .184, 558, 564	
8:23 184	3:29 564	**Hebrews**
8:28–30 564	4:4–6 564	1:1–3 .359
8:32 415	4:5 184	1:1–2 209
9–11 . . . . .461, 463, 564	4:9 474	1:2 . . . . .339, 564
9:1 401	4:29 475	1:3 . . . . 271, 340, 564
9:5 271	5:13 236	1:5 313
9:17 411	5:22 . . . . .239, 242	1:8 271
10:3 468	6:2 236	1:9 401
10:9 357	6:15 . . . . 184, 337, 474	2:1–3 267
10:16 . . . . .302, 410		5:5 313
11 564	**Ephesians**	6:6 242
13 563	1:5 184	9:12 454
13:1 450–51	1:7 454	11 .221, 564
15:8 438	2:1–5 384	11:5 388
16:23 98	2:8–9 .512	11:17 . . . . .381, 409
	2:20 264	12:2 235
1 Corinthians	4:1–6 249	13:12 .454
1:12 496	5:21–33 503	
1:14 98	6:12 222	

James

1:17 . . . . 265, 474
1:22–27 237
3:15, 17 474

1 Peter

1:1 88
1:6 235
1:8 565
1:11–12 565
1:19 . . . . 414, 419, 565
1:22 565
2:8 565
2:13–4:2 565
2:17 565
2:21–25 . . . . 414, 565
2:25 565
3:17–18 565
3:18 565
4:8 565
5:1 88
5:2–4 565
5:2–3 496
5:14 565

2 Peter

1:1 271
1:19 340
2:22 266

1 John

1 367
1:1–5 . . . . 96, 116
1:1–4 . . . . 88, 97, 171, 173, 263
1:1–3 . . . . 51, 479, 488
1:1–2 . . . . 342, 344–45, 454
1:1 . . . . 76, 86, 88, 263–64, 266, 284, 337–38
1:2 . . . . 86–88, 285, 337, 379
1:3 . . . . . . 88, 133, 322, 379–80, 392
1:4 . . . . 88, 133, 264
1:5–2:27 . . . . 172–73, 264
1:5–2:11 268
1:5–2:2 . . . . 173, 454
1:5–10 . . . . 265, 455
1:5–7 . . . . 166, 284
1:5 . . . . 87–88, 91, 166, 264, 268, 283, 337, 339, 345, 367, 369
1:6–10 96
1:6–7 . . . . 264, 283
1:6 . . . . 86–88, 266, 367, 455
1:7–8 292
1:7 . . . . . 88, 337, 345, 380, 392, 402, 466–67, 537
1:8–2:2 481
1:8–10 467
1:8 . . . . . 87–88, 265, 281, 341, 401, 455, 466
1:9 . . . . 87, 133, 265, 402, 466–67, 523
1:10 . . . 88, 263, 265, 281, 341, 466
2 . . . . 171, 367, 379
2:1–2 . . . . 265, 433, 467–68
2:1 . . . . 88, 91–92, 97, 126, 133, 267, 322, 379, 396–97, 466, 523
2:2 . . . . 226, 265, 267, 281, 341, 369, 415, 454–55, 463, 466, 520, 536–37, 539
2:3–11 . . . . 173, 265
2:3–8 519
2:3–5 523
2:3 88
2:4–6 455
2:4–5 97
2:4 . . . . 87, 95, 455
2:5–6 . . . . 481, 565
2:5 . . . . 88, 263, 367, 455
2:6 . . . . 134, 265
2:7–11 . . . . 268, 518
2:7–8 . . . . 93, 271
2:7 . . . . 263, 266–68
2:8–10 . . . . 166, 284, 345
2:8 . . . . 285, 337, 455
2:9–11 290–91
2:9–10 . . . . 94, 290
2:9 . . . . 95, 266, 271, 290, 337
2:10 . . . . 337, 471
2:11 271
2:12–17 173
2:12–15 97
2:12–14 . . . . 89, 94, 97
2:12 . . . . 126, 133, 266, 466
2:13 . . . . 133, 266–67
2:14 . . . . 263, 266–67, 367
2:15–17 . . . . 248, 266, 288, 454
2:15 379
2:16 . . . . 86, 379, 454
2:17 . . . . 171, 367
2:18–27 . . . . 173, 266
2:18–19 266
2:18 . . . . . . 88, 95, 126, 133–34, 269, 292, 296, 298, 401, 455
2:19 . . . . 92, 94, 98, 126, 133, 264, 266, 290, 322, 370, 400–401, 467, 481, 493, 520
2:20–21 481
2:20 . . . . 91, 267, 269, 400, 402
2:21 . . . . 87, 267, 455
2:22–23 95
2:22 . . . . . . 95, 267, 269–70, 291–92, 298, 322, 379–80, 386, 392, 400–401, 455, 456
2:23 . . . . 96, 267, 379–80, 392
2:24 . . . . . . 97, 267–68, 379–80, 392
2:25 . . . . 86, 268, 337, 344
2:26 . . . . 95, 97, 133
2:27 . . . . . . 86, 91, 97, 133, 264, 269, 402, 455
2:28–3:24 . . . . 172–73, 267
2:28–3:10 . . . . 173, 267
2:28–3:3 . . . . 91, 298
2:28 . . . . 97, 133, 171, 267
2:29 . . . . . 171, 267, 369, 479–80, 523
3–5 370
3 . . . . 367, 379
3:1–3 380
3:1–2 . . . . 177, 472
3:1 . . . . 267, 367, 369, 379, 454
3:2 . . . . 267, 287, 337, 367, 369
3:4–10 523
3:4–9 467
3:4 . . . . 87, 298, 466–67
3:5 466–67
3:6 . . . . 298, 466–67, 523
3:7–15 . . . . 365, 374, 398
3:7 523
3:8–15 281
3:8–10 . . . . 279, 367, 398
3:8 . . . . . . 87, 267, 281, 367, 380, 386, 456, 466–67
3:9 . . . . . . 91, 184, 267–68, 367, 369, 466–67, 471, 479–80
3:10–15 96
3:10 . . . . . . 50, 87, 94, 96, 177, 268, 281, 367, 369, 523
3:11–24 . . . . 125, 173, 268, 481
3:11–15 87
3:11 . . . . 87–88, 171, 242, 268, 292, 467, 520

3:12 . . . . . . 87, 91, 268, 281, 454, 523
3:13–15 290–91
3:13 . . . . 268, 291, 454
3:14–15 . . . . 342, 344
3:14 . . . . . . 87–88, 97, 268, 285, 291, 337, 342, 520
3:15 . . . . 86, 268–69, 291, 337
3:16–18 520
3:16–17 271
3:16 . . . . 88, 268–69, 367, 519
3:17–18 . . . . 268, 270
3:17 . . . . 86, 97, 133, 367
3:18 . . . . 88, 133, 455
3:19 . . . . 88, 268–69, 455
3:20–21 367
3:20 88
3:21–23 541
3:21 88
3:22 88
3:23 . . . . 88, 269, 322, 380, 392, 467, 470, 479, 518
3:24 . . . . 88, 269, 398
4:1–5:12 . . . . 172, 173, 269
4 367
4:1–6 . . . . 173, 269, 401
4:1–3 . . . . 341, 367
4:1 . . . . 94, 171, 455, 470, 479
4:2–3 . . . . . 51, 96, 269–70, 322, 401
4:2 . . . . . . 96, 291, 322–23, 386, 401
4:3 . . . . 292, 296, 298, 401, 455
4:4–6 367
4:4–5 269
4:4 . . . . 133, 433, 455
4:5 86
4:6–8 367
4:6 . . . . . . 86, 88, 269, 398, 401, 440, 455, 456
4:7–21 . . . . 125, 481
4:7–12 173
4:7 . . . . . . 88, 94, 171, 184, 242, 369, 467, 479–80
4:8 . . . . 87, 369
4:9–10 455
4:9 . . . 86, 88, 342, 367, 380–82, 392
4:10 . . . . 88, 269, 281, 341, 369–70, 380, 392, 415, 466–68, 537
4:11 . . . . 88, 269, 368, 467
4:12 . . . . 88, 269–70, 368, 467
4:13–21 173
4:13 . . . . 86, 88, 97, 269, 398
4:14 . . . . . 88, 116, 369, 379–80, 392, 415, 454–55, 488, 539
4:15 . . . . 96, 368, 380, 386, 402
4:16 . . . . 87–88, 269, 368–69, 470, 479
4:17 . . . . . 88, 134, 298, 455, 468–69
4:18 269
4:19–21 . . . . 270, 518
4:19–20 291
4:19 . . . . 88, 269
4:20–21 . . . . 368, 524
4:20 290–91
4:21 88
5 367
5:1–12 173
5:1 . . . . 96, 184, 270, 291, 317, 322, 368–69, 386, 470, 472, 479–80
5:2–3 . . . . 270, 368, 518
5:2 . . . . 88, 369
5:3 88
5:4–5 . . . . 281, 368, 455
5:4 . . . . . . 87, 130, 184, 369, 470, 479–80
5:5 . . . . 96, 269, 368, 380, 386, 470, 479
5:6–11 454
5:6–10 432
5:6–8 . . . . 96, 401, 419, 475
5:6–7 . . . . 164, 270, 401
5:6 . . . . . . 93, 270, 440, 455–56, 537
5:7–8 270
5:8 537
5:9–13 389
5:9–12 270
5:9–11 369
5:9–10 368
5:9 . . . . 88, 133, 380, 392
5:10 . . . 87, 133, 380, 386, 392, 401, 470, 479
5:11–13 344
5:11–12 384
5:11 . . . . . . 86, 88, 337, 368, 380, 392
5:12–13 386
5:12 . . . . 337, 380, 386, 392
5:13–21 . . . . 171, 173, 270
5:13 . . . . 85–86, 95, 97, 270, 337, 368, 380, 386, 470, 479, 481

5:14–15 541
5:14 . . . . 88, 270, 367
5:15 . . . . 88, 270
5:16–18 467
5:16–17 . . . . 270, 467, 471
5:16 . . . . 133, 337, 344, 466
5:17 466–67
5:18 . . . . 88, 184, 271, 281, 367, 369, 466–67, 471, 479–81
5:19 . . . . . 88, 281, 288, 369, 455, 479
5:20 . . . . 86, 88, 271, 322, 337, 344, 368–70, 380, 386, 392, 455
5:21 . . . . 133, 271, 368

2 John

1–3 . . . . 173, 271
1–2 271
1 . . . . 94, 97–98, 271–72
2 88
3 . . . . 271, 322, 368, 380, 392
4–11 . . . . 173, 271
4–6 173
4 . . . . 88, 98
5 . . . . 88, 98, 271, 467
6 . . . . 88, 271
7–11 . . . . 98, 173
7–8 . . . . 89, 271
7 . . . . 94, 96, 292, 322, 341, 401, 455
8–11 98
8–9 96
8 88
9–11 271
9 . . . . 97, 267, 323, 368, 380, 392
12–13 . . . . 173, 272

3 John

1–4 . . . . 173, 272
1 . . . . 94, 97, 272
2 . . . . 264, 272, 285
3 . . . . 272, 368,
4 272
5–12 . . . . 173, 272
5–8 173
7 272
8 . . . . 88–89, 272
9–10 . . . . 98, 116, 173
9 272
10 . . . . 88, 132, 272

11–12 . . . . .173, 272
11. 368
12. . . . . .88, 98, 116
13–14 . . . . .173, 272
14. 88, 272

Revelation

1:1–3. 88
1:7 .255, 302
1:9–10. 88
1:13 388
1:14, 16 340
2–3 .53, 126
2:28 340
5:5–6. .415
5:6. 414–15
5:9 415
5:12 414–15
5:12–13. 415
7:15 185
7:17 414–15
11:15 448
12:10 279
12:11 415
12:12 185
13:6 185
13:8 415
14:14 388
15:3 523
16:5, 7 523
17:14 415
19:2 523
19:7, 9 415
19:11 523
19:12 340
19:13 338
20:7–10. . . . . .281, 470
21–22 337
21. 433
21:3 . . . . .185, 424
21:22–23. 415
21:22 424
21:23 340
22:1–3. .415
22:1–2. . . . . 348, 421
22:5 340
22:11 523
22:16 340
22:17 421
22:18–19. . . . . .88, 119
22:20 357

Index of Extrabiblical Literature

Old Testament Apocrypha

2 Esdras (4 Ezra)
12:32 319
13:13–38 319

2 Maccabees
2:7–8 426
7:9–14 348

4 Maccabees
1:7–8 121

Sirach
24:19–21 421
36:19 426
51:23–24 421

Tobit
12:9–10 348

Wisdom of Solomon
7:26–30 339
15:11 400
16:20 416

Old Testament Pseudepigrapha

Apocalypse of Abraham
25 69

2 (Syriac) Baruch
14:6–7, 17–19 69
46:4–5 69
48:3–4 475
59:2 . . . . 166, 339
77:3–6 69

1 (Ethiopic) Enoch
37–71 . . . . 391, 469
41:3 475
49:4 . . . . 391, 469
60:12 475
61:9 . . . . 391, 469
62:2–6 . . . . 391, 469
63:11 469
90:9–12 414
105:2 384

4 Ezra
3:28–36 69
4:10–11 69
4:23–24 69
6:57 69
6:58 . . . . 381, 409
7:28–29 384
7:72 69
7:137 348
9–10 65
13:52 384
14:9 384
14:22 348

Jubilees
1:23–25 . . . . 350, 475
18:2, 11, 15 . . . . 350, 409

Psalms of Solomon
14:7 348
17:21–27 . . . . 391, 469
17:21–22 411
17:25 319
17:32 314
17:36 411
18:4 . . . . 381, 409
18:7 314

Pseudo-Philo
Biblical Antiquities 110
Assumption of Moses 110

Sibylline Oracles
3:702–13 69
4 69
4:9 69
5 59

Testament of Abraham
12:13–18 69

Testament of Benjamin
3:8 414

Testament of Joseph
19:8 414

Testament of Judah
20:1–5 398

Rabbinic Writings

Babylonian Talmud

b. Berakot
47a 475

b. ʿErubin
31b–32a 391

b. Ketubbot
66b 69
99b 391

b. Megillah
31a 421

b. Sukkah
48b 421

b. Taʿanit
2a 391

b. Yebamot
22a 475
48b 475
62a 475
77a 382
97b 475

Jerusalem Talmud

y. Berakot
5a 66

Mishnah

m. ʾAbot
1:12 462
3:16 462

Index of Extrabiblical Literature

m. Berakot
5:5 391

m. ʾOhalot
3:5 419

m. Pesaḥim
5:5–8 .419

m. Roš Haššanah
1.2 443

m. Šabbat
7:2 350
10:5 350
18:3 351
19:2–3 351

m. Sukkah
4:1, 9–10 421
5:2–4 420
5:6 421

m. Yebamot
4.13 221

Tosefta
t. Sukkah
3:3–12 421

Other Rabbinic Works
Pesiqta Rabati
52:3–6 421

Rabbah Exodus
30:9 350

Rabbah Genesis
11:10 .350

Rabbah Leviticus
15:2 419

Qumran/Dead Sea Scrolls
1QH
4:40 440
16:4–40 421

1QM 277, 283, 339
11:8 313

1QS
3:13–4:26 277
3:14–4:5 462
3:18–19 440
3:18 . . . . .398, 401, 455
3:21 339
4:9–14 339
4:20–21 440
4:23–26 . . . . .398, 401, 455
4:23 440
6:16, 19, 22 461
8:6 440
8:14 407
9:3–4 64
9:10–11 314
9:15–16 461
11:13–14 461

1QSa (1Q28) 314
2:11–12 384

4Q176
Frag. 1–2 col. 6–7 407

4Q259
3:4–5 407

4QFlor
1:5 426
1:6–7 384

4QTest
9–13 .166

11QMelch
2:24–25 358

11QT
29.7–10 64

CD
6:11–15 64
12:22–23 314

Miscellaneous
4Q174 . . . . .66, 313
4Q246 384
4Q252 313
4Q266 314
4Q534 363
4QMMT 64
4QpIsa 319

Papyri
p^{52} 82, 83
p^{66} .381
p^{75} .381

Josephus
Against Apion
1.26 121
1.47–50 119
2.193–98 62

Jewish Antiquities
1.22 381
2.68–69 116
8.4.1 .421
13.245 421
13.255–56 429
18.2.3 36 83
18.13, 16, 18 462

Jewish War
2.162–65 462
2.647–7.455 64
7.341–88 64

Life
407–23 64

Philo
Abraham
4 121

On the Changes of Names
259–60 416

On the Creation of the World 139

Moses
1.155–158 358

Allegorical Interpretation
3:169–76 416

Questions and Answers on Genesis
2.62 358

Who Is the Heir?
79 416
191 416

That the Worse Attacks the Better
118 416

That Every Good Person Is Free
42–44 358

Classical Writers

Aesop
Phaedrus
2.prol.8 123

Apollonius
Life of Tyana 106

Aristotle
Poetics
17.6–11 120
24.4 120
9.2 123

On Marvelous Things Heard
846b.27 382

Arrian
Alex.
4.10.8 122

Cicero
De invention rhetorica
2.53.161 437

De natura deorum
1.67 437

Demosthenes
Orat.
47.58 382

Dio Cassius
1.5.4 122
62.11.3–4 120

Diodorus Siculus
31.10.2 122

Dionysius of Halicarnassus
De compositione verborum
9 123

De Demosthene
58 116

Ars rhetorica
7.65.2 ....

De Thucydide
8 121

Epicetus
Diatribai
1.923–25 123
3.22.49 437

Isocrates
Evagoras 113

Longinus
De sublimitate
11.1 123

Lucian
Vera historia
7 108
7–13 123
16 108
48 108
55 120

Marcus Aurelius
9.1.2 437

Menander
2.3 123
279.2–4 123

Philostratus
Apollonius of Tyana 113–15

Plato
Apology of Socrates
1.70–71 123

Pliny the Younger
Letters
10.96 63

Plutarch
Alexander
37.4 108
56.1 108

Flatterer
16 437

De Herodoti malignitate
20 123

Moralia
58E 437
859b 123

Polybius
1.25.1–10 122
38.5.1–8 120

Porphyrus
Life of Plotinus 124

Quintilian
7.1.1 120
10.1.21 120

Satyrus
Euripedes 113, 115

Suetonius
Domitian
12.2 63

Tacitus
Histories
5.5 .... 357, 373

Theon
Progymnastia
1.172–75 123
4.37–42 123
4.80–82 123

Church Fathers

Augustine
Tractate 2.1 118

Apostolic Constitutions
7.46.9 98

Clement of Alexandria
Stromata
2.15.66 90

Hypotyposeis
6.14 .... 38, 51

Didache
8:1 418

Eusebius
Church History
3.1.1 .... 83, 93
3.23.3–4 93
3.31.3 94
3.39.4–5 74

3.39.4 90
3.39.5–7 88
5.24.2 94
6.14 . . . . .38, 51
6.14.7 74
6.25.10 89
7.25.7–8.11 90

Ignatius
Smyrneans
2.1 95
5.2 95
Trallians
10.1 95

Ephesians
7.1 95

Irenaeus
Against Heresies
3.1.1 94
3.1.2 . . . . 53, 74, 83, 93
3.3.4 .93, 95
3.11.1 95
3.16.8 89

Jerome
De viris illustribus
9 93

Justin Martyr
First Apology
63.15 358

Dialogue with Trypho
56:4 358

Martyrdom of Polycarp
7:1 418

Polycarp
Letter to the Philippians. . . 88, 89

Tatian
Diatessaron 79

Subject Index

above and below, 151, 287–88
aesthetic theology, 43
allusions, *see* Old Testament, allusions
ancestry, 112
anointing
    language, 400–401
    of Jesus, 230–32
antichrists, 269–70
aporias, 115, 145–50, 239, 554
apostolic authorship, 53–55, 72–79, 86–93
arrangement, 120
asides, 135–41
assurance, 480–81
atmosphere, 117–18
atonement, 226, 230, 417, 534, 537
authorship
    of John's gospel, 72–79
    of John's letters, 86–93

back-reference, 250; *see also* asides
balkanization of Johannine studies, 41
believing
    and unbelief, 178, 214, 220, 234, 245, 292–93
    and the new birth, 470–80
    theme, 179, 191–92, 197, 205, 211, 213, 225–26, 258, 260
Beloved disciple, the
    and apostolic authorship, 72–79
    and Peter, 491–96
biblical theology, 38–50
biography, 106–8
birkat ha-minim, 56–58, 60, 62, 67
Bread of Life discourse, 209–13, 416–17
bread symbolism, 165–67
burial, 254–57

Cana cycle, 191–206
characterization, 118, 490–500
chronology of Jesus in John's gospel, 79–82

commissioning scene, 259, 399–400
conclusion, *see* dual conclusion
corporate metaphors, 500–504
cosmic conflict, 279–81
cosmic drama, 293–94
cosmic trial motif
    in John's gospel, 244, 253, 437–54
    in John's letters, 454–56
cosmology, 277–79
covenant and creation, 405–6
creation, 176–79, 208, 219, 336–54, 405–6
critical realism, 42
cross, *see* theology of the cross
crucifixion, 254–56; *see also* theology of the cross

date
    of John's gospel, 82–83
    of John's letters, 93–94
Davidic typology, 411–12
death
    and consequences, 113
    and life, 268, 284–87
    of Jesus, 231
deity
    of Christ, 357–60, 431–32
    of the Word, 338–39
demythologization, 43, 51
descent-ascent theme, 236, 526–28, 531
destination
    of John's gospel, 84
    of John's letters, 94
destruction of the temple, 60–71
disciples
    characterization of, 482–96
    task of, 504–7
divine election, *see* election
divine sovereignty and human responsibility, 410–11, 458–60
double meaning, 132, 250
drama, 49–50, 124, 168–70, 293–94

dual conclusion, 119, 149–50

early use of subject's name, 114
ecclesiology, 481–508
eclipse of biblical narrative, 43
election, 218, 242, 247, 270, 458–64
elusive Christ, 223, 233
emphasis and content, 113
empty tomb, 257–59
Ephesus, 83–84, 93–94
eschatology, 285, 295–98
eternal life, *see* life
ethic, 509–24
external features, 118–24
eyewitness testimony, 46, 75–76, 79, 88, 123–24, 555, 561–62

faith, *see* believing
Farewell discourse, 238–46
Father, the, 177–79, 186, 208, 220, 235, 246, 255, 259, 370–80, 540
feeding of the multitude, 209–13
festal symbolism, 413–21
Festival cycle, 206–28
festivals, 182, 194, 214
final prayer of Jesus, 246–49
flesh and spirit, 287
footwashing, 235–37
foreknowledge of God, 234, 237, 249
format, 119–20
fulfillment, *see* festal symbolism

genre
    of John's gospel, 104–24
    of John's letters, 125–26
glory, 176–79, 185–86, 191, 223, 233–34, 247, 255, 294–95, 350, 406, 408–9, 418, 534
God, 177, 179, 247, 271, 339, 361–69
Good Shepherd discourse, 225–28; *see also* shepherd and his flock
great deeds and words, 112–13
greater works, 489, 504–5

healing
  of the lame man, 206–9
  of the man born blind, 223–25
Hebrews and John, 564
hermeneutical triad, 42–44
historical reliability of John, 38–40, 123–24, 550–53
historical setting, 51–99
historical-critical method, 43
historiography
  Greco-Roman, 107–8, 111–24
  Jewish, 108–11
holy space, 66
Holy Spirit, the, 190, 217, 238, 241, 248, 259, 270–71, 440; *see also* Spirit, the

incarnational angle of John's ethic, 516–17
inclusio, 73–74, 147, 168–69, 289
introduction, 176–78
introductory matters, *see* historical setting
irony, 150–55, 192, 198, 201, 208, 212, 216, 229–30, 252

James and John, 564–65
Jesus, characterization of, 447–52
Jewish leaders, the, 441–44
Johannine community hypothesis, 51–58, 90–93, 282, 404, 514–15
Johannine dualism, 277–79
Johannine theology
  and canon, 547–65
  historical framework, 35–99
  literary foundations, 101–272
  major themes, 47–50, 273–546
journey theme, 528
judgment, 177, 208, 233, 280, 468–70

kingdom of God, 286
kingship of Jesus, 253, 285–86, 318

Lamb of God, 189–90, 221, 230, 255, 318, 414–15, 464
language, 115–17
Lazarus, *see* raising of Lazarus
length, 120

life
  and death, 268, 284–87
  and light, 341–49, 337–49
  theme, 177, 180, 209, 219, 260, 270–71, 286, 317, 342–49
light
  and darkness, 179–80, 206, 219–20, 235, 264–65, 278, 283–84
  symbolism, 166–67
  theme, 178–81, 200, 219, 223, 317, 344–49
literary devices, 135–67
love
  and hate, 289–92
  and mission, 522–23
  ethic, 268, 509–24
  theme, 200, 208, 236, 239–50, 262, 268–69, 271

Messiah, 177, 182, 192, 202, 206, 216, 224, 231, 234, 255, 270, 312–23, 340
messianic expectations, 70–71, 215–17, 233, 313–14, 318–19
minor characters, 497–99
mission, 177, 183, 202, 239, 242, 245–46, 248, 539–46
misunderstandings, 141–45, 192, 194, 203, 211–12, 214, 229, 233, 236, 240, 242–43, 245, 250–51, 253, 256, 258, 443
monotheism, 356–60
moral vision, *see* ethic
myth, 43

new birth, 184, 198, 206, 242, 267, 270, 350, 470–80
new commandment, 291–92
new covenant community, 179; *see also* new messianic community
new creation
  and salvation history, 353–54
  theme, 219, 259, 336–54
new epistemology, 42
new look, 554–55
new messianic community, 176–77, 183, 187, 213, 238, 259, 481–508
new tabernacle, 425–27

new temple, 416, 422–35
Nicodemus, 197–200

obduracy, 218
occasion
  of John's gospel, 84–85
  of John's letters, 94–95
Old Testament
  allusions, 307–10
  quotations, 299–307
One and Only Son, 177–78, 186, 381–82, 409–10
orthodox Johannophobia paradigm, 52, 74–75

Passion narrative, 249–60
Passover
  symbolism, 414–20
  theme, 189–90, 194, 210, 235, 255
Paul and John, 563–64
pericope of the adulterous woman, 147–48, 219
Peter and John, 565
Pilate, 444–47
postmodernism, 44, 277
postscript, 119
predestination, 218, 229, 234, 247, 252, 256, 270, 410, 458–64
preexistence, 222, 263
preface, 118–19
promotion of a hero, 114
provenance
  of John's gospel, 83–84
  of John's letters, 94
purpose
  of John's gospel, 85–86, 120, 260, 311
  of John's letters, 97

quotations, *see* Old Testament, quotations

raising of Lazarus, 228–30
range of topics, 112
reading
  of John's gospel, 175–262
  of John's letters, 263–72
redemption, 177, 265; *see also* atonement

resurrection
  and new creation, 353
  appearances, 257–62
revelation
  and/or salvation, 534–37
  of God in Jesus, 177, 387, 427

Sabbath controversy, 207–8, 350–51
salvation history, 176, 178–79, 181, 184, 188, 202, 212, 240–41, 255–56, 403–35
Samaritan woman, 201–5, 400
Satan, 281, 455–56
seams, *see* aporias
secessionists, 94–97, 264–67
semantic domains, 129–30
sending Christology, 224, 243, 294
Servant of the Lord, 231, 408
shepherd and his flock, 500–502; *see also* Good Shepherd discourse
signs
  in the Old Testament, 325–26
  in John's gospel, 178, 191, 198, 204–6, 209–12, 216, 219, 223–24, 228, 234, 238, 243, 255, 260, 319, 323–25, 326–33
sin
  that leads to death, 270–71
  theme, 280, 464–68
Son, the, 179, 208, 246, 255, 380–93, 540–42; *see also* Son; One and Only Son

Son
  of God, 191–92, 255, 270, 382–86
  of Man, 191, 216, 220, 350, 386–89, 529–31
sovereignty of God, 222, 237, 252, 458–60
Spirit, the, 240, 244, 393–402, 440, 542–43
spiritual gospel, 38–40, 550–51
structure
  of John's gospel, 118, 167–70, 333–35
  of John's letters, 171–73
style, 115, 130–34
symbolism, 155–67
Synoptics and John, 549–62

Tabernacles, 214–22, 420–22, 430–31
temple, 176, 206, 223, 230; *see also* destruction of the temple, new temple
temple clearing, 193–97
theodicy, 218, 243
theology
  of mission, *see* mission
  of the cross, 235, 525–38
titles of Christ approach, 316–17
tragedy, 117
transposition proposal, 555–63
trial before Pilate, 252–54
trickster, 150

Trinity and mission, 543–44
triumphal entry, 232
trust and unbelief, 292–93
truth
  and falsehood, 288–89
  and the cosmic trial motif, 437–41
  theme, 187, 240, 253, 267, 271–72, 455
Twelve, the, 485–86
two-level hermeneutic, 159–61
type of material, 114

unbelief, *see* believing and unbelief
use of Scripture, 298–310
use of sources, 121–22

variation in detail, 122–23
vindication scene, 113
vine and the branches, 502–4
vocabulary, 127–28

water symbolism, 162–64
witness, 177, 181, 194, 201, 206, 209, 220, 244, 248, 253, 439, 455
women in John's gospel, 499–500
Word, the, 178–79, 184, 219, 255, 263, 317, 338–41, 425–27
world, the, 178, 182, 281–82, 340–41, 454–55
worldview, 277–97
worship, 209, 360, 429–32

Author Index

Aalen, S., 436, 438
Abbott, Edwin A., 130
Abrams, M. H., 152
Achtemeier, Elizabeth, 283
Achtemeier, Paul J., 95–96, 98, 172
Agourides, Savas, 492
Akin, Daniel L., 96, 171, 263
Albani, Matthias, 70
Albertz, Rainer, 63
Alexander, Loveday C. A., 103–4, 110–11, 114, 118
Alexander, Philip S., 57, 61–62, 67, 84, 103, 109
Alexander, T. Desmond, 422
Alter, Robert, 109, 371
Anderson, Hugh, 123
Anderson, Paul N., 76, 550, 563
Arens, Eduardo, 319, 527
Ashton, John, 275, 371
Asiedu-Peprah, Martin, 207, 436
Attridge, Harold W., 52
Aune, David E., 103, 106, 110, 114, 119–20, 125–26, 283
Avemarie, Friedrich, 64

Baird, William, 39–40, 43, 54
Ball, David M., 161, 355, 359
Balla, Peter, 45
Balthasar, Hans Urs von, 48, 293
Balz, Horst, 171, 509
Bampfylde, Gillian, 321, 530
Barclay, William, 450
Barnett, Paul W., 82, 182, 554
Barr, James, 438
Barrett, C. K., 72, 132, 196, 275, 277, 280, 282, 284, 287–88, 326–27, 331, 340, 351, 361, 384–85, 397, 399–400, 410, 415, 417, 419, 430, 438, 446, 461, 474, 496, 505, 536, 549, 555
Barrosse, Thomas, 336, 349
Bass, Christopher D., 457, 480
Bassler, Jouette M., 369, 491

Bauckham, Richard, 37, 39, 46, 52, 58–59, 73, 75–79, 84–85, 103–5, 107, 114, 116, 122, 124, 135–36, 159–60, 184–85, 190, 218, 244, 250, 261, 275, 278, 283, 355–60, 362, 365, 382, 399, 497–98, 515, 543, 549, 551–53, 555–56, 560–62, 565
Bauder, Wolfgang, 486
Bauer, Walter, 75
Baumbach, Günther, 482
Baumeister, Theofried, 495–96, 537
Beale, G. K., 195, 298, 311, 336
Beasley-Murray, George R., 72–73, 82–83, 184, 275, 296, 328–29, 333, 340, 397, 399, 414, 437–38, 448, 450, 474, 496, 505, 507, 530
Beck, David R., 175, 181, 499
Becker, Jürgen, 323, 439
Behr, John, 341
Bennema, Cornelis, 175, 436
Bernard, John Henry, 449
Betz, Hans-Dieter, 484
Betz, Otto, 323, 329, 396, 440
Beutler, Johannes, 533–34, 536
Bieringer, Reimund, 336, 353, 436, 443, 448, 453
Billings, J. S., 396, 491, 498
Bittner, Wolfgang J., 311, 320–21, 323, 325
Black, David Alan, 172
Blaine, Bradford B., Jr., 496
Blenkinsopp, Joseph, 408
Blomberg, Craig L., 37, 52, 60, 103–4, 106–8, 194, 314, 418, 499, 549, 551–52
Blount, Brian K., 510
Bock, Darrell L., 77, 297, 431, 438, 443, 448, 450, 545, 555
Bockmuehl, Markus N., 37–38
Boda, Mark J., 313
Boismard, Marie-Émile, 130, 349
Bolyki, János, 510

Bond, Helen K., 444, 446, 449
Booth, Wayne C., 151
Borchert, Gerald L., 72, 397, 399, 414, 461–62, 472–73
Borgen, Peder, 529
Borig, Rainer, 503
Boring, M. Eugene, 396
Bosch, David J., 539
Botha, J. E., 117
Bouchoc, Raymond, 116, 127, 129, 289
Bowen, Clayton R., 106
Bowersock, G. W., 123
Brant, Jo-Ann A., 103–4, 293
Braun, François-Marie, 38, 172, 494, 536
Bray, Gerald, 263
Bretschneider, Karl Gottlieb, 39–40, 51, 54, 551
Brodie, Thomas L., 440
Brooke, A. E., 86–87, 93, 98
Brooke, George J., 64
Brown, Jeannine K., 336–38, 353
Brown, Raymond E., 52, 57–58, 68, 78, 83, 88–89, 91–93, 98, 106, 125, 127, 158, 171, 270, 278, 295, 311, 321, 323, 326, 329, 331, 351, 382, 396, 399–400, 410, 414, 419, 425, 428, 440, 448–49, 457, 461, 474, 482, 493–94, 499, 502, 514, 536, 549, 554
Bruce, F. F., 172, 263, 307, 397, 562
Brunson, Andrew C., 275
Bryan, Steven M., 207, 433
Bryant, Michael, 541
Büchsel, H. M. F., 439
Bultmann, Rudolf, 40, 43–44, 47, 51, 54–55, 60, 121–22, 132, 141, 147, 153, 171, 177, 180–81, 183, 201, 238, 253, 275, 277, 295–96, 326, 329, 361, 396, 399, 439, 445–49, 468, 472, 493, 496, 529, 534–35, 537, 549

Burge, Gary M., 58–59, 127, 146, 171, 263, 396, 399, 415, 461, 549, 550–51, 553
Burkett, Delbert, 355, 529–30
Burridge, Richard, 103–7, 111–22, 509, 511–12
Bush, L. Russ III, 438
Buth, Randall, 116, 131
Byrskog, Samuel, 124

Caird, G. B., 178
Calvin, John, 399, 472, 475
Campbell, Ken M., 391
Carey, George L., 536
Carlyle, Thomas, 158
Carmichael, Calum M., 336
Carroll, R., 314
Carson, D. A., 40–41, 45, 51, 53, 60–61, 74–75, 78, 82–86, 93–94, 98, 105, 107, 122, 127, 141–42, 148–49, 160, 168, 176, 194, 237, 275, 277, 292–93, 298–99, 301, 305, 309–11, 323, 325, 328–33, 340, 349–51, 358, 363, 373–74, 382–86, 388, 390–92, 394, 397, 399, 406, 408, 410–11, 414, 416–19, 422, 425, 457–61, 463–64, 469, 471–72, 474–75, 480, 488–89, 496, 501–2, 504, 507, 512, 536, 549, 551, 554, 556
Carter, Warren, 28, 37, 60, 175
Casey, Maurice, 39, 52, 194, 358
Cassem, Ned H., 281, 436
Casurella, Anthony, 396
Celsor, Scott, 564
Chaine, Joseph, 171
Charlesworth, James H., 275, 277, 283, 311, 314, 363, 384, 398–99
Chennattu, Rekha M., 457
Chevalier, Haakon M., 151
Clavier, H., 150, 330
Clements, Ronald E., 356
Coetzee, J. C., 347
Cohen, Shaye J. D., 56, 70
Cohon, S. S., 373
Collins, Adela Yarbro, 483
Collins, John J., 311, 314
Collins, Raymond F., 127, 319, 482, 486, 491–92

Coloe, Mary L., 72, 195, 329, 372, 403, 423, 509
Colwell, Ernest C., 132
Combs, William W., 265
Connick, C. Milo, 106
Conway, Colleen M., 457, 499
Cook, Robert W., 28, 37, 178, 275, 295
Corell, Alf, 441, 482, 503
Cotterell, Peter, 198, 201, 229, 236, 474–75
Cowan, Christopher, 377
Credner, Karl August, 127, 130, 133, 135
Cribbs, F. Lamar, 82
Croteau, David A., 82, 86, 105, 292, 410, 457, 470–71, 545
Crump, D. M., 438–39
Cullmann, Oscar, 52, 132, 158, 425, 482, 494
Culpepper, R. Alan, 38, 40, 43, 66–67, 109, 114, 117, 119, 127, 135–36, 141–45, 150–53, 155–59, 161–63, 165–67, 175, 177, 180, 341, 361, 369, 371, 444–46, 482, 491–92, 494, 497–98, 509, 555

Dahl, Nils A., 369, 482
Daise, Michael A., 217, 413
Daly-Denton, Margaret, 275, 302, 305–6, 385, 411
Daube, David, 419
Davey, F. N., 416, 435
Davies, Margaret, 103–4, 106, 108, 117, 127, 396
Davies, W. D., 61, 66–67, 311, 323, 325, 329, 331, 364, 372–73, 403, 416, 425, 427
De Boer, Martinus C., 525
Denaux, Adelbert, 549, 550
Dennis, John A., 113, 226, 230, 525–26, 537
Dietzfelbinger, Christian, 505
Dobschütz, Ernst von, 171
Dodd, C. H., 91, 93, 132, 155, 158, 166, 295–96, 324, 328–30, 332–33, 439–40, 536, 554
Domeris, W. R., 106
Donfried, Karl P., 493

Draper, J. A., 65–67, 84
Dschulnigg, Peter, 122, 128, 131, 133, 146
Duke, Paul D., 117, 127, 150, 152, 155, 341, 452
Dumbrell, William J., 275, 297, 426
Dunn, James D. G., 28, 47, 57, 65, 67–68, 158, 358, 555
DuRand, Jan A., 336–37, 352
Dvoøák, James D., 549–50, 556

Edwards, M. J., 110
Edwards, Ruth B., 172, 263
Ego, Beate, 403
Ellingworth, Paul, 133
Endo, Masanobu, 336
Enz, Jacob J., 502
Erdmann, Martin, 539
Erickson, Millard J., 362, 544
Eshel, Esther, 64
Eshel, Hanan, 64
Evans, Craig A., 195, 234, 275, 299, 301, 306, 309, 325, 411
Evanson, Edward, 51, 54

Fee, Gordon D., 85
Ferreira, Johan, 457
Filson, Floyd V., 285, 342, 347
Fisher, Matthew C., 355, 362, 370
Fitzmyer, Joseph A., 381
Flanagan, Neal, 106
Forestell, J. Terence, 177, 329, 534–37
Fornara, Charles William, 108, 120–21
Fortna, Robert T., 121–22, 323–24, 329, 535, 554
France, R. T., 107, 276, 307, 312, 533
Freed, Edwin D., 276, 299, 319
Freedman, William, 158
Frei, Hans, 43
Frerichs, Ernest, 312, 314
Frey, Jörg, 64, 127, 165, 226, 276, 295, 525
Friedman, Norman, 157

Gaffney, J., 471
Gardner-Smith, Percival, 550, 554
Gathercole, Simon, 422

Gaugler, Ernst, 483
Gerhardsson, Birger, 76
Giblet, Jean, 438
Giblin, Charles Homer, 444, 447
Gibson, David, 520
Giesbrecht, Herbert, 483
Giles, Kevin J., 391
Glasson, T. Francis, 109, 502
Gloer, W. Hulitt, 337
Gnuse, Robert K., 356
Goodman, Martin, 62–63, 67, 69, 84
Goppelt, Leonhard, 285
Grant, Robert M., 82
Grayston, Kenneth, 91, 93, 125, 396
Green, Joel B., 95–96, 98, 172
Green, William S., 312, 314
Grenz, Stanley J., 377
Griffith, Terry, 95
Grigsby, Bruce H., 329, 525, 534–35
Grillmeier, Alois, 38
Groussow, W., 528
Guelich, Robert, 103–6
Guericke, Heinrich Ernst Ferdinand, 130
Gundry, Robert, 95, 103, 107, 278
Gunther, John J., 493
Guthrie, Donald, 90, 97, 172, 312, 323, 326
Guthrie, George H., 41

Haacker, Klaus, 483, 502, 503
Haenchen, Ernst, 112, 180
Hägerland, Tobias, 106, 159, 175
Hahn, Johannes, 65, 403
Hamid-Khani, Saeed, 127
Hamilton, James, 276, 309
Hanson, A. T., 427
Hare, Douglas R. A., 529
Harner, Philip B., 161, 355, 359
Harris, W. Hall, 28, 276, 282
Harris, Murray J., 112, 216, 271, 355, 362, 367, 381
Hartin, Patrick J., 493
Hasitschka, Martin, 457, 464
Hatina, Thomas R., 399, 400
Hawkin, David J., 436, 438
Hays, Richard B., 509–10, 514–16, 518–20, 524
Hedrick, Charles W., 135, 193
Hemer, Colin, 106

Hengel, Martin, 37, 52, 58, 74, 90, 103–4, 106–8, 120, 194, 227, 385, 551
Hess, Richard S., 312–14
Hesselgrave, David J., 515, 539
Hill, Charles E., 37–38, 51–52, 74–75, 83, 89
Hills, Julian V., 125
Hirsch, E. D., 104
Hitchcock, F. R. M., 106
Hoehner, Harold W., 37, 80, 444
Hofius, Otfried, 382
Holloway, Paul A., 113, 518
Holmes, Michael W., 89
Holtzmann, Heinrich Julius, 86
Horbury, William, 56, 166, 182, 312–13, 340
Hort, F. J. A., 55, 171
Hoskins, Paul M., 59, 71, 84, 195, 403, 415, 423–24, 426–27, 429
Hoskyns, Edwyn, 416, 435
Howard, J. K., 418
Howard, W. F., 91, 131, 158
Houlden, J. L., 515
Hubbard, Moyer V., 337
Hubbard, Robert L., 107
Hudson, Bob, 563
Humphrey, Edith M., 336
Humphreys, Colin J., 81
Hunter, W. Bingham, 541
Hurtado, Larry W., 103, 110–13, 118, 204, 312, 355, 357–60, 362, 365, 373
Hüttenmeister, Frowald G., 64

Ito, Hisayasu, 223, 225

Jackson, Howard J., 116, 124
Jackson, Howard M., 37
Janowski, Bernd, 306
Jeremias, Joachim, 418
Johnston, George, 396
Jones, Larry Paul, 127, 162
Jonge, Marinus de, 312, 319, 322–23, 326, 331, 482, 502

Kant, Immanuel, 40
Käsemann, Ernst, 216, 278, 361, 510, 515, 534
Katz, Steven T., 56

Kealy, Seán P., 37, 45
Keefer, Kyle, 37
Keener, Craig S., 37, 103–6, 108, 110–11, 114–15, 119–23, 163, 166, 168, 175, 193, 283, 297, 341, 347–48, 390, 408, 421, 437, 444, 452
Kellum, L. Scott, 72, 87, 115, 127, 130–31, 134, 146–47, 149, 171, 173, 239, 285, 292
Kerr, Alan R., 60, 64, 67, 69–70, 72, 82, 84, 195, 372, 403, 423–24, 426–27
Kidner, Derek, 412
Kieffer, René, 158
Kierspel, Lars, 374, 436
Kiley, Mark, 323
Kim, Stephen S., 207
Kimelman, Reuven, 56
Kinzer, Mark, 423–24
Klein, William W., 107
Klink, Edward W. III., 37, 44, 52, 59, 85, 276, 280, 287, 293
Knöppler, Thomas, 525, 537
Koester, Craig R., 28, 37, 59, 127, 155, 157, 162, 166, 336, 353, 355, 426, 471, 525
Kopas, Jane, 499
Köstenberger, Andreas J., 28, 37, 40, 42–43, 51–54, 57–58, 60, 72–73, 75–76, 78, 80, 82–84, 105, 111–12, 116–17, 119, 121, 127, 129, 132, 135, 147–50, 152–53, 155–56, 159, 161, 164, 166–68, 175–80, 184–86, 188–89, 191–94, 196–99, 201–3, 206, 208, 210–11, 213–14, 216–17, 219, 224, 227, 229–32, 234, 245, 247, 250–54, 256, 259, 261–62, 276, 278, 280–82, 284, 289–90, 292, 297, 334, 337–39, 349–51, 353, 355–56, 360, 362–63, 365, 371–72, 374–77, 379–80, 385–86, 388, 394–96, 398–99, 402, 404–7, 409, 418, 420, 422, 424, 426–28, 433–34, 436, 441, 445–46, 449, 455, 463, 465, 473, 484, 498–500, 513–15, 521–24, 526, 528, 539–40, 546, 549–52, 558

Köstenberger, Margaret Elizabeth, 231, 499
Krafft, Eva, 497
Kragerud, Alv, 493
Kruse, Colin G., 98, 171, 175, 263, 401, 449, 467
Kümmel, Werner G., 83, 88, 94
Kupp, David D., 359
Kurz, William S., 492
Kuyper, Lester J., 438, 441
Kynes, W. L., 475
Kysar, Robert, 52, 56, 58–59, 122

Laato, Antti, 313
Lacomara, Aelred, 238, 347, 501
Ladd, George E., 276–78, 348, 549
Lake, Kirsopp, 83
Lamarche, Paul, 533
Lamouille, Arnaud, 131
Lane, William, 104
Laney, Carl, 475
Lang, Bernhard, 357
Lange, Armin, 70, 403
Larkin, William J. Jr., 545
Larsson, Tord, 370
Law, Robert, 480
Lea, Thomas D., 172
Leal, Juan, 158
Leaney, A. R. C., 396
Lee, Aquila H. I., 355, 360
Lee, Dorothy A., 127, 158
Lee, E. Kenneth, 106
Lemcio, Eugene, 194, 395
Leroy, Herbert, 127, 141
Levin, Harry, 157–58
Levinsohn, Stephen H., 131
Lichtenberger, Hermann, 64–65, 69, 314
Lierman, John, 317
Lieu, Judith M., 95, 423–24
Lightfoot, J. B., 55, 555
Lincoln, Andrew T., 194, 289, 385, 396, 407, 436, 439–40, 453–54
Lindars, Barnabas, 493, 496, 530, 554
Lindemann, Andreas, 482
Lindsay, Dennis R., 436–37, 439–40
Loader, William, 355, 535
Lohse, Eduard, 312, 323
Longacre, Robert, 97, 171
Longman, Tremper, 313

Lorenzen, Thorwald, 492, 495
Louw, Johannes P., 127, 474
Lücking, Stefan, 61

Maccini, Robert G., 499
Machinist, Peter, 356
MacDonald, Nathan, 356
Macgregor, G. H. C., 120, 156
Maggay, Melba P., 438, 449
Malatesta, Edward J., 38, 238, 501, 503
Malina, Bruce J., 278
Manning, Gary T., Jr., 276, 309
Maritz, Petrus, 165
Marrow, Stanley B., 281, 436, 457
Marshall, I. Howard, 95, 98, 171, 263, 315, 401, 545
Martin, Troy W., 499
Martínez, Florentino García, 64
Martyn, J. Louis, 52, 55–58, 62, 67–68, 70, 83, 106, 159, 226, 293, 321, 482, 502, 514–15, 554
Marxsen, Willi, 105
Matera, Frank J., 510, 525, 536
Mburu, Elizabeth W., 92, 398
McCabe, Robert V., 350, 475
McCaffrey, James, 423–24
McConville, J. Gordon, 426
McKelvey, Robert J., 423, 427, 434
McKnight, Scot, 555
McNamara, Martin, 528
McPolin, James, 532, 539
McRae, George W., 128, 150
Mealand, David L., 207
Meeks, Wayne A., 57–58, 109, 156, 158, 278–79, 282, 482, 502, 509, 510–13, 530–31
Melick, Richard R., 471
Menken, Maarten J. J., 276, 299, 303, 306
Metzger, Bruce M., 207, 215
Metzner, Rainer, 183, 226, 457, 464, 525, 537
Meyer, Heinrich August Wilhelm, 449
Meyer, Paul W., 355, 361, 369, 370–72, 376
Michaels, J. Ramsey, 474, 498
Middlemas, Jill, 63
Miller, Ed L., 181

Minear, Paul S., 492
Mlakuzhyil, George, 529
Mohler, R. Albert, 398
Moloney, Francis J., 48, 167, 168, 175, 229, 295, 355, 361–62, 397, 419, 461–62, 476, 529
Montgomery, David A., 190
Moo, Douglas J., 74, 82–83, 85–86, 93–94, 98, 105, 107, 337
Moody, Dale, 381
Moore, Stephen D., 40, 175
Mörchen, Roland, 527
Moreland, J. P., 398
Moreton, M. B., 492
Morris, Leon, 28, 38–39, 51, 82, 128, 194, 253, 278, 312, 323–24, 328–29, 338, 340, 355, 370, 382–84, 386, 388, 390–91, 397, 399–400, 407, 410, 415, 427, 438–39, 441, 461, 474–75, 509, 515, 525, 534, 537, 549, 551, 553, 556
Morton, A. Q., 120
Motyer, J. A., 407
Motyer, Stephen, 56, 67–70, 72, 84, 374, 435, 440
Moule, Charles F. D., 347, 501, 527
Moulton, James Hope, 116, 128–29, 132
Mournet, Terence C., 555
Mowvley, Henry, 382
Muecke, D. C., 151–52
Muilenburg, James, 189
Müller, Christoph G., 181
Müller, Theophil, 533, 535
Müller, Ulrich B., 84, 525, 527, 534, 536

Nauck, Wolfgang, 171
Neill, Stephen, 43–44, 298
Nereparampil, Lucius, 329–30, 332, 423
Neusner, Jacob, 56, 61, 65, 69, 312, 314
Newsom, Carol, 258
Ng, Wai-yee, 128, 158, 162, 165
Nicholson, Godfrey Carruthers, 158, 216, 355, 525–26, 528, 530, 535, 538
Nicol, Willem, 312, 323, 329
Nicole, Roger, 438

Nietzsche, Friedrich, 445
Niewalda, Paulm, 158
Nun, H., 83
Nuttall, A. D., 449

O'Brien, Peter T., 539
O'Day, Gail R., 59, 75, 372
O'Neill, J. C., 171
O'Rourke, John, 128, 135
Obermann, Andreas, 276
Oegema, Gerbern, S., 314
Okure, Teresa, 58, 499, 539
Olsson, Birger, 171, 361
Olyan, Saul M., 357
Onuki, Takashi, 58, 282, 482
Osborne, Grant R., 104, 463–64, 537
Osten-Sacken, Peter von der, 525, 533
Oswalt, John N., 408
Owing, T. L., 457, 464

Painter, John, 88–89, 91, 157–58, 166, 336, 338
Pamment, Margaret, 178, 493, 528
Pancaro, Severino, 483
Panzram, Sabine, 62
Pao, David W., 113
Parsenios, George L., 117
Patterson, Richard D., 42, 151, 191
Pendrick, Gerard, 381
Peterson, David, 545
Peterson, Peter M., 492, 497
Peterson, Susan Lynn, 89
Phillips, Thomas E., 336–37, 349
Phythian-Adams, W. J., 336
Pilhofer, Peter, 403
Piper, Ronald A., 559
Plantinga, Cornelius, 371
Plumer, Eric, 559
Plummer, Alfred, 444
Pohlmann, Karl-Friedrich, 63
Poirier, John C., 227, 431
Pollard, T. E., 38, 51, 355
Pollefeyt, Didier, 374, 436, 453
Popkes, Enno Edzard, 509
Porter, Stanley E., 90, 299, 312, 315, 403, 414–19
Potterie, Ignace de la, 172, 438–40
Poythress, Vern S., 87, 131
Pryor, John W., 47, 177–78, 238, 298, 325, 332, 347, 403–4, 435, 462, 483, 490, 501, 503, 513

Quarles, Charles L., 72, 292
Quast, Kevin, 78, 457, 485, 492–93

Ramelli, Ilaria, 262
Reim, Günther., 276, 299
Reinhartz, Adele, 293
Rengstorf, Karl Heinrich, 325, 391, 483
Rensberger, David, 58, 278, 282, 482
Resseguie, James L., 128
Reumann, John, 493
Richard, Earl J., 128, 132, 158
Richter, Georg, 534
Ridderbos, Herman N., 148–49, 159, 168, 175, 180, 374, 384, 386, 394, 397, 399, 410, 415–16, 451, 461–62, 471–72, 474–76
Riedl, Johannes, 533
Riesenfeld, Harald, 396
Riga, Peter J., 312, 323
Rissi, Mathias, 528
Roberts, Colin, 149
Robinson, James M., 82, 110, 113, 554
Robinson, John A. T., 60, 70, 502
Rohrbaugh, Richard L., 278
Roose, Hanna, 119
Rosner, Brian S., 45
Ruckstuhl, Eugen, 122, 128, 131, 133, 146, 296, 531
Rudel, P., 128
Ruwe, Andreas, 63

Salier, Bill, 422, 424, 426, 433–34
Salier, Willis Hedley, 312
Sanday, William, 551
Sanders, J. N., 38, 45, 83, 324
Sanders, Jack T., 515
Sandnes, Karl Olav, 198
Satterthwaite, Philip E., 313
Schaff, Philip, 94
Schäfer, Peter, 56
Scheiber, Alexander, 419
Schiffman, Lawrence H., 56, 64
Schlatter, Adolf, 28, 42, 52, 82, 84, 132, 176, 188–89, 276, 404, 414, 438–39, 472, 475, 549
Schleiermacher, Friedrich, 40, 54
Schlund, Christine, 403, 419, 525
Schmidt, Karl Ludwig, 106

Schnabel, Eckhard J., 539
Schnackenburg, Rudolf, 94–95, 98, 130–31, 171, 263, 312, 323, 326, 328, 331, 347, 399, 401, 411, 439, 457, 461–62, 472, 474, 482–85, 487, 494–95, 501–3, 534, 536, 549
Schneiders, Sandra M., 157–58, 499
Schnelle, Udo, 323, 457, 483
Schrage, Wolfgang, 510
Schreiner, Thomas R., 28, 418
Schrenk, Gottlob, 371
Schröter, Jens, 525
Schuchard, Bruce G., 276, 299
Schulz, Anselm, 484–86, 536
Schürer, Emil, 391
Schwartz, Eduard, 145, 483
Schweizer, Eduard, 503
Scobie, Charles H. H., 45, 47
Segovia, Fernando F., 293, 509
Seim, Turid K., 457
Semler, Johann S., 40
Shafaat, A., 396
Shedd, Russell, 128, 132
Sheeley, Steven M., 135–36
Shuler, Philip L., 123
Sidebottom, Ernest M., 528–29
Siegert, Folker, 60
Sikeler, Jeffrey, 483, 487, 491
Simon, U. E., 284–85, 348
Smalley, Stephen S., 28, 125, 171, 263, 324, 329, 396
Smit, Peter-Ben, 191
Smith, D. Moody, 28, 39, 52, 56, 59, 76, 159, 171, 296, 398, 509–10, 549–50, 556, 563
Smith, Dennis E., 59, 350, 518
Smith, Jonathan Z., 162
Smith, Mark S., 357
Smith, Robert H., 276, 326, 502, 525
Snyder, Graydon F., 492
Söding, Thomas, 436, 438, 525–26
Spicq, Ceslas, 509
Sproston North, Wendy E., 105, 281
Stählin, Gustav, 276, 296
Staley, Jeffrey L., 208
Stamps, Dennis L., 103, 116–17, 128
Stanton, Graham N., 57, 114, 549
Stegemann, Ekkehard W., 66–67
Steinmetz, David, 41

Stemberger, Günter, 156, 166, 509
Stevens, George B., 38, 347, 464
Stibbe, Mark W. G., 48, 68, 78, 103–4, 109, 111, 150, 165, 169, 175, 189, 208, 341, 355, 361–63, 370–73, 376, 414, 416, 441, 444, 449
Stolz, Fritz, 325
Stott, John R. W., 98, 172, 263, 270, 488, 515
Stout, Stephen O., 76, 185
Strachan, R. H., 444
Strauss, David Friedrich, 39, 51, 54–55, 551
Strecker, Georg, 97, 263
Streeter, B. H., 86, 130, 553
Streett, Daniel R., 92, 164, 263, 291, 322, 337, 365, 401, 432, 467, 565
Stuhlmacher, Peter, 226, 306, 525, 537
Suggit, John, 336
Swain, Scott R., 42, 51, 76, 179, 184, 216, 355–56, 360, 398, 436–37, 439, 546
Swain, Simon, 110
Swartley, Willard M., 104, 108

Talbert, Charles H., 106, 120, 169, 400, 411, 474, 528–29
Tate, Marvin E., 411
Taylor, Michael J., 28, 38
Teeple, Howard M., 108
Tenney, Merrill C., 128, 135, 371, 470, 565
Teppler, Yaakov Y., 57
Thatcher, Tom, 38, 40, 43, 53, 60, 104, 122, 128, 135, 175, 276, 286, 554–55
Theobald, Michael, 510
Thielman, Frank, 51, 95, 97, 116, 128, 147, 474
Thiselton, Anthony C., 436, 438, 440, 446
Thomas, John Christopher, 208, 236
Thompson, L. A., 63, 278
Thompson, Marianne Meye, 39, 51, 88, 95–96, 98, 172, 216, 263, 312, 323, 328, 356, 358, 361–62, 370–71, 534, 551, 553

Thüsing, Wilhelm, 329, 525, 528, 530
Tidball, Derek, 336, 352
Timmins, Nicholas G., 128
Tolmie, Donald François, 356, 361, 364, 370, 373, 375–76, 379
Tomoi, K., 171
Torrey, C. C., 82
Tovey, Derek, 128
Trebilco, Paul, 83
Trites, Allison A., 436
Trobisch, David, 90
Trotter, Andrew H., 208, 549, 564
Trudinger, Paul, 492
Turner, George Allen, 60
Turner, Max, 198, 201, 229, 236, 399, 526, 534, 536–37
Turner, Nigel, 129, 132
Twelftree, Graham H., 559

Van Belle, Gilbert, 38, 122, 135, 165, 526, 554
Van den Bussche, Henri, 482
Van der Watt, Jan G., 127–28, 342, 509–10, 514, 518
Van Staden, Peter J., 171
Vandecasteele-Vanneuville, Frederique, 374, 436, 453
Vanhoozer, Kevin J., 43, 48, 72, 293, 316, 359, 398
Vellanickal, Matthew, 488
Vergote, Antoine, 530
Via, Dan O., 501
Viviano, Benedict T., 338
Vogel, Manuel, 65
Volf, Miroslav, 277–80, 436, 445, 452, 454, 510–11, 513
Volfing, Annette, 38
Vorster, Willem S., 492
Vos, Geerhardus, 438
Votaw, C. H., 104, 105
Vrede, Wilhelm, 171

Waddington, W. G., 81
Wahlde, Urban C. von., 551
Walker, Peter W., 55, 60, 195, 372, 403, 423, 425–27, 429–33, 435
Walker, W. O., Jr., 381
Wallace, Daniel B., 60, 362, 364, 382

Watson, Francis, 104–5
Watts, Rikki E., 113
Watty, William W., 493
Wead, David W., 128, 132, 150, 158
Webster, Jane S., 165
Welck, Christian, 312
Wellhausen, Julius, 130
Wenham, Gordon J., 313
Westcott, B. F., 54, 55, 72, 77, 438, 444
Wheelwright, Philip E., 161, 166
Whitacre, Rodney A., 121, 400, 453
White, John L., 125
Whiteley, D. E. H., 77
Wifall, Walter R., 306
Wilckens, Ulrich, 449, 537
Wilder, A. N., 172
Wilkens, Wilhelm, 323
Willi-Plein, Ina, 64
Williams, Catrin H., 161, 356, 359
Williams, P. J., 104, 118, 175–76
Wilson, W. G., 91
Windisch, Hans, 125, 128, 396, 550
Winter, Paul, 381
Witherington, Ben III, 114, 336, 382, 399–400, 452, 461–62, 471–72, 475
Wolters, Al, 314
Woodbridge, Paul, 436, 507
Wright, Christopher J. H., 356–57, 359, 539
Wright, George Ernest, 439
Wright, N. T., 42–44, 47, 294, 298, 336, 400, 422, 426
Wyatt, Nicolas, 337

Yarbrough, Robert W., 263, 271, 281, 289–91, 298, 373, 401, 403–4, 454–55, 457, 461, 463–64, 467–68
Yassif, Eli, 110
Yee, Gale A., 60, 68, 403
Young, Franklin W., 276, 306, 309

Zagzebski, Linda, 510
Zenger, Erich, 70
Zimmermann, Ruben, 127
Zumstein, Jean, 534